Revised Second Edition

Masterplots

1,801 Plot Stories and Critical Evaluations of the World's Finest Literature

Revised Second Edition

Volume 2
Bet – Con
615 – 1238

Edited by
FRANK N. MAGILL

Story Editor, Revised Edition
DAYTON KOHLER

Consulting Editor, Revised Second Edition
LAURENCE W. MAZZENO

SALEM PRESS
Pasadena, California   Englewood Cliffs, New Jersey

96-275

Editor in Chief: Dawn P. Dawson
Consulting Editor: Laurence W. Mazzeno   *Managing Editor:* Christina J. Moose
Project Editors: Eric Howard   *Research Supervisor:* Jeffry Jensen
Juliane Brand   *Research:* Irene McDermott
Acquisitions Editor: Mark Rehn   *Proofreading Supervisor:* Yasmine A. Cordoba
Production Editor: Cynthia Breslin Beres   *Layout:* William Zimmerman

Library of Congress Cataloging-in-Publication Data
Masterplots / edited by Frank N. Magill; consulting editor, Laurence W. Mazzeno. — Rev. 2nd ed.
    p.   cm.
Expanded and updated version of the 1976 rev. ed.
Includes bibliographical references and indexes.
1. Literature—Stories, plots, etc. 2. Literature—History and criticism. I. Magill, Frank Northen, 1907-   . II. Mazzeno, Laurence W.
PN44.M33   1996
809—dc20   96-23382
ISBN 0-89356-084-7 (set)   CIP
ISBN 0-89356-086-3 (volume 2)

Revised Second Edition
First Printing

LIST OF TITLES IN VOLUME 2

page

The Betrothed—*Alessandro Manzoni* 615
Between the Acts—*Virginia Woolf* 620
Bevis of Hampton—*Unknown* 624
Beyond Good and Evil—*Friedrich Wilhelm Nietzsche* 629
The Big Rock Candy Mountain—*Wallace Stegner* 632
The Big Sky—*A. B. Guthrie, Jr.* 636
The Big Sleep—*Raymond Chandler* 640
The Biglow Papers—*James Russell Lowell* 644
Billy Budd, Foretopman—*Herman Melville* 647
Biographia Literaria—*Samuel Taylor Coleridge* 652
The Birds—*Aristophanes* 656
The Birthday Party—*Harold Pinter* 660
The Black Arrow—*Robert Louis Stevenson* 664
Black Boy—*Richard Wright* 669
Black Elk Speaks—*Black Elk* 673
Black Lamb and Grey Falcon—*Rebecca West* 676
The Black Swan—*Thomas Mann* 679
Black Thunder—*Arna Bontemps* 682
Bleak House—*Charles Dickens* 686
Bless Me, Ultima—*Rudolfo A. Anaya* 691
Blithe Spirit—*Noël Coward* 695
The Blithedale Romance—*Nathaniel Hawthorne* 699
Blood Wedding—*Federico García Lorca* 703
The Bohemians of the Latin Quarter—*Henri Murger* 707
The Book of Laughter and Forgetting—*Milan Kundera* 712
Book of Songs—*Heinrich Heine* 716
The Book of the Courtier—*Baldassare Castiglione* 720
The Book of the Dead—*Unknown* 725
Book of the Duchess—*Geoffrey Chaucer* 729
The Book of the Ladies—*Christine de Pizan* 733
The Book of Theseus—*Giovanni Boccaccio* 737
Boris Godunov—*Alexander Pushkin* 742
The Borough—*George Crabbe* 746
The Bostonians—*Henry James* 750

MASTERPLOTS

page

Boswell's London Journal—*James Boswell* 755
The Braggart Soldier—*Plautus* 758
Brand—*Henrik Ibsen* 762
Brave New World—*Aldous Huxley* 766
Bread and Wine—*Ignazio Silone* 771
Break of Noon—*Paul Claudel* 775
The Bride of Lammermoor—*Sir Walter Scott* 779
The Bride's Tragedy *and* Death's Jest-Book—*Thomas Lovell Beddoes* 784
Brideshead Revisited—*Evelyn Waugh* 788
The Bridge—*Hart Crane* 793
The Bridge of San Luis Rey—*Thornton Wilder* 796
The Bridge on the Drina—*Ivo Andrić* 800
Britannicus—Jean Baptiste Racine 804
Broad and Alien Is the World—*Ciro Alegría* 809
The Broken Jug—*Heinrich von Kleist* 813
The Bronze Horseman—*Alexander Pushkin* 817
Brother Ass—*Eduardo Barrios* 821
The Brothers—*Terence* 825
The Brothers Ashkenazi—*Israel Joshua Singer* 829
The Brothers Karamazov—*Fyodor Dostoevski* 833
The Browning Version—*Terence Rattigan* 838
Brut—*Layamon* 842
Buddenbrooks—*Thomas Mann* 846
Bullet Park—*John Cheever* 851
The Bulwark—*Theodore Dreiser* 855
A Burnt-Out Case—*Graham Greene* 860
Bury My Heart at Wounded Knee—*Dee Brown* 864
Bus Stop—*William Inge* 867
Bussy d'Ambois—*George Chapman* 871

Cadmus—*Unknown* 876
Caesar and Cleopatra—*George Bernard Shaw* 879
Cain—*George Gordon, Lord Byron* 883
The Caine Mutiny—*Herman Wouk* 887
Cakes and Ale—*W. Somerset Maugham* 891
Caleb Williams—*William Godwin* 895
Call It Sleep—*Henry Roth* 899
The Call of the Wild—*Jack London* 903
Camel Xiangzi—*Lao She* 907
Camille—*Alexandre Dumas*, fils 911
Cancer Ward—*Aleksandr Solzhenitsyn* 915
Candida—*George Bernard Shaw* 919

page

Candide—*Voltaire* 923
Cane—*Jean Toomer* 927
The Cannibal—*John Hawkes* 931
The Canterbury Tales—*Geoffrey Chaucer*.................. 935
Canto general—*Pablo Neruda*........................ 939
Cantos—*Ezra Pound*............................. 943
Captain Horatio Hornblower—*C. S. Forester* 946
Captains Courageous—*Rudyard Kipling* 950
The Captain's Daughter—*Alexander Pushkin* 954
The Captives—*Plautus*............................ 959
The Caretaker—*Harold Pinter*....................... 963
Carmen—*Prosper Mérimée* 967
Carmina—*Catullus*.............................. 971
The Case of Sergeant Grischa—*Arnold Zweig* 974
Cass Timberlane—*Sinclair Lewis* 978
The Castle—*Franz Kafka* 982
The Castle of Otranto—*Horace Walpole* 986
Castle Rackrent—*Maria Edgeworth*.................... 990
Cat and Mouse—*Günter Grass* 995
Cat on a Hot Tin Roof—*Tennessee Williams* 999
Catch-22—*Joseph Heller* 1003
The Catcher in the Rye—*J. D. Salinger* 1007
Catiline—*Ben Jonson* 1010
Cawdor—*Robinson Jeffers*......................... 1014
Cecilia—*Fanny Burney* 1018
Celestina—*Fernando de Rojas* 1023
The Cenci—*Percy Bysshe Shelley* 1028
Ceremony—*Leslie Marmon Silko*..................... 1032
Ceremony in Lone Tree—*Wright Morris* 1036
The Chairs—*Eugène Ionesco* 1040
Chaka—*Thomas Mofolo*........................... 1043
The Changeling—*Thomas Middleton* and *William Rowley* 1047
The Changing Light at Sandover—*James Merrill*............. 1052
Charles Demailly—*Edmond de Goncourt* and *Jules de Goncourt* 1056
Charms—*Paul Valéry* 1061
The Charterhouse of Parma—*Stendhal* 1065
Chéri—*Colette* 1070
The Cherokee Night—*Lynn Riggs* 1074
The Cherry Orchard—*Anton Chekhov*................... 1078
The Chevalier de Maison-Rouge—*Alexandre Dumas*, père 1082
Chicago Poems—*Carl Sandburg* 1087
The Chickencoop Chinaman—*Frank Chin* 1090

page

Child of God—*Cormac McCarthy* 1094
Childe Harold's Pilgrimage—*George Gordon, Lord Byron* 1098
Children of a Lesser God—*Mark Medoff* 1102
The Children of Herakles—*Euripides* 1106
The Children's Hour—*Lillian Hellman* 1110
The Chimeras—*Gérard de Nerval* 1114
Chita—*Lafcadio Hearn* 1118
The Chosen—*Chaim Potok* 1121
A Christmas Carol—*Charles Dickens* 1125
Chronicles—*Jean Froissart* 1129
The Cid—*Pierre Corneille* 1132
Cinna—*Pierre Corneille* 1136
Cinq-Mars—*Alfred de Vigny* 1140
The City of God—*Saint Augustine* 1144
The City of the Sun—*Tommaso Campanella* 1147
Civilization and Its Discontents—*Sigmund Freud* 1150
Clarissa—*Samuel Richardson* 1154
The Clayhanger Trilogy—*Arnold Bennett* 1158
Cligés—*Chrétien de Troyes* 1162
A Clockwork Orange—*Anthony Burgess* 1167
The Closed Garden—*Julien Green* 1171
The Clouds—*Aristophanes* 1176
The Clown—*Heinrich Böll* 1179
The Cocktail Party—*T. S. Eliot* 1183
Cold Comfort Farm—*Stella Gibbons* 1188
Collected Poems—*Marianne Moore* 1192
The Collector—*John Fowles* 1196
Color of Darkness—*James Purdy* 1200
The Color Purple—*Alice Walker* 1203
The Comedy of Errors—*William Shakespeare* 1207
Commentaries—*Julius Caesar* 1212
The Company of Women—*Mary Gordon* 1215
The Compleat Angler—*Izaak Walton* 1219
The Complete Poems of Emily Dickinson—*Emily Dickinson* 1222
Comus—*John Milton* 1231
The Concubine—*Elechi Amadi* 1235

Revised Second Edition

THE BETROTHED

Type of work: Novel
Author: Alessandro Manzoni (1785-1873)
Type of plot: Historical
Time of plot: Seventeenth century
Locale: Milan, Italy
First published: I promessi sposi, 1827; revised, 1840-1842 (English translation, 1828; revised, 1951)

Principal characters:
LORENZO, a young Italian peasant
LUCIA, his betrothed
DON RODRIGO, an arrogant nobleman
THE UN-NAMED, a powerful outlaw nobleman
DON ABBONDIO, a parish priest
FRA CRISTOFORO, a Capuchin and a friend of the betrothed couple

The Story:

On the day before he was to have performed the marriage ceremony for Lorenzo and Lucia, two young peasants, Don Abbondio, parish priest at Lecco, was warned by two armed henchmen of Don Rodrigo, a tyrannical noble, not to marry the pair. In fear for his life, Don Abbondio refused to perform the marriage when asked to do so by the young couple. When they tried to trick him into being present while they exchanged vows, he dashed away into hiding.

The reason for the warning given to the priest was that Don Rodrigo wished to seduce Lucia. He was not in love with the young woman, but he had wagered his cousin that he could have her for his enjoyment while she was still a virgin. Toward this end, he sent a crew of his henchmen to abduct the girl from her home. Appearing at Lucia's home, they were frightened away by the tumult aroused when the priest caused the alarm to be sounded by tolling the church bell.

Frightened, Lucia sought aid from a saintly Capuchin, Fra Cristoforo, who gave her, her mother, and Lorenzo temporary haven within the walls of the monastery while he made arrangements for the safety of all three, away from the wrath and wickedness of Don Rodrigo. He sent the girl to seek sanctuary with a Capuchin chapter at Monza, along with her mother. He sent Lorenzo to another monastery in Milan.

Arriving at Monza, Lucia was put under the care of a nun who belonged to a noble family that had placed her in the convent rather than pay a dowry. The nun was a headstrong woman and, in some ways, wicked, but the Capuchins thought Lucia would be safe under her care. Lucia remained hidden for some weeks.

Don Rodrigo initiated a search for her until his henchmen discovered her place of refuge. Fearing that he could never take her from the sanctuary, Don Rodrigo enlisted the aid of a powerful noble called the Un-named. The Un-named, grateful for past services by Don Rodrigo, agreed to aid his vassal in abducting the woman and in teaching a harsh lesson to peasants who thought they could defy the nobility.

The Un-named learned that one of his men living near the convent had undertaken to murder a nun who had displeased the woman to whom the Capuchins had sent Lucia. As a result of the murder committed for her benefit, the nun was forced to enter into the scheme and send Lucia out of the convent. Once out of the sanctuary, Lucia was kidnapped by the Un-named's men and taken in a coach to his mountain retreat.

Meanwhile, Lorenzo had failed to reach the Capuchin monastery in Milan. Upon his arrival in the city, he had found the populace in a turmoil because of a shortage of bread. He took part in a riot, and afterward he became drunk in a tavern. While drunk, he had babbled to a police spy that he had incited a crowd to riot, and the spy had him arrested by the police. Another mob released Lorenzo from the police. With a price on his head, he fled from the Duchy of Milan into territory controlled by Venice. There he located a distant relative who found work for him in a silk mill. When the authorities of Milan tried to have him returned to that city, Lorenzo fled again and assumed a fictitious name in another Venetian community.

The Un-named was moved by Lucia's beauty and innocence and refused to turn her over to Don Rodrigo. Instead, he went to Cardinal Federigo and announced that he had suffered a change of conscience and wished to end a career of tyranny and oppression. The churchman welcomed him as an erring parishioner. Lucia was released from her imprisonment in the noble's mountain castle and returned once again to the keeping of her mother. Rather than send the woman to her home and the persecution of Don Rodrigo, Cardinal Federigo sent Lucia and her mother to the home of a noblewoman known for her charity. There Lucia would be safe.

Don Rodrigo, angry because Fra Cristoforo had been able to aid the young woman and so preserve her honor, caused the removal of the Capuchin to Rimini. More than a year passed; Lorenzo was unable to return to the Duchy of Milan because of his banishment. Corresponding with Lorenzo through letter writers, Lucia told him that in her period of duress she had vowed to the Virgin that she would never marry if released from the clutches of the ruffians who held her. Finally, because of the time that had intervened and the confusion that had arisen because of a plague, Lorenzo decided to return to Milan, where Lucia was staying with the charitable noblewoman. While searching for her in a city desolated by the plague, he contracted the disease. After his recovery, he continued his search, only to learn that Lucia had become ill and had been sent to the pesthouse, along with thousands of other unfortunates who had contracted the disease.

At the pesthouse, he found Fra Cristoforo, who had gone to Milan to aid the sick. Among his patients the Capuchin had Don Rodrigo, who had caught the plague and was near death. Fra Cristoforo made Lorenzo pardon Don Rodrigo and promise to pray for his soul. Continuing his search for Lucia, Lorenzo found her convalescing in the women's section of the pesthouse. After their reunion, Fra Cristoforo told Lucia that her vow to the Virgin was not valid, inasmuch as she had previously exchanged betrothal vows with Lorenzo.

When the plague subsided, Lorenzo went back to their village and found that the plague had almost wiped out its population as well, although sparing Don Abbondio and Lucia's mother. While he was there, the new heir to the estate arrived, Don Rodrigo having succumbed to the plague. With the new incumbent's aid, for he was a friend of the cardinal who had befriended Lucia, the betrothed couple returned to Lecco and were at last married by Don Abbondio.

After their marriage, the couple moved, again with the nobleman's aid, to a new home in the Venetian territory, where Lorenzo plied his trade in a silk mill, and he and Lucia reared a large and healthy family.

Critical Evaluation:

The Betrothed, one of the world's great historical novels, established its author as the leading Italian Romantic novelist of the nineteenth century. It was the work of Alessandro Manzoni, and *The Betrothed* in particular, that raised Italian fiction from the low estate to which it had fallen and made it, in the nineteenth century, assume a high place in European fiction. The simple, adventurous story that Manzoni told has captivated readers ever since it first appeared. In the best tradition of historical fiction, Manzoni presents many facets of life and culture in Milan during the 1620's, when much of Italy was under Spanish domination. In this novel, there are not only peasants and villainous nobles, who are the chief characters, but also the bravos, citizens, nuns, petty officials, churchmen, and scores of other types typical of seventeenth century Italy.

The complex and involuted history of Manzoni's revisions of his work and the drama of his artistic self-consciousness in their elaboration are as Romantic, in essence, as the story itself. *The Betrothed* underwent its first massive revision from 1823, the date of its first completion, until its eventual publication in 1827 as *Fermo e Lucia*, a revision overseen by the author's friend and advisor, Flauriel. The revision witnessed changes in the names and roles of most of the major characters, the modification of their motivation and psychology, and the excision of numerous digressions, such as the story of Gertrude, as well as endless linguistic and stylistic changes. Nevertheless, a second major revision of the retitled novel took place between its publication as *Fermo e Lucia* and its definitive form as *I promessi sposi*, which reflected not only Manzoni's concern about such issues as the work's commitment to doctrinal and historical truth but also his scrupulousness toward the language of the novel, down to its spelling, typography, and punctuation. The work underwent changes not only from edition to edition but also from copy to copy within the edition as whole pages were removed and reinserted. It would seem that the arbitrariness of time, more than artistic inevitability, governed the novel's final form. Manzoni did not stop revising it until he died.

Manzoni's Milan was alive with new ideas largely imported from France but lacked commanding figures to propound them. Milanese culture was undergoing a tumultuous change from the ideals of the Enlightenment to those of Romanticism, as the last waves of the French Revolution and the Napoleonic era ebbed. The Italians of Manzoni's time were painfully aware of their disunity, which found its most potent symbol in the absence of a national language. The creation of this national language became one of Manzoni's goals in writing *The Betrothed*, and both literary and ethical concerns would converge on it. The novel demanded a language that would be current, literary, and rich enough to express the profoundest values and ideas of seventeenth century Italy. The language also needed to remain accessible to the common reader, for whom it was intended. Manzoni found this language in Florentine during his 1827 sojourn in Florence. Thus began the linguistic revision that would eliminate from his novel the archaisms, stilted literary language, and regionalisms that impeded his goal for a national language.

Many of Manzoni's revisions illustrate his personal rejection of the Enlightenment literary tradition and his espousal of Romanticism. The first version of *The Betrothed* yokes much of the picaresque violence of Voltaire to the rustic idylls popular at the time. These passages were fated for early excision. Sir Walter Scott's *Ivanhoe* (1819) replaced the influence of Voltaire's *Candide* (1759) in the later versions. Scott's conception of the use of poetic invention for a better understanding of history impressed Manzoni. Yet history in Scott's work is essentially the picturesque background for tales of adventure, but in Manzoni's it becomes the means to an essentially moral end: understanding the limits of human freedom in the struggle between good and evil, and the particular nature of that struggle in a given age. Manzoni made the historical novel illuminate the nature of being in the world; the novel concerns itself with particular men and women and with minutely studied historical situations. If Manzoni appears obtuse about the larger historical and political implications of a major event, such as, for example, the siege of Casale, it is largely because of his concern with the individual.

Manzoni's Romanticism and his Catholicism dictated the democratic ends and themes of the work. The novel is for and about the humble folk of the world—artisans, peasants, and laborers. Such an audience conditioned both the choice of spoken Florentine as the language of the novel as well as the characterization of the protagonists. They represent their class well in their spontaneity, naturalness, thirst for justice, and sincere religiosity. By making the poor the heroes of moral struggle, Manzoni showed that they need not merely suffer history, but, by realizing the Christian message, create it. The social and ethical struggle of the work is accordingly the central struggle of Christianity: the struggle between pride and humility. In Christianity, Adam fell in pride and, in so doing, damned humanity, which had to await its redemption in the humble Christ. In *The Betrothed*, pride is represented by Don Rodrigo and the Governor of Milan, whose lives are circumscribed by an irrationality that their high positions seem to impose on them. This is typified by their code of honor, which leads them to seek Lorenzo's destruction. Humility is virtually personified by Lorenzo, Lucia, and Fra Cristoforo, who realize in their lives the values of gentleness, charity, and brotherhood. On a higher level, the struggle between pride and humility translated itself for Manzoni into the struggle between the oppressive Austrians and the subjugated Italians.

Criticism of *The Betrothed* has centered about the degree to which the novel can be said to create new values and meanings that are not reducible to a simplistic catechism. The question for critics has often been, then, whether the novel does or does not have a Christian moral. An event such as the conversion of the Un-named would then display the violence of the miraculous on the development of plot and character. Others have argued that it is the extraordinary coherence of character that is at issue, since the Un-named's fear of death and damnation conform perfectly to his previous behavior and virtually assure his conversion. Manzoni's choice of weak characters such as Don Abbondio and ultimately perhaps the Un-named himself sets into relief Manzoni's concern with the loneliness of moral choice. The authorial voice that tells the story and is aware of its outcome is unavailable to the character who must make his choice in anxiety. Manzoni's Christianity may moralize reality and offer itself as the ultimate key to the understanding of human nature, but it does so only in the end; the novel is also artistically whole, independent of Christian doctrine.

"Critical Evaluation" by James Thomas Chiampi

Bibliography:
"Alessandro Manzoni." In *Nineteenth-Century Literature Criticism*. Vol. 29, edited by Laurie DiMauro. Detroit: Gale Research, 1991. Contains a brief biography, an overview of *The Betrothed*, and excerpts form the criticism of numerous Manzoni critics. Includes bibliographic citations. An excellent starting place.

Barricelli, Gian Piero. *Alessandro Manzoni*. Boston: Twayne, 1976. The most thorough introduction to Manzoni in English. Provides a biography that focuses more on his life after his conversion to Catholicism in 1810 than on his life preceding the conversion. Examines his poetry and essays. Analysis of *The Betrothed*: its characters, styles, and themes.

Chandler, S. B. *Alessandro Manzoni: The Story of a Spiritual Quest*. Edinburgh: Edinburgh University Press, 1974. An insightful investigation of Manzoni's works, showing how the works demonstrate Manzoni's spiritual development and his movement toward a spiritual view of life.

Matteo, Sante, and Larry Peer, eds. *The Reasonable Romantic: Essays on Alessandro Manzoni.* New York: Peter Lang, 1986. A collection of critical essays on the range of Manzoni's works. Some of the essays are excerpted in *Nineteenth-Century Literature Criticism.*

Wall, Bernard. *Alessandro Manzoni.* New Haven, Conn.: Yale University Press, 1954. Provides an overview of the life of Manzoni and his role as poet and dramatist before examining *The Betrothed*, its place in literature, and the controversies of Manzoni's religion, of his use of the Italian language, and of the novel's relationship to Romanticism. Sometimes criticized for its brevity.

BETWEEN THE ACTS

Type of work: Novel
Author: Virginia Woolf (1882-1941)
Type of plot: Psychological realism
Time of plot: June, 1939
Locale: England
First published: 1941

> *Principal characters:*
> BARTHOLOMEW OLIVER, the owner of Pointz Hall
> GILES, his son
> ISA, his daughter-in-law
> MRS. LUCY SWITHIN, his widowed sister
> MRS. MANRESA and
> WILLIAM DODGE, the guests at the pageant
> MISS LA TROBE, the writer and director of the pageants

The Story:

Pointz Hall was not one of the great English houses mentioned in the guidebooks, but it was old and comfortable and pleasantly situated in a tree-fringed meadow. The house was older than the name of its owners in the county. Although they had hung the portrait of an ancestress in brocade and pearls beside the staircase and kept a watch under glass that had stopped a bullet at Waterloo, the Olivers had lived only a little more than a century in a district where the names of the villagers went back to the Domesday Book. The countryside still showed traces of the ancient Britons, the Roman road, the Elizabethan manor house, and the marks of the plow on a hill sown in wheat during Napoleon's time.

The owner of the house was Bartholomew Oliver, retired from the Indian Civil Service. With him lived his son Giles, his daughter-in-law Isa, two small grandchildren, and his widowed sister, Mrs. Lucy Swithin. Bartholomew, a disgruntled old man who lived more and more in the past, was constantly snubbing his sister, as he had done when they were children. Mrs. Swithin was a woman of careless dress, good manners, quiet faith, and great intelligence. Her favorite book was an *Outline of History*; she dreamed of a time when Piccadilly was a rhododendron forest in which the mastodon roamed. Giles Oliver was a London stockbroker who had wanted to be a farmer until circumstances decided otherwise. A misunderstanding had lately developed between him and his wife Isa, who wrote poetry in secret. She suspected that Giles had been unfaithful and fancied herself in love with Rupert Haines, a married gentleman farmer of the neighborhood. Isa thought that Mrs. Haines had the eyes of a gobbling goose.

On a June morning in 1939, Pointz Hall awoke. Mrs. Swithin, aroused by the birds, read again in the *Outline of History* until the maid brought her tea. She wondered if the afternoon would be rainy or fine, for this was the day of the pageant to raise funds for installing electric lights in the village church. Later, she went to early service. Old Bartholomew walked with his Afghan hound on the terrace where his grandson George was bent over a cluster of flowers. When the old man folded his newspaper into a cone to cover his nose and jumped suddenly at the boy, George began to cry. Bartholomew grumbled that his grandson was a crybaby and went back to his paper. From her window, Isa looked out at her son and the baby, Caro, in her perambulator that a nurse was pushing. Then she went off to order the fish for lunch. She read in Bartholomew's discarded newspaper the story of an attempted assault on a girl in the barracks at Whitehall. Returning from church, Mrs. Swithin tacked another placard on the barn where the pageant would be given if the day turned out rainy; regardless of the weather, tea would also be served there during the intermission. Mocked again by her brother, she went off to make sandwiches for the young men and women who were decorating the barn.

Giles was expected back from London in time for the pageant. The family had just decided not to wait lunch for him when Mrs. Manresa and a young man named William Dodge arrived unexpectedly and uninvited. They had intended, Mrs. Manresa explained, to picnic in the country, but when she saw the Olivers' name on the signpost, she had suddenly decided to visit her old friends. Mrs. Manresa, loud, cheerful, and vulgar, was a woman of uncertain background married to a wealthy Jew. William Dodge, she said, was an artist. He was, he declared, a clerk. Giles, arriving in the middle of lunch and finding Mrs. Manresa's showy car at the door, was furious; he and Mrs. Manresa had been having an affair. After lunch, on the terrace, he sat hating William Dodge. Finally, Mrs. Swithin took pity on Dodge's discomfort and took him off to see her brother's collection of pictures. The young man wanted to tell her that he was married but his child was not his child, that he was a pervert, that her kindness had healed his wretched day; but he could not speak.

The guests, arriving for the pageant, began to fill the chairs set on the lawn, for the afternoon was sunny and clear. Behind the thick bushes that served as a dressing room, Miss La Trobe, the author and director of the pageant, was giving the last instructions to her cast. She was something of a mystery in the village, for no one knew where she came from. There were rumors that she had kept a tea shop and had been an actress. Abrupt and restless, she walked about the fields, used strong language, and drank too much at the local pub. She was a frustrated artist. Now she was wondering if her audience would realize that she had tried to give unity to English history in her pageant and to give something of herself as well.

The pageant began. The first scene showed the age of Chaucer, with pilgrims on their way to Canterbury. Eliza Clark, who sold tobacco in the village, appeared in another scene as Queen Elizabeth. Albert, the village idiot, played her court fool. The audience hoped he would not do anything dreadful. In a play performed before Gloriana, Mrs. Otter of the End House played the old crone who had saved the true prince, the supposed beggar who fell in love with the duke's daughter. Then Miss La Trobe's vision of the Elizabethan age ended, and it was time for tea during the intermission.

Mrs. Manresa applauded; she had seen herself as Queen Elizabeth and Giles as the hero. Giles glowered. Walking toward the barn, he came on a coiled snake swallowing a toad, and he stamped on them until his tennis shoes were splattered with blood. Isa tried to catch a glimpse of Rupert Haines. Failing, she offered to show William Dodge the greenhouses. They discovered that they could talk frankly, like two strangers drawn together by unhappiness and understanding.

The pageant began again. This time the scene showed the Age of Reason. Once more, Miss La Trobe had written a play within a play; the characters had names like Lady Harpy Harraden, Sir Spaniel Lilyliver, Florinda, Valentine, and Sir Smirking Peace-be-with-you-all, a clergyman. After another brief interval, the cast reassembled for a scene from the Victorian Age. Mr. Budge, the publican, was made up as a policeman. Albert was in the hindquarters of a donkey, while the rest of the cast pretended to be on a picnic in 1860. Then Mr. Budge announced that the time had come to pack and be gone. When Isa asked Mrs. Swithin what the Victorians were like, the old woman said that they had been like Isa, William Dodge, and herself, only dressed differently.

The terrace stage had been left bare. Suddenly, the cast came running from behind the bushes, each holding a mirror in which the men and women in the audience saw themselves reflected in self-conscious poses. The time was the present of June, 1939. Swallows were sweeping homeward in the late light. Above them twelve airplanes flying in formation cut across the sky, drowning out all other sounds. The pageant was over; the audience dispersed. Mrs. Manresa and William Dodge drove away in her car. Miss La Trobe went on to the inn. There she drank and saw a vision and tried to find words in which to express it—to make people see once more, as she had tried to do that afternoon.

Darkness fell across the village and the fields. At Pointz Hall, the visitors had gone, and the family was alone. Bartholomew read the evening paper and drowsed in his chair. Mrs. Swithin took up her *Outline of History* and turned the pages while she thought of mastodons and prehistoric birds. At last, she and her brother went off to bed.

Now the true drama of the day was about to begin, ancient as the hills, secret and primitive as the black night outside. Giles and Isa would quarrel, embrace, and sleep. The curtain rose on another scene in the long human drama of enmity, love, and peace.

Critical Evaluation:

Between the Acts was completed without final revision before Virginia Woolf's suicide in 1941; in it, she returns to the tightly controlled structure, the classical unities of time and place, used before in *Mrs. Dalloway. Between the Acts* takes place all in a single day, the day of the annual village pageant, and in the house or on the grounds of Pointz Hall.

In the novel, Woolf presents a critique of patriarchy, militarism, and imperialism, themes familiar from her earlier fiction and nonfiction. Woolf's critique of male socialization becomes clear when George, Isa's small son, searches the flowerbeds and grasps a flower "complete," only to have his moment of being with the natural world shattered by the insistent presence of his grandfather Bartholomew, "a terrible peaked eyeless monster." George must identify with the patriarchal forces embodied in his Grandfather, who waves the same newspaper in which Isa will later read of the rape of a young girl carried out by soldiers.

Isa's husband, Giles, and Bartholomew are particularly identified with the powers of imperialism and male dominance, especially when Giles stamps on the snake eating a toad in a moment of parody of the militaristic man-of-action. To Woolf, the cult of masculinity contributes to the causes of war. It is against the background of a possible German invasion of England that Woolf sets the central event of the novel: Miss La Trobe's historical pageant.

Like Lily Briscoe in *To the Lighthouse*, Miss La Trobe represents Woolf's ideal of the androgynous artist, a creator who is "woman-manly." As a lesbian, however, Miss La Trobe knows a level of personal frustration and artistic anguish over the success of her pageant that is foreign to the more tranquil and asexual Lily Briscoe.

Struggling to impose an artistic unity on the chaos around her and on the tendency of the audience to "split up into scraps and fragments," Miss La Trobe's vision of history seeks to show how the past informs and shapes the present. At the pageant's conclusion, she has her actors flash mirrors before the audience in which they glimpse their own faces and forms. This suggests that the present can only be understood in the context of the past. Miss La Trobe's project in presenting her pageant is strikingly similar to Woolf's own project in all her fiction, which is to insist on the world's being both unified and fragmentary, on the persistence of the past in the present, and on an understanding that only through art can the world become conscious of itself.

The title of the novel suggests some of the ironic possibilities Woolf thought existed in the interplay between art and life. *Between the Acts* refers to the precarious time between World War I and World War II. It also refers to the events, relationships, and conversations that take place between the acts of the village pageant. Finally, the story occurs between the times when the estranged couple Giles and Isa truly communicate. Significantly, and novel's last lines are: "Then the curtain rose. They spoke." The couple's performance together merges with Miss La Trobe's artistic vision to suggest that all human lives are concerned with role playing and illusion.

The impending war, although seldom mentioned directly, is always in the background in the novel; it is briefly referred to in the spectators' conversations and more directly in the sound of airplanes at the end. The reality of war does not trivialize the efforts of the villagers to put together their amateur pageant, but instead stresses the power of art to give humanity order and meaning in times of crisis.

World War I had fragmented Western civilization both socially and psychologically, and the spectators see themselves in the pageant's mirrors as fragmented and isolated. For a moment, however, Miss La Trobe creates a unity in the audience by means of music. A state of harmony is reached wherein male and female, the one and the many, the silent and the speaking, are joined. Woolf was always searching for such a unity in her art, a way to reconcile opposites.

The novel is filled with cryptic and portentous symbolism. Written during the early years of World War II, it presents with poetic and fragmentary vision an outline of stark human drama against the backdrop of history. In Woolf's handling of background there is always an awareness of the primitive and historical past, conveyed in images of the flint arrowhead, the Roman road, or the manor house, which is the scene of the novel. England, rather than time, gives the novel its underlying theme. The pageant that presents a picture of English history from the Middle Ages to 1939 is only an interlude between the acts. The true drama is found in the lives of the trivial, selfish, stupid, frustrated, and idealistic people who watch the pageant and in the end are brought face-to-face with themselves. These people are actors in a drama that is older than Miss La Trobe's pictures out of the past. They are more important than the threat of war to come in the planes droning overhead. The novel represents Woolf's final affirmation of the artist's vision, the ability to distinguish between the false and the true.

"Critical Evaluation" by Roberta M. Hooks

Bibliography:
Gordon, Lyndall. *Virginia Woolf: A Writer's Life.* New York: W. W. Norton, 1984. An analytical biography that integrates events in Woolf's life with a thematic study of her works.
Hanson, Clare. *Virginia Woolf.* New York: St. Martin's Press, 1994. A sophisticated study of gender in Woolf's novels with specific attention to Woolf's feminism and its consequences for her works. An unusual reading of *Between the Acts* focuses on gender tensions in the novel.
Rose, Phyllis. *Woman of Letters: A Life of Virginia Woolf.* New York: Oxford University Press, 1978. A critical biography of the writer's life and works. Includes extended discussions of all her works.
Rosenman, Ellen Bayuk. *The Invisible Presence.* Baton Rouge: Louisiana State University Press, 1986. Informed by psychological theory, this study examines the bonds between mothers and daughters in Woolf's novels and her representations of the female artist. Includes a detailed chapter on Miss La Trobe in *Between the Acts.*
Rosenthal, Michael. *Virginia Woolf.* New York: Columbia University Press, 1979. Focuses on Woolf's preoccupation with form. Includes an excellent chapter on *Between the Acts.*

BEVIS OF HAMPTON

Type of work: Poetry
Author: Unknown
Type of plot: Romance
Time of plot: c. tenth century
Locale: England, the Holy Land, and Western Europe
First transcribed: c. 1200-1250

> Principal characters:
> BEVIS, a knight, heir to the estate of Hampton
> JOSYAN, a Saracen princess
> SIR MURDOUR, the usurper of Hampton
> ASCAPARD, a giant
> SABER, a knight, Bevis' uncle
> ERMYN, a Saracen king, Josyan's father
> INOR and
> BRADMOND, Saracen kings and enemies of Bevis

The Story:

The bold spirit of Bevis was first displayed when he was only seven years old. His father had been treacherously murdered, and now his mother and the assassin were engaged in shameless revelry. Bursting into the castle hall, Bevis cudgeled his mother's paramour, Sir Murdour, into senselessness. The mother, fearing future outbursts, sold him into slavery.

Honor, not slavery, awaited the courageous youth. Taken by slave merchants from England to a Saracen court, Bevis so impressed the king, Ermyn, that the monarch made the youth a chamberlain. After holding this position for eight uneventful years, Bevis began a series of remarkable exploits. The first was his single-handed slaughter of sixty Saracen warriors who made the error of deriding his Christianity. Next, he attacked and killed a man-eating boar and, to retain his trophy, beat out the brains of twelve keepers of the forest. These successes of the fifteen-year-old boy led Ermyn to place him in charge of a small troop that was to defend the kingdom against the aggression of Bradmond, a rival king. Bevis, astride his incomparable horse Arundel and wielding his good sword, Morglay, laid waste to the enemy forces. To his later misfortune, however, he spared Bradmond's life.

Bevis' valor had not escaped the attention of Josyan, the king's daughter. In fact, this fair young girl became so enamored of him that she agreed to renounce her religion and become a Christian if he would marry her. Hitherto reluctant, Bevis, under this condition, consented. When news of his daughter's apostasy reached Ermyn, the incensed king determined to get rid of her corrupter. To accomplish this task, he sent Bevis unarmed to the court of Bradmond with a sealed letter requesting the bearer's execution. Only after a considerable number of men were slain was Bevis subdued and thrown into a dungeon.

For seven long years Bevis remained in the dungeon, and during that time he grew in Christian virtue. At last divine intercession, as a reward for his piety, plus his own initiative, led to an escape in which Bevis killed two jailers and a dozen grooms. Immediately, he headed for Jerusalem to confess his sins and give thanks to God. Killing a sturdy knight and a thirty-foot giant on the way, he reached the Holy City and there received absolution, accompanied by an injunction never to marry a woman who was not a virgin.

Then, in order to be reunited with Josyan, he started toward Ermony, but on the way he learned that the maid, during his imprisonment, had married King Inor of Mounbraunt. To have one last look at his beloved, he dressed himself as a palmer and went to Mounbraunt. There Josyan, discovering his true identity, implored him to take her away. He at first refused; but when she revealed that, though seven years married, she had by magic avoided defloration, he relented.

After they had escaped from the city by trickery, Bevis turned his thoughts toward returning to England and avenging his father's death. Several years before he had learned that Saber, his uncle, was waging war against Sir Murdour and needed his nephew's help to gain the victory. Imprisonment, however, had detained Bevis, and he was to encounter other obstacles before he again saw England.

Killing two lions with one blow and subduing a thirty-foot giant, Ascapard, who then became his page, the indomitable Bevis, accompanied by his mistress, made his way to the coast. In a ship taken from the Saracens, they set sail for Germany. In Cologne, Josyan was at last baptized. Near this city, Bevis had the most perilous adventure of his life. A burning dragon was his opponent on this occasion. Only after suffering a broken rib, being knocked unconscious, and falling into a miraculous healing well, was Bevis able to defeat his enemy.

Leaving Ascapard to protect Josyan and taking with him a hundred men, Bevis finally sailed to England. Posing as a French knight, he tricked Sir Murdour, who was now his stepfather, into providing him with arms and horses. These supplies he then carried to his uncle and they prepared to make war on Sir Murdour.

Back in Cologne, meanwhile, Josyan was in trouble, for a German earl had conceived a great lust for her. After tricking the giant into leaving, he fancied that she was at his mercy. The resourceful Josyan insisted that he marry her; then on the wedding night she calmly made a slip knot in her girdle, strangled the unsuspecting German, and hung the corpse over a beam. The next day, when the deed was exposed, the unrepenting widow was sentenced to be burned; but before the sentence could be carried out, Ascapard and Bevis arrived, rescued her from the stake, and killed all who opposed them.

Taking Josyan and Ascapard with him this time, Bevis returned to England to pursue his war against Sir Murdour. Although Sir Murdour had a large army from Germany and another from Scotland, Bevis, assisted by Ascapard, Saber, and a moderate number of knights, won the battle. Sir Murdour was thrown by the victors into a caldron filled with boiling pitch and molten lead; Bevis' mother, on hearing the news, threw herself from a lofty tower.

Bevis now had avenged his father's death and regained his heritage. To complete his happiness, he married Josyan. He was not destined, however, to settle down in peace. In London, where he had gone to receive investiture, an event occurred that led him into further adventures after the son of King Edgar tried to steal Bevis' horse and had his brains knocked out by the animal's sudden kick. King Edgar was inconsolable over the loss of his son and intent on revenge, so Bevis proposed, in expiation of the crime, to settle his land on Saber and to banish himself and his horse from England.

Ascapard, after pondering this change in his master's fortunes, decided to betray him. Hastening to Mounbraunt, he made an agreement with King Inor to bring back Josyan. When the giant discovered her in a forest hut, she had just given birth to twin boys. Leaving the babies, he seized Josyan and started for Mounbraunt. Bevis, returning to the hut, took up the children and began searching for Josyan. Arriving at a large town, he decided to stay there and await news of his wife. While waiting, he entered a tournament and overcame all adversaries. The prize was the hand in marriage of a young lady, daughter and heiress of a duke. Bevis agreed to wed her after seven years, if Josyan had not by then appeared.

Saber, meanwhile, had learned, through a dream, of Josyan's plight. Accompanied by twelve knights, he overtook the giant on the road to Mounbraunt, killed him, and freed Josyan. Then began a long search for Bevis. After nearly seven years of wandering, they came to the town where Bevis was residing, and Josyan was reunited with her husband and children. Presently, news arrived that Josyan's father was in trouble: King Inor was attacking his kingdom. Bevis went to his rescue, defeated King Inor, and reached a reconciliation with his father-in-law. When Ermyn died a short time later, Bevis' son Guy became King of Ermony. A second empire came to the family soon after; in another fight with King Inor, Bevis killed him and became the ruler of Mounbraunt. To both these countries, Bevis, by the method of rewarding converts and butchering recalcitrants, brought Christianity.

Again he was not destined to rule in peace. News came that his uncle's lands had been taken by King Edgar. Hurrying to the assistance of Saber, Bevis and his two sons led an attack on the city of London in which sixty thousand men were killed. To end the slaughter, Edgar agreed that his only daughter should marry Mile, son of Bevis.

Guy, Bevis' other son, resumed his rule of Ermony; and Bevis and Josyan returned to Mounbraunt. There Josyan, stricken by a mortal disease, died in her husband's arms. A few minutes later the peace of death descended also on that incomparable knight, Sir Bevis of Hampton.

Critical Evaluation:
Readers accustomed to the tightly constructed plots of modern novels and narrative poems may find the plethora of action, the wandering story line, the frequent digressions, and the disregard for verisimilitude that characterize *Bevis of Hampton* strange, and even disturbing. The hero of this thirteenth century metrical narrative is able to slay men and monsters alike with virtual impunity; a one-man army, he appears invincible against forces considerably larger and often better armed. He engages frequently in adventures that can only be classified as fantastic. His unswerving devotion to his beloved Josyan and to his Christian faith survive every test. There seems to be nothing he cannot accomplish to rectify the wrongs done to him and to his family.

Such are the elements of the medieval romance, and *Bevis of Hampton* is typical of the genre. Its appearance in numerous manuscript versions and in a number of languages, as well as its presence among the first printed texts in England in the late fifteenth century, attest its popularity among audiences for over three centuries. The poem is one of the most important of those that celebrate Britain in describing the exploits of heroes such as King Horn, Guy of Warwick, and King Arthur and the knights of his Round Table. While most versions treat Bevis as an English hero, some scholars have noted parallels between his story and that of a number of Continental figures; it may be that earlier stories were recast by an Anglo-Norman scribe to create a heroic story that would satisfy audiences in the land conquered by French invaders little more than a century before *Bevis of Hampton* was composed. Such an explanation would be consistent with the pattern followed by many authors of medieval works, who placed less value on invention than on pleasing audiences with variations on well-known stories about characters with whom they could identify.

The adventures Bevis experiences are typical of those described in romances of the period: He is wrongfully denied his patronage and inheritance, he is exiled from his homeland, he overcomes monumental odds in battle, he falls in love with a beautiful maiden from whom he is separated and whom he must win by force of deeds. Like so many of the knights celebrated in romances of the period, Bevis is engaged, throughout his many adventures, on a quest—here, the quest to regain his rightful place as head of his family and lands, and to claim as his bride the woman he loves. Thirteenth century audiences seem to have been less concerned about unity of plot than they were in hearing about the adventures of individuals engaged in exploits of personal daring.

One of the principal distinguishing characteristics of *Bevis of Hampton* is the hero's devotion to his Christian faith. It is not uncommon for heroes in romances to struggle against pagan infidels; the real-life exploits of European knights in the various Crusades provided an abundance of material for the fertile imagination of scribes and storytellers wishing to please audiences made up of the nobility by creating an ancestry for them that included heroic figures both real and fictional. Unfortunately, many modern readers may find the attitude expressed in the poem disturbing, since the non-Christians are presented in a highly unfavorable light. The hero's exploits in slaying Saracen warriors are treated with great relish, and presumably were met with great approval by medieval audiences. The hatred with which Christian Europe looked upon the Islamic nations, which in the European view had transgressed on the most holy lands of Christendom, was a commonplace on which authors could count to evoke feelings of admiration and sympathy for knights who furthered the cause of Christianity and who remained constant to their faith. Unquestionably, the bounds of realism are strained in this poem, since the young Bevis is snatched away from his Christian home when he is only seven, yet he remains constant to the tenets of his faith while living among people who have only disdain for that creed. Even after he has committed himself to Josyan and demonstrated his determination to maintain his fidelity to her despite temptation and hardship, his commitment to his faith holds a higher place in his system of values, as he makes clear when he insists that she must convert to Christianity before he can marry her.

Like the young hero of Wolfram von Eschenbach's *Parzifal* (c. 1200-1210), a work contemporary with *Bevis of Hampton*, the title character of this romance is presented as a model of the Christian knight, fighting not only for himself but also for his Church, exhibiting the virtues one should emulate. The audiences of romance expected such instruction, and the entertainment they gained from hearing of the knight's exploits simply reinforced the lesson they gained from seeing Christianity triumph over other religions. The ability of knights such as Bevis to overcome great odds in serving his faith simply gave evidence to them that God, who had come down to earth to establish the Christian faith, would always support those who fought for His cause. This theme explains both the action and motivation of heroes who were much beloved by audiences of centuries ago.

Bevis of Hampton is of special importance because it also contains typically English elements and thus serves as a fine example of the transition from the rude Anglo-Saxon tales to the more refined French romances that prevailed after 1066. This quality of the poem may be seen by the later additions of much foreign material to a typically English celebration of a local hero. Although early romances are seldom found to have great unity of plot, *Bevis of Hampton* probably violates this principle as much as such a form can. As a metrical romance, *Bevis of Hampton* is not a success, but it is historically significant and contains that most common charm of early tales: the exuberant force of great events told in a fast-moving, sometimes even humorous, fashion.

Bevis of Hampton is often spoken of and linked together with Guy of Warwick: both English heroes upholding the Christian faith in Saracen lands, valiant youths from a very early age. They are both Crusades knights, although the romance of *Bevis of Hampton* is far more Christian in theme and characterization.

The story of Bevis probably originated in France; there are three different versions in verse and one in prose. The poem was translated into Italian, Scandinavian prose, Dutch verse, and Celtic versions. Its popularity is further attested by the numerous references in other medieval works.

From studies of the dialect, it appears that the work was composed in the south of England, probably near Southampton, where Bevis is supposed to have been born.

The narrative encompasses a longer period of time than many medieval romances; it begins when Bevis is sold into slavery at the age of seven, continues through the time when his grown sons fight alongside him, to the moment when both he and his faithful wife die within a few minutes of each other, presumably at a mature age.

Although there is little character differentiation, there are realistic touches such as detailed description of hand-to-hand combats, of weapons, and of military engines. The author also shows his knowledge of London in the passages where Bevis and his sons resist the inhabitants aroused by the king's evil steward.

The author uses an entire arsenal of the material of romance: typical expressions of grief, pious benedictions, greetings, oaths, similes, transitional phrases, promises, character traits, methods of wounding and slaying enemies. Much of this repetition is necessitated by demands of the rhyme scheme of metrical romance. *Bevis of Hampton* begins with the oral formula of the typical metrical romance, probably used by traveling minstrels to gather crowds in a market place: "Lordinges, herkneth to me tale!" This tale moves rapidly, has a Christian theme carefully adhered to, and, not unlike other such romances, has comic touches in several scenes. It celebrates one of England's earliest and most stalwart heroes.

"Critical Evaluation" by Laurence W. Mazzeno

Bibliography:
Billings, Anna Hunt. *A Guide to the Middle English Metrical Romances*. New York: Haskell House, 1965. Dated in its commentary, but this study contains useful details about the date of composition, authorship, and poetic qualities of *Bevis of Hampton*. Helpful as a starting point for further scholarly study.
Loomis, Laura Alandis Hibbard. *Medieval Romance in England: A Study of the Sources and Analogues of the Non-Cyclic Metrical Romances*. Rev. ed. New York: Burt Franklin, 1963. Discusses the sources of *Bevis of Hampton* and its international flavor, achieved through the wanderings of the hero. Includes a bibliography of secondary sources.
Holmes, U. T. *A History of Old French Literature from the Origins to 1300*. New York: F. S. Crofts, 1938. Discusses *Bevis of Hampton* as one of several *chansons de geste* that were immediately popular and that influenced subsequent literature in a number of countries. Believes the work is misclassified as a romance.
Mehl, Dieter. *The Middle English Romances of the Thirteenth and Fourteenth Centuries*. London: Routledge & Kegan Paul, 1968. Describes the form of the work and traces its popularity with medieval audiences. Notes that the writer achieves unity by focusing on the hero; the emphasis throughout is on action rather than ideology.
Rickard, P. *Britain in Medieval French Literature, 1100-1500*. Cambridge, England: Cambridge University Press, 1956. Links the Continental version of *Bevis of Hampton* with other French works dealing with the theme of "rebellion against English domination."

BEYOND GOOD AND EVIL

Type of work: Philosophy
Author: Friedrich Wilhelm Nietzsche (1844-1900)
First published: Jenseits von Gut und Böse: Vorspiel einer Philosophie der Zukunft, 1886
(English translation, 1907)

In *Thus Spake Zarathustra* (1883-1884) Friedrich Nietzsche proclaims in parable and pseudo-prophetical cries the philosophy of the Superman, the being who would transcend humanity in having the will to power, going beyond conventional morality and making one's own law. *Beyond Good and Evil* carries forward, in a somewhat more temperate style, the same basic ideas, but with particular attention to values and morality. The central thesis of the book is that the proud, creative individual goes beyond good and evil in action, thought, and creation.

Ordinary people are fearful, obedient, and slavelike. The true aristocrat of the spirit, the noble, is neither slave nor citizen, but rather is a lawmaker, the one who determines by acts and decisions what is right or wrong, good or bad. The aristocrat is what the novelist Fyodor Dostoevski in *Crime and Punishment* (1886) calls the "extraordinary" person. To sharpen his image of the noble, Nietzsche describes two primary types of morality: master-morality and slave-morality. Moral values are determined by either the rulers or the ruled. Rulers naturally regard the terms "good" and "bad" as synonymous with "noble" and "despicable." They apply moral values to the individual, venerating the aristocrat; but those who are ruled apply moral values primarily to acts, grounding the value of an act in its utility, its service to them. For the noble, pride and strength are virtues; for the "slaves" patience, self-sacrifice, meekness, and humility are virtues. The aristocrat scorns cowardice, self-abasement, and the telling of lies; as a member of the ruling class he or she must seek the opposite moral qualities. According to Nietzsche:

> The noble type of man regards himself as a determiner of values; he does not require to be approved of; he passes the judgment: "What is injurious to me is injurious in itself"; he knows that it is he himself only who confers honour on things; he is a creator of values. He honours whatever he recognizes in himself: such morality is self-glorification.

Those who are ruled, the slaves, construct a morality that will make their suffering bearable. They are pessimistic in their morality and come to regard the "good" person as the "safe" person, one who is "good-natured, easily deceived, perhaps a little stupid, un *bonhomme.*"

Nietzsche concludes that in slave morality "language shows a tendency to approximate the significations of the words 'good' and 'stupid.'" Perhaps because Nietzsche regarded love considered "as a passion" as of noble origin, he maintained in the chapter titled "Apophthegms and Interludes" that "What is done out of love always takes place beyond good and evil."

A proper interpretation of Nietzsche's work is possible only if one remembers that Nietzsche is not talking about actual political rulers and the ruled, although even in this particular case something of his general thesis applies. He is speaking instead of those who have the power and will to be a law to themselves to pass their own moral judgments according to their inclinations, and of those who do not: The former are the masters, the latter, the slaves. A revealing statement of the philosophical perspective from which this view becomes possible is the apophthegm, "There is no such thing as moral phenomena, but only a moral interpretation of phenomena."

Nietzsche must be given credit for having anticipated to a considerable extent many of the prevailing tendencies in twentieth century philosophy. He is sophisticated about language: He understands the persuasive function of philosophy, and he is unrelenting in his naturalistic and relativistic interpretation of human values and moralities. If he errs at all in his philosophic objectivity, it is in endorsing the way of power as if, in some absolute sense, that is the way, the only right way. This flaw in Nietzsche's disdain of dogmatism, this capitulation to dogmatism in his own case, is one cause of the ironic character of his book.

Another weakness in the author that makes something of a mockery out of his veneration of the Superman is his fear of failure and rejection. The fear is so strong that it comes to the surface of certain passages despite what must have been the author's desire to keep it hidden. Certainly he would not have appreciated the irony of having others discover that he himself is the slave he so much despises. For example, in the last few pages of the book Nietzsche writes that "Every deep thinker is more afraid of being understood than of being misunderstood." A little later, in describing the philosopher, he writes: "A philosopher: alas, a being who often runs away from himself, is often afraid of himself." He ends the book with a passage which begins, "Alas! what are you, after all, my written and painted thoughts!" and ends, "but nobody will divine . . . how ye looked in your morning, you sudden sparks and marvels of my solitude, you, my old, beloved-evil thoughts!" Although in context such passages seem to be part of Nietzsche's pose of superiority, it is interesting that out of context they take on another, revealing meaning.

Nietzsche begins his book with a chapter on the "Prejudices of Philosophers." He claims that philosophers pretend to doubt everything, but in the exposition of their views they reveal the prejudices they mean to communicate. Philosophers of the past have tried to derive human values from some outside sources; the result has been that what they reveal is nothing more than their own dogmatic "frog perspective." Nietzsche, on the other hand, prides himself on being one of the "new" philosophers, one who suggests that the traditional values may be intimately related to their evil opposites.

Nietzsche chides traditional philosophers for scurrying after Truth as if she were a woman. He argues that false opinions are often better than true ones, that the only test of an opinion is not whether it is true or false but whether it is "life-furthering, life-preserving, species-preserving, perhaps species-rearing." This is the point at which his own dogmatism shows itself: In making "species-rearing" the criterion of a worthy idea he shows his own prejudice in favor of the man of power. He is unabashed in his preference and argues that the recognition of the value of untruth impugns the traditional ideas of value and places his philosophy beyond good and evil. Nietzsche, declaring himself one who wishes to bring about a transvaluation of all values, argues that there is no more effective way than to begin by supposing that conventional morality is a sign of slavery and weakness. The free person, the one strong enough to be independent, sees through the pretenses of philosophers and moralists; such a person laughs, and creates a new world.

According to Nietzsche himself, there is danger in his philosophy. In fact, he takes pride in that danger. He identifies himself with the "philosophers of the dangerous 'Perhaps'"—that is, with philosophers who insist that "perhaps" everyone else is mistaken. He offers certain "tests" that one can use to determine whether he is ready for independence and command, and he says that one should not avoid these tests, "although they constitute perhaps the most dangerous game one can play." He chooses a dangerous name for the new philosophers: "tempters."

Speaking for the "philosophers of the future," the "opposite ones," Nietzsche writes: "We believe that severity, violence, slavery, danger in the street and in the heart, secrecy, stoicism, tempter's art and deviltry of every kind,—that everything wicked, terrible, tyrannical, preda-tory, and serpentine in man, serves as well for the elevation of the human species as its opposite."

Considered coolly, what is this danger and deviltry of which Nietzsche is so fond? It is nothing more than the possibility of new lines of development for the human spirit. The danger and the deviltry are such only in relation to the rule-bound spirits of conventional people. Nietzsche is philosopher enough to know that the human being is too complex an organism ever to have been confined or exhausted by ways of life already tried and endorsed. He calls attention to the value of revolt by playing the devil or tempter. The "most dangerous game," or the "big hunt," is humanity's free search for new ways of being. The hunting domain is extensive; it is the entire range of human experience, both actual and possible. Furthermore, there is no need or use in taking "hundreds of hunting assistants," Nietzsche points out, for each person must search alone; people must do everything for themselves in order to learn anything.

Nietzsche's objection to Christianity is that it has been a major force in limiting humanity by imposing a static morality. Since Nietzsche thinks of humanity's most important creative function as the creation of a new self, since he would urge each person, as an artist, to use himself or herself as material and fashion a new self, he rejects as life-defeating any force that works against such a creative function. He argues that people with neither the strength nor the intelligence to recognize the differences among people, to distinguish the nobles from the slaves, have fashioned Christianity with the result that humanity has become nothing more than "a gregarious animal, something obliging, sickly, mediocre."

Whether one agrees with Nietzsche in his estimate of Christianity and philosophy, no one can justifiably deny his claim that to look beyond good and evil, to throw away conventional modes of thought, is to provide oneself with a challenging, even a liberating, experience. The old "tempter" tempts readers into a critical consideration of their values, and that is all to the good.

Bibliography:
Chessick, Richard D. *A Brief Introduction to the Genius of Nietzsche.* Lanham, Md.: University Press of America, 1983. One section deals specifically with *Beyond Good and Evil.* A wonderful primer for understanding the concepts of nihilism and eternal recurrence.
Kaufman, Walter Arnold. *Nietzsche: Philosopher, Psychologist, Antichrist.* 4th rev. ed. Prince-ton, N.J.: Princeton University Press, 1974. Underscores the radical nature of Nietzsche's philosophy, especially given the Christian focus of the European literary world of his time.
Mencken, H. L. "Beyond Good and Evil." In *Friedrich Nietzsche.* New Brunswick: Transac-tion, 1993. A sympathetic treatment of Nietzsche's work. Probes Nietzsche's attacks on conventional morality.
Solomon, Robert C., ed. *Nietzsche: A Collection of Critical Essays.* Garden City, N.J.: Anchor Press, 1973. A valuable collection of essays by such greats as Thomas Mann, George Bernard Shaw, and Hermann Hesse. Discusses Nietzsche's views on nihilism, moral change, and eternal recurrence.
Stack, George J. *Nietzsche: Man, Knowledge and Will to Power.* Durango, Colo.: Hollowbrook Publishing, 1994. A modern and critical analysis of the major tenets of *Beyond Good and Evil.* Easy to follow and elucidating. Extended bibliography, detailed index, and footnotes.

THE BIG ROCK CANDY MOUNTAIN

Type of work: Novel
Author: Wallace Stegner (1909-1993)
Type of plot: Historical realism
Time of plot: 1905-1932
Locale: North Dakota, Washington, Saskatchewan, Montana, Utah, and Nevada
First published: 1943

> *Principal characters:*
> HARRY (BO) MASON, a bootlegger
> ELSA (NORGAARD) MASON, his wife
> CHESTER (CHET) and
> BRUCE, their sons
> LAURA BETTERTON, Chet's wife

The Story:

After her mother died and her father married her best friend, Elsa Norgaard, not yet nineteen, left her home in Minnesota to live with her uncle in Hardanger, North Dakota. In 1905, Hardanger was a little town on the edge of the frontier. There she met Harry Mason, better known as Bo, who ran a combination bowling alley, pool hall, and blind pig (an illegal bar).

Several years older than Elsa, Bo had run away from his abusive father when he was fourteen. Restless and ambitious, he was looking for a place that was just opening up where he could make his fortune. Elsa was attracted to Bo, who could be charming. Despite misgivings about his temper, when Bo proposed, Elsa accepted. Bo and his partner bought a hotel in Grand Forks, North Dakota, and ran it for seven years. Bo and Elsa had two boys: Chester (Chet) and Bruce.

When a customer paid his bar bill with gold dust from the Klondike, Bo and his partner decided to move to Alaska. While in Seattle waiting to sail, Chester and Bruce came down with scarlet fever. The partner went while Bo, chaffing and impatient, stayed. Bo and Elsa bought a café near a lumber camp. After Elsa's arm was injured, Bo was increasingly impatient with the café, which made little money, and with Bruce, who clung to his mother. When Bo lost his temper and mistreated Bruce, Elsa locked him out.

Elsa could not run the café by herself. She placed Chet and Bruce in an orphanage, swallowed her pride, and moved back to her father's home.

Bo went to Canada and opened a boardinghouse for railroad workers, selling them bootleg liquor at night. Prospering but lonely, he begged Elsa to come back to him. In 1914, Elsa and the boys went with him to Whitemud, Saskatchewan. For the next five years, they lived in town during the winters and on their homestead during the summers. The price of wheat was high but yields were low. In 1918, they ended the summer without enough money to live on that winter.

In late October, there were rumors of a flu epidemic. Alcohol, although illegal, was considered good medicine. Bo drove to Montana on primitive roads and bought enough to fill his car. On the way back, a blizzard hit. Badly frostbitten, he soon had pneumonia as well. When Elsa and Bruce got the flu, Chet sold the liquor. Profits were good, and Bo went into bootlegging on a steady basis.

The next year, when prohibition went into effect in the United States, Bo bought a faster car and they moved to Great Falls, Montana. When a large operation pressured Bo into working for them, he moved his family to Salt Lake City. Here Chet and Bruce attended high school. A gifted athlete, Chet excelled at baseball. Bruce was more academically inclined. He skipped a couple of grades and was graduated from high school with Chet.

At seventeen, Chet hoped to play professional baseball and was increasingly serious about a young woman, Laura Betterton, who was twenty-one. Concerned, Bo and Elsa arranged for Chet to work for a local semi-pro team in the hope that he would eventually play for them. One evening the police raided the house. Chet was home alone but Bo soon arrived. Both were taken to the police station, though Chet was not charged. Embarrassed, Chet gave up hopes for a baseball career and eloped with Laura. Both fathers insisted on an annulment, but Chet and Laura soon ran off again and moved to Rapid City, South Dakota.

After completing college, Bruce went to law school at the University of Minnesota. Elsa was stricken with breast cancer and had a mastectomy. In 1931, Chet lost his job and moved home with Laura and their child. Chet was washed up at twenty-three, and even Laura left him. Shortly after, he succumbed to pneumonia.

Bo invested in a casino in Reno, Nevada, his most profitable venture ever. Afraid that it would not last, he sold his share after a few months. When Elsa's cancer returned, they moved back to Salt Lake City. Bruce left school to help take care of her. Bo, unable to deal with her illness, was gone much of the time. When Elsa died, they buried her beside Chet.

Bruce returned to the University of Minnesota. Bo invested the last of his money in a mine deal that did not pay off. Old and lonely, his money gone, Bo had no more grand schemes for the future, no more places to move toward. As Bruce was being graduated from law school, he learned that his father had shot the mistress who had spurned him and then shot himself. While arranging the funeral, Bruce tried to make sense of his father's life and death. Although he had hated Bo and revered Elsa, he realized that both parents were a part of him.

Critical Evaluation:
The Big Rock Candy Mountain, Wallace Stegner's fifth novel, was his first commercial success. All of Stegner's fiction starts from his own experience, but *The Big Rock Candy Mountain* is the most autobiographical. Bo Mason is modeled after Stegner's father, Elsa after his mother, Chet after his older brother, and Bruce after himself. Stegner, who did not finish the book until after his father's death, says that writing about the father-son relationship was a way to exorcise his father.

Often categorized as regional literature, *The Big Rock Candy Mountain* is set in the West, in places in which Stegner had lived and which he knew intimately. His is an accurate, detailed picture of the language, the customs, and the psychology of the people who lived there. A major theme of the book is the attraction of the mythic West, the place where a person can start over and build a new, more prosperous life. *The Big Rock Candy Mountain*, described in an old song, is a symbol of such a place, and Bo's whole life is devoted to finding it.

The novel depicts a period of time between the old days, when the West was still a frontier, and the modern period, which had not yet begun. Bo comes from a long line of pioneers who had been moving farther west with each generation. Like his ancestors, he was born with an "itch in his bones" to find a place where he could realize the great American dream of success and independence, but he was born too late and the best opportunities have been taken. Many who migrated west did so to homestead farmland, and Bo does homestead in Canada, but the only land left is marginal and produces a good crop only occasionally. The only real opportunities Bo finds are outside the law.

Elsa's father also felt the lure of the frontier. He left Norway because he hoped to do better in America, but he wandered only as far as Minnesota and settled down. Elsa rejects her father and his way of life because his marrying her best friend is intolerable. Perhaps she finds Bo attractive because he is different from her father, and when her father objects to the match, she plunges ahead with the marriage. Although she rejects her father, what Elsa wants most is a home and a family and roots. The desires of the restless man and the nesting woman will always be in conflict.

As a result of their vagabond existence, the Mason family is doomed to be rootless. Toward the end of the book, Bruce realizes that having lived so many places, he does not know where home is, but it is someplace west of the Missouri River. The Mason family is isolated socially because Bo's bootlegging activities keep them outside respectable society. They have broken the ties with their own families. Bo, Elsa, Chet, and Bruce have only one another—and the relationships in this family are uneasy. Bo loves Elsa and the boys but feels his family obligations are holding him back from realizing his dream. Elsa loves Bo but feels she is a burden to him. Just as Bo and Elsa left home at a young age, so too do Chet and Bruce escape from their parents' way of life as soon as possible. The Mason family is like many other American families: The urge to move ever westward results in the social disruption of the family and the absence of community.

At the beginning of the book, Elsa and Bo's points of view dominate. As Chet and Bruce grow up, their voices are heard as well, and the relationship between father and sons is another important theme. Chet is more like Bo, athletic, a man of action, independent. Embarrassed by Bo's bootlegging activities, he runs away from home at seventeen but cannot make it on his own. A failure, he dies at twenty-three.

Bruce, who is small, unathletic, and bookish, has mixed feelings about his father. As a boy, he admires some of Bo's talents, but he is most often the target of Bo's temper when things go wrong. The only time he feels close to his father is in Saskatchewan when Bo kills a snake: Death is the one thing they share. As he grows older, he escapes to school and books. Eventually he chooses to study law—a direct rejection of Bo's lifelong habit of living outside it. When Elsa is dying, Bruce cannot understand Bo's self-centeredness, and his hatred grows more intense. After Elsa dies and he discovers that Bo has given her clothes to his mistress, he walks out. He never sees Bo alive again.

Elsa's and Bo's points of view dominate the first three-fourths of the book, dramatizing the conflict between the restless man and the nesting woman. Bruce's point of view, which controls the latter one-fourth, is much more reflective and tends toward a stream-of-consciousness narration. Bruce's sections, the ones most associated with Stegner's own voice, are more authoritative. Much of his perspective makes Elsa seem like a saint while Bo is condemned for his shortcomings.

Only when Bruce is making arrangements for Bo's funeral does he take a more enlightened view of his father. He acknowledges that Bo was a competent carpenter, mechanic, and story-teller, that "his qualities were the raw material for a notable man," and that in an earlier time he might have been great. He also realizes that family was important to Bo. Bruce comes to understand that he is the product not only of Bo and Elsa but of all his other ancestors. He cannot disown any part of himself. Instead, he must find a way to synthesize the restless chaser of dreams with the socially responsible person to become a complete man.

Eunice Pedersen Johnston

Bibliography:
Arthur, Anthony, ed. *Critical Essays on Wallace Stegner*. Boston: G. K. Hall, 1982. Includes two reviews of *The Big Rock Candy Mountain* written when it was first published and several critical essays that analyze themes, point of view, and autobiographical influences.

Lewis, Merrill, and Lorene Lewis. *Wallace Stegner*. Boise, Idaho: Boise State College, 1972. A brief overview of Stegner's life and work.

Robinson, Forrest Glen, and Margaret G. Robinson. *Wallace Stegner*. Boston: Twayne, 1977. Includes biographical information and a discussion of Stegner's fiction and nonfiction, including *The Big Rock Candy Mountain*.

Stegner, Wallace, and Richard W. Etulain. *Conversations with Wallace Stegner on Western History and Literature*. Salt Lake City: University of Utah Press, 1983. Stegner discusses his life and his writing as well as his views on literature and history.

Willrich, Patricia Rowe. "A Perspective on Wallace Stegner." *The Virginia Quarterly Review* 67 (Spring, 1991): 240-259. An overview of Stegner's life and work. Discusses the autobiographical material in his writings and his role as a Western writer.

THE BIG SKY

Type of work: Novel
Author: A. B. Guthrie, Jr. (1901-1991)
Type of plot: Adventure
Time of plot: 1830-1843
Locale: Western United States
First published: 1947

> *Principal characters:*
> BOONE CAUDILL, a mountain man
> TEAL EYE, his Indian wife
> JIM DEAKINS, his friend
> DICK SUMMERS, an old hunter
> JOURDONNAIS, a keelboat captain
> POORDEVIL, a half-witted Blackfoot
> ELISHA PEABODY, a Yankee speculator

The Story:

In 1830, Boone Caudill set out alone for St. Louis and the West after a fight with his father. Taking his father's rifle with him, he headed for Louisville to get out of the state before his father could catch him. On the road, he met Jim Deakins, an easygoing redhead, and the two decided to go west together. At Louisville, where the sheriff and Boone's father were waiting for the runaway, he and Jim were separated. Boone escaped by swimming the Ohio River to the Indiana shore.

When Boone was falsely accused of attempted theft and jailed, Jim, who had followed him after their separation, stole the sheriff's keys and released him. Together the boys continued west.

In St. Louis, they signed on as part of the crew of the keelboat *Mandan*. Most of the crew were French, as was the leader, Jourdonnais. The boat was headed for the country of the Blackfeet with a store of whiskey and other goods to trade for furs. Teal Eye, the young daughter of a Blackfoot chief, was also on board the ship. She had been separated from her tribe for some time; Jourdonnais hoped to gain the friendship of the Indians by returning the young woman to them.

The keelboat moved slowly upstream by means of poles, a tow rope, and oars. Boone and Jim found a friend in Dick Summers, the hunter for the *Mandan*, whose job was to scout for Indians and keep the crew supplied with meat. He made Boone and Jim his assistants. Jourdonnais was worried about getting to Blackfoot country before winter, and he worked the crew hard. At last, they passed into the upper river beyond the mouth of the Platte River. All the greenhorns, including Boone and Jim, were initiated by being dunked in the river and having their heads shaved.

At last they were in buffalo country. Summers took Boone with him to get some fresh meat. Attacked by a hunting party of Sioux, the white men escaped unharmed, but Summers expected trouble from the hostile Indians farther along the line. A few days later, the *Mandan* was ambushed by a large Indian war party. Only the swivel gun on the deck of the boat saved the men from death.

Shortly before the *Mandan* arrived at Fort Union, two men tried to sabotage the cargo. At Fort Union, Jourdonnais accused the American Fur Company trader McKenzie of trying to stop him. McKenzie denied the charge, but he tried to argue Jourdonnais out of continuing upriver and offered to pay double value for the *Mandan*'s cargo. Jourdonnais refused. At Fort Union, Boone met his Uncle Zeb, an old-time mountain man. He predicted that the days of hunting and trapping in open country were nearly gone. Boone and Jim, however, did not believe him.

When the *Mandan* arrived in Blackfoot country, Teal Eye escaped. The crew began to build a fort and trading post. One day, Indians attacked and killed all but the three hunters: Boone, Jim, and Summers. For seven years these three hunted together, and Summers made real mountain men out of the other two. In the spring of 1837, the three headed for a rendezvous on the Seeds-Kee-Dee River, where they could sell their furs and gamble, drink, and fight with other mountain men. They took with them a half-witted Blackfoot named Poordevil.

At the rendezvous, Boone killed a man who said that he was going to take Poordevil's scalp. Then, after they had had their fill of women and liquor, the three friends left the camp. Summers, however, did not go hunting with them. No longer able to keep up the pace of the mountain men, he went back to settle in Missouri. Boone, Jim, and Poordevil headed up the Yellowstone toward Blackfoot country. The journey was Boone's idea. He knew that Teal Eye was now a grown woman. Her beauty had remained in his memory all those years, and he wanted her for his wife. On the way to the Three Forks, Boone stole a horse from the Crow Indians and took a Crow scalp, two actions that would help him make friends with the Blackfoot Indians.

They came upon a Blackfoot village ravaged by smallpox, but Boone refused to stop until he was certain that Teal Eye was dead. At last he located her. She was with a small band led by Red Horn, her brother, who sold her to Boone.

Life was good to Boone. For five years he lived happily among the Blackfoot Indians with Teal Eye as his wife. Jim lived in the Blackfoot camp also, but he often left for months at a time to go back down the Missouri. He craved companionship, while Boone enjoyed living away from crowds. On one of his trips, Jim met Elisha Peabody, a shrewd Yankee speculating upon the future prosperity of the Oregon Territory, who wanted someone to show him a pass where wagons could cross the mountains. Jim and Boone contracted to show him a suitable pass. Before Boone left, Teal Eye told him that he would have a son when he returned.

The expedition had bad luck. Indians stole all the horses and wounded Jim badly. Then snow fell, destroying all chances to get food. Finally, Boone was able to shoot some mountain goats. Jim recovered from his wound, and the party went ahead on foot. Boone and Jim showed Peabody the way across the mountains and into the Columbia Valley. It was spring when Boone returned to Teal Eye and his son.

The child, born blind, had a tinge of red in his hair. The baby's blindness brought a savage melancholy to Boone. Then some of the old Indians hinted that the red hair showed the child was Jim's baby. Boone laid a trap to catch Jim with Teal Eye. Jim, suspecting nothing, found Teal Eye alone in her lodge; he tried to comfort her about her child's blindness and the ugly mood of her husband. Boone mistook the intent of Jim's conversation. Entering the lodge, he shot Jim in the chest, killing him. He cursed Teal Eye and left the Blackfoot camp. Then he headed back to Kentucky to see his mother before she died.

In Kentucky, he found his brother married and taking care of the farm. Boone grew restless. Slowly it came to him that he had been wrong about Jim and Teal Eye, for he noticed that one of his brother's children had a tinge of red hair. His mother said that there had been red hair in the family. When a neighbor girl insisted that he marry her because he had made love to her, Boone started back to the West. He longed both for freedom and for Teal Eye.

637

In Missouri, he visited Summers, who now had a wife and a farm. Over their whiskey, Boone revealed to Summers that he had killed Jim. He knew now that he had made a mistake. Everything was spoiled for him—Teal Eye and all the West. The day of the mountain man was nearly over; farmers were going to Oregon. Without saying good-bye, he stumbled out into the night. Summers could see him weaving along the road for a short distance. Then the darkness swallowed him, and he was gone.

Critical Evaluation:

In the tradition of James Fenimore Cooper's Leatherstocking romances, *The Big Sky* is distinguished among other fine historical novels for its realism and sharp insight into the psychology of the American Western pioneer. Like Cooper's adventure fiction, A. B. Guthrie's book explores the clash between two cultures: that of the retreating Indian tribes and that of the advancing Yankee frontiersmen. As the frontier expands westward, the Indians are forced to surrender their lands, their freedom, and their spiritual heritage. In the unequal struggle, the white pioneer, too, loses a portion of his heritage: a sense of idealism.

The "big sky" of Guthrie's title is the vast open land of the frontier, once teeming with wildlife, but slowly—even within the chronology of the novel, 1830 to 1843—changing, with the slaughter of buffalo, beaver, and other creatures of the forest and plains. In his descriptions of the land, its vegetation, and its animals, as well as of the rough frontiersmen, Guthrie has the eye of a naturalist; the smallest detail does not escape his attention. From *The Big Sky*, one learns how deer, elk, and mountain goats survive in the wilderness, how rivermen operate a keelboat, how fur hunters kill and strip game, and how mountain men endure the bitter northern winters. Unlike many other adventure stories treating the West, Guthrie's novel is without sentimentality. For the hunters, traders, and marginal farmers of the outlying territories, life is hard and often brutal. In his realism, Guthrie does not gloss over the harsh truths of the time. Trapped in a winter storm without food, Beauchamp becomes a cannibal and devours his dead companion, Zenon. Boone Caudill murders his best friend, Jim Deakins, whom he wrongly suspects of fathering his son. Guthrie's treatment of the Indians is similarly unsentimental. The squaws who mate with the white hunters are described, for the most part, as dirty, complaisant whores; whole tribes, like the Piegans, are wiped out by smallpox; others are reduced to the condition of drunkards. Poordevil, the Blackfoot who accompanies Boone, Jim, Dick Summers, and the other trappers, is a hopeless alcoholic. Thus, to Guthrie, the clash between the two cultures brutalizes both the white people and the native Indians.

In his analysis of the characters' motivations, the author is also a tough-minded realist. His protagonist, Boone, is a violent, headstrong, mostly insensitive man whose redeeming virtue is his loyalty. Throughout most of his adventures, he trusts, with good reason, his longtime friend Jim. Yet, at the last, he kills Jim when he fears, mistakenly, that his friend has betrayed him. In a similar vengeful action, he abandons his beloved Indian wife, Teal Eye, when he suspects her of adultery. From these impulsive actions he brings about the ruin of his dreams. Guthrie once wrote that the theme of *The Big Sky* (paraphrasing Oscar Wilde) is that each man destroys the thing he loves best. Nevertheless, Boone's destructive impulse results as much from his early experiences as from his conscious will. Abused by his father, robbed by the clever rascal Jonathan Bedwell, cheated by the law, Boone has come to regard men warily, as objects of his revenge. His passions, too elemental to be curbed by reason, run their course, as in Greek tragedy. In a larger sense, however, his personal defeat is insignificant compared to the greater tragedy of the dwindling American frontier. Although Boone and his fellow frontiersmen love the land, they are at least partly responsible for ravaging it. By 1843, the year when the novel ends, much of the frontier still remained, but the pattern for its destruction had already been established. The "big sky," like the mountain men's idealistic ambitions, would henceforth be diminished.

Bibliography:

Astro, Richard. "*The Big Sky* and the Limits of Wilderness Fiction." *Western American Literature* (Summer, 1974): 105-114. Reasons that *The Big Sky* fails as a nostalgic historical novel depicting a tragic hero falling. Boone Caudill, a one-dimensional character who is ignorant of the effect of time on historical details, cannot learn from friends or enemies, cannot gain wisdom, and symbolizes bankrupt primitivism.

Cracroft, Richard H. "*The Big Sky:* A. B. Guthrie's Use of Historical Sources." *Western American Literature* 6 (Fall, 1971): 163-176. Says Guthrie augments authenticity by writing into *The Big Sky* language, scenes, and incidents from works by Henry Marie Brackenridge, John Bradbury, Washington Irving, and George Frederick Ruxton, among others.

Ford, Thomas W. *A. B. Guthrie, Jr.* Boston: Twayne, 1981. Critical biography, chapter 3 of which treats *The Big Sky* in terms of its plot, Guthrie's purposes (to present facts about mountain men; to convey his love of the West), the novel's landscape pictures, its themes, (destructive violence and encroachment of civilization), its Calvinistic meditations, and its unadorned handling of time and space.

Gale, Robert L. "Guthrie's *The Big Sky.*" *Explicator* 38 (Summer, 1980): 7-8. Sees Jim Deakins' offer of his own flesh to feed Boone Caudill and the goat's gift of blood to Boone as forming a Holy Eucharist which Boone ignorantly spurns, resulting in unsociablity and natural desolation.

Stewart, Donald C. "The Functions of Bird and Sky Imagery in Guthrie's *The Big Sky.*" *Critique: Studies in Modern Fiction* 19, no. 2 (1977): 53-61. Presents interlocking bird and sky similes and metaphors as transforming a well-organized novel into coherent, imaginative art. Images individualize characters and actions, underline moods, and elucidate themes.

THE BIG SLEEP

Type of work: Novel
Author: Raymond Chandler (1888-1959)
Type of plot: Detective and mystery
Time of plot: 1930's
Locale: Los Angeles
First published: 1939

>*Principal characters:*
>PHILIP MARLOWE, a private detective
>GENERAL GUY STERNWOOD, a sick, old rich man who employed Marlowe
>VIVIAN STERNWOOD (MRS. REGAN), Sternwood's immoral oldest daughter
>CARMEN STERNWOOD, General Sternwood's lascivious younger daughter
>EDDIE MARS, a casino operator and racketeer
>ARTHUR GEIGER, a pornographer and blackmailer
>BERNIE OHLS, an assistant district attorney and Marlowe's friend
>CANINO, a paid killer

The Story:

Set among the dissolute rich, seedy hustlers, and the underworld of Los Angeles in the 1930's, *The Big Sleep* is Philip Marlowe's story of pornography, blackmail, and murder. A tough, cynical, independent, thirty-three-year-old private detective, Marlowe, recommended by his friend, Assistant District Attorney Bernie Ohls, agreed to interview wealthy General Guy Sternwood at Sternwood's lush West Hollywood estate.

Old and dying, Sternwood hoped to salvage the last remnants of family pride nearly destroyed by his two immoral daughters. Sternwood hired Marlowe to thwart Arthur Geiger, a blackmailer. Ostensibly, Geiger was squeezing Sternwood over a gambling debt incurred by Sternwood's disturbed younger daughter, Carmen. Dim-witted, spoiled, and a whore, Carmen had unsuccessfully thrown herself at Marlowe when he first arrived at the estate, only to be disdainfully rejected.

Before leaving, Marlowe was summoned by the General's older daughter, Vivian (Mrs. Regan). A seductive, blackhaired beauty, Vivian sought to discover whether Marlowe had been hired to locate her missing husband, Rusty Regan. Marlowe already knew from the General that Regan, a former bootlegger and Irish Republican Army officer, had been Sternwood's companion and protector—the bright spot in his waning life. Unimpressed by Vivian's rich-bitch style, Marlowe, with his trademark insouciance, refused to reveal his client's wishes. Vivian seemed relieved, however, that Marlowe apparently was not looking for Rusty. Nonetheless, displeased by Marlowe's blunt talk and lack of servility, she haughtily dismissed him. Marlowe left feeling he had emerged from a decadent loony bin.

Marlowe began his assignment by casing Geiger's bookstore and by tracking Geiger, who soon confirmed his hunch that the bookstore fronted for the sale of pornography. On a rainy night, he next trailed Geiger home. While he watched the house, Carmen's Packard arrived and a woman entered Geiger's.

Events then moved swiftly. Light from a flashbulb was followed by a scream inside the house, which drew Marlowe closer. His knock on Geiger's door was followed by three shots. Someone pounded down Geiger's backstairs and there were sounds of a car starting. Breaking in, Marlowe found Geiger dead. Virtually naked and obviously drugged, Carmen, babbling incoherently, appeared unaware of what had happened. Marlowe bundled her home in her Packard and left her with a trusted maid. Quickly returning to the murder scene, Marlowe found that Geiger's body had disappeared. Since the killer had fled, it was apparent that someone else wanted Geiger missing. Searching the house, Marlowe located a notebook listing hundreds of potential blackmail victims, leaving the police plenty of suspects.

The following day, Marlowe accompanied Ohls while Vivian Sternwood's Buick was dredged from the water. Inside was a murdered man whom Marlowe identified as Owen Taylor, an ex-con who had once run off with Carmen, but who at the end of his imprisonment was retained as the Sternwoods' chauffeur. After this incident, Marlowe returned to Geiger's store in time to observe someone removing Geiger's books. Following the cargo, Marlowe discovered the recipient was Joe Brody, a hustler who earlier had successfully blackmailed General Sternwood over Carmen.

Later at his office, Marlowe was unexpectedly met by Vivian. Troubled and apologetic, she displayed a blackmail note including a pornographic photograph of Carmen accompanied by a demand for five thousand dollars. A woman had phoned her, she reported, demanding payment that night or else the negative would be given to the scandal sheets. Not yet vouchsafed her inheritance, Vivian proposed that she get the money from Eddie Mars, a racketeer in whose casino she often gambled. Marlowe agreed. Vivian, meantime, disclosed nothing about her Buick or her murdered chauffeur inside. She revealed, however, why Mars was likely (as he soon did) to lend her the money. Her missing husband, Rusty, it seemed, had run off with Mona, Mars's missing wife.

Returning to Geiger's, Marlowe found Carmen lurking about. Inside with Marlowe, she named Brody, her former blackmailer, as Geiger's killer. Eddie Mars and his goons then arrived, demanding to know why Marlowe was there. In their ensuing exchanges, Mars denied killing Geiger. Warned off by Mars, Marlowe then located Brody and his girlfriend, Agnes, whom he scared by implying that the police might find Brody a prime suspect in Geiger's still undisclosed murder. Having shadowed Marlowe, Carmen suddenly broke in and tried to kill Brody. Terrified, Brody surrendered the photos of Carmen to Marlowe, who promptly sent Carmen packing. Brody, called to the door moments afterward, was fatally shot. Marlowe caught the killer, a youth who had been Geiger's homosexual lover and the person responsible for moving Geiger's corpse.

Marlowe delivered the photos to Sternwood's trusted servant and Brody's killer to the police. Though hassled by them, he maintained the integrity of his client, despite having withheld evidence. The same day, Sternwood offered to pay Marlowe to find Rusty, but Marlowe, refusing the money, decided to proceed unassigned. At home, Marlowe found Carmen, naked, waiting to seduce him, and angrily ousted her. In the evening, ignoring Mars's warnings, he visited Mars's casino. In their tough exchanges Mars again denied killing anyone. Vivian too was present and winning heavily. As she left, Marlowe prevented one of Mars's thugs from robbing her of her winnings. While being escorted home, Vivian, aping Carmen, failed either to seduce Marlowe or to gain information.

New connections materialized when another hustler, Harry Jones, desperate for money to leave town with Brody's ex-girlfriend, Agnes, sold Marlowe vital evidence. Jones confirmed that Vivian Sternwood knew Canino, a Mars hitman, and that Canino knew where to locate Mars's wife. Subsequently checking Jones's story, Marlowe, hidden in Jones's office, witnessed Canino poisoning Jones.

With these leads, Marlowe uncovered Mona Mars's hideaway, but in the process a flat tire landed him in Canino's hands. Slugged, captured, and bound, Marlowe briefly was guarded by the beautiful blonde, Mona, whom Marlowe persuaded to release him, although he was still handcuffed. Reaching his car and a pistol, he killed Canino in an ensuing shootout, all of which he swiftly reported to the police.

Marlowe's evidence then allowed him to solve key parts of the mystery. Since everyone knew of bad blood between Mars and Regan, Mars, with Mona's connivance and Canino's aid, faked Mona's disappearance to allay suspicions that Mars might have killed Regan. In the meantime, Mars, through Geiger, ran an elaborate blackmail scheme. First, he blackmailed the ever-vulnerable Carmen. Later, after Vivian had received her millions, Mars planned to blackmail her too. Vivian and Mars were aware that Carmen had killed Rusty Regan for refusing to sleep with her and that Vivian then had persuaded Mars to dispose of Regan's body. In love with Carmen, and loathing what Geiger had done to her, chauffeur Owen Taylor had shot Geiger. Marlowe never clarified who killed Taylor. It was because Geiger's death ultimately threatened to lead to Mona's whereabouts that Canino poisoned Jones.

Finally, employed officially by Sternwood to find Regan, Marlowe, agreeing to teach Carmen to shoot, conned her into trying to kill him on the site where Regan's body had been dumped. To save Sternwood's pride, Marlowe then remanded Carmen to Vivian, urging that she seek help for her now psychotic sister. Mars, his blackmail scheme aborted, was questioned and released by the police. Although guilty, he neither directly blackmailed nor killed anyone. Justice for Marlowe meant honoring Sternwood's wishes. Sooner or later, after all, everyone succumbed to the big sleep—but not without first having dreamed, as Marlowe did, of the gorgeous Mona.

Critical Evaluation:

The Big Sleep was Raymond Chandler's first novel. Many critics have considered it a classic. Arguably it was the best of Chandler's seven novels, and unquestionably it ranked above the writing of Dashiell Hammett as among the finest examples of its genre in the twentieth century. As such, it proved extremely influential. Other mystery writers, such as Ross Macdonald, Robert Parker, and Mickey Spillane, have acknowledged Chandler's influence. Mystery readers into the mid-1980's listed Chandler as their third favorite, just behind Sir Arthur Conan Doyle and Agatha Christie. In addition, writers such as Alistair Cooke and Bernard De Voto regarded Chandler as an important literary figure. Chandler may have been all the more respected and influential because of his ardent belief that fine mystery writing deserved full acceptance as respectable literature by the world of letters. Moreover, many critics believed that when other writers elevated the value of style, Chandler would doubtless merit a front rank.

In Philip Marlowe, *The Big Sleep*'s narrator, Chandler created a new species of hard-boiled private detective whose character continued evolving in his subsequent novels. Previous private-eye fiction had been freighted with square-jawed heroes who resolved matters with guns and fists. Encased in a cynic's armor, Marlowe, however, beneath all, was a knight, his name itself drawn by Chandler from Sir Thomas Malory's fifteenth century tales of chivalry.

Marlowe was an honest man in a sleazy trade, which he plied amid the tacky superficialities of Los Angeles and Southern California, a sump where the American Dream was going bad. In a world of money worshipers, Marlowe reflected Chandler's own hatred of the rich and their decadent influences. A romantic at heart, like the reasonably honest cops he encountered, Marlowe had learned to flense his expectations about American justice to the bone. He asserted his independence, however, and remained loyal to his clients, pragmatically attending to his craft. Thus, he managed to bring forth justice of a sort.

Chandler's storymaking was affected by his gift for near-total recall. Marlowe, for instance, was constructed from characters in four of his early short stories. The private investigator's more distant predecessors in American literature include James Fenimore Cooper's Natty Bumppo, Mark Twain's Huckleberry Finn, and Ernest Hemingway's Nick Adams, all of whom, a Chandler biographer observed, believed in the incorruptibility of at least a part of the population. Chandler kept the scenes in the novel's thirty-two brief chapters simple, acknowledging he had difficulty getting characters in and out of rooms. His plot, on the other hand, which also contained elements from previous work, is Byzantine. Indeed, *The Big Sleep* might well have been two stories, one of which ends when Marlowe decides to discover Regan's fate. Chandler's fresh stylistic verve, however, moves his complicated tale successfully.

Filled with social criticism, another Chandler first for mystery novels, *The Big Sleep* is also rich in the metaphors that laced its tough-guy talk and keen repartee. Chandler's metaphors reflect, as perceptive critics have noted, a mechanistic world measured in time, space, mass, and inertia. This world is described with comparisons of size, speed, impact, and balance. Moral absolutes are conspicuous by their absence. Critical of himself, Chandler, hence Marlowe, as *The Big Sleep* confirmed, approached life as an ambiguous mixture of the romantic and the realist. Marlowe lives almost existentially, taking independent action in regard to people and institutions, refining his own values, resisting temptations that would destroy his self-esteem, and taking responsibility for his actions—knowing that nobody cared.

Clifton K. Yearley

Bibliography:

Durham, Philip. *Down These Mean Streets a Man Must Go: Raymond Chandler's Knight.* Chapel Hill: University of North Carolina Press, 1963. An outstanding study of Chandler's work including *The Big Sleep.*

Gross, Miriam, ed. *The World of Raymond Chandler.* London: Weidenfeld & Nicolson, 1977. A superb collection of critical essays on Chandler's work by writers and scholars who provide ample discussion of *The Big Sleep.*

MacShane, Frank. *The Life of Raymond Chandler.* New York: E. P. Dutton, 1976. This is the best biography of Chandler's character as well as an informed analysis of his writings. Mentioned throughout, *The Big Sleep* is the subject of chapter 4.

Marling, William. *Raymond Chandler.* Boston: Twayne, 1986. An excellent critical survey of Chandler's life and writings. Although there are many references to *The Big Sleep*, chapter 5 is devoted entirely to the novel.

Speir, Jerry. *Raymond Chandler.* New York: Frederick Ungar, 1981. A thoughtful survey that contains frequent comments on *The Big Sleep.*

THE BIGLOW PAPERS

Type of work: Poetry, with editorial prose
Author: James Russell Lowell (1819-1891)
First published: first series, 1848; second series, 1867

> *Principal characters:*
> HOSEA BIGLOW, the Yankee author of the poems in *The Biglow Papers*
> BIRDOFREDUM SAWIN, his correspondent, a Massachusetts militiaman (first series), an adopted Rebel (second series)
> HOMER WILBUR, A.M., parson of the First Church of Jaalam, author of the editorial comments in *The Biglow Papers*

The Biglow Papers is political satire, and, as such, cannot be understood or appreciated until the reader is acquainted, first, with the policies and ideas being satirized and, second, with the conditions of publication. In short, like all satire, it must be seen in their historical perspective before it can be evaluated.

There are two series of *The Biglow Papers*. The first is an attack, from the Whig-Abolitionist point of view, on the Mexican War and the policies of President James Polk and the proslavery forces that authorized it; the second—all but the last paper—is an attack, from the Northern Republican point of view, on the rebellious, slaveholding South, the Democrats, and the interventionist policies of England during the first years of the American Civil War; the last paper is a condemnation of the "retrograde movement" of President Andrew Johnson.

The history of the papers is rather complex. In one sense, it dates back to 1840 and the beginning of Lowell's relationship with Maria White, who became his wife in 1844, for it was this visionary and forceful young woman who first converted him to the abolitionist cause. In any case, by the time of the outbreak of the Mexican War in 1846, Lowell had identified himself with the movement by contributions to the National Anti-Slavery Standard, which he edited for a short time. Such a radical position was more in keeping with the spirit of the Emersonians than with that of the aloof Brahmins with whom Lowell was allied by birth, and the strong influence of his wife's personality and ideals may be inferred from the fact that Lowell grew more and more conservative in the years following her death. By the time of his own death he was once more a conservative, but, in the 1840's, his radical leanings brought him into the camp of those idealistic New Englanders who preached freedom vociferously (and at times effectively) and those shrewd and stubborn rural Yankees who supported them for more practical reasons. The first series of *The Biglow Papers* arose from the interaction of these two elements. Abolitionist idealism gave it motivation; Yankee shrewdness gave it form.

The first Biglow paper appeared as a letter to the editor of the *Boston Courier,* a weekly Whig newspaper, in June of 1846. The letter was signed by one Ezekiel Biglow of Jaalam, Massachusetts, and its ostensible purpose was to introduce a poem by Mr. Biglow's son, Hosea. The important thing here was the poem, an attack, in the Yankee dialect, on the recruiting of the Massachusetts regiment for service in a war which the abolitionists and their sympathizers claimed was being fought only to extend the borders of slavery.

The response to this first letter prompted Lowell to continue the poetic exertions of young Mr. Biglow. "The success of my experiment," wrote Lowell later in the introduction to the second series, "soon began not only to astonish me, but to make me feel the responsibility of knowing I had in my hand a weapon instead of the mere fencing stick I had supposed." Lowell, clad in the rustic armor of Hosea Biglow, entered the fray with this newfound weapon eight more times in the following two years. Five of these dialect poems were direct political attacks on the war party group and their sympathizers, the Democrats and the "Cotton-" Whigs (those Whigs, as opposed to the "Conscience-" Whigs, who favored the war and were more or less tolerant of slavery), particularly those to be found in Biglow's—and Lowell's—own Bay State. The other three provided a more general satire of the progress of the war, of the ignorance, inefficiency, and immorality of those in command, and of the mistreatment of the Massachusetts enlisted man, both as soldier and as disabled veteran.

This general satire was presented through a new character, Birdofredum Sawin, whom Lowell introduced in his second letter to the *Courier*. Sawin was a ne'er-do-well Yankee from Jaalam who, succumbing to the blandishments of the recruiting officer, had enlisted as a private in the Massachusetts regiment. From Mexico, he wrote back to Hosea, who turned his letter into the Eastern Massachusetts equivalent of iambic heptameter couplets. Birdofredum's complaints and caustic observations supplied the material for Papers Two, Eight, and Nine. In the second paper, he is engaged in combat. In Papers Eight and Nine, he has been released from service minus one eye and one arm; he still has two legs, though by this time one of them is wooden.

The third character of these papers did not come upon the scene until the poems were published in book form late in 1848. This character is the pastor of the First Church of Jaalam, the Reverend Homer Wilbur, A.M., who is presented as the editor of the volume. Lowell admitted eighteen years later that he needed a character who would present the more cautious side of the New England character, expressing simple common sense enlivened by conscience.

The pedantry and the long-winded self-centeredness of Mr. Wilbur add much to the book— literally, for the learned churchman's remarks take up more space in the volume than do the nine original poems. His verbose expatiations do, undoubtedly, allow Lowell to express those more cautious elements of the Yankee character and to extend his satire by poking fun at the excessive and distracting paraphernalia that encumber learned works. Most amusing, perhaps, are the "Notices of an Independent Press" that Mr. Biglow admittedly wrote himself and included the lengthy material at the beginning of the volume. Besides offering amusing material, Mr. Wilbur can become eloquent in his own right in defense of freedom. For the most part, however, Lowell's imitation of pedantry is too realistic. Rather than acting as ballast, Mr. Wilbur almost causes the book to sink. In the end, this character's main contribution is that of making the poems, when they finally appear, more delightful because of their contrast to his wordy prose.

The addition of Parson Wilbur was a sign of the innate conservative caution in Lowell's character as artist, critic, and political figure. This caution and conservatism betray themselves still more in the second series of *The Biglow Papers*. By the time the slavery question reached its climax, Lowell was no longer the outspoken young abolitionist radical of the 1840's. By then he had been for six years professor of belles-lettres at Harvard (having succeeded his friend Henry Wadsworth Longfellow to that chair in 1855), had founded and was still editor of the *Atlantic Monthly*, and, perhaps most important of all, had lost his wife, Maria White Lowell, and had remarried. Occasionally he is effective in the second series, especially in the letters from Birdofredum Sawin (who, after having been falsely imprisoned in the South for two years, marries a slaveholding widow and becomes a sympathizer with the Southern cause) and in the last part of the second paper, an attack on England which ends with a piece bearing the title of "Jonathan to John."

In these he rises to the satirical heights of the original collection, but for the most part, as Lowell himself admitted, the papers of the second series are more studied, less spontaneous, more cautious and less biting than those of the first. Even the quaintness of the old Yankee diction was intentionally diminished, excused by the claim that Hosea was being tutored by Parson Wilbur and was learning proper spelling and academic phraseology.

Lowell kept the Yankee dialect to the last, but in the end his apparent need to defend its use is another indication of the dying out of his earlier satiric fire. The individual numbers of the second series were first printed in the *Atlantic Monthly*; when, in 1867, they were collected in book form, Lowell wrote a lengthy introduction for them. A brilliant contribution to linguistic knowledge, the preface is made concrete by Lowell's sensitive ear for dialect, and it is documented by his voluminous reading in English and American literature. Valuable as it is in its own right, however, it is still an apology, and, when satire is apologized for, it loses much of its force, much of its reason for being.

As a whole, however, despite this decreasing force, *The Biglow Papers* remain an important American literary monument. First, they are important historically as vivid expressions of public opinion in a particular section of the country during an especially critical stage in the health of the United States. Second, they are important in American literary history as one of the earliest examples of dialect writing and as the very earliest example of the Yankee dialect. Most of all, they are intrinsically important as outspoken examples of independent thought, of that Yankee independence, outspokenness, and ironic humor that are a part of national tradition.

Bibliography:

Arms, George. *The Fields Were Green: A New View of Bryant, Whittier, Holmes, Lowell, and Longfellow, with a Selection of Their Poems.* Stanford, Calif.: Stanford University Press, 1948. Places Lowell and his production in the context of the best popular poetry of the times. Downgrades *The Biglow Papers* in comparison to Lowell's other poetry.

Duberman, Martin. *James Russell Lowell.* Boston: Houghton Mifflin, 1966. Largely concerned with the objects of satire in *The Biglow Papers*: the recruiting of Massachusetts troops for the Mexican War, the institution of slavery, shoddy politicians, and American expansionism. Criticizes the poem for its prose interruptions, tiresome repetitions, and inconsistent tone and point of view.

McGlinchee, Claire. *James Russell Lowell.* New York: Twayne, 1967. Summarizes *The Biglow Papers*; stresses the youthful, zestful satire of the first series and the sagacious patriotism, vivified by the profuse use of Yankee dialect, expressed in the second series.

Wagenknecht, Edward. *James Russell Lowell: Portrait of a Many-Sided Man.* New York: Oxford University Press, 1971. Relates *The Biglow Papers* to Lowell the writer and the man, including his love of tobacco, lack of interest in drama, fondness for both Latinate and colloquial diction, vast reading experience, and political beliefs.

Wortham, Thomas. "Introduction." In *James Russell Lowell's The Biglow Papers, First Series: A Critical Edition.* DeKalb: Northern Illinois University Press, 1977. Details the political background inspiring Lowell to start *The Biglow Papers* and accounts for the immense popularity of the work. Analyzes Lowell's skillful handling of characterization, his use of pervasive irony, and the poetic and narrative structure of the poem.

BILLY BUDD, FORETOPMAN

Type of work: Novel
Author: Herman Melville (1819-1891)
Type of plot: Symbolic realism
Time of plot: 1797
Locale: Aboard a British man-of-war
First published: 1924

> *Principal characters:*
> BILLY BUDD, a young British sailor
> CAPTAIN VERE, commanding officer of HMS *Indomitable*
> CLAGGART, master-at-arms aboard the *Indomitable*

The Story:

In 1797, the British merchant ship *Rights-of-Man*, named after the famous reply of Thomas Paine to Edmund Burke's criticism of the French Revolution, was close to home after a long voyage. As it neared England, the merchant vessel was stopped by a man-of-war, HMS *Indomitable*, and an officer from the warship went aboard the *Rights-of-Man* to impress sailors for military service. This practice was necessary at the time to provide men to work the large number of ships that Britain had at sea for protection against the French.

The captain of the *Rights-of-Man* was relieved to have only one sailor taken from his ship, but he was unhappy because the man was his best sailor, Billy Budd. Billy was what his captain called a peacemaker; because of his strength and good looks, he was a natural leader among the other sailors, and he used his influence to keep them contented and hard at work. Billy Budd seemed utterly without guile, a man who tried to promote the welfare of the merchant ship because he liked peace and was willing to work hard to please his superiors. When informed that he was not to return to England but was to head for duty with the fleet in the Mediterranean Sea, he did not appear disturbed; he liked the sea, and he had no family ties. He was an orphan who had been left as a tiny baby in a basket on the doorstep of a family in Bristol.

As the boat from the warship took him away from the merchant ship, Billy called farewell to the *Rights-of-Man* by name, a deed that greatly embarrassed the naval officer who had impressed him. The remark was unwittingly satirical of the treatment to which Billy was being subjected by the navy.

Once aboard the *Indomitable*, Billy quickly made himself at home with the ship and the men with whom he served in the foretop. As a result of his good personality and his willingness to work, he soon made a place for himself with his messmates and also won the regard of the officers under whom he served.

At first, the master-at-arms, a petty officer named Claggart, seemed particularly friendly to Billy, a fortunate circumstance, Billy thought, for the master-at-arms was the equivalent of the chief of police aboard the warship. The young sailor was rather surprised, therefore, when he received reprimands for slight breaches of conduct that were normally overlooked. The reprimands came from the ship's corporals who were Claggart's underlings. Since the reprimands indicated that something was wrong, Billy grew perturbed; he had a deadly fear of being the recipient of a flogging in public. He thought he could never stand such treatment.

Anxious to discover what was wrong, Billy consulted an old sailor, who told him that Claggart was filled with animosity for the young man. The reason for the animosity was not known, and because the old man could give him no reason, Billy refused to believe that the master-at-arms was his enemy. Claggart had taken a deep dislike to Billy Budd on sight, however, and for no reason except a personal antipathy that the young man's appearance had generated. Sly as he was, Claggart kept, or tried to keep, his feelings to himself. He operated through underlings against Billy.

Not long after he had been warned by the old sailor, Billy spilled a bowl of soup in the path of Claggart as he was inspecting the mess. Even then, Claggart smiled and pretended to treat the incident as a joke, for Billy had done the deed accidentally. A few nights later, however, someone awakened Billy and told him to go to a secluded spot in the ship. Billy went and met a sailor who tried to tempt him into joining a mutiny. The incident bothered Billy, who could not understand why anyone had approached him as a possible conspirator. Such activity was not a part of his personality, and he was disgusted to find it in other men.

A few days later, the master-at-arms approached the captain of the ship and reported that he and his men had discovered that a mutiny was being fomented by Billy Budd. Captain Vere, a very fair officer, reminded Claggart of the seriousness of the charge and warned the master-at-arms that bearing false witness in such a case called for the death penalty. Claggart persisted in his accusations, however, and Captain Vere stopped the interview on deck, a place he thought too public, and ordered the master-at-arms and Billy Budd to his cabin. There Captain Vere commanded Claggart to repeat his accusations. When he did, Billy became emotionally so upset that he was tongue-tied. In utter frustration at being unable to reply to the infamous charges, Billy hit the master-at-arms. The petty officer was killed when he fell heavily to the floor.

Captain Vere was filled with consternation, for he, like everyone except the master-at-arms, liked Billy Budd. After the surgeon had pronounced the petty officer dead, the captain immediately convened a court-martial to try Billy for assaulting and murdering a superior officer. England was at war, and two mutinies had already occurred in the British navy that year, so action had to be taken immediately. The captain could not overlook the offense.

The court-martial, acting under regulations, found Billy Budd guilty and sentenced him to be hanged from a yardarm the following morning. Even under the circumstances of Claggart's death, there was no alternative. The only person who could have testified that the charge of mutiny was false was the man who had been killed.

All the ship's company were dismayed when informed of the sentence. Billy bore no animosity for the captain or for the officers who had sentenced him to die. When he was placed beneath the yardarm the following morning, he called out a blessing on Captain Vere, who, he realized, had no other choice in the matter but to hang him. It was quite strange, too, that Billy Budd's calm seemed even to control his corpse. Unlike most hanged men, he never twitched when hauled aloft by the neck. The surgeon's mate, when queried by his messmates, had no answer for this unique behavior.

Some months later, Captain Vere was wounded in action. In the last hours before his death, he was heard to murmur Billy Budd's name over and over again. Nor did the common sailors forget the hanged man. For many years, the yardarm from which he had been hanged was kept track of by sailors, who regarded it almost as reverently as Christians might revere the Cross.

Critical Evaluation:

According to Harrison Hayford and Merton M. Sealts, the editors of the novel, Herman Melville began the novel in 1886, developed and revised it through several stages, and then left it unpublished when he died in 1891. The Hayford-Sealts text, published in 1962, differs considerably from earlier ones published in 1924 and 1948. Among the noteworthy differences is the change of name for the ship on which the action occurs, from *Indomitable* to *Bellipotent*.

The symbolism of the latter name relates it to the emphasis that Melville places in the novel on war, human involvement in it, and the effects of war on the individual.

That Melville did not wish his readers to mistake the nature or the general intent of his novel is clear in his statement that Billy "is not presented as a conventional hero" and "that the story in which he is the main figure is no romance." The story itself is extremely simple. A young sailor on a British merchant ship is impressed for service on a British warship. He offers no resistance but accepts his new assignment with good will and attempts to be an ideal sailor. The ship's master-at-arms takes an immediate and unwarranted dislike to the sailor, plots to cause him trouble, and then accuses him to the captain of having plotted mutiny. The captain summons the sailor, asks him to defend himself, and sees him strike and accidentally kill his accuser. The captain imprisons him, convenes a court-martial, condemns him to death, and has him hanged. This plot is the vehicle for Melville's extended use of moral symbolism throughout the novel.

Billy Budd, Claggart, and Captain Vere are all clearly symbolic characters, and Melville brings out the symbolism through information supplied about their backgrounds, language used to describe them, and authorial comment of moral, theological, and philosophical import.

Melville employs a double symbolism for Billy: He is a Christ figure and a representation of innocent or Adamic man. Before Billy is removed from the merchant ship, the captain explains to the lieutenant from the warship that Billy has been most useful in quieting the "rat-pit of quarrels" that formerly infested his forecastle. "Not that he preached to them or said or did anything in particular; but a virtue went out of him, sugaring the sour ones." The captain's words echo Luke, 6:19: "And the whole multitude sought to touch him: for there went virtue out of him, and healed them all." When the lieutenant is adamant about Billy's impressment, the captain's last words to him are: ". . . you are going to take away my peacemaker." There is no mistaking the reference to the Prince of Peace. In describing Billy as he appears to the men and officers on the warship, Melville mentions "something in the mobile expression, and every chance attitude and movement, something suggestive of a mother eminently favored by Love and the Graces." An officer asks, "Who was your father?" and Billy answers, "God knows, sir." Though Billy explains that he was told he was a foundling, the hint has already been given of a divine paternity. Melville drops the Christ symbolism of Billy until the confrontation with Claggart when Billy, unable to reply to Captain Vere's request that he defend himself, shows in his face "an expression which was as a crucifixion to behold." At the hanging, Billy's last words are, "God bless Captain Vere!" and the reader recalls Christ's words on the Cross, "Father, forgive them; for they know not what they do." The symbolism continues with the hanging. Captain Vere gives a silent signal and "At the same moment it chanced that the vapory fleece hanging low in the East was shot through with a soft glory as of the fleece of the Lamb of God seen in mystical vision, and simultaneously therewith, watched by the wedged mass of upturned faces, Billy ascended; and, ascending, took the full rose of the dawn." In the final chapter, Melville adds that

> The spar from which the foretopman was suspended was for some few years kept trace of by the bluejackets. . . . To them a chip from it was as a piece of the Cross. . . . They recalled a fresh young image of the Handsome Sailor, that face never deformed by a sneer or subtler vile freak of the heart within. This impression of him was doubtless deepened by the fact that he was gone, and in a measure mysteriously gone.

Even in the verses which close the novel, with Billy's words, "They'll give me a nibble—bit o' biscuit ere I go./ Sure a messmate will reach me the last parting cup," one cannot miss the reference to the Last Supper.

Billy is Christlike, but he belongs to the human race. Melville repeatedly employs him as an archetype. Billy's complete innocence is first suggested in Melville's comment that "Billy in many respects was little more than a sort of upright barbarian, much such perhaps as Adam presumably might have been ere the urbane Serpent wriggled himself into his company." Later, Captain Vere thinks of the handsome sailor as one "who in the nude might have posed for a statue of young Adam before the Fall." Innocence does not protect Billy. As Adam's human imperfection led to his fall, so an imperfection in Billy leads to his destruction. In times of stress, Billy stutters or is even speechless and, says Melville, "In this particular Billy was a striking instance that the arch interferer, the envious marplot of Eden, still has more or less to do with every human consignment to this planet of Earth."

The innocence that is his "blinder" causes Billy (or "Baby" as he is called) to fail to see and be on guard against the evil in Claggart, and his "vocal defect" deprives him of speech when he faces his false accuser. He strikes out as instinctively as a cornered animal, and his enemy dies. Billy did not intend to commit murder but, as Captain Vere tells his officers, "The prisoner's deed—with that alone we have to do." Billy does not live in an animal's instinctive world of nature. His life is bound by social law and particularly by naval law in a time of war. As Captain Vere explains, innocent Billy will be acquitted by God at "the last Assizes," but "We proceed under the law of the Mutiny Act." That act demands death for Billy's deed, and he dies in order that discipline may be maintained in the great navy that protects Britain against its enemies.

As Billy symbolizes innocent man, Claggart represents the spirit of evil, the foe of innocence. There is a mystery in Claggart's enmity toward harmless Billy. For, says Melville, "what can more partake of the mysterious than an antipathy spontaneous and profound such as is evoked in certain exceptional mortals by the mere aspect of some other mortal, however harmless he may be, if not called forth by this very harmlessness itself?" Claggart's evil nature was not acquired, "not engendered by vicious training or corrupting books or licentious living, but born with him and innate." He can recognize the good but is "powerless to be it." His energies are self-destructive; his nature is doomed to "act out to the end the part allotted to it." Although he destroys an innocent man, he is destroyed as well.

As Billy at one extreme is Christlike and childishly innocent and Claggart at the other is satanic, Captain Vere represents the kind of officer needed to preserve such an institution as the navy he serves. He is a man of balance, "mindful of the welfare of his men, but never tolerating an infraction of discipline; thoroughly versed in the science of his profession, and intrepid to the verge of temerity, though never injudiciously so." His reading tastes incline toward "books treating of actual men and events . . . history, biography, and unconventional writers like Montaigne, who, free from cant and convention, honestly and in the spirit of common sense philosophize upon realities." More intellectual than his fellow officers, he seems somewhat "pedantic" to them, and Melville hints that, in reporting Vere's long speech to his junior officers of the drumhead court, he has simplified the phrasing of the argument. Yet elsewhere Captain Vere's speech is simple, brief, and direct.

Although Captain Vere is a thoughtful, reserved man, he is not without feeling. Quickly recognizing Billy's inability to speak when he has been ordered to defend himself, he soothingly says, "There is no hurry, my boy. Take your time, take your time." He is even capable of momentary vehemence as when he surprises the surgeon with the outburst, "Struck dead by an angel of God! Yet the angel must hang!" The captain quickly regains control. Melville does not report what Captain Vere says to Billy when he informs him privately of the death sentence, although Melville suggests that Vere may have shown compassion by catching Billy "to his heart, even as Abraham may have caught young Isaac on the brink of resolutely offering him up." Vere is seemingly overcome after Billy's last words, "God bless Captain Vere!" and the echo from the crew, since "either through stoic self-control or a sort of momentary paralysis induced by emotional shock," he stands "rigidly erect as a musket." The final view of a man whose heart balanced his mind is given in the report of Captain Vere's dying words, "Billy Budd, Billy Budd," spoken not in "the accents of remorse." Though capable of fatherly feeling toward an unfortunate young man, he had caused to be carried out a sentence he believed was needed if the strength of order was to be maintained in the turmoil of war.

Although *Billy Budd, Foretopman* has occasionally been read as a veiled attack on the unjust treatment of a hapless man by an impersonal, authoritarian state, a close reading of the novel makes it seem more likely that Melville's intent was to show, especially through Captain Vere, that the protection of a state during a time of war must inevitably involve on occasion the sacrifice of an individual. Melville includes scattered satiric comments on the imperfections of men and organizations, but his overwhelmingly favorable portrait of Captain Vere as a principled and dedicated representative of the state leaves the reader with the final impression that Melville had at last become sadly resigned to the fact that imperfect people living in an imperfect world have no guarantee against suffering an unjust fate. That Billy uncomplainingly accepts his end, even asking God's blessing upon the man who is sending him to death, suggests that Melville too had become reconciled to the eternal coexistence of good and evil in the world.

"Critical Evaluation" by Henderson Kincheloe

Bibliography:

Browne, Ray B. *Melville's Drive to Humanism.* West Lafayette, Ind.: Purdue University Press, 1971. The last chapter examines *Billy Budd, Foretopman* as a "provocative" and "disturbing" book that grew out of a ballad-like story. Sees the novel as an assertion of a democratic "gospel" and of a humanistic perspective.

Chase, Richard. *Herman Melville: A Critical Study.* New York: Hafner Press, 1971. The last chapter, devoted to *Billy Budd, Foretopman,* calls Melville's final acceptance of life as tragic. Excellent analysis of the book's balance between action and philosophizing.

Scorza, Thomas J. *In the Time Before Steamships: "Billy Budd," the Limits of Politics, and Modernity.* DeKalb: Northern Illinois University Press, 1979. Approaches the "political dimension" of the novel. Argues that modern people find tragedy rather than glory in the limits of politics. Argues that Melville's analysis led him to see modern tragedy as the result of prideful rational philosophy.

Stafford, William T., ed. *Melville's "Billy Budd" and the Critics.* 2d ed. Belmont, Calif.: Wadsworth, 1968. Discussion of the text and early critical views. Treats acceptance and resistance themes, spiritual autobiography, myth, art, social commentary, and Christian and classical parallels. Recent criticism focuses on the limits of human perception.

Vincent, Howard P., ed. *Twentieth Century Interpretations of Billy Budd: A Collection of Critical Essays.* Englewood Cliffs, N.J.: Prentice-Hall, 1971. Varied and excellent essays on innocence, irony, justice, tragedy, and acceptance in *Billy Budd, Foretopman.* Part 2 gives the viewpoints of major critics.

BIOGRAPHIA LITERARIA

Type of work: Literary criticism
Author: Samuel Taylor Coleridge (1772-1834)
First published: 1817

Samuel Taylor Coleridge's *Biographia Literaria* begins as an account of the major influences on the development of the author's philosophy and literary technique, but the total effect of the work is considerably less coherent than this plan would indicate. As he progressed, Coleridge apparently altered his purpose, and he discussed at considerable length intellectual problems of special interest to him and gave some of his standards of literary criticism, with comments on specific works. In his opening paragraph, he speaks of his work as "miscellaneous reflections," and such a description seems appropriate.

The loose, rambling structure of the *Biographia Literaria* accords well with the picture of Coleridge that has been handed down: that of a man with great intellectual and poetic gifts who lacked the self-discipline to produce the works of which he seemed capable. Charles Lamb and William Hazlitt both characterized him as an indefatigable and fascinating talker, full of ideas; this trait, too, plays its part in the creation of the *Biographia Literaria*, which is, in essence, a long conversation ranging widely over the worlds of poetry, drama, philosophy, and psychology. The lack of a tight organizational plan in no way prevents the book from being both readable and profound in its content; Coleridge's comments on the nature of the poetic imagination have never been surpassed, and his critique of William Wordsworth's work is still perhaps the most balanced and judicious assessment available, a model for all scholars who seek to form general views on the basis of close examination of individual texts.

In the opening chapter, Coleridge pays tribute to his most influential teacher, the Reverend James Bowyer of Christ's Hospital, who insisted that his students learn to think logically and use language precisely, in poetry as well as prose. Coleridge also discusses the poetry he preferred in the years when his literary tastes were being formed; he turned toward the "pre-Romantic" lyrics of minor writers rather than to the terse, epigrammatic intellectual poems of the best-known of the eighteenth century literary men, Alexander Pope and his followers. At an early stage, Coleridge developed sound critical principles, looking for works that gained in power through rereading and for words that seemed to express ideas better than any phrases substituted for them could. He quickly learned to distinguish between the virtues of works of original ideas and the faults of those that made their effect through novel phraseology. He confesses, however, that his critical judgment was better than his creative talent: His own early poems, though he thought highly of them when he wrote them, left much to be desired.

The harshness of the critics of his time is a theme that recurs throughout Coleridge's biography. In his second chapter, he ponders the tendency of the public to side with the critics rather than with the poets, who are considered to be strange, irritable, even mad. Yet the greatest writers—Geoffrey Chaucer, William Shakespeare, Edmund Spenser, and John Milton—seem to him unusually well balanced, and he suggests that the popular heresy results from the frustrations of the second-rate writer who pursues fame without real talent. These general comments are closely linked to Coleridge's sense of outrage at the vituperative attacks on him that issued regularly from the pages of the popular reviews, partly as a result of his association with Wordsworth and Robert Southey. The three poets were accused of trying to revolutionize, to vulgarize, poetry; they were avowedly interested in freeing poetry from the limitations of the eighteenth century poetic tradition. Coleridge denies that they deserved the abuses hurled at them.

After commenting on the works of Wordsworth and Southey, Coleridge turns to a number of philosophical problems that fascinated him, among them questions of perception, sensation, and the human thought processes. It is this section of the work that provides the greatest difficulty for the uninitiated reader, for Coleridge assumes considerable familiarity with the works of German philosophers and English psychologists and mystics. He surveys the theories of Thomas Hobbes, David Hartley, Aristotle, René Descartes, and others as they relate to problems of perception and of the development of thought through the association of ideas, and he assesses the influence of Immanuel Kant on his own philosophy.

Coleridge digresses from the complex history of his intellectual growth to describe his first literary venture into the commercial side of his world, his publication of a periodical called *The Watchman*. His attempts to secure subscriptions were ludicrous, and his project met with the failure that his friends had predicted; one of them had to pay Coleridge's printer to keep Coleridge out of debtors' prison.

One of the most important episodes of Coleridge's life was his 1798 trip to Germany, where he widened his knowledge of the literature and philosophy of that country. He returned to England to take a position with a newspaper, writing on literature and politics; he attacked Napoleon Bonaparte so vehemently that the French general actually sent out an order for his arrest while Coleridge was living in Italy as a correspondent for his paper. Coleridge evidently enjoyed his journalistic work, and he advises all would-be literary men to find some regular occupation rather than to devote all of their time to writing.

Returning to his philosophical discussion, Coleridge lists several of his major premises about truth and knowledge. He is particularly concerned about distinguishing between the essence of the subject, the perceiver, and of the object, that which is perceived. Related to this distinction is the nature of the imagination, which Coleridge divides into two parts. The primary imagination is the human power that perceives and recognizes objects; the secondary imagination acts on these initial perceptions to produce new thoughts: "It dissolves, diffuses, dissipates, in order to re-create."

Coleridge next turns to a presentation of his literary standards, referring especially to the *Lyrical Ballads* (1798), the revolutionary volume that contained much of Wordsworth's poetry and some of his own. He tries to define poetry, pointing out that it has as its "immediate object pleasure, not truth," and that it delights by the effect of the whole as well as of individual parts. In one of the book's most famous passages, he discusses the function of the poet who, by the power of his imagination, must bring unity of diversity, reconciling "sameness, with differences; of the general, with the concrete; the idea, with the image; the individual, with the representative; the sense of novelty and freshness, with old and familiar objects; a more than usual state of emotion, with more than usual order; judgment ever-awake and steady self-possession, with enthusiasm and feeling profound or vehement."

Coleridge applies these general tenets to specific works, analyzing Shakespeare's early poems *Venus and Adonis* (1593) and *The Rape of Lucrece* (1594) to determine what in them reveals genius and what is the result of the poet's immaturity. He praises particularly Shakespeare's musical language and his distance from his subject matter, saying, with reference to the latter point, that the average youthful writer is likely to concentrate on his own sensations and experiences. Shakespeare's greatness seems to him to lie, too, in the vividness of his imagery and in his "depth, and energy of thought."

Although he was closely associated with Wordsworth, Coleridge does not hesitate to indicate the points at which he differed from his colleague. He takes issue most strongly with Wordsworth's assertion that the speech of low and rustic life is the natural language of emotion and therefore best for poetry. Coleridge stresses rather the choice of a diction as universal as possible, not associated with class or region, and he says that it is this kind of language that Wordsworth has, in fact, used in almost all of his work. He argues that in the famous preface to the *Lyrical Ballads*, Wordsworth was, to a certain extent, exaggerating in order to make clear the advantages of natural, simple language over the empty poetic diction typical of the poetry of the time.

Coleridge's comments on Wordsworth lead him to an extended attack on the practices of the critical reviews, which published commentary on his friend's works that seemed to him both biased and absurd. He ridicules the tendency of anonymous reviewers to offer criticism without giving examples to support their assertions; they hardly seem to have read the works they lampoon. To counteract their ill-tempered, inconsistent judgments, he sets down his own views on Wordsworth's most serious flaws and outstanding talents. He criticizes Wordsworth's "inconstancy of the style," a tendency to shift from a lofty level to a commonplace one; his occasionally excessive attention to factual details of landscape or biography; his poor handling of dialogue in some poems; his "occasional prolixity, repetition, and an eddying instead of progression of thought" in a few passages; and, finally, his use of "thoughts and images too great for the subject."

With these defects in mind, Coleridge commends Wordsworth's work for the purity and appropriateness of its language, the freshness of the thoughts, the "sinewy strength and originality of single lines and paragraphs," the accuracy of the descriptions of nature, the pathos and human sympathy, and the imaginative power of the poet.

The major portion of the *Biographia Literaria* ends with a final assessment of Wordsworth's work; Coleridge thereupon adds a section of letters written to friends while he was traveling in Germany. The letters contain amusing accounts of his shipboard companions, a description of his meeting with the poet Friedrich Gottlieb Klopstock, and some of his literary opinions. To show how little his critical standards had changed, he also includes a long and devastating critique of a contemporary melodrama, *Bertram, or the Castle of St. Aldobrand*. Coleridge's concluding chapter, as rambling in subject matter as the rest of the book, treats briefly the harsh critical reaction to his poem *Christabel*, then turns to his affirmation of his Christian faith and his reasons for holding it. He makes no attempt to summarize his volume, which has presented a remarkably full portrait of his wide-ranging, questioning mind.

Bibliography:
Barfield, Owen. *What Coleridge Thought*. Middletown, Conn.: Wesleyan University Press, 1971. A lucid exposition of Coleridge's philosophy, which is explained in its own terms rather than in its relations to other systems of thought. Emphasizes Coleridge's concept of "Polar Logic" and thoroughly discusses such key concepts as fancy and imagination, understanding and reason.
Eilenberg, Susan. *Strange Power of Speech: Wordsworth, Coleridge, and Literary Possession*. New York: Oxford University Press, 1992. Chapters 6 and 7 are principally concerned with the *Biographia Literaria*. Extensive bibliographic notes and index.
Gravil, Richard, et al., eds. *Coleridge's Imagination: Essays in Memory of Pete Laver*. Cambridge, England: Cambridge University Press, 1985. Fifteen collected essays treating one of the central aspects of Coleridge's thought. Jonathan Wordsworth's " 'The Infinite I AM': Coleridge and the Ascent of Being" and Lucy Nelwyn's "Radical Difference: Coleridge and Wordsworth, 1802" give particular attention to the *Biographia Literaria*.
Holmes, Richard. *Coleridge: Early Visions*. New York: Viking Press, 1990. The first volume of

a projected two-volume biography; covers Coleridge's life up to his departure for Malta in 1804. Well-researched, lively, and sympathetic to its subject. Fully captures Coleridge's brilliant, flawed, fascinating personality.

Richards, I. A. *Coleridge on Imagination*. New York: Harcourt, Brace, 1935. A landmark of Coleridge scholarship, still valuable despite its age. Richards, the father of the New Criticism, delves especially into Coleridge's anticipation of modern psychology.

THE BIRDS

Type of work: Drama
Author: Aristophanes (c. 450-c. 385 B.C.E.)
Type of plot: Social satire
Time of plot: 431-404 B.C.E.
Locale: Athens and Nephelo-Coccygia, the city of the birds
First performed: Ornithes, 414 B.C.E. (English translation, 1824)

> *Principal characters:*
> EUELPIDES, an Athenian
> PISTHETAERUS, his friend
> EPOPS, the hoopoe, formerly a man
> THE BIRDS

The Story:

Euelpides and Pisthetaerus, two disgruntled citizens, wanted to escape from the pettiness of life in Athens. They bought a jay and a crow, which Philocrates, the bird seller, told them could guide them to Epops, a bird not born of birds; from Epops they hoped to learn of a land where they could live a peaceful life.

The jay and the crow guided the pair into the mountains and led them to a shelter hidden among the rocks. They knocked and shouted for admittance. When Trochilus, Epops' servant, came to the door, Euelpides and Pisthetaerus were prostrated with fear; they insisted that they were birds, not men, a species the birds intensely disliked. Epops, a hoopoe with a triple crest, emerged from the shelter; he did not present a very colorful aspect, since he was molting. Epops informed the Athenians that he had once been a man named Tereus, whom the gods had transformed into a hoopoe.

When the Athenians revealed the purpose of their visit, Epops suggested that they move on to the Red Sea, but they said they were not interested in living in a seaport. Epops suggested several other places, but on one ground or another the pair rejected them all. The truth was that they wanted to stay among the birds and establish a city. Interested in this novel idea, Epops summoned the birds, that they too might hear of the plan.

The birds swarmed to the shelter from all directions until every species of Old World bird was represented at the gathering. The leader of the birds, fearful of all men, was dismayed when he learned that Epops had talked with Euelpides and Pisthetaerus, and he incited all the birds to attack, threatening to tear the Athenians to pieces. To defend themselves, Euelpides and Pisthetaerus took up stewpots and other kitchen utensils. Epops rebuked the birds for their precipitous behavior. Finally, heeding his suggestion that perhaps they could profit from the plan of the two men, they settled down to listen. Epops assured the birds that Euelpides and Pisthetaerus had only the most honorable of intentions.

Pisthetaerus told the birds that they were older than human beings. In fact, the feathered tribes had once been sovereign over all creation, and even within the memory of people birds were known to have been supreme over the human race. For that reason, Pisthetaerus declared, people used birds as symbols of power and authority. The eagle, for example, was Zeus's symbol, the owl was Athena's symbol, and the hawk, Apollo's.

Seeing that the birds were interested in his words, Pisthetaerus propounded his plan: The birds were to build a wall around their realm, the air, so that communication between the gods and human beings would be cut off. Both gods and people would then have to recognize the supremacy of the birds. If human beings proved recalcitrant, the sparrows would devour their grain and crows would peck out the eyes of their livestock. If they acceded, the birds would control insect plagues and would help them store up earthly treasures.

The birds were delighted with his plan. Epops ushered the Athenians into his shelter, where the pair momentarily forgot their project when they saw Epops' wife, Procne, who bore an uncanny resemblance to a desirable young maiden. Meanwhile the leader of the birds spoke of humankind's great debt to the birds. Urging human beings to look upon the birds as the true gods, he invited them to join the birds and acquire wings.

Pisthetaerus, winged like a bird, organized the building of the wall and arranged all negotiations with gods and human beings. As he prepared to make propitiatory offerings to the new gods, he was beset by opportunists who had heard of the great project. An indigent poetaster offered to glorify the project in verse. A charlatan offered worthless prophecies. When Meton, a surveyor, offered to divide the realm of the air into the principal parts of a typical Greek city, Pisthetaerus thrashed him. An inspector and a dealer in decrees importuned him and were likewise thrashed and dismissed. Annoyed by these money-seeking hangers-on, Pisthetaerus retreated into Epops' shelter to sacrifice a goat. The leader of the birds again sang the praises of his kind and told how the birds were indispensable to the welfare of humankind.

The sacrifice was completed, and shortly thereafter the wall was finished. All the birds, using their various specialized organs, had cooperated in the construction. Then a messenger reported that a winged goddess, sent by Zeus, had penetrated into the bird kingdom in spite of the wall. Pisthetaerus issued a call to arms—the birds would war with the gods. When Iris, the goddess of the rainbow, made her appearance, Pisthetaerus was enraged at the ineffectualness of his wall. Oblivious of the importance assumed by the birds under Pisthetaerus' influence, Iris declared that she was on her way to ask human beings to make a great sacrifice to the Olympian gods. When Pisthetaerus inferred that the birds were now the only gods, Iris pitied him for his presumption and warned him not to arouse the Olympians' ire.

A messenger who had been sent as an emissary from the birds to human beings returned and presented Pisthetaerus with a gift, a golden chaplet. Apparently they were delighted with the idea of the bird city; thousands were eager to come there to acquire wings and to live a life of ease. Pleased and flattered, the birds welcomed the human beings as they arrived.

First came a man with thoughts of parricide, who felt that he would at last be free to murder his father. Pisthetaerus pointed out to him that the young bird might peck at his father, but that later it was his duty to administer to his father. He gave the youth wings and sent him off as a bird-soldier in order to make good use of his inclinations. Next a poet arrived and asked for wings so that he might gather inspiration for his verse from the upper air. Pisthetaerus gave him wings and directed him to organize a chorus of birds. An informer arrived and asked for wings the better to practice his vicious profession; Pisthetaerus whipped him and in despair removed the baskets of wings that had been placed at the gate.

Prometheus, the friend of humankind, made his appearance. Although he still feared the wrath of Zeus, he raised his mask and reported to Pisthetaerus, who recognized him, that human beings no longer worshipped Zeus since the bird city, Nephelo-Coccygia, had been founded. He added that Zeus was deeply concerned and would send a peace mission to the city; he was even prepared to offer to Pisthetaerus one of his maidservants, Basileia, for his wife.

Poseidon, Heracles, and the barbarian god Triballus came upon Pisthetaerus as he was cooking a meal. Pisthetaerus, visibly impressed by their presence, greeted them nonchalantly. They promised him plenty of warm weather and sufficient rain if he would drop his project. Their argument might have been more effective had they not been so noticeably hungry.

Pisthetaerus declared that he would invite them to dinner if they promised to bring the scepter of Zeus to the birds. Heracles, almost famished, promised, but Poseidon was angered by Pisthetaerus' audacity. Pisthetaerus argued that it was to the advantage of the gods that the birds be supreme on earth since the birds, who were below the clouds, could keep an eye on humankind, while the gods, who were above the clouds, could not. The birds could, in fact, mete out to men the justice of the gods. The envoys agreed to this argument, but they balked when Pisthetaerus insisted upon also having Basileia as his wife.

After a heated discussion, Pisthetaerus convinced Heracles, a natural son of Zeus, that he would receive nothing on the death of Zeus, and that Poseidon, as brother of Zeus, would get Heracles' share of Zeus's property. Heracles and Triballus prevailed over Poseidon in the hot dispute that followed and Basileia was conceded after much argument. The envoys then sat down to dinner. Pisthetaerus, having received the scepter of Zeus, became not only the king of the birds but also the supreme deity.

Critical Evaluation:

First shown at the City Dionysia festival in 414 B.C.E., *The Birds*, although it only won second prize at the festival, is commonly regarded as Aristophanes' finest work. Richly imaginative and full of scintillating wit and lovely lyrical songs, *The Birds* is unquestionably a comic masterpiece. In it, Aristophanes takes a fantastic and amusing idea and quite literally soars into infinity with it. The entire play is a sustained and wonderful joke.

Some critics have concluded that this play satirizes the airy hopes of conquest that gripped Athens at the time the comedy was being written. In 415 B.C.E., a huge military expedition had sailed to subdue Sicily and establish an empire in the west. Two years later, the expedition was proved to have been a fiasco, but in the meantime Athens was rife with grand rumors and expectations. The grand, crazy scheme proposed in *The Birds* seems to convey some of the ebullience of the time. Aristophanes also uses the fantasy as a means of delivering several well-aimed kicks at contemporary figures, at Athens, and at human beings and gods in general. Yet later readers and audiences with no knowledge of its topical allusions could appreciate the work simply for its comedy and its beautiful language. The important facts are contained in the play itself.

In *The Birds*, Aristophanes adapts an idea he used earlier in *The Clouds* (423 B.C.E.), where Socrates explores the starry heavens in a basket. Debt-ridden, plagued by lawsuits in Athens, and seeking a restful retirement community, the hero, Pisthetaerus, conceives the ingenious idea of founding a kingdom in the sky. By organizing the birds to intercept the offerings made by human beings to the gods, he could starve the gods into submission. He could bring human beings to their knees by using the birds to control harvests and livestock. Elderly, quick-witted, and confident, Pisthetaerus is likable as well, a kind of supersalesman. He convinces the birds to collaborate with him and, by his through-the-looking-glass logic, he gains absolute mastery of the cosmos, winning a goddess for a bride in addition.

Yet his true glory rests in the kingdom to which he gives birth—Nephelo-Coccygia, or Cloudcuckooland. It is the equivalent of the Big Rock Candy Mountain, a place where all one's dreams come true. This utopia is in harmony with nature, as represented by the birds, but it attracts idlers, parasites, and nuisances. Bad poets, a false prophet, a magistrate, a process server, an informer, a surveyor, and a sycophant flock to Cloudcuckooland, which gives Pisthetaerus the chance either to reform or to repel them. Even the gods are not really welcome. Pisthetaerus' own companion, Euelpides, leaves of his own accord, sick of being ordered about. The hero exercises his power mainly to exclude undesirables, with the result that when he is finished, his only comrades are the birds.

This rejection of human pests allows Aristophanes' satirical gift free play. The parasites in *The Birds* are the types the dramatist often lampooned, including representatives of the legal profession, fake seers, awful poets, toadies, cowards, pederasts, scientists, informers. Aristophanes is not just saying that without these types a community could be a paradise. He goes further than this. The birds, particularly the chorus, sing exquisitely beautiful and lyrically virtuosic songs that are vastly superior to anything the poets in the play invent. Almost all the birds have beautiful plumage, whereas by contrast the human beings are shabbily dressed. Moreover, whereas the birds are friendly once Pisthetaerus wins them over, the human beings are typically rapacious or looking for a handout. In short, the birds are altogether more desirable as companions than human beings. Even the gods come off poorly by comparison, for they are merely immortal "humans," full of greed and anxious to take advantage of their position.

The Birds is not completely misanthropic, for it pays ample tribute to the eternal human desire to achieve birdlike freedom and beauty. It suggests that human beings can best gain a utopia by their own wits and in friendly communion with nature. The stage called for in the play is singularly bleak, with a single bare tree and a rock, yet it is precisely here that Pisthetaerus founds his fabulous empire. It is a realm of sheer imagination, where anyone can erect castles in the air, fashioned of daydreams and free of life's demands. This is the place where Pisthetaerus can find peace with friends of his own choosing, the kingdom where he can win out over the gods and his human foes alike. Imagination is the single area where a human being can enthrone himself as ruler of the universe. In a sense, *The Birds* is a dramatic hymn to schizophrenia. All the shackles of reality and of human limitation are in abeyance, while the play sails straight up into the wild blue yonder. It is escapist of course, but a daring, witty, songful, exhilarating kind of escape.

"Critical Evaluation" by James Weigel, Jr.

Bibliography:
Dearden, C. W. *The Stage of Aristophanes*. London: Athlone Press, 1976. The work is an overview of Greek theatrical conventions that uses the plays of Aristophanes as models. It discusses form, staging, settings, the chorus, and the use of actors and masks. Each of the plays is discussed individually.
Dover, K. J. *Aristophanic Comedy*. Berkeley: University of California Press, 1972. Textual criticism of the plays of Aristophanes. Discusses *The Birds* as fantasy and as one of the few by the writer that does not point toward a didactic change in politics. Includes a discussion of the sexual humor of the time and the role of women in Greek society as reflected in the plays.
Ehrenberg, Victor. *The People of Aristophanes*. London: Methuen, 1974. Discussion of the creation of types as caricatures of Athenian society. An analysis of old Attic comedy from a sociological perspective.
Lord, Louis E. *Aristophanes: His Plays and His Influence*. New York: Cooper Square, 1963. Traces Aristophanes' influence on Athenian society as well as on later German, French, and English writers. Also presents an overview of Greek comedy as the origin and model for later sociological and political satire.
Spatz, Lois. *Aristophanes*. Boston: Twayne, 1978. A discussion of the evolution of Greek plays and their religious connection to the festival of Dionysus. Presents each play chronologically and depicts the historical context in which it was created.

THE BIRTHDAY PARTY

Type of work: Drama
Author: Harold Pinter (1930-   )
Type of plot: Absurdist
Time of plot: Mid-twentieth century
Locale: England
First performed: 1958; first published, 1959

> *Principal characters:*
> PETEY BOLES, a man in his sixties
> MEG BOLES, his wife, a woman in her sixties
> STANLEY WEBBER, their boarder, a man in his late thirties
> LULU, a neighbor, in her twenties
> GOLDBERG, a man in his fifties
> McCANN, a man of thirty

The Story:

Petey Boles and his wife Meg were the proprietors of a dilapidated boardinghouse in a seaside town in England. One morning, as they were discussing the local news over breakfast, Petey mentioned that two men had approached him on the beach the previous night and asked him for a room. He said the men had agreed to drop by later that day to see if the room were available. Meg told Petey that she would have the room ready if the men arrived.

When their only lodger, Stanley, joined Petey and Meg for breakfast, he complained that he "didn't sleep at all." As soon as Petey left for work as a deck chair attendant on the promenade, Meg began her morning chores, telling Stanley about the two men who spoke to Petey. This news upset Stanley at first, but, after reflection, he dismissed the incident as a "false alarm."

When Lulu, a young neighbor, dropped by to deliver a package, she questioned Stanley about his morning activities and complained that his appearance made her feel depressed. In response, Stanley first lied about what he had done that morning, then asked her to "go away" with him, though they both agreed that there was nowhere for them to go. Lulu called Stanley "a bit of a washout" and left.

When two men named Goldberg and McCann arrived, Stanley avoided them by slipping out the back door. The men reminisced about "the golden days" and the "old school" and suggested that an informant had provided important information regarding their "present job" which, according to Goldberg, was "quite distinct" from their "previous work." Meg told them that if they took the room they could join the household in celebrating Stanley's birthday that night. She explained that he was formerly a pianist and that she hoped he would play at the party. She promised to invite Lulu and to wear her party dress, hoping that the party would improve Stanley's attitude; he had been "down in the dumps lately." Goldberg and McCann decided to take the room and to attend the party.

As soon as they left, Stanley returned and asked Meg about the men. When Meg told him that they were the "ones that were coming," Stanley was visibly dejected. To cheer him up, Meg opened the package Lulu had delivered. It contained a drum that Meg then gave to Stanley for his birthday present. Stanley slung the drum around his neck and marched around the room, beating the drum frantically.

That night, Stanley came downstairs to find McCann "sitting at the table tearing a newspaper into five equal strips." Stanley tried to leave, but McCann stopped him. When Stanley picked up the pieces of paper, McCann became violent and warned Stanley to leave the paper alone. Then Stanley tried to convince McCann that it was not his birthday, and the argument escalated into violence. When Goldberg joined McCann again, Stanley, desperate, claimed that the room Meg had promised the two men was not available, that it was taken, and that they would have to find lodging elsewhere. He told them to "get out," but instead they began to interrogate Stanley, alternating comically nonsensical statements with serious accusations, until their tirade became an existential inquisition questioning Stanley's identity. Finally, both men concluded that Stanley was dead.

The interrogation was interrupted by Meg, who brought Stanley his drum. As Meg began toasting Stanley, Lulu joined the party, flirting with Goldberg, sitting on his lap, and embracing him. Meg then made a play for McCann, and soon all of them were playing blindman's buff. Blindfolded, McCann stumbled around the room until he found Stanley and removed his glasses. In turn, Stanley began to strangle Meg, the lights went out, and, in the confusion, Stanley tried to rape Lulu. When McCann finally found a flashlight, Stanley was backed up against the wall, giggling hysterically.

The next morning Petey, who had missed the party, sat at the table as usual, reading his paper. Meg complained that the drum she bought for Stanley was broken, but she did not remember it being broken at the party. She told Petey that the men were upstairs in Stanley's room "talking" and that the "big car" she had seen in front of the house was probably Goldberg's.

When Goldberg came downstairs, he informed Petey and Meg that he and McCann were taking Stanley with them because Stanley had suffered a "nervous breakdown." McCann came downstairs and explained that Stanley had stopped talking and had broken his glasses trying "to fit the eyeholes into his eyes."

McCann began tearing strips of newspaper again, which so irritated Goldberg that he started shouting for him to stop, and when McCann called him "Simey" he became even more agitated, calming down only when McCann blew into his mouth. Lulu dropped by and accused Goldberg of seducing her after the party, but Goldberg countered that she wanted him to do it. Insulted, Lulu claimed that she had a "pretty shrewd idea" about what was going on and left.

When Stanley was finally brought downstairs, he was dressed in a well-cut suit and a bowler hat. Goldberg and McCann began another sequence of absurd statements regarding Stanley's situation, and by the time they had finished, Stanley could only respond in unintelligible noises. Petey tried to stop them from taking Stanley, but Goldberg told him they were delivering Stanley to "Monty" for "special treatment" and left in a car with McCann and Stanley. While Petey resumed his breakfast, Meg insisted that at the party that night she had been "the belle of the ball" but was so confused that she still believed Stanley was upstairs in his room asleep.

Critical Evaluation:

The Birthday Party, which opened in 1958 to terrible reviews, was Pinter's first full-length play. Neither the public nor the critics were aesthetically or culturally prepared for Pinter's style. Pinter's willful obscurity was often viewed as a breach of contract between the playwright and his audience, leaving many theatergoers feeling dissatisfied, cheated, or foolish, as if they had missed something, while critics and scholars attacked Pinter for his frustrating dismissiveness regarding the meaning of his plays. Later, however, after the success of *The Caretaker* (1960), *The Birthday Party* was revived in London and became a commercial success. Subsequently, it was televised by the British Broadcasting Corporation (BBC) and, in 1968, it opened on Broadway. Along with *The Caretaker* and *The Homecoming* (1965), *The Birthday Party* is generally considered one of Pinter's most significant plays.

A lyrical dramatist, Pinter was impatient with epic plays involving multiple scene changes and large casts, preferring instead to use one set with a small cast. Pinter was also skeptical of "message" plays, which he believed were aesthetically compromised by social didacticism. Pinter explored the formal, structural properties of theater, developing meaning more by design than by plot or characterization. Misunderstood by the general public and professional critics alike, Pinter was accused of intentionally teasing viewers into expecting revelations that were never delivered. Much of the confusion surrounding early public reaction to his work stems from the fact that his plays are neither clearly absurd nor clearly realistic; his style derives its distinctiveness from its quirky combination of elements from both schools. Pinter blends the authentic, mimetic behavior usually associated with realism, evoking a world the audience recognizes as the everyday world they inhabit, with the absurdist vision of a senseless, purposeless world to create, out of seemingly ordinary situations, symbolic overtones that both invite and frustrate interpretation. Frequently labeled an absurdist, Pinter distances himself from any school of theater. He has, however, acknowledged the influence of Irish novelist and playwright Samuel Beckett. The lyrical dialogue, the meaningful silences, the intentional obscurity, the mordant humor, and the cryptic plots are all Beckettian techniques that Pinter has assimilated into his own style.

The Birthday Party represents a turning point in Pinter's career. Not only did he prove he could sustain a full-length work, but he also demonstrated an uncanny control of suspense, a sense of horror which is sustained throughout the play. *The Birthday Party* also marks a change in Pinter's approach to his material, from his cerebral, often abstract, early plays to plays that were less about ideas than they were about people. It was this shift in focus, from the philosophical concerns of the playwright to the human concerns of the characters, that assured Pinter his later critical and commercial success.

In the play, Stanley Webber is hiding from some unspecified event in his past which has forced him into exile, isolated from the world outside the confines of his room. The uneventful, monotonous life at the house seems to be exactly what Stanley needs to maintain his isolation. The order of his routine provides him a measure of security against the contingent outside forces that he fears, while Petey and Meg are like surrogate parents and Lulu is the girl next door.

Stanley's dream of infantile security turns to nightmare when McCann and Goldberg arrive to "do a job." The job, it appears, is to break down Stanley's defenses, both the tactical strategies he has devised to hide from his past and the psychological barriers he has erected against his own sense of guilt, until finally Stanley is unable to answer even the childish riddle of why the chicken crossed the road. A broken man, compliant, no longer able to speak, he is forced to accept his role as a sacrificial victim caught up in a fate he can no longer deny. In his refusal to act and in his withdrawal from the world, Stanley is not, as he hoped, free; he is still a man with a past that must be acknowledged. He is not excused from responsibility for this past simply because he is no longer either active or vital.

While the play is designed to suggest an open-ended set of possible allegorical interpretations—the forced socialization of a reclusive personality, a demand for conformity from a nonconformist, the abstract visiting of justice upon a man guilty of unnamed crimes, the persecution of an artist hounded and ruined by his critics—the significance of the play as drama is in the action itself. Dramatic tension is created and sustained during the play by Pinter's masterful handling of menacing surface details that defy simplistic symbolic interpretations. Of all the suggested meanings, the immediate situation is the most compelling: A man is discovered in hiding; hoodlums brutally reduce him through psychological techniques from a pianist to a babbling idiot, changing him from a man once capable of language and logic to a pliable creature capable only of nonsensical utterances. The inevitability of his dilemma, the hapless and innocent ineffectiveness of Petey and Meg, and the methodical brutality of Goldberg and McCann suggest a disturbing commentary on life concerning the existential suffering of a man desperately searching for certainty and comfort in the face of inexplicable destructive forces.

Jeff Johnson

Bibliography:
Bloom, Harold, ed. *Modern Critical Views: Harold Pinter*. New York: Chelsea House, 1987. An eclectic collection of essays by various critics. Comprehensive analysis of general themes as well as selected specific texts.
Burkman, Katherine H. *The Dramatic World of Harold Pinter: Its Basis in Ritual*. Columbus: Ohio State University Press, 1971. An analysis of Pinter's work viewed through Freudian, Marxist, and myth analysis. Heavy on theory with solid literary analysis of individual plays.
Esslin, Martin. *Theatre of the Absurd*. New York: Viking Penguin, 1987. Overview of the avant-garde and how the term relates to selected dramatic works. Includes an excellent discussion of Pinter's early work.
Gale, Stephen H., ed. *Harold Pinter: Critical Approaches*. Rutherford, N.J.: Fairleigh Dickinson University Press, 1986. A collection of essays by various critics on a wide range of Pinter's work. Places the material in the context of contemporary critical theories.
Merritt, Susan H. *Pinter in Play: Critical Strategies and the Plays of Harold Pinter*. Durham, N.C.: Duke University Press, 1990. Excellent discussion of current and past debates on critical theory as it relates to Pinter's work. Provides scrupulous textual examination.

THE BLACK ARROW
A Tale of the Two Roses

Type of work: Novel
Author: Robert Louis Stevenson (1850-1894)
Type of plot: Adventure
Time of plot: Fifteenth century
Locale: England
First published: 1888

Principal characters:
SIR DANIEL BRACKLEY, a political turncoat
RICHARD "DICK" SHELTON, his ward
JOANNA SEDLEY, Lord Foxham's ward
SIR OLIVER OATES, Sir Daniel's clerk
ELLIS DUCKWORTH, an outlaw
LAWLESS, another outlaw and Dick's friend
RICHARD, duke of Gloucester

The Story:

One afternoon in the late springtime, the Moat House bell began to ring. A messenger had arrived with a message from Sir Daniel Brackley for Sir Oliver Oates, his clerk. When the peasants gathered at the summons of the bell, they were told that as many armed men as could be spared from the defense of Moat House were to join Sir Daniel at Kettley, where a battle was to be fought between the armies of Lancaster and York. There was some grumbling at this order, for Sir Daniel was a faithless man who fought first on one side and then on the other. He had added to his own lands by securing the wardships of children left orphans in those troubled times, and it was whispered that he had murdered good Sir Harry Shelton to make himself the guardian of young Dick Shelton and the lord of the Moat House estates.

As guardian, Sir Daniel planned to marry Dick Shelton to the orphaned heiress of Kettley, Joanna Sedley. He had ridden there to take charge of the girl. Dick, knowing nothing of these plans, remained behind as one of the garrison of the manor. Old Nick Appleyard, a veteran of Agincourt, grumbled at the weakness of the defense in a country overrun by stragglers from warring armies and insisted that Moat House lay open to attack. His prophecy came true. While he stood talking to Dick and Bennet Hatch, Sir Daniel's bailiff, a black arrow whirred out of the woods and struck Nick between the shoulder blades. A message on the shaft indicated that John Amend-All, a mysterious outlaw, had killed old Nick.

Sir Oliver Oates trembled when he read the message on the arrow. Shortly afterward, he was further disturbed by a message pinned on the church door, announcing that John Amend-All would kill Sir Daniel, Sir Oliver, and Bennet Hatch. Dick learned from the message that the outlaw accused Sir Oliver of killing Sir Harry Shelton, Dick's father; but Sir Oliver swore that he had had no part in the knight's death. Dick decided to remain quiet until he learned more about the matter and in the meantime to act in all fairness to Sir Daniel.

It was decided that Hatch should remain to guard Moat House while the outlaws were in the neighborhood. Dick rode off with ten men-at-arms to find Sir Daniel. He carried a letter from Sir Oliver telling of John Amend-All's threats.

At Kettley, Sir Daniel was awaiting the outcome of a battle already in progress, for he intended to join the winning side at the last minute. Sir Daniel was also upset by the outlaw's threats, and he ordered Dick to return to Moat House with a letter for Sir Oliver. He and his men left to join the fighting; but not before he roundly cursed his luck because Joanna Sedley, whom he held hostage, had escaped in boy's clothing. He ordered a party of men-at-arms to search for the girl and then to proceed to Moat House and strengthen the defenses there.

On his return journey, Dick met Joanna, still dressed as a boy, who told him that her name was John Matcham. Dick, unaware that she was Sir Daniel's prisoner, promised to help her reach the abbey at Holywood. As they hurried on, they came upon a camp of the outlaws led by Ellis Duckworth, another man ruined by Sir Daniel. Running from the outlaws, they saw the party of Sir Daniel's retainers shot down one by one. The cannonading Dick heard in the distance convinced him that the soldiers of Lancaster were faring badly in the day's battle. Not knowing on which side Sir Daniel had declared himself, he wondered whether his guardian was among the victors or the vanquished.

Dick and his companion slept in the forest that night. The next morning, a detachment of Sir Daniel's men swept by in disorderly rout. Soon afterward, they saw a hooded leper in the woods. The man was Sir Daniel, attempting to make his way back to Moat House in disguise. He was dismayed when he heard that the outlaws had killed a party of his men-at-arms. When the three arrived at Moat House, Sir Daniel accused Dick of distrust. He claimed innocence in the death of Dick's father and forced Sir Oliver to do the same. Another black arrow was shot through a window into a room in which the three were talking. Sir Daniel gave orders to defend Moat House against attack. Dick was placed under close watch in a room over the chapel, and he was not allowed to see his friend John Matcham.

That night, when John Matcham came secretly to the room over the chapel, Dick learned that the companion of his adventures in the forest was really Joanna Sedley, the girl to whom Sir Daniel had betrothed him. Warned that he was in danger of his life, Dick escaped into the forest. There, he found Ellis Duckworth, who promised him that Sir Daniel would be destroyed.

Meanwhile, the war went in favor of Lancaster, and Sir Daniel's fortunes rose with those of the house he followed. The town of Shoreby was full of Lancastrians all of that summer and fall, and there Sir Daniel had his own house for his family and followers. Joanna Sedley was not with him; she was kept in a lonely house by the sea under the care of the wife of Bennet Hatch. Dick and an outlaw companion, Lawless, went to the town, and while reconnoitering Joanna's hiding place, Dick encountered Lord Foxham, enemy of Sir Daniel and Joanna's legal guardian. Lord Foxham promised that if Joanna could be rescued she would become Dick's bride. The two men attempted a rescue by sea in a stolen boat; but a storm almost sank their boat, and Lord Foxham was injured when the party attempted to land.

That winter, Dick and his faithful companion, Lawless, returned to Shoreby. Disguised as priests, they entered Sir Daniel's house and were there protected by Alicia Risingham, Joanna's friend and the niece of a powerful Lancastrian lord. When Dick and Joanna met, she told him that the following day she was to marry Lord Shoreby against her will. An alarm was given when Dick was forced to kill one of Lord Shoreby's spies. Still in the disguise of a priest, he was taken to Sir Oliver Oates, who promised not to betray Dick if he would remain quietly in the church until after the wedding of Joanna and Lord Shoreby. During the night, Lawless found Dick and gave him the message that Ellis Duckworth had returned and would prevent the marriage.

As the wedding procession entered the church, three archers discharged their black arrows from a gallery. Lord Shoreby fell, two of the arrows in his body. Sir Daniel was wounded in the arm. Sir Oliver Oates denounced Dick and Lawless, and they were taken before the Earl of Risingham. Aided by Joanna and Alicia, Dick argued his cause with such vigor, however, that the earl agreed to protect him from Sir Daniel's anger. Later, learning from Dick that Sir Daniel was secretly plotting with the Yorkist leaders, the earl set him and Lawless free.

Dick made his escape from Sir Daniel's men only to be captured by the old seaman whose skiff he had stolen on the night he and Lord Foxham had attempted to rescue Joanna from Sir Daniel. It took him half the night to escape the angry seaman and his friends. In the morning he was in time to meet, at Lord Foxham's request, young Richard of York, duke of Gloucester. On his arrival at the meeting place, he found the duke attacked by bandits. He saved Richard's life and later fought with the duke in the battle of Shoreby, in which the army of Lancaster was defeated. He was knighted for his bravery in the fight. Afterward, when Richard was giving out honors, Dick claimed as his portion only the freedom of the old seaman whose boat he had stolen.

Pursuing Sir Daniel, Dick rescued Joanna and took her to Holywood. The next morning, he encountered Sir Daniel in the forest near the abbey. Dick was willing to let his enemy escape, but Ellis Duckworth, lurking nearby, killed the faithless knight. Dick asked the outlaw to spare the life of Sir Oliver Oates.

Dick and Joanna were married. They lived quietly at Moat House, withdrawn from the bloody disputes of the houses of Lancaster and York. Both the old seaman and Lawless were cared for in their old age, and Lawless finally took orders and died a friar.

Critical Evaluation:

Robert Louis Stevenson has often been discussed as a children's author, and to some extent this description is justified. Many of his works can be enjoyed by children, and some of them were written with such an audience in mind. *The Black Arrow* was serialized in *Young Folks*, a magazine intended for boys, in 1988, five years after Stevenson's success with *Treasure Island*, which had been written for the same publication.

These novels are also part of a very old tradition of historical romance, dating back at least as far as Sir Thomas Malory and his *Le Morte d'Arthur* (1485). Closer to Stevenson's own time, Sir Walter Scott wrote *Ivanhoe* in 1819, and the two authors are often compared. In his handling of characters and motives, Stevenson clearly broke with the traditions of historical romance.

The Black Arrow is set in the fifteenth century, during the War of the Roses, a civil war among the British aristocracy. This setting presents an author with problems in terms of motivation. Unlike the many stories of Robin Hood, or the adventures of heroes battling ferocious monsters, there is no clear delineation between good and evil in this novel. The various noblemen of the rival houses of York and Lancaster are all ruthless, out for their own advantage. There is never the slightest suggestion that one branch of the royal family is morally superior to the other.

Dick Shelton, the young hero of *The Black Arrow*, begins by being completely uncertain of which side he will support in the war. His guardian, Sir Daniel, also wavers, determined to wait until the last minute and to join the winning side. When Dick becomes convinced that his guardian conspired in the murder of his father, he casts his lot with the side opposing his guardian; the choice is a matter of Sir Daniel's badness, not the side's goodness. Sir Daniel decides to join the Lancasters and Dick joins up with the Fellowship of the Black Arrow, who are Daniel's enemies and are siding with the House of York.

When Dick meets a major leader of that faction, he is suddenly catapulted to great importance in the war, because that leader, Richard, Duke of Gloucester (later to become King Richard III), has a superstitious tendency to support anyone who shares his first name. Richard is obviously a cruel, almost inhuman individual, and Dick Shelton finds it very hard to reconcile his own feelings with his support of such a leader.

The members of the Fellowship of the Black Arrow are also far from pleasant. They are bandits, but not the sort of romantic bandits found in stories of Robin Hood. They steal from people of all classes, for their own gain, and are quite willing to commit murder if necessary. This causes Dick Shelton's final dilemma, and the one that forces him to lose all interest in the adventure in which he has taken part.

At the end of the novel, Dick has the chance to do away with his wicked guardian, but decides to spare his guardian's life. Ellis Duckworth, the chief of the Fellowship of the Black Arrow, kills Sir Daniel instead. Dick marries Joanna, the woman his guardian wanted him to marry (a break with tradition, certainly), and retires from the war.

The Black Arrow works as an exciting adventure story, but it leaves something to be desired as an historical romance. There are certainly villains, including Sir Daniel and Duke Richard, but they are on both sides of the dispute. More important, Dick Shelton is not the romantic hero readers expect in such stories. He makes mistakes, he can never seem to make up his mind, and he "lives happily ever after" without resolving any of his problems.

The Black Arrow is somewhat difficult for a modern reader, because the language is deliberately archaic. A greater difficulty is that Stevenson was working within the framework of Victorian morality. Sex was practically nonexistent in most writings of the time, and violence was relatively tame. The story was written for a children's magazine, which meant that even by Victorian standards, it had to be especially clean. As a result, passionate love scenes and delightfully gory executions are not to be found in the book.

Stevenson was a great writer in this genre, perhaps the last. The term "romance" has changed its meaning over time, and now almost always refers to a formulaic love story rather than to an adventure story. Apart from books intended for children, there are few stories about knights in shining armor being written today, and actual history has largely been replaced by fantasy in adventure stories.

The Black Arrow should not be dismissed because it is children's literature. Like many books for children, this story must be considered within a greater context. Presenting readers with a hero who has difficulty in deciding where his loyalties lie, and villains who seem willing to join whatever side is winning, Stevenson provides a realistic vision of humanity. Dick Shelton, Sir Daniel, and even Richard Crookback are more human than Ivanhoe or Robin Hood. The heroes of *The Black Arrow* are not perfect. Readers can therefore identify with them in a personal way.

"Critical Evaluation" by Marc Goldstein

Bibliography:
Calder, Jenni. *Robert Louis Stevenson: A Life Study.* New York: Oxford University Press, 1980. A study of the works of Stevenson and the circumstances in his life that influenced his books. The emphasis is on the works, rather than on the author's life. Includes analyses of many of Stevenson's novels.
Green, Martin. *Dreams of Adventure, Deeds of Empire.* New York: Basic Books, 1979. A discussion of the genre of romantic adventure in English literature, particularly focusing on the nineteenth century. An excellent source for placing works such as *The Black Arrow* in their literary context.
Kiely, Robert. *Robert Louis Stevenson and the Fiction of Adventure.* Cambridge, Mass.: Harvard University Press, 1964. A discussion of Stevenson's adventure stories, their antecedents in English literature, and their effects on later works. Particular emphasis is placed on *Treasure Island* and *The Black Arrow.*

McLynn, Frank J. *Robert Louis Stevenson: A Biography*. London: Hutchinson University Library, 1993. A highly detailed biography of the author, covering his life from early childhood to his death in Samoa in 1894. Emphasizes the author's extensive travels and their influence on his work.

Pope-Hennessy, James. *Robert Louis Stevenson*. London: Jonathan Cape, 1974. A biography, including a detailed discussion of the times and places in which the works were written and the circumstances that inspired them. Includes many illustrations.

BLACK BOY
A Record of Childhood and Youth

Type of work: Autobiography
Author: Richard Wright (1908-1960)
First published: 1945

> *Principal characters:*
> RICHARD WRIGHT, the narrator
> ELLA, his mother
> NATHAN, his father
> MARGARET and
> RICHARD WILSON, Richard's grandparents
> AUNT MAGGIE and
> UNCLE HOSKINS, Ella's sister and her husband
> CLARK and
> JODY, Richard's aunt and uncle
> ROSS, a member of the Communist Party

The Story:

Richard Wright was a bored and frustrated young boy growing up in Natchez, Mississippi, in a household that he believed neither understood nor appreciated him. At the age of four, he demonstrated his boredom and frustration by setting his house on fire, thus incurring the wrath of his mother, Ella, who beat him into unconsciousness.

When the family moved to Memphis, Tennessee, Richard's father deserted the family, leaving them in poverty. Richard's mother was forced to put her two sons in an orphanage, where they remained for six weeks before being reunited with their mother. They then moved to Elaine, Arkansas, to live with Ella's sister and her husband. En route to Arkansas, they stayed for a brief time in Jackson, Mississippi, with Ella's parents, Margaret and Richard Wilson. Margaret (called Granny), the matriarchal head of the house, was a stern ruler, intolerant of the love of fiction demonstrated by a schoolteacher who boarded with her. The schoolteacher introduced fiction to Richard. From Granny's intolerance, Richard learned lessons about familial rigidity and cruelty that he carried with him throughout his youth.

When they arrived in Elaine, Arkansas, to stay with Aunt Maggie and Uncle Hoskins, it appeared that the Wrights' lives of constant mobility and poverty were over. They finally got the food they needed and the security they had lacked. This sustenance and stability were short-lived, however. Uncle Hoskins was murdered by whites who wanted his saloon, thus compelling the Wright family to leave. They fled to West Helena, a town near Elaine.

The mobility continued when Richard's mother suffered a stroke. Granny took her and the two boys back to Jackson, Mississippi. Even this move was temporary, because Granny could not afford to provide for the three Wrights. She sent Richard's brother to stay with their Aunt Maggie, who had moved to Detroit, and she sent Richard to Greenwood, Mississippi, to live with Uncle Clark and Aunt Jody. This sojourn in Richard's life was a miserable time for him because of his uncle's brutality. In the early 1920's, Richard returned to Jackson, Mississippi.

During his four years in Jackson, from 1921 to 1925, Wright went to two schools, graduating as valedictorian from Smith-Robinson Public School. Although this was his only formal education, he made the most of this brief schooling and immersed himself in all types of literature. He also published his first work, "The Voodoo of Hell's Half Acre," which appeared in the *Southern Register* in 1924.

Despite the fulfillment he discovered in literature, Richard's life in Jackson was painful because of the religious fanaticism of his grandmother and his Aunt Addie, who lived with them. When he could no longer tolerate those surroundings, Richard first got a job to earn money for his escape from Jackson, then stole money so that he would have enough support to go to Memphis, where he stayed for two years.

In 1927, Richard followed his dream to Chicago, to what he envisioned as the promised land of the North. He arrived there looking for the freedom he had been denied in the South, and he believed he had found that freedom as well as solidarity with others in the John Reed Club, which was a Communist literary organization, and then in the Communist Party itself. This was only a momentary stop on his journey toward self-realization, however, for Richard learned that the Communist Party was not the organization he had thought it was. It wished to rob him of his individuality, his unique gifts as a writer, and his desire to be an individual who used words to create a new world. As he observed what the Communist Party did to people, including a man named Ross who was tried as a traitor to the party, Wright realized that he needed to leave the party. Having learned that his calling was not to be a member of an organized group but to be a solitary individual whose strength was his identity as a wordsmith, he accepted his vocation. He was a writer.

Critical Evaluation:

When *Black Boy* was first published in 1945, it did not include Wright's conclusion, intended to be a critical part of the book. This section, published separately in 1977 under the title *American Hunger*, focuses on an important theme of the book—Richard's growth as a writer—and places the first part of the book—his challenging adventures en route to his acceptance of himself as a writer—within this context. The complete edition of the autobiography is now published as two parts, the first titled "Southern Night" and the second titled "The Horror and the Glory." In the concluding paragraph of this self-portrait, Wright announces his vocation as a writer and points, with hope, to the strength of his language:

> I would hurl words into this darkness and wait for an echo, and if an echo sounded, no matter how faintly, I would send other words to tell, to march, to fight, to create a sense of hunger for life that gnaws in us all, to keep alive in our hearts a sense of the inexpressibly human.

Quotations from the Book of Job signal this theme, serving as epigraphs for the entire book and for the first part of the autobiography. The first quotation suggests the struggle that will characterize Richard's flight from the South to the North and his fight to find himself: "They meet with darkness in the daytime/ And they grope at noonday as in the night." The second quotation suggests that "Southern Night" will narrate the Job-like struggle Richard will endure as he moves from adventure to adventure, from home to home, from one stage of his childhood and youth to the next: "His strength shall be hunger-bitten/ And destruction shall be ready at his side." The subtitle of *Black Boy* captures this movement, for the book is indeed "A Record of Childhood and Youth" that is also a portrait of an artist as a young man.

This developing artist re-creates his childhood and youth through dialogue, the use of details, and the selection of symbolic scenes. All these techniques combine to demonstrate the ability of the child and youth to survive, to endure the challenges of his environment so that he can emerge from those surroundings a thoughtful, sensitive writer.

An example of Wright's effective use of dialogue is the conversation between Richard and a white woman whom Richard approaches about doing chores for her. The woman asks if he wants the job, and, learning that he does, poses what she believes is an important question: "Do you steal?" Richard bursts into a laugh and tells the woman that if he were a thief, he would never tell anyone. The woman is enraged by this response, and Richard realizes that he has made a terrible mistake, that he has demonstrated to the woman that he is "sassy," and that he must resume the mask that white people expect of blacks, the mask of respect and deference. Through the dialogue between the woman and Richard, the issue of black-white relations is revealed dramatically and without any need for editorial comment by the narrator.

The use of details also reveals thematic ideas, one of which is the paradoxical situation of destruction as a means of bringing about new growth. The detailed use of fire suggests this paradox, beginning with the opening scene in which Richard sets fire to the house, nearly destroying it and, more important, nearly destroying himself, because his mother had come close to killing him for his action. This act of potential destruction serves as a paradoxical opportunity for growth insofar as Richard learns, at the age of four, that his family is a destructive force in his life, one from which he must flee if he is to be free to pursue his dreams. He is reminded of this lesson at the end of the chapter, when he goes to see his father to request money so that he, his brother, and his mother can go to Arkansas. When Richard arrives at his father's house, he sees not only his father but also a strange woman with him, both sitting before a fire. Once again, detailed use of the image of fire reinforces the theme of destruction and its role in the education process. Richard sees the fire and understands that it represents the destructive force of his father, a force from which he must run if he is to mature.

Wright uses dialogue and details as techniques to plot the journey of his childhood and youth; symbolic scenes act as markers along the trip to self-knowledge. The opening scene and the conversation with the white woman who gives Richard a job doing chores for her are powerful markers. Another symbolic scene occurs in the second half of the self-portrait, when Richard describes his job in a medical research institute in a large, wealthy hospital in Chicago. On Saturday mornings, Richard assists a doctor in slitting the vocal cords of dogs, so that their howling will not disturb the hospital patients. Richard describes the sight of the dogs being rendered unconscious as the result of an injection, then having their vocal cords severed, and finally awakening and being unable to wail. Wright calls this "a symbol of silent suffering," clearly not confined to the canines.

As a book that gives testimony to the transformation of silent suffering into creative growth and as an autobiography that shows the development of a struggling artist who seeks to find words to describe that suffering, *Black Boy* is one of the most significant autobiographies created by an American, black or white. When it was first published in 1945, it was the fourth best-selling nonfiction title that year, and it has continued to be read, reviewed, and respected as a classic study of the growth of a young man and the environment in which he develops. It is both a portrait of an individual and a portrait of a culture, the two struggling with each other and meeting each other "with darkness in the daytime" to illustrate a way to survive, to endure, and to thrive.

Marjorie Smelstor

Bibliography:
Butterfield, Stephen. *Black Autobiography in America*. Amherst: University of Massachusetts Press, 1974. Essays on slave narratives and other influences upon black autobiography as

well as essays on specific writers including Richard Wright, James Baldwin, and Frederick Douglass.

Fabre, Michel. *The Unfinished Quest of Richard Wright.* Translated by Isabel Barzun. Rev. ed. New York: William Morrow, 1973. A significant, and probably the definitive, biography, with much useful information about Wright's literary works, including *Black Boy.*

Felgar, Robert. *Richard Wright.* Boston: Twayne, 1980. A useful overview of the author and his works.

Mack, Richard, and Frank E. Moorer. *Richard Wright: A Collection of Critical Essays.* Englewood Cliffs, N.J.: Prentice-Hall, 1984. A collection of essays examining the writer and his works, including a chronology of important dates in Wright's life.

Margolies, Edward. *The Art of Richard Wright.* Carbondale: Southern Illinois University Press, 1969. A general study, including a brief discussion of *Black Boy* as a film documentary.

BLACK ELK SPEAKS

Type of work: Autobiography
Author: Black Elk (1863-1950), with John G. Neihardt (1881-1973)
First published: 1932

Black Elk Speaks is the work of two collaborators: Black Elk, an Oglala Sioux holy man who tells his life story, and John G. Neihardt, a white man sensitive to Indian culture, who interviewed Black Elk at the Pine Ridge Reservation in 1931 and fleshed out and gave artistic form to Black Elk's account. Black Elk tells the adventure story of a young Sioux boy as he grows into manhood. He had early memories of a father wounded in the Fetterman Fight against the Wasichus (white men), which at first seemed only like a bad dream that he did not understand. Then had come a growing awareness of the white man and first seeing one when he was ten years old. His grandfather made him a bow and arrows when he was five, and with the other boys he had played at killing Wasichus. There were the times when an older man named Watanye took him hunting or down to a creek woods to go fishing, or told him funny stories like that of the misadventures of High Horse in his courtship of a chief's daughter. He had memories of playing pranks with the other boys—chopping off the top of the flagpole at Fort Robinson, teasing the people during a dance—and of endurance contests such as the breast dance, in which the boys burned sunflower seeds on their wrists and tried to keep them there without crying.

Black Elk's account includes memories of famous chiefs he had known: Red Cloud, who was too friendly with the white men, the defiant but always cautious Sitting Bull, and Black Elk's cousin, Crazy Horse, whom he idolized. Black Elk listened to the stories about Crazy Horse and how he became a great and daring warrior. He also heard about Crazy Horse's idiosyncrasies, but he especially remembered Crazy Horse's sense of humor. Crazy Horse had sometimes teased him, and one time he had invited him into his tent to eat with him.

The book is a rich source of information about Sioux customs. The psychologist Carl Jung called it a storehouse of anthropological data. Dances of various kinds were frequent, preceded by elaborate rituals. A comic dance was the heyoka ceremony, which involved considerable horseplay and clowns circulating throughout the crowd, provoking laughter. At the age of nine, Black Elk, with five other boys, had gone through the puberty rite of purification—his body and face painted yellow, a black stripe on either side of his nose, his hair up to look like a bear's ears, and eagle feathers on his head. Even the bison hunt, so necessary for the meat supply and survival, had a ritual that was preceded by the smoking of the sacred pipe and a prayer to the Great Spirit and Mother Earth. The hunters attacked in a special order, with the soldier band first.

Black Elk's account documents events from much of the second half of the nineteenth century as witnessed by a young Indian boy. These include the series of battles in the Indian War and the sufferings of the Sioux as they were displaced from their lands by the white people. When Black Elk was eleven, tensions with the whites mounted as news arrived of the coming of Pahuska (literally, Long Hair, the name given to Custer). Many chiefs gathered in a council to discuss a strategy to deal with the whites, a gathering avoided by Crazy Horse and Sitting Bull, who were suspicious of any agreement with the whites. Black Elk's people did not hear of the subsequent attack on Crazy Horse's village for quite a while, but when they did, they joined the huge gathering of tribes on the Rosebud River. Chaos ensued when the Wasichus attacked, and Black Elk ran from place to place and even killed one of the soldiers.

Custer, eager to avenge the defeat on the Rosebud, decided to attack the Sioux at the Little Big Horn. Black Elk was not yet of age to fight. He watched with the women from the top of a hill, but all he could see was a cloud of dust. When it cleared, he rode down to where a vast army of Wasichus lay dead. He did not see Custer, and no one knew which of the corpses was his. When Black Elk saw a quivering soldier, he shot him with an arrow; he scalped another. He was not sorry, since the Wasichus had come to kill them, but he got sick at the sight of so much blood and went home.

The victory had done no good, however, and the Sioux began to travel the Black Road of suffering. Some went to the white agencies, but most tribes scattered in different directions, pursued by the soldiers. Sitting Bull and Gall went to Canada, but Crazy Horse stayed. Black Elk's tribe moved from one place to another, setting fire to the grass behind them to stave off pursuing soldiers. It was a hard winter. Most of their land had been burned, and there were no bison. One day, when Black Elk was fourteen years old, Dull Knife came with what was left of his starving and freezing people. Black Elk's tribe gave them clothing but not much food because they themselves had only their frozen ponies to eat.

Then came the news of the arrest of Crazy Horse. Black Elk was in the crowd and could not see him, but he heard him struggle. When he heard that he had been killed, all he could do was mourn with the others and watch the next morning as Crazy Horse's father and mother put the body on a drag and bore it away, nobody knew where. After that, Black Elk's tribe went to Canada for a while. When they returned home, they found the people in despair, but soon after they heard about the Messiah and his Ghost Dance, with its mission for a spiritual revitalizing of the Indian nation and restoration of the old Indian culture. Because the Messiah seemed to promise the eventual defeat of the whites, the whites became alarmed and took the offensive again. Black Elk was a grown man when he heard that Sitting Bull had been killed. The Messiah went to the soldiers at Wounded Knee to attempt conciliation. Black Elk, nearby at Pine Ridge, hearing that violence might occur, rode over and arrived to see the result of the Massacre at Wounded Knee: the land covered with the bodies of men, women, and children.

Black Elk Speaks, however, is primarily an account of a man's vision and what became of it. Black Elk first saw his vision when he was nine years old and lying in a coma for twelve days. In his vision he had flown to a council of his grandfathers, where he had been given a hoop representing his people. In its center there was a flowering tree that promised they would flourish. The tree stood at the crossing of a red road, the road of good on which his nation would walk, and a black road, a road of troubles and war, on which he would also walk and where he would have the power to destroy his people's foes.

As a result of having seen the vision, Black Elk became a visionary seeker of salvation for his people. He was troubled because they were threatened not only by the destruction of their culture but by their willingness to adopt the worst habits of their white conquerors. At intervals he sank back into the routines of Sioux life, but the vision recurred periodically throughout his life, for example, after the purification ceremony of puberty and again on his family's journey back from Canada, when he sat alone on a hillside. There, he experienced a strange foreboding that lingered until he had returned home. When a medicine man urged him to tell others of his vision with a dance, he discovered he could heal the sick, and for three years he practiced curing. He felt, however, that his mission was greater than that: It was to save the nation's hoop.

When Buffalo Bill approached the tribe to recruit members for his Wild West Show, Black Elk joined. This, he concluded, was an opportunity to bring the whole world into the sacred hoop. His people had sunk back into selfish pursuits, everybody concerned only about himself. If the Wasichus had a better way, maybe his people should live that way. The travel with the show took him to many places, including into the presence of Queen Victoria, and although it was a happy time, he was in strange world. One night, he experienced another vision and returned to his people. Things there were even worse, however, and he had lost his power. At first, he could hardly remember the vision, but when people came to him for help, the power returned. This was about the time when he heard of the Messiah and for some time he believed that this was the answer to his vision. He soon discovered though, that it, too, was a mistake. At Wounded Knee, he found that his and the Messiah's vision of peace and unity was not to be. When Black Elk looked over the horror of Wounded Knee, he realized that something besides people had died in that bloody mud: a dream.

As the interview ends, Black Elk says to Neihardt: "He to whom a great vision was given is now a pitiful old man who has done nothing. His nation's hoop was there broken and scattered. There was no center any longer, and the sacred tree was dead." After the interview, Black Elk and Neihardt made a trip to Harney Peak in the Black Hills. Black Elk pointed out the spot where he had stood in his vision. He stopped, dressed and painted himself as he was in his vision, faced the west, held the sacred pipe before him in his right hand, and prayed to the Great Spirit: "The tree is withered. Maybe some little root of that tree still lives. Hear me that my people may once more go back into the sacred hoop and find the red road." The old man stood weeping in the drizzling rain. Then the sky cleared again.

Black Elk Speaks reflects Black Elk's and Neihardt's affection for the Oglala Sioux and their sorrow for the Black Road the Sioux had had to travel and for the way of life they had lost. At the same time, the book is permeated by a genuine mysticism, a belief in the unity of all humankind under one great Being. It is about the failure to accomplish a mission but also about a hope that that mission could yet be accomplished.

Thomas Amherst Perry

Bibliography:
Aly, Lucile F. *John G. Neihardt*. Boise, Idaho: Boise State University, 1976. Presents a synopsis of *Black Elk Speaks*, with emphasis on the vision, which Aly finds similar to apocalyptic visions in the Bible and to poems by William Blake.

Dunsmore, Roger. "Nicholaus Black Elk: Holy Man in History." In *A Sender of Words*, edited by Vine Deloria, Jr. Salt Lake City: Howe Brothers, 1984. Concludes that Black Elk's life story and the wisdom of Ogalala Sioux traditions are not merely a romantic longing for a lost way of life but the story of the responsibility imposed on those who have had a great vision.

McCluskey, Sally. "Black Elk Speaks: And So Does John Neihardt." *Western American Literature* 6 (Spring, 1972), 231-242. Discusses *Black Elk Speaks* as literature. Notes the effective use of the first person and control of verbal rhythms.

Rice, Julian. *Black Elk's Story. Distinguishing Its Lakota Purpose*. Albuquerque: University of New Mexico Press, 1991. Points out that Black Elk's story unfolds symbolically like sophisticated fiction, with an intuitive selection of details that create a coherent narrative. Black Elk draws on a wide range of religious metaphors, some of them Christian.

Whitney, Blair. *John G. Neihardt*. Boston: Twayne, 1976. The author concludes that *Black Elk Speaks* is a tragic book about a man who is too weak to implement his vision. The book's function is to preserve that vision for other men.

BLACK LAMB AND GREY FALCON
A Journey Through Yugoslavia

Type of work: Travel writing
Author: Rebecca West (Cicily Isabel Fairfield, 1892-1983)
First published: 1941

Principal personages:
REBECCA WEST, a journalist
HENRY ANDREWS, her husband
CONSTANTINE, a Yugoslav poet
GERDA, Constantine's German wife

The Story:

Rebecca West had not seen Yugoslavia until 1936 when she made a lecture tour in that country; it impressed her so greatly that she decided to travel throughout the country as a tourist in 1937. She also felt that it was important to know something of the country because of the effect it might have upon world politics after the death of its king, Alexander, in 1937. It had been of great importance twenty-three years before, when the assassination of Franz Ferdinand in Sarajevo had precipitated a world conflict.

The author and her husband entered Yugoslavia by railroad on the line which ran from Munich, Germany, to Zagreb, Yugoslavia. Their journey was not a very interesting one, except for the antics of four portly German tourists who shared their compartment and told of the advantages of Germany over the barbaric country they were entering. Zagreb was interesting because it was inhabited mainly by Croats, one branch of the southern Slavic racial group.

In Zagreb, they met Constantine, a Yugoslav poet who had become a friend of the author on her previous trip to his country. Constantine showed them around the city, introduced them to various interesting people, and promised to travel with them during part of their journey. In Zagreb, the tourists were surprised at the depth of feeling and the frequent arguments between the various Yugoslav groups. There were Serbs, Slovenes, and Croats, all under the government at Belgrade, and all disagreeing heartily on government policies. The country was also divided internally by religious beliefs. There were three main religious groups, the Roman Catholics, the Orthodox Catholics, and the Muslims. The latter were either Turks who had remained in the country when the Turkish regime had been driven out more than a century before or Yugoslavs who had accepted the religion of the Muslims during the five centuries of Turkish occupation of that part of Europe. West noted that in Zagreb the people lived in physical comfort, if not in political comfort. She thought that the city had a warm and comfortable appearance but that the Austrian influence had deprived it of much of its originality and naïveté.

From Zagreb the travelers went to visit a castle which had been turned into a sanatorium. They found the place spotlessly clean for such an old castle. The sanatorium was one of the few places in Yugoslavia in which there was little political speculation or argument. The doctors were too busy for politics. Patients were forbidden to discuss such matters.

Returning to Zagreb, the author and her husband went next to Sushak on the Dalmatian coast. Their first impression of the coast was one of bare, treeless hillsides and shouting, angry men; it was poor country. While at Sushak, they crossed the river to Fiume, which seemed to be the kind of city one would find in a bad dream. What struck the travelers as being the worst aspect of this town was the number of officials throughout the city who demanded to see their passports.

After visiting Fiume, they traveled by steamer to Senj, a city which interested them because it had played a decisive part in keeping the Turks from overrunning Western Europe in the sixteenth and seventeenth centuries. The town had financed pirate vessels which had terrorized the Turks and had kept them from using the western part of the Mediterranean and the Adriatic.

Farther south on the Dalmatian coast they visited Split, and found it to have an almost Neapolitan air. The town was also famed for the palace Diocletian had built there. West learned that eighteenth century British architects had borrowed the Georgian style so popular in England and in some parts of the American colonies from Diocletian's palace.

This informaton came to her from a young Englishman she met in Split. The young man was making a living in the city by teaching English. For him, the Dalmatian coast was the closest thing to a terrestrial heaven. West was surprised at the number of old buildings still in use. Diocletian's mausoleum, for example, had been turned into a Christian cathedral. At Split, West disclosed that she had little respect for the Romans and thought far more highly of the Croats and Slavs. She hoped that schoolchildren were not being impressed with the idea that the Romans had been a great and glorious influence on the Yugoslav territory and people, for she saw that their poverty and their reputation as barbarians were the result of the Roman attitude toward their forebears, an attitude maintained by Central Europeans in the twentieth century.

The last stop on the Dalmatian coast was Dubrovnik, a disappointment to the travelers. There they wired their friend Constantine to meet them at Sarajevo, to which they were going by automobile from Dubrovnik. On the way to Sarajevo, they passed a valley which West could describe only as something out of Baron Munchausen's tales. This valley was a lake in the wintertime, but in the spring the water went out of the valley through some unknown outlet to the sea, leaving fertile fields in which peasants planted crops during the summer months.

At Sarajevo they met Constantine and his German wife, Gerda. The German woman made the air about the party a bit tense because of the deprecating attitude which she, like most Germans, took toward Yugoslavs. While at Sarajevo they wandered throughout the town and were able to visit the family of the man who had killed Franz Ferdinand in 1914.

The next phase of their journey was a rail trip to the capital city of Belgrade, where they were impressed by the large supply of good food available and the provincial air of the capital and its people. The part of the journey by rail from Belgrade to Skoplje was almost as uninteresting as the trip from Munich to Zagreb. More enjoyable was a stay at Lake Naum, on the southern edge of Yugoslavia near Greece and Albania. It was a wild and beautiful part of the country, despite the poverty of the land and its people.

From the Lake Naum area, they went back part of the way to Belgrade on the railroad and then motored to Kotor on the Dalmatian coast. There Constantine and his German wife bade them goodbye. The author and her husband took a ship at Kotor and traveled up the coast, returning to Zagreb by rail. They visited the Plivitse Lakes on the way. The last leg of the journey was by rail from Zagreb to Budapest, Hungary.

The sadness of the plight of the Yugoslavs was impressed on West one last time in Budapest. There she met a university student who wanted to write a paper about West's work. The girl tried to prevent West from discovering that her family had come from the Balkans, for the girl wanted to be a part of the Central European culture rather than a part of the one she had inherited.

Critical Evaluation:

Black Lamb and Grey Falcon is a travelogue of epic sweep through Yugoslavia and its many cultural regions: Croatia, Dalmatia, Herzegovina, Bosnia, Serbia, Macedonia, Old Serbia, and Montenegro. Rebecca West re-created the experience of her journey through culture and history, intertwining the near and distant past in a narrative which possesses something of the flavor of the great works of Marcel Proust. Her guide, the poet Constantine, speaks as the poetic imagination of the Yugoslav people in this cultural dialogue between Eastern and Western Europe.

The book's focus is on the folk culture of Yugoslavia and the reactions and impressions of the narrator. The black lamb in the title refers to an incident in the book in which a lamb is sacrificed as part of an ancient religious custom; the grey falcon alludes to an old and popular Slavic folk song. Set in the years just prior to World War II, *Black Lamb and Grey Falcon* evokes the political attitudes of the period, somewhat sentimental expressions of the Marxist leanings of Constantine and the humanism of West and her husband, ironically counterposed by history, with Nazism and Fascism nascent in the background. The philosophical digressions on love and jealousy, for instance, are interesting though less than profound. The tone of the book throughout is polite, almost to a fault, for it disguises a patronizing and sentimental stance toward the "picturesque" life of the peasants.

Rebecca West's style is elegant, witty, and rhetorically grand. Her first-person narrative permits frequent and delightful digressions into entertaining personal vignettes. The book is a compendium of intellectual and historical reactions to a personal experience, relayed through the highly literate consciousness of West. It is literature of the literate experience, a highly elaborate curio, which despite its condescension does not fail to entertain.

Bibliography:
Glendinning, Victoria. *Rebecca West: A Biography*. New York: Knopf, 1987. Several pages on the sources and critical reception of *Black Lamb and Grey Falcon* defending West's approach against the charges of several critics. Glendinning explores West's politics and provides a helpful discussion of West's interpretation of Yugoslav history and the aftermath of World War II.

Orel, Harold. *The Literary Achievement of Rebecca West*. New York: St. Martin's Press, 1986. The last chapter is an extensive, critical examination of West's work, emphasizing her anticipation of World War II. He takes issue with some of her historical judgments but regards the book as her "finest contribution to literature."

Rollyson, Carl. *Rebecca West: A Saga of the Century*. New York: Scribner, 1995. This biography contains several chapters on the sources of *Black Lamb and Grey Falcon*. It also provides a new, comprehensive interpretation, surveying previous criticism and treating the book as a "self-correcting masterpiece."

Tillinghast, Richard. "Rebecca West and the Tragedy of Yugoslavia." *The New Criterion* 10 (June, 1992): 12-22. Although marred by inaccurate comments on West's biography, Tillinghast's discussion of her work is sympathetic and insightful, showing how relevant it is to contemporary history. He is particularly helpful in pointing out West's biases—such as her animus against the Turks.

Wolfe, Peter. *Rebecca West: Artist and Thinker*. Carbondale: Southern Illinois University Press, 1971. The beginning and end of the book treat *Black Lamb and Grey Falcon* as West's most important work. Wolfe pays special attention to the book's style and structure and to how the influence of Saint Augustine colors much of what she writes.

THE BLACK SWAN

Type of work: Novella
Author: Thomas Mann (1875-1955)
Type of plot: Symbolism
Time of plot: 1920's
Locale: Düsseldorf, Germany
First published: Die Betrogene, 1953 (English translation, 1954)

Principal characters:
FRAU ROSALIE VON TÜMMLER, a middle-aged widow
ANNA, her spinster daughter
EDUARD, her teenage son
KEN KEATON, a young American who tutors Eduard in English

The Story:

During the 1920's, Frau Rosalie von Tümmler was living in Düsseldorf with her unmarried daughter Anna and her teenage son Eduard. Widowed for more than a decade, Frau von Tümmler had been the wife of a German lieutenant general who was killed in action in 1914. After his death, she had retired to a small villa in Düsseldorf, partly because of the beautiful parks in which she could indulge her love for nature. She had many friends of her own age and older, and she believed her life quite happy. She had always been attractive to men, but as the time for her change of life neared, she and Anna were drawn closer to each other. Anna, who had always been cut off from companions of her own age because of her clubfoot, was an abstract painter. Rosalie was often dismayed by her daughter's canvases of mathematical or symbolic designs, but she tried to understand what Anna was trying to express. On their walks together, they had many long talks on nature and art. Sometimes Rosalie complained that nature was cheating her by taking away her function as a woman while her body remained youthful and her mind as active as ever. Anna tried to convince her that body and soul would soon be brought into harmony by psychological changes following physical ones.

Rosalie was fifty years old when she hired Ken Keaton, a young American, to give Eduard lessons in English. Keaton was a veteran who had chosen to live in Europe after the war. Like most expatriates of his generation, he spoke of his own country as a place of shoddy materialism, a land that in its pursuit of money had lost all respect for the art of living. His interest in Rhineland history had brought him to Düsseldorf, where he supported himself by tutoring the wives and children of the well-to-do.

Keaton brought a new spirit of youthfulness and vitality into the Tümmler household. Rosalie often listened outside her son's room to the snatches of conversation and the bursts of laughter she could hear from within; after a time, the young American was accepted as a friend of the family and soon thereafter Rosalie realized that she was falling in love with the virile young man. Anna, watching what was happening, was greatly disturbed by this promise of her mother's autumnal romance, especially when Rosalie announced triumphantly that nature had given her a second period of physical flowering by renewing her fertile cycles. Rejoicing in what she believed a miracle of rejuvenation, Rosalie refused to listen to her daughter's warnings.

Early in the spring, the Tümmlers and Keaton went on an outing to Holterhof Castle, a rococo structure not far from the city. Rosalie was pleased to show the young American the castle and

679

the park, in which the spirit of earlier German culture had been preserved. Keaton had brought stale bread to feed the black swans on the castle lake. Rosalie took some of the bread and nibbled at it playfully while one of the giant swans hissed indignantly for his dinner. In an alcove of the chilly, musty old castle, she threw her arms about the young man and embraced him. On the way home, she decided that she would give herself to Keaton without reserve.

That night, she was taken suddenly ill and rushed to the hospital, where an examination revealed that she was suffering from cancer. Nature had played on her the cruelest of jokes—the signs of renewed fertility had been nothing more than the symptoms of coming death.

Critical Evaluation:
  The Black Swan is a slight work that followed the vast, complicated novels of Thomas Mann's later period—such works as *Joseph and His Brothers* (1933-1943) and *Doctor Faustus* (1947). Mann had previously worked successfully in the brief narrative form of the novella in *Tonio Kröger* (1903) and *Death in Venice* (1912). As he demonstrates in *The Black Swan* and the earlier stories, he does not need breadth to give his writing the effect of depth and insight.

  In this work, there are reminiscences of *Death in Venice*, that wonderful short novel dealing with the dissolution of personality and with death in a plague-stricken pleasure resort on the Adriatic. *The Black Swan* presents on several planes of meaning the writer's favorite themes of life and death, body and soul, nature and spirit, art and decay, love and death. At the same time, his sense of ironic detachment and the deliberate parody of eighteenth century style make this one of the most puzzling books of his career.

  The plot of *The Black Swan* is simple almost to the point of banality. Yet by manipulating symbols and repeating key words and phrases that linger in the memory like motifs in music, Mann infuses multiple levels of meaning. In one sense, *The Black Swan* is a fable of one of the ways in which the creative spirit sometimes dies, in a late-flowering resurgence that is often no more than a prelude to death. The symbolism of death and decay also points to an interpretation of Rosalie as twentieth century Europe, an aging continent weakened by disease from within but finding in the symptoms of its corrupted state an urge to self-destructive vitality. Images of death are everywhere apparent in the novel: in the picture of the black swan stretching its wings and hissing for the stale crust that Rosalie withholds, in the decaying ancient castle moldering with dampness where Rosalie declares her love for the young American, in the corpse of the small animal that Rosalie and Anna find during one of their walks.

  In *Tonio Kröger*, the leading character remarks that once an idea takes hold of him, he finds it all about him, so that he can even smell it. *The Black Swan* creates its atmosphere of the charnel house in its sensuous effects. The novel begins as the story of a sentimental matron who loves nature, but the atmosphere surrounding the characters grows almost suffocating as the situation unfolds. What seems at first a light, playfully humorous parody of the eighteenth century sentimental story becomes a grotesque, almost diabolical fable when the reader realizes the contrast between the story being told and the manner of its telling. The book becomes a caricature and a brutal exposure of modern attitudes and failings. Perhaps Mann's intention was better illustrated in the original German title of the book—*Die Betrogene*, "the deceived." The novel is a study of deception and self-deception, of betrayal and death.

  In spite of its disturbing and sometimes repellent details and somberness of vision, *The Black Swan* is a miniature work of art. Mann wrote it at an age when most writers are content with the place they have won by their performances in the past. Though the novel was written in a diminished tone, it probes deeply into areas of the strange and the perverse for its reflection of an age divided between the opposing forces of nature and the spirit.

Bibliography:

Feuerlicht, Ignace. *Thomas Mann.* New York: Twayne, 1968. A brief treatment of *The Black Swan* in chapter 9 calls for a broader, more sympathetic reception. Views the story structurally as a novella—with its trademark turning point, dominant image, and strange occurrence—and not as a short story.

Latta, Alan. "The Reception of Thomas Mann's *Die Betrogene*: Tabus, Prejudices, and Tricks of the Trade." *Internationales Archiv für Sozialgeschichte der Deutschen Literatur* 12 (1987): 237-272. Painstakingly thorough studies of the novella's reception, including detailed documentation.

_____. "The Reception of Thomas Mann's *Die Betrogene*: Part II, The Scholarly Reception." *Internationales Archiv für Sozialgeschichte der Deutschen Literatur* 18 (1993): 123-156. Latta demonstrates how the initial lack of understanding for the novella has been superseded in recent years by more open, thoughtful, and less taboo-determined interpretations.

Mileck, Joseph. "A Comparative Study of *Die Betrogene* and *Der Tod in Venedig.*" *Modern Language Forum* 42 (December, 1957): 124-129. Though Mann himself claimed these novellas are unrelated, Mileck compares the theme of death through love (*Liebestod*) in both novellas.

Schoolfield, George C. "Thomas Mann's *Die Betrogene*." In *Thomas Mann*, edited by Harold Bloom. New York: Chelsea House, 1986. A scholarly, positive, and balanced treatment of the work, though it does not reflect the feminist concerns of more recent readings. Excellent on influences and the mythological background of the characters.

Straus, Nina Pelikan. Introduction to *The Black Swan*, by Thomas Mann, translated by Willard R. Trask. Berkeley: University of California Press, 1990. A female-centered, though not necessarily a feminist, positive reading of the novella. An excellent place to begin an in-depth interpretive study. Contains a brief description of earlier negative readings. No notes or bibliography.

BLACK THUNDER

Type of work: Novel
Author: Arna Bontemps (1902-1973)
Type of plot: Historical realism
Time of plot: 1800
Locale: Henrico County, Virginia
First published: 1936

> *Principal characters:*
> GABRIEL, a slave who leads a rebellion
> JUBA, his girlfriend
> THOMAS PROSSER, his cruel master
> BUNDY, an old slave whom Prosser abuses
> MOSELEY SHEPPARD, a slave owner, inherently decent
> BEN and
> PHAROAH, Sheppard's slaves who betray the rebellious slaves
> MINGO and
> MELODY, freed slaves

The Story:

In 1800, in Henrico County, Virginia, a slave rebellion grew out of Thomas Prosser's beating of his aging slave Bundy, whom he considered to be more of a liability than an asset. Bundy's main wish had been to die free, but the beating resulted in his death. He had dreamed of a rebellion like the Toussaint L'Ouverture uprising in Santo Domingo, which had drawn enough public support to succeed.

A group of French liberals in Richmond, espousing the ideals of the recent French Revolution, opposed slavery. They thought that slave owners oppressed both blacks and poor whites. These liberals, labeled as Jacobins and revolutionaries, sought to enlighten Americans and bring about greater equality for oppressed groups throughout the world. Despite their high ideals, the Jacobins were too small a group to be effective in protecting the blacks, who were considered chattel, in their rebellion against involuntary servitude. The Jacobins did, however, circulate abolitionist ideas and ideals, as did Alexander Biddenhurst, a Philadelphia abolitionist who was making plans to smuggle black slaves to Canada and to freedom.

Following Bundy's death and funeral, Gabriel, another slave, solidified plans for a rebellion to protest this senseless killing. Gabriel was a man of singular leadership and organizational ability, but was limited in what he could do for the cause he espoused. Obsessed with a bedeviling dream of freedom, he always understood the odds against his succeeding. Despite these odds, he mustered a rebellious army of eleven hundred blacks. They planned to overrun Richmond's arsenal and take control of that city, nearby Petersburg, and, eventually, Norfolk. Gabriel thought that most slaves shared his obsession, except for those who had been beaten down and co-opted to the point that their spirit and will were broken. Mingo, a freed slave, strongly supported the freeing of all slaves, saying that it was no good to be free if one's people, in his case his wife and children, still were slaves.

Gabriel believed that right would triumph in the end, although his chances of personally witnessing that triumph were remote. He had that unique sense of destiny that motivates great leaders and demanded basic human rights for all people, regardless of race and social position. Although the dominant society was against his cause, Gabriel had the conviction that God and universal codes of human conduct were on his side and would eventually prevail.

Gabriel approached his task of leading blacks to freedom fearlessly, yet matter-of-factly. His fight was futile, however, in part because unusually bad weather had caused extensive flooding that made it impossible for his full army to assemble. Recognizing a task he was called upon to do, he was determined to carry it out, regardless of what personal consequences might ensue. Gabriel was imbued not so much with a special stripe of courage as with a consuming zeal for the liberation of his people. At times, he was naïve in his belief that he could change the system.

The slave rebellion was suppressed. Ben and Pharoah, two slaves belonging to Moseley Sheppard, were caught between loyalty to their owners and to their fellow slaves. After the rebellion erupted, Gabriel remained steadfast. Ben and Pharoah, however, fearing for their lives if the rebellion failed, fled to Richmond in terror to report the uprising to the whites.

The result was crushing defeat, and the hanging of countless innocent black slaves. Six weeks after the uprising, Gabriel was executed, going to the gallows convinced that his actions and his death were necessary steps toward the eventual liberation of his people. Thomas Prosser flogged Juba, Gabriel's girlfriend, who had accompanied Gabriel throughout the rebellion, then sold her down the river.

Critical Evaluation:

Black Thunder is often compared to William Styron's *The Confessions of Nat Turner* (1962), which focuses on a similar rebellion in Virginia. *Black Thunder*, which was called the best novel by an African American writer in its time, possesses a verity that is not consistently present in Styron's celebrated book, excellent though it is in its own right. Perhaps Bontemps succeeds more completely because, like his characters, he is an African American. He understands subtleties relating to the black experience to which persons of other races may not fully relate.

A notable characteristic of this novel is the dispassion of Bontemps' presentation. He never suggests that all slave owners were bogeymen or that all slaves or free blacks were saints. He writes with detachment, restraint, and balance, always permitting the facts to speak for themselves. This approach adds force to the topic that concerns Bontemps centrally. The telling of his tale, unbiased as it is, strikes with incredible force.

Bontemps presents his story in small segments, each dominated by a central character or event. This technique provides differing points of view and adds to the detachment with which the story unfolds. Segmenting the narrative also gives the reader a sense of immediacy as it is recounted.

Bontemps places slavery in an interesting social and historical perspective by including a report of the Virginia legislature that called for its members of Congress to promote federal legislation calling for the resettlement of all slaves in Louisiana as a means of ameliorating the racial problems that threatened the social structure of their state and of the South. He also writes about the Federalist press, which used the rebellion on which this story is based as a means of supporting a second term for President John Quincy Adams, citing the rebellion as something related to the radical social ideas of his opponent, Thomas Jefferson. By including this material, Bontemps conceptualizes the rebellion to an arena larger than the area in which it occurred, larger than Henrico County and its environs, larger, indeed, than Virginia or the South.

Bontemps' understanding of black folkways, many of them harking back to Africa, is apparent in *Black Thunder*. Bundy's funeral is pervaded with folkways relating to death and burial, such as roasting a pig and putting it on the grave. Still more telling is the fact that Bundy's spirit invades the being of one of his fellow slaves, which is in keeping with folklore conventions relating to one's departure from life.

In several instances, the rebels have long discussions about the stars and their meaning. Such an acceptance of signs and portents is well established in the traditions of African folklore. The rebels also attribute the success of the Toussaint rebellion in Santo Domingo to the fact that a hog was killed and its blood drunk before the uprising. Gabriel takes no part in this superstition, for which some of his followers later blame him.

A prediction of the death of one of the slaves is strengthened when the female house slaves shoo from the house a bird that has flown in. Birds are common harbingers of death in folk literature. In the course of the uprising, several of the slaves use charms as forms of protection, and countercharms against their oppressors.

A striking example of Bontemps' use of folklore has to do with "conjure-poisoning," which is akin to the use of voodoo in some African and Caribbean societies. Pharoah, whose death has already been foretold by the bird in the house, is in a state of panic. He has betrayed his fellow slaves. After spreading the news of the rebellion among the white community, he falls sick, convinced that he is the victim of conjure-poisoning, a conviction that, added to his other pressures, quickly drives him mad.

These folk elements in *Black Thunder* lend a great deal to its authenticity. Such elements help readers to understand how the rebels could initially be galvanized into action as a group. Their belief in spirits, signs, portents, and conjuring all impose a unity upon the community of slaves who engage in the uprising.

By never deviating from his controlling theme, which concerns the basic need for living creatures to be free, Bontemps achieves a focus that results in a book of unique and remarkable credibility. Bontemps' presentation of Gabriel is psychologically convincing. If readers come away from the novel thinking that Gabriel is bigger than life, it is not because Bontemps has said that he is. Gabriel wins the trust of those who know him. Neither notably superstitious nor fervently religious, he is single-minded in his quest for freedom, which he realizes will not be likely to result in his personal freedom but that, over time, may result in the liberation of his people. It is only in this broader context that his actions, which are suicidal, make sense. He knows the risk, but he proceeds anyway. Psychologically, Gabriel is more akin to Martin Luther King, Jr., than to any other major twentieth century African American leader, because King knew that he had embarked upon a course that was likely to prove fatal. Gabriel knows this too, but he continues to strive for the good of his people.

R. Baird Shuman

Bibliography:

Baker, Houston A., Jr. *Black Literature in America.* New York: McGraw-Hill, 1971. Places Bontemps within the broad context of twentieth century black literature. Asserts that Bontemps is more skilled as a poet than as a fiction writer. Clearly identifies significant symbols and images Bontemps used in his fiction.

Bone, Robert A. *The Negro Novel in America.* Rev. ed. New Haven, Conn.: Yale University Press, 1965. Argues that Bontemps is a transitional black writer whose work is rooted in the Harlem Renaissance and in the Depression era. Good discussion of the structure of *Black Thunder,* which Bone considers Bontemps' finest novel.

Bontemps, Arna. *Arna Bontemps-Langston Hughes Letters, 1925-1967.* Selected and edited by Charles H. Nichols. New York: Paragon House, 1990. Extensive collection of letters between

Bontemps and his friend and sometime collaborator, Langston Hughes, reveals a great deal about both artists' aesthetics. The 1935-1937 letters are particularly relevant.

Davis, Arthur P. *From the Dark Tower: Afro-American Writers, 1900-1960*. Washington, D.C.: Howard University Press, 1974. Chapter on Bontemps deals insightfully with *Black Thunder* and several of his other novels, making thoughtful comparisons among them. Illuminates the psychological validity of Bontemps' characterizations.

Gloster, Hugh M. *Negro Voices in American Fiction*. Chapel Hill: University of North Carolina Press, 1948. Still illuminating assessment of *Black Thunder*. Acknowledges the novel's shortcomings, but takes no exception to A. B. Spingarn's contention that *Black Thunder* is the best historical novel written (up to the mid-1940's) by an African American.

BLEAK HOUSE

Type of work: Novel
Author: Charles Dickens (1812-1870)
Type of plot: Social realism
Time of plot: Mid-nineteenth century
Locale: London, Lincolnshire, and Hertfordshire, England
First published: 1852-1853

Principal characters:

JOHN JARNDYCE, the owner of Bleak House
RICHARD CARSTONE and
ADA CLARE, his cousins
ESTHER SUMMERSON, his ward and companion to Ada
ALLAN WOODCOURT, a young physician
LADY DEDLOCK, Sir Leicester Dedlock's wife
TULKINGHORN, a solicitor
WILLIAM GUPPY, Tulkinghorn's clerk
SNAGSBY, a law-stationer
KROOK, the owner of a rag-and-bottle shop
JO, a young street sweeper

The Story:

The suit of *Jarndyce vs. Jarndyce* was a standing joke in the Court of Chancery. Beginning with a dispute as to how the trusts under a Jarndyce will were to be administered, the suit had dragged on, year after year, generation after generation, without settlement. The heirs, or would-be heirs, of suits like *Jarndyce vs. Jarndyce* spent their lives waiting. Some, like Tom Jarndyce, blew out their brains. Others, like tiny Miss Flite, visited the court in daily expectation of some judgment that would settle the disputed estate and bring her the wealth of which she dreamed.

Among those involved in the Jarndyce suit were John Jarndyce, grandnephew of the Tom Jarndyce who had shot himself in a coffeehouse, and his two cousins, Richard Carstone and Ada Clare. Jarndyce was the owner of Bleak House in Hertfordshire, a country place by no means as dreary as its name. His two young cousins lived with him. He had provided Esther Summerson as a companion for Ada. Esther had suffered an unhappy childhood under the care of Miss Barbary, her stern godmother, and a servant, Mrs. Rachel. The two had told the girl that her mother was a wicked woman who had deserted her. Miss Barbary was now dead, and Mr. Jarndyce had become Esther's benefactor. Upon arriving in London on her way to Bleak House, Esther Summerson had found an ardent admirer in William Guppy, a clerk in the office of Kenge and Carboy, Jarndyce's solicitors.

It was Guppy who first noticed Esther's resemblance to Lady Dedlock, who was also tenuously concerned in the Jarndyce suit. Sir Leicester and Lady Dedlock divided their time between their London home, where Lady Dedlock reigned over society, and Chesney Wold, their country estate in Lincolnshire. One day, when Lord Dedlock's solicitor, Tulkinghorn, was in the Dedlocks' London home, Lady Dedlock swooned at the sight of the handwriting on a legal document. Immediately suspicious, the lawyer traced the handwriting to its source, the stationer Mr. Snagsby, who could, however, tell him only that the paper had been copied by a man named Nemo, a lodger in the house of the junk dealer Mr. Krook. When Mr. Tulkinghorn went there, he found Nemo dead of an overdose of opium. He was convinced that Nemo was not the dead man's real name, but he could learn nothing of the man's identity or connections.

Allan Woodcourt, a young surgeon who had been called to minister to the dead Nemo, requested an inquest. One of the witnesses called was Jo, a crossing sweeper whom Nemo had often befriended. A short time later, Jo was found with two half crowns on his person. He explained that they had been given to him by a lady he had guided to the gate of the churchyard where Nemo was buried. Jo was arrested, and as a result of the cross-examination that followed, Mr. Guppy questioned the wife of an oily preacher named Chadband and found that the firm of Kenge and Carboy had once had charge of a young lady with whose aunt Mrs. Chadband had lived. Mrs. Chadband was the Mrs. Rachel of Esther Summerson's childhood. She revealed that Esther's real name was not Summerson, but Hawdon.

The mystery surrounding Esther Summerson began to clear. A French maid who had left Lady Dedlock's service identified her former mistress as the lady who had given two half crowns to the crossing sweeper. It was established that the man who had called himself Nemo was a Captain Hawdon. Years before, he and the present Lady Dedlock had fallen in love. Esther was their child, but Lady Dedlock's sister, Miss Barbary, angry at her sister's disgrace, had taken the child and moved to another part of the country. Esther's mother later married Lord Dedlock. She was afraid of exposure but also guiltily overjoyed that the child her unforgiving sister had led her to believe dead was still alive.

Mr. Guppy informed Lady Dedlock that a packet of Captain Hawdon's letters was in the possession of the junk dealer, Krook. Lady Dedlock asked Guppy to bring them to her, and the wily law clerk agreed, but on the night he was to obtain the letters the drunken Krook exploded of spontaneous combustion; presumably the letters burned with him.

In the meantime, Richard Carstone had become completely obsessed by the Jarndyce case and had abandoned all efforts to establish his career. Living in the false hope that the Chancery suit would soon be settled, he spent the little money he had on an unscrupulous lawyer named Vholes. When Jarndyce remonstrated, Richard thought that his cousin's advice was prompted by selfish interests. Ada Clare was worried about Richard's behavior, but she remained loyal to him and secretly married him so that her own small fortune might stand between Richard and his folly.

When Esther Summerson fell desperately ill of a fever, Lady Dedlock felt all of a mother's terror. When Esther gradually recovered, Lady Dedlock went to Hertfordshire and revealed herself to her daugher. As a result of her illness, Esther lost her beauty and thus her resemblance to Lady Dedlock. John Jarndyce felt free for the first time to declare his love for her and asked her to marry him; she accepted.

Tulkinghorn was murdered, and several nights later, when she knew her secret was about to be revealed to her husband, Lady Dedlock fled. It was discovered that Tulkinghorn had been murdered by the French maid through whom he had learned of Lady Dedlock's connection with Jo. The maid had attempted to blackmail the lawyer, and when he threatened her with imprisonment, she killed him. Inspector Bucket, who solved the mystery of the murder, also informed Lord Dedlock of his wife's past. The baronet, who had suffered a stroke, told the detective that his feelings for his wife were unaltered and that he was to employ every means to bring her back. It was Esther Summerson, however, who found her mother dead at the gate of the churchyard where Captain Hawdon was buried.

Among Krook's effects was a Jarndyce will made at a later date than the one that had been disputed in Chancery for so many years. It settled the question of the Jarndyce inheritance forever. Richard and Ada were declared the heirs, but the entire fortune had been consumed in court costs. Richard did not long survive this final blow; he died, leaving his wife and infant son in the care of John Jarndyce.

When John Jarndyce discovered that Esther's true love was young Doctor Woodcourt, he released her from her promise to marry him and in his generosity brought the two lovers together. Before her wedding, Jarndyce took her to see a country house he had bought in Yorkshire. He had named it Bleak House, and it was his wedding present to the bride and groom. There Esther lived, happy in the love of her husband and her two daughters and in the lasting affection of John Jarndyce, the proprietor of that other Bleak House that would always be her second home.

Critical Evaluation:

Bleak House was first published as a serial and appeared in book form in 1853 at the height of Charles Dickens' career. Preceded by *Martin Chuzzlewit* and followed by *Hard Times*, the work comes early in the group of Dickens' great novels of social analysis and protest. A major critical anatomy of mid-nineteenth century England, *Bleak House* shows some signs of concessions to audience taste in the use of pathos, melodrama, and a somewhat strident moralism. Yet Dickens manages to weave out of these a controlled assessment of the corruption at the heart of his society.

At the center of the novel's intricate plot is the lawsuit of *Jarndyce vs. Jarndyce*. To this frame, Dickens adds an interlocking structure of subplots. On one level, the plot is a series of thin detective stories woven together so as to involve all strata of society. Character after fascinating character appears in episodes that are each of gripping interest; in Dickens' masterly resolution, no earlier action or detail remains extraneous.

The third-person narrator of most of *Bleak House* is a sharply ironic commentator on the political, social, and moral evils that abound in the book. There is no ambiguity in the narrator's stance toward the selfishness and irresponsibility he recounts (though he is not quite as sardonic or homiletic as the narrator of *Hard Times*), but this stern tone is both relieved and reinforced by the introduction of a second first-person narrator, Esther Summerson. While some critics have seen the dual narration as an aesthetic flaw, they concede that the two voices contribute different perspectives. Esther represents a sympathetic and morally responsible attitude that is rare in the world of *Bleak House*. She is a compassionate insider who represents a model that is, if sometimes sentimental, a corrective to the false values of society.

As the lawsuit of *Jarndyce vs. Jarndyce* lumbers to a close after years of litigation, a gallery of characters emerges, each revealing how the moral contagion has spread. With his talent for caricature, Dickens has created memorable minor characters to people the corrupt world. There is Mr. Chadband, the preacher enamored of his own voice; Mrs. Pardiggle, who would feed the poor Puseyite tracts rather than bacon; Mr. Turveydrop, who is the model of deportment and little else; Mrs. Jellyby, who supports noble causes while neglecting her own children; and Mr. Skimpole, the model of unproductivity. Many of these characters betray the varieties of egoism and irresponsibility that have left society stagnant and infected. Perhaps the most striking is Krook, the junk dealer and small-scale surrogate of the Lord Chancellor, who dies of what Dickens calls spontaneous combustion. Krook is a microcosm of the self-destructive tendency of a diseased society.

Despite Dickens' talent for plot and character, *Bleak House* is primarily a novel of image and symbol. The first chapter insistently sets the moral tone as it repeats its images of fog and mud that surround the Court of Chancery and, by extension, all of English society. As the fog, which surrounds all in a miasma from which there seems no escape, is a symbol of Chancery, the court itself, with its inert, irresponsible, and self-destructive wranglings, is a symbol of the calcified social and economic system strangling English life. The case of *Jarndyce vs. Jarndyce* is the model of the social canker. Characters sacrifice their lives to its endless wrangling, and in succumbing to the illusory hope of instant riches, they forfeit the opportunity to accept individual responsibility and make something of themselves. The conclusion of the suit is Dickens' ironic commentary on the futility of such vain hopes.

People and places in *Bleak House* so consistently have symbolic value that the novel occasionally verges on allegory. The cloudiness and rain that surround Chesney Wold symbolize the hopelessness of the nobility. Even the name of its inhabitants, Dedlock, is a sign of the moral deadlock and immobility of the ruling class. At the other end of the social spectrum, the dirty and disease-ridden part of town known as Tom-all-alone's is a symbol of the vulnerability and victimhood of the lowest classes. In gloom of one sort or another, many characters act as detectives searching out the guilty secrets and hypocrisies that permeate this world.

On the more positive side is Bleak House itself, where the kindly John Jarndyce, who keeps aloof from involvement in the lawsuit, presides over a more orderly and benevolent demesne; but the contagion cannot be kept even from there, as is symbolized by the admirable John Jarndyce's periodic fits of depression and frustration, which he attributes to the east wind instead of the real cause, conditions in the world at large. Moreover, Ada and Richard bring the lawsuit into their uncle's house; Richard is another victim of the anachronistic system that destroys those who participate in it and feeds on the inertia, complacency, and hypocrisy of the whole society. Finally, when Esther contracts smallpox from Jo as a result of having been kind to him, Dickens is showing the interrelatedness of all levels of society. Jo is at the bottom but his misfortune becomes the misfortune of many as his contagion spreads through the social fabric. The implication is that the unfeeling society that creates Jo and Tom-all-alone's cannot protect itself from those victims.

Dickens offers no programmatic, revolutionary solution. If there is a solution, it is to be found in people like John Jarndyce, Esther Summerson, and Allan Woodcourt. Jarndyce symbolizes the selflessness that is needed if injustice is to be rectified. Esther Summerson, as her name implies, is a bright antidote to the fog and rain. Her housekeeping keys are a sign of her commitment to domestic duties and an acceptance of responsibility. Allan Woodcourt, too, is the kind of active individual society needs. The marriage of Esther and Woodcourt is a vindication of what they have to offer, as is Jarndyce's generous acceptance of their love. The new Bleak House in which they live is full of the joy and goodness that can reform society. The novel does not offer the easy optimism of radical political solutions, because it is only this revolution in the heart of humankind that Dickens believes can cure society.

"Critical Evaluation" by Edward E. Foster

Bibliography:

Dyson, A. E., ed. *Dickens: "Bleak House": A Casebook*. New York: Macmillan, 1969. A collection of criticism and supplemental readings. Includes historical information about the working class in England and other social concerns of the novel, several early reviews and comments, and eight very readable studies.

Nelson, Harland S. *Charles Dickens*. Boston: Twayne, 1981. After four chapters of overview, Nelson uses *Bleak House* as a model to demonstrate how Dickens wrote all of his novels. This accessible guide includes plot summaries of other novels discussed.

Newsom, Robert. *Dickens on the Romantic Side of Familiar Things: "Bleak House" and the Novel Tradition*. New York: Columbia University Press, 1977. Discusses the implications of Dickens' comment in the novel's preface that he "purposely dwelt on the romantic side of familiar things."

Shatto, Susan. *The Companion to "Bleak House."* Boston: Unwin Hyman, 1988. Lengthy but very useful to have while reading the novel. Detailed explanations, including allusions to earlier literature, definitions of unusual terms, and identifications of proper names from history—things Dickens' first readers would have known but with which later readers need help.

Storey, Graham. *Charles Dickens, "Bleak House."* New York: Cambridge University Press, 1987. An excellent introduction, intended as a textbook. Focuses on the novel as a social commentary. Includes a chronology that pairs events from Dickens' career with dates from history and a guide to further reading.

BLESS ME, ULTIMA

Type of work: Novel
Author: Rudolfo A. Anaya (1937-   )
Type of plot: Bildungsroman
Time of plot: 1943
Locale: Rural New Mexico
First published: 1972

> *Principal characters:*
> ANTONIO "TONY" JUAN MÁREZ Y LUNA, the narrator
> GABRIEL MÁREZ, his father
> MARIA LUNA, his mother
> ULTIMA, the *curandera* who lives with Antonio's family
> TENORIO TREMENTINA, her enemy
> NARCISO, the town drunk, a good friend of the Márez family

The Story:

Tony dreamed of his own birth. In the dream, his mother's brothers, the Lunas (*luna* means "moon"), blessed him and offered him fruit, calling him a "man of the people." Then his brothers, on horseback, came and, shouting, shooting, and laughing, smashed the fruit and broke up the gathering. They claimed Antonio for the Márezes (*mar* means "sea"). Antonio sensed that Ultima (*última* means "the last one"), who was present at the birth, was connected to his future.

Ultima came to stay with the narrator's family the summer he was "almost seven." Antonio was living with his parents and sisters, Deborah and Theresa; his three older brothers were away in the war. Ultima was a *curandera*, or healer. One evening, Tony witnessed horrible violence. Lupito, whom people claimed World War II had made crazy, had killed Chavez, the sheriff of the town. Antonio secretly followed his father to town when his father went to investigate the killing and, hiding on the river bank, saw the fugitive gunned down by a mob of pursuers. Narciso, the Márez family friend and peacemaker, pleaded with the posse but could not save Lupito. "'Bless me,'" Lupito said to Antonio as Lupito died. Later, Antonio realized that he had been protected that night by Ultima's owl, who had always been close by and who seemed to carry the powerful spirit of the *curandera* and to watch over Antonio.

Antonio started school in Guadalupe that fall. From his first teacher Miss Maestas he learned the magic of letters, and how to write. He also experienced disorientation and humiliation in the English-only classroom. From Ultima, however, he learned equally important lessons, such as the healing power of the herbs and roots they gathered as they walked along the river banks, and about the spirits of the natural world. "I knew she held the secret of my destiny," he thought. From his friends, Antonio learned about the golden carp that lived in the river surrounding the town and that would also form a part of this destiny. With his friend Cico he would later see the beautiful and sacred fish.

Antonio's three brothers—Andrew, Leon, and Eugene—returned home, but not for long. The war had given them a taste for the larger world, and soon Leon and Eugene left the family to work in it. Only Andrew remained.

Tony accompanied Ultima when she went to El Puerto to heal Uncle Lucas, his mother's brother, who was sick from a curse laid on him by the witchlike daughters of Tenorio Trementina, a satanic saloonkeeper and barber. Ultima cured Lucas with her powerful folk medicines, and laid a curse on the three witches; she thus earned the enmity of the evil Tenorio. When one of his daughters died and the priest refused her burial in holy ground, Tenorio began his deadly campaign against the *curandera*.

Antonio entered third grade. Tenorio was still threatening Ultima, and Antonio witnessed a fight between him and Narciso, who was trying to protect her. When Narciso and Antonio tried to save Ultima by enlisting the help of his brother Andrew, who was at that moment in the bordello, Antonio wondered whether through all his experiences so far—both bad and good—he had not already become an adult. Andrew refused to help, thus dishonoring the Márezes and leaving Narciso to fight a more powerful enemy.

Tenorio murdered Narciso, and, for the second time, a dying man acted as if Antonio were a priest, for Narciso whispered "Confess me" to Antonio before dying. Antonio heard his confession. After that terrible death, Antonio developed a fever and had one of his many dreams, each one of these visions seeming to teach him something, or to show him the way through his childhood. Antonio was not only learning magical powers from Ultima; he also went through his catechism, and, at Easter that year, he made his first confession and took his first communion. He was learning about the religion and culture of the Catholic church and about the older, folk traditions represented by Ultima, his father, and the belief in the golden carp.

After school that summer Antonio accompanied Ultima to the house of Tellez, where a curse by Tenorio caused stones to rain down on his house. Ultima saved Tellez. Antonio's friend Cico warned him that he must choose between the church (the religion of his mother) and the lessons of Ultima and his father (which included belief in the power of the golden carp). After this conversation, Antonio's friend Florence drowned, the third death Antonio had personally witnessed.

When Tenorio's second daughter died, he came looking for Ultima, and Antonio had to run ten miles to Guadalupe to warn her. This was his test of initiation. He could not save her, however: Tenorio killed the owl (which was Ultima's spirit) and was shot and killed in turn by Antonio's Uncle Pedro, who redeemed the Márez family after Andrew's refusal to help. Ultima died, but Antonio had become a man in the process of trying to save her. Ultima's lessons would stay with the young boy. He had learned that he should embrace life and know that the spirit of the *curandera* would always watch over him.

Critical Evaluation:

Bless Me, Ultima is one of the best novels of initiation in the Chicano tradition. The novel presents a powerful story of a young boy moving toward adulthood; Antonio's choices on that journey reveal the rich and diverse traditions of the Mexican Americans of the American Southwest. Ultima helps Antonio heal the split into which he was born, pulled as he is between the heritage of his father, who had been a cowboy, and that of his mother, whose family have been farmers. This spiritual split between the Márez and Luna families, between the plains and the town, and between Ultima's magical folk religion and Catholicism, is the central conflict of Antonio's childhood.

In the end, Antonio is not forced to choose between the two traditions of the horsemen and the farmers, but rather blends them into a workable identity for himself. It also becomes clear, as a result of his association with Ultima and his use of words to influence the events of the novel, that he will use his gift for words, imagination, and learning to become not a priest but rather a writer. He achieves this fusion only through the aid of Ultima.

Ultima is a spiritual guide who teaches the young boy and directs him toward his future. Antonio will have to reach it himself, but Ultima is the guide who aims him in the right direction and who protects him even after her death. Ultima not only helps Antonio reach adulthood but also teaches him a number of important lessons along the way—the healing arts of nature, for example, and the power of love. As Antonio says toward the end of his journey: "And that is what Ultima tried to teach me, that the tragic consequences of life can be overcome by the magical strength that resides in the human heart."

When Antonio looks back on his youth toward the end of the novel, he realizes what he has gained from the adults in his life. From his mother he learned how close people are to the earth. From his father and Ultima he learned that "the greater immortality is in the freedom of man, and that freedom is best nourished by the noble expanse of land and air and pure, white sky." From these important lessons Antonio's adult self emerges.

Ultima helps Antonio to achieve his own identity; at the end of the novel, he directs his mother to take his sisters to their room. "It was the first time I had ever spoken to my mother as a man; she nodded and obeyed." Ultima also helps Antonio to heal the split in his own heritage; he can be a Catholic (as his mother wants) and a believer in the golden carp as well. Anaya's novel is important in the way it uses the literary and folk traditions of the American Southwest. The religious symbolism of the novel can be understood only in the context of that cultural geography. Anaya is tapping a rich vein of Southwestern folklore and history.

Characterization is rather two-dimensional, although the major characters (particularly Ultima) have shadings: For example, is she a *bruja* or witch, or just a healer? This question receives a somewhat noncommittal answer when she demonstrates that she is not a witch by walking through a door marked with a cross, but the cross, made of needles, falls apart as she does so. The characterization works in terms of the point of view of the novel, which is that of a naïve young boy growing up in rural New Mexico.

Much more complex are the symbolic aspects of the novel. Antonio's dreams have a rich significance; they reflect and predict actions in the novel. They are, in the truest sense, revelations. Likewise, the literary symbolism of the novel—the importance of water, for example (the golden carp, the drowning), and the religious rituals (of both Christian and native spiritual traditions)—is complex and effective. A reading of the oppositions of the novel (Luna/Márez or moon/sea, female/male, agrarian/pastoral) points out its complexity and its final reconciliations. Anaya has produced a novel of deep and subtle meaning, and one that reveals some of the rich literary traditions of the American Southwest.

David Peck

Bibliography:
Bruce-Novoa. *Portraits of the Chicano Artist as a Young Man: The Making of the "Author" in Three Chicano Novels.* Albuquerque, N.Mex.: Pajarito Press, 1977. This important early analysis of *Bless Me, Ultima* reveals the novel to be "the apprenticeship of a writer who fulfills his training with Ultima by becoming a novelist, the author of his own text."

Calderón, Héctor. "Rudolfo Anaya's *Bless Me, Ultima*: A Chicano Romance of the Southwest." *Critica* 1, no. 3 (Fall, 1986): 21-47. Argues that the novel is actually a highly crafted romance.

Gonzalez-T., Cesar A., ed. *Rudolfo A. Anaya: Focus on Criticism.* La Jolla, Calif.: Lalo Press, 1990. Includes useful essays on *Bless Me, Ultima* by Roberto Cantu, Jean Cazemajou, and others.

Lamadrid, Enrique R. "The Dynamics of Myth in the Creative Vision of Rudolfo Anaya." In *Paso por aquí: Critical Essays on the New Mexican Literary Tradition, 1542-1988*, edited by Erlinda Gonzales-Berry. Albuquerque: University of New Mexico Press, 1989. Shows the ways in which Anaya uses Southwestern myth in his novel.

Saldivar, Ramon. "Romance, the Fantastic, and the Representation of History in Rudolfo Anaya and Ron Arias." Chapter 5 in *Chicano Narrative: The Dialectics of Difference*. Madison: University of Wisconsin Press, 1990. Argues that Anaya's book "creates a uniquely palatable amalgamation of old and new world symbolic structures."

BLITHE SPIRIT
An Improbable Farce in Three Acts

Type of work: Drama
Author: Noël Coward (1899-1973)
Type of plot: Comedy
Time of plot: Late 1930's
Locale: Kent, England
First performed: 1941; first published, 1941

> *Principal characters:*
> CHARLES CONDOMINE, a novelist
> RUTH, his wife
> ELVIRA, his former wife, now deceased
> MADAME ARCATI, a spiritualist medium and writer
> EDITH, the Condomines' new maid
> DOCTOR BRADMAN and
> MRS. BRADMAN, neighbors of the Condomines

The Story:

The Condomines were awaiting three dinner guests, one of whom was the celebrated medium Madame Arcati, who was to hold a séance after dinner. The purpose of this séance—although Madame Arcati had not been told this—was to allow Charles to gather background material for his new thriller, *The Unseen*. While waiting, Ruth attempted to teach the new maid, Edith, some discipline and decorum. Conversation turned to the subject of Charles's former wife, Elvira, who had died of a heart attack brought on by a fit of uncontrollable laughter.

Ruth, who had also been married before, claimed that she did not mind in the least being thought less attractive than Elvira, although the manner in which she brought the subject up, and Charles' determination to avoid making any such judgment, suggested that she did mind. It seemed that Ruth felt that she was still, in some sense, competing with her predecessor for her husband's affections. She suggested to Charles that he had been dominated by women throughout his life and still remained under Elvira's spell. He denied this but said that if it were so then Ruth was obviously the one presently running his life.

When the Condomines' friends the Bradmans arrived, the discussion switched to the topic of Madame Arcati, whom all knew only by sight and reputation. Charles was dismissive of her literary endeavors, which included fantasies for children and biographies of minor members of the royal families of Europe. Madame Arcati eventually arrived on her bicycle.

Before the séance began, Madame Arcati put the popular song "Always" on the gramophone because her spirit guide—a child name Daphne—liked music. The séance was rather chaotic to begin with, producing a good deal of table-rapping and an abundance of sarcastic remarks that began to annoy the medium. Charles's mood underwent a dramatic change, however, when he heard Elvira's voice speaking to him—a voice that, as became clear, no one else (except, of course, the audience) could hear. Madame Arcati fainted, and when she regained consciousness everything seemed normal. As soon as Charles showed her to the door, the conversation between Ruth and the Bradmans became casual again. They were unable to see the ghost of Elvira enter the room and sit down.

When Charles returned he joined in the lighthearted conversation. Not until the Bradmans had gone did he move to a position from which Elvira was visible. Because Ruth was unable to see or hear Elvira, Charles's reaction to her presence and his subsequent dialogue with the ghost seemed to be evidence of madness. Ruth soon stalked off to bed, leaving Charles to sleep in a chair.

When Charles awoke the next day he assumed that he had been the victim of a hallucination. He had almost made his peace with Ruth when Elvira's ghost strolled in from the garden. As misunderstandings multiplied once again, Charles prevailed upon Elvira to prove she existed by moving various inanimate objects. As soon as Ruth was convinced, she summoned Madame Arcati with a view to exorcising the ghost, but the medium was not at all certain whether this could be done.

The problem became urgent when Ruth became convinced that Elvira was trying to kill Charles in order to secure a permanent reunion on equal terms. Charles was initially skeptical about Elvira's murderous intentions, in spite of her constant sniping at Ruth. He was, however, forced to see the truth when one of Elvira's traps caught the wrong victim and killed Ruth instead of him.

At this point Elvira decided that perhaps she would be better off where she came from. Madame Arcati managed to locate a spell that might do the trick and told her spirit guide that Mrs. Condomine now wished to return. Because of her careless ambiguity, the Mrs. Condomine who "returned" was Ruth, brought back to earth exactly as Elvira had been.

With two ghostly wives constantly bickering around and over him, Charles became increasingly desperate to exorcise both of them. He strenuously denied that it was the power of his desire—conscious or subconscious—that had materialized the two ghosts. Nevertheless, it was necessary to identify the psychic power that was responsible in order to reverse the process. Madame Arcati set out to determine how the psychic energy had been provided. She conjured the deeply entranced Edith from her bed and mobilized her newly revealed powers in the task of sending the ghosts back from where they had come. They finally vanished, taunting Charles as they went. Their disappearance, however, was not absolute. The house remained subtly haunted, prone to mysterious rappings and movements of furniture that revealed that the wives, now invisible and inaudible even to Charles, were still present. Charles had by now gained sufficient insight into the characters of both his wives that he no longer felt morally or emotionally bound to either one of them. He left the house—and them—bidding them a sarcastic farewell as he set forth to live the rest of his life in splendid isolation from all womankind.

Critical Evaluation:

For two years before he wrote *Blithe Spirit*, Noël Coward had been involved in "war work." The British government, acutely aware of the fact that most of the public did not support the war, had recruited the literary establishment to the cause of building morale and disseminating propaganda. Coward had written the deeply sentimental and fervently patriotic *This Happy Breed* (1939), which was first performed in 1942, and the unproduced *Time Remembered*. He had also undertaken a grueling schedule of personal appearances, which took him to Australia and New Zealand as well as continually back and forth across the Atlantic. When he got the chance of a holiday he settled down to write a light comedy without any references to the war. *Blithe Spirit* is essentially a work of pure self-indulgence, written for the fun of it.

It may be that when writers are at their most self-indulgent and have no other intention than to please themselves they are most inclined to reveal something of themselves. On the surface,

Blithe Spirit does not seem to differ much in style or substance from Coward's previous comedy, *Present Laughter* (written before *This Happy Breed* in early 1939 but likewise not produced until 1942). There, Coward used a protagonist who is an actor and unrepentant egomaniac as well as a writer, which would have enabled some "autobiographical" elements. Given that Coward was as openly homosexual as it was possible to be in his day—that is to say that it was no secret in the theatrical community—it does not seem that the theme of second marriages, which are often haunted by the ghosts of the former spouse, can have been of much relevance to him. If therefore there is any personal significance in *Blithe Spirit*, it is buried beneath the surface of glittering artifice.

The artifice of *Blithe Spirit* works to greatest effect in the character of Madame Arcati, who is a wonderful grotesque. Although she is clearly drawn from stereotypical images of spiritualist mediums, her idiosyncratic deviations from that stereotype provide a constant stream of amusing lines. Her insistence on traveling by bicycle, her observations on how various foods affect her psychic powers, her reasons for preferring a child to the more conventional Red Indian as a spirit guide, and so on, fuel the undercurrent of polite absurdity that sustains the pace of the play.

Even when she is not actually on stage, the other characters' remarks about Madame Arcati are essential to the flow of wit. When she is absent from the stage or from the conversation, the tempo is markedly different. Charles Condomine's dialogues with Elvira sparkle, but the only really funny scene that does not involve Madame Arcati is the one in which Charles's exchanges with Elvira are continually misinterpreted by Ruth, to whom Elvira is invisible and inaudible— a near-slapstick device that diverges sharply from Coward's usual method of raising laughs.

The mischievous Elvira, whose amorality is intensified rather than redeemed by her personal charms, is the kind of female character Coward loved to create. Her disregard for convention— which certainly warrants the description of "blithe"—is indicated in a fashion so subtle as to be sketchy, but any admirer of Coward's work would immediately recognize the precise tenor of her naughtiness. The same admirer might, however, have difficulty in recognizing Charles as another in the series of Cowardian alter egos who serve as his male protagonists. By comparison with Gary Essendine in *Present Laughter*, who is the epitome of the breezily appalling hams Coward loved to design and play, Charles is not merely restrained but positively ordinary. Ruth's role is largely that of playing sober foil to the mercurial Elvira, but she too is forced to exercise that sobriety with an uncommon restraint.

The relative quietness of the two leading players is counterbalanced by the fact that they are enmeshed in a structured plot. Many of Coward's characters had to be larger than life because they had to carry the plays forward by the sheer force of personality, but *Blithe Spirit* stands almost alone among Coward's comedies in having an element of mystery and narrative suspense. This is probably the reason that it has proved to be the most popular of all his plays with audiences, although connoisseurs often prefer *Private Lives* (1930). Significantly, when the play was filmed in 1945 the plot was considered so weak as to require a modified climax; the director evidently felt that Charles's casual farewell to his invisible spouses was disappointingly anticlimactic and added an extra "accident" to reunite the three of them beyond the grave. The fact that Coward felt that no such move was necessary or desirable in the play may provide the key to such personal significance as it has.

Coward spent his entire life performing in a calculatedly flamboyant manner that helped create the notion of "campness." His declared justification for this was, of course, that he was not just a man of the theater and a genius but a homosexual who was only permitted to acknowledge the fact within certain circles and thus forced to conduct his social life as a performance; his calculated exaggeration of that performance was, to some extent, a commentary on the absurdity of his situation. Of all the parts he wrote for himself, Charles Condomine is the least prone to exaggerated performance (Coward's "straight" parts were, of course, performances precisely because they pretended to set aside the kind of ostentation he employed in real life). The ending of Charles's story qualifies as a uniquely happy ending because his release from the various social pressures put upon him by his successive wives offers him the promise, or at least the possibility, of being able to stop performing altogether.

Charles is the one character Coward wrote for himself who is allowed the hope of being himself in being by himself. It was the kind of notion that the relentlessly gregarious Coward could probably never have contemplated had he not been temporarily surfeited with unusually onerous social responsibilities, but given the circumstances in which he conceived and wrote *Blithe Spirit* it is certainly understandable.

Brian Stableford

Bibliography:
Gay, Frances. *Noël Coward.* London: Macmillan, 1987. A critical study of Coward's work. Discusses *Blithe Spirit* as a farcical comedy with "a darker dimension."
Lahr, John. *Coward the Playwright.* London: Methuen, 1982. The fullest and most detailed critical study of Coward's plays. *Blithe Spirit* is extensively discussed in the chapter "Ghosts in the Fun Machine."
Lesley, Cole. *The Life of Noël Coward.* London: Cape, 1976. A useful memoir by Coward's longtime secretary and companion.
Mander, Raymond, and Joe Mitchenson. *Theatrical Companion to Coward.* New York: Macmillan, 1957. A comprehensive and detailed reference work dealing with Coward's plays.
Morley, Sheridan. *A Talent to Amuse.* Garden City, N.Y.: Doubleday, 1969. A sensitive and wide-ranging critical and biographical study.

THE BLITHEDALE ROMANCE

Type of work: Novel
Author: Nathaniel Hawthorne (1804-1864)
Type of plot: Psychological realism
Time of plot: Mid-nineteenth century
Locale: Massachusetts
First published: 1852

> *Principal characters:*
> MILES COVERDALE, a resident of Blithedale Community
> ZENOBIA, a worldly woman
> PRISCILLA MOODIE, a simple maiden
> HOLLINGSWORTH, beloved of Zenobia and Priscilla
> WESTERVELT, an evil conjurer
> OLD MOODIE, Priscilla's father

The Story:

As Miles Coverdale prepared to journey to Blithedale, where he was to join in a project in community living, he was accosted by Old Moodie, a seedy ancient who seemed reluctant to state his business. After much mysterious talk about having Coverdale do him a great favor, Old Moodie changed his mind and shuffled off without telling what it was that he wanted. It was April, but Coverdale and his companions arrived at Blithedale in a snowstorm. There they were greeted by a woman called Zenobia, a well-known magazine writer. Zenobia was a beautiful, worldly woman of wealth and position. At all times she wore a rare, exotic flower in her hair. Zenobia spent most of her energy fighting for "woman's place in the world."

On the evening of Coverdale's arrival, another of the principals arrived at Blithedale. He was Hollingsworth, a philanthropist and reformer. In fact, philanthropy was to him a never-ceasing effort to reform and change humanity. He brought Priscilla with him, a simple, poorly dressed, bewildered young girl. Priscilla went at once to Zenobia and, falling at the proud woman's feet, never took her eyes from that haughty face. There was no explanation for such behavior. Hollingsworth knew only that he had been approached by Old Moodie and asked to take Priscilla to Blithedale. That was the request Old Moodie had tried to make of Coverdale. Such was the community of Blithedale that the inhabitants made the girl welcome in spite of her strange behavior.

It was soon evident to Coverdale that Hollingsworth's impulse to philanthropy had reached such an extreme that the man was on the way to madness. Hollingsworth was convinced that the universe existed only in order for him to reform all criminals and wayward persons. The dream of his life was to construct a large edifice in which he could collect his criminal brothers and teach them to mend their ways before doom overtook them. To Coverdale, he was a bore, but it was obvious that both Zenobia and Priscilla were in love with him. Priscilla blossomed as she reaped the benefits of good food and fresh air, and Zenobia viewed her as a rival with evident but unspoken alarm. Hollingsworth seemed to consider Priscilla his own special charge, and Coverdale feared the looks of thinly veiled hatred he frequently saw Zenobia cast toward the vulnerable young Priscilla, who was, ironically, devoted to Zenobia. When Old Moodie appeared at Blithedale to inquire of Priscilla, Coverdale tried to persuade him to reveal the reason for his interest in the girl. The old man slipped away without telling his story.

Shortly after this incident, Professor Westervelt came to Blithedale to inquire about Zenobia and Priscilla. Coverdale saw Westervelt and Zenobia together and was sure that even though Zenobia hated him now, she once had loved and been made miserable by this evil man. Coverdale knew that all the pain that he sometimes saw in Zenobia's eyes must surely have come from this man. Coverdale felt also that there was still some bond between them.

After Westervelt's visit, Zenobia was short-tempered and more vehement than usual about the poor lot of women. She was so much in love with Hollingsworth that even the misery, or perhaps terror, caused by Westervelt did not deter her from literally worshiping at his feet. Hollingsworth, in his egotism, believed that women were placed on earth only to serve men, he being one, and so great was Zenobia's passion that she accepted his words without protest, not proclaiming her real thoughts in his presence. It was clear to Coverdale that Hollingsworth intended to use Zenobia's money to build the school for criminals of which he never ceased to talk. When Coverdale refused to join him in this project, Hollingsworth became quite cool in his dealings with Coverdale.

Tiring of the life at Blithedale, Coverdale took a vacation in town. He was greatly surprised when Zenobia, Priscilla, and Westervelt also arrived in the town shortly afterward. He called on the ladies and was disturbed by the tension that was apparent. When he chided Zenobia about Priscilla and Hollingsworth, she warned him not to interfere lest he cause serious trouble. Priscilla did not know why she was there. She told Coverdale that she was like a leaf blown about by the wind. She had no will of her own, only the will of Zenobia. Then Westervelt called for the two women, and the three left Coverdale standing as if they did not know he was there.

Determined to uncover the mystery surrounding the three, Coverdale sought out Old Moodie and pried from him the story. Once Moodie had been a wealthy and influential man until, through dishonest business practices, he had been ruined. Then, leaving his wife and daughter, Zenobia, he wandered about in poverty and disgrace. His wife died and he married again. To them Priscilla was born, as different from his first child as it was possible to be. Zenobia was beautiful and proud, Priscilla plain and shy. Neighbors thought Priscilla had supernatural powers, but her kindness and her goodness made everyone love her.

Zenobia, after Moodie's disgrace, was reared by his brother; and since Moodie was believed dead, Zenobia, as the next heir, inherited her uncle's wealth. She grew up a wild and willful girl; it was whispered that she had made a secret marriage with an unprincipled man. No one, however, knew anything definite. Such were her beauty and wealth that no one criticized her. Moodie called her to his home and, not telling her who he was, cautioned her to be as kind as a sister to Priscilla.

During his vacation, Coverdale chanced upon a magician's show in a nearby village. There he found Hollingsworth in the audience and Westervelt on the stage. Westervelt produced a Veiled Lady, an ethereal creature whom he said would do his bidding. At the climax of the act, Hollingsworth arose from the audience and strode to the platform. He called to the Veiled Lady to remove her veil, and Priscilla lifted her veil and fled into the arms of Hollingsworth with a cry of joy and love. She looked like one who had been saved from an evil fate.

Coverdale returned to Blithedale. There he witnessed a terrifying scene between Zenobia, Priscilla, and Hollingsworth. Hollingsworth admitted his love for Priscilla to Zenobia. Zenobia reviled him and warned her half sister against the emptiness of his heart. She said she knew at last the complete egotism of the man and saw that he had deceived her only to get her fortune for his great project. After the lovers left her, Zenobia sank to the ground and wept, and that night drowned herself in the river flowing close by. Westervelt came to view her dead body, but his only sorrow seemed to be that he could no longer use Zenobia in his schemes.

After Zenobia's tragedy, Coverdale left Blithedale. Priscilla and Hollingsworth lived quietly, he giving up his desire to reform criminals because he felt himself to be one—Zenobia's murderer. In his twilight years Coverdale confessed his real interest in these ill-fated people. He had from the first been in love with Priscilla.

Critical Evaluation:

The self-conscious ironical tone of *The Blithedale Romance* is one of the first things that strikes the reader, and this tone is set by the first-person narrator, Miles Coverdale, an independently wealthy poet. In spite of his expressed desire to participate in the experimental paradise of Blithedale, Coverdale's implicit attitude is that of a dilettante, someone who loves his creature comforts but who, through boredom, is pursuing an idealistic alternative to his privileged artificial life. If Coverdale typifies those who, like Hawthorne, participated in the Brook Farm experiment of 1841, the reader can understand why the project failed.

Coverdale is essentially an observer of life. He is able to situate the socialistic experiment of Blithedale historically: It is a successor of the Puritan attempt to make one's principles the foundation of daily living. Coverdale notes that group living requires a sacrifice of individual development, and the prime leaders—Hollingsworth and Zenobia—are individualists incapable of such a sacrifice. Perhaps because of the first-person narrative mode, none of the three main characters described by Coverdale ever comes to life on the page.

Hollingsworth is the type of the single-minded philanthropist who has channeled all of his considerable energy into founding an institute for the reformation of criminals. This apparently selfless devotion endears him to the two female protagonists: the dark and sensual Zenobia and the pale and spiritual Priscilla.

Like true romantic heroines, Zenobia and Priscilla are initially shrouded in mystery. The proud, wealthy Zenobia chafes at the restrictions society places on her sex. Priscilla, on the other hand, a seamstress before coming to Blithedale, possesses an essentially dependent character, devoting herself first to Zenobia and later to Hollingsworth. According to their father, the impoverished Old Moodie, his daughter Zenobia represents the wealth and power that her father abused and lost through some unnamed crime, while Priscilla is the child of his poverty, a reclusive person who fills her imagination with her father's stories. Zenobia possesses many social qualities; Priscilla is rumored to be psychic.

Irony dominates the narration of *The Blithedale Romance*. For example, the judgmental narrator Coverdale finally acknowledges that if it is true, as he believes, that Hollingsworth's life is empty of human warmth because he cares only about his criminal project, so it is also true that Coverdale's own life is empty because he has no real interests beyond his own comfort. Also ironically, Zenobia, a dominant personality who espouses the rights of women to receive equal treatment in society, is so devastated when Hollingsworth turns away from her to propose to the subservient, adoring Priscilla that she commits suicide. Again ironically, because of this suicide, Hollingsworth is so haunted by feelings of guilt he no longer pursues his great project of criminal reform and becomes a recluse devoted to converting one murderer, himself. Furthermore, the once powerful but now debilitated Hollingsworth is cared for by the weak Priscilla. Finally, Coverdale, who fills his narration with the wonders of Zenobia, admits in the final sentence of the novel he was in love with Priscilla all along.

Irony also envelops the account of the Blithedale experiment itself. These participants who aspire to improve the world are unable to handle their personal lives. Their condescension toward their managing farmer Silas Foster certainly undermines the professed sincerity of this democratic project. Ironically, Foster tells them that if they wish to succeed as farmers they must compete with more market-experienced farmers. Such competition seems a direct contradiction to their socialist goals. Coverdale, who like a true Transcendentalist rhapsodizes over communing with nature in his special treehouse, at the conclusion of the romance concedes nature is indifferent to the death of one of its noblest products, Zenobia.

In keeping with his practice of using characters as types, Nathaniel Hawthorne gives them names that suggest their symbolic role. Coverdale is a felicitous name for the narrator, who is adept at covering his personal feelings and motives while he attempts to uncover the hidden motives of others. Coverdale notes that Zenobia uses her exotic name like a mask. The name Zenobia recalls Queen Zenobia, a proud and capable ruler who ultimately fell victim to the all-too-male Roman Empire. The name Priscilla evokes the wan, enervated wraith who somehow inspires the love of Hollingsworth and Coverdale. The name Hollingsworth also reveals the person's character; he is hollow in worth, since the suicide of Zenobia effectively destroys his project and his spirit. When the protagonists meet by Eliot's pulpit, the name of the rock recalls the work of this idealistic Puritan apostle of the Indians; the irony is that his converts were massacred in King Philip's War. The name, therefore, effectively prophesies the unsuccessful conclusion of the idealistic experiment in improving the world. Old Moodie is called Fauntleroy in the fairy-tale-like narrative describing his fabulous wealth and power prior to his crime and flight. That name is the same as that of a well-known contemporary English forger. Hawthorne probably expected his readers to be able to identify Moodie's crime.

The most effective use of a name is the title of the work, apparently the name of the place. Any suggestions of the members to choose another name provoke objections; they feel Blithedale (happy valley) is appropriate. Madness, suicide, and depression soon find their way to Blithedale. Designating the work a romance in the title expresses Hawthorne's purpose of creating a work of mystery and fantasy, not a realistic work. The use of the word "romance" is ironic; the novel is all about disillusionment. The novel is filled with veilings and coverings; the author effectively shrouds his real-life adventure in utopian living at Brook Farm in 1841 in a fantasy of titanic star-crossed lovers. It remains for the reader to separate truth from fiction.

"Critical Evaluation" by Agnes A. Shields

Bibliography:

Hawthorne, Nathaniel. *The Blithedale Romance*. Edited by Seymour Gross and Rosalie Murphy. New York: W. W. Norton, 1978. Contains the text, background information, sources, criticism, and bibliographies.

Johnson, Claudia D. *The Productive Tension of Hawthorne's Art*. Tuscaloosa: University of Alabama Press, 1981. Chapter 4 contends that Hawthorne attacks the romantic tendency toward artist-centered art in *The Blithedale Romance*. Bibliography.

Kaul, A. N., ed. *Hawthorne: A Collection of Essays*. Englewood Cliffs, N.J.: Prentice-Hall, 1966. Kaul's analysis of *The Blithedale Romance* identifies the author's theme as social regeneration. Chronology and bibliography.

Lee, A. Robert, ed. *Nathaniel Hawthorne: New Critical Essays*. New York: Barnes & Noble Books, 1982. Depicts Hawthorne as looking back to the Puritans and forward to modernist themes and concerns.

Pearce, Roy Harvey, ed. *Hawthorne Centenary Essays*. Columbus: Ohio State University Press, 1964. Includes essays dealing with the reception of Hawthorne's work in the nineteenth century. Suggests that the author's complex, ambiguous feelings about the idealistic social experiment are evident.

BLOOD WEDDING

Type of work: Drama
Author: Federico García Lorca (1899-1936)
Type of plot: Tragedy
Time of plot: Early twentieth century
Locale: Spain
First performed: 1933; first published, 1935 as *Bodas de sangre* (English translation, 1939)

> Principal characters:
> THE BRIDEGROOM
> THE BRIDEGROOM'S MOTHER
> THE BRIDE
> THE BRIDE'S FATHER
> LEONARDO FELÍX, former suitor of the Bride
> LEONARDO'S WIFE

The Story:

The Bridegroom's Mother was unhappy when she learned that he wished to be married and that he had found a woman whom he desired. In spite of her sorrow at losing him, she commanded him to go buy fine presents for the Bride. The Bridegroom's Mother was also unhappy because the Bridegroom was her only surviving child. Her husband and her older son had been killed many years before in fights with members of the Felíx family. Since then, the Bridegroom's Mother had lived in fear that the only surviving man in her family, the Bridegroom, might also fall a victim to someone's knife or gun. She told her son that she would much rather that he had been born a girl, to sit in the house and knit instead of going out among men.

After the Bridegroom had left the house to go buy gifts for the Bride, gifts to be presented when the parents met, a neighbor stopped to see his Mother. The neighbor told the Bridegroom's Mother that there was bad blood in the Bride's veins, inherited from her mother. She also said that Leonardo, a member of the hated Felíx family and a cousin of the Bride, had wooed the Bride unsuccessfully before his own marriage three years earlier. The Bridegroom's Mother grew uneasy at the news, but she determined to carry through her part in the marriage customs because her son was in love and because the Bride's Father owned rich vineyards comparable to those of her own family.

Meanwhile word of the proposed marriage had reached Leonardo, who still was in love with the Bride. In fact, he rode many miles to her house to see her whenever he had the chance. For some time both Leonardo's Wife and her mother had realized that something was wrong. Leonardo was curt and sharp with his Wife for no reason at all, and he failed to take much notice of their child.

The next day the Bride's servant prepared her to meet with her father, the Bridegroom, and the Bridegroom's Mother in order to make plans for the wedding. The servant accused the Bride of permitting Leonardo to visit late at night. The Bride, without denying the fact, merely indicated that she was not very happy at the prospect of marrying the Bridegroom.

After the arrival of the Bridegroom and his Mother, it was decided to have the wedding take place on the following Thursday, the Bride's twenty-second birthday. The Bride said that she would welcome the chance to shut out the world from her life and devote herself to the Bridegroom. A short time after the Bridegroom and his Mother had departed, Leonardo's horse was heard neighing beneath the Bride's window.

The day of the wedding arrived, and early in the morning the servant began to prepare the Bride for the ceremony. The Bride was not happy. When the servant began to speak of the bliss that would soon be hers, the Bride commanded the woman to be quiet. She even threw her wreath of orange blossoms to the ground.

A short time later the guests began to arrive. The first to make his appearance was the Bride's cousin and former wooer, Leonardo. He and the Bride, despite the servant's pleas, had a talk in which bitter recriminations were flung back and forth. Neither wished to be married to anyone else, but each blamed the other for the unhappiness to which they were apparently doomed. Only the arrival of other guests broke up the argument.

The guests having arrived, the party set out for the church. Only the most vigorous language on the part of his Wife convinced Leonardo that he ought to ride in the cart with her, in order to keep up appearances. When the wedding ceremony was over, Leonardo and his Wife were the first guests to return to the Bride's Father's house. Leonardo had driven like a madman.

Shortly after the guests had gathered at the house, the Bridegroom went quietly up behind the Bride and put his arms about her. She shrank from his embrace. Complaining that she felt ill, she went to her room to rest after asking the Bridegroom to leave her alone. As the wedding feast continued, some of the guests proposed that the Bridegroom and the Bride dance together. The Bride, however, was nowhere to be found. Searchers discovered that she and Leonardo had ridden away on his horse. The Bridegroom, furious at being so dishonored and filled with desire for revenge, organized a posse of his relatives and immediately started out after the fugitives. All day they searched without finding the pair.

On into the night the Bridegroom continued his search and came at last into the wood where the runaways had stopped. The Bride, meanwhile, had had a change of heart; refusing to give herself to Leonardo, she said that it was enough that she had run away with him. Leonardo, becoming angry, reminded her that it was she who had gone down the stairs first, who had put a new bridle on the horse, and who had even buckled on his spurs. Nevertheless, the Bride said she had had enough. She did not want to stay with him, but she had no greater desire to return to her husband.

While they argued, the Bridegroom met Death, disguised as a beggarwoman. Death insisted upon leading him to the place where he would find his escaped bride and her lover. By the light of the moon they searched until they found the pair. When they met, Leonardo and the Bridegroom fought, killing each other.

After they had died, Death, still disguised as a beggarwoman, went back to spread the evil tidings. When she heard of her son's death, the Bridegroom's Mother took the news stoically, not wanting her neighbors to see her overwhelming grief. Returning to her mother-in-law, the Bride was told to remain at the door without entering the room. The Bride tried to explain her actions, saying also that she had come so that the Bridegroom's Mother could kill her. No one paid any attention to the Bride's argument that neither Leonardo nor her husband had ever slept with her.

The Bridegroom's Mother was joined in her lamentations by Leonardo's Wife when searchers carried in the bodies of the two men. The grief-stricken women, joined by the Bride, complained bitterly that an instrument as small as a knife could take away the lives of two such men, lives that were so much greater than the instruments which caused their deaths.

Critical Evaluation:

In the three plays—*Blood Wedding*, *Yerma* (1934), and *The House of Bernarda Alba* (1936)—that culminated his poetic and dramatic career, Federico García Lorca succeeded brilliantly where a host of modern poet-dramatists had failed; he created a true poetry of the theater. The twentieth century is dotted with half-successful attempts at poetic drama by playwrights who lacked the requisite verbal facility for writing poetry or by versifiers whose theatrical efforts are very difficult to accomplish onstage. Even successful verse dramatists such as T. S. Eliot, Christopher Fry, and Archibald MacLeish offer self-consciously "poetic" and "literary" efforts that lack the impact or even the "poetry," of the best prose dramas of the period. García Lorca, who was both a great lyric poet and a practical man of the theater, fused all of the elements of the stage—language, movement, ritual, color, lighting, spectacle, and music—into a single dramatic presentation.

Much of the power of these plays comes from the way García Lorca combines a complex, sophisticated theatrical style with extremely simple dramatic situations. Although the original impulse for *Blood Wedding* came from a real incident, the basic plot—a bride stolen from her wedding by a lover—is a perennial one. Leonardo Felíx and the Bride are victims of their own uncontrollable emotions. He has a wife and child; she fervently desires the social and financial stability that marriage to the Bridegroom will bring. Since the entire society favors that match, they know that their passionate act will have fatal consequences. These logical and moral considerations, however, are irrelevant to them in the face of their powerful, passionate feelings.

García Lorca develops and expands the meanings of this tragedy with a dynamic synthesis of realistic, poetic, and symbolic theatrical devices. On the realistic level, he presents vivid, intense characterizations. The Bridegroom's Mother is an impressive, anguished woman who, having lost both husband and son, expects tragedy, but resolutely pursues the family destiny all the same. The Bridegroom is likable, sensitive, but hesitant, perhaps frightened by his pending marriage to a woman who is more strong-willed and passionate than he. The Bride's passion for Leonardo and clear disappointment at having lost him are evident from her first scene; her fervent desire for security and social respectability are doomed from the start and her troubled attempt to keep her emotions under control excites fear and pity in the audience. Leonardo—the only character in the play individualized by a name—is vital, volatile, frustrated, and overtly sexual; the intensity of his passion and the power of his attraction suggest energies and drives that are more than human. The Bride refers to him as "a dark river, choked with brush, that brought near me the undertone of its rushes and its whispered song."

All of this realistic characterization and conflict are then reinforced and extended by García Lorca's use of color, light, music, poetry, and symbolism. Even in the most realistic scenes there are patterns of imagery, both verbal and visual, that underscore the play's action. The Bridegroom's Mother broods over knives. Leonardo's mother-in-law sings a lullaby with images of "frozen horses" and "blood flowing like water." The Bride wears black. Leonardo identifies himself with his horse—a traditional symbol of sexual passion—and the Bridegroom is likened to "a dove/ with his breast a firebrand."

The masterful third act offers a full realization of García Lorca's stage poetry. The relative realism of the first two acts gives way to a stylized forest landscape, and symbolic figures replace "real" ones. The final violence is previewed by a "debate" between the Moon—a sexually ambiguous young man—and the Beggar Woman, an image of death. The Moon stands for the primal emotion that has driven the fated couple together; the Beggar Woman represents the inevitable consequence of that passion. The scene culminates with the last meeting between Leonardo and the Bride as the realistic and the symbolic fuse into a powerful acknowledgment of unbridled love, desperate loss, and heroic defiance. The play's finale, when the bodies of Leonardo and the Bridegroom are brought in to be mourned by a stage full of bereaved women, leaves the audience completely drained of emotion—a tragic catharsis reminiscent of the greatest classical dramas.

Bibliography:

Crow, John A. *Federico García Lorca*. Berkeley: University of California Press, 1945. Examines the biographical, thematic, formalistic, and historical elements of García Lorca's poetry and drama. An excellent source for serious study.

Duran, Manuel, ed. *Lorca: A Collection of Critical Essays*. Englewood Cliffs, N.J.: Prentice-Hall, 1962. Extensive examination of the aspects of poetry and drama and how they complement each other in García Lorca's writings. Reveals how *Blood Wedding* is deeply rooted in Spanish folk and literary traditions. Principal plays are analyzed in great detail.

Edwards, Gwynne. *Lorca: The Theater Beneath the Sand*. Boston: Marion Boyars, 1980. Discussion of García Lorca's dramatic technique and innovation in the theater. Includes a thorough treatment of themes and characteristics and an intensive discussion of *Blood Wedding*. Excellent source for an understanding of García Lorca's scope, technique, and talent for dramatic expression.

Gibson, Ian. "Blood Wedding." In *Federico García Lorca: A Life*. New York: Pantheon Books, 1989. The chapter gives a historical and psychological discussion of the people of the Andalusia region of Spain. Analysis includes examination of the Spanish Fascist political response to the play and a discussion of the play as a timeless tragedy.

Honig, Edwin. *García Lorca*. Rev. ed. New York: New Directions, 1980. An excellent source for discussion of García Lorca's works. A critical guidebook of his life and work; treats in detail all the available writings of García Lorca. Provides insight into how his poetry matured into full-scale drama.

THE BOHEMIANS OF THE LATIN QUARTER

Type of work: Novel
Author: Henri Murger (1822-1861)
Type of plot: Sentimental
Time of plot: Mid-nineteenth century
Locale: Paris
First published: Scènes de la vie de Bohème, serial, 1847-1849; book, 1851 (English
translation, 1901)

Principal characters:
RUDOLPHE, a poet
MARCEL, a painter
SCHAUNARD, a musician and painter
COLLINE, a philosopher
JACQUES, a sculptor
MIMI, Rudolphe's beloved
MUSETTE, Marcel's beloved
FRANCINE, Jacques's lover
PHEMIE, Schaunard's lover

The Story:

Alexander Schaunard, a poor musician and painter, was unable to pay the rent for his cold
and windy top-floor room in the Latin Quarter of Paris. Eluding the porter who was on watch
to keep Schaunard from moving his few pieces of furniture, the musician tried in vain to borrow
money from his impecunious friends. Shortly after he left the tenement, Marcel, a painter, came
to take over the room Schaunard had vacated. The painter had no furniture except his canvas
flats, and he was pleased to find that his quarters contained Schaunard's table, chairs, bed, and
piano.

Although Schaunard approached all of his friends in alphabetical order, he was unable to
borrow more than three of the seventy-five francs he needed to satisfy his landlord. At
dinnertime, his stomach led him to Mother Cadet's, famous for her rabbit stew. He arrived too
late, however; his table companion, Colline, had ordered the last stew of the evening. Colline,
barricaded behind a pile of books, kindly offered to share the stew with Schaunard. Not to be
outdone, Schaunard ordered extra wine. Colline ordered yet another bottle, Schaunard called
for a salad, and in conclusion Colline ordered dessert. By the time they left Mother Cadet's,
they were well pleased with the world. Stopping by a café for coffee and liqueurs, they fell into
conversation with Rudolphe, who, to judge by his clothes, could only have been a poet.

Rudolphe soon became as expansive as they. Forgetting that he no longer had a room,
Schaunard offered to take Colline and Rudolphe home with him, for the hour was late and they
lived at the far ends of Paris. As they reeled into the house, the porter too forgot that Schaunard
had been dispossessed. The musician was a bit taken aback when he found another key in his
door, but the three made so much noise that Marcel opened the door to them and gladly accepted
the supper they had brought with them. Schaunard and Marcel decided to stay together, since
the musician owned the furniture and the painter had paid the rent. The other two were surprised
to find themselves in a strange room the next morning. After another day and night of convivial
treating, when all but Schaunard still had a few francs in their pockets, the four decided to meet
daily.

One day, Marcel received an invitation to dine with a patron of the arts. He was famished and yearned to go, but he realized that he had no dress coat. Just then a stranger appeared at the door asking for Schaunard, whom he wanted to hire to paint his portrait. Marcel pointed to the caller's coat, and Schaunard, preparing to begin the painting, asked the man to doff his coat and put on a borrowed dressing gown because the picture, intended for the man's family, ought to be as informal as possible. Marcel appropriated the coat and went to the dinner. Schaunard persuaded his sitter to send out for a fine dinner and kept the man entertained until Marcel returned.

One evening in Lent, Rudolphe was disturbed to find that everywhere he looked people and birds were pairing off. Schaunard told him that he was in love with love and offered to find him a girl. Schaunard did produce a fresh-colored, pleasing girl, but she refused to stay with Rudolphe more than a few days. She did not understand his poetizing.

Lacking money for his rent, Rudolphe turned to his stove-maker uncle, who wanted him to write a manual on stove-making. Having learned that an advance to Rudolphe meant that he would disappear until the money had been spent, the uncle kept the young man locked up. The manual proved to be slow and boring work. Rudolphe struck up an acquaintance with an actress on the floor below, and she promised to get his play produced. When a letter arrived with word that Rudolphe had won three hundred francs, the uncle refused to let him go. Rudolphe made a knotted rope out of his quilt and slid down to the actress' apartment. She provided a disguise for him, enabling him to leave the house. Later, she did have his play produced, but it brought the young writer neither fame nor fortune. Before long, his address, as he said, was Avenue St. Cloud, third tree as you go out of the Bois de Boulogne, fifth branch.

Mademoiselle Musette was a friend of Rudolphe's, but she was never more than a friend, though neither knew why. When he asked leave to introduce Marcel, Musette invited them both to a party. She had just been jilted by her lover, the councilor of state. On the day of her party, her creditors took her furniture from her rooms and put it in the courtyard to be sold the following morning. Unabashed, Musette had her party in the courtyard and invited all the tenants. They were still laughing and singing when the porters came to take the furniture away. It was such a successful party that Rudolphe and Marcel carried Musette off to the country for the day.

On their return to Paris, Rudolphe allowed Marcel to take Musette home. Soon after he had left her at her doorway, he felt a tap on his shoulder. There stood Musette, who told him that she no longer had a key to her room and that it was after eleven o'clock at night. Calling her the goddess of mirth, Marcel took her home with him. The next morning, he bought her a pot of flowers. She said that she would stay with him until the flowers faded. He was surprised at their continued freshness until the day he found Musette watering them carefully.

M. Benoit was dunning Rudolphe for three quarters of rent, three pairs of shoes, and additional loans of money, for he was landlord, shoemaker, and moneylender all in one. Rudolphe walked the streets all day in the hope that providence would provide. When he returned, the room had already been rented to someone else, but the landlord allowed Rudolphe to go upstairs to claim his papers. A young woman named Mimi was the new tenant. After one look at Rudolphe, she told M. Benoit that she had been expecting the gentleman.

On Christmas Eve, the four friends, accompanied by Mimi and Musette and Schaunard's Phemie, repaired to the Café Momus, whose owner and his wife had a weakness for the arts; relying on that weakness, the bohemians ordered a fine supper. In their high holiday spirits, they ran up a huge bill before they drew lots to see who should be the one to speak diplomatically to the proprietor. Schaunard was having no success on that errand when a stranger, Barbemuche, asked to be introduced and offered to pay the bill. Schaunard suggested a game of billiards to settle the matter. Barbemuche had the good taste to lose the match, and the bohemians' dignity was saved.

Neither Mimi nor Musette could resist going off with other lovers. One time, Mimi and Rudolphe quietly agreed to separate, but it was not long before Mimi came to call, ostensibly to take away her belongings. Instead, she stayed with Rudolphe again.

Jacques, a sculptor, and the dressmaker Francine were tenants in the same apartment building. They met one evening when Francine's candle was extinguished by the wind and she came to Jacques to relight it. In doing so, she also lost her key and the two played a lovers' game in looking for it (since Jacques, who found it right away, had been so clever as to hide it quickly in his pocket). Francine, ill with tuberculosis and suffering terribly in the cold Paris winter, as a last request, asked Jacques for a muff to warm her hands. Jacques bought her the muff, but Francine died the next day. Upon her death, Jacques was distraught, and although he recovered somewhat from the heartbreak, he became ill and died not long after in a pauper's hospital.

Musette was said to alternate between blue broughams and omnibuses. While she was living with M. Maurice, she received a letter from Marcel asking her to come for dinner, for the friends even had wood for a fire. She received the note in a roundabout way but left the bewildered M. Maurice immediately. Because snow was beginning to fall, she stopped at a friend's house and met an interesting young man there. Five days later, she arrived at Marcel's room. The fire was dying out, and the food was gone. She stayed one day before returning to M. Maurice with the announcement that she had quarreled with Marcel. She told M. Maurice that each of her loves was the verse of a song, but Marcel was the refrain.

The second time Mimi and Rudolphe separated, she went to live with Paul, a young viscount. Meeting by chance on the street, Mimi and Rudolphe bowed. The poet went home and wrote a long poem for Mimi, which so irritated the young nobleman that he put Mimi out of his house.

On another Christmas Eve, as Marcel and Rudolphe were trying to forget their sorrows, Mimi came back, so ill that a doctor insisted that she be taken at once to a hospital. She was afraid to go, even though her friends tried to encourage her with the hope that she would be well by spring. Rudolphe went to see her on the first visiting day. Before the next day for calling, he heard that she was dead. A few days later, his correspondent admitted that he had been mistaken, that Mimi had been moved to a different ward. Rudolphe hurried to the hospital, only to have his hopes shattered forever. Mimi, grieved because Rudolphe had failed to appear for the expected visit, had died that morning.

One year later, Rudolphe had written a book that was receiving much critical attention. Schaunard had produced an album of songs. Colline had married well, and Marcel's pictures had been accepted for the annual exhibit. Musette came to spend a final night with Marcel before marrying the guardian of her last lover.

Critical Evaluation:

Henry Murger's *The Bohemians of the Latin Quarter*, which is also sometimes translated as *Scenes of Bohemian Life*, is not a literary masterpiece in the traditional sense, but it is a classic work. Murger, the son of a tailor/concierge and a man of little formal education, learned about writing from reading such popular nineteenth century French authors as Victor Hugo and Alfred de Musset, as well as from absorbing what he could from his associates.

Life in mid-nineteenth century Paris was a mixture of many elements. Louis-Philippe, who ruled from 1830 to 1848, had limited appreciation for the arts and literature, and the days of patronage for artists had faded. Murger's first literary attempts, mostly poetry and bits of prose, met with little success and he lived meagerly, experiencing firsthand the poverty, hunger, and illness that afflicted so many people in Paris. It was not until 1845, when he began to write the short episodes for the French publication *Le Corsaire*, a newspaper that was read avidly by the artist population of the Latin Quarter, that he began to gain a reputation. However, because the remuneration for one such article was a mere fifteen francs, his poverty continued.

By the end of 1846, more than two dozen of Murger's vignettes had been published in *Le Corsaire*, and he had established a small following. In 1849, Théodore Barrière, a successful Parisian theatrical producer, joined with Murger to produce a musical play, *La Vie de Bohème*, based on the experiences of Murger's characters. It was as a result of this play that Murger gained true recognition. His characters, positioned halfway between reality and fantasy, won the hearts of French readers who were tired of the drudgery of revolution and political strife.

In 1851, Murger published the combined episodes in book form. The value of *The Bohemians of the Latin Quarter* lies less in the work's literary style than in the fresh, unusual, expressive way in which Murger created his characters and situations. Murger's scenes, which do not really constitute a novel, contrast the cruel realities of daily life defined by unrelieved material need with fantasies of wealth, comfort, and delightful suppers in the Latin Quarter. Probing social margins and testing society's rules of propriety, Murger's characters, not being able to afford other entertainment, turn facets of everyday life into art. Although poverty and its resultant hunger, illness, and desperation are never far from the surface, the book is filled with humorous scenes created by the characters themselves in their attempt to keep life bearable.

The Bohemians of the Latin Quarter is fundamentally an autobiographical work. Murger was born in the Latin Quarter, and it was there that he struggled to achieve literary success in his early adulthood. The Café Momus where the bohemians met was a place Murger too frequented. His friends from that time, called the "Water-Drinkers," appear in his work as members of the "Bohemian Club." The Water-Drinkers were a group that included poets, a painter, a philosopher, and a sculptor, and Murger's fictional characters closely parallel them in their professions and personalities, though in some instances he combined the traits of different people to create a single character. The poet Rudolphe represents Murger himself, however, and his painter friend Marcel remains Marcel in the book.

Murger's first love, Marie Fonblanc, and his later beloved, Lucile Louvet, serve as models for Mimi, Musette, and Francine. It was Lucile's death that served as the model for the death of the character Mimi, which many consider the most poignant moment in the book. The women are categorized as "grisettes," poor young women of nineteenth century Paris who were unencumbered by middle-class restrictions. They were known for their gaiety, capriciousness, frugality, and fastidious lovemaking. Unwilling to sell their favors unless driven to it by need, they are portrayed as being not promiscuous but valiant.

Murger depicts the picturesque details of everyday life in the Latin Quarter in a nonchalant and often conversational style that easily draws the readers into the lives of the characters. Readers feel a kinship with the youthful spirited artists, and they empathize with their pain as well as their delight. Certain recurrent themes unify the work, perhaps most important exposure to cold and hunger. Many of the episodes center around the characters' efforts either to alleviate their want or, if that is not possible, to find a way to forget about it. The freezing garret, snowy Parisian scenes, and Mimi's cold hands all arouse a longing for spring, the sun, or enough wood for a fire. The healing capacity of warmth becomes a familiar reference.

The term "bohemian" to refer to the carefree and impoverished lifestyle of the struggling artists of nineteenth century Paris did not exist at the time of Murger's writing. It was in fact this collection of sketches that, more than any other single work, forged the concept of "bohemian" artistic life, which within a few years became a permanent part of literary and social history. By the 1890's, Murger's play had been revived five times, and in 1896 in Turin, Italy, one of the most enduring operatic masterpieces, Giacomo Puccini's *La Bohème*, which is based on Murger's book, was given its premiere. It is the pervading spirit of the youthful resilience that makes *The Bohemians of the Latin Quarter* a classic of French literature.

"Critical Evaluation" by Sandra C. McClain

Bibliography:
Baldick, Robert. *The First Bohemian: The Life of Henry Murger*. London: Hamish Hamilton, 1961. Definitive biography of Murger with an introduction giving background on the period and an extensive (although mostly French) bibliography. Offers biographical information about Murger and his literary career and discusses Murger's style and the basis of characters and situations in his book.
Josephs, Herbert. "Murger's Parisian Scenes and Puccini's *La Bohème*." In *La Bohème*, by Henry Murger, translated by Elizabeth Ward Hughes. Salt Lake City: Peregrine Smith Books, 1988. Addresses specific aspects of Murger's writing, as well as the transformation of the book into a libretto for Puccini's opera.
Lewis, D. B. Wyndham. Introduction to *La Bohème*, by Henry Murger, translated by Elizabeth Ward Hughes. Salt Lake City: Peregrine Smith Books, 1988. The introduction to the first translation, which discusses the history of the book, aspects of Murger's style, and the value of his writing.
Moss, Arthur, and Evelyn Marvel. *The Legend of the Latin Quarter: Henry Murger and the Birth of Bohemia*. New York: Beechhurst Press, 1946. Gives an excellent overview and background information to *The Bohemians of the Latin Quarter*.
Seigel, Jerrold. *Bohemian Paris: Culture, Politics, and the Boundaries of Bourgeois Life, 1830-1930*. New York: Viking, 1986. Discusses the history of the concept of bohemian lifestyle in Paris; includes background and specific discussion of Murger's writing and his influence; credits Murger with having defined bohemia in his writing.

THE BOOK OF LAUGHTER AND FORGETTING

Type of work: Novel
Author: Milan Kundera (1929-   )
Type of plot: Political; psychological realism
Time of plot: 1948-1980
Locale: Czechoslovakia and France
First published: Le Livre du rire et de l'oubli, 1979 (English translation, 1980)

Principal characters:
MIREK, a political dissident
ZDENA, his onetime mistress
MARKETA, a young woman
KAREL, her husband
EVA, Marketa and Karel's lover
MOTHER, Karel's mother
GABRIELLE, an American schoolgirl
MICHELLE, an American schoolgirl
MADAME RAPHAEL, their teacher
R., an editor
MILAN KUNDERA, the author
TAMINA, a Czech defector
BIBI, her friend
HUGO, a writer
KRISTYNA, a provincial woman
THE STUDENT, her boyfriend
KUNDERA'S FATHER
JAN, a doctor
EDWIGE, his lover
PASSER, Jan's dying friend

The Story:

Lost Letters. Disregarding his friends' advice to destroy his diaries recording dissident political meetings, Mirek traveled by car to meet Zdena. She was ugly, so he was ashamed of having had an affair with her twenty-five years earlier. He realized that he was being followed by another car, most likely the secret police. Mirek asked Zdena to return his old love letters to him. She refused. On the way back to his apartment, Mirek managed to elude the car following him. When he arrived home, he found his apartment being searched by the police, who confiscated his diaries. Mirek was arrested and sentenced to jail for six years.

Mother. Marketa and her husband Karel asked his aging, nearly sightless mother to stay with them for a week. Mother refused to leave on the day planned, insisting on staying another day. Eva arrived to stay with them that night, and Mother was told that Eva was Marketa's cousin. Marketa accused Karel of infidelity, and they began to fight, but Eva intervened and smoothed things over. As Mother was telling Karel that Eva reminded him of one of her old friends, Eva and Marketa emerged from their bath half-naked. After Mother retired for the evening, the three slept together. Karel, thinking himself a superb tactician for having arranged the ménage à trois,

712

called himself Bobby Fisher, after the chess master. In truth, his wife had arranged that they sleep with his lover. The next morning at the train station, Karel invited his mother to move in with them, but she refused.

The Angels. Gabrielle and Michelle discussed the play *Rhinoceros*, by Eugène Ionesco, with Madame Raphael. The author, Milan Kundera, recalled that, after the Soviet invasion of Czechoslovakia in 1968, he lost his job and wrote under a pseudonym for a living. R., the editor of the magazine for whom Kundera wrote an astrology column, illegally covered up the fact that he was the author. Her boss requested that the "astrologer" write a personal astrological reading for him. Kundera, as a prank, predicted an awful future for the boss. Kundera then recalled that, in 1950, the French writer Paul Éluard, to show his solidarity to the communist movement, did not protest the unjust death sentence of his friend, the Czech artist Zavis Kalandra. Kundera imagined Éluard rising in the air while dancing with other communists. R. sent a letter to Kundera informing him that it had been discovered that he was the author of the column. Kundera met with R., who had been fired from her job and was going to be interrogated by the police. After their class presentation on *Rhinoceros* was ridiculed by their classmates, Gabrielle and Michelle ascended through the ceiling with Madame Raphael.

Lost Letters. Tamina and her husband had defected from Czechoslovakia but left behind their notebooks and letters to each other. Tamina's husband fell ill while abroad and died. She wanted to retrieve the notebooks to help preserve her memories of her husband and their life together. Bibi agreed to get the notebooks on her trip to Prague, but Bibi then canceled her trip. Tamina's brother, who still lived in Prague, was persuaded to get the notebooks, which her in-laws had opened and read. Tamina had sex with Hugo, in part because he offered to travel to Prague to bring the notebooks back. While they made love, Tamina tried to remember her husband's image. After Hugo refused to go to Czechoslovakia, Tamina resolved to forget her memories.

Litost. Kristyna traveled to Prague from the countryside to see the student, who was embarrassed over her provincial dress and manners. Though invited to an important gathering of famous writers, the student declined so that he could be with Kristyna. She persuaded him to attend, requesting that a famous poet sign his book for her. At the gathering, the student witnessed the drunken carousing of the poets, and the famous poet wrote a personal message in his book for Kristyna. Upon his return, she refused to have sex with him, ashamed to tell him directly that another pregnancy could kill her. The student interpreted her vaguely worded excuse to mean that she would die from love. He found this message inspiring. The next morning, she explained more fully, and he was dejected once he realized his self-deception.

The Angels. Kundera's father, slowly dying, gradually lost the power of speech. Kundera recalled speaking with his father about his ideas on Ludwig van Beethoven's sonatas, which prompted Kundera's comments on the writing of the novel in terms of musical structure. Tamina was taken to an island inhabited only by children. She played their games, but the children physically and sexually abused her. She attempted to escape, but they captured her. Attempting to escape a second time, she swam into the water and drowned.

The Border. Jan reflected on his erotic life with Edwige, which had lost meaning for him. Jan visited his dying friend Passer at a sanatorium, where they discussed their different views of the meaning of life. At Passer's funeral, the wind blew a mourner's hat into the open grave. As the mourners shoveled some dirt into the pit and onto the hat, they struggled to restrain their inappropriate laughter. Afterward, at a group orgy, Jan was struck at the ridiculousness of the scene and was asked to leave when he laughed out loud. At a nude beach, Jan and Edwige discussed but misunderstood each other's interpretations of the myth of Daphnis and Chloë.

Critical Evaluation:

The Book of Laughter and Forgetting marked a new direction in Milan Kundera's development as a novelist. The novel is a synthesis of the major themes and narrative techniques of his previous fiction, but its structure is radically different. *The Book of Laughter and Forgetting* is divided into seven sections, most of which concern different characters (including Kundera) and different situations. The connections between the sections are primarily thematic and cluster around the shattering political and social impact of the Soviet invasion of Czechoslovakia, and the key words of the title. *The Book of Laughter and Forgetting* is, as Kundera writes in the novel, "a novel about laughter and forgetting, about forgetting and Prague, about Prague and the angels," but it is also a testimony to the tragedy of Soviet totalitarianism in Czechoslovakia.

The major theme of *The Book of Laughter and Forgetting* is the importance of memory to individual and collective lives. Kundera juxtaposes individual battles between memory and forgetting with Czech culture's battle to retain its identity in the face of Soviet domination. Mirek, the main character in the first section, "Lost Letters," justifies keeping a written record of incriminating facts, names, and dates by saying, "the struggle of man against power is the struggle of memory against forgetting." For individuals such as Mirek and Tamina as well as for the Soviets in control of Czechoslovakia, "the past is full of life, eager to irritate us, provoke and insult us, tempt us to destroy or repaint it."

The novel's other major theme is the paradox of laughter. Kundera distinguishes between skeptical, questioning laughter and self-righteous, joyful laughter throughout the novel. In a subsection entitled "On Two Kinds of Laughter," Kundera refers to these types of laughter as devils' and angels' laughter. He writes: "If there is too much uncontested meaning on earth (the reign of the angels), man collapses under the burden; if the world loses all its meaning (the reign of the demons), life is every bit as impossible." He complicates this relationship considerably, however, by asserting that "one and the same external phenomenon embraces two completely contradictory internal attitudes." In the last section of *The Book of Laughter and Forgetting*, Kundera uses the metaphor of the border to describe the instability of dualities in general. Although Kundera in *The Book of Laughter and Forgetting* portrays both extremes—fanaticism on one side and nihilism on the other—with distance, he is especially critical of angelic laughter, which he perceives as the laughter of communist zealotry.

In *The Book of Laughter and Forgetting* erotic and sexual scenes play a dominant role. In every section of the novel, characters (though male characters profit more than female ones) learn something about themselves through failed sexual relations, but this self-knowledge is bitter and disillusioning. The two scenes of group sex in the novel are comically ridiculous, providing exaggerated examples with which to strip away any sense of human sexuality as essentially meaningful and life-affirming.

In terms of Kundera's development as a novelist, *The Book of Laughter and Forgetting* marks a breakthrough in Kundera's ideas about novelistic structure. Its formal discontinuity has led some critics to be reluctant to describe the book as a novel. John Updike is representative when he calls it "more than a collection of seven stories yet certainly no novel." Early in *The Book of Laughter and Forgetting*, Kundera gives the reader explicit advice on how to unify the book's disparate parts while outlining his new aesthetic ambitions for the novel: "This entire book is a novel in the form of variations. The individual parts follow each other like individual stretches of a journey leading toward a theme, a thought, a single situation, the sense of which fades into the distance."

Kundera's structural method in *The Book of Laughter and Forgetting* is based on an analogy with formal musical composition. References to music in *The Book of Laughter and Forgetting* and in Kundera's textual comments reflect his interest and early training in classical music. Each section of the novel contains very different kinds of discourse: autobiographical fragments, historical facts and anecdotes, philosophical reflection, and fantasy. In one section, for example, Kundera juxtaposes a dreamlike tale of Tamina on an island inhabited only by children, the story of Kundera's father's dying days, and mini-essays concerning the demolition of Czech monuments and history. The essays cover Czech leader Gustav Hasak ("the president of forgetting"), time in Franz Kafka's novels, Beethoven's use of theme and variation, and the inanity of popular music. All these reflections are unified in that they refer to the same theme: Communism makes everyone into children by promising the future in exchange for the past. This kind of juxtaposition of thematically related fragments is characteristic of the entire structure of *The Book of Laughter and Forgetting*, and the result is a tour de force of narrative skill that has established Kundera's reputation as a major writer.

Glen Brand

Bibliography:
Banerjee, Maria Nemcova. *Terminal Paradox: The Novels of Milan Kundera*. New York: Grove Weidenfeld, 1990. Thorough summary and discussion of the major themes of the novel.
Bell, Pearl K. "The Real Avant-Garde." *Commentary* 70, no. 6 (December, 1980): 66-69. Places Kundera in a tradition of dissident Eastern European writing and praises *The Book of Laughter and Forgetting*'s originality.
Lodge, David. "Milan Kundera, and the Idea of the Author in Modern Criticism." *Critical Quarterly* 26, nos. 1/2 (Spring/Summer, 1984): 105-121. Compares the narrative technique of Kundera's first novel, *The Joke* (1967), to that of *The Book of Laughter and Forgetting*, calling the latter "a masterpiece of postmodernist fiction."
Misurella, Fred. *Understanding Milan Kundera: Public Events, Private Affairs*. Columbia: University of South Carolina Press, 1993. Good discussion of the novel in the wider contexts of Kundera's thought, life, and career.
Updike, John. "Czech Angels." In *Hugging the Shore: Essays and Criticism*. New York: Vintage Books, 1984. An often-cited enthusiastic review/essay that focuses on the themes of forgetting and eroticism in the novel.

BOOK OF SONGS

Type of work: Poetry
Author: Heinrich Heine (1797-1856)
First published: Buch der Lieder, 1827 (English translation, 1856)

Although it is generally conceded that Heinrich Heine's finest poetry was not written until his last years, the *Book of Songs*, which assembled his entire lyrical output to the age of twenty-six, remains the core of his poetic work. The book gained immediate popularity and appeared in a new edition every other year for decades. German critical opinion of the period cited Heine for writing in the spirit and with the simple accents of German folk song, but he soon became a controversial figure. His merits are still fiercely disputed in German territories, much of the controversy centering on his later prose writings, in which the unquenchably poetic nature of his approach to religion and political philosophy yielded, along with chilling prophetic insights, considerable rhetorical muddle.

His own feelings toward Germany were intensely ambiguous. He later became, through his Paris exile, "a link that spanned the Rhine"; but the French influences that surrounded him in his first sixteen years (during which time the Rhineland was mostly under French military occupation or French civil rule) apparently had little effect. In his memoirs, he said that early school experiences imbued him with a permanent prejudice against French literature, and he went through a phase of nationalistic fervor that ended only when he discovered that he breathed more freely under the French than the Prussian regime; ultimately he denounced Gallophobia and German national egotism. "The Grenadiers," one of his earliest poems, expresses his boyish admiration for Napoleon—typically an admiration not for the deeds but only for the genius of the man. When Heine lived among the French, however, his admiration was chiefly directed toward their freedom from the idealism, prudery, and sentimentality that he deplored in the German philistines, at whose expense his satirical wit waxed especially brilliant.

In the North Sea cycle that closes his *Book of Songs*, Heine describes his deep love of Germany, a love that flourished in spite of the fact that Germany's "pleasant soil" was "encumbered with madness, hussars, and wretched verses." There are passages, especially in the early poems, in which he expresses identification with the German character, either lamenting the passing of old Germany's nobility and virtues or praising the oak that stands for the essential hardihood and "holiness" of the fatherland. There is, however, something in his love for Germany that resembles his commitment to the lost beloved, the false fair, the maiden with flowering beauty and decaying heart, and this constitutes his poetic stock in trade and is, in fact, almost his whole *Nibelungenhort*. Nevertheless, he considered himself from first to last a German, and his poetry is deeply rooted in the German Romantic movement. He liked to refer to himself as the last of the Romantics, marking the close of the old lyric school of the Germans, but he attacked the political, realist, engagé "Young Germany" group with much the same exuberance as he did the old "poesy" and regressive spiritualism.

Heine, experimenting in most of the modes of Romanticism but ultimately taking from the movement only what suited him, provided finally one of the paths by which the Romantic spirit was deflected toward Symbolism. Individual lyrics of the *Book of Songs* sometimes suffer from a facile outpouring of stock diction and sentiment, but here is poetry that from the beginning avoids either the heights or the depths of the abysmal absolute. Its dealings with the absolute are rather directed at maintaining a perilous equilibrium, buoyed by Heine's fresh, vigorous idiom, his delicate music, with its constant play of assonance, and his frequent ironic twists. Reacting to the artifice of eighteenth century diction, Heine sympathized with the Romantic interests in a return to the German folk tradition and a poetic approximation to the supposedly purer aesthetic impact of music. Nevertheless, in spite of the fact that some of his ballads ("The Lorelei," for example) were actually admitted into the canon of German folk song, Heine himself insisted of his poetry that it was only the form that was somewhat akin to the folk song; the subject matter was that of conventional society. Perhaps more important to Heine's poetry than the Romantic exaltation of the *Volk* was the concern, distinctive to the German Romantic school, with developing a rationale of the comic. This concern provided a sympathetic climate for Heine's particular form of mockery, itself partially a product of the satirical wit native to his Jewish cultural inheritance.

The Romantic movement itself was later to provide one of the most obvious targets for Heine's irony, and the lyrical preface to the third edition of the *Book of Songs* contains an implicit comment on that subject. It was Heine who once defined the German Romantic school as a return to the medieval poetry that sprang from the Catholicism in which men derived voluptuous pleasure from pain. The prefacing verses satirically summarize that pleasure as it finds expression in his own lyrics. It is the "old enchanted wood" through which the poet wanders, listening to the nightingale singing "of love and the keen ache of love." He comes to a gloomy castle before which lies a marble sphinx, half lion, half woman, which the song of the nightingale prompts him to kiss. The kiss awakens the statue, who proceeds to embrace him rapturously in return at the same time that she sinks her claws into him, kissing and rending simultaneously. As the poet submits to this "exquisite torture," the nightingale sings, "O wondrous sphinx, O love,/ Why this always distressing/ Mingling of death-like agony/ With every balm and blessing?" The whole effect involves the same burlesque by exaggeration that is operative at the end of the "Lyrical Intermezzo," in which Heine describes the enormity of the coffin that would be required for him to lower all his sorrows into the Rhine—a facetious note not entirely confined to his earliest poems. On the whole, the *Book of Songs* contains Heine's exploration of the Romantic movement rather than his rejection of it, if only because it contains expressions of the sentimental attachments of various adolescent periods.

The first section, titled "Junge Leiden" (sorrows of youth), represents roughly Heine's *Sturm und Drang* period. It contains such characteristic pieces as "The Minnesingers" in which, with "word for sword," the singers engage in a tournament whose victor is the one who enters the fray with the deadliest wound. The section is subdivided into Dream Pictures, Songs, Romances, and Sonnets; the romantic decor of the poet's sensibility is rendered in its most studied garishness and most rollicking meter. Images include the enchanted garden and the graveyard vision; the wedding festivities and attendant corpse conjuring; the shining dream that turns to nightmare or to day-lit delusion; and Poor Peter, alias the clumsy knight, alias "King Heinrich"—a primordial Prufrock. Not all of the skeleton-rattling in this group is as delightful as that of "I came from my love's house." Here a minstrel sits on his crumbling tombstone and plays a delirious dance to arouse the graveyard's other inhabitants, and each tells how he came to be there—"How he fared, and was snared in love's mad and furious chase."

By the time of the "Lyrical Intermezzo" and the "Homecoming" sequence, which follow "Junge Leiden," Heine had largely abandoned his supernatural baggage in favor of a more natural imagery and a more personal, direct form of address:

> God knows where I'll find that silly
> Madcap of a girl again;

717

I have searched this endless city,
Wet and cursing in the rain. . . .

The imagery of sea, storm, seasonal change, and the like is never employed for its own richness, but for its directly evocative effect, as in the famous "Der Tod, das ist die kühle Nacht." Heine also proves himself capable of a restraint and lightness of touch in the most ageless tradition:

The golden flame of summer
Burns in your glowing cheek;
But in your heart lies winter,
Barren and cold and bleak.
Soon it will change, my darling,
Far sooner than you seek;
Your heart will harbor summer,
While winter lines your cheek.

In the "Lyrical Intermezzo," a subtle spring to autumn progression is threaded through the whole sequence.

Max Brod noted the remarkable cohesion revealed by assembling the whole of Heine's early poetry into a single book. The experiences of the hero of the poem sequences form a consistent whole in which the action develops with almost the progression of a verse novel. A biographical basis for these experiences is easy to establish, but it is detracting from its value to do so. Heine himself was extremely opposed to any biographical reading.

A unity less restricted to the theme of the rejected lover is attempted in the two North Sea cycles. Short, parallel sequences that exhibit a kind of symphonic development, they are often discounted as set pieces because they were written partly to escape the confines of a reputation for "lyrical, mordant, two-stanza" verse. They are not without rewarding moments, however, and their parallelism is curious and revealing. In the beginning the poet invokes the sea, the great symbol of inhuman immensity and constant change. In the poems that follow, the poet is actually at sea, witnessing and participating in various phenomena—storm, calm, seasickness, sunset, the progression of twilight, and night. There are also apostrophes to the ancient gods. Finally the poet comes to port, in the first sequence to the Peace of Christ, and in the final sequence, in a poem that parodies Christian metaphor throughout, to the haven of the wine cellar of Bremen. In a final burst of exuberance he writes:

Well, I have always declared
That not among quite common people,
Nay, but the best society going,
Lived for ever the King of Heaven!

Bibliography:
Brod, Max. *Heinrich Heine: The Artist in Revolt.* Translated by Joseph Witriol. New York: New York University Press, 1957. An English version of Brod's 1934 biographical study, offering a post-Holocaust historical assessment. Emphasizes Heine's loneliness and restlessness as a Diaspora Jew, to which Brod paradoxically attributes the universality of his verse.
Prawer, S. S. *Heine: Buch der Leider.* London: Edward Arnold, 1960. Stresses the significance of the *Doppelgänger* motif in the *Book of Songs*, resulting in ironization as Heine assumes various guises throughout the work. Considers the collection's influence on German literature disastrous because Heine's imitators lacked his complexity.

Reeves, Nigel. *Heinrich Heine: Poetry and Politics*. London: Oxford University Press, 1974. Traces apparently contradictory elements in Heine to a transitional historical context. Concludes that Heine's experiment with folk song failed largely because cultural refinement in Germany, with its subsequent loss of spontaneity and immediacy, was irreversible.

Sammons, Jeffrey L. *Heinrich Heine: The Elusive Poet*. New Haven, Conn.: Yale University Press, 1969. Argues that if Heine is taken seriously, the *Book of Songs* must not be dismissed, as many critics have done. Finds the work extraordinary in its concentration on a single theme and its revelation of the growth of a fictive persona.

Spencer, Hanna. *Heinrich Heine*. Boston: Twayne, 1982. Offers close analysis of most popular pieces in the *Book of Songs*, as well as a consideration of Heine's organization of the whole. Identifies a sudden change of mood, or *Stimmungsbrechung*, as the characteristic feature of the work.

THE BOOK OF THE COURTIER

Type of work: Didactic
Author: Baldassare Castiglione (1478-1529)
First published: Il libro del cortegiano, 1528 (English translation, 1561)

Principal personages:
    LADY ELISABETTA GONZAGA, duchess of Urbino
    LADY EMILIA PIA, her witty friend and attendant
    COUNT LEWIS (LUDOVICO) OF CANOSSA,
    SIR FREDERICK (FEDERICO) FREGOSO,
    LORD OCTAVIAN FREGOSO,
    LORD JULIAN (GIULIANO) DE MEDICIS,
    M. BERNARD BIBIENA,
    LORD GASPAR PALLAVICIN, and
    PIETRO BEMBO, Italian noblemen, courtiers to the duke of Urbino
    FRANCESCO MARIA DELLA ROVERE, heir to the duke of Urbino

The Story:

The duchess, Elisabetta Gonzaga, asked the gentlemen of the court to choose a topic of conversation for the evening's entertainment. They settled on "what belongeth to the perfection of Courtiership." The resulting conversation, with digressions, addressed that topic. Lewis, count of Canossa, began the discussion.

His ideal courtier must be, he said, nobly born, with a pleasant disposition, wit, and "a comely shape of person and countenance." Since his chief profession was to be a soldier, he needed training in all the skills that would make him an able warrior for his prince: riding, handling weapons of all sorts, wrestling, swimming, and other sports that increase strength and agility. The courtier also needed certain social talents, easy conversation, wit, the ability to dance, and, above all, a certain grace that made all his activities seem effortless and unconscious.

The conversation turned to language, a burning issue in the Renaissance, when the vernaculars were struggling with Latin for supremacy. The count recommended that the courtier avoid using antiquated or unfamiliar words and that he take his vocabulary from those familiar Italian words "that have some grace in pronunciation." Sir Frederick Fregoso argued that the count depended too much on custom; the courtier should shun "vices of speech," even if they have been adopted by the multitude. The count concluded the argument by stating that it was the courtier's knowledge, rather than his diction, that would ultimately be important. The first evening's conversation ended with a brief consideration of the importance of a courtier's having some skills in music and art.

On the second night Sir Frederick Fregoso was instructed to discuss the proper times and places for the courtier to exercise those virtues that have been declared essential for him. Frederick pointed out that most of all an ideal gentleman needed discretion to determine when to speak, when to be silent, and how to act so as to win praise and avoid envy. Fregoso recommended "little speaking, much doing, and not praising a man's own self in commendable deeds." He cited as a bad example an uncouth courtier who on one occasion entertained a lady with a description of his prowess with a two-handed sword and terrified her with a demonstration of various strokes.

All courtiers were expected to be able to entertain ladies gracefully, and the ability to sing was a particularly valuable accomplishment. Sir Frederick noted that a gentleman needed the wisdom to recognize that time in his life when his age made it ludicrous for him to perform in public; if such a man must sing, let him do it privately.

This point led to a general consideration of the proper demeanor for the young and the old. Fregoso praised mildness, deference, and hesitancy on the part of the fledgling courtier, but he suggested that the more restrained older man should strive for a little liveliness. A golden mean was the ideal.

After a serious discussion of the value of friendship with loyal, honorable men, Sir Frederick turned, at the request of the cynical Lord Gaspar Pallavicin, to a consideration of court entertainments. In this area, too, Fregoso pleaded for moderation; too great a concern with dice or cards could become a vice, and a man could waste the better part of his days in becoming a brilliant chess player. The best entertainment came from a courtier's wit, as Castiglione showed by weaving into his narrative a number of anecdotes and "merry pranks." M. Bernard Bibiena, who told many of the witty tales, cautioned the company to be mindful of the time, the place, and the individuals in jesting; maliciousness and cruelty should have no part in court life.

The conversation then turned to the character of women, whose honor and trustworthiness were wittily attacked by Lord Gaspar and defended by the Lady Emilia. Lord Julian de Medicis was instructed to imagine an ideal court lady for the next evening's amusement. The position of women was eloquently defended in part 3; one of the gentlemen asserted that "no court, how great so-ever it be, can have any sightliness or brightness in it, or mirth without women, nor any Courtier can be gracious, pleasant or hardy, nor at any time undertake any gallant enterprise of Chivalry, unless he be stirred with the conversation and with the love and contentation of women."

Lord Julian wanted for his ideal woman sweetness, tenderness, and womanliness, a pleasing disposition, noble birth, and a certain amount of beauty; she needed the same virtues of courage, loyalty, and discretion that the courtier required, and her position, too, could be enhanced by pleasant conversation and modesty. She needed to avoid that common feminine failing, a fondness for gossiping about other women. The ladies, as well as the gentlemen, of the court needed some skill in the arts, so that they could dance, sing, or play musical instruments with ease. Lord Julian said that the court lady should at least be acquainted with literature and philosophy.

Lord Gaspar, who had injected antifeminist sentiments throughout Lord Julian's discourse, scoffed at the notion of educated women and proclaimed that the sex is an imperfection in nature. Lord Julian countered by enumerating those qualities in which he found women superior to men and by relating stories of famous women in history.

Sir Frederick asked Lord Julian to consider what he thought was most important for women: "what belongeth to the communication of love." The latter answered that a lady must first distinguish between true and false protestations of affection. A good Christian, he could approve only of love that could lead to marriage. To the objection that an aged, unattractive, or unfaithful husband might justify favors to a lover, Lord Julian replied: "If this mishap chance to the woman of the palace, that the hatred of her husband or the love of another bendeth her to love, I will have her to grant her lover nothing else but the mind; not at any time to make him any certain token of love, neither in word nor gesture, nor any other way that he may be fully assured of it."

The fourth part opens with a brief reflection on mortality. Castiglione relates the fates of members of the court of Urbino during the years between the nights he is describing and the time he completed his book. He turns then to the topic of the final evening's discussion, the courtier's role as adviser to his prince. Lord Octavian Fregoso pointed out that this role was often made difficult by the arrogance and pride of rulers, who considered that their power automatically brings wisdom. The courtier was obliged to lead his prince gently and subtly toward goodness, courage, justice, and temperance, mingling moral instruction with pleasure, one justification for the courtier's acquiring skills in the "polite arts." Lord Gaspar questioned Fregoso's basic premise, that virtue can be taught, but the latter affirmed his conviction that if moral virtues were innate, a man would never become evil. Morality is acquired, rather than inborn, and education is therefore of inestimable value.

The discussion shifted to government itself, and arguments about the relative value of the kingdom and of the commonwealth were weighed. The group concluded that the rule of the virtuous prince, a man attuned to both the active and the contemplative life, was best. Lord Octavian suggested that a council of the nobility and a lower advisory house, chosen from the citizens of the land, might increase the virtue and knowledge of the prince; such a government would combine the best aspects of monarchy, aristocracy, and the commonwealth.

Finally, Pietro Bembo discoursed on Platonic love. The passions of youth were unfitting for the older courtier; he had to recognize that all love is, in fact, a yearning for beauty, and he must raise his thoughts from admiration of a single lovely woman to contemplate the idea of beauty. Purified of his human faults by this contemplation, he could reach "the high mansion place where the heavenly, amiable and right beauty dwelleth, which lieth hidden in the innermost secrets of God." Bembo's discourse became more and more enraptured, and when he broke off at last the others realized that it was daybreak. The courtiers and ladies dispersed for the last time.

Critical Evaluation:

Baldassare Castiglione's *The Book of the Courtier* was one of the most widely read books in sixteenth century Europe. Noblemen and poets looked upon it as a portrait of the ideal man of the Renaissance, and such men as Sir Philip Sidney are said to have modeled themselves on Castiglione's imaginary courtier. There is, perhaps, no finer or more appealing picture of life in the Italian Renaissance than that in *The Book of the Courtier*. Castiglione had a brilliant dramatic gift that enabled him to bring to life his friends at Urbino and to express their ideals clearly and powerfully in natural, rapidly moving dialogue.

The Book of the Courtier became a handbook for the English gentleman. Queen Elizabeth's teacher, Roger Ascham, said a young man could learn more by reading the book than he would be spending three years in Italy. It seems ironic that Castiglione should find his most enthusiastic readers in England, for he distances himself from the original conversation in Urbino by pretending to have been in England at the time. His name appears in the dialogue only because he sends a glowing report about the education of Prince Henry, the future Henry VIII and the father of Elizabeth I.

Castiglione wrote *The Book of the Courtier* between 1508 and 1518. He kept adding to the text for another decade, during which it circulated among courts in the city states of what became Italy. Only when he got word of the circulation of an unauthorized copy did he finally prepare the text for publication. He presented specially bound volumes to surviving members of the group featured in the book. The group had gathered at the Palace of Urbino in March, 1507. The courtly ideal (or ideology) that Castiglione upheld was already dead in the Italian-speaking world, replaced by the power politics of the Medicis as described in *The Prince* (1513) by Niccolò Machiavelli. Castiglione's son was forced to remove jokes about monks in order to keep later editions from being banned by the Catholic church. Castiglione found an appreciative audience in England when Thomas Hoby translated the text.

Castiglione presents the book as an extended treatise for Alfonso Ariosto, a relative of the epic poet Ludovico Ariosto. In the opening of the first book, he addresses Alfonso directly, responding to his friend's request for an account of the ideal life at court. Rather than offer his own opinion, he says he is repeating what he heard about a famous exchange at Urbino. He says he is following classical tradition, and his closest model is Cicero's account of the ideal orator in *On Oratory* (55 B.C.E.), also set as a dialogue in the past. Indeed, the courtier seems to be the Renaissance equivalent of the ancient Roman orator, a man of knowledge, influence, and eloquence. When Castiglione addresses Alfonso more briefly, at the outset of each succeeding book, he offers rhetorical proofs that public life is no worse in the Renaissance than it was in antiquity, that it has reached its recent perfection at the court of Duke Guidobaldo, and that it may again flourish at Urbino. Each major speaker gives a rhetorical declamation; together the speakers argue what a courtier should be, how he should act, how he should advise the prince, and what his female counterpart should be like.

The rules of the discussion that Lady Elisabetta proposes are the rules of rhetoric, as well as the rules of good manners, and everyone observes them. The rhetorical dimension of *The Book of the Courtier* was unmistakable to readers in the sixteenth century, when classical rhetoric was a central subject of education. Much of the dramatic interest, in what might easily have become a series of set speeches, derives form the rhetorical moves that the speakers make as they offer to be concise or beg each other to continue, as they challenge each other and reply to the challenges. Much of the pleasure that readers have had with the book is that of hearing genuine conversation among highly civilized people. Frederick Fregoso, who leads the discussion on the second evening, is especially concerned with metaphor, irony, and other figures of speech. It is not necessary, however, to know the names of all the rhetorical figures. It is enough to realize that Castiglione is not digressing or contradicting himself when he piles figure on figure and story on story; he is representing the twists and turns of a conversation.

Those twists and turns can be tiresome for modern readers who want to get on with the story. *The Book of the Courtier* is less a story about four evenings in Urbino than a book of stories about the courtly or courteous life. The chief method of proof that the various speakers use is the illustrative anecdote or exemplum, and there are even examples of good and bad practical jokes as the second evening draws to an uproarious end. Castiglione's model here may be *The Decameron* (1349-1351) by the great Italian storyteller Giovanni Boccaccio, a tale about people who tell tales. Castiglione's tales are in summary form, many of them no longer than a paragraph; they never use the street language that makes Boccaccio's tales so vivid, but they say much about the tellers. In the dedication to the Bishop of Viseu, Castiglione rejects the comparison to Boccaccio that readers immediately made. His most fully realized characters, such as Emilia and Julian, nevertheless step out of the pages and live on their own. The advantage of a dialogue is that many points of view can be expressed, even if some are put down.

The villain in the piece is the sickly young Gaspar Pallavicin, who is thoroughly cynical about men and especially cynical about women. His views are barely tolerated, but they are forcefully expressed and belong to *The Book of the Courtier* as much as Bembo's encomium on love. Castiglione's *The Book of the Courtier* is inevitably paired with Machiavelli's *The Prince*, not only because the prince needs the courtier but because idealism needs an antidote of realism. The Elizabethans saw the two works as poles apart. They coined the term "Machiavellian" to describe the rogues they feared in politics and cultivated the ideals of courtesy in the heroic courts of Sir Philip Sidney's *Arcadia* (1593) and Edmund Spenser's *The Faerie Queene* (1596).

"Critical Evaluation" by Thomas Willard

Bibliography:

Castiglione, Baldassare. *The Book of the Courtier*. Translated and with an introduction by George Bull. New York: Penguin Books, 1967. Renders the Italian names more faithfully than Sir Thomas Hoby's classic translation. Includes a lively introduction, useful notes, and an index.

Finucci, Valeria. *The Lady Vanishes: Subjectivity and Representation in Castiglione and Ariosto*. Stanford, Calif.: Stanford University Press, 1992. A feminist and psychoanalytic perspective. Includes separate chapters on the discourse, the women, and the jokes in *The Book of the Courtier*. Draws comparisons to a popular epic of the same era.

Frye, Northrop. *Myth and Metaphor: Selected Essays, 1974-1988*. Edited by Robert D. Denham. Charlottesville: University Press of Virginia, 1990. Contains a lucid account of Castiglione's importance in Renaissance literature, written by one of the twentieth century's most influential literary critics.

Hanning, Robert W., and David Rosand, eds. *Castiglione: The Ideal and the Real in Renaissance Culture*. New Haven, Conn.: Yale University Press, 1983. Includes a chronology of Castiglione's life and essays on language, women, and humanism and an essay on Renaissance portraiture.

Rebhorn, Wayne A. *Courtly Performances: Masking and Festivity in Castiglione's "Book of the Courtier."* Detroit: Wayne State University Press, 1978. Considers Castiglione's book in the light of courtly customs and entertainments.

Woodhouse, John Robert. *Baldesar Castiglione: A Reassessment of "The Courtier."* Edinburgh: Edinburgh University Press, 1978. A new appraisal of Castiglione's work, emphasizing the artistic creation rather than the historical account.

THE BOOK OF THE DEAD

Type of work: Religious
Author: Unknown
First transcribed: Papyrus Ani, 4500 B.C.E.-200 C.E. (English translation, 1895)

Principal characters:
OSIRIS, the judge and special god of the dead
ISIS, his sister goddess and mate
HORUS, twice-born, son of Osiris and Isis
ANUBIS, protector of dead; allotted destiny
SET, the principle of evil, murderer of Osiris
TEMU, spirit of creation; inspired Ptah
PTAH, author of creation; spoke First Word
RA, with Ptah, the principle of light; sun
NUT, sky goddess, great mother

The Story:

The god Temu, the spirit of creation, became manifest first as Ptah, and then as the word spoken by Ptah, which brought creation into existence. Ptah created first himself, then the other gods, and finally created Egypt, by speaking the divine words that made the gods aware of themselves; thus, all of creation exists as different aspects, or "faces," of Ptah, and of his words. Immediately after he spoke these first powerful magic words, while the earth and the waters of primordial chaos were still in the process of separating themselves, Ptah promised eternity to the dead who had not yet been born. On that same day, the god Anubis, protector of the souls of the dead, allotted to each person a destiny and held all these fates in readiness.

For mortals, the immediate earthly manifestation of Ptah was Ra, the sun, and it was in this form that they most often contemplated the one God. Priests used many names to refer to the different faces of God; these names varied from place to place, but the names which the gods gave themselves were hidden, because in their names lay their essence, and so their power. By a stratagem, Isis learned the hidden name of Ra and, with a power derived from his, became queen of the goddesses. Her power is illustrated by the story of her healing of her mate, the god Osiris.

Osiris was murdered by Set, his brother, who in his malice cut the body of Osiris into pieces and scattered them across northern Africa. Isis, weeping, gathered these pieces together and rejoined them, and from the corpse conceived Horus, their son. Then she brought Osiris back to life, led him before the gods, and brought him into new forms, with new powers. It was through this rebirth that Osiris became the principle of birth and rebirth. He was the fountainhead through which the earth received life, from the first new life of sprouting corn and all the life it brought in its turn, to the rebirth in the afterlife of the pharaohs.

All the dead who received the proper rites and who performed the sacred rituals were reborn in the afterlife as new forms of Osiris and shared his glory. Like him, their bodies were made whole and perfect when they were resurrected in Osiris' name and in accordance with the prescribed formalities. The secrets of embalming, the processes and forms for charms and incantations and funereal rites, were given to mortals by Isis, who thus gave them a means of being reborn. As she recreated Osiris' body, so it was for the dead reborn in Osiris' name. As the dead approached Osiris in the afterlife, they recited the ritual incantations learned in life, and their impurities, manifestations of Set, fell away from them. Meanwhile the living, left to perform rites of ablution and purification, sprinkled cleansing water on the dead and made offerings. One after another the dead approached Osiris, and those who were justified were rejuvenated and were blessed by Isis and by Horus, who held a special position within the hierarchy of immortals.

Horus, one of the greatest of the Egyptian panoply of gods, had as many as twenty different forms. In a sense he was one aspect of Osiris; in another sense he was an aspect of Ra. In most of his aspects, however, and perhaps because of his relationship to Ra, he was closely associated with light. In a battle with Set, Horus lost one eye, but pursued Set, the spirit of evil, and castrated him, making Set powerless. Horus was therefore especially revered by the dead, for by Horus' victory over the darkness of Set the dead could see to approach eternity, and by Horus' victory over the evil of Set the dead could be made sanctified. Horus' face, in the aspect called Harmachis (translated as "Horus on the Horizon"), was immortalized as the face of the great Sphinx of Gizeh.

Horus led the dead into the presence of Osiris and acted as intermediary for the dead during the process of judgment. Horus was especially suited for this role by virtue of his aspect as an avenger of his father, and of the miraculous circumstances surrounding his conception. Making his petitions for the dead to his father in the presence of his mother, his pleas were granted. Then the dead made a special appeal to Osiris to restore the physical body and protect it from decay, as he had renewed his own after it had been dismembered by his brother Set.

The gods lived in a paradise in the sky, and there the justified dead lived with them. When Nut, the goddess of the sky, bent over forward and placed her palms flat on the earth before her, her arms and legs formed the pillars which upheld the sky. Across this sky passed the sun and moon, and through it sailed the Celestial Boat, carrying the gods and the dead permitted to join them. Their souls arrived by ascending a ladder or by passing through a gap in the mountains. There they lived in peace and serenity in the presence of the gods, renewed daily by the power of Osiris.

Critical Evaluation:

For five thousand years, those who lived along the Nile and across northern Africa believed that when they died, they would be resurrected in body and spirit by the power of Osiris and would live forever in the presence of the majesty of the One God in all his different forms. Death was an untying of the knot that held the soul on the mortal plane, and was more a cause for methodical care and preparation than for fear. The precepts on which the Egyptians built their convictions are recorded in what has come to be known, somewhat inaccurately, as *The Book of the Dead.*

The literal translation of the title by which the Egyptians referred to this remarkable work is "the book of coming forth by day." Its influences on Western culture have been significant, and various editions and forms of the book have been continuously available for study since long before the time of Cleopatra. Some "chapters" were inked on the sarcophagi of the pharaohs; others were carved into the stones of the secret and sacred chambers of the pyramids. Copies on papyrus of the spells, hymns, and incantations were buried with the dead for ready use in the trials that the departed soul would face in the netherworld. Whatever translation one reads, however, one finds that the book is a vehicle for profound feeling, from the weeping of Isis as she searches for the severed limbs of her beloved Osiris to the joy of the dead whose spirits awaken to a fresh northern breeze in the light from Ra.

Recorded editions exist in three forms; the earliest are the Pyramid texts, dating from 2400 B.C.E., hieroglyphics carved in the stones of the pyramids of the fifth, sixth, and eighth dynasty rulers. These texts are clearly derived from much older oral versions. Later, when coffins became shaped to conform to the body within, papyrus scrolls replaced the carvings or inked symbols; gradually the use of hieratic script, a more abstract form of writing, replaced the earlier hieroglyphics. Finally, after the Roman conquest, scraps of spells or charms, their meanings largely forgotten, were written in contemporary script on small squares of papyrus and tossed into the coffins before they were sealed.

There is no authoritative version of the book, although a reasonably complete compilation appeared in German translation in 1842 and was widely available in English translation after 1895. The various chapters, of which there are now known to be over 300, include hymns of adoration, charms, rituals of purification and passage, and devotional poems written over a period spanning five millennia. Copies were eventually mass produced by priests and scribes for sale to individuals for burial use, though the text was not standardized until the Ptolemaic period, which began in 322 B.C.E. Various "recensions," authoritative versions of which multiple and various editions exist, have been identified and studied extensively, but no comprehensive ancient version has been found to contain all of the chapters.

The influence this rich and vital book of scripture has had on other cultures is incalculable. The religion of Osiris was flourishing while the Israelites were captive in Egypt, and there can be little doubt that some of the images and symbols, as well as some of the more powerful precepts of faith and spirituality, were incorporated from the Egyptian cult of Osiris into the holy Hebrew writings that later formed the bases of the Talmud, the Koran, and the Bible. Hymns to Ra and Osiris have much in common with the Psalms, both in image and theme. The image of King David dancing before God, for example, mirrors that of Seti I dancing before the assembled deities of the netherworld.

The most significant parallels, however, are in the coincident views on a single, all-powerful father/creator and on a redeemer, part man and part God, who will come to afford the souls of the sanctified resurrection and eternal life. All three of the major modern religions to originate in Northern Africa share these basic views; all three revere the power of ritual worship; all three believe in the existence of a paradise to which the justified dead may aspire, and all three have elaborate funereal procedures during which prayers are made to intercede for the departed souls. The Egyptian cult of Osiris significantly predates all three of the other main North African religions, and when the Romans introduced Christianity to the Egyptians they found fertile soil already prepared. Osiris and Horus, father and son, easily became identified with God and Christ, while the statues of Isis suckling Horus could be seen as Mary with the infant Jesus. Other parallels too numerous to mention may be noted.

The Book of the Dead is an affirmation of faith and joy. All such works are beautiful, allegories reconciling seeming contradictions of light and darkness, good and evil, multiplicity and unity, and life and death. New generations of readers will bring new interpretations, but what is timeless will remain so, and *The Book of the Dead* will continue to be a subject of study.

Andrew B. Preslar

Bibliography:
Budge, E. A. Wallis. *The Book of the Dead: The Papyrus of Ani in the British Museum: The Egyptian Text with Interlinear Transliteration and Translation.* Reprint. New York: Dover Publications, 1967. An extensive introduction describes the gods, their roles, and their realms, along with the funeral ceremonies and their importance. Clear interpretations by chapter.

_____. *Egyptian Religion: Egyptian Ideas of the Future Life*. Reprint. London: Routledge & Kegan Paul, 1975. Explores conceptual and symbolic parallels between the beliefs of the Osirians and the modern Christians. Classification by subject imposes a degree of order on the diverse topics.

Černý, Jaroslav. *Ancient Egyptian Religion*. London: Hutchinson University Library, 1952. A timetable matches dynastic periods with dates. Describes Osirian beliefs. Learned without being difficult.

Champdor, Albert. *The Book of the Dead, based on the Ani, Hunefer, and Anhaï Papyri in the British National Museum*. Translated by Faubion Bowers. New York: Garrett, 1966. Arranges material chronologically, from creation to modern times. Weaves interpretation with text to capture the substance and grandeur of the work. Extensive, beautiful illustrations provide visual context.

Hornung, Erik. *Conceptions of God in Ancient Egypt: The One and the Many*. Translated by John Baines. Ithaca, N.Y.: Cornell University Press, 1971. An exhaustive treatment of the subject. Outlines the Egyptian solution to the paradox of unity in multiplicity. An invaluable chronology. Glossary of gods and index.

BOOK OF THE DUCHESS

Type of work: Poetry
Author: Geoffrey Chaucer (c. 1343-1400)
Type of plot: Allegory
Time of plot: Indeterminate
Locale: Idealized dream landscape
First published: c. 1370

> *Principal characters:*
> DREAMER, a dying man who has a vision
> BLACK KNIGHT, a dying lover who has lost his beloved
> WHITE, the beloved who has died

The Story:

The Dreamer of the poem was lamenting his terrible loss, a loss which only one physician might heal. He had lost his beloved lady, either through rejection or through death. In either case, the Dreamer was unable to sleep, fearful that death might come upon him. There seemed to be no hope for him.

He decided to pass a lonely night by reading in a collection of tales, and there he found the story of King Ceyx and Queen Alcyone. When Ceyx sailed away, his wife waited patiently yet eagerly for his return, but she was unaware that his ship was caught in a storm and all hands were lost. As the days went by, Alcyone began to despair, and, like the Dreamer, she was unable to sleep and finally prayed to Juno for relief. Juno sent a messenger to the god Morpheus, who inhabited Ceyx's drowned body and told Alcyone of his death. Alcyone died four days later of despair.

The Dreamer regretted Alcyone's pain but responded to the story of the god of sleep, Morpheus, and he imagined what rich gifts he would give to that god if only he would confer sleep upon him. In fact, his head began to nod and he fell asleep over his book. He was instantly transported to a dream landscape. It was May; the flowers had bloomed and had begun to rival the stars in the sky in number. The fairies had made their abode in the forest, and the whole place resembled a landscaped garden.

The Dreamer found himself in a beautiful chamber filled with paintings and glazed windows that told stories of love and romance. Then suddenly he was outside, watching the Emperor Octavian in a royal hunt. The hounds found the scent, but the hart was clever and escaped the dogs. The hunt was recalled, but the Dreamer, who had been stationed by a tree, found one of the young, untrained dogs coming up to him. He followed the whelp, which took him deeper into the woods. The forest was beautiful, orderly, and full of deer.

There the Dreamer found the Black Knight, who lay beneath a huge oak singing a song of sorrow over the death of his lady. In fact, his sorrow was so deep that as the Dreamer watched, the Black Knight seemed to be dying, the blood draining from all of his limbs and leaving him green and pale. The Dreamer greeted him, and though the Knight seemed unaware of the Dreamer's presence at first, soon his courteous nature asserted itself and he greeted the Dreamer gently. When the Dreamer offered to help bear his sorrow and asked the Knight to reveal its cause, the Knight was at first reluctant, but then began a diatribe against Fortune and its wiles. It was Fortune that had brought him low, he argued, by playing chess with him and stealing his lady.

The Dreamer did not seem to understand this image and encouraged the Knight to stand firm against Fortune, arguing that no loss of a love should lead to this kind of woe. The Knight responded that the Dreamer did not understand how much he had indeed lost, for, since his youth, he had been wholly subject to love, and now that to which he had devoted himself had been destroyed.

The Black Knight told how he first met his lady, dancing on a green with a company of ladies. She was by far the fairest, the most beautiful and courteous, the best of speech and manner, gentle, good, steadfast, and simple. She was faithful and temperate, unable to do wrong because she loved right so much. The Dreamer concluded that the Black Knight could not have bestowed his love on a better woman and asked to hear of their first words together. The Black Knight confessed that for a long time he did not tell her of his love; he simply composed songs about her. His woe increased, however, and finally he approached her and swore his love. At first, she rejected him, and for a year he lived in despair until, gathering his courage, he approached her again. This time he was accepted because of his virtue, and for years they lived happily.

Then, the Knight moaned, death took her. At that word, the Dreamer saw the hunters returning through the woods and the king riding homeward to a long castle with white walls. The Dreamer woke up in his bed and resolved to put his dream into rhyme.

Critical Evaluation:

Geoffrey Chaucer is best known for his *Canterbury Tales* (1380-1390). *Book of the Duchess* is one of his minor works, probably his first fully polished long poem. It is generally understood that the poem is meant to commemorate the death of Blanche, the Duchess of Lancaster and the wife of John of Gaunt, one of Chaucer's patrons. If this is true, then the poem was probably meant not only to celebrate her physical and spiritual virtues but also to console John in some measure over the loss of his own beloved. The frequent references to the color white, including the principal woman's name, suggest that Chaucer was punning on the name Blanche.

If the poem is connected to a specific individual, it is still very much a genre poem. When Chaucer was writing this poem, he was heavily influenced by French poets who frequently used allegories in which a dreamer was suddenly transported to a beautiful, gardenlike setting, as though he had entered into a tapestry. There the lover learns something about the nature of love, usually by meeting a lover who has been rejected by his lady or who has suffered the lady's death. There are some indications, such as a reference to an eight-year illness, that Chaucer adds to these conventions specific references to the despair of John of Gaunt; nevertheless, he remains firmly within the convention of the dream allegory.

The story of *Book of the Duchess* is one of increasing woe and a search for consolation. The story begins with the Dreamer's own undefined loss and his suggestion that only one physician will help, suggesting that the physician is in fact his lady, who either will not or cannot help him. (The same image is later used to describe White.) His hopeless despair is so deep that he cannot sleep and fears that he will die.

In fact, the second story of loss suggests that this indeed might happen. The loss of King Ceyx is a mirror image of the loss of the Dreamer's lady, only here the despair does indeed drive Alcyone first to a lack of sleep, then to a telling dream, and then to death. The story has the potential of leading to a tragic conclusion for the Dreamer. However, this is a poem about consolation, and it does not end with tragedy. Some have gone so far as to suggest that Chaucer is using the story of Ceyx and Alcyone to encourage John of Gaunt to move past his grief, rather than to yield to it.

The third story of grief is that of the Black Knight and his lady, and the Dreamer learns of it as he encourages the Black Knight to tell of his lady, of their first meeting, and of his loss. Like the Dreamer, the Black Knight is physically devastated by his loss, and he can think of nothing else. In fact, it seems that for him to think of anything else would be a betrayal of his lady. The Dreamer leads him to the point of revealing the totality of his loss.

With this admission comes a vision of the return of the king to his white-walled castle set upon a rich hill, and, while the description may once again be a reference to John of Gaunt, it also suggests a heavenly vision, there lying the ultimate—and only—consolation. The recurring theme of each of the stories of loss is that "too little while our bliss lasts," that happiness is fleeting. The suggestion at the conclusion, however, is that, though this is true while on earth, it is not true in an eternal sense.

If the central issue of the poem is loss and consolation, it deals with that issue on several levels. The poem could be read as an idealized allegorical biography in which the Black Knight clearly represents John of Gaunt and White represents Blanche. The poem could also be read as an elegy meant principally to console John, encouraging him to keep intact his wife's memory but to move beyond his grief. (Certainly there is no other forum in which Chaucer, the son of a merchant, could have given advice like this to one of the most powerful men in England.) The poem could also be read as an examination of grief in which each of the characters represents an attitude toward loss: the Dreamer representing reason, the Black Knight symbolizing passion.

Chaucer does seem to suggest an inevitable progress in the ways characters respond to grief. Anxiousness leads to despair, leading to sleeplessness, leading, eventually, to sleep with troubled dreams that seem to accentuate the loss. When the Dreamer enters the dreamworld, it is hardly surprising that he comes upon a figure much like himself—not in terms of his social position but in terms of his psychological position. In his dream situation, the role of the Dreamer is suddenly reversed; whereas in the beginning of the poem, he was dying and in need of consolation, he is now the one to offer consolation to one who is also dying over the loss of a beloved.

The character of the Dreamer in this role has been variously interpreted. On the one hand, he seems something of a dunce. He hears the Black Knight sing a song in which he laments the death of his beloved lady, yet later he seems unable to understand that the Black Knight is sorrowing over his lady's death. In fact, he gives him what appears to be callous advice, suggesting that the loss of a lady is not worth intemperate grief. Perhaps the Dreamer means well, but he is an inept comforter.

Yet, on the other hand, the Dreamer may be quite psychologically astute. In his apparent clumsiness, he leads the Black Knight into a recitation of joyful and happy memories—quite different from the Knight's initial moanings and groanings. At first, the Knight cannot make an open declaration of the cause of his grief, though he hints at it. Finally he is led to a point at which he declares his lady's death. Only now, when the words are stated boldly and accepted as true, does the Black Knight confront his own pain. As he confronts pain, so too does the Dreamer. It is at this point that consolation comes and the Dreamer awakes, for the dream is no longer necessary.

The poem, then, is a recognition that this is a world of real pain and real loss. Such loss and pain lead to real sadness that cannot simply be wiped away; in fact, remembering a loved one, even though it may bring pain, is good and valid. Pain must be accepted rather than denied, for even though the long and white castle suggests a heavenly reunion, in this world it is only natural to feel grief in the face of inevitable loss.

Gary D. Schmidt

Bibliography:

Bronson, Bertrand H. "*The Book of the Duchess* Re-Opened." In *Chaucer: Modern Essays in Criticism*, edited by Edward Wagenknecht. London: Oxford University Press, 1959. Bronson focuses on the apparent inconsistencies and ignorance of the narrator, arguing that these are not flaws but are actually built into the meaning and narrative structure of the poem.

Corsa, Helen Storm. *Chaucer: Poet of Mirth and Morality*. Toronto: Forum House, 1970. In a chapter examining Chaucer's early work, Corsa argues that, though the occasion of *Book of the Duchess* is a sad one, the general tone is one of gladness and mirth.

Hieatt, Constance B. *The Realism of Dream Vision: The Poetic Exploitation of the Dream-Experience in Chaucer and His Contemporaries*. The Hague: Mouton, 1967. Hieatt examines the ways in which Chaucer raises and uses reader expectations to create meaning in his dream visions.

Lawlor, John. "The Pattern of Consolation in *The Book of the Duchess*." In *Chaucer Criticism*, edited by Richard J. Schoek and Jerome Taylor. Notre Dame, Ind.: University of Notre Dame Press, 1961. Lawlor examines the complex system of consolation which the narrator offers to the bereaved Black Knight, moving from apparent ignorance to assertion of his loss.

Lumiansky, R. M. "The Bereaved Narrator in Chaucer's *The Book of the Duchess*." *Tulane Studies in English* 9 (1959): 5-17. Lumiansky focuses on the role of the narrator in terms of his parallel bereavement with that of the Black Knight.

Millar, Robert P. *Chaucer Sources and Backgrounds*. New York: Oxford University Press, 1977. Millar supplies translations of the French and Latin sources that Chaucer used for his dream visions, though this book deals with the entire range of Chaucer's work.

Muscatine, Charles. *Chaucer and the French Tradition*. Berkeley: University of California Press, 1957. Muscatine focuses on the dream vision tradition from French literature and Chaucer's adaptations of those forms.

Robertson, D. W., Jr. "*The Book of the Duchess*." In *Companion to Chaucer Studies*, edited by Beryl Rowland. New York: Oxford University Press, 1968. Robertson provides a general study of the background, thematic meanings, and critical understandings of *Book of the Duchess*.

Spearing, A. C. *Medieval Dream-Poetry*. Cambridge, England: Cambridge University Press, 1976. In a chapter on *Book of the Duchess* within this general study of medieval dream visions, Spearing argues that, though the poem demonstrates many of the traditional elements of the dream vision, it differs from them in that it was written for a specific occasion and has a great deal of material not included in the actual vision. These differences affect the operation of the dream vision in terms of its overall meaning for the reader.

Windeatt, Barry A., ed. and trans. *Chaucer's Dream Poetry: Sources and Analogues*. Totowa, N.J.: Rowman & Littlefield, 1982. Examines the mostly French sources upon which Chaucer drew for *Book of the Duchess*.

THE BOOK OF THE LADIES

Type of work: Biography
Author: Christine de Pizan (c. 1365-c. 1430)
Type of plot: Allegory
Time of plot: Early fifteenth century
Locale: Paris and the allegorical City of Ladies
First published: Le Livre de la Cité des Dames, c. 1405 (English translation, 1521, 1982)

> *Principal characters:*
> CHRISTINE DE PIZAN, the narrator
> LADY REASON, the first allegorical guide
> LADY RECTITUDE, the second allegorical guide
> LADY JUSTICE, the third allegorical guide

The Story:

Christine de Pizan was sitting in her study reading when her mother called her to supper. The next day, as Christine resumed reading *The Lamentations of Mathéolus*, which slandered women's character, she reflected on the behavior of the female sex. While she was lost in thought, a vision of three ladies appeared to her. They told Christine that they had come to correct the erroneous impressions that men had created about women by helping her build a city where virtuous women would reside. They identified themselves as Lady Reason, Lady Rectitude, and Lady Justice.

Christine accepted their commission to build the City of Ladies by writing about worthy women. With Lady Reason's guidance, she laid the foundations. Christine first asked Lady Reason why male authors had maligned women. Reason offered several explanations and affirmed that these accounts of women's behavior were false. Christine inquired why women did not hold positions of governmental authority. Reason recounted the lives of several women who ruled after the death of their husbands, including Nicaula, empress of Ethiopia in antiquity, and French queens such as the Merovingian Fredegund and Blanche of Castile in the thirteenth century.

When Christine asked about women's strength, Reason told how the ancient Assyrian Queen Semiramis led armies after her husband's death. Reason related the feats of strength of the Amazons in ancient Greece and cited instances of other women from antiquity who acted with bravery. Lady Reason answered Christine's queries about learned women by mentioning two Roman poets, Cornifica and Proba, and the Greek poet Sappho. Other women such as Manto, Medea, and Circe from Greek antiquity excelled in magical sciences. Several women from ancient times including Nicostrata, Minerva, Ceres, and Isis discovered arts, sciences, and technologies. Women contributed to the arts and crafts of textiles and painting. To Christine's inquiry if women behaved prudently, Lady Reason, explaining qualities of prudence based on the biblical book of Proverbs, adduced the lives of the Romans Gaia Cirilla and Lavinia, Queen Dido of Carthage, and Queen Ops of Crete.

Lady Rectitude then assumed the guidance of Christine's work in completing the city walls and building edifices within the city. Rectitude instructed Christine on the wisdom of women by telling about the ten sibyls and their gifts of prophecy. She cited several biblical women— among them, Deborah, Elizabeth, and the Queen of Sheba—whose understanding made them prophetic. Other women, such as the Greek Cassandra and the Byzantine Antonia, had prophetic powers. When Christine asked why parents preferred sons to daughters, Lady

733

Rectitude demonstrated that many daughters took care of their parents. The Roman virgin Claudine defended her father from attack, and another Roman woman nursed her imprisoned mother.

Rectitude announced that the buildings of the City of Ladies were complete and ready to be inhabited. In response to Christine's inquiries about women's role in marriage, Rectitude brought to the city Queen Hypsicratea, who showed such devotion to her husband that she accompanied him on military campaigns and into exile after his defeat. The city was filled with married women who counseled their spouses wisely and commemorated their deceased husbands. Of women who had saved their people, Rectitude mentioned Hebrew women such as Judith and Esther, the Sabine women of ancient Rome, and the Frankish queen Clotilda who converted her husband Clovis to Christianity. Many women were noted for chastity, including the biblical Susanna and the Greek Penelope, wife of Ulysses. The Roman Lucretia tried to protect herself from rape. Women such as Griselda and the Roman empress Florence endured extreme hardships in remaining faithful to their husbands. Rectitude praised the virtues of French queens who were Christine's contemporaries, among them Queen Isabella, wife of Charles VI, and the duchesses of Berry, Orléans, and Burgundy.

Lady Justice took up the task of completing the high towers and selecting their residents. The Virgin Mary became the queen of the City of Ladies. Justice led in female martyrs for the Christian faith by recounting the acts of martyrdom of more than thirty saints. Christine finally declared that the city was complete and exhorted women to follow the virtuous examples of the residents of the City of Ladies.

Critical Evaluation:

Christine de Pizan was known as the first professional woman writer in France. She was Italian by birth, but her family moved to Paris when her father became court astrologer to King Charles V. Christine married a French notary, Estienne de Castel. His premature death left her a widow at the age of twenty-five, with responsibility for raising three children and caring for her mother.

Over her mother's objections, Christine's father had encouraged her literary education, and she began to write to support herself. Initially, she composed verses that were popular with the French nobility. By dedicating her works to prominent individuals, Christine was able to acquire patrons in a male-dominated literary world.

Around 1400, after Christine had developed a secure reputation, she began to expand the range of topics about which she wrote. She began to pursue the problem of misogyny, addressing her defense of women in a number of literary arenas. Between 1401 and 1403, she participated in an epistolary debate on the *Roman de la Rose*, a famous French literary work of the thirteenth century. She objected to its vulgar language and explicit misogyny. In the two allegorical prose works *The Book of the Ladies* and its sequel, *The Book of Three Virtues* (also known as the *Treasury of the City of the Ladies*), she attempted to correct the misogynistic views about women found in many works of literature by male authors.

The compositional structure of *The Book of the Ladies* is based on the allegory of building a city in which worthy women are to reside. The construction of the city is an image for Christine's writing about women. Her task is guided by the three female allegorical personifications of Reason, Rectitude, and Justice, who command her to "take the trowel of your pen" and "mix the mortar in your ink bottle" to build the City of Ladies.

The Book of the Ladies is divided into three sections or books. The first sets up the frame for the allegory by situating Christine in her study reading a misogynistic book. Her allegorical guides appear to her as she contemplates the implications of the depiction of women by male authors. With the aid of the personification of Reason, Christine narrates the lives of women who made positive contributions in various ways and thus lays both the allegorical foundation of the city and the literal foundation of her literary work.

In the second book, Rectitude becomes Christine's guide. The image of city building is continued as the city walls are finished, edifices are built, and the city is populated. Justice guides Christine's work in the third book, where the high towers are completed and inhabited by the Virgin Mary, the queen of the city, and by a host of female saints.

This framework provides a narrative scaffolding for a series of biographical sketches of women drawn from antiquity and from French history up to the time when Christine was writing just after 1400. Christine arranges the lives of these women by topics introduced as queries to the allegorical guides. As Christine asks about subjects such as women's strength, their contributions to the sciences, and their faithfulness in marriage, Reason, Rectitude, and Justice illustrate women's conduct with examples drawn from particular women's lives. In effect, *The Book of the Ladies* is a collective biography of famous women united within the allegorical convention of building a city.

Christine drew on many sources to create *The Book of the Ladies*. The idea of an allegorical vision was used in such medieval literary works as Boethius' *Consolation of Philosophy* (c. 523-524; where Lady Philosophy, who is similar to Reason, is his guide), Dante's *Divine Comedy* (c. 1320), and the *Roman de la Rose* that Christine had criticized. The tripartite structure was also used frequently in medieval literature, for example in *The Divine Comedy*, which Christine acknowledges as one of her models. The image of a city was developed in one of the most influential works of early medieval theology, St. Augustine's *The City of God* (413-427).

The biographies of women for the most part come from stories that had been retold many times from antiquity through the Middle Ages. Christine especially drew on the fourteenth century author Giovanni Boccaccio, who had written a collective *Concerning Famous Women* (c. 1361-1375). The saints' lives came from compendia such as Vincent of Beauvais' thirteenth century French encyclopedic history, *Speculum historiale*. This reliance on sources should not obscure the originality of Christine's composition. From a twentieth century perspective, what seems like borrowing or compiling from other sources, drawing on traditional sources, was precisely what medieval writers were expected to do. It was not a question of inventing original material but rather of demonstrating what they could do with preexistent material.

Christine reworks her sources to emphasize women's positive qualities and contributions. As she recounts incidents in the lives of women, she recasts the narratives derived from Boccaccio, Ovid, and others. In her description of Queen Semiramis of Assyria, for example, she focuses on the queen's strength in military campaigns and governing her territories, while downplaying an incident of incest with her son. Christine's topical rearrangement of her material enables her to address such universal issues of concern as rape.

Feminist readings of *The Book of the Ladies* have criticized Christine for her conservative stance on the French political situation in the early fifteenth century, her acceptance of the social hierarchy, and her emphasis on female submissiveness to husbands. These criticisms fail to account for the historical context in which Christine wrote. Because her ability to support herself depended on patronage from the nobility, her criticism of the political and social order of her times had to be muted and contained within the prevalent code of conduct.

One of the few female voices in the Middle Ages to be expressed directly through writing, Christine de Pizan's *The Book of the Ladies* is an important literary achievement. Through the well-sustained allegorical structure and the subtle reworking of sources, Christine created a literary work that stands on its own merits and redresses the misogynistic imbalance created by the preponderance of male authors in the Middle Ages.

Karen Gould

Bibliography:
Quilligan, Maureen. *The Allegory of Female Authority. Christine de Pizan's "Cité des Dames."* Ithaca, N.Y.: Cornell University Press, 1991. The only book devoted exclusively to *The Book of the Ladies*. Explains how Christine de Pizan transformed many of her sources and offers feminist approaches to the material.

Richards, Earl Jeffrey, trans. *The Book of the City of the Ladies*. New York: Persea Books, 1982. A modern English translation of Christine de Pizan's *The Book of the Ladies*. Contains a substantial introduction to the work and helpful notes on the text.

_____, ed. *Reinterpreting Christine de Pizan*. Athens: University of Georgia Press, 1992. A collection of essays about the literary works of Christine de Pizan, several of which focus on *The Book of the Ladies*.

Willard, Charity Cannon. *Christine de Pizan: Her Life and Works*. New York: Persea Books, 1984. A thorough biography of Christine de Pizan that analyzes her literary works and places them in historical context. Also contains a chapter on *The Book of the Ladies*.

Yenal, Edith. *Christine de Pizan: A Bibliography*. 2d ed. Metuchen, N.J.: Scarecrow Press, 1989. An extensive bibliography on Christine de Pizan. The section on *The Book of the Ladies* contains entries on primary manuscript sources as well as secondary books and articles.

THE BOOK OF THESEUS

Type of work: Epic
Author: Giovanni Boccaccio (1313-1375)
Type of plot: Romance
Time of plot: Antiquity
Locale: Athens
First transcribed: Teseida, c. 1340-1341 (English translation, 1974)

Principal characters:
THESEUS, ruler of Athens
HIPPOLYTA, his wife
EMILIA, her sister
ACHATES, Theseus' kinsman
CREON, the leader against Theseus
ARCITES and
PALAEMON, cousins and soldiers of Creon
PEIRITHOUS, a nobleman, friend to Theseus

The Story:

While Aegeus was king of Athens, the women of Scythia rebelled against the men and elected Hippolyta queen. Theseus proposed to purge this sin and set sail with an army to fight the Amazons. When Theseus attacked the fortress of Queen Hippolyta, he received a message from her saying that he should desist or be driven away. He in turn told her that she must surrender or die. Hippolyta decided to surrender under a pact whereby she became Theseus' bride. After the wedding, Theseus was struck by the beauty of Hippolyta's sister Emilia.

Two years later, Theseus, Hippolyta, and Emilia sailed to Athens. On his return Theseus learned that Creon had attacked Thebes and, hating the Greeks, had prohibited the burial of the dead Thebans. Theseus vowed to defeat Creon so that the dead men of the weeping Athenian women could have a proper burial. Theseus and his men followed the women to the scene of battle and confronted Creon. After the warriors had challenged one another, the two armies fought. During the battle Theseus encountered Creon and killed him. Creon's men fled to the mountains. Theseus then told the women to collect the bodies of their men and burn them in proper ceremony.

Meanwhile, some Athenian soldiers had found two wounded youths of Creon's army, Palaemon and Arcites, whose armor showed them to be of royal blood. When they were brought before Theseus, he had them cured and taken as prisoners back to Athens. Several days after his triumphant return to Athens, Theseus summoned Palaemon and Arcites and sentenced them to eternal imprisonment in the palace where, because of their station, they would be treated well.

On a day in the following spring, as Arcites was opening the window of his prison chamber, he saw Emilia in the garden below. He was so overwhelmed by her beauty that he believed her to be Venus. Arcites summoned Palaemon; both immediately acknowledged their love for her. Emilia heard them and left, but every morning she returned and, because of her vanity, sang in the garden below their window. Each day the youths became more in love with her. In the autumn, however, she ceased her morning stroll, and Palaemon and Arcites became desperate.

At that time Theseus was visited by his friend Peirithous. When Theseus mentioned his two prisoners to Peirithous, the visitor asked to see them. Peirithous, recognizing Arcites as an old friend, requested that Theseus release him. Arcites left Athens with great sadness, for he did not wish to leave his companion Palaemon in prison, nor did he want to lose his opportunity of seeing Emilia. Palaemon believed that Arcites was fortunate in being able to travel and alleviate his pain while he was forced to be confined.

Later, calling himself Pentheus, Arcites returned to Athens in disguise. He managed to obtain a position with Theseus and became his favorite servant. He was not able to keep his identity secret from Emilia, but she did not reveal what she knew and he was able to contain his desire for her by sleeping in a field three miles from the city. There he prayed each night to Venus to encourage Emilia to love him. One morning, as Arcites was returning to the palace from his abode, one of Palaemon's servants heard Arcites' lamentations and discovered his true identity. He returned to the prison and told Palaemon that Pentheus was actually Arcites. This information enraged Palaemon. He decided to escape and win Emilia by armed force.

With the help of his servant, who intoxicated the guards, Palaemon escaped and went to an inn. The next morning he armed himself and went to the place where Arcites slept. After professing their love for Emilia, the kinsmen decided that a sword fight would determine who should vie for her hand. They began to fight savagely.

Theseus and Emilia, who were hunting with some companions, chanced to pass the field where the battle was taking place, and Emilia summoned Theseus to stop the fight. After Theseus confronted the youths, they informed him of their mutual love for Emilia. Believing that both men were qualified to be her husband, Theseus proposed a battle in the theater to decide who should have her hand. The conditions of the battle were that one year from that day the cousins should each bring one hundred chosen soldiers.

During the next year Arcites and Palaemon passed the time with lavish feasts, hunts, jousts, and finally with preparations for the battle. As the day approached, great noblemen and warriors came to the city, all elaborately dressed and armed. There was one last great feast for all the soldiers and nobility.

On the day before the battle Arcites and Palaemon prayed to the gods. Arcites prayed to Mars, promising that if he should be made victor, he would give great honor to Mars and his temples. To this plea, Mars gave a sign that the vow had been heard. Palaemon, on the other hand, went to the temple of Cytheraea, where he prayed not for victory, but for the hand of Emilia, and he too received a sign. Emilia, not wishing harm to either suitor, prayed to the goddess Diana in whose temple she kindled two fires. She asked that the desires of the two lovers be quenched. If she had to accept one, however, she prayed that it would be the lover who desired her most. She received a sign that she would have one of the two, but that the outcome could not yet be revealed.

The next day the spectators and soldiers gathered in the great theater. Arcites and his men entered from the east, Palaemon and his men from the west. At the sound of the third call to battle, the fight began, with many noblemen wounding one another. The sight of the battlefield wet with blood and so many men dying for her caused Emilia to wish that Theseus had let the two finish the fight in the grove. Shortly, the warriors became tired and perplexed, but Arcites, spurred on by Mars, fought more fiercely than ever, causing Emilia's affection to turn to him. Arcites, victorious, circled the field with his men.

Venus, who had watched the battle with Mars, each concerned for their respective champions, told Mars that his part was over, for he had granted Arcites' prayer. She then directed Erinys to frighten Arcites' steed. The horse reared and Arcites fell mortally wounded. Emilia and Palaemon were grief-stricken at the sight of dying Arcites. A doctor was summoned and Arcites was carried to the palace and placed on a great bed. There he and Emilia were married by

Theseus, and Palaemon was set free. Knowing that he would die with his love unconsummated, Arcites summoned Palaemon and told him that he should take Emilia. Emilia refused to accept Palaemon. She told Arcites that she would die a virgin.

After nine days of great suffering, Arcites died, and Theseus ordered a great funeral ceremony for the dead warrior. Later Palaemon had a temple built to Juno to contain Arcites' ashes. In it were represented all the adventures of Arcites' life. Emilia's grief for her dead husband caused her to become sickly, and it was therefore agreed that her lamentation should cease and that she would be wedded to Palaemon. Theseus told them that Arcites lived well and had been mourned enough. Palaemon and Emilia were then married. A great feast was held for fifteen days to celebrate their wedding.

Critical Evaluation:

The Book of Theseus is an epic poem composed in Italian and written in stanzas of eight verses (octavos). The poem is divided into twelve cantos or books, the traditional number of books in classical epics. Boccaccio wrote this poem as the first epic in the Italian language, and the poem recounts the deeds of warriors. Boccaccio followed Dante Alighieri, who, a generation earlier with his *Divine Comedy* (c. 1320), had established Italian as a legitimate vehicle for literary work of a serious intent, as opposed to the Middle Ages' established literary language, Latin.

The structure of *The Book of Theseus* is straightforward. Book 1 explores how Emilia came to be in Athens, and book 2 shows how Arcites and Palaemon arrived there—none of them being a native Athenian. The first six books lead up to the tournament fought between the two rivals for Emilia's love, and the second six books present the exploits of the contest and its aftermath. The work opens with the events surrounding the marriage of Theseus and Hippolyta, and it closes with the nuptials of Palaemon and Emilia.

Boccaccio's work reflects the literary influence of the "sweet new style," the poetic style popularized by Dante by which the Italian language was advanced as an avenue for the sophisticated expression of an emerging Italian culture. Boccaccio intended the work as a new type of vernacular literature, but much of it also reflects his medieval heritage. The romance epic was a well-established genre. Even though the principal figures of *The Book of Theseus* are ancient Greeks, they think and behave as medieval knights, demonstrating two medieval literary types. First, they strive for the courtly love of the unobtainable woman. As Arcites explains to Palaemon in book 5, Arcites can never expect to reveal his love for Emilia. Arcites is living in disguise as a servant to Theseus, someone customarily unworthy of Emilia's noble status. Palaemon, as an escaped prisoner and a former enemy of the Athenians, likewise cannot openly solicit her love. Second, after Arcites' and Palaemon's passions for Emilia become known to Theseus, they engage in a medieval joust, a tournament involving them and their soldiers.

Theseus, the ruler of ancient Athens, is the namesake of the work, and he plays an important role. He is the force that moves the tale along, first by bringing all the participants together in Athens and then by supervising the unfolding of its various episodes. Books 1 and 2 establish Theseus as an ideal medieval knight. Twice he resolves to sacrifice himself in order to right a perceived wrong by marching off to war. In ensuing battles, he proves his soldierly competence, and afterward he demonstrates his generosity and wisdom. Readers might judge the other figures by his image.

The action of *The Book of Theseus* centers on the relationship between Arcites and Palaemon. Having proven their noble origins and knightly valor in book 2, they then individually seek the love of Emilia. Even though they compete directly for her and each attempts to defeat the other physically—even to death—they both also show concern and sympathy for each other. Arcites chooses not to slay Palaemon in the heat of battle while Palaemon lies unconscious, and Palaemon tends to Arcites' wounds after the tournament. The most poignant episode of their story is when Arcites, having been mortally wounded, wishes that his new bride, Emilia, should next marry Palaemon, and Palaemon resolves to follow through on Arcites' wish more out of love for him than for love of Emilia.

The Book of Theseus is much more than a simple story of two knights striving for the love of a lady. The travails of Arcites and Palaemon compose an allegory for the tension between reason and passion. Arcites repeatedly offers prayers to Mars, the god of war. Palaemon is aided by Venus, the goddess of love and sexual appetite. Mars and Venus are participants in the action and they are equal in degree to Arcites and Palaemon. They compete between themselves and at times involve themselves directly in the action of the human players. The two young men are their proxies, both literally and metaphorically as two competing impulses in human nature.

Emilia and Hippolyta demonstrate a traditional role for women in medieval romance epics; they also reflect medieval society's perspective on women. Both are major figures in the tale; Hippolyta is queen of the self-governing Amazons, and Emilia is the object of the desires of the two principal antagonists. Both women also serve the literary purposes of their corresponding male figures, rather than having their own purposes. Hippolyta is the occasion for an illustration of Theseus' military skill, personal courage, and gentle benevolence. Emilia likewise exists to serve the literary purposes of male figures. Early in her youth (and in the work), she becomes aware of Arcites' and Palaemon's admiration of her beauty, but she never exhibits a voice of her own in their competition for her love. Theseus, with the full agreement of the two young men, declares that she will be the prize to the victor in their tournament. Emilia does not resist this plan, and she does not even reveal any preference between the two men.

Reflecting a familiarity with classical literature (from antiquity), Boccaccio uses the ancient Roman author Statius as an inspirational model. Boccaccio adapts the tale, according to his own words in the work, from the Byzantine (medieval Greek) heritage. Ancient epics had been popular throughout the Middle Ages. Boccaccio frequently mentions stories and characters from ancient history and mythology. These references would have been readily recognized by Boccaccio's contemporaries. A modern reader may find these references esoteric, but they reinforce the story and increase its impact for readers.

According to Boccaccio's own words within *The Book of Theseus*, he intended this as a major epic to bolster the vernacular and culture of Italians. *The Book of Theseus* is narrative and epical, and the tale is entertaining, yet it did not achieve the renown for which Boccaccio had hoped. A crucial reason was its lack of a distinctly Italian nature. The setting and the characters are, after all, Grecian.

"Critical Evaluation" by Alan Cottrell

Bibliography:
Anderson, David. *Before the Knight's Tale: Imitation of Classical Epic in Boccaccio's "Teseida."* Philadelphia: University of Pennsylvania Press, 1988. A literary analysis. Asserts that Boccaccio's *Teseida* is a creative imitation of the work of a classical writer Statius. Emphasizes Boccaccio's own sources of inspiration.
Boccaccio, Giovanni. *The Book of Theseus-Teseida delle Nozze d'Emilia.* Translated by Bernadette Marie McCoy. New York: Medieval Text Association, 1974. A translation of the work

with an introduction. Includes (placed at the end of each of the *Teseida*'s twelve books) a slightly abridged translation of Boccaccio's own marginal glosses to the text.

Branca, Vittore. *Boccaccio: The Man and His Works*. Translated by Richard Monges. New York: New York University Press, 1976. Authoritative biography of Boccaccio by a preeminent Italian scholar. Also includes specific discussion of the *Teseida*.

Branch, Eren Hostetter. "Rhetorical Structures and Strategies in Boccaccio's *Teseida*." In his *The Craft of Fiction: Essays in Medieval Poetics*, edited by Leigh A. Arrathoon. Rochester, Mich.: Solaris Press, 1984. Examines various rhetorical devices employed by Boccaccio. Discusses the intellectual and stylistic traditions—for example, classical, Christian, vernacular—into which Boccaccio's rhetorical devices fit.

Wallace, David. *Chaucer and the Early Writings of Boccaccio*. Woodbridge, Suffolk: D. S. Brewer, 1985. Examines the relationship between Boccaccio and Geoffrey Chaucer. Discusses *The Book of Theseus* in chapter 7.

BORIS GODUNOV

Type of work: Drama
Author: Alexander Pushkin (1799-1837)
Type of plot: Historical
Time of plot: 1598-1605
Locale: Russia
First published: 1831 (English translation, 1918); first performed, 1870

Principal characters:
BORIS GODUNOV, the czar of Russia
FEODOR, his son
GRIGORY OTREPYEV, the pretender
MARYNA, Grigory's beloved
BASMANOV, a military leader

The Story:

Boris Godunov, a privy councilor, was a schemer. He had planned the assassination of Czarevitch Dmitri so that the actual assassins had been caught and promptly executed by a mob, and no suspicion fell on Boris. He even ordered the nobleman Shuisky to investigate the crime. Shuisky returned and told with a straight face the version of the murder that Boris had suggested to him.

When the people began to clamor for Boris to become czar, Boris and his sister took refuge in a monastery, ostensibly to escape the pressure of the populace who had acclaimed him their ruler. With a great show of humility and hesitation, he finally accepted the great honor. In spite of his initial popular appeal, Boris proved to be a cruel ruler, binding the serfs more firmly than ever to their masters and crushing ruthlessly nobles who might have opposed him. There were a few, however, who did not forget that Boris had murdered Dmitri.

Father Pimen was an old monk, a writer of chronicles. At night he wrote his observations of Russia's troubled times, while a young monk named Grigory Otrepyev slept nearby. Grigory was troubled by grandiose dreams. It seemed to him that he was mounting a great staircase from the top of which all Moscow was spread out before him. When he awoke, Father Pimen counseled him to forget the call of the world, for lust and power were illusory. Grigory scarcely listened, for he knew that in his youth Pimen had been a soldier and had had his fill of secular life.

When a wicked monk tempted Grigory by reminding him that he was the same age as the murdered Dmitri would have been, Grigory quickly resolved that he would indeed be Dmitri. To get support for his enterprise Grigory went to Lithuania, where, so as to pass unnoticed through the country, he attached himself to two beggar monks. Somehow Boris heard of the impostor's intentions. A description of Dmitri was broadcast, and the czar's agents were instructed to arrest him on sight. In a remote tavern, several officers came upon Grigory and his two companions. Grigory drew his dagger and fled.

Both the Lithuanians and the Poles were delighted to help Grigory march on Moscow. The Poles, especially, were eager to attack the hated Muscovites. As rumors of the impending rebellion spread, many Russians came into Poland to join the swelling ranks of Grigory's supporters. Before long, Grigory found another powerful ally in a Jesuit priest who promised to throw the influence of Rome behind the pretender. Grigory at the head of a rebellious army in Poland was a real menace to Boris' throne and life.

Yet Grigory, comfortably installed at an estate near the Russian border, lingered in Poland. He could not bring himself to give orders to advance because Maryna, the daughter of the house, had captured his heart. She had been cold to him and finally asked him outright whether he was really Dmitri or an unfrocked monk, as some people were saying. When Grigory, unnerved by love, confessed that he was a baseborn monk, Maryna haughtily refused to ally her noble blood with his. Stung by her actions, Grigory thereupon proudly declared that he would be czar, and if Maryna denounced him, he would use his power to punish her. Satisfied that he had an indomitable spirit, Maryna overlooked his birth and agreed to be his czarina.

The next morning, Grigory began his conquering march, and for a while all went well. Towns and villages joined his campaign willingly, for the name of Dmitri was a powerful one. In Moscow, Boris was greatly perturbed and asked the patriarch to give his best counsel. He was told that Dmitri's grave had become noted for its cures; the patriarch himself knew of an old man who had been blind for many years before a visit to the tomb restored his sight. If Dmitri's remains were brought into the Kremlin and a miracle were to happen before all the people, Moscow would have proof that Dmitri was dead and the pretender was a fraud. Boris paled at the suggestion. Tactfully Shuisky proposed another course. Rather than appear to use religious means in a political quarrel, he would go before the people and denounce Grigory. Surely, when the people knew the truth they would desert the baseborn monk who called himself Dmitri.

For a time, events seemed to favor Boris. Grigory was beaten back in several attacks on strongholds held by Boris' troops. Nevertheless, Grigory remained cheerful and confident, even after his forces had been defeated.

Boris entrusted the command of his whole defense to Basmanov, an able leader though not of noble birth. Basmanov was gratified at the honor, for he had as little patience with the intrigues of the court as he did with the fickle loyalties of the mob. His conference with Boris was interrupted by the arrival of a delegation of foreign merchants. Boris had hardly left the room before an alarm was sounded; the czar had suddenly been taken ill. Blood gushed from his mouth and ears.

Before his death, Boris had time formally to name his son Feodor the next czar. As his life ebbed away, he advised Feodor to name Basmanov the military leader, to retain all the stately court procedures that gave dignity to the government, and to preserve strictly the discipline of the Church. After the last rites were administered, Boris died.

At army headquarters, Pushkin, a supporter of Grigory, had an interview with Basmanov. Pushkin admitted that Grigory's army was only a rabble and that Cossacks and Poles alike were not to be trusted. If, however, Basmanov would declare for Grigory, the new czar would make him commander of all the Russian armies. At first, Basmanov hesitated, but Pushkin reminded him that even if Grigory were an impostor, the magic name of Dmitri was enough to ensure that Feodor had no chance of retaining his czardom. Basmanov, convinced, publicly led his troops to Grigory's side.

Basmanov's defection spread. The people of Moscow listened to Pushkin when he made an inflammatory speech in the great square. As he reminded them of all they had suffered under Boris and of the justice of Dmitri's accession, the crowd shouted their allegiance to the false Dmitri. Impassioned, the mob surged into Boris' palace to seek out Feodor.

Feodor looked hopelessly out of the window. Some in the crowd felt pity, but their voices were overruled. The boyars forced their way inside, presumably to make Feodor swear allegiance to Dmitri. Out of the uproar came screams. At last the door opened. One of the boyars made an announcement: Feodor and his mother had taken poison. He had seen the dead bodies. The boyar urged the people to acclaim Dmitri, but the people stood silent, speechless.

Critical Evaluation:

Alexander Pushkin began to work in earnest on *Boris Godunov* in November, 1824, and finished the play one year later. He was at the time turning away from Lord Byron as a literary model and toward William Shakespeare. The complexity and variety he found in Shakespeare's characters had a strong appeal for him, as did the English playwright's willingness to treat both history and tragedy with more freedom than had been allowed by the formal constraints of the French neoclassicism that had until then been the dominant influence on the Russian theater.

Boris Godunov consists of twenty-three loosely connected scenes. Of the dramatic unities (time, place, and action) Pushkin observed only the unity of action, and he cast the poetry in iambic pentameter, which is closer to natural speech than the hexameters of neoclassic drama, and intermixed poetry with prose. A large number of speaking characters is further augmented by crowd scenes. Though the play is a historical tragedy, Pushkin includes snatches of comedy. In short, Pushkin exhibited in *Boris Godunov* the romantic sensibility of his day in creating a poetic drama that placed the arresting confusions of history above the theoretic requirements of art. Russian history in the early seventeenth century was somewhat confused, but Pushkin chose to set up several definite determinants. He took as the source for his play Nikolay Karamzin's *History of the Russian State* (1816-1829), which maintained that Boris Godunov was culpable in the death in 1591 of Dmitri, the half brother of the ruling czar, Feodor. There is in fact no clear evidence for this, Boris Godunov was first called to be czar after Feodor died in 1598, and initially he seems to have been a popular ruler. When the situation changed, however, people began to remember that Godunov had not been part of any ruling dynasty and that he had achieved power because, as Feodor's brother-in-law, he was strategically placed at a moment when Russia needed a ruler. This led many to suspect that he may have engineered his own rise to power by evil means.

Karamazin also claimed that the false Dmitri was an ambitious monk with determination and ability but no legitimate claim to power. This put Pushkin in a difficult spot, for in order to remain faithful to his source, he could not develop a dramatic opposition of good and evil in his characters. A Boris Godunov who was a vicarious assassin and a Dmitri who was a crass imposter did not provide effective theater. Pushkin could of course have altered the historical premise, but that would have conflicted with his motive in writing the play, which was to record a critical epoch in Russia's past. Pushkin resolved his dilemma by finding the point in the story where history gives way to tragedy. He made his title character, Boris Godunov, a man who was capable and even in many ways honorable but in whose internal struggle between conscience and ambition, ambition had been the victor. Dmitri, on the other hand, is shown to possess few admirable traits so that in the conflict between the two ambitious men, Boris Godunov is the likeliest figure who can be seen as a tragically flawed hero.

Another problem Pushkin had to surmount was the unexciting nature of Godunov's death. He resolved this difficulty by concluding the play with the death of Boris Godunov's children at the hands of Dmitri's agents. Having shown that Godunov was responsible for the death of the true Dmitri, Pushkin implied a rough justice in showing Godunov's children being destroyed by the agency of the false Dmitri.

For the purposes of theater, history is more readily married to tragedy than to comedy. The dramatist must try to find in history patterns of human conduct that are somehow heroic, even if flawed. Shakespeare, Pushkin's model, often chose historical figures sufficiently remote in time or clouded in circumstance so that he could revise the past to fit a tragic mold. Plays treating more recent history could be shaped to gratify contemporary political sentiments. Boris Godunov, in many ways an excellent subject for dramatic treatment, posed a certain problem for Pushkin because it was Godunov's failure, as well as the failures of various pretenders (for eventually more than one man claimed to be Dmitri), that led to the emergence of the Romanov dynasty, which held power in Pushkin's lifetime. Insofar as the poet needed to write a play that would secure the approval of rulers in his own era, there was an advantage to showing both Boris Godunov and the pretender to possess great flaws.

The title character nevertheless exhibits enough of the qualities of a tragic hero to allow the audience's attention to center on Boris Godunov. The play is not exclusively a tragedy of ambition, but it is far more than a simple chronicle of history. Moreover, it proved a suitable record of a difficult moment in Russia's past.

"Critical Evaluation" by John Higby

Bibliography:

Bayley, John. *Pushkin: A Comparative Commentary.* Cambridge, England: Cambridge University Press, 1971. One of the best English-language studies of Pushkin. A long chapter on drama treats *Boris Godunov* in relation to Shakespeare, the German poet Friedrich Schiller, and others.

Briggs, A. D. P. *Alexander Pushkin.* New York: Barnes & Noble Books, 1983. In the chapter on drama, Briggs argues that Pushkin's success as a dramatist was limited, but that his plays are more interesting than is sometimes allowed. Discusses such aspects of *Boris Godunov* as the work's historical background, Shakespearean influence, structure, characters, language, and poetry.

Magarshack, David. *Pushkin.* New York: Grove Press, 1969. This biography of Pushkin places *Boris Godunov* in the context of the poet's life and literary career. A good starting place for the general reader.

Sandler, Stephanie. *Distant Pleasures: Alexander Pushkin and the Writing of Exile.* Stanford, Calif.: Stanford University Press, 1989. Scholarly and subtle, this book is better suited to the serious student of Pushkin than to the general reader. *Boris Godunov* is discussed at considerable length.

Vickery, Walter N. *Alexander Pushkin Revisited.* Rev. ed. New York: Twayne, 1992. A brief but clear account of the historical circumstances leading to Boris Godunov's rule is useful to those not familiar with the background for Pushkin's play. Many of the established topics in the study of *Boris Godunov* are included.

THE BOROUGH
A Poem in Twenty-four Letters

Type of work: Poetry
Author: George Crabbe (1754-1832)
First published: 1810

> *Principal characters:*
> PETER GRIMES, a fisherman
> ELLEN ORFORD, a pauper
> SWALLOW, a grasping lawyer
> BLANEY, an inhabitant of the Alms-House
> THE MAYOR OF THE BOROUGH
> THE VICAR OF THE PARISH
> A BURGESS, who writes the letters

George Crabbe was a writer of provincial background who had made good in the capital by using his provincial material. His initial success in London with *The Library*, published in 1781, made it possible for the son of a fisherman and petty customs officer to enter the Church in 1782 and be given a respectable living as an Anglican clergyman. For a time he gave up poetry after publishing *The Newspaper* in 1785. His next publication, *Poems*, was not until 1807. In the decades between his two periods of composition, much had changed in English poetry; Crabbe's continuation of his original style and matter makes it difficult to place him in the Romantic period.

He was really the last and best representative of the host of adventuring, provincial poetasters who flocked to London to make their fortunes in the eighteenth century—these included Thomas Chatterton, Oliver Goldsmith, David Mallet, and Samuel Johnson, to name but a few. This is to repeat a truism in Crabbe criticism—that Aldeburgh, where he was born, is all his material—but it also places Crabbe in literary history and shows his strength, and perhaps accounts for his durability. The most obvious manifestation of that is the initiation of the Aldeburgh Festival and Benjamin Britten's opera *Peter Grimes* (1945), derived from letter 22 of *The Borough*.

The Village, published in 1783, and *The Borough* contain and are contained by a seaside community in which the folk are at the mercy of the elements, their only salvation against bad times being native prudence. In their world, no help comes from the outside, only temptation and danger. Despite his absence from Aldeburgh after the age of twenty-six, Crabbe was unable to forget youthful privation and misery by adopting a tourist's attitude to provincial society and nature, an increasingly common mid-Victorian attitude of which Balmoral is the symbol. Few of his heroes and heroines have private incomes, and if caught in a storm at sea they are more likely to perish than to find themselves washed up on the sand.

Crabbe's realism was reinforced by parish duties; it is not the pessimism of which his mid-Victorian and Romantic critics accused him. Later readers appreciated the salt in his stories more than the sugar in the work of other poets writing at the same time as Crabbe but equipped with a less immediate experience of people and place. His second importance in the history of English poetry is the fact that he casts a shadow beside the major figures of his second period and prepares the narrative form in English poetry for the genre work of Alfred, Lord Tennyson's *Enoch Arden and Other Poems* (1864), Robert Browning's *Men and Women* (1855), and Thomas Hardy's local-color sketches in verse. In the early years of the nineteenth century

Crabbe's work was paralleled in prose by Maria Edgeworth's Irish *Castle Rackrent* (1800) and John Galt's Scottish *Annals of the Parish* (1821), rather than the country novels of Jane Austen. All the foregoing is summed up in Crabbe's best-known line from *The Village*—"I paint the Cot, as Truth will paint it, and as Bards will not"—and illustrated in *The Borough*, the most unified of his works.

To "paint the Cot" Crabbe used the pentameter couplet, a meter noted for its wit and music and not for the narrative use to which Crabbe put it; that *The Borough* is made up of twenty-four letters or "epistles" to some extent restricts the narrative and encourages general observation, conventional in the eighteenth century verse epistle. In place of wit and music, Crabbe relied on rugged and compact language that reflects that of his characters, especially that of the burgess who is supposed to be writing the letters. The most tiring feature of the succession of couplets is the regular placing of the caesura, which makes too obvious the antithesis and balance supporting the lines:

> Then he began to reason and to feel
> He could not dig nor had he learn'd to steal;
> And should he beg as long as he might live,
> He justly fear'd that nobody would give:

Crabbe arranged the letters in a certain order, preceded each with a curt prose argument, added a long preface, and subscribed a brief envoi. After the "General Description" of letter 1, Crabbe arranges his aspects in the proper order, beginning with the most important person in the borough and its center, the vicar and his church, but concluding with the schools. His arrangement falls into two major divisions, the provident and the improvident, of the adult world, with the children bringing up the rear. The provident come under three headings or activities in order of importance: religion, work, and play. The improvident are divided into those in the almshouse and hospital and the poor outside parish relief, with a final letter on those in prisons. Seven of these letters narrate the miserable histories of those in or out of the almshouse. Within each of the three sections of the first division, Crabbe also observes a declining order of importance: After the church and the vicar have been described, Crabbe turns to the "Sects and Professions of Religion," which he defends at length in his preface as a strong but essentially true picture of the "Calvinistic" and "Armenian" Methodists who so disturbed the parson and his church, as Crabbe knew from bitter experience. The professions of law and physic are followed by the "Trades." The third section begins with "Amusements," followed in descending order by "Clubs and Social Meetings," "Inns," and "Players," which last leads straight down the path of destruction to the whole division on the improvident. The strength of this division is the seven narratives, but many readers will prefer the first division for the extraordinarily vivid scenes briefly sketched there, especially in "Elections" and "Players." These include brief portraits such as that of the lawyer Swallow, who lives up to his name.

Crabbe's preface, like his arguments, outlines what is to come in each letter but also deals with the work as a whole. The whole scheme of *The Borough* is that Crabbe has apparently written to "an ideal friend," a burgess in an unnamed large seaport, asking him to describe his borough. The letters sometimes begin with a brief question that the correspondent answers. Crabbe admits that the resulting picture of the borough is uneven, but the envoi provides the answer:

> Man's vice and crime I combat as I can, . . .
> (The giant-Folly, the enchanter-Vice) . . . I point the powers of rhyme,
> And, sparing criminals, attack the crime.

Here the country parson drops his mask and admits that he is preaching one of his regular sermons to encourage industry and thrift and to avoid the enticements of riches and city life. Most of the preface, including the long passage on the Methodists, is taken up with apologizing for the satire of religions, professions, and amusements in the first division and for the repetitious falls from fortune in the second. An exception is letter 20, "Ellen Orford," which ends in resigned piety. Crabbe's justification is that of "fidelity," that he did know such a person or instance, as when in letter 5 he cites a rich fisherman who had never heard, until a friend told him, of the practice of lending money at interest, with this result:

> Though blind so long to interest, all allow
> That no man better understands it now: . . .
> Stepping from post to post, he reach'd the chair,
> And there he now reposes—that's the mayor.

Crabbe is the bard who will paint his borough "as Truth will paint it," and in the envoi to letter 24 he looks forward to his readers' reaction: "This is a likeness," may they all declare,/ "And I have seen him but I know not where. . . ."

It is sometimes difficult to see the "likeness" in the seven narratives of the poor and the almshouse because they all seem to decline with celerity into remorse and destitution. It may be, however, that time has removed such objects from what must have been Crabbe's daily observation both as a boy in Aldeburgh and as a country parson. Certainly the most surprising decline is that of Peter Grimes, which is at the same time the most convincing, partly because in this account Crabbe uses nature to much greater effect than in the other narratives. More than nature, society is his object, and especially the quirks of character and turns of fate in family histories well known to those who stay long in any place. If Crabbe seems to relish the misery and vice exhibited in the citizens of his borough, he is adopting what is often the provincial's revenge against his native town: a scarifying of its mean soul and low manners in gripping detail. This is not the whole effect of *The Borough*, but what there is marks it as a forerunner of that supremely provincial novel, James Joyce's *Ulysses* (1922).

Bibliography:
Bareham, Tony. *George Crabbe*. London: Vision, 1977. Analyzes Crabbe's work against the backdrop of his life, emphasizing his experience as an ordained Anglican minister and as a magistrate. Examines his position during turbulent times, when he became a voice for sane, rational, reliable English thought and custom. Includes frequent references to *The Borough*.
Blackburne, Neville. *The Restless Ocean*. Lavenham, Suffolk, England: Terence Dalton, 1972. An excellent biography. Identifies the various prejudices and influences underlying Crabbe's poetry. In chapter 10, Blackburne discusses *The Borough* as "the peak of Crabbe's poetic achievement." Includes illustrations and bibliography.
Chamberlain, Robert L. *George Crabbe*. New York: Twayne, 1965. Discusses the works in chronological order, showing Crabbe's development as a master of poetic diction and as a superb creator of character. A twenty-page section of the book is devoted to *The Borough*. Also includes an annotated bibliography and a helpful index.
Pollard, Arthur, comp. *Crabbe: The Critical Heritage*. London: Routledge & Kegan Paul, 1972. A collection of excerpts from reviews and essays dating 1780-1890. Includes eight contemporary reviews of *The Borough*. A separate index to the works indicates other critical comments. Pollard's introduction is an excellent starting point for any study of Crabbe.

Sigworth, Oliver. *Nature's Sternest Painter: Five Essays on the Poetry of George Crabbe.* Tucson: University of Arizona Press, 1965. Focuses on Crabbe's relationship to the eighteenth century and to the Romantic movement, his interest in nature, his use of narrative, and his reputation. Many comments about *The Borough* are scattered throughout. Bibliography.

THE BOSTONIANS

Type of work: Novel
Author: Henry James (1843-1916)
Type of plot: Psychological realism
Time of plot: Early 1870's
Locale: Massachusetts and New York City
First published: serial, 1885-1886; book, 1886

> *Principal characters:*
> OLIVE CHANCELLOR, a woman of modest means
> MRS. ADELINE LUNA, her sister
> BASIL RANSOM, her cousin from Mississippi
> VERENA TARRANT, Olive's protégée and a platform prodigy
> "DOCTOR" SELAH TARRANT, Verena's father and a mesmeric healer
> MRS. TARRANT, the daughter of Boston abolitionists and Verena's mother
> MISS BIRDSEYE, a veteran of New England reform movements
> DR. PRANCE, a woman doctor attending Miss Birdseye
> MRS. FARRINDER, a campaigner for women's rights
> MRS. BURRAGE, a New York society hostess
> HENRY BURRAGE, her son, a Harvard undergraduate who courts Verena

The Story:

Olive Chancellor, a Boston activist in the women's movement, was entertaining her cousin Basil Ransom, a Mississippian who lived in New York City. She invited him to join her at a gathering at the home of Mrs. Birdseye, a leader in the movement. Though he disagreed with the ideals of the feminists, Ransom accepted, partly out of curiosity and partly to meet Mrs. Farrinder, a national spokesperson for women's rights. At Mrs. Birdseye's, Ransom expressed his views on the movement to Dr. Prance, a woman who had become successful in a traditionally male profession. Olive, becoming aware that Basil opposed all she stood for, developed a strong animosity toward her cousin.

Also in attendance at Mrs. Birdseye's were the Tarrants, a family supported by the father's lectures on mesmerism; the Tarrants claimed that their daughter Verena had a special gift for oratory, and they persuaded Mrs. Birdseye to let her speak to the group about the women's movement. Everyone was captivated by Verena's performance. Olive immediately recognized that the young woman had a future as a public figure promoting women's rights. Basil was smitten with Verena's beauty and charm. Both spoke briefly to Verena after her performance.

Basil was forced to return immediately to New York, but Olive went to the Tarrants' home in Cambridge on the following day to try to persuade Verena to become active in the women's movement in Boston. The Tarrants were anxious to comply, Mr. Tarrant seeing this as a way to make money, and Mrs. Tarrant believing that it would provide an opportunity for her daughter to move into high society. Although Verena was being wooed by several young men, including the Harvard student Henry Burrage and the journalist Matthias Pardon, she agreed to collaborate with Olive. Over time, the two became inseparable, and Olive eventually entered into a financial arrangement with the Tarrants to permit Verena to live at the Chancellor home. There, Olive educated her protégée in feminist doctrine. Olive was insistent that Verena abandon all thoughts of marriage and devote her energies to the cause. After years of dominating women, she declared that "men must take *their* turn" as objects of domination and that "they must pay!"

During this time, Basil was struggling to practice law in New York. He spent his spare time writing Carlylean tracts against modern times, but no one would publish them. He managed to make ends meet by working for Mrs. Luna, Olive's sister, who made amorous advances that he consistently rejected. She was the first to recognize that Basil had fallen in love with Verena, whom she considered a sham.

Basil decided to go back to Boston to woo Verena. Outside Olive's house, Basil met Mrs. Birdseye, who was under the impression that he supported the women's movement and therefore told him that Verena was now staying with her parents in Cambridge. Basil went to see her, and though she rejected his advances, Verena nevertheless took him on a tour of Harvard and agreed to keep the meeting secret from Olive.

Sometime later, after Basil had returned to New York, he received an invitation to attend a meeting at the home of Mrs. Burrage, a socialite, who was sponsoring a public appearance by Verena. Basil attended, knowing that Verena had arranged for the invitation. Before Verena's speech, he had an ugly encounter with Mrs. Luna, who accused him of impropriety in his relationship with Verena. While she was in New York, Verena agreed to see Basil socially. When he tried to persuade her to give up her work in the movement and marry him, Verena balked. She had received an invitation to stay on in New York with the Burrage family, whose son, Henry, had been courting her in Cambridge and wanted to marry her. Knowing that Olive had a special influence over Verena, Mrs. Burrage tried to convince her that such an arrangement would be good for women's rights, but Olive was not persuaded. When Verena insisted that she could not stay in New York, Olive took her back to Boston.

Months later, Basil traveled to New England again, this time to Cape Cod, where Olive and Verena were staying together with Mrs. Birdseye and Dr. Prance. Olive was preparing Verena for a triumphant public engagement at Boston's Music Hall. Basil once again ingratiated himself with Mrs. Birdseye and Dr. Prance, but though he stayed with them for a month, he made no headway against his cousin's dislike or in convincing Verena to marry him. Everyone was greatly saddened when Mrs. Birdseye, who had been ailing, died.

The party returned to Boston, where Mrs. Birdseye was buried. Little time was spent on mourning, however, as Verena's big night at the Music Hall was approaching. Basil was kept away from her. Olive even sent Verena into hiding so that he would not be able to divert her attention from her mission, and when he attempted to see her backstage at the Music Hall before her performance, he found a policeman barring his way. He was finally able to see Verena in her dressing room, where he confronted Olive, Verena's parents, and Matthias Pardon and accused them of expecting to profit in some way from Verena's newfound notoriety. Verena was hesitating to go before the crowd in the Music Hall, and Basil sensed that she was finally coming around to his way of thinking. He made a final impassioned plea to her to abandon this scheme devised by others to use her talents for their ends. Finally persuaded, Verena refused to go on stage and left with Basil to start a new life outside the spotlight and away from political wrangling.

"The Story" by Laurence W. Mazzeno

Critical Evaluation:
The Bostonians is the longest of Henry James's novels in an American setting, and in spite of his later dissatisfaction with its middle section or the high promise given to the unfinished *The Ivory Tower* (1917), it is his most important fictive statement on America. The name and setting of the novel are significant; two other American novels, *Washington Square* (1880) and

The Europeans (1878), are set in New York City and Boston respectively, and though *The Bostonians* begins in Charles Street and ends in the Music Hall in Boston, its second half begins in New York, which James always claimed as his native city. James had difficulty selecting a title for the work, but when he had settled on *The Bostonians*, he knew it precisely suited the contents and his meaning.

The best commentary on the work is found in James's preface to the New York edition. James had several times tried to clarify a passage he had written in his life of Nathaniel Hawthorne, on what he believed that America offered and lacked with respect to writers. *The Bostonians* was James's attempt to write on a subject that was at once local and typical, a local manifestation of a national trait. James chose that distinguishing feature of American life, the American woman, whom he had earlier encapsulated in Isabel Archer and other heroines. The settings he chose were the Boston of the early 1870's and postabolitionist New York, with its atmosphere of exhausted triumph and its hectic pursuit of new reform movements, especially that of women's rights. James's general distaste for the reformers if not for their proposals may be sensed in his portraits in the novel.

The "Bostonians" may be variously identified as one, two, or more characters, but James uses the term only once to refer to Olive Chancellor and Verena Tarrant. Although James referred to Verena as the heroine, the true Bostonian is Olive, the embodiment of the clash between discrimination and undiscriminating action in Boston of the 1870's. Destined by nature and appearance to be what was called a New England Nun, she becomes a Boston battler in the very last paragraph of the novel, haranguing a capacity crowd in Boston's largest auditorium. She does so in place of Verena, who has been carried away by Basil Ransom. These three characters play out an ironic and psychologically penetrating form of the eternal triangle.

James seems to approve Verena's fate, largely because she is unawakened throughout almost the whole novel; she remains a pretty young girl with no mind, and James shows little interest in her. Basil Ransom is a Mississippian trying to revive the family plantation by practicing law in New York; he does not have ideas (until he begins to write reactionary articles) but lives by a code: Everyone must do his or her work well in one's appointed station in life. When he tries to express this idea to Verena as they sit in Central Park, she is horrified and fascinated because there is no "progress" in his code. In the end, however, Basil and Verena pair off as a fairly normal couple. What would become of Verena would have made a superb sequel to this work, but James did not know the South, and he treats it simply as the last reservoir of acceptable masculinity from which to pluck his hero.

Olive Chancellor was more of a known quantity for James. With no other family ties except those to her sister, comfortably settled in Charles Street, she had time, intelligence, taste, and money that she diffused quietly through twenty committees and reform groups. She is the very portrait of a Boston lady; her tragic flaw is to allow her desire for real action to overrule her taste: She falls in love with Verena's sweet stream of humbug as Basil falls in love with Verena's voice. This is not wholly Olive's fault, as is shown by the gallery of Bostonians introduced at the suffragist party in Miss Birdseye's tasteless apartment at the beginning of the novel. The two male Bostonians are a hack journalist and "Doctor" Selah Tarrant, a mesmeric healer and a fake not only to Basil's eyes but also to those of Dr. Prance, a woman doctor who is active in her role as "new woman" and who has little time for talking about the subject. As the real and fake doctors are contrasted, so is Dr. Prance contrasted with the suffragist campaigner Mrs. Farrinder, who is not a Bostonian and who is also suspicious of Tarrant and Verena's "inspirational" views. Mrs. Farrinder's weak husband shows what men will amount to and what Basil is fighting in the new regime; Mrs. Farrinder, in thinking that talk will achieve the revolution Dr. Prance quietly demonstrates, shows the possible and probable results of Olive's degeneration.

Also ranged about Olive in contrasting positions are three other Bostonians: Mrs. Luna, completely worldly and contemptuous of any womanly activity except that of the salon; Verena's mother, equally worldly but totally vulgar; and Miss Birdseye, James's favorite creation in the novel. At the age of eighty, she is still a compulsive reformer in a completely selfless and ineffectual manner that contrasts with the practical Dr. Prance and Mrs. Farrinder and with the worldly creatures of Boston and New York. She appears only three times in the novel: at the initial party that introduces most of the characters; when she plays the part of destiny in giving Ransom Verena's Cambridge address; and at Olive's summer cottage at Marmion, where she dies happily, mistakenly believing that Verena has enlisted Ransom in the cause. She stands for Boston's true nature, which Olive ignores in trying to achieve a triumph through Verena.

In the second part of the novel, Olive compounds her failure of discrimination by accepting the invitation of Mrs. Burrage, a New York society hostess, to show off Verena in New York. Olive thinks she has triumphed in securing Verena's promise not to marry and in diverting young Henry Burrage's attentions from Verena, but she overreaches herself.

Verena is the fulcrum of the plot, and her affection first for Olive, then for Ransom, is reflected in the structure of the novel. The first twenty chapters contain Olive's dinner with Basil, Miss Birdseye's party, Basil's call on Olive and Verena the next morning, and some months later a tea party at the Tarrants for Olive and, as it turns out, Henry Burrage. This first half of the novel concentrates on Olive's developing affection for Verena. Verena, however, is incapable of decision or independent action, and in the second half of the novel, as Basil Ransom takes the center of the stage, she gradually falls under his influence.

Throughout the novel, the characteristic devices of James's late middle style are apparent: lengthening paragraphs, alternating direct and indirect colloquy, and the use of idiomatic terms to carry nuances of meaning. More obvious, especially in the dramatic close, is the growing dependence on set scenes to show the stages of the drama. Over all these is the play of James's irony and pity directed at the latter-day Bostonian Olive Chancellor, the local representation of a national type and the heroine of this distinctly American novel.

Bibliography:

Bell, Millicent. "The Determinate Plot: *The Bostonians*." In *Meaning in Henry James*. Cambridge, Mass.: Harvard University Press, 1991. Bell compares *The Bostonians* with other James novels and argues that it serves as an ironic rejection of naturalism.

Bowen, Janet Wolf. "Architectural Envy: A Figure Is Nothing Without a Setting in Henry James's *The Bostonians*." *New England Quarterly* 65, no. 1 (March, 1992): 3-23. By focusing on the architectural imagery of the novel, Bowen points out that the novel depicts conflicts between inner life and public persona.

Faderman, Lillian. "Female Same-Sex Relationships in Novels by Longfellow, Holmes, and James." *New England Quarterly* 51, no. 3 (September, 1978): 309-332. A feminist perspective on the novel that focuses on the contrasting treatment James gives to Verena's relationships with Basil and with Olive.

Jacobson, Marcia. "Popular Fiction and Henry James's Unpopular *Bostonians*." *Modern Philology* 73, no. 3 (February, 1976): 264-275. Focuses on the novel as a political work and examines it in the context of the social and political consequences of the Civil War and the emerging women's movement.

Wagenknecht, Edward. "Explorations: *The Bostonians*; *The Princess Casamassima*; *The Tragic Muse*; and *Reverberater*." In *The Novels of Henry James*. New York: Felix Ungar, 1983. This chapter, in a book which provides general background on James's life and works, places the novel in a biographical context.

BOSWELL'S LONDON JOURNAL: 1762-1763

Type of work: Diary
Author: James Boswell (1740-1795)
First published: 1950

> *Principal personages:*
> JAMES BOSWELL, the author, a young Scotsman
> SAMUEL JOHNSON, the great critic, lexicographer, essayist, and poet
> WILLIAM TEMPLE, Boswell's friend, a sensible young law student
> LORD EGLINTON, a wealthy young nobleman, another of Boswell's friends
> THE HON. ANDREW ERSKINE, a Scotsman who befriends Boswell in London
> LADY ANNE ERSKINE, his sister

James Boswell left his family at home near Edinburgh in the autumn of 1762 to spend the winter in London, where he hoped to obtain a commission in the Guards. He was convinced that the military life, which would allow him to live in the city he loved so much, would suit him far better than the legal profession chosen for him by his father, a noted Scottish jurist. He recorded the activities, the hopes, and the disappointments of this year in London in a diary, which he sent in regular installments to a young friend who remained in Scotland. This journal, which miraculously survived for two hundred years and came to light in the twentieth century, is a remarkably revealing document, for reticence was not one of Boswell's characteristics. The frankness of his account of his activities brings him vividly to life.

Boswell was only twenty-two when he traveled south into England. He had passed his legal examinations, and his father had at last grudgingly agreed to give his son an allowance to allow him to pursue the career he thought he wanted. Lord Auchinleck's decision proved to be a wise one, for, after months of discouragement, Boswell finally realized that he was not going to obtain the desired commission, even with the help of noble friends, and he agreed to take up law again, on the condition that he might travel on the Continent before he returned to Scotland to begin his practice.

These experiences were frustrating to Boswell, but they provide fascinating reading. The author's youth is evident in many of the actions and impressions he records. He goes to the city to turn himself into a polished gentleman, and the pages of his diary are filled with resolutions for the improvement of his character and manners. At times this desire for sophistication manifests itself as a rather unattractive snobbery. Boswell records his disgust at the familiarity with which some of his Scottish friends treated him, at the provincialism of their conversation, and at the lack of restraint in their manners. In these moods he overlooks the fact that these hospitable people, especially Captain Andrew Erskine and his sister, did much to alleviate his loneliness.

Boswell is, however, usually perceptive about his relationships. He knows that William Temple, an old comrade from university days and a reserved and studious young man, is a good influence on him and that Lord Eglinton, who introduces Boswell to various dissipations during his first trip to London in 1760, encourages those vices for which his inclination is already too strong. Toward the end of the journal Boswell comments that Temple and Johnston, the Scottish friend to whom he was sending the diary, were those in whom he could confide his deepest feelings, while he feared to expose his sentiments to Erskine and Eglinton, though he valued their company for amusement. Boswell did, on occasion, lay himself open to their scorn with his sensitivity regarding his own dignity. He violently resents criticism of his writing, and he sends indignant letters to Lord Eglinton when he gets the feeling that he has not been treated with the civility to which he thinks he is entitled. This overblown sense of his own importance is perhaps the hardest of Boswell's faults for him to recognize. It never occurs to him even to doubt that courtiers, ladies, and distinguished literary figures would consider themselves privileged to make his acquaintance.

Boswell is, however, acutely aware of many of his other shortcomings. His daily memoranda constantly remind him to correct them. His resolutions are short-lived. A vow of increased economy is sure to be followed by some extravagance, generally charitable but prodigal. Intense remorse over his profligate relations with women generally precedes new debauchery. Promised rejection of his more frivolous acquaintances often leads only to renewed amity. His later works show him still at his youthful routine, repenting and renewing his wrongdoing with equal fervor.

He was often the victim of his essentially trusting nature, especially in his relations with women, as the first entries of his diary show in the account of his affair with Louisa, an actress. Anxious to see himself as a romantic hero, he trusted her protestations of affection, fidelity, and morality, lent her money, pursued her ardently, and as a reward spent five weeks in his rooms convalescing from the venereal disease with which she infected him.

For all Boswell's bravado and his apparent self-assurance, he suffered at times from a deep sense of melancholy and inferiority, probably the lingering result of a nervous disorder that had struck him when he was in his late teens. He had a childish fear of ghosts, and in his darker fits, when he could not bear to sleep alone in his lodgings, he would seek refuge for the night with one of his friends. This melancholy strain in his personality may have been one of the things that drew Boswell close to the great lexicographer, critic, and essayist, Samuel Johnson, whom he met for the first time during the winter of the time of the London journal. Johnson was himself subject to inexplicable terrors, and throughout his life he showed great compassion for this type of human weakness.

It is sometimes difficult to understand just what drew Boswell and Johnson together, but the account of their early acquaintance shows the appealing quality of Boswell's easygoing, candid nature, however brash it might be at times. Boswell's hero-worship for Johnson, his anxiety to please, and his eagerness for the older man's counsel are also clearly evident. Johnson's attitude toward Boswell, as scholars have pointed out, is in many respects paternal. He responded warmly to both the adulation and the appeals for help, and he seems to have found Boswell's enthusiasm refreshing. His insistence on accompanying his young friend to Harwich to see him sail for his studies in the Netherlands provides touching testimony of the older man's affection.

Boswell's friendship with Johnson changed the character of the London journal to a degree. From the time of their meeting, Boswell records more and more about Johnson's opinions on life and literature and less about his own feelings, although the latter were never ignored. Boswell's widening interests tend to decrease his introspection.

The London journal is not simply jottings of the day's activities, but a conscious literary effort. Boswell seems to have composed the account of several days at a time, basing the diary on sketchy memoranda, and this practice allowed him to build some dramatic suspense. His ability to capture the conversations of his day, the remarks of London citizens at Child's coffee house, or the discussions of Johnson and his circle, shows the gift for narration that makes the

Life of Johnson a masterpiece. Spurred on by Johnson's praise of the practice of keeping a journal, Boswell strove with great diligence to improve the literary quality of the latter portions of his work. As a result the book presents a remarkably lively and accurate picture of life in Boswell's time.

Bibliography:

Boswell, James. *The Heart of Boswell: Six Journals in One Volume.* Edited by Mark Harris. New York: McGraw-Hill, 1981. A compendium of Boswell's writings, along with various reviews, essays, and analysis that appeared in response to the 1950 publication of Frederick Albert Pottle's comprehensive edition of the London journal.

Finlayson, Iain. *The Moth and the Candle: A Life of James Boswell.* New York: St. Martin's Press, 1984. Exactingly researched, this illustrated volume draws on the letters between Boswell and his contemporaries and serves as an insightful factual counterpoint to Boswell's journal.

Ingram, Allan. *Boswell's Creative Gloom: A Study of Imagery and Melancholy in the Writings of James Boswell.* London: Macmillan, 1982. Combines literary criticism and psychoanalytic interpretation, exploring the process of thought and the method of creative expression employed by Boswell in his journal.

Pottle, Frederick Albert. *Pride and Negligence: The History of the Boswell Papers.* New York: McGraw-Hill, 1982. Considered to be the most authentic account published of the loss, reacquisition, and publication of the missing Boswell papers. Informative on the factual accuracy of the London journal.

Wimsatt, William K., Jr. "James Boswell: The Man and the Journal." *Yale Review* 49, no. 1 (September, 1959): 80-92. Discusses Boswell's autobiographical technique, his skills as a diarist from a literary perspective, and the distinction between the author as a society man and the image he portrays of himself in the London journal.

THE BRAGGART SOLDIER

Type of work: Drama
Author: Plautus (c. 254-184 B.C.E.)
Type of plot: Comedy
Time of plot: Third century B.C.E.
Locale: Ephesus, in Asia Minor
First performed: Miles gloriosus, c. 200 B.C.E. (English translation, 1767)

> *Principal characters:*
> PYRGOPOLINICES, a braggart army captain
> PLEUSICLES, a young Athenian
> PERIPLECOMENUS, an old gentleman, Pleusicles' friend
> SCELEDRUS, a servant of Pyrgopolinices
> PALAESTRIO, another servant of Pyrgopolinices, former servant
> of Pleusicles
> PHILOCOMASIUM, Pyrgopolinices' mistress
> ACROTELEUTIUM, an Ephesian courtesan

The Story:

Pleusicles, a young Athenian, was in love with and loved by Philocomasium, a young woman of Athens. While he was away on public business in another city, a captain of Ephesus, Pyrgopolinices, came to Athens and, in order to get Philocomasium into his power, worked his way into the confidence of her mother. As soon as the opportunity presented itself, he abducted the daughter and carried her off to his home in Ephesus.

News of ravished Philocomasium soon reached Pleusicles' household, and Palaestrio, a faithful servant, immediately embarked for the city in which his master was staying, intending to tell him what had happened. Unfortunately, however, Palaestrio's ship was taken by pirates; he was made captive and was presented by chance to Pyrgopolinices as a gift. In the captain's house, Palaestrio and Philocomasium recognized each other but tacitly agreed to keep their acquaintance a secret.

Perceiving that the woman bore a violent hatred for Pyrgopolinices, Palaestrio privately wrote to Pleusicles, suggesting that he come to Ephesus. When the young man arrived, he was hospitably entertained by Periplecomenus, an old gentleman who was a friend of Pleusicles' father and who happened to live in a house adjoining that of Pyrgopolinices. Since Philocomasium had a private room in the captain's house, a hole was made through the partition wall, enabling the two lovers to meet in the approving Periplecomenus' house.

One day Sceledrus, a dull-witted servant appointed to be the keeper of Philocomasium, was chasing a monkey along the roof of the captain's house when he happened to look through the skylight of the house next door and saw Pleusicles and Philocomasium at dalliance together. He was observed, however, and before he could report his discovery to the captain, Periplecomenus told Palaestrio how matters stood. Palaestrio then developed an elaborate hoax to convince Sceledrus that he had not seen what he thought he had. Philocomasium was to return immediately through the hole in the wall and pretend never to have left the captain's house. In addition, she was to make a reference at the proper time to a dream she had had regarding the sudden advent in Ephesus of a pretended twin sister. This ruse was carried out before the ever more confused Sceledrus, Philocomasium first playing herself and then changing clothes, going through the hole to the other house, and playing her nonexistent twin sister. The dull Sceledrus

758

was slow in taking the bait, but at last he swallowed it and became as unshakably convinced that he had not seen Philocomasium as he had previously been to the contrary.

The danger of discovery temporarily averted, Palaestrio, Periplecomenus, and Pleusicles conferred together on how they might trick Pyrgopolinices into giving up Philocomasium and Palaestrio. The servant again formulated an elaborate ruse. Since the captain was ridiculously vain regarding his attractiveness to women as well as his pretended prowess in battle, it was decided that the plotters would use an Ephesian courtesan to undo him. Periplecomenus, a bachelor, was to hire her to pretend to be his wife but so infatuated with Pyrgopolinices that she was willing to divorce her aging husband for the captain's favor.

This plan was executed. Acroteleutium, chosen as the courtesan and using her maid and Palaestrio as go-betweens, sent the ring of her "husband" to the captain with word of her infatuation. Pyrgopolinices was immediately aroused, but as he was discussing the situation with Palaestrio, it occurred to him that he would be compelled to get rid of Philocomasium before he could take advantage of Acroteleutium's offer. When Palaestrio informed him that Philocomasium's mother and twin sister had just arrived in Ephesus looking for her and that the captain could easily put her out and let her return to Athens with them, Pyrgopolinices eagerly accepted this suggestion. Overwhelmed by Palaestrio's flattery, he even agreed to let Philocomasium keep the gold and jewels he had given her.

When Pyrgopolinices went in to tell her to leave, however, she feigned immense grief. Finally she agreed to leave quietly but only after he promised that she might take Palaestrio with her as well as the gold and jewelry. The captain, amazed at this sudden display of affection, attributed it to his irresistible masculine charm. When he returned to Palaestrio he was given to understand that Acroteleutium wanted him to come to her in Periplecomenus' house. Although he was at first reluctant to do so for fear of the old man's wrath, he was told that Acroteleutium had put her "husband" out and that the coast was clear.

At that moment Pleusicles, disguised as the master of a ship, appeared and said he had been sent to take Philocomasium and her effects to the ship where her mother and sister were waiting. Pyrgopolinices, overjoyed that the matter was being handled with such dispatch, sent Philocomasium and Palaestrio off as soon as he could manage it.

After their departure he hurried into Periplecomenus' house in expectation that Acroteleutium would be waiting for him. Much to his dismay, however, Periplecomenus and his servants were waiting instead, armed with rods and whips and intent on giving Pyrgopolinices the beating that a real husband would have inflicted under such circumstances. This punishment they accomplished with great alacrity, extorting from the captain, under threat of even more dire punishment, the promise that he would never retaliate against any of the persons involved.

When they were finished, Sceledrus came up and crowned the captain's beating with the news that the ship's master was Philocomasium's lover and that he had seen them kissing and embracing each other as soon as they were safely outside the city gate. Pyrgopolinices was overwhelmed with rage at the way he had been tricked, but as Sceledrus and he entered the house the servant observed that the captain had received only what he deserved.

Critical Evaluation:

Miles gloriosus, or *The Braggart Soldier*, provided the prototype of the vainglorious, cowardly soldier for many characters in later drama, not the least of whom is William Shakespeare's Falstaff. Pyrgopolinices' character, however, is not worked out with nearly the depth that Falstaff's is. Plautus tends in this play to fail to integrate character development with plot development: The action is frequently brought to a full stop while discussions take place that have little function other than to give the audience a notion of what the characters are like. Nevertheless, the action is ingeniously contrived. Even though the trickery seems in excess of that required by the situation, the tone of the play is sufficiently light to prevent the audience from feeling any strong desire for verisimilitude.

The Braggart Soldier is one of Plautus' most successful and rollicking comedies. He adapted the play from a Greek original, and possibly he combined two different sources. This is probably an early work by Plautus, judging by the lack of variety in the meter and by the reference to Naevius, the poet and dramatist. The comedy was most likely very popular when it was first presented, because repeat performances were given.

In staging it must have resembled the American musical comedy, with song and dance used to enliven the dramatic action. Masks and Greek costumes may have been employed. The backdrop consisted of two adjoining houses, one belonging to Pyrgopolinices and the other to Periplecomenus. The play itself is rich in buffoonery, parody, punning, comic names, and verbal ingenuity. The action is lively, and the characters—stock types of farce—exhibit great energy in playing out their predestined roles. There is a unity of time as well as of place, since the action occurs in less than a day. Moreover, despite what many critics say, there is a unity of dramatic movement, not to mention suspense, in the way the play is constructed. The overall effect is one of exuberance carried to its utmost limits.

When Plautus wrote his plays during the early Roman Republic, Roman morality was still quite strict, and his audiences must have been titillated by the spectacle of lecherous generals, courtesans, rascally servants, and indolent lovers, all of whom were Greek. The Romans would never have allowed such characters to appear as Romans at that period, but the fact that they were Greeks must have added largely to their enjoyment. The theater, and particularly the comic theater, has often served as a liberating force, a kind of psychic safety valve, by exposing private daydreams on the stage.

The Braggart Soldier is a comedy of deception with a highly intricate plot. Superficially it has two distinct sections, the duping of Sceledrus into thinking Philocomasium is two different women, and the duping of Pyrgopolinices into voluntarily releasing Philocomasium and Palaestrio. Both schemes are closely related, and the one follows from the other.

The opening scene, in which the vain, supremely boastful, and lewd Captain Pyrgopolinices appears with his toady, makes it clear that Pyrgopolinices is going to be the butt of the intrigue. Then the slave Palaestrio, in his prologue, explains he is going to play a trick on the slave Sceledrus in order to make Philocomasium's meetings with Pleusicles safer. Since Sceledrus has already seen the lovers together, the scheme becomes a matter of necessity. It takes a lot of elaborate guile to prove to the stupid, pig-headed Sceledrus that Philocomasium is two people. Even though he is intimidated by Palaestrio and Periplecomenus, he is never truly convinced of it. He says he is leaving until the trouble blows over, but in fact he sticks around and gets drunk, which poses a threat to the later scheme to trick Pyrgopolinices.

Having subdued Sceledrus into temporary silence, Palaestrio has to invent a plan for freeing himself and Philocomasium from the intolerable Pyrgopolinices. If his first deception had failed, any new one would be impossible. The connection between the two schemes is further strengthened when Palaestrio incorporates the idea for the first (Philocomasium being twins) into the second. Yet the crux of the new plan occurs to him in a supposedly irrelevant scene where old Periplecomenus pontificates on the joys of bachelorhood: Why not give Periplecomenus a fake wife infatuated with Pyrgopolinices?

The characters involved talk over this plan extensively, but the audience does not know how it will work until Philocomasium and Palaestrio are almost freed, which maintains suspense.

Suspense is also maintained tactically, when we learn that Sceledrus is getting drunk, when Palaestrio and Milphidippa nearly burst out laughing in Pyrgopolinices' face, when Philocomasium and Pleusicles almost begin making love before Pyrgopolinices' eyes, and when Palaestrio dangerously delays his escape in saying good-bye to Pyrgopolinices. All these things give excitement to the intrigue, making the audience forget how improbable it really is.

However, it is not enough to swindle Pyrgopolinices of his courtesan and his slave woman— he must be put in a position where retaliation becomes impossible. To do that he must be completely humiliated and deflated. Hence, the scheme by which he is enticed into Periplecomenus' house to ravish the phoney wife makes it possible for Periplecomenus to drag him in his underwear out into the street to be beaten and threatened with castration, the punishment for adultery. The threat is enough to get the desired result from the lascivious Pyrgopolinices, securing the safety of Palaestrio and Philocomasium. At the end Pyrgopolinices is left standing on the stage in his underwear, vanity collapsed, asking the audience to applaud. This conclusion is unique among comedies of deception in the way merry practical joking has led up to such a brutal, shaming finish.

This whole complex story revolves around a few simple elements of character—the colossal vanity and lust of Pyrgopolinices, the desire of Philocomasium to be free and reunited with her lover, and Palaestrio's ingenuity in securing their mutual freedom. In keeping with the martial nature of Pyrgopolinices' profession, the strategy against him is spoken of in military terms. Pyrgopolinices is one of a long line of cowardly, conceited, boastful, lecherous soldiers in the theater, not the least of which is Shakespeare's Falstaff. Palaestrio, the wily slave, is the forerunner of the artful servant from Renaissance theater to the present.

"Critical Evaluation" by James Weigel, Jr.

Bibliography:
Anderson, William S. *Barbarian Play: Plautus' Roman Comedy*. Toronto: University of Toronto Press, 1993. A well-written scholarly work. In his discussion of Plautus' *The Braggart Soldier*, Anderson suggests that in this play the quality of "heroic badness" is transferred from a conventional hero to the clever slaves who outwit their masters. Exhaustive bibliography.

Hanson, J. A. S. "The Glorious Military." In *Roman Drama*, edited by T. A. Dorey and Donald R. Dudley. London: Routledge & Kegan Paul, 1965. Plautus' egotistical soldier is the most famous use of a military stereotype in Roman drama. This essay is an excellent examination of the subject.

Hunter, R. L. *The New Comedy of Greece and Rome*. Cambridge, England: Cambridge University Press, 1985. The chapter on "Plots and Motifs: The Stereotyping of Comedy" explores the use of the comic soldier in Roman comedy. An index also points to specific passages discussed. Detailed notes and bibliography.

Segal, Erich. *Roman Laughter: The Comedy of Plautus*. Cambridge, Mass.: Harvard University Press, 1968. Numerous references to the play, noted in the index to passages from Plautus, as well as useful comments on "military heroes" and relevant discussions of slaves. Extensive notes.

Slater, Niall W. *Plautus in Performance: The Theatre of the Mind*. Princeton, N.J.: Princeton University Press, 1985. Approaches Plautus' works from a different perspective. Some specific comments and notations about *The Braggart Soldier* suggest the subtleties that may be missed in a casual reading.

BRAND

Type of work: Drama
Author: Henrik Ibsen (1828-1906)
Type of plot: Social criticism
Time of plot: Nineteenth century
Locale: West coast of Norway
First published: 1866 (English translation, 1891); first performed, 1885

Principal characters:
BRAND, a priest
HIS MOTHER
AGNES, his wife
EINAR, a painter
THE MAYOR
THE DOCTOR
THE DEAN
THE SEXTON
THE SCHOOLMASTER
GERD, a gipsy girl

The Story:

Brand, a young priest, met three types of people as he made his way down the mountainside to the tumbledown church in his home valley. The first was a peasant who would not give his own life for his dying daughter. The second was Einar, a young painter returned from travel overseas, and Agnes, his betrothed, who were gaily on their way to the town of Agnes' parents. The third was a half-gipsy girl named Gerd, who taunted him to climb up to her church of ice and snow. In the peasant, Einar and Agnes, and Gerd—the fainthearted, the lighthearted, and the uncontrolled—Brand saw exemplified the triple sickness of the world, and he vowed to heaven to bring about its cure.

In the village, Brand gained the admiration of the crowd when he risked his life to aid a man. Later he saw Agnes sitting by the shore disturbed and uplifted by new powers awakening in her when she experiences a vision of God urging her to choose another path. He saw his aged mother, who offered him all her savings on condition that he preserve them for family use. Brand refused and urged her to give up all her earthly possessions. The mother left unrepentant, unwilling that her lifetime savings should be scattered. By these encounters Brand was convinced that his mission lay close at hand in daily duties, even if he were unapplauded by the world. Just as he was going to return to the village, Einar suddenly appeared and demanded that Agnes come back to him. Agnes, having seen her vision, refused to go with Einar, even though Brand warned her it would be gray and sunless in his fissure between the mountains; he demanded all or nothing.

Three years passed. Although success had marked Brand's work, he realized that, married to Agnes and blessed with her love and that of their son Alf, he had yet made no real sacrifices. The tests soon came. First his mother died, still unrepentant. Then his child became ill, and the doctor advised them to leave their icy home or the child would die. When Brand agreed, the doctor pointed out that, in leaving, Brand would give the lie to his own stern attitude toward others. Agnes prepared to go, but Brand was plagued by indecision. Brand thought that Agnes, as the child's mother, should make the decision. When Agnes said that she would abide by her husband's choice, Brand chose the only way he thought was compatible with his beliefs, though he knew his decision meant death for the child they loved.

A year later, the mayor, with elections near, arrived to seek Brand's aid in building a house for the poor. When Brand said he himself was going to build a new church that would cost the people nothing, the mayor left.

Agnes felt that she must challenge her husband with what he demanded of others, all or nothing. If she were to return to her old life, Agnes asked, would he choose her or his holy work? When she realized that there could be only one answer, Agnes rejoiced, knowing that for the husband she loved it was indeed all or nothing. Soon afterward she died, leaving Brand alone.

A year and a half later the new church was complete and a great throng gathered for the consecration. The mayor and the dean congratulated Brand on his great accomplishment. Einar appeared, emaciated. He had become a fanatic missionary, and he brushed aside as unimportant the news that Agnes and her child had died; his only interest was the faith in which she died.

Einar left, but the encounter had made things clear to Brand. He exhorted the people to lead a new life. It had been wrong, he said, to lure the spirit of God to their heart by building a larger church. There should be no compromise. It must be all or nothing. He waved them away from the church and locked the door.

When he called the people to the greater Church of Life where every day was dedicated to God, they lifted Brand on their shoulders. Up toward the mountains he urged them. As the rain began to fall, the sexton warned them they were on the way to the ice-church. The older ones complained of feeling faint and thirsty. Many cried out for a miracle. They felt the gift of prophecy was on Brand and called on him to speak. Uplifted, he told them they were waging a war that would last all their lives; they would lose earthly wealth but gain faith and a crown of thorns. At this, the crowd cried out that they had been misled, betrayed, and they were ready to stone and knife the priest.

Brand toiled upward, followed far behind by a single figure, Gerd. He heard an invisible choir that mocked him, saying his work on earth was doomed. The apparition of Agnes appeared, saying he could be reunited with his wife and son if he would blot out from his soul the three words that had characterized his old life: all or nothing. When Brand spurned the tempter, the phantom vanished. Gerd, with her rifle, caught up with him. She saw that Brand's hands were pierced and torn, his brow marked with thorns. To Gerd he was the Lord, the Redeemer. Brand bade her go, but Gerd told him to look up. Above him towered the ice-church. Brand wept, feeling utterly forsaken. With his tears came sudden release. His fetters fell away, and he faced the future with renewed youth and radiant faith.

In the snow from the mountain heights Gerd saw a mocking sprite, and she raised her rifle and shot. With a terrible, thunderous roar an avalanche swept down. As it was about to crush him, Brand called out to God. Above the crashing thunder a voice proclaimed that God was a god of love.

Critical Evaluation:

Immensely popular when first published, the verse drama *Brand*—a play in poetry—took the whole Scandinavian world by storm and launched Henrik Ibsen's European fame. Four editions appeared in the year of its publication; by 1889, the eleventh edition had appeared. Four translations were published in Germany between 1872 and 1882. Though not intended for the stage, the work's fourth act was played repeatedly (only in Sweden has the whole drama been performed). The play was written in Italy, where the author had exiled himself in protest against Norway's national shame in remaining neutral and failing to support Denmark in its war against invading Prussia. From Italy, Ibsen was able to catch in clearer perspective the strengths and weaknesses of his native land. The writing of *Brand* seemed to be a personal catharsis, and he was able thereafter to return to his northern home and produce in regular succession, almost every two years for the rest of his life, his original and stirring dramas. Though *Brand* is addressed to the people of Norway, it is universal in its appeal, depicting the never-ending and tragic struggle of the soul in its search for uncompromising truth.

Brand was written in the first phase of Ibsen's career, when his plays dealt mainly with historical themes, folklore, and romantic pageantry, and before the playwright turned to prose and social issues in the second phase of his career. *Brand* was the first of Ibsen's masterpieces, foreshadowing his best-known plays of social criticism. The play vitalized the Norwegian theater, which had been languishing under the shadow of the Danish theater in Copenhagen even after Norway's separation from Denmark in 1814. *Brand* thus has historical significance as well as artistic importance.

The play combines poetry and moral passion in a grim Norwegian landscape of jagged mountains, deep-fissured valleys, and cruel cold. The setting is an apt complement to the solemn, tragic atmosphere of the play and to the dour cynicism of many of Brand's parishioners and fellow villagers. Indeed, gloom pervades the play. At the beginning of the play, Einar and Agnes appeared to Brand as symbols of lightheartedness that the priest deplored as evil. Soon after, Agnes breaks off her engagement to Einar to marry Brand and live a life of great sacrifice, which ends with her early death. Einar, too, subsequently forsakes his lighthearted ways and becomes a religious fanatic. It is the stern image of Brand, however, that dominates the play.

Brand is the tragedy of a supreme idealist misled by an image of holiness. His uncompromising attitude in his dealings with others—even with his wife and in matters relating to the survival of their son—reveals his conviction that the path to holiness is too narrow for concessions or backsliding. Brand is so sure of his own judgment that even his mountain-climbing injuries appeared as vindicating stigmata. Ironically, his epiphany is shattered by the rifle shot of Gerd, his one remaining follower and a social outcast. The manifestation of the transcendent mercy of God, however, just before the avalanche engulfs Brand and Gerd, is not a validation of his beliefs. Rather, Ibsen is showing that even the most pious and dedicated priest can do and be wrong and thus stand in need of the divine solace Brand had earlier exhorted his sinful parishioners to seek. Brand depicts the fate of a proud man whose ideals and idealism had blinded him to his own pride.

Bibliography:
Bellquist, John E. "Ibsen's *Brand* and *Når vi døde vågner*: Tragedy, Romanticism, Apocalypse." *Scandinavian Studies* 55, no. 4 (Autumn, 1983): 345-370. A discussion of Brand's extreme idealism, which causes him to sacrifice the interests of his family members as well as his own life and happiness. Bellquist regards Brand as a typical Aristotelian tragic hero.
Eikeland, P. J. *Ibsen Studies*. New York: Haskell House, 1934. A collection of four essays. The essay on *Brand*, a particularly good introductory discussion for the general reader, emphasizes Brand's Christianity, his willingness to admit to error, and his commitment to following his conscience.
Hurt, James. *Catiline's Dream: An Essay on Ibsen's Plays*. Urbana: University of Illinois Press, 1972. A survey of Ibsen's works. Contains a good discussion of Brand's spiritual struggles and the opposition between love and will as organizing principles in life.

Lyons, Charles R. *Henrik Ibsen: The Divided Consciousness*. Carbondale: Southern Illinois University Press, 1972. A volume with studies of seven Ibsen plays. The essay on *Brand* discusses the play's tension between the spiritual and the carnal.

Sohlich, Wolfgang. "Ibsen's *Brand*: Drama of the Fatherless Society." *Journal of Dramatic Theory and Criticism* 3, no. 2 (Spring, 1989): 87-105. A discussion of Brand's family relationships as a key to Ibsen's depiction of the social transformation at the time. The article relies heavily on the critical theory of the Frankfurt School.

BRAVE NEW WORLD

Type of work: Novel
Author: Aldous Huxley (1894-1963)
Type of plot: Dystopian
Time of plot: 632 years After Ford
Locale: London and New Mexico
First published: 1932

Principal characters:
BERNARD MARX, an Alpha Plus citizen
LENINA CROWNE, a worker
JOHN, the Savage
MUSTAPHA MOND, a World Controller

The Story:

One day in the year 632 After Ford (A.F.), as time was reckoned in the brave new world, the Director of the Central London Hatchery and Conditioning Centre took a group of new students on a tour of the plant where human beings were turned out by mass production. The entire process, from the fertilization of the egg to the birth of the baby, was carried out by trained workers and machines. Each fertilized egg was placed in solution in a large bottle for scientific development into whatever class in society the human was intended. The students were told that scientists of the period had developed a Bokanovsky Process by means of which a fertilized egg was arrested in its growth. The egg responded by budding, and instead of one human being resulting, there would be from eight to ninety-six identical humans.

These Bokanovsky Groups were employed whenever large numbers of people were needed to perform identical tasks. Individuality was a thing of the past. The new society made every effort to fulfill its motto—Community, Identity, Stability. After birth, the babies were further conditioned during their childhood for their predestined class in society. Alpha Plus Intellectuals and Epsilon Minus Morons were the two extremes of the scientific utopia.

Mustapha Mond, one of the World Controllers, joined the inspection party and lectured to the new students on the horrors and disgusting features of old-fashioned family life. To the great embarrassment of the students, he, in his position of authority, dared use the forbidden words "mother" and "father"; he reminded the students that in 632 A.F., everyone belonged to everyone else.

Lenina Crowne, one of the workers in the Hatchery, took an interest in Bernard Marx. Bernard was different—too much alcohol had been put into his blood surrogate during his period in the prenatal bottle, and he had sensibilities similar to those possessed by people in the time of Henry Ford.

Lenina and Bernard went by rocket ship to New Mexico and visited the Savage Reservation, a wild tract where primitive forms of human life had been preserved for scientific study. At the pueblo of Malpais, the couple saw an Indian ceremonial dance in which a young man was whipped to propitiate the gods. Lenina was shocked and disgusted by the filth of the place and by the primitive aspects of all she saw.

The pair met a white youth named John. The young man disclosed to them that his mother, Linda, had come to the reservation many years before on vacation with a man called Thomakin. The vacationers had separated, and Thomakin had returned alone to the brave new world. Linda, marooned in New Mexico, gave birth to a son and was slowly assimilated into the primitive society of the reservation. The boy educated himself with an old copy of William Shake-speare's plays that he had found. Bernard was convinced that the boy was the son of the Director of Hatcheries, who in his youth had taken a companion to New Mexico on vacation and had returned without her. Bernard had enough human curiosity to wonder how this young savage would react to the scientific world. He invited John and his mother to return to London with him. John, attracted to Lenina and anxious to see the outside world, went eagerly.

Upon Bernard's return, the Director of Hatcheries publicly proposed to dismiss him from the Hatchery because of his unorthodoxy. Bernard produced Linda and John, the director's son. At the family reunion, during which such words as "mother" and "father" were used more than once, the director was shamed out of the plant. He later resigned his position.

Linda went on a soma holiday, soma being a drug which induced euphoria and forgetfulness. John became the curiosity of London. He was appalled by all he saw—by the utter lack of any humanistic culture and by the scientific mass production of everything, including humans. Lenina tried to seduce him, but he was held back by his primitive morality.

John was called to attend the death of Linda, who had taken too much soma drug. Maddened by the callousness of people conditioned toward death, he instigated a mutiny of workers as they were being given their soma ration. He was arrested and taken by the police to Mustapha Mond, with whom he had a long talk on the new civilization. Mond explained that beauty caused unhappiness and thus instability; therefore, humanistic endeavor was checked. Science was dominant. Art was stifled completely; science, even, was stifled at a certain point, and religion was restrained so that it could not cause instability. With a genial sort of cynicism, Mond explained the reasons underlying all of the features of the brave new world. Despite Mond's persuasiveness, the Savage continued to champion tears, inconvenience, God, and poetry.

John moved into the country outside London to take up his old way of life. Sightseers came by the thousands to see him; he was pestered by reporters and television men. At the thought of Lenina, whom he still desired, John mortified his flesh by whipping himself. Lenina visited John and was whipped by him in a frenzy of passion. When he realized that he, too, had been caught up in the "orgyporgy," he hanged himself. Bernard's experiment had failed. Human emotions could end only in tragedy in the brave new world.

Critical Evaluation:

Utopian—and dystopian (anti-utopian)—fiction is not really about the future; it is an indirect view of the present. The authors of such works begin with aspects of their own society that they like, dislike, desire, or fear, and by extrapolating them into a possible future, they demonstrate the likely consequences of such tendencies or pressures developed to extremes. If readers do not see their own society reflected in an exaggerated, distinctive, but recognizable form, it is unlikely that the projected world will offer more than amused distraction. *Brave New World* has endured as a classic of the genre because Aldous Huxley's vision not only was frighteningly believable when first presented but also has become more immediate since its initial appearance. Indeed, in *Brave New World Revisited* (1958), an extended expository gloss on the original, Huxley suggests that his only important prophetic error was the assumption that it would take six centuries to implement fully the brave new world; a scant twenty-six years after the novel's publication, Huxley revised his estimate of the time needed to less than a century.

The most disturbing aspect of *Brave New World* is the suspicion that many, perhaps most, people would like to live in such a society. After examining the modern Western world in general and America in the 1920's in particular, with its assembly-line techniques, its consumerism, its hedonistic tendencies, its emphasis on social conformity, and its worship of childhood and youth, Huxley projected his observations to their logical conclusions and then asked himself how a "sane" man would react to such an environment: the result was *Brave New World*.

Given modern industrial and scientific "progress," Huxley saw that the time would soon arrive when humanity would possess the knowledge and equipment to "solve" all of its material and social problems and achieve universal "happiness," but at a very high price—the sacrifice of freedom, individuality, truth, beauty, a sense of purpose, and the concept of God. The central question is this: How many people would really miss these things? Do they constitute enough of an intellectual, emotional, and moral force to alter the direction of modern society, and do they possess the requisite will, conviction, and energy to do so?

Compared to such earlier efforts as *Antic Hay* (1923), *Those Barren Leaves* (1925), and especially *Point Counter Point* (1928), *Brave New World* is a model of structural simplicity. The dynamics of a brave new world are presented in a long introductory tour of Huxley's futuristic society that takes up almost the first half of the book. Then a catalytic character, John the Savage, is introduced, who directly challenges the social system that has been described. This conflict leads to a confrontation between John, the representative of "sanity," and Mustapha Mond, who speaks for the brave new world. Their extended debate serves as the novel's ideological climax. The book ends as the Savage experiences the inevitable personal consequences of that debate.

The long opening sequence begins with assembly-line bottle births, in which the individual's potential is carefully regulated by a combination of genetic selection and chemical treatments and then follows the life cycle to show how all tastes, attitudes, and behavior patterns are adroitly controlled by incessant conditioning. The net result of the conditioning is a society that is totally and deliberately infantile. All activities are transitory, trivial, and mindless—promiscuity replaces passion, immediate sensory stimulation (feelies) replaces art, hallucinatory escape (soma) replaces personal growth.

At this point John, the Savage, enters the narrative. Reared among primitives by a mother who loved him in spite of her conditioning, John has known the beauty of great art, because of his reading of Shakespeare, and the pain of loneliness, having been ostracized by the natives because of his light skin and his mother's loose morals. Primed by Linda's nostalgic memories of her former life, the Savage is ready for contact with the outside world when Bernard Marx discovers him on the reservation and connives to use him in a revenge scheme against the Director of the Hatcheries (John's natural father). At first, John is feted as an interesting freak, but, given his "primitive" moralism, a clash is inevitable. Reacting emotionally to the events surrounding Linda's death, John provokes a violent social disruption—the most serious crime in the brave new world—which leads to the discussion with Mustapha Mond, a World Controller.

In a bitterly funny way, this extended debate between John and Mond resembles the Grand Inquisitor passage in Fyodor Dostoevski's *The Brothers Karamazov* (1879-1880) and is the rhetorical center of the book. Like Dostoevski's Inquisitor, Mond justifies his social vision as the only one compatible with human happiness, and like his literary predecessor, he indicates that he, along with the other World Controllers, has taken the pain of life's ambiguities and indecisions upon his own shoulders in order to spare those less capable from having to endure such emotional and psychological pressures. The major difference between the Inquisitor's society and the brave new world is that Dostoevski's hero-villain had only a vision, but, with the aid of modern science and industry, the World Controllers have succeeded in making the vision a permanent reality—providing all distractions such as beauty, truth, art, purpose, God, and, ironically, science itself are suppressed. The Savage rejects Mond's world out of hand, for he demands the right to be unhappy, among other things.

Unfortunately, however, the brave new world cannot allow the Savage that right, nor, if it would, is he fully capable of exercising it. His designation as "savage" is ironical and true. He is civilized compared to the dehumanized infantilism of most brave new worlders, but he is also still the primitive. Shakespeare alone is not enough to equip him for the complexities of life. His upbringing among the precivilized natives, who practice a religion that is a form of fertility cult, has left him without the emotional and religious resources needed to face a brave new world on his own. Denied a chance to escape, the Savage tries to separate himself from its influence, but it follows him and exploits him as a quaint curiosity. Frustrated and guilt-ridden, he scourges himself and is horrified to discover that the brave new worlders can incorporate even his self-abasement into their system. Caught between the insanity of utopia and the lunacy of the primitive village, John reacts violently—first outwardly, by assaulting Lenina, and then inwardly, by killing himself.

It therefore remains for the other "rebellious" characters in the book to establish alternatives to the brave new world. In this aspect, perhaps, the book is artistically inferior to Huxley's previous works. One of the most impressive qualities in the novels that immediately preceded *Brave New World* is the way in which the author pursues and develops the qualities that he had given to his major characters. Unfortunately, in *Brave New World*, he does not fully develop the possibilities latent in his primary figures.

One of the sharpest ironies in *Brave New World* lies in the way Huxley carefully demonstrates that, in spite of mechanistic reproduction and incessant conditioning, individualistic traits and inclinations persist in the brave new world. As a result of alcohol in his prenatal blood surrogate, Bernard Marx shows elements of nonconformity. As a result of an overdeveloped I.Q., Helmholtz Watson is dissatisfied with his situation and longs to write a book, although he cannot imagine what he wants to say. Even Lenina Crowne has dangerous tendencies toward emotional involvement; but Huxley largely fails to develop the potential of these deviations. After repeatedly showing Marx's erratic attempts to conform to a society in which he feels essentially alienated, Huxley abandons him once the Savage enters the narrative. On the other hand, Helmholtz Watson's character is hardly explored at all; and after her failure to seduce John, Lenina is almost completely forgotten except for her fleeting reappearance at the book's conclusion. Unlike the Savage, Marx and Watson are allowed a chance to travel to an isolated community and experiment with individualism, but the reader never sees the results of their austere freedom.

Although the "positive" side of *Brave New World* is never developed and all of the artistic possibilities are not fully exploited, the novel remains a powerful, perceptive, and bitterly funny vision of modern society; but let readers fervently hope, along with the author, that the final importance of *Brave New World* does not come from its prophetic accuracy.

"Critical Evaluation" by Keith Neilson

Bibliography:
Bowering, Peter. *Aldous Huxley: A Study of the Major Novels.* New York: Oxford University Press, 1969. Devotes a chapter to *Brave New World*, concentrating particularly on its themes of technological slavery and the limits of freedom. Includes substantial character analysis.
Firchow, Peter. *Aldous Huxley: Satirist and Novelist.* Minneapolis: University of Minnesota Press, 1972. Devotes most of chapter 5 to discussion of *Brave New World* as a dystopian

novel. Considers it as a satirical parable modeled on the Grand Inquisitor episode in *The Brothers Karamazov*.

Meckier, Jerome. "Debunking Our Ford: *My Life and Work* and *Brave New World*." *South Atlantic Quarterly* 78, no. 2 (Autumn, 1979): 448-459. Examines the relationship between Henry Ford's autobiography and Huxley's dystopia. Huxley was alarmed by the parts of the American ethos that he thought Ford represented.

Nance, Guinevera. *Aldous Huxley*. New York: Continuum, 1988. Chapter 3 offers a critical summary and evaluation of the novel. Considers its themes and gives particular attention to the moral implications of the Savage.

Watts, Harold H. *Aldous Huxley*. Boston: Twayne, 1969. One chapter discusses the novel as dystopian fiction, examines its themes, structures, and characterizations, and considers its artistic value. A good general introduction to the novel.

BREAD AND WINE

Type of work: Novel
Author: Ignazio Silone (Secondo Tranquilli, 1900-1978)
Type of plot: Social realism
Time of plot: 1930's
Locale: Italy
First published: German translation, 1936 as *Brot und Wein*; Italian original, 1937 as *Pane e vino*; revision, 1955 as *Vino e pane* (English translation, 1962)

Principal characters:

DON BENEDETTO, a liberal priest
PIETRO SPINA, a former pupil and a political agitator
BIANCHINA GIRASOLE, a peasant girl befriended by Spina
CRISTINA COLAMARTINI, Bianchina's schoolmate

The Story:

In the Italian village of Rocca dei Marsi, Don Benedetto, a former Catholic teacher, and his faithful sister, Marta, prepared to observe the don's seventy-fifth birthday. It was April, and war with the Abyssinians was in the making. Benedetto had invited several of his old students to observe his anniversary with him. Three appeared, and the group talked of old acquaintances. Most of Benedetto's students had compromised the moral precepts that the high-minded old scholar had taught them. Benedetto asked about Pietro Spina, his favorite pupil, and learned from his guests that the independent-minded Spina had become a political agitator, a man without a country. It was rumored that Spina had returned to Italy to carry on his work among the peasants.

One day Doctor Nunzio Sacca, one of those who had been at the party, was summoned by a peasant to come to the aid of a sick man. Sacca, upon finding the man to be Spina, was filled with fear, but the sincerity and fervor of Spina made him ashamed. Spina, only in his thirties, had used iodine to transform his features to those of an old man. Sacca administered to Spina and arranged for the agitator's convalescence in a nearby mountain village. Later, he furnished Spina with clerical clothes. Disguised as a priest and calling himself Don Paolo Spada, Spina went to the Hotel Girasole in Fossa, where he brought comfort to a young woman who was believed dying as the result of an abortion.

In the mountains, at Pietrasecca, Paolo—as Spina called himself—stayed at the inn of Matelena Ricotta. In his retreat, Paolo began to have doubts concerning the value of the life he was leading, but the brutal existence of the peasants of Pietrasecca continued to spur him on in his desire to free the oppressed people.

Bianchina Girasole, the woman whom Paolo had comforted at Fossa, appeared, well and healthy. Attributing her survival to Paolo, she said that the man was surely a saint. Disowned by her family, Bianchina went to Cristina Colamartini, a school friend who lived in Pietrasecca. The two women, discussing school days and old friends, concluded that most of their schoolmates had taken to ways of evil in one way or another. When Bianchina seduced Cristina's brother, Alberto, the Colamartinis were scandalized. Paolo lost his respect for Cristina, who showed only too plainly that her devotion to God excluded all reason and any humanity; she avowed that a Colamartini could never marry a Girasole because of difference in caste.

Paolo began to visit more frequently among the peasants. Soon he had a reputation as a wise and friendly priest. In his association with those simple people, he learned that no reformer

771

could ever hope to be successful with them by use of abstractions; the peasants accepted only facts, either good or bad. He left the valley. At Fossa, he again sought out potential revolutionary elements. He spoke of revolution to Alberto and Bianchina, who had moved to Fossa, and to Pompeo, son of the local chemist. The youths were delighted. Paolo enlisted Pompeo in the movement.

Paolo next went to Rome. There, in the church of Scala Santa, he discarded his clerical dress to become Spina once again. In Rome, he found an air of futility and despair. Romeo, his chief contact, told him that peasant agitators did not have a chance for success. Spina explained that propaganda by words was not enough; success could be achieved only by living the truth to encourage the oppressed. Spina saw student demonstrations in favor of the leader and of the projected war. He talked to Uliva, who had become completely disillusioned. Then he looked for Murica, a youth from his own district who, perhaps, could direct him to dependable peasants. Murica, however, had returned to his home. Before Spina left Rome, he heard that an explosion had killed Uliva in his apartment. The police learned that Uliva had been preparing to blow up a church at a time when many high government officials were to be in it.

Back at the Hotel Girasole in Fossa, Spina, again disguised as Don Paolo, was sickened by the enthusiasm of the peasants for the success of the Abyssinian war. He sent Bianchina to Rocca to seek out Murica. During the prowar demonstrations, he went about the village writing antiwar and antigovernment slogans on walls. Pompeo, who had gone to Rome, returned during the excitement and revealed that he had been won over by the glory of the new war; he had enlisted for service in Africa. Paolo's charcoaled slogans soon had the village in an uproar. Pompeo, who suspected Paolo, announced publicly that he would disclose the culprit's identity, but Bianchina persuaded the youth not to expose her beloved Paolo.

Paolo went to visit his old schoolmaster, Don Benedetto, at Rocca. He appeared before the venerable old priest as himself, not as Paolo, and the two men, although of different generations, agreed that theirs was a common problem. They asked each other what had become of God in the human affairs. Neither could offer any solution to the problem, but they both agreed that any compromise to one's belief was fatal not only to the individual but also to society.

Paolo gave Bianchina money and letters and sent her to Rome; he himself went to Pietrasecca. There a young peasant brought him a letter from Don Benedetto. The messenger was Murica, the man he had been seeking. When Spina revealed his true identity to Murica, the two men swore to work together. News of Murica's work with Paolo circulated in Pietrasecca, and Paolo found himself playing the part of confessor to Pietraseccans. What they disclosed to him disgusted him but at the same time convinced him more than ever that the peasants must be raised from their squalor. Paolo renewed his acquaintance with Cristina, who had been asked by Don Benedetto to give Paolo help whenever he should need it.

Don Benedetto had been threatened because of his candid opinions. Called to officiate at a mass, he was poisoned when he drank the sacramental wine. At the same time Paolo, having received word that Romeo had been arrested in Rome, went to the Holy City, where he found that Bianchina had become a prostitute. She confessed her undying love for the priest. Paolo, now Spina, found the underground movement in Rome in utter chaos after Romeo's arrest. Despairing, he returned to his home district, where he learned that Murica had been arrested and killed by government authorities. He fled to Pietrasecca to destroy papers he had left in the inn where he had stayed during his convalescence. Learning that he was sought throughout the district, he fled into the snow-covered mountains. Cristina followed his trail in an attempt to take him food and warm clothing. Mists and deep snow hindered her progress. Night fell. Alone and exhausted, she made the sign of the cross as hungry wolves closed in upon her.

Critical Evaluation:

Ignazio Silone, Italy's chief novelist of the 1930's and 1940's, was attracted to communism in the 1920's but by 1930 he had become disillusioned with the party's hypocrisy and tyranny. *Bread and Wine*, his best novel, is in part a study in political disillusionment. The novel reveals that reaction to social injustice is at the root of Silone's impulse to write fiction. He has said, "for me writing has not been, and never could be except in a few favored moments of peace, a serene aesthetic enjoyment, but rather the painful continuation of a struggle."

The central question in *Bread and Wine* is whether one can satisfy the demands of the soul and of social betterment at the same time. At the beginning of the novel, Pietro Spina is a full-fledged political propagandist and organizer for the Communists. He opposes the private ownership of land and he seems to believe that the world's wealth will eventually be shared equally. Forced to hide and rest in an out-of-the-way village in the garb of a priest, he begins to change his views. He asks himself whether he has not lost his sincerity in his wholehearted pursuit of party ideology. He asks whether he has not fled "the opportunism of a decadent church to fall into the Machiavellianism of a sect?" In his self-examination, the question of good faith is paramount. Political action in Silone's belief demands as much honesty and composure of soul as does a true religious vocation.

Two factors in particular contribute to Spina's change. The first is his assumption of the role of Don Paolo. As a priest, people come to him in trust, and his own instinctive love of truth and justice is, ironically, rekindled. The second has to do with the peasants he encounters and the region in which they live. The Abruzzi region is central in Silone's fiction. It is bleak and poverty-stricken, but its peasants are tough and basic. They and their land bring Spina back to the basic problems governing the individual's relationships with others.

Spina's problem can be put another way: As he becomes more and more influenced by his role as Don Paolo, he must not lose sight of Pietro Spina. He must keep Don Paolo and Spina together and integrated. His old schoolteacher Don Benedetto helps him here. Don Benedetto has moral authority and candor. His advice to Spina confirms him in his way. His death is a further sign to Spina that he must not back away from social problems. In his dialogues with Cristina Colamartini, Spina is also confirmed in his spiritual change. She too is sacrificed at the end of the novel. For Silone, such sacrifices are necessary to the pursuit of political justice and spiritual wholeness.

Two scenes in particular reveal Pietro's independence and help to define his rejection of party politics. In the first scene, Pietro refuses to follow the party line as enunciated by a character named Battipaglia. He points out that if he conforms to an edict in which he does not believe, he will be committing the same sin of which the Communists accuse the Fascists. The second scene follows directly after the first and is really a continuation of the argument begun in the first. Uliva, an old friend of Pietro, says he already foresees the corruption of their movement into orthodoxy and tyranny. The enthusiastic ideas they had as students have hardened into official doctrine. The party cannot stand any deviation, even if it leads to the truth. Uliva's disillusionment is great: "Against this pseudolife, weighed down by pitiless laws," he cries out, "the only weapon left to man's free will is antilife, the destruction of life itself." Later, he is killed in his apartment by a bomb that police evidence showed he meant for high government officials gathered in a church. This was his physical end, but he had really been destroyed by the dialectical process. Between Battipaglia's cynical rigidity and Uliva's honest but misguided nihilism, Spina must find a way to perpetuate the cause. He succeeds because his faith cannot dry up and because he is able to pass on his belief to two or three others. The process of simple communion replaces the idea of the Communist state, and the revolutionary spirit is saved.

Silone's communism is the primitive communism of the earliest Christianity. Poverty is its badge of honesty, and its heroes are men who travel in disguise from place to place looking for kindred souls. They like to listen to peasants and simple people rather than to the learned.

In a scene that is repeated throughout Silone's work, Spina meets one such man and says he wants to talk with him. The man proves to be a deaf mute but that does not prevent Spina from communicating with him. Indeed, it is the wordless nature of their communication that is important, for words can neither confuse nor betray them. Their spiritual communion is the most solid base on which to build a relationship. Spiritual communication is, Silone seems to be saying, the one thing absolutely necessary for successful political action, the only thing which should never be betrayed.

The humanistic basis of Silone's politics is stated most fully by Spina when he says to Uliva, "man doesn't really exist unless he's fighting against his own limits." At the end of *Bread and Wine*, the spirit of clandestine rebellion is abroad in the land. As in early Christian times, the history of martyrdoms and miracles has begun.

"Critical Evaluation" by Benjamin Nyce

Bibliography:
Brown, Robert McAfee. "Ignazio Silone and the Pseudonyms of God." In *The Shapeless God: Essays on Modern Fiction*, edited by Harry J. Mooney, Jr., and Thomas F. Staley. Pittsburgh: University of Pittsburgh Press, 1968. Notes the underlying Christian symbolism in this novel of failed revolution. Suggests that God is not dead but hidden, revealed not through religion but through sacrifice for others.
Howe, Irving. "Silone: A Luminous Example." In *Decline of the New*. New York: Harcourt, Brace & World, 1970. Traces Pietro Spina's spiritual anguish and his ultimate rejection of Marxism in favor of the primitive Christianity of the Abruzzi peasants. Explores the possibility of modern heroism through contemplation rather than action.
Lewis, R. W. B. "Ignazio Silone: The Politics of Charity." In *The Picaresque Saint: Representative Figures in Contemporary Fiction*. Philadelphia: J. B. Lippincott, 1959. Identifies Spina, with his alter ego Paolo Spada, as a picaresque saint, part hero and part rogue. Analyzes his encounters with other symbolic figures.
Scott, Nathan A., Jr. "Ignazio Silone: Novelist of the Revolutionary Sensibility." In *Rehearsals of Discomposure: Alienation and Reconciliation in Modern Literature*. New York: King's Crown Press, 1952. Characterizes *Bread and Wine* as a revolutionary novel, citing its disenchantment with all political parties. Examines the inevitable isolation of a revolutionary such as Spina.
Silone, Ignazio. *Bread and Wine*. Translated by Harvey Fergusson II, with an afterword by Marc Slonim. New York: Atheneum, 1962. Comments on significant changes in Silone's 1955 revision. Views the novel as a kind of ethical *Bildungsroman*.

BREAK OF NOON

Type of work: Drama
Author: Paul Claudel (1868-1955)
Type of plot: Problem
Time of plot: Early twentieth century
Locale: Far East
First published: Partage de midi, 1905 (English translation, 1960); first performed, 1948

> *Principal characters:*
> FÉLICIEN DE CIZ, a French businessman
> YSÉ, his wife
> ALMARIC, a former lover
> MESA, a disenchanted young man

The Story:

De Ciz and his wife, Ysé, were chatting one morning with their fellow passengers Almaric and Mesa on the forward deck of a liner on the Indian Ocean bound for the Far East from France. The married couple and their two children had only recently embarked at Aden, and De Ciz, like Almaric, was traveling to China to seek new business opportunities. Mesa, a former seminarian, was returning to China where he had previously achieved success as an influential customs official.

Ysé flirted with Mesa, teasing him about his gold rocking chair and extracting a promise that she might use it whenever she wished. De Ciz and Ysé went below to attend to their luggage, and Almaric suggested to Mesa that Ysé had a romantic interest in him. Though Mesa protested that she was too vulgar and a brazen flirt, Almaric implied that the romantic interest might very well be mutual.

When De Ciz and Ysé returned, De Ciz and Mesa went for a stroll. Ysé and Almaric reminisced about old times. By coincidence, they had been lovers ten years earlier. They recalled their affair with a regretful wistfulness. However, although Ysé did not particularly appreciate the life her husband had provided for her, she insisted that she loved him.

Almaric went for a solitary smoke just as Mesa returned from his stroll. He found Ysé alone, reclining in the rocking chair and reading a love story. Mesa told Ysé that he knew she was attracted to him. She forced him to swear that he would not love her, thereby arousing his ardor. When Almaric and then De Ciz returned with drinks for all, the four discussed their various prospects for making their fortunes in the Far East. In the glaring noon heat in the middle of the ocean they enjoyed their drinks.

In Hong Kong, Mesa and Ysé arranged a rendezvous in an obscure corner of an old Chinese cemetery. Mesa, arriving early enough to get cold feet, left. Shortly afterward, Ysé and De Ciz arrived. They were arguing over his latest business deal, which required that he leave her for a time. Despite her pleas that he take her with him, he left without her.

Mesa returned, unable to keep away from the rendezvous. Ysé told him that De Ciz would be gone for one month but that Mesa should not come to see her during that time. Mesa found her irresistible, even with her husband nearby. Ysé made Mesa swear before a cross that she was no less desirable as a married woman, even though she was forbidden to him. She also told him that he must help her become free of De Ciz, even if it meant his death. Mesa balked at that, just as De Ciz unexpectedly returned. Ysé remained cool and left the two men discussing

De Ciz's plans to undertake some shady dealings in Manila. Mesa encouraged De Ciz to take a desk job in a customs house, which would require that De Ciz remain away from Ysé for several years. De Ciz, apparently unaware that Mesa was cuckolding him, agreed to accept the offer.

Some time later, Ysé and Almaric were hiding out in a ruined Confucian temple in a Chinese port where a bloody rebellion was raging. Almaric had once again become Ysé's lover. Ysé had left Mesa to save him from her, and she did not know where De Ciz or their children were. She and Almaric had with them the child she had had with Mesa, a sickly child who died shortly after.

Almaric set a time bomb that would take their lives as well as the lives of the rampaging mob slaughtering any Europeans left in the city. As the sun began to set, he and Ysé were philosophical at the thought that they would not survive the coming night. Almaric had left Ysé to make the rounds of their hideaway when Mesa showed up at the door. She said nothing when he protested that he still loved her and that, because De Ciz was dead, they could now marry. When Almaric returned, Mesa announced that he had come to take Ysé and their child away. Almaric laughed in his face, but Mesa pulled a revolver and in the ensuing struggle, Mesa was knocked unconscious and his shoulder dislocated.

Almaric found a safe passage marker on Mesa's person. Thrilled that they would now be able to escape with their lives, Almaric went off with Ysé. Soon, Mesa regained consciousness. Ysé, who accidentally missed the boat that would have meant her salvation, returned to comfort the injured Mesa. Knowing that they were soon going to die together, she apologized to him for the pain she had caused him, but she declared that none of it was her fault.

Critical Evaluation:

Paul Claudel, whose dramas have been compared to the works of Aeschylus and William Shakespeare, is regarded as one of the major writers of the first half of the twentieth century. A traditionalist in his religious beliefs after a life-altering conversion to Catholicism in 1886, he was nevertheless very much a product of and spokesperson for his time in his efforts to find themes and an idiom expressive of love and faith in contemporary terms.

The economy of action in *Break of Noon*, which many critics regard as Claudel's most realistic play, makes clear that the work's drama resides in the internal moral and spiritual struggles of the characters. These struggles are broadly drawn. Mesa, who is generally equated with Claudel's alter ego in this somewhat autobiographical work, falls in love with a married woman, arranges for her husband's absence from the scene, and has a child by her, fully aware at all times that he is flirting with his own eternal damnation.

In the characters of De Ciz and Almaric, Claudel provides plausible foils to Mesa's highly refined spiritual sensibilities. The adventurous De Ciz is incapable of perceiving any action as right or wrong, good or evil. Almaric, on the other hand, is an atheist and recognizes wrongdoing only to the extent of reveling in it. Mesa, the former seminarian who confesses to a belief in God as the only significant other, is the most culpable of the play's characters because he believes in sin and then knowingly commits it.

Only Ysé seems capable of recognizing the limits of her own moral authority and tries to exercise that power effectively for the better. In the first act, Ysé forces Mesa to swear that he will not love her; in the second, she begs De Ciz to take her with him, and in the third, she leaves Mesa for his own good. With these actions, she is trying to do the right thing, although she knows that there is no solution to the problem posed by the desire between her and Mesa. Ysé is not sure that there is a God, but she believes in the real presence and power of the spirit more than Mesa does.

Mesa's fatal flaw is his inability to share either guilt or salvation with others, a result precisely of his belief in, and failed relationship with, God. By thinking that he is the only person with a spiritual relationship with God, he cuts himself off from the spiritual growth he could have realized through Ysé. The lesson Mesa should have learned is that others, for better or for worse, exist.

Ysé, as she tells him, is that embodiment of otherness that is finally only self. Early in the play she had reminded him of how two were made from one in the myth of Adam and Eve, and she tells Mesa bluntly that she is his soul. Mesa could only have grown from this relationship, however, if he had been prepared to make a full commitment, soul and body, to Ysé's soul and body. "And that's what you don't like, Mesa," Ysé tells him at the end, "to pay dearly for something." Ironically, he pays dearly nevertheless by failing to recognize the seed of salvation that even forbidden fruit must contain for it to be fully savored.

To achieve the combination of narrative economy and ambitious spiritual theme, Claudel used symbolist techniques. A primary symbol is the passage of the day from mid-morning to midnight, which is already suggested in the title. The original French title, *Partage de midi*, is even more telling, however, for *partage* is a geological term denoting the separation of rainwater as it runs off a hill, in other words, a watershed. On the one side of the play's watershed, which occurs at the end of the first act, is light and life and youthful hopefulness; on the other side, the play descends into darkness, night, despair, and death. Only Mesa's raised hand is visible as the play ends, and the audience is left in the dark as to the significance of that gesture.

Another symbolic device is developed with the gold rocking chair, which in Act I symbolizes the vainglory of Mesa's squandered spirituality, his selfish self-possession. In Act II, as the Omega-shaped entrance into an empty tomb, it portends the doom, both physical and moral, that is looming over the lovers, as well as the contrary emblem of the redemption each is capable of achieving, Christ-like, through sacrifice of self. In Act III, it has become what Omega denotes, the last letter, the final note, or, as Ysé puts it, the pincers closing around them. No doubt, Omega connotes as well the higher vision of the Gospels: divine judgment and, for the receptive heart, forgiveness. Because the audience cannot be certain what Mesa is reaching for—the stars, as Ysé has asked of him; the noon light that is gone; the desirable flesh that is still present; the otherness of God that eludes him, or that he has eluded—the Omega symbol remains ambiguous, as a good symbol must.

In the moral universe described in *Break of Noon*, there are a number of certainties: the necessity of choice, death, and the need to work out personal spiritual redemption through interrelationship with others. That redemption, however, remains only the promised grace.

Russell Elliott Murphy

Bibliography:
Berchan, Richard. *The Inner Stage: An Essay on the Conflict of Vocations in the Early Works of Paul Claudel.* East Lansing: Michigan State University Press, 1966. Describes Claudel's early works, taking into consideration the conflicts caused by his being drawn to both a religious and a poetic vocation following his 1886 conversion to Roman Catholicism. *Break of Noon* is seen as a regression, intensified by personal experience, to earlier love-quest motifs.
Caranfa, Angelo. *Claudel: Beauty and Grace.* Lewisburg, Pa.: Bucknell University Press, 1989. Places Claudel in the twentieth century trend in French literature toward transcendent

themes. The contrasts in *Break of Noon* between light and darkness, and the flesh and the spirit exemplify the attempt to harmonize physical and spiritual impulses.

Fowlie, Wallace. Introduction to *Break of Noon*, by Paul Claudel. Chicago: Henry Regnery, 1960. Translator Fowlie's introduction to the play is informative and perceptive. Provides background to the 1948 production overseen by Claudel and discusses the work's place in Claudel's corpus.

Russell, John, trans. *The Correspondence 1899-1926 Between Paul Claudel and André Gide*. London: Secker & Warburg, 1952. The insightful and revealing comments and opinions on their work, lives, and beliefs shared by these two giants of French literature put the autobiographical *Break of Noon* as much in focus as any critical interpretation.

Waters, Harold A. *Paul Claudel*. New York: Twayne, 1970. A thorough general introduction to Claudel's life and work. Asserts that *Break of Noon* rectifies the paradox Claudel often witnesses regarding the existence of sin and the loving nature of God.

THE BRIDE OF LAMMERMOOR
A Legend of Montrose

Type of work: Novel
Author: Sir Walter Scott (1771-1832)
Type of plot: Gothic
Time of plot: Late seventeenth century
Locale: Scotland
First published: 1819

Principal characters:

EDGAR, the master of Ravenswood
SIR WILLIAM ASHTON, Lord Keeper of Scotland
LUCY ASHTON, his daughter
LADY ASHTON, his wife
CALEB BALDERSTONE, Ravenswood's old servant
FRANK HAYSTON OF BUCKLAW, a young nobleman
THE MARQUIS OF A——, Ravenswood's powerful kinsman
ALICE, an old, blind tenant on the Ravenswood estate

The Story:

Sir William Ashton, the new master of the Ravenswood estate, was delighted to hear of the disturbances at the late Lord Ravenswood's funeral. He hoped that the brave stand of Edgar, the young and former master of Ravenswood, which made it possible for the previously prohibited Episcopal service to take place in Scotland, would put Edgar in disfavor with the Privy Council and prevent his attempt to reclaim his family's property. However, when the Lord Keeper and his daughter Lucy visited old Alice, a tenant on the estate, they were warned about the fierce Ravenswood blood and the family motto, I Bide My Time.

The Ashtons' first encounter with Edgar seemed fortunate; he shot a bull as it charged Sir William and Lucy, saving them from serious injury. The sheltered, romantic girl was fascinated by her proud rescuer, who left abruptly after he identified himself. Her more practical father gratefully softened his report of the disturbances at Lord Ravenswood's funeral and asked several friends to help Edgar.

On the evening of the rescue, Edgar joined Bucklaw, the heir to a large fortune, and the adventurer-soldier Captain Craigengelt at a tavern where he told them that he would not go with them to France. As he started home, Bucklaw, who thought himself insulted, challenged him to a duel. Edgar won, gave his opponent his life, and invited him to Wolf's Crag, the lonely, sea-beaten tower that was the only property left to the last of the once-powerful Ravenswoods.

Old Caleb Balderstone did his best to welcome his master and his companion to Wolf's Crag in the style befitting the Ravenswood family, making ingenious excuses for the absence of whatever he was not able to procure from one of his many sources. The old man provided almost the only amusement for the two men, and Edgar thought often of the girl whom he had rescued. Deciding not to leave Scotland immediately, he wrote to his kinsman, the Marquis of A——, for advice. The marquis told him to remain at Wolf's Crag and hinted at political intrigue, but he offered no material assistance to supplement Caleb's meager findings.

One morning, Bucklaw persuaded Edgar to join a hunting party that was passing by the castle. An ardent sportsman, Bucklaw brought down a deer, while his friend watched from a

779

hillside. Edgar offered Wolf's Crag as shelter against an approaching storm for an elderly gentleman and a young girl who had come to talk to him.

Poor Caleb's resourcefulness was taxed to its limit with guests to feed. When Bucklaw thoughtlessly brought the hunting party to the castle, Caleb closed the gate, saying that he never admitted anyone while a Ravenswood dined. The old servant sent them to the village, where Bucklaw met Captain Craigengelt again.

At Wolf's Crag, Edgar soon realized that his guests were Sir William and Lucy; Sir William had planned the hunt with the hope of securing an interview with Edgar. Lucy's fright at the storm and Caleb's comical excuses for the lack of food and elegant furnishings made relations between the two men less tense. When Edgar accompanied Sir William to his room after a feast of capon cleverly procured by Caleb, the older man offered his friendship and promised to try to settle certain unresolved questions about the estate in Edgar's favor.

An astute politician, Sir William had heeded a warning that the Marquis of A—— was likely to rise in power, raising his young kinsman with him, and he feared the loss of his newly acquired estate. He felt that Edgar's goodwill might be valuable, and his ambitious wife's absence allowed him to follow his inclination to be friendly. A staunch Whig, Lady Ashton was in London, where she was trying to give support to the falling fortunes of her party.

Although Edgar's pride and bitterness against the enemy of his father kept him from trusting Sir William completely, the Lord Keeper had an unexpected advantage in the growing love between Edgar and Lucy. Anxious to assist the romance, he invited Edgar to accompany them to the castle where the young man had once lived.

Edgar and Lucy went together to see old Alice, who prophesied that tragedy would be the result of this unnatural alliance of Ravenswood and Ashton. Edgar resolved to break off his relationship with Lucy, but at the Mermaiden Fountain, he asked her to marry him instead. They broke a gold coin in token of their engagement but decided to keep their love a secret until Lucy's much-feared mother arrived.

Sir William correctly interpreted the confusion of the pair when they returned, but he overlooked it to tell them of the approaching visit of the Marquis of A—— to Ravenswood. He urged Edgar to stay to meet his kinsman.

Sir William's elaborate preparations for his distinguished guest left Edgar and Lucy alone together much of the time, to the great disgust of Bucklaw, who had inherited the adjoining property. He unfairly resented Edgar, thinking that he had ordered Caleb to dismiss him summarily from Wolf's Crag. Bucklaw confided to his companion, Captain Craigengelt, that a cousin of his had become intimate with Lady Ashton and had made a match between himself and Lucy. He sent the captain to tell Lady Ashton of Edgar's presence and of the Marquis of A——'s impending visit. Bucklaw hoped that she would return and intervene on his behalf.

Lady Ashton was so upset by the news that she left for home immediately, arriving simultaneously with the marquis and striking fear into the hearts of her husband and daughter. She immediately sent Edgar a note ordering him to leave, thereby incurring the displeasure of his kinsman. She became still more furious when Lucy told her of her engagement.

As Edgar passed the Mermaiden Fountain, traditionally a fateful spot for his family, he saw a white figure which he recognized as old Alice or her ghost. When he went to her cottage and found her dead, he realized that her appearance had been her final warning to him.

The marquis joined his young cousin, who had been helping with the funeral preparations, and reported that all his entreaties had failed to make Lady Ashton tolerate the engagement. He asked Edgar to let him spend the night at Wolf's Crag, insisting over the young man's protests about the lack of comfort there. When the two approached the old castle, however, they saw the tower windows aglow with flames. Later, after the people of Wolf's Hope had provided a bountiful feast for the marquis and his retinue, Caleb confessed to Edgar that he had set a few fires around the tower to preserve the honor of the family. Henceforth, he could explain the absence of any number of luxuries by saying that they had been lost in the great conflagration.

Edgar went to Edinburgh with his kinsmen, who quickly acquired their expected power when the Tories took over Queen Anne's government for a short time. In prospect of better fortunes, Edgar wrote to Sir William and Lady Ashton asking permission to marry Lucy. Both answered negatively—the lady with insults and the gentleman in careful phrases, hopefully designed to win favor with the marquis. A brief note from Lucy warned her lover not to try to correspond with her; however, she promised fidelity. Edgar, unable to do anything else, went to France for a year on a secret mission for the government.

Bucklaw, whose suit was approved by the Ashtons, requested an interview with Lucy and learned from Lady Ashton, who insisted upon being present, that the girl had agreed to marry him only on the condition that Edgar would release her from her engagement. Lucy had written to ask him to do so in a letter dictated by her mother, but Lady Ashton had intercepted it, hoping that her daughter would give in if she received no answer. Lucy confessed, however, that she had sent a duplicate letter with the help of the minister and that she expected an answer before long.

She was not the same young woman with whom Edgar had fallen in love, for she had been held almost a prisoner by her mother for weeks. Unable to stand the constant persecution, she had grown gloomy and ill. Lady Ashton hired an old woman as nurse for her, and at the mother's instigation, she filled the girl's wavering mind with mysterious tales and frightening legends about the Ravenswood family. Sir William, suspecting the reason for his daughter's increasing melancholy, dismissed the crone, but the damage had already been done.

Edgar, who had finally received Lucy's request that their engagement be ended, came to Ravenswood Castle to determine whether she had written the letter of her own free will; he arrived just as she was signing her betrothal agreement with Bucklaw. Unable to speak, the girl indicated that she could not stand against her parents' wishes, and she returned Edgar's half of the gold coin.

Lucy remained in a stupor after this encounter. Meanwhile, her mother continued making plans for the wedding. Old women outside the church on the marriage day prophesied that a funeral would soon follow this ceremony. Lucy's younger brother was horrified at the cold clamminess of the girl's hand. Later, she disappeared during the bridal ball, and Lady Ashton sent the bridegroom after her. Horrible cries brought the whole party to the girl's apartment, where they found Bucklaw lying stabbed on the floor. After a search, Lucy was discovered sitting in the chimney, gibbering insanely. She died the next evening, reaching vainly for the broken coin that had hung around her neck.

Bucklaw recovered, but Edgar, who appeared silently at Lucy's funeral, perished in quicksand near Wolf's Crag as he went to fight a duel with Lucy's brother, who blamed him for her death. Lady Ashton lived on, apparently without remorse for the horrors her pride had caused.

Critical Evaluation:

This novel of seventeenth century Scotland has a driving psychological as well as political, religious, and social determinism. The conflict between Presbyterian (Lord Ashton and family) and Episcopalian (Edgar) is influential in the plot. So, to a lesser degree, is the political-social turmoil that involves disintegration of old-order Tory values before the energetic ambitions of the Whigs. Popular superstition thus thrives upon the inevitable confusion, disorder, and decay resulting from these changes. This power of the supernatural—manifest in omens, dreams, hidden fears, prophecies, visions, specters, and other phenomena—directs the thoughts and actions of both major and minor characters.

Sir Walter Scott, however, does not impose such superstitious paraphernalia directly upon the story; he employs them more subtly, so that they seem the result of psychological conflicts within the characters. The young master of Ravenswood, deprived of his castle and hereditary rights, can only, by submerging his proud loyalty, ally himself with the Ashtons, who have usurped all he holds significant in life. In his own eyes, his sudden, almost unconscious love for Lucy Ashton, although a solace and partial fulfillment of loss, still demeans him. He knows he cannot betray the values of the past, yet he has within him youth and ardor, which force him into an engagement with Lucy. All the characters in the novel, and the reader as well, know that such an alliance will lead to doom. Old Alice tells him this, and Caleb Balderstone, Ravenswood's faithful, ingenious manservant, also warns him about the marriage. The apparition at Mermaiden's Fountain confirms Ravenswood's fears; even Lucy's passive affection and terror of her mother all underline the young man's own perception, but he remains psychologically divided, unable to free himself emotionally from what he realizes intellectually is a disastrous union.

The schism within young Ravenswood, a truly Byronic hero, finds its dark expression in the ugly prophecies of the village hags, the superstitious talk of the sexton, the mutterings of the peasants, and Henry Ashton's shooting of the raven near the betrothed couple at the well. However, step-by-step, Ravenswood almost seeks his fate, driven relentlessly by factors deep within his personality.

Lucy is equally torn. She loves Ravenswood but is paralyzed before the dominating force of her mother. She submits to marriage with Bucklaw, but her divisive emotions drive her to murder, insanity, and death. Lord Ashton also has commendable motives in spite of his political chicanery, but he, like Lucy, is rendered ineffective by his wife's mastery.

To keep the novel from sinking into grotesque morbidity and gothic excess, Scott provided comic relief through specific character action. Balderstone in his bizarre methods of replenishing the bare tables of Wolf's Crag and the rallying of all in the village to provide adequately for the marquis during his visit furnish this needed humor. Scott's sense of timing and ability to tie supernatural elements to psychological divisions within personality manage to hold the novel together and to make it a controlled and well-structured work.

Bibliography:

Brown, David. *Walter Scott and the Historical Imagination.* Boston: Routledge & Kegan Paul, 1979. A thorough discussion of Scott's tragic plot and comic subplot. Compares the novel to other Scott novels and notes, focusing in particular on the similarities between *The Bride of Lammermoor* and *Guy Mannering.*

Johnson, Edgar. *Sir Walter Scott: The Great Unknown.* 2 vols. New York: Macmillan, 1970. The standard biography of Scott. Regards the novel as a tragedy of character and fate—one in which the love affair is surrounded by an atmosphere of foreboding.

Kerr, James. *Fiction Against History: Scott as Storyteller.* Cambridge, England: Cambridge University Press, 1989. Considers the most fascinating feature of the novel to be its merging of pessimistic historical narrative with complex love story. Notes how the novel is a lament for the decline of the feudal order and a critique of the new order. Emphasizes the way in which Scott deploys gothic elements to develop a historical lesson found often in the Waverley novels.

Lauber, John. *Sir Walter Scott*. Rev. ed. Boston: Twayne, 1989. An excellent introduction. Has a chronology of Scott's life, chapters on Scott's career, poetry, and fiction, and a selected bibliography. Refers to the novel as a one of oaths and omens, signs and warnings.

Milgate, Jane. *Walter Scott: The Making of the Novelist*. Toronto: University of Toronto Press, 1984. Discusses the legend surrounding the novel's composition. Explores the importance of the dating of its action. Notes that the novel depicts a particular historical moment, one with which both Ravenswood and Sir William Ashton are out of step.

THE BRIDE'S TRAGEDY and DEATH'S JEST-BOOK

Type of work: Poetry
Author: Thomas Lovell Beddoes (1803-1849)
First published: The Bride's Tragedy, 1822; *Death's Jest-Book,* 1850

Thomas Lovell Beddoes spent his life as a perpetual medical student, even after he qualified for his degree at universities in Germany and Switzerland; he ended it by poison at the age of forty-five. Apart from two books of juvenile poems, Beddoes published only one work in his lifetime, *The Bride's Tragedy,* which became a best-seller in London when he was a nineteen-year-old undergraduate at Oxford. Early success with this poetical drama suggested to him the notion of "reviving" the English drama, a desire shared by many English writers between the successes of John Dryden and William Butler Yeats or T. S. Eliot—witness the impossible verse dramas of William Wordsworth, Percy Bysshe Shelley, Robert Browning, Alfred, Lord Tennyson, and Thomas Hardy. The shadow of William Shakespeare and the Elizabethans lay long across the centuries, but unlike the Elizabethans the great English poets had very little practical experience of the stage. Thus it is that Beddoes' two most complete works are verse dramas, *The Bride's Tragedy* and *Death's Jest-Book,* which he completed in the four years ending in 1828 and spent the rest of his life revising.

Beddoes enjoyed a competent income all his life and suffered no attachments. He seems to have spent his years on the Continent, between 1825 and 1848, as a graduate student and political radical; a favorable rate of exchange and the reputation of a free Englishman made him a well-known figure among students and the secret police abroad. He seems to have been fortunate in his friends, especially his literary executor, Thomas Forbes Kelsall, but to have suffered a grand dyspepsia for life, of which he was thoroughly conscious:

> For death is more "a jest" than Life, you see
> Contempt grows quick from familiarity,
> . . . Few, I know,
> Can bear to sit at my board when I show
> The wretchedness and folly of man's all
> And laugh myself right heartily.

Beddoes' long self-exile is perhaps the clearest indication of his malaise and the cause of his fragmentary work. He was unable to grasp the realities of life around him. A gentleman, a student, a foreigner, he sought an effective means of communication in a totally unrealistic medium, the poetic drama. Having little to say and no way of saying it, he turned ever inward, exploring his own melancholy and recording it in an outworn medium he acquired not from the stage but from books.

Yet for all this perversity, eccentricity, and tragedy, no anthology of nineteenth century English poetry can afford to omit at least two of Beddoes' lyrics: "Old Adam, the carrion crow" from the final scene of *Death's Jest-Book,* and "Dream-Pedlary" from *The Ivory Gate,* the title of a collection of the poems written on the Continent. Remote as he was from the country of his speech, the events and literature of his time, that may have been the precondition of his unique tone, which escapes finer definition as does that of his place in English literature. The situations of his lyrics are always slightly freakish, for it is the style that marks their individuality. Along with much conventional language there are turns in the lines that can only be crass or inspired phrasing: "And through every feather/ Leaked the wet weather. . . ." The second line is ironic and realistic. This is the effect Beddoes was always trying to bring off, a *danse macabre* in polka time that forces his lines to try to outdo one another, often in a succession of compounds. When inspiration fails, crassness results. These terrible alternatives are more or less described in the words of Wolfram, which introduce the lyric:

> When I am sick o' mornings,
> With a horn-spoon tinkling my porridge-pot,
> 'Tis a brave ballad: but in Bacchanal night,
> O'er wine, red, black, or purple-bubbling wine,
> That takes a man by the brain and whirls him round,
> By Bacchus' lip! I like a full-voiced fellow,
> A craggy-throated, fat-cheeked trumpeter,
> A barker, a moon-howler. . . .

There is more triumph than failure of these startling effects in the last poems of "The Ivory Gate," and the range is much larger. Beddoes can satirize Britannia from a penny:

> O flattering likeness on a copper coin!
> Sit still upon your slave-raised cotton ball,
> With upright toasting fork and toothless cat.

He concludes "Silenus in Proteus" with the wit of: "I taught thee then, a little tumbling one,/ To suck the goatskin oftener than the goat?" "An Unfinished Draft," beginning "The snow falls by thousands into the sea," shows his lyric powers, as does the striking image in "The Phantom-Wooer": "Sweet and sweet is their poisoned note,/ The little snakes of silver throat, . . ."

Similarly, it is the lyrics in the verse dramas that are now best remembered. The larger effect Beddoes was trying for by constructing plot, character, and situation never quite comes off; the fault mainly lies in the plots of the dramas together with their settings and the distrait emotions of the speakers. The two brides of *The Bride's Tragedy* are Floribel and Olivia; the latter's brother, Orlando, has forced Floribel's wooer, Hesperus, to promise marriage to Olivia so that Orlando himself can wed Floribel. Hesperus decides that both shall be the "brides" of death. In Act III, he stabs Floribel when she keeps her tryst; as Olivia is preparing for her wedding to Hesperus his deed is discovered, and the duke orders his arrest at the marriage feast. When he is condemned to die, Olivia dies, too, and Floribel's mother (having poisoned Hesperus with the scent of flowers at the place of execution) precedes Hesperus to the grave in a general holocaust that includes the fathers of Floribel and Hesperus. Most of the action takes place offstage, the characters making the most of the marvelous situations, such as a suicide's grave, for verbal arias that furiously imitate the clotted passages of witty exchange in the Elizabethan play. The play is effective from moment to moment, but as a whole it is impossible. Much the same can be said for *Death's Jest-Book* or "The Fool's Tragedy." Wolfram goes to the Holy Land to rescue Duke Melveric from the Saracens. The two fight over the love of Sibylla, and Melveric kills Wolfram, whose body is returned to Grussau accompanied by the duke, in the disguise of a friar, and Sibylla. There the duke finds his two sons, Adalmar and Athulf, plotting rebellion against the duke's governor, Thorwald, and fighting each other for the love of Thorwald's daughter. The rebellion is led by Isbrand, Wolfram's vengeful brother, who has substituted a clown, Mandrake, for Wolfram's corpse, so that when the duke, despairing of his present troubles, asks his African slave to raise the dead, first Mandrake, then Wolfram come from the sepulchre. The wedding of Adalmar and Thorwald's daughter is planned. Isbrand agrees to marry Sibylla; Athulf appears to commit suicide by drinking poison as the musicians, come to lead Thorwald's daughter to her marriage, sing the beautiful song, "We have bathed, where none have seen us." The scene ends with Athulf killing Adalmar. In the fifth act, the events are most complicated, for the ghost of Wolfram is seeking revenge and the conspirators have decided to kill Isbrand. Sibylla dies but Athulf does not. The conspiracy first succeeds and then is overthrown. In the end, the duke loses both his sons, resigns his crown to Thorwald, and makes a marvelous final exit, going into the sepulchre with Wolfram. The play is saturated with echoes of Shakespeare, both in the language ("O Arab, Arab! Thou dost sell true drugs") and in the situation of a duke in disguise, and but for Beddoes' obvious gravity the situation would amount to a parody. Many of the situations and passages play on death, but apart from a soliloquy by Isbrand, the "Fool" of the subtitle, they do little more than weave around the subject. The soliloquy in Act V, scene i, begins:

> How I despise
> All you mere men of muscle! It was ever
> My study to find out a way to godhead,
> And on reflection soon I found that first
> I was but half created; that a power
> Was wanting in my soul to be its soul,
> And this was mine to make.

This passage carries the ring of reality and makes it clear that Isbrand is a *persona* for Beddoes, one of the rare moments when he speaks recognizable truth. In the "Lines written in Switzerland," after a passage that plays with the notion of truth, Beddoes again speaks out in what may well be his epitaph:

> Not in the popular playhouse, or full throng
> Of opera-gazers longing for deceit; . . .
> May verse like this e'er hope an eye to feed on't.
> But if there be, who, having laid the loved
> Where they may drop a tear in roses' cups,
> With half their hearts inhabit other worlds; . . .
> Such may perchance, with favorable mind,
> Follow my thought along its mountainous path.

Bibliography:

Donner, H. W. *Thomas Lovell Beddoes*. Oxford, England: Basil Blackwell, 1935. Extensive critical examination of the writer's career that includes lengthy chapters on both *The Bride's Tragedy* and *Death's Jest-Book*. Discusses technical merits, sources, and themes for each verse drama.

Frye, Northrop. "Yorick: The Romantic Macabre." In *A Study of English Romanticism*. New York: Random House, 1968. Extensive analysis of *Death's Jest-Book*, establishing its place in the Romantic canon and discussing Beddoes' handling of themes common to Romantic writers.

Snow, Royall H. *Thomas Lovell Beddoes: Eccentric and Poet*. New York: Covici, Friede, 1928. Scholarly investigation of the writer's life and works. Includes chapters on *The Bride's Tragedy* and *Death's Jest-Book*. Points out Beddoes' problem in meeting the requirements of the stage in both works, but acknowledges the author's ability to create powerful scenes.

Thompson, James R. *Thomas Lovell Beddoes*. Boston: Twayne, 1985. Introductory survey of the writer that contains a chapter on each play. Describes *The Bride's Tragedy* as a derivative of Jacobean drama. Claims that *Death's Jest-Book* is a satiric *danse macabre*. Explains why Beddoes chose drama as a form of artistic expression.

Wilner, Eleanor. *Gathering the Winds: Visionary Imagination and Radical Transformation of Self and Society*. Baltimore, Md.: The Johns Hopkins University Press, 1975. Though somewhat eccentric in approach, this study provides significant insights into Beddoes' works and shows how his dramas may serve to counter typical notions of the Romantics' apocalyptic vision.

BRIDESHEAD REVISITED
The Sacred and Profane Memories
of Captain Charles Ryder

Type of work: Novel
Author: Evelyn Waugh (1903-1966)
Type of plot: Social realism
Time of plot: Twentieth century
Locale: England
First published: 1945

Principal characters:
CHARLES RYDER, an architectural painter and the narrator
LORD MARCHMAIN, the owner of Brideshead
LADY MARCHMAIN, his wife
BRIDESHEAD (BRIDEY),
SEBASTIAN,
JULIA, and
CORDELIA, their children
CELIA, Charles Ryder's wife
ANTHONY BLANCHE and
BOY MULCASTER, Oxford friends of Charles and Sebastian
REX MOTTRAM, Julia's husband
CARA, Lord Marchmain's mistress

The Story:

Captain Charles Ryder of the British Army and his company were moved to a new billet in the neighborhood of Brideshead, an old estate he had often visited during his student days at Oxford. Brideshead was the home of the Marchmains, an old Catholic family. Following World War I, the Marquis of Marchmain went to live in Italy. There he met Cara, who became his mistress for life. Lady Marchmain, an ardent Catholic, and her four children, Brideshead, Sebastian, Julia, and Cordelia, remained in England. They lived either at Brideshead or at Marchmain House in London.

When Charles Ryder met Sebastian at Oxford, they soon became close friends. Among Sebastian's circle of friends were Boy Mulcaster and Anthony Blanche. With Charles's entrance into that group, his tastes became more expensive, and he ended his year with an overdrawn account of £550.

Just after returning home from school for vacation, Charles received a telegram announcing that Sebastian had been injured. He rushed off to Brideshead, where he found Sebastian with a cracked bone in his ankle. While at Brideshead, Charles met some of Sebastian's family. Julia had met him at the station and later Bridey, the eldest of the Marchmains, and Cordelia, the youngest, arrived. After a month, his ankle having healed, Sebastian took Charles to Venice. There they spent the rest of their vacation with Lord Marchmain and Cara.

Early in the following school year, Charles met Lady Marchmain when she visited Sebastian at Oxford. Her famous charm immediately won Charles, and he promised to spend his Christmas vacation at Brideshead. During the first term, Sebastian, Charles, and Boy Mulcaster were invited to a London charity ball by Rex Mottram, a friend of Julia. Bored, they left early and were later arrested for drunkenness and disorderly conduct. Rex obtained their release.

As a consequence of the escapade, Charles, Sebastian, and Boy were sent back to Oxford, and Mr. Samgrass, who was doing some literary work for Lady Marchmain, kept close watch on them for the rest of the term. Christmas at Brideshead was spoiled for almost everyone by the presence of Samgrass. Back at Oxford, Charles began to realize that Sebastian drank to escape his family. During the Easter vacation at Brideshead, Sebastian became quite drunk. Later, when Lady Marchmain went to Oxford to see Sebastian, he again became hopelessly drunk. Shortly afterward, he left Oxford. After a visit with his father in Venice, he was induced to travel in Europe under the guidance of Samgrass.

The next Christmas, Charles was invited to Brideshead to see Sebastian, who had returned from his tour. Sebastian told Charles that during their travels Samgrass had completely controlled their expense money so as to prevent Sebastian from using any for drink. Before coming down to Brideshead, however, Sebastian had managed to circumvent Samgrass and get liquor by pawning his valuables and by borrowing. He had enjoyed what he called a happy Christmas; he remembered practically nothing of it. Lady Marchmain tried to stop his drinking by locking up all the liquor, but her efforts proved useless. Instead of going on a scheduled hunt, Sebastian borrowed two pounds from Charles and got drunk. Charles left Brideshead in disgrace and went to Paris. Samgrass was also dismissed when the whole story of the tour came out. Rex Mottram was given permission to take Sebastian to a doctor in Zurich, but Sebastian slipped away from him in Paris.

Rex Mottram, a wealthy man with a big name in political and financial circles, wanted Julia not only for herself but also for the prestige and social position of the Marchmains. Julia became engaged to him despite her mother's protests but agreed to keep the engagement secret for a year. Lord Marchmain gave his complete approval. Rex, wanting a large church wedding, agreed to become a Catholic. Shortly before the wedding, however, Bridey informed Julia that Rex had been married once before and had been divorced for six years. They were married in a Protestant ceremony.

When Charles returned to England several years later, Julia told him that Lady Marchmain was dying. At her request, Charles traveled to Fez to find Sebastian. When he arrived, Kurt, Sebastian's roommate, told him that Sebastian was in a hospital. Charles stayed in Fez until Sebastian had recovered. Meanwhile, word had arrived that Lady Marchmain had died. Charles returned to London. There, Bridey gave Charles his first commission; he was to paint the Marchmain town house before it was torn down.

Charles spent the next ten years developing his art. He married Celia, Boy Mulcaster's sister, and they had two children, Johnjohn and Caroline, the daughter born while Charles was exploring Central American ruins. After two years of trekking about in the jungles, he went to New York, where his wife met him. On their way back to London, they met Julia Mottram, and she and Charles fell in love. In London and at Brideshead, they continued the affair they had begun on the ship.

Two years later, Bridey announced that he planned to marry Beryl Muspratt, a widow with three children. When Julia suggested inviting Beryl down to meet the family, Bridey informed her that Beryl would not come because Charles and Julia were living there in sin. Julia became hysterical. She told Charles that she wanted to marry him, and they both made arrangements to obtain divorces.

Cordelia, who had been working with an ambulance corps in Spain, returned at the end of the fighting there and told them of her visit with Sebastian. Kurt had been seized by the Germans and taken back to Germany, where Sebastian followed him. After Kurt had hanged himself in a concentration camp, Sebastian returned to Morocco and gradually drifted along the coast until he arrived at Carthage. He tried to enter a monastery there but was refused. Following one of his drinking bouts, the monks found him lying unconscious outside the gate and took him in. He planned to stay there as an underporter for the rest of his life.

While Bridey was making arrangements to settle at Brideshead after his marriage, Lord Marchmain announced that he was returning to the estate to spend his remaining days. He did not arrive until after he had seen Bridey and Beryl honeymooning in Rome. Having taken a dislike to Beryl, Lord Marchmain decided that he would leave Brideshead to Julia and Charles. Before long, Lord Marchmain's health began to fail. His children and Cara, thinking that he should be taken back into the Church, brought Father Mackay to visit him, but he would not see the priest. When he was dying, however, and Julia again brought Father Mackay to his bedside, Lord Marchmain made the sign of the cross. That day Julia told Charles what he had known all along—that she could not marry him because to do so would be living in sin and without God.

Critical Evaluation:

Evelyn Waugh's official biographer, Christopher Sykes, asserts that the author relied upon metaphor to a greater extent in *Brideshead Revisited* than he had ever done before. Sykes further suggests that metaphor can be a perilous device. A principal characteristic of this novel is certainly its richness of language, yet some critics regard the language as the novel's chief sin. Foremost among these detractors is Edmund Wilson, who had profusely praised Waugh's earlier novels and described him as the greatest comic genius since George Bernard Shaw. In his review of *Brideshead Revisited*, however, Wilson claimed that the novel tends toward romanticism and sentimentalism. Critics who consider the structure of the novel to be its greatest flaw argue that too much of the novel is devoted to the Oxford section and too little to Ryder's crucial love affair with Julia. Still others dislike the tone set by the protagonist and first-person narrator, Charles Ryder, who strikes them as smug and snobbish.

Despite the adverse criticism the work received—far more than was leveled at any of Waugh's previous novels—*Brideshead Revisited* was easily the most popular of Waugh's books. It was so popular in America that it brought the author downright celebrity, a level of attention that, in the role of curmudgeon that he played from his middle years until his death, he claimed not to enjoy.

Political aspects of *Brideshead Revisited* were controversial. Certainly Waugh's portrayal of the incompetent Lieutenant Hooper, who complains constantly about the army's inefficiency but cannot be trusted to perform the simplest task, was interpreted as hostility toward the working class. Indeed, Waugh has Ryder state that he considers Hooper the symbol of Young England, a typical product of the awful age of the Common Man. Also controversial was the fact that *Brideshead Revisited* was regarded as the first novel in which Roman Catholicism is at the heart of the narrative.

The far-from-ideal Marchmain family is certainly a curious device if, as some have charged, Waugh's novel is indeed an apologia for Catholicism. Lord Marchmain has been separated from his wife for many years and lives with his mistress in Venice. Lady Marchmain is lovely, kind, and good, but she is also enigmatic. Her saintliness makes her into a kind of vampire, who unintentionally sucks the lifeblood from her husband and second son. The eldest child, heir to Lord Marchmain's title, is Brideshead (Bridey), who is as stolid as his younger brother is charming, irresponsible, and doomed. Sebastian becomes a hopeless alcoholic. Perhaps Lady Marchmain is intended to represent God's demands on Sebastian and his father; the harder they struggle against those demands, the more complete becomes their ruin. Julia, who willfully marries the abominable Rex Mottram, later, when she falls in love with Ryder, decides she cannot marry him because of the Church's prohibition of divorce. Cordelia, the youngest, who is devout in a natural, unaffected way, is the most normal.

In book 2, the Marchmains submit severally to God's will. After Lady Marchmain's death, Lord Marchmain—in the most roundly condemned scene of the novel—returns and experiences in the opulent Chinese drawing room a deathbed reconciliation with the Catholic faith. Bridey marches pompously on, unimaginatively practicing his Catholicism to the letter and marrying a middle-aged widow whom no one in the family likes but to whom he is "ardently attracted." Sebastian, overwhelmed and ravaged by alcoholism, ends up living the austere life of a porter in a monastery near Carthage. Julia remains the wife of the unloved and unlovable Rex Mottram. Cordelia is destined for a life of service and self-abnegation. Charles Ryder gains a faith but loses the woman he loves. It is not possible to say that any of these characters achieve "happiness"; if Waugh was writing about the Catholic life, at least he did not err on the side of glamorizing its earthly rewards.

The charges of romanticism laid against the book center on the way Waugh treats Ryder's Oxford days and his love affair with Julia. Yet while Waugh sometimes employs metaphor recklessly in the serious sections of the book, he shows an admirable restraint in the comic sections. The passages featuring Charles in conversation with his eccentric father are among the funniest Waugh ever wrote.

The significance of Waugh's shift to the first-person narrative can hardly be overemphasized. Every theme in *Brideshead Revisited* is implicit in the earlier novels, as is every prejudice and every antipathy of the author. It is as if Waugh is not directly associated with the ideas of his narrator until the narrator becomes a character in the novel. Then such is the power of suggestion in the first-person narrative that Charles Ryder suddenly reveals himself to be very like Evelyn Waugh.

It would be misleading to suggest that the adverse criticism of *Brideshead Revisited* resulted merely from personal disapproval of the author's attitudes. The criticism concentrates on two major areas of weakness in the novel—its structure and its tone—both of which had been considered areas of great strength in the preceding novels. Negative response to the novel's structure must have stung, for Waugh had every right to be proud of his skill in architectonics. His 1960 revision of the novel attests the fact that he came to take this criticism seriously.

The problems with the novel's tone must finally be attributed to the first-person narrator. In *Brideshead Revisited*, Waugh does, however, succeed in creating a style that allows him to do more than merely criticize the modern world he has been humorously denouncing for a decade and a half. The snobbish but sensitive artist who narrates *Brideshead Revisited* makes explicit the social, political, and religious attitudes that are merely implicit in the earlier novels. Waugh proves that he can easily master the conventions of the realistic novel, and through the device of his first-person narrator, he proves that he is not limited to the point of view of the detached (or frequently sardonic) narrator.

Critical opinion remains quite mixed on this best-known of Waugh's novels. Some influential critics have judged the book an artistic failure, and there is evidence to suggest that Waugh himself came to the same conclusion. If *Brideshead Revisited* is a failure, however, it must be considered one of literature's most magnificent failures.

"Critical Evaluation" by Patrick Adcock

Bibliography:
Cook, William J., Jr. *Masks, Modes, and Morals: The Art of Evelyn Waugh.* Rutherford, N.J.: Fairleigh Dickinson University Press, 1971. A valuable source because Cook analyzes the point of view employed in each of the novels. It is a commonplace observation that Waugh's style changed in mid-career (just before publication of *Brideshead Revisited*); Cook argues that the altered point of view accounts for the stylistic change.

Davis, Robert M. "Imagined Space in *Brideshead Revisited.*" In *Evelyn Waugh: New Directions,* edited by Alain Blayac. New York: St. Martin's Press, 1992. This essay confronts the problem of a sometimes unlikable narrator who is at the center of the entire novel.

Lygon, Lady Dorothy. "Madresfield and Brideshead." In *Evelyn Waugh and His World,* edited by David Pryce-Jones. Boston: Little, Brown, 1973. An essay by one of Waugh's intimate friends. Discusses the country house that was the model for the fictional Brideshead.

Quennell, Peter. "A Kingdom of Cokayne." In *Evelyn Waugh and His World,* edited by David Pryce-Jones. Boston: Little, Brown, 1973. A reminiscence of the Waugh whom the author knew at Oxford. Provides excellent background information for the Oxford segment of *Brideshead Revisited.*

Wilson, Edmund. "Splendors and Miseries of Evelyn Waugh." In *Critical Essays on Evelyn Waugh,* edited by James F. Carens. Boston: G. K. Hall, 1987. After having praised the young Evelyn Waugh as a comic genius, Wilson in this essay reflects his disappointment with *Brideshead Revisited.*

THE BRIDGE

Type of work: Poetry
Author: Hart Crane (1899-1932)
First published: 1930

A serious student of poetry during the 1920's, Hart Crane saw himself as one whose poetry would celebrate rather than denigrate the modern experience. His was to be a poetry of hope in the future and in the poet's ability to transcend shortcomings. He sought to counteract the cultural despair that was typified, particularly, in T. S. Eliot's influential *The Waste Land* (1922), a poem that Crane described as "good, but so damned dead."

Crane consciously intended *The Bridge* to provide an antidote to the spiritual despair of modern life by holding up to its readers, as the emblem of the modern world's own inspiriting accomplishments, John Augustus Roebling's great technical achievement, the Brooklyn Bridge, which was completed in 1883. Crane had first essayed the long poem form in the three-part "For the Marriage of Faustus and Helen" (1923), which utilizes jazz rhythms and a wide range of classical, biblical, and historical allusions in its exhortation to his contemporaries to "unbind our throats of fear and pity."

The initial idea for *The Bridge* was the direct result of Crane's insight that the contemporary world was the product, and therefore more likely the fulfillment rather than the negation, of the world's previous effort toward understanding. By 1924, Crane had, for inspiration, taken up residence in the same Columbia Heights apartment that Roebling had occupied during the bridge's construction. By then, too, Crane's circle of literary friends, among them fellow poets and critics Gorham Munson, Waldo Frank, and Allen Tate, anticipated the completion of Crane's great modernist epic with much the same excitement as he continuously shared its progress with them.

A sudden spurt of productivity occurred when the banker and art patron Otto Kahn advanced Crane $1,000, with the promise of an additional $1,000, so that he might leave his job as an advertising copywriter to devote his full attention to *The Bridge*. During the summer of 1926, on the Isle of Pines, off Cuba, Crane composed nearly half of the fifteen individual pieces that constitute the completed poem, including, along with the first three sections, "Cutty Sark," "Three Songs," and the final section, "Atlantis"—in sum, much of the poem's most lyrical passages as well as its visionary heart.

The work then became bogged down as a result of Crane's philosophical doubts after his having read Oswald Spengler's *Der Untergang des Abendlandes* (1918-1922; *The Decline of the West*, 1926). Crane joined the American expatriate scene in Paris from December, 1928, to July, 1929, but rather than the experiences serving as a source of renewed inspiration, he gained a considerable notoriety by indulging in assorted debaucheries. Back in New York, he finally completed *The Bridge*, which was published in a limited edition in Paris by the Black Sun Press in January, 1930, and by Liveright in New York in March.

The finished work might appear at first to be no more than a series of loosely connected individual poems, disparate in tone, voice, and style from one another. In fact, however, *The Bridge* is orchestrated much like a symphony, in which a progressive series of interrelated lyrics create a narrative sequence that achieves greater intensity of vision as history and common experience give way to the mythic quest for an overarching identity and purpose—hence Crane's ruling metaphor of a bridge.

In the opening poem "To Brooklyn Bridge," the reader begins at the foot of that noteworthy structure in Manhattan, from there to be transported, in vision, back in time to the deck of the *Santa Maria* as Columbus, unbeknown even to himself, approaches the discovery of a new world.

The hero and speaker of *The Bridge* identifies openly with a "bedlamite" who "speeds to thy parapets," the only difference being that the hero knows that he must not make any literal leap but wait for the visionary moment to descend. The madman and the poet are the same, nevertheless, in spirit. Both recognize, as Columbus, yet another visionary, does in the poem's next section, "Ave Maria," that there will always be "still one shore beyond desire."

Part 2, "Powhatan's Daughter," a section composed of five individual poems, duplicates the poem's structure thus far by beginning again in a contemporary setting in "Harbor Dawn" but then moving back through time, locating literary and other historical landmarks. "Van Winkle" returns to the earlier New Amsterdam of the original Dutch settlers. "The River" takes the reader into the heartland of the continent in a collage of nineteenth century American folklore. "The Dance" recalls the Native American culture embodied in Powhatan's daughter, Pocahontas of Jamestown. She and John Smith become an American Helen and Faustus, the representative wedding of European yearnings with a native Indian wisdom. "Indiana," the closing poem of part 2, sends their spiritual descendant, young Larry, the son of pioneers, off to sea. America returns its new spirit to the Old World.

Part 3, "Cutty Sark," characterizes this uniquely American contribution as the settlers' capacity to subdue not only nature by mastering a continent, but time and space as well. This section celebrates the speedy clipper ships by which the early settlers' descendants spread American commerce, and so the pervading influences of American culture, everywhere. The seagoing "bridge" formed by those vessels takes to the air in part 4, "Cape Hatteras," an appropriate venue since it is not only a hazard for shipping but also the locale from which Wilbur and Orville Wright's heavier-than-air vessel took off in 1903.

In part 5, "Three Songs," there is a momentary lyric interlude in praise of the female, left behind in the closing section of "Powhatan's Daughter." Venus, Eve, and Magdalen, she is ultimately reincarnated in "Virginia" in both the fated Indian princess Pocahontas and the Judeo-Christian tradition's Mary.

A sort of quiescent domesticity is established as the energies that tamed a continent subside, and so part 6, "Quaker Hill," conveys, as the name implies (although the ghosts of Emily Dickinson and Isadora Duncan inhabit its pages), the placid suburban neatness of middle-class America. That surface quiet is deceptive, however, and part 7, "The Tunnel," is part 6's necessary companion piece, a descent, via the New York subway, into the sprawling urban nightmare that has also become, by Crane's time, another part of the American experience. There we meet another ghost from America's literary, and mythic past, Edgar Allan Poe.

Naturally, this darkest hour is just before the visionary dawn, and this subway ride, for all its urban squalor and inchoate terror, stops in the Battery at the Brooklyn Bridge, site of Walt Whitman's old Brooklyn Ferry, and in part 8, "Atlantis," we conclude where the epic hero began, by rising out of the darkness of the urban nightmare into the bright nightlife of a modern city enlightened by the sight of the Brooklyn Bridge: "Through the bound cable strands, the arching path/ Upward, veering with light, the flight of strings. . . ." The hero-speaker has arrived back where he started, immeasurably wiser for the experience of spiritually living his nation's becoming. He hopes to see the fulfillment of the old European dream of Atlantis, the perfected human community. Columbus had, after all, sought a better world. The poet has already told the reader that there will always be that one shore beyond desire, and so the hero can only wonder if he has indeed reached the vision's source.

So concludes Hart Crane's *The Bridge*, and there is perhaps no more sustained or ambitious a lyric undertaking from Crane's time. *The Bridge* has, nevertheless, generally been received as a flawed epic, grander in the scope of its design and of its central metaphor of America as the dynamic bridge between the past and the future than in the fulfillment of its execution. Crane later would comment, "So many true things have a way of coming out all the better without the strain to sum up the universe in one impressive little pellet."

Crane, committed to the visionary aspects of poetry, settled on an apotheosis of the American experience as a theme equal to his talents and ambitions. What Crane accomplishes, however, rather than a vision of America, is a vision of the poet as the dreamer who will not give up his dream, even if its realization is private or obscure. It is Crane's hero's recognition of these vulnerabilities, of the fact that he lets the world make a fool out of him, that realizes his heroism.

Crane apparently committed suicide by leaping into the Atlantic Ocean somewhere north of Cuba on April 24, 1932. Although he was only thirty-two, he thought himself a failure and a has-been. His poetic achievement fell far short of his aims, but his aims for his masterwork, *The Bridge*, were quite lofty. Its poetry will continue to echo in the American experience.

Russell Elliott Murphy

Bibliography:
Brunner, Edward. *Splendid Failure: Hart Crane and the Making of "The Bridge."* Champaign: University of Illinois Press, 1985. Despite its title, this work sets out to disprove the conventional wisdom that Crane's was a largely undisciplined and reckless talent. *The Bridge* is the culmination of Crane's continuing effort to hone his craft.
Clark, David R., ed. *Studies in "The Bridge."* Westerville, Ohio: Charles E. Merrill, 1970. A compilation of fourteen essays, providing a road map of critical responses to the poem virtually from the time of its publication to the 1960's. Most of the major commentators are represented.
Crane, Hart. *The Letters of Hart Crane, 1916-1932.* Edited by Brom Weber. Berkeley: University of California Press, 1952. Crane was an astute critic of his own work and that of others. Offers many insights into *The Bridge*.
Horton, Phillip. *Hart Crane: The Life of an American Poet.* New York: Viking Press, 1957. Written with the cooperation of Crane's mother, this biography is like a novel in its sense of drama. It does not stint on insightful analyses of Crane's poetry.
Paul, Sherman. *Hart's Bridge.* Champaign: University of Illinois Press, 1972. The first book-length treatment of Crane's masterwork. *The Bridge* required Crane to achieve the maturity of vision and technique required of epic poetry.

THE BRIDGE OF SAN LUIS REY

Type of work: Novel
Author: Thornton Wilder (1897-1975)
Type of plot: Philosophical realism
Time of plot: Early eighteenth century
Locale: Peru
First published: 1927

Principal characters:

BROTHER JUNIPER, a Spanish friar
THE MARQUESA DE MONTEMAYOR, a lonely old woman
PEPITA, her maid
THE ABBESS MADRE MARÍA DEL PILAR, the directress of the Convent of
 Santa María Rosa de las Rosas
UNCLE PIO, an actor-manager
LA PÉRICHOLE, an actress
MANUEL, a foundling
ESTEBAN, his brother

The Story:

On Friday, July 20, 1714, the bridge of San Luis Rey, the most famous bridge in Peru, collapsed, hurling five travelers into the deep gorge below. Present at the time of the tragedy was Brother Juniper, who saw in the event a chance to prove, scientifically and accurately, the wisdom of that act of God. He spent all his time investigating the lives of the five who had died, and he published a book showing that God had had a reason to send each one of them to his death at exactly that moment. The book was condemned by the church authorities, and Brother Juniper was burned at the stake. He had gone too far in explaining God's ways to humanity. Through a strange quirk of fate, one copy of the book was left undestroyed, and it fell into the hands of the author. From it, and from his own knowledge, he reconstructed the lives of the five persons.

The Marquesa de Montemayor had been an ugly child and was still homely when she matured. Because of the wealth of her family, she was fortunately able to marry a noble husband, by whom she had a lovely daughter, Doña Clara. As she grew into a beautiful young woman, the Marquesa's daughter became more and more disgusted with her crude and unattractive mother, whose possessive and overexpressive love left Doña Clara cold and uncomfortable. The daughter finally married a man who took her to Spain. Separated from her one joy in life, the Marquesa became more eccentric than ever and spent her time writing long letters to her daughter in Spain. In order to free herself of some of her household cares, the Marquesa went to the Abbess Madre María del Pilar and asked for a girl from the Abbess' school to come and live with her, so Pepita, unhappy that her beloved teacher was sending her away from school, went to live with the Marquesa.

When the Marquesa learned by letter that Doña Clara was to have a child, she was filled with concern. She wore charms, bought candles for the saints, said prayers, and wrote all the advice she could discover to her daughter. As a last gesture, she took Pepita with her to pay a visit to a famous shrine from which she hoped her prayers would surely be heard. On the way, the

Marquesa happened to read one of Pepita's letters to her old mistress, the Abbess. From the letter, the Marquesa learned just how heartless she had been in her treatment of the girl, how thoughtless and egotistic. She realized that she had been guilty of the worst kind of love toward her daughter, love that was sterile, self-seeking, and false. Aglow with her new understanding, she wrote a final letter to her daughter, telling her of the change in her heart, asking forgiveness, and showing in wonderful language the change that had come over her. She resolved to change her life, to be kind to Pepita, to her household, to everyone. The next day she and Pepita, while crossing the bridge of San Luis Rey, fell to their deaths.

Esteban and Manuel were twin brothers who had been left as children on the doorstep of the Abbess' school. She had brought them up as well as she could, but the strange relationship between them was such that she could never make them talk much. When the boys were old enough, they left the school and took many kinds of jobs. At last they settled down as scribes, writing letters for the uncultured people of Lima. One day Manuel, called in to write some letters for La Périchole, fell in love with the charming actress. Never before had anything come between the brothers, because they had always been sufficient in themselves. For his brother's sake, Manuel pretended that he cared little for the actress. Shortly afterward, he cut his leg on a piece of metal and became very sick. In his delirium, he let Esteban know that he really was in love with La Périchole. The infection grew worse and Manuel died.

Esteban was unable to do anything for weeks after his brother's death. He could not face life without him. The Abbess finally arranged for him to go on a trip with a sea captain who was about to sail around the world. The captain had lost his only daughter, and the Abbess believed he would understand Esteban's problem and try to help him. Esteban left to go aboard ship, but on the way, he fell with the others when the bridge broke.

Uncle Pio had lived a strange life before he came to Peru. There he had found a young girl singing in a tavern. After years of his coaching and training, she became the most popular actress of the Spanish world. She was called La Périchole, and Uncle Pio's greatest pleasure was to tease her and anger her into giving consistently better performances. All went well until the viceroy took an interest in the vivacious and beautiful young actress. When she became his mistress, she began to feel that the stage was too low for her. After living as a lady and becoming prouder and prouder as time went on, she contracted smallpox. Her beauty was ruined, and she retired to a small farm out of town to live a life of misery over her lost loveliness.

Uncle Pio had a true affection for his former protégée and tried time and again to see her. One night, by a ruse, he got her to talk to him. She refused to let him help her, but she allowed him to take Jaime, her illegitimate son, so that he could be educated as a gentleman. The old man and the young boy set off for Lima. On the way, they came to the bridge and died in the fall when it collapsed.

At the cathedral in Lima, a great service was held for the victims. Everyone considered the incident an example of a true act of God, and many reasons were offered for the various deaths. Some months after the funeral, the Abbess was visited by Doña Clara, the Marquesa's daughter. Doña Clara had finally learned what a wonderful woman her mother had really been. The last letter had taught the cynical daughter all that her mother had so painfully learned. The daughter, too, had learned to see life in a new way. La Périchole also came to see the Abbess. She had given up bemoaning her own lost beauty, and she began a lasting friendship with the Abbess. Nothing could positively be said about the reason for the deaths of those five people on the bridge. Too many events were changed by them; one could not number them all. The old Abbess, however, believed that the true meaning of the disaster was the lesson of love for those who survived.

Critical Evaluation:

The Bridge of San Luis Rey marked the beginning of a key stage in Thornton Wilder's development and also revealed the essential dimensions of the artistic program he would follow. His first novel, *The Cabala* (1926), had viewed the decadent aristocracy of contemporary Rome through the eyes of a young American student. In the tradition of Henry James and Edith Wharton, the highly autobiographical work suffered by comparison and was not praised by the critics. *The Bridge of San Luis Rey*, however, which vividly evoked a forgotten era and a type of society utterly foreign to Wilder's experience, sold three hundred thousand copies in its first year and made its author a celebrity. This success confirmed Wilder's intention to make abundant use of historical materials, and he set his next novel, *The Woman of Andros* (1930), in postclassical Greece. *The Bridge of San Luis Rey* also served notice that a major philosophical and theological writer had entered the literary scene. The engaging simplicity of the book drew its readers toward problems no less recondite than those of the justice of God, the possibility of disinterested love, and the role of memory in human relationships. Wilder's subsequent works consistently returned to these themes.

The Christianity that inspires and informs *The Bridge of San Luis Rey* is existential and pessimistic. "Only one reader in a thousand notices that I have asserted a denial of the survival of identity after death," Wilder once remarked of the book. He also denied the value of the apologetic task that Brother Juniper undertakes. For even if human reason could scientifically demonstrate God's Providence—a proposition Wilder rejects—humanity would inevitably employ this knowledge in a self-aggrandizing manner. The inherent mystery of the divine intention is a check to human pride, and pride is Wilder's overriding concern, especially that pride which cloaks itself in the guise of unselfish love. If there is Providence, Wilder suggests, it most clearly operates as something that exposes the egoistic taint in all love and reveals to the lover his need to be forgiven both by the one he loves and by the social community.

Despite the ostensible importance of Brother Juniper, Uncle Pio, and Esteban, only Wilder's female characters develop sufficiently to gain awareness of the meaning of the novel's action. The Marquesa undergoes the clearest transformation. The maternal love that she cultivates so assiduously is neither spontaneous nor generous. Rather, the Marquesa craves her daughter's affection as an antidote to her own insecurity. Her imagination first magnifies the daughter's virtues and prestige; then, to assuage a deep self-loathing, she demands from her a meticulous and servile devotion. Although the Marquesa is aware of her manipulative impulses, she is nevertheless powerless to conquer them. She is not aware of how her distorted passion causes misery to those around her. The revelation of Pepita's agonized loneliness shames and humiliates her, but she thereby gains the strength to eliminate the element of tyranny in the love she bears for her daughter.

Because La Périchole (Camila) appears in each of the three tales, she is the novel's most real character. Her satirical attack on the Marquesa becomes ironic when, later on, her own ugliness and avarice also make her the object of gossip and scorn. Like the Marquesa, she does not believe herself to be intrinsically valuable. Yet Uncle Pio, who first treated Camila as something to dominate and in whom to take aesthetic delight, now loves her unconditionally. Her willingness to accept this fact and to express her love causes him to suffer and isolates her unnaturally from society. Such a painful yet liberating acceptance is made possible both by Pio's persistence and by La Périchole's love for Jaime. Her grief, and the possibility of disinterested love that it implies, moves her at last to present her disfigured self to society.

Even though her moral insight makes the Abbess the standard against which all in the novel are measured, she too must suffer and grow. Unlike the abstract and detached Brother Juniper, she makes herself vulnerable to the pains that love and service involve. Unlike the Marquesa, she does not demand instant expressions of servile devotion from those who love her. She does, however, yearn to have her work remembered, to gain that (in Wilder's view, illusory) immortality which comes to those who labor for great causes. Consequently, she manipulates Pepita much as Uncle Pio manipulates Camila. That Pepita died lonely and forsaken reveals to the Abbess the results of her misguided passion. Her faith undergoes a purification when she confronts the fact that "Even memory is not necessary for love."

The episode of Esteban and Manuel does not fit neatly into the pattern Wilder generally establishes. Some critics have suggested that Wilder here meant to deal with homosexual love. This view is partially refuted by the heterosexual activity of both youths and by Esteban's evident unwillingness to stand between Manuel and Camila. Does Esteban, however, unconsciously attempt to retain possession of his brother, communicating his feelings through the uncanny channels of sympathy that bind these twins? Even if this were so, there remains the fact that Manuel is also unable to conceive of a separation. The tale thus seems to constitute a digression, one which serves to underscore the enormous mystery and intensity of all relationships of love. It is linked to the central thematic pattern by Esteban's deep feelings for the Abbess, which enables him to reach out to another human being despite his tragic sorrow.

For Wilder, it is almost impossible for human beings to live serenely and faithfully knowing that their personalities will neither be remembered by society nor allowed to survive death in a hereafter. This prospect creates an anxiety that pervades all their efforts to love. They persistently use the beloved to prove themselves worthy and immortal. Then to love are added additional, degrading elements. People never realize, in the Abbess' words, that "the love will have been enough." Wilder's views could have led him to enormous sentimentality, but, in truth, *The Bridge of San Luis Rey* is extraordinarily stark. It is sustained only by the single hope that "all those impulses of love return to the love that made them."

"Critical Evaluation" by Leslie E. Gerber

Bibliography:
Anderson, M. Y. *"The Bridge of San Luis Rey": A Critical Commentary*. New York: American R. D. M., 1966. Provides concise background details on Wilder and effective commentary about the book's plot structure, characterizations, and major themes.
Burbank, Rex J. *Thornton Wilder*. New York: Twayne, 1961. An insightful introduction to Wilder and his writings. Explores the humanism of *The Bridge of San Luis Rey* and concludes that this novel, despite weaknesses, "has all the intellectual scope, depth of feeling, and complexity of character that make a mature and aesthetically satisfying vision."
Castronovo, David. *Thornton Wilder*. New York: Ungar, 1986. An excellent brief introduction to Wilder and his works. Sees *The Bridge of San Luis Rey* as a study "of isolation and chaos" which attempts to show how "to rise above the disasters of the modern world into a sustaining, if not always clear, spirituality."
Goldstone, Richard H., and Gary Anderson. *Thornton Wilder: Annotated Bibliography of Works By and About Thornton Wilder*. New York: AMS Press, 1982. An excellent source for finding works by and about Wilder. Includes many bibliography entries for sources and reviews dealing with *The Bridge of San Luis Rey*.
Harrison, Gilbert A. *The Enthusiast: A Life of Thornton Wilder*. New Haven, Conn.: Ticknor and Fields, 1983. Includes important information surrounding the writing of the novel, as well as emphasizing its purpose, reception, and contribution.

THE BRIDGE ON THE DRINA

Type of work: Novel
Author: Ivo Andrić (1892-1975)
Type of plot: Historical realism
Time of plot: 1516-1914
Locale: Višegrad, Bosnia
First published: Na Drini ćuprija, 1945 (English translation, 1959)

Principal characters:
MEHMED PASHA SOKOLLI, a Grand Vezir in the sixteenth century
ABIDAGA, the first builder of the bridge
ALIHODJA MUTEVELIĆ, hodja and shopkeeper
LOTTE ZAHLER, an innkeeper
SALKO CORKAN, a Gipsy

The Story:

The "blood tribute" was a most cruel practice of the Turkish rulers during the several hundred years of their occupation of the Balkans. It meant taking young boys away from their parents and rearing them as the sultan's obedient servants, called janissaries. One of the boys, taken from a Serbian village called Sokolovici in Bosnia in 1516 when he was only ten years old, would later become Mehmed Pasha Sokolli and rise to the office of the Grand Vezir, the highest position a non-Turk could reach in the Ottoman Empire. In memory of his childhood, he decided to build a bridge across the Drina River by the town of Višegrad, the last place where he had seen his mother when he was taken away and where he had felt a sharp pain in his breast as the last memory of his home.

The building of the bridge began in 1566. The first builder, Abidaga, was famous for his efficiency and the strict, at times cruel, methods of accomplishing his tasks. The bridge was built by slave labor conscripted from the nearby Serbian villages. The peasants not only resented having to work as slaves; they saw in the building of the bridge a sinister symbol of Turkish might. For that reason, they sabotaged the bridge's progress, often destroying at night what was built during the day. To frighten the distrusting and rebellious populace into submission and obedience, Abidaga caught one of them, Radisav, and had him impaled on the site of the bridge. The excruciatingly painful process of his death lasted several days.

The bridge was finally completed in 1571, a beautiful structure of eleven arches rising above the turbulent Drina, with the *kapia,* an elevated fixture in the middle of the bridge where people could sit, as a focal point. A caravansary was also built next to the bridge for tired travelers. Thus began the bridge's long influence on every aspect of life for the people on the shores as they finally resigned themselves to the bridge, learning to like it because of its usefulness and its uncommon beauty. Mehmed Pasha was stabbed to death by a deranged dervish only a few years after the construction, without having seen the object of his dreams fully completed. As he was dying, he felt again a sharp pain in his breast. Although he had accomplished many other things as a vezir, his name in Bosnia would forever be remembered by this bridge.

Years and decades passed, life kept changing, the floods came, and the Muslims, the Christians, and the Jews mingled, but the bridge survived everything, shining "clean, young and unalterable, strong and lovely in its perfection, stronger than all that time might bring and men imagine to do." As Serbia began to rise against the Turks at the beginning of the nineteenth century, the bridge witnessed the beheading of two Serbs, Jelisije and Mile, at the *kapia* as a warning to the rebels—the first of many acts of intimidation and revenge. Yet the bridge remained unchanged and unchangeable. The Turks withdrew gradually from Serbia from 1825 to 1850, cholera and plague visited the inhabitants on the shores, and the unquiet waters kept passing beneath the bridge's smooth and perfect arches, but nothing changed the bridge itself. It became a focal point of life in the town and surrounding villages. A beautiful young girl named Fata jumped from the *kapia* to her death during her wedding procession because her father was about to force her to marry a man whom she did not love. When Bosnia was placed under the Austrian protectorate, Alihodja Mutevelić, a shopkeeper, was nailed by his ear at the *kapia* by his town rival only because he did not believe that the Austrians would come or that the people of Višegrad should resist them if they did.

The Austrian presence brought important changes in Višegrad and to the bridge as the new began to replace the old. Trees were cut down and new ones planted, streets were repaired, drainage canals dug, public buildings built, permanent lighting installed, and a railway built. The caravansary was rebuilt into an army barracks, and the bridge itself seemed to be forgotten. The *kapia*, however, continued to witness interesting events. For the first time, women were allowed to sit on it. Milan Glasicanin, an inveterate gambler, was cured of his vice by being challenged to gamble for his life by a mysterious gambling partner. Gregor Fedun, a young sentry from Galicia, committed suicide after having been tricked by two Serbian rebels, one of them a beautiful girl, into allowing them to cross the bridge. Salko Corkan, a powerful young Gipsy, danced precariously on the bridge railing and almost fell to his death after a drinking bout and the unsuccessful wooing of a girl. Lotte, a Galician Ashkenazi, built a hotel next to the bridge, bringing a new aspect to life around the bridge.

The Austrian annexation of Bosnia in 1908 ushered in yet another new age and more changes. The bridge was mined in case a war with neighboring Serbia began. The Serbian triumphs in the Balkan Wars brought new hopes for the Serbian population and fears for the Muslims. Most important, the new generation of young people gathered regularly around the *kapia* and held endless discussions about the current events, reflecting a sharp rise in national-istic feelings, as they defended their nationalist points of view. As Lotte's fortunes declined and the young Serbian teachers Zorka and Glasicanin dreamed of emigrating to America, the first bombs of World War I fell on the bridge. Yet the bridge still stood between the two warring sides. When it was finally destroyed, it took along Alihodja as a witness of the centuries-old history of the town, the people, and the bridge itself.

Critical Evaluation:

Ivo Andrić, a leading Yugoslav writer for four decades and the only Nobel Prize winner among the southern Slav writers, was always interested in his native Bosnia, and many of his works have Bosnia as a background. *The Bridge on the Drina* is a perfect example. The story of the bridge can be seen as a survey of Bosnian history between 1516 and 1914.

The story is completely historical. As a lifelong diplomat of the kingdom of Yugoslavia, Andrić was also an astute student of history, and he often studied historical facts and documents in preparation for the writing of his works. Even his doctoral thesis, "The Development of the Spiritual Life of Bosnia Under the Influence of Turkish Sovereignty" (1924), reveals his passion for history; it also served him well while writing this novel and other works. *The Bridge on the Drina* encompasses the entire period of the Turkish rule of the Balkans, mirroring the birth and death of the Ottoman occupation of Bosnia. It is a broadly conceived panorama of cultural changes brought about by the Turkish reign and of the multicultural and multireligious nation resulting from it. It also depicts the inevitable and multifaceted conflicts of the area. The novel is, therefore, a good source of general information about Bosnia, although not a substitute for a scholarly history.

On a personal level, *The Bridge on the Drina* serves its author as a tribute to his childhood. As a little boy, he was brought to Višegrad after the death of his father and left there by his mother to live with relatives. It is no wonder that the mentor of the bridge, Mehmed Pasha Sokolli, ordered the bridge built as a memory of his childhood. Thus, the story of the bridge embodies a return to one's roots and a monument to one's childhood.

Another symbolic connotation of the bridge lies in its long life, outlasting many generations and all the changes through the centuries since its construction. Andrić concludes no fewer than twelve chapters out of twenty-four with a short paragraph extolling the bridge as a symbol of the permanence of all life. Considering the constant changes taking place around the bridge, its permanence serves as a comforting and life-affirming value.

Andrić imparts yet another symbolic meaning to the bridge by calling it a thing of beauty, a reflection of humanity's age-old desire to create beauty and to enrich life. The inborn need of humanity to express itself in the arts found its fulfillment in the creation of this beautiful edifice that defies transience.

The final symbolic interpretation of the bridge lies in its spanning of the two shores, as if connecting two worlds, the east and the west, and the different nationalities, religions, and cultures of Bosnia. Himself a diplomat who saw the main key to success in the art of compromise, Andrić used the metaphor of the bridge to underline the need for minimizing differences for the sake of living in harmony. The tragic events of Bosnia over the centuries clearly show what happens when this plea for harmony goes unheeded. In this sense, *The Bridge on the Drina* manifests an eerie mystical quality uncommon for a work of literature.

Andrić's narrative is characterized by a measured realistic style, reflecting the stoic firmness and beauty of the bridge. Yet beneath that calm exterior, life manifests itself in many forms and events are never static. As his translator, Lovett F. Edwards, notes, Andrić's style has "the sweep and surge of the sea, slow and yet profound, with occasional flashes of wit and irony." The novel is unusual in that it covers a long period of time, making it difficult to concentrate on character development. The episodic nature of narration, however, lends itself to the creation of individual pieces that stand by themselves. When put together, they create a remarkable mosaic, echoing the principal message of Andrić's entire philosophy that life is an incomprehensible miracle that is constantly being consumed and eroded, yet one that lasts and stands firmly like the bridge on the Drina.

Vasa D. Mihailovich

Bibliography:
Bergman, Gun. *Turkisms in Ivo Andrić's "Na Drini ćuprija." Examined from the Point of View of Literary Style*. Uppsala, Sweden: Almqvist & Wiksell, 1969. The author examines the use of Turkisms in *The Bridge on the Drina* from both the linguistic and the literary point of view.
Goy, E. D. "The Work of Ivo Andrić." *Slavonic and East European Review* 41 (1963): 301-326. One of the best introductions to Andrić in English. Goy dwells on the main points in Andrić's life and creativity, specifying in each work its most important characteristics. In *The Bridge on the Drina*, for example, Andrić has solved the dilemma of existence through the beauty of creation.

Hawkesworth, Celia. *Ivo Andrić: Bridge Between East and West*. London: Athlone Press, 1984. An excellent overall portrait of Andrić the man and the writer. The author discusses in detail every important feature of his works, underlining the importance of *The Bridge on the Drina* as his seminal work.

Mihailovich, Vasa D. "The Reception of the Works of Ivo Andrić in the English-Speaking World." *Southeastern Europe* 9 (1982): 41-52. A survey of articles and reviews on Andrić in English through 1980. Useful for both beginners and established scholars.

Mukerji, Vanita Singh. *Ivo Andrić: A Critical Biography*. New York: MacFarland, 1990. Another general introduction to Andrić. Not as significant and exhaustive as Hawkesworth's volume, but still useful for finding out about the basic features of Andrić's works.

BRITANNICUS

Type of work: Drama
Author: Jean Baptiste Racine (1639-1699)
Type of plot: Tragedy
Time of plot: 55 C.E.
Locale: Rome, the palace of Néron
First performed: 1669; first published, 1670 (English translation, 1714)

Principal characters:
BRITANNICUS, Claudius' son by the wife who preceded Agrippine
AGRIPPINE, Claudius' widow
NÉRON, Agrippine's son, Emperor of Rome
JUNIE, betrothed to Britannicus
NARCISSE, Britannicus' tutor
ALBINA, Agrippine's confidante
BURRHUS, Néron's tutor

The Story:

In the anteroom of the imperial palace Agrippine waited to speak with Néron, her son. The impatient nature of his character had at last revealed itself in antagonistic behavior toward Britannicus, and Agrippine feared that she would next incur his disfavor. Albina was convinced of the emperor's continued loyalty to his mother. Agrippine felt that if Néron were indeed noble, the fact that she had won the throne for him would ensure his devotion; but if he were ignoble, the fact of his obligation would turn him against her.

On the previous night Néron had abducted Junie, to whom Britannicus was betrothed, a deed possibly motivated by resentment against Agrippine, who had begun to support Britannicus in an attempt to preserve her position in the future if Néron were to turn against her. Albina assured Agrippine that her public power and honor, at least, had not decreased. Agrippine, however, needed the assurance of a more personal trust. She confided that once Néron had turned her aside from the throne on which she customarily sat in the Senate. She was also denied all private audience with him.

Agrippine, reproaching Burrhus for disloyalty to her, accused him of attempting to gain power over Néron. Burrhus was convinced that his prime loyalty was to the emperor who ruled well by his own authority. Néron feared that Britannicus' children would inherit the throne if he married Junie. Britannicus, distracted by his loss of Junie, complained of Néron's harshness. Agrippine sent him to the house of Pallas, the freedman, where she would meet him later. Britannicus told Narcisse, who encouraged him to join Agrippine, that he still wished to claim the throne.

Néron decided to disregard his mother's reproaches, which he called unjust, and to banish Pallas, the friend and adviser of Agrippine, who, he thought, had corrupted Britannicus. Narcisse assured him that Rome approved of his abduction of Junie, and Néron confessed that when he had seen her he had fallen in love with her. He was convinced by Narcisse that Britannicus was devoted to Junie and that she probably loved him in return. Narcisse insisted that the love of Junie would be won by a sign of favor from the emperor. Narcisse advised Néron to divorce Octavia, Britannicus' sister, and marry Junie. Néron feared Agrippine's wrath if he did so; only when he avoided her completely did he dare defy her wishes, for in her presence he was powerless. Narcisse informed Néron that Britannicus still trusted him; he was therefore dispatched to bring Britannicus for a meeting with Junie. Junie asked Néron what her crime had been and insisted that Britannicus was the most suitable person for her to marry, as he was the only other descendant of Augustus Caesar at court. When Néron said that he himself would marry her, Junie, appalled, begged him not to disgrace Octavia by doing so. Finally she realized that she could save Britannicus' life only by telling him, when they met, that he was to leave Rome. Néron intended to listen to their conversation.

At their interview, Britannicus was bewildered by Junie's coldness toward him and by her praise of the emperor. When he left, Néron reappeared, but Junie fled, weeping. Néron sent Narcisse to comfort Britannicus. Burrhus reported that Agrippine was angry at Néron, and he feared that she might plot against the emperor. When Néron refused to listen to Burrhus as he begged him not to divorce Octavia, the tutor realized that the emperor's true character was at last appearing.

Meanwhile, Agrippine planned to take Britannicus before the Roman army and to declare that she had wronged him by exalting Néron to the throne. By this action she hoped to win their allegiance to Britannicus. Burrhus told her that her scheme was impossible. Agrippine told Albina that if Néron married Junie and banished Britannicus, her own power would be ended. That condition she would never accept. Although Britannicus did not trust her, she planned with his cooperation to prevent Néron's marriage to Junie.

Although Narcisse had persuaded Britannicus that Junie was faithless, she nevertheless managed to see him and insisted that he flee to save his life. Accused of unfaithfulness, she explained that Néron had been listening during their previous meeting. Britannicus fell at her feet in gratitude for her continued love. In this situation Néron came upon them and demanded from Britannicus the obedience that through fear he intended to extort from all Rome. Later Néron ordered Britannicus arrested and Agrippine detained in the palace.

Burrhus advised Agrippine, before her audience with Néron, to be affectionate and even apologetic, and to make no demands on him. Instead, she explained to him exactly how she had procured the throne for him and reproached him for his present behavior. Néron, infuriated by her continued claims on him, realized that she had made him emperor only for her own glory. Accused of being a plotter, Agrippine denied that she had attempted to replace Néron with Britannicus; all she wanted was that Junie should be allowed to choose her own husband and that she herself should be able to see Néron when she wished. When Néron appeared to yield, Burrhus congratulated him. Néron had merely deceived Agrippine, however; he still intended to punish Britannicus. Burrhus then implored him to continue his just reign and be reconciled with Britannicus. Néron, again wavering, decided to meet Britannicus.

Narcisse had already prepared poison for Britannicus, but Néron declared he would not now use it. Narcisse, counseling him against clemency, said that Agrippine already publicly boasted of her regained control. He also insinuated that Burrhus was not to be trusted. Néron decided to plan his future actions with Narcisse.

Britannicus informed Junie that he was to be reconciled with Néron and voiced his conviction that she would be returned to him, but Junie, doubting Néron's sincerity, feared that Narcisse had deceived them. Agrippine, on the other hand, believed that her words had changed Néron completely and that her plans would be executed. Sometime after Britannicus had left for his audience with Néron, Burrhus returned and informed the women that Narcisse had poisoned Britannicus and that Néron, unmoved, had watched him die. Appalled by Néron's callousness, Burrhus determined to leave Rome.

Although Néron declared that the death of Britannicus had been inevitable, Junie fled from the palace. When Agrippine accused Néron of murder, Narcisse attempted to explain that Britannicus had been a traitor. Agrippine foretold that Néron had now set the pattern for his reign. After a public disturbance, Albina informed the court that at the statue of Augustus Junie had pledged herself to become a priestess of Vesta and that the crowd, to protect her, had killed Narcisse. Agrippine and Burrhus went to Néron to try to console him in his despair.

Critical Evaluation:

Jean Baptiste Racine's third play, *Andromache* (1667), established his mastery of the sentimental drama. In his fifth, *Britannicus*, he intended to prove his ability to write a Roman political tragedy to rival, and if possible surpass, the work of Pierre Corneille. The first performance was only moderately successful. Later its reputation improved after Louis XIV spoke highly of it. The play is constructed in keeping with Aristotle's unities, as was obligatory in seventeenth century French drama after the success of Corneille's neoclassic plays. The theme is Néron's first crime, which sets the pattern for the rest of his reign. Burrhus attempts to keep uppermost the good elements of Néron's character, while Narcisse, a supreme opportunist, works on the emperor's baser instincts. Although other plays by Racine have greater emotional insight and poetic beauty, *Britannicus* is a fine example of his command of verse and language and of his dramatic perception of the motivation of his characters.

Esteemed by many critics to be France's greatest composer of neoclassical tragedies, Racine was elected to the French Academy in 1673, after having established his concept of tragedy in *Bérénice* (1670). Racine's excellent education enabled him to brilliantly adapt Greek and Roman history to seventeenth century French plays; he composed eleven tragedies and one comedy in the style approved by the French Academy. Established in 1635, the French Academy had borrowed from Aristotle's *Poetics* (c. 334-323 B.C.E.) to create the French neoclassical style, with its emphasis on reason, order, clarity, and the unities of time, place, and action. The observance of decorum and verisimilitude aided the spectator in empathizing with the characters who represented the universality of the human condition.

Racine surpassed in popularity his rival Corneille, who preferred to modify Roman tragedies into plots with exterior action. Racine showed his genius for creating inner drama, a genius which culminated in 1677 with *Phaedra*, his masterpiece taken from Euripides. After *Phaedra*'s success, he was named the king's historiographer. Racine wrote his last two plays, *Esther* (1689) and *Athaliah* (1691), for Saint-Cyr's school, which was affiliated with Mme de Maintenon, in order to accommodate Louis XIV, who then appointed him to an advisory position.

After the success of *Andromache* in 1668, Racine responded to his rivals' criticism that he was incapable of treating subjects other than love by composing *Britannicus*. The principal theme of *Britannicus* is Agrippine's extreme domination of her son Néron and his destructive effort to extract himself from her powerful web. In fact, the French meaning of Agrippine's name refers to "gripping."

Agrippine's excessive attachment to the idea of controlling the thoughts and actions of her son Néron causes her to misinterpret situations. She tends to ascribe the wrong motives for her conduct. For example, Agrippine thinks her husband's murder was for her son's benefit. Agrippine's obsessive will to control others prevents her from loving anyone; she therefore becomes the victim of her tragic flaw. Agrippine reveals her inhumane appetite for power through the treatment of her son. She tries to destroy him mentally and physically. First, she tries to place guilt upon him when she tells him that he owes her a debt because she stole and murdered for him. She also speaks of the wonderful past, when a younger Néron left all the matters of state to her. Agrippine's second way to thwart her son's emotional development is to belittle him. She tells him that when he was still quite young, he exhibited unacceptable behavior and was noted for his anger, pride, and deceit. In order to break his spirit, his mother reinforces her negative attitude about his behavior by telling him that she kept his evil nature a secret. Agrippine then tries to have her son castrated; but Burrhus, Néron's tutor, tries to explain to her that since the people already revere her, she can release her control over her son. Burrhus' reasonable manner contrasts with her compulsive desire to dominate.

Agrippine's third attempt to cause her son's demise stems from jealousy. After her discovery of Néron's love for Junie, Agrippine, despite Burrhus' suggestion that she act in moderation, frantically summarizes her motherly sacrifices to secure her son's royal authority: her marriage to Claudius, her desire for Néron to be king, her consent from Claudius for Néron to marry Octavia, her insistence on Claudius' adoption of Néron, and her husband's murder. Disoriented, Agrippine accuses her son of deception and ingratitude. In order to subdue his mother's controlling behavior, Néron lies about allowing her to win in the affairs of state and in his personal life, declaring that he would become reconciled to Britannicus. Agrippine's reaction of excessive joy to Néron's pretended transformation contrasts with Junie's great sense of impending doom, producing a frightening atmosphere of suspense, which ends with the announcement of Britannicus' death. Agrippine is then able to see Néron as an individual rather than a part of her own personality.

Burrhus, who advocates the stoic values of self-control and resignation, has tried to teach Néron virtuous behavior, but Burrhus realizes he has misjudged the effectiveness of his teaching when Néron says that he would hug his rival in order to deceive him. Néron proceeds to erase the past from his mind and decides to gratify his present instincts. His next tutor, the evil Narcisse, encourages Néron to pursue his courtship of Junie despite her love for Britannicus. Narcisse is also instrumental in the murder of Britannicus. The evil character of Néron is further developed when he impassively observes Junie's pain of having to tell Britannicus she does not love him. Observing pain allows Néron to feel a sense of power. Néron experiences the same feelings of control as his mother.

On the other hand, Britannicus and Junie portray the concept of virtuous behavior, as does Burrhus. Britannicus serves in the plot as an object for Agrippine's machinations and a reason for Narcisse to be in the palace; he also thwarts Néron's plans because of his love for Junie. The conversation that takes place between Britannicus and Néron depicts this contrast in character. Néron's frantic insistence upon obedience reflects his feeling of weakness and leads to the evil poisoning of Britannicus.

Linked to the play's thematic exploration of good and evil are symbols. The palace, for example, is endowed with a past history and various chambers; it is a labyrinth, disorienting the characters. The personification of the palace as being able to sigh, hear, and see conveys a monstrous image of evil. The protagonists all meet their doom: Agrippine and Burrhus do not succeed in their endeavors; Britannicus and Narcisse die, Junie renounces the world, and Néron, unable to face reality, looks inward with despair.

"Critical Evaluation" by Linda Prewett Davis

Bibliography:
Abraham, Claude. *Jean Racine.* Boston: Twayne, 1977. Intended for the general reader; all quotations are in English. Gives a brief biographical sketch and discusses Racine's major works.

Butler, Philip. *Racine: A Study*. London: Heinemann, 1974. Introduction to Racine, with a section on how to read his works. Indicates the traditional approach to literary criticism as well as nontraditional approaches.

Lapp, John C. *Aspects of Racinian Tragedy*. Toronto: University of Toronto Press, 1955. Contains excellent thematic analyses. An informative account of Racine's dramatic art.

Turnell, Martin. *Jean Racine, Dramatist*. London: Hamish Hamilton, 1972. Shows how Racine may be considered the greatest French tragic dramatist. Gives an interesting analysis of Racine's imagery and illuminating study on each of his plays.

Weinberg, Bernard. *The Art of Jean Racine*. Chicago: University of Chicago Press, 1963. Presents Racine's tragedies arranged chronologically in order to show how his dramatic art evolved. Refers to neoclassicism to explain Racine's plays.

BROAD AND ALIEN IS THE WORLD

Type of work: Novel
Author: Ciro Alegría (1909-1967)
Type of plot: Social realism
Time of plot: 1912-1926
Locale: Peru
First published: El mundo es ancho y ajeno, 1941 (English translation, 1941)

> *Principal characters:*
> ROSENDO MAQUIS, mayor of a community of Indians
> DON AMENABAR, the tyrannical owner of a neighboring ranch
> BISMARCK RUIZ, a rascal lawyer
> CORREA ZAVALA, a lawyer friendly to the Indians
> FIERO VASQUEZ, a highwayman friendly to the Indians
> BENITO CASTRO, an Indian who had lived away from the village

The Story:

Rosendo Maquis was the mayor of Rumi, a small Indian town in the Peruvian uplands. The village was a communal organization, as it had been for centuries. Its life was peaceful, for the Rumi Indians were an agricultural people. Rosendo's only troubles were personal. His wife was dying, and he had been sent into the mountains to find herbs to be used in making medicine for the sick woman. On his way back to the village, he saw an evil omen in the passage of a snake across his path. Troubled times, he felt, lay ahead.

That same night, Rosendo's wife died, and her death marked the beginning of many misfortunes for the mayor and his people. A few days later, it became known that Don Amenabar, whose ranch bordered the Indian village, was filing suit to take away the best of the land belonging to Rumi. Rosendo and his selectmen saddled their horses and rode to the nearby town to get a lawyer to defend them. They hired Bismarck Ruiz, a man who had a poor reputation in the town because of his love affair with La Castelana, a notorious woman of very expensive tastes. In return for a large fee, Ruiz promised to win the suit for the Indians.

Life went on as usual in the village during the days before the trial. There was a cattle roundup, to which Don Amenabar sent men to collect the cattle belonging to him. Although he did not pay the grazing fee, and the Indians knew it would be futile to ask it of him, he charged them a high fee to redeem any cattle that accidentally wandered onto his lands. The Indians were also busy building a school, for the commissioner of education of the province had promised them a schoolmaster as soon as they had a hygienic place for the school to convene.

In an effort to learn what Don Amenabar was plotting against them, the Indians sent one of their number to the ranch to sell baskets and woven mats. When Don Amenabar saw the Indian on his ranch, he ordered his overseers to give the unlucky fellow a hundred lashes, a punishment that would have killed many men.

Finally, the case came to court. The Indians felt at first that they would win. Don Amenabar's men had removed the stones marking the community boundaries, but the Indians had returned them. The return, they felt, was indicative of their success. The case was soon over, however, thanks to a large number of perjuring witnesses who testified against the Indians by claiming that the people of Rumi had encroached on Don Amenabar's land. Even the judge had received money and preferment from the rancher.

The Indians' lawyer immediately made up a brief for an appeal to a higher court, but Don Amenabar's men, disguised as the followers of Fiero Vasquez, the outlaw, stole the mailbag containing the documents as the mail carrier passed through a desolate part of the Andes. Don Amenabar did not want the authorities in Lima to hear of the affair because he wished to send his son to the legislature and, eventually, to become a senator himself.

Correa Zavala, a young lawyer fired with zeal for the cause of the Peruvian Indians, took up the villagers' case. It had become clear to the Indians that Bismarck Ruiz was not helping them, and they had evidence that he was really in the pay of Don Amenabar. The young lawyer made up a long brief that included many documents from the history of the village. These were sent to the capital with a guard of troops and Indians, for their loss would have made it difficult to prove the village's legal existence as a community.

All was to no avail, however, for at last the day came when the court order, enforced by troops, was delivered to the Indians. They were to leave the most fertile of their lands and move to what was left to them in the higher areas. When one of the village women went to her lover, Fiero Vasquez, the notorious highwayman and bandit, he came with his band of cutthroats to help the Indians drive off the people who were forcing them to leave. Rosendo refused aid from the outlaws because he knew that resistance would have been useless. His point was made when a villager was machine-gunned to death for daring to kill one of Don Amenabar's men with a rock.

Even in the highlands the Indians were not safe from Don Amenabar, who wanted to make them slaves to work a mine that he owned on another piece of property. He had resolved never to be satisfied until they were delivered into his hands. His men raided the Indians' cattle herds, even creeping up to the corrals in the village at night. At last, the prize bull of the village disappeared. The Indians found the animal on Don Amenabar's ranch. In spite of the brand, Don Amenabar refused to return the bull and ordered Rosendo off the ranch. That same night the mayor returned, determined to regain the animal for his people. He found the bull, but as he was leading the animal away, he was captured. Taken into town, Rosendo was jailed on a charge of thievery. At his trial, he was found guilty and sentenced to a long term in prison.

While Rosendo was in jail, Fiero Vasquez was captured and placed in the cell with Rosendo. Having plenty of resources to make bribes, the highwayman made arrangements to break out of prison. When he escaped, Rosendo was blamed. The prison guards beat the old man so severely that he died within a few hours.

Not long after the death of Rosendo, a young Indian he had reared came back to the village after an absence of many years. Benito Castro, a soldier and a gaucho, was quickly accepted as a leader by the Indians, who needed the wisdom and aid of someone who had been outside the mountain village. Under Castro's leadership, the people drained swampy meadows and rebuilt their village in a better location in the highlands. Their relative prosperity, however, was short-lived, for Don Amenabar still planned to enslave them or drive them into hiding. At last, a large detachment of troops, augmented by men convinced that the Indians were mutinous against the government, attacked the village. In a long battle with the forces sent against them, the Indians were utterly defeated, their leaders were killed, and the village was destroyed. The few survivors, told by the dying Benito Castro to save themselves, had no idea where they could go to seek a refuge in that harsh, lawless land.

Critical Evaluation:

Ciro Alegría's panoramic novel mirrors life in the Peruvian Andes early in the twentieth century. Its many themes include defense of the downtrodden, justice, injustice, the tragedy of human life, dishonest lawyers and courts, litigation over land boundaries, suffering, villainy and heroism, and racism.

The novel's power lies in its defense of the abused Indian populace of Rumi. The reader lives with Rumi's people throughout the story and identifies with them. Unforgettable is the noble old leader of Rumi, Rosendo Maquis, and his efforts, ideals, character, misfortunes, and death. Grave and good like the community of Rumi itself, Rosendo incarnates his people, who are idealized by Alegría. The dark night and demise of Rumi itself is ably painted by Alegría, giving the novel an epic reach. Besides its many regionalist qualities, moreover, *Broad and Alien Is the World* has a well-developed plot and generally convincing characterization that rank it as one of the better contributions to the literature of *indianismo*, which defends the Indian peoples of Latin America. The plot reaches a final crescendo with the destruction of Rumi and all that the recently murdered Rosendo stood for; but the noble Rosendo, his wife the pathetic Pascuala, black-clad Fiero Vasquez, and Benito Castro still live and stand out in the reader's memory.

Alegría's language is poetic, lively, and colorful. He uses standard Spanish laced with occasional regionalisms, including Quechua words, to good effect. Dialogue is authentic. The novel is also unwieldy, structurally chaotic, and lacking in careful planning (owing to its hasty composition; it was completed in a matter of months).

Geography is always a silent presence in the novel. At times, it is almost a dominant character, reflecting the fact of the importance of geography in Peru's culture. One sees the lofty Andean sierra with its crisp, thin air, its gaunt landscapes, sparse vegetation, and rocky soil, and pastel Rumi with its cobbled, windswept streets and huddled houses. Rumi's people grow potatoes and tend their llamas, but they chew coca to cope with hunger and the cold, and their chests are like those of pouter pigeons since the air has so little oxygen.

Alegría was born and reared on a *hacienda* in the same region in which he set his novel. Although his parents were his first teachers, he later credited the whole Peruvian people with having molded him and caused him to understand their grief. An Indian wet nurse cradled him in her arms and taught him to walk; he played as a child with Indian children, and later "saw things that he couldn't forget." In *Broad and Alien Is the World*, thus, Alegría penetrates the Indian mind, revealing the native's feeling for the soil, his poverty, stoicism, dignity, superstition, and occasional lapsing into alcoholism or sexual license. Unfortunately, Alegría ladled out some crude propaganda in his lambasting of such types as white men, priests, and landowners. These stock, one-dimensional figures are reminiscent of Diego Rivera's murals with their pasty-faced, evil whites, bloated priests, cruel-faced landowners, and clean-cut Indians. Thus, Don Amenabar, Bismarck Ruiz, and the cowardly, servile priest are not convincingly drawn. Alegría reveals unconscious prejudice in this respect, although his own family owned land and was Caucasian in appearance. As is often the case in Spanish American literature, the novel is inspired and sincerely motivated but betrays the fact that its author belongs to a privileged social class and has not been as truly a member of the working classes as, say, John Steinbeck, Jack London, or José Antonio Villarreal.

One of Alegría's great contributions is his pictorial depiction of rural Peruvian society. The reader experiences many social types and their folkways, traditions, mentality, society, and sorrows. In Rumi, readers see the kaleidoscopic results of four centuries of blending between Inca and Spaniard. One of the finest examples is the colorful sketch of Rumi's village meeting, with its touches of imagery wherein bronzed Indian faces mingle with lighter mestizos and an occasional white face, against a background of Inca and Spanish dress, manners, postures, and gestures. The novel is thus a storehouse of all that has happened to Peru, from the days of the Inca Empire, through the dramatic conquest by the Spaniards, and the four ensuing centuries of racial and cultural blending. It is said that all of Alegría's works demonstrate a determination to create an original literature that not only interprets the Peruvian reality but also expresses contemporary Peru's peculiarities. He therefore draws the mestizo, whose heart is rooted to the Peruvian soil and in whose soul exists a harmonious mixture. A mestizo is the central personality in all of Alegría's novels, with the possible exception of *Broad and Alien Is the World*, and even in that work, the mestizo, Benito Castro, inherits Rosendo Maquis' role and develops into the most significant personality of the latter part of the novel.

Broad and Alien Is the World is essentially a novel of the high sierra as other Spanish American novels are novels of the pampa, llanos, desert, jungle, or city. It nevertheless broadens the social and human conflict beyond the boundaries of the community of Rumi to Peru's coast and jungle—nowhere under the Peruvian flag is there a place that is not hostile to the Indian. Benito Castro is regarded as an extremist agitator in Lima; one of Rosendo's sons is blinded by the explosion of a rubber ball in the eastern jungles; Calixto Paucar dies in a mine shaft; other emigrants from Rumi meet misfortune in many parts of the Peruvian Republic, demonstrating that, for the Indian at least, broad and alien is the world. Alegría's great achievement, thus, is that his masterpiece has undoubtedly helped to implement reform in favor of the mountain-dwelling Indians and mestizos of central Peru, for their lot has slowly but surely improved since the day when, while writing a scene for another novel concerning the expulsion of some Indians from their community, Alegría was struck with such force "by an intense gust of ideas and memories" that the inspiration for his masterpiece was born.

The novel is a veritable storehouse of Peruvian lore, giving as it does a detailed picture of the social structure of the Indian community, its innate dignity, its traditions, and its overwhelming tragedy. Alegría was exiled from Peru in 1934 because of his political views.

"Critical Evaluation" by William Freitas

Bibliography:
Aldrich, Earl M., Jr. *The Modern Short Story in Peru*. Madison: University of Wisconsin Press, 1966. Historical survey introducing major writers, styles, and themes of the Peruvian short story of Alegría's day. Alegría's short story production is analyzed within the context of the author's literary contributions.
Early, Eileen. *Joy in Exile: Ciro Alegría's Narrative Art*. Lanham, Md.: University Press of America, 1980. Survey of Alegría's short stories and novels. Traces Alegría's major literary motifs within the context of Peruvian literature.
Flores, Angel. "Ciro Alegría." *Spanish American Authors: The Twentieth Century*. New York: H. W. Wilson, 1992. Surveys Alegría's production, including bibliographical sources. Written primarily in Spanish. An excellent starting point to Alegría's works.
Foster, David William, and Virginia Ramos Foster. "Alegría, Ciro." In *Modern Latin American Literature*, edited by David William Foster and Virginia Ramos Foster. New York: Frederick Ungar, 1975. Excerpts from critical studies. An excellent starting point to Alegría's best-known works.
González-Pérez, Armando. *Social Protest and Literary Merit in "Huasipungo" and "El mundo es ancho y ajeno."* Milwaukee: University of Wisconsin-Milwaukee, Center for Latin America, 1988. Alegría's two most well-known novels are analyzed in terms of his ideological views. Alegría is presented as an influential intellectual who participated in social movements that promoted the advancement of the indigenous population.

THE BROKEN JUG

Type of work: Drama
Author: Heinrich von Kleist (1777-1811)
Type of plot: Farce
Time of plot: Late eighteenth century
Locale: A village in The Netherlands
First performed: 1808; first published, 1811 as *Der zerbrochene Krug* (English translation, 1830)

Principal characters:
ADAM, the village judge
WALTER, a counselor-at-law
LICHT, the clerk of the court
MARTHE RULL, a villager
EVE, her daughter
RUPRECHT, Eve's suitor
BRIGITTE, Ruprecht's aunt
VEIT TUMPEL, Ruprecht's father

The Story:

Licht, clerk of the court of Huisum, a village near Utrecht in The Netherlands, appeared in the courtroom one morning to prepare for the day's proceedings. He discovered Adam, the village judge, in a generally disreputable state, nursing a badly lacerated face and an injured leg. When he asked the judge how he came to be in such a condition, he received a highly questionable story about an altercation with a clothesline and a goat. Licht, sensing that there had been some philandering involved, hinted as much to Adam, but the judge naturally denied the clerk's suggestions.

There were more important matters to discuss. A peasant passing through Holla, a neighboring village, had heard that Counselor Walter, of the High Court at Utrecht, had inspected the courts in Holla and was preparing to come to Huisum on a tour of inspection this very day. That was serious business, particularly when Adam learned that in Holla both the clerk of the court and the judge had been suspended because their affairs were not in order; the judge had almost succeeded in killing himself when he tried to hang himself in his own barn. Needless to say, Adam's affairs were in no better shape than those of his unfortunate neighbors. Before he could get his clothes on and make an attempt to restore order, however, a servant came to announce that Counselor Walter had arrived. Adam tried to defer immediate action by telling an even more unlikely story about his accident and begging that the inspection be delayed. Licht was calmer, however, and insisted that Adam receive the counselor.

At the height of the chaos, Adam, discovering that he could not find his wig, was informed by a spying servant girl that he had come home without it after eleven o'clock the night before. He naturally denied this claim also and told the servant girl that she had lost her mind; he suddenly remembered that the cat had kittened in his wig and therefore he could not use it. The girl was sent to borrow a wig from the verger's wife, after being reminded not to mention the matter to the verger himself. Before the girl could return, Counselor Walter appeared, expressing regrets that he had not been able to announce himself in advance and assuring Adam and Licht that he knew matters would be only tolerably in order but that he expected little more. He then demanded that the court proceedings get under way, just as the servant girl returned bearing the calamitous news that she could not borrow a wig. Though it was highly irregular for a judge to sit without his wig, Walter insisted that the petitions begin, wig or no wig.

When the doors were opened, Marthe Rull and her daughter Eve charged in accompanied by Veit Tumpel and his son Ruprecht; all were in a high state of agitation over a broken pitcher. Marthe accused Ruprecht, who was engaged to marry Eve, of breaking the pitcher, but Ruprecht denied doing so. Eve was having a mild case of hysterics because she was about to lose Ruprecht, who swore that he never wished to see her again and kept calling her a strumpet. Marthe vociferously demanded that justice be done because she felt that Eve's good name had been destroyed along with the pitcher.

In the middle of this confusion, Judge Adam, wigless, appeared in his robes to open his court; he was visibly shaken at the scene before him. Eve pleaded with her mother to leave well enough alone, while Adam tried unsuccessfully to talk with Eve about a piece of paper. Counselor Walter finally insisted that court begin. Marthe, brought to the stand, accused Ruprecht of breaking the pitcher. He denied the charge and demanded that she prove her accusation. Adam agreed completely with Marthe and tried to dismiss the case, but the counselor would not let him. So the trial proceeded.

As the evidence was presented, it came out that the pitcher had been broken at eleven o'clock the night before. Marthe had heard voices coming from Eve's room and had rushed in to find the pitcher smashed, Eve in tears, and Ruprecht standing in the middle of the room. Ruprecht was the obvious suspect, but according to him a third party had been present whom he could not identify. According to Marthe, Eve too had admitted that there was a third party in the room, but she refused to identify him. When Ruprecht finally took the stand, he testified that he had come to make a late call on Eve and had found her near the gate to her house with another man. He had watched until they went to Eve's room; then, overwhelmed by fury, he had rushed after them and broken down the door, smashing the pitcher just as someone jumped out of the window and got caught in the grapevine. He had seized the door latch and beaten the culprit over the head with it, in return receiving a handful of sand in the face. He thought the man was the village cobbler, but he could not be sure.

Adam was quite anxious to assign the blame to the cobbler and thereby prevent Eve from giving testimony, but his attempts were unsuccessful. When Eve took the stand, she cleared Ruprecht of smashing the pitcher but refused to identify the third party.

There had however been another participant in the evening's affair—Brigitte, Ruprecht's aunt. She appeared in court with a wig that was identified as Adam's and a story of having seen the devil leave Eve's house around eleven o'clock the night before. She had followed the tracks in the snow the next morning in order to find the devil's abode, and the tracks had led to the judge's very door. Adam, declaring that this account had nothing to do with the case, proceeded to sentence Ruprecht.

The judge's decision prompted Eve to confess the whole story. It seemed that Adam had told Eve that Ruprecht would be drafted and sent to India but that he had the power to save Ruprecht from this fate; and he had forged a certificate that Eve had gone to her room to sign. He had taken the occasion to try to seduce her, at which time Ruprecht burst in, smashed the pitcher, and beat Adam, who had jumped out of the window. Before the whole story was out, however, Judge Adam had run off to escape a beating. The only person left unsatisfied was Marthe, who planned to take her pitcher to the High Court in Utrecht and demand justice.

Critical Evaluation:
Heinrich von Kleist wrote the one-act comedy *The Broken Jug* at the request of friends who

had seen a French copper engraving entitled *La Cruche cassée*, which depicted a pair of lovers, a scolding older woman holding a broken jug, and a judge. In the original manuscript, Kleist also alluded to the influence of Sophocles' *Oedipus Tyrannus* (429 B.C.E.). In both plays, the crime has already been committed and the audience knows the identity of the culprit. The action on the stage, therefore, consists of unraveling various past events for the purpose of naming this person. Johann Wolfgang von Goethe was the first to produce the play in 1808 in Weimar, where it proved a dismal failure. Goethe blamed the unkind reception on the play's slow action, not realizing that his own arbitrary division of the thirteen scenes into three acts had destroyed the unity of the work. Staging it after a long opera had not helped matters either. Perhaps the German playwright Friedrich Hebbel pronounced the most appropriate judgment on it after its 1850 Vienna production when he said that the only failure the play could have was that of its audience.

The Broken Jug derives its humor from the ridiculous situation involving a country judge holding court proceedings for a case in which he is guilty of the crime. The plaintiff, the defendants, and his superior all depend on him to preside over the case, yet all the while he himself—and soon too the audience—knows full well that it is he who broke the jug. Judge Adam's ability effortlessly to tell outrageous lies is one important source of the play's comedy. Adam is a bald old man with a clubfoot who feels attracted toward Marthe Rull's sweet, innocent daughter Eve. In creating a physically repulsive Adam, Kleist does not intend to provoke laughter at physical shortcomings. Rather, Adam's deformities are meant to symbolize his disgusting character and his decadence. Yet Adam's looks also arouse pity, for it is because of them that the audience realizes how all too human he is. His talent for inventing lies, which he uses to postpone the discovery of his complicity in the case, makes him into a stage clown putting up a show.

Kleist employed a colloquial language to re-create the realistic village scene. The characters use rough language with clever double meanings, thus creating a bawdy atmosphere. Their coarse sense of humor probably contributed to the lack of appreciation of the Weimar audience, which was used to seeing sentimental dramas.

Adam immediately wants to pronounce Ruprecht guilty, as he wants the potentially dangerous situation to end as soon as possible. The district judge Walter intervenes, however, to let the accused defend himself. As a higher official of the court he feels responsible for ensuring that the case is heard properly. Whenever Adam veers into irrelevant descriptions, Walter uses his authority to bring him back to the trial. Kleist thus creates an extended and very comical tug-of-war between Adam and his chief on the one hand, and Adam and the plaintiff Marthe on the other. A further source of merriment is that Marthe is more concerned about her jug than her daughter's reputation. She pursues the culprit relentlessly, without considering that while doing so she may be destroying her daughter's good name. At the play's conclusion, she is still pursuing the vain hope of recompense for her jug; she hardly seems to notice that her daughter and Ruprecht have reconciled.

In Eve, Kleist has created a strong, positive female character. She embodies his ideal of a sensitive woman who believes that trust is the ultimate component of a relationship. Because of her love for Ruprecht, she silently endures all kinds of aspersions on her character. Ruprecht's jealousy may make him disown her, but she staunchly refuses to expose Adam, as that would mean she would not get the medical certificate from him that is needed to save Ruprecht from military conscription. On the other hand, she cannot let Ruprecht appear as the culprit, because he would then be justified in believing that she had been unfaithful to him. Only after Adam has hurriedly pronounced a jail sentence for Ruprecht, does Eve break her silence.

Kleist not only wrote one of the best German comedies, he also presented a social critique of his time. The description of the village courtroom, with its leftover food and drinks strewn amidst various documents, hardly resembles a place of justice. On the other hand, Judge Adam's superior, the district judge Walter, is so bent on maintaining the dignity of the court that he refuses to pronounce Adam guilty even though he knows he has committed the crime. It is more important for him to maintain respect for the authority residing in a judge's position than to uphold the truth. Instead of being jailed, Adam is therefore merely suspended; his ambitious clerk, Licht, is promoted to the level of judge. In Kleist's treatment, the theme that justice matters just as little to the people at the courthouse, who all have their individual concerns, becomes yet one more source of hilarity in *The Broken Jug*.

"Critical Evaluation" by Vibha Bakshi Gokhale

Bibliography:
Doctorow, E. L. Introduction to *Plays by Heinrich von Kleist*, edited by Walter Hinderer. New York: Continuum, 1982. Doctorow discusses the farcical nature of *The Broken Jug*. The translation in this volume remains true to nineteenth century colloquial English, which imparts a rustic tone to the play.

Greenberg, Martin, trans. *The Broken Jug*. In *Five Plays by Heinrich von Kleist*. New Haven, Conn.: Yale University Press, 1988. Excellent translation of *The Broken Jug* into colloquial English that successfully brings out the coarse and bawdy sense of humor of the original. The volume also contains a fine introduction to the plays.

Maass, Joachim. *Kleist: A Biography*. Translated by Ralph Manheim. New York: Farrar, Straus & Giroux, 1983. A light treatment of the writer, written in an anecdotal, humorous style. Discusses the psychological torment of Kleist's characters. Presents a succinct analysis of Adam's corrupt but likable character.

McGlathery, James M. *Desire's Sway: The Plays and Stories of Heinrich von Kleist*. Detroit, Mich.: Wayne State University Press, 1983. Refers to *The Broken Jug* as a sexual comedy. Cleverly interprets Adam's various statements as expressions of his sexual fantasies.

Reeve, William C. *Kleist on Stage: 1804-1987*. Montreal: McGill-Queen's University Press, 1993. An excellent reference source for a history of productions of Kleist's plays. Gives an account of various interpretations of *The Broken Jug* and discusses the merits of actors who have played the part of Adam.

THE BRONZE HORSEMAN

Type of work: Poetry
Author: Alexander Pushkin (1799-1837)
Type of plot: Historical realism
Time of plot: 1703 and 1824
Locale: St. Petersburg, Russia
First published: Medniy vsadnik, 1837 (English translation, 1899)

> *Principal characters:*
> PETER THE GREAT, czar of Russia, 1672-1725
> THE BRONZE HORSEMAN, a statue of Peter
> EVGENY, a clerk
> PARASHA, the woman Evgeny loves

The Story:

Peter the Great stood on the desolate Baltic shore on the northwest borders of his domain and gazed off into the distance. The very landscape around him seemed unformed, unclear; the land was soft and marshy, the sun shrouded in mist, the Finnish huts flimsy and temporary. Peter's design, however, was quite clear. Here, on the delta of the river Neva, out of nothing, he would build St. Petersburg, a fortress against the powerful Swedes, a new capital, a magnet to ships of all nations, a "window into Europe."

One hundred years had passed, according to the narrator, and the city had grown not just into a busy port, a strategic fortress, but also into a network of granite-faced rivers and canals lined with palaces, parks, and gardens, a metropolis whose power and elegance put dowdy old Moscow, the "dowager" capital, decidedly in the shade. It was all Peter's creation: the majesty of the architecture, the vast expanses of the city lit by the "white nights" of early summer, the sounds of winter—of sleighs and lavish balls—the sights and sounds of Imperial troops on parade. Let the city flaunt its beauty, and let Peter's eternal sleep go undisturbed, said the narrator. However, there was a certain, terrible time and a sad story to be told.

On a dark November evening in 1824, a young man named Evgeny lay in his rented rooms in an unfashionable suburban quarter and listened to the rain and wind. He could not sleep, and he thought idly that it would have been nice to have had more brains and money, or at least someone else's better luck. However, he did not bother mourning his more illustrious ancestors or envying them either. Instead, his thoughts turned to his beloved Parasha, whom he hoped to marry one day. They would find a little place to live, and they would have children; a peaceful, humdrum life would go on until those children's children would, one day, bury him and faithful Parasha. Vaguely troubled by the storm, Evgeny fell asleep while the river rose and rose. By morning, it had turned back on itself and, flowing upstream from the gulf, had inundated the city.

Evgeny managed to save himself from the floodwaters by straddling one of a pair of stone lions on the portico of a nobleman's house. There he sat, pale, motionless, and trapped, as he watched the waves do their worst precisely where, far out toward the gulf, stood Parasha's house. He feared for her more than for himself. Not far away, its back toward him, the Horseman rose high above the waves.

Finally the Neva River began to recede. Evgeny climbed down from his perch and found a ferryman to take him to Parasha's island, where he found familiar houses collapsed or wrenched off their foundations. Of Parasha's house—and its inhabitants—there was not a trace. The city began to recover and go about its business, but Evgeny did not. He never returned to his rooms, and weeks stretched into months as he wandered the streets, oblivious to everything around him. He slept wherever he could find shelter, until one day, waking up on the quay near the stone lions that had saved him, he recognized where he was. His bewilderment seemed to clear as he caught sight of the Horseman, and he walked round its base, muttering. He clenched his fists, whispering a furious threat. At that moment, it seemed that the czar's face changed, and, as Evgeny turned to run, he heard the statue galloping after him, its ponderous hooves ringing on the city's cobblestones all night long.

From then on, he gave the Horseman wide berth, doffing his cap and lowering his eyes whenever he happened to be on that particular square. Not long after, Evgeny's body was found on a barren island in the river; he lay at the threshold of a small house wrecked and cast ashore by the flood, and that is where they buried him.

Critical Evaluation:

A poet who ranks with William Shakespeare, Johann Wolfgang von Goethe, and Dante Alighieri, Alexander Pushkin virtually created Russian literature. He was not the first Russian writer with talent or even genius, but he was the first (and some might say the only one) of such enormous range and brilliance, for he left models in lyric poetry, long narrative poems (the Russian poèma), drama, and fiction. Translated often but not always well, Pushkin is less known outside his homeland than the writers named above; the clarity and seeming simplicity of his style, its compactness and economy, its combination of unpredictability and inevitability make him surprisingly difficult to translate. His place in his national literature is unique, and the Russian habit of referring to Pushkin in the present tense is not just literary convention, but rather a sense of him as a living presence, a continuing source of ideas and images. The characters seen in *The Bronze Horseman* and *Evgeny Onegin* (1823-1831), for example, have reappeared in various forms and guises in Russian literature ever since their creation, as has the idea of the artificial, "premeditated" city of St. Petersburg first evoked in Pushkin's poem.

Generally considered Pushkin's finest work, *The Bronze Horseman* was written in the autumn of 1833. It was not published until after Pushkin's death, and even then with some changes to pacify the censors, who, among other things, found the reference to a czar's statue as an idol disturbing. The work consists of an introduction and an exposition in two parts, a total of 481 lines of iambic tetrameter, freely rhymed. Though the shortest of Pushkin's serious narrative poems, it varies widely in style, tone, and tempo: Measured and majestic passages with archaic or rhetorical vocabulary (as in parts of the introduction) give way to straightforward conversational speech and even a slightly flippant tone, seen in the choice of Evgeny's name (familiar and easy because Pushkin had used it in his great verse novel *Evgeny Onegin*) and his lineage (so similar to Pushkin's own), for example. The poet varies his rhyme scheme as well as his vocabulary, now speeding the action with couplets, now slowing it with quatrains and longer rhyming units. Violent similes and metaphors dominate in the description of the flood; jagged line breaks and a deliberately jumbled rhyme scheme that has nothing in common with anything preceding it depict Evgeny's increasing derangement and panic. Pushkin's deftness at modulating from one tone to another keeps his devices from overwhelming the story itself.

For all the straightforward simplicity of the story, the poem is a tightly woven web of theme and reference, drawing in multiple historical, philosophical, and social strands so tightly that they are sometimes hard to separate. Pushkin drew on many sources: Polish poet Adam Mickiewicz's satiric indictment of Peter the Great and his city in his long poem *Forefathers'*

Eve (1925-1946) is an immediate and important one, as were contemporary accounts of the disastrous flood. Pushkin had long been fascinated with Peter's life and times and had already written about them in his story of his great-grandfather, *The Negro of Peter the Great* (1828), and in his narrative poem *Poltava* (1828). There were personal complications as well. Pushkin's ancestors had been prominent and influential, but his own financial and social positions were precarious. Czar Nicholas I's "patronage" was a dubious honor, since it meant that the czar himself was Pushkin's personal censor. Then there were the Decembrists, conspirators who, in 1825, had attempted a palace coup d'état to overthrow the autocracy and to prevent Nicholas from ascending to the throne. The armed struggle resulting in their surrender took place in Senate Square, in the very shadow of Peter's statue; a number were hanged, and many more were exiled. Among them were some of Pushkin's closest friends. Though they are nowhere mentioned in the poem, no reader could fail to make the association between the place, the statue, and the revolt.

While differing in their interpretations of the poem, most commentators at least agree that the pattern is one of polarity, of seemingly irreconcilable opposites juxtaposed. Some of these pairings are specific to Russia, while others are universal: East versus West, the ongoing Russian preoccupation with national identity either inside or outside European culture, and the wisdom of Peter's forced Westernization of Russia. Peter's decision to "hack" out a window on Europe was an unresolved question in Pushkin's time and remains so in the post-Soviet era. That question involves yet other conflicting notions: Moscow versus St. Petersburg, religious tradition versus secular change, the organic versus the artificial. Unresolved, too, is the question of Russia's traditional preference for the strong hand that will impose order on a vast, chaotic land. What will that order bring, and what is its price? Is the Horseman reining in his steed on the edge of an abyss, or is he urging it on? Pushkin clearly celebrates Peter's—and Russia's—greatness in the introduction, but the fate of Evgeny does not bode well for the ordinary citizen, let alone the dissenter. What kind of overlord is it who will not brook even a ragged madman's muttered threat but descends from his pedestal to chase him down?

The question Pushkin poses about the relationship of the ruler to the ruled goes beyond Russia, as does the question of humankind's relationship to nature. Here, Peter indeed brings Cosmos out of Chaos, in lines that are deliberately suggestive of the blank formlessness of the world before creation. However, Peter builds in spite of the natural order, not in harmony with it, and his creation is vulnerable to destruction by the very elements he claims to have mastered—a point that his successor Alexander I briefly and poignantly makes before sending troops out to aid victims. At the same time, Alexander is portrayed as rueful, not ridiculous. The poet's irony is never facile or cheap—only tragic.

Russia versus Europe, state versus citizen, historical destiny versus individual fate, Peter's grand vision versus Evgeny's humble daydreams, humankind versus nature—these are some of the opposing principles Pushkin presents. He reconciles them poetically, creating a unified whole, but never resolves them. Just as the statue's pose is ambiguous, so is Pushkin's attitude, and it is quite deliberately so.

"Critical Evaluation" by Jane Ann Miller

Bibliography:
Bayley, John. *Pushkin: A Comparative Study*. Cambridge, England: Cambridge University Press, 1971. This study looks at Pushkin in the context of both Russian and European literature, with special attention given to Shakespeare and the English poets. The chapter on

Pushkin's narrative and historical poetry uses *The Bronze Horseman* as a standard of comparison both with Pushkin's own earlier poems such as *Poltava* and with Lord Byron's treatment of some of the same themes. There is an extensive discussion of *The Bronze Horseman* in its own right.

Briggs, A. D. P. *Alexander Pushkin: A Critical Study.* Totowa, N.J.: Barnes & Noble, 1983. A thorough introduction to Pushkin's work, with an entire chapter devoted to *The Bronze Horseman*. Briggs gives an overview of the poem's sources, themes, devices (including rhyming patterns), and structure.

Gregg, Richard. "The Nature of Nature and the Nature of Eugene in *The Bronze Horseman*." *Slavic and East European Journal* 21 (1977): 167-179. Offers a slightly different view of Evgeny as an individual caught between two opposing forces, and argues for the notion that character as much as circumstance dictates individual fate.

Lednicki, Wacław. *Pushkin's "Bronze Horseman": The Story of a Masterpiece.* Berkeley: University of California Press, 1955. The only book-length study in English and still an invaluable resource. Appendices include a translation of the poem itself, of the works of Adam Mickiewicz, and of other sources.

Vickery, Walter N. *Alexander Pushkin.* Rev. ed. New York: Twayne, 1992. A revised edition of an earlier book by the same author, it incorporates new scholarship and is a brief but highly readable introduction to Pushkin's life and work. The section on *The Bronze Horseman* includes a synopsis, brief comments on style, and a discussion of major themes.

BROTHER ASS

Type of work: Novel
Author: Eduardo Barrios (1884-1963)
Type of plot: Psychological realism
Time of plot: Twentieth century
Locale: A rural town in Chile
First published: El hermano asno, 1922 (English translation, 1942)

> *Principal characters:*
> FRAY RUFINO, a friar with the reputation of a saint
> FRAY LÁZARO, narrator and Fray Rufino's best friend
> MARÍA MERCEDES, a friend of Fray Lázaro
> GRACIA, María Mercedes' older sister

The Story:

Fray Lázaro had celebrated his seventh anniversary as a Franciscan friar. His major concern, that he had never had a true call to the priesthood, led him to write a diary. The diary focused on his life and on the life of Fray Rufino, a friar who had earned the reputation of a saint.

Both men had been under considerable stress because of life at the monastery. Fray Rufino had trained cats and mice to eat from the same plate. The monks celebrated this event as a miracle. It soon became a curse, however, as the cats stopped hunting mice, and rodents invaded the monastery. As secret punishment for that "miracle," Fray Rufino began to flagellate himself and maintain a heavy work schedule; he frequently took upon himself the chores of his fellow friars.

Fray Rufino's reputation kept growing outside the monastery. People from faraway places started coming to the monastery in order to meet the monk, whose miracles included cures of dying animals and the restoration of a blind woman's sight. Such personal attention created in him a fear of losing his true Franciscan vocation to achieve total humility.

Fray Lázaro's fragile confidence in his religious calling suffered a great blow the day he saw in church a beautiful young woman who reminded him of a past love. To his surprise, the woman, María Mercedes, was the sister of Gracia, the former girlfriend, now a married woman living in town. Against his will, Fray Lázaro felt an attraction to María Mercedes, who appeared to love him. Her constant visits caused him severe depression as he began to debate whether he had fallen in love. In desperation, and in order to stop seeing María Mercedes, Fray Lázaro pretended to be ill.

Suddenly Fray Rufino warned Fray Lázaro to be careful; Fray Rufino told him that he could see that Fray Lázaro was losing his religious vocation. Fray Lázaro, surprised by the advice because he had not confided his secret to anyone, decided that Fray Rufino was right. That very day he would tell María Mercedes that they could not see each other anymore. When he saw the young woman, however, he could not resist her innocence and beauty. He also experienced jealousy when he noticed that a handsome young man had been trying to attract María Mercedes' attention. Fray Lázaro happily withdrew to the monastery when he realized that María Mercedes did not respond to the young man's flirtation.

Fray Lázaro became more interested in Fray Rufino's well-being. He had recognized that something unusual was happening to Fray Rufino. His suspicions were confirmed one night when he discovered that Fray Rufino had increased his physical punishment to the point of crawling on his knees while carrying a heavy wooden cross. The crawling produced heavy bleeding in the weak old man. At last Fray Lázaro confronted Fray Rufino with the knowledge of the secret physical punishment. In turn, Fray Rufino confessed more terrible news: He claimed that an apparition, the ghost of a monk who claimed to have come from Purgatory, had visited him several times in order to warn him about his weaknesses as a monk. Fray Lázaro made him promise to stop the intense punishment and to seek advice from higher religious authorities.

One day María Mercedes came to mass accompanied for the first time by her sister Gracia. María Mercedes' aloofness toward Fray Lázaro made him suspect that her family had discovered their relationship and had forbidden her to speak to him. When María Mercedes spoke to Fray Lázaro, she confirmed the monk's fears. She also insisted upon seeing Fray Rufino. Fray Lázaro promised her a visit with Fray Rufino early the next morning.

Fray Lázaro arrived late for that meeting with Fray Rufino and María Mercedes. As he walked into the reception room, he was horrified by María Mercedes' screams for help as she was sexually attacked by Fray Rufino. In desperation, she managed to run away from Fray Rufino, who was screaming that he was not worthy of his saintly reputation. He also claimed that the ghost of the monk had made him behave in such a brutal fashion. To avoid a scandal, Fray Lázaro assumed all guilt for the attack, and he was transferred to a monastery far from the town.

Critical Evaluation:

Eduardo Barrios was born in Valparaiso, Chile, the son of a Chilean father and a Peruvian mother. He lived in Peru and in various other countries of Latin America, where he traveled extensively and worked at odd jobs. He was a prolific writer of short stories, plays, and novels. Such versatility may have contributed to his careful, detailed literary style.

Brother Ass initiated in Latin America a literary trend that may be called the psychological novel. Within the realist mode focused on social critique, the psychological novel presents an analytical study of the human psyche by means of well-delineated characters, each of whom represents traits common to all people. The interaction and the clash of these types illustrate how human behavior works, including the ways in which people relate to each other in friendship. Psychological analysis such as this also includes a didactic approach to improvement of life in society at large. As a by-product of the carefully orchestrated case study, the psychological novel offers a strong social comment on a particular problem in contemporary society.

In an analytical approach, Barrios' characters are important components of what could be viewed as a psychological behavior experiment, with close documentation of their reactions toward each other. Characters, therefore, stand as abstractions of the impact of strong personality traits when people find themselves together in society. The title, *Brother Ass*, incorporates the concept of human beings viewed as animals in their personal interaction. Life in a formal social setting, along with the rules and restrictions imposed by groups, clashes against people's animal-like feelings and emotions. That conflict reveals the metaphorical message: Each human being's struggle to keep "Brother Ass" under control constitutes the greatest challenge for all members of society.

The choice of setting, a Franciscan monastery in an isolated town, illustrates Barrios' intention to create a controlled environment for his psychological experiment. One could argue that Barrios' intentions are twofold. One is to show how characters behave when removed from society. The second is to show how, once isolated from civilized rules, characters reconstitute societal values. The odd, unexpected behavior of the characters and the surprising ending constitute Barrios' social comment.

Barrios moves away from examination of Latin American society as it was practiced by most of his contemporary realist fellow writers. Instead, Barrios attempts to achieve a universal message through contemplation of the human psyche and its function in the shaping of life within a social group. Unlike animals, human beings respond to one factor in particular that makes them relate to one another, making the social fabric of interpersonal relationships more apparent to the reader. Love and its opposite feeling, hatred, stand out as those forces that promote social cohesiveness. In *Brother Ass*, love is presented in three forms: fraternal, religious, and sexual. These loves, however, are interconnected, and their carefully maintained balance makes a well-rounded individual. Fraternal love makes people want to live together in a social group, as demonstrated by life at the monastery. The desire for companionship comprises the basic foundation of life in society. As demonstrated by the frantic behavior of Fray Lázaro and Fray Rufino, however, deprivation or overcommitment to the other two equally strong forms of love may result in a personal crisis.

In regard to sexual love, Barrios treats the roles of women in contemporary society in a new way. His contemporary fellow writers often take extreme positions in their representations of women. Either women represent evil vices (prostitution, for example) or they become ethereal beings, subjected to great stress from their immediate reality. In Barrios' novel, women protagonists, such as María Mercedes, are affected by the same strains in life that men are. María Mercedes shares with Fray Lázaro his doubt about his vocation for the religious because they both understand that such a choice opposes a natural desire for reproduction. Women, therefore, share equally with men the inherent human task of establishing themselves as members of a larger social group.

The function of yet another inherent human feeling is the ability to love a supernatural being, known in Western cultures as God. Barrios depicts love for a divine being as the most sublime expression because this loving relationship does not require physical reciprocity, yet he does not preach acceptance of the existence of God. Instead, he proposes life as observed by the Franciscan order as an example of simpler societal values. Life in a community with close attachment to nature is seen as a refreshing relief from the chaotic modern society at the beginning of the twentieth century. When life in the monastery loses its spiritual purpose, however (as it happened to Fray Rufino), an existentialist crisis takes place.

Barrios' most important contribution to contemporary Latin American literature is his work with such modern psychological theories as Freudian psychoanalysis. Rather than bewildering his reader with macabre descriptions of situations in society, as most realist writers are doing, Barrios prefers a more in-depth critical analysis of the possible causes of those problems. His characters are also real, and they face psychological problems similar to those experienced by his readers.

Rafael Ocasio

Bibliography:

Brown, James. "El hermano asno: When the Unreliable Narrator Meets the Unreliable Reader." *Hispania* 71, no. 4 (December, 1988): 798-805. In-depth study of the various modern literary techniques displayed in the novel. Stresses the relationship between the reader and the novel's narrator. Discusses the use of irony in the plot.

Foster, David William, and Virginia Ramos Foster. "Barrios, Eduardo." In *Modern Latin American Literature*, edited by David William Foster and Virginia Ramos Foster. New York: Frederick Ungar, 1975. A survey study of Barrios' work. Provides excerpts of critical studies by various critics. An excellent starting point to Barrios' works.

Souza, Raymond. "Indeterminacy of Meaning in *El hermano asno*." *Chasqui* 13, nos. 2/3 (Febrero, Mayo, 1984): 26-32. An in-depth analysis of Barrios' literary craft and the treatment of rape as a literary motif. Focuses on women's issues.

Walker, John. *Gálvez, Barrios, and the Metaphysical Malaise. Symposium: A Quarterly Journal in Modern Foreign Literatures* 36, no. 4 (Winter, 1982/1983): 352-358. Comparative study of Barrios and novelist Manuel Gálvez; both authors were interested in metaphysical subjects. Stresses their interest in metaphysical issues as ways to improve contemporary society.

_____. *Metaphysics and Aesthetics in the Works of Eduardo Barrios*. London: Tamesis, 1983. Studies the relationship between Barrios' novel and his strong interest in metaphysics.

THE BROTHERS

Type of work: Drama
Author: Terence (Publius Terentius Afer, c. 190-159 B.C.E.)
Type of plot: Comedy
Time of plot: Second century B.C.E.
Locale: Athens
First performed: 160 B.C.E.

Principal characters:
    MICIO, an aged Athenian
    DEMEA, his brother
    AESCHINUS, Demea's son, adopted by Micio
    CTESIPHO, Demea's other son
    SOSTRATA, an Athenian widow
    PAMPHILA, Sostrata's daughter
    SANNIO, a pimp and slave dealer
    HEGIO, an old man of Athens

The Story:

Micio was an aging, easygoing Athenian bachelor whose strict and hardworking brother Demea had permitted him to adopt and rear Aeschinus, one of Demea's two sons. Unlike his brother, Micio had been a permissive parent, choosing to let pass many of Aeschinus' small extravagances on the assumption that children are more likely to remain bound to their duty by ties of kindness than by those of fear.

Micio came to wonder if his policy had been the best. One day, shortly after Aeschinus had told him he was tired of the Athenian courtesans and wanted to marry, Demea came to Micio and informed him angrily that Aeschinus had broken into a strange house, beaten its master, and carried off a woman with whom he was infatuated. It was a shameful thing, Demea said, especially since Aeschinus had such a fine example of continence and industry in his brother Ctesipho, who dutifully spent his time working for Demea in the country. It was also shameful that Aeschinus had been reared the way he had, Demea suggested; Micio was letting the youth go to the bad by failing to restrain his excesses.

After quarreling about their methods for rearing children, the two men parted. Demea agreed not to interfere and Micio, although confused and grieved by Aeschinus' apparent change of heart and failure to inform him of the escapade, determined to stand by his adopted son.

As it turned out, however, Demea's report of Aeschinus was correct only in outline. The house into which the young man had broken belonged to Sannio, a pimp and slave dealer, and the woman carried off was a slave with whom, ironically, the model son Ctesipho had fallen in love, but whom he could not afford to buy. Demea's restraint had been more than Ctesipho could bear, and because he was afraid to indulge himself before his father, he had chosen to do so behind his back. Aeschinus had agreed to procure the woman for his brother but had kept his motives secret in order to protect his brother from Demea's wrath.

Sannio, furious at the treatment he had received, hounded Aeschinus for the return of the slave. Sannio was soon to leave on a slave-trading expedition, so he had no time to prosecute the case in court; moreover, an obscure point of law created the possibility that the slave might be declared free and that Sannio could lose his entire investment. In consequence, he finally consented to sell her for the price he had paid for her.

Meanwhile, other complications arose. Long before the slave episode, Aeschinus had fallen in love with Pamphila, the daughter of Sostrata, a poor Athenian widow. Aeschinus had promised to marry Pamphila and they had anticipated this union, with the result that she was about to be delivered of his child. Then, while she was in labor, it was reported that he had abducted the slave girl and was having an affair with her. The mother and daughter were of course extremely upset at Aeschinus' apparent faithlessness, and in despair Sostrata related her dilemma to her only friend, Hegio, an impoverished old man who had been her husband's friend and who was also a friend of Demea. Hegio, indignant, went to Demea to demand that justice be done. Demea, having just heard that Ctesipho had played some part in the abduction and assuming that Aeschinus had seduced the model son into evil ways, was doubly furious at Hegio's news. Immediately he went off hunting for Micio, only to be misdirected by one of Aeschinus' slaves, who was attempting to prevent the old man from discovering that Ctesipho and his mistress were both in Micio's house.

A short time later Hegio encountered Micio, who, having learned the truth regarding the abduction, promised to explain everything to Sostrata and Pamphila. As he was leaving the widow's house, he met Aeschinus, who was himself coming to try to explain to the women the muddle he was in. Pretending ignorance of Aeschinus' situation, Micio mildly punished the young man for his furtiveness by pretending to be at Sostrata's house as the representative of another suitor for Pamphila's hand; but when he saw the agony which the prospect of losing Pamphila produced in Aeschinus, Micio put an end to his pretense and promised the grateful and repentant youth that he could marry Pamphila at once.

Demea, finally returning from the wild-goose chase that the servant had sent him on, accosted Micio in front of his house. Although Micio calmed his brother somewhat by telling him how matters really stood, Demea still retained his disapproval of Micio's parental leniency. The crisis occurred shortly afterward when Demea learned the full truth about Ctesipho—that the model son had not only been a party to the abduction, but that the whole affair had been conceived and executed for his gratification. At first the knowledge nearly put him out of his wits, but Micio gradually brought him to a perception of the fact that no irreparable harm had been done. Also, since Demea's strictness and severity had ultimately not succeeded, perhaps leniency and generosity were most effective after all in dealing with children. Demea, realizing that his harshness had made Ctesipho fearful and suspicious of his father, decided to try Micio's mode of conduct, and he surprised all who knew him by his cheerful resignation. Indeed, he even went so far as to have the wall between Micio's and Sostrata's houses torn down and to suggest, not without a certain malice, that the only truly generous thing Micio could do for Sostrata would be to marry her. At first Micio hesitated, but when the suggestion was vehemently seconded by Aeschinus, Micio at last gave in.

Demea also persuaded Micio to free Syrus and his wife Phrygia, his slaves, and to give Hegio some property to support him in his old age. Then he turned to his sons and gave his consent to their amorous projects, asking only to be allowed in the future to check them when their youthful passions threatened to lead them astray. The young men submitted willingly to his request.

Critical Evaluation:
The Brothers is one of Terence's most popular comedies, probably because it approaches in such a good-humored manner a subject that affects every member of a family. Responsible parents worry about the best way to bring up their children, and their offspring worry about how to live up to their parents' expectations.

Although both fathers love the young men for whom they are responsible, Demea and Micio could hardly differ more in their philosophies of child rearing. Demea believes in governing by fear, and Micio believes in governing by love. Ctesipho, who has been raised by Demea's strict rules, has been made to work hard, and, at least in his father's opinion, has been kept away from temptation, while Aeschinus, who has been raised by Micio, has been allowed total freedom, excused for his misdeeds, and easily forgiven.

As Micio explains his ideas in his opening monologue, his ideas seem extremely appealing, while Demea's ideas seem old-fashioned and unenlightened. By appearing to side with Micio, however, Terence is placing his audience off guard. In fact, neither brother has a foolproof solution to the problem of raising and educating the young. As the story progresses, it becomes evident how little the two fathers really know about their sons and how easily the fathers can be deceived.

When Terence looks at the outcomes of these two educational experiments, the young men have entered the most critical time in their lives. They are old enough to get into serious trouble, but they are too young to govern their actions by reason. Each has become involved with a woman, and as the customs of comedy dictate, these relationships have been concealed from the older generation. In fact, since one woman is a slave, and the other comes from a poor family, neither relationship seems likely to win parental approval.

Meanwhile, the fathers remain ignorant, not only of what the young men are doing, but also of what their sons are really like. Demea thinks that he has created a boy in his own stern and upright image. He has no idea that Ctesipho is sneaking away whenever he can. As for Micio, though he knows that Aeschinus is sowing his wild oats, he cannot imagine that his son would ever fail to confide in him. It is doubly ironic, then, that Aeschinus not only deceives his father about seducing Pamphila but, in addition, that he admits to an involvement of which, in fact, he is innocent and then accepts his lenient father's forgiveness for it.

Even though *The Brothers* has a dual plot, as do all but one of Terence's plays, and though there are two love stories, this play is different from the other works because it does not focus on the love interest. The important pairings are not those of the lovers. The comparisons are between the two fathers; between the two sons, who, though so different in character, behave so much alike; and between the two fathers and sons.

Critics differ in their assessments of Micio and Demea. Some critics find Micio the more sympathetic of the two men and these critics feel that his final punishment, losing money and property and acquiring an unwanted wife, is too harsh. Other critics agree with Demea that Micio is motivated not by true generosity but, instead, by laziness and a desire for popularity. These critics argue that he deserves what has happened to him.

Another question is just how Terence wishes Demea to be viewed. If Demea actually chooses popularity over principle, he can hardly be respected. On the other hand, if he is merely tricking his brother in order to make a point, he goes too far. In either case, Demea seems to forfeit the sympathy of the audience. For some reason, however, Terence chooses him as the spokesman for moderation and, presumably, for the author.

There are, however, no problems of interpretation concerning the sons. Obviously, Ctesipho, the younger, is the weaker of the two, either by nature or perhaps because he has not been given a chance to make his own decisions. Certainly his willingness to let his brother take the blame for his own scheme does not say much for Demea's force-feeding of moral principles. Most audiences find Aeschinus much more appealing. He is loyal to his brother, and if he lacks the courage to face his imminent fatherhood, at least he cannot allow the woman he loves to be married to another.

The father-son relationships in *The Brothers* resemble each other because both of them are based on illusion on the part of the fathers, and deception on the part of the sons. The relationships are also similar, however, because they are based on real affection. The fathers would not feel so strongly about their sons' conduct if they were not genuinely concerned about their future welfare. As for the sons, it seems unlikely that Ctesipho really dislikes his father, as Demea suggests in his bitterness. Although he does not appear in the last part of the play, Ctesipho has previously shown no signs of callousness. It seems reasonable to assume that a youth so responsive to his brother's kindness also appreciates his father's efforts. As for Aeschinus, one need only look at his fourth act soliloquy to ascertain the depth of his feeling for Micio. This speech may be as important a key to Terence's own attitude as Demea's final comments, which argue that in the rearing of children, the middle way between harshness and indulgence is best. It may be that even more important than commitment to any educational theory is children's assurance that they have their parents' unconditional love.

"Critical Evaluation" by Rosemary M. Canfield Reisman

Bibliography:
Arnott, W. Geoffrey. *Menander, Plautus, Terence*. Oxford, England: Clarendon Press, 1975. After a short summary of Terence's environment and career, Arnott explores such major critical issues as Terence's "contamination" of his Greek sources, his use of innovation, and the quality of his work. The chapter on Plautus and Terence begins with a bibliographical essay.
Forehand, Walter E. *Terence*. Boston: Twayne, 1985. Chapters on Terence's life, his literary career, and the theater of his day are followed by analyses of the plays. *The Brothers* is treated at length, with special attention given to its themes. Extensive notes, select bibliography, and index are included.
Goldberg, Sander M. *Understanding Terence*. Princeton, N.J.: Princeton University Press, 1986. Several references to *The Brothers*. Topically organized and well indexed. Discusses the implications of the education theme and includes a discussion of the play's political significance.
Sandbach, F. H. *The Comic Theatre of Greece and Rome*. London: Chatto & Windus, 1977. The chapter on Terence is an excellent starting point for study of the dramatist. Includes discussion of Terence's use of sources in *The Brothers*. Appendix includes useful glossary of Greek and Roman terms, as well as a brief bibliography.
Sutton, Dana F. *Ancient Comedy: The War of the Generations*. New York: Twayne, 1993. Analyzes *The Brothers* and shows the unique quality of Terence's comedy, in contrast to that of Menander or Plautus. Agrees with Goldberg that Terence lacks a spirit of fun but asserts that Terence's basic problem is philosophical. Includes bibliographical suggestions.

THE BROTHERS ASHKENAZI

Type of work: Novel
Author: Israel Joshua Singer (1893-1944)
Type of plot: Historical realism
Time of plot: Late nineteenth and early twentieth centuries
Locale: Poland
First published: Di brider Ashkenazi, 1936 (English translation, 1936)

> *Principal characters:*
> SIMCHA MEYER ASHKENAZI, an enterprising Jew
> JACOB BUNIM, his twin brother
> ABRAHAM, their father
> DINAH, Simcha's wife
> PEARL, Jacob's wife
> GERTRUDE, the daughter of Simcha and Dinah
> TEVYEH, a revolutionary weaver
> NISSAN, a revolutionary

The Story:

Abraham was a pious Jew and a good businessman. General agent for the Huntze mills, he was greatly respected by the community. He always spent the Passover season with his beloved rabbi in a town some distance from Lodz. One year, his wife protested more than usual at being left alone because she expected to be confined soon. She knew the child would be a boy, for she felt stirrings on her right side. Abraham paid no attention to her.

When he returned, he found two sons. The older by several minutes was Simcha, the younger Jacob. Simcha was the smaller of the two and showed a meaner spirit. As they grew older, Jacob was the happy leader of neighborhood games, the favorite of all. Dinah, a neighbor girl, worshiped him for years. Simcha seldom played with anyone, and he had no stomach for even minor physical pain.

In school, however, Jacob was an amiable dunce, whereas Simcha was the scholar. Before long, Simcha was recognized as a genius. At an early age, he could cite the Talmud and dispute with his teacher. When he was ten years old, he was sent to a more learned rabbi, Nissan's father. His new teacher was more moral and uncompromising, and Simcha's glib smartness often led him into disfavor. Moreover, here he had to take second place to Nissan.

Simcha kept his leadership by running gambling games during class hours, and on holidays he led his schoolmates into gambling houses. Simcha always won, even from the professional gamblers. Nissan had no time for gambling, but his sin was even greater: He read secular books on chemistry, astronomy, and economics. When Simcha betrayed him and his father cast him out, Nissan became an apprentice weaver.

Because of Simcha's growing reputation for acuity, a marriage broker was able to arrange an advantageous engagement. At the age of thirteen, Dinah and Simcha were betrothed. Dinah was miserable. She was blonde and educated in languages; Simcha was unprepossessing and educated only in the Talmudic discipline. The marriage, which took place several years later, was never a happy one, for Dinah could never forget Jacob.

Simcha, with a clever head for figures, kept the accounts at the mill belonging to his easygoing father-in-law. By convincing the older man to sign promissory notes, Simcha soon became a partner. Although the family resented Simcha's hard dealing, he was grimly intent on making money. By shrewdness and trickery, he became sole owner of the mill in a short time. His father-in-law's mill, however, was only a handloom establishment; Simcha set his sights higher.

The biggest steam mill in Lodz was owned by a crusty German named Huntze. Simcha's father was general agent, and the mill had a high reputation. Huntze's profligate sons wanted a title in the family, but old Huntze would not spend the money for one. Wily Simcha lent great sums to the Huntze boys, enough to buy a title and more. When their father died, the sons recognized the debt by appointing Simcha their agent. Abraham was dismissed and thereafter counted his oldest son among the dead.

Jacob had married Pearl, the anemic daughter of the great Eisen household in Warsaw. Pearl had seen Jacob at Simcha's wedding and had fallen in love with the ebullient younger brother. Jacob easily shed his Jewish ways and became Europeanized. Because Pearl was sickly, she could not keep up with her vigorous husband, and Jacob spent much time in Lodz. Eventually, to Simcha's chagrin, Jacob was made agent for the Flederbaum mills, a rival establishment.

When a depression came, Simcha adulterated his goods to keep going and then decided to cut wages. Under the leadership of Tevyeh, a fanatic, and Nissan, now a well-educated weaver, the men struck. Simcha resisted for a long time and then broke the strike by bribing the police to arrest Nissan and Tevyeh. The two were sentenced to exile in Siberia.

By paying close attention to sales and by sweating his labor, Simcha made money. He traveled to the East and increased his market enormously. He was recognized as the merchant prince of Lodz. During the Russo-Japanese War, he made great profits by selling to the military. Throughout these years, the trade union movement was growing, however, and Nissan, back in Lodz, had become a highly placed official in the revolutionary society. When the workers struck again, the unionists were too strong for Simcha, and his factory stayed closed for months. This time the strike was broken only by military action, which turned into a pogrom against the Jews. Nissan was again sent to prison.

To increase his holdings and to get sufficient capital to buy the entire ownership of the Huntze mills, Simcha divorced Dinah and married a rich widow. Jacob, matching his brother's affluence by becoming the lover of one of the Flederbaum girls after Pearl divorced him, was made director of the rival mill. Simcha's daughter Gertrude, a headstrong modern young woman, willed Jacob to fall in love with her. He married her because she reminded him of Dinah.

When World War I broke out, Simcha moved his factory to Petrograd and so missed the German occupation of Lodz. Russia went through a revolution, however, and the workers came to power. Once again, Nissan met Simcha, but this time Nissan was the master, and his party confiscated Simcha's property. When the ruined Simcha tried to get out of Russia, he was betrayed by a fellow Jew, arrested, and jailed.

Back in Lodz, Jacob still maintained some position in the community, and Simcha's second wife had managed to hold on to some wealth. Jacob went to Russia and by judicious bribery freed his brother, who was now a broken man. When the two brothers attempted to reenter Poland, anti-Jewish feeling was strong. The border guards forced Simcha to dance and grovel and shout a repudiation of his religion and race. Refusing to truckle, Jacob struck a captain. Jacob was shot to death, but Simcha was permitted to live.

Simcha apathetically stayed for a time with his wife, his divorced wife Dinah, his daughter Gertrude, and his granddaughter. Gradually, his cunning returned. He made a trip to England and arranged for a substantial loan to rebuild his looted factory. He induced his long-forgotten son to come back from France. Ignatz brought his French wife with him. Simcha suspected darkly that she was not even Jewish, but he did not inquire. When the postwar depression struck, Simcha was reviled by his fellow merchants for bringing in English capital. Commercially, Lodz was almost dead when Simcha died.

Critical Evaluation:

At first glance, Israel Joshua Singer's *The Brothers Ashkenazi* appears to have many of the qualities typical of the historical fiction of writers such as Sir Walter Scott and Alexandre Dumas, who intermingle the lives of fictional characters with those of real personages, usually during periods when important events were affecting the future of a region or a nation. Seen in that light, the novel is a study of what happens to individuals when they are forced to act in response to, or in an attempt to influence, larger historical forces. Such a description could be misleading, however, since Singer's work is not simply a historical novel. Rather, it is a novel about history, a study of the way the historical process affects, or fails to affect, the lives of the Jewish people. Singer contrasts the prevalent view of world history, which is often described as a linear process, with that of Jewish history, which Singer represents as being cyclical. Anita Norich has said that in *The Brothers Ashkenazi* Singer tries "to come to terms not only with the tension between Jewish society and the Jew but also between Jewish society and its broader environment," thus highlighting "the similarity of Jewish experience in every age."

The lives of the brothers Jacob and Simcha Ashkenazi mirror the linear notion of history. Though radically different in temperament, both prosper in the city of Lodz, which is itself undergoing a renaissance as a result of the influx of foreigners who bring with them technological improvements. Whereas Jacob succeeds by looks and luck, Simcha relies on his cunning and his renunciation of traditional Jewish and family values to manipulate others to his advantage. In fact, Simcha is almost a stereotype of the Jew as he has been viewed by Gentiles throughout history, one who takes advantage of others' misfortunes, including those of close relations. Trying to distance himself from his heritage and become accepted by the non-Jewish community where he sees the opportunity to make his fortune, Simcha engages in a conscious attempt to achieve assimilation, a phenomenon rejected by more conservative Jews for centuries. He glibly changes his name to the more Germanic "Max," and with almost equal ease puts aside his wife when he learns that he can gain monetary and social advantage by taking a Russian bride.

What both Jacob and Simcha learn is that regardless of their actions, it is their fate to be Jews. When both are threatened by the Russian guards during World War I, they learn that their social status is no shield for anti-Semitism. Jacob is heroic in accepting his fate; he dies celebrating his Jewishness. Max, on the other hand, denies his heritage and escapes death but then finds little solace upon his return to Lodz, where he cannot avoid his lineage. His final, poignant scene in the novel shows him near death, sitting under a portrait of a satyr (the symbol of pagan pursuits of pleasure), reading from an old Hebrew Bible the words of the writer of Ecclesiastes about the vanity of human wishes.

Singer's lesson is not intended simply as a critique of Simcha Ashkenazi. Readers are to understand that the novelist is making a comment on a much larger issue, the fact that there is no safe place for Jews in the larger world. Certainly Max is intended as a symbol of the fate of Jews who, no matter how hard they try, find that assimilation is a pipedream. For Singer, the Jewish heritage is both a blessing and a curse.

Singer reinforces his message through effective use of symbolism. The presence of the portrait of the satyr over the dying Simcha is only one example of his inclusion of signs that provide silent commentary on the significance of his protagonist's futile struggle. Even more telling are references to Mephistopheles, repeated throughout the novel at key points when Max has made some further attempt to promote himself at the expense of his own people. Max is a Faustian figure, willing to sell his soul for personal enhancement; like Faust, his fate is sealed, for anyone who gives in to temptation of this magnitude is doomed.

Adding to the symbolic resonance of the novel is Singer's representation of the city of Lodz and its inhabitants. The rise and fall of the Ashkenazi brothers are paralleled in the history of the city. Lodz stands in the novel as a symbol of the fate of the Jews when they interact with the outside world. The sleepy village undergoes a false renaissance when outside forces introduce the marvels of technology, but the city's prosperity quickly disappears when manufacturing ceases to be profitable; the collapse of industry returns Lodz to its former state, wiser perhaps for its experience but no better off than it was before the Germans brought their machinery and modern methods of production. So it is, Singer suggests, with the Jews. They may interact with the forces of history, but they will never be able to achieve permanent benefit from them. They will always be outsiders. For Singer, that represents strength as well as struggle, for that which is permanent in Jewish heritage will always permit the Jews to transcend sorrow to achieve both personal and social dignity.

"Critical Evaluation" by Laurence W. Mazzeno

Bibliography:
Howe, Irving. Introduction to *The Brothers Ashkenazi*, by Israel Joshua Singer. 1st ed. New York: Atheneum, 1980. Provides an assessment of the work as a historical novel and relates it to other examples of the genre. Claims that Singer adopted the Marxist notion that the sweep of history determines the lives and actions of individuals.
_____. *World of Our Fathers*. New York: Harcourt Brace Jovanovich, 1976. Links Singer with Scholem Asch as being Yiddish writers who achieved fame by writing in the tradition of European novelists of the nineteenth and twentieth centuries. Compares his techniques in *The Brothers Ashkenazi* with those used by Thomas Mann.
Norich, Anita. *The Homeless Imagination in the Fiction of Israel Joshua Singer*. Bloomington: Indiana University Press, 1991. Focuses on cultural dimensions of Singer's writing. Offers a sensitive reading of *The Brothers Ashkenazi* and discusses the tensions Singer creates by contrasting the "extraordinary changes of the period he is depicting" with the static nature of the Jewish fate.
Schulz, Max F. "The Family Chronicle as Paradigm of History in *The Brothers Ashkenazi* and *The Family Moskat*." In *The Achievement of Isaac Bashevis Singer*, edited by Marcia Allentuck. Carbondale: Southern Illinois University Press, 1969. Compares Singer's novel to one by his more famous brother, Isaac Bashevis Singer, showing how each adapts the conventions of the family epic to the demands of a public attuned to the complexities of the historical process.
Sinclair, Claire. *The Brothers Singer*. London: Allison & Busby, 1983. Extensive analysis of major characters in *The Brothers Ashkenazi*. Pays special attention to the political and historical dimensions of the work.

THE BROTHERS KARAMAZOV

Type of work: Novel
Author: Fyodor Dostoevski (1821-1881)
Type of plot: Psychological realism
Time of plot: Nineteenth century
Locale: Russia
First published: Bratya Karamazovy, 1879-1880 (English translation, 1912)

> *Principal characters:*
> FYODOR KARAMAZOV, a profligate businessman
> DMITRI, his sensual oldest son
> IVAN, his atheistic, intellectual son
> ALEXEY or ALYOSHA, his youngest son
> GRUSHENKA, a young woman loved by Fyodor and Dmitri
> SMERDYAKOV, an epileptic servant of Fyodor
> ZOSSIMA, an aged priest
> KATERINA, betrothed to Dmitri

The Story:

In the middle of the nineteenth century in Skotoprigonyevski, a town in the Russian provinces, Fyodor Karamazov fathered three sons, the eldest, Dmitri, by his first wife, and the other two, Ivan and Alexey, by his second. Fyodor, a good businessman but a scoundrel by nature, abandoned the children after their mothers died. A family servant, Grigory, saw that they were placed in the care of relatives.

Dmitri grew up believing he would receive a legacy from his mother's estate. He served in the army, where he developed wild ways. Becoming a wastrel, he went to his father and asked for the money that he believed was due him. Ivan, morose but not timid, went from a gymnasium to a college in Moscow. Poverty forced him to teach and to contribute articles to periodicals, and he achieved modest fame when he published an article on the position of the ecclesiastical courts. Alexey, or Alyosha, the youngest son, a boy of a dreamy, retiring nature, entered a local monastery, where he became the pupil of a famous Orthodox Church elder, Zossima. When Alyosha asked his father's permission to become a monk, Fyodor, to whom nothing was sacred, scoffed but gave his sanction.

When the brothers had all reached manhood, their paths met in the town of their birth. Dmitri returned to collect his legacy. Ivan, a professed atheist, returned home for financial reasons.

At a meeting of the father and sons at the monastery, Fyodor shamed his sons by behaving like a fool in the presence of the revered Zossima. Dmitri, who arrived late, was accused by Fyodor of wanting the legacy money in order to entertain a local adventuress to whom he himself was attracted. Dmitri, who was betrothed at this time to Katerina, a colonel's daughter whom he had rescued from shame, raged at his father, saying that the old man was a great sinner and in no position to judge others. Zossima fell down before Dmitri, tapping his head on the floor, and his fall was believed to be a portent of an evil that would befall the oldest son. Realizing that the Karamazovs were sensualists, Zossima advised Alyosha to leave the monastery and go into the world at Zossima's death. There was further dissension among the Karamazovs because of Ivan's love for Katerina, the betrothed of Dmitri.

Marfa, the wife of Grigory, Fyodor's faithful servant, had given birth to a deformed child. The night that Marfa's deformed baby died, Lizaveta, an idiot girl of the town, also died after giving birth to a son. The child, later to be called Smerdyakov, was taken in by Grigory and Marfa and was accepted as a servant in the household of Fyodor, whom everyone in the district believed was the child's true father.

Dmitri confessed his wild ways to Alyosha. He opened his heart to his brother and told how he had spent three thousand rubles of Katerina's money in an orgy with Grushenka, a local woman of questionable character with whom he had fallen passionately in love. Desperate for the money to repay Katerina, Dmitri asked Alyosha to secure it for him from Fyodor.

Alyosha found Fyodor and Ivan at the table, attended by the servant, Smerdyakov, who was an epileptic. Entering suddenly in search of Grushenka, Dmitri attacked his father. Alyosha went to Katerina's house, where he found Katerina trying to bribe Grushenka into abandoning her interest in Dmitri. Grushenka, however, could not be compromised. Upon his return to the monastery, Alyosha found Zossima dying. He returned to Fyodor, to discover his father afraid of both Dmitri and Ivan. Ivan wanted Dmitri to marry Grushenka so that he himself could marry Katerina. Fyodor wanted to marry Grushenka. The father refused to give Alyosha any money for Dmitri.

Spurned by Dmitri, Katerina dedicated her life to watching over him, although she felt a true love for Ivan. Ivan, seeing that Katerina was pledged to torture herself for life, nobly approved of her decision.

Later, in an inn, Ivan disclosed to Alyosha that he believed in God but that he could not accept God's world. The young men discussed the dual nature of humankind. Ivan disclosed that he hated Smerdyakov, who was caught between the wild passions of Dmitri and Fyodor and who, out of fear, worked for the interests of each against the other.

The dying Zossima revived long enough to converse once more with his devoted disciples. When he died, a miracle was expected. In the place of a miracle, however, his body rapidly decomposed, delighting certain of the monks who were anxious that the institution of the elders in the Orthodox Church be discredited. They argued that the decomposition of his body proved his teachings had been false.

In his disappointment at the turn of events at the monastery, Alyosha was persuaded to visit Grushenka, who wished to seduce him. He found Grushenka prepared to escape the madness of the Karamazovs by running off with a former lover. The saintly Alyosha saw good in Grushenka; she, for her part, found him an understanding soul.

Dmitri, eager to pay his debt to Katerina, made various fruitless attempts to borrow the money. Mad with jealousy when he learned that Grushenka was not at her home, he went to Fyodor's house to see whether she were there. He found no Grushenka, but he seriously injured old Grigory with a pestle with which he had intended to kill his father. Discovering that Grushenka had fled to another man, he armed himself and went in pursuit. He found Grushenka with two Poles in an inn at another village. The young woman welcomed Dmitri and professed undying love for him alone. During a drunken orgy of the lovers, the police appeared and charged Dmitri with the murder of his father, who had been found robbed and dead in his house. Blood on Dmitri's clothing, his possession of a large sum of money, and passionate statements he had made against Fyodor were all evidence against him. Dmitri repeatedly protested his innocence, claiming that the money he had spent on his latest orgy was half of Katerina's rubles. He had saved the money to ensure his future in the event that Grushenka accepted him, but the testimony of witnesses made his case seem hopeless. He was taken into custody and placed in the town jail to await trial.

Grushenka fell sick after the arrest of Dmitri, and she and Dmitri were plagued with jealousy of each other. As the result of a strange dream, Dmitri began to look upon himself as an innocent man destined to suffer for the crimes of humanity. Ivan and Katerina, in the meantime, worked on a scheme whereby Dmitri might escape to America.

Before the trial, Ivan interviewed Smerdyakov three times. The servant had once told Ivan that he was able to feign an epileptic fit; such a fit had been Smerdyakov's alibi in the search for the murderer of Fyodor. The third interview ended when Smerdyakov confessed to the murder, insisting, however, that he had been the instrument of Ivan, who by certain words and actions had led the servant to believe that the death of Fyodor would be a blessing for everyone in his household. Smerdyakov, depending on a guilt complex in the soul of Ivan, had murdered his master at a time when all the evidence would point directly to Dmitri. He had felt that Ivan would protect him and provide him with a comfortable living. At the end of the third interview, he gave the stolen money to Ivan, who returned to his rooms and fell ill with fever and delirium, during which he was haunted by a realistic specter of the devil that resided in his soul. That same night, Smerdyakov hanged himself.

The Karamazov case had attracted widespread attention throughout Russia, and many notables attended the trial. The prosecution built up what seemed to be a strong case against Dmitri, but the defense, a city lawyer, refuted the evidence piece by piece. Doctors declared Dmitri to be abnormal; in the end, however, they could not agree. Katerina had her woman's revenge by revealing to the court a letter Dmitri had written to her, in which he declared his intention of killing his father to get the money he owed her. Ivan, still in a fever, testified that Smerdyakov had confessed to the murder. Ivan gave the money to the court, but he negated his testimony when he lost control of himself and told the court of the visits of his private devil.

Despite the defense counsel's eloquent plea in Dmitri's behalf, the jury returned a verdict of guilty amid a tremendous hubbub in the courtroom. Katerina was haunted by guilt because she had revealed Dmitri's letter; furthermore, she felt that she was responsible for the jealousy of the two brothers. She left Ivan's bedside and went to the hospital where Dmitri, also ill of a fever, had been taken. Alyosha and Grushenka were present at their interview, when Katerina begged Dmitri for his forgiveness.

Later, Alyosha left Dmitri in the care of Grushenka and went to the funeral of a schoolboy friend. Filled with pity and compassion for the sorrow of death and the misery of life, Alyosha gently admonished the mourners, most of them schoolmates of the dead boy, to live for goodness and to love the world. He himself was preparing to go with Dmitri to Siberia, for he was ready to sacrifice his own life for innocence and truth.

Critical Evaluation:

Fyodor Mikhailovich Dostoevski's budding literary career was interrupted in 1849 by a nine-year exile in Siberia and Asian Russia for political subversion, a charge never fully substantiated. When he resumed his career, at the age of thirty-eight, he began to work at a frenetic pace—as novelist, journalist, and editor—a pace that he maintained until his death, only one year after the publication of *The Brothers Karamazov*. Dostoevski was an inveterate gambler, frequently indulging gambling binges of up to two weeks in duration; when his gambling debts mounted and his other creditors became insistent, he wrote, in a furiously intense burst of energy, to pay his bills. In addition, other catastrophes punctuated his hectic life. His first wife died; he began to have epileptic seizures; he got into further trouble with the government; he found it impossible to resist beautiful women; and woven through all this were the epiphanic flights of imagination, which culminated in his superb novels and the agonized soul searching of a man deeply concerned with truth, peace of mind, and religious faith. Indeed, the turbulence of Dostoevski's life never really subsided, although he did enjoy a relative calm of sorts during the last few years of his life under the careful ministrations of his second wife. That turbulence is reflected in Dostoevski's novels, particularly *The Brothers Karamazov*, his last novel and presumably the most mature expression of his style and his thought.

Like the other novels, *The Brothers Karamazov* is a psychological novel: Less emphasis is placed on plot, action, and setting (although Dostoevski was a master craftsman at all three) than on emotions and thoughts. In fact, Dostoevski's psychological insights are so sharp that Sigmund Freud selected *The Brothers Karamazov* as one of the three greatest works in world literature. (The other two he picked were *Oedipus Rex* and *Hamlet*. All three involve a death of a father and an intergenerational love triangle.) Moreover, Freud's essay on *The Brothers Karamazov*, "Dostoevsky and Parricide," is considered a classic in psychology and literary criticism. In it, Freud gives a thorough explanation of the strong Oedipal theme in the novel, which echos, according to Freud, Dostoevski's own unresolved Oedipal conflicts. In this Freudian age, it is most difficult not to cast Dmitri's hostility toward Fyodor in any other light. Each son resents his father in his own fashion and for his own reasons. All three legitimate sons, however, have less reason to despise Fyodor than his illegitimate son, Smerdyakov, does. All four sons have some justification—stemming largely from greed or vengeance—for wanting Fyodor dead.

It is evident, then, that the story proceeds from something more profound than plot. The loose structure of the novel, however, is offset by its intensity. It is frequently lurid, but Dostoevski never avoids a difficult question; he amalgamates thinking and feeling in a carefully planned interplay between the two. One of the consequences of this technique is an early foreshadowing of events that later come to pass—the creation of an atmosphere of premonition, as it were. There is, for example, frequent and early mention of patricide, especially in the scenes between Ivan and Smerdyakov, revealing a pathological obsession that besets both father and sons. Furthermore, the selection of details and their accretion contribute not only to the novel's verisimilitude but also to its psychological depth and profundity. Even so seemingly trivial a matter as numerous references to time sequence—all of them accurate—indicates Dostoevski's meticulous orchestration of his characters' emotions. Yet these techniques serve only to enhance a novel whose impact ultimately derives from its head-on confrontation with the larger issues of human existence.

In *The Brothers Karamazov*, Dostoevski's search for truth leads him to the question, "What is the nature of humanity?" The answer takes shape in the characterization of three of the brothers. Dmitri is dominated by sensuality; Ivan prizes the intellectual; Alyosha represents spirituality, although his asceticism sometimes clashes with his incipient sensuality. Together, the three personalities (together with the evil, twisted, and victimized Smerdyakov) are symbolic of humanity. Another question, "Is there a God?" is less easily answered because neither "The Grand Inquisitor" story nor "The Devil: Ivan's Nightmare" definitively resolves the matter. Likewise, the question of humanity's relationship to God remains nebulous for the same reasons, Father Zossima notwithstanding. The questions about one's relationship to another and one's relationship to society, however, are more concretely dealt with: Hostility, fear, and resentment, commingled with morbid curiosity, characterize the relationship of one to another, appearing to mirror the same qualities in the relationship of the individual to society. Thus, when Dostoevski poses the question "Does humanity have free will?" the tentative answer is that free will, if it exists at all, is very limited. One can hardly see one's destiny, much less exert substantial control over it, as Dmitri, among others, so tragically learns. Finally, Dostoevski wonders whether human intellect is capable of development or change; but since the entire novel is an exposition of the predestined Karamazov family, the answer is a foregone conclusion. These deeply felt philosophical considerations permeate the book without dwarfing its characters. Indeed, what could diminish the operatic rages and the petty buffoonery of Fyodor Karamazov, the screaming frustrations of Dmitri, the barely repressed seething indignation of Ivan, and the incredible shock of Alyosha's losing his spiritual innocence? Thus, philosophy and psychology go hand in hand in *The Brothers Karamazov* to shape a tale of immense emotional range and profound philosophical depth. *The Brothers Karamazov* is one of the masterpieces of the world's literature.

"Critical Evaluation" by Joanne G. Kashdan

Bibliography:
Belknap, Robert L. *The Genesis of "The Brothers Karamazov": The Aesthetics, Ideology, and Psychology of Text Making*. Evanston, Ill.: Northwestern University Press, 1990. Considers the reading and experiences of Dostoevski that appear in the novel. A study of the mind behind the book.
Bloom, Harold, ed. *Fyodor Dostoevsky's "The Brothers Karamazov."* New York: Chelsea House, 1988. Selection of critical interpretations of the text. Essays printed in chronological sequence from 1971 to 1977. Includes an extended chronology of Dostoevski.
Leatherbarrow, William J. *Fyodor Dostoyevsky—The Brothers Karamazov*. Cambridge, England: Cambridge University Press, 1992. Provides background for understanding, including historical, intellectual, and cultural influences. Discusses the major themes of the novel.
Terras, Victor. *A Karamazov Companion: Commentary on the Genesis, Language, and Style of Dostoevsky's Novel*. Madison: University of Wisconsin Press, 1981. Discusses the moral and religious philosophy that underlies the text, the use of language and symbolism, subtexts, and relevant myths.
Thompson, Diane Oenning. *"The Brothers Karamazov" and the Poetics of Memory*. Cambridge, England: Cambridge University Press, 1991. A psychological interpretation of the text based on meaning and memory. Connects the text to aesthetics and poetics.

THE BROWNING VERSION

Type of work: Drama
Author: Terence Rattigan (1911-1977)
Type of plot: Problem
Time of plot: The first half of the twentieth century
Locale: A public school in the south of England
First performed: 1948; first published, 1949

> *Principal characters:*
> JOHN TAPLOW, a student
> FRANK HUNTER, a science master
> ANDREW CROCKER-HARRIS, a classics master
> MILLIE CROCKER-HARRIS, his wife
> DR. FROBISHER, the headmaster
> PETER GILBERT, Crocker-Harris' successor
> MRS. GILBERT, his wife

The Story:

John Taplow, who was about sixteen years old and in the lower fifth form of an English public school, appeared at the flat of Andrew Crocker-Harris for an end-of-term tutorial in the hope of being advanced to the upper fifth. Seeing a box of chocolates, he helped himself to two pieces, ate one, and then, either out of conscience or fear of being caught, replaced the other.

Shortly thereafter, Frank Hunter arrived, and in the course of the conversation between the two it became clear that Crocker-Harris was retiring because of ill health. Known for his strict discipline, students had dubbed him the "Crock" and "Himmler of the lower fifth." Hunter, on the other hand, enjoyed easy rapport with students, as could be seen in Taplow's readiness to share confidences with him. While they waited for "the Crock" to appear, Hunter instructed Taplow in a proper golf swing. Taplow admitted that, although like most students he had had his share of fun at Crocker-Harris' expense, he did have sympathy for him.

Taplow was in the midst of mimicking the classics master when Millie Crocker-Harris entered and overheard the mimicry. She dispatched Taplow on an errand to the druggist for Crocker-Harris' heart medicine so that she could be alone with Hunter, with whom she had been having an affair.

Crocker-Harris appeared, only to find that Taplow was not there. When Taplow returned, Millie left to prepare dinner, and Hunter left pupil and master to their work on a translation of Aeschylus' *Agamemnon.* As with the earlier incident with the chocolates, Taplow's schoolboy-ish nervousness emerged in the form of a thoughtless comment about the master's inability to pass his love for the Greek play on to the boys. Frightened by his own audacity, Taplow attempted to make amends by encouraging Crocker-Harris to talk about the rhymed translation he had made of the play at the age of eighteen. Then, overcome by emotion for the first time in years, Crocker-Harris cut short the session and abruptly dismissed Taplow.

The next visitor, Dr. Frobisher, added to Crocker-Harris' long-repressed sense of failure as a teacher when he informed him that the board had voted to deny him a pension. In an attempt to be considerate, he requested that Crocker-Harris precede, rather than follow, a more popular master, whom the students would noisily applaud. When told about the denial of a pension, Millie was visibly annoyed and wondered how they would manage on the reduced salary her husband would receive in his new position at a crammer's school.

Dr. Frobisher's departure was followed by the arrival of Crocker-Harris' successor, Peter Gilbert, who came with his wife to look over the quarters that were to be their new home. The Gilberts seemed to be headed for the same kind of life as their predecessors. Mrs. Gilbert was as materialistic as Millie Crocker-Harris and, like Millie, had brought money to her marriage.

After the Gilberts left, Taplow reappeared unexpectedly, bringing a gift for Crocker-Harris, a second-hand copy of Browning's translation of *Agamemnon* that Taplow had inscribed with a Greek line from the play, translated roughly as "God from afar looks graciously upon a gentle master." The emotional strain on Crocker-Harris was obvious, but his delight in the gift was cut short when Millie taunted him cruelly by telling him that Taplow had earlier mimicked him; she added that the gift was probably only a bribe for a passing grade.

Hunter faced Millie with the truth that both had realized all along, that their affair was a purely physical one. He told her that he intended to end their affair, partly because of her cruelty to her husband. He also told her that he would not visit her at her parents' home in the summer as they had planned.

Hunter then insisted on telling the classics master the truth about his relationship with Millie, only to be informed that Crocker-Harris had known of the affair since its inception and that Millie was the one who had told him. Hunter mentioned that he was only the last of Millie's several affairs over the years. As Taplow had done earlier, Hunter attempted to make amends to Crocker-Harris, telling him of Taplow's liking for him and insisting that Taplow's gift of the Browning version of *Agamemnon* was a genuine gesture. He promised to visit Crocker-Harris in the fall in his new home, even naming the specific date on which he would come. Crocker-Harris seemed tentative in his acceptance of Hunter's offer, but expressed his recovered dignity by granting Taplow his advancement and by accepting Hunter's offer of a visit. Most important, however, he phoned Dr. Frobisher to inform him that he would, after all, as was his due as the older of the two retirees, speak after the popular younger retiree at the commencement ceremony, for, as he noted, "occasionally an anticlimax can be surprisingly effective." Having made that decision, he sat down to dinner, saying to Millie that they must not let their dinner get cold.

Critical Evaluation:

As one of two short companion plays, *The Browning Version* rapidly gained favor as one of Terrence Rattigan's best plays. Coming from the same tradition as James Hilton's famous schoolmaster, Mr. Chips, the figure of the "Crock" became almost as well known to English audiences as Hilton's schoolmaster. An award-winning Oxford University graduate, Crocker-Harris had come to his career at a public school with great enthusiasm about teaching the classics, especially *Agamemnon*. Gradually habit took over, and gradually he developed into a strict disciplinarian no longer able to communicate his enthusiasm to students.

His marriage to a woman whose family had provided her with an annuity was loveless from the start. He describes himself as having been unable to give his wife the type of sexual love that she required. Their relationship had soon turned to hatred. The play is about the failures of a career and a marriage, with both failures attributed to the conflict between private need and public behavior, a major theme in all of Rattigan's plays. The destructive disguising of inner feelings with outward decorum is an English character trait Rattigan had dubbed the "vice Anglais." Thus Crocker-Harris aptly describes his uncontrollable burst of emotion at Taplow's gift as the muscular twitchings of a corpse.

The fast-moving events on this last day of the school term serve to revive that living corpse. Crocker-Harris' emotional reaction to Taplow's gift, his confession to Gilbert of his initial excitement about teaching, and his admission to Hunter that he has known all along about his wife's infidelities, in conjunction with the denial of a pension and being forced to take a teaching position at an inferior school, free him from the emotional prison erected by the years of habitual responses to his wife, students, and colleagues. Hard truths emerge from Rattigan's diagnosis of his schoolmaster's life. Both Millie and her replacement, Mrs. Gilbert, seem spiritually vacuous, and Dr. Frobisher has realized success at the expense of compassion. Only Taplow and Hunter display compassion.

Criticized by some for its sentimentality, the drama is seen by others as a hard, if sympathetic, view of a failed life that offers hope of recovery. Crocker-Harris is at the end able to look back on the mockery of the students and to advise Gilbert that even a single success can atone for many failures. To Millie and Hunter, he is able, for the first time in his married life, openly to acknowledge the failure of his marriage. To Dr. Frobisher, he courageously insists on speaking after rather than before a more popular retiree at the commencement exercises.

The play is much more tightly concentrated than most of Rattigan's other plays. The conversations among Taplow, Hunter, and Millie serve to introduce the schoolmaster before he makes his first entrance. All the characters serve to impel the action of the play, which consists of Crocker-Harris' emotional reserve cracking in a series of confrontations with Taplow, Hunter, Frobisher, Gilbert, and Millie. The action of the play spans a twenty-four-hour period, occurs in one location, and consists of a tightly knitted sequence of entrances and exits that lead inevitably to the conclusion. These are the unities of time, place, and action about which Aristotle wrote in his *Poetics* (c. 334-323 B.C.E.).

In fact, the play's concentration resembles that of Sophocles' *Oedipus Tyrannus* (c. 429 B.C.E.), in which, one after another, important characters from Oedipus' life put together the pieces of his past. He must confront that past before he can know himself. Unlike Oedipus, however, Crocker-Harris has known his past all along, and it merely remains for him to acknowledge that past openly and to deal with what is left of his career and of his marriage. The marital plot in *The Browning Version* actually resembles that in *Agamemnon*. Both plays are about deceived husbands, though again, like Oedipus, Agamemnon discovers the pieces of his past, whereas Crocker-Harris has lived with the knowledge of his past during his eighteen years at the public school.

Susan Rusinko

Bibliography:

Darlow, Michael, and Gillian Hodson. *Terence Rattigan: The Man and His Work*. London: Quartet Books, 1979. This biography by the award-winning film and television director Michael Darlow and the film and television researcher Gillian Hodson is the definitive source of information about Rattigan's life and art. Also contains photographs and concludes with a bibliography, an index, a valuable appendix of original casts in important British and American stage productions (with dates, theaters, casts, directors, and numbers of perfor- mances), and a list of principal film and television productions.

Rusinko, Susan. *Terence Rattigan*. Boston: Twayne, 1983. Includes a chronology, biographical chapter, footnotes, bibliography, and index. A chronological treatment of Rattigan's plays; one chapter is devoted to his radio, television, and many film plays.

Smith, Kay Nolte. "Terence Rattigan." *Objectivist* 10 (March, 1971): 9-15. Defends Rattigan against accusations of mediocrity and provides a useful overview of Rattigan's plays, including an assessment of *The Browning Version* as his finest work.

Taylor, John Russell. "Terence Rattigan." In *The Rise and Fall of the Well-Made Play*. New York: Hill and Wang, 1967. Places Rattigan as the last of a group of dramatists in the tradition of well-made English plays that went out of fashion in the 1950's.

Young, Bertram A. *The Rattigan Version: Sir Terence Rattigan and the Theatre of Character*. London: Hamish Hamilton, 1986. A memoirist more than a biographer or literary critic, Young creates a portrait of Rattigan and his times drawn from his many years as theater critic for *Punch* and *The Financial Times*. Contains photos, a selected list of play openings, and an index.

BRUT

Type of work: Poetry
Author: Layamon (fl. twelfth century)
Type of plot: Epic
Time of plot: c. 409-689
Locale: Britain
First published: c. 1205

Principal personages:
UTHER PENDRAGON, the king of the Britons
MERLIN, a wizard and friend of Uther
ULFIN, an adviser to Uther
ARTHUR, the son of Uther, king of the Britons
GRACIEN, the Roman governor of Britain
YGAERNE, the mother of Arthur
COLEGRIM, the Saxon leader
CHILDRIC, an ally of Colegrim
GORLOIS, the earl of Cornwall and an enemy of Uther
MODRED, the nephew of, and traitor to, Arthur

The Story:

Gracien, Roman governor of Britain, was known throughout the land for terror and destruction. He was given orders by Roman emperor Maximian to defeat the Picts and the Scots. Only a few months after his arrival in Britain, he was brutally slain by the army of two noblemen, the twins Ethelbald and Aelfwald. Great joy and celebration broke out throughout Britain.

Meanwhile, Uther Pendragon, king of the Britons, fell madly in love with a noblewoman, Ygaerne, the wife of his enemy Gorlois. Uther sent for Merlin, his wizard, to help him win Ygaerne's love. To this end, Merlin cast a spell that made Uther appear to be Gorlois. Uther then went to the castle of his enemy and slept with the beautiful Ygaerne. Nine months later, Ygaerne gave birth to Arthur.

Uther Pendragon did not know that the Saxons had sent spies into his court and planned to kill him. He soon found himself ill and could not eat or drink anything but water. He never knew that the water was poisoned, and he soon died, along with a hundred men that had drunk of the water with him.

The Saxons continued their attacks upon the Britons for years. Colegrim, the Saxon leader, had conquered all of the north of Britain, from the river Humber to Caithness-shire. Soon his forces met the army of the young Arthur. The battle was bloody and costly, causing Arthur's forces to retreat. Colegrim thought Arthur had given up the battle when Arthur once again attacked Colegrim's forces viciously. Colegrim began to flee with his men across the river, but the deep water was too much for their horses and seven thousand Saxons were drowned. Colegrim survived the battle and took refuge in the walled city of York.

Many battles were to follow the defeat of Colegrim. The Saxon Childric, an ally of Colegrim, brought as many as six hundred ships of warriors to fight the forces of Arthur. Together, he and his men ravaged entire villages, killing all the men and then raping and killing the women and children. He destroyed churches and castles alike, setting fire to all wooden structures. Then came the great battle of the city of Bath, in which King Arthur and Colegrim once again stood face to face on the battlefield. Colegrim, his brother Baldulf, and Childric all attacked Arthur simultaneously, but their armies were no match for the knights of King Arthur. Colegrim died from the blade of King Arthur's sword, his head split into two by its blow. His brother, Baldulf, lay dead by his side. Childric escaped, but was later slain by Duke Cador on the Isle of Thanet.

Twelve years of peace followed the battle of Bath, and King Arthur brought the land to wealth and prosperity. He called for a meeting of his allies on Yule day (Christmas day) in London. Seven kings attended, their queens, seven hundred knights, and their companions. All were peaceful and merry. King Arthur sat down, his queen Wenhaver (Guinivere) at his side, and the winter feast began. The knights were seated according to rank; the highest were placed near Arthur, with the lowest at the end. Soon the company became angry with one another and fights began. King Arthur vowed vengeance on those who disturbed his feast and sought a way to prevent this jealousy and bickering among knights. He concluded that there was only one way: a table without a head—the round table.

Arthur was to fight many battles and perform many deeds of chivalry. He fought for the Celts in France against the Romans. He fought the giant of Brittany and met Lucius Hiberius, a Roman, on the battlefield. Victory after victory was won, and Arthur's reputation grew with each blow of his sword. One day, he dreamed that Modred, his nephew whom he had left in charge in Britain, would defeat him on the battlefield. He put this out of his mind and continued with his campaign against the Romans. Having defeated Lucius Hiberius, he commanded that Lucius' body be carried to a pavilion he had built and covered with golden clothes. There it was to remain for three days. He then had all the bodies of the dead—kings, nobles, and commoners—brought together and buried with dignity. He did not know that the battle he had just won would not end the war.

King Arthur had yet another dream and called for an interpretation of it. He had dreamed that his nephew, Modred, raised an army against him. That morning, a knight came to bring him news from Modred. This knight told the king that Modred had allied himself with the Picts, Scots, and Saxons and had taken Arthur's lands and his queen, Wenhaver, as his own. Arthur vowed vengeance and death upon any who would ally themselves with Modred. He would kill Modred and Wenhaver. Immediately, he set forth for Britain with his armies poised for battle. He did not know that a spy among his men had sent word to Modred that the king was on his way home.

Modred's armies met Arthur on the shores of Britain. Arthur's armies pushed Modred and his men into Winchester and then to Cornwall. Two hundred thousand men were slain in battle, including the evil Modred. Only three men stood at the battle's end, Arthur and two of his knights. The queen, meanwhile, was hiding in York, afraid of what would become of her. She soon fled west into Wales and was never heard of again. King Arthur surrendered his kingdom to the young Constantine, son of Cador, and went to Avalon, promising to return.

Critical Evaluation:

Brut, one of the earliest accounts of the Arthurian legend, is the work of a secular monk of Worcestershire, southern England. Layamon's name is the Middle English equivalent of "lawman," leading to the belief that this poet-monk was educated in the king's law and that he might have been a legal adviser to the town's gentry. Layamon based his work on a verse chronicle by Wace, *Roman de Brut* (c. 1155), a Norman version that in turn was based on the prose history composed by Geoffrey of Monmouth, who was the first to draw the elements of the Arthurian legend together in his *History of the Kings of Britain* (c. 1136). Layamon followed the outline of Wace's verse chronicle but nearly doubled its length with the addition of imaginative passages and selections from Welsh tradition. By emphasizing the Saxon character of the Arthurian period and by incorporating fanciful Celtic additions to the narrative, Layamon added considerably to the dimensions of the Arthurian story inherited from Geoffrey and Wace. It was from his *Brut* that later writers such as Chrétien de Troyes and Sir Thomas Malory borrowed the essential elements of their own masterpieces.

Layamon's poem adopts a style and an approach that better represents Old English poetry than Middle English poetry. Its vocabulary, tone, and meter all reflect the style of the early English poets of the early Middle Ages and the Anglo-Saxon style of epic poetry. The lines of the poem, for example, are divided into half-lines so that alliteration (the repetition of initial consonant sounds) stands out as a major poetic device. This is the style of *Beowulf* (c. 1000) and other Anglo-Saxon poems written in Old English between 500 and 1100. Rhyme is almost completely absent from *Brut*, though it was a common device in Middle English poetry.

The absence of rhyme from Old English poetry was a result of the guttural nature of the language. The favoring of consonants over vowels made it next to impossible to achieve the sounds necessary for rhyme. The French and Latin influences following the Norman invasion in 1066, however, altered the language enough to change the arrangement of letters in favor of vowel sounds. Thus the style of *Brut* is probably deliberate on behalf of the poet, who, though he had the full use of a rhyming language, either had a fondness for the alliterative style of Old English poetry or felt that the style, reflecting the time during which the story takes place, would be better appreciated by his audience.

Layamon used several sources of information upon which to base *Brut*. However, there are two he seems to have relied upon most heavily. *The Ecclesiastical History of the English People* (731), by Bede, was one of his two major sources. This work was originally written in Latin. It is surprising that Layamon looked to this source because he had several Arthurian poems from which to draw his material. The other, more extensively used source was the Anglo-Norman work, *Roman de Brut* by Wace. This was originally written in French, and Wace provides much more detail regarding the legend of King Arthur than Bede does. Bede merely mentions the possibility of such a Celtic king during the early history of Britain.

The style of *Brut* is often interpreted as rough and vulgar, descending from popular forms rather than more stylized forms of Old English poetry. Celtic mythology can also be found throughout *Brut*. Merlin, for example, is presented as a pagan priest, possibly a druid. He shows power over nature itself and has the power to take on other forms at will. He is a mystic and a soothsayer. Even the death of Arthur is full of mysticism. King Arthur, being one of only three survivors from his last battle with Modred, sails off with Argante (Morgan La Fey) to Avalon, a mystical island from Celtic folklore. It is to its rough, old-fashioned style, however, that Layamon's *Brut* may owe its popularity. Unlike the French and Latin accounts of King Arthur, which focus on presenting Arthur and his knights as heroes, Layamon places Arthur in history. Only about one third of *Brut* actually deals with Arthurian legend. The rest chronicles the history of the time before and after Arthur. Layamon, unlike Wace, avoids the subtleties of character and personality and spends little time on love, romance, and chivalry. Rather, he leans toward violence, action, and brutality. This, again, is an attribute more often found in Old English verse than in Middle English writings. He deals with the brutal murder of King Gracien, the treachery surrounding the conception of King Arthur by Uther Pendragon and the beautiful Ygaerne, several bloody battles, and Arthur's departure. There is an overwhelming sense of tragedy to Layamon's poem. Lust, greed, and the horror of battle prevail over chivalry and glory. The reader is presented with a King Arthur whose very birth was the result of lust and deception, a leader who lacks most of the approved qualities of a king. His life is primitive, and his power is tribal. Thus, he is presented as a Celtic chieftain rather than as a heroic Anglo-Norman king. He is powerful and even cruel, as can be seen in his handling of those who rebel against his authority. It may be possible that there is more truth about the legendary King Arthur in *Brut* than in any other Arthurian tale.

Gordon Robert Maddison

Bibliography:
Garbaty, Thomas J., ed. *Medieval English Literature*. Lexington, Mass.: D. C. Heath, 1984. A full study of Old and Middle English poetry with great emphasis on Arthurian legends. Presents *Brut* without translation.
Layamon. *Brut*. Translated by Rosamund Allen. New York: St. Martin's Press, 1992. A very clear translation with well-developed notes and a good introduction. Contains a complete bibliography.
———. *Layamon's "Brut": A History of the Britons*. Translated by Donald G. Bzdyl. Binghamton: Center for Medieval and Early Renaissance Studies, State University of New York at Binghamton, 1989. A fine prose translation with good explication and a complete index.
O'Neal, Michael. *King Arthur: Opposing Viewpoints*. San Diego, Calif.: Greenhaven Press, 1992. A good primer for students of the Arthurian legends. Presents conflicting theories with both legend and historical evidence.
Wilhelm, James J., ed. *The Romance of Arthur*. New York: Garland, 1994. Prose and poetry translations of Arthurian tales, including parts of *Brut* and all of Layamon's source material.

BUDDENBROOKS

Type of work: Novel
Author: Thomas Mann (1875-1955)
Type of plot: Social realism
Time of plot: Nineteenth century
Locale: Germany
First published: Buddenbrooks: Verfall einer Familie, 1901 (English translation, 1924)

Principal characters:
> JEAN BUDDENBROOK, the head of a German business house
> FRAU BUDDENBROOK, Jean's wife
> ANTONIE (TONY), their daughter
> CHRISTIAN and
> TOM, their sons
> HERR GRÜNLICH, Tony's first husband
> ERICA, the daughter of Tony and Grünlich
> GERDA, Tom's wife
> HANNO, the son of Tom and Gerda
> HERR PERMANEDER, Tony's second husband

The Story:

In the year 1875, the Buddenbrook family was flourishing. Johann had maintained intact the business and wealth he had inherited from his father, and the Buddenbrook name was held in high esteem. Johann's oldest son, Jean, inherited the business when old Johann died. Antonie (Tony), Jean's first child, who was born in the family home on Mengstrasse, had aristocratic tendencies by nature and temperament. The next child was Tom, followed by Christian, who from birth seemed somewhat peculiar. Tom displayed an early interest in the Buddenbrook business, but Christian seemed indifferent to all family responsibilities.

Tony grew into a beautiful woman. When Herr Grünlich, obviously interested in Tony, came to call on the family, Jean investigated his financial status. The headstrong Tony despised Grünlich and his obsequious manner. Going to a nearby seaside resort on the Baltic Sea to avoid meeting him when he called again, she fell in love with a young medical student named Morten. When they learned of this, Tony's parents hurriedly brought her home. Tony, having been raised to feel a sense of her family duty, was unable to ignore their arguments in favor of Grünlich when he asked for her hand. Once the wedding date was set, Grünlich received a promise of a dowry of eighty thousand marks. Grünlich took his twenty-year-old bride to the country and refused to allow her to call on any of her city friends. Although she complained about this in her letters to her parents, Tony resigned herself to obeying her husband's wishes.

Tom held an important position in the business, which continued to amass money for the Buddenbrook family. Christian's early distaste for business and his ill health had given him the privilege of going to South America. When Grünlich found his establishment floundering, his creditors urged him to apply to his father-in-law for help. Only then did Jean Buddenbrook discover Grünlich's motive for marrying Tony: The Buddenbrook reputation had placed Grünlich's already failing credit on a sounder basis, but only temporarily so. Actually, Grünlich was hoping that Jean's concern for Tony would help him avoid financial failure. Tony herself assured her father that she hated Grünlich but that she did not wish to endure the hardships that bankruptcy would entail. Jean brought Tony and his granddaughter, Erica Grünlich, back to the Buddenbrook home. The divorce, based on Grünlich's fraudulent handling of Tony's dowry, went through easily.

Jean Buddenbrook loved his family dearly and firmly believed in the greatness of the Buddenbrook heritage. Tony was once again happy in her father's home, although she bore her sorrows so that everyone would notice. She had grown quite close to her brother Tom and took pride in his development and in the progress of the Buddenbrook firm.

Christian failed in his enterprises in South America and when he returned home his father gave him a job in the firm and an office, which Christian avoided as much as possible. His manners were still peculiar and his health poor. Serious Tom was able to handle the business as well as Jean, and he remained attached to family customs. When Jean died and left the business to Tom, Tony felt that the family had lost its strongest tie. Tom, too, was greatly affected by his father's death, but the responsibility of following in his father's footsteps became his principal goal.

Because Christian could not adjust to Buddenbrook interests, the ever-patient Tom sent him to Munich for his health. Reports from Munich that he was seen often in the company of a notoriously loose actress distressed the family. Then Tom made a satisfactory marriage with the daughter of a wealthy businessman. Gerda, whose dowry was added to the Buddenbrook fortune, was an attractive woman who loved music. Once again, parties were held at the Buddenbrook mansion on Mengstrasse.

Tony returned from a trip hoping that a new acquaintance, Herr Permaneder, would call, and soon he did. He was a successful beer merchant in Munich. Tom and Frau Buddenbrook thought that Permaneder, in spite of his crude manners and strange dialect, would make a satisfactory husband for Tony. Fortified with her second, smaller dowry, Tony went to Munich as Frau Permaneder. She sent Erica off to boarding school.

Soon, however, Tony was once again writing passionate appeals to her family and complaining of her married life. When Permaneder betrayed her by making love to a servant, she came home. Tom protested against a second divorce, but Tony insisted. She was surprised to learn that her husband would not fight the proceedings, that he felt the marriage had been a mistake, and that he would return the dowry, which he did not need.

Tom and Gerda had produced a son to carry on the family name. Little Johann, or Hanno, as he was called, inherited his mother's love for music, but he was pale and sickly from birth. Tom tried to instill in his son a love for the family business, but Hanno was too shy to respond to his father.

After the death of Frau Buddenbrook, Christian, Tony, and Tom haggled over the inheritance. Christian demanded his share outright, but Tom, as administrator of the estate, refused to take it out of the business. Christian thereupon quarreled bitterly with Tom, all the pent-up feeling of the past years vented in a torrent of abuse against what he considered to be the cold, mercenary actions of Tom Buddenbrook.

Tom was not mercenary; he merely worked hard and faithfully. Despite his efforts, however, the business had begun to decline because of larger economic changes. Now suffering from poor health, Tom felt that sickly Christian who had refused to take on any responsibility would outlive him.

Tony found a fine husband for her daughter, but, like hers, the marriage of Erica and Herr Weinschenk ended in disaster when Weinschenk was caught indulging in foul business practices and sent to prison for three years. Accustomed to public scandal, Tony bore that new hardship with forbearance. Erica also adopted her mother's attitude.

Tom died suddenly. He had fallen in the snow and had been brought to his bed, where he died a few hours later, babbling incoherently. His loss meant more to Tony than to any of the others. Christian, arriving from Munich for the funeral, had grown too concerned over his own suffering to show grief over the death of his brother. Gerda too felt deep sorrow, for her marriage with Tom had been a true love match.

After the will was read, Christian returned to Munich to marry the woman he had been unable to marry when he was under Tom's financial control. Soon afterward, Christian's wife wrote to Tony that his illness had poisoned his mind and that she had placed Christian in an institution. Life at the Buddenbrook home continued. Little Hanno never gained much strength. Thin and sickly at fifteen years old, he died during a typhoid epidemic.

So passed the last of the Buddenbrooks. From the days of the first Johann, whose elegance and power had produced a fine business and a healthy, vigorous lineage, to the last pitiably small generation, which died with Hanno, the Buddenbrook family had decayed.

Critical Evaluation:

Buddenbrooks, Thomas Mann's first novel, was a great and immediate success, and it is still one of his most popular works. Though not as complex or problematic as his later novels, it develops most of the major themes that occupied him throughout his career. The work had originally been planned as a novella about the boy Hanno Buddenbrook, but in assembling the material, Mann found himself tracing the story back four generations. Thus the novel became a family chronicle with a broad social milieu. This type of novel was rare in German literature, which tended to concentrate on the *Bildungsroman*, which traces the growth of a single character. *Buddenbrooks* further departs from that tradition in reversing the emphasis on growth and development to concentrate on decay and decadence. This fascination with the conflict between the life force and the death wish, especially as it appears in the artist type, represents a typical aspect of Mann's work. Mann's artist figures are the product of robust bourgeois stock, families whose drive for work and achievement has led to prosperity and comfort. As the family attains greater refinement and sensitivity, however, the life force slackens. At this stage, the artist figure appears, estranged from the bourgeois world and its values and curiously drawn toward disease and death. It is no accident that several of Mann's works take place in sanatoriums, or that typhus, syphilis, and tuberculosis figure prominently in his work.

This theme was not only important to Mann the writer but to Mann the human being. Indeed, *Buddenbrooks* is the most thoroughly autobiographical of his novels. Every character in it can be traced to an actual prototype. Certainly the people of Mann's hometown, Lübeck, were shocked when the novel appeared and protested what amounted to an invasion of privacy. The streets and houses of the town, the nearby seashore and countryside were all easily identifiable, and the Buddenbrooks could easily be identified as, in fact, being the Mann family. Thomas Mann was an artist, working in words rather than in music, and he rejected the values of his family, a middle-class career, and the expectations of his community. He had left Lübeck for Italy, where, in fact, he began to write the chronicle of the Buddenbrook family, and the stuff of the novel was intensely personal to him. Indeed, he drew largely on family documents and stories. Despite these autobiographical aspects, however, Mann carefully structured the work so that the process of family decay proceeds in a clear and almost inevitable movement, by stages through the four generations, gathering momentum and expressing itself simultaneously in the business fortunes and the physical characteristics, mannerisms, and psychological makeup of the four eldest sons of their respective generations: Johann, Jean, Tom, and Hanno.

At each stage there is both a descent and an ascent. Vitality and physical vigor decline and the business skills atrophy, as is evidenced by the steadily declining capital. This external decline, reflected even in such details as increasing susceptibility to tooth decay, is however counterbalanced by an increase in sensitivity, an inclination toward art and metaphysics, and an increasingly active interior life. Johann may indeed play the flute—a necessary social grace for the eighteenth century gentleman—but he is not given to introspection. He lives to a ripe old age, and although he is an honest man, he has no scruples about the validity of running a business and making a profit; he also has a sure sense of the economic situation of his time and showed sound judgment in his investments. His son Jean is already far more concerned with moral principles, and business is no longer for him a natural drive but a responsibility. His health suffers and his life is shorter, but his capacity for artistic enjoyment and religious emotion is greater. A tension between inner and outer begins to manifest itself, which becomes even more evident in Tom. In him, refinement becomes elegance, and an inclination for the exotic manifests itself in his choice of a wife. Yet the strain of preserving the exterior forms—a new house, social position, and the fortunes of the business—shows in his weakened physical constitution and in his attraction, late in his short, forty-eight-year life, to the philosophy of Arthur Schopenhauer, in which he sees the possibility of his embattled individuality dissolving into an eternal impersonal spiritual existence. Hanno, the last of the Buddenbrooks, dies while he is still a boy, his life filled with pain but rich in inner creativity that is expressed in his Wagnerian flights of musical composition. For Mann, Wagner was always linked with decadence and the death wish.

Many of the elements of this sequence recur in Mann's other works, especially his early works. It is also clear that Mann is absorbed by the psychological development of his figures. The novel dwells more and more intensely on the inner states of the later characters. Hanno, the starting point of Mann's conception, retains a disproportionately large share of the novel's pages and remains one of Mann's most engaging and memorable creations. Yet it is also clear that Mann, for all of his understanding and sympathy toward the artistically inclined temperaments of the declining Buddenbrook family, drew a clear line between that sympathy and his own allegiance. Not only does he dwell on the increasingly difficult lives and demeaning deaths of the later characters—as when the eloquent and self-possessed Tom collapses and dies in a pool of filth on the street, or when Hanno dies suddenly of typhus—but, in the case of Hanno, he also unequivocally attributes the death to a failure of the will to live. In one of the most remarkable chapters of the book, the narrator, who has generally retained his omniscience in chronicling the fortunes of the family, describes the course of a typical case of typhus and raises it to a mythical encounter between life and death: At the crisis, victims may either exert their will to live and return or they can proceed onward on the path to self-dissolution in death. Hanno, whose music has expressed this longing for release from the demands of life to which he is not equal, takes the latter course and dies. Here, any similarity between Mann and his characters ends. Although Mann as an artist felt himself estranged from the social world of the bourgeois, for him, unlike Hanno, art itself is the means by which he can retain his focus on life. *Buddenbrooks* may describe a family's loss of will to live, but in so doing, it affirms the writer's most profound love of life.

"Critical Evaluation" by Steven C. Schaber

Bibliography:
Furst, Lilian. "Re-Reading *Buddenbrooks*." *German Life and Letters* 44, no. 4 (July, 1991): 317-329. Emphasizes the place of aesthetic, rather than traditional sociohistorical, readings

of the novel. Points out how important it is that readers are able to imagine the novel's internal world now that that actual historical world is gone.

Hatfield, Henry. "Thomas Mann's *Buddenbrooks*: The World of the Father." In *Thomas Mann: A Collection of Critical Essays*, edited by Henry Hatfield. Englewood Cliffs, N.J.: Prentice-Hall, 1964. A useful introduction, showing how the novel is still indebted to the style of naturalism but also already pointing toward modernism. Contains a clear, brief analysis of Mann's use of the leitmotif in the novel.

Heller, Erich. "Pessimism and Sensibility." In *Thomas Mann: The Ironic German*. 1958. Reprint. South Bend, Ind.: Regnery/Gateway, 1979. This classic study explains the philosophical influences on the novel. Heller finds nearly all the elements of Mann's later masterpieces already present in this first novel.

Ridley, Hugh. *Thomas Mann: "Buddenbrooks."* Cambridge, England: Cambridge University Press, 1987. A basic, well-balanced, and useful introduction to all aspects of the novel. Especially good on psychological interpretation. Brief bibliography.

Swales, Martin. *"Buddenbrooks": Family Life as the Mirror of Social Change*. Boston: Twayne, 1991. Perhaps the best available treatment for nonspecialists, this is a thorough overview of sources, criticism, and reception, followed by a balanced essayistic reading that emphasizes philosophical aspects. Includes a brief annotated bibliography of primary and secondary literature.

BULLET PARK

Type of work: Novel
Author: John Cheever (1912-1982)
Type of plot: Psychological realism
Time of plot: Mid-twentieth century
Locale: Suburban New York
First published: 1969

Principal characters:
  ELIOT NAILLES, an advertising executive
  NELLIE NAILLES, his wife
  TONY NAILLES, his son
  PAUL HAMMER, the crazed would-be murderer of Eliot Nailles
  SWAMI RUTUOLA, a mystic
  GRETCHEN OXENCROFT, Hammer's mother

The Story:
  Paul Hammer was being shown around the village of Bullet Park by a real estate agent. The foibles and residents of Bullet Park, which was connected to New York City by a commuter railroad, were the subject of the real estate agent's babble. Little or nothing was learned about the mysterious Mr. Hammer, who was about to buy a house.
  Eliot Nailles was introduced to Paul Hammer and his wife at church. Nailles was mildly irritated by the priest's pun upon their names (Hammer and Nailles), which struck him as having a kind of inevitability about it. The two most important people in Nailles's life were his wife, Nellie, and his son, Tony, whom he dearly loved but had trouble approaching. Though she had pretensions in the arts, Nellie, coming home from a disastrous day in New York, had been shocked there by the sexual crudity of a play and other threats to her sensibilities. For Nellie and Tony, Bullet Park was a sanctuary. Nailles won for his family this sanctuary by setting off daily for the city on the 7:56 to write copy for a mouthwash, Spang.
  One day Tony refused to get out of bed. The doctor found nothing wrong with him. A psychiatrist gave Nellie a moral lecture about the lack of values of her class. A somnambulist expert gave Tony a series of tests and submitted a bill for five hundred dollars. Nailles was distraught and could not understand what was wrong with his son.
  Mr. and Mrs. Hammer invited the Nailles to a dinner party, though they had been no more than introduced. The evening was a disaster. Mrs. Nailles insulted her husband and ridiculed suburban life: "All you have to do is to get your clothes at Brooks, catch the train and show up in church once a week and no one will ever ask a question about your identity."
  That lack of identity appeared to be illustrated a few days later when a man named Shinglehouse, a regular on the 7:56, committed suicide by throwing himself under an express train. Though the rhythm of life seemed barely disturbed by the event, Nailles was deeply shaken. Returning home, he tried harder to communicate with Tony about what he felt, but Tony only slept. In his mind he reviewed difficult episodes in his attempts to be a parent. Nailles remembered the time Tony had been arrested for attacking a teacher who denied him the privilege of playing football. He recalled another time when Tony briefly disappeared over-night, having stayed with a Mrs. Hubbard, whom he met in a bookstore. Later, Tony invited Mrs. Hubbard to dinner in a grotesque parody of social convention. Nailles further remembered

the confrontation with his son that had immediately preceded his son's taking to bed, in which he had been told: "The only reason you love me . . . is because you can give me things."

Desperate to do something about Tony's strange illness, Nellie took the advice of a former cleaning woman and looked up Swami Rutuola, who lived above a funeral parlor in Bullet Park. The Swami visited Tony, asked him to repeat "Love" and "Hope" hundreds of times, and, as if by magic, Tony would thereby be cured.

Paul Hammer, writing in his journal, revealed his madness in his own words, and a long interpolated letter from his mother showed her madness as well. Hammer first became aware of Nailles by a small article in a dental journal announcing his promotion to the head of the mouthwash division of his company. From that moment, Hammer settled on Nailles as his target for assassination, though he would later focus on Tony as the best way of hurting the father.

Hammer's account revealed his life as a lonely drifter. He had been born out of wedlock and was hidden away at school. Until he settled upon Nailles, he was wholly without purpose and almost entirely cut off from normal human contact. In one passage, for instance, he described his travels about the world in terms of the furniture of his hotel rooms. His mother, Gretchen Oxencroft, laid out the entire conspiracy on one of his infrequent visits: Hammer should settle in a place like Bullet Park, fix upon an advertising executive like Nailles (who represented the shallowest aspects of modern culture), and then nail him to the door of Christ's church as a statement that would wake up the world. With a purpose in his life, Hammer followed the plan like the dedicated assassin he had become. His marriage was an emotionally meaningless event that became part of his disguise as he moved into Bullet Park.

Nailles sponsored Hammer as a member of the volunteer fire department and accompanied him on a fishing trip. Hammer settled upon Tony's death as the best way of injuring Nailles. As Tony worked directing traffic at a neighborhood party, Hammer knocked him out and dragged him off to church. Hammer, however, had told Swami Rutuola of the intended murder, and the Swami came running to Nailles. With a chain saw, Nailles cut through the door of the church and rescued his son from the altar where he was about to be sacrificed.

Critical Evaluation:

Bullet Park is John Cheever's third novel. His long and distinguished writing career was capped by many honors, including two National Book Awards, the Pulitzer Prize for Literature (1979), and the Edward McDowell Medal in the Arts (1979). Much of his work, including the first chapter of *Bullet Park*, appeared originally in the magazine *The New Yorker*. His subject matter centers largely on the suburban types of *Bullet Park*. His stature as a writer, however, is greater than that of a journalistic social satirist.

Bullet Park proved problematic to early reviewers, who were disappointed that it veered away from the satirical humor with which Cheever had become identified, told a preposterous story without narrative logic, and plunged without warning into absurdist melodrama. Yet criticism over time has reclaimed the novel's reputation. Difficult and complex, *Bullet Park* is a fine and rewarding novel.

A comparison of its two major figures, Eliot Nailles and Paul Hammer, defines the conflicts that shape this apparently malformed story. The suburbanite Nailles carries his share of psychological baggage. He gets through the day anesthetized with drugs and alcohol. His son, Tony, resents him deeply. His wife, Nellie, seems to have lost her way. His prayers and his opinions are perfunctory and shallow. He is, moreover, an advertising executive for Spang mouthwash. Readers of Cheever know what to think of admen. Nailles's supposed lack of substance, judged from the article in the dental journal, induces Hammer to select him as his victim. Nailles proves to be more than a stereotype, however, in the way he understands his world. He is deeply committed to his wife, and especially to his son. He wins his living in the hostile city to preserve the domicile where his wife and son have retreated for protection, and where he returns with gratitude each evening. When the snapping turtle appears on the lawn, Nailles goes out to shoot it, just as primitive man defended his home against the woolly mammoth. Cheever nevertheless uses the expectation of the stereotype of the suburbs to shape his paradox. Nailles is the one who loves; he thereby possesses a generous share of goodness.

Hammer, on the other hand, parodies the defeated person of existential literature. Nellie, in a thematic echo, is reading the works of the French philosopher and novelist Albert Camus in her book club. Mersault, in Camus' *L'Étranger* (1942; *The Stranger*, 1946) for example, is so psychologically empty that he shoots an unknown person to demonstrate to himself that he has the will to make a choice. Reading Hammer's own words in his journal, the reader discovers his moral emptiness in the texture of the prose: "Have you ever waked on a summer morning to realize that this is the day when you will kill a man? . . . Hammer mowed his lawns that day. The imposture was thrilling. Look at Mr. Hammer cutting his grass. What a nice man Mr. Hammer must be." The reader will probably recall the string of political murders of the 1960's committed by assassins with vague and forlorn motives. Hammer is equally evil, crazed, and alone.

Bullet Park contrasts the moral states of Nailles and Hammer, revealing them in images and in the texture of language. Although flawed and foolish, Nailles celebrates his humanity. He loves Tony with a love that continues to flow although he gets very little in return. He describes the scene in which he almost kills his son in anger on a miniature golf course when Tony declares that he is going to quit school: "I said that even if he wanted to be a poet he had to prepare himself to be a poet. So then I said to him what I've never said before. I said: 'I love you, Tony.'"

A third character is also important to the book. The narrator, especially in the early part of the story, provides the commentary and wit that make up the characteristic Cheever voice: "The diocesan bishop had suggested that church-goers turn on their windshield wipers to communicate their faith in the resurrection of the dead and the life of the world to come." Such humor is brittle and risks silliness (in one of Cheever's stories, the zoning laws do not allow anyone to die; a body has to be removed to another place before a death certificate can be issued). Here that voice is carefully modulated to serve a purpose within the story. People generally are foolish and limited, and Nailles is only one example. With love and hate such people blunder into good and evil, in one mixture or another. The suburbs prove to be as good a place as any to look for fulfilling love.

Bruce Olsen

Bibliography:
Coale, Samuel. "The Resurrection of *Bullet Park*: John Cheever's Curative Spell." In *The Critical Response to John Cheever*, edited by Francis J. Bosha. Westport, Conn.: Greenwood Press, 1994. Finds that *Bullet Park* arose from creative tensions within the writer himself, which find expression in his journals.
Donaldson, Scott. *John Cheever*. New York: Random House, 1988. A standard biography with a critical discussion of all Cheever's work.
Gardner, John. "Witchcraft in *Bullet Park*." In *Critical Essays on John Cheever*, edited by Robert G. Collins. Boston: G. K. Hall, 1982. Asserts *Bullet Park* to be a first-rate novel and takes early reviewers to task for misunderstanding it.

Hunt, George. *John Cheever: The Hobgoblin Company of Love*. Grand Rapids, Mich.: Wm. B. Eerdmans, 1983. Contains a chapter on *Bullet Park* that relates it to the time in which it was written and offers a strong defense of its value.

Waldeland, Lynne. *John Cheever*. Boston: Twayne, 1979. Defends the style and plotting of *Bullet Park* as appropriate to its exploration of good and evil.

THE BULWARK

Type of work: Novel
Author: Theodore Dreiser (1871-1945)
Type of plot: Social realism
Time of plot: 1890 to the mid-1920's
Locale: Dukla and Philadelphia, Pennsylvania; New York City; and Atlantic City
First published: 1946

Principal characters:
SOLON BARNES, a Quaker banker
BENECIA (NÉE WALLIN), his wife
CYNTHIA BARNES, Solon's sister
RUFUS BARNES, Solon's father
HANNAH BARNES, Solon's mother
PHOEBE KIMBER, Hannah's sister
RHODA KIMBER and
LAURA KIMBER, Phoebe's daughters
JUSTUS WALLIN, Benecia's father
ISOBEL, the oldest child of Solon and Benecia
ORVILLE, the second child of Solon and Benecia
DOROTHEA, the attractive third child of Solon and Benecia
ETTA, the fourth child of Solon and Benecia
VOLIDA LA PORTE, Etta's friend
HESTER WALLIN, Justus' sister
WILLARD KANE, an artist and Etta's lover
STEWART, the youngest child of Solon and Benecia
VICTOR BRUGE and
LESTER JENNINGS, Stewart's friends
PSYCHE TANZER, a young girl

The Story:

Rufus Barnes was a farmer and tradesman living near Segookit, Maine. He and his wife, Hannah, were good Quakers. When Hannah's sister, Phoebe Kimber, living in Trenton, New Jersey, lost her husband, she asked Rufus to come to New Jersey to help settle her husband's affairs. Rufus, finding himself the executor of a rather large estate, did a thorough and competent job. In gratitude for his help and in hopes that he would move his family close to her, Phoebe offered Rufus one of her properties, an old, rundown, but elegant house in Dukla, Pennsylvania, just across the Delaware River from Trenton. Rufus was willing to restore the house and try to sell it, but Phoebe was eager to give the house to him. At last, Rufus agreed to take the house and move his family to Dukla. He and his wife had the house restored with great taste and beauty.

Rufus and Hannah became somewhat more worldly in Dukla. Rufus went into business, dealing in real estate, but he applied his Quaker principles to his business and helped the poor farmers make their land yield more profit so that he would not have to foreclose. Respected and prosperous, he and his wife still followed their faith and taught it carefully to their two children, Cynthia and Solon.

Solon Barnes cut his leg with an ax. An incompetent doctor bungled the treatment, and for a time, they all feared that the boy might die. His mother prayed devoutly, however, and Solon recovered, an event that kept the family strictly loyal to their faith.

Sent to school with their cousins, Laura and Rhoda (Phoebe's children), Cynthia and Solon began to acquire more polish and knowledge of the world. At school, Solon met Benecia Wallin, the daughter of a wealthy Quaker. Cynthia, Laura, Rhoda, and Benecia were all sent to a Quaker finishing school at Oakwold, but Solon chose to remain at home and help his father in the real estate business.

Justus Wallin, Benecia's father, was impressed by the Barnes family. He admired the way Rufus and Solon conducted their business; he was impressed with Hannah's faith and her behavior at Quaker meetings. The families became friendly, and Justus asked Rufus and Solon to become the agents for his extensive holdings. Solon and Benecia fell in love. Justus found a job for Solon in his Philadelphia bank and, although Solon had to start at the bottom, it was clear that he had both the talent and the influence to rise quickly to the top. Solon and Benecia were married, to the delight of both families, in a Quaker ceremony.

The years passed. Solon and Benecia were happy and successful. Solon did well at the bank in Philadelphia; Benecia was a quiet, principled, and religious woman. After the death of Solon's parents, Solon and Benecia moved into the house in Dukla. Although Solon occasionally experienced metaphysical doubts, he lived in complete adherence to the moral principles of the Quakers. He became a bulwark of the community, an honest and forthright man who did not approve of smoking, drinking, art, music, literature, or dancing. He and Benecia brought up their five children in accordance with these strict Quaker principles.

Each of the children reacted differently to this upbringing. The oldest daughter, Isobel, unattractive and unpopular in school, found it difficult to make friends. She began to read books and decided, against the ideas implanted by her parents, that she wanted to avoid the Quaker finishing school and go to college. Solon managed to compromise and send her to Llewellyn College for Women, a Quaker institution, where she remained to do postgraduate work. Orville, the oldest son, inherited Solon's severity, although not his kindness. Orville became interested in business at an early age, although his materialism was not tempered by any principle deeper than respectability. He married a wealthy socialite and went into her father's pottery business in Trenton. The third child, Dorothea, was the beauty of the family. She had been taken up by her father's cousin Rhoda, who had married a wealthy doctor, one of Benecia's cousins, in the Wallin family. More worldly than the Barnes family, Rhoda gave elegant parties, approved of dancing, and soon had Dorothea married to a wealthy and socially acceptable young man. None of these three children, however, overtly abandoned the Quaker faith or caused their parents serious concern.

The fourth child, Etta, was more interesting. Sensitive, pretty, highly intelligent, she soon began to read forbidden books. She became friendly with a young girl named Volida La Porte, who introduced her to French novels and gave her the idea of studying literature at the University of Wisconsin. When Solon insisted that his daughter attend the Llewellyn College for Women, Etta ran away to a Wisconsin summer session after pawning her mother's jewels to provide the fare. Solon went after her, and the two were reconciled. Etta acknowledged the theft and returned the jewels. In the meantime, old Hester Wallin, Justus' sister, had died and left Etta, as well as each of her sisters, a small income.

Solon allowed Etta to remain in Wisconsin for the summer session. After she left the university, Etta moved to Greenwich Village to continue her studies. There she met Willard Kane, an artist, and eventually had an affair with him, even though she realized that he had no intention of jeopardizing his artistic career by marriage. The Barnes family knew of the affair—Orville had discovered it—and they highly disapproved.

The youngest child, Stewart, was the wildest of all. He lacked the essential honesty of his brother and sisters. Spoiled by his cousin Rhoda, who took him up as she had taken up Dorothea, and sent him to a snobbish private school, Stewart was interested only in his conquests of lower-class girls on riotous trips to Atlantic City. With his friends Victor Bruge and Lester Jennings, Stewart would pick up girls and take them off for the weekend. He often had to steal money from his parents or his brother to finance his escapades. His reckless life was paralleled by wild financial speculations in the business world that increasingly worried Solon. Solon's bank was involved in some questionable activities, but Solon, true to his religious principles, felt he could not pull out of the situation without hurting others who depended on him. Similarly, he could not abandon Stewart.

One weekend, Stewart's friend Bruge gave a young girl, Psyche, some of his mother's "drops" because Psyche had not yielded to Bruge, and he felt the "drops" might make her comply. They did, but they also killed Psyche. The boys, frightened, left her body on the road. The police soon apprehended them and charged all three with rape and murder. Unable to face his family and feeling some vestiges of religious guilt, Stewart killed himself in jail.

The shock of Stewart's suicide caused Benecia to suffer a stroke. Etta left her lover and returned home shortly before her mother's death. She found Solon greatly changed. In his despair, he had lost his severity and no longer believed he had the right to judge others. Realizing that his concern with business and with strict standards had cut him off from the kindness and light at the center of his faith, he had learned to love all things, all creatures of nature. Etta, who often read to him, found herself more and more attracted to the central "Inner Light" of the Quaker belief. Always the most understanding child, she and her father developed a genuine closeness and affection for each other before Solon died of cancer six months later. Etta, left alone and removed from the commercial contemporary world, became the embodiment of essential Quaker principles.

Critical Evaluation:

Theodore Dreiser devoted the last year of his life to completing *The Bulwark*, a project that he had started numerous times before then but never completed. The idea for the novel was given to him in 1912 by a young woman named Anna Tatum, who told Dreiser about her Quaker father. Despite having an early outline and draft of the novel and promising several publishers the work, Dreiser did not publish it during his lifetime; it was not published until 1946, a year after his death. While the novel is no longer in print and still receives only mixed reviews, *The Bulwark* is noteworthy not only because it is Dreiser's final, complete novel but also because its prose style marks a significant deviation from Dreiser's previous fiction. The novel also explores and resolves thematic issues raised in all of Dreiser's works.

Stylistically, Dreiser wrote *The Bulwark* in a simple and concise style, not a technique for which he was known. *The Bulwark* is also the shortest of Dreiser's eight novels, even though the plot follows the Barnes family for three generations. In some passages, the prose reads like a plot summary devoid of detail and dialogue, a mere outline of events. An example of this simple, direct prose is evidenced at the beginning of chapter 26, in which the births of Solon and Benecia's first three children are recounted in three brief paragraphs. In comparison to Dreiser's other novels, the syntax and diction are also streamlined. *The Bulwark* lacks the masses of detail, the complex diction, and the melodramatic pronouncements on life that can be found in Dreiser's other works. When Etta claims at the end of the novel that she is crying not for herself or for her father but for life, this denouement seems reserved when compared to the conclusion of *Sister Carrie* (1900). Dreiser's age and failing health may have contributed to this change in style. It should be noted, however, that the sparse style fits the austere Quaker characters.

While this simple style is unusual for Dreiser, it is the unique exploration of themes commonly found in Dreiser's work that especially marks this book as significant. *The Bulwark* is an anomaly in that it is Dreiser's only extended exploration of his favorite themes from the point of view of the older, nineteenth century generation. Solon and Solon's father, Rufus, represent this older generation, and their rigid religious beliefs result in a spiritual dilemma for Solon and his children. On the one hand, Solon is a Quaker who believes, and whose ancestors believed, in an agrarian, spiritual, stoic, self-sacrificing existence. On the other hand, Solon is a wealthy banker who must exist in a society concerned with money, consumer goods, and pleasure. In previous fiction, Dreiser showed sympathy for those who held the agrarian, spiritual ideal of the nineteenth century, but only in *The Bulwark* does Dreiser tell an extended tale from what would have been the older generation's point of view.

In *The Bulwark*, Dreiser is asking: What happens to a human being who is raised to believe in a Christian, agrarian world but who is placed in an urban, materialistic setting? Dreiser raised the same question in other novels. Carrie Meeber, in *Sister Carrie*, leaves her rural hometown of Columbia City, Wisconsin, for Chicago and New York. Clyde Griffiths, in *An American Tragedy* (1925), abandons the poverty and religion of his parents' mission to enter the wealthy environment of the Green-Davidson hotel. *The Bulwark* reenacts this same transplantation, but the story is told from the perspective of the older generation; the devout parent, Solon Barnes, reflects on his own failings and on his children's inability to live by Quaker values.

It is Solon's children, not Solon himself, who embody the consequences of the relocation from a rural farm in Maine to a mansion in Pennsylvania, from an isolated agrarian lifestyle to an urban, materialistic mode of existence. Each of Solon's five children, like characters in an allegory, represents a different response to this clash between the father's values and his or her own experiences. None can maintain the Quaker belief system. Isobel, the first daughter is not beautiful, and in an increasingly materialistic society where appearance is as important as social position and devotion, she abandons both her father's religion and secular society to become a scholar. Orville, the first son, inherits his father's severity and work ethic, but he adopts his father's religion only as a means of maintaining good appearances. Dorothea, the second daughter, is beautiful and charming; she marries well, and high society becomes her domain. While not openly denouncing the Quaker faith, Dorothea and Orville, through their actions, have embraced material wealth and social success as their ideals. Etta, the third daughter, embodies one more reaction to her father's inflexible code; she embraces art and moves to Greenwich Village. Stewart, the youngest, is ironically named because he, in the Quaker sense, is the worst "steward." He rejects his father's religion, embracing a destructive life of hedonism.

Each child, in a crescendo of tragedy, symbolizes the possible consequences of attempting to maintain Quaker beliefs strictly in an increasingly secular environment. By the end of the novel, however, Etta and Solon, unlike the other characters, have changed. They gain a tragic vision, a vision that allows them to accept both the good and evil in life. They achieve this vision, not by abandoning their Quaker roots, but by adjusting their beliefs to new circumstances, by becoming more flexible, and by more closely associating themselves with the creative force found in nature.

After losing his son and his wife, Solon encounters a snake, a symbol of evil in Christianity. Yet Solon communes with the snake. Dreiser, like Solon, had a similar experience. Discovering a puff adder, Dreiser killed it, believing it to be poisonous. Later, learning it was not a dangerous snake and experiencing great guilt, Dreiser reassuringly spoke to the next puff adder he encountered, causing the snake to uncoil and retreat. Like Solon, Dreiser believed in a creative force, one that he associated with a divine plan that he observed in nature. Just as Solon finds peace through a resigned acceptance of life's beauty and pain, so Dreiser must have found peace by writing *The Bulwark*, a novel that resolves many of the philosophical questions with which he wrestled throughout his life.

"Critical Evaluation" by Roark Mulligan

Bibliography:
Gerber, Philip L. *Theodore Dreiser Revisited*. New York: Twayne, 1992. Provides a good introduction to the life and writing of Dreiser. In addition, the book contains a cogent chapter on *The Bulwark*.

Hussman, Lawrence E., Jr. *Dreiser and His Fiction: A Twentieth-Century Quest*. Philadelphia: University of Pennsylvania Press, 1983. Hussman's thesis is that Dreiser's beliefs changed toward the end of his life and that his fiction reflects this change. Thus, *The Bulwark* becomes a final sign that Dreiser was more interested in spiritual matters.

Lehan, Richard. *Theodore Dreiser: His World and His Novels*. Carbondale: Southern Illinois University Press, 1969. Offers thoughtful insights into Dreiser's writing and thinking. Lehan notices a gradual shift in Dreiser's late fiction toward communism and nature, away from technology and capitalism.

Lingeman, Richard. *Theodore Dreiser: An American Journey, 1908-1945*. New York: G. P. Putnam's Sons, 1990. The second volume of a biography on Dreiser. Besides recounting the events in Dreiser's life, Lingeman analyzes Dreiser's fiction.

Pizer, Donald. *The Novels of Theodore Dreiser: A Critical Study*. Minneapolis: University of Minnesota Press, 1976. Pizer is a recognized authority on Dreiser and naturalism. He offers both a solid reading of *The Bulwark* and important background information on the novel.

A BURNT-OUT CASE

Type of work: Novel
Author: Graham Greene (1904-1991)
Type of plot: Bildungsroman
Time of plot: Mid-twentieth century
Locale: The Congo
First published: 1961 (first published in Swedish translation from manuscript, 1960)

>   *Principal characters:*
>   QUERRY, a retired Catholic architect
>   DR. COLIN, a doctor
>   RYCKER, a factory manager
>   MARIE, Rycker's young wife
>   DEO GRATIAS, Querry's servant, a leper
>   PARKINSON, a journalist
>   FATHER THOMAS, a doubting priest

The Story:

Querry took the long boat ride into the African jungle, traveling deeper and deeper into the Congo and escaping farther and farther from the misery of his life in Europe. When the boat reached its ultimate point—a leper colony run by Catholic missionaries—Dr. Colin and the priests invited Querry to stay. Settling in at the colony, Querry asked only for solitude. "So you thought you could just come and die here?" Dr. Colin asked him. "Yes, that *was* in my mind," he responded. "But chiefly I wanted to be in an empty place, where no new building or woman would remind me that there was a time when I was alive, with a vocation and a capacity for love." Querry explained to Dr. Colin that he was figuratively like the lepers—the burnt-out cases—who had lost their toes and fingers to the disease, but once mutilated, no longer suffered pain. "The palsied suffer, their nerves feel, but I am one of the mutilated, doctor," Querry said. After a month at the leper colony, Querry offered to drive to Luc, the capital city, to pick up some medical equipment for Dr. Colin. While in the city, Querry was accosted by Rycker, who recognized the famous architect from an old cover photo in *Time* magazine. After picking up the doctor's equipment, Querry agreed to spend the night at Rycker's house, near the palm oil factory that Rycker managed. At the house, Querry met Rycker's childlike young wife, Marie, and witnessed firsthand the misery of her marriage to Rycker.

While Marie was preparing a drink for her guest, Rycker explained to Querry that he had married a very young woman because women aged rapidly in the tropics and he wanted a wife who would still be sexually attractive when he was an old man. He added that young women are more easily trained and that he had trained Marie to "know what a man needs." Rycker, who had spent six years in the seminary, complained that Marie was ignorant of Catholic rituals and that she could not understand his spiritual needs the way Querry could. Querry insisted he no longer believed, but Rycker refused to listen. Appalled by Rycker's insensitivity and disgusted by his hollow professions of faith, Querry left hurriedly the next morning.

For a time, Querry felt at ease only in the company of Dr. Colin. Dr. Colin respected Querry's need for peace and quiet, but Rycker, the failed priest, and Father Thomas, the doubting priest, refused to respect Querry's privacy. Although Querry protested, they saw him as the great Catholic architect, the famous builder of monuments to God, and they tormented him with their spiritual problems. After two months at the leper colony, Querry felt more secure, and he began the long journey back from his emotional breakdown. At Dr. Colin's urging, he began to draw up plans for a new leper hospital. When his leper-servant, Deo Gratias, became lost in the jungle, he rescued him. Querry and Dr. Colin talked often about God—Dr. Colin happy in his atheism and Querry tormented by his half-belief.

Just as Querry was beginning to enjoy a rebirth of interest in life, he suffered a setback with the arrival of the journalist Parkinson. Querry had begun to believe he had truly escaped his past, hidden in the jungle where few knew or cared that he had once been famous, but the journalist's arrival shattered this sense of security. Parkinson, a lonely and bitter man, knew he could achieve fame for himself by publishing the whereabouts of the famous architect. He dug up painful events of Querry's past, including the suicide of a mistress who had killed herself for Querry's love. He sought out Rycker, who pretended intimacy with Querry and fed Parkinson a pack of lies. Angered by Rycker's lies to Parkinson, Querry traveled to Rycker's house, determined to confront him and convince him to stay away from the journalist. Arriving at Rycker's home, Querry found Rycker ill in bed and Marie in a state of panic, fearing she was pregnant and knowing her husband wanted no children. Touched by her helplessness and moved by her tears, Querry offered to take Marie to the doctor in Luc. That night in the hotel in Luc, Querry heard Marie crying in the room next door and went in to comfort her. He told her a story about a famous Catholic jeweler who had lost his faith in God, a story which Marie quickly recognized as the story of Querry's own life. In the morning, Marie saw the doctor, who told her she would have to wait two days for her pregnancy test results.

That same morning at the hotel, Querry and Marie met Parkinson, and they were soon joined by Rycker, who insisted that Querry and Marie had slept together the night before. Querry tried to convince Rycker of the truth, but Rycker refused to believe him. Disgusted with Rycker once again, Querry promptly left Luc and returned to the colony. Three days later, the priests held a party to celebrate the completion of the new hospital. Querry, Dr. Colin, and the priests toasted their accomplishment with champagne. Querry felt warm and happy, planning his future there among his new friends.

His joy, however, was interrupted with the news that Marie had shown up at the nearby convent school, exposing her pregnancy and falsely claiming that Querry was the father. No amount of coaxing on Querry's part could persuade the young woman to tell the truth. She stubbornly clung to her lie, perhaps for love of Querry, or perhaps seeing her chance to escape from Rycker. Though Dr. Colin and some of the priests believed in Querry's innocence, others did not, and Querry sadly prepared to leave the colony. That very night, however, Rycker showed up in a rage. As Querry attempted to pacify him, Rycker shot and killed Querry in a fit of jealous passion.

Critical Evaluation:

Considered by many critics to be the greatest British writer of the twentieth century, Graham Greene was made a British Companion of Honour in 1966 and awarded the Order of Merit in 1986. In a literary career that spanned sixty years, he published twenty-five novels, dozens of short stories and plays, two autobiographies, and countless critical and journalistic pieces. Unlike many great writers, Greene enjoyed not only critical acclaim but also popular success. Many of his fictional works were made into films, and a great number were best-sellers. Upon Greene's death in 1991, William Golding proclaimed him "the ultimate chronicler of twentieth-century man's consciousness and anxiety," and Sir Alec Guinness hailed him as "a great writer who spoke brilliantly to a whole generation."

During his long and varied career, Greene was a journalist, a film critic, and, for a time, a British spy. In 1926, he converted to Catholicism, and many of his works have Catholic themes. Also important to Greene's fiction were his endless travels throughout the world, often to places of political unrest. With the journalist's eye for character and detail, Greene exposed the dark side of political intrigue in places like Papa Doc's Haiti and Vietnam at the start of the conflict between Vietnam and the United States. For Greene, external political and religious conflicts were a reflection of the greater conflict within the human soul. Greene's characters—particularly in his later novels—struggle to find their identity in a ravaged and alienating world and fight to find meaning in lives where none is apparent.

Like most of Greene's later novels, *A Burnt-Out Case* is strong on characterization, rich in symbolism, and heavy with irony. Greene's third-person omniscient narration offers readers insights into each character's motivation, making the characters seem authentic and compelling. Greene's skillful use of symbol and metaphor gives the story emotional and psychological depth, and his masterful use of irony lends the story poignancy and immediacy.

In *A Burnt-Out Case*, Greene develops the theme of the individual's search for identity and for meaning by using two controlling metaphors, the "journey" and the "burnt-out case." As the story opens with Querry's river voyage, the narrator refers to Querry as "the cabin passenger"—a nameless, faceless traveler on an unknown journey. On the trip, Querry speaks little, insulating himself from the other passengers and wallowing in his self-imposed isolation. The boat travels far down the river, deep into the jungle, stopping finally at the leper colony. On a literal level, the river voyage is simply Querry's means of escape from his sad and sordid past. On a metaphorical level, however, Querry is seeking death, trying to "bury" himself in the jungle. Like the leper who has lost his extremities and suffers from numbness, Querry is numb to joy and pain and longs to withdraw from a world he finds meaningless.

When he arrives at the leper colony, Querry disembarks because the boat "goes no farther." Metaphorically, though, his journey has just begun. On the deeper symbolic level, Querry's river voyage is a journey of self-discovery. The farther he travels into the jungle, the deeper he delves into himself. With an irony characteristic of Greene's work, what Querry finds at the end of his journey is not the death he seeks but a symbolic rebirth he once thought impossible. Surrounded by the peace and safety of the colony, Querry begins to lose his fear of the world. Strengthened by his friendship with Dr. Colin and his affection for Deo Gratias, he begins to think of others before himself. Stirred by compassion for Marie Rycker, he travels the long road back to the world of the emotionally alive. Once burnt out, Querry eventually regains the ability to feel, to care, and to love. Once a stranger to himself and the world around him, Querry learns to find meaning in the human community. Traveling to the Congo, Querry wants to lose himself in darkness and anonymity; paradoxically, he finds himself and his life's meaning by doing so. Having lost the ability to feel, he seeks symbolic death and burial; paradoxically, he finds a rebirth of interest in life. In one of Greene's fine ironic twists, Querry finds literal death at the moment he is reborn into the world of those who feel and care.

Karen Priest

Bibliography:

Bloom, Harold, ed. *Graham Greene*. New York: Chelsea House, 1987. Contains critical essays on all the major novels, with three essays dedicated to *A Burnt-Out Case*. Contains a chronology of Greene's life and works and a brief bibliography.

Kurismmootil, K. C. Joseph. *Heaven and Hell on Earth: An Appreciation of Five Novels of*

Graham Greene. Chicago: Loyola University Press, 1982. Kurismmootil sees *A Burnt-Out Case* as the last of Greene's religious novels and addresses the novel's "Christian insights." Offers good coverage of characterization. Includes a bibliography of Greene's works and Greene criticism.

O'Prey, Paul. *A Reader's Guide to Graham Greene*. New York: Thames and Hudson, 1988. An excellent source for discussion of Greene's major works. Analyzes plot, character, and theme, and includes a bibliography of all Greene's publications.

Thomas, Brian. *An Underground Fate: The Idiom of Romance in the Later Novels of Graham Greene*. Athens: University of Georgia Press, 1988. An outstanding exploration of eight Greene novels in terms of the romance myth (in which the hero descends into the underworld but then emerges reborn and triumphant). Thomas' work is remarkable in its argument that Greene's later works end in hope rather than despair. Offers an extensive bibliography of criticism about Greene's works.

Van Kaam, Adrian, and Kathleen Healy. *The Demon and the Dove: Personality Growth Through Literature*. Pittsburgh: Duquesne University Press, 1967. Written from the perspective of psychological criticism, the chapter "Querry in Greene's *A Burnt-Out Case*" offers an outstanding analysis of characterization and symbolism in the novel.

BURY MY HEART AT WOUNDED KNEE

Type of work: History
Author: Dee Brown (1908-   )
First published: 1970

The title of this book, a poetic line from Stephen Vincent Benét's "American Names," introduces Dee Brown's history of the Indians in the American West. Brown presents a factual as well as an emotional account of the relationship between the Indians, American settlers, and the U.S. government. The massacre at Wounded Knee Creek in South Dakota on December 29, 1890, provides the backdrop for the narrative. In his introduction, Brown states the reason for his work. Thousands of accounts about life in the American West of the late nineteenth century have been written. Stories are told of the traders, ranchers, wagon trains, gunfighters, and gold-seekers. Rarely is the voice of the Indian heard. The pre-European occupant of the land was classified only as a hindrance to the spreading of American civilization to the West Coast. In this book, Brown seeks to remedy the historical injustice done to the Native American. The author declares that the reader will not finish the book with a cheerful spirit, but will come away with a better understanding of what the American Indian is and was. Punctuating the book throughout are photographs of and quotations from those whose story is being told.

The opening chapter of Brown's chronological account begins with the attitudes of different groups of Europeans toward the natives they encountered in America. Although Christopher Columbus expressed admiration for the natives of the West Indies, the Spanish were often brutal. The English, capable of brutality when the occasion called for it, usually tried subtler methods. Included in this chapter are the initial relationships between the Indians and the government of the United States. Brown relates early indignities against Indian leaders, including that of the skeleton of Black Hawk, a Sauk and Fox chief who resisted American expansion, being on display in the office of the governor of the Iowa Territory. Black Hawk was the grandfather of Jim Thorpe, an Olympic gold medal athlete in 1912.

The remaining chapters of *Bury My Heart at Wounded Knee* are a survey of the western Indians, tribe by tribe, event by event, and leader by leader. The story begins with the Navajo of the Southwest, led by Manuelito. Like many later Indian leaders, Manuelito at first tried to be realistic and to accept the presence of Americans in their territory on reasonable terms. When those terms were violated by the Americans, the Navajo retaliated. The result was war that involved atrocities on both sides. Brown supports his narrative by direct quotes from participants in the conflict, such as a white soldier's account of a massacre of Navajos at Fort Wingate in New Mexico in September, 1861.

Brown next turns to Little Crow, a chief of the Santee Sioux in Minnesota. After many years of trying to adopt the white man's lifestyle and dress, even visiting President James Buchanan in Washington, Little Crow became disillusioned and angry during the summer of 1862. The result of that anger was Little Crow's War. The war ended with the Santee Sioux moving west to the Great Plains and with Little Crow's scalp and skull being put on display in St. Paul.

Chapter 4 begins with a meeting at Fort Laramie, Wyoming, in 1851. Leaders of the Cheyenne, Arapaho, Sioux, Crow, and several smaller tribes met with United States government representatives. The agreements made there permitted the building of roads and military posts in Indian territory, but no land was surrendered by the Indians. The Pikes Peak gold rush in 1858 resulted in the arrival of thousands of white prospectors, ranchers, and farmers to the lands of the Cheyenne and Arapaho. In spite of the loss of much land, the Indians remained peaceful until 1864. Black Kettle, the Cheyenne chief, had heard about the experiences of the Navajo and the Sioux; he hoped to spare his people that suffering. War did break out in the spring of 1864, when soldiers attacked some Cheyenne on the South Platte River. The fighting ended in November with the well-planned Sand Creek Massacre of Black Kettle's Cheyenne by a United States Army force under the command of Colonel John M. Chivington.

In the next two chapters, Brown's account returns to the Sioux. It is centered on Red Cloud, chief of the Oglala Sioux. It describes the Powder River Invasion of the northern Great Plains by white gold-seekers, traders, and United States Army regiments in 1865. Red Cloud was trying to keep the area between the Black Hills of South Dakota and Big Horn Mountain in Montana as the domain of the Indians, including bands of Cheyenne and Arapaho, as well as the Sioux. In 1866, the United States government began preparation for a road through the Powder River country into Montana. The result was Red Cloud's War (1866-1868), beginning with the Fetterman Massacre of a contingent of soldiers in an ambush in December, 1866. After two years of conflict, Red Cloud triumphantly signed a treaty at Fort Laramie, Wyoming, that closed the Powder River road. The exact terms of the treaty after ratification by the United States Senate were disputed, but it did result in several years of peace.

Chapter 7 continues in the recounting of the struggle of Black Kettle of the Cheyenne and other Indians of the central Great Plains against white occupation of their lands. This includes the great council at Medicine Lodge Creek in Kansas in October, 1867. Although Black Kettle could only bring a few Cheyenne, more than four thousand Kiowa, Comanche, and Arapaho were present to negotiate an honorable peace with the United States government. At this meeting, Ten Bears of the Comanche gave an eloquent appeal on behalf of the Indians. Brown later includes a quote from that speech. The saddest incident in this chapter is the death of Black Kettle, who had survived the Sand Creek Massacre, in another massacre led by George Custer in November, 1868. This chapter also includes the infamous words of General Phil Sheridan: "The only good Indians I ever saw were dead," which over time became "The only good Indian is a dead Indian."

After discussing the visit to Washington by Red Cloud and other Sioux chiefs, and attempts to clarify terms of the Fort Laramie Treaty of 1868, Brown moves to the Southwest and Cochise with the Apache warriors. The story, now becoming all too familiar, begins with Cochise welcoming white soldiers to his territory, even allowing a mail route and a stage station to be established. False accusations by an army officer and attempted arrest in 1861 convinced Cochise that all whites had to be driven from Apache territory. After his father-in-law, Mangas Colorado, was murdered by soldiers while a prisoner, open war broke out. The Camp Grant Massacre of unarmed Apaches in 1871 revealed the futility of Cochise's efforts. Although other Apache chiefs remained on the warpath, Cochise made peace in 1872.

In Chapter 10, the scene moves to the West Coast and the Modoc leader, Captain Jack. The account begins with attempts at cooperation and ends with Captain Jack's being hanged in 1873. The next chapter, "The War to Save the Buffalo," is an excellent account of the last major effort by the Indians of the Great Plains to preserve their traditional life. Brown includes part of the emotional speech given at the Council of Medicine Lodge Creek in 1867 by Ten Bears, who best tells his own story: "I was born upon the prairie, where the wind blew free and there was nothing to break the light of the sun. I was born where there were no enclosures and where everything drew a free breath. I want to die there and not within walls." This chapter includes more accounts of abuse by George Custer. The story of Quanah Parker, the Comanche war chief whose mother was captured as a small child and raised as a Comanche, is another highlight of the chapter.

Chapter 12 of Brown's chronology returns the reader to the Sioux in the Black Hills of South Dakota. Red Cloud is joined in this narrative by Sitting Bull, Crazy Horse, and other Sioux leaders. In 1874, after the discovery of gold, the Black Hills were invaded by white miners. The miners were followed by soldiers under George Custer. The war that followed ended in July, 1876, with the death of Custer and his men in the Battle of the Little Bighorn River in Montana.

The next four chapters record the flight of Chief Joseph and his Nez Perce from their home in the northwest, the final Cheyenne subordination, the troubles of the Poncas and Standing Bear, and the removal of the Utes from their Rocky Mountain homes to undesirable land in Utah. Chapter 17 is a good account of the last Apache resistance, first by Victorio, then by Geronimo. After years of violent rebellion, Victorio was killed by Mexican soldiers in 1880. Geronimo then led the opposition until his surrender in 1886, after which the once-fierce Apache were in subjection to the United States.

The last two chapters are a fitting conclusion to a fascinating and disturbing story. Brown describes the Ghost Dance, a ritual attributed to Wovoka, a Paiute from Nevada. The dance was supposed to bring back dead Indians and the buffalo and eliminate whites from Indian lands. Sitting Bull of the Sioux, after years of Canadian exile, imprisonment in the United States, and appearances as a feature in Buffalo Bill's Wild West Show, became an advocate of the Ghost Dance. Growing despair among the Sioux intensified interest in the dance and led to Sitting Bull's death on December 15, 1890.

In the confusion that followed Sitting Bull's death, one group of his followers joined Big Foot, also a Ghost Dance advocate. On December 28, Big Foot's group was taken into custody by the U.S. Army and forced to camp along Wounded Knee Creek in southwestern South Dakota. The next day, as the Sioux were being disarmed, a minor incident involving one deaf warrior led to the massacre of the Sioux by the soldiers. Of about 350 people in the group, 51 wounded were left to be taken to the Pine Ridge Sioux Agency.

Bury My Heart at Wounded Knee is a factual account that needs no artificial elaboration. The pages of history are opened to many examples of the United States' inhumanity. The wounded from Wounded Knee were taken to the Episcopal Mission at Pine Ridge. Above the pulpit, four days after Christmas, a sign declared, "Peace on Earth, Good Will to Men."

Glenn L. Swygart

Bibliography:
Beal, Merrill. *"I Will Fight No More Forever":* *Chief Joseph and the Nez Perce War.* Seattle: University of Washington Press, 1963. Using the words of Chief Joseph, Beal makes the account of the Nez Perce in *Bury My Heart at Wounded Knee* easier to understand. Emphasizes Nez Perce efforts to live peacefully with white settlers. Photographs and sketches.
Brown, Dee. *Tepee Tales of the American Indian.* New York: Holt, Rinehart and Winston, 1979. Describes the culture and heritage of the Indians. Good illustrations throughout by Louis Mofsie.
Hyde, George. *Red Cloud's Folk.* Norman: University of Oklahoma Press, 1937. Covers the history of the Sioux from 1650 to 1878. Provides background on the dominant tribe of *Bury My Heart at Wounded Knee*, including the history of Red Cloud's family.
Underhill, Ruth. *The Navajos.* Norman: University of Oklahoma Press, 1956. Covers the origin of the Navajo, the first tribe discussed in *Bury My Heart at Wounded Knee*, up to the time of publication. Good photographs, maps, and bibliography.

BUS STOP

Type of work: Drama
Author: William Inge (1913-1973)
Type of plot: Comedy
Time of plot: 1950's
Locale: Kansas, thirty miles west of Kansas City
First performed: 1955; first published, 1955

> *Principal characters:*
> CHERIE, a singer from Kansas City
> BO DECKER, a cowboy from Montana
> VIRGIL BLESSING, Bo's guardian and close friend
> DR. GERALD LYMAN, a has-been professor
> CARL, a bus driver
> GRACE HOYLARD, a middle-aged waitress
> ELMA DUCKWORTH, a young waitress, Grace's helper
> WILL MASTERS, a sheriff

The Story:

Grace Hoylard and her helper, Elma Duckworth, were alone in a crossroads restaurant of a small Kansas town thirty miles west of Kansas City. They were keeping a lonely vigil in expectation of the arrival of the Kansas-City-to-Wichita bus that was due at 1:00 A.M. A raging blizzard left the restaurant deserted. Shortly before the bus was due, Will Masters, the sheriff, came in.

Grace and Elma's conversation with Will made it clear that, when the bus arrived, it would be unable to go farther before morning. The roads to the west were closed by the heavy snowfall. Grace speculated on who might be driving the bus, suggesting to Elma that if Carl was driving, she wanted to wait on him herself. At that moment, the door flew open and, snow swirling around her, Cherie asked if there was someplace she could hide. She suggested going into the powder room to escape the lanky cowboy she was trying to avoid, but when Grace told her that the powder room was outside, she rejected that possibility, more emphatically when she learned that the bus would be stranded for the night.

Elma suggested that Cherie go to a hotel down the street, but Cherie, protesting that she was not a millionaire, rejected that idea. When Will introduced himself as the local sheriff, Cherie declared that she did not want to have anyone arrested but that she wanted protection from the man who was after her. She told Will that he was on the bus asleep, hardly suggesting a dangerous pursuit on his part. Cherie insisted, nevertheless, that she was being abducted. Cherie was a chanteuse (she pronounced it "chantoosie") at the Blue Dragon, a Kansas City nightclub. When she sang "That Old Black Magic," it drove Bo, one of the club's patrons, wild. (Cherie would later reveal that he met her and ended up losing his virginity to her.) What was a one-night stand for Cherie was a mandate for marriage to Bo, the innocent, ingenuous cowpoke. He loaded Cherie onto the bus and the two of them, accompanied by Bo's guardian of eleven years, Virgil Blessing, were heading to Montana, where Bo owned a ranch. Cherie did not want to go, even though her life in Kansas City seemed to be heading nowhere.

Before Bo appeared, Dr. Lyman, a former college professor who drank too much and had a fondness for young girls, emerged from the bus and immediately began to charm the unworldly and nubile Elma. Before long, he had told Elma his life story. He expressed his eagerness to cross the state line. Will Masters and Carl had a whispered conversation about Dr. Lyman, suggesting that perhaps the old man was fleeing from prosecution. Bo and Virgil were still asleep in the bus, and Carl preferred to leave them undisturbed because of the trouble Bo had already caused. When Bo and Virgil finally entered the restaurant, rumpled and half asleep, Bo scolded Cherie for leaving them on the cold bus and told her that was no way to treat the man she was going to marry. Will asked Bo to shut the door, but Bo was concentrating on Cherie and did not hear him. After Bo gave a thumbnail sketch of his background, he ordered a staggeringly large meal and chided Cherie for eating only a doughnut. As Bo and Cherie bickered, Grace asked Elma to look after the restaurant. She and Carl stole upstairs to Grace's living quarters. By the end of Act I, Bo was forced to face the possibility that perhaps his love for Cherie was not reciprocated.

At the beginning of Act II, Dr. Lyman was trying to impress Elma with his vast learning and experience. Dr. Lyman tried to arrange a meeting with Elma in Topeka the following day. Bo revealed to Virgil the loneliness he had been feeling and, in so doing, he emerged as a sympathetic character. Cherie told Elma about her life and, as her story unfolded, it began to seem that marrying Bo might be the most reasonable way out for Cherie, despite her reluctance. At Elma's suggestion, some passengers were conscripted into acting in a floor show to pass the hours they were stranded in the restaurant. Dr. Lyman and Elma reenacted the balcony scene from Romeo and Juliet, during which Dr. Lyman demonstrated his extreme selfishness as an actor and as a person. This selfishness was what had led to his loneliness and personal isolation. His weakness for young women was clearly related to his isolation.

Viewing the balcony scene inflamed Bo's passion to the point that he lifted Cherie off her feet, whereupon Will Masters came to Cherie's rescue, lunging at Bo and, in so doing, enabling Cherie to get loose of him. Bo and Will engaged in fisticuffs, and Will finally subdued Bo, slapping handcuffs on him. Will asked Cherie if she wanted to press charges. If not, he said, he would release Bo and let him return to the bus. Virgil, revealing to Cherie that she was the first woman Bo had ever made love to, promised Cherie that he would control Bo if she did not press charges. The act ended with Cherie seemingly touched by Bo's innocence.

In Act III, after Bo made forced apologies to everyone and was released, he offered Cherie money to return to Kansas City. He became solicitous about her comfort. His actions began to touch her; her emotions toward him softened. Finally, she decided to continue to Montana with Bo. Virgil, knowing that Bo and Cherie were likely to do better without his presence, remained behind. Grace set about closing the restaurant when the bus pulled out at five in the morning. She had said earlier that she hated to go up to her lonely apartment by herself. On this night, however, her needs having been satisfied early, she closed up and left Virgil—quite literally— out in the cold. This bittersweet ending suggests that Bo and Cherie might have a chance to escape the selfish loneliness of people like Virgil, Grace, and Dr. Lyman. Inge holds out no real hope for these three, but he suggests with considerable optimism that Bo's innocence would rub off on Cherie and that she would find fulfillment and contentment with Bo in Montana. Bo observed, when he learned of some of Cherie's sexual exploits, that he was pure enough for both of them.

Critical Evaluation:

Bus Stop, which grew out of Inge's one-act play, *People in the Wind* (which was published after *Bus Stop* in 1962), is essentially an anatomy of love. The themes of innocence and ultimate acceptance that it explores grew out of the theme of loneliness that had pervaded a great deal of Inge's earlier work. Loneliness is a pervasive element in *Bus Stop*, growing out of a variety of causes. In the case of Dr. Lyman, who is, in many ways, an autobiographical character, the loneliness stems from an uncontrolled egocentricity, from an inability to give of himself. Dr. Lyman's closest and most reliable companion is his bottle. Unable to hold a teaching job, he spends his life on buses riding through the countryside, with life to the right and left of him but never a part of him. The bus, confined and warm, has become his womb, his retreat from a world with which he cannot cope.

Virgil Blessing, in some ways an allegorical character whose name suggests quite a bit about his personality, devotes his life to raising Bo, who lost his parents at age ten. Virgil gives unstintingly of his time and affection, but when Bo matures to the point of considering marriage, Virgil bows out of the picture gracefully, blessing Bo and Cherie's anticipated union. Virgil once was in love with a woman, but he feared offending her with his crude manners. He only felt comfortable back in the bunkhouse with his fellow cowboys, so he never pursued marriage.

Grace has reached middle age devoid of any real attachments. She works hard and lives upstairs over the restaurant and dreads going alone to her empty apartment. She overcomes her loneliness during the hours when someone like Carl is in her bed, but she apparently has no hope of forming any permanent union. The love she experiences is physical, and it satisfies her for long enough to keep her from getting irritable, as she admits to Elma.

Elma, at age sixteen or seventeen, is not popular with boys. Grace points to Elma's problem. Elma is too bright; boys do not like girls to be smarter than they are. Elma is at the point in her life when things might change for her, but she is so innocent and unworldly that she likely will face some difficult choices in her immediate future. As outgoing as Dr. Lyman is selfish, Elma might eventually have a satisfactory life.

Cherie has survived by her looks and limited talent, but she is not getting any younger and her future is not promising. Bo offers her a reasonable way out, particularly in view of the fact that he is quite financially stable and that she finds him attractive. Her early reluctance is probably the result of her never before having met a man who genuinely loved her. The previous men in her life have used her sexually and discarded her. Cherie has no reason initially to think Bo is any different from them. When she learns, however, of Bo's virginity, she is touched, and when she begins to realize that Bo truly loves her and wants to protect her, she begins to love him. Inge seems to suggest that the Bo-Cherie relationship has a good chance of flourishing.

R. Baird Shuman

Bibliography:
Dusenbury, Winifred L. *The Theme of Loneliness in Modern American Drama*. Gainesville: University of Florida Press, 1960. Focuses mostly on *Come Back, Little Sheba*. Much about the theme of loneliness can be applied to most of Inge's plays, and most notably to *Bus Stop*.
Inge, William. "Interview with William Inge." In *Behind the Scenes: Theatre and Film Interviews from the "Transatlantic Review,"* edited by Joseph McCrindle. New York: Holt, Rinehart and Winston, 1971. A seven-page interview with William Inge is searching and revealing. It provides valuable insights into Inge's major dramas, including *Bus Stop*.
Kansas Quarterly 18, no. 4 (1986). This entire issue of *Kansas Quarterly* is devoted to William Inge. The dozen articles cover most of his plays and both of his novels. Although no single article is devoted to *Bus Stop*, at least half of them give some interpretive consideration to the play.

Lewis, Allan. *American Plays and Playwrights of the Contemporary Theatre*. New York: Crown, 1965. Compares *Bus Stop* to Maxim Gorky's *Na dne* (1902; *The Lower Depths*, 1912).

Shuman, R. Baird. *William Inge*. 2d ed. New York: Twayne, 1989. Offers a complete reevaluation of all of Inge's plays and of his two novels. A major interpretive section on *Bus Stop*.

Voss, Ralph F. *A Life of William Inge: The Strains of Triumph*. Lawrence: University Press of Kansas, 1989. Voss's is the most thorough critical biography of William Inge. His analytical considerations of all the plays are strong, and his comments on *Bus Stop* have particular merit.

BUSSY D'AMBOIS

Type of work: Drama
Author: George Chapman (c. 1559-1634)
Type of plot: Tragedy
Time of plot: Sixteenth century
Locale: Paris
First performed: 1604; first published, 1607; revised, 1641

> *Principal characters:*
> BUSSY D'AMBOIS, a soldier of fortune
> HENRY III, king of France
> MONSIEUR, the king's brother
> THE DUKE OF GUISE
> THE COUNT OF MONTSURRY
> TAMYRA, his wife
> A FRIAR

The Story:

In Paris, Bussy d'Ambois was a soldier and gentleman too poor to gain favor at the court. He met Monsieur, brother of King Henry III, by appointment in a side street. Monsieur, chiding Bussy for his downcast countenance, reminded him that some of the greatest men in history had endured obscurity and exile before becoming renowned. Anxious to have ambitious and ruthless young men about him, Monsieur invited Bussy to be his man and to become a courtier. Later, Maffe, Monsieur's steward, came to Bussy and, seeing the wretched state he was in, gave him only one hundred crowns of the thousand that Monsieur had sent Bussy. Bussy, perceiving that Maffe was a proud scoundrel and knowing Monsieur's reputation for generosity, was able to talk Maffe out of the remaining nine hundred crowns. With the money in his possession, Bussy struck Maffe in payment for his insubordination. Maffe hinted that he would be avenged.

Monsieur introduced Bussy, dressed in fine new clothes, at court. As he was presented to various noble people of the court, he impressed them with his directness. The Duke of Guise jealously noted that Bussy was being quite free with the duke's wife, Elenor, and suggested that Bussy not be so forward. Bussy, in conduct unlike what would be expected of a courtier, answered Guise sharply. Although warned by Monsieur, Bussy still persisted in dallying pleasantly with Elenor. Having offended Guise, Bussy also bluntly incurred the enmity of three courtiers, Barrisor, l'Anou, and Pyrrhot.

In the duel that followed, the three courtiers and two of Bussy's friends were killed; Bussy was the only survivor. He later went to the court with Monsieur, who successfully won a pardon for Bussy from King Henry. Bussy thanked the king and declared that he could not avoid defending his honor. Guise was deeply offended by the royal pardon Bussy had received.

Tamyra, Countess of Montsurry, met Bussy and fell in love with him. At the same time, Monsieur, making every attempt to seduce the noblewoman, gave her a pearl necklace. Later, Tamyra entered a secret chamber in back of her bedchamber. A friar, in league with her, brought Bussy by a secret passageway to the chamber on the pretext that Bussy was to explain to Tamyra a false report that he had killed Barrisor because the dead man had been interested in the

871

countess. The friar, after hinting of Tamyra's love for Bussy and cautioning him to be discreet, left Bussy and Tamyra together.

After Tamyra's passion for Bussy was consummated, she expressed a deep feeling of guilt and feared that she might be discovered. Bussy assured her that he would protect her from all dishonor. As he took leave of her, again accompanied by the friar, she gave him the necklace Monsieur had given her. At daybreak, Montsurry returned home to find his wife awake and fully clothed. She explained that she had not been able to sleep while he had been away on business. When he asked her to come to bed with him, she begged off, saying that the friar did not approve of making love by daylight.

Bussy, having become a great favorite of the king, declared to the court that he would be the king's own right arm in exposing sycophants, rascals, and any other unprincipled men in the realm. Grown heady with favor, he taunted Guise, who retorted that Bussy was the illegitimate son of a cardinal. The two men were ready to settle their grudge in a duel, but the king managed to reconcile them momentarily.

Monsieur realized that he had sponsored a man who could not be manipulated. He and Guise plotted Bussy's downfall by gaining the confidence of the serving-women of the chief ladies of the court. Pero, Tamyra's maid, disclosed to Monsieur that her mistress had given herself to Bussy, but the servant was unable to reveal the identity of the person who had acted as go-between in the illicit affair.

Bussy, at the height of his power in the court, reminded his patron of Monsieur's ambition to be king. He declared that he would assist Monsieur in everything short of actually killing King Henry. Monsieur asked Bussy for his honest opinion of him; Bussy said he would give it in return for Monsieur's opinion of Bussy. Monsieur thereupon declared that Bussy was a vain, pompous, ruthless, and inconsistent man. Bussy, in return, said that Monsieur was a liar, a gossip, and the fountainhead of all cruelty and violence in France. The two, having made their disclosures of each other's worth, went together to a banquet given by the king.

During the banquet, Monsieur suggested to Bussy that he pay court to Tamyra, who was reputed to be unapproachable. When Bussy pretended to have only the slightest acquaintance with her, Monsieur hinted that he knew more than he would tell. The king, sensing that violence was in the offing, beckoned to his favorite to join him, and he and Bussy left the banquet hall.

Monsieur offered to show Montsurry a letter that would reveal to him the perfidy of his wife. The trusting Montsurry refused to take the letter, but his suspicions had been aroused. Tamyra, aided by Pero, was able to convince Montsurry that he had no cause to suspect his wife of faithlessness.

Later, Bussy and Tamyra met in the secret chamber and Tamyra revealed to her lover that Monsieur knew of their meetings. The friar invoked spirits so that the two could foresee what the future might hold. Behemoth, the chief spirit invoked, re-created an image of Monsieur, Guise, and Montsurry in conference. Monsieur and Guise, having convinced Montsurry of Tamyra's passion for Bussy, urged him to force Tamyra to reveal the identity of the go-between so that Bussy might more easily be ambushed and killed. Pero came to the conferring lords and gave Monsieur a letter written by Tamyra. Montsurry, utterly confused by that time, and not knowing whom to trust, stabbed Pero. Behemoth forecast a violent end for the friar, Tamyra, and Bussy unless they were able to act with the greatest wisdom.

Montsurry returned to his house and seized Tamyra, who was in the company of the friar. Despite the friar's warning to him not to act with violence, Montsurry ordered Tamyra to write her confession. She resisted, whereupon he stabbed her repeatedly. When she still persisted in her refusal to write, he had her placed on a rack. The friar, who had left that scene of violence, returned with a sword and killed himself with it. Tamyra, tortured on the rack, confessed that the friar had been the go-between. She wrote to Bussy in her own blood that he was to come to her in the secret chamber.

Montsurry, disguised as the friar, brought hired murderers to his friends Monsieur and Guise; then he left them to lure Bussy to a carefully plotted doom. The ghost of the friar appeared to Bussy and predicted a dire fate for him. When the ghost left, after declaring that it would meet Bussy in Tamyra's secret chamber, Bussy apprehensively invoked the spirit of the underworld. The spirit appeared and told him that the friar was really dead and that Bussy should not heed his next summons from Tamyra. Bussy wanted to know who would deliver the summons. The spirit could not answer because a stronger spirit, Fate, controlled by Monsieur and Guise, prevented that disclosure.

Montsurry, dressed as the friar, brought the letter written in blood to Bussy. Duped by the disguise and defying the malign predictions he had heard, Bussy followed Montsurry back to Tamyra.

The ghost of the friar, meanwhile, appeared to Tamyra and advised her to shout a warning to Bussy as he was brought into the secret room. When Bussy and Montsurry entered the chamber, she did indeed warn Bussy. As his enemies and the hired murderers closed in on their victim, the ghost of the friar unnerved the murderers and Bussy was given time to collect himself. Having killed one of the murderers, he was about to kill Montsurry when he was shot down. Bussy, propping himself on his sword so that he might die in a defiant attitude, forgave those who had brought him to his death. After Bussy's death, Montsurry banished Tamyra, his unfaithful wife.

Critical Evaluation:

George Chapman, an acquaintance of Christopher Marlowe and Ben Jonson, was a jack-of-all-trades among Elizabethan writers, turning out poetry and translations as well as plays. His reputation was first established as a poet with his *The Shadow of Night* (1594) and *Ovid's Banquet of Sense* (1595), but his only poem much read today was begun by another man: When Christopher Marlowe's *Hero and Leander* (1598) was left unfinished at his death, Chapman completed the poem by adding the final four books.

By about 1595, Chapman had begun writing for the theater, supplying plays to Philip Henslowe's company of actors, the Lord Admiral's Men. Although a contemporary source cites Chapman as a tragic author, whatever works led to that opinion have been lost; some comedies, written by Chapman alone and in collaboration with John Marston and Ben Jonson, are all that survive of his early dramas. In 1599, he left the Lord Admiral's company, but continued to write for the stage until 1614. His translations of Homer's the *Iliad* and the *Odyssey* were published in 1616. He may have had financial troubles in his later years; he died in 1634.

Chapman wrote *Bussy d'Ambois* about 1604. Surprisingly, given the play's subject, it was probably first acted by Paul's Boys, a children's company. Paul's Boys was one of the then-popular groups of child actors, in this case an outgrowth of the choir school at St. Paul's Cathedral. The play exists in two printed versions, one produced in 1607 and a later one, printed in 1641, that is noticeably different. Most critics believe the 1641 version to derive from a revision of the play made by Chapman himself. The play was extremely successful: It continued to be performed until the closing of the theaters in 1642. After the Restoration of Charles II, the play was revived, and its last performance is recorded in 1691.

Chapman's play is based on the actual career of Louis de Clermont, Sieur de Bussy d'Amboise, a minor courtier during the reign of Henry III of France. The historical Bussy was widely known in his time, and seems to have been every bit the swaggering bravo who appears in Chapman's play. Known for his dueling, his poetry, and his love affairs, Bussy was murdered by a jealous husband when he was about thirty years old. One might wonder how meaningful tragedy could be made from such unpromising material, but Bussy d'Ambois' life furnished Chapman with a scarecrow on which to drape his philosophy.

In one respect, Bussy d'Ambois represents a decadent, rather cynical comment on the Renaissance individual whose ambition and self-confidence know no bounds. Having achieved status in a ruthless and utterly corrupt court, he offended at every hand and dallied with abandon in illicit love. What the quarto of 1607 refers to as *Bussy d'Ambois: A Tragedy* appears to be as much satire as tragedy. Even Bussy's determination, after he has been shot, to die while he supports himself on his sword seems comic in its futility, considering the despicable nature of his antagonists and his mistress.

On the other hand, Bussy embodies the Renaissance ideal of the man who, by virtue of his physical, mental, and moral powers, is a law unto himself. In this sense, Bussy is a relative of the heroes found in Marlowe's *Tamburlaine the Great* (1587-1590) and *Doctor Faustus* (1588). Although not bent on evil, Bussy resembles William Shakespeare's Richard III, in that neither recognizes any moral force higher than himself, nor submits to anything but his own will. Just exactly what virtues Bussy possesses are not always clear. Indeed, what he calls his honor leads him to kill in a duel three men who have insulted him by snickering at the wrong time. That same honor does not prevent him from speaking bawdily to strange women at court or committing adultery when the opportunity presents itself. Yet Bussy is steadfast in his belief that he owes obedience to no one, not even to the king, as he states to the king's face in the scene in which he is pardoned for dueling.

Chapman often seems to sacrifice the plausibility of the plot to show his hero flouting society: Bussy's lover succumbs to an overwhelming passion for him at first sight. This, in itself, is not so hard to believe, but that Bussy should have the same desire for her is harder to accept, because he ignored her a few scenes earlier at court. In the play's least convincing moment, this adulterous passion is approved by a friar, who then consents to act as their go-between. Clearly, who the characters are and the reasons for their actions are of less interest to Chapman than are illustrations of Bussy's independence of customary morality.

The play is skillfully constructed, the language at times poetic and compelling. The style of the play, however, is rhetorical in the extreme, with long passages of obscure philosophizing that often bring the action to a halt. When Chapman's contemporaries accused him of obscurity, he defended himself by claiming that the language was appropriate to the gravity and nobility of the subject. In some speeches, however, the grammar breaks down entirely. In view of these and similar difficulties, the taste of the audiences that made the play so popular for so long a time might be questioned.

The play, however, retains more than enough elements of the Elizabethan tragedy to satisfy those who desire action, and plenty of it. Duels and murder fill the stage. The betrayed husband tortures his wife; the friar drops dead, providing the requisite ghost at the end of the play; and, in a scene harking back to the miracle plays of the fifteenth century, a devil is raised by Bussy in an attempt to discover his enemies' plots. The final scene shows Bussy and the ghost holding off a pack of paid killers, when an assassin with more sense than superstition draws a pistol and shoots Bussy down. With action like this, a good part of the audience must have simply endured the moralizing in the knowledge that something exciting would soon happen.

"Critical Evaluation" by Walter E. Meyers

Bibliography:
Bartlett, Phyllis B. *Poems of George Chapman*. New York: Modern Language Association of America, 1941. Discusses Chapman's use of drama and poetry as a vehicle for philosophy. Excellent starting point for studying the debate over the frequently difficult language and ambiguous thematic elements of Chapman's plays.
Ferguson, A. S. "The Plays of George Chapman." *Modern Language Review* 13 (1918): 1-24. Concise and still useful essay on Chapman's indebtedness to Seneca.
Rees, Ennis. *The Tragedies of George Chapman*. Cambridge, Mass.: Harvard University Press, 1954. Reads Bussy's view of himself as subjective; argues that, given the protagonist's actions, the play must be read ironically. Demonstrates one of the interpretative extremes the play has provoked.
Schwartz, Elias. "Seneca, Homer, and Chapman's *Bussy d'Ambois*." *Journal of English and Germanic Philology* 56 (1957): 163-176. Accepts the protagonist's estimate of himself and his situation as basically correct. With Rees's essay, suggests the widely divergent poles of criticism on the play.
Wieler, John. *George Chapman: The Effect of Stoicism upon His Tragedies*. New York: King's Crown Press, 1949. Excellent introduction to the philosophical background of the play. Asserts the play should be read as a straightforward Christian tragedy; however one reads it, the influence of Stoicism appears throughout the play.

CADMUS

Type of work: Short fiction
Author: Unknown
Type of plot: Adventure
Time of plot: Antiquity
Locale: Greece
First published: Unknown

> *Principal characters:*
> CADMUS, the founder of Thebes
> JUPITER, the king of the gods
> MINERVA, the daughter of Jupiter
> MARS, the god of war
> HARMONIA, the wife of Cadmus

The Story:

Jupiter, in the form of a bull, carried away Europa, who was the daughter of Agenor, the king of Phenicia. When her handmaidens told Agenor of the kidnapping, he commanded his son Cadmus to look for Europa and not to return until he had found her. Cadmus searched for his sister for many years and in strange lands. Although he searched diligently, killing many monsters and endangering himself many times in his quest, he could not find her. Afraid to return to his father, he consulted the oracle of Apollo at Delphi and asked where he should settle. The oracle told him that he would find a cow in a field, and that he should follow her, for she would lead him to a good land. Where the cow stopped, Cadmus was to build a great city and call it Thebes.

When Cadmus soon thereafter saw a cow, he followed her. Finally, the cow stopped on the plain of Panope. In order to give thanks to the gods, Cadmus sent his slaves to find pure water for the sacrifice. In a dense grove, they found a wonderful clear spring, which was, however, guarded by a terrible dragon sacred to Mars. His scales shone like gold, his body was filled with a poisonous venom, and he had a triple tongue and three rows of huge, ragged teeth. The servants, thinking only to please their master, dipped their pitchers in the water, whereupon all were instantly destroyed by the monster.

After waiting many hours for the return of his servants, Cadmus went to the grove and found the mangled bodies of his faithful slaves and, close by, the terrible monster of the spring. Cadmus threw a huge stone at the dragon, but the stone did not dent his shining scales. Then, he drew back his javelin and heaved it at the serpent. It went through the scales and into the entrails. The monster, trying to draw out the weapon with his mouth, broke the blade and left the point burning his flesh. He swelled with rage as he advanced toward the hero, and Cadmus retreated before him. Cadmus then threw his spear at the monster, and the weapon pinned him against a tree until he died.

As Cadmus stood gazing at the terrible creature, he heard the voice of the goddess Minerva telling him to sow the dragon's teeth in a field. Hardly had he done so when a warrior in armor sprang up from each tooth. Cadmus started toward the warriors, thinking he must slay them all or lose his own life, but again Minerva spoke to him and told him not to strike. The warriors began to do battle among themselves. All were slain but five, who then presented themselves to Cadmus and said that they would serve him. Together with these five warriors, Cadmus built the city of Thebes.

Jupiter gave Cadmus Harmonia, the daughter of Mars and Venus, to be his wife, and the gods came down from Olympus to honor the couple. Vulcan forged a brilliant necklace with his own hands and gave it to the bride. Four children were born, and for a time Cadmus and Harmonia lived happily with their children. Yet doom hung over Cadmus and his family for the killing of the serpent. Eventually, Mars revenged himself by causing all of Cadmus' children to perish.

In despair, Cadmus and Harmonia left Thebes and went to the country of the Enchelians, who made Cadmus their king. However, Cadmus could find no peace because of Mars's curse on him. One day, he told Harmonia that if a serpent were so dear to the gods he himself wished to become a serpent. No sooner had he spoken the words than he began to grow scales and to change his form. When Harmonia beheld her husband turned into a serpent, she prayed to the gods for a like fate. Both became serpents, but they continued to love human beings and never did injury to anyone.

Critical Evaluation:
The story of Cadmus follows a typical pattern of the Greek hero-myth: The young man is sent on a quest (in this case to find his lost sister), receives instructions from a god to found a new city, proves himself by killing a dragon, and endures the hostility of a god, who kills all of his children. The Cadmus myth is somewhat unusual in its combination of elements from both Eastern and Western mythological traditions. This is reflected in the Phoenician connections of Cadmus' lineage and the probable derivation of his name from a Phoenician or Semitic word meaning "the one from the east."

Cadmus' search for his missing sister is reminiscent of other famous mythological quests, such as that of Jason for the Golden Fleece and Odysseus' attempt to return to his home and family. The success of the hero in these cases represents the return of order to a disordered home, city, and, by extension, world. The monsters and obstacles that have to be overcome in the process indicate the difficulties of restoring order.

The story of the building of Thebes is reminiscent of the stories of other cities, for example the founding of Rome by the Trojan exile Aeneas and the closely related tale of Ilus and his cow and the founding of Troy. In these two cases, the cow, a symbol of female fecundity, seems to represent the earth goddess. In all of these stories, the hero must subdue the local inhabitants and make the land safe for the new city. The foundation of a city is accompanied by violence and death, out of which new life arises: In the case of Thebes, Cadmus must first kill the dragon that guards a spring of clear water. The dragon, sacred to the god of war, Mars, also represents the primeval forces of the earth goddess. When Cadmus kills the creature and from its teeth harvests warriors, with whom he founds Thebes, this indicates that the earth has been tamed and is prepared to cooperate with the hero in the creation of a new city.

Mars's curse on Cadmus for killing the dragon is another stock element in mythology, similar to the curse on the house of Atreus. The persistence of the Theban curse is remarkable for extending all the way down to Oedipus and his descendants. Cadmus himself loses all of his children, suggesting once again that the foundation of a city involves much personal suffering and sacrifice for the founder. To a certain extent, Cadmus is reincarnated in his descendant Oedipus, who likewise consults the oracle of Apollo, is driven to leave his city because of a divine curse, and is fated to lose his children to violent deaths.

The marriage of Cadmus and Harmonia, daughter of Mars and Venus, is likewise an ill-starred affair: Harmonia is the product of an adulterous relationship (Venus was married to Vulcan) and, despite the fact that the wedding celebration is attended by all the Olympian gods, Vulcan's gift of a beautiful necklace to the bride brings bad fortune with it, and the harmony that Cadmus and his wife enjoy is short-lived. The marriage recalls that of Menelaus and Helen, which set in motion the events of the Trojan war. Like Helen, Harmonia is beautiful, but her beauty holds the seeds of destruction for the hero who marries her. It might be argued, of course, that Harmonia is an essentially positive figure, devoted to her husband and prepared to stay with him throughout all his vicissitudes. Some have seen an analogy with the marriage of Dushyanta and Sakuntala in Hindu mythology. Others view Harmonia as a version of Pandora or Eve, the archetypal woman who brings trouble to man in patriarchal myths. The fact that Cadmus' children are all girls, and that they all die unpleasant deaths, tends to strengthen a negative association with women that underlies this legend.

The story of Cadmus closes with the metamorphosis that transforms Cadmus and Harmonia into serpents. This represents a reconciliation with Mars as well as with the earth goddess from whom serpents spring. The serpent generally occupied a significant place in Theban mythology: Tiresias the seer is changed from a man into a woman and back again when he encounters two serpents in the forest, and Dionysus, the new god whom Pentheus tries to keep out of the city, is often associated with snakes. The fearsome dragon of the beginning of the founding myth is eventually transformed into a beneficial entity, for Cadmus and Harmonia do no harm to human beings. After their deaths, Jupiter carries both of them to the Elysian fields in recognition of their self-sacrifice and devotion to the gods.

The myth of Cadmus is a complex patchwork of several mythological archetypes and of Eastern and Western influences. It has enduring literary value in its presentation of a hero driven by forces beyond his control and victimized by hostile deities. The hero is also a man who must reap what he sows, yet his sufferings and sacrifices are ultimately beneficial and necessary for the growth of civilization, for Cadmus is responsible for the foundation of one of the greatest of all Greek cities.

"Critical Evaluation" by David H. J. Larmour

Bibliography:
Calasso, Roberto. *The Marriage of Cadmus and Harmony.* Translated by Tim Parks. New York: Knopf, 1993. An imaginative exploration of the Greek myth cycles, ending with a discussion of the Cadmus story in chapter 12. Offers an interpretation of the complex and troubled relationship between gods and humans.
Edwards, Ruth B. *Kadmos the Phoenician: A Study in Greek Legends and the Mycenaean Age.* Amsterdam: Adolf M. Hakkert, 1979. Discusses the origins of the Cadmus story and locates such myths in the context of the Mycenaean civilization.
Euripides. *The Adorers of Dionysus (The Bakchai).* Translated by James Morgan Pryse. Los Angeles: J. M. Pryse, 1925. This edition contains an interpretation of the myth of Cadmus that shows him as a man who devotes his soul to the quest for divine wisdom.
Fontenrose, Joseph. *Python: A Study of Delphic Myth and Its Origins.* Berkeley: University of California Press, 1959. A useful study of the mythological context in which the Cadmus story exists; there are many similarities between Cadmus' slaying of the dragon and Apollo's killing of the Python and between the foundation myths of Thebes and Delphi.
Green, Roger L. *The Tale of Thebes.* New York: Cambridge University Press, 1977. Tells the Theban myths in a narrative, simplified format that is suitable for nonspecialists.

CAESAR AND CLEOPATRA

Type of work: Drama
Author: George Bernard Shaw (1856-1950)
Type of plot: Comedy
Time of plot: October, 48 B.C.E., to March, 47 B.C.E.
Locale: Egypt
First published: 1901; first performed, 1906

>*Principal characters:*
>JULIUS CAESAR
>CLEOPATRA, the queen of Egypt
>PTOLEMY DIONYSUS, her brother and husband, the king of Egypt
>FTATATEETA, Cleopatra's nurse
>BRITANNUS, a Briton, Caesar's secretary
>RUFIO, a Roman officer
>POTHINUS, the king's guardian
>APOLLODORUS, a Sicilian

The Story:

Act I. Caesar was alone at night in the Egyptian desert, apostrophizing a statue of the Sphinx. Caesar was startled when a young girl, Cleopatra, addressed him from the paws of the Sphinx. He climbed up to her, thinking he was dreaming. She was full of superstitions about cats and Nile water. She told Caesar she was there because the Romans were coming to eat her people. Caesar saw that he was not dreaming and identified himself to Cleopatra as a Roman. She was terror-stricken, but Caesar told her that he would eat her unless she could show herself to him as a woman, not a girl. Cleopatra put herself in the hands of this Roman and they moved to her throne room. Caesar tried to persuade Cleopatra to act like a queen; Ftatateeta entered and began to order Cleopatra about until the nurse was chased from the room. Caesar ordered Cleopatra's servants to dress her in her royal robes. When Roman soldiers entered and saluted Caesar, Cleopatra finally realized who he was and, with a sob of relief, fell into his arms.

Act II. The ten-year-old king Ptolemy was delivering a speech from the throne in Alexandria, prompted by his tutor and guardian. Caesar entered and demanded taxes, then called for Cleopatra. Rufio reminded Caesar that there was a Roman army of occupation in Egypt, commanded by Achillas and supporting the Egyptians, while Caesar had only four thousand men. Achillas and Pothinus suggested that they held the upper hand, but when Roman troops entered, the Egyptians backed off. Lucius Septimius and Pothinus reminded Caesar that they had decapitated Pompey in order to ingratiate themselves with Caesar, who was horrified to hear of the act. All the Egyptians but Ptolemy left, and Rufio again protested against Caesar's clemency. Ptolemy was escorted out. Cleopatra and Caesar discussed how much Cleopatra had grown up, and Caesar promised to send strong young Mark Antony to Cleopatra. A wounded Roman soldier entered to inform Caesar that the Roman army of occupation had come; Caesar ordered that all the ships be burned except those that were to carry the Romans to the lighthouse on an island in the harbor. As Caesar started to arm himself, Pothinus entered, followed by Theodotus with the news that the great library in Alexandria was burning. After Pothinus and Theodotus left, Cleopatra helped Caesar put on his armor and made fun of his baldness. Caesar and Rufio left to lead the troops to the Pharos.

Act III. On a quay in front of Cleopatra's palace, Apollodorus, who had brought carpets for Cleopatra to look at, argued with the Roman sentinel. Cleopatra wanted to be rowed to the lighthouse, but the sentinel refused to allow it. Cleopatra thereupon said she would make a present of a carpet to Caesar, and secretly she had herself rolled up in one and put in a boat that was sailing for the lighthouse that the Egyptians had begun to attack. When Apollodorus entered with the carpet, which was unrolled and revealed Cleopatra, Caesar regarded the young woman as a nuisance. The Egyptians had cut off the Romans and were approaching. Several Roman ships approached, whereupon Apollodorus, Caesar, and Rufio dove into the sea to swim to them. Cleopatra was tossed into the sea as well and carried along.

Act IV. Six months later, Cleopatra and her serving women were discussing Caesar when Ftatateeta brought in Pothinus, who was now a prisoner of the Romans and wanted to make a deal with Cleopatra. After Rufio and Caesar entered, Rufio brought Pothinus to talk to Caesar privately. Pothinus finally blurted out that Cleopatra wanted Caesar out of the way so that she could rule alone. Cleopatra denied this, but Caesar knew it was true. When Pothinus left, Cleopatra ordered Ftatateeta to kill him. Caesar, Rufio, and Apollodorus had just returned for a banquet when a terrible scream was heard. Apollodorus, sent to investigate, reported that Pothinus had been assassinated and that the city, in an uproar, was blaming Caesar. Cleopatra admitted that she had given the order, but Caesar could not make her understand that this was not his way of governing. Lucius Septimius approached Caesar and told him that the relief army under Mithridates was near. Realizing that the Egyptian army had left to fight Mithridates, Caesar left, intending to meet Mithridates and fight the Egyptian army. When Rufio learned that Ftatateeta had killed Pothinus, he killed her.

Act V. Having won the battle, Caesar prepared to return to Rome. He appointed Rufio to be the Roman governor of Egypt, praised Britannus for his conduct in the battle, and left Apollodorus in charge of Egyptian art. Cleopatra, in mourning for Ftatateeta, pleaded for revenge against Rufio, who had admitted to killing Ftatateeta; since it had been a justified slaying, Caesar denied Cleopatra's plea. He said that Cleopatra had learned little from him but again promised to send her Mark Antony. Caesar boarded the ship to a salute from the Roman soldiers. Cleopatra remained behind, saddened but content.

"The Story" by Gordon N. Bergquist

Critical Evaluation:

Ever since the publication in 1579 of Sir Thomas North's translation of Plutarch's *Parallel Lives*, Cleopatra has been one of the great romantic figures of English literature. To be sure, Dante had briefly glimpsed her, "tossed on the blast," in Hell's Circle of the Lustful in his *Inferno* (c. 1320), but he had hurried on to give the famous story of Paolo and Francesca. It remained for William Shakespeare, in *Antony and Cleopatra* (1606-1607), to make her immortal as "the serpent of old Nile," the epitome of the eternal and irresistible female. Even the neoclassic John Dryden, in 1678, still found her the archetype of an all-consuming passion, for whose sake Antony held "the world well lost."

As for Caesar, his imprint has been upon the European mind since 44 B.C.E. To Dante—who saw him in Limbo as "Caesar armed, with the falcon eyes"—he was the founder of the Roman empire, and his murder was so terrible an example of treachery to lords and benefactors that Cassius and Brutus, his asssassins, were placed with Judas in the jaws of Satan in the lowest pit of Hell. To Shakespeare, he was a man who in spite of arrogance and a thinly disguised ambition for absolute power actually bestrode "the narrow world like a Colossus." These are the figures of world history and world legend whom George Bernard Shaw chose to bring together in a comedy.

So strongly has Shakespeare stamped his interpretation of Cleopatra on Western literary consciousness that Shaw's heroine inflicts a distinct shock when audiences meet a girl of sixteen, crouched, on a moonlit October night, between the paws of the Sphinx in the desert where she has fled to escape the invading Romans. She is the typical schoolgirl: high-strung, giggly, impulsive, terrified of her nurse, ready to believe that Romans have trunks, tusks, tails, and seven arms, each carrying a hundred arrows. She has the instinctive cruelty of a child; after encountering Caesar—whom she does not recognize and who forces her nurse to cringe at her feet—she is eager to beat the nurse and can talk gleefully of poisoning slaves and cutting off her brother's head. Shaw has set his plot at the moment in history when Egypt is divided. Ptolemy Dionysus has driven Cleopatra from Alexandria, and while the two foes—Ptolemy represented by Pothinus and Cleopatra by Ftatateeta—are at swords' points, Egypt is ready to fall into the conqueror's hand. It is the familiar situation of an immensely old and decadent civilization at the mercy of a rising world power, represented by Caesar.

Audiences with memories of Caesar's commentaries on the Gallic War and Mark Antony's funeral oration receive another shock when Caesar appears. The conqueror of the world is presented as a middle-aged man, painfully conscious of his years, somewhat prosaic, very far indeed from "Caesar armed, with the falcon eyes." He is past fifty, and the fateful Ides of March is less than four years away. As most men of his age in any period of history would be, he is somewhat amused and yet wholly fascinated by the lovely child he has met under such strange circumstances. Since he is quite aware of his weakness for women, the audience begins to anticipate a romantic turn to the plot. Shaw was not, however, a romantic dramatist. When Caesar returns Cleopatra to her palace, reveals his identity, and forces her to abandon her childishness and to assume her position as queen, he is revealed as a man who is eminently practical, imperturbable in moments of danger, and endowed with the slightly cynical detachment of a superior mind surrounded by inferiors.

The outline that Shaw used for his somewhat rambling plot is to be found in Plutarch's *Life of Caesar* and in Caesar's *Civil War*. Shaw followed his sources quite faithfully, except in inventing a meeting between Caesar and Cleopatra in the desert and calling for Pothinus to be killed by Ftatateeta at Cleopatra's instigation after Caesar had promised him safe conduct from the palace. There is also a possible debt to the almost forgotten drama, *The False One*, written by John Fletcher and Philip Massinger around 1620, which deals with the same story. Certainly Shaw's blunt-spoken Rufio appears to be a reworking of that play's Sceva.

Shaw also added two characters of his own to the story: the savage Ftatateeta, who is eventually killed by Rufio; and Britannus, Caesar's secretary. The latter is Shaw's picture of the eternal Englishman—conventional, easily shocked, unable to understand any customs but those of his own island. It is in characterization, rather than in plot, that the play excels, and it also excels through the element of surprise, created by the device of presenting familiar literary figures from new angles, for it is obvious that Shaw intended to rub some of the romantic gilding from them. Cleopatra, although under Caesar's influence she becomes a precocious adult, loses her girlish charm without becoming a particularly attractive woman. She never really loves Caesar, nor he her, for Shaw rearranged history in this aspect of their relationship, and her one thought is of the arrival of Antony, whom she has met before and never forgotten. She has a presentiment of her coming tragedy, yet, eternally childish, is poised to run to meet it.

The critic James Huneker maintained that this drama "entitled [Shaw] to a free pass to that pantheon wherein our beloved Mark Twain sits enthroned." Yet this play is no *Connecticut*

Yankee in King Arthur's Court (1889), which was based on a conviction of the vast progress achieved since the Middle Ages. It was Shaw's conviction that there had been no perceptible progress since Caesar's day. Caesar himself knew that history would continue to unroll an endless series of murders and wars, always disguised under high-sounding and noble names. He was a great man, not because he was "ahead of his age" but because he stood outside it and could rule with mercy and without revenge. Such a leader would be great in any period of history.

Bibliography:
Crompton, Louis. "*Caesar and Cleopatra.*" In *Shaw the Dramatist.* Lincoln: University of Nebraska Press, 1969. Discusses the social, philosophical, and especially historical backgrounds. A clear and accessible presentation of Shaw's ideas and their sources in the nineteenth century intellectual tradition.
Dukore, Bernard F. "The Center and the Frame." In *Bernard Shaw, Playwright: Aspects of Shavian Drama.* Columbia: University of Missouri Press, 1973. Concentrates on the formal aspects of the play and discusses how certain central scenes contribute to the whole. Deals at length with the prologues (which are seldom played) and Act III, which Shaw had suggested could be omitted but which Dukore claims is important and even necessary.
Evans, T. F., ed. *Shaw: The Critical Heritage.* London: Routledge & Kegan Paul, 1976. A useful collection of generally brief early reviews and notices of Shaw's plays, including *Caesar and Cleopatra.* Interesting to compare these early reviews with later scholarly views.
Holroyd, Michael. *Bernard Shaw: The Search for Love.* New York: Random House, 1988. In this first volume of the standard and indispensable biography of Shaw, Holroyd relates Shaw's life and thought to his works.
Whitman, Robert F. "Plays for Realists." In *Shaw and the Play of Ideas.* Ithaca, N.Y.: Cornell University Press, 1977. Discusses the play's conflict between *realist* and *idealist.* Caesar's grasp of reality makes him immune to the temptations of vengeance and to Cleopatra's sensuality. Caesar is the representative of the future.

CAIN

Type of work: Drama
Author: George Gordon, Lord Byron (1788-1824)
Type of plot: Tragedy
Time of plot: The period of Genesis
Locale: Outside Eden
First published: 1821

> *Principal characters:*
> ADAM, the first man
> EVE, the first woman
> CAIN and
> ABEL, their sons
> ADAH, Cain's wife
> ZILLAH, Abel's wife
> LUCIFER, the fallen angel

The Story:

While Adam, Eve, Abel, Zillah, and Adah prayed to God, Cain stood sullenly by and complained that he had nothing to pray for, since he had lost immortality when Eve ate the fruit from the tree of knowledge. He could not understand why, if knowledge and life were good, his mother's deed had been a deadly sin. Abel, Adah, and Zillah urged him to cast off his melancholy and join them in tending the fields. Alone, Cain deplored his worldly toil. Tired of the repetitious replies to all his questions, replies which refused to challenge God's will, he was no longer sure that God was good.

At the conception of this thought, Lucifer appeared to explain that Cain's mortality was only a bodily limit. He would live forever even after death. Cain, driven by instinct to cling to life, at the same time despised it. Lucifer admitted that he also was unhappy in spite of his immortality, which was a cursed thing in his fallen state. He launched into a bitter tirade against God, whom he described as a tyrant sitting alone in his misery, creating new worlds because his eternity was otherwise expressionless and boring to him. Lucifer exulted that his own condition was at least shared by others. These words echoed for Cain his own beliefs about the universe. Long had he pitied his relatives for toiling so hard for sustenance, as God had decreed when he had banished Adam and Eve from Eden.

Lucifer confessed that the beguiling snake had not been a disguise for himself; the snake was merely a snake. He predicted, however, that later generations of humanity would array the fall of Adam and Eve in a cloak of fable. Cain then asked his mentor to reveal the nature of death, which held great terrors for Cain. Lucifer promised to teach Cain true knowledge if Cain would worship him. Cain, however, having refused to worship even God, would not worship any being. His refusal was, according to Lucifer, in itself a form of worship.

Adah came to ask Cain to go with her, but he claimed that he must stay with Lucifer, who spoke like a god. She reminded Cain that the lying serpent, too, had spoken so. Lucifer insisted that the serpent had spoken truly when it had promised knowledge from the fruit of the forbidden tree; humanity's grief lay not in the serpent's so-called lie but in humanity's knowledge of evil. Lucifer said he would take Cain with him for an hour, time enough to show him the whole of life and death.

Traveling with Lucifer through the air, Cain, watching with ecstasy the beauty around him, insisted upon viewing the mystery of death, which was uppermost in his mind. The travelers came at last to a place where no stars glittered and all was dark and dreadful. As they entered Hades, Cain voiced again his hatred of death, the end of all living things.

In the underworld he saw beautiful and mighty shapes which, Lucifer explained, had inhabited the world and died by chaotic destruction in an age before Adam had been created. When Lucifer taunted Cain with his inferiority compared to those other beings of an earlier age, Cain declared himself ready to stay in Hades forever. Lucifer confessed, however, that he had no power to allow anyone to remain in Hades. When he pointed out to Cain that the spirits of the former inhabitants of the earth had enjoyed a beautiful world, Cain said that earth was still beautiful. His complaint was against human toil for what the earth bore, human failure to obtain knowledge, and the unmitigated human fear of death. Cain, bewailing the trade humanity had made of death for knowledge, asserted that humanity knew nothing. Lucifer replied that death was a certainty and therefore truth and knowledge. Cain thought that he had learned nothing new from his journey, but Lucifer informed him that he had at least discovered that there was a state beyond his own.

They discussed Cain's relative state of happiness in life, which, Cain asserted, was dependent upon his love for his family. Lucifer hinted that Abel, favored by the others and by God, caused Cain some jealousy. Cain then asked his guide to show him where Lucifer lived, or else God's dwelling place. It was reserved for those who died, Lucifer claimed, to see either one or the other, not both. As Lucifer prepared to return his pupil to earth, Cain complained that he had learned nothing. He had, Lucifer said, discovered that he was nothing. With a warning to distinguish between real good and evil and to seek his own spiritual attachment, Lucifer transported the mortal back to earth.

Standing over their son Enoch, who was asleep under a tree, Adah and Cain discussed their ever-present sorrow: They must all die. When Adah said she would gladly die to save her parents, Cain agreed only if his own death might save everyone else. Adah prophesied that such a gift might some day be rendered. Seeing the pair of altars Abel had erected for a sacrifice, Cain uttered his first evil thought by muttering a denial that Abel was his brother.

Abel insisted that Cain share in the sacrificial rites he was about to perform. While Cain impiously stood by, Abel knelt in eloquent prayer. Cain's prayer was a defiant challenge to the omnipotent to show his preference for one of the altars. His own offerings were scattered to the earth, while Abel's sacrifice burned in high flames toward the heavens. In anger Cain attacked his brother's altar, and when Abel protested that he loved his God more than life, Cain struck him a mortal blow.

Adam, Eve, Adah, and Zillah, rushing to the scene of the murder, accused Cain of murdering his brother. Eve uttered loud imprecations against her guilty son. Adam ordered him to depart. Only Adah remained by his side. The Angel of the Lord then appeared to confront Cain and ask the whereabouts of his brother. The Angel predicted that henceforth Cain's hand would cultivate no growing things from the earth and that he should be a fugitive. Lest the man guilty of fratricide be the cause of another murder, the Angel branded Cain with a mark on his forehead, to warn the beholder that to kill Cain would engender a sevenfold vengeance. Cain blamed his evil deed upon Eve, who bore him too soon after her banishment from Eden, when her own mind was still bitter over the lost paradise. Adah offered to share her husband's fate. Carrying their children with them, she and Cain traveled eastward from Eden.

Critical Evaluation:

The first European drama was that of classical Greece and Rome, but this tradition was lost during the Dark Ages. Drama was then reinvented in medieval times as an elaboration of the Mass, in which priests would act out brief scenes to emphasize their emotional power. As these scenes became more popular, they gradually moved out of the church and into the churchyard. They became whole plays in which biblical stories were recounted with a great deal of freedom. Such works are called mystery plays.

The term "mystery play" has nothing to do with crime and detection. As originally applied, it meant a play based on any of the fifteen events to be meditated upon during a saying of the rosary. Such plays were performed in cycles by members of craft guilds that also came to be called mysteries (because they concealed the secrets of their trades). By the sixteenth century, mystery plays became less popular and were eventually superseded by secular drama. Mystery plays were ignored as a form of drama until the form was revived by George Gordon, Lord Byron in *Cain* and in *Heaven and Earth*, both of which were published in 1821. *Heaven and Earth* is a sequel to *Cain* and ends with the Flood. Unlike the earliest medieval mystery plays, Byron's derive from the Old Testament rather than the New Testament.

The scriptural basis for *Cain* is the fourth chapter of Genesis. Eve gives birth to Cain and Abel, who become a tiller of the soil and a keeper of flocks, respectively. Both present offerings to the Lord; for an unexplained reason, God accepts Abel's but rejects Cain's. Crestfallen, Cain then leads Abel into the field and kills him. When the Lord asks Cain where Abel is, Cain asks: Am I my brother's keeper? The Lord then banishes Cain, condemning him to restless wandering, and places a mark upon him to prevent his being slain by others.

Just who these "others" and who Cain's wife might be have long been regarded as problems. In Byron's version, both Cain and Abel have wives—their sisters—who are named Adah and Zillah, respectively. Byron found these names in the fourth chapter of Genesis also. They are, in the Bible, the two wives of Lamech, and they are the first women other than Eve to be named in the Old Testament.

Byron was the object of scandal and ostracism because of his incest with his half sister, Augusta. He was not a practicing Christian, did not attend religious services, did not pray, did not write religious works, did not believe in saints or miracles, and did not desire any form of religious burial. He believed strongly that whatever form of "salvation" might follow death would be achieved not by any kind of ritual or priestly intervention but by strength of will. The Bible, for Byron, was not so much a record of God's dealings with humanity as of humanity's failure to understand God. It follows from this position that Byron would tend to side with Cain and against the God of Genesis. Note that the fallen angel in Byron's play is called Lucifer (the bringer of light) rather than Satan (the enemy). Under the guidance of Lucifer, Cain—or modern man—is led to reject a theological worldview in favor of one derived from skepticism and science. Exhausting the fourth chapter of Genesis as source material, Byron adds two important newer ideas to *Cain*. In a letter to his friend and fellow poet Thomas Moore, dated September 19, 1821, Byron identified the creatures that Cain sees in Act II, scene ii of his play as "rational Preadamites, beings endowed with a higher intelligence than man, but totally unlike him in form." The idea that there were beings on earth before Adam was a common, although heretical, speculation. If human, Preadamites could have accounted for the existence of Cain's wife. Byron made it clear, however, that the Preadamites of his imagination are neither human nor inferior. He regularly saw history as devolution (a getting worse) with the present being inferior to the past.

In the same letter to Moore, Byron explained the prehistoric past that Cain describes, also in Act II, scene ii. "I have gone upon the notion of Cuvier," Byron wrote, "that the world has been destroyed three or four times, and was inhabited by mammoths, behemoths, and what not; but not by man" until the time of the story in Genesis. In 1821, dinosaurs had yet to be discovered, and, as he was aware, no ancient human fossils had yet been discovered. He took for granted that humanity was a recent creation. The book from which Byron derived his ideas about the prehistoric past was written by Georges Cuvier. Cuvier's *Recherches sur les ossements fossiles de quadrupèdes* (1812) and *Discours sur les révolutions de la surface du globe* (1825) present the history of life on earth as a series of catastrophes, with change being abrupt rather than gradual. The idea that past life was grander than present (the mammoth being larger and more ferocious than the mere elephant of today, for example) had been advocated by an earlier French theorist named Georges-Louis Leclerc de Buffon. Neither theory was universally accepted in 1821, and Buffon's was rather out of fashion, but it is notable that Byron turned to science to supplement scripture. It is not surprising that he chose those scientific theories that coincided with his own feelings and convictions. As an exile banished from his homeland by scandal over his incest and marked by an obvious limp, Byron unquestionably identified with the biblical Cain to a considerable extent. *Cain* marks an attempt on Byron's part to establish a new, post-biblical relationship between modern man and the cosmos. It is certainly the most thoughtful of his works.

"Critical Evaluation" by Dennis R. Dean

Bibliography:
Chew, Samuel Claggett. *The Dramas of Lord Byron: A Critical Study.* New York: Russell & Russell, 1964. Despite its age, Chew's study remains the best place to begin any study of Byron and his writing for the theater.
Lowes, John Livingston. *The Road to Xanadu.* Boston: Houghton Mifflin, 1927. This famous study includes background material useful for the study of Romantic literature as a whole. Lowes's treatment of the legend of Cain is still one of the best.
Marchand, Leslie. *Byron: A Biography.* 3 vols. New York: Knopf, 1957. Byron, one of the most autobiographical of all poets, led a fascinating life. In many instances, his works are largely an idealized version of his own experiences. Marchand's biography is the standard one and reliably illuminates autobiographical elements in *Cain.*
Thorslev, Peter L. *The Byronic Hero: Types and Prototypes.* Minneapolis: University of Minnesota Press, 1962. Probably the most helpful book that a student confronting Byron for the first time can read. Thorslev describes seven well-known types of heroes in Romantic literature before turning specifically to Byron's. Depictions of Cain in legend and literature are summarized. Byron's Cain is usefully compared with John Milton's Satan and Johann Wolfgang von Goethe's Faust.

THE CAINE MUTINY

Type of work: Novel
Author: Herman Wouk (1915-   )
Type of plot: Bildungsroman
Time of plot: 1942-1945
Locale: New York City, San Francisco, and the Pacific Ocean
First published: 1951

Principal characters:

WILLIE KEITH, a young Naval Reserve officer
TOM KEEFER, an intellectual and Keith's communications officer
CAPTAIN DE VREISS, Keith's first commanding officer on the *Caine*
STEVE MARYK, Keith's fellow officer
CAPTAIN PHILIP FRANCIS QUEEG, the *Caine*'s second captain and a focus
   of controversy
LIEUTENANT BARNEY GREENWALD, the mutineers' defense attorney
MAY WYNN (MARIE MINOTTI), Keith's girlfriend

The Story:

Wealthy and sheltered, Willie Keith had just graduated from Princeton. To avoid Army service, he entered the Navy Reserve Officers' Training Program shortly after Japan's attack on Pearl Harbor. A spoiled adolescent, his distinctions were limited to amusing friends by playing piano and inventing clever ditties. Straying from his social reservation, he had also begun an infatuation with May Wynn (born Marie Minotti), a hardworking nightclub singer and the daughter of immigrants. In the first of *The Caine Mutiny*'s six parts, Keith passes into the bizarre world of the Navy, war, and authority. During the next three years, the once callow Ensign Keith acquired the skills of his trade, learned self-reliance, acquiesced to cabals against his superior, became a party to a mutiny, and ultimately captained the final voyage of the U.S.S. *Caine*.

At the outset, however, Keith had difficulty comprehending that there was "a right way, a wrong way, and the Navy way." Loaded with demerits for his blunders, unclear about the meaning of service or sacrifice, and close to expulsion, he survived his midshipman's training at Columbia University only by mustering a surprising amount of inner determination. Expecting a soft billet thereafter, he was dismayed by his assignment to the *Caine*, a lowly, World-World-I-era destroyer that had been converted to a minesweeper.

Keith's first tour aboard the battle-scarred *Caine* was a study in mixed signals. Boarding ship as it was being refitted in San Francisco Bay, he met the aspiring novelist-intellectual Tom Keefer, a communications officer and Keith's superior officer. Keefer immediately defined himself as a sneering, acerbic critic of the Navy. Keith also met Steve Maryk, soon to be the ship's executive officer, who admired Captain De Vreiss. Having just imbibed respect for Navy regulations, Keith, however, was appalled by De Vreiss' lax discipline and slovenly shipkeeping, despite Maryk's stress on De Vreiss' superb seamanship and the respect he enjoyed among the weary crew. Keith's estimate of De Vreiss dropped lower when Keith's failure to deliver an important message to De Vreiss led him to reprimand Keith. Upon transfer of command from De Vreiss to Lieutenant Commander Philip Francis Queeg, Keith therefore felt relieved and hopeful.

In his mid-thirties, Queeg, though physically unimpressive, was a Naval Academy graduate and a believer in strict adherence to regulations. Behind Queeg lay fourteen years at sea and extended combat duty, so to the officers things looked promising under their new captain.

Part 3 chronicles the growing estrangement between Queeg and his officers. As the *Caine* alternated in the Pacific between training exercises, routine convoy duty, and then Keith's first combat during the Marianas invasion, her officers, led on by Keefer, awakened to mounting evidence of Queeg's indecision, ineptitude in shiphandling, personal quirkiness, and preoccupation with minor disciplinary matters.

A series of episodes cast doubt on Queeg's fitness for command. Initially maneuvering his ship in harbor, he grazed another vessel and ran the *Caine* aground. Called to account by his superior, Queeg blamed the accident on crewmen. Later, while the *Caine* conducted a target towing exercise, Queeg, busy reprimanding a seaman for a flapping shirttail, allowed the *Caine* to turn full circle, sever a towline, and sink a valuable target. Again, Queeg laid blame elsewhere. Returning his ship to San Francisco for repairs, Queeg sequestered his officers' liquor rations and illegally tried smuggling them ashore for himself. The liquor was lost overboard by a boat party in Keith's charge, and Keith was blamed.

Worse was to come. Responsible for guiding landing craft to an invasion beachhead, Queeg, frightened, dropped a yellow marker before the *Caine* reached its designated turning point, abandoning troop-filled small craft under fire. Shortly afterward, he failed to aid another ship busy suppressing enemy artillery. Keith and others, in addition, observed Queeg's habit of seeking the safest place on the bridge during combat. For a minor infraction, Queeg deprived the crew of water for days. Theft of a gallon of Queeg's strawberries resulted in turning the *Caine* inside out in a fruitless search that continued even after the culprits were known. Meanwhile, at Keefer's urging, Maryk began a record of Queeg's behavior.

At last, convinced that Queeg was psychologically unbalanced, Maryk, citing Navy law and joined by Keith and others, relieved Queeg of command as the *Caine* threatened to founder in a typhoon. Subsequently charged with mutiny, Maryk (who accepted full responsibility), Keith, Keefer, and other officers were defended reluctantly by Lieutenant Barney Greenwald, an experienced Jewish lawyer. Greenwald, with ruthless brilliance, discredited the Navy's psychological experts who testified to Queeg's sanity and then led Queeg to discredit himself thoroughly on the stand. Morally, however, it was a hollow victory. Amid the acquitted officers' celebratory party, Greenwald denounced them, damning Keefer in particular as the real cause of the mutiny and the person responsible for making Greenwald ruin Queeg.

Justice was done in the novel's final section. Queeg was reassigned to ignominious service as executive officer of a Navy depot in Kansas. Placed in command of the *Caine*, Tom Keefer demonstrated cowardice when he leaped overboard, his manuscript in hand, after a Japanese kamikaze plane crashed into his ship. Willie Keith, by then seasoned and commanding, became the last captain of the *Caine*, sailing her home to decommissioning and destruction, and, despite his mother's doubts, to renewed romance with May Wynn.

Critical Evaluation:

Retrospectively, many critics, even those not well disposed toward some of Herman Wouk's later writings, considered *The Caine Mutiny* his best work and one of the finest war novels to emerge from World War II. Wouk was awarded a Pulitzer Prize for it in 1952. Certainly the reading public affirmed this decision, for it became one of the best-selling novels published in the twentieth century. By 1960, sales in the United States exceeded three million copies and the novel had been translated into sixteen languages. In addition, adapted for theater, *The Caine*

Mutiny Court-Martial became a hit play, and, buoyed by actor Humphrey Bogart's superb performance as Captain Queeg, the screen version of *The Caine Mutiny* earned multiple awards that presaged recognition of it as a film classic.

Although Herman Wouk served several years in the Pacific during World War II as an officer aboard a minesweeper much like the *Caine*, his novel was not autobiographical. *The Caine Mutiny* certainly reflected elements of Joseph Conrad's *The Nigger of the "Narcissus"* (1897) and of Herman Melville's *Billy Budd, Foretopman* (1924) in the sense that both of these major literary works were stories of seamen trapped by implacable nature and unbending authority, of mutinies, and of trials. These similarities ought not, however, obscure *The Caine Mutiny*'s differences from them.

Philosophically, Wouk's themes are conservative and moralistic. The moral lesson he emphasized by following spoiled Willie Keith through his rite of passage to genuine maturity was that Keith's maturation had demanded sacrifice. Part of that sacrifice entailed the acceptance of an almost unquestioning obedience to properly constituted authority, along with the assumption of responsibility for making decisions. Wouk stressed how Keith, Maryk, even Keefer in his own manner, and not the least Greenwald, eventually realized, first by observation and then by the experience of rising to command themselves, that Captains De Vreiss and Queeg were subject to crushing pressures. These pressures in their instances were worsened by their extended wartime sea duty and combat. Ultimate authority, and the accountability that went with it, could not be shared, the lives of those in command were marked by loneliness and alienation. Their actions were open to constant denunciation and their peccadilloes to ridicule. Such burdens and circumstances alone, Wouk implied, entitled authority to strict obedience and to substantial respect. Although he was disturbed about Queeg's performance, Steve Maryk initially demonstrated this point when, after becoming the detested Queeg's executive officer, he refused to participate further in his fellow officers' daily fulminations against their captain.

A Keith put through the rigors of a maturation process becomes Wouk's metaphor for America's coming-of-age, a consequence of its involvement in World War II. In a confessional deathbed letter from his father that Keith opens at sea, his father, indeed, compares Willie to his country, young, naïve, and spoiled but still possessing sufficient pioneer determination to create a better life.

Keith's search for a father figure constitutes another minor theme. Keith's father nominally had been a successful physician; his final letter burdens Keith with the disclosure of a life of high-minded dreams betrayed by wasted opportunities, concessions to social status, and many unnecessary compromises. Thus, an irresolute Keith, harboring his own dreams of literary scholarship, confronts a number of surrogate fathers: two of his training instructors, a kindly admiral who likes his piano playing, Captain De Vreiss, Maryk, Keefer, and, eventually Queeg.

There are other minor themes. *The Caine Mutiny* is full of tensions that existed during World War II between former civilians, often innately contemptuous of the seemingly arbitrary nature of military authority, and the disciplined, underpaid, and socially demeaned officers like Queeg, who began their careers in the peacetime Navy. It was also difficult for reserve officers to cope with the entrenched Navy bureaucracy or with the Naval Academy's old boy network. It was also unusual for reservists to get respectful hearings for their ideas. Wouk remained a reserve officer long after 1945. Emphasizing the virtues of both regulars and reservists, he frequently called for their greater mutual understanding.

Stylistically, Wouk's third-person narrative moves his story swiftly and satisfactorily, sometimes with passion and often with humor, if without true distinction. His dialogue varies from touching and insightful to comic and clichéd. His exclusion of the obscenities that composed the bulk of servicemen's speech appeared timorous to many authors, an error to some editors, and unrealistic to readers. Furthermore, even Wouk's admirers criticized his handling of Keith's romance and his trite characterization of May Wynn. Yet despite such flaws, *The Caine Mutiny* appears destined for longevity. Wouk's skill ensures that characters such as Keith, Keefer, and certainly Queeg will remain memorable ones. More than good entertainment, the novel represents a fresh address, particularly for war novels, to sensitive social and moral issues.

Clifton K. Yearley

Bibliography:
Beichman, Arnold W. *The Novelist as a Social Historian*. New Brunswick, N.J.: Transaction Books, 1984. Concentrates on Wouk's conservatism. There are useful observations on *The Caine Mutiny* and the problems it raises about authority versus individualism.
Darby, William. *Necessary American Fiction: Popular Literature of the 1950's*. Bowling Green, Ohio: Bowling Green State University Press, 1987. An insightful analysis of how popular novels such as *The Caine Mutiny* reflect American values of the decade.
Jones, Peter G. *War and the Novelist*. Columbia: University of Missouri Press, 1976. Jones uses *The Caine Mutiny* as an exemplar of how war novels deal with problems of wartime military command.
Mazzeno, Laurence W. *Herman Wouk*. New York: Twayne, 1994. The best study of Wouk and his writings. Chapter 3 is devoted entirely to the novel.
Waldemeir, Joseph T. *American Novels of the Second World War*. The Hague: Mouton, 1971. Emphasizes how *The Caine Mutiny*, among a minority of war novels, commends the subordination of civilian individualism to military authority.

CAKES AND ALE
Or, The Skeleton in the Cupboard

Type of work: Novel
Author: W. Somerset Maugham (1874-1965)
Type of plot: Social satire
Time of plot: Late 1920's
Locale: London and Kent
First published: 1930

> *Principal characters:*
> ASHENDEN, a writer
> ALROY KEAR, a popular novelist
> EDWARD DRIFFIELD, a great Victorian
> ROSIE, Driffield's first wife
> AMY, Driffield's second wife
> GEORGE KEMP, Rosie's lover

The Story:

Alroy Kear, the most popular novelist of the day, arranged to have lunch with his friend Ashenden, another writer. Ashenden was fond of Kear, but he suspected that his invitation had been extended for a purpose. He was right. Kear wanted to talk about the late Edward Driffield, a famous English author of the past century. Kear had nothing but praise for the old man's books, but Ashenden said that he had never thought Driffield exceptional. Kear enthusiastically told how well he had known Driffield in his last years and said that he was still a friend of Driffield's widow, his second wife. Luncheon ended without a request for a favor. Ashenden was puzzled.

Returning to his room, Ashenden fell into a reverie. He recalled his first meeting with Driffield. Ashenden was then a boy, home for the holidays at Blackstable, a Kentish seacoast town, where he lived with his uncle, the local vicar. Ashenden met Driffield in the company of his uncle's curate, but the boy thought the writer a rather common person. He learned from his uncle that Driffield had married a local barmaid after spending a wild youth away from home.

Two or three days after Ashenden had lunched with Kear, he received a note from Driffield's widow. She wished him to visit her in Blackstable. Puzzled, Ashenden telephoned to Kear, who said that he would come to see him and explain the invitation.

Ashenden had seen Mrs. Driffield only once. He had gone to her house with some other literary people several years before, while Driffield was still alive. Driffield had married his second wife late in life, and she had been his nurse. In the course of the visit, Ashenden had been surprised to see old Driffield wink at him several times as if there were some joke between them. After that visit, Ashenden recalled how Driffield had taught him to bicycle many years before. Driffield and his first wife, Rosie, had taught him to ride and had taken him with them on many excursions. He liked the Driffields, but he was shocked to find how outspoken they were with those below and above them in social station.

One evening, Ashenden found Rosie visiting his uncle's cook, her childhood friend. After Rosie left, he saw her meet George Kemp, a local coal merchant. The couple walked out of town toward the open fields. Ashenden could not imagine how Rosie could be unfaithful to her husband.

Ashenden went back to school. During the Christmas holiday, he often joined the Driffields for tea. Kemp was always there, but he and Rosie did not act like lovers. Driffield sang drinking songs, played the piano, and seldom talked about literature. When Ashenden returned to Blackstable the following summer, he heard that the Driffields had fled, leaving behind many unpaid bills. He was ashamed that he had ever been friendly with them.

Kear arrived at Ashenden's rooms and explained that he was planning to write Driffield's official biography. He wanted Ashenden to contribute what he knew about the author's younger days. What Ashenden told him was not satisfactory, for the biography should contain nothing to embarrass the widow. Kear insisted that Ashenden write down what he remembered of Driffield and go to Blackstable to visit Mrs. Driffield. Ashenden agreed.

Ashenden remembered how he had met the Driffields again in London when he was a young medical student. By chance, he saw Rosie on the street; he was surprised that she was not ashamed to meet someone from Blackstable, and he promised to come to one of the Driffields' Saturday afternoon gatherings. Soon he became a regular visitor in their rooms. Since Driffield worked at night, Rosie often went out with her friends. Ashenden began to take her to shows. She was pleasant company, and he began to see that she was beautiful. One evening, he invited her to his room. She offered herself to him and remained for the night; after that night, Rosie visited his room regularly.

One day, Mrs. Barton Trafford, a literary woman who had taken Driffield under her care, invited Ashenden to tea. He learned from her that Rosie had run away with Kemp, her old lover from Blackstable. Ashenden was chagrined to learn that Rosie cared for another man more than she did for him.

Ashenden then lost touch with Driffield. He learned that the author had divorced Rosie, who had gone to New York with Kemp. Mrs. Barton Trafford continued to care for Driffield as his fame grew. Then he caught pneumonia. He went to the country to convalesce and there married his nurse, the present Mrs. Driffield, whom Mrs. Trafford had hired to look after him.

Ashenden went down to Blackstable with Kear. They talked with Mrs. Driffield of her husband's early life. She and Kear described Rosie as promiscuous. Ashenden said that she was nothing of the sort. Good and generous, she could not deny love to anyone, that was all. Ashenden knew this to be the truth, now that he could look back at his own past experience. The others disagreed and dismissed the subject by saying that, after all, she was dead.

Rosie, however, was not dead. When Ashenden had last been to New York, she had written him and asked him to call on her. He found her now a wealthy widow; Kemp had died several years before. She was an old woman who retained her love for living. They talked of old times, and Ashenden discovered that Driffield, too, had understood her—even when she was being unfaithful to him.

Rosie said that she was too old to marry again; she had had her fling at life. Ashenden asked her if Kemp had not been the only man she really loved; she said that it was true. Then Ashenden's eyes strayed to a photograph of Kemp on the wall. It showed him with a waxed mustache; he was dressed in flashy clothes, carried a cane, and flourished a cigar in one hand. Ashenden turned to Rosie and asked why she had preferred Kemp to her other lovers. Her reply was simple. He had always been the perfect gentleman.

Critical Evaluation:

Cakes and Ale is a characteristic Maugham novel, a combination of social satire, autobiography, and *roman à clef*. It is a masterfully structured story, told largely in retrospect, with the Maugham touch of the unanticipated ending. Like many of the author's plays, novels, and stories, it underscores his conviction that human morals are relative, rather than absolute.

The title is taken from William Shakespeare's *Twelfth Night: Or, What You Will* (c. 1600-1602), in which the happy libertine, Sir Toby Belch, upbraids the priggish, hypocritical Malvolio with the pronouncement: "Dost thou think, because thou art virtuous, there shall be no cakes and ale?" Sir Toby's question applies to all who would shape the world around them to fit a preconceived, narrow code of conduct and behavior in which joy and earthy pleasure play little or no part. Maugham's *Cakes and Ale* offers a response to Sir Toby's question. The novel is about the self-discovery that comes through a young man's awareness of joy and carnal passion. Maugham sees these elements of life as vitally important. To those for whom human nature is more a failing than a triumph, joy and passion are subsumed by respectability and conformity to arbitrary standards of social conduct. Initially, young Willie Ashenden, the narrator and Maugham's persona, is a petty snob, one who without thought or consideration embraces the strictures and prejudices of class-obsessed Victorian England. To young Ashenden and to those with whom he shares a certain stratum of society, outspoken and uninhibitedly good-natured working-class people are considered beneath any social interaction beyond the most rudimentary formal politeness—men like George Kemp, the coal merchant, for example, whose friendly camaraderie serves only to demonstrate to young Ashenden that Kemp is a man "who doesn't seem to know his place." Rosie's intrinsic goodness and the love she offers—of a nature entirely different from anything Ashenden has previously experienced—break through his barriers and teach him how shallow his preconceptions of human nature are.

Maugham's social satire in the novel centers on the contemporary literary society of the late 1920's, taking to task, in particular, its often shallow and self-serving pretensions, as well as its subservience to contemporary trends of fashionable literature. Created for particular parody in this regard is the character of Alroy Kear, the popular novelist with a decided penchant for managing the commercial and public relations side of his career, undoubtedly to compensate for the limitations of his creative ability. At the behest of Amy Driffield, Kear has undertaken to create a literary icon. He is in the preliminary stages of writing the authorized biography of the late Edward Driffield, Amy's recently deceased husband and a highly acclaimed Victorian author. As Driffield's second wife, it has long been her chosen task in life to be the "keeper of the flame," the curator of all that his life and work have become. She is determined to reconstruct—or at least censor—that life, with Kear's aid and compliance, into an acceptable portrait for public view, devoid of scandal and above reproach. Kear's motives, however, fall far short of scholarly interest and integrity. He envisions his work on Driffield, as he explains it to Ashenden, as "a sort of intimate life, with a lot of those little details that make people feel warm inside . . . woven into this a really exhaustive criticism of his literary work, not ponderous . . . although sympathetic"—in brief, an insubstantial formula biography tailored to the mass market.

The character of Alroy Kear was based on Hugh Walpole, a highly popular novelist of the late 1920's; Walpole is now relegated to the occasional footnote in English literary history. Edward Driffield is largely drawn from Thomas Hardy. Although for many years Maugham denied the *roman à clef* identifications, in later years he admitted to the Kear-Walpole creation. Walpole, according to Maugham, was a man he found "easy to like but difficult to respect." Literary posterity has generally agreed with Maugham and has credited Walpole with being a man who made the most of a moderate talent, even to the point of parlaying it into a knighthood, in 1937, for his service to literature.

The Driffield-Hardy conception is largely creative conjecture based on contemporary gossip. Hardy was a widower who married a second time late in life; he lived until 1928. Driffield's novel, *The Cup of Life*, seems to be a composite drawn from the public outcry associated with two Hardy novels, *Tess of the D'Urbervilles* (1891) and *Jude the Obscure* (1895).

The enduring heart of the novel, however, is Rosie, the warm center in the otherwise dreary lives of the men of Blackstable. She is a generous and loving woman whose childlike amorality and *carpe diem* philosophy enable her to endure and survive her own hidden suffering (the loss of the daughter she had with Driffield). She is a woman, the mature Ashenden tells the incredulous and contemptuous Alroy Kear and Amy Driffield, who "gave herself as naturally as the sun gives heat or the flowers their perfume."

In intellectual circles in the 1920's, it was fashionable to be in revolt against all things Victorian. One of the immutable laws of Victorian fiction decreed that "a woman who falls may never rise." Lost virtue may never be supplanted by regained respectability. Hardy himself was subjected to considerable criticism for permitting Sue Bridehead, in *Jude the Obscure*, to return to her husband; she had been insufficiently punished after her long sojourn with Jude Fawley, despite the fact that her children had all died tragic deaths. Rosie, whose love is readily available to any man who would be made happy by it, remains triumphantly unrepentant into old age, living in relative prosperity, with no regrets. She is Somerset Maugham's literary prototype of the twentieth century liberated woman, a free spirit who lives her life unfettered by pointlessly repressive convention.

"Critical Evaluation" by Richard Keenan

Bibliography:

Cordell, Richard. *Somerset Maugham: A Biographical and Critical Study*. Bloomington: Indiana University Press, 1961. Thorough analysis of Maugham as a writer proficient in all genres of literature.

Curtis, Anthony. *The Pattern of Maugham: A Critical Portrait*. New York: Taplinger, 1974. Analysis of Maugham's more prominent works, with insights into the role of his insecurities and his frequent digressions in *Cakes and Ale* and other novels, when he offers personal commentary on the state of society and the world of arts and letters.

Curtis, Anthony, and John Whitehead, eds. *W. Somerset Maugham: The Critical Heritage*. London: Routledge & Kegan Paul, 1987. Particularly valuable for tracing the critical reception of *Cakes and Ale* since its initial publication. Contemporary reviews by noted literary figures such as Ivor Brown, Evelyn Waugh, and Leslie Marchand.

Loss, Archie K. *W. Somerset Maugham*. New York: Frederick Ungar, 1987. An in-depth analysis of the *roman à clef* aspects of the novel, emphasizing Maugham's disparaging treatment of Hugh Walpole and Thomas Hardy.

Morgan, Ted. *Maugham*. New York: Simon & Schuster, 1980. A comprehensive overview of Maugham's life and career, with an extended discussion of the character of Rosie in *Cakes and Ale*. Morgan emphasizes her pragmatic morality and adaptability in a socially repressive atmosphere.

CALEB WILLIAMS

Type of work: Novel
Author: William Godwin (1756-1836)
Type of plot: Detective and mystery
Time of plot: Eighteenth century
Locale: England
First published: Things As They Are: Or, The Adventures of Caleb Williams, 1794

> *Principal characters:*
> CALEB WILLIAMS
> FERDINANDO FALKLAND, Caleb's employer
> COLLINS, Falkland's servant
> BARNABAS TYRREL, Falkland's enemy
> GINES, Caleb's enemy
> EMILY MELVILE, Tyrrel's cousin

The Story:

Caleb Williams was engaged as secretary by Mr. Ferdinando Falkland, the wealthiest and most respected squire in the country. Falkland, although a considerate employer, was subject to fits of distemper that bewildered Caleb. These black moods were so contrary to his employer's usual gentle nature that Caleb soon investigated, asking Collins, a trusted servant of the household, about them and learning from him the story of Falkland's early life.

Studious and romantic in his youth, Falkland lived many years abroad before he returned to England to live on his ancestral estate. One of his neighbors was Barnabas Tyrrel, a man of proud, combative nature. When Falkland returned to his family estate, Tyrrel was the leading gentleman in the neighborhood. As a result of his graceful manners and warm intelligence, Falkland soon began to win the admiration of his neighbors. Tyrrel was jealous and showed his feelings by speech and actions. Falkland tried to make peace, but the ill-tempered Tyrrel refused his proffered friendship.

Miss Emily Melvile, Tyrrel's cousin, occupied the position of a servant in his household. One night, she was trapped in a burning building, and Falkland saved her from burning. Afterward, Emily could do nothing but praise her benefactor. Her gratitude annoyed her cousin, who planned to revenge himself on Emily for her admiration of Falkland. He found one of his tenants, Grimes, a clumsy ill-bred lout, who consented to marry Emily. When Emily refused to marry a man whom she could never love, Tyrrel confined her to her room. As part of the plot, Grimes helped Emily to escape and then attempted to seduce her. She was rescued from her plight by Falkland, who for the second time proved to be her savior. Further cruelties inflicted on her by Tyrrel finally killed her, and Tyrrel became an object of disgrace in the community.

One evening, Tyrrel attacked Falkland in a public meeting, and Falkland was deeply humiliated. That night, Tyrrel was found dead in the streets. Since the quarrel had been witnessed by so many people just before the murder, Falkland was called before a jury to explain his whereabouts during that fatal night. No one really believed Falkland guilty, but he was hurt by what he considered the disgrace of his being questioned. Although a former tenant was afterward arrested and hanged for the crime, Falkland never recovered his injured pride. He retired to his estate, where he became a moody and disconsolate recluse.

For a long time after learning these details, Caleb pondered over the apparent unhappiness of his employer. Attempting to understand Falkland's morose personality, Caleb began to wonder whether Falkland suffered from the unearned infamy that accompanied suspicion of murder or from a guilty conscience. Determined to solve the mystery, Caleb proceeded to talk to his master in an inquisitive way, to draw him out in matters concerning murder and justice. Caleb also began to look for evidence that would prove Falkland guilty or innocent. Finally, the morose man became aware of his secretary's intent. Swearing Caleb to secrecy, Falkland confessed to the murder of Barnabas Tyrrel and threatened Caleb with irreparable harm if he should ever betray his employer.

Falkland's mansion became a prison for Caleb, and he resolved to run away no matter what the consequences might be. When he had escaped to an inn, he received a letter ordering him to return to defend himself against a charge of theft. When Falkland produced some missing jewels and bank notes from Caleb's baggage, Caleb was sent to prison in disgrace. His only chance to prove his innocence was to disclose Falkland's motive, a thing no one would believe. Caleb spent many months in jail, confined in a dreary, filthy dungeon and bound with chains. Thomas, a servant of Falkland and a former neighbor of Caleb's father, visited Caleb in his cell. Perceiving Caleb in his miserable condition, Thomas could only wonder at English law that kept a man so imprisoned while he waited many months for trial. Compassion forced Thomas to bring Caleb tools with which he could escape from his dungeon. At liberty once more, Caleb found himself in a hostile world with no resources.

At first, he became an associate of thieves, but he left the gang after he had made an enemy of a man named Gines. When he went to London, hoping to hide there, Gines followed him, and soon Caleb was again caught and arrested. Falkland visited him and explained that he knew every move Caleb had made since he had escaped from prison. Falkland told Caleb that although he would no longer prosecute him for theft, he would continue to make Caleb's life intolerable. Wherever Caleb went, Gines followed and exposed Caleb's story to the community. Caleb tried to escape to Holland, but just as he was to land in that free country, Gines appeared and stopped him.

Caleb returned to England and charged Falkland with murder, asking the magistrate to call Falkland before the court. At first, the magistrate refused to summon Falkland to reply to the charge, but Caleb insisted upon his rights, and Falkland appeared. The squire had now grown terrible to behold; his haggard and ghostlike appearance showed that he had not long to live.

Caleb pressed his charges in an attempt to save himself from a life of persecution and misery. So well did Caleb describe his miserable state and his desperate situation that the dying man was deeply touched. Demonstrating the kindness of character and the honesty for which Caleb had first admired him, Falkland admitted his wrongdoings and cleared Caleb's reputation. In a few days the sick man died. Although remorseful, Caleb was determined to make a fresh start in life.

Critical Evaluation:

William Godwin titled his novel *Things As They Are: Or, The Adventures of Caleb Williams*, but it survives under the name of its hero. It is a novel of divided interests, as it was written to criticize society and to tell an adventure story. All the elements that contribute to Caleb's misery are the result of weaknesses in eighteenth century English laws, which permitted the wealthy landowners to hold power over poorer citizens.

Historians of the novel have always encountered great difficulty in categorizing Godwin's *Caleb Williams*. It has been called a great tragic novel, the first pursuit novel, a crime or mystery novel, a chase-and-capture adventure, a political thesis fiction, a gothic romance, a terror or sensation novel, even a sentimental tale. To some extent, it is all of these—and none of them. The novel has, like most enduring works of art, taken on many shapes and meanings as new readers interpret the narrative in terms of their own personal, cultural, and historical experiences.

Godwin had no doubts about his book's meaning or about the effect he hoped to achieve with it: "I will write a tale that shall constitute an epoch in the mind of the reader, that no one, after he has read it, shall ever be exactly the same man that he was before." Having achieved fame in 1793 with his powerful, influential, and controversial political treatise *Enquiry Concerning the Principles of Political Justice*, he sought a form in which to dramatize his ideas. At the most obvious level, then, *Caleb Williams* can be seen as a fictional gloss on Godwin's previous political masterpiece.

Caleb Williams, however, is no simple political tract. Godwin knew that he must first develop a narrative, in his words, "distinguished by a very powerful interest," if he expected readers to absorb and seriously consider his philosophical and social ideas, so he took the most exciting situation he could conceive, creating, as he said, "a series of adventures of flight and pursuit; the fugitive in perpetual apprehension of being overwhelmed with the worst calamities, and the pursuer, by his ingenuity and resources, keeping his victim in a state of the most fearful alarm." Having first decided on the outcome of his adventure, Godwin then worked backwards, like a modern mystery story writer, to develop a sequence of events leading up to his climax. The result is a well-constructed narrative in which each of the three volumes are tightly connected, both structurally and thematically, the action developing logically and directly with ever-mounting tension to a powerful, even tragic, denouement.

In Godwin's words, Ferdinando Falkland has the ability to "alarm and harass his victim with an inextinguishable resolution never to allow him the least interval of peace and security," because of an unjust and fundamentally corrupt society. The worst villain is a legal system that gives too much power to the rich and victimizes the poor, all in the name of justice. Falkland fears Caleb's knowledge, because Falkland has committed the only crime that an aristocrat could commit in eighteenth century England—an injury to a social equal. Had Tyrrel been poor, the issue would never have been raised. Caleb's alleged crime—stealing from his master and accusing the master of conspiracy against him—arouses such extreme repugnance because it challenges the social hierarchy and the assumptions that support it.

The problem, however, is not one of simple, conscious tyranny. The rich and the poor are unaware of the injustice and cruelty that their social institutions foster. They have been conditioned by their environment to accept the system as necessary, proper, and even benevolent. It is not the willful malevolence of a few but society itself that distorts and dissipates the best qualities of men, regardless of their social class, although the poor suffer the most obvious physical oppression. Falkland is not an example of deliberate evil; he is a good man who, because of his social role, has accepted a body of attitudes and moral values that are destructive. His passion to conceal his crime and his persecution of Caleb are the result not of any fear of legal punishment but of his obsessive concern for his aristocratic honor. "Though I be the blackest of villains," he tells Caleb, "I will leave behind me a spotless and illustrious name. There is no crime so malignant, no scene of blood so horrible in which that object cannot engage me."

There are no human villains in this novel; social institutions are Godwin's targets. This explains the novel's strange ending, which seems to reverse all of the book's previous assumptions. Having finally succeeded in turning the law against his tormentor, Caleb realizes, as he faces a broken Falkland, that he, Caleb, is the real enemy. Falkland, for his part, admits his guilt and embraces Caleb; but, to Godwin, neither man is guilty. Both have been caught up in a series of causal circumstances created by their environment and resulting in their inevitable mutual destruction. Only when the environment can be altered to allow people's natural capacities to emerge, undistorted and unfettered by artificial, malevolent environmental conditioning, can such self-destruction be avoided and human potential realized.

Bibliography:
Boulton, James T. *The Language of Politics in the Age of Wilkes and Burke*. London: Routledge & Kegan Paul, 1963. Discusses the "inexorable deliberateness" of Godwin's novel, the way he builds up a systematic chain and combination of events. Godwin's weakness is a lack of dramatic immediacy. Too often Godwin speaks about psychological states rather than dramatizing them.

Godwin, William. *Things As They Are: Or, The Adventures of Caleb Williams*. Edited by Maurice Hindle. New York: Penguin Books, 1988. Hindle's introduction discusses the novel's origins, the politics and history informing its narrative, and its place in the genre. Notes, bibliography, and appendices.

Kiely, Robert. *The Romantic Novel in England*. Cambridge, Mass.: Harvard University Press, 1972. Considers how Godwin's philosophy influences his novel and compares him to his contemporaries. Discusses his fascination with fantasy and romance writing.

Miyoshi, Masao. *The Divided Self: A Perspective on the Literature of the Victorians*. New York: New York University Press, 1969. Considers the novel as part of the gothic tradition. Analyzes Caleb's motivations for spying on Falkland, discusses the differences between Godwin's novel and his great work of political philosophy, *Political Justice*, and addresses differences between the imaginative and discursive process.

Ousby, Ian. *Bloodhounds of Heaven: The Detective in English Fiction from Godwin to Doyle*. Cambridge, Mass.: Harvard University Press, 1976. Discusses the novel as the first work of English fiction to take a sustained interest in detection. Other critics have emphasized how the structure of the novel influenced later detective fiction, but Ousby points out that the main character, Caleb, is equally important because he is an original detective in the English novel.

CALL IT SLEEP

Type of work: Novel
Author: Henry Roth (1906-1995)
Type of plot: Bildungsroman
Time of plot: 1907-1913
Locale: Lower East Side, New York City
First published: 1934

> *Principal characters:*
> DAVID SCHEARL, a young Jewish immigrant boy
> GENYA, his mother
> ALBERT, his father
> JOE LUTER, a print shop foreman
> BERTHA, Genya's sister and David's aunt
> YUSSIE MINK, David's friend
> ANNIE MINK, his sister
> LEO DUGOVKA, another of David's friends
> NATHAN STERNOWITZ, a widower and later Bertha's husband
> POLLY and
> ESTHER, his daughters
> RABBI YIDEL PANKOWER, David's teacher

The Story:

In 1907, David Schearl, then about two years old, and his mother, Genya, were on a steamer leaving Ellis Island, the last leg of their journey to America. David's father, Albert, had come to America earlier, and the family was now to be reunited. Albert displayed a coldness, however, that was in marked contrast to the joy pervading other reunions taking place around him. His remarks to his wife and son were contemptuous and accusatory; because he did not want his boy to look like an immigrant, he snatched David's old-country hat off his head and hurled it into the river.

Like the other immigrants, the Schearls were people in an alien culture. Unlike most of the other families, however, there was a deep alienation in the family, particularly between father and son: David was the immigrant in life who had to seek his own meanings in maturity.

By the time David was six years old, his attachment to his mother was important not only for the relationship between them but also for the shelter she provided him from his father's icy contempt. Where Genya was placid and beautiful, Albert was aloof, suspicious, gullible, and eaten away by a tragic pride. Albert was at war with the world. His great fear—partly based on an awareness of his own foreignness and partly based on a deeper insecurity—was of being laughed at, cheated, or made to look a fool. David's immature but meticulous consciousness recorded that Albert's foreman, Luter, flattered Albert only in order to be with Genya. He also experienced a repugnant sexual encounter with a neighborhood girl, and a terrible thrashing by Albert. In the second book, David watched the courting of Aunt Bertha by the laconic Nathan Sternowitz and listened in confused fascination to his mother's account of an earlier love affair in Russia. Through these experiences, David became uneasily aware of sexuality, particularly of the disturbing fact that his mother was also a sexual being.

899

In the Hebrew school, the cheder, David's intellect was awakened by Rabbi Yidel Pankower, a tragicomic figure of classic proportions. David learned rapidly, but one afternoon he was puzzled by a verse from Isaiah in which Isaiah, seeing the Lord seated on a throne, was afraid; then a seraph touched a fiery coal to Isaiah's lips, and he heard God speak. David yearned to ask about that coal but was not given an opportunity to do so. At home, he asked his mother to explain God. He is brighter than day, she told him, and He has all power.

On the first day of Passover there was no school, and David wandered toward the East River. He stared at the river, meditating on God's brightness. The experience was almost a mystical trance, but the dazzling contemplation was broken by three boys who taunted him. They told him that he would see magic if he were to go to the train tracks and drop a piece of scrap metal in the groove between the tracks. When David did so, there was a sudden blinding light that terrified him. His child's mind connected the thought of God's power and light with the electric flash.

David sometimes did not get along with the rough boys of the neighborhood. One day, he discovered the roof of the flat as a place of refuge. From there, he saw a boy with blond hair flying a kite. Leo Dugovka, a confident and carefree boy, also owned skates. He was surprised to learn that David did not know anything about the Cross or the Mother and Child. David desperately wanted Leo to like him.

The next day, David walked the long distance to Aunt Bertha's candy shop to see if she had any skates he could use. The living quarters behind the store were cramped, dark, and filthy. Bertha told him to get Esther and Polly out of bed while she watched the store, but she had no skates. David thereupon went to Leo's flat. There he was attracted to a picture of Jesus and to a rosary. When Leo heard about David's two cousins, he became interested in seeing them. The next day, Leo promised to give David the rosary if he would take him to see the girls. Though uncomfortable with the proposal, David agreed. Leo was successful with Esther, but they were caught by Polly, who tattled.

David was terrified at the thought he might be implicated. At cheder in the afternoon, he was nervous when he read before a visiting rabbi. Bursting into tears, he entangled himself in hysterical lies fabricated out of the secret in his mother's past. He said that his mother was dead and that his father was a gentile organist in Europe. When the puzzled rabbi went to David's parents to try to clear up the matter, Nathan angrily blamed David for what had happened to Esther. The rabbi learned that David had lied, but mention of the organist had aroused Albert's suspicion. He accused his wife of unfaithfulness and believed David to be the child of another man. Genya could not convince him that he is wrong.

When Bertha arrived, the adults began to argue violently. David, terrified, ran into the street. Images, recollections, and fears spun through his mind. Finding a steel milk-dipper, he desperately decided to produce God again at the tracks. At first, nothing happened when he inserted the dipper; then, he received a terrific electric shock that knocked him out. The flash drew a crowd of anxious people, but David had not been seriously hurt. Even his father seemed somewhat relieved to find that he was all right. David reflected that soon it would be night and he could go to sleep and forget everything. In sleep, all the images of the past—sights, sounds, feelings—become vivid and alive. Life was painful and terrifying, but in sleep he could triumph.

Critical Evaluation:

When Henry Roth's first novel, *Call It Sleep*, appeared in 1934, its critical reception was predominantly positive. The novel sold fairly well, going through first and second editions totaling four thousand copies, a large number for the depths of the Depression. Yet the novel soon fell into obscurity. Then in 1964, the book was republished in hardcover and paperback, and its sales and critical reputation soared. *Call It Sleep* came to be recognized as a masterpiece and one of the great works of American literature. Not until 1994 did Roth publish his second novel, *A Star Shines over Mount Morris Park*, the first volume of a projected series of books to be entitled *Mercy of a Rude Stream*. Roth seems to have conceived this later series as a kind of continuation of *Call It Sleep*. Many critics argue that the long time between Roth's first and second novels resulted in part from his dismay that the public seemed to have forgotten his first book.

After 1964, critics began to praise *Call It Sleep* for being a tightly knit, stylistically excellent piece of literary art. Roth uses imagery to give the novel a kind of organic unity that points inexorably to its ending. Especially important are the images Roth associates with the titles of the four books of the novel, "Cellar," "Picture," "Coal," and "Rail." "Cellar" is associated with David Schearl's fear, initially, of the dark cellar in the tenement where he lives and ultimately of a series of things that include his violent father and sex.

"Picture" points to Genya's picture of cornflowers, which reminds her of her home in Austria. The picture represents her European past, especially her affair with a Christian before she met Albert. Balancing Genya's picture is Albert's pair of bull's horns, which he associates with the cattle he tended in Eastern Europe and with the accusation that he watched passively while a bull gored his father to death. Significantly, he is bitterly unhappy with every job he has in America until he works as a milkman. The horns also represent his fear that he has been cuckolded and that David is not his biological child.

"Coal" refers to the physical object, the source of heat and power. For David, it represents what he does not have, power, and he associates it with the passage in Isaiah in which an angel touches coal to Isaiah's lips and gives him divine knowledge.

"Rail" is a reference to the third rail, which provides power to streetcars. David is tricked into touching a piece of scrap metal to the third rail, which creates a blinding light that he associates with the power of God. He tries to draw on that power near the end of the novel when he runs from his apartment in fear that his father will kill him. This time, David uses a milk ladle against the third rail, which connects his actions with his mother, who gives him milk, and his father, who delivers milk. Knocked unconscious and near death, he has a vision full of religious and sexual imagery. When the policeman who revives him carries him into his home, his father talks "in a dazed, unsteady voice," and David listens to "him falter and knew him shaken." In fact, David sees that his father, whom Genya has reassured that David is his son, is genuinely concerned about him. This suggestion of a reconciliation has important implications for David's future growth.

Stylistically, *Call It Sleep* is a triumph. Roth often enables his readers to enter David's mind by using a stream-of-consciousness technique reminiscent of James Joyce. Roth also draws on Sigmund Freud's theories about dreams and their relationship to waking life when he combines surrealistic or dreamlike episodes with highly realistic, tangible impressions of life on the Lower East Side of New York between 1907 and 1913.

In *Call It Sleep*, the reader becomes immersed in the sights, smells, and especially sounds of the Lower East Side. When Roth's Jewish characters speak Yiddish, their language is represented by lyrical English. When they speak English, however, Roth shows their strong accents and the difficulty they have making themselves understood. He also reproduces Italian, Irish, and Hungarian accents and the English dialect associated with the streets of New York that David and his young companions speak.

Central to the story is David's growing up. Not only is it remarkable that he survives in an atmosphere of violence, it is a miracle that he manages to grow in spite of all the things that conspire to thwart his growth. It is Roth's magnificent achievement that David's growth is believable. Although the novel gives an extraordinarily good picture of Jewish life in New York City during the first part of the twentieth century, it simultaneously tells a universal story of maturation and reconciliation.

"Critical Evaluation" by Richard Tuerk

Bibliography:
Dembo, L. S. *The Monological Jew: A Literary Study*. Madison: University of Wisconsin Press, 1988. Argues that Roth uses an imagist technique of perceiving reality: David senses but never understands life.
Farber, Frances D. "Encounters with an Alien Culture: Thematic Functions of Dialect in *Call It Sleep*." *Yiddish* 7 (1990): 49-56. Analyzes the way Roth masters the "cacophony" of street dialects of immigrants becoming acculturated in early twentieth century New York City and how he uses speech to show "young David's temptations and terrors."
Guttmann, Allen. *The Jewish Writer in America: Assimilation and the Crisis of Identity*. New York: Oxford University Press, 1971. Analyzes David's agony as representative of the experience of first-generation Jews as they take their place in American culture. Also recognizes the novel's universality.
Lyons, Bonnie. *Henry Roth: The Man and His Work*. New York: Cooper Square, 1976. In this extensive treatment of Roth, Lyons discusses *Call It Sleep* in the context of the author's life and shows that it is a unified work of art.
Sherman, Bernard. *The Invention of the Jew: Jewish-American Education Novels (1916-1964)*. New York: Thomas Yoseloff, 1969. Treats the book as primarily a Depression novel but recognizes that central to it is the maturing of a young mind.

THE CALL OF THE WILD

Type of work: Novel
Author: Jack London (1876-1916)
Type of plot: Adventure
Time of plot: 1897
Locale: Alaska
First published: 1903

> *Principal characters:*
> BUCK, a dog
> SPITZ, his enemy
> JOHN THORNTON, his friend

The Story:

Buck was the undisputed leader of all the dogs on Judge Miller's estate in California. A crossbreed of St. Bernard and Scottish shepherd, he had inherited the size of the first and the intelligence of the latter. Buck could not know that the lust for gold had hit the human beings of the country and that dogs of his breed were much in demand as sled dogs in the frozen North. Consequently, he was not suspicious when one of the workmen on the estate took him for a walk one night. The man took Buck to the railroad station, where the dog heard the exchange of money. Then a rope was placed around his neck. When he struggled to get loose, the rope was drawn so tight that it shut off his breath, and he lost consciousness.

He recovered in a baggage car. When the train reached Seattle, Washington, Buck tried to break out of his cage while he was being unloaded. A man in a red shirt hit him with a club until he was senseless. After that, Buck knew that he could never win a fight against a club. He retained that knowledge for future use.

Buck was put in a pen with other dogs of his type. Each day, some of the dogs went away with strange men who came with money. One day, Buck was sold. Two French-Canadians bought him and some other dogs and took them on board a ship sailing for Alaska. The men were fair, though harsh, masters, and Buck respected them. Life on the ship was not particularly enjoyable, but it was a paradise compared to what awaited Buck when the ship reached Alaska. There he found men and dogs to be little more than savages, with no law but the law of force. The dogs fought like wolves, and when one was downed, the pack moved in for the kill. Buck watched one of his shipmates being torn to pieces after he lost a fight, and he never forgot the way one dog in particular, Spitz, watched sly-eyed as the loser was slashed to ribbons. Spitz was Buck's enemy from that time on.

Buck and the other dogs were harnessed to sleds on which the two French-Canadians carried mail to prospectors in remote regions. It was a new kind of life to Buck but not an unpleasant one. The men treated the dogs well, and Buck was intelligent enough to learn quickly those things that made him a good sled dog. He learned to dig under the snow for a warm place to sleep and to keep the traces clear and thus make pulling easier. When he was hungry, he stole food. The instincts of his ancestors came to life in him as the sled went farther and farther north. In some vague manner, he sensed the great cunning of the wolves who had been his ancestors in the wilderness.

Buck's muscles grew firm and taut and his strength greater than ever. Yet his feet became sore, and he had to have moccasins. Occasionally, one of the dogs died or was killed in a fight, and one female went mad. The dogs no longer worked as a team, and the two men had to be on guard constantly to prevent fights. One day Buck saw his chance; he attacked Spitz, the lead dog on the sled, and killed him. After that, Buck refused to be harnessed until he was given the lead position. He proved his worth by whipping the rebellious dogs into shape, and he became the best lead dog that the men had ever seen. The sled made record runs, and Buck was soon famous.

When they reached Skaguay, the two French-Canadians had official orders to turn the team over to a Scottish half-breed. The sled was heavier and the weather bad on the trip back to Dawson. At night, Buck lay by the fire and dreamed of his wild ancestors. He seemed to hear a faraway call that was like a wolf's cry. After two days' rest in Dawson, the team started back over the long trail to Skaguay. The dogs were almost exhausted. Some died and had to be replaced. When the team arrived again in Skaguay, the dogs expected to rest, but three days later, they were sold to two men and a woman who knew nothing about dogs or sledding conditions in the northern wilderness. Buck and the other dogs started out again, so weary that it was an effort to move. Again and again, the gallant dogs stumbled and fell and lay still until the sting of a whip brought them to their feet for a few miles. At last, even Buck gave up. The sled had stopped at the cabin of John Thornton, and when the men and the woman were ready to leave, Buck refused to get up. One of the men beat Buck with a club and would have killed him had not Thornton intervened, knocking the man down and ordering him and his companions to leave. They left Buck with Thornton.

As Thornton nursed Buck back to health, a feeling of love and respect grew between them. When Thornton's partners returned to the cabin, they understood this affection and did not attempt to use Buck for any of their heavy work. Twice, Buck saved Thornton's life and was glad that he could repay his friend. In Dawson, Buck won more than a thousand dollars for Thornton on a wager, when the dog broke loose a sled carrying a thousand-pound load from the ice. With the money won on the wager, Thornton and his partners went on a gold-hunting expedition. They traveled far into eastern Alaska, where they found a stream yellow with gold. In his primitive mind, Buck began to see a hairy man who hunted with a club. He heard the howling of the wolves. Sometimes he wandered off for three or four days at a time, but he always went back to Thornton. At one time, he made friends with a wolf that seemed like a brother to Buck.

Once Buck chased and killed a great bull moose. On his way back to the camp, he sensed that something was wrong. He found several dogs lying dead along the trail. When he reached the camp, he saw Indians dancing around the bodies of the dogs and Thornton's two partners. He followed Thornton's trail to the river, where he found the body of his friend full of arrows. Buck was filled with such a rage that he attacked the band of Indians, killing some and scattering the others.

His last tie with humanity broken, he joined his brothers in the wild wolf packs. The Indians thought him a ghost dog, for they seldom saw more than his shadow, so quickly did he move. Had the Indians watched carefully, however, they could have seen him closely. Once each year, Buck returned to the river where Thornton had died. There the dog stood on the bank and howled, one long, piercing cry that was the tribute of a savage beast to his human friend.

Critical Evaluation:

Jack London's adventure stories made him one of the most popular writers of his day. In works such as *The Call of the Wild, White Fang* (1906), and *Jerry of the Islands* (1917) London made animals into compelling leading characters, as engaging and sympathetic as any human protagonists. London's animal stories do not anthropomorphize animals simply to play on the heartstrings of his audience. Some of his contemporaries criticized him for writing maudlin beast fables suitable only for children, but these critics misrepresented London's books and misunderstood his literary aims. London resisted the sentimental beast fables of his day, which personified animals in order to manipulate the reader's emotions. London's stories, instead, reflect more substantial scientific and philosophical issues. His goal was not to make animals appear human, but to emphasize the hereditary connection that humans have with animals.

London was heavily influenced by the works of Charles Darwin (*On the Origin of Species by Means of Natural Selection*, 1859, and *The Descent of Man and Selection in Relation to Sex*, 1871). In *The Call of the Wild*, Buck's experience follows Darwinian principles. He is molded by the changes in his environment, thriving because he possesses the necessary genetic gifts of strength and intelligence to adapt to his mutable circumstances. He is an example of a popular understanding of Darwin's theories: survival of the fittest. Although raised in the domestic ease of Judge Miller's estate, Buck learns quickly what it takes to endure the brutal world of dog-sledding—the "law of club and fang." When Buck first learns to steal food from one of his French-Canadian masters, readers are told that this "theft marked Buck as fit to survive in the hostile Northland environment. It marked his adaptability, his capacity to adjust himself to changing conditions." *The Call of the Wild* also reflects London's admiration for the works of nineteenth century German philosopher Friedrich Nietzsche. In the North, might makes right, and Buck proves to be the animal equivalent of Nietzsche's superman, possessing superior physical and mental abilities to those of the other dogs.

Buck, however, does not experience only raw nature. With John Thornton he returns to a more civilized existence. London's dog stories shuttle between the poles of domesticated and the wild, of the civilized and the natural. *The Call of the Wild* begins in a domesticated environment and ends in the wild. (Conversely, *White Fang* begins in nature and ends in civilization.) Thornton's compassionate influence helps temper the savage ferocity Buck developed to survive in a crueler world. The wild instinct still remains. Buck's love for Thornton compels Buck to be obedient, loyal, and altruistic, but his wild half keeps calling to him. Buck's romp in the woods with the wolf that seems like a brother to him anticipates his complete surrender to nature when Thornton dies. In the end, Buck hearkens to the call of the wild.

The Call of the Wild suggests that the reader draw a corollary between the divided nature of Buck and that of every human being. Inspired by Darwin, London believed in the evolutionary continuity between animals and human beings. If human beings evolved from animals, then what exists on a lower level in animals must hold true on a higher level for human beings. London does not give Buck human qualities, but suggests that animals and humans share common traits and experiences because of their evolutionary connection. Buck's vision of the short-legged, hairy man sleeping restlessly near the fire symbolizes the primitive beast lurking within all civilized beings. Being an animal, Buck can completely surrender to his primitive half. London seems to celebrate the primordial throughout the book, lauding the "surge of life" Buck experiences when he hunts down prey, the "ecstasy" of tasting living meat and warm blood. For human beings the rift between nature and civilization is much more complicated. People cannot and should not revert completely to their animalistic ancestry. In *White Fang*, for example, human beings dominated by their primitive halves are degenerates and criminals. London deals more directly with this human struggle in *The Sea-Wolf* (1904), suggesting that for humans a balance between the brutish and the civilized is best.

Readers can also see how *The Call of the Wild* reflects London's socialism. No single philosophical system satisfied London, so he accepted bits and pieces of many different, even contradictory ideas. When the ideas of Darwin or Nietzsche fell short in his estimation, those of Karl Marx seemed attractive. From a Marxist perspective, Buck can be interpreted as a representative of the oppressed, subject to the whims of cruel masters and their corrupt use of power. Under these brutal conditions Buck must do what he has to do in order to survive. He becomes a brute and a thief himself, struggling individually to fend for himself. Thornton's benevolent, more equitable treatment encourages socialistic values in Buck. He cooperates with the other dogs, becoming productive and working for the good of the group. Without Thornton's guidance Buck once again is left with his instinct for survival. Under corrupt power the Darwinian and Nietzschean principles of "survival of the fittest" and "might makes right" apply. Under such conditions, the primitive brute, the evolutionary residue of millions of generations, takes control out of necessity. With a less oppressive system, cooperation can flourish; the civilized half is nurtured and is able to contain the brute. Whether read as a demonstration of Darwinian ideas, a homage to Marxist socialism, or an engaging adventure, *The Call of the Wild* is considered by many critics to be the best of London's dog tales. The story of Buck is the most popular of London's many books.

"Critical Evaluation" by Heidi Kelchner

Bibliography:
Labor, Earle, and Jeanne Campell Reesman. *Jack London*. Rev. ed. Boston: Twayne, 1994. Analyzes the elements that went into the stories that London wrote. Recognizes London's use of mood and atmosphere. Discusses *The Call of the Wild* chapter by chapter.
O'Conner, Richard. *Jack London: A Biography*. Boston: Little, Brown, 1964. Delves into London's childhood and formative experiences. Chapter 7 covers the writing and success of *The Call of the Wild*.
Perry, John. *Jack London: An American Myth*. Chicago: Nelson-Hall, 1981. Discusses the validity of London's works, including London's misleading depiction of wolves. Covers the issue of the accusations of plagiarism that haunted London.
Roden, Donald. *Jack London's "The Call of the Wild" and "White Fang."* New York: Simon & Schuster, 1965. Begins with a brief overview of Jack London's life. Then follows with an in-depth discussion of *The Call of the Wild*.
Walcutt, Charles Child. *Jack London*. Minneapolis: University of Minnesota Press, 1966. Gives a well-rounded overview of the life and works of Jack London. Covers the effect of Darwinism and the other philosophies that London studied on his works. Discusses the use of the dog's point of view in the story.

CAMEL XIANGZI

Type of work: Novel
Author: Lao She (Shu Qingchun, 1899-1966)
Type of plot: Naturalism
Time of plot: 1930's
Locale: Beijing, China
First published: Lo-T'o Hsiang-tzu, 1936 (English translation, 1945 as *Rickshaw Boy*; 1979
  as *Rickshaw*; 1979 as *Camel Xiangzi*)

> *Principal characters:*
> XIANGZI, a rickshaw boy
> HUNIU (TIGRESS), Xiangzi's wife
> XIAO FUZI (JOY), a prostitute
> LIU SI YE (FOURTH MASTER LIU), Tigress' father
> MR. CAO, a professor
> ER QIANZI, Joy's father, a drunkard
> RUAN MING, a false revolutionary

The Story:

After Xiangzi's parents died, he went to the city of Beijing, bringing with him a country boy's
sturdiness and simplicity. He rented a rickshaw from Fourth Master Liu, who owned the
Harmony Rickshaw-renting Yard, to make a living. Unlike the other rickshaw pullers, who were
addicted to smoking, drinking, and visiting prostitutes, Xiangzi led a decent, frugal life. His
only dream was to have a rickshaw of his own. After three or four years of struggle and
hardship, he saved enough money to buy a rickshaw, believing that the rickshaw would bring
him freedom and independence. No sooner had he bought the rickshaw than he was drafted into
the army and his rickshaw was confiscated. Later Xiangzi escaped from the barracks during a
night attack, taking with him three army camels. He sold the camels and got back to Beijing,
starting another round of saving money to buy himself a rickshaw. For his theft of the camels,
he became known as Camel Xiangzi.

Xiangzi deposited the money he had made from the sale of the camels at Fourth Master Liu's
place and worked even harder. One night Fourth Master Liu's daughter Tigress seduced him.
Ashamed of himself, he left Liu's place to work as a private rickshaw puller for Mr. Cao. Even
so, he was repeatedly bothered by Tigress, who pretended to be pregnant. Around the same time,
Ruan Ming informed the police of Mr. Cao's socialist ideas as a revenge for Ruan Ming's
academic failure under Mr. Cao. During the police raid of Mr. Cao's home, Xiangzi surrendered
all his savings, including the camel-sale money he had just gotten back from Tigress, to a secret
policeman who was formerly the lieutenant Xiangzi had waited on in the barracks. Tigress then
took advantage of Xiangzi's misfortune, tricking him into marriage. As a result, Fourth Master
Liu disowned his daughter for her determination to marry a penniless coolie and looked down
upon Xiangzi, believing that he had married Tigress for money. Xiangzi and Tigress moved to
a slum.

Counting on her father's eventual forgiveness, Tigress lived an easy life on her savings. She
treated Xiangzi as a plaything and forbade him to work pulling a rickshaw. Xiangzi became
depressed. He was frustrated when Tigress accused him of marrying her for her money. When
Tigress learned that her father had sold the Harmony Yard and gone into hiding with all the

money, she finally had to let Xiangzi buy a rickshaw with the rest of her savings. Xiangzi hoped the rickshaw would enable him to assert his independence. He worked furiously day and night. Then he caught a disease after pulling rickshaw in a summer storm. His health was impaired. Worse still, he was constantly tortured by his wife's nagging. He could only seek solace from Joy, the neighboring woman who was supporting her drunken father and two little brothers on her meager earnings as a prostitute. Tigress was terribly jealous of the friendship between Xiangzi and Joy. The two women became reconciled when Tigress gained some understanding of Joy's plight and her forced prostitution. When Tigress got pregnant, the prospect of being a father gave Xiangzi a new hope in life. Tigress ate excessively and did not exercise, resulting in her death when she gave birth to an oversized baby. After Tigress' death, Joy wanted to marry Xiangzi. For fear of supporting her large family, Xiangzi turned her down but promised to come to her someday.

Xiangzi was forced to sell his rickshaw to pay for the funeral of his wife and son. After the loss of this, his second rickshaw, he lost faith in the value of hard work. He began smoking and drinking, even contracting venereal disease from the mistress of a house where he worked temporarily. He indulged himself shamelessly in dissipation and grew pugnacious. One day Fourth Master Liu happened to ride by in a rickshaw and asked about Tigress. Xiangzi said she was dead, but refused to tell Liu where she was buried. Depriving the old rich man of his only relative, Xiangzi felt that he had won a spiritual victory. He had a sudden urge to recover his old self, "that unfettered, unburdened, decent, ambitious and hard-working Xiangzi." He believed that Mr. Cao and Joy would help him succeed in establishing a decent life. As expected, Mr. Cao offered him a job and even agreed to let Joy come and work. Xiangzi then went in search of Joy in high spirits. After a few days of inquiries, however, Xiangzi discovered that Joy had hanged herself after being forced by economics to enter a low-class brothel. His mind went blank and life suddenly lost its meaning. He did not return to Mr. Cao's family but instead degraded himself by becoming lazier, dirtier, and more shiftless day by day. He delighted not only in the small gains of petty thievery but also in the monetary reward he received for betrayal of a revolutionary. He finally degenerated into an automaton, parading for a pittance in Beijing's endless wedding and funeral processions.

Critical Evaluation:

Camel Xiangzi was first published serially in *Cosmic Wind* from September, 1936, to May, 1937. It was first translated into English by Evan King in 1945. The first English version is titled *Rickshaw Boy*, an apt title that reveals the intimate relationship between Xiangzi and the rickshaw. To own a rickshaw of his own seems to Xiangzi to be a moderate and practical ambition. Like a white bird gliding above the dark crows, the dream of owning his own rickshaw keeps Xiangzi's hope alive. Xiangzi's dream also helps him to maintain moral integrity and drives him to seek beauty even in the manner of pulling a rickshaw. Xiangzi does not comprehend that in his unjust society any effort to accomplish an idealistic goal is a joke. The degree of Xiangzi's demoralization corresponds to his repeated deprivation of a rickshaw. Whenever he tries to pull himself up, the dream of keeping a rickshaw fades. The death of his dream reduces Xiangzi to a living dead man. Lao She conveys the importance of holding on to one's dream, even if it is delusional.

The title of the novel, *Camel Xiangzi*, conveys another important theme: the degradation of an individual. The theft of the camels marks Xiangzi's first spiritual lapse. Xiangzi had justification for his theft of the three army camels in the confiscation of his rickshaw, but his adultery with Tigress destroys his self-respect and leads to his subsequent moral downfall.

According to the tenets of naturalism, and this novel may be considered naturalistic, Xiangzi's downfall is not his individual responsibility but that of the society. Lao She, for example, makes it a point in the novel to criticize individualism. The grandfather of Little Ma compares an individual to a helpless grasshopper caught and tied by a child and believes that only swarms of grasshoppers can defeat the victimizing hand. Lao She ends the novel by denouncing the degenerated Xiangzi as "a lost soul at the end of the road to individualism." Although *Camel Xiangzi* is the first novel to reveal Lao She's inclination toward socialism, his socialism should be called Confucian socialism. Mr. Cao, a mild socialist who provides a moral oasis in the society's desert of evil, has Confucian aesthetic taste and individual integrity. He upholds Lao She's ideal. The novel negates selfish individualism; Xiangzi's tragedy is also caused by his abandonment of positive individualism, or personal responsibility. He is defeated by relying on Mr. Cao and on Joy for his salvation.

Tigress and Joy are two unforgettable female characters. They represent two traditional types in literature: the vicious scourge and the nursing angel. Tigress, ugly, seductive, and vampirish, threatens Xiangzi's independence, whereas Joy, pure and innocent although forced to be a prostitute, nurtures his spiritual and bodily wounds. Lao She's favor for Joy's meek sacrifice and loathing of Tigress' aggressiveness are obvious. Joy represents the traditional type of woman whose identity equals self-annihilation. Tigress, at least, pursues her own happiness and struggles for status and economic independence among men. Lao She's fiction very often reveals his phobia of assertive women as well as of young revolutionaries because of their self-interested motives. It was not surprising that he committed suicide at the beginning of the Cultural Revolution in 1966 after a humiliating confrontation with the Red Guards.

Camel Xiangzi was Lao She's masterpiece, praised by the eminent critic C. T. Hsia as "the finest modern Chinese novel before the second Sino-Japanese War." The first piece of realistic modern fiction introduced to the West from China, as *Rickshaw Boy*, Evan King's translation, it was an instant best-seller. People all over the world enjoy *Camel Xiangzi*; Xiangzi's tragic fate appeals to everyone, and the rickshaw world is a microcosm of human society. *Camel Xiangzi* also demonstrates Lao She's sophisticated humor and mastery of the Beijing dialect. Although Lao She was influenced by English and American literature, his *Camel Xiangzi* is uniquely Chinese.

Qingyun Wu

Bibliography:
Birch, Cyril. "Lao She: The Humorist in His Humor." *China Quarterly* 8 (1961): 51-55. An insightful discussion of Lao She's humor and Chaplinesque characterization.
Hsia, C. T. *A History of Modern Chinese Fiction.* New Haven, Conn.: Yale University Press, 1971. Contains a survey of Lao She and his fiction. Lucid and comprehensive; an excellent introduction to a serious study of *Camel Xiangzi*.
Kao, George, ed. *Two Writers and the Cultural Revolution: Lao She and Chen Jo-hsi.* Hong Kong: Chinese University Press, 1980. Contains five pieces translated from Lao She's fiction as well as several critical essays. Sheds light on Lao She's life and literary career in England and America. Examines the cause of Lao She's suicide in 1966. Includes a brief summary of the Western reception of *Camel Xiangzi*.
Lau, Joseph. "Naturalism in Modern Chinese Fiction." *Literature East and West* 2 (1970): 148-160. Discusses the naturalist dimension of *Camel Xiangzi*, attributing Xiangzi's downfall to his social environment.

Vohra, Ranbir. *Lao She and the Chinese Revolution*. Cambridge, Mass.: East Asian Research Center, Harvard University, 1974. A chronological study of Lao She's life and works, with bibliography, notes, and index. Discusses Lao She's childhood and political development in the 1920's and his artistic maturity and theme of alienation in the 1930's. Analyzes Lao She's humor and treatment of women characters.

Wang, David Der-wei. *Fictional Realism in Twentieth-Century China: Mao Dun, Lao She, She Congwen*. New York: Columbia University Press, 1992. The fourth chapter is devoted to the study of Lao She's fiction. Deals with the formal structure of *Camel Xiangzi*, focusing on the melodramatic and farcical aspects of the story. A good study of Lao She.

CAMILLE

Type of work: Drama
Author: Alexandre Dumas, *fils* (1824-1895)
Type of plot: Sentimental
Time of plot: Nineteenth century
Locale: France
First performed: 1852; first published, 1852 as *La Dame aux camélias* (English translation, 1856)

> *Principal characters:*
> MARGUERITE "CAMILLE" GAUTIER, a woman of Paris
> NANINE, her maid
> COUNT DE VARVILLE, who desires Camille
> ARMAND DUVAL, who loves her
> M. DUVAL, Armand's father
> MADAME PRUDENCE, Camille's friend

The Story:

Marguerite Gautier was a courtesan in the city of Paris. The symbol of her character was the camellia, pale and cold. She had once been a needleworker who, while taking a rest cure in Bagneres, had been befriended by a wealthy duke whose daughter she resembled. After the death of his daughter, the duke had taken Marguerite back to Paris and introduced her into society. Somehow the story of Marguerite's past life had been rumored on the boulevards, and society frowned upon her. She was respected only by a few friends who knew that she longed for a true love and wished to leave the gay life of Paris. She was heavily in debt for her losses at cards and had no money of her own to pay her creditors.

The Count de Varville, her latest admirer, offered to pay all of her debts if she would become his mistress. Before she gave her consent, however, she met Armand Duval. Armand had nothing to offer her but his love. He was presented to Marguerite by her milliner, Madame Prudence, who pretended to be her friend but who was loyal to her only because Marguerite was generous with her money.

At first Marguerite scorned Armand's love, for although she longed for a simple life she thought she could never actually live in poverty. Armand was persistent, and at last Marguerite loved him and told him she would forsake her present friends and go away with him. She had a racking cough. Armand wanted Marguerite to leave Paris and go to a quiet spot where she could rest and have fresh air.

Marguerite, Armand, and Nanine, her maid, moved to a cottage in the country. For many weeks Armand was suspicious of Marguerite and feared she missed her former companions. Convinced at last of her true love, Armand lost his uneasiness and they were happy together. The garden flowers he grew replaced the camellias she had always worn in Paris.

Their happiness was brief. Armand's father called on Marguerite and begged her to renounce his son. He knew her past reputation, and he felt that his son had placed himself and his family in a disgraceful position. Marguerite would not listen to him, for she knew that Armand loved her and would not be happy without her. Then Armand's father told her that his daughter was betrothed to a man who threatened to break the engagement if Armand and Marguerite insisted on remaining together. Moved by sympathy for the young girl, Marguerite promised Armand's father that she would send his son away. She knew that he would never leave her unless she betrayed him, and she planned to tell him that she no longer loved him but was going to return to her former life. Armand's father knew then that she truly loved his son, and he promised that after her death, which she felt would be soon, he would tell Armand she had renounced him only for the sake of his family.

Marguerite, knowing that she could never tell Armand the lie directly, wrote a note declaring her dislike for the simple life he had provided for her and her intention to return to de Varville in Paris. When Armand read the letter, he swooned in his father's arms.

He left the cottage and then Paris, and did not return for many weeks. Meanwhile Marguerite had resumed her old life and spent all her time at the opera or playing cards with her former associates, always wearing a camellia in public. Count de Varville was her constant companion, but her heart was still with Armand. Her cough was much worse. Knowing she would soon die, she longed to see Armand once more.

When Marguerite and Armand met at last, Armand insulted her honor and that of the Count de Varville. He threw gold pieces on Marguerite, asserting they were the bait to catch and hold her kind, and he announced to the company present that the Count de Varville was a man of gold but not of honor. Challenged by de Varville, Armand wounded the count in a duel and left Paris. He returned only after his father, realizing the sacrifice Marguerite had made, wrote, telling him the true story of Marguerite's deception, and explaining that she had left him only for the sake of his sister's honor and happiness.

By the time Armand could reach Paris, Marguerite was dying. Only Nanine and a few faithful friends remained with her. Madame Prudence remained because Marguerite, even in her poverty, shared what she had. Marguerite and Nanine had moved to a small and shabby flat, and there Armand found them. He arrived to find Marguerite on her deathbed but wearing again the simple flowers he had once given her. He threw himself down beside her, declaring his undying love and begging for her forgiveness. The once beautiful Marguerite, now as wasted as the flowers she wore on her breast, died in the arms of her true love.

Critical Evaluation:

Camille established the artistic reputation of Alexandre Dumas, *fils*. Although Dumas initially could not find a theater to produce *Camille* because of its scandalous subject, the play caused a sensation as soon as it was performed in Paris. It went on to become one of the most popular plays of the nineteenth century in Europe and in America; nothing Dumas later wrote ever matched its phenomenal success.

There are many reasons for the play's great appeal. First, the play presents an intimate and realistic view of a segment of French society that has long fascinated respectable folk—the demimonde of high-class courtesans and their many wealthy protectors. Audiences may take vicarious pleasure in a world of private boxes at the opera, fancy-dress balls, high-stakes gambling, late-night suppers of oysters and champagne, fabulous clothes, and dazzling jewelry. The younger Dumas knew this world quite well; he and his father amused themselves at least on its fringes. Moreover, he had the keen eye of a born social anthropologist, and he focused on the details of this life—its pleasures, costs, and self-deceptions—with rapt attention.

At the same time, *Camille*, unlike Dumas' later thesis plays, brims with romantic sentiments not to say sentimentality. Marguerite earns her livelihood as a courtesan and leads a dissipated life that is literally killing her, but she finds redemption through the power of true love. Vice and redemption appear in their most audience-pleasing forms. Marguerite renounces her glamorous life in Paris. Without a backward glance, she sells off her fine possessions in order to pay her debts and begin a new life with Armand. When she realizes that all her efforts to reform will not redeem her in the eyes of the world and that her reputation will harm Armand and his family, she sacrifices the love of her life, although it means making him hate her. She knows that she will soon die of consumption; she gives up those last few months of happiness and peace for his sake. The sharp contrast between the inspiring generosity of her actions and the world's harsh view of fallen women places Marguerite safely in Romanticism's pantheon of the beautiful and the doomed—redeemed sinners who die as they are saved. The poignant irony of her situation appeals irresistibly to the romantically inclined.

Camille derives much of its power from the intensity of Dumas' deep emotional commitment to the subject. In 1844, at the age of twenty, he had met and fallen in love with Marie Duplessis, who became the model for Marguerite Gautier in both his play and his earlier novel of the same name (1848). Like Armand, he lured his beautiful demimondaine to simpler pleasures for a time, but she soon returned to her old life and died of tuberculosis not long after. In real life, Marie had nothing to do with Dumas' father (who was anything but a provincial prude), nor did she renounce her lover for the sake of his family, nor was he present at her deathbed. The idealized version of their affair that appeared in his novel proved popular with French readers, although not nearly so popular as the dramatization a few years later.

A remarkably skillful piece of theatrical writing, especially for a first play, *Camille* resembles and differs from Dumas' later works. Even in this tender romantic drama, audiences can discern traces of the preachiness that would soon dominate his work in Marguerite's frustration with a society that countenanced a sexual double standard and refused to forgive women who had strayed from the path of middle-class virtue. In part, that theme reflects Dumas' life, for he remained devoted to his mother all his life, despite the prevailing condemnation of women who bore children out of wedlock as she had done. In his later plays, the moralism, while well intentioned, becomes overt and fairly predictable. In *Camille*, however, the message comes through much more subtly, as a result of the audience's sympathetic emotional response to the characters. His most affecting play was written from the heart, not the head.

The image of Camille has permeated Western culture as an emblem of redemptive, self-sacrificing, romantic love. At least six cinematic versions of the play exist, and, up through the 1930's, the play itself was performed frequently. After that, however, it almost disappeared from the stage, except in the form of Giuseppe Verdi's popular opera *La traviata* (1853). In part, this reflects the more internalized styles of acting that developed in the twentieth century, such as the realistic psychological approach of Konstantin Stanislavski. The visible tears, audible sobs, full-body shudders, and racking coughs popular with earlier audiences seem overdone today. Melodramatic climaxes, as when Armand throws his gambling winnings in Marguerite's face, now probably would produce laughter rather than a horrified gasp. Such extravagant gestures may work well in an opera house but seem out of scale with more modern theatrical expectations.

In a sense, *Camille* appears destined to become, at best, a museum piece. Yet Dumas' urgent passion shines through the old-fashioned dramatic structure, probably because of the total conviction with which he portrays the young lovers. Novelist Henry James called it "an astonishing piece of work" that evokes the extreme joys and sorrows of the springtime of life. As he put it, *Camille* abounds in "fresh perversity, fresh credulity, fresh passion, fresh pain." While the literary artifact may fade because of being too closely tied to the period of its creation, the story, the characters, and, above all, the passionate emotions remain vivid and powerful. Unlike its heroine, the play, in this sense, will surely survive.

"Critical Evaluation" by Susan Wladaver-Morgan

Bibliography:

Chandler, Frank Wadleigh. *The Contemporary Drama of France*. Boston: Little, Brown, 1920. Sees Dumas as an important precursor of early twentieth century French drama and insists that Dumas saw himself primarily as a realist.

Matthews, J. Brander. *French Dramatists of the Nineteenth Century*. London: Remington, 1882. Presents Dumas in the context of his contemporaries; describes Dumas as not part of any tradition but his own. Sees *Camille*'s treatment of a scandalous subject as neither poetic nor unpleasantly realistic. Instead, considers *Camille* to be merely vulgar melodrama, fit only for the opera house.

Maurois, André. *The Titans: A Three-Generation Biography of the Dumas*. Translated by Gerard Hopkins. New York: Harper, 1957. Lively literary biography of *Camille*'s playwright, his father, and his grandfather. Gives the flavor of their lives and times. Abundant use of personal letters, illustrations, and notes. Bibliography.

Schwarz, H. Stanley. *Alexandre Dumas, fils, Dramatist*. New York: New York University Press, 1927. Focuses on Dumas' place in nineteenth century French literature, comparing his work with that of Eugène Scribe and Honoré de Balzac. Provides descriptions of the plays' productions and detailed analysis of Dumas' ideas on social problems.

CANCER WARD

Type of work: Novel
Author: Aleksandr Solzhenitsyn (1918-   )
Type of plot: Social realism
Time of plot: 1955-1956
Locale: An unnamed city based on Tashkent in Kazakhstan, Soviet Union
First published: Rakovy korpus, 1968 (English translation, 1968)

> *Principal characters:*
> OLEG FILIMONOVICH KOSTOGLOTOV, a political exile with stomach
>   cancer
> PAVEL NIKOLAYEVICH RUSANOV, a bureaucrat with a tumor on his neck
> LYUDMILA AFANASYEVNA DONTSOVA, the head of the radiology
>   department
> VERA KORNILYEVNA GANGART, a radiotherapist who takes a special
>   interest in Kostoglotov
> VADIM ZATSYRKO, a geology scholar with cancer in his leg
> ZOYA, a young nurse who is attracted to Kostoglotov
> DYOMKA, a teenage cancer patient
> ASYA, a teenage athlete and cancer patient

The Story:

In February, 1955, Pavel Nikolayevich Rusanov was admitted into the cancer ward of a Soviet hospital. His wife, upon examining conditions in the hospital, immediately tried to bribe one of the nurses to offer him superior care. Rusanov was a Party official in charge of labor relations—a euphemism for being a government informer—and used to having privileges. He had chosen this hospital rather than one in Moscow because his doctor, Lyudmila Afanasyevna Dontsova, had insisted that he receive treatment as quickly as possible for the large tumor on his neck. Dontsova, fifty years old and one of the older doctors, was the head of the radiology department at the hospital.

Rusanov quickly sized up the other eight patients in the ominously named ward no. 13 and decided that they were his inferiors. He took a particular dislike to Oleg Filimonovich Kostoglotov, a former labor camp inmate whom he nicknamed Ogloyed, or "lout," even though the man appeared to be an avid reader. Dyomka, a teenage student with cancer in his leg, also revealed that he enjoyed reading, now that he had the time to do so. Kostoglotov told him that education does not necessarily make a person smarter, but Dyomka disagreed.

Kostoglotov asked Zoya, an attractive young nurse, whether he might borrow one of her medical books. His doctors had never told him what was wrong with him, and he wanted to know. He had been near death when he arrived at the hospital less than two weeks earlier, and six months prior to that, a doctor had told him that he had less than three weeks to live. Once he discovered the type of cancer he had, he asked Dontsova whether he might get a year of peace, rather than undergoing the radiation treatments that would make him sick and not necessarily cure him. Dontsova became attached to him, in part because she was writing a professional thesis on cancers similar to his; the hospital had too many difficult cases to allow her to take a leave to finish the thesis. She recognized the danger of radiation treatment and sympathized with Kostoglotov.

Dyomka met Asya, a beautiful girl, in a recreation area shared by male and female patients. She was an athlete, and she told Dyomka that she was in the hospital for a checkup. In her opinion, she said, it would be better for him to be dead than to have his leg amputated. Dyomka received contrary advice from Vadim Zatsyrko, another patient. Zatsyrko studied intensely in the ward and wanted to go back to his research on a geological theory about radiation. He knew that he had less than a year to live, but he wanted to leave behind his method of finding ore deposits.

Rusanov learned from the newspaper that the entire Supreme Court of the Union had been replaced, and he had a nightmare that the people he had denounced were being called to the new Supreme Court. His wife earlier had revealed that amnesty had been granted to Rodichev, a former neighbor whom Rusanov and his wife had denounced, partly to get a larger living space.

Kostoglotov became friends with Vera Kornilyevna Gangart, a radiotherapist who was about his age. He had been taking a diluted poison made from a mushroom that grows on birch trees, a folk cure for his cancer. She persuaded him to pour out the poison. Kostoglotov found Gangart attractive, but he also pursued Zoya. He persuaded Zoya to kiss him, and she told him that he was getting hormone therapy that would eventually render him impotent. She briefly withheld the hormone treatments. When he stopped pursuing her, she became more distant.

Dontsova began having pains in her stomach. Like many of the other medical personnel, she had been exposed to more X rays than was safe; the doctors chose to operate the X-ray machines according to patients' needs rather than according to recommendations for their own exposure. She later visited Dormidont Tikhonovich Oreshchenkov, an older doctor who was allowed to have a private practice as a reward for having saved the son of a local politician. She asked him to examine her, and they discussed the merits of a private system of medicine. Later, because the doctors at the cancer ward were uncertain of her diagnosis, they sent her to Moscow. If she had been a regular patient, they would have cut her open to examine her, because that would have been less expensive and more expedient.

Asya came to visit Dyomka, who had decided to have his leg amputated. She looked like the other patients, disheveled and in an old dressing gown. She revealed that she had breast cancer and asked him to kiss the breast that would be removed; she wondered if anyone would ever like her, once it was gone.

Rusanov and Kostoglotov were discharged. Because his neck tumor had shrunk, Rusanov believed that he was cured, but the doctors expected new tumors to grow and were not sure whether he would live a year. Gangart offered to let Kostoglotov stay briefly at her apartment; as a political exile, he was not allowed to stay in a hotel. Unless someone took him in, he would have had to sleep at the railway station. Zoya also invited him to stay with her. He traveled around the city, trying various things that he had not experienced before. He decided not to see Zoya again and went to Gangart's apartment, but she was not home. Rather than wait for her or return later, he went to the railroad station and wrote letters to Dyomka, Zoya, and Gangart.

Critical Evaluation:

Like *One Day in the Life of Ivan Denisovich* (1943), *The First Circle* (1968), and other works by Aleksandr Solzhenitsyn, *Cancer Ward* has a close connection to the author's life. Like Kostoglotov, he had been diagnosed with cancer and had had to find his own way to a hospital. Also like Kostoglotov, he had taken a folk cure that may have kept him alive until he reached the hospital. Kostoglotov is most clearly the author's mouthpiece, although the other patients also express his views. Rusanov and a few minor characters present contradictory views and show, through citing examples, the flaws of the Soviet system.

On the surface, *Cancer Ward* is an examination of the patients, and to a lesser degree the doctors, in a cancer treatment ward of a Soviet hospital. The novel is far more about the characters than about the setting; the experience of cancer forces them to come to terms with their beliefs. The novel could be analyzed as a political allegory, but it is not apparent that Solzhenitsyn meant it to be read as such. Politics figure in the novel primarily because they were so much a part of Soviet life at the time, not because it is an overtly political novel.

Rusanov, a Party bureaucrat introduced in the opening sections, sets the scene. The disparaging view of the hospital and of the other patients, coming from an obviously officious and snobbish man, induces the reader to sympathize with the other patients and defend the hospital.

Rusanov later fades into the background. When he is mentioned, it is to show his metamorphosis. Particularly telling is the section in which the technologist and supply agent Maxim Petrovich Chaly joins the ward. Rusanov becomes friends with Chaly, an operator in the black market who brings in numerous luxury food items, even though this is contrary to Party principles; through Chaly, he comes to see the value of letting people act in their own best interests. He is still chagrined, however, when his son, acting as a government investigator, fails to charge a truck driver for losing a case of macaroni from his truck. The truck had broken down in a snowstorm, and the man had left it for his own safety; when he returned, the macaroni was gone. Rusanov believed that the man should have risked death to guard his cargo and that he should be punished for not having done so.

The political exile Kostoglotov is the novel's primary character. One of the patients reads an essay on the subject of what it means to be a human being, which starts a general discussion. Kostoglotov illustrates various aspects of that discussion in his own life. He clings to the hope offered by the folk cure from the birch tree mushroom, even though the cure is unproven and potentially dangerous. He struggles literally with the meaning of being a man; the hormone treatment recommended for him would render him impotent, and he desires, for a while, a sexual relationship with Zoya. He also discusses with Dr. Gangart the relative merits of living a few more months in peace against the option of undergoing treatment that will make him weaker and sicker, with only a hope of prolonging his life.

The setting of *Cancer Ward* is important. Facing death, the characters are free to rebel. Few of them, perhaps only Kostoglotov, would have dared to express their opinions in front of Rusanov in any other setting. Although discussions focus on the meaning of life, they also touch on political principles. With the exception of Rusanov, the patients agree that personal choice is important; the question becomes how people should choose to live. Characters offer different interpretations of what gives meaning to life. Many give materialistic answers: One mentions his homeland, and another suggests that creative work makes a worthwhile life. Only Dyomka mentions love.

Political subtexts do enter the story. The doctors argue that they have the right to prescribe treatment that potentially will save lives, even though the patient may prefer to die a peaceful death. Although this argument is a statement of medical principles, it also touches on political themes in the era of de-Stalinization. Rusanov reflects on the meaning of de-Stalinization in his life, wondering what the changes will mean for him as a denouncer of many people who may now be freed. His concern is narrow, but his view offers one of many interesting perspectives on a period of social upheaval.

A. J. Sobczak

Bibliography:
Allaback, Steven. *Alexander Solzhenitsyn*. New York: Taplinger, 1978. The chapter on *Cancer Ward* focuses on various characters' journeys toward self-discovery and on the degree to which they represent Soviet society. Offers brief comparisons with other works by the author.

Burg, David, and George Feifer. *Solzhenitsyn*. Briarcliff Manor, N.Y.: Stein & Day, 1972. There are references to *Cancer Ward* throughout this biographical volume. Well indexed. Includes a bibliography and a brief chronology of the author's life.

Kodjak, Andrej. *Alexander Solzhenitsyn*. Boston: Twayne, 1978. Several chapters describe the author's major works. The chapter on *Cancer Ward* highlights the use of dialogue to present various philosophies.

Rothberg, Abraham. *Aleksandr Solzhenitsyn: The Major Novels*. Ithaca, N.Y.: Cornell University Press, 1971. Discusses the book's use of cancer as a metaphor for the problems of Soviet society and institutions. Describes major characters and the plot lines involving them, as well as an overview of themes.

Scammell, Michael. *Solzhenitsyn: A Biography*. New York: W. W. Norton, 1984. An impressive text of more than a thousand pages. Includes notes and an extensive index. The chapter entitled "Cancer Ward" compares Solzhenitsyn's own hospitalization for cancer with that of Kostoglotov.

CANDIDA

Type of work: Drama
Author: George Bernard Shaw (1856-1950)
Type of plot: Comedy
Time of plot: 1894
Locale: London
First performed: 1897; first published, 1897

> *Principal characters:*
> THE REVEREND JAMES MORELL, a Christian Socialist clergyman
> CANDIDA MORELL, his intelligent, vivacious wife
> EUGENE MARCHBANKS, a poet in love with Candida
> MR. BURGESS, Candida's father
> THE REVEREND ALEXANDER MILL, Morell's idealistic, admiring young
> curate
> PROSERPINE GARNETT, "PROSSY," Morell's secretary

The Story:

Act I. In his London home, the Reverend James Morell, a popular speaker for Christian Socialist causes, was arranging lecture dates with his secretary, Prossy, who is secretly in love with him. His curate, the Reverend Alexander Mill, entered and announced that Morell's father-in-law, Mr. Burgess, was coming to see him. While Morell briefly left the room, Mill and Prossy argued about Mill's tendency to idealize Morell and his wife, Candida. When Burgess entered, Mill left. Burgess had not seen Morell, whom he regarded as a fool, for three years. Morell despised Burgess for being interested only in money and for paying low wages to his help. Morell had been instrumental in getting the county council to turn down Burgess' bid for a construction contract. Burgess said that he had changed his ways and now paid higher wages, but Morell suspected that Burgess only wanted to bid on other contracts. Candida returned from a vacation with her children, accompanied by Eugene Marchbanks; Burgess, impressed to discover that he was the nephew of a peer, left, promising to return that afternoon. Candida too went out, and Morell invited Marchbanks to stay for lunch. Marchbanks announced that it was incredible that Morell should think his marriage to Candida a happy one; he himself loved Candida, and he dared Morell to tell Candida what he had said. Morell began to get angry when Marchbanks asserted that Candida was too fine a spirit for a life with Morell. Saying that he would not tell Candida of their talk, Morell told the young man to leave. Candida returned and invited Marchbanks to stay for lunch.

Act II. Later that same afternoon, Prossy berated Marchbanks for fiddling with her typewriter. Marchbanks talked poetically of love until Prossy, who was at first exasperated, admitted that she too was in love. Burgess entered and asserted that Morell was mad. When Morell came in with the news that Candida was cleaning the house and the lamps, Marchbanks was horrified to think that his idealized woman was getting her hands dirty doing mundane chores. This amused Candida, who took Marchbanks out to peel onions. Morell left to answer a telegram brought to him by Prossy, who told Burgess that Marchbanks was mad. When Morell returned, Burgess complained that Prossy had insulted him and went out; that upset Prossy, who also rushed out. Candida returned and began to baby Morell. She told him of "Prossy's complaint," and that women were in love with him and not with his preaching and ideas. Saying that Morell was spoiled with love and worship, she claimed that Marchbanks was the one who needed love. Marchbanks, she said, was always right because he understood Morell and Prossy and her. She ended by telling Morell to trust in her love for him. Mill came in with the news that The Guild of St. Matthew was very upset that Morell had canceled his lecture. Candida said that they should all go to hear Morell, but her husband, resolved to put matters to the test, decided that he would give the lecture but that Candida and Marchbanks should stay at home together.

Act III. Later that evening, when Candida and Marchbanks were alone by the fire, Marchbanks read poetry to her until Candida told Marchbanks she would rather talk. Marchbanks sat on the floor with his head against her knees. Candida wanted him to speak of his real feelings and not to indulge in attitudes, but Marchbanks only repeated Candida's name over and over. She asked him if he were happy and if he wanted anything more. Marchbanks said that he was happy. When Morell entered and Candida left to talk to the maid, Morell and Marchbanks argued about their differing views of Candida; Marchbanks said that he loved Candida so much that he wanted nothing more than the happiness of being in love. Then he became very excited and begged Morell to send for Candida so that she could choose between them. Candida came back into the room, followed by Mill, Prossy, and Burgess, who had returned from a supper after the lecture. All were full of praise for Morell. Prossy had had a bit too much champagne, and Morell told Mill to see her home; Burgess, satisfied with having made contact for business purposes with a member of the County Council Works Committee, also left. When Morell told Candida that Marchbanks was in love with her, Candida scolded them both. Morell finally said that Candida had to choose between them. He himself offered strength, honesty, ability, and industry. Marchbanks offered his weakness and desolation. When Candida said that she chose the weaker of the two, Marchbanks immediately realized that she meant Morell. Candida explained that Morell had been spoiled from birth and needed support, whereas Marchbanks was a rebel and really self-sufficient. Candida kissed Marchbanks on the forehead and he left. Morell and Candida embraced.

"The Story" by Gordon N. Bergquist

Critical Evaluation:

Some of George Bernard Shaw's critics bring the twofold charge against him that his characters are too academic and lifeless, and that his plays are merely tracts for expressing Shaw's ideas on love, war, property, morals, and revolution. This charge is not, however, often leveled at *Candida*. Generally the harshest critics concede that here is one play that is, aside from a few comments on socialism and corruption in government, free from really revolutionary ideas. In fact, in *Candida*, Shaw is saluting that old, established institution, marriage. Of course, as he salutes, he does wink at the audience.

Candida belongs to the group of his *Plays, Pleasant and Unpleasant* published in 1898. It was given its first public London production in 1904, after a private presentation in 1897, and went on to become one of the most popular plays in the Shaw repertory. It was an early favorite with Shaw himself, and he held on to it for some time before allowing its production, preferring to read it privately to his friends, who, it is said, would weep aloud at the more touching scenes.

Candida is put together in a masterly way and has a uniformity that is often lacking in some of Shaw's other works. Here is a play that gives an audience intensely comic scenes as well as moments of serious insights. Moreover, it is a very actable play. Candida herself is one of the great roles in twentieth century theater, that of the self-possessed woman who, as in many homes, subtly runs the household while appearing to be subservient to her husband. The Reverend James Mavor Morell is also an excellent role: the hearty Christian Socialist clergyman, the popular speaker always in demand, the unintimidated man who is happy and secure in his important position until a young, wild, seemingly effeminate friend of the family, the poet Eugene Marchbanks, threatens his security. The role of Marchbanks, the eighteen-year-old worshiper of Candida, has also been a favorite of many stage juveniles. As the boy who grows faint at the thought of Candida's peeling onions, who rants, raves, and whines over the thought that the earthly, boorish Morell is married to such a poetic delight and inspiration as Candida, Marchbanks bears striking resemblances to the young and ethereal Shelley; possibly he is a younger Bernard Shaw.

A resemblance between *Candida* and Henrik Ibsen's *A Doll's House* (1879) is also evident, though in his play Shaw reversed Ibsen's situation. In Ibsen's play, Nora is the doll, but in *Candida* it is Morell, the likable, high-principled husband, who is the doll. As he eventually learns, it is his wife who is responsible for his success. When Candida is "forced" to choose between Marchbanks and Morell, she chooses Morell, the weaker of the two. This is, supposedly, Shaw's Virgin Mother play; certainly Candida plays the role of Morell's wife, mother, and sisters rolled into one. She is the one who arranges his affairs, who keeps him happy and content, and who peels his onions for him. Morell eventually comes to realize her true status, though later he might try to rationalize his way out of his paradoxical victory. Many regard this, a husband and wife coming to a fuller understanding of each other, as the central aspect of the play.

This aspect bears a certain resemblance to romantic drama, which may be the secret of the play's success among non-Shavian theatergoers. Shaw indulged in tirades against romanticism, but *Candida* is infused with romantic ideas and situations. Although Candida discovers a typical Shavian thought—that service and not necessarily contentment is the greatest triumph in life—the play and its celebration of the wife-mother role is romantic in comparison with other Shavian drama.

In the growing awareness between the husband and wife, Marchbanks serves as the catalyst who brings about the final result. Because of Marchbanks' poetic railings, Morell begins to wonder if he might actually be too commonplace for Candida. Yet when Morell is chosen and the poet spurned, Marchbanks leaves as a more mature being with a secret in his heart, and he seems quite eager to go out into the night. It may well be that Marchbanks realizes that this mundane domesticity is not for him—his is a greater destiny. Candida has revealed the average happy marriage to him, and he realizes there is no poetry in it. A poet must go out into the night, and on to greater and more exalted triumphs.

The force of the concept that the man of genius is out of place in conventional society is somewhat weakened by the fact that Marchbanks' role is somewhat overdrawn. Through his excessive behavior, the conflict between Marchbanks and Morell fails to convince many readers and viewers; to some, there is no choice at all between the likable clergyman and the effeminate boy. Others, however, are willing to overlook this flaw and to ignore the charge that Candida, in the "choosing" scene, behaves in a most conceited fashion. Audiences have generally preferred simply to delight in the high comedy of *Candida*, its amusing situations, and the consistently witty, sparkling dialogue throughout. There is no doubt that its great popularity is due not only to its tight construction but also to the fact that in *Candida* we have Shaw's safest play.

Bibliography:
Carpenter, Charles A. "Critical Comedies." In *Bernard Shaw and the Art of Destroying Ideals: The Early Plays*. Madison: University of Wisconsin Press, 1969. Treats *Candida* as a sentimental comedy and discusses the conflict of ideals in the play. Devotes much space to an analysis of Candida's character and to her ability to use sympathy to dominate the other characters in the play.

Crompton, Louis. "*Candida*." In *Shaw the Dramatist*. Lincoln: University of Nebraska Press, 1969. Discusses the social, philosophical, and especially historical backgrounds of *Candida*. A clear presentation of Shaw's ideas and their sources in the nineteenth century intellectual tradition.

Holroyd, Michael. *Bernard Shaw: The Search for Love*. New York: Random House, 1988. This first volume of the standard biography of Shaw details the connections between Shaw's life and thought and his works. Indispensable.

Merritt, James D. "Shaw and the Pre-Raphaelites." In *Shaw: Seven Critical Essays*, edited by Norman Rosenblood. Toronto: University of Toronto Press, 1971. Focuses on the character of Marchbanks and on the various references in the play to art, which Merritt relates to the Pre-Raphaelites and the art-for-art's-sake movement of the 1890's.

Stanton, Stephen. *A Casebook on Candida*. New York: Thomas Y. Crowell, 1962. Very useful as an introduction to the play. Contains not only the text of the play and its sources but also selected prefaces and notes by Shaw and a wide variety of brief interpretations and criticism.

CANDIDE
Or, The Optimist

Type of work: Novel
Author: Voltaire (François-Marie Arouet, 1694-1778)
Type of plot: Social satire
Time of plot: Eighteenth century
Locale: Europe and South America
First published: Candide: Ou, L'Optimisme, 1759 (English translation, 1759)

>   *Principal characters:*
>   CANDIDE, Baroness Thunder-ten-tronckh's illegitimate son
>   MADEMOISELLE CUNEGONDE, Baron Thunder-ten-tronckh's daughter
>   PANGLOSS, Candide's friend and tutor
>   CACAMBO, Candide's servant

The Story:

Candide, the illegitimate son of Baron Thunder-ten-tronckh's sister, was born in Westphalia. Dr. Pangloss, his tutor and a devout follower of Liebnitz, taught him metaphysico-theologo-cosmolonigology and assured his pupil that this is the best of all possible worlds. Cunegonde, the daughter of the baron, kissed Candide one day behind a screen, whereupon Candide was expelled from the noble baron's household.

Impressed into the army of the king of Bulgaria, Candide deserted during a battle between the king of Bulgaria and the king of Abares. Later, he was befriended by James the Anabaptist. He also met his old friend, Dr. Pangloss, now a beggar. James, Pangloss, and Candide started for Lisbon. Their ship was wrecked in a storm off the coast of Portugal. James was drowned, but Candide and Pangloss swam to shore just as an earthquake shook the city. The rulers of Lisbon, both secular and religious, decided to punish the people whose wickedness had brought about the earthquake, and Candide and Pangloss were among the accused. Pangloss was hanged, Candide thoroughly whipped.

He was still smarting from his wounds, when an old woman accosted Candide and told him to have courage and to follow her. She led him to a house where he was fed and clothed. Then Cunegonde appeared. Candide was amazed because Pangloss had told him that Cunegonde was dead. Cunegonde related what had happened to her since she last saw Candide. She was being kept by a Jew and an Inquisitor, but she held both men at a distance. Candide killed the Jew and the Inquisitor when they came to see her.

Together with the old woman, Cunegonde and Candide fled to Cadiz, where they were robbed. In despair, they sailed for Paraguay, where Candide hoped to enlist in the Spanish army then fighting the rebellious Jesuits. During the voyage, the old woman told her story. They learned that she was the daughter of Pope Urban X and the princess of Palestrina.

The governor of Buenos Aires developed a great affection for Cunegonde and caused Candide to be accused of having committed robbery while still in Spain. Candide fled with his servant, Cacambo; Cunegonde and the old woman remained behind. When Candide decided to fight for the Jesuits, he learned that the commandant was Cunegonde's brother. The brother would not hear of his sister's marrying Candide. They quarreled, and Candide, fearing that he had killed the brother, took to the road with Cacambo once more. Shortly afterward, they were captured by the Oreillons, a tribe of savage Indians, but when Cacambo proved they were not Jesuits, the two were released. They traveled on to Eldorado. There life was simple and perfect, but Candide was not happy because he missed Cunegonde.

At last he decided to take some of the useless jeweled pebbles and golden mud of Eldorado and return to Buenos Aires to search for Cunegonde. He and Cacambo started out with a hundred sheep laden with riches, but they lost all but two sheep. When Candide approached a Dutch merchant and tried to arrange passage to Buenos Aires, the merchant sailed away with all his money and treasures, leaving him behind. Cacambo then went to Buenos Aires to find Cunegonde and take her to Venice to meet Candide. After many adventures, including a sea fight and the miraculous recovery of one of his lost sheep from a sinking ship, Candide arrived at Bordeaux. His intention was to go to Venice by way of Paris. Police arrested him in Paris, however, and Candide was forced to buy his freedom with diamonds. Later, he sailed on a Dutch ship to Portsmouth, England, where he witnessed the execution of an English admiral. From Portsmouth he went to Venice. There he found no Cacambo and no Cunegonde. He did, however, meet Paquette, Cunegonde's waiting maid. Shortly afterward, Candide encountered Cacambo, who was now a slave and who informed him that Cunegonde was in Constantinople. In the Venetian galley that carried them to Constantinople, Candide found Pangloss and Cunegonde's brother among the galley slaves. Pangloss related that he had miraculously escaped from his hanging in Lisbon because the bungling hangman had not been able to tie a proper knot. Cunegonde's brother told how he survived the wound that Candide had thought fatal. Candide bought both men from the Venetians and gave them their freedom.

When the group arrived at Constantinople, Candide bought the old woman and Cunegonde from their masters and also purchased a little farm to which they all retired. There each had his own particular work to do. Candide decided that the best thing in the world was to cultivate one's garden.

Critical Evaluation:

Candide, Voltaire's tour de force, surpasses most other famous satires. Like Alexander Pope's *Rape of the Lock* (1714), it takes a swipe at the pretentiousness of the upper classes; like George Orwell's *Animal Farm* (1945), it undercuts political systems; like Jonathan Swift's ambitious *Gulliver's Travels* (1726), it sheds sharp light on the grossness, cupidity, and stupidity of human beings, as well as on their crude and frequently cruel institutions. Voltaire's satire goes beyond human beings and their society, however, to examine the entire world in which they find themselves. Its thesis is contrived in explicit response to the Leibnitzian optimism that this is "the best of all possible worlds."

The existence of evil in the world has been a problem for human beings ever since they began to speculate about the nature of things. It is treated in the literature of the West at least as early as the book of Genesis, which attributes evil to human beings' disobedient nature. St. Augustine and, later, John Milton enlarged on this theory, claiming that God limited his own interference in the world when he created people "sufficient to stand though free to fall." The book of Job in the Bible centers more specifically on the problem of suffering. Its answer is essentially no answer, a restriction to an overwhelming (some have said obscene) demonstration of God's power, which humbles Job into acceptance. A third century Persian philosopher, Mani, devised the theory that earth is a field of dispute between two nearly matched powers—one of light, one of darkness—with human beings caught in the middle.

Most later explanations appear to be variations on these three approaches. The seventeenth century Frenchman Blaise Pascal believed, like the author of Job, that human vision cannot perceive the justice in God's overall plan. Gottfried Wilhelm von Leibnitz developed this explanation further. In his *Theodicée*, published in 1710, he described a harmonious universe in which all events are linked into a chain of cause and effect, and in which apparent evil is compensated by some greater good that may not be evident to the limited human mind. The English poet Alexander Pope expressed similar views.

In his early life, Voltaire was generally optimistic. Beginning in 1752, however, his writings evidence growing pessimism. On November 1, 1755, an earthquake in Lisbon, Portugal, killed between thirty and forty thousand people. This catastrophe provided Voltaire with a perfect springboard for his skepticism about the basic goodness of the world. "If Pope had been at Lisbon," he wrote, "would he have dared to say *All is well*?" His fellow Frenchman Jean Jacques Rousseau responded that human beings, not God, are to blame for evil, including earthquakes: that human beings bring misfortune upon themselves by congregating in cities instead of living naturally in the country.

Voltaire continued the debate in *Candide*, where he created a young, impressionable protagonist and set him upon an incredible string of adventures, many of which he drew from real life. Historical events include the Lisbon earthquake and subsequent *auto-da-fé*, the political chaos of Morocco, and the execution of an admiral (Voltaire had tried to intercede in just such a situation). Like such other wandering heroes as Gulliver and Huckleberry Finn, Candide is naïve. For a time, like a schoolboy, he reacts to such events as torture, war, and catastrophe by recalling the favorite sayings of his tutor, Pangloss, among them "Every effect has a cause" and "All is for the best in this best of all possible worlds." As horror piles on horror, however, his doubts increase. Pangloss reappears periodically to soothe his pupil with further examples of illogical logic, but harsh experience begins to have its effect.

Candide's visit to Eldorado, the famed lost city of the New World, is a high-water mark. Here all is placid and serene. People live in absolute harmony. Suffering and poverty are unknown. There is no greed, and the natives smile at Candide's interest in the gold and jewels that lie on the ground as "clay and pebbles." Eldorado is utopia. Because of his desire to regain his lost love, Cunegonde, Candide leaves Eldorado; having however seen a truly harmonious world, he can no longer accept cruelty, catastrophe, and suffering as necessary ingredients for a universal good.

In the final chapter, Candide and his little band, including Pangloss, his more recent friend, the pessimistic Martin, and Cunegonde, who has now grown old and ugly, settle on a small farm "till the company should meet with a more favorable destiny." There they become almost as distressed by boredom as previously they had been by disaster until two neighbors bring enlightenment to them. A dervish, questioned about the existence of evil, responds, "What signifies it whether there be evil or good? When his highness sends a ship to Egypt does he trouble his head whether the rats in the vessel are at their ease or not?" This echo of a metaphor that Voltaire had contrived as early as 1736 briefly asserts the notion that the world may in the view of the "divine architect" be excellent indeed, but it is not designed for human beings, the "mice" in the hold. The second neighbor, a contented old farmer, advises Candide's group of the worthwhileness of labor, which "keeps off from us three great evils—idleness, vice, and want." For once, those philosophical opposites, Pangloss and Martin, agree; the little community settles down to work in earnest, each member doing his part with a good will and deriving satisfaction therefrom.

Candide, although it is an attack on philosophical optimism, is not a pessimistic work. Its ending, with the hero remarking that "we must cultivate our garden," reminds the reader of the words of another realistic but hopeful man, Anton Chekhov, who was to observe more than a century later, "If everyone in the world did all he was capable of on his own plot of land, what a beautiful world it would be!"

"Critical Evaluation" by Sally Buckner

Bibliography:

Aldridge, Alfred Owen. *Voltaire and the Century of Light.* Princeton, N.J.: Princeton University Press, 1975. A thoughtful study that describes Voltaire's extraordinarily diverse literary career. Compares Voltaire's 1759 "philosophical tale" *Candide* with Jonathan Swift's masterful satire *Gulliver's Travels.*

Besterman, Theodore. *Voltaire.* 3d ed. Chicago: University of Chicago Press, 1976. An admirable and reliable biography of Voltaire that focuses on his development as a writer. In the discussion of *Candide*, Besterman explains the moral and emotional transformation of the protagonist from an immature and selfish adolescent into a sensitive, responsible adult.

Mason, Haydn. *Voltaire: A Biography.* Baltimore: The Johns Hopkins University Press, 1981. The chapter on *Candide* describes the philosophical and ethical motivation for Voltaire's criticism of excessive optimism.

Pearson, Roger. *The Fables of Reason: A Study of Voltaire's "Contes philosophiques."* New York: Oxford University Press, 1993. An insightful literary study of Voltaire's use of satire, irony, and understatement in his many philosophical tales. The lengthy chapter on *Candide* includes an explanation for the appropriateness of viewing *Candide* as a tale on moral education and on the search for human honesty.

Richter, Peyton, and Ilona Ricardo. *Voltaire.* Boston: Twayne, 1980. Excellent general study on Voltaire's life and career. Describes several different levels of satire in *Candide* and Voltaire's other major philosophical tales, including *Zadig* (1748) and *Micromégas* (1752). Also includes a well-annotated bibliography of significant critical studies on his work.

CANE

Type of work: Poetry and short fiction
Author: Jean Toomer (1894-1967)
Type of plot: Experimental
Time of plot: Early twentieth century
Locale: Georgia, Washington, D.C., and Chicago
First published: 1923

> *Principal characters:*
> KARINTHA, a beautiful young woman in Georgia
> BECKY, a white woman with two black sons
> ESTHER, who becomes obsessed with King Barlo
> KING BARLO, a man whom Esther thinks is a prophet
> LOUISA, an African American woman loved by two men
> TOM BURWELL, a man who loves Louisa
> BOB STONE, a white man who loves Louisa
> RHOBERT, a man obsessed with home ownership
> PAUL JOHNSON, a student in Chicago
> BONA HALE, a student to whom Paul is attracted
> RALPH KABNIS, a teacher from Washington, D.C.
> FATHER JOHN, a former slave, living in Halsey's basement

The Story:

The title character of "Karintha" was a woman whose beauty captivated men, making her like "a growing thing ripened too soon." She had a child, whom she apparently killed, and became a prostitute. Becky was a white woman cast out by the community because she had two black sons. Townspeople built her a cabin and took food to her, but never saw her. The boys grew up, caused trouble, and left, cursing people of both races. When Becky's chimney collapsed, burying her, someone threw a Bible onto the rubble.

The title character of "Carma" had affairs when her husband was away; he found out and accused her. She took a gun into the cane field. Hearing a shot, her husband gathered men and found her. The men carried her home and searched for a wound, waking her. Realizing that he had been deceived by his wife again, her husband became irrational and cut one of the searchers. He was sent to work on the chain gang.

"Fern" tells of a young woman whose eyes attracted men. They wanted to do great things for her, but she tired of them. A Northerner visiting relatives in Georgia met Fern. During a walk, he held her, but she broke away, sang a pained song, then fainted. He could think of nothing to do for her, and he went back North.

"Esther" follows its title character for eighteen years. When she was nine, she saw King Barlo appear to go into a trance and talk about an African's coming to the United States to redeem people. Years after Barlo left town, Esther dreamed of having a child who was rescued from a fire. At first, she dreamed the child was immaculately conceived; when Esther imagined normal conception, the child became ugly like Barlo. Barlo returned when Esther was twenty-seven years of age; she visited him, but he repulsed her, making her feel empty.

Louisa, in "Blood-Burning Moon," worked for the family of her white admirer, Bob Stone, who wished she were his slave. Tom Burwell, a black laborer, also loved her. One night, Stone found Burwell talking with Louisa and challenged him. When Stone drew a knife, Burwell killed him. White townspeople burned Burwell in an old factory under a full, red moon.

In "Reapers," the narrator watched workers sharpen scythes and saw a horse-pulled mower cut a rat, then continue mowing. "November Cotton Flower" describes misery caused by drought and boll weevils; the untimely beauty of a cotton flower blooming in November caused people to lose fear. In "Cotton Song," cotton rollers sang of making a path to God's throne. In "Georgia Dusk," sawmill workers sang while walking home through the cane, combining music of African heritage with Christian hymns.

"Seventh Street" describes a street in Washington, D.C., that showed the influence of Prohibition and World War I. "Rhobert" is about a man who suffered the burdens of home ownership. "Calling Jesus" is about a woman whose soul followed her like a dog throughout the city, finding her only in dreams of hay and cane.

In "Avey," a man loved Avey from childhood, although he found her indolent. After returning to Washington, D.C., from school, he ran into her again, and they went to a park, where he talked and she fell asleep.

"Theater" tells the story of a dancer, Dorris, who felt the attraction of the cabaret manager's brother, John. John dreamed of Dorris, but believed the difference between them was too strong for a relationship, so he did not pursue her. His rejection caused her pain. Dan Moore, in "Box Seat," felt anger toward a society that would not let him be its savior. He loved Muriel, a teacher, but she could not become involved with such an unrooted man. Dan followed her to a vaudeville show, during which two dwarves fought; then one sang and offered a bloody rose to Muriel, who rejected it. Dan rose, shouted, and stormed out, angering a man who challenged him to a fight. By the time Dan got outside, he had forgotten the man.

"Bona and Paul" tells of two students. Paul's dark complexion caused rumors that he was a black; everyone else in the school was white. He became attracted to Bona, a Southerner, and a friend invited them on a double date. Their attraction was mutual, and they left the nightclub together. Paul stopped to tell the doorman of their love, and Bona left.

In "Beehive," a man likened himself to a honey-drinking drone in a crowded hive, wishing he could fly to a farmyard flower. "Her Lips Are Copper Wire" uses urban electrical objects to describe a woman's sexuality. "Storm Ending" compares thunder to bell-like flowers. "Prayer" is about the soul's separation from body and mind, and its paradoxical strength and frailty. "Harvest Song" describes a tired, thirsty, hungry reaper who distracted himself with pain.

"Kabnis" tells of Ralph Kabnis, a Washingtonian with Southern roots, who came to a small Georgia town to teach. Unable to sleep, he killed a noisy hen in the next room. The next day he went to church, then talked with his friends Halsey and Layman about lynchings. Through the window came a stone with a note telling the black man from the North to go home. Kabnis was terrified. That evening, Halsey and Layman brought moonshine to calm him. Hanby, the principal, fired him for drinking, and Halsey offered him a job in his blacksmith's shop. Lewis came to Kabnis' cabin and said the note was meant for him, not Kabnis. Kabnis, Lewis, and some women accompanied Halsey to his basement to visit a former slave they called Father John. The next morning, Kabnis and Carrie Kate, Halsey's sister, heard the old man say "sin" several times. He explained that the sin was white people's making the Bible lie. Kabnis replied with contempt, but Carrie seemed uplifted and calmed Kabnis.

Critical Evaluation:

Cane is a collection of stories, poems, and sketches in three sections. *Cane* appeared in 1923, receiving favorable reviews although it was not widely read. Rediscovered during the 1960's, it has become one of the best-known and most respected African American works. Oddly, Jean Toomer was only a fraction African American; his ancestry was so mixed that some laws considered him white.

Cane is important in African American literature no matter what Toomer's ethnic background was because it describes the black Southern rural experience, the black Northern urban experience, and intellectuals' attempts to understand the connection between the two. It also uses experimental techniques to portray traditional experiences.

The first section, set in rural and small-town Georgia, contains stories about women and men's attraction to them. The poems generally concern workers and landscape and often describe farm labor. Other poems in the first section are portraits. "Face" is a word picture of an old, sorrow-filled woman. "Portrait in Georgia" uses lynching imagery to describe a woman: "Hair—braided chestnut,/ coiled like a lyncher's rope. . . ." "Nullo" is a portrait of rural Georgia, describing pine needles falling.

Three poems do not fit in any of these categories: In "Song of the Son," the narrator realized that all former slaves would soon be dead, but he would sing their song, as a tree grows from a seed; in "Evening Sun," the narrator spoke of love at nightfall; "Conversion" describes negatively Africans' conversion to Christianity in the Americas.

The second section, set in cities, primarily Washington, D.C., contains poetry, short stories, and cryptic word sketches. Many short stories in section two continue male-female relationship themes; some of the poems relate to city life, such as "Her Lips Are Copper Wire."

Toomer's word sketches combine the cryptic imagery of poetry with the flowing quality of prose. This is true especially in "Calling Jesus," in which someone comes in "soft as a cotton boll brushed against the milk-pod cheek of Christ." Similar descriptions appear in the short stories. In "Karintha," for example, the title character carries "beauty, perfect as dusk when the sun goes down."

In the short stories, the author often portrays people on society's fringes to reveal the society itself. Becky, the white woman with sons of mixed race, is exiled by both communities. Townspeople are torn between their Christian duty to help her—to bring her food, build her a cabin—and their antagonism toward the mixing of races. The reader knows Becky only through townspeople's reactions.

Toomer's poetry often combines two aspects of African American experience: work songs and spirituals. "Cotton Song," for example, begins like a work song: "Come, brother, come. Lets lift it." A later stanza brings in elements of the spiritual: "Weary sinner's bare feet trod,/ Softly, softly to the throne of God. . . ." Other poems are more traditional, such as "Song of the Son," in which the narrator promises to sing his slave ancestors' song when they are gone.

The final section of *Cane*, "Kabnis," is a story originally written as drama. "Kabnis" is the most problematic part of *Cane*, but it also is the story that pulls the book together. The African American experience is displacement. Slavery displaced Africans from their homeland; emancipation freed slaves, but also often displaced them. To escape the horrors of Southern persecution, many African Americans moved to Northern cities, again displacing themselves. Those who stayed in the South lived a way of life that was ending, as factories replaced farming. Ralph Kabnis is one of those displaced persons. An educated man from Washington, D.C.— considered Northern by any Southerner—Kabnis had returned to his ancestral land to teach. There, however, he was frightened and did not fit in. He lost his position and became a blacksmith's apprentice, despite his education. He was afraid that both white people and black would think he was uppity and attack him. When the ancient former slave reminded him of the sin of slavery, Kabnis refused to identify with the pain of his ancestors. Only Carrie Kate, still rooted in her home, found profundity in the old man's talk; only she could comfort Kabnis.

Much of *Cane* is beautiful; other parts are disturbing. Toomer offers little solace, for human relationships fail; religion is portrayed as a sham; and escape seems impossible. The beauty almost intensifies the pain.

M. Katherine Grimes

Bibliography:

Benson, Brian Joseph, and Mabel Mayle Dillard. *Jean Toomer*. Boston: Twayne, 1980. Discusses Toomer's writing, especially *Cane*. Bibliography.

Kerman, Cynthia Earl, and Richard Eldridge. *The Lives of Jean Toomer: A Hunger for Wholeness*. Baton Rouge: Louisiana State University Press, 1987. Contains a long chapter about *Cane*, discussing autobiographical elements, the circumstances of its writing, and other authors' reactions.

McKay, Nellie Y. *Jean Toomer, Artist: A Study of His Literary Life and Work, 1894-1936*. Chapel Hill: University of North Carolina Press, 1984. Includes a long chapter on each section of *Cane*.

O'Daniel, Therman B., ed. *Jean Toomer: A Critical Evaluation*. Washington, D.C.: Howard University Press, 1988. This lengthy work includes essays about influences on *Cane*, interpretations of the book, male-female relationships, female characters, and other elements, as well as about Toomer himself. Useful bibliography.

Toomer, Jean. *Cane*. 1923. Reprint, edited by Darwin T. Turner. New York: W. W. Norton, 1988. Includes notes throughout the text, letters, essays, and bibliography on Toomer and *Cane*.

THE CANNIBAL

Type of work: Novel
Author: John Hawkes (1925-   )
Type of plot: Allegory
Time of plot: Twentieth century
Locale: Germany
First published: 1949

> *Principal characters:*
> ZIZENDORF, the narrator
> MADAM STELLA SNOW, a singer, wife of Ernst
> ERNST, Stella's husband
> CROMWELL, an English germanophile
> JUTTA, Stella's sister

The Story:

Part One—1945. In 1945, at the end of World War II, asylum inmates were released in the city of Spitzen-on-the-Dein in Germany. The Allied victors had left only a few overseers. One of these, Leevey, an American Jew, patrolled one-third of the country on his motorcycle and was about to travel through the city. Zizendorf, the editor of the town's newspaper, *The Crooked Zeitung*, was planning to kill Leevey, liberate Germany, and found a neo-Nazi state.

Zizendorf was the lover of Jutta, the wife of the previous editor, a Nazi soldier, who was lost in Siberia during the war. Jutta and her two children lived in a room on the fifth floor of Madam Stella Snow's boardinghouse. Madam Snow was Jutta's older sister. Herr Stintz, the schoolteacher, lived on the fourth floor, the Census-Taker on the third. The roomer who lived on the second floor, the Duke, was out, following Jutta's son through the rubble of the city. Madam Snow lived on the first floor, consulting her tarot cards every day. Balamir, a former inmate of the asylum, was put to work by Madam Snow, unearthing furniture in the basement.

Madam Snow's son, who returned from the war physically disabled, lived with his wife in the moving-picture house, where, each day, he showed the same film to an empty theater. The Mayor, his memory obliterated, was too blind to tend the chronicles of history. He was haunted by dreams of Pastor Miller, an innocent man who was executed because of the Mayor's betrayal. In the newspaper office, drinking with the Census-Taker, Zizendorf thought about the Mayor's situation while he waited to kill Leevey. He had placed a log across the road where Leevey would be passing through town. Jutta's son fled for his life from the Duke, who was following him, as Jutta's daughter, Selvaggia, watched from her window.

Part Two—1914. Stella and Ernst were inspired by their parents with romantic dreams of conquest and heroism. Singing for the soldiers in the *Sportswelt Brauhaus*, Stella, "the sorceress, sent them boiling and held them up for joy." Herman Snow, proprietor of the *Sportswelt*, urged Ernst, his son, to win Stella, to become the conquering hero. When Cromwell took Stella home from the *Sportswelt*, Ernst ran after them down the "avenue of heroes." He appeared at the side of the carriage, told Stella he would come back, and fled to the university, where he dueled with the Baron. Wounded in the groin, he went to Stella's, and she welcomed him. World War I began the next day. Stella witnessed her mother's death when an English airplane fell from the sky, sending a "splinter" into her body.

After her father, the old Prussian General, also died, Stella married Ernst. They went to the mountains on their honeymoon, where Ernst became obsessed with Christ. He began to collect wooden crucifixes and longed for death. Cromwell came to their hotel with news of the war. He told Ernst "everything he did not want to know." When Stella and Ernst returned to Spitzen-on-the-Dein, they found Germany on the verge of defeat. Herman Snow had become a "bare shell of the man." Finding Ernst dying, unable to admit to this death, Herman roared: "He's not sick!" Just before he died, Ernst expressed hatred for his father and "was reprieved from saintliness."

After her parents died during the early part of World War I, Jutta was placed in a nunnery. She feared the nuns, especially the Mother Superior, who crossed off from the human list each night the names of those who had submitted to "the slovenly captivity of forgiveness." When the Mother Superior came to Jutta's cell, Jutta told her she had nothing to confess. Wasting away with disease, Jutta began to recover when the Oberleutnant, director of the nunnery, became her lover. After using him to fulfill her needs, Jutta abandoned the Oberleutnant to marry a man who was to become a Nazi soldier in World War II.

Part Three—1945. Zizendorf and two henchmen waited by the side of the road. The Duke followed Jutta's son into the theater. Zizendorf remembered the day the Allies set up their headquarters in Madam Snow's apartment and the Mayor betrayed Pastor Miller. Leevey had fastened the red cloth about Miller's eyes. The Colonel gave Zizendorf the only rifle containing a live cartridge. The Duke faced the boy in the theater. Herr Stintz watched a light circle along the autobahn. Leevey sped up to go past the town. When the Duke reached out his hand, the boy did not move.

Leevey was killed immediately when his motorcycle hit the log. With his henchmen, Zizendorf took Leevey's body to the swamp. They were watched by Herr Stintz and Salvaggia. Zizendorf knew someone saw them with Leevey. The Duke took Jutta's son toward the asylum. When Zizendorf went back to Jutta's room, Selvaggia told him that she had seen Leevey get killed. Zizendorf went to Stintz's room and murdered him. Then he set up the press in Madam Snow's chicken coop and printed his "Indictment of the Allied Antagonists, and Proclamation of the German Liberation."

The Duke killed Jutta's son with his sword and dismembered him. He tied the organs and mutilated pieces in the boy's jacket. Zizendorf decided to make Madam Snow's house the National Headquarters. He thought the Duke would make a good chancellor and the Census-Taker could be secretary of state. Zizendorf and the Census-Taker went to kill the Mayor. The Duke came to Madam Snow's apartment. When she read Zizendorf's pamphlet, thrust under her door, tears of joy ran down her cheeks. She went to dine with the Duke. Zizendorf returned to Jutta's room and got in bed with her. When her daughter opened the door, Zizendorf said "draw those blinds and go back to sleep." She did as she was told.

Critical Evaluation:

In *The Cannibal,* the cannibalistic processes of nature, including human nature, dominate life when institutions of order have been destroyed in war. These institutions, however, are also destructive in their efforts to repress or control the processes of life. Zizendorf's plan to assassinate Leevey and to establish a neo-Nazi state parallels the nationalistic dream of Germany in 1914 and the Nazi goals of the 1930's. Each past dream has been destructive, resulting in war, and each has been abortive, destroyed by the war it provoked.

The parallel expressions of the cannibalistic life force in nature, in human beings, and in institutions are implied when Stella wonders how cannibals "could bear, in only their feathers, this terrible sun." She saw them, "carrying victims high over their heads, as tall vengeful crea- tures who sang madly on their secret rock." Stella senses the "terrifying similarity" between the cannibalism of nature, represented by the "terrible sun," and the cannibalism of people. Their need to protect themselves from death by feeding off the life of others parallels the need of the visible world to perpetuate itself. The cannibals secure a rock, an enclave of order, to facili- tate their feeding and to protect themselves from the natural world and from other cannibals. The cannibals and their rock parallel the world's nations and their institutions of protective- repressive order.

The disorder and the threats of destruction which confront Zizendorf and the other characters are mirrored for the reader in the apparent incoherence of the novel and in John Hawkes's focus on seemingly gratuitous horrors. The central enormity is the butchering of Jutta's son by the cannibalistic Duke. Hawkes's surrealistic style contributes a nightmare quality to the novel. Like a literal nightmare, the novel is also characterized by disruption of chronology, abrupt transition in place, and fragmentation of action. The narrative of the first and third sections is interrupted by the narrative of the second section. Similar interruptions occur within each section as Hawkes carries several actions forward simultaneously.

Confronted with these disruptions, the reader attempts to order his or her experience of the novel, just as Zizendorf attempts to impose order on his experience. The success of the reader's effort depends on the perception of parallels in image, statement, character, and action, as well as the perception of historical parallels. Herman Snow is identified with Kaiser Wilhelm II, the ruler of Germany during World War I. His personal desires parallel the nationalistic aspirations of Germany in 1914. The historical counterpart to Ernst is Gavrilo Princep, the assassin of the Austrian archduke. Ernst's desire to win Stella for himself parallels the Serbian desire for independence. His appearance at the side of Stella's carriage corresponds to Princep's assassi- nation of Archduke Francis Ferdinand, the act which began World War I.

After Stella and Ernst become disillusioned with dreams of conquest and heroism, they seek protection from life in the institution of religion. Belief in another world, in the immortality of souls, parallels in the novel the illusion that human beings can create a paradise of protective order in this world. Both dreams are cannibalistic: The institutions of aggression destroy life; the institutions of religion deny life. After Ernst dies, Stella abandons religion. During World War II, she sides with the Nazis and sacrifices her son to war, just as Herman and the old general, Stella's father, were willing to sacrifice their children in 1914.

In 1914, Cromwell and Jutta are disillusioned with their parents' dreams. Cromwell is associated with technological power and dehumanizing order. He is the prototype of Zizendorf in the 1945 sections of the novel. Jutta is imaged as an architect. She worships people "in the abstract." Her concern with "angles and structures" associates her with Cromwell's "Techno- logical Revolution" and, later, with Zizendorf's plans to "build the house" of his neo-Nazi state. It is Jutta whom Zizendorf takes as his mistress. In another parallel, Madam Snow nurses Balamir in the 1945 sections, just as she comforted Ernst on the first night of World War I. She abandons Balamir and accepts the Duke's invitation to dinner, just as she left the dead Ernst to side with the Nazis in World War II.

When the inmates of the "ordered institution," literally a madhouse symbolizing the Nazi state, are released at the end of World War II, the pattern begins again. Zizendorf believes he can succeed where those before him have failed because his plans are founded on a disillusioned view of reality, on his recognition that "life is not the remarkable, the precious or necessary thing we think it is." Zizendorf is identified with both the Duke and Balamir. His disregard for other human lives parallels the Duke's cannibalism. Zizendorf's belief that he can succeed mirrors Balamir's illusion that he can rebuild the old Germany. Zizendorf fails to recognize that there is really no division between the Germany of 1914, the Germany of 1945, and his new state; there is only a continuity. One abortive system of destructive order has spawned another.

John Hawkes has said that *The Cannibal* is in the future. Zizendorf writes that he has had to leave the town—"a garden spot; all of our memories are there"—but he assures the reader: "I am waiting, and at the first opportunity I will, of course, return."

James Green

Bibliography:

Berry, Eliot. *A Poetry of Force and Darkness: The Fiction of John Hawkes.* San Bernardino, Calif.: R. Reginald, the Borgo Press, 1979. Discusses the link between historical time and the unconscious in *The Cannibal* and finds repression the link between the sexual and the political in the novel.

Busch, Frederick. *Hawkes: A Guide to His Fictions.* Syracuse, N.Y.: Syracuse University Press, 1973. Presents a close analysis of the novels. Discusses Hawkes's style and social concern in *The Cannibal.* Also discusses animal imagery in relation to the theme of sterility and hopelessness.

Greiner, Donald J. *Comic Terror: The Novels of John Hawkes.* Memphis, Tenn.: Memphis State University Press, 1973. Analyzes Hawkes's comedy in terms of "black humor" and discusses his use of poetic techniques and concern for structural coherence.

Kuehl, John. *John Hawkes and the Craft of Conflict.* New Brunswick, N.J.: Rutgers University Press, 1975. Discusses the tension between Eros and Thanatos in Hawkes's novels in relation to setting, myth, structure, characterization, and narrative focus. Also analyzes Hawkes's use of characters to represent ideas.

Reutlinger, D. P. *"The Cannibal*: The Reality of Victim." *Critique* 6, no. 2 (Fall, 1963): 30-37. Sees the characters as victims of romantic politics and discusses Hawkes's antirealistic art as a way of evoking sympathy through intellectual apprehension of horror.

THE CANTERBURY TALES

Type of work: Poetry
Author: Geoffrey Chaucer (c. 1343-1400)
Type of plot: Romance, farce, fable
Time of plot: Late fourteenth century
Locale: Pilgrimage road between London and Canterbury
First transcribed: 1387-1400

> *Principal characters:*
> CHAUCER, the narrator
> HARRY BAILLY, the host
> THE KNIGHT
> ROBIN, the miller
> ALISON, the wife of Bath
> THE NUN'S PRIEST

The Story:

One April, a group of pilgrims gathered at the Tabard Inn in Southwark near London to embark on a pilgrimage to the shrine of St. Thomas at Canterbury. After dinner, Harry Bailly, the host, proposed a storytelling competition on the journey. The host would judge, and the winner would receive a dinner at the Tabard Inn. The following morning, as they departed, they drew lots to begin. The Knight drew the shortest lot and told his tale.

The Knight's Tale. As Duke Theseus returned to Athens victorious over the Amazons with their queen, Hippolyta, as his wife and with her sister Emily, they encountered women mourning because the Theban king, Creon, refused burial for their husbands, who had besieged Thebes. Duke Theseus then conquered Thebes. He captured two knights, Palamon and Arcite, and imprisoned them.

One May morning, both Palamon and Arcite fell in love with Emily when they saw her walking in the garden. Duke Perotheus, a friend of Duke Theseus, negotiated Arcite's release on the condition that he never return to Athens. Arcite longed for Emily, however, so he disguised himself as a squire, Philostratus, serving at the court of Duke Theseus. Palamon escaped by sedating his jailor.

By chance, Palamon and Arcite met in the woods outside Athens. Duke Theseus found them as they battled over Emily. He decreed that Palamon and Arcite should return in a year to wage a tournament for Emily. Palamon and Arcite gathered with their knights at the new stadium built by Duke Theseus. Palamon was defeated, but Arcite was mortally injured while riding in victory around the stadium. After mourning Arcite, Duke Theseus arranged for the marriage of Palamon and Emily.

After commending the Knight's story, Harry Bailly asked the Monk to continues but Robin, the drunken Miller, insisted on telling his bawdy tale next.

The Miller's Tale. John, an older carpenter who was married to Alison, a pretty young woman, was afraid of her attractiveness to other men. Nicholas, a student who boarded in their house, proposed a tryst with Alison. Absalom, a parish clerk, also tried to court her.

Nicholas contrived a plan to deceive the carpenter. He convinced the carpenter of an impending flood and instructed John to provide tubs and provisions for them. At night, when they retired to their tubs in the attic to await the deluge, the carpenter fell asleep and Nicholas stole away with Alison to her bedroom.

Meanwhile, Absalom wooed Alison outside her room. In the darkness, he asked for a kiss. She stuck her backside out the window. He kissed her backside. Realizing that he had been duped, Absalom obtained a red-hot iron. Absalom returned and asked for another kiss. Nicholas, amazed at Absalom's foolishness and wishing to participate in the jest, stuck his backside out the window while Alison said it was she, and Absalom branded Nicholas with the iron. Nicholas' screams of pain awakened the carpenter, who fell to the ground and broke his arm. Nicholas and Alison convinced the neighbors that the carpenter was delusional about the flood.

After the Reeve, the Cook, and the Man of Law told their stories, the Wife of Bath offered her tale. She prefaced the story with a discourse on marriage, based on her experiences with five husbands.

The Wife of Bath's Tale. There was a knight in King Arthur's court who raped a young woman. The queen interceded and agreed to save the knight's life if he searched for a year to ascertain what women most desire. As he was about to return after an unsuccessful search, he encountered an ugly old woman. She agreed to tell him the answer if he would grant her next request. The knight agreed, was told what women want, and returned to court. When the knight revealed to the queen that women desire power, his answer was accepted. The old woman appeared and demanded that the knight marry her. The knight was reluctant, but changed his mind after the old woman lectured him on the true character of nobility. After the marriage, the old woman was transformed and became young and beautiful.

The Friar, the Summoner, the Clerk, the Merchant, the Franklin, the Physician, the Pardoner, the Shipman, the Prioress, the Monk, and even "Chaucer" himself told their tales as the pilgrims continued toward Canterbury. Because the Monk's Tale was a tragedy that saddened the company, Harry Bailey asked the Nun's Priest to lighten their hearts with a merrier tale.

The Nun's Priest's Tale. Chauntecleer was a vain rooster. One night as Chauntecleer slept beside his favorite hen, Pertelote, he dreamed about a fox. Pertelote did not believe in dreams and chided him for cowardice. Although Chauntecleer thought dreams had veracity, he flew down into the yard the next morning. Sir Russel, the fox, arrived and flattered Chauntecleer into singing. The fox seized Chauntecleer and ran into the woods. Chauntecleer advised the fox to eat him immediately. When the fox opened his mouth to reply, Chauntecleer escaped.

The Nun's Priest's Tale was followed by the Second Nun's Tale, the Canon's Yeoman's Tale, the Manciple's Tale, and finally the Parson's Tale, a long prose tract.

Critical Evaluation:

The Canterbury Tales, Geoffrey Chaucer's last major work, was written between the mid-1380's and his death in 1400, although some of the stories, such as the Knight's Tale, were composed earlier. It is considered to be one of the greatest works of English literature. Most of the work is a poem, but a few of the tales are written in prose. In the twenty-four tales, Chaucer demonstrates mastery of almost every literary genre known in the Middle Ages. These selections include romance (Knight, Wife of Bath), farce (Miller), and beast fable (Nun's Priest). Although many of the stories are not new, Chaucer transforms this material with an originality that makes the tales unique. He imbues his characters with vivacity by skillfully playing types of social classes and occupations against individual details of appearance and mannerisms.

The general prologue sets up the frame narrative of the pilgrimage that provides the rationale for the stories and introduces the pilgrims. The concept of a story collection has antecedents in medieval literature, including the *Decameron*, written in the fourteenth century by the Italian Giovanni Boccaccio. The frame of telling stories on a pilgrimage, however, was unprecedented and creates interaction among the storytellers, which Chaucer exploits. The descriptions of the pilgrims show how well Chaucer combines the typical with the particular. While the "true, perfect, gentle knight" represents the ideal estate of medieval knighthood, the Wife of Bath, a middle-class textile maker, comes to life with more individual details about her appearance and her ability to laugh and gossip.

The Knight's Tale is a romance, a medieval literary genre in which the setting is the distant past, the protagonists are from the nobility, and the plot stems from deeds based on love and chivalry. The Knight's Tale is set in ancient Athens; the principal characters are knights, Palamon and Arcite; and the plot unfolds from their contest to win the love of the noble lady, Emily. Although Boccaccio's *Book of Theseus* (c. 1340-1345) provided the idea, Chaucer shortened and changed the emphasis of Boccaccio's narrative. He also introduced new elements, particularly about the role of fate, from diverse sources. Individual character development is subordinated to maintaining the conventions of the romance genre.

With the drunken Miller's outburst, Chaucer poses a dramatic contrast between the Knight's Tale and the Miller's Tale. The fable told by the Miller is the exact opposite of the Knight's refined, noble romance. Characters in a fable typically are from a lower social class, as is the Miller. John, the husband, is a carpenter; his young wife, Alison, is a pretty, but common, damsel. Her suitors are the student Nicholas and the clerk Absalom. The action takes place in the Oxford of Chaucer's time. The plot generates humor from sexual exploits as Nicholas and Absalom vie for Alison's favors. Chaucer's inspiration came from similar themes that characterize medieval fabliaux. He creates lively characters through their appearance and actions. For example, his lengthy description of Alison utilizes comparisons with animals ("skittish as a colt") to emphasize her playful attractiveness. The fast-moving plot, the contemporaneous setting, and the earthy characters make the Miller's Tale memorable.

With the Wife of Bath, Chaucer returns to the romance genre. The Wife of Bath prefaces her tale with a lengthy discourse on marriage, in which she recounts her life with her trials and triumphs over five different husbands. The prologue allows Chaucer to develop her garrulous character. This passage is famous for the Wife of Bath's diatribe against medieval misogyny.

In contrast, her tale about a knight at King Arthur's court is restrained. Its source is probably English folklore, but it follows the requirements of romance with its setting in Arthurian England and a plot based on a love quest. The tale deals with nobility, not only in the social position of its main characters, including the knight and King Arthur's queen, but also in the old woman's discussion of nobility's true nature. While its point about a wife's dominion over her husband supports the Wife of Bath's position on marriage, the courtly setting and economical narration diminish the impact of its message when compared to the Wife of Bath's vivid discourse and opinions in her prologue.

The Nun's Priest tells a beast fable, in which animal protagonists provide a human moral. The tale of the cock, Chauntecleer, and the fox, Sir Russel, was a well-known beast fable, which Chaucer transforms. First, he amplifies the plot with an extended commentary on the nature of dreams that draws on varied literary sources. Second, the full description of Chauntecleer, "the courtly cock," and his animated conversations with his favorite hen, Pertelote, create characters more real than the humans within the story or even the storyteller. Chaucer again uses his literary talents to create a memorable and distinctive story.

These selections provide only a glimpse into the variety that makes *The Canterbury Tales* such an intriguing literary work. This variety also introduces a question about the unity of *The Canterbury Tales*. The issue is complex because Chaucer died before finishing the work, and the order of the tales, in part, results from editorial efforts made from the fifteenth through the twentieth centuries. Many crucial elements contribute to the artistic integrity of *The Canterbury*

Tales as a complete concept. The frame of the pilgrimage is maintained throughout, and dialogue among the pilgrims links some of the tales, as seen in the transition between the Knight's and Miller's tales. Particular themes repeat themselves; the Wife of Bath's Tale, for example, is one of a "marriage group." In its entirety, *The Canterbury Tales* provides an infinite source for entertainment and enlightenment and remains as engrossing a work of English literature in the twentieth century as when Geoffrey Chaucer first composed it during the fourteenth century.

Karen Gould

Bibliography:
Brown, Peter. *Chaucer at Work: The Making of "The Canterbury Tales."* New York: Longman, 1994. Designed as an introduction to *The Canterbury Tales*, it includes questions for discussion to guide the reader about the workings of Chaucer's literary method. A good place to start a study of *The Canterbury Tales*.
Cooper, Helen. *The Canterbury Tales*. Oxford, England: Clarendon Press, 1989. A complete reference for all basic points about the literary character of *The Canterbury Tales*.
Howard, Donald R. *The Idea of the Canterbury Tales*. Berkeley: University of California Press, 1976. Discusses the concept of *The Canterbury Tales* in terms of style and form as an unfinished but complete literary work.
Leyerle, John, and Anne Quick. *Chaucer: A Bibliographical Introduction*. Toronto: University of Toronto Press, 1986. A bibliographical guide to Chaucer's work with sections on *The Canterbury Tales*, the facts of Chaucer's life, and his rich literary sources.
Pearsall, Derek. *The Canterbury Tales*. Winchester, Mass.: Allen & Unwin, 1985. Approaches *The Canterbury Tales* by genre of stories. Includes helpful discussions of the surviving manuscripts and the reception of *The Canterbury Tales* from 1400 to modern times.

CANTO GENERAL

Type of work: Poetry
Author: Pablo Neruda (Neftalí Ricardo Reyes Basoalto, 1904-1973)
First published: 1950

When Pablo Neruda succumbed to cancer in his sixty-ninth year, he left behind nine unpublished manuscripts: one prose memoir and eight collections of poetry. He had already earned world recognition as one of the most important and prolific poets of his generation. One of the works that had brought him recognition was *Canto general* (general song), which appeared almost exactly at the midpoint of his career. His poetic career spanned about five decades. *Canto general* is a work of immense scope and poetic ambition such as has been accomplished by few poets of any time or place.

The collection is divided into fifteen sections, each section containing from a dozen to more than forty individual poems. The sheer immensity of the work may be intimidating to the uninitiated, but it is a fine place for readers new to Neruda to become acquainted with his work. It provides a compendium of the poet's wide range of interests and gathers in one volume the forms he regularly explored during periods throughout his career. Neruda's passionate interests in history, politics, and nature, and his stunning ability to show the sublime within the mundane are all present in *Canto general* in full working order.

Neruda's emotional and spiritual history and his evolution as a poetic thinker become entwined with the natural history and political evolution of the southern half of the American continent. "A Lamp on Earth," the opening section, begins with "Amor America (1400)." This poem, as do most in this section, operates much in the manner of Neruda's numerous odes. The book's first poem conjures the beauty and relative peace of America prior to the arrival of the conquistadores. The succeeding poems of the opening section sing respectively to "Vegetation," "Some Beasts," "The Birds Arrive," "The Rivers Come Forth," "Minerals," and finally, "Man."

"A Lamp on Earth" is something of a contemporary *Popol Vuh*, the sequence of ancient Mayan creation myths. Neruda's work may be more accurately dubbed a re-creation myth. As in the Mayan vision, each separate element of the natural world is treated to its own individual tale of creation. The creation of the world is described as a series of smaller creations—landscape, vegetation, animals, minerals, people—all of which finally exist together as though by way of some godly experiment. The destruction of Mayan culture by the Spanish is detailed in the third section, which concentrates on a selection of names and places. Before moving into that cataclysmic period, however, Neruda inserts one of the most highly regarded works of his career, "The Heights of Macchu Picchu."

From the age of twenty-one until illness curtailed his ability to travel, Neruda served as diplomatic consul for his native Chile, living in a variety of nations throughout the world. In the years preceding "The Heights of Macchu Picchu," he had been acting consul to Spain, during the unfortunate time when fascism was gaining momentum. Neruda relinquished his post and returned to the Americas. Soon after, during the early 1940's, he traveled to the Andes and saw Macchu Picchu. His journey proved to be a revelatory one, forming the basis of one of his masterpieces.

"The Heights of Macchu Picchu" is a numbered sequence of twelve poems. Taken as an entity separate from the larger work, it is the product of classic poetic inspiration and indicates a turning point in Neruda's work. It is a richly imagistic chronicle of the rebirth of the poet's imagination and heart. The grave disillusion brought about by the tragedy of Spain leads to a renewal of Neruda's recognition of his need for political action. Neruda's renewal is told somewhat in the diction of a manifesto:

> Rise up to be born with me, my brother.
> Give me your hand from the deep
> zone of your disseminated sorrow . . .
> . . . show me the stone on which you fell
> and the wood on which you were crucified. . . .
> Throughout the earth join all
> the silent scattered lips
> and from the depths speak to me all night long,
> as if I were anchored to you. . . .
> Hasten to my veins and to my mouth.
> Speak through my words and my blood.

Neruda's outrage is arguably at its most eloquent in "The Heights of Macchu Picchu." The sequence is equally powerful either in or out of the context of *Canto general.*

His political anger finds an increasingly explicit enunciation in succeeding sections. The work launches into a broad historical epic. "The Conquistadors," another section, includes a series of lyric narrative poems that recall the exploits of Cortés and a selection of his lieutenants. There are also poems of lament, eulogizing and grieving for a lost way of life, and poems about several legendary native resistors.

"The Liberators" and "The Sand Betrayed," the fourth and fifth sections, tell of the political rebels and freedom fighters of the eighteenth and nineteenth centuries. Neruda invokes the reader to join his lamentations for the noble spirits of murdered figures such as José Miguel Carrera, a Chilean rebel of the nineteenth century. Carrera holds a particular place of honor in Neruda's esteem. Carrera's life and work are the focus of a sequence of seven poems within "The Liberators."

Neruda's homage to freedom fighters of the past does not, however, confine itself to those of his native country. Nor are these rebels always soldiers. There is Castro Alves, a Brazilian poet of the nineteenth century, whose voice Neruda assumes throughout the greater portion of one of the fourth section's most eloquent poems:

> Castro Alves from Brazil, for whom did you sing?
> "I sang for the slaves who sailed aboard the ships
> like a dark cluster from the sea of wrath . . .
> I sang in those days against the inferno . . .
> I wanted man's deliverance from man . . .
> My voice knocked on door closed until then
> so that, fighting, Freedom might enter."

There are also tributes to Toussaint-Lóuverture, the eighteenth century liberator of Haiti, the first Latin American nation to become independent; to Emiliano Zapata, the farmer who became an instrumental leader of the Mexican Revolution in the early twentieth century; and to Augusto César Sandino, leader of the war against U.S. military presence in Nicaragua.

Neruda's preferences for communism and freedom are explicit in these poems, and there is little to suggest any distinction in the poet's mind between the two. His communist ideals are rooted in a purer Marxist view than have been practiced in reality. For Neruda, freedom means self rule, regardless of the method, even at mortal costs. More than to any political ideology, Neruda was committed to the notion of class equalization.

Canto general's historical and political poems do not follow a rigid pattern. Neruda' scheme suggests a thematic sense of structure. From "America, I Do Not Invoke Your Name in Vain," the sixth section, and through succeeding sections, the poems become more directly autobiographical. The titles often include dates, focusing on the late 1930's through the late 1940's, just before the book's initial publication in Mexico.

The latter sections of *Canto general* extend the concerns and poetics of "A Lamp on Earth." Nature is seen more often as an entity separate from politics and war. The settings are less likely to appear as battlefields or the hometowns of martyred rebels, but places for solitary reflection, where the poet's personal and aesthetic epiphanies meld with the natural essence of creation at large. Neruda turns more often to the concept of the ode, as in "Hymn and Homecoming," an intensely passionate song of praise to his native land, which appears in the book's seventh section, "Canto General de Chile." This section often returns to specific points of Chilean topography and wildlife. As in earlier sections, several pieces express the poet's admiration of the characteristics of individual species. The "Red-Breasted Meadowlark" and "House Wrens" are described in anthropomorphic terms in comparatively simple lyrics. The creatures Neruda invokes are a source of consolation, an answer to the disappointments dealt with elsewhere.

The seventh section opens with "Eternity," which takes a panoramic view of Neruda's native landscape. The poet conjures himself as a product of his region, becoming integrated with it in dreams. "Eternity" is followed by "Hymn and Homecoming," in which his sad return from Spain brings him to reexamine his country as a source of spiritual nourishment. This is the section in which Neruda takes the opportunity to describe the more personal and confessional facets of the regeneration he writes of in "The Heights of Macchu Picchu."

Neruda specifically mentions numerous places and people high in his esteem throughout the poem. In the fourteenth section, "The Great Ocean," he turns to the lives of mariners and coastal communities. Nowhere is Neruda as openly autobiographical as in the book's closing section, "I Am." A smattering of all the book's formal and thematic components appears in closing, and the poet assumes a more prominent presence in the poems. Again, the land, nature, youth, and the passions for travel and common people are sung to by way of odes, reminiscences, laments, and confessions. Two of the poems, "The War" and "Love," examine Neruda's experience in Spain.

Neruda had turned forty-six by the time *Canto general* was published, having finished the writing at age forty-four. The final poems begin to look at his life as an artist, expressing his state of mind over arriving at the completion of such a monumental work. The poem "I End Here" describes *Canto general* as having been "written on the run." Allowing Neruda his moment of self-deprecation, one cannot avoid the immensity and deeply passionate drive of *Canto general*, even considering the work as part of the canon of a poet known for producing immense and passionate volumes.

Canto general is remarkable for its employment of a free sense of form, an idiomatic eloquence, and its musicality, which owes much to the treasures of the ballad tradition in Spanish. Works such as *Canto general* make one wonder not that Neruda won a Nobel Prize in Literature but rather that he did not win it sooner.

Jon Lavieri

Bibliography:
Bloom, Harold, ed. *Pablo Neruda*. New York: Chelsea House, 1989. A collection of writings

on various aspects of Neruda's work. Includes Federico García Lorca's "Introduction of Pablo Neruda to the School of Philosophy and Letters, Madrid."

Costa, René de. *The Poetry of Pablo Neruda*. Cambridge, Mass.: Harvard University Press, 1979. Analyzes themes and techniques in a selection of Neruda's main works. Among the best sources for a detailed study of *Canto general*.

Duran, Manuel, and Margery Safir. *Earth Tones: The Poetry of Pablo Neruda*. Bloomington: Indiana University Press, 1981. A straightforward overview of Neruda's work, organized thematically.

Teitelboim, Volodia. *Neruda: An Intimate Biography*. Translated by Beverly J. DeLong-Tonelli. Austin: University of Texas Press, 1991. A Chilean novelist, politician, and close personal friend of Neruda provides an excellent and accessible understanding of Neruda's life. Highly recommended.

CANTOS

Type of work: Poetry
Author: Ezra Pound (1885-1972)
First published: 1917; complete edition, 1948

Ezra Pound may be considered one of the most powerful, disturbing, and enigmatic literary figures of the twentieth century. Often his public persona overshadowed his interest in being a poet who would be remembered for his poetry, but part of that was due to Pound's own un-flagging energies and ambitions as an editor, as a friend to writers in exile from America, and as the "foreign correspondent" for Harriet Monroe's 1912 publication *Poetry: A Magazine of Verse.* He was responsible for the final version of T. S. Eliot's *The Waste Land* (1922), he influenced William Carlos Williams, he was instrumental in getting James Joyce published, and he spent time with Ernest Hemingway in Italy. He was the guiding voice behind the Imagist movement in poetry early in the twentieth century, and his association with Benito Mussolini still stands in infamy. Pound's time in a temporary detention center in Pisa, Italy, also still stands in infamy—and led to *The Pisan Cantos*—as does his later imprisonment in St. Elizabeths Hospital in Washington, D.C., from 1945 to 1970.

Many who attempt to analyze Pound's literary career are so struck by its richness that they miss the kernel at the core of his poetry: the *Cantos.* While Pound worked on other types of poetry and poetic movements, his mind and his focus remained on the *Cantos*, which he conceived of as a twentieth century epic. Pound worked on the *Cantos* for nearly fifty years, weaving scores of subjects and themes into the longest important poetic work of the modern era. When he set out on his poetic odyssey, Pound conceived of his poem as a modern version of Dante Alighieri's *The Divine Comedy* (c. 1320); his intention was to mirror Dante's epic organization into "inferno," "purgatory," and "heaven." Pound, following Dante, called the individual units of the epic cantos. Small press publications of parts of the *Cantos* appeared upon occasion, but the poem as a whole was not published until 1948. The publication date was, perhaps, meant to coincide with the availability of *The Pisan Cantos* (1948).

After his release from St. Elizabeths, Pound returned to Italy, where he had about five years of peace. Some who visited him there related that he continued to work on his masterpiece, but there is little, if any, of that work remaining.

Pound's poem *Hugh Selwyn Mauberley* (1920), also considered a classic in the English language, is often discussed in reference to the style of the *Cantos*, although the *Cantos* are much more ambitious. In *Hugh Selwyn Mauberley*, Pound uses a rhetorical persona who reflects on a wide variety of experiences. In many similar ways, the first sixteen cantos use a reactive rhetorical narrator, and at times these two figures have similar interests—not surpris-ing, since the poems began to be composed at about the same time.

There is another influence on Pound's work, that of Eliot's narrator in *The Waste Land.* The difference between Eliot and Pound is clear: Eliot presents a rhetoric rich in narrative, while Pound presents a rhetoric steeped in speculation, myth, and ancient history. Some critics see the first canto as a reflection on Odysseus, and they believe that the Odysseus references are broad rather than specific, but if readers follow the Odysseus beginning, they are able to become grounded in specific myth.

In the *Cantos*, Pound displays his knowledge and his ability to present it without introduc-tions, borders, or transitions. The poem is as much instructive as it is reflective, and it is in part the breadth of Pound's knowledge that has caused so much continued study of the *Cantos.* To as great a degree as may be possible in English or American poetry, this poem is about everything.

Many sections of the poetic discourse written in English are interrupted by quotations from Provençal, Italian, German, French, Latin, and Greek, not to mention Anglo-Saxon and Middle English. There are quotations from the prosy diplomatic correspondence of John Adams, phrases more than a century old and deader in intrinsic interest than that. There are quotations from the fiscal regulations of Leopold of Hapsburg-Lorraine, who instituted good financial conditions in Tuscany before the disaster of Napoleon Bonaparte's arrival. There are abundant references to historical and literary figures good and bad, Oriental and Western. There are references to many people, both well-known and obscure. These people include contemporaries familiar to Pound; through them he memorializes the literary crusades and battles of the first half of the twentieth century. Further, there are many pages adorned with the completely enigmatic ideograms that Pound derived from classical Chinese, which he used to symbolize ideas that were important to him. Pound also translated some foreign-language sources, among which his translations of Japanese poems are considered exemplary.

All this is included and woven into a tight but anecdotal structure that Pound introduces and embroiders with great metrical variety and dexterity. His language varies from noble simplicity and elegance through imitations of the banality (with which people of all ages have conducted the affairs of the world) to the argot of the illiterate. A special interest appears in the section entitled *The Pisan Cantos*, in which Pound describes his life in a prison camp at Pisa, working on an installment of his masterwork.

Many of the sections of the poem are highly musical, and Pound was virtuosic in his use of forms, but he never forgot the lessons of his early villanelles and of his poem "Sestina: Altaforte," which some see in the *Cantos*, in smaller form. Pound also used the technique of the theatrical mask, taken from Greek tragedy. His speakers are often half-revealed or not revealed at all. This adds a dramatic texture and a certain richness to the poem and, once again, satisfies Pound's need to say as much as possible, to be as allusive as possible.

Most versions of the *Cantos* rely heavily on footnotes to direct the reader elsewhere, often to moments or events in the poet's life. Just as often the footnotes fill in historical or mythological information. When reading the *Cantos*, it must be remembered that Pound was attempting to write an epic poem and that he was very aware of his ambition and the requirements for an epic. He did not follow these requirements, however, because they would not have worked—and that lesson is as important as any other lesson about this work.

To a great degree, the *Cantos* are Pound's reactions to and reflections of his own almost limitless reading and to his broad knowledge and curiosity about his world and the worlds that had preceded him. There are references to influences noted elsewhere, to Homer, to Ovid, and to Remy de Gourmont. Contemporary literary figures and occasions in Paris and London, his important meetings with William Butler Yeats in 1908 and later are also included, as are earlier poems by Pound.

Strange and without many literary parallels in its lack of plan and in its preference for jumble rather than clarity, the continuing poem that is the *Cantos* is a record of the workings of a sophisticated and ingenious mind that conducted a decades-long war with a world out of joint. In this work, language is in decay, social life is ebbing, and the economic system is a center of rot. The *Cantos* represents a break with the going social order and the modes of literary expression grateful to that order. Pound, in a phrase he derives from the Chinese, must "make things new." The techniques of confusion, blending, and non sequitur in the poem are techniques of assault; indurated sensibility must be awakened, and new habits of direct, nonabstract apprehension must be set up. Pound gathers hints from Homer, Confucius, the Provençal poets, and countless other writers who managed to be "human." By tearing apart the tapestry of the conventionally viewed past and weaving the threads into a new pattern of his own, Pound assaults ingrained and complacent sensibilities.

Pound also startles conventional and unreflective moral tastes by expressing admiration for such "natural" monsters as Sigismundo Malatesta, whose evil was at least direct and not transmogrified into a neutral entry in a ledger. One must have, in the world of the *Cantos*, a considerable amount of sin; in "good" ages, unlike the poet's own, sin and virtue declare themselves for what they are and do not masquerade as something else.

Thus the organized confusion of the *Cantos* becomes the pattern of Pound's own outraged and crusading sensibility. What the poem expresses is always clear to that sensibility. If it is not clear to those of his readers, then, according to the poet, so much the worse for them and their responses and blindness. Such, at any rate, is the intransigent accent of many a canto.

Many critics consider the *Cantos* to be flawed, but even such critics marvel at what Pound was able to do in an epic poem of the twentieth century. This poem shows what can be done within the poetic medium, and Pound will always be one of the great literary masters because of it.

Updated by John Jacob

Bibliography:
Baumann, Walter. *A Rose in the Steel Dust: An Examination of The Cantos of Ezra Pound.* Coral Gables, Fla.: University of Miami Press, 1970. A revisionist examination of the *Cantos*, with a view toward the post-industrial age seen through Pound's extreme interest in Dante and the French Provençal troubadours.
Emery, Clark. *Ideas into Action: A Study of Pound's Cantos.* Coral Gables, Fla.: University of Miami Press, 1958. One of the original sources on the *Cantos*, written well after *The Pisan Cantos* but well before Pound's release from St. Elizabeths and the official ending of the poetry sequence. Analyzes the active in relation to the passive.
Goodwin, K. L. *The Influence of Ezra Pound.* New York: Oxford University Press, 1976. Places the poet firmly in the pantheon of modern poets, largely because of his having attempted the epic poem the *Cantos*.
Kenner, Hugh. *The Poetry of Ezra Pound.* Norfolk, Conn.: New Directions, 1951. With Donald Davie, Kenner is the foremost authority on Pound, his work, and his influence. Chapters are devoted to the *Cantos*, but Kenner explains how the sequence drew together common threads in all Pound's work.
Leary, Lewis, ed. *Motive and Method in The Cantos of Ezra Pound.* New York: Columbia University Press, 1954. Early treatment of the epic poem. Explores both political statements, prosody, and technique in Pound's fusion of myth and personal statement.

CAPTAIN HORATIO HORNBLOWER

Type of work: Novel
Author: C. S. Forester (1899-1966)
Type of plot: Historical
Time of plot: Early nineteenth century
Locale: Pacific Ocean, South America, the Mediterranean, Spain, France, England, and the
 Atlantic Ocean
First published: 1939: *Beat to Quarters*, 1937; *Ship of the Line*, 1938; *Flying Colours*, 1939

>*Principal characters:*
>CAPTAIN HORATIO HORNBLOWER, the captain of HMS *Lydia* and HMS
> *Sutherland*
>BUSH, the first lieutenant
>BROWN, the captain's coxswain
>DON JULIAN ALVARADO (EL SUPREMO), a rich plantation owner in
> Central America
>MARIA, Hornblower's wife
>LADY BARBARA WELLESLEY, the sister of the duke of Wellington
>ADMIRAL LEIGHTON, Hornblower's immediate commander and Lady
> Barbara's husband

The Story:

Captain Horatio Hornblower, the commander of the thirty-six-gun frigate HMS *Lydia*, was sailing under sealed orders from England around the Horn to the Gulf of Fonseca on the western shores of Spanish America. He had been ordered to form an alliance with Don Julian Alvarado, a large landowner, and assist in raising a rebellion against Spain. The *Lydia* carried the necessary munitions with which to start the revolution. In addition, Hornblower had fifty thousand guineas in gold, which he was to give for the support of the rebellion only if the revolt threatened to fail without English gold to back it. If he did otherwise, he would be court-martialed. His orders also casually mentioned the presence in Pacific waters of a fifty-gun Spanish ship called the *Natividad*, which he was ordered to take, sink, burn, or destroy at the first opportunity.

After the *Lydia* had anchored in the Gulf of Fonseca, a small boat appeared with emissaries from Don Julian, who now called himself El Supremo. They told Hornblower that El Supremo required the captain's attendance. Hornblower was not pleased with evidences of El Supremo's tyranny. What he observed made him all the more cautious. He refused to hand over to El Supremo the arms and ammunition that he had until his ship had taken on food and water. The ship was loaded with stores as rapidly as possible, and the operation was going forward when a lookout on the mountain announced the approach of the *Natividad*.

Deciding to try to capture her in the bay, Hornblower hid the *Lydia* behind an island as the *Natividad* approached. At the moment of greatest advantage, Hornblower ordered the ship to sail alongside the *Natividad* and rake her decks with grapeshot. The British sailors lashed the two ships together and boarded the *Natividad*. El Supremo demanded the captured ship as his own. Hornblower hesitated to turn over his prize to El Supremo, but if he were to fulfill his orders he dared not antagonize the dictator.

Hornblower sailed away and shortly afterward learned that upon Napoleon's deposition of King Ferdinand, England was now an ally of Spain. He also received further orders, one from his admiral and one from an Englishwoman in Panama, Lady Barbara Wellesley, the duke of Wellington's sister, who requested transportation to England. During this period, the *Lydia* met and defeated the *Natividad*, now commanded by El Supremo. The long period together on board ship led to a deep love between Lady Barbara and Hornblower, but the captain could not bring himself to act on that love because of his wife, Maria, at home. Lady Barbara was carried safely to England.

Captain Horatio Hornblower was next ordered to command HMS *Sutherland*, a seventy-four-gun battleship. He sailed with the *Pluto* and the *Caligula* to protect a convoy of merchant ships as far as the latitude of North Africa. They then met French privateers and beat them off. Before parting company with the merchantmen, Hornblower impressed sailors from the convoy. Sailing along the coast, he captured the *Amelie*, attacked the battery at Llanza, burned and destroyed supply vessels, and shelled two divisions of cavalry on a highway passing near the seashore.

Admiral Leighton, now the husband of Lady Barbara, ordered Hornblower to join and take charge of Spanish forces at the siege of French-held Rosas, but the operation failed because the Spaniards did not cooperate. After his retreat, Hornblower met the *Cassandra*, a British frigate, and he learned that four French ships were bearing down upon them. Hornblower decided to fight, even though the odds were four to one, and he sent the *Cassandra* to seek the *Pluto* and the *Caligula*. The *Cassandra* came back with a message to Hornblower to engage the enemy, an order that indicated the presence of the admiral's flagship. Hornblower engaged the French ships one at a time. The fourth French ship, however, came upon him as he was fighting a two-decker and forced him to surrender.

After his surrender, Hornblower and Bush were imprisoned at Rosas. Admiral Leighton sailed into the bay with the *Pluto* and the *Caligula* and completed the destruction of the French squadron. Hornblower watched the battle from the walls and saw the *Sutherland*, which had been beached, take fire as a raiding party of British seamen burned her to prevent her use by the French. He learned from a seaman that Admiral Leighton had been injured by a flying splinter.

Colonel Caillard, Napoleon's aide, came to Rosas to take Hornblower and the wounded Bush to Paris. Bush was seriously ill as a result of losing a foot in the battle; therefore, Hornblower requested a servant to attend Bush on the long journey. He selected Brown, the coxswain, because of his strength, his common sense, and his ability to adapt himself to every situation. In France, their stagecoach was halted by a snowstorm near Nevers. Hornblower had noticed a small boat moored to the bank of a river and, as he and Brown assisted the French in trying to move the coach, he laid his plans for escape. He himself attacked Colonel Caillard, and Brown tied up the Frenchman and threw him into the bottom of the coach. They lifted Bush out of the coach and carried him to the boat. The whole operation required only six minutes.

In the dead of night, the fugitives made their way down the river; Hornblower rowed while Brown bailed the icy water from the boat. When the boat crashed against a rock, Hornblower, thinking he had lost Bush and Brown, swam ashore in the darkness. Brown, however, brought Bush safely to shore. Shivering with cold, the three men made their way to a farmhouse nearby, where they announced themselves as prisoners of war and were admitted.

Throughout the winter, they remained as guests of its owner, Comte de Gracay, and his daughter-in-law. Brown made an artificial foot for Bush and, when Bush was able to get around well, he and Brown built a boat in which to travel down the Loire. In early summer, Hornblower disguised himself as a Dutch customs inspector. To complete his disguise, the comte gave him the ribbon of the Legion of Honor that had been his son's. That decoration aided Hornblower in his escape.

When Hornblower and his two men arrived in the harbor at Nantes, Hornblower cleverly took possession of the *Witch of Endor*, taking with him a group of prisoners to be the crew, and made his way back to England. Upon his arrival, Hornblower was praised for his exploits, knighted, and whitewashed at a court-martial. His sickly wife had died during his absence, and Lady Barbara had become guardian of his young son. Hornblower went to visit Lady Barbara and to see his son. Admiral Leighton had died of wounds at Gibraltar, and Barbara was now a widow. Hornblower realized from the quiet warmth of her welcome that she was already his. He was grateful to life for having given him fame and fortune and Barbara.

Critical Evaluation:

C. S. Forester's *Captain Horatio Hornblower*, itself composed of three short novels—*Beat to Quarters*, *Ship of the Line*, and *Flying Colours*—falls in the middle of a series that begins with the intrepid officer's sea apprenticeship and concludes with *Commodore Hornblower* (1945), *Lord Hornblower* (1946), and *Admiral Hornblower in the West Indies* (1958). For its broad scope and sustained vigor, the whole series has appropriately been described as a modern saga. While Forester's Hornblower stories lack the philosophical and moral dimension of the sea fiction of Joseph Conrad, Richard Henry Dana, and Herman Melville, they certainly are the equal of sea-adventure novels by Captain Frederick Marryat or James Fenimore Cooper. Forester's novels combine meticulous historical reconstruction with a flair for storytelling. In 1932, he began writing screenplays for Hollywood. Unlike many other distinguished novelists who either failed or were only moderately successful in adapting their skills to this medium, Forester excelled as a scriptwriter and thereby learned how to use certain cinematic techniques in his fiction. Lively and fast-paced, the Hornblower stories, in which each scene builds to a climax, are easy to visualize. They are also based on historical information. The celebrated battle scenes bristle with sharp, concrete details that capture the excitement of the moment, and in Forester's descriptions of English manners, customs, and topical interests during the early nineteenth century, the robust age comes alive.

A realist, Forester does not gloss over the unpleasant truths about warfare at sea or the rigors of nautical life. Early in *Captain Horatio Hornblower*, readers learn that Hankey, the previous surgeon attached to HMS *Lydia*, died of the complications of drink and syphilis. Hornblower must perform several grisly operations on his wounded men. After one battle in *Beat to Quarters*, he cuts out a great splinter of wood lodged in a seaman's chest. Forester does not spare his readers the terrible details of Hornblower's crude operation, in which he uses no anesthetic. In *Flying Colours*, Hornblower must relieve the gangrenous pressure on the stump of his friend Bush's amputated leg. Applying cold vinegar to the stump to reduce the inflammation, he opens, cleans, and then sews up the victim's wound. Many such similar scenes of grim realism impart a sense of truth to the plots. In *Beat to Quarters*, Hornblower sees a man horribly tortured by the cruel El Supremo for no reason but that the man has been judged "one of the unenlightened." Hornblower also witnesses the aftermath of battle: "dirty bodies with blood and pus and vomit." Forester creates realistic touches not only in the stark scenes of battle but also in the smallest details. He describes how ships are loaded with provisions, how the officers and crew function in a hierarchy of responsibilities, and how the ships operate in calm or storm. At one point, Hornblower's friend Gailbraith describes a poem that he admires, "The Lay of the Last Minstrel," whose author is "an Edinburgh lawyer." Instead of identifying the author as Sir Walter Scott, Forester thus creates a sense of contemporaneity, for at the time of the action, Scott was not yet famous and might easily have been known primarily as a lawyer who dabbled in poetry.

In his characterization of Horatio Hornblower, Forester provides sharp, realistic details that make his hero seem human. Although he is high-minded, courageous, and capable, Hornblower is not without frailties. He is vain, sometimes squeamish, and—strange to say—naturally indolent. Near the beginning of *Beat to Quarters*, Hornblower views himself critically in a mirror, noting all of his physical liabilities as well as his strengths. He does not like his "rounded belly" and fears that he is growing bald. Several times in the book he reflects unhappily on his receding hairline. For a hero, he has a weak stomach for scenes of squalor or bloodshed. He must be shamed by Lady Barbara Wellesley before he allows her to dress the wounds of the injured. Furthermore, he is, by his own admission, lazy. After a battle involving the *Lydia*, Hornblower retires to his hammock to sleep. Although he feels "a prick of shame" that the other officers and men have to clean up the bodies and wreckage, he confesses to his physical limitations. Again, in *Flying Colours*, he wishes "to be idle and lazy." When his gentle wife, Maria, dies, he is plunged into grief; when he holds his child in his arms, he feels paternal elation; and when he courts Lady Barbara, he is an ardent yet awkward lover. Forester humanizes Hornblower, making him a man as well as a hero and thus a hero worthy of his victories.

Bibliography:
Forester, C. S. *The Hornblower Companion*. Boston: Little, Brown, 1964. The fullest account Forester left of the creative processes that led to the inception of the Hornblower series. In two parts, the first a useful atlas of thirty annotated maps depicting events in the Hornblower saga, and the second the essay "Some Personal Notes," in which Forester explains how he came to write each novel.

_____. *Long Before Forty*. Boston: Little, Brown, 1968. Posthumously published autobiography that Forester completed before he began the Hornblower saga. An appendix contains "Some Personal Notes," the memoir he wrote for *The Hornblower Companion*.

Parkinson, C. Northcote. *The Life and Times of Horatio Hornblower*. London: Joseph, 1970. A pseudobiography of Forester's fictional character by a trained naval historian. Parkinson's creative solutions to gaps in the Hornblower saga have little to do with Forester; however, his knowledge of British naval history helps place Hornblower's fictional adventures in a broader historical context.

Sternlicht, Sanford. *C. S. Forester*. Boston: Twayne, 1981. The only scholarly work on C. S. Forester, a lucidly written book that devotes a long chapter to the Hornblower saga. Using Forester's "Some Personal Notes" as his starting point, Sternlicht examines Hornblower as Forester's most fully realized "man alone." He suggests that the historical British naval hero Thomas Cochrane (1775-1860) may have served as a model for Hornblower, and he discusses the significance of the Hornblower stories in bolstering British morale during World War II, when the "Captain" books first appeared.

CAPTAINS COURAGEOUS

Type of work: Novel
Author: Rudyard Kipling (1865-1936)
Type of plot: Adventure
Time of plot: 1890's
Locale: Grand Banks of Newfoundland
First published: 1897

> *Principal characters:*
> HARVEY CHEYNE, a spoiled young rich boy
> DISKO TROOP, the owner and captain of the *We're Here*
> DAN TROOP, his son
> MR. CHEYNE, Harvey's father

The Story:

Harvey Cheyne was a rich, spoiled fifteen-year-old boy, bound for Europe aboard a swift ocean liner. He was so seasick that he hardly realized what was happening to him when a huge wave washed him over the rail of the ship into the sea. Luckily, he was picked up by a fisherman in a dory and put aboard the fishing schooner *We're Here*. The owner and captain of the boat, Disko Troop, was not pleased to have the boy aboard but told him that he would pay him ten dollars a month and board until the schooner docked in Gloucester the following September. It was then the middle of May. Harvey insisted that he be taken to New York immediately, asserting that his father would gladly pay for the trip, but the captain, doubting that Harvey's father was a millionaire, refused to change his plans and hazard the profits of the fishing season. When Harvey became insulting, Disko Troop promptly punched him in the nose to teach him manners.

The captain's son, Dan, was glad to have someone his own age aboard the fishing boat, and he soon became a friend of the castaway. Harvey's stories about mansions, private cars, and dinner parties fascinated him. Dan recognized that Harvey was telling the truth and that he could not possibly have made up so many details of a wealthy person's life.

Harvey began to fit into the life aboard the schooner. All the fishermen took an interest in his nautical education, and Long Jack taught him the names of the ropes and the various pieces of equipment. Harvey learned quickly, partly because he was a bright young lad and partly because Long Jack whipped him with the end of a rope when he gave the wrong answers. He also learned how to swing the dories aboard when they were brought alongside with the day's catch, to help clean the cod and salt them away below the decks, and to stand watch at the wheel of the schooner as they moved from one fishing ground on the Grand Banks to the next. Even Disko Troop began to admit that the boy would be a good hand before they reached Gloucester in the fall.

Gradually, Harvey became accustomed to the sea. There were times of pleasure as well as work. He enjoyed listening while the other eight members of the crew talked and told sea yarns in the evenings or on the days when it was too rough to lower the dories and go after cod. He discovered that the crew came from all over the world. Disko Troop and his son were from Gloucester, Long Jack was from Ireland, Manuel was a Portuguese, Salters was a farmer, Pennsylvania was a former preacher who had lost his family in the Johnstown flood, and the cook was a black man who had been brought up in Nova Scotia and swore in Gaelic. These men fascinated Harvey, for they were different from anyone he had ever known. What pleased the boy most was that they accepted him on his own merits as a workman and a member of the crew and not as the heir to millions. Of all the crew, only Dan and the black cook believed Harvey's account of himself.

One day, a French brig hailed the *We're Here*. Both vessels shortened sail, and Harvey and Long Jack were sent from the schooner to the brig to buy tobacco. Much to Harvey's chagrin, he discovered that the sailors on the French boat could hardly understand his schoolboy French but that they understood Long Jack's sign language perfectly.

The French brig figured in another of Harvey's adventures. He and Dan went aboard the ship at a later time to buy a knife that had belonged to a deceased sailor. Dan bought the knife and gave it to Harvey, thinking it had added value because the Frenchman had killed a man with it. While fishing from a dory several days later, Harvey felt a weight on his line and pulled in the Frenchman's corpse. The boys cut the line and threw the knife into the sea; it seemed to them that the Frenchman had returned to claim his knife.

Although they were the same age, Harvey was not nearly as handy on the schooner or in the dory as Dan was, who had grown up around fishing boats and fishermen, but Harvey surpassed Dan in the use of a sextant. His acquaintance with mathematics and his ability to use his knowledge seemed enormous to the simple sailors. So impressed was Disko Troop that he began to teach Harvey what he knew about navigation.

Early in September, the *We're Here* joined the rest of the fishing fleet at a submerged rock where the cod fishing was at its best, and the fishermen worked around the clock to finish loading the holds with cod and halibut. The vessel that first filled its holds was not only honored by the rest of the fleet, it also got the highest price for the first cargo into port. For the past four years, the *We're Here* had finished first, and it won honors again the year Harvey was aboard. All canvas was set, the flag was hoisted, and the schooner made the triumphant round of the fleet, picking up letters to be taken home. The homeward-bound men were the envy of all the other fishermen.

As soon as the *We're Here* had docked at Gloucester, Harvey sent a telegram to his father informing him that he had not been drowned but was well and healthy. Mr. Cheyne wired back that he would take his private car and travel to Gloucester as quickly as he could leave California. Disko Troop and the rest of the crew, except Dan and the black cook, were greatly surprised to discover that Harvey had been telling the truth.

Mr. Cheyne and Harvey's mother were overjoyed to see their son, and their happiness was further increased when they observed how much good the work aboard the fishing schooner had done him. It had changed Harvey from a snobbish adolescent into a self-reliant young man who knew how to make a living with his hands and who valued people for what they were rather than for the money they had. Mr. Cheyne, who had built up a fortune after a childhood of poverty, was particularly glad to see his son's improvement.

Disko Troop and the crew of the *We're Here* refused to accept any reward for themselves. Dan was given the chance to become an officer on a fleet of fast freighters that Mr. Cheyne owned. The cook left the sea to become a bodyguard for Harvey. In later years, when Harvey had control of the Cheyne interests, the man got a great deal of satisfaction out of reminding Dan, who was by then a mate on one of Harvey's ships, that he had told the two boys years before that some day Harvey would be Dan's master.

Critical Evaluation:

Captains Courageous was written in 1896 while Rudyard Kipling was living in the forests of Vermont. The period during which Great Britain's poet laureate—who wrote during Britain's imperial heyday when "the sun never set" on an empire stretching "from palm to pine"—wrote a sea story while living in the North American woods is a little known phase of the writer's career. Kipling loved Vermont's forests, especially during the colorful Indian summer season, but he also deeply appreciated the vital kinship between America and Great Britain. He equated such Captains Courageous of the Grand Banks as Disko Troop with the pioneers who journeyed into the American-Canadian West (Daniel Boone, George Vancouver, and Kit Carson, as well as railroad magnates like King Cheyne) with Sir Francis Drake, Sir John Hawkins, Sir Martin Frobisher, Sir Walter Ralegh, Sir Philip Sidney, and other bold Elizabethan adventurers. He believed that the Elizabethan spirit of adventure and accomplishment survived in the modern fishing captains and railroad magnates and that they were blood brothers of the earlier Anglo-Saxon adventurers, displaying the same spirit of freedom, free enterprise, and bravery against odds.

Kipling had lived for many years among Asian peoples, where he believed that people of his kind could never exist naturally and thus could never be more than a dissolving white drop in a colored ocean. Partly for that reason, Kipling experienced great relief to find himself in Vermont. It must, however, be conceded that in *Captains Courageous* Kipling reveals a certain typical respect for all sturdy breeds. The British poet implies that men and the civilizations they create need challenges, not security, and must maintain healthy folk instincts while rearing each generation of their own kind in hardiness. In *Captains Courageous*, the representatives of European, expansionist, seafaring races—British, French, German, Portuguese—who have braved the Grand Banks for centuries are favorably presented, as is the black cook. His nineteenth century racist belief in a white man's burden notwithstanding, Kipling sometimes praised members of other races such as the tough Sudanese.

The novel stresses traditional virtues like those of Horatio Alger. Harvey Cheyne learns practical skills and escapes emasculating luxury. He also learns the salutary value of hard work, sweat, and plain living, and he returns to nature and healthy simplicity by recapturing his self-reliance amid the sheer beauty of the high seas. The physical environment of sea and shore is thus a character in the story, and it has been pointed out that *Captains Courageous* concerns the environment more than it does the protagonist. Even the theme of the boy's conversion stems from environment, though it is also linked to individual will and hereditary character. The driving ambition of Harvey's father, King Cheyne, is paralleled in Kipling's eulogy of the redoubtable fishermen who brave cold storms and fogs off the Grand Banks to fish for cod in their small dories. A millionaire's son becomes a man through enduring hardships on a fishing boat and through sharing the lot of toiling fishermen from Massachusetts, Canada, Germany, and Portugal.

The very pith of Kipling's story can be found in King Cheyne's conversation with the redeemed young Harvey when the father relates the story of his life—how he had to toil for everything he earned; how he fought Indians and border ruffians before the West was tamed; how he encountered deadly struggles against odds; and how he built his railroad empire. He stresses the progress that railroads represented, enabling families to cross the immense and mountainous continent without suffering for months in covered wagons, sometimes having to bury their children along the way, as they had been forced to do before Cheyne built his railroads. Infused with the pride at his heritage, young Harvey returns to Gloucester, borrows money from his father, and invests it in fishing boats. Hiring some of the friends he had made on his first fishing expedition, Harvey starts his own fishing empire in the true Anglo-American tradition of creative enterprise.

Kipling's familiarity with the sea is evident. His descriptions of life on a fishing vessel, of how fish are caught and processed, and of the abrupt tragedies that sometimes overtake the "captains courageous" are not superficial. He evidently familiarized himself with the Gloucester accents and the idiom as well, for they are reproduced with the idiomatic skill for which Kipling is noted. Like so many Kipling works, *Captains Courageous* is easy for children to read, enjoy, and understand, but its meanings are subtle and its literary virtues considerable.

After experiencing personal troubles and an unfortunate lawsuit, Kipling left Vermont. It is interesting to note that shortly after this military poet wrote one of the better novels of North Atlantic sea literature, he composed his famous *Recessional* honoring Queen Victoria's Diamond Jubilee in London in 1897. On this august occasion, rather than vaunting Great Britain's military might, however, Kipling shocked Empire enthusiasts by worrying over the fact that England's regiments were shedding their blood over the entire earth and that Royal Navy ships were sinking on distant headland and dune. Fearing "lest we be one with Nineveh and Tyre," Kipling wrote "Lord God of hosts, be with us yet, be with us yet." Retroactively, he shed light on the beliefs underlying his reasons for having written *Captains Courageous*.

"Critical Evaluation" by William Freitas

Bibliography:
Gross, John, ed. *Rudyard Kipling: The Man, His Work, and His World*. London: Weidenfeld & Nicolson, 1972. Presents interesting background on *Captains Courageous* based on earlier materials and sketches that Kipling developed in the book. Argues that different sections of the novel fail to mesh.
Kipling, Rudyard. *Something of Myself: For My Friends Known and Unknown*. 3d ed. New York: Doubleday, Doran, 1937. Fascinating autobiography that provides insight into Kipling's detailed preparations for writing, which included his having boarded ships, prepared fish, and analyzed fishing charts and railway timetables.
Mason, Philip. *Kipling: The Glass, the Shadow, and the Fire*. New York: Harper & Row, 1975. Studies Kipling's development as a man and an artist. Argues that the plot and characters are weak but praises the atmospheric portrayal of the fisherman's world on the ship, where hard physical work is in conflict with the natural power of the seas.
Moss, Robert. *Rudyard Kipling and the Fiction of Adolescence*. New York: St. Martin's Press, 1982. Good introduction discussing thematic contrast between the crew of *We're Here*, whose codes of behavior and values are based on years of tradition, and the self-centered world of Harvey and the new industrial age represented by his father. Concludes that Kipling admires values in both but finds the former more sympathetic.
Shahane, Vasant. *Rudyard Kipling: Activist and Artist*. Carbondale: Southern Illinois University Press, 1973. Excellent introductory study. Argues that the novel breaks traditional form and excels in observation and descriptive detail, which sweep the reader into the world of the sea, a microcosm of the larger world. Also analyzes Kipling's treatment of character, theme, and setting.

THE CAPTAIN'S DAUGHTER

Type of work: Novel
Author: Alexander Pushkin (1799-1837)
Type of plot: Historical
Time of plot: c. 1774
Locale: Russia
First published: Kapitanskaya dochka, 1836 (English translation, 1846)

Principal characters:
PETER ANDREITCH GRINEFF, a young Russian officer
MARIA IVANOVNA, his sweetheart
ALEXEY IVANITCH SHVABRIN, Peter's fellow officer
SAVELITCH, Peter's servant
EMELYAN POUGATCHEFF, a rebel Cossack leader

The Story:

Although Peter Andreitch Grineff was registered as a sergeant in the Semenovsky regiment when he was very young, he was given leave to stay at home until he had completed his studies. When he was nearly seventeen years old, his father decided that the time had come for him to begin his military career. With his parents' blessing, Peter set out for distant Orenburg in the company of his faithful servant, Savelitch.

One night, the travelers put up at Simbirsk. There, while Savelitch went to make some purchases, Peter was lured into playing billiards with a fellow soldier, Zourin, and quickly lost one hundred rubles. Toward evening of the following day, the young man and Savelitch found themselves on the snowy plain with a storm approaching. As darkness fell, the snow grew thicker, until finally the horses could not find their way and the driver confessed that he was lost. They were rescued by another traveler, a man with such sensitive nostrils that he was able to scent smoke from a village some distance away and lead them to it. The three men and their guide spent the night in the village. The next morning, Peter presented his sheepskin jacket to his poorly dressed rescuer. Savelitch warned Peter that the coat would probably be pawned for drink.

Late that day, the young man reached Orenburg and presented himself to the general in command. The general decided that there was a danger that the dull life at Orenburg might lead the young man into a career of dissipation; therefore, he sent him to the Bailogorsk fortress garrison under Captain Mironoff.

The Bailogorsk fortress, on the edge of the Kirghis steppes, was nothing more than a village surrounded by a log fence. Its real commandant was not Captain Mironoff but his lady, Vassilissa Egorovna, a lively, firm woman who saw to the discipline of her husband's underlings as well as the running of her own household.

Peter quickly made friends with a fellow officer, Shvabrin, who had been exiled to the steppes for fighting a duel. Peter spent much time with his captain's family and grew deeply attached to the couple and to their daughter, Maria Ivanovna. After he received his commission, he found military discipline so relaxed that he was able to indulge his literary tastes.

The quiet routine of Peter's life was interrupted by an unexpected quarrel with Shvabrin precipitated by his having shown his friend a love poem he had written to Maria. Shvabrin criticized the work severely, and when he made derogatory remarks about Maria they quarreled and Peter found himself challenged to a duel for having called him a liar. The next morning, they met in a field to fight but were stopped because Vassilissa Egorovna had learned of the duel. Peter and Shvabrin, although ostensibly reconciled, nevertheless intended to carry out their duel at the earliest opportunity. Discussing the quarrel with Maria, Peter learned that she had once rejected Shvabrin.

Having assured themselves that they were not watched, Shvabrin and Peter fought their duel the following day. Wounded in the breast, Peter lay unconscious for five days after the fight. When he began to recover, he asked Maria to marry him. Shvabrin had been jailed. Peter's father wrote to say that he disapproved of a match with Captain Mironoff's daughter and that he intended to have his son transferred from the fortress so that he might forget his foolish ideas. Savelitch denied having written a letter home, so Peter concluded that Shvabrin had been the informer.

Life would have become unbearable for the young man after his father's letter arrived if Captain Mironoff had not one evening informed his officers that the Yaikian Cossacks, led by Emelyan Pougatcheff, who claimed to be the dead Emperor Peter III, had risen and were sacking fortresses and committing outrages everywhere. The captain ordered his men to keep on the alert and to ready the cannon.

The news of Pougatcheff's uprising quickly spread through the garrison. Many of the Cossacks of the town sided with the rebels, so Captain Mironoff did not know whom he could trust or who might betray him. It was not long before he received an ultimatum from the leader of the Cossacks ordering him to surrender. The Mironoffs decided that Maria should be sent back to Orenburg, but the attack came early the next morning before she had left. Captain Mironoff and his officers made a valiant effort to defend the town, but with the aid of Cossack traitors inside the walls, Pougatcheff was soon master of the fortress.

Captain Mironoff and his aides were hanged. Shvabrin deserted to the rebels. Peter, at the intercession of old Savelitch, was spared by Pougatcheff. The townspeople and the garrison soldiers had no scruples about transferring their allegiance to the rebel leader. Vassilissa Egorovna was slain when she cried out against her husband's murderer.

When Pougatcheff and his followers rode off to inspect the fortress, Peter began his search for Maria. To his great relief, he found that she had been hidden by the wife of the village priest and that Shvabrin, who knew her whereabouts, had not revealed her identity. He learned from Savelitch that the servant had recognized Pougatcheff as the man to whom he had given his hareskin coat months before. Later, the rebel leader sent for Peter and acknowledged his identity. He tried to persuade Peter to join the Cossacks but respected his wish to rejoin his own forces at Orenburg. The next day, Peter and his servant were given safe conduct, and Pougatcheff gave Peter a horse and a sheepskin coat for the journey.

Several days later, the Cossacks attacked Orenburg. During a sally, Peter received a disturbing message from one of the Bailogorsk Cossacks that Shvabrin was forcing Maria to marry him. Peter went at once to the general and tried to persuade him to raise the siege and go to the rescue of the village. When the general refused, Peter and Savelitch started out once more for the Bailogorsk fortress. Intercepted and taken before Pougatcheff, Peter persuaded the rebel to give Maria safe conduct to Orenburg.

On the way, they met a detachment of soldiers led by Captain Zourin, who persuaded Peter to send Maria to Savelitch's family under his protection, while he himself remained with the troops in Orenburg. The siege of Orenburg was finally lifted, and the army began its task of tracking down rebel units. Some months later, Peter found himself near his own village and set off alone to visit his parents' estate. Reaching his home, he found the serfs in rebellion and his family and Maria captives. That day, Shvabrin swooped down upon them with his troops. He was about to have all of them except Maria hanged, when they were rescued by Zourin's men. The renegade was shot during the encounter and taken prisoner.

Peter's parents had changed their attitude toward the captain's daughter, and Peter was able to rejoin Captain Zourin with the expectation that he and Maria would be wed in a month. Then an order came for his arrest. He was accused of having been in the pay of Pougatcheff, of spying for the rebel, and of having taken presents from him. The author of the accusations was the captive, Shvabrin. Though Peter could easily have cleared himself by summoning Maria as a witness, he decided not to drag her into the matter. He was sentenced to spend the rest of his life in exile in Siberia.

Maria, however, was not one to let matters stand. Leaving Peter's parents, she traveled to St. Petersburg and went to Tsarskoe Selo, where the court was located. Walking in the garden there one day, she met a woman who declared that she went to court on occasion and would be pleased to present her petition to the empress. Maria was summoned to the royal presence the same day and discovered that it was the empress herself to whom she had spoken. Peter was pardoned, and soon afterward he and the captain's daughter were married.

Critical Evaluation:

The longest of Alexander Pushkin's completed prose tales, *The Captain's Daughter* was based on true events that Pushkin wrote as history in his 1834 *Istoria Pugachev* (*The History of the Pugachev Rebellion*). The most astonishing aspect of *The Captain's Daughter* is that, though written in 1836, it possesses a brisk, lean style more suggestive of the twentieth century than of the mid-nineteenth century. Pushkin wastes no words, yet his scenes are vivid, his characters fully fleshed and remarkably alive, and his tale recounted in a suspenseful and moving manner. The realistic first-person narration adds to the verisimilitude of the story. The entire story is seen through Peter's eyes, allowing the reader to share his enthusiasms, impetuousness, and fears, as well as his youthful ardor and romantic spirit. The naïve, romantic illusions of the young protagonist are described by the narrator in a thoroughly disarming and often humorous manner. A sense of the vitality of youth pervades the book.

Pushkin recounts action, such as the duel or the siege of the Bailogorsk fortress, in a vivid, well-paced manner. Throughout the novel, he writes with extraordinary vitality, bringing situations and characters to life in a few strokes. Sly humor is an integral part of the narrative. When the hero notes that his French tutor was sent from Moscow with the yearly supply of wine and olive oil, readers know precisely where that unlucky tutor fit into the household. Many of the characters possess a humorous side to their nature. The ill-fated, henpecked captain and his talkative but kindly tyrant of a wife are both portrayed with a light touch. Old Savelitch, Peter's servant, is the truest comic figure in the novel; devoted to his young master, as earlier he had been to Peter's father, the old man would willingly sacrifice his life for Peter but never hesitates to talk back to Peter or to the rebel Cossack leader if he feels that he is in the right. Even Pougatcheff, the self-styled claimant to the throne, is presented with a great deal of humor; in a sense, he is the only character in the book who does not take himself completely seriously, and this, at least in part, is because he has an ironic realization of the precariousness of his existence.

Many scenes in the novel possess double-edged humor, from the absurd, aborted, and then completed duel between Peter and Shvabrin to the moment, in the midst of horror, when old Savelitch dares to present an itemized list of destroyed and stolen goods to the man who holds all of their lives in his hands. The deaths of the captain and his wife are handled with a certain grotesque humor. As in Shakespeare's tragedies, humor serves to heighten the horror of such dramatic scenes as the fall of the fortress and the murders of the innocent at the hands of the rebels. At the same time, there are shockingly realistic portrayals of the duplicity of human nature, Shvabrin's traitorous villainy, the garrison's cowardice when they all throw down their arms in the face of the enemy, and the pettiness displayed by many of the minor characters. Despite the terrible events portrayed in the novel, the book is, however, not grim. It is a romantic tale of action and romance, with an appropriate happy ending. Even the conclusion, with its scenes of mistaken identity, possesses a charming humor. The brilliant construction of the novel, with its alternating light and dark scenes, sweeps readers along, never letting them be quite sure of where they are. Pushkin seems to delight in catching readers off guard, making them laugh and gasp with horror, and then to hurl a piece of slapstick at them before they have recovered from the surprise. The scene of the captain's fat wife being dragged naked from her house to the gallows, screaming and shouting abuse at the Cossacks, is both funny and horrible. Shvabrin, completely despicable, is shown to be absurd as he struts and postures during his brief glory, and then, even more so, when he falls. Pushkin is extremely deft at showing both sides of human beings, the noble and the phony, the absurd and the courageous, the hateful and the loving.

The Russian land is an important part of this novel. The vast spaces become another charac-ter, as the hero flies across them in sleds and carriages or on horseback. Pushkin carefully builds a sense of intense patriotic fervor throughout the narrative, culminating in the scenes with the empress. The empress is seen as the mother figure of all Russia, wise and warm, quick to understand and forgive and to come to the aid of her "children." Frequently in the course of the book, words and phrases refer to the Russian people as one large family; underlings call their masters and mistresses "Father" and "Mother," and the land is referred to as the great mother of them all. The empress and the land are inseparable. In the light of this powerful sentiment, the daring of Pougatcheff to attempt to usurp the throne becomes all the more shocking, as Pushkin intended, because to attack the throne is to attack all of Russia and to undermine the structure of the entire country.

The Captain's Daughter exerted a tremendous influence on Russian fiction; it showed novelists the possibilities of Russian themes and Russian settings, and, above all, it illustrated the narrative capabilities of the Russian language. Never before had Russian prose been used in fiction in such a lean, vigorous, and completely unpretentious manner. The perfection of the book was inspiring to the writers who followed. It can be said that the great period of Russian fiction begins with *The Captain's Daughter*. (The other great influence on Russian fiction, Nikolai Gogol's *Dead Souls*, did not appear until 1842.) The great tragedy for Russian literature and the world is that the year after writing this novel, Pushkin was killed at the age of thirty-seven in a duel.

"Critical Evaluation" by Bruce D. Reeves

Bibliography:
Bayley, John. *Pushkin: A Comparative Commentary*. Cambridge, England: Cambridge Univer-sity Press, 1971. A good introduction to Pushkin's work, with a particularly fine analysis of the later prose tales. Integrates biographical information with analysis of basic themes and structures of the major works. Also discusses Pushkin's works in the context of European romanticism.
Debreczeny, Paul. *The Other Pushkin: A Study of Alexander Pushkin's Prose Fiction*. Stanford, Calif.: Stanford University Press, 1983. The only complete survey of Pushkin's prose work.

Includes a gloss of previous discussions and a thorough study of *The Captain's Daughter*. Extensive notes on the contemporary context of the works, combined with detailed narrative analysis.

Driver, Sam. *Pushkin: Literature and Social Ideas*. New York: Columbia University Press, 1989. Considers the poet as an engaged social thinker rather than an alienated romantic poet. Traces the development of Pushkin's social ideas and his involvement in contemporary politics. Devotes considerable discussion to issues of censorship and to Pushkin's relationship with the Czar as it is revealed in his prose.

Richards, D. J., and C. R. S. Cockerell, eds. and trans. *Russian Views of Pushkin*. Oxford, England: Willem Meeuws, 1976. A wide-ranging collection of Russian essays about Pushkin's verse and prose spanning the nineteenth and twentieth centuries. Includes important discussions of his major works and covers contemporary social issues, narrative structure, and thematic organization.

Simmons, Ernest J. *Pushkin*. Cambridge, Mass.: Harvard University Press, 1937. A solid survey of Pushkin's life and some discussion of his major works. Also discusses Pushkin's manuscript and includes facsimile pages. Considered the standard biography of the writer.

THE CAPTIVES

Type of work: Drama
Author: Plautus (c. 254-184 B.C.E.)
Type of plot: Farce
Time of plot: War between Aetolia and Elis
Locale: Aetolia
First performed: Captivi, second century (English translation, 1767)

Principal characters:
    HEGIO, a wealthy Aetolian
    ERGASILUS, a parasite
    PHILOCRATES, a wealthy Elian and prisoner of war
    TYNDARUS, son of Hegio and Philocrates' slave
    PHILOPOLEMUS, elder son of Hegio
    ARISTOPHONTES, a prisoner of war and Philocrates' friend
    STALAGMUS, a runaway slave

The Story:

Hegio was a wealthy Aetolian who many years before had lost a son, Tyndarus, when a runaway slave named Stalagmus had carried the boy off at the age of four years. Later, during a war with Elis, his other son, Philopolemus, was captured and made a slave by the Elians. In an effort to rescue Philopolemus, Hegio bought up prisoners of war captured by the Aetolian army, hoping to find a wealthy young Elian whom he could exchange for his own son. He spent a great deal of money without finding a suitable prisoner. Mourning his son's loss with him was a parasite, Ergasilus, a favorite of Hegio's son and the recipient of many free meals.

One day, entirely by accident, Hegio bought a pair of prisoners of whom one, unbeknownst to him, was the son stolen years before. Tyndarus was now the slave of Philocrates, a wealthy Elian prisoner. Philocrates and Tyndarus had changed clothing and names, hoping by that ruse to get Philocrates set free to return to Elis. The ruse worked, for Hegio allowed Philocrates to return to Elis and arranged for an exchange of his own son for Philocrates' "master." Shortly afterward, Hegio, while visiting at his brother's home, found a slave there named Aristophontes, who claimed to be a friend of Philocrates. To satisfy himself as to the identity of his hostage and to do a kindness to both prisoners, Hegio took Aristophontes home with him. At Hegio's home, Aristophontes laid bare the ruse that had been played on Hegio. At first, Tyndarus, still posing as Philocrates, tried to complete the plan by claiming that Aristophontes was mad, but Hegio soon became aware that Tyndarus was not Philocrates. In his anger, Hegio had Tyndarus, actually his own son but whom his father did not recognize, sent to the stone quarries, with orders that he was to be worked hard for the trick he had played on his new owner.

The parasite Ergasilus, meanwhile, was going hungry in the absence of his patron, Philopolemus, although Hegio occasionally gave him a frugal meal. Ergasilus was the victim of a move on the part of the wealthy Aetolians to pay no attention to parasites, thus forcing those unwelcome individuals to earn an honest living in some way or other.

Elian Philocrates was an honest man who loved his slave Tyndarus, for the two had been companions since childhood. Upon his return to Elis, therefore, he arranged for the exchange of Philopolemus in return for his own freedom. He also decided to go with Philopolemus to Aetolia to regain his slave Tyndarus. He had promised, through the false Philocrates (Tyndarus), to pay a sum of money as bail for Tyndarus' return.

The first person to see Philocrates and Philopolemus was the parasite Ergasilus. Realizing that the news was money in his wallet and food in his stomach, he rushed off to tell Hegio the tidings. Overjoyed, Hegio promised to give Ergasilus his board for the rest of his life and, for one meal, to give Ergasilus free rein in the kitchens. While Ergasilus rushed to have a feast prepared, Hegio went to the harbor to meet Philopolemus and the former prisoner, Philocrates. Hegio's joy knew no bounds when he embraced his son.

As soon as he returned to his house, Hegio sent for Tyndarus, whom he still did not recognize, and had him released to his master Philocrates, without demanding the payment he had initially set for Tyndarus' freedom. While they were waiting for Tyndarus, Hegio questioned Stalagmus, his former slave, who had been recaptured at Elis and returned by Philocrates. Hegio hoped to discover what had happened to Tyndarus. Stalagmus told how he had kidnapped Hegio's son and taken him to Elis. There, he said, he had sold the young boy to Philocrates' father. Philocrates then related how the little boy had been given to him as a companion and playfellow and had later become his valet. By the time Tyndarus returned from the quarry, the riddle had been solved. He was welcomed, not as a slave, but as a free man, the brother of Philopolemus and Hegio's son.

Tyndarus was overjoyed by his good fortune. Hegio, anxious to punish Stalagmus for the kidnapping and to make amends to his long-lost son, gave the kidnapper over to Tyndarus to be punished. Tyndarus sent immediately for a blacksmith to strike off his chains, which were exceedingly heavy, and had them placed on Stalagmus; he promised that unworthy person a life of hard labor and harsh treatment. Stalagmus philosophically accepted his fate; he had been born a slave, and he expected to die a slave.

Critical Evaluation:

Information about the life of Plautus survives primarily in the writings of other Latin writers, which suggests the impact of his theatrical success even on his contemporaries. His critical reputation remained high after his death. It is likely that the reason he was credited with more than one hundred plays was because his name was such a guarantee of popular success. How many plays he actually wrote remains a mystery; it is commonly agreed that twenty plays and a fragment of another are his. As a group, they represent the Plautine contribution to New Comedy, the most influential comedic formula to survive to this day. His earthiness was frowned upon at certain stages of Western history, such as the Middle Ages, when the more decorous works of his younger contemporary, Terence, were favored. During the Renaissance, in the rebirth of all things classical, Plautus came into his own again, however, and he inspired many of the greatest English dramatists, including William Shakespeare.

The Latin comedy of Plautus' time was based on the new Greek Comedy, whose best-known practitioner was the Greek dramatist Menander. *Comoediae palliatae* was the name given to the category of Roman plays based on Greek originals. Most of these have not survived, so what is known about Plautus' originality and contribution is sometimes a matter of conjecture. By the number of Roman references in his plays, however, it is clear that Plautus did not simply translate his Greek sources. A man who had to live by his words, he was evidently adept at writing what would please his Roman audiences. Still, the illusion that he was writing about another time and place was useful when he poked fun at Roman values.

The Captives has an unusual position among Plautus' works. It appears to have a highly moral tone and is almost tragic in some aspects. The prologue and epilogue seem intended to assure audiences that this play is different from the others, without the usual comic stereotypes.

Critics have pointed out that the play does toy with some traditional comic features and they have identified several reversals. It is common in both Greek and Roman plays of the New Comedy, for example, to have a climactic recognition scene, when, for example, the children who have been lost or thought dead are revealed to their parents. At times, this section of the plot unravels the knotty problems that have prevented a young man from marrying the young woman he loves. The young woman is frequently of a lower class, perhaps a slave, and unfit for the young man of a higher class until something happens to change that gap in social position. The young man, with the help of his clever servant, may manage to find the money to free the woman, or the woman may be revealed to have been of high birth or to have been stolen away from her family as an infant.

The Captives has these plot elements, but with a twist. The servant who is helping his master is actually a peer; the character who turns out to be of higher birth is not the young female character but the male servant. The love that is demonstrated in the play is not between a young man and young woman, but between two men.

Some critics have argued that Tyndarus' great love and sacrifice for his master shows the remnants of a more obviously homoerotic Greek original. If so, this change would be an excellent example of what Plautus could allow himself through the expediency of pretending that the setting was Greek. Yet Erich Segal has noted that the surviving examples of New Comedy seldom refer to homosexuality; moreover, a Roman audience steeped in the usual love plot could very well have welcomed this new twist to an old plot.

One feature of *The Captives* that is typical of Plautus is the character of Ergasilus. According to some scholars, Plautus tends to favor the underdog in his plays and is most successful in his portrayal of clever slaves. The parasite figure is not intrinsic to the plot, and the play has been criticized for such a superfluous role. Without Ergasilus, however, the play could barely be amusing. As is typical of a parasite, he moans about his stomach, setting up a nice comic counterpoint to the more serious themes of the play. The emphasis on Ergasilus' down-to-earth physicality is typical of comedy, which traditionally focuses on what is necessary for survival and shows less concern for how that survival is achieved.

The Captives is not considered to be the most perfectly constructed of Plautus' plays. The parasite is an intrusion on a logical plot, and there are other inconsistencies that have caused some critics to call the play a failure. One eighteenth century critic, however, called it the most beautiful play ever to come to the stage. It has also been one of the popular choices for study, because its high-minded themes of loyalty and sacrifice seem more suitable in an educational context than Plautus' more ribald plays. *The Captives* also exhibits some of the features that have made Plautus endure, among them comic, entertaining features of plot and language. As Segal has pointed out, Plautus' irrepressible high spirits may have seeped into the title itself: In the original, it is ambiguous, meaning "take prisoner" or "take in," leaving the audience to wonder just how far the joking goes.

"Critical Evaluation" by Shakuntala Jayaswal

Bibliography:
Beacham, Richard C. *The Roman Theatre and Its Audience*. London: Routledge & Kegan Paul, 1991. Explains the physical aspects of Roman theater with illustrations and speculates on the nature of the ancient audience. Useful for production ideas.
Duckworth, George. *The Nature of Roman Comedy: A Study in Popular Entertainment*. Princeton, N.J.: Princeton University Press, 1952. The classic study on the subject of Roman comedy. Provides a comprehensive introduction to Latin playwrights, including Plautus.

Konstan, David. "*Captivi:* City-State and Nation." In *Roman Comedy*. Ithaca, N.Y.: Cornell University Press, 1983. Examines the plays of Plautus and Terence in the light of the ancient city-states' cultural system. This play is seen to bring up the question of Greek national identity.

Leach, Eleanor Winsor. "Ergasilus and the Ironies of the *Captivi*." *Classica et Mediavalia* 30 (1969): 145-168. Examines situations in the play such as the handling of the traditional recognition scene.

Segal, Erich. *Roman Laughter: The Comedy of Plautus*. Cambridge, Mass.: Harvard University Press, 1968. Organized by topics rather than by plays, this book presents an argument about Plautus' comedy as a whole. An appendix includes a twenty-three-page discussion of *The Captives*.

THE CARETAKER

Type of work: Drama
Author: Harold Pinter (1930-   )
Type of plot: Psychological realism
Time of plot: Twentieth century
Locale: London, England
First performed: 1960; first published, 1960

> *Principal characters:*
> MICK, a man in his late twenties
> ASTON, his brother, a man in his early thirties
> DAVIES, an old man

The Story:

Mick and his brother Aston lived alone together in a West London house until one night Aston brought home Davies, who had just left his job as a kitchen helper at a restaurant. The old man proved to be a violent, selfish bigot, uncharitable himself but quick to exploit the kindness of others. He told Aston that "Blacks, Greeks, Poles" were "treating him like dirt" and that "nobody's got more rights than I have." He also vowed to get revenge on another employee at the restaurant. In contrast to Davies' vulgar, abrasive, vengeful attitude, Aston was quiet, gentle, and accommodating. In addition to offering Davies a bed for the night, he tried to give him a comfortable pair of shoes. Davies, ungrateful, refused the shoes, claiming they did not fit. When Aston offered him money, however, Davies accepted it, insisting that he had to "get down to Sidcup," where he could get his papers and resume his true identity as Mac Davies, instead of living as he had been under the assumed name of Bernard Jenkins.

Davies stayed the night, and in the morning Aston complained that Davies had been making noises. When he suggested that perhaps Davies had been dreaming, Davies countered by saying that he never dreamed and became angry when Aston said his "jabbering" kept him from sleeping. Nevertheless, Aston suggested that Davies stay on longer if he wanted and gave him a key to the room. Before going out to shop for a jigsaw, Aston recalled an encounter he had recently with a woman he met in a café, who offered "to have a look" at his body. Davies asked him for money, but Aston reminded him that he had given him some money the previous night.

Left alone, Davies began to rummage through items scattered around the room but was surprised by Mick, who grabbed him in a hammerlock and threw him on the floor, asking "What's the game?" and demanding to know Davies' real name. Davies lied, saying his name was Jenkins, and, as if to punish him for lying, Mick aggressively interrogated Davies, undercutting his confidence, confusing the old man, critiquing his motives, and questioning his racism, ethnocentrism, suspicions, and arrogance. Mick finally accused Davies of being "a born fibber" and began teasing him by not giving him his trousers. He was interrupted, however, by Aston returning with a valise—Davies having claimed to have left his at the restaurant the previous night. When Aston handed Davies the bag, however, Mick grabbed it and continued teasing Davies.

Once Mick finally gave Davies the bag, the old man was so startled and frightened that he staggered back and dropped it. Mick then left Aston alone with Davies, who, shaken and angry, called Mick "a real joker." He also complained that the bag Aston had brought him was not his, and though the bag contained some clothes Aston had bought him, Davies was indignant, rejecting the gear—except for a smoking jacket which he put on, claiming that it was not "a bad piece of cloth."

When Aston suggested the old man could become the caretaker around the house, Davies became evasive, reciting a list of excuses. Later, Davies returned to the room alone in the dark. Frightened upon discovering that the lights were not working and thinking that he heard an intruder, he pulled a knife, but the intruder turned out to be Mick, who chased Davies around the room with a vacuum cleaner. After sparring mentally with Davies, Mick pretended to befriend him, offering him a sandwich. Once he had gained Davies' trust, however, Mick again set a trap for him. Suggesting that his brother was odd and lazy, Mick got Davies to join in the criticism of Aston, calling him a "funny bloke." Mick then demanded that Davies clarify his statement, confusing the old man. To compound Davies' confusion, Mick asked him to become the caretaker, provided that Davies could produce references. Davies again asserted that his references—his papers—could be verified only if he could get to Sidcup.

The next morning Aston complained again that Davies was making so much noise that he could not sleep. Aston recalled being arrested for having hallucinations and being sent to a doctor, who told him he would "do something" to his brain. Aston claimed that he had written to his mother hoping to prevent the treatment, but his mother signed the forms and allowed the doctor to perform shock therapy on him. After the treatment, Aston said his thoughts "had become very slow." He said that he suffered from headaches and that he had learned to stay out of public places. He also admitted that he would like to find the doctor who administered the treatment.

Two weeks later, Davies, alone in the house with Mick, began to list a series of complaints against Aston. Aston was not talking to him, he was not being "straight forward," he would not provide him with a clock, and he would not let him sleep. By the time Aston joined the other two, Davies was trying to conspire against him with Mick. That night, awakened by Aston's complaints about the old man's noises, Davies lost his temper and yelled that Aston was "half-off." When Aston made a move toward Davies, the old man pulled his knife, convincing Aston that it was time for Davies to leave. Davies appealed to Mick for help, but Mick defended his brother's position. Smashing a bust of Buddha, Mick launched into a tirade against Davies' selfishness. When Aston noticed the broken Buddha, Davies reversed himself against Mick and again appealed to Aston, hoping that Aston would allow him to stay at the house. This time, Aston refused to help the old man, telling him he could not stay because he made "too much noise."

Critical Evaluation:

Pinter's second full-length play, *The Caretaker*, opened in London in 1960 and, after a twelve-month run, moved to Broadway, where it was acclaimed as a critical, if not commercial, success. *The Caretaker* has been described as Pinter's most naturalistic play. The British theater critic Kenneth Tynan called it "a play about people," which, in Pinter's case, marked a significant turn in his approach to theater. His early work, such as *The Room* (1957) and *The Dumb Waiter* (1959), was laden with symbolism and was heavily influenced by the absurdist theater of Irish playwright Samuel Beckett and Russian-born French playwright Eugène Ionesco. In *The Caretaker*, however, Pinter eschews latent meanings and focuses instead on the lives of the three characters, presenting the action realistically and in a naturalistic fashion. The setting, a cluttered room, has no overt symbolic significance. It is, as is often the case in Pinter's plays, a realistic vision of isolation and withdrawal. Nor does Pinter force any allegorical message into the story. The characters are readily identifiable as local people in ordinary circumstances.

Nevertheless, the play is anything but conventional. The characters seem unfinished, inde-terminate, with no stable, verifiable stake in life. Davies, an inveterate liar, claims he has "papers" in Sidcup that will establish his identity, but it is never made clear exactly who he is, where he has been, or what the papers in Sidcup would prove. Aston, the benevolent brother who befriends Davies, recites a poetic soliloquy that describes his incarceration and treatment in a mental institution, but why he was committed is never established. He says only that, at some point in his life, he saw things too clearly and talked too much where he worked. His brother, Mick, who is more hostile to Davies, seems to improvise his past, whimsically concocting stories that confuse Davies while providing no real information regarding his identity. Their plans about the future are especially vague. Davies hopes to get his papers from Sidcup but makes no real effort to go. Aston hopes to build a shed, but the idea sounds more like a pipe dream than any project he could actually complete. Mick mentions several projects involving renovation and a van, but he is never specific; when he offers details, no conclusions can be drawn from what he says.

Another characteristically unconventional tactic Pinter uses in *The Caretaker*, giving it a quality of uncertainty that has become the trademark of his plays, is the way the meager plot belies the psychological complexities of the characters as they strive to discover and maintain their separate identities. Aston finds Davies one night after the homeless tramp has been fired from his job and offers to share his living quarters with him. Davies is a self-righteous bigot, a cantankerous reprobate, ungrateful, untrustworthy, and exceedingly selfish. Aston, who is laconic, withdrawn, and passive to a fault, overlooks the old man's negative traits and tries, inexplicably, to make him comfortable, offering him money, a bed, and a key to the house. As soon as Aston leaves the room, however, Davies is assaulted by Mick, who has been trying to develop Aston's interest in some projects, hoping to help him adjust after his treatment at the mental institution. Mick sees Davies as a manipulator who is trying to take advantage of Aston's condition. He immediately engages Davies in a series of verbal encounters that serve to disorient the old man and to protect Aston, realizing that Aston must reject Davies voluntarily to assure himself that he can deal independently with people and situations in his life. In the end, after talk of Davies becoming "caretaker" of the property, Aston sees through the tramp's machinations and tells him to leave.

The irony in the title of *The Caretaker* evolves from Davies' being offered a job as caretaker when, in fact, he is capable neither of caring for himself nor of expressing care for others. It is his rejection of basic human kindness, his need to manipulate instead of trust, and his choice of lies over honesty that finally result in his being rejected by the brothers. Cynically, the play suggests that the innocents of the world are at risk and that to survive without being threatened one must develop the defensive tactics that Aston is still learning, but that Mick has already mastered.

Jeff Johnson

Bibliography:
Bloom, Harold, ed. *Modern Critical Views: Harold Pinter.* New York: Chelsea House, 1987. An eclectic collection of essays by various critics. Comprehensive analyses of early and late writings and selected specific texts.
Burkman, Katherine H. *The Dramatic World of Harold Pinter: Its Basis in Ritual.* Columbus: Ohio State University Press, 1971. An analysis of Pinter's work viewed through Freudian, Marxist, and myth analyses. Heavy on theory with solid literary analyses of individual plays.

Esslin, Martin. *Pinter the Playwright*. Portsmouth, N.H.: Heinemann Educational Books, 1988. Precise and exhaustive critical study combining biographical details with critical analysis to identify sources of style and theme in Pinter's work. Written with the assistance of Pinter, it includes discussion of previously unpublished material.

Gale, Steven H., ed. *Harold Pinter: Critical Approaches*. Rutherford, N.J.: Fairleigh Dickinson University Press, 1986. A collection of essays by various critics on a wide range of Pinter's work. Places the material in the context of contemporary critical theories.

Merritt, Susan H. *Pinter in Play: Critical Strategies and the Plays of Harold Pinter*. Durham, N.C.: Duke University Press, 1990. Excellent discussion of current and past debates on critical theory as it relates to Pinter's work. Provides scrupulous textual examination.

CARMEN

Type of work: Novella
Author: Prosper Mérimée (1803-1870)
Type of plot: Psychological
Time of plot: Early nineteenth century
Locale: Spain
First published: 1845; revised, 1847 (English translation, 1878)

> *Principal characters:*
> DON JOSÉ, a soldier
> CARMEN, a cigarette worker
> GARCIA, Carmen's husband
> LUCAS, a toreador

The Story:

Don José was a handsome, young cavalryman from Navarre. The son of a good Basque family, he had excellent chances of being quickly promoted and making his name as a soldier. A short time after arriving at his post in Seville, however, he happened to meet a beautiful, clever young gypsy named Carmen. Don José fell in love with her at once and allowed her to escape after she had been taken into custody for attacking another worker with a knife in a cigarette factory.

One night, she persuaded him to desert his post and go with her. He was punished by being ordered to stand guard. When she went to him again, and again urged him to come with her, he refused. They argued for more than an hour, until Don José, exhausted by his struggle between anger and love, succumbed to her. After he became her lover, she caressed him and ridiculed him by turn. Carmen was independent, rebellious, and tormenting. The more fickle she was, the more madly Don José loved her.

One night, having agreed to a rendezvous with Carmen, he went to her apartment. While they were together, a lieutenant who was also Carmen's lover entered. He and Don José began to argue and swords flashed. In the struggle, Don José killed the lieutenant after himself suffering a head wound. Carmen, who had remained in the room throughout the fight, accused Don José of being stupid. She went out and returned a few minutes later with a cloak, which she told him to wear, as he would be a hunted man. Don José's hopes for a brilliant career were shattered as a result of this impetuous act. His love had led him to murder, and he was doomed to live the life of an outlaw with a woman who was a pickpocket and a thief.

Carmen had many friends and acquaintances who were outlaws. Because Don José had no choice in the matter, he agreed to go with her to join a small band of smugglers and bandits for whom Carmen was a spy. By that time, a reward had been posted for Don José's capture. He and Carmen set out and eventually found the smugglers. For a long time, Don José lived with them, throwing himself into his new, lawless life with such vigor and enthusiasm that he became known as a desperate and ruthless bandit. All the time, however, he was deeply unhappy. By nature, he was kind and had nothing of the desperado in him. His wild life was not the type of existence he had envisioned. Worst of all, he knew that Carmen was unfaithful to him, and he grew silent and sullen.

His anger and jealousy increased when he discovered that Garcia, the one-eyed leader of the gang, was Carmen's husband. By that time, the band had been reduced in numbers. One day, while Carmen was absent, Don José killed Garcia. A fellow outlaw told Don José that he had been very stupid and that Garcia would have given Carmen to him for a few dollars. When Carmen returned, he informed her that she was a widow. The death of Garcia also meant that there were only two of the band left on the eve of a dangerous raid they had planned.

Don José and a smuggler named Dancaire organized a new band. Carmen continued to be useful to them. She went to Granada, and there she met a toreador named Lucas. Jealous of his rival, Don José asked her to live with him always, to abandon the life they were leading, and to go off with him to America. Carmen refused, telling him that nobody had ever successfully ordered her to do anything, that she was a gypsy, and that she had read in coffee grounds that she and Don José would end their lives together. Her words half convinced Don José that there was no reason for him to worry.

A short time later, Carmen defied him again and went to Cordova, where Lucas was appearing in a bullfight. Don José followed her, but he caught only a glimpse of her in the arena. Lucas was injured by a bull. Outside the arena, Don José met Carmen. Once more he implored her to be his forever and to go with him to America, but she only laughed and jeered at him.

Don José went to a monk and asked him to say a mass for a person who was in danger of death. He then returned to Carmen and told her to follow him. She responded that she would go with him, even to her death, though she knew that he was about to kill her. Resigned to her fate, she told him that she no longer loved him and that she would not love him any more even if Lucas did not love her. Their affair was ended. In desperation, Don José took out his knife and killed her. With the same knife, he dug her grave and buried her in a grove of trees. Then he went to the nearest constabulary post and surrendered. The monk said the mass for the repose of Carmen's soul.

Critical Evaluation:

Prosper Mérimée is one of a handful of French writers credited with inventing the *nouvelle*, something more than a short story but less than a novel. His first exercise in this genre had been *Colomba* (1841), a much-acclaimed tale about a vendetta set in Corsica. *Carmen* may be seen as an attempt to repeat the success of the earlier story by mixing similar ingredients: an exotic and colorful setting; a central character who operates outside the law but with reference to some definite code of honor; and, of course, a bewitching femme fatale.

The thematic materials in *Carmen* are somewhat reminiscent of the gothic novels that had flourished a generation before, novels that had often been set in wild places haunted by colorful characters. The form of its plot and the manner of its narration are, however, very different from the florid excesses of gothic melodrama. The plot of *Carmen* is borrowed from the Abbé Prévost's *Manon Lescaut* (1731), which tracks the moral decline of a supposedly honorable man who has become infatuated with an altogether unsuitable woman. Mérimée's narrative style is laconic and rather clinical, full of anthropological asides regarding the customs and language of the gypsies. Most of these asides, as Mérimée admits, are lifted from the early works of the English writer George Henry Borrow, author of *The Zincali: Or, An Account of the Gypsies of Spain with a Collection of Their Songs and Poetry and a Copious Dictionary of Their Language* (1841). The result of Mérimée's syncretic amalgamation is a work delicately suspended between realism and Romanticism, a kind of work that had not previously existed and that Mérimée was to make his own.

In *Manon Lescaut*'s account, a worthy man's descent into ruin is attributed to an oppressive, almost tangible force operating within a context defined by the author's Jesuitical Catholicism.

Carmen, too, is marked by fatalism, but the fate that pursues Don José is no dark, oppressive one. His decline, which occurs over a series of dispirited failures, begins even before he meets Carmen, for he has fled his homeland after killing a man in a duel fought over a tennis match. When Carmen tempts him, Don José knows precisely where his duty lies, yet by capitulating again and again, he eventually becomes so casual in his immorality as to plot and execute the murder of Carmen's supposed husband on a whim rather than as an act of true desperation.

The only resistance Don José can raise against his temptress is displayed in the frame narrative, when he refuses to murder the archaeologist to whom he eventually tells his life story. He is restrained by the fact that the archaeologist has previously saved him from being captured. This raises the doubt as to whether Don José is entirely reliable as a narrator or whether his matter-of-factness represents the state of mind instilled by the imminence of his execution. Most of the events he describes speak for themselves, however, and they make sense only if one accepts that they happened as casually as he describes them.

Don José's fatalism is matched by Carmen's, especially in the remarkable conclusion of the story, which differs sharply not only from that of *Manon Lescaut* but also from those of such nineteenth century recapitulations of that plot as *La Dame aux camélias* (1852), by Alexandre Dumas, *fils*. Carmen knows that Don José will kill her, but she refuses to save herself by lying, even though she has built her entire career on conscienceless deception. In effect, she not only invites destruction but insists on it, and she does so not out of principle or passion but out of a basic inability to care.

Those who know the story of Carmen only through Georges Bizet's famous 1875 opera of that name would hardly recognize the story, because the composer and his librettist carefully obliterated the very elements that make the story unique. Lucas the picador, who hardly figures in the story, becomes a much more powerful figure in the opera so as to justify Carmen's desertion and Don José's jealousy. Yet the point of Mérimée's story is that the motivation for murder was so slight. In his story, Carmen is fickle and Don José weak, and that is all there is to it; their infatuation is not a grand passion of the kind whose erotic ecstasy might explain—perhaps even justify—acts of reckless violence. Carmen is certainly a femme fatale in the great tradition of French literary femmes fatales, but she has neither the secret capacity for honest passion that marks the tragic heroines of Romanticism nor the cold callousness of the anti-heroines of the Decadent movement. She is a gypsy (or perhaps, if one of her seeming lies is in fact the truth, a changeling adopted by gypsies), and she has a different way of feeling as well as a different way of behaving.

The clinical tone of Mérimée's description of the doomed affair is no mere pastiche of scientific objectivity; it expresses an authentically scientific view of the mechanisms of human behavior. Unlike the Abbé Prévost, who might have been a bad Catholic but was nevertheless a Catholic through and through, Mérimée is an agnostic who clearly considers that the soul—if it exists at all—is an irrelevance, and that judgment is a purely human business. He does record that Carmen is sometimes described as a sorceress and a "child of Satan," and he even concedes her a measure of magical and prophetic power, but he never endorses the evaluation to the point of regarding her death as predestined damnation.

Mérimée's objectivity secures his place as an original writer despite his tendency to borrow all his plots and much of his local color from any sources that came conveniently to hand. *Carmen* embodies this attitude of mind and manner of execution most strikingly and forcefully, and that is one of the reasons for the work's enduring position as a literary landmark.

"Critical Evaluation" by Brian Stableford

Bibliography:

Cogman, Peter. *Mérimée: Colomba and Carmen*. London: Grant & Cutler, 1992. A detailed account of the two texts, paying particular attention to their use of the exotic and their deployment of femmes fatales.

Horrocks, Gillian. "A Semiotic Study of *Carmen*." *Nottingham French Studies* 25 (1968): 60-72. A brief but interesting structuralist analysis of the story.

Raitt, A. W. *Prosper Mérimée*. London: Eyre & Spottiswoode, 1970. A comprehensive study of the author's life and works. Includes a detailed discussion of *Carmen*.

Segal, Naomi. *Narcissus and Echo: Women in the French Récit*. Manchester: Manchester University Press, 1988. A feminist analysis that discusses *Manon Lescaut* and *Carmen* as classic instances of women being blamed by male narrators for their own shortcomings.

Tilby, Michael. "Language and Sexuality in Mérimée's *Carmen*." *Forum for Modern Language Studies* 15 (1979): 255-263. An analysis of the way in which Mérimée employs his borrowings from George Henry Borrow to establish Carmen's alluring sexual exoticism.

CARMINA

Type of work: Poetry
Author: Catullus (Gaius Valerius Catullus, c. 85-c. 54 B.C.E.)
First transcribed: c. 50 B.C.E. (English translation, 1894)

Catullus, greatest of the Latin lyric poets, was born in Verona in northern Italy, only a few years after it had been taken from the Celts. Some scholars believe him to have been Celtic, not only because of his name but also because of his use of such Celtic words as *basium* (kiss) instead of the Latin *osculum.*

Catullus was one of the so-called New Poets, whose leader was Valerius Cato. Beginning about 90 B.C.E., these writers revolted against the conservative poets who treated only wars, history, and mythology. Instead, they experimented with Greek meters and Greek words, and their work reveals the inspiration of Sappho, Archilochus, and especially the Alexandrians. It is not known how radical Catullus' fellow poets were, for most of their work has been lost. Indeed, the poetry of Catullus survived only by chance.

Catullus probably published a number of books—*libelli*, the Latins called them—made by pasting together sheets of parchment or papyrus into a long strip and rolling it on a stick. About a thousand lines constituted a book. All 116 of Catullus' poems were on one roll, arranged by length rather than by subject or chronology. It could not have been the poet himself who arranged them thus, because the dedication provided was hardly suitable for such a volume. This roll of poems was disregarded for fourteen centuries, for Catullus was not considered an important classical poet like Ovid, Martial, or his friend Vergil. Yet Vergil's indebtedness to Catullus is evident both in Vergil's earlier poetry and in the *Aeneid* (c. 29-19 B.C.E.), and Ovid and Martial both praised him highly.

The roll of Catullus' poems came to light briefly in his native city in the fourteenth century, when two admirers made complete copies of the works before the roll was lost forever. It is from the two copies that later ages learned to admire the lyric genius of Catullus. Petrarch owned and used one copy.

Once the poems, the *Carmina*, appeared in print, the cult of Catullus began to spread. The pious François de Salignac de La Mothe-Fénelon, overlooking Catullus' occasional obscenities, accounted with two words for his greatness: *simplicité passionée.* The critical judgment of the poet ever since has been that he was one of the supreme poets of love and a singer of ardent and sincere passion, a passion that he expressed with fiery earnestness but also with simplicity.

The date of Catullus' first poems cannot be determined. It is known that he went to Rome when he was about twenty. There he met the object of an overpowering love, a woman whom he addressed in his verses as Lesbia, a name suggested by the homeland of Sappho, whose meter he used in several of the poems. Scholars later identified her as Clodia, wife of the praetor Quintus Caecilius Metellus, a talented, cruel beauty described as ox-eyed (a compliment: oxen have beautiful, large eyes) even by her enemies. She was married when Catullus, meeting her, was so struck that he could not speak. He thereupon wrote for her one of the most famous of all love poems, in which he declared that a man becomes godlike "who sits and constantly in your presence watches and hears you laugh." Possibly about this same time he courted her in the charming and well-known lyric addressed to her pet sparrow, who could be happy although its mistress and the poet were miserable and thwarted.

Before he had progressed very far in his courtship, his older brother, a diplomat in the east, suddenly died. Perhaps it was he who had financed Catullus' literary career in Rome. Certainly the poet never mentioned assistance from his father. At any rate, Catullus returned home in 60 B.C.E. Once back in Verona, the poet, finding no kindred spirits, was frankly bored. In one rhyme to a friend he complained that he found no poetic inspiration. In another lyric he begged a fellow poet to come and visit him. Julius Caesar is known to have lodged with his father several times when traveling from his Gallic campaigns to Rome, but Catullus did not like him.

In 57 B.C.E., apparently believing it was time for him to get into politics, the poet secured an appointment to the staff of Memmius, the governor of Bithynia, in northern Africa. Judging by Catullus' satirical poems, his superior there appropriated all the art treasures and the gold. All that fell to the poet was a yacht:

> Stranger, the bark you see before you says
> That in old times and in her early days
> She was a lovely vessel that could make
> The quickest voyages and overtake
> All her competitors in sail or oar.

This vessel brought him home the following year. On the way he stopped to visit the tomb of his brother near the site of Troy, where he wrote one of the most beautiful of his elegiac poems (number 101):

> By ways remote and distant waters sped,
> Brother, to thy sad graveside am I come
> That I may give the last gifts to the dead
> And vainly parley with thy ashes dumb. . . .
> Take them, all drenched with a brother's tear,
> And, Brother, for all time, hail and farewell.

Back in Rome, Clodia, after her husband's suspiciously sudden death, had become the mistress of Caelius. When his ardor cooled, she tried to destroy his political career by bringing all sorts of charges against him. Cicero, the greatest orator of his time, defended Caelius in an oration, still extant, that completely demolished Clodia's reputation and character. The returning Catullus still felt some of "Lesbia's" old charm, however, and again he wrote impassioned lyrics to her. Some scholars have tried to arrange the score or more in a pattern to show the growth of their love, their quarrels, charges of infidelity, reconciliations, and the final break, but these arrangements are mere suppositions. There is not, for example, any chronological clue to the shortest and most memorable poem about her (number 85): "I hate and love. You ask perhaps how that could be?/ I know not, but I feel its agony." Determined to leave her, Catullus wrote in poem 8:

> She-devil, damn you! What life's left for you? . . .
> Whom will you kiss? In whose lips set your teeth?
> Stop, Catullus! It's over; don't give in.

He did, however, write one more poem about her, in Sapphic meter, asking several friends to take her a message, "short and not kindly," bidding farewell to her and her "hundreds of lovers, whom she exhausts sexually."

Poets ever since have been inspired to translate and adapt these love lyrics. Robert Herrick has been called an English Catullus, though he certainly lacks the Latin poet's depth of passion. Nearer in spirit was John Donne, who claimed that Catullus was only one of the "1,400 authors" the English poet had analyzed.

Among Catullus' 116 poems are themes other than love. About twenty-five deal with friendship in various forms. Some, fewer but fiercer, poetize his hates: false friendship, pretension, infractions of the moral code, and corruption in high places. His dislike of Julius Caesar he expressed in the invective of poem 93. Later, however, he felt more kindly toward Caesar and made amends by praising Caesar's undoubted personal charm and military ability.

Among Catullus' works are several long poems, including two wedding hymns and two epyllia, or little epics, modeled on those of the Alexandrian poets. One, celebrating the marriage of Peleus and Thetis, includes the story of Theseus and Ariadne. The other, a translation of Callimachus' "Lock of Berenice," is one of the sources for Alexander Pope's "The Rape of the Lock."

Most of the *Carmina* were satiric poems, sometimes with invective or humor so vulgar that they shocked readers of later centuries. Perhaps forty-six can be so considered, but those are not the verses for which Catullus will be remembered. He is immortal because of his expressions of passion and love and for his inspired poems of sadness, which, though only few in number, are enough to have made Alfred, Lord Tennyson, refer to Catullus as the tenderest of Latin poets.

Bibliography:

Conte, Gian Biagio. *Latin Literature: A History.* Translated by Joseph B. Solodow and revised by Don Fowler and Glenn W. Most. Baltimore: The Johns Hopkins University Press, 1994. An excellent introduction to Catullus and his works in this comprehensive volume. Despite the relatively limited space, Catullus' verse is explored in some detail.

Ferguson, John. *Catullus.* New York: Oxford University Press, 1988. Examines the life, career, and achievements of Catullus. Helpful on Catullus' style and its influence on later writers.

Janan, Micaela Wakil. *"When the Lamp Is Shattered": Desire and Narrative in Catullus.* Carbondale: Southern Illinois University Press, 1994. Examines various approaches to Catullus' work in terms of culture and sex. Sees Catullus as setting up "oscillations" between contradictory elements in human beings.

Martin, Charles. Introduction to *Poems of Catullus,* by Catullus. Baltimore: The Johns Hopkins University Press, 1990. In his introduction, Martin notes that Catullus was a technically accomplished poet who influenced modern writers such as Robert Frost and Ezra Pound.

Stuart Small, G. P. *Catullus: A Reader's Guide to the Poems.* Lanham, Md.: University Press of America, 1983. A close-reading explication of Catullus' works. Helpful in resolving textual problems.

Zetzel, James E. Z. "Catullus." In *Ancient Writers: Greece and Rome.* New York: Charles Scribner's Sons, 1982. An excellent starting point for study of the poet. Provides a fairly comprehensive survey of Catullus' accomplishments, set within the context of Latin literature.

THE CASE OF SERGEANT GRISCHA

Type of work: Novel
Author: Arnold Zweig (1887-1968)
Type of plot: Social realism
Time of plot: 1917
Locale: Russia
First published: Der Streit um den Sergeanten Grischa, 1927 (English translation, 1928)

Principal characters:
GRISCHA, a Russian soldier
BABKA, his mistress
GENERAL VON LYCHOW, a divisional general
SCHIEFFENZAHN, an administrative general
WINFRIED, a German lieutenant

The Story:

In the year 1917, the Russians were nearly beaten, and the Germans contented themselves with consolidating their hold on Russian territory from Riga south through Poland. With the end of the bitter fighting, a camaraderie grew up between the German soldiers and their Russian prisoners. Even so, Sergeant Grischa Iljitsch Paprotkin was determined to escape. His work was not difficult, and his cheerful strength had made him foreman of the labor gang and a general favorite with his German captors. Grischa, however, thinking of his wife and son far to the east, made his plans as he loaded lumber into freight cars on the railroad siding. He made a tunnel in the car, a wooden tunnel about the size of a coffin. That night, he succeeded in concealing himself in his hideout. Before daybreak, the train pulled out of the station. Grischa did not know it, but his train went far to the south. After four days, the train came to a stop. With his stolen pliers, Grischa opened the door and walked cautiously away from the railroad tracks. Guided only by his small compass, he set his path toward the east.

The thick underbrush made traveling difficult. Somewhere along the route Grischa picked up an old umbrella. By binding several ribs together with a string and using a long thong, he had a serviceable bow. Another rib made an arrow. With patient waiting, he could shoot rabbits in the snow, and he seldom went hungry. One day he came to the blasted area of a battlefield, where he built a fire in a ruined dugout and heated snow to make water for a bath. Taking off his upper clothes, Grischa stretched out and began to wash himself.

Two people, attracted by his fire, surprised him in his retreat. One was a Russian soldier, a deserter, and the other was Babka, a small, dirty woman whose gray hair justified her name, "Grandmother." Both were armed. After they became acquainted, Grischa knew he was in luck, for they were the leaders of a band of refugees camped comfortably nearby in a wooden house made from old German dugouts. Grischa stayed with the refugees the rest of the winter. He cut wood energetically and traded in the villages of friendly peasants. He slept with Babka, who was young and vital under her misshapen clothes. Three years of war had turned her hair gray. Under the shrewd leadership of Babka by day, and warmed in her bed at night, Grischa became strong again.

The band of refugees scattered in the spring. Grischa and two companions were the first to leave. Grischa felt reasonably safe. Babka had given him the identification tag of a dead Russian soldier, and he called himself by a new name. He was no longer Grischa Paprotkin, an escaped prisoner, but Sergeant Pavlovitsch Bjuscheff, a deserter from the Russian army who was trying to get back to the Russian lines.

In Mervinsk, the Germans had established military headquarters. With little fighting to be done, the rivalry between field troops and the military police grew more bitter. The troops under old General von Lychow were technically in charge of the town, but the military police under General Schieffenzahn had been stationed in Mervinsk so long that Schieffenzahn had consolidated his hold on the whole district. Von Lychow was a Prussian, a stern man but just and compassionate; Schieffenzahn was an upstart more concerned with power.

Outside the city stood several rows of small wooden villas. Many of them now housed German officers. Grischa, gaunt and dirty, came upon these villas one day and hid in an empty one. A few days later, alert military police discovered him there. The man called Bjuscheff was not really afraid at his trial. Even when they said he must be a spy because he had spent so many months behind the German lines, he was easy in his mind. They would merely hold him prisoner a little while in the town of Mervinsk. Surely the war would end soon. The court, however, declared that a Russian deserter who, according to his own story, had wandered about in German territory for nearly two years was by definition a spy. Sergeant Bjuscheff was condemned to die. Scarcely understanding what he was told, Grischa was led back to his cell. When the truth dawned on him, he called out so violently that an officer came to quiet the disturbance. Grischa told the officer his whole story. He was not Bjuscheff the deserter, but Grischa the escaped prisoner.

Ponsanski, a famous Jewish lawyer and aide to General von Lychow, questioned the prisoner. Impressed by the story of changed identity but interested only from a legal point of view, Ponsanski collected all the evidence he could and went to von Lychow. With the general's permission, two guards who had known Grischa in his former prison camp went all the way to Mervinsk and identified him. With legal logic, Ponsanski claimed that the court-martial decision should be set aside. All the evidence, depositions, and signatures were put in a neat packet and forwarded to Schieffenzahn with a request that the Komandatur indicate which military court now had jurisdiction over the case of Sergeant Grischa.

In some way, Babka learned where Grischa was imprisoned. Walking barefoot, she went to Mervinsk in the disguise of a peddler woman. She was now carrying Grischa's child. Her plan was simple: She would bring berries and fruit to the post to sell to the Germans. She would get in to see Grischa. Then, after she had become a familiar visitor, she would poison the guards' schnapps. With the Germans dead, Grischa could walk out a free man once more. Grischa, however, would not agree to her plan. He knew that all of his papers had been sent away for final judgment. Anyway, the war would soon be over.

When Grischa's papers went to the Komandatur, they came before Wilhelmi, his aide. Knowing the temper of Schieffenzahn, Wilhelmi recommended that Grischa be executed. When that advice became known in Mervinsk, von Lychow was indignant. A new request was forwarded to Schieffenzahn. Schieffenzahn grew weary of the affair. Hearing that von Lychow was coming to see him, he sent a telegram ordering Grischa's execution within twenty-four hours. Von Lychow protested. Because the old Prussian had influence at court, Schieffenzahn telegraphed a reprieve.

That telegram was never delivered in Mervinsk because of a snowstorm. Grischa knew at last that he would be shot. When Babka brought in the poisoned schnapps, he poured the drink down the drain. He was shot according to Schieffenzahn's orders, and he died like a soldier after digging his own grave. His child with Babka was born just after his death. In Berlin, von

Lychow smarted. He drew up the full particulars of the case and presented his report to the emperor. The kaiser promised to demote Schieffenzahn, but his mind was distracted by a present of a jeweled casket. Because of the kaiser's joy in a new toy, Schieffenzahn got off with a light reprimand. The case of Sergeant Grischa was closed.

Critical Evaluation:

The plot of *The Case of Sergeant Grischa*, an absorbing account of the last months of World War I, appeared first as a play in 1921. Its great and deserved popularity led Arnold Zweig to recast his characters in the larger framework of a novel. A brilliant novel, it is one of the best in any language to emerge from World War I. Zweig has a strong narrative sense, an excellent grasp of physical detail, and a fine ability to portray characters. Additionally, the novel relates the particular setting of the German Eastern Front in World War I to the historical and social forces, in the army and outside it, that bring Sergeant Grischa to his fate.

The story itself begins in a primitive setting, where Grischa is impelled to escape imprisonment by the most basic human feelings: the need for wife, child, and home. The story moves forward into progressively more richly textured social and political settings, where human emotions became more disguised and elaborate through their contact with the institutions of society and of war. Throughout this movement, the story itself remains prominent. Sergeant Grischa's career remains of interest because he is so appealing as a character and because he encounters such a broadly representative spectrum of forces and circumstances in his life.

The physical details of the labor camp, forests, towns, offices, trenches, battlefields, and prisons are especially rich and provocative. Zweig is compelling in his presentations of places, using both panoramas and in-depth descriptions. This intense realism is heightened by Zweig's superb characterizations. Grischa himself, despite his lowly status (or perhaps because of it) and despite his naïveté, is clearly of heroic proportions. He has courage, endurance, deep feelings, and, above all, great human potential. It is his potential that impresses those around him and that makes his final and seemingly inevitable fate all the more significant. As he grows more heroic, especially in contrast to the corruption around him, he still never ceases to be a victim. This heroic doubleness, perhaps the central feature of European, American, and British literature of the interwar period, marks *The Case of Sergeant Grischa* as an undeniably modern novel.

Unlike much literary work of this period, however, *The Case of Sergeant Grischa* remains firmly embedded in actual history and society. There is no sliding into the abstract; everything is rooted in social and political actuality. Real institutions and their functionaries never disappear or become merely parable; instead, they retain their particular historical features. Yet, precisely because the officials, bureaucrats, officers, and guards are so authentic and because Sergeant Grischa is himself so authentic, *The Case of Sergeant Grischa* retains its life and relevance.

Bibliography:
Feuchtwanger, Lion. "*The Case of Sergeant Grischa:* Germany's First Great War Novel." *Chicago Tribune*, December 1, 1928, sec. 2, p. 21. An insightful review by a noted German novelist. Concentrates on Grischa as a symbolic character of the age, the little man whose experience stands for that of all soldiers caught in the jaws of war.
Fishman, Solomon. "The War Novels of Arnold Zweig." *Sewanee Review* 49, no. 4 (October/December, 1941): 433-451. A basic thematic and contextualizing overview of *The Case of Sergeant Grischa* and Zweig's other war novels published before 1941. Provides the best

place for the general reader to begin further study. Situates Zweig's ideas in their interwar historical context and argues positively for his firm moral stance.

Pfeiler, Wilhelm K. "Arnold Zweig." In *War and the German Mind: The Testimony of Men of Fiction Who Fought at the Front*. New York: Columbia University Press, 1941. A good introduction to *The Case of Sergeant Grischa* and other war novels in the context of German attitudes toward war in general. Though dated, the points made here are still valid. Good index.

Salamon, George. *Arnold Zweig*. New York: Twayne, 1975. The only comprehensive treatment of Zweig's works in English, the bulk of the book explores *The Case of Sergeant Grischa* and Zweig's other war novels. An excellent overview for the general reader, it also contains biographical information on Zweig and a brief bibliography.

White, Ray Lewis. *Arnold Zweig in the USA*. New York: Peter Lang, 1986. Not a critical treatment, but a collection of contemporary reviews of Zweig's works in English in the United States. The thirteen reprinted reviews of *The Case of Sergeant Grischa*, though excerpted, give a good sense of the novel's reception at the time of its publication.

CASS TIMBERLANE
A Novel of Husbands and Wives

Type of work: Novel
Author: Sinclair Lewis (1885-1951)
Type of plot: Social realism
Time of plot: 1940's
Locale: Grand Republic, Minnesota
First published: 1945

> *Principal characters:*
> CASS TIMBERLANE, a district judge
> JINNY MARSHLAND TIMBERLANE, his wife
> BRADD CRILEY, Jinny's lover

The Story:

After his divorce from his wife, Blanche, Judge Cass Timberlane continued to meet his old friends socially and to hold court in his usual honest and effective manner. It was not until Jinny Marshland appeared in his court as witness in a routine case, however, that Cass once more began to find his life interesting. Cass was forty-one years old and Jinny in her early twenties, so he told himself that he was foolish to think of her in a romantic manner. In spite of his logical reasoning, Cass thought more and more about Jinny. Within a few days of their first meeting, he had arranged to see her again. Dignified Judge Cass Timberlane was falling in love.

He had no smooth romance. His friends thought him stupid to become involved with a young woman of the working class. It seemed strange to Cass that his friends would dare to criticize anyone. For example, there was Dr. Roy Drover, who openly made love to any and every cheap woman he could, without bothering to conceal his infidelities from his wife. In the same class were Boone and Queenie Havock, both loud, brassy, and vulgar; Jay Laverick, a rich, lustful drunkard; and Bradd Criley, notorious for his affairs with the wives of his best friends.

Cass's friends were not the only ones opposed to the affair. Jinny's young radical friends thought Cass a stuffy conservative. The only two people who were sympathetic with Cass were Chris Grau, who also wanted to marry him, and Mrs. Higbee, his housekeeper.

What his friends thought of Jinny did not matter; it was what Jinny would think of them that worried Cass at the time of their marriage. After the honeymoon, they lived in his old family home, although Jinny would have preferred a new house in the country club section. They went out seldom, for they were happy enough to stay at home together. It was the first year of World War II, and Jinny found work to do in various civic activities. Cass hoped that the work would keep her stimulated. When he noticed that she was beginning to be bored by civic duties, he encouraged her to accept a part in a little theater production. Later, he was sorry that he had encouraged her, for the town began to talk about Jinny and various male members of the cast, particularly Jay Laverick. When Cass spoke to her about the gossip, Jinny accused him of being unreasonably jealous and then apologized. Cass loved her more than ever.

Cass sold some property at an unexpectedly high price and bought the new house that Jinny had desired in the country club district. While waiting for it to be finished, they took a trip to New York. At first, Jinny was enchanted with the size and brightness of the city, but soon she was bored by the unfriendliness of everyone she met. After Bradd Criley arrived in New York and took them under his wing, Jinny enjoyed herself. Cass was not so happy.

Shortly after Cass and Jinny returned home, they learned that Jinny was pregnant; but their happiness was marred by the knowledge that Jinny had diabetes. Roy Drover, her doctor, assured Cass that there was no cause for worry if Jinny followed her diet and got plenty of rest. Bradd Criley seemed to amuse her, so Cass often invited him to the house.

Jinny went through her delivery safely, but the baby died. For many weeks afterward, she would see no one but Cass. Then, for no apparent reason, she wanted to have a party almost every night. Cass tried to be patient with her, for he knew that she was still reacting to the death of the baby, and that the restrictions placed on her by her illness were irritating. When his friends once again warned him about allowing Jinny to see so much of Bradd, his patience wore thin; he almost ordered Jinny to stop seeing Bradd, and he told Bradd to stay away from Jinny. Later, Bradd apologized to Cass and the three were friends once more.

After Bradd moved to New York, all tension between Jinny and Cass seemed to disappear for a time. Then Jinny grew restless again and began to talk of moving to a larger city. Although Cass prized his judgeship and hated to give it up, he was still willing to do anything for his wife. They took another trip to New York, where Cass hoped to find a partnership in an established law firm. They met Bradd during their visit. Although he trusted his wife, Cass was relieved when Jinny told him that she knew she would not really like living in New York and that she wanted to go home. They left hurriedly, without seeing Bradd again before their departure.

On their first night at home, Jinny told Cass that she loved Bradd and that he had become her lover while she was in New York. When Cass refused to give her a divorce until she had had ample time to consider her own wishes carefully, she went back to New York to stay with Bradd's sister until Cass would free her. For Cass, the town, the house, his friends, and his work were now meaningless. He could think only of Jinny. Then he received a telegram from her. After failing to follow her diet, she was desperately ill and she wanted Cass. He flew to New York that night. He found Jinny in a coma, but she awakened long enough to ask him to take her home.

After Jinny could be moved, Cass took her to a seashore hotel and then home. He had forgiven her completely, but he warned her that she would have to work hard to win back their friends. They still had to make their own private adjustment. It was not until Bradd returned to Grand Republic that Jinny was able to see him as the charming philanderer that he really was. That night, she went to Cass's room. He received her as if she had never been away.

Critical Evaluation:

Published only five years before Sinclair Lewis' death, *Cass Timberlane* is one of two late works (the other being *Kingsblood Royal*, 1947) that compare favorably with his five major novels of the 1920's. As in earlier novels such as *Babbitt* (1922) and *Elmer Gantry* (1927), Lewis uses a memorable character to dramatize a particular social problem.

Lewis' subtitle, *A Novel of Husbands and Wives*, reveals the major theme and basic structural pattern of *Cass Timberlane*. The novel examines the institution of marriage through numerous comparisons and contrasts. Interrupting the main narrative of Cass and Jinny are fifteen brief accounts of other husbands and wives. Some are friends of the Timberlanes; others are residents of Grand Republic who have little or no connection with the main plot. In some cases, these accounts—labeled collectively "An Assemblage of Husbands and Wives"—are character sketches with little action. Others are narratives with economical but well-developed plots.

Among the marriages portrayed by Lewis, no more than five are successful. The others range from quietly desperate to violently destructive. For example, Nestor and Fanny Purdwin have been married for fifty years, but their time together has been as monotonous as the unvaried breakfasts of porridge they have eaten every morning for all those years. Roy and Lillian Drover are considered one of the happiest couples in Grand Republic, but Roy is repeatedly unfaithful, Lillian considers suicide, and their two sons enjoy killing things. To escape from a truly vicious wife, Allan Cedar attempts suicide, but she defeats him even in this grim effort. In response to his marital problems, Vincent Osprey becomes a drunk and eventually succeeds in jumping to his death from a hotel window.

By late twentieth century standards, Lewis' depiction of sexuality is modest, but he documents the power of passion and displays a range of behaviors without resorting to graphic details. He alludes at times to the ideas of Sigmund Freud and Richard von Krafft-Ebing, and some of the accounts of husbands and wives sound like case studies of psychosexual problems. In George Hame's case, incestuous desire for his own daughter threatens his marriage. Sabine Grossenwahn is a nymphomaniac who spends part of her wedding night with a man other than her husband. Norton Trock calls his mother "sweetheart" from the age of three and later discovers that his homoerotic attraction to his chauffeur far surpasses the sexual allure of his wife.

Although these relationships are glimpsed in passing, that of the Timberlanes is developed in detail. The pairing of Jinny and Cass is not exactly a May-December romance, but at the ages of twenty-three and forty-one, respectively, they could almost be daughter and father. This disparity in age leads to two motifs in Lewis' main narrative. For the disillusioned older man, the romance leads to spiritual awakening. For the inexperienced younger woman, the courtship and subsequent marriage lead to education and maturing.

As the novel begins, Cass is clearly in a state of stagnation. After his divorce from Blanche, he was briefly a vagabond and an alcoholic. Now he is a responsible judge, but he battles sleep in the courtroom just as he struggles against lethargy in life. The dramatic appearance of Jinny Marshland as a witness in a minor case is the first step in his gradual reawakening. When he meets her young friends at the boarding house, he experiences the concerns of a new generation and a different social class.

In plotting Jinny's education, Lewis uses many standard devices, some of which parallel those used in developing the character of Carol Kennicott in *Main Street* (1920). By traveling away from her provincial environment, Jinny learns about her place in the larger world. Taking part in amateur theatrical productions enables her to explore new roles, on the stage and in real life. In hunting for a new house, she searches for a new identity. Suffering from diabetes, she plunges into a coma but awakens with a more mature vision of reality.

Although the main focus of *Cass Timberlane* is an examination of marriage, Lewis includes much incidental satire of provincial smugness and hypocrisy. He pokes fun at those who consider the *Reader's Digest* to be highly intellectual literature. At one point, Lewis includes a reference to his own novel *Main Street*, but the character who mentions this title in order to appear learned has never read it and thinks the author is Upton Sinclair. Lewis satirizes local organizations such as the Junior Chamber of Commerce, whose members routinely eat together at six o'clock, listen placidly to an invited speaker at seven-fifteen, and return home to their families by eight-thirty. In passages that recall *Babbitt*, Lewis portrays the local Rotarians as slightly higher in social rank but equally vacuous.

In this satire of Grand Republic, Lewis intends to point out the superficiality of an entire culture. Grand Republic sounds more like the name of a country than that of a city, and Lewis says that this midwestern metropolis is interchangeable with at least thirty other U.S. cities. The role of Cass in the context of satire of provincial narrowness is ambiguous. Like Lewis himself, Cass is both attracted to and repelled by the values and behavior of his hometown. This ambiguity is demonstrated best in Cass's attitude toward Bradd Criley. Bradd has been Cass's best friend since childhood but becomes Jinny's seducer. Cass condemns Bradd's immoral behavior but still treasures him as a friend. Cass similarly deplores the hypocrisy and shallowness of Grand Republic but continues to embrace those who blatantly display those qualities.

The conclusion of *Cass Timberlane* is somewhat contrived, but in the return to Grand Republic from New York City, Lewis proclaims the triumph of Midwestern values over those of the effete East. At the same time, he suggests that the Timberlane marriage, having been tested in both the provincial town and the big city, can survive further trials and achieve success.

"Critical Evaluation" by Albert E. Wilhelm

Bibliography:
Dooley, D. J. *The Art of Sinclair Lewis*. Lincoln: University of Nebraska Press, 1967. Reviews major criticism and considers arguments that the novel's contrived ending is more ironic than sentimental. Analyzes the contrapuntal effect of the brief accounts from " An Assemblage of Husbands and Wives."
Geismar, Maxwell. *The Last of the Provincials: The American Novel, 1915-1925*. Boston: Houghton Mifflin, 1947. Argues that *Cass Timberlane* displays Lewis' return to the values of his native Midwest. Asserts that Judge Timberlane is a true aristocrat, whose values are in contrast to corrupt East Coast values.
Grebstein, Sheldon Norman. *Sinclair Lewis*. New York: Twayne, 1962. Intelligent commentaries on Lewis' major novels, along with useful annotated bibliography. Praises the economical sketches in "An Assemblage of Husbands and Wives" as some of Lewis' best writing. Acknowledges that *Cass Timberlane* degenerates at times to soap opera, but argues that Lewis' aim is realism rather than satire.
Schorer, Mark. *Sinclair Lewis: An American Life*. New York: McGraw-Hill, 1961. An authoritative biography. Points out parallels between Lewis' own life and that of Cass Timberlane; suggests that both were victims of a matriarchal complex. Sums up early reviews of the book, including comments by H. L. Mencken. Identifies similarities in structure with *Main Street*.
Wilson, Edmund. "Salute to an Old Landmark: Sinclair Lewis." *The New Yorker*, October 13, 1945, 94, 96-97. One of the most perceptive early reviews. Sees *Cass Timberlane* as significantly different from earlier Lewis novels in its treatment of Midwestern values and of liberated young women.

THE CASTLE

Type of work: Novel
Author: Franz Kafka (1883-1924)
Type of plot: Allegory
Time of plot: Early twentieth century
Locale: Europe
First published: Das Schloss, 1926 (English translation, 1930)

Principal characters:
  K., a seeker and land surveyor
  FRIEDA, a barmaid
  BARNABAS, a young man
  OLGA and
  AMALIA, his sisters
  ARTHUR and
  JEREMIAH, K.'s assistants

The Story:

It was late in the evening when K. arrived in the town that lay before the castle of Count Westwest. After his long walk through deep snow, K. wanted to do nothing so much as to go to sleep. He went to an inn and fell asleep by the fire, only to be awakened by a man wanting to see his permit to stay in the town. K. explained that he had just arrived and had come at the count's request to be the new land surveyor. A telephone call to the castle established the fact that a land surveyor was expected, and K. was allowed to rest.

The next morning, K. decided to go to the castle to report for duty, although his assistants had not yet arrived. He set off through the snowy streets toward the castle, which as he walked seemed further and further away. He became tired and stopped in a house for refreshment and directions. As he left, he saw two men coming from the castle. He tried to speak to them, but they refused to stop. As evening came on, K. got a ride back to the inn in a sleigh.

At the inn, he met the two men he had seen, who introduced themselves as Arthur and Jeremiah and said they were his old assistants. They were not, but K. accepted them because he knew they had come from the castle and must therefore have been sent to help him. Because the two men closely resembled each other, K. could not tell them apart and therefore called both of them Arthur. He ordered them to take him to the castle the next morning by sleigh. When they refused, he telephoned the castle. A voice told him that he could never come to the castle. Shortly afterward, a messenger named Barnabas arrived with a letter from Klamm, a chief at the castle. K. was ordered to report to the mayor of the town.

K. arranged for a room at the inn. He asked to accompany Barnabas on a walk, to which Barnabas, a kind young man, agreed. He took K. to his home to meet his two sisters, Olga and Amalia, and his sickly old mother and father. K. was ill at ease, however; it was Barnabas, not he, who had come home. When Olga left to get beer from a nearby inn, K. went with her. At the inn, it was made clear to him that he would be welcome only in the bar, as the other rooms were reserved for the gentlemen from the castle.

In the bar, K. quickly made friends with the barmaid, Frieda, who seemed to wish to save him from Olga and her family. She hid K. under the counter. K. did not understand what was happening. He learned that Frieda had been Klamm's mistress.

982

Frieda was determined to stay with K., if K. were willing. K. thought he might as well marry her. He was determined to get to the castle and thought his chances would improve if he married the chief's former mistress. When Arthur and Jeremiah entered the room and watched him and Frieda, K. sent them away. Frieda decided to go to the inn where K. was staying.

K. went to call on the mayor, whom he found sick in bed with gout. K. learned that a land surveyor had been needed several years earlier but that nobody knew why K. had come now to fill the unnecessary post. When K. showed him Klamm's letter, the mayor said that it was not important. The mayor convinced K. that his coming to the town was the result of confusion. K. decided to remain and find work, so that he would become an accepted resident of the town.

By the time K. returned to the inn, Frieda had made his room comfortable. The schoolmaster came to offer K. the job of janitor at the school. At Frieda's insistence, K. accepted. That night, K., Frieda, and the two assistants moved to the school to live there. The next morning, the assistants tricked K. into so many arguments with the teachers that K. dismissed them both. After he had finished his day's work, he slipped away and went to Barnabas' house to see if there was a message for him from the castle.

Barnabas was not at home. Olga explained that her family had been rejected by the town because Amalia had refused to become the mistress of one of the gentlemen of the castle, who had written her a crude, obscene letter. Amalia had destroyed the letter, and afterward the whole town had turned against them. K. was so interested in the story that he did not realize how late he had stayed. When he finally prepared to leave, he saw that Jeremiah was outside spying on him.

K. slipped out the back way but then returned and asked Jeremiah why he was there. The man sullenly replied that Frieda had sent him. She had gone back to her old job as barmaid and never wanted to see K. again. Barnabas arrived with the news that one of the most important gentlemen of the castle was awaiting K. at the inn.

At the inn, K. learned that the gentleman had gone to sleep. As he stood in the corridor, he saw Frieda going down another corridor. He ran after her to explain why he had stayed away so long and to ask her to come back to him. She seemed about to relent, when Jeremiah came up to them and persuaded her to go with him. Frieda left K. forever.

At this point in chapter 18, the first edition of the novel ends. The remaining eighty pages were found among Kafka's papers and included in the definitive fourth edition. In this portion, K. intrudes on a sleeping gentleman in a corridor of the pub, only to fall asleep himself in the corridor. After sleeping for twelve hours, he has a lengthy conversation with Pepi, the substitute barmaid, and criticizes the landlady for her old-fashioned clothing.

Critical Evaluation:

The fragmentary work *The Castle* was published posthumously, against Franz Kafka's instructions, by his friend Max Brod. Critics have ever since debated all aspects of it, from the textual problems to the interpretation of the highly suggestive, symbolic structure. It is typical of Kafka's works that a final and convincing definition of his symbols is impossible; like dreams, they combine reference to the everyday world with absurd fantasies, seemingly coherent mythic structure with a discontinuity that frustrates attempts to develop a rational interpretation. The images Kafka conjures up are compelling, but they seem ultimately to stand for themselves and not for any symbolic message.

A knowledge of Kafka's circumstances in 1922 is germane to an understanding of *The Castle*. The author's tuberculosis was already so far advanced that he knew not only that he had not long to live but also the manner of his death. Placed by disease in the position of an outsider,

Kafka could for the first time view personal and professional concerns with detachment. His immanent death gave him the freedom to rise above manner and restraint and through his novel's main character, K., to indulge his sense of humor with outrageous observations. K., who calls himself a land surveyor, takes a sharp look at his surroundings. Like Kafka himself, K. too suffers from those paradoxical effects of advanced disease that leave a patient at once exhausted and impatient.

K.'s main counterpart in the novel is Frieda. Her name connotes *Frieden*, or peace, an irony because the couple has hardly a quiet moment together. Critics have seen in Frieda the fictional representation of Milena Jesenka-Polak, one of Kafka's translators, who professed to love Kafka but ultimately would not leave her husband. The affair in the novel also reflects Kafka's lifelong attitude toward marriage: Although conditioned by society to feel that he should marry, he repeatedly broke off relationships when it became evident that they would interfere with his writing.

In *The Castle*, Kafka criticizes the roles imposed on men and women by the society of his time. Too often, women were perceived mainly as sexual objects and expected to be subservient to and dependent on men. Kafka chose to make his strongest female character in his novel a liberated woman. Set up by her parents (in a frilly blouse and garnet necklace) to attract a husband, Amalia instead repudiated the direct sexual advance of a "gentleman" from the castle. Amalia is portrayed as a capable and talented individual, a person who does not need affiliation with a man to realize her potential.

Just as Kafka criticizes the societal reduction of women to a secondary role, so too does he criticize the expectation that men automatically fulfill a dominant role. Using the device of satire, he represents all figures of male authority and the bureaucracies in which they operate as hopelessly and ludicrously inept, thus exposing the reverence in which they are held as all the more ridiculous. His first example is the most memorable: The mayor, who has let unorganized files accumulate, increases the disorder with every new and frantic search for information. Yet this is the man who solemnly assures K. that there is no possibility of error in the system. K. is not impressed and to the mayor's face calls it "ludicrous bungling."

While no such direct confrontation occurs with the more distant and respected "gentlemen" of the castle—mainly because K. during his one chance interview is overcome by sleep—these officials too are portrayed as being completely out of touch with the affairs of the village they purportedly control and influence. This is no idle criticism. Kafka, who held a doctorate in law and had been a valued employee of an insurance company, knew what bureaucracies were like. By keeping the exact nature of the castle unspecific, Kafka uses that image to demystify arbitrary and illusory authority in all its forms. By having K. continually try to meet Klamm face to face, he shows that it is in the interests of the citizen to pierce the façade of authority.

K. in fact never does reach the castle. Perhaps it is enough that he had his say on important issues and thereby pointed the way for others to take. Kafka indicated to his friend and later executor of his estate, Max Brod, that had he finished the novel he would have had K. die of exhaustion without reaching the castle. Exhaustion is, in fact, a strong factor in the book. The entire four-hundred-page novel takes place in a winter landscape. The days are very short, and the people are exhausted by the cold and spend much of their time sleeping indoors. In choosing this setting, Kafka drew on the literary convention of using winter as a metaphor for death.

The spiritual message of *The Castle* gains in impact by being merely suggested and allowed to continue independently of K.'s physical limitations. Where the mind is free, as it most certainly is in this dreamlike novel, a survey of the land yields new truths. Kafka shows that the castle is a jumble created by people themselves and in need of rearrangement.

Thomas Mann defined Kafka as a religious humorist. While Kafka's meaning has perhaps eluded the attempts of critics to define it, his portrayal of the experiences of individual isolation and frustration, and of the ambivalence toward the community and the vague forces that dominate the individual and human society, remains compelling.

"Critical Evaluation" by Jean M. Snook

Bibliography:
Fickert, Kurt J. "Chapter IV: Castle and Burrow." In *Kafka's Doubles*. Bern, Switzerland: Peter Lang, 1979. A short but substantial work that provides new insights into Kafka's careful creative process. Interprets *The Castle* as the author's self-analysis.

Kraft, Herbert. "Being There Still: K., Land Surveyor, Stable-Hand, . . ." In *Someone Like K.: Kafka's Novels*, translated by R. J. Kavanagh. Würzburg, Germany: Königshausen & Neumann, 1991. A positive assessment of K. as the antitype. Since there is no mass resistance, individuals must stand alone, but they can be perceived to be powerful. K. knows what Amalia knows, but he also has the courage to act.

Neumeyer, Peter F., ed. *Twentieth Century Interpretations of "The Castle": A Collection of Critical Essays*. Englewood Cliffs, N.J.: Prentice-Hall, 1969. Part 1 contains ten so-called Interpretations; part 2 contains shorter View Points. A testimony to the astounding number of diverse and conflicting interpretations that *The Castle* has inspired.

Sheppard, Richard. *On Kafka's Castle: A Study*. London: Croom Helm, 1973. A close reading of the novel, which is in many aspects convincing. A bourgeois interpretation; like the German critic Wilhelm Emrich, whose study of Kafka's writing appeared in English translation in 1968, Sheppard tends to take the viewpoint of the villagers and is critical of K. for not settling down with Frieda.

Spann, Meno. "Chapter 9: The Castle." In *Franz Kafka*. Boston: Twayne, 1976. A lucidly written essay that places the novel in the context of Kafka's personal and literary development. Spann, one of the few critics receptive to Kafka's sense of humor, offers a convincing interpretation of *The Castle* as a satire on bureaucracy.

THE CASTLE OF OTRANTO

Type of work: Novel
Author: Horace Walpole (1717-1797)
Type of plot: Gothic
Time of plot: Twelfth century
Locale: Italy
First published: 1765

Principal characters:
    MANFRED, the prince of Otranto
    MATILDA, Manfred's daughter
    CONRAD, Manfred's son
    ISABELLA, Conrad's fiancée
    FATHER JEROME, a priest
    THEODORE, a young peasant and the true heir to Otranto

The Story:

Manfred, the prince of Otranto, planned to marry his fifteen-year-old son Conrad to Isabella, the daughter of the marquis of Vicenza. On the day of the wedding, however, a servant ran into the hall and informed the assembled company that a huge helmet had appeared mysteriously in the courtyard of the castle. When Count Manfred and his guests rushed into the courtyard, they found Conrad crushed to death beneath a gigantic helmet adorned with waving black plumes. Theodore, a young peasant, declared the helmet was like that on a statue of Prince Alfonso the Good, which stood in the chapel. Another spectator shouted that the helmet was missing from the statue. Prince Manfred imprisoned the young peasant as a magician and charged him with the murder of the heir to Otranto.

That evening, Manfred sent for Isabella. He informed her that he intended to divorce his wife so that he himself might marry her and have another male heir. Frightened, Isabella ran away and lost herself in the passages beneath the castle. There she encountered Theodore, who helped her to escape through an underground passage into a nearby church. Manfred, searching for the girl, accused the young man of aiding her. As he was threatening Theodore, servants rushed up to tell the prince of a giant who was sleeping in the great hall of the castle. When Manfred returned to the hall, the giant had disappeared.

The following morning, Father Jerome came to inform Manfred and his wife that Isabella had taken sanctuary at the altar of his church. Sending his wife away, Manfred called on the priest to help him divorce his wife and marry Isabella. Father Jerome refused, warning Manfred that heaven would punish him for harboring such thoughts. The priest unthinkingly suggested Isabella might be in love with the handsome young peasant who had aided in her escape.

Manfred, enraged at the possibility, confronted Theodore. Although the young man did not deny having aided the princess, he claimed never to have seen her before. The frustrated Manfred ordered him to the courtyard to be executed, and Father Jerome was called to give absolution to the condemned man; however, when the collar of the lad was loosened, the priest discovered a birthmark that proved the young peasant to be Father Jerome's son, born before the priest had entered the Church. Manfred offered to stay the execution if the priest would deliver Isabella to him. At that moment, a trumpet sounded at the gates of the castle.

The trumpet signaled the arrival of a herald from the Knight of the Gigantic Sabre, champion of Isabella's father, who was the rightful heir to Otranto. Greeting Manfred as a usurper, the herald demanded either the immediate release of Isabella and Manfred's abdication or the satisfaction of mortal combat. Manfred invited the Knight of the Gigantic Sabre to the castle, hoping to get his permission to marry Isabella and keep the throne. The knight entered the castle with five hundred men at arms and a hundred more carrying one gigantic sword.

During the feast, the strange knight kept silence and raised his visor only to pass food into his mouth. Later, Manfred broached the question of marrying Isabella, telling the knight he wished to marry again to ensure himself of an heir. Before he had finished, Father Jerome arrived with the news of Isabella's disappearance from the church. After everyone had gone to look for Isabella, Manfred's daughter, Matilda, assisted Theodore to escape from the castle.

In the forest, Theodore met Isabella and promised to protect her. Shortly thereafter, they met the Knight of the Gigantic Sabre. Fearing the knight meant harm to Isabella, the young man overcame him in combat. The knight, thinking he was about to die, revealed to Isabella that he was her father. They returned together to the castle, where Isabella's father confided to her that he had discovered the gigantic sword in the Holy Land. It was a miraculous weapon; on the blade was written that only the blood of Manfred could atone for the wrongs committed on the family of the true ruler of Otranto. When Manfred returned to the castle, he found Theodore dressed in armor. It seemed to Manfred that the young man resembled the prince whose throne Manfred had usurped.

Manfred still hoped to wed Isabella, and he craftily won her father's consent by allowing that nobleman's betrothal to Matilda. At that point, a nearby statue dripped blood from its nose, an omen that disaster would follow the proposed marriages.

Manfred saw only two courses open to him. One was to surrender all claims to Otranto; the other was to proceed with his plan to marry Isabella. In either case, it appeared that fate was against his success. Nor did a second appearance of the giant in the castle ease the anxiety he felt. When Isabella's father heard of the giant, he decided not to court disaster by marrying Matilda or by permitting Manfred to marry his daughter. His resolution was strengthened when a skeleton in the rags of a hermit exhorted him to renounce Matilda.

Hours later, Manfred was told that Theodore was in the chapel with a woman. Jealous, he went to the chapel and stabbed the woman, who was his own daughter Matilda. Over the body of Matilda, Theodore announced that he was the true ruler of Otranto. Suddenly, the giant form of the dead Prince Alfonso appeared, proclaiming Theodore to be the true heir. Then he ascended to heaven, where he was received by St. Nicholas.

The truth now became known that Theodore was the son of Father Jerome, when he was still prince of Falconara, and Alfonso's daughter. Manfred confessed his usurpation, and he and his wife entered neighboring convents. Theodore married Isabella and ruled as the new prince of Otranto.

Critical Evaluation:

Horace Walpole's *The Castle of Otranto* is among the best-known, best-loved, and best-crafted novels of the gothic genre in English. It is also one of the first. Gothic fiction was representative of the late eighteenth century rejection of the rational, realistic creed of neoclassicism, which asserted the superiority of the familiar and contemporary for literary purposes. This reaction was but a phase of the revival of interest in the recondite past, an interest that focused on medieval life and manifested itself in pseudoscholarly antiquarianism, imitation Gothic castles, artificial ruins, balladry, and contrived narratives.

These narratives, permeated with fashionable melancholy, attempted to portray human conduct and sentiment with psychological realism while setting the action in remote and mysterious places and times. The emotional thrills of adventure provided the reader an escape from humdrum existence; hence, the villain was characteristically somber and restless, and the heroine—beautiful, innocent, young, and sensitively perceptive—waited dutifully to be rescued by a brave and courageous lover. The obligatory setting was a haunted castle, a cloister, or a ruined abbey, fortuitously furnished with underground passages, secret doors, and locked and unused rooms, and surrounded by wild and desolate landscape. The action inevitably included strange and deliberate crimes (often accompanied by rattling chains and other inexplicable phenomena), incidents of physical violence, and emotional anguish orchestrated with supernatural manifestations. A strong erotic element usually underscored the plot, and comic relief, following William Shakespeare's model, was confined to servants. In a bogus historical setting, chronologically and geographically remote, novels of mystery and passionate emotion depicted the trials and misfortunes of sentimental love with an overlay of ghosts, prescience, and preternatural forces, as well as the titillating horror of violence and crime.

The author of *The Castle of Otranto*, which stood at the very forefront of this gothic revival, seemed personally ideally suited to his book (rather than the more usual obverse). Horace Walpole was a nobleman who was respected for his antiquarian scholarship, and he was a fussy bachelor in precarious health, unable to join his peers in hunting, tippling, and wenching. He escaped the demands of this world by psychologically and physically retreating into the past. He built himself a pseudo-Gothic retreat at Strawberry Hill, and there he displayed his collection of antiques and led an active fantasy life, imagining himself at one time a feudal lord and at another time a learned monk. One evening, he reportedly climbed his narrow Gothic staircase to his library so that he could dream—possibly with the aid of opium—of the romantic past.

The Castle of Otranto was spawned out of dreams, illustrating two major themes of the gothic genre. The story unites a baroque view of architecture and sentiment and a repudiation of neoclassical ideals of proportion, balance, and harmony. The physical appearance of the Castle of Otranto, therefore, was an exaggeration of genuine Gothic style, carrying the visual image to such excessive lengths that the structure bore hardly any resemblance to authentic examples of medieval Gothic architecture. Yet the effectiveness of the description in the novel is undeniable. Similarly, the emotional overreaction of the characters—in defiance of all neoclassical canons of moderation—served to transcend the mundane realities of common life on the wings of fancy. In the very uncommon life of this story, Walpole sought to liberate imagination and allow it to rove freely in what he characterized as "the boundless realms of invention . . . creating more interesting situations." Simultaneously (and without any sense of contradiction), Walpole claimed to strive for naturalness and probability in his character development. Nevertheless, fanciful setting and untrammeled emotion were the hallmarks of his as well as many other gothic novels.

Walpole employed supernatural devices to create his interesting situations, and the totally immersed reader can become so wrapped up in the plot that inconsistencies escape notice. The plot is actually plausible, but the events that surround and to some extent precipitate it are more than a little suspect. The story opens with the ambiguous prophecy that "the castle and lordship of Otranto should pass from the present family, whenever the real owner should be grown too large to inhabit it." Intrigue thickens with Conrad's peculiar death and Manfred's frantic attempts to sire another heir. In due course, other supernatural manifestations intervene: Two menservants see a strange apparition, which also appears to Bianca, Matilda's maid. Manfred's reasonable objections notwithstanding, these events very nearly unseat his reason; but even as Manfred argues with Hippolita to annul their marriage so that he can marry Isabella and produce an heir, three drops of blood fall from the nose of the statue of Alfonso, the original prince of Otranto who won the principality through fraud and deceit. Manfred is thus given supernatural warning to desist from his wicked plan. He is still undeterred, but his intended father-in-law also sees an apparition when he goes to the chapel to pray for guidance. In the end, after many such scenes of terror, violence, and bewilderment, the true heir of Otranto is unexpectedly discovered amid a thunderclap, a rattling of armor, and a disembodied pronouncement about legitimate succession.

Although in retrospect these contrivances may strain the credulity of today's reader, the chain of events is so engrossing that the reader's normal skepticism is effectively held at bay. It is only after the fact that the reader begins to examine the logic and question the veracity of Walpole's highly convincing tale. Therein lies the art of the story.

"Critical Evaluation" by Joanne G. Kashdan

Bibliography:

Day, William Patrick. *In the Circles of Fear and Desire: A Study of Gothic Fantasy.* Chicago: University of Chicago Press, 1985. A study of the themes and conventions of gothic fantasy from the publication of Walpole's novel up through the twentieth century. Discusses Manfred as an example of the typical gothic male protagonist.

Kallich, Martin. *Horace Walpole.* New York: Twayne, 1971. Discusses the formal style and period-piece conventions of the novel. Suggests a reading of the story as a version of the Freudian family romance, with such Oedipal themes as desire for the mother, anger toward the father, and fear of punishment.

Mehrotra, K. K. *Horace Walpole and the English Novel.* Oxford, England: Basil Blackwell, 1934. A detailed discussion of the novel that analyzes the work from the perspective of the readers of its time and places the work in the context of the realistic novel and the tale of terror.

Sabor, Peter, ed. *Horace Walpole: The Critical Heritage.* London: Routledge & Kegan Paul, 1987. A valuable collection of reviews, introductions, contemporary discussions, and letters relating to Walpole's works. Includes eighteen items discussing *The Castle of Otranto.*

Varma, Devendra. *The Gothic Flame.* New York: Russell & Russell, 1966. A well-known history of the English gothic novel that discusses both the origins and the influences of the genre. Clarifies the various gothic conventions originated by *The Castle of Otranto*, particularly its surrealistic style and gothic hero.

CASTLE RACKRENT
An Hibernian Tale

Type of work: Novel
Author: Maria Edgeworth (1767-1849)
Type of plot: Regional
Time of plot: Eighteenth century
Locale: Ireland
First published: 1800

> *Principal characters:*
> HONEST THADY QUIRK, the narrator
> SIR KIT RACKRENT, the owner of Castle Rackrent
> SIR CONDY RACKRENT, Sir Kit's heir
> ISABELLA, Condy's wife
> JUDY QUIRK, Thady's niece
> JASON, Thady's son

The Story:

After the death of Sir Patrick O'Shaughlin, his fine and generous master, Honest Thady Quirk found himself working at Castle Rackrent for the heir, Sir Murtagh, a penny-pinching owner with a vicious temper. Lady Murtagh was also more interested in money than in the happiness of her tenants. After Sir Murtagh died in a fit of temper, she stripped Castle Rackrent of its treasures and went to live in London. The estate passed to her husband's younger brother, Sir Kit Rackrent, a wild, carefree man. Finding the estate in debt and heavily mortgaged, Sir Kit went to England to marry a rich wife who would repair the estate and bring a dowry for his support.

At last, he came back with a wealthy wife, a Jewess he had married while staying in Bath. It was soon apparent to Honest Thady that there was no love between the honeymooners. One serious difficulty arose over the presence of pig meat on the dinner table. Lady Kit had insisted that no such meat be served, but Sir Kit defied her orders. When the meat appeared on the table, Lady Kit retired to her room, and her husband locked her in. She remained a prisoner for seven years. When she became very ill and appeared to be dying, Sir Kit tried to influence her to leave her jewels to him, but she refused. It was assumed she would die shortly, and all eligible ladies in the neighborhood hoped to become the next Lady Kit. Amid the controversy over his possible choice, Sir Kit was challenged and killed in a duel. Miraculously recovering from her illness, Lady Kit went to London. The next heir was Sir Condy Rackrent, a distant cousin of Sir Kit.

Sir Condy Rackrent was a spendthrift but a good-natured master. Although the estate was more deeply in debt than ever, he made no attempt to improve the condition of his holdings. Sir Condy soon began a steadfast friendship with the family who lived on the neighboring estate. The youngest daughter, Isabella, took a fancy to Sir Condy, but her father would not hear of a match between his family and the owner of Castle Rackrent. Sir Condy really loved Judy, the grandniece of Honest Thady. One day, in Thady's presence, Sir Condy tossed a coin to determine which girl he would marry. Judy lost, and soon after Sir Condy eloped with Isabella.

He had expected that Isabella would bring some money to the estate, but she was disinherited by her father when she married Sir Condy. While the newlyweds lived in careless luxury, the house and grounds fell further into neglect, to the distress of the servants and tenants. Learning of a vacancy in the coming elections, Sir Condy decided to stand for Parliament. He won the election, but too late to save himself from his creditors.

Honest Thady's son, Jason, a legal administrator, helped a neighbor buy up all Sir Condy's debts. With so much power in his hands, Jason scorned his own father. When Lady Condy learned that her husband's debtors were closing in on him, she complied with the demands of her family and returned to her father's house. Sir Condy wrote a will, in which he willed his wife all the land and five hundred pounds a year after his death. When Jason demanded payment for the Rackrent debts, Sir Condy explained that he could not do so because he had given an income of five hundred a year to Lady Condy. Jason thereupon insisted that Sir Condy sell Castle Rackrent and all the estates to satisfy his creditors. Having no other recourse, Sir Condy agreed. The five hundred a year was still guaranteed for Isabella. Thady was grief-stricken that his son had maneuvered in this way against Sir Condy, and it came to a break between them. When Lady Condy's carriage was upset and she was nearly killed, Jason, assuming she would surely die, hurried to Sir Condy with a proposal that he sell him Lady Condy's yearly income. Sir Condy, needing the cash, complied with Jason's proposal.

Judy Quirk had married in the meantime, and her husband had died. She paid a call on Sir Condy, who was staying at Thady's lodge. The old servant felt certain that Judy would now become Lady Rackrent, but Judy told her uncle that there was no point in becoming a lady without a castle to accompany the title. She also hinted that she might do better to marry Jason, who at least held the lands. Thady tried to dissuade her from such a thought, but Judy was bent on acquiring a fortune.

Sir Condy, who had long indulged in an excess of food and drink, suffered from gout. One night at a party, he drank a large draught too quickly and died a few days later. After Sir Condy's death, Jason and the now-recovered Lady Condy went to court over the title of the estate. Some said Jason would get the land, and others said Lady Condy would win. Thady could only guess the results of the suit.

Critical Evaluation:

Maria Edgeworth was famous in her day as the author of seven novels and as a writer interested in the education of children. She shared this interest with her father, Richard Lovell Edgeworth, an Irish landowner who had settled his large family in Ireland in 1782 when Maria was at the impressionable age of fifteen. He was an intellectual and a believer in social and political reform. Throughout his life, Maria Edgeworth deferred to his tastes, seeking not only his guidance but also his collaboration in much of her writing.

Castle Rackrent is the author's first novel, written sometime between 1797 and 1799 and published in 1800. It is a distinguished piece of work in several ways. A successful first novel, generally regarded as her best, it is also one of the few works in which her father had no part. The author herself declared that "it went to the press just as it was written."

In addition, *Castle Rackrent* holds a distinction in the history of the English novel as the first regional novel, a significance noted by Sir Walter Scott in the preface to his first historical novel, *Waverley* (1814), in which he stated his purpose of creating a Scottish milieu with the same degree of authenticity as "that which Miss Edgeworth so fortunately achieved for Ireland." In her own preface, Edgeworth takes pains to indicate the realistically Irish quality of the novel. Her first-person narrator, Thady Quirk, is a character based on her father's steward; he speaks in Irish idiom because "the authenticity of his story would have been more exposed to doubt if it were not told in his own characteristic manner." Moreover, the subject is peculiarly Irish:

"Those who were acquainted with the manners of a certain class of the gentry of Ireland some years ago, will want no evidence of the truth of Honest Thady's narrative."

In the use of certain devices, Maria Edgeworth anticipates the historical novel later developed by Scott—for example, in the historicity suggested by the subtitle: "An Hibernian Tale Taken from Facts, and from the Manners of Irish Squires, Before the Year 1782." More explicitly, Edgeworth assures her readers that "these are 'tales of other times'; . . . the manners depicted . . . are not those of the present age: the race of the Rackrents has long been extinct in Ireland." Similar to the kind of documentation Scott was to employ is her anecdotal glossary of Irish "terms and idiomatic phrases." The convention of the "true story," of course, is an eighteenth century legacy, and, like many eighteenth century novels, *Castle Rackrent* purports to be an original memoir for which the author is merely the editor.

The theme of the novel adumbrates Scott's characteristic theme, the conflict between a dying culture and one coming into being; the resemblance, however, stops there. Lacking historical events and personages, the Rackrent story is not too remote in time from the date of composition. Although the Rackrents indulge in gloriously absurd deeds—such as the sham wake staged by Sir Condy in order to spy on his own mourners—there are no heroic deeds in their past. The name "Rackrent," referring to the exorbitant rents exacted by landlords from their tenants, reveals their main trait.

The novel is a satire on the Irish ruling class. With the sustained irony behind Thady's blind "partiality to the family in which he was bred and born," the author presents one Irish family's reprehensible history. Except for Sir Murtagh, who wastes his fortune in lawsuits, all the Rackrents ruin themselves and their estates through extravagance and dissipation. Whether they are squires in residence or absentee landlords dealing through agents "who grind the face of the poor," they increase the misery of the common Irish people. Concealed behind Thady's comical anecdotes is the judgment that the Rackrents represent the destructive arrogance and irresponsible stupidity of landowners who answer to no one except, eventually, moneylenders such as Thady's ruthless son Jason, who finally takes possession of the Rackrent estates.

The novel is centered on Thady himself, however, despite the title of the novel and Thady's own unwavering focus on the Rackrents, despite even several unforgettable comic episodes of Rackrent peccadilloes. His voice reveals his self-importance:

> Having out of friendship for the family, upon whose estate, praised be Heaven! I and mine have lived rent free time out of mind, voluntarily undertaken to publish the Memoirs of the Rackrent Family, I think it my duty to say a few words, in the first place, concerning myself.

His self-importance is based on his illusions of living in the family's reflected grandeur and glory. If he lives by his professed loyalty, he acts on the example of his masters, exploiting his privileges as they do and just as blind to the inevitable outcome. Throughout the novel, for example, Thady boasts of various strategies to push forward "my son Jason," who acquires his first lease on Rackrent land because "I spoke a good word for my son, and gave out in the county that nobody need bid against us." As the opportunistic Thady comments, "Why shouldn't he as well as another?" Yet he complains bitterly of Jason grown rich that "he is a high gentleman, and never minds what poor Thady says, and having better than 1500 a-year, landed estate, looks down upon Honest Thady, but I wash my hands of his doings, and as I have lived so will I die, true and loyal to the family."

Thady's praise of the Rackrents is often coupled with his appreciation of money. When a new heir neglects Thady, the old man is hostile, but the first casual attention produces a characteristic response: "I loved him from that day to this, his voice was so like the family—and he threw me a guinea out of his waistcoat pocket." Another trait incompatible with honest devotion is Thady's evasive habit of silence at crucial moments, a silence very much at odds with his characteristic garrulity. There is a self-serving tone in the recurring motif, "I said nothing for fear of gaining myself ill will."

On the other hand, Thady's talkativeness, urged by vanity, contributes to the downfall of his favorite, Sir Condy, the last of the Rackrents. It is Thady's son who seizes the property, but it is Thady who made the young Condy his "white-headed boy" and fed his imagination with the disastrous "stories of the family and the blood from which he was sprung." He proudly takes credit for the adult Condy's unfortunate gambling habits, boasting, "I well remember teaching him to toss up for bog berries on my knee." The ultimate irony is that his teachings indirectly bring about Sir Condy's death; for the family legend of Sir Patrick's prodigious whiskey-drinking feat, which the last Rackrent fatally duplicates, is "the story that he learned from me when a child."

Torn between his son and his master and called by his niece an "unnatural fader," he confesses, "I could not upon my conscience tell which was wrong from the right." He is unaware, even as he explains it, that Rackrent rights derive from money just as Jason's pretensions do. Even the designation "ancient" is not appropriate for the Rackrents, since the estate had come into "the family" in Thady's great-grandfather's time when Sir Patrick, by act of Parliament, took the surname in order to receive the property. Thady's dilemma is treated comically, but there is also pathos in the position in which he finds himself in the end: "I'm tired wishing for any thing in this world, after all I've seen it—but I'll say nothing; it would be a folly to be getting myself ill will in my old age."

Thady Quirk is a masterful characterization, requiring none of the apologies that Edgeworth as fictitious editor appended to his memoirs. However, those remarks served the purpose not so much of the author of fiction but of the daughter of Richard Lovell Edgeworth when she offered her thoughts concerning a political resolution as her last word on the moral dilemma so convincingly portrayed in this short novel: "It is a problem of difficult solution to determine whether an Union will hasten or retard the amelioration of this country." Sir Walter Scott later praised her fictional Irish, England's "gay and kind-hearted neighbours," as having "done more towards completing the Union" than any subsequent legislation. Fortunately, Thady Quirk lives on as a fictional character, independent of the long-standing tumultuous relations between England and Ireland.

"Critical Evaluation" by Catherine E. Moore

Bibliography:
Butler, Marilyn. *Maria Edgeworth: A Literary Biography.* London: Oxford University Press, 1972. The standard biography, eloquent and reflecting scrupulous research in Edgeworth family papers and correspondence. Includes information on the Edgeworth family's relationship with their retainers and tenants, and on the reception of the novel.
Flanagan, Thomas. *The Irish Novelists: 1800-1850.* New York: Columbia University Press, 1959. An elegant and witty discussion of Maria Edgeworth that places her in the context of her Irish contemporaries. The analysis of regional and native elements set the standard for much subsequent discussion of *Castle Rackrent.*
Harden, Elizabeth. *Maria Edgeworth.* Boston: Twayne, 1984. A fine survey of Edgeworth's life and work that stresses her theme of "the education of the heart" through the various phases

of her development. Close analysis of the narrative strategies of *Castle Rackrent*. Includes a useful annotated bibliography.

McCormack, W. J. *Ascendancy and Tradition in Anglo-Irish Literary History from 1789 to 1939*. Oxford: Clarendon Press, 1985. A wide-ranging discussion of the political circumstances of the composition of *Castle Rackrent*, Maria Edgeworth's use of family chronicles, and the architecture of the Big House.

Owens, Cóilín, ed. *Family Chronicles: Maria Edgeworth's "Castle Rackrent."* Totowa, N.J.: Barnes & Noble, 1987. A casebook of fourteen selections from the best formal and historical criticism on the novel. Includes essays on biographical backgrounds, the Irish and English novel, the reliability of Thady's account, and Irish folklore. Also includes an annotated bibliography.

CAT AND MOUSE

Type of work: Novella
Author: Günter Grass (1927-   )
Type of plot: Bildungsroman
Time of plot: World War II
Locale: Danzig, Germany
First published: Katz und Maus, 1961 (English translation, 1963)

> *Principal characters:*
> PILENZ, the narrator
> JOACHIM MAHLKE, his schoolmate
> TULLA POKRIEFKE, a young girl
> FATHER GUSEWSKI, a practical-minded priest
> WALDEMAR KLOHSE, the headmaster of the boys' school, the Conradium

The Story:

Encouraged by his confessor, Pilenz wrote down his recollections about the complicated cat-and-mouse relationship he had with Mahlke, his friend from school. He began with a sunny day on the baseball field, when he had set a cat on Mahlke's enormous Adam's apple; unable to resist, the cat had scratched Mahlke, embarrassing him. Pilenz identified himself with the "eternal cat" that would be Mahlke's undoing.

A group of boys that included Pilenz, Mahlke, Hotten Sontag, and Schilling spent their summers swimming around the abandoned wreck of a Polish minesweeper in the Danzig harbor. Mahlke went to a great deal of trouble to learn to swim, and soon he swam and dove better than any of the other boys. He often swam down into the minesweeper, bringing back a variety of objects, including a medallion of the Virgin Mary, a fire extinguisher, and a Victrola. Sometimes the boys were joined by Tulla Pokriefke, a girl who greatly admired Mahlke.

Because of his enormous Adam's apple, Mahlke wore a variety of objects around his neck, including the medallion and a screwdriver he had brought up from the minesweeper. Once he even started a fashion trend by wearing yarn pom-poms as if they were a bow tie. These objects, according to Pilenz, did as much to draw attention to as they did to distract from Mahlke's Adam's apple.

One summer, Mahlke, exploring the insides of the minesweeper, found that he could reach a radio room that was not underwater. This became Mahlke's sanctuary, and he transported many of his treasures to the room, cleverly protecting them from water damage on the way. He took the Victrola and several records to his secret room, where he would play music while the boys sunned themselves on top of the minesweeper.

Mahlke, a Roman Catholic, was remarkably devoted to the Virgin Mary, although he professed no faith in God or Christ. This excessive devotion set him apart from the other boys, even from Pilenz, who was often an altar boy at the church Mahlke attended. Mahlke sometimes dreamed of being a clown when he grew up, and he was certainly very conscious of himself as a spectacle at school. With his odd looks, religious fanaticism, and collection of bizarre objects hanging from his neck, Mahlke was the object of alternating ridicule and admiration from his schoolmates.

The boys attended the Conradium, an elitist all-boys school run by the headmaster Klohse, who was a member of the National Socialist Party. After an alumnus of the school who had been

995

awarded the Iron Cross for his service in the air force came to speak to the student body, all of Mahlke's energy became focused on the Iron Cross. He began to dream of earning one for himself; the Iron Cross would be the perfect counterbalance to his Adam's apple.

Another speaker came, and although Mahlke did not want to go, Pilenz dragged him along. This speaker, although extremely boring, also had the Iron Cross around his neck; after the speech, in the school locker room, Mahlke stole the medal. He wore it to school under his shirt and tie. Eventually Mahlke confessed to headmaster Klohse, who expelled him from school.

For a while, Mahlke attended the nearby Horst Wessel School. He spent a summer in paramilitary training and then joined the army in an effort to gain his own Iron Cross. Eventually he succeeded in doing so and returned to Danzig in triumph. He expected that he, like other illustrious alumnae, would be asked to give a speech at the Conradium. When he approached Klohse, however, his speech already written, Klohse refused to allow him to speak to the student body. Mahlke, frustrated, sought out Klohse near his home, confronted him, and slapped him in the face. Because of this, and because he had overstayed his furlough from the army, Mahlke became a fugitive. When his old priest, Father Gusewski, was unable to help him, he turned to Pilenz for help.

Pilenz took advantage of Mahlke's total dependence on him. He refused to harbor him in his basement, instead suggesting that Mahlke hide in the old minesweeper. Even though it was not summer time, Mahlke and Pilenz rowed out to the minesweeper with two cans of pork and a can opener. When they arrived, Mahlke removed and carefully folded his uniform, put on the Iron Cross, and wearing his old gym shorts from the Conradium, dove into the water with the tins. Pilenz, noticing that he had left the can opener behind, pounded on the side of the minesweeper, shouting, "Can opener!" There was no response.

For years afterward, Pilenz searched for Mahlke among the clowns at circuses or at reunions for recipients of the Iron Cross. He never found Mahlke and ultimately concluded that Mahlke, the eternal mouse, had finally fallen prey to the eternal cat, which Pilenz perceived as a combination of forces that included school, society, the army, and Pilenz himself.

"The Story" by Kelly C. Walter

Critical Evaluation:

After World War II, the spiritual recovery of Germany lagged far behind its economic recovery, and nowhere was this lag more apparent than in the failure of German literature to regain the eminence it had attained before the war in the work of such authors as Heinrich and Thomas Mann, Franz Kafka, and Hermann Hesse. These writers and many others diagnosed the spiritual malaise of the society, which reached its culmination in the horrors of the Nazi regime. In the 1960's, the emergence of several writers of the first rank indicated a spiritual rebirth in Germany. Perhaps the most notable of these young writers, certainly the most heralded, was Günter Grass, whose first novel, *The Tin Drum* (1959), established him as a major figure in the postwar rehabilitation of German literature. In *Cat and Mouse*, his second novel, he reinforces his claim to that status by perceptively probing into what was continuing to ail the German spirit.

Although narrated in 1961 by an adult named Pilenz, who works as a secretary for a parish settlement house, *Cat and Mouse* is set in the years during World War II, when Pilenz was a teenager and schoolboy. Caught up in the dull round of secular life in postwar Germany and poignantly aware of a great spiritual emptiness in his world (he is a Catholic who has lost his belief in God), Pilenz feels compelled to tell the story of his boyhood friend Joachim Mahlke, who disappeared, after deserting the army, by diving into a sunken minesweeper where they played as boys and where Mahlke had a secret retreat. Though fifteen years have elapsed since then, Pilenz has looked for Mahlke ever since and everywhere he could possibly appear; he has never given up hope that his friend will "resurface." *Cat and Mouse* is dedicated, as it were, to resuscitating the spirit of Mahlke and thereby to rediscovering a spiritual basis for German life and art.

The resuscitation—that is, Pilenz's writing of the novel—is a complicated matter. Time has dimmed and confused his memory, so his story is as much a reconstruction of the past as a recollection of it; it is as much the re-creation of Mahlke, and of that part of himself Mahlke represents, as it is memory. A self-conscious artist, Pilenz realizes that his story, written out of inner necessity, is like all art: a fusion of reality and imagination. What he remembers most vividly, providing him with a grip on the past and himself, is a boyhood scene in which he or one of his friends—he remembers it differently each time he returns to it—encouraged a black cat to pounce on Mahlke's mouse, that is, his Adam's apple, while he lay asleep. About this fablelike incident, Pilenz constructs his tale of how the beast of death eventually kills Mahlke's mouse. *Cat and Mouse* is a definition and revival of the spiritual qualities that were lost with Mahlke's disappearance, the dialogue of recollection being a way of making him reappear to the narrator and his public.

Endowed with an abnormally large and active Adam's apple and lacking physical grace, Joachim Mahlke was an unnoticed figure among the children of the neighborhood until at the age of fourteen he learned to swim. Thereafter, he was a moral force—leading them to the sunken boat, diving into dangerous depths and staying beneath the surface for long periods while collecting trophies, and being modest and considerate. He was not, however, nature's darling: Besides being clumsy in looks and manner, he never tanned, and the cold water chilled him blue and coarsened his skin. Furthermore, he had no interest in girls or in displays of virility. Rather, he was driven by self-consciousness to use the power with which he was blessed to hide his Adam's apple, to redeem his natural being and shortcomings. For that purpose, he devoted himself to self-transcending ideals, represented alternately by the Virgin Mother and military heroes. These provided him with religious idols before which he could kneel in purifying devotion.

Growing up audience-conscious, Mahlke originally wanted to be a clown so that he could make people laugh and help them be happy, but the Catholic Church, the German state through its heroes and schools, and the war sapped his faith and channeled his power toward destructive ends. Eventually, he who had been called the Redeemer by a classmate caricaturist, is refused recognition for his military exploits by the school that had taught him that heroes are made by slaughter in the name of the state, and he is led to betray his initial religious and humanistic impulses by the pressure of social and political circumstances. Frustrated in his aspiration to reveal the truth to schoolchildren, he is left with nothing in which to believe, with no honorable task to perform. His disappearance into the minesweeper comes as a final gesture of knowledge and repudiation, perhaps an awareness of his inability to hide his Adam's apple, certainly a recognition of the inability of his society to harbor his spiritual talents and aspirations or to acknowledge their source. His was the hero's dilemma: He was the victim of the contradictions between his inordinate desire to serve and the refusal of the common order to tolerate him and his idol.

The disappearance and absence of the heroic is what ails Germany in Günter Grass's diagnosis. It is not, however, the loss of the traditional heroes that he laments. What Grass resuscitates is the Christian-chivalric vision in which masculine power is bound in service to feminine tenderness, in which nature is tamed and saved from its inherent evil through devotion to purifying spiritual values, and in which the magnetism of love replaces domination by tyrannical force.

Mahlke's ultimate defeat hinges on the triviality of a medal stolen from a war hero at school, a circumstance that at first glance seems a narrative weakness, but is actually the novel's strength. Though in places the novel is reminiscent of Franz Kafka's allegory and Thomas Mann's irony, the demoniac powers that haunt and doom the characters in the works of those writers are conspicuously absent in *Cat and Mouse*. Pilenz, though he cannot be sure he incited the cat to pounce on Mahlke's mouse, knows he is implicated in his disappearance and so writes out of guilt, using art as a vehicle to redeem his sin. Recognition of what he has lost, of how far he has fallen, implies a spiritual awakening sufficient for the first steps toward freedom from necessity and from the bondage of the past. Grass's fablelike story, with its blend of symbolism and irony with realism, expresses the power of the imagination to transform the "real." Only by forgetting enough of the past can Pilenz entertain ideals again; only by believing in the spiritual origins and power of art, as Mahlke believed in the Virgin Mother, is genuine art again possible. Lyric and comic as well as tragic, the novel expresses Grass's belief that the German spirit could again face its past, avoid possession by its demons, and be aware of the spiritual power and transcendent values necessary for a truly new and healthy life.

Bibliography:

Cunliffe, W. Gordon. *Günter Grass*. New York: Twayne, 1969. This basic study places Grass's work in its historical and political context. Includes one chapter on *Cat and Mouse*.

Hayman, Ronald. *Günter Grass*. New York: Methuen, 1985. A survey of Grass's work that places *Cat and Mouse* in the context of Grass's aesthetic ideas and emphasizes the unreliable narrator. Also compares the text to other works by German writers who have focused on the clown archetype.

Keele, Alan Frank. *Understanding Günter Grass*. Columbia: University of South Carolina Press, 1988. This general study of Grass's work examines *Cat and Mouse* primarily as a political allegory, drawing parallels between Mahlke and Germany, as well as between Pilenz and Grass himself.

Lawson, Richard H. *Günter Grass*. New York: Frederick Ungar, 1985. This survey of Grass's work includes a chapter on *Cat and Mouse* that discusses the text from a variety of perspectives. Includes a good discussion of the novella genre and traces the quest motif in the work.

Reddick, John. *The Danzig Trilogy of Günter Grass: A Study of "The Tin Drum," "Cat and Mouse," and "Dog Years."* London: Secker and Warburg, 1975. A good in-depth study of *Cat and Mouse* that examines the structure, imagery, setting, themes, and symbols of the work and relates it to the other elements of the Danzig trilogy.

CAT ON A HOT TIN ROOF

Type of work: Drama
Author: Tennessee Williams (Thomas Lanier Williams, 1911-1983)
Type of plot: Psychological realism
Time of plot: Mid-twentieth century
Locale: Mississippi
First performed: 1955; first published, 1955

Principal characters:
BIG DADDY POLLITT, a plantation owner
BIG MAMA, his wife
BRICK and
GOOPER, their sons
MAGGIE, Brick's wife
MAE, Gooper's wife

The Story:
The Pollitt family had assembled to celebrate Big Daddy's sixty-fifth birthday. While Brick showered, Maggie described the birthday dinner, telling how badly Gooper's five children had behaved and how their mother, Mae, used them to impress Big Daddy. Brick came out of the bathroom on crutches, having broken his ankle jumping hurdles.

Maggie informed Brick that a medical report had arrived that day with the news that Big Daddy was dying of cancer. She also explained that Mae and Gooper wanted to send Brick to a hospital for alcoholics so that they could control Big Daddy's money. Maggie believed, however, that Big Daddy disliked Gooper and his family and that he had a "lech" for her.

Maggie admitted that she had become "catty" because Brick refused to sleep with her and she was lonely. She did, however, intend to win back his love. After hinting that Brick's problems stemmed from someone named Skipper, she asked Brick to drink less. He replied that he needed to drink until he heard a "click" in his head that gave him peace. Maggie complained that her current situation made her as tense as "a cat on a hot tin roof."

Big Mama entered to say how happy she was; she had been told that Big Daddy had a spastic colon, not cancer. Brick retreated to the bathroom as she entered. After asking about Brick's drinking, Big Mama told Maggie that sexual problems must have caused their marital troubles and childlessness.

When Big Mama left, Maggie again urged Brick to sleep with her; he suggested a divorce instead. Maggie returned to the subject of Big Daddy's cancer, explaining that the family would tell Big Mama the truth later. Then, ignoring Brick's anger, she recounted the story of Skipper, Brick's college friend whose homosexual love Brick could not or would not return. Maggie said that she had forced Skipper to face his feelings for Brick. To prove her wrong, Skipper tried to make love to her but could not. He later died of drink. Maggie reminded Brick that although Skipper was dead, she, Maggie, was alive and able to conceive a child. Brick asked how she planned to do that when he hated her.

At that moment, the family entered, bearing Big Daddy's birthday cake. Big Daddy became annoyed that others, especially Big Mama, appeared to be trying to run his life. Since he no longer believed he was threatened by a terminal illness, he announced that he was resuming control of the family. Hurt, Big Mama realized that Big Daddy had never believed she loved him. When she told him that she loved even his hatefulness, Big Daddy said to himself that it would be funny if that were true.

Eventually, the others drifted out, leaving Brick and Big Daddy alone. Although he had wanted a serious discussion with Brick, Big Daddy talked instead about his trip to Europe. Brick wondered why communication was so difficult between him and Big Daddy. Big Daddy admitted that he had been afraid of cancer and that he was not ready to die. When Brick acknowledged his alcoholism, Big Daddy asked why he drank. Because of disgust with the world's "mendacity," Brick answered, a reason Big Daddy did not accept. Most lives were based on lies, he said, and Brick must live with this fact. Big Daddy suggested that Brick was actually drinking because of guilt over Skipper's homosexuality and death. Brick angrily protested that he had not shared Skipper's feelings or even discussed them; when Skipper had tried to explain over the telephone, Brick had hung up. That, then, was the real reason for Brick's drinking, Big Daddy said: Brick was disgusted with himself because he had refused to face his friend's truth. Brick retaliated by telling Big Daddy the truth about his cancer. Shattered, Big Daddy left, damning all liars as he went.

In the original ending, the family and the doctor entered to tell Big Mama about Big Daddy's cancer. She at first refused to believe them. Brick, meanwhile, had gone to the balcony to drink, but he returned as Gooper tried to persuade Big Mama to sign legal control of the plantation over to him. Angrily, Big Mama refused. As her final answer, she shouted Big Daddy's favorite word, "crap."

Big Mama then urged Brick to give Big Daddy a grandson. To everyone's surprise, Maggie announced that she was pregnant. Though Mae and Gooper disbelieved the news, they could not disprove it and finally left. At that moment, Brick heard the "click" in his head. Maggie refused to allow him this escape and threw away his crutch, pointing out that she had emptied the liquor cabinet. As she turned out the light, Maggie assured Brick that she did love him. Brick said to himself that it would be funny if that were true.

In the Broadway production ending, the family, after much preparation, told Big Mama the truth about Big Daddy's cancer. While she tried to digest the news, Gooper explained why Big Mama should give him legal control of the estate. After dismissing Gooper's legal plans with Big Daddy's favorite word, "crap," Big Mama reminded Brick and Maggie that Big Daddy hoped they would have a son.

The loud talk brought Big Daddy back to the room. He related a crude joke about a fornicating elephant, perhaps to remind Brick that sex was natural and necessary. Maggie then announced her pregnancy. Although Mae and Gooper refused to believe her, Big Daddy professed to do so. When Brick and Maggie were at last alone, Maggie threw his liquor off the balcony while he watched with growing admiration. Finally, both Brick and Maggie sat together on the bed as Maggie vowed to use her love to help restore Brick to life.

Critical Evaluation:

As the author of *The Glass Menagerie* (1944), the Pulitzer Prize-winning *A Streetcar Named Desire* (1947), and many other plays, Tennessee Williams was one of the leading American dramatists of the twentieth century. Born in Mississippi, Williams used the South and southerners as a vehicle for exploring the confusing and even inexplicable minds and relationships of human beings. Although his plays have been criticized as too symbolic and theatrical, as well as philosophically murky, no one disputes his success in creating a gallery of memorable characters who grapple with some of humankind's most significant issues: love, sex, power, age, family, self-awareness, honesty, the past, dreams, and death.

At once tragic and comic, *Cat on a Hot Tin Roof*, which won the Pulitzer Prize in drama, examines the mysterious and even grotesque interconnections that define a family. The play also delineates the struggle of individuals within the family to define a self. On the surface, the play is realistic: The lapsed time of the story is equal to the time of performance; the characters are complex and human; the situation, a family birthday party, is ordinary. Yet despite the surface realism, the play can better be described as expressionistic. The set Williams calls for is dominated by a large bed and large liquor cabinet symbolizing sex and escape. The language is poetic, and the characters have nearly as many monologues as conversations. The action, too, is episodic and symbolic. The specific tensions of the Pollitt family are staged in a series of emblematic confrontations: husband and wife, youth and age, past and present, wealth and poverty, homosexuality and heterosexuality, truth and lies, love and hate, life and death.

Williams does not, however, allow the audience to choose one option over another or even to define each term clearly. Although he favors life and honesty, for example, he never promises that either is possible or even always desirable. Each side has its allure and validity. Big Daddy and Maggie are most directly associated with life and truth, yet both have important limitations. Maggie yearns for a child and vows to restore Brick to life; she insists that Brick must value her honesty if nothing else. In many respects, she is the healthiest and most appealing character in the play. In the end, though, she must pretend to be pregnant in order to affirm life, and that affirmation has as much to do with her need for financial security as with any real desire for children. Nor do the fertile Mae and Gooper represent a viable commitment to life: They have produced only rude, screeching "no-neck monsters" who function as a sort of Greek chorus of futility.

Big Daddy, in the words of Dylan Thomas that Williams uses as an epigram, does not "go gentle into that good night" of death; instead, he clings to life and to truth so fiercely that his energy overflows into the vulgarity and garrulity that make him larger than life. He refuses to allow Brick the refuge of drink and dissembling. Yet despite his powerful life force, Big Daddy is dying; his physical cancer mirrors the metaphorical corruption that touches the whole family and, by extension, the entire South. His dedication to honesty is complicated by his own lifelong "mendacity." Ironically, it is the self-destructive Brick, whose broken ankle symbolizes his broken spirit and who must rely on both literal and figurative crutches, who voices perhaps the most pertinent questions about honesty: "Who can face truth?" he asks Big Daddy. "Can you?"

Closely connected with the question of life are the topics of sex and homosexuality, topics that made *Cat on a Hot Tin Roof* controversial in the 1950's and 1960's but that had come to seem tame by the 1970's. In this play, Williams neither condemns nor explicitly approves of either homosexuality or heterosexuality. For the most part, he merely shows that society offers no livable place for homosexuals; he suggests, moreover, that sex of any kind is as likely to push people apart as it is to draw them together.

The two endings complicate the final effect of the play. Williams explained that he wrote the second version of Act III at the request of Elia Kazan, who directed the 1955 Broadway production. Kazan wanted Maggie to be more sympathetic and Brick to be more obviously changed by his confrontation with Big Daddy in Act II. He also believed that Big Daddy was too important and dynamic a character to disappear after one act. Although the new ending offers slightly more hope for a reconciliation between Brick and Maggie, it is less consistent with the development of the first two acts. Williams' first version works better: Big Daddy, though certainly a powerful character, does not belong in Act III. His last words in Act II—"Christ—damn—all—lying sons of—lying bitches!! Lying! Dying! Lying!"—provide a more fitting thematic end to Big Daddy than his elephant story and his unconvincing acceptance of Maggie's pregnancy. The change in Brick is even less effective. Williams' reasons for initially resisting this change make sense: He did not "believe that any conversation, however revelatory, ever effects so immediate a change in the heart . . . of a person of Brick's state of spiritual disrepair."

Ultimately, *Cat on a Hot Tin Roof* presents, rather than corrects, several portraits of "spiritual disrepair." Although Williams may offer little hope of eventual repair, he does offer a sympathetic understanding of the human condition.

Kathleen R. Chamberlain

Bibliography:
Bloom, Harold, ed. *Tennessee Williams.* New York: Chelsea House, 1987. A collection of critical essays that includes thorough discussions of *Cat on a Hot Tin Roof* by Ruby Cohn, who examines themes and characters; Robert Heilman, who explores different "levels" of the play; and Esther Jackson, who focuses on the play's symbolism.
Falk, Signi Lenea. *Tennessee Williams.* 2d ed. Boston: Twayne, 1978. A useful introduction to Williams and his works. Summarizes critical assessments of *Cat on a Hot Tin Roof.*
Hirsch, Foster. *A Portrait of the Artist: The Plays of Tennessee Williams.* Port Washington, N.Y.: Kennikat Press, 1979. An overview of Williams' work and career. Concludes that *Cat on a Hot Tin Roof* is "dishonest" but well crafted.
Spoto, Donald. *The Kindness of Strangers: The Life of Tennessee Williams.* Boston: Little, Brown, 1985. A thorough biography that includes critical commentary. Argues that *Cat on a Hot Tin Roof* is a deliberately ambiguous yet "compassionate" play.
Williams, Tennessee. *Cat on a Hot Tin Roof.* New York: New Directions, 1955. A useful edition that contains both versions of Act III and commentary by Williams in which he explains why he wrote the second ending.

CATCH-22

Type of work: Novel
Author: Joseph Heller (1923-   )
Type of plot: Metafiction
Time of plot: 1944
Locale: Pianosa, a mythical island eight miles south of Elba, and Rome, Italy
First published: 1961

>
> *Principal characters:*
> CAPTAIN JOHN YOSSARIAN, a United States Air Force bombardier
> COLONEL CATHCART, the group commander
> MAJOR MAJOR MAJOR, the 256th Squadron commander who was
>   promoted by an I.B.M. machine
> MAJOR —— DE COVERLEY, the squadron executive officer
> LIEUTENANT MILO MINDERBINDER, the mess officer, who turns black
>   marketing into big business
> CAPTAIN BLACK, the squadron intelligence officer
> CHIEF WHITE HALFBOAT, an American from Oklahoma and the assistant
>   intelligence officer
> DOC DANEEKA, the flight surgeon
> CAPTAIN R. O. SHIPMAN, the chaplain
> NURSE SUE ANN DUCKETT
> CLEVINGER,
> ORR,
> HAVERMEYER,
> KID SAMPSON,
> MCWATT,
> AARDVAARK (AARFY),
> HUNGRY JOE,
> DOBBS, and
> NATELY, pilots, bombardiers, and navigators of the 256th Squadron
> NATELY'S WHORE
> GENERAL DREEDLE, the wing commander
> GENERAL PECKEM, the commanding officer of Special Services
> EX-PFC WINTERGREEN, a goldbrick who controls 27th Air Force
>   Headquarters because he sorts, and unofficially censors, all
>   the mail

The Story:

The events took place in Pianosa, a small Italian island where an Air Force bombing group was sweating out the closing months of World War II, and Rome, where the flyers went on leave to stage latter-day Roman orgies in a city filled with prostitutes. Men who behaved like madmen were awarded medals. In a world of madmen at war, the maddest—or the sanest—of all was Captain John Yossarian, a bombardier of the 256th Squadron. Deciding that death in war is a matter of circumstance and having no wish to be victimized by any kind of circumstance, he tried by every means he could think of—including malingering, defiance, cowardice, and irrational behavior—to get out of the war. That was his resolve after the disastrous raid over Avignon, when Snowden, the radio-gunner, was shot almost in two, splashing his blood and entrails over Yossarian's uniform and teaching the bombardier the cold, simple fact of man's mortality. For some time after that, Yossarian refused to wear any clothes, and when General Dreedle, the wing commander, arrived to award the bombardier a Distinguished Flying Cross for his heroism, military procedure was upset because Yossarian wore no uniform on which to pin the medal. Yossarian's logic of nonparticipation was so simple that everyone thought him crazy, especially when he insisted that "they" were trying to murder him. His insistence led to an argument with Clevinger, who was bright and always had an excuse or an explanation for everything. When Clevinger wanted to know who Yossarian thinks was trying to murder him, the bombardier said that all of "them" were, and Clevinger said that he had no idea who "they" could be.

Yossarian went off to the hospital, complaining of a pain in his liver. If he had jaundice, the doctors would discharge him; if not, they would send him back to duty. Yossarian spent some of his time censoring the enlisted men's letters. On some, he signed Washington Irving's name as censor; on others, he crossed out the letter but added loving messages signed by the chaplain's name. The hospital would have been a good place to stay for the rest of the war if it had not been for a talkative Texan and a patient so cased in bandages that Yossarian wondered at times whether there was a real body inside. When he returned to his squadron, he learned that Colonel Cathcart, the group commander, had raised the number of required missions to fifty. Meanwhile, Clevinger had dipped his plane into a cloud one day and never brought it out again. He and his plane simply vanished.

It was impossible for Yossarian to complete his tour of combat duty because Colonel Cathcart wanted to get his picture in *The Saturday Evening Post* and to become a general. Consequently, he continued to increase the number of required missions for his outfit beyond those required by the 27th Air Force Headquarters. By the time he had set the number at eighty, Kraft, McWatt, Kid Sampson, and Nately were dead, Clevinger and Orr had disappeared, the chaplain had been disgraced (the C.I.D. accused him of the Washington Irving forgeries), and Aarfy had committed a brutal murder. Hungry Joe screamed in his sleep night after night, and Yossarian continued looking for new ways to stay alive. It was impossible for him to be sent home on medical relief because of Catch-22. As Doc Daneeka, the medical officer, explained, he could ground anyone who was crazy, but anyone who wants to avoid combat duty is not crazy and therefore could not be grounded. This is Catch-22, the inevitable loophole in the scheme of justice, the self-justification of authority, the irony of eternal circumstance. Catch-22 explains Colonel Cathcart, who continued to raise the number of missions and volunteer his men for every dangerous operation in the Mediterranean theater. Cathcart also planned to have prayers during every briefing session but gave up that idea when he learned that officers and enlisted men must pray to the same god. Catch-22 also explained the struggle for power between General Dreedle, who wanted a fighting outfit, and General Peckem of Special Services, who wanted to see tighter bombing patterns—they looked better in aerial photographs—and issued a directive ordering all tents in the Mediterranean theater to be pitched with their fronts facing in the direction of the Washington Monument. It explained Captain Black, the intelligence officer who compelled the officers to sign a new loyalty oath each time they got their map cases, flak suits and parachutes, paychecks, haircuts, and meals in the mess. It explained, above all, Lieutenant Milo Mindbinder, the mess officer, who parlayed petty black-market operations into an international syndicate in which every man, as he said, had a share. By the time he had his organization on a paying basis, he had been elected mayor of half a dozen Italian cities, Vice-Shah of Oran, Caliph of Baghdad, Imam of Damascus, and Sheik of Araby. Once he almost made a mistake by cornering the market on Egyptian cotton, but after some judicious bribery, he unloaded it on the United States government. The climax of his career came when he rented his fleet of private planes to the Germans and from the Pianosa control tower directed the bombing and strafing of his own outfit. Men of public decency were outraged until Milo opened his books for public inspection and showed the profit he had made. Then everything was all right, for in this strange, mad world, patriotism and profit are indistinguishable; the world lives by Milo's motto, the claim that whatever is good for the syndicate is good for the nation.

Eventually, Yossarian took off for neutral Sweden, three jumps ahead of the authorities and less than one jump ahead of Nately's whore, who for some reason blamed him for her lover's death and tried to kill him. He spent the last night in Italy wandering alone through wartime Rome.

Critical Evaluation:

Catch-22 was the first of the post-World War II novels to convey the sense of war as so insane and so negligent of humane values that it can be treated only through exaggerated ridicule. One means whereby Joseph Heller suggests the ways in which war violates humanity is by violating the conventions of realistic fiction. The individual chapters are, for example, named after the different characters, although the character for whom a chapter is named may or may not be important in that chapter, or anywhere in the book. The chapters follow no evident plan; time in the novel is confused because there is no narrative line. Such structure as exists is based on recurrent references to specific situations. Only toward the end is there a progression in time from one chapter to the next.

The salient element that distinguishes *Catch-22* from more conventional war novels is its outrageous humor, much of it black and having to do with death and injury. In the late twentieth century, the term "metafiction" began to be applied to this kind of novel, suggesting a kind of fiction that does not pretend to portray reality and continually calls attention to its fictive nature. The cruel joke that gives the novel its title typifies its humor and the situation of the aviators. Each man is required to fly a certain number of missions against the Germans before he can be rotated home. Each time, however, a significant number of men approach that number, Colonel Cathcart, the commanding officer, raises the required number. Those in command are uniformly corrupt and have the power to force their subordinates to do whatever they wish; they plan dangerous missions, choose the most beautiful nurses, and make monetary profits from the war. The subordinate officers, led by Yossarian, have no choice but to act subversively in order to try to survive.

Many of the episodes of the novel reflect outrageous humor. There are many instances of wordplay, puns, and jokes the characters tell and play on one another. Yet underlying the humor, there are always constant reminders of death and the grisly business of war. One of the threads that holds the novel together is found in the frequent references to a character named Snowden. His death is alluded to very early in the novel and in the description of his funeral and burial midway through the book there is a description of an unnamed character who sits naked in a tree while the ceremony is performed. Later in the novel, it becomes clear that the naked man was Yossarian, who had returned in shock from a mission, covered with Snowden's blood and flesh. He had been so horrified by Snowden's death that he could not bear to wear anything, but he felt compelled to attend the funeral. Only very late in the novel is Snowden's death described in grisly detail, but with the same tone of outrageous humor. Snowden's death carries the novel's most overt message: "Man was matter, that was Snowden's secret. . . . The spirit gone, man is garbage." The novel's satiric targets include not only the mechanized destruction of modern war but many aspects of civilian society in the postwar world that are linked, with satiric intent, with the war itself. Heller mocks the business ethic and the economic arrangements of American society in the sections dealing with the machinations of Milo Minderbinder; he savagely parodies the good-guy image of the typical American boy in the casual cruelty of Aarfy; he ridicules the scant attention paid to religion through his use of a chaplain, a good-hearted innocent whose ministrations have no effect on the problems of the men in the squadron; he sees modern medicine only as it is used to patch up wounded men so as to return them to battle. Above all, Heller mocks the sheeplike way in which ordinary humans follow orders even when they know those orders will lead to their destruction and that those who give them are idiotic or stupid.

In the world Heller describes, values are of little account. Love has been reduced to lustful sexual encounters in which women are barely human. The only absolutes in this world are human mortality and the corruption of the world, as depicted in the chapter "Eternal City," where the "holy" city of Rome is depicted in nightmarish terms as a kind of hell on earth. The choices in this world are few. The men may be killed at any time. They can take life as they find it, as most people do. They can try to fight against the forces that control them, knowing that their efforts are doomed. They can, if they are desperate enough, try to find a way out. Improbably, at the end of the novel, Yossarian chooses the latter in imitation of his friend Orr. After accidentally killing his friend Kid Sampson, Orr has managed to row from Italy through the Mediterranean Sea around the west coast of Europe and through the North Sea to a safe haven in neutral Sweden. This unbelievable journey is perhaps the novel's most bitter joke.

Catch-22 was a pioneering work of metafiction. Of Heller's later novels, only *God Knows* (1984) takes similar liberties with fact, and none of his subsequent works measured up to the high standard set by *Catch-22*. Most critics considered the book's sequel, *Closing Time* (1994) to be a distinct disappointment. *Catch-22* nevertheless deserves its continuing reputation as one of the four or five most memorable novels to come out of World War II.

"Critical Evaluation" by John M. Muste

Bibliography:
Karl, Frederick R. *American Fiction 1940-1980: A Comprehensive History and Evaluation.* New York: Harper & Row, 1983. The judgment of an outstanding critic and biographer on forty years of American novels. Judges *Catch-22* as an outstanding product of its time.
Martine, James J. *American Novelists.* Detroit: Gale Research, 1986. Contains the most comprehensive bibliography of works by and about Heller.
Merrill, Robert. "The Structure and Meaning of *Catch-22*." *Studies in American Fiction* 14, no. 2 (August, 1986): 139-152. Detailed discussion of the effect of the novel's unusual structure on the message it conveys about society.
Potts, Stephen W. *Catch-22: Antiheroic Antinovel.* Boston: Twayne, 1989. The first single volume devoted exclusively to *Catch-22*. Discusses most of the major aspects of the novel.
Ruas, Charles. *Conversations with American Writers.* New York: Alfred A. Knopf, 1985. Contains a section on Heller in part 2 with a detailed interview on his life and intentions that focuses on *Catch-22*.

THE CATCHER IN THE RYE

Type of work: Novel
Author: J. D. Salinger (1919-   )
Type of plot: Social realism
Time of plot: Late 1940's
Locale: Pennsylvania, New York City
First published: 1951

Principal characters:

HOLDEN CAULFIELD, a seventeen-year-old boy
PHOEBE CAULFIELD, his ten-year-old sister
MR. SPENCER, a prep school teacher
MR. ANTOLINI, a prep school teacher
ROBERT ACKLEY, a schoolmate
WARD STRADLATER, Holden's roommate
MAURICE, a hotel elevator operator

The Story:

Holden Caulfield was expelled from Pencey Prep, in Agerstown, Pennsylvania, just before Christmas. Before leaving his preparatory school, Holden said good-bye to Mr. Spencer, one of the Pencey teachers with whom he had good rapport, and had an altercation with his roommate, Ward Stradlater, and a dormitory neighbor, Robert Ackley. A disagreement over a composition Holden had agreed to write for Stradlater and Holden's anger with Stradlater's treatment of the latter's weekend date, whom Holden knew and liked, precipitated a fight in which Holden was cut and bruised. Holden set out by train to New York City. Since he was not expected at his home in the city for Christmas vacation for a few days, he decided to stop at a city hotel and contact some friends.

Holden tried to pick up some women in the hotel bar, took in a show at Radio City Music Hall, and visited a local café. Upon returning to his hotel, he was approached by the elevator man, Maurice, who arranged for a prostitute to come to Holden's room. Holden preferred conversation to sex, however, and after he refused to pay the woman for her services, Maurice arrived and beat Holden. After attending a play with a former girlfriend, Sally, Holden got drunk in a bar and sat alone in Central Park, thinking, as he often did, about how lonely and depressed he was.

Finally, late at night, Holden went home. His parents were out for the evening, and he spent some time talking with his ten-year-old sister, Phoebe, with whom he had always been very close. Phoebe expressed her disappointment with Holden's having been expelled from school, and brother and sister talked at length about what Holden truly believed in and what he would do with his life. Holden told Phoebe of his idealistic vision of being a "catcher in the rye," protecting innocent children from disaster. He imagined children playing in a field of rye, and himself catching them whenever they were in danger of falling over a cliff. He avoided seeing his parents on their return home and went to see another former teacher, Mr. Antolini. Holden intended to seek advice.

Mr. Antolini and his wife received Holden warmly, and he was invited to spend the night. He listened carefully to Mr. Antolini's ideas on Holden's future. To Holden's shock and dismay, however, Mr. Antolini made what Holden understood to be sexual advances, and he left the Antolini apartment hurriedly. He spent the rest of the night in Grand Central Station.

The next day, Holden visited Phoebe at her school and told her of his plans to begin a new life in the West. Holden's story ended with his good-bye to Phoebe, but the novel's first and last chapters indicate that he had a nervous breakdown of sorts. He told the story while in a hospital, apparently in California.

Critical Evaluation:

J. D. Salinger's *The Catcher in the Rye* has become, since its publication, one of the enduring classics of American literature. The novel is a favorite because of its humor, its mordant criticism of American middle-class society and its values, and the skill with which Salinger has captured colloquial speech and vocabulary. *The Catcher in the Rye*, ironically enough, has received some criticism over the years because of its rough language, which Holden cites in order to denounce. The novel's story is told in retrospect by the main character, Holden Caulfield, apparently while staying in a psychiatric hospital in California.

What Holden tells is the story of his disenchantment with his life and the direction it was taking him. Throughout the novel, Holden speaks of his loneliness and depression; the story of a few days in his life indicates how sad and lonely his search for moral values is in a society in which he finds them sorely lacking. As the novel begins, Holden has been expelled, immediately before Christmas, from an exclusive preparatory school in Pennsylvania. He knows his parents will be angry with him, so he decides to spend a few days in New York City before going home. In New York, Holden endures several adventures before explaining to his only real friend, his sister, Phoebe, just what it is he believes in. This discovery of some moral identity does not, however, save Holden from hospitalization.

From the beginning of the novel, readers see Holden as the champion of the downtrodden: children, for example (whom he sees as essentially innocent, fragile, and uncomplicated) and those who have been persecuted by others. At the same time, Holden shows no patience with hypocrisy and self-delusion (except his own; readers need to keep in mind that the narrator is institutionalized), as seen in any number of his acquaintances. Caulfield's idealism does not spare even his own older brother, D.B., whom Caulfield accuses of prostituting his writing talent as a screenwriter in Hollywood. Holden admires courage, simplicity, and authenticity. He is preoccupied with the lack of justice in life, a point that leads him to defend a girl's honor in a fight with his Pencey roommate, Ward Stradlater, and results in another beating in New York, when Holden refuses to be cheated by a pandering hotel elevator operator. Moreover, Holden was devastated by the death of his younger brother, Allie, and it turns out that one of Holden's heroes is a former schoolmate named James Castle, who committed suicide rather than contradict his beliefs. In a well-known passage late in the novel, Holden sees obscene graffiti on the walls of Phoebe's school. He is enraged that someone would affront children in this way, and he manages to efface one set of obscenities. Later, however, he finds more such graffiti and depressedly comes to the conclusion that one can never erase all obscene scribblings from the walls of the world.

Salinger's novel takes its title from two key episodes that involve children. The first of these is Holden's chance observation of a little boy, who, with his parents, is strolling along a city street. Evidently, the happy boy is singing to himself, humming a song Holden calls "If a body catch a body coming through the rye." Holden is impressed with the fact that the boy is simply enjoying his own music, pleasing only himself in naïve artistic integrity.

Much later, when Holden spends an evening with Phoebe, he defends himself against his sister's charge of moral bankruptcy by indirectly alluding to the little boy. Holden tells Phoebe that he would like to be a "catcher in the rye," a man who watches over children, protecting them from falling from a cliff while they play. Holden's fantasy elaborates his obsession with innocence and his perhaps surprisingly traditional moral code.

It is important to realize that Holden's intention of making a new life for himself in the West places Holden Caulfield in a tradition of American literature in which young people seek out a better life away from the corruptions of civilization. Such characters seek to realize the American Dream of justice, purity, and self-definition on the country's frontiers, away from cities. Unfortunately, Holden's move westward takes him only to a mental hospital; one wonders if this development is cruel irony or, perhaps, a real start on a new life for Holden.

Gordon Walters

Bibliography:
Grunwald, Henry Anatole, ed. *Salinger: A Critical and Personal Portrait*. New York: Harper & Row, 1962. Contains two important articles on *The Catcher in the Rye*. One deals with Holden Caulfield as an heir of Huck Finn; the other is a study of the novel's language.

Laser, Marvin, and Norman Fruman, eds. *Studies in J. D. Salinger: Reviews, Essays, and Critiques of "The Catcher in the Rye" and Other Fiction*. New York: Odyssey Press, 1963. Includes an intriguing essay by a German, Hans Bungert, another by a Russian writer, and one of the best structural interpretations of the novel, by Carl F. Strauch.

Marsden, Malcolm M., ed. *If You Really Want to Know: A "Catcher" Casebook*. Glenview, Ill.: Scott, Foresman, 1963. Contains reviews of the original publication of the novel. Examines Holden from opposing points of view, as "saint or psychotic."

Pinsker, Sanford. *"The Catcher in the Rye": Innocence Under Pressure*. Boston: Twayne, 1993. A sustained study of the novel. Contains a helpful section on the body of critical literature on the novel.

Salzman, Jack, ed. *New Essays on "The Catcher in the Rye."* Cambridge, England: Cambridge University Press, 1991. Provides an unusual sociological reading of the novel as well as an essay that firmly places the novel in American literary history.

CATILINE

Type of work: Drama
Author: Ben Jonson (1573-1637)
Type of plot: Political
Time of plot: First century B.C.E.
Locale: Ancient Rome
First performed: 1611; first published, 1611 as *Catiline His Conspiracy*

> *Principal characters:*
> CATILINE, the leader of a conspiracy against Rome
> LENTULUS and
> CETHEGUS, his lieutenants
> CURIUS, a conspirator and spy
> CICERO, the defender of the state
> CATO, the "voice of Rome"
> JULIUS CAESAR, a shrewd politician and friend of the conspirators
> FULVIA, a courtesan and spy
> SEMPRONIA, a conspirator
> AURELIA, Catiline's wife

The Story:

Under the sinister influence of Sulla's ghost, the reckless patrician Catiline organized a conspiracy to overthrow the Roman Republic. The conspirators, among them the rash Cethegus and the outcast senators Lentulus and Curius, gathered at Catiline's home. Catiline and his wife pandered to the weaknesses of each and skillfully manipulated them without allowing them to realize that they were puppets. The conspirators concluded their meeting with a gruesome sacrament and pledged their faith by drinking the blood of a murdered slave.

The first step in their plan was to have Catiline elected as one of the two consuls. Success seemed probable after four of the candidates withdrew in favor of Catiline. That left only two competitors in the race, Antonius, impecunious and lukewarm, and Cicero, a new man but a dangerous antagonist. A Chorus of Roman citizens gathered and discussed the uncertainty of the survival of great national powers, which often seem to carry in themselves seeds of their destruction: Luxuries and vices soften nations and leave them easy prey to their own malcontents or to alien invaders.

Fulvia, the profligate wife of an elderly fool, numbered among her lovers the conspirator Curius and, on a very casual basis, Julius Caesar. As she was interested in wealth, not romance, she forbade her servants to admit the down-at-heels Curius on future visits. She was being readied for her social day when Sempronia visited her, a politician well past the bloom of youth. Sempronia was an eager supporter of the patrician Catiline and a scorner of "that talker, Cicero," who presumed to be more learned and eloquent than the nobility. When Curius arrived to interrupt their gossip, Sempronia overrode Fulvia's objections, ushered him in, and made great play of leaving the lovers alone. Fulvia's reception of Curius was so hostile that he became enraged and dropped threats and hints of future greatness and power. Fulvia immediately shifted to the tactics of Delilah and wheedled information about the conspiracy from him.

The Chorus gathered before the election and prayed for wisdom to choose consuls worthy of Rome's great past. Antonius and Cicero won the election, which shocked and infuriated

Catiline and his party. Cato praised Cicero warmly, but Caesar and other sympathizers of Catiline regarded the new consul with veiled hostility or open contempt. Catiline masked his fury in public, but in private he planned rebellion and civil war. Fulvia, partly because of self-interest and partly because of a vain dislike of playing second fiddle to Sempronia, carried information about the conspiracy to Cicero. He used it to intimidate Curius, appealing to his greed and winning him as a spy. Fulvia served the same purpose among the women conspirators. Alone, Cicero bemoaned the low estate of Rome, which was reduced to dependence on such tools as Fulvia and Curius for safety. He strengthened his position still further by giving a province to Antonius.

Caesar showed Catiline favor and gave him advice, but he did not join the assemblage of conspirators. At the conspirators' next meeting, plans were laid for setting fire to the city at strategic points and starting local uprisings to be timed with an invasion from outside. The first move was to be the murder of Cicero that very night. The women conspirators entered with Catiline's wife, Aurelia. Under cover of their excited chatter, Curius whispered to Fulvia the plan to assassinate Cicero. She left the meeting and warned Cicero in time for him to gather protecting friends and impartial witnesses. Although the attempt on Cicero's life failed, the threat of civil violence terrified senators and citizens. The Chorus expressed horror at the danger, which seemed brought about by the city's guilt.

In the Senate, Cicero delivered an impassioned oration against Catiline and disclosed detailed information about the conspiracy. Catiline thereupon lost control of himself, threatened Cicero and Rome, and left to join his army outside the city. Lentulus and Cethegus remained in charge of the internal organization of the conspirators. Cato warned Cicero of the danger from Caesar and other concealed supporters of Catiline, but Cicero chose to avoid a break with them. He persuaded the ambassadors from the Allobroges, who had been approached by Catiline's men, to pretend to join the conspiracy and to secure incriminating documents. When the ambassadors were arrested, as prearranged, a conspirator taken with them turned state's evidence to save his life. With the evidence of the conspirator and the ambassadors, the Senate approved the arrest and execution of the conspirators remaining in Rome. Because Caesar tried to save their lives, he was accused by Curius, but Cicero chose to pretend that this dangerous man was innocent, allowing him to remain alive and uncurbed.

After the execution of the conspirators, the leader of the Roman forces arrived and reported the defeat of Catiline and his "brave bad death" while leading his troops. Honored and rewarded by the Senate and the Roman people, Cicero pronounced thanks for Rome's rescue.

Critical Evaluation:

Ben Jonson's two tragedies based on Roman history, *Sejanus* (1603) and *Catiline* (1611), were critical failures when they were first presented, and they have remained the object of scholarly reservation, even of disapproval. *Catiline* in particular has been dissected for its rhetorical presentation, undramatic staging, and unsympathetic characters. In his essay on Ben Jonson, T. S. Eliot dismissed the play as "that deadly Pyrrhic victory of tragedy," and his judgment has been generally accepted.

To be fully appreciated, however, *Catiline* must be judged according to its author's intentions and his own self-imposed conventions, drawn largely from classical drama and Senecan closet drama, both genres that are very different from the more popular works of Elizabethan and Jacobean playwrights, including Jonson himself. In addition, it may well be that the real subject of *Catiline* is not the actual historical conspiracy that nearly overthrew the Roman Republic in 63 B.C.E. The real subject, instead, may be a broader topic: the state of England during Jonson's lifetime, politics in general, or even language as a means of human communication and control.

The immediate influences on the play are simple enough. Jonson intended to write a drama conforming to the strict considerations of classical drama; in particular, he is careful to exclude all violent action from the stage, so that battles and deaths, including Catiline's, are reported but never seen. In this way, Jonson is working in the style and traditions of Senecan closet drama, where the language of the play takes precedence over action.

In addition, and as part of this adherence to the classical patterns, Jonson makes extensive use of a chorus, which comments upon the actions of other characters and which itself functions as a character. Unlike Shakespeare's solitary chorus in *Henry V* (1598-1599), Jonson's chorus is thought to be modeled on the classical Greek chorus, which consisted of a group of characters who speak and act in unison.

As T. S. Eliot and others have long noted, the traditions and conventions of classical and Senecan drama were important influences on English playwrights during the Renaissance. When, however, presented in the severe, almost undiluted form Jonson employs in *Catiline*, those conventions run counter to the normal direction and impulse of English stagecraft. Unless *Catiline* is recognized as belonging to a different genre, the play cannot be appreciated or even understood. It is a meditation on the consequences of political actions rather than a presentation of the actions themselves.

In depicting those actions, Jonson drew upon ancient historical record, but he may also have been commenting on more recent events. In writing *Catiline*, Jonson was careful to remain close to his historical sources, most notably the Roman historian Sallust, whose *The Conspiracy of Catiline* (43-42 B.C.E.) is the fullest account of the conspiracy and its defeat. In addition, Jonson drew on a number of details from the historians Plutarch and Dio Cassius, including the hint that Julius Caesar was involved in the conspiracy. In particular, Jonson turned to the writings of Marcus Tullius Cicero, the consul at the time of the conspiracy, who was largely responsible, through his brilliant orations, for its exposure and defeat. Indeed, long passages of Jonson's play are simply paraphrases (or, more accurately, translations) of Cicero's *Orations Against Catiline* (60 B.C.E.).

Perhaps the outstanding example of this close dependence on original sources comes at the climax of the play, in the long speech in Act IV when Cicero reveals and denounces Catiline's conspiracy. The words here are taken almost verbatim from Cicero's own record. As Eliot and other critics have noted, however, what Jonson gains in historical accuracy is won at the expense of dramatic effectiveness. The audience sees and hears Catiline verbally rebuked in the Senate, but it is only told about his actual defeat and death on the battlefield.

Jonson's purpose in adhering so closely to the historical record, and his insistence on a strict classical form, may have been based on a desire to transcend the specifics of history and politics to reveal the underlying fundamental laws and principles and thereby to connect republican Rome and Jacobean England. Jonson presents these parallels either as specific instances or more general themes.

Some similarities have been noted between Jonson's presentation of the Catilinarian conspiracy and the Gunpowder Plot of 1605, in which Guy Fawkes and other Catholic dissidents attempted to kill King James I and the English Parliament. The explosion was timed to take place on November 5, and in his denunciation of Catiline during the play, Cicero thunders:

> I told too in this Senate that they purpose
> Was on the fifth, the kalends of November,
> T'have slaughter'd this whole order.

These lines, and repeated variants of the word "blow" in the dual sense of a sudden, violent overthrow and an explosion, suggest a deliberate connection between the ancient and the modern conspiracy.

Jonson's purpose in *Catiline* may well have been more general, however, serving to present an overview of the political processes in the abstract. During a period in which the political and social structures of England were being severely tested both by religious factionalism and dynastic change, there was an increased desire for stability and order. The villains in *Catiline* are those who seek to create disorder and to profit from it: Catiline himself, deeply ambitious, seeks to dominate Rome; Caesar, already aspiring to power, is implicated in the conspiracy, but manages to escape censure; Fulvia, a courtesan and spy, mingles her own concerns with political intrigue. The common thread that links these figures is a desire for social and political revolution.

By contrast, Cicero, seen by many critics as the heroic protagonist of the play, is dedicated to upholding and defending the established principles of republican Rome. Although a "new man" himself (that is, not coming from a long-established patrician family), Cicero is more loyal to the traditions and principles of Roman life than is the patrician Catiline. Significantly, Cicero's victory is accomplished not on the battlefield but in the Senate chamber, and his victory is won by the power of language rather than by the strength of weapons.

Cicero's victory over Catiline through the mastery of language is central to both the content and the form of the play. As a Senecan closet drama, and as a play, *Catiline* is forced by convention to rely upon linguistic, rather than dramatic, resources. It may well be, however, that Jonson was impelled to use the classical and Senecan models precisely because the subject matter of his drama, and the key events which it chronicles, are concerned with power and consequences of language itself and with its influence on human beings and their actions.

"Critical Evaluation" by Michael Witkoski

Bibliography:
Barton, Anne. *Ben Jonson, Dramatist*. Cambridge, England: Cambridge University Press, 1984. In a manner similar to T. S. Eliot but more extended in scope, Barton examines the play in terms of its relationship to Jonsonian comedy, especially in its use of the characters' names to define and describe their nature and roles.
Bloom, Harold, ed. *Ben Jonson*. Edgemont, Pa.: Chelsea House, 1987. Contains several perceptive essays on various aspects of *Catiline*.
De Luna, Barbara. *Jonson's Romish Plot: A Study of "Catiline" and Its Historical Context*. Oxford, England: Clarendon Press, 1967. Argues that the play was a retelling of the Gunpowder Plot of 1605. De Luna's most controversial conjecture is that Jonson himself may have been implicated in, or at least have had prior knowledge of, the plot.
Eliot, T. S. "Ben Jonson." In *Selected Essays*. Winchester, Mass.: Faber & Faber, 1932. First published in 1919, this essay asserts that *Catiline* failed primarily because Jonson could not place his theme, characters, and subject in the proper vehicle. T. S. Eliot sees some parts of the play as similar to satiric comedy.
Miles, Rosalind. *Ben Jonson: His Craft and Art*. New York: Barnes & Noble Books, 1990. A general study of Jonson's artistry. Includes an examination of *Catiline*.

CAWDOR

Type of work: Poetry
Author: Robinson Jeffers (1887-1962)
Type of plot: Psychological realism
Time of plot: 1900
Locale: Carmel Coast Range, California
First published: 1928

> *Principal characters:*
> CAWDOR, a farmer
> HOOD CAWDOR, his son
> GEORGE CAWDOR, another son
> MICHAL CAWDOR, a daughter
> MARTIAL, a neighbor
> FERA, Martial's daughter
> CONCHA ROSAS, Cawdor's Indian servant

The Story:

In 1899 a terrible fire devastated many of the farms along the Carmel coast, but Cawdor's farm was untouched. Early one morning he saw two figures approaching his house: a young woman leading a blind old man. They were the Martials, who held the land bordering his, and with whom Cawdor had an old feud. Martial had been blinded by the fire, his farm destroyed. His daughter Fera had only Cawdor to turn to for relief. Cawdor took them in and sent his servant, Concha Rosas, to live in a hut. When the old man was well enough to walk around, Cawdor spoke of sending the two away unless Fera would marry him. She agreed.

Hood Cawdor had left home after a fight with his father. On the night of the wedding he dreamed that the old man had died, and he decided to return to the farm to see if all were well. When he reached a hill overlooking the farm, he camped and lit a fire. His sister Michal saw him and went to tell him of their father's marriage. Cawdor received his son in a friendly manner. For a wedding present, Hood gave Fera a lion skin.

Fera found in Hood the same quality of hardness which had drawn her at first to Cawdor. She openly confessed to Hood that although she had loved his father when she married him, she no longer cared for him. She was jealous, too, of Concha Rosas, who had been Cawdor's mistress before he married Fera, and whom he again seemed to prefer to his wife. Disturbed by Fera's advances, Hood resolved to leave. After a prowling lion killed one of the farm dogs, he decided to stay, however, until he had killed the animal. A terrible storm arose which prevented his hunting for several days.

Fera's father was dying. On the pretext that Martial wished to talk to Hood, Fera called him into the sick room. Openly, before her unconscious father, she confessed her passion. That night Fera asked Concha to watch with her by the old man's bedside. Toward morning Martial died. Instead of summoning her husband, Fera went to Hood's room, where Cawdor found them. Fera tried to lull his suspicions by declaring that she had tried to awaken him but could not, and so she had gone to rouse Hood.

The next morning the men dug a grave for the old man. Fera, who had been watching them, called Hood into the wood to help her pick laurels for the grave. Again she begged for his love. Suddenly he drew his knife and stabbed himself deep in the thigh. Once more he had been able to resist her. The funeral service for her father was short but painful. Afterward Fera found her way home alone.

Desperate now, she covered herself with the lion skin Hood had given her and hid in the bushes. Hood shot at her, his bullet entering her shoulder. He carried Fera to her room, where Cawdor attempted to set the bones that had been fractured. Fera begged him to stop torturing her. Then, as if it were wrenched out of her because of the pain, she said that Hood had seduced her by force. Her lie was a last resort to prevent Hood's leaving. Hood, however, had already left the farm and was camped once more on the top of the hill. There the infuriated father found him. In the fight that followed Hood was pushed off the cliff, his body falling upon the rocks below. Cawdor met Michal on his way down the cliff and told her that Hood had fled. Meanwhile Fera sent Concha from the room to get some water. Quickly she unfastened the strap around her arm, and slung it over the head of the bed and around her own neck. When Concha returned, Fera was almost dead. For many days she lay in bed, slowly recovering. Neither George nor Michal would visit her. They hated her for what they knew must have been false charges against Hood.

Cawdor was haunted by his secret sin. Fera tried to destroy him with her own death wish. She told him the truth about Hood; how, rather than betray his father, he had stabbed himself with his knife. Cawdor's grief was uncontrollable. When Fera taunted him, demanding that he kill her, his fingers fastened around her throat. When she began to struggle, he released her and ran into Hood's old room. There he thought he saw Hood lying on the bed, and for a moment he imagined all that had passed had been a dream.

He was aroused when Fera came to tell him that everyone knew he had killed Hood, that soon the authorities were bound to hear of his crime. Again she urged him to seek the peace that death would bring. They were walking near her father's grave, with George and Michal nearby. Cawdor suddenly declared to them that their suspicions were correct, that he had killed Hood, and that they were to send for the authorities. Then he reached down and picked up a flint. Without warning, he thrust it into his eyes. Then, patiently, he asked them to lead him back to the house, to wait for whatever fate his deed would merit. Fera followed him weeping. Once again she felt that she had failed. She had tried to get Cawdor to kill her and then himself; instead, he had shown the courage to face his crime and pay for it.

Critical Evaluation:

Robinson Jeffers, poet of the beautiful and often wild and harsh California coast, believed that the Big Sur, California, landscape in which he lived revealed the truth about both people and the rest of nature. That truth is that all existence is in a constant process of flux, driven by, in the case of inorganic nature, great physical and chemical forces, and, in the case of living beings, in the desire to survive and to seek pleasure.

Sexuality is a source of pleasure for people. This pleasure is also the way in which nature survives and continues in the form of new life. People respond to some sexual acts with punishment because people are dependent on one another and on the survival of the social order. People must define some sexual activity as wrong and not only condemn it but punish it.

Jeffers examines such sexual aberrations as incest in *Tamar* (1924) and loveless coupling in *The Roan Stallion* (1925). An obvious question is, can pain and misery be avoided by avoiding wrongful sex? In *Cawdor*, which Jeffers regards as part of a trilogy which includes *Tamar* and *The Women at Point Sur* (1927), he investigates the same questions, and he concludes that sexuality is a trap from which there is no escape; even abstinence only leads to trouble and suffering.

Jeffers was well educated in the classics, and the Greek tragedies were his favorite form of literature. His model for the story of the house of Cawdor is Euripides' *Hippolytus* (fifth century B.C.E.). In that dramatic account of a myth, Theseus' son, Hippolytus, rejects the sexual advances of Aphrodite, the goddess of love, because he prefers, instead, Artemis, the goddess of the hunt. This relationship is doomed, however, because Artemis cherishes her virginity. Although Artemis' views would seem to be enough to punish Hippolytus, vengeful Aphrodite also clouds the mind of his stepmother, Phaedra, and causes her to fall in love with him. When Hippolytus rejects her too, Phaedra sets Theseus against his son. Theseus has Poseidon send a sea monster to frighten Hippolytus' horses as the boy rides by the shore. He is thrown from his chariot and dragged to his death.

Jeffers was drawn to this story, not only by the themes of sexuality and incest, but also by the fact that the characters are manipulated by forces that they cannot control. The Greeks personified these forces as gods and goddesses; in the twentieth century, Jeffers thinks, people are not certain what to call these forces, but people are, nevertheless, at the mercy of such forces. The Greek myth is a good reference point for his story.

In *Cawdor*, Fera Martial (whose name means "wild beast," a connection which is reinforced when she puts on the skin of the mountain lion which Hood has given her) plays the part of Phaedra; Cawdor plays the part of Theseus; and Hood Cawdor plays the part of Hippolytus. Fera feels that her sexuality is wasted in the service of, on the one hand, her much older husband, and on the other hand, her injured, invalid father. She reaches out to Hood, who stabs himself in the thigh as a gesture of self-condemnation for even considering betraying his father in a liaison with a woman who has replaced his mother. He does not tell his father, however, what this woman has done. Hood is trapped by his own sense of honor. He can neither yield to temptation nor inform his father of Fera's advances, lest he break the old man's heart. Like Othello, another possible model, Cawdor chooses to believe Fera's false reports. He attacks Hood, causing him to fall to his death. When Cawdor learns that he has attacked his son and has caused Hood's death because of Fera's lies, he blinds himself in imitation of Oedipus; in this case, however, the sin is of father against son, rather than son against father. Hood accidentally shoots Fera, mistaking her for a mountain lion while she is wearing the lionskin. All the major characters die or are wounded as a result of passion, whether the passion is acted upon or whether it is avoided.

Jeffers' description of Hood's self-mutilation, which he calls an "Attis-gesture," is an indication of another level of meaning. *Cawdor* is based not only on the Greek tragedies, but also on the myths behind those tragedies. Attis destroyed himself, but he merged into a larger reality by doing so, and he was reborn in a different form when spring returned. The idea that death is neither an end nor a gateway to immortality, but, instead, is part of an ongoing cycle of reformation and synthesis appears in three passages: When old Martial dies; when Hood dies; and when George Cawdor shoots the caged, broken-winged eagle which Michal Cawdor has kept as a pet. In each section, Jeffers describes the dissolution of consciousness after death, as if death itself is not a final event but a process which continues after the one who dies is lost to the living. Critics consider the passage about the eagle's death one of Jeffers' best. Like many other artists, Jeffers uses the dream as a means of connection between the ordinary waking world and the larger process of which people are all a part; each of the "death dreams" grows more intense until the caged eagle's consciousness soars above the coast where its body has died; Cawdor blinding himself is only a small part of a great spectacle. The agony of the Cawdor family, which the rest of this long poem describes, becomes only a tiny incident in the great evolving, revolving, and returning cycle of things, and then the eagle can "see" no more, as its consciousness becomes merged into another type of life which no one, not the eagle, not Jeffers, can describe.

"Critical Evaluation" by Jim Baird

Bibliography:
Brophy, Robert J. *"Cawdor."* In *Robinson Jeffers: Myth, Ritual, and Symbolism in His Narrative Poems.* Hamden, Conn.: Archon Books, 1976. An analysis of *Cawdor* as a restatement of mythic themes and patterns. Brophy has done the most work in this field. Bibliography.
Carpenter, Frederic I. *"Cawdor."* In *Robinson Jeffers.* New York: Grosset & Dunlap, 1962. Analyzes *Cawdor* along with the rest of Jeffers' early long narratives as part of a chapter on Jeffers' early poetic career. Also the best short introduction to all of Jeffers' work. Bibliography.
Coffin, Arthur B. *"Cawdor."* In *Robinson Jeffers: Poet of Inhumanism.* Madison: University of Wisconsin Press, 1971. An examination of the poem by a critic who is primarily interested in the philosophical underpinnings of Jeffers' work, specifically such thinkers as Arthur Schopenhauer and Friedrich Nietzsche. Bibliography.
Houston, James D. "Necessary Ecstasy: An Afterword to *Cawdor." Western American Literature* 19, no. 2 (Summer, 1984): 99-112. An analysis of the poem that links it to the California coast in which it was set.
Zaller, Robert. "The Bloody Sire." In *The Cliffs of Solitude.* Cambridge, England: Cambridge University Press, 1983. Treats *Cawdor* along with a number of Jeffers' other poems, particularly the other long narratives, from a psychological, specifically Freudian, perspective. Bibliography.

CECILIA
Or, Memoirs of an Heiress

Type of work: Novel
Author: Fanny Burney (Madame D'Arblay, 1752-1840)
Type of plot: Social realism
Time of plot: Eighteenth century
Locale: England
First published: 1782

> *Principal characters:*
> CECILIA BEVERLEY, a beautiful and virtuous heiress
> MR. HARREL, her profligate guardian
> MR. BRIGGS, her miserly guardian
> MR. DELVILE, a proud aristocrat and also a guardian
> MRS. DELVILE, his wife
> MORTIMER DELVILE, their son
> MR. MONCKTON, Cecilia's unscrupulous counselor
> MR. BELFIELD, a pleasing but unstable young man
> HENRIETTA BELFIELD, his modest sister

The Story:

Cecilia Beverley, just short of her majority, was left ten thousand pounds by her father and an annual income of three thousand pounds by her uncle, the latter inheritance being restricted by the condition that her husband take her name. Until her coming of age, she was expected to live with one of her guardians, the fashionable spendthrift Mr. Harrel, husband of a girlhood friend. One who warned her against the evils of London was Mr. Monckton, her clever and unscrupulous counselor. His secret intention was to marry Cecilia; at present, however, he was prevented by the existence of an old and ill-tempered wife, whom he had married for money.

The constant round of parties in London and the dissipation of the Harrels were repugnant to Cecilia. Kind but unimpressive Mr. Arnott, Mrs. Harrel's brother, fell hopelessly in love with the girl, but Harrel obviously intended her for his friend, insolent Sir Robert Floyer, whom Cecilia detested. After vainly begging Harrel to pay a bill, which Arnott finally paid, Cecilia became so disgusted with the Harrels' way of life that she decided to leave their household; but she found the abode of her miserly guardian, Mr. Briggs, so comfortless, and was so repulsed by the pride and condescension of her third guardian, Mr. Delvile, that she decided to remain with the Harrels.

At a masquerade party, she was pursued by a man disguised as the devil. He was Monckton in disguise, attempting to keep others away from her. She was rescued first by a Don Quixote and later by a domino whose conversation pleased her greatly. At first, she believed the domino was Mr. Belfield, a young man she had met before. Later, she was surprised to learn that Don Quixote was Belfield. Angered at Cecilia's courtesy to Belfield, Sir Robert insulted him at the opera; a duel resulted, and Belfield was wounded. A young man, Mortimer Delvile, who was courteously attentive to Cecilia, proved to be the domino and the only son of her guardian. He was the pride and hope of his family, whose fortune he was to recoup by marriage. Cecilia visited his mother and was charmed by her graciousness and wit. She was disturbed, however, by the knowledge that she was universally believed to be betrothed to either Sir Robert or Belfield. Monckton, feeling that the Delviles were the only threat to him, attempted to destroy her friendship with them.

Cecilia met and immediately liked Henrietta Belfield. When she visited her new friend, she found Henrietta nursing her wounded brother, whom Mortimer wished to aid. Seeing Cecilia there, Mortimer believed that she was in love with Belfield. Having been educated above his station, Belfield had grown to feel contempt for business. He was clever and pleasant but unable to settle down to anything. Although Cecilia had refused Sir Robert's proposal, she saw that Harrel was still bent on the marriage. Monckton's constant warnings against the Delviles disturbed her, for she was now in love with Mortimer. Knowing his father's pride, however, she determined to conquer her feelings.

Cecilia, who had previously discharged some debts for Harrel, was now so alarmed by his threats of suicide that she pledged herself to a total of seven thousand additional pounds. Since Briggs would not advance the money, she was forced to borrow from a usurer.

Mortimer, learning that Cecilia loved neither Sir Robert nor Belfield, betrayed his own love for her—and then avoided her. Cecilia discovered that Henrietta had also fallen in love with Mortimer. Mrs. Belfield, believing that Cecilia loved her son, constantly urged him to propose to her.

Cecilia lent another thousand pounds to Harrel, who was to escape his creditors by leaving the country. Meanwhile, his wife was to live with her brother until Cecilia's house was ready. Harrel shot himself, however, leaving a note for Cecilia in which he revealed that her marriage to Sir Robert was to have canceled a gambling debt. Monckton discharged Cecilia's debt with the usurer; she was to repay him on coming of age. Against his wishes, she went with the Delviles to their castle. Only Mrs. Delvile was agreeable there. The family was too proud to encourage visitors, and Mortimer still avoided Cecilia. Much later, during a thunderstorm in which he contracted a fever, he betrayed his true emotions. Cecilia was puzzled and hurt; her emotions intensified when Mrs. Delvile, who had guessed the feelings of both Mortimer and Cecilia, let Cecilia know that they were not for each other. Mortimer, before going away for his health, told Cecilia that his family would never accept the change-of-name clause in the will.

Cecilia then went to live with an old friend. There she was surprised to see Mortimer's dog, sent, she discovered later, as a joke, unknown to the Delviles. She spoke aloud of her love for its master and turned to discover Mortimer beside her. She agreed to a secret wedding, but Monckton, chosen as their confidant, persuaded her of the wrongness of the act. Cecilia went on to London with the intention of breaking off the match; but discovery made her feel she was compromised, and she agreed to go through with the wedding. She could not continue, however, after a disguised woman interrupted the ceremony. Later, Mrs. Delvile, whose family pride exceeded her love for Cecilia, made her promise to give up Mortimer. She renounced him in a passionate scene during which Mrs. Delvile burst a blood vessel. Cecilia consoled her misery by acts of charity which Monckton, feeling that she was squandering his money, tried in vain to prevent.

Finally of age, Cecilia went to London with the Moncktons. There she discharged her debt to Monckton. Abused by Mr. Delvile, she was sure that someone had slandered her. When Cecilia went to visit Henrietta, Mr. Delvile saw her there. Having just heard Mrs. Belfield say that Cecilia loved her son, his suspicions of Cecilia's impurity were confirmed. Mrs. Harrel and Henrietta moved with Cecilia into her new home. Mortimer came to tell her that both his parents had agreed to a plan. If she would renounce her uncle's fortune, he would marry her, although she would have only the ten thousand pounds inherited from her father. Mr. Delvile knew, however, that she had already lost her father's money. Enraged at his father's treachery, Mortimer was determined to marry Cecilia, even though she was portionless. She agreed, but only if his mother would consent. Again, a secret wedding was planned, this time with Mrs. Delvile's approbation. They were married; Cecilia returned to her house, and Mortimer went to inform his father.

A woman Cecilia had befriended identified Mrs. Monckton's companion as the person who had stopped the first wedding. Mortimer was prevented from telling his father of the marriage by the scandals with which Delvile charged Cecilia. Upon learning that the slanderer was Monckton, Mortimer fought and wounded him and was forced to flee. The man who was to inherit Cecilia's fortune, since her husband had not taken her name, demanded his rights. Cecilia determined to join her husband. Mrs. Harrel took Henrietta with her to Arnott's house. Cecilia hoped that Henrietta, as miserable in her hopeless love for Mortimer as Arnott was in his for Cecilia, would comfort and be comforted by him.

In London, Cecilia consulted Belfield about her trip. Mrs. Belfield, hoping to get her son married to Cecilia, had left them alone when Mortimer entered. The meeting seemed to confirm his father's accusations, and he sent her to wait for him at his father's house. Mr. Delvile refused to admit her. Wild with fear that Mortimer would fight a duel with Belfield, she began a distracted search for her husband. Fevered, delirious, and alone, she was locked up by strangers. When Mortimer found her, convinced of her purity by Belfield, she was too sick to know him.

After many days of uncertainty, Cecilia eventually recovered. Monckton also was out of danger and grudgingly admitted that he had deliberately lied to Mr. Delvile about Cecilia's moral character. Mr. Delvile then accepted her as his daughter. Mrs. Delvile recovered her health, and Mrs. Harrel married again and resumed her life of careless frivolity. Arnott and Henrietta married. With Mortimer's help, Belfield finally settled down to an army career. Monckton lived on in bitterness and misery. Impressed by Cecilia's unselfishness and sweetness, Mortimer's aunt willed her a fortune. Cecilia was then able to continue her charities, though never extravagantly. She did occasionally regret the loss of her own fortune but wisely recognized that life cannot be absolutely perfect.

Critical Evaluation:

Following the phenomenal success of Burney's first novel, *Evelina: Or, The History of a Young Lady's Entrance into the World* (1778), *Cecilia: Or, Memoirs of an Heiress* shares thematic elements with its predecessor but demonstrates a marked shift in technique and style. Burney abandoned the epistolary form of her first novel, adopting a third-person, omniscient narrative. This narrative approach provides a distant perspective that allows the author to delve into more diverse personal viewpoints and to cross various social boundaries. Critics have traditionally viewed this novel as flawed compared to Burney's earlier effort, but *Cecilia* was nevertheless admired by the great Samuel Johnson. Although the novel lacks the sentimental happy ending characteristic of eighteenth century fiction, thereby provoking much complaint among her readers, the novel was commercially highly successful. The novel's literary influence was considerable. Novelist William Godwin first parodied it and then tried to emulate it in *The Adventures of Caleb Williams: Or, Things as They Are* (1794); Jane Austen's classic novel *Pride and Prejudice* (1813) is also indebted to *Cecilia*.

The novel combines two major themes, that of romantic love and the destructive power of the love of money. These themes are interwoven in the major plot line and in the numerous subplots involving characters who come in and out of Cecilia's life. The tension of the novel derives from Cecilia's attempt to reconcile two impulses in her life: the desires to marry the man she loves and to have independence and meaningful work. The great irony of the novel is that in order to have one, she must surrender the other.

When Cecilia arrives in London, her country upbringing has prepared her to see through the sham of society, and she is aware that her well-attended reception springs more out of interest in her wealth than out of genuine regard for her personally. With a too trusting nature, at first Cecilia finds the frivolous nature of the upper classes merely amusing. When the flighty Miss Larolles, for example, recalls how a friend's fortunate illness allowed her to attend a party in her place, Cecilia does not realize, as she later learns through the course of the novel, that such insensitivity can and often does lead to downright cruelty. As Cecilia gradually discovers the true nature of some of the people she trusts, Burney exposes the hypocrisy and materialism of London society in increasingly harsh terms.

Understandably, Cecilia is repeatedly disappointed by these people. Cecilia considers Mrs. Harrel an old and close friend and looks forward to living with her; however, Mrs. Harrel is entirely absorbed with her own vain pursuits, caught up in her husband's irresponsible insistence on living beyond their means and allowing him to take advantage of Cecilia, thus exhausting his ward's fortune. When Cecilia discovers the utter destitution of the family of Mr. Hill, a laborer whom Harrel refuses to pay, the young woman must face the extreme, tragic consequences of this reckless disregard for others. Mrs. Delvile, seemingly gracious and kind, withdraws her friendship when learning of her son's interest in marrying Cecilia, whom she considers socially inferior. Mortimer listens to malicious gossip and jumps to conclusions about Cecilia's behavior regarding men and money. Furthermore, he weakly surrenders to his family's vain rejection of Cecilia as an appropriate bride. His careless actions lead to Cecilia's madness, homelessness, and complete isolation. Her trusted confidante, Mr. Monckton, turns out to be the one responsible for spreading the false rumors about Cecilia and most deliberately sabotaging her happiness. Finally, none of Cecilia's guardians cares for her. One squanders her fortune, one advises her out of his own miserliness, and the other considers her a nuisance and socially inadequate.

Society's obsession with wealth and related superficial concerns is at the root of all of this deceit. Mrs. Belfield, in educating her son to be part of the upper class, destroys him by distorting his values and ignores her other children, including Henrietta, the most loyal and noble character in the entire novel and Cecilia's only true friend. The Delviles' obsession with their family name, despite the fact that it has long ceased reflecting any real power or wealth, is the most frustrating example of the emptiness of society's values. Such vanity leads to much suffering and ultimately threatens to ruin the lives of Cecilia and Mortimer.

Although the plot contains an excess of coincidences, and the novel presents a number of minor characters who serve no plot function and who do not generate much interest, the novel does contain some memorable, well-crafted scenes. The masquerade ball intrigues, in which Cecilia makes mistakes about the identities of her disguised suitors, provide suspense and irony. The suicide of Harrel at Vauxhall is dramatic and affecting. His note, naming Cecilia's refusal to marry Sir Robert Floyer as the cause of his financial ruin, is a final revelation into the character of Cecilia's selfish guardian.

Although much of the dialogue is stilted and artificial and the authorial narrative intrusive, some of Burney's colorful characters emerge vividly. The miserly Mr. Briggs's speech is abbreviated, reflecting his stinginess, as if he does not want to waste words any more than he does money. Captain Aresby sprinkles his speech with French phrases self-consciously, a detail that allows Burney to provide humor to the novel as well as satirically expose such social pretenses.

Critical assessment of Cecilia diverges significantly. Some critics argue that *Cecilia* and subsequent works by Burney are inferior to *Evelina* and that Burney lost her spontaneity and abandoned her genuine voice as she yielded to the pressures of fame and the expectations of her readership. Others insist that Burney progressively improved, and that the later novels demonstrate a maturity and a growing sophistication of thought. This discrepancy can be attributed to the position of *Cecilia* in the development of the novel. Less conventional in theme as well as structure than *Evelina*, Burney's second novel is a product of some risk-taking. The unsatisfying, perhaps unconvincing, reconciliation of Cecilia with Mortimer and his mother, which ends the novel, and Cecilia's acceptance of human love as being by nature imperfect, does not correspond to that of any previous genre. The philosopher Edmund Burke, who otherwise admired Burney's work, wished for either a happier or a more miserable ending to *Cecilia*, not the compromise with which it ends. Frances Burney insisted that her characterizations and her novel's conclusion are more realistic in their ambiguity. As Burney attempted to mirror a society she viewed with an increasingly mature and critical eye, such innovations were perhaps inevitable.

"Critical Evaluation" by Lou Thompson

Bibliography:
Cutting-Gray, Joanne. *Woman as "Nobody" and the Novels of Fanny Burney*. Gainesville: University Presses of Florida, 1992. Explores the recurring theme of names and namelessness as it relates to female identity; Cecilia's madness is the only rational response to an irrational society.

Epstein, Julia. *The Iron Pen: Frances Burney and the Politics of Women's Writing*. Madison: University of Wisconsin Press, 1989. Defends Burney's reputation as a major writer, citing her influence on later writers and characterizing her prose as representative of women in late eighteenth century fiction. The prevalence of aggression and violence in Burney's work derives from the societal conflict between the public and the private self.

Rogers, Katherine M. *Frances Burney: The World of "Female Difficulties."* New York: Harvester Wheatsheaf, 1990. Looks at the novel as social satire, as depicting an awkward blending of individuality and conformity, and as accepting and resisting society. Burney's intense depiction of the psychology of women is perhaps the author's greatest contribution to the development of the novel.

Simons, Judy. *Fanny Burney*. New York: Barnes & Noble Books, 1987. Comprehensive study of Burney's works, including journals and plays. Argues that the novel, although lacking spontaneity, demonstrates a maturing of vision and incisive social criticism. Cecilia is not a typical eighteenth century heroine of sensibility, but a rationalist, a woman who wants independence.

Straub, Kristina. *Divided Fictions: Fanny Burney and Feminine Strategy*. Lexington: University Press of Kentucky, 1987. Drawing on feminist criticism, Straub focuses on what are traditionally observed as flaws in Burney's work, and establishes new criteria by which Burney's work may be judged.

CELESTINA

Type of work: Novel
Author: Fernando de Rojas (c. 1465-1541)
Type of plot: Tragicomedy
Time of plot: Fifteenth century
Locale: Spain, probably Toledo
First published: Comedia de Calisto y Melibea, 1499; revised edition, 1502 as *Tragicomedia
de Calisto y Melibea* (English translation, 1631)

> *Principal characters:*
> CALISTO, a young nobleman
> MELIBEA, his beloved
> PLEBERIO, her father
> ALISA, her mother
> CELESTINA, a procuress
> ELICIA and
> AREUSA, the girls in Celestina's house
> SEMPRONIO and
> PÁRMENO, Calisto's servants

The Story:

One day, while pursuing his stray falcon, Calisto entered a strange garden where he saw and fell in love with a beautiful young woman named Melibea. His eagerness to take advantage of her gentle innocence shocked her, and she angrily drove him away. Calisto went home desolate and ready to die; his only comfort was the melancholy tunes he played on his lute. One of his servants, Sempronio, let him suffer for a time before he suggested that his master seek the aid of Celestina, a procuress, with whose servant, Elicia, Sempronio himself was in love. At Calisto's command, the servant hurried to Celestina's house to summon the old bawd. He and the procuress agreed to work together to cheat lovesick Calisto. The young nobleman had another servant, Pármeno, who had once worked in Celestina's house. He told his master of the bawd's evil reputation throughout the city and warned him against her.

Ignoring the warning, Calisto welcomed Celestina and offered her gold to act as a go-between in his suit. While he was upstairs getting the money for her, Celestina tried to win Pármeno to her side by assuring him that she was interested in his welfare because of her fondness for his mother. She also promised to help him in winning the affections of Areusa, whom he coveted. Pármeno, knowing her tricks, was not entirely convinced.

Unable to control his impatience to make Melibea his own, Calisto sent Sempronio to hurry Celestina in her efforts. Refusing to consider Pármeno's suggestion that he court Melibea honorably instead of trusting a notorious go-between, he did, however, order his horse so that he could ride past her house. He rode away after further criticism of Pármeno for trying to cross his desires, harsh words which made the servant regret his decision to remain faithful to his young master.

When Sempronio arrived at Celestina's house, he found her making a love charm. While she was busy, he and Elicia made love. Then Celestina, who had weighed the threat to her life from Melibea's father against the gold that a grateful Calisto would pay her, went to talk to Melibea. Lucrecia, a servant in the household, saw the go-between coming and warned Melibea's mother against Celestina, but Alisa thought the woman no more than a vender of sewing materials, hair nets, and feminine makeup. Trustingly, she asked Celestina to stay with Melibea while she herself went to visit a sick sister.

Celestina first told Melibea that she had come on behalf of a sick man. After purposely confusing Melibea, she finally explained that all Calisto wanted was a rope belt that had been taken on pilgrimages to Rome and Jerusalem and a copy of a prayer by Saint Polonia, supposed to cure toothaches. Ashamed of what she thought had been unjust suspicions of the old bawd, Melibea gave her the rope girdle and promised to copy off the charm so that it would be ready by the next day. Before she left the house, Celestina won Lucrecia to her side by promising to sweeten the maid's breath and to make her a blonde. Going to Calisto's house, the procuress boasted of her success, and the grateful lover promised her a new cloak. By that time, Pármeno had decided to accept Celestina's offer and help her in her scheme. He suggested that he accompany her home. On the way he demanded that she make arrangements to have him spend the night with Areusa. Celestina took him to her house, where Areusa was in bed, and persuaded the woman that Pármeno would comfort her during her sweetheart's absence.

The next day, while the servants were dining at Celestina's house, Lucrecia arrived with word that her mistress was ill and wished to see the procuress. The bawd went at once to Pleberio's house, where she discovered that Melibea's disease was lovesickness for Calisto. Celestina promised to cure the malady by having Calisto call at Melibea's door at midnight.

When she reported this latest development to Calisto, her news won his regard so completely that he gave her a gold chain. Having no intention of dividing it with her partners, she refused to agree when Sempronio and Pármeno demanded their share. While they quarreled, she screamed for the police. The servants silenced her forever, but her screams had been heard. Sempronio and Pármeno tried to escape through a window but were injured in the fall. The authorities beheaded them on the spot.

In the meantime, Calisto had gone to Pleberio's house, where he found Melibea eagerly awaiting him. While the lovers talked through the door, his cowardly attendants, who were supposed to be guarding him, ran away from imaginary enemies. The confusion awoke her parents, but Melibea explained that Lucrecia had made the noise while she was getting a drink for her mistress.

The next morning, Calisto awoke happy, only to be saddened by news of Sempronio's and Pármeno's fate. The thought of seeing Melibea in her garden that night was enough to make him forget what had happened, however, except for a fleeting thought that Celestina's bawdry was now punished. With another servant to carry a ladder, he went that night to the garden and climbed over the wall. Melibea was waiting for him. When the time for parting came, hours later, she lamented the loss of her maidenhood. Calisto mourned only the shortness of their time together.

Grieved by the loss of their servant sweethearts, Elicia and Areusa were determined to avenge their deaths. By pretending to be in love with Sosia, another of Calisto's servants, Areusa learned that the lovers were meeting secretly each night in Pleberio's garden. Eager for her favors, Sosia was willing to join in the plot. Neither he nor the women were prepared for violence, however, and so they played up to a scoundrelly soldier and murderer named Centurio. Elicia, who had taken over Celestina's house after the old bawd's death, had Areusa offer herself to Centurio if he would go into the garden and kill, or at least beat up, Calisto. At first the bully agreed, but prudent reconsideration convinced him that he would be unwise to meddle in the affair. Instead, he arranged to have several friends go to the garden and make a noisy but harmless commotion.

Meanwhile, Pleberio and Alisa talked over plans to marry off their daughter. Overhearing their conversation and conscience-stricken because she had spent every night of the past month with Calisto, Melibea almost confessed her wrongdoing to her unsuspecting parents. Once more Calisto went to the garden with his servant and ladder and made his way over the wall. A short time later, Centurio's friends arrived and pretended to get into a fight with Sosia in the street outside. Calisto was aroused by the disturbance. Despite Melibea's fears, he started hastily over the wall in order to go to the aid of his servant.

He fell from the wall and was killed. Lucrecia, frightened by the vehemence of her mistress' sorrow, awoke Pleberio and Alisa. Meanwhile, Melibea had climbed to the roof of the house. There she reflected upon the effect her actions would have on her parents. Her resolve to die unweakened by their pleadings, she compared herself to many parricides of antiquity, confessed her misdeeds, and bade them farewell. Then she leaped to her death. Pleberio carried her shattered body into the house, where he and Alisa sat alone in their grief.

Critical Evaluation:

Although written in dramatic form, with conventional division into acts, this work is regarded as a novel in dialogue because its excessive length and frequently shifting scenes make performance, without significant editing, impossible on any stage. In the 1499 version, the story consists of sixteen acts, which were increased to twenty-one in 1502, and at a considerably later date, to twenty-two. Some doubt has been cast upon the authenticity of certain of these additions. Although the work was published anonymously, Fernando de Rojas is generally accepted as the author, the chief evidence being an acrostic poem containing his name to which one of his early publishers first called attention, as well as several legal depositions made about 1525. The writer declared that he found the first act and amused himself by completing the story at the rate of an act a day during a two-week vacation at the University of Salamanca. Rojas was the mayor of Talavera as well as an educated lawyer who enjoyed the humanistic learning of the Renaissance.

The book has appeared in many editions and a number of translations. It was the first translation into English (originally translated as *The Spanish Bawd*, 1631) of any Spanish book, and it has had a tremendous influence upon all succeeding writing in Spain. Modern critics agree that *Celestina* is among the best novels in Spanish literature. Rojas demonstrates the tendency of Renaissance writers to refer to the texts of the ancient writers and to borrow subjects from ancient writers. The plot stems from an anonymous thirteenth century Latin poem, *Pamphilus* (the protagonist's name, which Rojas converted to Calisto), which is not readily available in English translation. The *Pamphilus* story was also incorporated as an episode in the *Libro de buen amor* by the "Archpriest of Hita," Juan Ruiz, in the fourteenth century. Rojas is known to have had access to both the original *Pamphilus* and the reduction in Juan Ruiz's *Libro de buen amor*; but Rojas greatly altered his source material. Classical literature also provides themes and motifs in the work. For example, there is an allusion to Pasiphae toward the beginning of the novel. This reference establishes desire as a principal theme of the work. According to Greek legend, Pasiphae mated with the minotaur because of lust. Pasiphae's daughter Phaedra was possessed with an illicit love like her mother, but Phaedra's passion was for her stepson. Rojas' portrayal of Phaedra's monstrous lust introduces Calisto's desire for Melibea. The idea of a cord leading Phaedra's future husband Theseus out of the labyrinth after he had killed the minotaur, Phaedra's half-brother, further suggests the confusion of the thread that Celestina uses in order to cause Melibea to be receptive to her message. In order to achieve this cooperation, Celestina invokes the god of Greek and Roman mythology, Pluto, who rules the underworld, urging him to wrap himself in the thread so that Melibea may buy it and entangle her heart in it, thereby causing her to become imbued with a strong and cruel love for Calisto.

Celestina also shows a Renaissance scholar's appreciation for varieties of language. A lover in the Petrarchan style, Calisto declares himself to be unworthy of Melibea and delights in the sensual image of his beloved. She is, as one may expect, a voluptuous Renaissance beauty, with lustrous pure white skin, big green eyes highlighted by her long, thick lashes, red full lips, and shapely figure. Melibea incarnates the traditional, naïve, proud, and imprudent young woman sparked by Calisto's wild delirium. The two young lovers, representing the upper classes, use high, periodic speech, and lace their expression of sensual desire with idealistic sentiment.

Deviating from the idealism of Calisto and Melibea, the proletarian characters present the themes of unsullied greed and desire. For example, Sempronio, Calisto's servant, connives with Celestina to profit monetarily from his master's passion. Sempronio introduces Calisto to Celestina, a witch shrewd in evil machinations, under the pretense that she may fix the affront to his master's honor, as well as to his ego, that occurs when Melibea initially rejects him in her garden. Celestina's great linguistic ability in the areas of persuasion and selling is linked to the devil. Frankness, superstition, and greed enable her to manipulate the other characters. Celestina's manipulative techniques are demonstrated in her dealings with the characters of both the upper and lower classes. In order to convince Melibea to give Calisto her girdle and a prayer, Celestina skillfully uses psychology; the procuress makes Melibea feel sorry for her advanced age and for Calisto's toothache. Celestina uses popular speech and proverbs to persuade Pármeno, Calisto's other servant, to join Sempronio and her in extracting money from Calisto.

Celestina, not the somewhat unsympathetic lovers, is the main character of the novel. The novel's concentration upon surreptitious matchmaking and witchcraft is, at least in part, a reflection of the interests of the times. Rojas (a Jew converted to Christianity under the threat of immolation at the hands of the Holy Inquisition) was distinctly aware of the fate of witches and other heretics. His portrait of Celestina is thus acutely sensitive and extraordinarily vivid.

Celestina has no religious identification; she could be Christian, Muslim, or Jew, for all three faiths coexisted in late medieval Spain. Her allegiance seems firmly rooted in the spirits of evil, judging from her imperious conjuration of the devil in Act III. Her affiliation with the occult is firmly established in the catalog of her pharmaceuticals detailed in Acts I, III, VII, and elsewhere. From her early sympathy for Areusa's abdominal cramps to her own susceptibility to fears of death, she remains a very human and humane criminal. Celestina truly recognizes the limitations of her powers, and in that recognition, she becomes a vulnerable, credible human being with relevance to her times and to any reader's own. Fernando de Rojas' creation of a dialogue novel, and of a character as singular as Celestina, became significant in the development of realism. The novel is a milestone in the development of literature. *Celestina* influenced the novel and drama in Spain and abroad.

Bibliography:

Barbera, Raymond. "*No puede creer que la tenga en su poder.*" *Romanic Review* 28, no. 1 (January, 1991): 105. A concise article in English that treats the relationship between the characters by developing the sentence that serves as the article's title. Describes the role of ambiguity in *Celestina*.

Dunn, Peter. *Fernando de Rojas*. New York: Twayne, 1975. Provides a detailed summary of each act in *Celestina* followed by a helpful commentary. Acquaints the reader with literary evaluation by discussing the genre, antecedents, characters, and structure of the work.

Gilman, Stephen. *The Spain of Fernando de Rojas*. Princeton, N.J.: Princeton University Press, 1972. Portrays the life of Fernando de Rojas. Depicts the difficult circumstances that his Jewish family, converted to Catholicism, had to face in Spain.

Martin, June Hall. *Love's Fools: Aucassin, Troilus, Calisto, and the Parody of the Courtly Lover*. London: Tamesis Books, 1972. Explains the late medieval tradition of moralistic satire. Shows how Calisto exemplifies the parody of courtly love.

Simpson, Lesley Byrd. Introduction to *The Celestina*, by Fernando de Rojas. Berkeley: University of California Press, 1971. The introduction to this translation by Simpson situates the work in literary history. Gives a brief synopsis of the plot and a character analysis.

THE CENCI
A Tragedy in Five Acts

Type of work: Drama
Author: Percy Bysshe Shelley (1792-1822)
Type of plot: Tragedy
Time of plot: 1599
Locale: Rome and the Apennines
First published: 1819; first performed, 1886

Principal characters:
COUNT FRANCESCO CENCI, a Roman nobleman
BEATRICE, his daughter
BERNARDO, his son
GIACOMO, his son
LUCRETIA, his wife, and stepmother to his children
ORSINO, a priest once loved by Beatrice
OLIMPIO and
MARZIO, assassins of Cenci
SAVELLA, a papal legate who discovers the murder of Cenci
CARDINAL CAMILLO, a merciful churchman

The Story:

Count Cenci was a cruel and brutal man whose greatest delight was to make people suffer. He had sent two of his sons to Salamanca in the hope that they would starve. His daughter, Beatrice, had been in love with Orsino, who had entered the priesthood. She did not know where to turn for solace. Her father was worse than cruel to her and her lover had become a priest. Orsino promised to present to the Pope a petition in which Beatrice begged relief from the sadistic abuses she and the rest of her family were suffering from her father. Beatrice told Orsino of a banquet her father was giving that night in celebration of some news from Salamanca and said that she would give him the petition at that time. After they parted, Orsino revealed his lust for her and resolved not to show the Pope her petition, lest she be married by the Pope's order and Orsino be left without a chance of winning her outside wedlock. He resolved also not to ask for special permission to marry lest he lose his own large income from the Church.

At the banquet that night, Cenci announced the purpose of his celebration: His two sons had been killed by accident in Salamanca. Since they had defied his tyranny, Cenci felt that this was well-deserved punishment. At first the guests could not believe their ears. Beatrice boldly begged that the guests protect her, her stepmother, and her remaining two brothers from further cruelties at the hands of her father. Cenci, telling them she was insane, asked the guests to leave. Then he turned on his daughter, threatened her with a new cruelty, and ordered her and his wife to accompany him to his castle in the Apennines on the following Monday.

At the Cenci palace, Beatrice then disclosed to her stepmother that Cenci had committed a crime against her which she dared not name. Orsino came to the women and proposed a plan for the assassination of Cenci. At the bridge on the way to the Apennines he would station two desperate killers who would be glad to murder Cenci. Giacomo entered to announce that he had lent his father his wife's dowry and had not been able to recover it. In fact, Cenci had suggested to Giacomo's wife that her husband was a wastrel who had spent the money in riotous living. Orsino assured Giacomo that the Pope, sympathizing with fathers, not children, would not restore his money. Egged on by Orsino, Beatrice and Giacomo conspired with him to murder their father.

Later Orsino came to report to Giacomo that his father had escaped from the plot and was safe within his castle in the Apennines. Giacomo then resolved to kill his father by his own hand, but Orsino said that he knew two men whom Cenci had wronged and who would be willing to rid the earth of their persecutor. At the castle in the Apennines, Cenci raged against the insolence of his daughter and confessed to Lucretia that he had tried to corrupt the soul of Beatrice. While he was sleeping, the two murderers, Olimpio and Marzio, appeared. Lucretia said she had put a sleeping potion in Cenci's drink to make him sleep soundly. The two men were hesitant. Olimpio reported that he could not kill an old man in his sleep. Marzio thought he heard the ghost of his own dead father speaking through the lips of the sleeping Cenci. Beatrice snatched a dagger from them and cried out that she herself would kill the fiend. Shamed into action, the assassins strangled Cenci and threw his body over the balustrade into the garden.

The Papal Legate, Savella, arrived with a warrant for the immediate execution of Cenci for his crimes. When Savella and his followers discovered that Cenci was already dead, they began an investigation. The guards seized Marzio, on whose person they found Orsino's note introducing the two murderers. Lucretia and Beatrice denied knowledge of the handwriting, but Savella arrested them in order to make them appear before the court in Rome. Giacomo, tricked by Orsino, fell into the hands of the Roman police. Orsino escaped in disguise.

Under torture, Marzio confessed, implicating the others. Threatened with torture herself, Beatrice swore to her purity and innocence, convincing Cardinal Camillo, but not the judge. Marzio, confronted by her impassioned plea, denied that Beatrice was guilty of parricide. The judge sent him back to the wheel, but he died with no further words. Camillo's pleas against further torture were futile, and Lucretia and Giacomo soon confessed. Beatrice, to avoid torture, ceased denying her guilt. As they awaited execution, she reasserted her family leadership, comforting the others, even the distressed Camillo.

Critical Evaluation:
The Cenci is Percy Bysshe Shelley's poetic tragedy of the moral depravity that he believed tyranny fosters. It treats Shelley's favorite theme: the moral imagination as the faculty that awakens, through its capacity to empathize with others, sympathetic love, which defeats despotism. In this play, however, Shelley renounces his typical visionary idealism wherein love conquers unjust power. Instead, he presents the realism, as he saw it, of a world in which victims of absolute power had no recourse to mitigating moral sympathies. The drama, in blank verse, follows Elizabethan tragic form.

As had Shakespeare and other tragedians, Shelley took his plot from historical events. The sordid tale of the Cenci family in late sixteenth century Rome had become a well-known legend through its many retellings. The story often has been structured to represent a political struggle for liberty from feudal and papal tyranny. Converting history to art, Shelley minimized the sensationalism of his source, emphasizing not the brutish details but the conflict between moral evil, which delights in the mental agony of its victims, and spiritual innocence, which can be violated by that evil. The play suggests that paternal tyranny succeeds only with the support of institutionalized powers of church and state. These powers were the causes, to Shelley, of a corrupt society. *The Cenci* is therefore a realistic representation of the same conflict that Shelly developed concurrently in the idealistic *Prometheus Unbound* (1820). Beatrice, the figure of defeated liberty erring tragically by seeking vengeance and perpetuating the cycle of violence, represents, mythically, a good that is helpless to overcome evil.

Dramatizing his revolutionary claim that power causes immoral abuse and only loving sympathy can create the conditions for justice, Shelley develops a rather bare historical account into fully motivated action. The tyranny of church and state produces the sadistic personal despot Francesco Cenci and the self-interested manipulator Orsino. The same unjust powers produce the weak, vacillating Giacomo, the helpless Lucretia, the broken-spirited Bernardo, the desperate hired killers, and the brutally victimized Beatrice. The kind Cardinal Camillo is Shelley's addition, for dramatic purposes, to history. The cardinal's fruitless appeals to Cenci show the limits of religion to convert diabolism, as his announcements of punishing fines enact Shelley's belief that the Church tolerated abuses in order to increase its wealth. Furthermore, Camillo's empathy for Beatrice balances the self-referential attitudes of Pope Clement VIII, who sees the murdered Cenci as another wronged father, justified in demanding total obedience. The dramatic contrast emphasizes Shelley's distinction between true empathy and sympathy, which extends only to others perceived as like oneself.

Unlike many closet dramas of the period, *The Cenci* was originally intended for stage production. Shelly sent detailed instructions to his friend Thomas Love Peacock concerning choices of actors for presentation at Covent Garden. He expected that the play's factual base would justify its content to the prudish and that its argument for liberty would appeal to revolutionary sympathies in England, but he reckoned without the strength of idealistic literary taste and reactionary Tory censorship, which, missing the moral tragedy, decreed incest and parricide unfit subjects. The play was first produced in 1886, privately, by the Shelley Society. Since then, post-Victorian responses to several productions have affirmed that *The Cenci* is among the best verse dramas since the Elizabethans. Although the ascendancy of literary realism has made the subject acceptable, it has also made verse drama become less popular.

Apart from early censorship, the major critical question the play evokes has concerned whether Beatrice's claims of innocence against the charge of conspiracy to murder her father are consistent with the character of a tragic protagonist, who, by classical standards, should assume responsibility for her actions. A related issue bears upon the larger question of tragedy in the modern world, in which human beings are often defined as helpless products of the circumstances that have molded them instead of creatures who freely make their tragic choices. Since Shelley's revolutionary politics led him to define social evil as resulting from tyrannical power and to present character as formed by conditions that surround it, the question is whether Beatrice, as a brutalized victim, can possess tragic stature. Most post-Victorian critics and reviewers have agreed that she can. Shelley carefully portrays her in the early acts as innocent and righteous, attempting every available solution for her family's protection from the fiendish paternal sadism that was known to church officials, including her former beloved, and to the social circle attending the banquet. All but the Pope fear Cenci too much to check his despotism, and Shelley motivates the Pope's inaction by the fines for Cenci's crimes that feed the Church coffers. When Beatrice's appeals fail and Cenci rapes her, his act temporarily deranges her natural nobility to a state of hysterical despair in which she chooses murder instead of believing, as Shelley did, that the act of another person could not dishonor her. That she maintains her innocence to the papal court is consistent with the moral conflict between her goodness and Cenci's hatefully wanton will to corrupt. Her sense that she has been a divine instrument ridding the world of monstrous evil is her tragic hubris. Shelley added to the historical source Savella's sudden appearance with a warrant for Cenci's death, contrasting papal power with the family's helplessness. That Beatrice regains her self-possession and goes to her execution expressing loving care for Bernardo and Lucretia demonstrates her reassertion of a dignity that rises above her vengeful hysteria induced by her father's perverted violence. This self-possession is consistent with the character of a tragic heroine.

Some scholars have conjectured that a biographical impulse underlies the parent-child conflict. Cenci's unpaternal avarice and tyranny toward his children echoes, one may argue, Shelley's experience with his father, Sir Timothy Shelley. Certainly Shelley's early experiences with a demanding father and an unaccepting society gave impetus to his works, which extol individual liberty of the spirit and argue for an end to social cruelties.

"Critical Evaluation" by Carolyn F. Dickinson

Bibliography:
Behrendt, Stephen C. "Beatrice Cenci and the Tragic Myth of History." In *History & Myth: Essays on English Romantic Literature*, edited by Stephen C. Behrendt. Detroit: Wayne State University Press, 1990. Argues that Beatrice's situation is like that of the English people in 1819. Shelley's play argues that the English needed to temper their urges toward violence in order to avoid self-destruction.

Cameron, Kenneth Neill. *Shelley: The Golden Years*. Cambridge, Mass.: Harvard University Press, 1974. Analyzes Shelley's transmutation of his source into *The Cenci*. Includes notes and bibliography.

Curran, Stuart. *Shelley's "Cenci": Scorpions Ringed with Fire*. Princeton, N.J.: Princeton University Press, 1970. Forms a basis for subsequent commentaries on the play, covering its historical context, Shelley's changes from his source, the play's critical reception, and its literary, philosophic, and mythic dimensions. Illustrations and notes.

Ferriss, Suzanne. "Reflection in a 'Many-Sided Mirror': Shelley's *The Cenci* Through the Post-Revolutionary Prism." *Nineteenth-Century Contexts* 15, no. 2 (1991): 161-170. Argues that Beatrice's succumbing to the urge toward vengeful violence is analogous to the French Revolution's descent to the Reign of Terror. Argues that the play reflects Shelley's skepticism concerning the achievement of revolutionary ideals.

Hammond, Eugene R. "Beatrice's Three Fathers: Successive Betrayal in Shelley's *The Cenci*." *Essays in Literature* 8, no. 1 (Spring, 1981): 25-32. Finds Beatrice betrayed successively by her father, the Pope, and God. References, notes.

Reiman, Donald H. *Percy Bysshe Shelley*. New York: Twayne, 1969. Offers an excellent interpretive synopsis of the play, including an analysis of Beatrice as a tragic protagonist. Bibliography and notes.

Wasserman, Earl R. *Shelley: A Critical Reading*. Baltimore: The Johns Hopkins University Press, 1971. The chapter on *The Cenci* discusses the play in full detail, focusing on Shelley's reference to the play's being based on "sad reality."

CEREMONY

Type of work: Novel
Author: Leslie Marmon Silko (1948-   )
Type of plot: Social realism
Time of plot: Just after World War II
Locale: Laguna, New Mexico
First published: 1977

> *Principal characters:*
> TAYO, a Laguna Pueblo veteran of World War II
> ROCKY, Tayo's cousin and best friend
> JOSIAH, Tayo's beloved uncle
> THE NIGHT SWAN, Josiah's lover
> TS'EH, Tayo's lover
> AUNTIE, Tayo's aunt who raises him
> GRANDMA, Tayo's grandmother
> KU'OOSH, a traditional Laguna healer
> BETONIE, a nontraditional healer in Gallup
> HARLEY,
> EMO, and
> LEROY, Tayo's war buddies

The Story:

Tayo and Rocky joined the Army because Rocky wanted to join and because they both wanted to travel. However, the young men had not planned on seeing the Philippine jungle and the death that occurred there. Tayo could not bring himself to shoot Japanese soldiers because they all resembled his uncle Josiah. Rocky was killed, and as the rain poured down incessantly, Tayo cursed it and begged for it to stop.

Back at Laguna, New Mexico, Tayo saw the result of his curse. The land was dry, and nothing was growing. Tayo was as sick as the land. He kept throwing up and could not eat. Tayo's family decided that he needed a healing ceremony, so the tribal healer, Ku'oosh, was called in to cure him. His ceremony, however, did not cure Tayo's sickness. Ku'oosh, knowing that Tayo needed a special ceremony, sent him to a medicine man named Betonie.

Betonie cured with elements from contemporary culture, such as old magazines and telephone books, as well as with native ceremonies. He explained Tayo's sickness to him. It was the witchery that was making Tayo sick, and it had the entire Native American population in its grip. The purpose of witchery was to prevent growth, and to grow was to survive. Betonie explained to Tayo that a new ceremony was needed and that he was a part of something much larger than his own sickness.

The Navajo medicine man made a sand painting for Tayo to sit in to reorient him. When the ceremony was over, Betonie remarked that it was not yet complete. There were a pattern of stars, some speckled cattle, a mountain, and a woman whom Tayo had yet to encounter.

The speckled cattle were of Mexican origin, designed for the hard existence of northern New Mexico. Uncle Josiah had bought them before he died, but when they had been set loose to graze, they had started south and kept moving, and neither Tayo nor Josiah could find them. Tayo realized that part of his ceremony was to find these cattle.

He began his search at the place where they had last seen the cattle and soon met a woman who lived in a nearby house. He ended up eating dinner and spending the night there. Later they made love. Tayo had already had an experience like this one when, before the war, he went to the home of The Night Swan, Josiah's lover, to tell her that Josiah could not make their appointment. After Tayo and The Night Swan made love, she said that he would remember this moment later.

While he was staying with the woman, he saw a pattern of stars in the north and decided to follow it. The search took him to a mountain named for the swirling veils of clouds that clung to the peaks. On the mountain Tayo came across the barbed wire of a ranch and found the speckled cattle. He cut the fence so they could escape toward Laguna. Two ranch hands caught Tayo but did not see the cattle in the distance. They were going to take him in but left him when they saw the tracks of a mountain lion. Still in search of the cattle, Tayo came across a hunter with a freshly killed buck across his shoulders. The hunter suggested that Tayo's cattle were probably down in the draw by his house. Tayo followed the hunter down to the house and met the hunter's wife, who was the same woman with whom he had slept at the beginning of the search. The cattle were held in the woman's corral; they had come down off the mountain the previous day. Tayo said good-bye to the woman and took the cattle back to Laguna.

Upon returning, Tayo told his grandmother that he was all right; the ceremony had worked. He decided to stay with the cattle at the ranch rather than live among other people. There he again met the woman, who this time called herself Ts'eh, claiming that her Indian name was too long. They spent much time together making love and talking. She taught Tayo about plants and rain, and he was immersed in her love.

Ts'eh left and told Tayo to remember everything she had taught him. He took a long walk and found himself at the uranium mine. There he realized the connection among all things of which Betonie had spoken. He saw the mining and use of uranium as a sand painting created by witchery and used for destruction. In the production and release of the atomic bomb, from the first test explosion at Trinity site to the southeast to the top-secret laboratories in Los Alamos, the witchery had joined everyone, Japanese, American, and Native American, into one clan united by one horrific fate. Tayo finally saw the pattern, the way all the stories fit together, and realized that he had not been crazy but was simply seeing things the way they truly were.

Critical Evaluation:

Leslie Marmon Silko's work is about the importance of stories, how they serve to orient one in the world and how they keep people and cultures alive. Her later work, *Storyteller* (1981), is an attempt to weave together legends from Laguna mythology and lore, stories told by her family, her own short stories and poems, and her father's photographs of the Laguna area. The themes that are developed in *Ceremony* regarding story and ritual are taken up in a different way in the labyrinthine and copious *Almanac of the Dead* (1991). In all of her work, however, Silko sees herself continuing what is essentially an oral tradition via the written word. The line breaks and spacing in *Storyteller* and in the verse portions of *Ceremony* are attempts to convey the pauses and stops in oral discourse, which is the way she heard these stories originally. Silko believes that stories are the lifeblood of a culture and can effect great changes in the world.

Ceremony is a multidimensional work in both form and content. The reader is immediately struck by the "interruptions" in the story. The opening pages of the novel are not prose, but verse, and speak of the mythological figure Thought-Woman "sitting in her room and whatever she thinks about appears." This figure, linked in the novel with the character Ts'eh, is associated with Grandmother Spider, a prominent figure in Laguna mythology; she is, in fact, the Creatrix herself. Versions of Laguna tales are woven into the narrative throughout the novel and parallel the story that Tayo is living. Silko's point is to show that which Tayo learns at the end of his ceremony, that "all the stories fit together—the old stories, the war stories, their stories—to become the story that was still being told."

Tayo is not so much finding himself as he is finding his place in the world. Native American writers and critics are careful to point out that finding one's place is a primary element of their culture and literature. Tayo is not the only sick one in this novel; Laguna society and the earth itself are out of sorts. Emo graphically depicts the attitude of the society when he remarks, "Look what is here for us, Look. Here's the Indians' mother earth! Old dried-up thing!" Tayo knows that Emo is wrong, but he feels disconnected from the earth as well. In fact Tayo blames himself for the drought that has made the earth an "old dried-up thing." He needs a ceremony that will restore his sense of place.

Women play a vital role in Tayo's ceremony. The encounter with The Night Swan foreshadows other ritualized encounters with women. Unlike his war buddies, who see women as conquests of war, Tayo experiences love and sex with the mysterious mountain woman, Ts'eh. Ts'eh is no doubt a shortened form of Ts'its'tsi'nako, or Thought-Woman, who begins the novel by thinking of a story. She appears in various forms but is always associated with Mount Taylor, which in Laguna is Tse'pina or Woman Veiled in Rain Clouds. She is the spirit of Mount Taylor and an extension of the earth itself. She is the feminine principle embodied and, thus, is Yellow Woman, Corn Woman, and other female figures from Laguna mythology. When Tayo makes love to these different expressions of Thought-Woman, he feels himself connected once again to a fertile and nurturing earth. He loses himself in the unity of all life and is no longer an invisible outcast; he has a place.

It is easy to see the importance of women in this novel, but an equal significance is given to language. In fact the image of the web, Spider-Woman's web, appears throughout the novel. The spinning of the web is the spinning of tales, and these tales, if understood in the appropriate way, can effect healing for individuals, society, and the earth. On the first page of the novel, the spider is thinking of a story, and the reader is told the story she is thinking. The stories are "all we have to fight off illness and death." The stories connect everything in a web that is paradoxically both strong and fragile. When Ku'oosh first comes to offer a ceremony for Tayo, he remarks, "But you know, grandson, this world is fragile." The reader is informed that the word "fragile" was "filled with the intricacies of a continuing process" and "with a strength inherent in spider webs." Tayo realizes that even one person, acting inappropriately, can tear away the delicate web and injure the world. These descriptions of storytelling as a web of words offer a profound explanation of the nature of language in oral cultures. Silko, in writing the novel, is continuing to spin the web.

Few Native American writers have so provocatively and dramatically woven oral tradition into her work as Leslie Marmon Silko has done. Hers is a powerful voice that offers a tribal interpretation of contemporary American culture and values.

Gregory Salyer

Bibliography:
Allen, Paula Gunn. "The Feminine Landscape of Leslie Marmon Silko's *Ceremony*." In *Studies in American Indian Literature: Critical Essays and Course Designs*, edited by Paula Gunn Allen. New York: Modern Language Association of America, 1983. A foundational essay that articulates the importance of the feminine in Tayo's healing, written by a Laguna Pueblo writer and critic.

Garcia, Reyes. "Senses of Place in *Ceremony.*" *MELUS: The Journal of the Society for the Study of the Multi-Ethnic Literature of the United States* 10, no. 4 (1983): 37-48. An exploration of the sense of place embodied by Tayo at the end of the ceremony. Also shows the importance of language and story in reorienting Tayo into his "place."

Manley, Kathleen. "Leslie Marmon Silko's Use of Color in *Ceremony.*" *Southern Folklore* 46 (1989): 133-146. Draws upon anthropology and Laguna mythology to explore the meanings of various colors in particular settings.

Nelson, Robert M. "Place and Vision: The Function of Landscape in *Ceremony.*" *Journal of the Southwest* 30 (1988): 281-316. A detailed examination of landscapes and Tayo's movement through them to reach his ultimate healing. Discusses the relationship between particular figures and particular landscapes. This essay is especially thorough and useful in interpreting the novel.

Ruppert, James. "The Reader's Lessons in *Ceremony.*" *Arizona Quarterly* 44 (1988): 78-85. Ruppert suggests that the reader, like Tayo, experiences the fusion of story and reality and can ultimately learn the same lesson Tayo learns, namely, that the world is unified through appropriate storytelling.

CEREMONY IN LONE TREE

Type of work: Novel
Author: Wright Morris (1910-   )
Type of plot: Psychological realism
Time of plot: Mid-twentieth century
Locale: Nebraska
First published: 1960

          Principal characters:
              TOM SCANLON, an elderly man
              LOIS MCKEE, his oldest daughter
              WALTER MCKEE, Lois' husband
              MAXINE MOMEYER, another daughter
              BUD MOMEYER, Maxine's husband, a postal worker
              LEE ROY MOMEYER, Bud's nephew, a high-school boy
              EDNA EWING, Tom's youngest daughter
              "COLONEL" CLYDE EWING, Edna's husband, a wealthy Oklahoman
              GORDON MCKEE, Walter's son
              CALVIN MCKEE, Gordon's son
              ETOILE MCKEE, Calvin's wife
              GORDON BOYD, Walter's boyhood friend and hero
              W. B. JENNINGS, a journalist and adventure story writer
              "DAUGHTER," a hitchiker who Gordon Boyd picks up

The Story:

Tom Scanlon had spent his life in the Lone Tree Hotel in Lone Tree, Nebraska, now a ghost town. The winter before he was ninety, his daughter Lois and her husband, Walter, took him on a trip to Mexico. There they ran into Walter's old friend Gordon Boyd, who had left Nebraska because he could not have Lois. Later, Walter wrote Boyd and invited him to a reunion in Lone Tree late in March, on Tom's ninetieth birthday.

After much soul-searching, Boyd left Acapulco in his dilapidated car and headed north. In a Nevada town, where tourists came to see nuclear bomb tests, Boyd offered a ride to a young, penniless girl. In Nebraska, after the car rolled into a ditch, Boyd and "Daughter" hopped a passing freight train.

The members of Tom's family shared several worries. One was the increasing violence around them. In Lincoln, Charlie Munger had shot ten people, and Bud Momeyer's nephew, Lee Roy Momeyer, had run his car over two boys, killing them. Lois was concerned about little grandson Gordon McKee, who loved guns and liked to torment women. Even the friendly Bud Momeyer had a sadistic streak; his hobby was shooting cats with a bow and arrow.

The women in the family also discussed the possibility of marriage between two cousins, the Momeyer girl, Etoile, and the older Gordon McKee's son, Calvin. Etoile's mother, Maxine, saw this as a chance for her daughter to catch a husband with money, but Etoile herself was primarily interested in sex. Calvin just wanted to be free, like a cowboy. Calvin was busy planning a birthday surprise for Tom. Etoile would dress up like Tom's late wife Samantha, and the two of them would ride into Lone Tree in a mule-drawn buggy, just as in the old days.

Unable to get into high school at home, Lee Roy Momeyer had gone to Lincoln, where he could stay with his uncle and take classes in shop and physical education. Lee Roy and Charlie

Munger, who worked with him repairing cars, were regularly bullied by some boys at school. Enraged, Charlie started shooting people at random, and when the boys blocked his way once too often, Lee Roy gunned his car and ran into them.

Interested in the case, the journalist W. B. Jennings looked up Lee Roy's parents, but they said he needed to talk to Maxine and sent him on to Lone Tree. On the freight train that went in that direction, Jennings was joined by Boyd and "Daughter."

In Lone Tree, "Colonel" Clyde Ewing, his wife, Edna, and their valuable dog, Shiloh, were living in comfort in their huge trailer. The rest of the family camped out in the hotel. When Boyd arrived, he did not explain his relationship to "Daughter," but everyone was polite. The family also made Jennings feel welcome. Maxine organized things, cooked, and cried about being the family workhorse. Boyd kept talking about the bomb.

At the dinner table, Walter and Boyd, who had been Walter's hero, squabbled about the past, and Walter called Boyd a fool for ruining his life. When little Gordon wandered in with his grandfather's loaded pistol, Jennings managed to get first the ammunition, then the weapon, away from the child. Tom had been asleep through all of this, but when Etoile appeared in costume, he rose up, calling for Samantha. The Colonel was looking for Shiloh. Some time later, Bud went out into the night with his bow and arrows.

The trip back to Lone Tree was more difficult than Calvin had expected it to be. At one point, Etoile was thrown out of the buggy. When Calvin ran to her, she pulled him down onto the grass and persuaded him to make love to her.

Boyd found a 1927 newspaper, announcing that Lindbergh was over the Atlantic, and brooded about time. Lois thought his notions were ridiculous. Her love was reserved for little Gordon; however, she was well aware that the child had an evil streak and enjoyed making her suffer.

In the middle of the night, the buggy came around the corner of the hotel, carrying Calvin and Etoile, entwined in each other's arms, and Bud with his trophy, the corpse of Shiloh. Lois shot off her pistol, Tom started toward the buggy and dropped down dead, and Etoile kept trying to announce that she and Calvin were married.

While the Colonel worried about his insurance and the rest of the family discussed what to do about their father, Calvin was hitching up the mules to the covered wagon in which Tom had been born. The Colonel and Edna drove off. Tom's corpse was loaded into the covered wagon; Boyd, "Daughter," Jennings, and Walter all climbed on; and as Lone Tree vanished in the dust behind them, Walter kept urging Boyd to come back home to Nebraska.

Critical Evaluation:

Although for decades many critics have considered him one of America's most important writers, Wright Morris has never attained the prominence he deserves. The reason may lie in the fact that much of his work is closely tied to a particular region of the United States, the rural Midwest, so some have misclassified Morris as a mere local-color writer. This myth should have been dispelled by his winning the National Book Award for *The Field of Vision* (1956). By this time, however, Morris was being accused of having too much to say, rather than too little. In *Ceremony in Lone Tree*, Morris juggles multiple themes, complex characters, and rapid shifts in time and focus in a way that some readers find dizzying. Others, however, are exhilarated by their excursion into Morris' sometimes comic, sometimes nightmarish world, in which the only certainty is constant change.

The inevitability of change is emphasized in the first section of Morris' novel, entitled "The Scene." Tom Scanlon's home, Lone Tree, is a ghost town, with dusty, deserted streets and a hotel littered with dead flies. In contrast to Lone Tree, Walter's boyhood home, Polk, is still very much alive. It has green, tree-shaded avenues and even a new supermarket. Polk also has maintained its links with the historical past, represented by the Civil War cannon in the park, and with the personal past of Walter McKee and Gordon Boyd, who carved their initials on the cannon and who rode the sled which, although no longer used, still sits under the house where Boyd once lived. In some ways, Polk is changing; in others, it is unchanged. Significantly, Walter no longer lives there. He is a resident of Lincoln, where Maxine, Bud, and Etoile also live, along with the killers, Lee Roy and Charlie.

Both Lone Tree, the ghost town, and Tom, who loves it and identifies himself with it, represent the Old West, both the reality and the illusion. Calvin thinks of Tom as a Western hero, a cowboy who has lived free and solitary, with just a horse and a gun for company. Threatened by Etoile's attractions and her mother's designs, Calvin goes west, as generations of restless men had done before. In making Tom a hero of the frontier, however, Calvin has ignored the realities of his great-grandfather's life. Even Tom's being born in a covered wagon, which was used to transport families, not individuals, indicates that the society of undomesticated men was already dying when Tom arrived on the scene. At least subconsciously, Calvin accepts this revised view of Tom's youth; when he re-creates it, he does not ride in on a horse, shooting a gun, but hitches mules to the covered wagon and puts Etoile, dressed as Tom's dead wife, on the seat beside him. Even Tom's funeral procession is certainly not what one would expect for a frontier hero. He is not laid to rest on the lone prairie, alone for eternity, but, with kinfolk and friends around him, he is loaded into the covered wagon to be taken to town.

Walter, too, finds that the person he had always admired was not, after all, a hero. Gordon Boyd left Nebraska not because he was courageous, but because he was too weak to face reality, and he has been drifting ever since. If he is to survive, he may have to accept Walter's generous offer, return home, and settle into a middle-class existence.

Such disillusionment is not the only result of the American male's continuing infatuation with the heroic ideal. The cowboy or the gunfighter was an individualist, who made his own rules, fled from the women who would trap him into domesticity, and, when pressed, spoke with his gun. When Calvin and Boyd act out this ideal, they do not endanger anyone but themselves, but not every hero is so harmless. Bud Momeyer ventures forth to kill domestic animals, and little Gordon has the same impulse in regard to human beings, especially women such as his doting grandmother.

In Charlie Munger and Lee Roy Momeyer, one can see how the Western ideal plays out in modern society. To be somebody, they believe, means to be feared, like a gunfighter in a Western movie. When such a hero encounters disrespect, he pulls out his gun, and his enemy either backs down or is killed. To Charlie, the obvious way to reestablish his worth is to shoot some people. Although Lee Roy's weapon is a car, not a gun, his will to kill heroically is the same as Charlie's.

In the myth, it is women who pose a threat to the hero; in *Ceremony in Lone Tree*, it is women who oppose the expression of the myth in the modern world. Ever since the murders in Lincoln, say Tom Scanlon's daughters and daughters-in-law, they have lived in fear, and they do not like it. It is no accident that the other prevailing topic of conversation among these women is the possibility of getting Calvin married to Etoile. Instinctively, they seem to sense that the only way to disarm would-be Western heroes is to cajole them into domesticity. Otherwise, Morris suggests, by acting out their ideal, they may well destroy civilized society.

Rosemary M. Canfield Reisman

Bibliography:

Crump, G. B. *The Novels of Wright Morris: A Critical Interpretation*. Lincoln: University of Nebraska Press, 1978. Argues that the primary theme of *Ceremony in Lone Tree* is the unhappy effects that the heroic ideal produces in individuals and in society. Crump's introductory discussion of earlier critical views is helpful. Extensive bibliography.

Harper, Robert D. "Wright Morris's 'Ceremony in Lone Tree': A Picture of Life in Middle America." *Western American Literature* 11 (November, 1976): 199-213. In this exceptionally lucid essay, the novel is placed within the context of traditional U.S. fiction. Unlike most of his contemporaries, Morris defines the hell of white, middle-class Americans.

Howard, Leon. *Wright Morris*. Minnesota Pamphlets on American Writers, no. 69. Minneapolis: University of Minnesota Press, 1968. A concise overview of Morris' work. In a brief discussion of *Ceremony at Lone Tree*, Howard points out how characters from earlier novels are fleshed out in this work.

Knoll, Robert E., ed. *Conversations with Wright Morris: Critical Views and Responses*. Lincoln: University of Nebraska Press, 1977. This unusual volume contains essays about Morris written by four major critics and an informal conversation between each of the critics and the author. Also includes an essay by Morris, a biographical summary, and a bibliography.

Madden, David. *Wright Morris*. New York: Twayne, 1964. The chapter on *Ceremony in Lone Tree* explores the symbolic importance of the major characters, as they represent stages in the eternal process of change. Justifies Morris' characteristic ambiguity as an honest reflection of the human condition. Annotated bibliography.

THE CHAIRS

Type of work: Drama
Author: Eugène Ionesco (1912-1994)
Type of plot: Absurdist
Time of plot: Indeterminate
Locale: An island
First performed: 1952; first published, 1954 as *Les Chaises* (English translation, 1958)

> *Principal characters:*
> THE OLD MAN, aged ninety-five
> THE OLD WOMAN, aged ninety-four
> THE ORATOR, hired by the Old Man to speak, aged 45 to 50

The Story:

The Old Man and his wife, the Old Woman, lived in a circular room in a tower in the middle of a circular island surrounded by nothing but a stagnant sea. The Old Man stood on a chair and peered out the window to look at the shadows of ships on the water, apparently waiting for someone, but the Old Woman scolded him to come down because she feared that he might fall and, besides, she told him, it was early morning and thus dark out, so he could not see the ships.

Reluctantly, the Old Man climbed down. The Old Woman begged him to entertain her by imitating the month of February, which he reticently did, and then she pleaded with him to tell her once more the story of how they had arrived on the island decades earlier. Reluctantly he agreed to, even though he had told it and she had heard it too many times before. When he mentioned that by coming to this deserted isle he had ruined his promising career, the Old Man began to weep and moan like a child. The sun had begun to rise.

The Old Woman, who called him Semiramis, took him on her lap and rocked him, as if he were a baby. She assured him that if they had remained in civilization, he could have been anything he had wanted, even Head Orator. Even though the Old Man protested that he had too much difficulty in communicating to ever become a great speaker, he insisted that he had something of such enormous importance to tell the world that he had hired a professional orator and invited the most important people to come to the island that very day so that they would all hear what the Orator would say on the Old Man's behalf.

Afraid that the guests would tire them, the Old Woman protested that he must call off this engagement. The Old Man wavered and began to panic. Yet no sooner had he declared that it was too late to cancel than the doorbell rang. Nervously, the old couple prepared themselves. Slowly, the Old Man went out of their tower room to the entry and, with the Old Woman following him, opened the door. Yet the Lady whom they brought into their circular room was invisible. They ushered this unseen woman into the room, greeted and spoke to her with extreme politeness, and offered her a chair. They even argued about what this invisible guest might have meant by a particular remark and talked behind her back. As they sat beside her, they paused to listen to what the Lady was saying—none of which could really be heard.

Then, the bell rang again and the sounds of a boat pulling away from the island could be heard. The Old Man jumped up, ordered his wife to bring in more chairs, and excusing himself to the invisible lady, ran for the door. Just as the Old Woman returned with a chair, the Old Man came back with another invisible guest, a Colonel, to whom he presented his wife and also the invisible Lady, already seated. The Old Woman admired the Colonel's uniform, and the Old Man asked him to sit down beside the Lady. The four of them—the two who were visible and the two who were not—became involved in a heated conversation. Once again, the doorbell sounded. The Old Man sprang to his feet and ran for the door while the Old Woman raced to find more chairs for these unseen guests.

More invisible people now arrived. The room soon began to fill with chairs, and the light grew brighter and brighter. As more and more unseen guests came in, the Old Man and the Old Woman spoke to them animatedly, entertaining them, sometimes individually, sometimes together. Outside they could hear more boats docking on the island. As the doorbell continued to ring, the Old Man opened the door and the Old Woman went for chairs. Finally, with the room completely packed with chairs and invisible guests, one more person arrived: the Emperor himself. Deeply moved by his majesty's unseen presence, the Old Man tearfully introduced his wife and then explained that this moment was the high point of their long lives. They thanked the Emperor for gracing them with his presence on this special night when all would be revealed. The couple agreed that they could not have wished for anything more. Content now to lie eternally together in death, they unexpectedly jumped from the window, both shouting "Long live the Emperor!"

Then, after a moment of silence, as the light in the room and through the windows suddenly dimmed, the Orator who had been hired by the Old Man came into the circular room. He faced the rows of empty chairs and began to make sounds—not words, merely meaningless noises. He then tried to scrawl a message on the blackboard, but the words he wrote were not words at all, just incomprehensible lines. He politely bowed to the chairs and then left.

Now from the chairs came the sounds of people—laughter, murmurs, coughs—all the different noises that a theater audience might have made. Gradually, these noises grew louder.

Critical Evaluation:

In Eugène Ionesco's plays, many ideas are presented very directly, through startling images that defy commonly accepted theatrical conventions. Setting, character, and story as they are usually understood are noticeably absent from *The Chairs*. The audience is asked to accept that the peculiar string of events that it witnesses throughout the play is something that, presumably, has meaning.

Ionesco's dramas are absurd. In the context of theater, "absurd" does not simply mean "silly" or "ridiculous." Rather, absurdity refers to the perception that in the modern world, where people are cut off from their traditional ties, all actions become useless, senseless. The absurdity of the absurd play is a reflection of the absurdity of the world. The emphasis of many absurd plays is on the emotional content, or lack thereof, of the moment. Often, nothing appears to be occurring onstage, and characters seem shallow, puppetlike creatures, but amid the frightening lack of communication come waves of humor and terror. Rejecting the logic and reason of earlier writers, Ionesco offers an illogical and irrational drama that expresses the often mystifying feeling of senselessness that pervades the awareness of many modernists.

The Chairs is very clearly concerned with communication among human beings, or perhaps the inevitable lack of communication among them. The Old Man, who has spent his life on an isolated island, feels he must share the message of his life with others before he dies. He invites an audience of notables to hear what he has to tell them. Yet instead of experiencing the presence of other people, he and the Old Woman experience the absence of others. The "people" who come to this secluded island are invisible and mute. Similarly, the Orator whom the Old Man has chosen to convey his message would be incapable of presenting it even if there were someone there because he can neither speak with any meaning nor can he write in intelligible signs. By the time the Orator has begun his futile attempts, both the Old Man and the Old Woman have killed themselves, convinced that they have reached the high point of their long lives.

Even between themselves, the old couple may talk a great deal throughout the play, but very little of what they have to say makes any sense. The story that the Old Woman begs the Old Man to tell her, of their arrival on the island, seems circular, insignificant. Moreover, the Old Woman has heard it so many times that she hardly even listens to what he says. Rather, she relates to the story as if it were a piece of music and seems more interested in the emotions that the Old Man's tale inspires rather than in gaining any meaning from the words.

Ionesco called *The Chairs* "a tragic farce," and indeed much of the play is extremely funny. The early scenes, for example, in which the Old Man and the Old Woman seem to shift from acting like old people to acting like small children, are especially humorous, and later in the play, with the arrivals of the unseen guests, the behavior of the old couple (who carefully observe all the social niceties without there being any guests to be seen) amounts to high comedy. Nevertheless, the failure of the Old Man to communicate what he seems to believe is the essence of his life's experience, even amid the bizarre absurdities of the play, turns *The Chairs* toward tragedy.

Instead of providing any readily understandable answers, the tragic farce provokes many questions. Is communication between people possible? How much of what a speaker says is genuinely understood? Do writers actually make contact with their readers, whom they never meet? Perhaps most significant, what role does a theater audience play in a drama as it is in progress? Are spectators, who sit by silently in the darkened auditorium, in fact rather similar to the unseen, unheard guests who come to the old couple's island?

Since *The Chairs* premiered in 1952, it has remained one of Ionesco's most respected and popular plays. Frequently revived all over the world, this play has contributed to Ionesco's reputation as a serious dramatist.

Kenneth Krauss

Bibliography:
Coe, Richard N. *Ionesco: A Study of His Plays*. Rev. ed. London: Methuen, 1971. Presents a careful study of *The Chairs*, offering information about the early productions of this work and discussing how confused and delighted critics were by this cryptic play.
Cohn, Ruby. *From "Desire" to "Godot": Pocket Theater of Postwar Paris*. Berkeley: University of California Press, 1989. Has a chapter devoted to the first production of *The Chairs*, with much informative material about what the play means and has meant to those who have seen it. Provides a very solid discussion of how one might respond to this perplexing masterpiece.
Dobrez, L. A. C. *The Existential and Its Exits: Literary and Philosophical Perspectives on the Works of Beckett, Ionesco, Genet, and Pinter*. New York: St. Martin's Press, 1986. Explores some of the possibilities of what is one of Ionesco's best pieces.
Esslin, Martin. *The Theatre of the Absurd*. 3d rev. ed. New York: Penguin, 1980. Long before other critics had a clue about what Ionesco's plays might mean, Esslin had placed Ionesco in a group with other writers, whom he called "absurdists." Esslin delivers an often moving interpretation of *The Chairs* and how Ionesco came to write it.
Guicharnaud, Jacques. *Modern French Theatre: From Giraudoux to Genet*. New Haven, Conn.: Yale University Press, 1967. The chapter on Ionesco and his work uses *The Chairs* as a centerpiece. Long an admirer of the absurdist playwright, Guicharnaud looks into the texts of Ionesco's one-act dramas and finds much to explain.

CHAKA

Type of work: Novel
Author: Thomas Mofolo (1875?-1948)
Type of plot: Historical realism
Time of plot: Nineteenth century
Locale: Lesotho (Zululand), Africa
First published: 1925 (English translation, 1931)

> *Principal characters:*
> CHAKA, a warlord and tribal king
> SENZANGAKHONA, his father
> NANDI, his mother
> ISANUSI, a sorcerer
> DINGISWAYO, a neighboring tribal king
> NDLEBE and
> MALUNGA, agents of Isanusi
> ZWIDE, a neighboring tribal king
> NOLIWA, Chaka's favorite wife
> NONGOGO, favorite and faithful servant to Chaka

The Story:

Senzangakhona, the tribal king, was without male children. He decided to marry again so that he could have a male offspring for the kingship. He was attracted to Nandi and, overcome by her beauty, took her when they were not yet married, in violation of tribal law. She became pregnant, whereupon the two were married secretly. Chaka was born. The other wives were jealous of Nandi and her son Chaka, and they threatened to expose Senzangakhona for impregnating Nandi before marriage. In the meantime, other male heirs to the throne were born.

Senzangakhona banished Nandi and Chaka to another village. At first, he sent them cattle and sheep to help, but when this was discovered by his wives he was forced to discontinue the presents. Chaka grew up lonely—an outcast from his father and from the other young boys, who tormented him as an outsider. He learned early to fight and to seek and take vengeance.

Chaka's courage and boldness grew, as did his strength. He performed deeds of heroism that made him a favorite in the village rather than an outcast. He killed a lion that was terrorizing the people. Later, he killed a hyena as it was dragging a girl away.

While bathing in the river, Chaka was visited by an ominous snake. The event foretold that Chaka was destined to greatness. His mother, having witnessed the event, tried to visit a sorcerer, but it was learned that the woman has died after arranging for Chaka and Nandi to consult her own master in sorcery, Isanusi.

Chaka had become the most likely successor to the tribal kingship, and a dispute of contention arose with Mfokanzana, the chosen heir. Chaka was forced to flee the village after his father, King Senzangakhona, arrived and ordered Chaka killed.

Upon fleeing the village, Chaka met the sorcerer Isanusi, who liked the young man and promised that if he would obey in all things that he would one day inherit his father's kingship, which was rightfully his own by birth. Chaka agreed. Isanusi made several different kinds of medicine with which he strengthened Chaka and his resolve.

Chaka, who had previously told his mother all things, did not report to her about his meeting with Isanusi. Chaka then, following Isanusi's instructions in all things, went to the kingship of Dingiswayo, where he quickly became a hero and king's favorite by killing a madman. He helped Dingiswayo in battle, immediately becoming by far the best warrior in the tribe. Chaka liked warfare and determined that he wanted to fight a war that had no end. Ndlebe and Malunga, sinister agents of Isanusi, appeared mysteriously to assist Chaka in all things. Chaka lied to Dingiswayo about their origins, claiming that they were childhood friends. The two possessed supernatural gifts that helped Chaka in all things, particularly war, marriage, and tribal politics. Chaka fell in love with Noliwa, Dingiswayo's daughter, but he was afraid to take up the matter with the king. With the help of the two agents of evil, Ndlebe and Malunga, the marriage was eventually made. Noliwa was to be Chaka's favorite wife.

Senzangakhona died, whereupon his son Mfokanzana claimed the throne. Following the instructions of Ndlebe and Malunga, Chaka fought Mfokanzana and killed him, whereupon Chaka was installed as his father's successor. An old enemy of Dingiswayo, Zwide (king of a neighboring tribe) made war against Dingiswayo and killed him. Chaka, after conquering Zwide, then became the new king of Dingiswayo's and Zwide's territories as well as that of his father.

Chaka, now with three kingships to his name, made numerous reforms in his new, combined kingdom. He made innovations to assure that his warriors were the most fierce and feared in all of Africa. Chaka was visited by Isanusi, who promised him that he could become even more powerful and that he could control more land than he could ever see or people than he could ever visit—all if Chaka would continue to follow Isanusi's orders. Chaka, lustful for power, agreed.

Chaka turned into a tyrant. He killed his own men without discretion, often killing even the most faithful of his own warriors for inconsequential reasons. The people came to fear him totally and wanted a new leader. Chaka responded by becoming more and more fierce, tyrannical, and arbitrary in controlling his growing kingdoms.

Chaka continued to follow Isanusi's instructions exactly. When he was told that he had to make medicine for his warriors with blood from his son, he did so. When he was told that he had to make more medicine with blood from his wife Noliwa, he killed her and made the medicine. Finally, when Isanusi gave him the order to kill his mother Nandi, he carried out that command as well. Each time he acquired more land and people, becoming the greatest leader in all of African history.

Finally, Chaka became sick. In his illness he had numerous dreams in which he was visited by the ghosts of those whom he had killed, particularly family members. When his own men came into his quarters with spears to stab him, he did not resist. He accepted his death with stoicism.

Critical Evaluation:

Written during the first two decades of the twentieth century and first published in English in 1931, *Chaka* was one of the first significant novels written by an African native to receive widespread attention and readership in Europe and the United States. Thomas Mofolo, with this book, provided the English-speaking world with a depiction of African life, culture, tradition, and mind-set before the coming of Europeans.

Unlike many African novels, *Chaka* is set in the eighteenth century, before the Europeans came. European forms of government and religion were not part of African life in the time in which the novel is set. Mofolo, himself educated by Christian missionaries, writes of a time previous to his own African existence, but he does so with a voice of authenticity and sincerity.

The story reveals much about human nature within a localized African setting. The soul-devouring nature of evil, the motive for revenge, the matters of love and war, the fall of a hero—all of these universal human stories are detailed in an African context.

As a result of circumstances of birth, Chaka is set apart from his family and his inheritance through no fault of his own. When he gives himself over to the evil of the sorcerer Isanusi, however, he morally takes things into his hands and assures his descent into evil. He slowly abandons all reason, love, and goodness in his life. He does so always for selfish reasons. In the beginning, it is reasonable and human that he would want to gain the throne that is rightfully his own and which he has been denied. His descent into evil, however, begins with his pact with the sorcerer and is confirmed in his actions, which become increasingly selfish and despotic.

As Chaka descends morally yet rises in power, he becomes given to atrocities, even killing members of his own family. He murders the most faithful of his servants and warriors; it is suggested that he participates in cannibalism and unspeakable sexual acts. His greatest violation, however, is his lust for blood: The more people he kills, the more it is necessary for him to kill again in order to feel that his life has direction. He conquers and controls more of the world than he can ever even see, yet he remains dissatisfied.

In Christian terms, Mofolo is writing about a character who sells his soul to the devil. No Christian elements, however, ever enter the story. The coming of the whites is mentioned in only one instance and their influence is totally absent in the work. Chaka is nevertheless comparable to other figures in literature who sell their souls, Christopher Marlowe's Dr. Faustus, for example. Chaka knows what he is doing when he is visited by Isanusi and enters into the agreement with him. Similarly, Isanusi knows exactly what he is doing and proceeds to tempt Chaka in his moral descent.

Mofolo records the story as history, making it read as factual biography. Elements of the supernatural, such as works carried out by Isanusi and his two agents Ndlebe and Malunga, are rendered in a matter-of-fact manner that never questions their credibility. The narrative itself is almost never interrupted with authorial intrusions. Nevertheless, the author is aware of the ignorance of Western readers (and twentieth century African readers) of the beliefs and culture of the eighteenth century Zulus. Accordingly, he weaves explanations and comments into the story.

The novel contains no preachy, moralistic attitude or outlook. It is clear to everyone that Chaka is evil long before his death. He dies, miserable not so much for his sins against human nature and whatever gods there be but because he can not find pleasure in anything except blood and death. His own family and warriors kill him in his illness. He is too weakened to fight for himself, and he succumbs to death willingly.

Carl Singleton

Bibliography:
Dathorne, O. R. *The Black Mind: A History of African Literature*. Minneapolis: University of Minnesota Press, 1974. Discusses *Chaka* as a product of tradition and African oral history. Argues that the work is more than the mere debunking of myth about the Zulu leader.
Gerard, Albert S. *Four African Literatures: Xhosa, Sotho, Zulu, Amharic*. Berkeley: University of California Press, 1971. Gerard discusses *Chaka* within the context of the religious beliefs (that is, Christianity) of the author. Biographical information about Mofolo is provided.
Ikonne, Chidi. "Thomas Mofolo's Narrator." In *Aspects of South African Literature*, edited by Christopher Heywood. London: Heinemann, 1976. Ikonne's criticism deals primarily with

narrative techniques in the novel; he finds a "double narrative" running throughout.

Kunene, Mazisi. *Emperor Shaka the Great: A Zulu Epic*. London: Heinemann, 1979. Written as a narrative in poetry, this poem details biographical elements and stands in contrast to the novel.

Wauthier, Claude. *The Literature and Thought of Modern Africa: A Survey*. Translated by Shirley Kay. New York: Praeger, 1964. Discusses the historical figure, Shaka, in the light of Mofolo's literary creation. Gives particular attention to paganism in the novel and to the character of Isanusi.

THE CHANGELING

Type of work: Drama
Authors: Thomas Middleton (1580-1627) and William Rowley (1585?-1642?)
Type of plot: Tragedy
Time of plot: Early seventeenth century
Locale: Alicante, a seaport on the east coast of Spain
First performed: 1622; first published, 1653

> *Principal characters:*
> VERMANDERO, governor of the castle of Alicante
> BEATRICE, his daughter
> ALSEMERO, her suitor and later her husband
> ALONZO DE PIRACQUO, another suitor of Beatrice
> ALIBIUS, a jealous doctor
> ISABELLA, his wife
> ANTONIO, the changeling
> DIAPHANTA, Beatrice's waiting-woman
> DE FLORES, Vermandero's servant
> JASPERINO, Alsemero's friend

The Story:

Alsemero, after glimpsing Beatrice at church, expressed to himself the hope that he could gain her hand in marriage. Outside, in the street, his musings were interrupted by Jasperino. To the latter's surprise, he learned that Alsemero, whose enthusiasm for travel was common knowledge, had become reluctant to undertake a projected voyage to Malta. While they were talking, Beatrice entered, accompanied by Diaphanta, and the four talked in friendly fashion. The mood of Beatrice changed, however, when she was angered by the arrival of De Flores, her father's servant, to whom she had a seemingly unconquerable aversion. She made no effort to hide her feelings from De Flores, who, nevertheless, remained unabashed and continued to follow her about.

Vermandero, Beatrice's father, passed by and met Alsemero for the first time. He was pleased to learn that the young man was the son of an old friend of his, a battle companion now dead. To Alsemero he gave an invitation to visit the castle of which Vermandero was governor. The invitation was eagerly accepted, but Alsemero's pleasure turned to dismay when he learned of Vermandero's determination to wed Beatrice to Alonzo De Piracquo within the next seven days. As they started for the castle, Beatrice dropped one of her gloves. In disdain she threw its mate after it rather than accept the glove from the hands of De Flores, who had picked it up and offered it to her.

Meanwhile, in another part of Alicante, Alibius was giving instructions to his servant Lollio. Alibius, a doctor, made Lollio promise to keep an eye on Isabella, the former's much younger wife. The doctor's establishment, which included facilities for the care of madmen and fools, soon increased with the arrival of a new patient. Antonio, enamored of Isabella, had chosen to pose as an idiot so that he could be near her. Lollio interrogated Antonio in an effort to establish his degree of stupidity, but Antonio cleverly parried the servant's questions.

With the help of Jasperino and Diaphanta, Beatrice and Alsemero communicated with each other and arranged a secret meeting. De Flores, coming to announce the arrival of Beatrice's suitor, Alonzo, was cruelly railed at but he equally prolonged the interview in order to be in

Beatrice's presence. His doggedness aroused in her a vague presentiment of evil, which was quickly dismissed when she rallied herself to face Alonzo. He and her father reluctantly agreed to her request for a three-day postponement of the wedding. Her behavior prompted Alonzo's brother, Tomaso, to utter the warning that Beatrice was not in love, but Alonzo shrugged off any intimation that the marriage was not wise.

Beatrice and Alsemero confessed their mutual affection. Beatrice, however, refused her lover's offer to engage Alonzo in a duel because she feared that his death or punishment would be the result of such an affair. Instead, she suggested another scheme to get rid of Alonzo, with De Flores serving as a possible tool through whom to work her will. Seeking him out, she gained his consent to help her, but she did not know the price which he expected her to pay. Fate took a hand in their plotting when Alonzo presently asked De Flores to guide him about the castle's obscure maze of passageways. De Flores cozened Alonzo into disarming himself, then killed him with a rapier previously hidden behind a door. Before disposing of the body, he cut off a finger adorned by a diamond ring.

Back at the house of Alibius, Isabella complained to Lollio about the strict watch under which she was kept. Out of curiosity, she prevailed upon him to let her visit the quarters reserved for the madmen and fools. There she met Franciscus who, like Antonio, was one of the gentlemen from the castle of Alicante with amorous designs upon Isabella. He managed to convey his feelings to her, and she reflected that, after all, a lady need not leave her home if she has any desire to stray from virtue. Lollio, infected by all this romantic intriguing, forgot his master's commission and made advances to Isabella; but she repulsed him.

De Flores, to prove that he had done her bidding, brought the finger of the murdered Alonzo to Beatrice. Refusing her offer of gold, he threatened her with exposure for her part in the crime if she refused to reward him with her love. Beatrice, twist and turn as she might, could find no avenue of escape from his relentless blackmail, and eventually she yielded to his desires.

Vermandero misunderstood the sudden disappearance of Alonzo; angered, he allowed his daughter to make a hasty marriage to Alsemero. Nevertheless, he began to wonder about the prolonged absence from the castle of Antonio and Franciscus; they were sent for, to be questioned about Alonzo. A few hours before her wedding night, Beatrice began to fear Alsemero's discovery that she was no longer a maid. Pleading timidity, she persuaded Diaphanta, who was still a virgin, to act as her substitute in Alsemero's bed during the early part of the night. Diaphanta was far from displeased to have been asked for this favor, even without the gold with which her mistress promised to reward her.

Elaborate nuptial celebrations had been planned for Beatrice and Alsemero. As part of the entertainment, Vermandero had requested Alibius to rehearse some of his madmen and fools so that they might perform a weird dance for the amusement of the assembly. Alibius decided that he would let Isabella accompany him to the castle for that event. Meanwhile that lady, attracted to Antonio, disguised herself briefly as a madwoman in order to converse with him. Lollio played a prank on Antonio and Franciscus by pretending, to each, that Isabella would reward him for getting rid of the other.

Diaphanta, pretending to be Beatrice, amorously overstayed her time with Alsemero, so that her impatient mistress became first dismayed, then suspicious, and at last vengeful. At the suggestion of De Flores, she agreed to Diaphanta's death. A fire was set, to create confusion and arouse Diaphanta from the marriage bed. The unfortunate young woman was followed to her own bedroom and slain by De Flores.

By that time Franciscus and Antonio had been apprehended and charged with the murder of Alonzo, since it was learned that they had entered Alibius' house in disguise on the day of

Alonzo's disappearance. Beatrice and De Flores finally brought about their own undoing, however, after Alsemero's discovery of their secret meetings made him suspicious. Under his questioning, Beatrice broke down and confessed. Although she pleaded her love for him as an excuse for the crime, Alsemero, shocked, took her and De Flores into custody. The pair were unwilling to face trial; De Flores gave Beatrice a fatal wound and then stabbed himself, unrepentant to the last.

Critical Evaluation:

Written in 1622, toward the end of an extraordinarily rich period in English drama that produced a substantial body of the finest plays written in English, *The Changeling* is widely considered to be one of the best non-Shakespearean tragedies. The opening and closing scenes and the subplot are generally attributed to William Rowley, and the remainder of the play to Thomas Middleton. Of the two authors, Middleton was the more prolific. He wrote at least twenty-five plays alone or in collaboration with other playwrights, such as Thomas Dekker, John Webster, and Francis Beaumont. Middleton's output was varied, including comedies, tragicomedies, and masques. He is best known for his political satire, *A Game at Chess* (1624), and for his two great tragedies, *The Changeling* and *Women Beware Women* (c. 1621-1627). Rowley was well known in his own time as an actor of comedy roles. He also wrote at least eleven plays in collaboration with others and four plays unaided.

The word "changeling" has three definitions relevant to the play: a changeable person, a person surreptitiously exchanged for another, and an idiot. Various characters are associated with the different senses of the word, and the last few speeches of the closing scene point to many of these. Although the subplot of the play, with its fools and madmen, is tiresome and in poor taste according to twentieth century sensibilities, it provides some commentary on the main theme of the play. There is a shared imagery of change. Antonio and Francisco undergo transformation in their pursuit of love, as do Alsemero, Beatrice, and De Flores. Isabella, who remains true to her marriage vows in spite of temptation, provides a comparison to Beatrice's increasing immorality. The madness and folly observed in Alibius' institution form a grotesque reflection of the madness and folly of the outside world. In the play's development of the characters of Beatrice and De Flores, as well as in some fine passages of dramatic rhetoric, the play achieves great stature.

In the course of the play, Beatrice is transformed from an apparently pious, dutiful young woman into a damned soul, stabbed to death by her murderous lover. This process occurs with terrifying ease and speed. Her downfall begins with her passion for Alsemero and her desire to marry him rather than Alonzo. On the face of it this seems a reasonable wish. Beatrice does not reason, however; she does not consider or question the means she employs to achieve her ends. She is utterly self-centered and this blinds her to the nature of the events she sets into motion. There is a willful irrationality about her initial loathing for De Flores and a selfish amorality in her determination to persuade her father to dismiss him. This is a foreshadowing of her later schemes. She is too intent on the gratification of her own desires to recognize that in instigating the murder of her unwanted fiancé, she participates in evil. When she realizes that the price she has to pay De Flores for his part in the crime is sexual surrender to him, she is horrified at the violation of her honor.

> Why, 'tis impossible thou canst be so wicked,
> Or shelter such a cunning cruelty,
> To make his death the murderer of my honor!

This "honor," the perception by others that her virtue is unsullied, remains, to her, a compelling value. The protection of this sham leads to the corruption and murder of Diaphanta. Beatrice's growing reliance, affinity, and then passion for De Flores are indicative of how she becomes accustomed to evil.

De Flores is a malcontent, resentful of his social status because he was born to a higher rank. His ugliness is an additional misfortune. Like Beatrice, he is motivated by passion, but unlike her, he acts in full consciousness of his own evil. He too puts his own desires above all other considerations. The moral values of the play clearly cast him as villainous. Not only does he commit murders but also he is clearly implicated in, although not wholly responsible for, Beatrice's downfall. In De Flores, as in Beatrice, there is a psychological complexity that allows the possibility for some measure of sympathy for him. He kills three times, but the first time is to win his beloved, the second to protect her honor, and the third because she has repudiated him. His loyalty to Beatrice makes him courageous and bold, as exemplified by his actions on the night of the fire. Having killed Beatrice, he kills himself, still glorying that she has been his:

> I thank life for nothing
> But that pleasure; it was so sweet to me
> That I have drunk up all;

De Flores speaks some of the finest lines in the play, for example in Act III, scene iv, when he claims his reward from Beatrice. His speeches display a stark and unflinching clarity of vision expressed plainly and forcefully.

The typical themes of English Renaissance tragedies are intrigue, murder, revenge, and sexual desire. The characters of these plays are often types, sometimes caricatures. The Machiavellian villain, one who is consciously evil and who delights in it, is an example, and so is the irresponsible aristocratic girl. *The Changeling* is clearly a tragedy of its age. Beatrice and De Flores are developed beyond the standard heroine and villain types, with well-observed, subtle, and believable characteristics. The tragedy of these two characters, both driven by obsessive wills, is a tragedy of universal relevance. The dissatisfaction and the desire that drive De Flores to his destruction, and the blind egocentricity of Beatrice, are as familiar to contemporary audiences as they were to the original seventeenth century audience.

"Critical Evaluation" by Susan Henthorne

Bibliography:
Bradbrook, M. C. *Themes and Conventions of Elizabethan Tragedy.* 2d ed. New York: Cambridge University Press, 1980. Analysis of the drama of the period, including its staging and conventions of plot and character. Chapter on Middleton finds him untypical in his simplicity of language, but subtlety of implication.
Brittin, Norman A. *Thomas Middleton.* New York: Twayne, 1972. A good basic guide to Middleton's drama. It claims that he is the most important writer of the Jacobean comedy of manners. Sensitive analysis of *The Changeling* and a useful summary of critical assessments.
Farr, Dorothy M. *Thomas Middleton and the Drama of Realism.* New York: Harper & Row, 1973. Traces Middleton's development, initiated with the aid of Rowley in *The Changeling*, toward a new form of tragic drama, which, Farr claims, is close to the modern theater.
Jump, J. D. "Middleton's Tragic Comedies." In *The Pelican Guide to English Literature.* Vol 2.

New York: Penguin Books, 1964. Focus is the two tragedies, *Women Beware Women* and *The Changeling*, with emphasis on the quality of the verse and the realism of the drama.

Mulryne, J. R. *Writers and Their Work: Thomas Middleton*. New York: Longman, 1979. Surveys the body of Middleton's work, including *The Changeling*. Useful bibliography.

THE CHANGING LIGHT AT SANDOVER

Type of work: Poetry
Author: James Merrill (1926-1995)
First published: 1982

The Changing Light at Sandover is an assemblage of three previously published books of poetry by James Merrill to which is added a new poem, "Coda: The Higher Keys." The trilogy, as the first three books are commonly known, begins with the 1976 "The Book of Ephraim," which was originally the second half of Merrill's Pulitzer Prize-winning book of poems, *Divine Comedies.* The next section of *The Changing Light at Sandover* is "Mirabell: A Book of Numbers." For inclusion in *The Changing Light at Sandover,* Merrill retitled his National Book Award-winning *Mirabell: Books of Number.* In 1980, *Scripts for the Pageant,* the third part of the trilogy, was separately published. In 1982, these three books plus "Coda: The Higher Keys" were collected for the one-volume book of poetry, *The Changing Light at Sandover.* Of the four parts, only "The Book of Ephraim" stands alone as a complete book of verse; the others are interconnected by characters and themes.

The Changing Light at Sandover, regularly labeled as an epic poem, covers such diverse topics as the writing of poetry, the threat of nuclear war, the destruction of the environment, death and reincarnation, and the role of the arts in a technological world. Merrill's accomplishment in this book has led him to be compared with Dante Alighieri, William Butler Yeats, and Marcel Proust. As a poet, Merrill also represents the New Formalism movement in American poetry as he questions the balance between language and poetic form, as well as the affects of both on readers of poetry.

The trilogy begins with "The Book of Ephraim," which comes to represent the first step in the process of discovering the answers to essential questions about the relationships between reason and imagination, truth and fiction, power and impotence, and time and wisdom. The story told in this book begins in 1955 with Merrill, who is labeled "JM" in the poems, and his friend, David Jackson, "DJ," sitting down on a hot summer evening in Merrill's Stonington, Connecticut, home to ask questions of a homemade Ouija board. They use a blue and white willowware china teacup to spell out the answers received from the spirit world. As they start, the answers are disjointed as many spirits pass by; then, Ephraim, the spirit of a Greek Jew, born in 8 C.E. who died in 39 C.E., becomes their clearest and principal conductor through the world they have conjured up. With Ephraim, JM and DJ are taught that the people now on earth house souls, called patrons in his world, who are promoted in a celestial hierarchy based on the deeds of their earthly hosts. As the conversations progress (Ephraim's speeches shown in capital letters and unpunctutated lines) JM and DJ are able to speak with poets Wallace Stevens and W. H. Auden, friends and relatives of both men, and people from Ephraim's world. Ephraim also describes the organization of the universe.

"The Book of Ephraim" comprises twenty-six cantos, one for each letter of the alphabet, from "Admittedly" to "Zero Hour." Merrill employs iambic pentameter, both rhymed and unrhymed, and he uses the meter to write cantos in couplets, quatrains, strophes, and sonnets. The language of the poem is clear and vivid. Nearly every line alludes to other literary works, opera, art, travel, or friends of JM. For example, *The Arabian Nights' Entertainments* (first transcribed, fifteenth century), opera singer Kirsten Flagstad, composer Richard Wagner, and writers Thomas Mann, Virginia Woolf, and Isak Dinesen have their places next to Merrill's friends Hans Lodeizen, Maria Mitsotaki, and Maya Deren, among others. "The Book of Ephraim" is also marked by the poet's use of irony, wit, bluntness, and a plot structure of searching and accepting what is found.

"The Book of Ephraim" provides the exposition of the tone, ideas, and major figures that create the limited unity of *The Changing Light at Sandover*. In the "A" poem, the poet describes his mission to write a poem that will reveal the unities of past and present. The "B" poem yields setting and background, and the "C" poem introduces Ephraim. In the "D" poem, twelve real and imaginary people are listed as the *dramatis personae* of "The Book of Ephraim." In the "W" poem, JM converses with a fictional nephew, Wendell Pincus, about the poet's ability to transcend his own self when writing to create a literary work that is universally significant. Finally, the "Z" poem describes a break-in at the Stonington house. Although nothing was taken, the family's possessions were disturbed. The symbolism of intrusion of the unknown into their lives is captured here:

> The threat remains, though of there still being
> A presence in our midst, unknown, unseen,
> Unscrupulous to take what he can get.

Supplementing the visits from Ephraim are two other plots in this first part of the trilogy: Merrill's incorporation of characters and partial story lines from his lost novel set in New Mexico and the poet's indication of how this book was written. Letter sections J, N, S, T, and X recount parts of Merrill's novel's plot as he rewrites how Leo Cade, a Vietnam veteran suspected of murdering a Vietnamese thought by his company to be a spy, falls under the influence of Eros, a sensual spirit, and how Joanna, an older woman with unclear motives, aims to seduce Matt Prentiss, a character reminiscent of DJ's father. Another character, Sergei Markovich, buys land from Rosamund Smith and is thought to parallel Merrill himself.

The third plot, on the writing of the poem, is described as the main activity of 1974. "The Book of Ephraim" spans about twenty years. The writing was completed mainly at Stonington, with trips to Greece and Italy. The Ouija board mentioned in the verse accompanied Merrill on these trips. The quests to define the differences between poetry and fiction and between the real and the imaginary give "The Book of Ephraim" its literary strengths as well as its complexity, as the fictional is designed to seem "real" by the confident, reliable voice of the poet.

"Mirabell: A Book of Numbers," the second book of the trilogy, is set in mid-1975 as Merrill and Jackson are residing in their second home, in Greece. Again, the Ouija board is with them. Their readings take them around the board's numbered sections, from 0 to 9. The poems in this part are further subdivided into ten separately numbered units, so that "Mirabell" contains ninety individual poems. The predominant theme of this section of the book is death of those much loved and those loved little. The name "Mirabell" is given to the primary spirit-seeker by JM; Mirabell describes himself to JM and DJ as a peacock.

In "Mirabell," other spirits, which are again combinations of the real and the imaginary, play roles in the poet's journey to write a poem merging reason and imagination. In this section, the spirits of JM and DJ's guides, Maria Mitsotaki and W. H. Auden, join the pair at the level of equals to explore cosmological and philosophical ideas. The spirits begin to urge JM to write a poem about science. Much of the section is devoted to an examination of how ordinary people see and come to understand scientific concepts. It is here that the "science" themes of *The Changing Light at Sandover* are addressed as the pair learn how "God B(iology)," described as "the accumulated intelligence of cells," operates through the "R/LAB" to conduct research into life, death, and reincarnation. Nature is presented as the powerful and constant force in the universe. Illustrations of the themes in this section include discussion of the biblical Fall of Man, the destruction of the lost civilization of Atlantis, and the retelling of the Faust legend. "The Book of Ephraim" weaves humor and irony into a loosely constructed plot; "Mirabell," in contrast, contains much more transcription (again all in capital letters and unpunctuated) with little interpretation to bring together ideas about science and pseudoscience and the role of the imaginary in the real.

"Mirabell" may be read as a representation of the raw materials from which poetry is made and as an assemblage of a variety of ideas, experiences, memories, and imaginings. In the course of this section, JM and DJ learn of the violent and destructive practices of civilization. As they try to acquire the keys to stopping these practices, the spirit guides are often silenced or punished by their bureaucracy, leaving large parts of the section unfocused and occasionally hard to follow. At the close of "Mirabell," the spirits awaiting rebirth are shown to be limited by their stage in the reincarnation process, so JM and DJ are made ready to meet the highest levels of the spirit world.

Scripts for the Pageant takes JM and DJ around the final section of the Ouija board, the "Yes," "&," and "No." "Yes" is a series of seven lyric poems, ten "lessons," and a commentary on "God B's" song spoken by the spirit of Auden. "&" features four titled lyric poems, five lessons, and five additional lyrics. "No" begins with ten lessons and ends with six lyric poems. In this last third of the trilogy, JM and DJ communicate directly with the archangels; God, Jesus, Buddha, and Muhammad; the Nine Muses of classical Greece; Akhenaton, Homer, Montezuma, Nefertiti, and Plato, collectively known as "The Five"; and a variety of poets and musicians. Ephraim and Mirabell are joined by a rather clumsy, comical spirit, Unice. Auden, Mitsotaki, George Cotzias (a biologist friend of Merrill), and Robert Morse (a musician friend and house guest at Stonington), whose recent deaths are recorded in *Scripts for the Pageant* along with those of DJ's parents, all have speaking parts.

In *Scripts for the Pageant*, the discussion of the poet's work continues and escalates as the mediums, JM and DJ, consider various elemental forces and how the self-destructive tendencies of humans might be stopped. By now, the writing of the poem of science has become known as "V" work, which refers to the number 5 (the halfway point in "Mirabell"), the Group of Five, and *vie*, which is the French word for "life." "Mirabell" was based on opposition and the tension opposites create; *Scripts for the Pageant*, is focused on the attraction of opposites to stress how order can be brought from chaos.

As the part titles of *Scripts for the Pageant* underscore, there is no precise answer to the question of halting self-destruction: Individuals are shown as being only limitedly able to control their fates. In *Scripts for the Pageant*, the apparent limitations on JM's abilities to draw information out of the Ouija board become blurred as the lines between the known and the unknown are drawn. Morse's death and impending reincarnation are the narrative events that hold this third part of *The Changing Light at Sandover* together. The title is derived from the pageant of luminaries who cross the Ouija board stage and give long speeches on the nature of the universe. Among its outstanding literary features are the use of the *canzone* in the poem "Samos," which is found in the "No" section of *Scripts for the Pageant*. Yeats' *A Vision* (1925), Dante's *The Divine Comedy* (c. 1320), John Milton's *Paradise Lost* (1667), and the poetry of W. H. Auden all provide models for the writing of *Scripts for the Pageant*. The magical realism of *The Changing Light at Sandover* is at its height as JM and DJ talk directly, through the board, to God. The insights they gain in this section allow them to set aside the limitations of the ordinary human, held back by fear, insecurity, and ignorance; this transcendence is symbolized in the breaking of the mirror, a recurring image in the poetry, in the poem "Finale."

"Coda: The Higher Keys" was written especially for the one-volume edition of *The Chang-ing Light at Sandover*. This section contains thirteen lyrics. Like "The Book of Ephraim," "Coda: The Higher Keys" is narrative in its structure as JM learns, on the board, of Robert Morse's reincarnation process. This section, set in Stonington in 1978, tells how DJ has painted a mural designed to fix in visual form the essence of the Ouija board personalities and what the two have learned in their manifold sessions. The body of the "Coda" has five poems titled "Ceremony" and they are numbered 1 through 5. These describe Morse's journey to a new life and the growing preparations for JM's reading of the poem the trilogy has led him to write. "The Ballroom at Sandover" completes *The Changing Light at Sandover* as Merrill imagines a return to his boyhood home, set here as "in the old ballroom of the Broken Home," so named because of the divorce of Merrill's parents when he was eleven. It is here that JM unveils the poem to the assembled and anxious spirits. When the poem is started, the spirits take their leaves of JM and DJ. The end of the poem begins with the first word of "The Book of Ephraim," "Admit-tedly," and it becomes clear to the reader that *The Changing Light at Sandover* is constructed as its own complete world, a mirror of itself.

The Changing Light at Sandover is a complicated philosophical and personal poem that requires study for full appreciation of its intricacies. It is unique among American poetry, and among American poets Merrill has few rivals. His poetic compositions are consistently ad-mired for their style, scope, and provocativeness. In *The Changing Light at Sandover*, Merrill asks readers to consider what they really know about life and death, human nature and self-destruction, the place of poetry in a technological and scientific world, and the differences between what is real and what is imaginary.

Beverly E. Schneller

Bibliography:
Labrie, Ross. *James Merrill*. Boston: Twayne, 1982. The first full-length reference book on Merrill. As part of Twayne's U.S. Authors Series, it provides an overview of Merrill's life and analysis of the poetry published before 1982.
Lehman, David, and Charles Berger, eds. *James Merrill: Essays in Criticism*. Ithaca, N.Y.: Cornell University Press, 1982. This collection of eleven essays ranges from analysis of unifying elements in Merrill's poetry to a memoir of the Ouija experiences by David Jackson. Two-thirds of the essays are on *The Changing Light at Sandover*.
McClatchy, J. D. "The Art of Poetry XXXI." *The Paris Review* 24 (Summer, 1982): 184-219. Poets Merrill and J. D. McClatchy discuss the genesis of the Ouija board's messages and their transformation into Merrill's verse. This frequently cited interview also features a photograph of the homemade board and sample transcripts from 1976.
Shetley, Vernon. *After the Death of Poetry: Poetry and Audience in Contemporary America*. Durham, N.C.: Duke University Press, 1993. Chapter 3, "Public and Private in James Mer-rill's Work," includes a useful discussion of *The Changing Light at Sandover*, especially regarding the interpretation of "The Book of Ephraim."

CHARLES DEMAILLY

Type of work: Novel
Authors: Edmond de Goncourt (1822-1896) and Jules de Goncourt (1830-1870)
Type of plot: Naturalism
Time of plot: Mid-nineteenth century
Locale: Paris
First published: Les Hommes de lettres, 1860 (*A Man of Letters,* 1862)

Principal characters:
 CHARLES DEMAILLY, a young author
 MARTHE MANCE, an actress whom he marries
 NACHETTE, a journalist and critic
 COUTURAT, another journalist
 REMONVILLE, a writer and Charles's friend
 CHAVANNES, Charles's boyhood friend

The Story:

A new kind of literary world came into being in Paris during the mid-nineteenth century, the world of the journals and little newspapers that thrived on gossip and superficial aesthetic criticism. By creating and catering to the shifting fads of the fashionable world through concentrating on personality, modishness, and sensationalism, they debased the public's taste.

Two young men among the writers for one of these journals, *Scandal,* were thoroughly immersed in their world. Nachette, a belligerent, clever man who had fled his father's bad name in his home province, enjoyed the power that he believed the journals possessed to create or ruin a reputation. Couturat, hiding behind a mask of innocence and gaiety, was a thorough opportunist. Also among the group was Charles Demailly, who disliked the dilettantes and their trivial gossiping but seemed unable to do anything more than observe them ironically as he accompanied them to cafés, salons, and balls.

After many illnesses as a child, Charles had grown up a nervous and acutely sensitive young man. The heightened perceptivity of all his senses extended to an unusual awareness of emotional nuances in those around him, but at the same time it prevented him from finding satisfaction in real life. His search for perfection always met his uncanny ability to perceive imperfection: Pleasure for him paled at the slightest false note. Even in writing, his real refuge, his hypersensitivity was a handicap, for his meticulously keen observation and attention to detail almost precluded true depth and greatness.

A letter from his old friend Chavannes urged Charles to visit him in the country and to settle down to serious writing. Although Charles declined the invitation, he did go into seclusion to work on his novel. At last his book, *La Bourgeoisie,* was finished, but his late friends of *Scandal,* who were irritated because he had deserted them and jealous of his potential success, decided to do their best to prevent that success. Scarcely bothering to read the book, they ignored its attempt to convey psychological reality. Instead, they used the title as an excuse to generalize wittily on it as an inept social document. Full of anguish at these reviews, Charles wandered about the streets until he met Boisroger, a poet who cared nothing for the superficialities of society. He recognized the novel's worth and introduced Charles to a circle of men who were true artists in various fields. Charles was happy among these vivid, intelligent people, and he greatly admired their individualism and their informed opinions on art and literature.

Charles's uncle died, leaving him feeling bereft. A discussion of the nature of love led some of his friends to assert that the artist cannot be a true husband or lover; other men seek in love what the artist finds only in creation. These two factors may have predisposed Charles to fall in love himself as a protest against the loneliness that his friends felt was unavoidable. At the theater, he saw a charming young ingénue, Marthe, and felt strongly attracted to her. At last he met her at a masquerade ball; three months later, they were married.

For a time, they created a blissful world in which only they existed. Marthe delighted Charles with her affection and endearing, childlike ways. Charles worked secretly on a play whose heroine captured Marthe's coquettish innocence. Finding his hidden work, Marthe was enraptured by it because the role was so well suited to her. Charles was delighted by her appreciation. Failing to look beneath the surface, he assumed, in his idealization of her, that she was actually the character he had created.

After Marthe read an article by the now fashionable Nachette, which criticized Charles's work, she suggested that he find a collaborator to help him with the play. Charles realized that she cared only for his reputation and its effect on her own and not for his work. With that, he began to see her as she really was: an insensitive chatterbox, full of false sentiment and other people's ideas. Marthe, too, had tired of her sweet role. Now she tried another, the woman who despises her husband for the love he bears her and who delights in violent changes of mood and in being wholly self-absorbed.

When his distress at his disillusionment in his wife's character made Charles ill, the couple went to a provincial spa so that he might recover. Charles rejoiced in the placid beauty of the country, but Marthe, bored, posed as the martyred wife. Refusing to leave, she showed her pique in subtle ways. Her banality and insincerity further tortured Charles, but the growing realization that she no longer loved him was even worse, for it threatened to destroy what remained of the image he had created.

At a country fête, they met the group from *Scandal*, and the visitors returned to dine with them. Nachette stayed on for a week. Shortly afterward, a mock play in which a sweet ingénue was held prisoner by a neurasthenic appeared in *Scandal*. Charles was hurt, not by the silly play but by knowing that Marthe had deliberately created the impression on which it was based.

After Charles grew well enough to return to Paris, events there combined to break him down again. He discovered that his wife had borrowed money, ostensibly because he was a madman who never gave her any. In retaliation for his indignation at her falsehoods, she then announced that she was leaving her role in his play, which had gone into rehearsal. At length, trying to create a scene, she told him that she loved Nachette. When he refused to give her the opportunity for histrionics, she left.

She returned the next day, however, full of remorse, and almost succeeded in captivating Charles again by her winsome affection. For two weeks, she behaved as if they were again on their honeymoon. When she asked to have her role back, however, Charles refused, saying truthfully that it was too late for any change before the opening night. At that, she broke into a furious tirade, saying that she had never loved him and that she had spread stories to dishonor him. Overcome with anguish, Charles wept. When she laughed at his tears, he ran into the street. Eventually, he regained enough self-control to return and to order her out of the house.

When Marthe left, she took the letters Charles had once written to her while gaily parodying some of his friends in the inner circle of artists into which he had been welcomed. Although innocuous, when lifted out of context and changed slightly the letters looked like malicious attempts to scoff at his friends. Marthe, unable to bear the thought that her husband's play might be a success without her, believed that if these influential gentlemen were offended, they might somehow contribute to its ruin.

Spitefully, she gave the letters to Nachette, who was engaged in a silent struggle with Couturat for control of *Scandal*. Nachette recognized the sensational value but told Marthe to leave him; she could do him no good, and her charms were wearing thin. Couturat, the opportunist, won the paper, however, and saw in the letters, set up on the front page, an excuse to fire Nachette and establish himself as a good fellow. He sent one copy of the front page to Charles and burned the rest.

Charles's friend Chavannes brought the news that Charles had suffered an attack when he saw the journal. At length, Charles himself, wraithlike but calm, appeared to hear Couturat's supposedly profound apologies. To Charles, the knowledge that Marthe had been behind the attempt to ruin him was intolerable. Loathing Paris, the theater, and life itself, he refused to allow the performance of his play and withdrew to another part of the city. There, only his old nurse cared for him as he sank into apathy and madness. Feeling his reason slipping away, he tried to write but could only scrawl his own name over and over.

Charles was taken to an asylum where treatment gradually restored him to health. When he was at last well enough to go outside, he rejoiced at the prospects of a new life. He felt able to attend a small theater, but when he saw his wife on the stage—for Marthe had descended to playing in second-rate theaters—madness overcame him once more. After months of violence, he became calm again, but with the calmness of an idiot or a beast. So he lived, little more than a heap of flesh, to the end of his days.

Critical Evaluation:

Charles Demailly, one of the early novels of Edmond and Jules de Goncourt, describes the world of journalism in which they were enmeshed as well as the world of belles lettres to which they aspired. Although the theme of venal journalism was common in nineteenth century fiction, the thinly veiled portraits of their acquaintances were regarded as exposé. In addition to describing the offices of the journal *Scandal* in detail, the Goncourts present portraits of the journal's directors. They show how the lives of struggle, the wounded egos, and the disappointments create the acrimonious and insensitive journalistic character. At the journalists' café, the conversation is inelegant and witless. At the writers' café, Charles Demailly meets fictionalized versions of Théophile Gautier and Gustave Flaubert, and the conversation reflects an authenticity and shows up the shoddiness of the first group.

The journalists of *Scandal* epitomize the duplicity and emptiness of the world of Parisian letters. Couturat doggedly pursues his ambitions while laughing and punning; Malgras preaches duty and honor while obviously repressing evil instincts; and Bourniche is merely an imitator with no inner self. The journal pretends to be a responsible publication even while its journalists invent stories. The Goncourts believed that the low estate of journalism resulted from writing having been transformed into a trade. The world of journalism is merely a microcosm of a society given over to false values while maintaining an illusion of virtue. Charles, a true writer, dedicates himself to art as an antidote to the hypocrisy of the age. He is at ease among the literati with their personal integrity and, as the pages of his journal reveal, agrees with their elitist view of art.

The novel's second story line explores the interactions of artist and woman. The love affair between Charles and Marthe was based on the experience of a friend of the Goncourts, who told them of his wife's physical abuse and defamatory scheming. The brothers regarded women as "hysterical animals" lurking behind a façade of beauty and as creatures of sensation who were morally bankrupt. They made an exception of the women of the salons, whose attitudes reflected those of their male contemporaries. In their own lives, the brothers preferred women without any education, titles, or power. Although they recognized female beauty as inspiration, they theorized that celibacy is indispensable for the true artist. Adopting the deterministic point of view of naturalist novels, the Goncourts blamed the hypocritical upbringing of bourgeois women for their destructiveness.

Marthe meets Charles at a masked ball and appears in costume at various points throughout the novel, which emphasizes her ability to create a false identity. The reality behind the illusion is soon revealed. Although the honeymoon of Charles and Marthe seems idyllic, the Goncourts suggest that, however delightful, it is merely a lie. Marthe utterly lacks appreciation for art. Her ideal literature is formulaic and sensational. She encourages Charles to work with a hack collaborator to insure greater success and profit. Although Marthe's beauty initially inspires Charles's art, her scheming destroys him.

Charles's mental instability begins when he retreats from the exterior world to an inner one of fragmentary visions. In a complete reversal, the exterior world becomes illusion and the interior one of nightmarish reality. The Goncourts treat Charles's illness with clinical precision. Charles's doctor explains his illness as the weakness of a contemporary man with an over-wrought nervous system. Motifs of the collapse of a decadent society pervade the end of the novel, and the beauty of nature is contrasted ironically with the horror of humanity.

The characters in *Charles Demailly* are representatives of traits the Goncourts wish to present rather than fully developed individuals. There is no explanation of Marthe's vicious-ness, or her reversal from love to villainy. Although the narrator suggests that she continues her role of a villainess from a play in which she stars, it is not developed within the story. Charles is never physically described and has no past, no family, no close friends; he exists in a vacuum. The dialogue, however, is successfully rendered with a combination of low and high discourse. The combinations of letters, diary entries, and plays taken from the newspaper contribute to the realistic detail assembled in the novel.

In the brothers' collaborations on their novels, Jules usually worked on the characters and dialogue while Edmond developed the architecture of the book. Like many of their works, *Charles Demailly* unfolds slowly in a succession of internally fragmented chapters, and the action culminates suddenly and explosively. The text oscillates between reality and fantasy. The fact that both brothers were artists is reflected in the attention they give to visual effect. As part of their "painterly writing," they frequently invented new words and combined unusual descriptive terms. In its emphasis on nuanced tone and gradations of light and color detached from a subject, their syntactical technique is comparable to that of the Impressionist painters. In general, the brothers favored abstraction as a means of creating visual effect.

Charles Demailly was greeted with little enthusiasm when it first appeared. Critics consid-ered the integration of styles unsuccessful, the relation of events disordered and confused, and the attack on journalistic circles of which they were members personally offending. Yet in its thematic coherence and stylistic invention the semi-fictional depiction of the Goncourts' literary world stands out from other novels of the time. *Charles Demailly* realistically portrays the process of establishing a career as a writer and it retains historical interest as a portrait of the literary scene of the period.

"Critical Evaluation" by Pamela Pavliscak

Bibliography:

Auerbach, Erich. *Mimesis: The Representation of Reality in Western Literature*. Translated by Willard Trask. New York: Doubleday, 1953. Auerbach considers the Goncourts, whom he classifies as second-tier writers, in the context of the naturalist school. Compares their novels with those of Émile Zola.

Baldick, Robert. *The Goncourts*. London: Bowes, 1960. Excellent survey that concentrates on biographical background to the novels. Analyzes *Charles Demailly* as a personal manifesto of the brothers' celibacy and misogyny.

Billy, Andre. *The Goncourt Brothers*. Translated by Margaret Shaw. New York: Horizon Press, 1960. The standard biography of the Goncourts. Discusses biographical events that are reflected in the novels and provides examples of contemporary reception.

Grant, Richard B. *The Goncourt Brothers*. New York: Twayne, 1972. A chronological survey that integrates the authors' biographies with detailed stylistic and thematic analysis of their novels. Includes a detailed analysis of *Charles Demailly* and elaborates on the Goncourts' critique of the world of journalism.

Nelson, Brian, ed. *Naturalism in the European Novel: New Critical Perspectives*. New York: Berg, 1992. A collection of essays by prominent scholars on the naturalist schools in England, France, Germany, and Spain. Includes several important discussions of the Goncourts' role in the development of social documentary as a literary genre.

CHARMS

Type of work: Poetry
Author: Paul Valéry (1871-1945)
First published: Charmes, 1922 (English translation, 1971)

Paul Valéry came rapidly to enduring prominence in French literature on the strength of his earliest work. His abstract poetry was widely noted for its unusually sensate quality, and he is arguably the most important figure in a transitional period of French poetry, forming a bridge from the prior Symbolist school to the subsequent Surrealist movement. Valéry was notably prolific not only as a poet but also as a philosopher and essayist who earned a firm reputation for dealing with a wide range of subject matter. Politics, science, the arts, and language were among the numerous concerns of his voluminous life's work. His greatest reputation, however, remains for his poetry, and he has been deemed by some critics to have been the greatest French poet of the twentieth century. *Charms* comprises poems written from 1917 through 1921, a period which proved to be a significant one in Valéry's artistic growth, and the volume is generally regarded as a seminal work.

The year *Charms* was published coincides with the death of Édouard Lebey, then director of the French press association and Valéry's employer since 1900. Having worked as Lebey's private secretary for more than twenty years, the poet's sudden state of unemployment caused him a brief period of serious concern as to how he would continue to earn a living. Trusting the encouragement and advice of friends as well as Gaston Gallimard, his publisher, Valéry seized this opportunity to begin earning his living solely from his literary work. This proved to be more easily accomplished than he had first expected, as his reputation was on the rise. *Charms* did much to enhance the poet's popularity and reputation, containing some of his best-known and most highly regarded work, highly regarded by critics and by the poet himself.

Poetic form held a high degree of importance to Valéry, and the twenty-one poems gathered in *Charms* indicate the diversity of traditional structures he explored. The book's title is the French derivation of the Latin word *carmina*, meaning song, and it includes several odes and ballads that draw from English structures in addition to French. Valéry came to poetry during World War I, finding in it a welcome distraction from the daily pressures of that time of great stress and uncertainty. Even after the war, the period during which he wrote these poems, he continued to perceive the solitary reflection afforded the poet in the act of writing to be of higher intellectual value than the mundane or tedious demands of day-to-day living. Poetry was a vehicle Valéry used to separate himself from those aspects of life. He believed that the higher level of concentration necessary to follow a given structure allowed him to retreat that much further, which may explain his claim that form is of greater importance than content. The manifestation of this concept in *Charms* is an engaging sense of intimacy between the poet and his work, a sort of private circle, into which the reader enters upon entering the poems themselves.

Valéry adamantly refuted critics who attempted to apply overall conceptual interpretations to *Charms*, insisting that the poems had been written at intervals spread too wide for this to have even been possible. One of his responses to these attempts by critics was that any particular meaning in his poetry was that which the individual reader may take. His intention was to capture his reader with a more eclectic range of interests and frameworks to house them. There are a number of sonnets, although the styles range from Spenserian to Elizabethan to Italian. There are also several ballads, but again the styles and lengths vary considerably. The first and final poems of the collection are an unusual instance of poems appearing in the same form, both being regular odes.

As such, the thematic map of the work is as multidirectional as the structures of the poems themselves. The reader will find a reworking of the Narcissus myth, along with deeply symbolic meditations on a random array of temperaments and locations. Given Valéry's attachment to form, however, the collection draws a sense of cohesion by way of a conceptual thread. However secondary an element the poet believed content to be, his subjects are undoubtedly distinguished by the varying rhythms and tones that inform them.

The opening poem, entitled, appropriately enough, "Dawn," begins as a simple ode to the breaking of day.

> . . . at the rosy
> Apparition of the sun.
> I step forth in my own mind
> Fully fledged with confidence.

Four stanzas later, the images of the awakening physical world become increasingly laden with deeper spiritual implications.

> These spiritual toils of theirs
> I break, and set out seeking
> Within my sensuous forest
> For the oracles of my song.

From here, it is difficult not to see the poem as reinventing itself into a metaphor for poetic inspiration. The poet's physical world possesses a growing sense of sensuality, embodied within a female presence. This presence bears qualities of both mother and mistress. The poet becomes the "ravisher" of the dawning "world."

> No wound however profound
> That is not to the ravisher
> A fecund wound . . .

The act of creation is couched in an atmosphere of turbulence, but the closing stanza imagines the nurturing sense of peace awaiting the poet at the other end of his creative journey.

At the end of the book is "Palm," which shares its formal structure with "Dawn." These poems do overlap in their subject matter and were in fact one single poem until the author chose to separate them for their divergent handling of their material. Again, at the core of the latter poem is the matter of mental process, yet there is immediately a very different sense of movement. Palm trees require an extremely limited variation in climate in order to live. In the poem, the palm tree becomes a metaphor for constancy and intellectual patience, unlike the inner passions of the creative process. The poem emphasizes the palm's immobility, its slight swaying in the wind signifying the image of its rooted permanence: "It simulates the wisdom/ And the slumber of a sibyl." Here is a more direct statement than may be found in "Dawn." In general, "Palm" is less given to ambiguity than "Dawn," and the notion of the steadfast pursuit of wisdom at the poem's center is rather explicit.

"The Bee" is a sonnet with which Valéry makes a clear, simple statement on the nature of sensation: "A vivid and a clear-cut pain/ Is better than a drowsy torment." The poem is a direct address to the bee. The poet invites, actually welcomes, the bee's sting as a deliverance from the numbing effects of complacency: ". . . let my senses be illumined/ By that tiniest golden alert/ For lack of which Love dies or sleeps!" To assume the poet means only romantic love would be to underestimate this work. It would not be a wholly inaccurate response, simply an incomplete one. In the word, "Love," Valéry really means to include a much more inclusive range of sensory and intellectual passions.

"The Footsteps," however, does bring out a more purely personal facet of the poet's work. The poem is baldly sentimental, dealing with romantic love in lyric simplicity that precludes ambiguous attachments. In juxtaposition to the more complex symbolism of the rest of the majority of the collection, this poem is bound to strike the reader as being deceptively simple. Considering Valéry's partiality to traditional form, however, it only seems fitting that this classically romantic lyric be included in such an eclectic collection.

Two of the most important pieces in the collection are those which later became regarded as the finest verses Valéry ever wrote; one considered so by the poet himself, the other considered so by critics.

"Fragments of Narcissus" is an extended, three-part monologue in the voice of the mythical character named in the title. Though he never fully completed this poem, Valéry believed it was his best. It employs the Alexandrine line characteristic of classical narrative poetry. The story of Narcissus was of particular interest to Valéry, and this poem is not the only example of the appearance of this myth in his writing. In 1938, his "Cantata for Narcissus" would be set to music, but "Fragments of Narcissus" would remain his most successful use of the myth, regardless of its unfinished state. The poet claimed he never completed this work because of a lack of time. It would not be the only work on which he may have intended to spend more time but did not after its initial publication in a periodical. In this regard, Valéry brings credence to the axiom that poems are never finished, simply abandoned. The opening lines of the second section are among Valéry's best-known and most frequently cited lines.

> Fountain, my fountain, water coldly present,
> Sweet to the purely animal, compliant to humans
> Who self-tempered pursue death into the depths,
> To you all is dream, tranquil Sister of Fate!
> Barely does it alter an omen to recollection
> When, ceaselessly reflecting its fugitive face,
> At once the skies are ravished from your slumber!
> But pure as you may be of the beings you have seen
> Water where the years drift by like clouds,
> How many things, nevertheless, you must know,
> Stars, roses, seasons, bodies and their amours!

While many critics have agreed with the poet's opinion that "Fragments of Narcissus" was his best effort, at least as many have defended the same opinion of "The Graveyard by the Sea." This poem's setting derives from Séte, where Valéry spent time as a child. The graveyard's reappearance in the poem indicates the lasting importance of the setting in the shaping of the poet's imagination. Correspondingly, the poem itself is a meditation on meditation as well as on the nature of artistic and intellectual imagination.

The sea and cemeteries are settings that poets of every era since Homer have found conducive to poetic meditation. The combination of these atmospheres allows Valéry an advantageous standpoint from which to move through diverse levels of consciousness as they are informed by the poem's dual senses of location. In terms of form, this poem is arguably the one in which Valéry is at his best, as the form—six, five beat lines per stanza—is hardly notice-able as one becomes engaged by his seemingly effortless language. The vehicle comes into as perfect a harmony with the journey it accommodates as the poet may have ever achieved. Ironically, the cemetery featured in this poem is the one in which Valéry was buried.

What has perhaps confounded critics the most was Valéry's assertion that the poems in *Charms* were written as exercises; he was experimenting with a greater diversity of forms than he had at any previous time. The considerable quality of these poems is what led critics to question the credibility of the author's claim. In all likelihood, the crux of the contention was semantic. Valéry was never overly fond of critics, to put it mildly, although it is certainly their valuable role to second-guess writers. Critics may feel the value of their work to be diminished when so much good attention has been expended on work the author casually passes off as "a collection of prosodic experiments" and not the product of some supposedly higher artistic goal. Had Valéry been a scientist, he would have been forgiven his use of the word experiment. These experiments, however, were to signal a key turning point in the career of a poet who would later be named the national poet of France.

Jon Lavieri

Bibliography:
Grubbs, Henry A. *Paul Valéry.* New York: Twayne, 1968. A comprehensive overview of Valéry's life and work. *Charms* receives close attention in several sections; for readers new to Valéry, this is perhaps the best place to begin detailed study.
Valéry, Paul. *The Art of Poetry.* Translated by Denise Folliot. Vol. 7 in *The Collected Works of Paul Valéry,* edited by Jackson Mathews. New York: Pantheon Books, 1958. This volume contains essays, one devoted specifically to *Charms,* in which Valéry discusses the original intentions at the base of his work. This is where one will find the main points of contention between the poet and his critics.
Weiss, Ted, and Renee Weiss, comps. *Quarterly Review of Literature: Special Issues Retrospective.* Princeton, N.J.: Quarterly Review of Literature, 1976. From the publishers of one of America's foremost literary quarterlies, this presents chronological sequences of critical works on an eclectic variety of poets. There are six essays on Valéry, beginning with T. S. Eliot's point of view.

THE CHARTERHOUSE OF PARMA

Type of work: Novel
Author: Stendhal (Marie-Henri Beyle, 1783-1842)
Type of plot: Historical
Time of plot: Early nineteenth century
Locale: Italy
First published: La Chartreuse de Parme, 1839 (English translation, 1895)

Principal characters:
FABRIZIO DEL DONGO, a young adventurer
GINA PIETRANERA, his aunt
COUNT MOSCA, Gina's lover
MARIETTA, an actress, Fabrizio's first lover
CLELIA CONTI, Fabrizio's mistress

The Story:

Early in the nineteenth century, Fabrizio, son of the marchese del Dongo, grew up at his father's magnificent villa at Grianta on Lake Como. His father was a miserly fanatic who hated Napoleon and the French, his mother a long-suffering creature cowed by her domineering husband. In his boyhood, Fabrizio was happiest when he could leave Grianta and go to visit his aunt, Gina Pietranera, at her home in Milan. Gina looked upon her handsome nephew as if he were her son.

When he was nearly seventeen years old, Fabrizio determined to join Napoleon. Both his aunt and his mother were shocked, but the boy stood firm. Fabrizio's father was too stingy to allow Fabrizio's mother or his aunt to give Fabrizio any money for his journey, but Gina sewed some small diamonds in his coat. Under a false passport, Fabrizio made his way to Paris as a seller of astrological instruments.

Following one of Napoleon's battalions out of Paris, Fabrizio was arrested and thrown into jail as a spy. His enthusiastic admiration for the emperor and his bad French were marks against him. Released from jail by the kindhearted wife of the turnkey, Fabrizio pressed on, anxious to get into the fighting. Mounted on a horse he bought from a good-natured camp follower, he rode by accident into a group of hussars around Marshall Ney at the Battle of Waterloo. When a general's horse was shot, the hussars lifted Fabrizio from the saddle, and the general commandeered his horse. Afoot, Fabrizio fell in with a band of French infantrymen and, in the retreat from Waterloo, killed a Prussian officer. Happy at being a real soldier, he threw down his gun and escaped.

Meanwhile, at home, Gina had succumbed to the romantic advances of Count Mosca, prime minister of Parma. They made a convenient arrangement. Old Duke Sanseverina badly wanted a diplomatic post. In return for Mosca's favor in giving him the post, he agreed to marry Gina and set her up as the Duchess of Sanseverina. Then the duke left the country for good, and Mosca became Gina's accepted lover. It was a good thing for Fabrizio that his aunt had some influence. When he returned to Grianta, the gendarmes came to arrest him on a false passport charge. He was taken to Milan in his aunt's carriage. On the way, the party passed an older man and his younger daughter, also arrested but condemned to walk. Graciously Gina and Fabrizio took General Conti and his daughter Clelia into the carriage with them. At Milan, Fabrizio's difficulties were easily settled.

1065

Gina was growing very fond of Fabrizio, who was a handsome youth, and she took him with her to Parma to advance his fortune. There, upon the advice of Mosca, it was decided to send the young man to Naples to study for three years at the theological seminary. When he came back, he would be given an appointment at court.

At the end of his studies, Fabrizio was a suave, worldly young monsignor, not yet committed to a life of piety despite his appointment as alternate for the archbishop. At the theater one night, the young cleric saw a graceful young actress named Marietta Valsera. His attention soon aroused the anger of a rascal called Giletti, Marietta's protector.

Fearing the consequences of this indiscretion, Mosca sent Fabrizio to the country for a while to supervise some archaeological excavations. While looking over the site, Fabrizio borrowed a shotgun and walked down the road to look for rabbits. At that moment, a carriage drove by, with Marietta and Giletti inside. Thinking that Fabrizio intended to take Marietta, Giletti leaped from the carriage and rushed at Fabrizio with his dagger. In the fight, Fabrizio killed Giletti. The alarmed Marietta took Fabrizio with her to Bologna. There his aunt's emissaries supplied him with ample funds, and Fabrizio settled down to enjoy his lovely Marietta.

News of the affair reached Parma. Political opponents of Mosca found an opportunity to strike at him through Gina, and they influenced the prince to try the fugitive for murder. Fabrizio was tried in his absence and condemned to death or imprisonment as a galley slave.

Fabrizio soon tired of Marietta. Attracted by a young singer named Fausta, he followed her to Parma. There he was recognized and imprisoned. In spite of his influence, Mosca could do little for Gina's nephew; but Fabrizio was happy in jail, for Clelia, the daughter of his jailer, was the girl to whom Fabrizio had offered a ride years previously. By means of alphabet cards, the two were soon holding long conversations.

Outside, Gina laid her plans for Fabrizio's escape. With the help of a poet named Ferrante, she arranged to have ropes smuggled to her nephew. Clelia was to carry them in to Fabrizio. Fabrizio escaped from the tower and fled to Piedmont. At Parma, according to Gina's instructions, Ferrante poisoned the prince who had condemned Fabrizio to imprisonment. In the resulting confusion, Gina and Fabrizio returned to Parma, now governed by the new prince. Pardoned, he was named coadjutor by the archbishop. Later, he became archbishop and attracted great crowds with his preaching. In the meantime, Clelia had married a rich marchese. One day, moved by curiosity, she came to hear Fabrizio preach. Her love finally led her to take him for a lover. Every night he came to her house. After their child was born, Fabrizio took the baby to his own house, and Clelia visited her small son there. Fabrizio, however, was to be happy only a short time. The infant died, and Clelia did not long survive her child. Saddened by her death, Fabrizio gave up his office and retired to the Charterhouse of Parma, a monastery on the river Po, where quiet meditation filled his days.

Critical Evaluation:

The Charterhouse of Parma, the second of Stendhal's great masterpieces, was written three years before his death. Written in its entirety over a seven-week period, the novel represented its author's return to his spiritual homeland of Italy. With its intensely beautiful landscapes and vividly detailed descriptive passages, the book is on one level a poetic hymn to the Italian spirit and land. On another level, it is the complicated story of the search of four people for happiness, a story rich in psychological revelations and social and historical insights. On whatever level *The Charterhouse of Parma* is read, it unfailingly impresses readers with its unmistakably magical quality and its pervasive atmosphere of happiness fraught with gentle melancholy and romantic yearning.

The Charterhouse of Parma has often been likened to a Mozart symphony; the important section at the beginning of the novel, in which the young Fabrizio runs away to join Napoleon's army, can easily be read as a musical prelude which contains the seeds of all the themes and action to follow. When Fabrizio, after a series of mishaps and near escapes, manages to find the scene of the Battle of Waterloo, it is already in progress. Instead of giving a panoramic, chronologically accurate account of the event, Stendhal fires a barrage of impressionistic detail at the reader, which leaves him or her overwhelmed and bewildered. The reader is as lost as Fabrizio, who, in his confusion, spends a whole day searching for the regiment from which he has been separated. He repeatedly stops soldiers and officers to ask them, amidst smoke and grapeshot, where the battle is. Slowly, however, the individual, seemingly random details accumulate. Fleeing soldiers, deafening noise, a corpse trampled in the grass, the incessant cannon booming, fire, smoke, and infantry crowded so close that all sense of direction and movement is lost, all of these images gradually coalesce to produce a total effect of the horror of war remarkable in its vividness and realism. At the same time, this portion of the novel serves as prelude by showing the crucial aspects of Fabrizio's personality which are to be focal points in the narrative's later action. Against the grimness of the war backdrop, the figure of Fabrizio stands in happy contrast. He is youthful, fresh, and innocent; he has boundless enthusiasm and natural curiosity; he enjoys invincible high spirits and is filled with innate courage and grace. Furthermore, although he is still very young, he will retain throughout the narrative these essential qualities, which make him the ideal protagonist to search tirelessly for happiness through a multitude of loves and adventures.

Surrounding Fabrizio are the twin heroines of *The Charterhouse of Parma*, Clelia Conti and Gina Pietranera. The two women provide an important contrast in their respective characters: Clelia is young and innocent, pure and idealistic, religious and superstitious; Gina is mature and worldly, witty and intelligent, beautiful and passionate. The fourth major character, Count Mosca, combines within his character the qualities of a supreme diplomat and an ideal knight. Among these four men and women grow the three love relationships that are the focal point of the novel: the love of Gina for Fabrizio, of Count Mosca for Gina, and of Fabrizio for Clelia.

Stendhal's portrait of Gina is a triumph of characterization. Charming, stubborn, astute, devoted, erotic, and intelligent, her richly varied personality is revealed through her relationship with Count Mosca and, most crucially, through her love for Fabrizio. What began as maternal affection for a small boy grows over the years into a love that is undefinable; Gina's feelings, which under acceptable circumstances would immediately flow into erotic channels, must be sublimated; she struggles to control her boundless energies, to guide them into outlets of devoted maternal concern and to disguise from herself all the while what she really feels. Ironically, Fabrizio is not genetically related to her, since a French soldier, rather than Gina's brother, was the hero's father; for all practical purposes, however, given their background and Fabrizio's attitude of boyish admiration for his aunt, any sexual relationship between the two would be psychologically incestuous.

The second love relationship in the book is that between Count Mosca and Gina. It is a one-sided affair insofar as the intensity of passion is all on the count's side; Gina feels a great affinity for Mosca and loves him in a certain fashion but not in the same way as he loves her. The count is a fascinating figure—intelligent, skilled in diplomacy, powerfully ambitious, warm, faithful, benevolent, yet capable of jealousy and anger. What draws Mosca and Gina together is their common wisdom tempered with skepticism, their basic love of humanity, and their fierce hatred of the petty tyrants who hold authority over the rest of humanity. In many ways, Stendhal wrote his own personality not only into Fabrizio but also into the character of the gallant Mosca; it has been said that within him Stendhal "deposited, with his artist's curiosity, the residue of his knowledge and his disappointments—the supreme irony of a too ambitious ego which 'set its nets too high.'" Significantly, at the close of the novel, only Mosca is strong enough to survive the pain of loss and intense suffering.

The love Fabrizio and Clelia will later feel for each other is foreshadowed very early when Fabrizio gives twelve-year-old Clelia and her father a ride in his carriage. When the hero saves Count Conti, who is traveling in disguise, from exposure to the police, the little girl does not fully understand what is happening but suspects that the young man is somehow noble and admires him shyly from a distance. Years later, when they meet again as adults, their love blossoms slowly as they move through phases of the process which Stendhal called "crystallization." For Fabrizio, the feeling is new in its degree of intensity and joy; his love is so vehement that, at one point, it causes him to wish for death and to refuse help in escaping rather than to lose it. On Clelia's side, the reaction to love is more complex. She becomes increasingly passionate and demanding, yet purer in the sense that into her love for Fabrizio she pours her entire soul, concentrating in him all of her capacity for feeling. Her commitment is so total that she can feel compassion toward Gina; yet, simultaneously, jealousy taints her pity, and she leans toward hatred for the older woman. Her love allows her to sleep with Fabrizio after he has become a bishop and she is married, yet superstition makes her cling to her vow to meet him only in darkness and never see his face. The lovers' depth of emotion extends to their child so strongly that when the child Sandrino dies, his mother follows him shortly afterward, while his father retires to the Carthusian monastery that gives the novel its title.

Behind these four extraordinary figures is ranged a gallery of minor characters, the most memorable being those associated with the court in Parma. People are paraded before the reader's eyes in all of their vanity and pomposity to instruct the audience in the venality and pettiness of humanity. The Grand Duke Ranuce-Ernest IV leads this gallery of comic figures; in quick flashes, Stendhal reveals a man at once cruel and terrified to indulge his cruelty, proud of his power yet ashamed that it is not greater, affected and overbearing but inwardly filled with fear and indecision. While the main characters are used to show how humans can commit themselves wholly to love, through the minor characters, Stendhal ridicules, in a comic fashion reminiscent of the works of Molière, all the vices and follies of humankind.

"Critical Evaluation" by Nancy G. Ballard

Bibliography:
Alter, Robert, in collaboration with Carol Cosman. *A Lion for Love: A Critical Biography of Stendhal*. New York: Basic Books, 1979. Despite its relative brevity, this is the best biography in English. Alter calls *The Charterhouse of Parma* the novel that Stendhal "had been gathering resources all his life to write" and skillfully relates the circumstances of its composition. Notes and illustrations, no bibliography.
Gutwirth, Marcel. *Stendhal*. New York: Twayne, 1971. A very readable if somewhat dated study of the writer's autobiographical and fictional works, developed in terms of several controlling images: "The Pistol Shot," "Brief Candle," and so on. Prefaced with a brief but useful chronology.
Talbot, Emile J. *Stendhal Revisited*. New York: Twayne, 1993. The best starting point for the beginning reader of Stendhal. Talbot profits from scholarship appearing since Gutwirth's survey but downplays the autobiographical element in Stendhal's fiction. Good annotated bibliography of secondary works.

Turnell, Martin. *The Novel in France*. New York: Vintage, 1958. A standard and highly acclaimed survey. Places Stendhal's three major novels in a tradition running from the seventeenth century through the early twentieth century. Turnell praises *The Charterhouse of Parma* for its "extraordinary poise and maturity."

Wood, Michael. *Stendhal*. Ithaca, N.Y.: Cornell University Press, 1971. An accessible study of Stendhal's major and some of his minor works. Wood is particularly good at identifying the many elements—personal, historical, social, and political—that contributed to the genesis of *The Charterhouse of Parma*.

CHÉRI

Type of work: Novel
Author: Colette (Sidonie-Gabrielle Claudine Colette, 1873-1954)
Type of plot: Psychological realism
Time of plot: c. 1910
Locale: Paris
First published: 1920 (English translation, 1929)

> *Principal characters:*
> LÉONIE VALLON, called Léa de Lonval
> FRED PELOUX, called Chéri
> MADAME PELOUX, Chéri's mother
> EDMÉE, the woman Chéri married
> MARIE-LAURE, Edmée's mother

The Story:

In the pink boudoir of Léa, a still lovely courtesan, Chéri, her handsome young lover, demanded her valuable pearls with which to play. She discouraged his mood, fearing that the removal of her pearls might cause him to notice that her neck was showing the wrinkles of age. Chéri cursed his luncheon engagement with his mother. Léa gently and teasingly helped him in his erratic dressing. Although he became lazily aroused at her touch, she managed to send him away.

Alone, Léa dressed with efficient care, choosing a white-brimmed hat for her visit to Madame Peloux. She ate a good lunch before joining Chéri at his mother's house. There she found Madame Peloux loud-voiced, gossipy, and inquisitive. Also there were Marie-Laure, an elegant woman of forty years, and her quiet daughter Edmée, whose looks nearly equaled her mother's. They left as soon as Léa arrived, and the degree to which mother and son then relaxed disgusted Léa. Despite Chéri's careless manners, he still looked to her like a young god.

She remembered him as a very beautiful and lonely child who had soon developed his mother's miserliness and her keen business sense. In his late adolescence, Chéri had been taken away by Léa to Normandy to feed him well and also to remove him from his dissipated life in Paris. Her offer to do so had been accepted with a kiss that had inflamed them both.

In Normandy, they had become lovers. Chéri was devoted to Léa for her passion and solicitude, and she to him for his youth, ardor, and faunlike freedom. At that point, Léa would still have been willing to abandon him because of the inconvenience he caused her; he was, in succession, taciturn and demonstrative, tender and spiteful. After they returned to Paris, however, Chéri still wanted Léa and he became her established lover. He had remained with her for six years.

When Chéri returned to Léa after the luncheon party, he told her that he was to marry Edmée. Since Léa had always known a marriage would be eventually arranged for Chéri, she did not outwardly react to this news. Chéri declared that his wife would influence him little and that she already adored him. Wounded by Léa's apparent lack of emotion, he declared that he would like her to hide herself in Normandy and grieve. He desperately wanted to be her last lover.

In the few weeks before Chéri's marriage, he and Léa were very happy, though at times she was appalled at his heartlessness toward his future bride and realized that by pampering him she had maintained in him the immaturity of a child. When Chéri chattered about his honeymoon, Léa reminded him that she would not be there. Chéri turned white and gave her great happiness by announcing ambiguously that for him she would always be there.

While visiting Madame Peloux during the honeymoon, Léa was suddenly overwhelmed by an ill-defined grief. Feeling ill, she returned home and went to bed. When she realized that she was for the first time really suffering from the loss of a great love, she fled from Paris and stayed away for a year.

Chéri and Edmée lived with Madame Peloux at Neuilly until their own house was finished. Chéri was also miserable and questioned his mother about Léa's uninformative parting note. No one knew where she had gone. Sometimes he fought viciously with his young wife, who loved him and bored him. Again, he would become obsessed with plans for their house and give many and contradictory orders for exotic decorations.

Edmée became so unhappy that at last she resorted to looking for love letters in Chéri's desk. When she accused him of loving only Léa and wept unrestrainedly, Chéri was unmoved but interested; Léa had never cried. Edmée deeply offended Chéri when she suggested that their own lovemaking was not really love. Chéri explained that no man could tolerate such remarks. Their quarrels finally forced Edmée to suggest a divorce. Chéri calmly rejected the suggestion because he knew that Edmée loved him and because divorce offered no real solution to his problem.

Chéri next went to Léa's house, but her servants had no news of her. In deep despair, he dined away from home for the first time. He stayed in Paris, living a miserable and silent life with a young man who had frequently lived on his money before. He recovered the strength to act when at last the lamps in Léa's house were again lighted. Then, without seeing Léa, he bought jewels for his wife and returned home.

Léa did not wholly regret her exile, but she was distressed to discover how much the year had aged her. Only her eyes remained as lovely as before. Although a visit from Madame Peloux restored her spirit, she was hurt by the news she received of Chéri, and she realized that she was not free of her love for him. While out walking, she twice saw young men who she was convinced were Chéri. Knowing that she was not yet strong enough to meet him unexpectedly, she returned home. She changed her street clothes for a peach-colored robe and paced about her room while trying to face the fact that she was alone.

About midnight Chéri arrived, sullen and disheveled, and declared that he had returned to her. She quarreled with him for a time but at last was so completely disarmed by his pleas that she kept him there. For the first time, that night, they declared to each other that they were in love.

In the morning, Léa, unknowingly watched by Chéri, made wild plans for their departure together. She looked old to Chéri, and he felt exhausted. Unable to draw him into her plans, she bitterly abused Edmée. He stopped her by insisting that she was not being the fine and lovely woman he had known. She told him gently that their fate had been to love and then part. Although he knew how he had hurt Léa, Chéri was unable to follow any course but return to his family. Léa begged him not to make Edmée miserable and told Chéri how she loved him. Having thus successfully sent him away, Léa last saw Chéri breathing in the air of the courtyard as if it were something that he could taste.

Critical Evaluation:

Colette is an enchantress when writing about the relations between the sexes. She has been criticized as being a writer whose main concern was the world of the superficial. Many of her characters are drawn from the world of the theater, the demimonde, and the arts, and many of her characters exist within the world of the cabaret and the brothel. Recent feminist theory has done much to portray Colette as a writer who wrote exquisitely about both sexes and who was especially adept at writing about the sensual natures of both men and women. In addition, she was one of the writers of her age who could see through the veil of patriarchal authority. While her characters have not always been able to free themselves of gender stereotypes, Colette's characters never indulge in self-pity or despair.

In *Chéri*, the interactions between the hopelessly young and beautiful Chéri and his much older lover, Léa, are defined along traditional gender lines. At the same time, these traditional gender divisions are subverted. Chéri, in his decision to marry Edmée, finds himself in the position of being bound to his young wife while still in love with Léa. For her part, Léa never betrays the dignity of her age. The marriage between Chéri and Edmée grieves Léa to the point that she leaves Paris for a year's travel in Europe, but she never reveals her sorrow to Chéri. In the end Chéri returns to declare his love for Léa; Léa maintains her superiority as the more experienced and comforting choice for Chéri.

Spoiled, petulant, and relying only on his beauty and social position, Chéri, not Léa, has the most superficial features that are stereotyped as "female." Léa, on the other hand, as a woman of great dignity, experience, reserve, and strength, in a sense reinvents female identity by showing that she is not dominated by the need to have the fidelity and the attention of a man. While Léa's situation is not tragic—Colette was careful to respect the gaming and humorous side to interpersonal relationships—neither is it possible to condemn Léa on the grounds of superficiality. She makes her bid, withstands the indignity of rejection, and lives with her sorrow by maintaining a stance of remove, if not acceptance. In the end, she wins out in character over the young man who can do nothing other than what he is told to do—and then only to his own destruction.

Chéri was a novel that gave Colette great satisfaction. It is also the first novel she wrote in the third person. Stylistically, the novel shows her at the apex of her craft. Written primarily in dialogue, *Chéri* captures the voices of its characters in haunting clarity. Chéri, the spoiled young man, sounds every bit the character that he is, and his mother's voice indicates the psychological origin for his haughty nature. Léa, on the other hand, is characterized by a carefully measured and precise choice of words. She teases Chéri, but always only to a point before her words will actually hurt him. As the older woman, she is gentle, a source of great comfort to the young Chéri. In the novel, Colette explores the dichotomy of a relationship between unequal characters.

Colette practiced her skills in many earlier novels and stories before she wrote *Chéri*. Many critics consider her best work to have been written in her short stories, vignettes, and prose poems. In the stories as well as in the novels, Colette takes her experience as a cabaret dancer and courtesan as the primary material for her fiction. Her world was the amorphous and amoral world of pre-World War I French society. Her fiction captures its time.

Colette never made any secret of her bisexuality, and she lived openly with men and women. This is an important factor to consider when making any critical evaluation of her work because it explains her adeptness at entering the minds of both her male and female characters and drawing so closely on the feelings of both. In *Chéri*, this bisexual perspective allows her to explore—outside the stereotypes of her time—the variations on the traditional sexual roles of both men and women.

Colette is a consummate writer of short stories as well as novels. The "game of love" that is played out in *Chéri* was frequently explored by Colette, especially in her short fiction. It is important to keep in mind that Colette, a writer of the *fin de siècle* era, was also a contemporary

Chéri / COLETTE

of Sigmund Freud. In her short stories and in her novels, Colette incorporates many Freudian ideas about sexual relations. She was especially capable, as a woman writer, of freeing her characters from the role of the "butt of the male joke" that Freud saw women as occupying in his conception of the joke as recorded in *Jokes and Their Relationship to the Unconscious* (1905). Freud posits woman as the butt of the male joke, that joke being obscenity. In Colette's writing, she often undermines this joke by reinstating a woman as a dominator of the joke structure. In *Chéri*, Léa, the butt of Chéri's joke of choosing a much younger woman as his wife, is vindicated by her dignity and resolve to abandon, however painful it may be for her, her pursuit of Chéri. In the novel, *Chéri*, Colette reverses the traditional roles of sexual relations between a younger man and an older woman and ultimately reveals Léa, the woman, to be of much greater strength.

"Critical Evaluation" by Susan M. Rochette-Crawley

Bibliography:

Dormann, Geneviève. *Colette: A Passion for Life.* Translated by David Macey and Jane Brenton. New York: Abbeville Press, 1985. An excellent collection of photos and pictures from Colette's life. Useful for an author whose work is as autobiographical as hers. Contains some illustrations for an edition of *Chéri* by artist Marcel Vertès.

Lottman, Herbert. *Colette: A Life.* Boston: Little, Brown, 1991. Biography accounting for all Colette's major works. Provides a summary of the autobiographical content of *Chéri* and the conditions of its creation.

Marks, Elaine. *Colette.* New Brunswick, N.J.: Rutgers University Press, 1960. Critical biography has remained authoritative over the years. Provides excellent close readings of *Chéri* and its sequels which Marks terms "parables of experience."

Sarde, Michèle. *Colette: Free and Fettered.* Translated by Richard Miller. New York: William Morrow, 1980. A definitive biography. Provides a strong feminist perspective on Colette's life and work.

Stewart, Joan Hinde. *Colette.* Boston: Twayne, 1983. A good introduction to Colette's work. Analyzes *Chéri* together with three works which continue its themes and use some of the same characters: *The Ripening Seed* (1923), *The Last of Chéri* (1926), and *The Break of Day* (1928). Contains a selected bibliography.

Ward Jouve, Nicole. *Colette.* Brighton, England: Harvester Press, 1987. A feminist analysis which addresses the question of "women's writing" in Colette's major works. *Chéri* illustrates an aspect of the power relationship between men and women.

1073

THE CHEROKEE NIGHT

Type of work: Drama
Author: Lynn Riggs (1899-1954)
Type of plot: Social realism
Time of plot: 1895-1931
Locale: Oklahoma
First performed: 1936; first published, 1936

Principal characters:

> VINEY JONES, a frontier schoolteacher
> BEE NEWCOMB, a prostitute
> HUTCH MOREE, a man of partial Cherokee ancestry
> ART OSBURN, a man of partial Cherokee ancestry
> GAR BREEDEN, a man of partial Cherokee ancestry
> OLD MAN TALBERT, a traditional Cherokee
> SARAH PICKARD, Viney's sister
> MAISIE PICKARD, Sarah's daughter
> KATE WHITETURKEY, an Osage Indian
> GEORGE MOREE, Hutch's brother
> CLABE WHITETURKEY, Kate's brother
> JOHN GRAY-WOLF, a full-blooded Cherokee
> EDGAR "SPENCH" BREEDEN, Gar's father
> MARTHY BREEDEN, Gar's mother
> FLOREY NEWCOMB, Bee's mother

The Story:

In the shadow of Claremore Mound, Oklahoma, a group of young people, all of whom were of mixed white and Cherokee ancestry, were having a frolicsome picnic one night in 1915. They quarreled among themselves, at first in a harmless fashion but later in a serious one. They verbally tormented one another with insults and references to one another's personality flaws. Viney Jones, who had been a schoolteacher, told of keeping Hutch Moree, an oil hand, after school for his stuttering. Bee Newcomb was rightly accused of being a prostitute. Other insults were exchanged. Noises made by another person were then heard in the night. Directly, Old Man Talbert appeared and informed the youth that he was collecting arrowheads, relics from the past with which he hoped to reestablish his own identity as an Indian, as well as to reestablish that of the part-Indians around him such as the members of the group. Talbert went mad, recalling the long-gone greatness of the Cherokee and Osage Indians who had once lived and fought on this very scene.

Some twelve years later, in the Rogers County Jail, Bee was hired by the sheriff to trick Art Osburn into confessing that he had murdered his wife, a white woman much older than he with children of her own. The sheriff placed Bee in the cell with Art, where she lied by claiming that she had been put in jail for being drunk. She produced whiskey to help loosen Art's tongue. Shortly, thinking no one could hear what he said, Art confessed that he had murdered his wife and that she had not drowned as he claimed. Art then discovered a tape recorder hidden in the cell by the sheriff, but it was too late. He attacked Bee, who was barely saved from his wrath. The sheriff then paid her for deceiving her fellow Indian.

In 1931, Viney Jones decided to visit her sister Sarah Pickard, who lived on a run-down farm within sight of Claremore Mound. Sarah was the mother of Maisie, a young girl of seventeen years who had recently married. The Pickard family was very poor and bordering on starvation. Viney, who had entirely hidden and denied her Cherokee heritage, lived in town where she passed for white—evidently because of her husband's money. Viney offered some money to her sister, but out of pride Sarah rejected it. The two sisters quarreled bitterly; each accused the other of being selfish and living a lie. As she exited the home, Sarah threw several coins at her sister and instructed her to use them to buy medicine. Maisie found them and held them gratefully.

The three youths—Gar, Hutch, and Art—as boys in 1906 were playing games in the absence of adults. In the woods in the summer, they had sought out the location where an African American man had been murdered by white men. The man had been chased there after murdering another African American in a card game. The three boys searched for blood and other evidence that they had found the right location. In so doing, they went into something of a frenzy, engaging in a war dance and even harming themselves to the point of bringing out their own blood.

A group of people, all of whom had varying amounts of Cherokee blood, were meeting in a small, primitive church for services in 1919. They sang and danced and chanted in a fashion reminiscent of Indian war ceremonies. Into their midst and up the mountainside came Gar, who was running from the white people for some unspecified reason. He had turned to his Indian brothers to help him in his attempt to escape. They refused, and rather than help him, they actually tied him to a tree so that he would be ready for the taking when the people who were chasing him arrived.

In 1919, George Moree came to visit his brother Hutch after an absence of many years; Hutch was then living with Kate Whiteturkey, a rich, eighteen-year-old, full-blooded Osage Indian. Evidently, the two were married. Kate had somehow come into money by denying her Indian heritage. Hutch, too, was living a white man's lifestyle, replete with ten silk shirts, six pairs of shoes, and a Studebaker car of his very own. Because of the differences in values, the two brothers verbally fought, and George left.

Gray-Wolf, one of the last purebred Cherokees and one of the last to know and hold somewhat to the traditions of his fathers, informed Gar Breeden (a very young boy) and Marthy Breeden (his mother) that the whites were after Edgar "Spench" Breeden for sundry acts of misconduct. Spench was chased to the cabin, where the conversation among the family members dealt with Florey Newcomb, recently impregnated by Spench. (Florey later gave birth to Bee Newcomb.) Tinsley, a white man, arrived at the cabin to shoot Spench, but he was too late. Spench was already dead.

Critical Evaluation:

Structurally, Lynn Riggs's drama *The Cherokee Night* is actually a series of seven "mini-plays" that the playwright calls "scenes." Each of the seven scenes is populated with different characters, although some do appear in as many as three of these episodes. Each of the seven scenes has a different plot. These scenes are not directly or even indirectly connected to each other. Moreover, each scene is set in a different time, and the sequence is not chronological. An "experimental" play for the 1930's, Riggs's work was well ahead of its time. Consequently, this deserving and worthy work was not generally well received by critics and has been produced only infrequently.

Thematically, the play does succeed as a unified whole. Riggs's main point is revealed by the title *The Cherokee Night*. He depicts the disintegration of the Cherokee nation as it was slowly consumed by white people's religion, government, agriculture, industry, and way of life. Most of all, however, the Cherokee nation has disintegrated primarily through its loss of bloodline; all of the characters except Gray-Wolf are of mixed ancestry. They have not been assumed into the white society, but they have chosen to leave the old ways behind—all to their own destruction. Viney Jones, educated in the schools of the white people's culture, is given over to the white culture's ways because of money; Kate and Clabe Whiteturkey are similarly bribed. Gar and Spench Breeden have assumed all of the vices of white people: drunkenness, theft, laziness, and materialism. Bee Newcomb is a prostitute who will sell out her Cherokee brothers for money, and a small amount at that.

The play is also unified by setting. All seven scenes are either on or in the shadow of Claremore Mound, Oklahoma, at once a burial ground for the Cherokee and Osage and the location of many important battles, both between the two tribes and against the white people. Claremore Mound, an embodiment of the past and a shroud of American Indian graves and history, ominously and perpetually casts its shadow over all activities of the present generation of Cherokee and Osage.

The older generation of Indians is represented by two characters. Old Man Talbert collects arrowheads, artifacts which to him can magically work to resurrect the dignity and integrity of his heritage. He must do this to keep his heritage alive. To the younger people of mixed ancestry, however, they serve only as symbols of times gone by, a life that is no more, and a way of being which is meaningless. Similarly, John Gray-Wolf survives as something on the order of the last person of character. He fully understands the white people and knows what has happened to the younger generation of American Indians. They have taken on all of the evil characteristics of the pervasive white society while simultaneously abandoning all that is good about their own traditions and heritage. The result is that they are in the worst of circumstances—both materially and morally—by actions of their own design.

Lynn Riggs, himself part Cherokee, understood very well the fallacy of blaming whites for all that was wrong with American Indian society. The settlers had taken the land and killed the buffalo and so on, but such offenses had not dealt the final death blow producing the "Cherokee night." Even the miscegenation between American Indians and white people, though perhaps a contributing factor, is not the ultimate reason that the Indian identity has been disintegrated into nothingness or, more correctly, transformed into decay and corruption. The Cherokees have brought "night" upon themselves.

This theme, revealed primarily through characterization, singularly holds together the play as a statement of politics as well as of morality. The chronological order of the seven scenes, though clear to persons reading the script, is entirely perplexing to viewers. Similarly, it is confusing for one watching the play to determine who the various characters are at different ages of their lives; moreover, three or four of the main characters have different marital names or nicknames, or are variously identified by such titles as "young man." Doubtlessly, all of this is by design on the part of the writer. Riggs is concerned with thematics, not readily discernible consistencies in plot. Such design reinforces the idea of "Cherokee night" as the last whimper of Cherokee death.

Carl Singleton

Bibliography:
Braunlich, Phyllis Cole. "*The Cherokee Night* of R. Lynn Riggs." *Midwest Quarterly* 30 (Autumn, 1988): 45-59. By far the best critical discussion of the play. Braunlich takes up

matters of characterization, experimentation in plot, and the main theme of the work itself: the disintegration of the Cherokee people.

_____. "The Oklahoma Plays of R. Lynn Riggs." *World Literature Today* 64, no. 3 (Summer, 1990): 390-394. The critic discusses *The Cherokee Night* as it relates to other plays written by Lynn Riggs during the same period. She finds this play to have a "dark mood" that makes for "haunting reading."

Scharine, Richard G. *From Class to Caste in American Drama: Political and Social Themes Since the 1930's.* New York: Greenwood Press, 1991. Scharine discusses *The Cherokee Night* within the context of biculturalism produced by the miscegenation of white people and Cherokees. He explores the problems of assimilation into mainstream culture.

Sievers, Wieder David. *Freud on Broadway: A History of Psychoanalysis and the American Drama.* New York: Cooper Square, 1955. Sievers provides something of a Jungian interpretation of the play, finding in it elements of racial memory which account for the basic conflicts of the work.

Sper, Felix. *From Native Roots.* Caldwell, Idaho: Caxton, 1948. Finding the play to be a "semifantasy," Sper claims that the play basically applauds the cause of the American Indians. He states that the American Indians of mixed ancestry are taking a position against the white people's God, a position from which they cannot win.

THE CHERRY ORCHARD

Type of work: Drama
Author: Anton Chekhov (1860-1904)
Type of plot: Impressionistic realism
Time of plot: Early twentieth century
Locale: An estate in Russia
First performed: 1904; first published, 1904 as *Vishnyovy sad* (English translation, 1908)

Principal characters:
MADAME RANEVSKAYA, a landowner
ANYA, her daughter
VARYA, her adopted daughter
GAEV, her brother
YASHA, a valet
DUNYASHA, a maid
FIERS, an old footman
LOPAKHIN, a merchant
CHARLOTTA, a governess
PISCHIN, a landowner
TROFIMOV, a student

The Story:

When Madame Ranevskaya's little son, Grischa, was drowned only a year after the death of her husband, her grief was so overwhelming that she was forced to go to Paris to forget, and she remained away for five years. The Easter before her return to her estate in Russia, she sent for her seventeen-year-old daughter Anya to join her. To pay the expenses of her trip and that of her daughter, Madame Ranevskaya had been forced to sell her villa at Mentone, and she now had nothing left. She returned home to find that her whole estate, including a cherry orchard, which was so famous that it had been mentioned in an encyclopedia, was to be sold at auction to pay her debts. Madame Ranevskaya was heartbroken, but her old friend Lopakhin, a merchant whose father had once been a serf on her ancestral estate, proposed a way out. He said that if the cherry orchard were cut down and the land divided into lots for rental to summer cottagers, she would be able to realize an income of at least twenty-five thousand rubles a year.

Madame Ranevskaya could not endure the thought that her childhood home with all its memories should be subjected to such a fate, and all the members of her family agreed with her. Her brother Gaev, who had remained behind to manage the estate, was convinced that there must be some other way out, but none of his ideas seemed feasible. It would be fine, he thought, if they all came in for a legacy, or if Anya could be wed to a rich man, or if their wealthy aunt could be persuaded to come to their aid. The aunt did not, however, entirely approve of Madame Ranevskaya, who, she felt, had married beneath her.

The thought that Gaev himself might do something never occurred to him; he went on playing billiards and munching candy as he had done all his life. Others who made up the household had similar futile dreams. Varya, an adopted daughter, hoped that God might do something about the situation. Pischin, a neighboring landowner, who had been saved financially when the railroad bought a part of his property, advised a policy of waiting for something to turn up.

Lopakhin, who had struggled hard to attain his present position, was frankly puzzled at the family's stubborn attitude. He had no illusions about himself; in fact, he realized that, compared with these smooth-tongued and well-mannered aristocrats, he was still only a peasant. He had tried to improve himself intellectually, but he fell asleep over the books with which he was supposed to be familiar.

As he gazed at the old cherry orchard in the moonlight, the cherry orchard that seemed so beautiful to Madame Ranevskaya, he could not help thinking of his peasant ancestors, to whom every tree must have been a symbol of oppression. Trofimov, who had been little Grischa's tutor, and who was more expressive than Lopakhin, tried to express this thought to Anya, with whom he was in love.

The cherry orchard was put up at auction. That evening, Madame Ranevskaya gave a ball in the old house, an act in keeping with the unrealistic attitude of her class in general. Even her aged servant, Fiers, supported her and remained loyal to her and her brother. Lopakhin arrived at the party with the news that he had bought the estate for ninety thousand rubles above the mortgage. When he announced that he intended to cut down the orchard, Madame Ranevskaya began to weep. She planned to return to Paris.

Others were equally affected by the sale of the cherry orchard. Gaev, on the basis of the transaction with Lopakhin, was offered a position in the bank at six thousand rubles a year, a position he would not keep because of his laziness. Madame Ranevskaya's servant, Yasha, was delighted over the sale because the trip to Paris would for him mean an escape from the boredom of Russian life. For Dunyasha, her maid, the sale meant the collapse of her hopes of ever marrying Yasha and instead a lifelong bondage to Yephodov, a poor, ineffectual clerk. To Varya, Madame Ranevskaya's adopted daughter, it meant a position as housekeeper on a nearby estate. To the landowner, Pischin, it was the confirmation of his philosophy. Investigators had found valuable minerals on his land, and he was now able to pay his debt to Madame Ranevskaya and to look forward to another temporary period of affluence. Fiers alone was unaffected. Departure of the family was the end of this old servant's life, for whatever it had been worth, but he was more concerned because Gaev, his master, had worn his light overcoat instead of a fur coat when he escorted the mistress, Madame Ranevskaya, to the station.

Critical Evaluation:

The Cherry Orchard, Anton Chekhov's best-known play, was published in 1904, the year Anton Chekhov died. The author's brief life had been a painful one. After an unhappy childhood he was forced, by his father's bankruptcy, to assume the responsibility of supporting his family. This he did by writing at the same time that he pursued a medical degree. By the time he earned his doctorate in 1884, his health was impaired by tuberculosis, which was to cut his life short at the age of forty-four. One might expect the final product of such an existence to reveal bitterness and rage. Instead, like most of Chekhov's work, *The Cherry Orchard* exemplifies his profound humanity.

The characters of *The Cherry Orchard* are not tragic in the usual sense of the word because they are incapable of any great heroic action. Chekhov shows them clearly in their frustrations, jealousies, and loves. Beyond his subtle characterizations, he catches in Madame Ranevskaya's household a picture of the end of an era, the passing of the semifeudal existence of Russian landowners on their country estates. Chekhov's fictional world is populated by persons who do not have the perception to understand their own lives, to communicate with those around them, or to bring their dreams to fruition. Most of the characters dream but only a few act. Madame Ranevskaya dreams that their estates will somehow be saved; her daughter, Anya, of a future without blemish; Fiers, the old valet, of the glories that used to be; Dunyasha, the maid, of becoming a fine lady; Trofimov, the student, of a magnificent new social order. Their predicament is summed up by Gaev, Madame Ranevskaya's somewhat unstable brother: "I keep thinking and racking my brains; I have many schemes, a great many, and that really means none." Only the merchant Lopakhin, the son of a serf, has the energy and will to make his dreams come true—but he does so with the single-mindedness of the ruthless manipulator he may well become.

The few characters who do not dream are perhaps more pitiable even than those who do. Yephodov, nicknamed "two-and-twenty misfortunes" because of his habitual bad luck, sees failure and despair everywhere. His only triumphant moments come when he fulfills his nickname. Charlotta, the governess, performs tricks to make others laugh because she herself is unable to laugh and views the future with empty eyes. Yasha, the young valet, a callous, self-centered cynic, is beyond dreams.

Only Varya, able to see her dreams for what they are, is realistic and fully human at the same time. Perhaps because she is the adopted daughter and unrelated to the ineffectual aristocrats, it is she who can look the future full in the face, who can see other characters—and accept them—for what they are. With the security of the estate crumbling, with prospects increasingly dim for her hoped-for marriage to Lopakhin, she finds salvation in work.

Madame Ranevskaya and her family have done nothing with their plot of land, which was once a grand and famous estate. Even the cherry orchard has become more dream than reality. Forty years before, the cherries made famous preserves, but the recipe has been forgotten. Lopakhin, the pragmatic merchant, points out, "The only thing remarkable about the orchard is that it's a very large one. There's a crop of cherries every alternate year, and then there's nothing to be done with them, no one buys them." Yet to the family the orchard continues to symbolize their former grandeur. When Lopakhin suggests that it should be cut down and the land developed into a summer resort, Gaev protests proudly, "This orchard is mentioned in the 'Encyclopaedia.'"

The Cherry Orchard, like Chekhov's other plays, is objectively written and may vary greatly in different productions. Madame Ranevskaya can be played as a dignified if somewhat inept woman caught in the vise of changing times, or as a silly lovesick female refusing to face truth. Lopakhin can be portrayed sympathetically—it is certainly easy to applaud his rise from menial to master of the estate—or as a villain, pretending to warn the family while knowing full well that they are incapable of action, gloating over his triumph, and heartlessly rejecting Varya. Trofimov has been interpreted as the perpetual student, given to long intellectual rumination and little else; after the 1917 Revolution, he was frequently portrayed as the spokesman for the new social order, a partisan of the common people.

Ambiguity is consistent with Chekhov's insistence that "to judge between good and bad, between successful and unsuccessful, would need the eye of God." The author himself chose not to play God but to be the eye of the camera, letting selected details speak for themselves. Madame Ranevskaya, exhorted by Trofimov to "face the truth," retorts, "What truth?" She and Chekhov are aware that there are many truths and that reality, like beauty, is frequently in the eye of the beholder.

Chekhov's friend Maxim Gorky once commented that "No one ever understood the tragic nature of life's trifles so clearly and intuitively as Chekhov did." Yet if Chekhov saw tragedy, he was also capable of recognizing the comedy in human experiments in living. "This was often the way with him," Gorky reported. "One moment he would be talking with warmth, gravity, and sincerity, and the next he would be laughing at himself and his own words." As with himself, so with the remainder of humanity.

Chekhov saw life with double vision that encompassed the tragic and the comic almost simultaneously. It is accurate therefore that *The Cherry Orchard* is classified as tragicomedy. The comedy is evident in stretches of apparently meaningless dialogue (which makes *The Cherry Orchard* a precursor of the theater of the absurd much later in the century), and in the superficial behavior typical of a comedy of manners. The tragedy lies in the lack of communication—much is said, but little is heard, let alone understood—and in the blindness of the characters as they blunder through their lives, hardly ever fully aware of what is happening to them. In the final speech, Fiers, the ill, elderly valet, mutters words that echo as a coda to the entire play: "Life has slipped by as though I hadn't lived."

"Critical Evaluation" by Sally Buckner

Bibliography:

Barricelli, Jean Pierre, ed. *Chekhov's Great Plays: A Critical Anthology*. New York: New York University Press, 1981. Seventeen essays that cover Chekhov's dramatic art and the individual plays. The essays on *The Cherry Orchard* include the editor's "Counterpoint of the Snapping String: Chekhov's *The Cherry Orchard*" and Francis Fergusson's "*The Cherry Orchard:* A Theater-Poem of the Suffering of Change."

Magarshak, David. *Chekhov the Dramatist*. New York: Hill and Wang, 1960. A thorough discussion of such topics as plays of direct action, transitions, and plays of indirect action, using Chekhov's development as a dramatist as the context.

Peace, Richard. *Chekhov: A Study of the Four Major Plays*. New Haven, Conn.: Yale University Press, 1983. A solid study of *Uncle Vanya* (1897), *Three Sisters* (1901), *The Seagull* (1896), and *The Cherry Orchard*. Excellent for basic information and knowledge about the plays.

Pitcher, Harvey. *The Chekhov Plays: A New Interpretation*. New York: Harper & Row, 1973. Offers bold new interpretations and nonstandard views, which make this study a valuable contribution to the understanding of Chekhov's plays. The chapter on *The Cherry Orchard* is particularly illuminating.

Valency, Maurice. *The Breaking String: The Plays of Anton Chekhov*. London, England: Oxford University Press, 1966. One of the best treatments of Chekhov's plays. Valency analyzes Chekhov's approach to theater, and individually discusses all the plays, including *The Cherry Orchard*.

THE CHEVALIER DE MAISON-ROUGE

Type of work: Novel
Author: Alexandre Dumas, *père* (1802-1870), with Auguste Maquet (1813-1888)
Type of plot: Historical
Time of plot: 1793
Locale: Paris
First published: Le Chevalier de Maison-Rouge, 1846 (English translation, 1846)

> *Principal characters:*
> GENEVIÈVE DIXMER, a young woman of aristocratic birth
> MAURICE LINDEY, an officer in the Civic Guard
> LOUIS LORIN, his faithful friend
> MONSIEUR DIXMER, a tanner and a Royalist conspirator
> MORAND, his friend and the Chevalier of the Maison Rouge
> MARIE ANTOINETTE, queen of France
> SIMON, a cobbler
> HÉLOÏSE TISON, an aide to the conspirators

The Story:

At the beginning of 1793, after the death of King Louis XVI on the guillotine, France was menaced at its borders by practically all of Europe. Internally, the political leadership was torn apart by dissensions between the Montagnards and the Girondins. One night in March, Maurice Lindey, a lieutenant in the Civic Guard, met a group of enlisted volunteers who were taking a woman to the guardhouse because she had no pass permitting her to be out at that time. The woman implored the officer for his protection against these men, who showed the effects of having drunk many toasts to their future victories. He decided to conduct her to the guardhouse himself, but she talked him into escorting her to her home.

Louis Lorin, Maurice's friend, had tried to persuade the lieutenant to avoid involving himself with an unknown woman who was so afraid of the guardhouse and who might well be a *ci-devant*, an aristocrat. Maurice, however, was already in love with her; he was afraid only that she was returning from a lovers' tryst. He escorted her home, but she refused to tell him her name. Once they had arrived in the old Rue Saint Jacques, in the center of the tanneries with their horrible smell, she ordered him to close his eyes, gave him a kiss, and, leaving a ring between his lips, disappeared. The next morning, he received a short note in which the woman gave him her thanks for his gallant conduct and said good-bye to him forever. He treasured this note with the ring.

Now that he had the lovely unknown woman on his mind he was not too upset to learn that the same night the Chevalier of the Maison Rouge, back in Paris, had attempted a new conspiracy to free Marie Antoinette. The immediate consequence was that the Dauphin was taken away from the apartment where he was imprisoned with his mother, sister, and aunt. The boy was given to Simon, a shoemaker, to receive a so-called republican education.

On another evening, Maurice went back to the same spot where the beautiful stranger had vanished. When he began reading all the names on the doors in the hope that love would prompt him to identify the right one, he was suddenly surrounded by seven men and thrown into an enclosed space with his hands tied and his eyes blindfolded. Behind the door he could hear the men deliberating to determine whether he was a spy and whether they should kill him. The name of Madame Dixmer was also mentioned. Maurice had gathered from their talk that she was the wife of one of the men, apparently the manager of a large tannery. The men continued talking, emphasizing that Madame Dixmer must know nothing of this happening. Maurice wondered why a tanner would want to assassinate him.

Meanwhile, he had succeeded in freeing himself from his bonds, and when the door was opened he jumped out, only to find himself in an enclosed garden where he found no visible means of escape. He leaped through a window and found himself in a room where a woman was reading. Dixmer followed him and ordered the woman to step aside so that he could shoot the intruder. Instead, she stretched out her arms to protect him. Geneviève Dixmer was the unknown woman of his previous encounter. Dixmer offered his apologies, explaining that he was using prohibited acids in his tannery business and that his smugglers had been afraid Maurice was an informer. Maurice was asked to stay for dinner, where he met Dixmer's business partner, Morand. At the end of the evening, he was invited to return.

One day in May, Maurice was on duty at the Temple—the apartment where Marie Antoinette was held—when Héloïse Tison came to visit her mother, the prisoner's keeper. She was accompanied by a friend who was allowed to go upstairs. After they had left, a letter was discovered in Marie Antoinette's pocket, a note confirming the death of a friend. The handwriting was familiar to Maurice, and he wondered how Geneviève Dixmer could have anything to do with the queen. The next day, Marie Antoinette asked to go to the top of the tower for a walk. After a while, turning to the east, she received signals from a window. Maurice thought he recognized Geneviève and immediately went to the Rue Saint Jacques, where he found everyone very busy with a new dye. He was amused at his own suspicions.

While he believed that Geneviève felt esteem rather than real love for her husband, Maurice was growing more and more jealous of Morand, whom for no reason at all he suspected of being in love with her. One day he did voice his jealousy; Geneviève pleaded with him to remain her friend. On the following day, he received a note from her asking him to send a letter to her husband giving any reason he might think of for stopping his visits. Once more he complied with her wish.

His action greatly upset Dixmer and Morand, whose tannery business was only a cover to hide their conspiracies. Morand was the Chevalier of the Maison Rouge. After Geneviève refused to write to Maurice or to invite him back to their home, Dixmer himself went to see him. True to his promise, Maurice refused to return. He became so lovesick that he could not do anything until he received a letter from Geneviève, in which, at her husband's insistence, she invited him to call once more. He had no suspicion that the conspirators had great need of him. They had bought a house close to the Temple and had worked all night to connect its caves with a trapdoor leading into the prison yard.

When Geneviève expressed a desire to see the queen, Maurice asked her to come to the Temple on the following Thursday. He also invited Morand. When a flower seller offered them some carnations, Maurice bought a bouquet for Geneviève. Later, as the queen walked by on her way to the top of the tower, she admired the flowers, and Geneviève offered her the bouquet.

Simon, who hated Lorin and Maurice because they protected the Dauphin against his cruelty, picked up a flower that had fallen from the bouquet and discovered a note hidden inside; but the note was blown away by the wind. After Simon had given the affair great publicity, the flower seller was found, tried, and condemned to death. The Chevalier of the Maison Rouge was unsuccessful in his efforts to rescue her; she was executed immediately. The flower seller was Héloïse Tison. Her mother had contributed to her doom by further substantiating Simon's accusations.

When the day set for the queen's escape arrived, Marie Antoinette asked to go into the yard for a walk. She was to sit by the trapdoor, then pretend to faint; during the confusion, she and her daughter and sister-in-law could be carried away through the tunnel; but as they were entering the yard, the queen's little black dog jumped forward and went barking toward the concealed tunnel. The conspirators were forced to retreat. The plot confirmed Simon's earlier charge, so he became the man of the day. Maurice fell under suspicion, together with his friend Lorin.

Determined to save his friend, Lorin insisted that he join the expedition which was to arrest the man who had bought the house to which the tunnel led. Maurice accepted, only to learn that Dixmer was the man. He realized that he had been a mere instrument in the hands of his alleged friends. When he arrived at the house, Geneviève said that she truly loved him, and she promised to be his if he would let the Chevalier go free. He revealed the password to them, and the conspirators escaped. The house was burned down. As Maurice ran everywhere desperately calling for Geneviève, Lorin realized the woman's identity. He followed his friend through the city on a fruitless search for his love and finally took him home after he had become completely exhausted. There they found Geneviève waiting for Maurice.

Maurice decided to leave France in order to take Geneviève away. She was left alone to pack her few belongings while Maurice went to see Lorin. During his absence, her husband came after her and forced her to go away with him.

In the meantime, Marie Antoinette had been transferred to the Conciergerie. The Chevalier managed to be hired as a turnkey there, replacing the former turnkey, whom he had bribed. Dixmer also had a plan for the queen's escape. His design was to introduce himself in the Conciergerie as a registrar. He hoped to get into Marie Antoinette's room with Geneviève and kill the two keepers. Geneviève would then persuade the queen to change clothes with her and leave with Dixmer.

The Chevalier of the Maison Rouge had introduced a small file into the queen's room with which she was supposed to cut the bars of her window. Meanwhile, he would keep the jailers busy at the other window. Unfortunately, the two attempts, taking place simultaneously, worked against each other, and Geneviève was arrested.

After having searched all Paris in order to find Geneviève again, Maurice had gone to live with Lorin after narrowly missing arrest in his own quarters. He and Lorin were definitely marked as suspects.

It was not until Marie Antoinette's trial, at which he met the Chevalier, that Maurice learned what had happened to Geneviève. He went to the Revolutionary Tribunal every day in the hope of finding her there. Finally she was brought in, and Maurice was surprised to see Lorin brought in as well. The commissary who had come to arrest Maurice had arrested Lorin instead when Maurice was not to be found. Geneviève and Lorin were sentenced to death.

Maurice had seen Dixmer in the audience. After the trial, he followed him and killed him during a quarrel. He took a pass which Dixmer, in order to harass his wife and accuse her of adultery, had secured for the purpose of entering the room where the prisoners were kept. Maurice ran to the waiting room and, handing the pass to Lorin, told him he, Lorin, was now free. Lorin, however, refused his friend's offer. Maurice was seized, and all three died on the scaffold.

Critical Evaluation:
    The Chevalier de Maison-Rouge takes as its subject matter the so-called carnation conspiracy, the attempt by the Chevalier de Rougeville to rescue Marie Antoinette from prison fol-

lowing the French Revolution. As a novel, it is an excellent example of Alexandre Dumas' ability to interest and enthrall his readers when the ultimate result of the action is a foregone conclusion. The title of the novel is taken from La Maison Rouge which, under the monarchy of pre-Revolutionary times, was one of the companies of the King's Household Guard, so named because of the brilliant red cloak which was part of the uniform.

The carnation conspiracy was a relatively little-known incident that occurred in September, 1793, while the French queen Marie Antoinette was in prison awaiting execution. An officer in the Household Guard, the Chevalier de Rougeville, entered the queen's cell in disguise, escorted by a municipal officer named Michonis. De Rougeville caught the queen's attention and then dropped a carnation behind a stove in the room. The flower contained a note which detailed the plans for a conspiracy to rescue her from captivity. Unfortunately for the plotters, the action was observed by a gendarme, Gilbert, assigned to watch the queen. The incident was reported, and the revolutionary government, under the impression that there was a widespread plot in Paris to rescue the queen, took severe protective measures, including the arrest and imprisonment of everyone deemed by the officials to have had a part in the conspiracy. The queen's guard was replaced by a new and more numerous force, and a number of the people around her were placed in prison themselves. The harsh measures were effective and, as every student knows, the queen went to her execution as planned.

This footnote to history constituted the framework on which Dumas chose to hang his plot. The author of a historical novel is certain to be somewhat hampered in his pattern making by the stubbornness of facts and events well-known to the reader and by the discrepancies of time and place. Yet in *The Chevalier de Maison-Rouge*, Dumas demonstrates small care for historical accuracy and the constraints of fact. At the same time, however, he exhibits a tremendous faculty for seizing the characters and situations that best render historical atmosphere. To write a good adventure story, an author must have rich materials with which he is naturally, and also by education, in sympathy. That these materials have been processed by other authors and are based on fact is of little consequence because adventure, not history, is the author's prime concern. In this novel, history provided the skeleton that depended on Dumas for life and development.

Dumas takes the reader into the open air of an extremely realistic world. His characters are active, not reflective. Their morality is that of the camp and field. Dumas never gloats over evil and shows no curiosity regarding vice and corruption. His heroes, Maurice and Louis, are moved by strong passions, their motives are universal and, as a rule, brave and honorable. Friendship, honor, and love are the trinity that governs their movements. In many respects, these two characters, like most of Dumas' protagonists, represent extensions of the author's own personality. Maurice is the romanticist and lover, an embodiment of the author, who went from mistress to mistress, frequented the society of actresses, and tended to pattern himself upon the flamboyance of the romantic author Lord Byron. Louis is the perfect gentleman and, like Dumas, the proponent of the virtues commonly found in aristocratic society.

Dumas' characterization, however, represents the most serious problem in the novel. Dumas was essentially aristocratic in temperament, and these qualities, when projected into the personalities of his protagonists—who ostensibly represent the post-Revolutionary common people—cause a serious contradiction in character delineation. Dumas' readers may wish simply to overlook such inconsistencies, concentrating instead on the action and adventure of the narrative.

The action and adventure of the narrative constitute the strength of Dumas' style in this as in the majority of his novels. The illusion of vitality comes across strongly to the reader. The author—a physically active man—reveled in his own physical exuberance and reveals this personal trait in the novel, especially in the two characters that are Dumas in disguise. In the era depicted in *The Chevalier de Maison-Rouge*, there was much material of a gruesome and painful character that could have found its way into Dumas' novel. The author, however, never dwells on the horrors of the torture chamber. He is all for the courage shown, not for the pain and cruelty inflicted and endured.

Accordingly, although his action scenes are not historical, Dumas is a master in depicting a duel or battle. The quarrel between Maurice and Dixmer, resulting in the mortal wound to Dixmer near the end of this novel, is an indication of that ability. The gusto of the novel's action scenes, however, is matched by the simplicity and yet the grandeur of his epic diction. Only such language is capable of portraying the enthusiasm of the protagonists, their loyalty, their courage, and the zest with which they approached a mystery or a beautiful woman.

On the other hand, *The Chevalier de Maison-Rouge* is not flawless, especially in terms of plot. The structure of the novel occasionally tends to be loose, and there are a number of inconsistencies in characterization. Yet, if judged in terms of the readers' reactions rather than according to codified mechanics, Dumas' novel has much unity and coherence.

"Critical Evaluation" by Stephen Hanson

Bibliography:
Dumas, Alexandre. *The Road to Monte Cristo: A Condensation from "The Memoirs of Alexandre Dumas."* Translated by Jules Eckert Goodman. New York: Scribner, 1956. Excellent, abridged translation of Dumas' memoirs that relate to his source material for his novels, including *The Chevalier de Maison-Rouge*.

Gorman, Herbert. *The Incredible Marquis, Alexandre Dumas*. New York: Farrar and Rinehart, 1929. Entertaining, popular biography of Dumas, *père* that chronicles the social circles in which he moved. Sheds light on biographical details of his life that enhance the readings of his novels.

Maurois, André. *The Titans, a Three-Generation Biography of the Dumas*. Translated by Gerard Hopkins. New York: Harper, 1957. Considered the authoritative biography of Dumas *père*, his father, and his son. Excellent bibliography. Approaches *The Chevalier de Maison Rouge* in a cursory fashion.

Schopp, Claude. *Alexandre Dumas: Genius of Life*. Translated by A. J. Koch. New York: Franklin Watts, 1988. A biographical and critical approach to the life and works of Dumas, *père*. Discusses Dumas' adaptation of *The Chevalier de Maison-Rouge* into a drama called *Les Girondins* to pay his bills.

Stowe, Richard S. *Alexandre Dumas (père)*. Boston: Twayne, 1976. An excellent starting point for an analysis of the life and works of Dumas, *père*, probably the best source in English. *The Chevalier de Maison Rouge* is analyzed in the chapter entitled "The Marie-Antoinette Romances," of which the novel is the fifth and final installment.

CHICAGO POEMS

Type of work: Poetry
Author: Carl Sandburg (1878-1967)
First published: 1916

The publication of *Chicago Poems* created a furor characteristic of the introduction of material that is new both in subject matter and in style. The subject matter frightened and infuriated the conservatives, who insisted that Carl Sandburg's topics were vulgar, indecent, and scarcely poetic. The poetry itself could not be scanned in the conventional way, was very free verse, and could not be called poetically beautiful. Liberal critics and readers, however, such as Harriet Monroe, the editor of *Poetry: A Magazine of Verse* who had "discovered" Sandburg as she had also "discovered" Vachel Lindsay, were convinced that Sandburg might be the great democratic poet called for by Walt Whitman and that his style of writing, his Whitmanesque barbaric yawp, was not only his own particular voice in poetry but also exactly the correction that conventional poetry needed.

Even Monroe's first reaction to Sandburg's totally new kind of writing was unsympathetic, so different was Sandburg from even the unconventional poets of the day. When Sandburg first submitted "Chicago," the title piece in the later volume, and eight other poems to Monroe for publication in *Poetry*, her first response was one of shock. As she read on, shock turned to admiration. She published the poems and subsequently championed the author, defending him against the criticism leveled against him after the appearance of *Chicago Poems.*

The some one hundred fifty poems in the volume, although of the same style and content, differ rather sharply in quality. At their best they are powerful, harsh when covering harsh subjects, but astonishingly gentle when discussing gentle subjects. At their worst they are chopped-up prose, sometimes duller than spoken language.

In the title poem, "Chicago," Sandburg looks at the boisterous capital of the Midwest, and with great love and admiration catalogs Chicago's glories as well as its degradation; or rather, in recognizing its weaknesses and seeing through and beyond them, he arrives at its greatness: the muscular vitality, the momentum, the real life that he loves. He shows Chicago as the capital of the meat-packing industry, the great manufacturer of the Midwest, the crossroads of rail lines. All of these are its glory. He also sees it as the city of wicked people, of crooks and gunmen, of prostitutes. Chicago is fierce, but it is a city of builders, proud of being sweaty, bareheaded, of destroying and rebuilding. Chicago, like the poet who sings its praises, is proud of being all these things.

The volume continues in this vein. Sandburg sees the city from its underbelly, the tenderloin, looking at it through the eyes of the men and women on the streets, the lost, the underprivileged, the exploited, the lonely, and the hated. In these poems he is, as he was called, the "mystical mobocrat." So comprehensive is his view that to read all the poems is to cover the whole seamy side of city life. Sandburg's feeling about these people and the conditions of their lives is not, however, one of despair. Although he sees the terror of poverty and lack of privilege, he believes in the happiness, the present, and the future of the poor of Chicago. His treatment of the people is optimistic and romantic.

"The Shovel Man" is a good example of this two-sided view of the same man. The laborer, as the poet sees him, is merely a person working with a shovel, a "dago," who works for very little money each day. This man's lot, however, is not discouraging, and does not fill him with despair. For to an Italian woman back in Tuscany, he is a much greater success than one could imagine.

Another successful man, glad to be alive and doing what he does for a living, is the "Fish Crier," a Jew down on Maxwell Street, who with his sharp voice daily cries out his herring to customers. Far from unhappy, he is delighted that God created the world as great as it is.

This theme is continued in the poem "Happiness." Sometimes there is a close approach to the mawkish and sentimental in Sandburg's sensibility. The democratic impulse sometimes carries him out of the realm of observation and common sense and into that of romanticized fantasy. In this poem Sandburg says he has asked professors and successful executives for the meaning of life, and they could not answer him, looking at him as though they felt he had meant to fool them. Then one Sunday afternoon he observed a group of Hungarians, with their beer and music, answering his philosophic question by unconsciously enjoying life merely by living it.

At times Sandburg quietly, in an undertone, states with telling effect the paradoxes and contradictions that exist in such a thriving city as Chicago, the city of the rich and the poor, the successful and the failures, the working and the jobless. In "Muckers," for example, he writes that twenty men are watching a group of men dig a ditch in preparation for new gas mains. Among the twenty are two distinctly different reactions. Ten men see the work as the sorriest drudgery, while the other ten wish desperately that they had the job.

The contrast in the ways of life in Chicago is furthered in "Child of the Romans." In this poem an Italian eats his noon meal of bread, bologna, and water beside the railroad track he is repairing. The poverty of his meal is spotlighted by the train that passes on the tracks he is repairing so that the ride on the train will be so smooth that nothing will disturb the wealthy passengers and their splendid living.

Another aspect of Chicago life, the lure of the city for the country woman, is brought out in the poem named simply "Mamie." The namesake of the poem comes from a small Indiana town, where she was bored and ached for the romance of the big city. Once in Chicago, however, working in a basement store, she continues to dream of another bigger and more romantic city where her dreams can be realized.

"Fellow Citizen" is another study of true happiness, in which Sandburg barks his belligerent democracy. The poet says he has associated with the best people in the best of clubs, with millionaires and mayors. The happiest man he knows is one who manufactures guitars and accordions. This man is happy because, in contrast with the rich and the powerful, he is not a money-grubber. He manufactures his accordions and guitars because he loves to, and he is so indifferent to money that he will scarcely mention price to someone who wants to buy his instruments. This man, says the poet, is the only person in Chicago for whom he ever held any jealousy.

There are other moods and other themes in this volume. Sandburg was familiar with the Imagist poets, their desire for simplicity and clarity, and although he disclaimed any influence from them, he did admit having been influenced by the Japanese poetry he had read. The section of his volume titled "Fogs and Fires" reveals characteristics of both types of verse.

"Nocturne in a Deserted Brickyard" is a gentle, hushed picture of a static moment of nature. Another quiet understatement is "Monotone." In "Monotone" the author is concerned with beauty and with what is beautiful. The monotone of the rain has this quality, as does the sun on the hills. Most beautiful of all, however, is a face that the poet knows, for it contains the aspects of beauty caught in all other bits of nature.

Perhaps one of the most deservedly popular of Sandburg's brief nature images is the six-line poem called simply "Fog." With compelling gentleness the noise and violence of blustery Chicago is diminished to a single image in which fog steals catlike up to the city, looks over it for a moment, and then moves on.

Other themes are evident in the volume. One, the weakness of words in conveying strong emotion, is revealed in "Onion Days," a poem concerning the Giovannitti family caught in the iron grip of an exploiting millionaire named Jasper. Although they are wracked by economic necessity, there is a dignity about the Giovannittis, a simple goodness that, says Sandburg, no novelist or playwright could adequately express.

Another theme is the transitoriness of life, the ultimate disappearance of all. "Gone" tells the story of Chick Lorimer, a "wild girl" whom everybody loved, but who finally disappeared. Nobody has even the vaguest idea where she went.

"Murmurings in a Field Hospital," in the "War Poems," tells of a soldier longing for what is past: a singing woman in the garden, an old man telling stories to children, and his own past. This theme of the stupidity and uselessness of war constitutes many of Sandburg's powerful statements.

Early readers found *Chicago Poems* a work of tremendous impact; its voice was that of people talking and protesting in a manner never before attempted; its smell was of sweat, of the stockyards. Though Sandburg's ultimate status in the history of poetry has not yet been established, there can be no doubt that this volume was a powerful influence on the poetic revival during and after World War I.

Bibliography:
Allen, Gay Wilson. *Carl Sandburg*. Minneapolis: University of Minnesota Press, 1972. Brief but useful introduction to Sandburg's poetry, with specific references to *Chicago Poems*.
Callahan, North. *Carl Sandburg: His Life and Works*. University Park: Pennsylvania State University Press, 1987. Overview of Sandburg's career, with sensitive readings of his poems. Chapters 5, 6, and 7 focus on Sandburg's Chicago experience and the poetry he produced during that period.
_____. *Carl Sandburg: Lincoln of Our Literature*. New York: New York University Press, 1970. A critical biography of Sandburg that includes comment on his Chicago years.
Crowder, Richard. *Carl Sandburg*. New York: Twayne, 1964. One of the best general discussions of Sandburg's life and career. Relates how Harriet Monroe arranged for the publication of "Chicago" and other poems in *Poetry: A Magazine of Verse* in March, 1914, and the literary establishment's negative reaction to this unconventional poetry. Useful chronology of Sandburg's life; selected bibliography.
Niven, Penelope. *Carl Sandburg: A Biography*. New York: Charles Scribner's Sons, 1991. A first-rate critical biography of Sandburg that includes a section on "The Chicago Years" and the poet's creative work during that period. Perhaps the best single work to date on Sandburg and his art.

THE CHICKENCOOP CHINAMAN

Type of work: Drama
Author: Frank Chin (1940-   )
Type of plot: Comedy
Time of plot: Late 1960's
Locale: Oakland district of Pittsburgh, Pennsylvania
First performed: 1972; first published, 1981

> *Principal characters:*
> TAM LUM, a Chinese American filmmaker
> KENJI, a Japanese American research dentist
> LEE, Chinese American possibly passing for white, Robbie's mother
> ROBBIE, Lee's son
> CHARLEY POPCORN, a former boxing trainer who runs a porno house in
>   Pittsburgh; Tam Lum has come to interview him for his latest movie
>   project
> THE LONE RANGER, a legendary hero of the Old West
> TONTO, the Lone Ranger's American Indian companion
> TOM, Lee's former husband and current fiancé

The Story:

Tam Lum, a Chinese American filmmaker and writer, went to Pittsburgh to interview Charley Popcorn for a documentary film. Tam believed that Popcorn was the father of famous light-heavyweight boxing champion Ovaltine Jack Dancer. In Pittsburgh, Tam Lum stayed with his childhood friend, "BlackJap" Kenji, a research dentist. Also living in Kenji's apartment were Lee and her son Robbie. They were awaiting the arrival of Lee's latest fiancé, another Chinese American, Tom. Tom was currently at work on his latest book, a cookbook entitled *Soul on Rice* (a play on Eldridge Cleaver's *Soul on Ice,* 1967).

Lee accused Tam, a caustic character, of hating his Chinese heritage, a charge that he immediately denied. She also accused Kenji of being prejudiced against African Americans. Tam answered that this was untrue because he and Kenji attended school with African Americans and Mexican Americans. If they had not dressed and behaved like the other students, they would have been beaten everyday. Now this antagonistic behavior toward African Americans and Latinos had become normal for them. Kenji joined the conversation, saying that he was not imitating African Americans. He lived with them and participated in their culture because he was as unsure of Japanese American culture as Tam was of Chinese American culture.

Although Tam pretended to hate everything that was part of the white culture, Lee reminded him that his former wife, Barbara, was white and that his children were biracial. She believed that his marriage to a white American was a further attempt to erase his Chinese identity.

Tam then declared that he did not like being part of the "model minority." This designation was yet another stereotype, though a positive one. Tam saw Asians as the type of immigrant the United States wanted: passive, hardworking, and highly educated. White Americans had praised Tam for being Americanized and for the absence of juvenile delinquency in Chinatown. There was no delinquency, he explains, because there were no children. There were no children because there were no women. There were no women because the terms of the 1882 Chinese

Exclusion Act prohibited the entry of Chinese women into the United States. Furthermore, under law, Chinese women born in the United States would lose their citizenship if they married a man from China.

In Act II, scene i, Tam had a strange dream that included the Lone Ranger and Tonto. Tam was reminiscing about his childhood spent listening to popular radio programs, including "The Lone Ranger." He also read about the Lone Ranger in the comic section of the Sunday newspapers. Tam, looking for the Chinese presence in American culture, identified very strongly with the Lone Ranger. The only evidence of "Chineseness" that he found in American culture was the Lone Ranger. Tam believed that the Lone Ranger wore a mask in order to hide his Asian identity by hiding his Asian eyes. In Tam's dream, while he was reminiscing about him, the Lone Ranger appeared and shot Tam in the hand, damaging his writing career.

The Lone Ranger could only identify Tam with the traditional Chinese occupation of launderer. He, like Kenji, associated Asian Americans with Helen Keller, claiming that she reminded him of the three Chinese monkeys that see no evil, hear no evil, and speak no evil. The Lone Ranger also reiterated the theory of Asian Americans as the model minority, fabled law-abiding citizens, and dubbed them "honorary whites."

After Tam awoke, he and Kenji went to meet Charley Popcorn at the movie theater. Their Asian appearance surprised Popcorn; he had expected them to be African American. He took an immediate dislike to them, but not necessarily because of racial bias. Popcorn had internalized the American stereotype of Asians, although Popcorn explained his dislike of Asian Americans as coming from their treatment of African Americans.

Tam and Kenji returned to the apartment with Tam symbolically carrying Popcorn on his back. Tom, Lee's fiancé, had also arrived at the apartment. Tom told the gathering that he was writing a book, not the Chinese cookbook, *Soul on Rice*, but a book on Chinese American identity. He apparently had accepted the definition of others who had made his group part of the model minority.

However, since Popcorn continued to deny fathering Ovaltine Jack Dancer, Tam decided to change his documentary to a straightforward professional boxing film. At the end of the play, Tam was in the kitchen wishing that his children knew and understood their history.

Critical Evaluation:

Frank Chin, essayist, novelist, short-story writer, and playwright, is probably the most prolific Chinese American writer of the late twentieth century. In *The Chickencoop Chinaman*, he brings together his ideas on the history and position of Chinese Americans in the society, history, and culture of the United States. In the first scene of *The Chickencoop Chinaman*, Chin establishes the play's themes: the absence of a Chinese American identity, the lack of respect for Asian women, and the emasculation of Asian American men by American culture. Chinese Americans, according to Chin, are not born. Instead, racists using various parts of the culture of the western United States created them. He writes that Americans manufactured Chinese American identity in a chicken coop " . . . nylon and acrylic . . . a miracle synthetic!"

The chicken coop in the title refers to Chin's perception of Chinatown as a zoo or a dirty, noisy, foul-smelling place occupied by people who speak an unintelligible language. In many of his works, Chin depicts the Chinese of Chinatown as insects or frogs. He does not regard Chinatown as an ethnic enclave where the Chinese congregated to preserve their culture. Instead, Chin sees it as a product of American racism, of discriminatory housing laws.

The Chickencoop Chinaman depicts the cultural and historical dilemma of Tam Lum, who is insecure in his cultural identity and his place in American history and society. Chin uses

Chinaman, an offensive term to some, because to him Chinese American suggests a split personality, half Chinese and half American; the phrase Chinese American also symbolizes assimilated Chinese Americans, not those who are aware of their history and culture.

The action takes place in Oakland, the mainly African American section of Pittsburgh, in the 1960's. This period was a time of protest against the inequities in American society. Chin uses this period because Asian Americans also began protesting their exclusion. He includes his frequently stated conviction that an Asian American sensibility cannot be found by imitating African Americans, although, in the play, Chin does recognize the groundbreaking efforts of African Americans in the Civil Rights movement.

Tam, who may be Chin's alter ego, is vitriolic about his Chinese American identity, insisting that Helen Keller is the metaphorical equivalent of Chinese Americans. Chinese Americans, like Keller, see no evil, hear no evil, and speak no evil about American racism. Keller overcame her disabilities not by rioting or protesting but by passively accepting them, becoming a model American citizen. Chinese Americans imitated Keller to overcome their racial impediments, becoming the model minority.

A western hero, the Lone Ranger, is ironically the idol of Tam's youth. Searching for the presence of his group in American culture, Tam discovered the Lone Ranger. He is Tam's hero not only because the mask supposedly hid the Lone Ranger's Asian eyes, but because he applies Chinese color symbolism in wearing a red shirt for good luck and riding a white horse to bring death. The Lone Ranger, as a westerner with a long history of anti-Chinese sentiment, arrogantly assigns Tam and all other Chinese Americans their place in American history as honorary whites. This assignment is unacceptable to Tam because the Chinese were an essential element of the history of the American West. Many Chinese Americans have ignored their history in the United States in their eagerness for acceptance.

Tom, Lee's fiancé, is the only character who accepts the designation model minority. He repeats the media hyperbole of Asians being the ethnic group with the lowest crime rate and highest education level.

Additionally, the emasculation and feminization of Chinese American males are favorite themes that Chin stresses in *The Chickencoop Chinaman*. The dominant culture has stereotyped Asian American men as effeminate. In the play, Chin seems to dramatize what he has written in his essays: that the stereotype of Chinese American men places them outside the John Wayne mold of white American masculinity. He adds that the dominant society considers African Americans and Latinos more masculine, therefore more threatening.

Chin classifies *The Chickencoop Chinaman* as a comedy. However, The *Chickencoop Chinaman* more appropriately fits the definition of a comedy of common sense. In this type of comedy, a character must maintain a careful balance between the theoretical standards of human conduct and the practical demands of society. Therefore, at the end of the play the conflict is unresolved because Tam has not maintained that balance. He is in the kitchen chopping green onions with a Chinese cleaver. He has rejected Cheerios, Aunt Jemima pancakes, and Chun King chop suey, all symbols of American culture. The issue of his identity is still unresolved. He is neither white American nor African American. He is something new, unique, a Chinaman.

Mary Young

Bibliography:
Chin, Frank, et al. *Aiiieeee! An Anthology of Asian American Writers*. New York: Mentor, 1991.
    Contains Act I of *The Chickencoop Chinaman* and some biographical information.

Davis, Robert Murray. "Frank Chin: Iconoclastic Icon." *Redneck Review of Literature* 23 (Fall, 1992): 75-78. A brief analysis of many of Chin's works, including *The Chickencoop Chinaman.*

Kim, Elaine H. *Asian American Literature: An Introduction to the Writings and Their Social Context.* Philadelphia: Temple University Press, 1982. Contains a synopsis and an evaluation of many of Chin's works, including *The Chickencoop Chinaman.*

Li, David Leiwei. "The Formation of Frank Chin and Formations of Chinese-American Literature." In *Asian Americans: Comparative and Global Perspectives.* Edited by Shirley Hune et al. Pullman: Washington State University Press, 1991. Explains Chin's reordering of Chinese American history and his application of that history to *The Chickencoop Chinaman.* Evaluates Chin's impact on Asian American literature.

McDonald, Dorothy Ritsuko. "An Introduction to Frank Chin's *The Chickencoop Chinaman* and *The Year of the Dragon.*" In *Three American Literatures: Essays in Chicano, Native American, and Asian-American Literature for Teachers of American Literature.* Edited by Houston A. Baker. New York: Modern Language Association of America, 1982. Probably the best critical analysis of *The Chickencoop Chinaman* and *The Year of the Dragon* (1974).

CHILD OF GOD

Type of work: Novel
Author: Cormac McCarthy (1933-   )
Type of plot: Social realism
Time of plot: Early 1960's
Locale: Sevier County, Tennessee, in the Appalachian Mountains
First published: 1973

Principal characters:
> LESTER BALLARD, a young, solitary man
> FATE TURNER, the high sheriff of Sevier County
> JOHN GREER, an outsider who buys Ballard's house
> REUBEL, a dumpkeeper, Ballard's drinking companion

The Story:

Under the supervision of Fate Turner, the high sheriff of Sevier County, a farm was being auctioned off for nonpayment of taxes. When the owner, Lester Ballard, threatened the auctioneer with a rifle, one of the men assembled at the auction hit Lester in the head with an ax and took him away. From that time on, Lester had difficulty holding up his head. The blow might also have affected his mind. Because of Lester's behavior, many local people were afraid to bid on the land, and it went to John Greer, an outsider. Lester Ballard was determined to kill Greer.

Lester had no home and no way to support himself, without even enough money to buy whiskey; but he was not defeated. Deep in the woods he found a deserted house, cleaned it up, brought his few possessions to it, and moved in. He survived by stealing food and shooting game. He had no way, however, to fulfill his sexual needs. One night he relieved himself while watching a couple having intercourse in a car, but when they saw him, they fled. Sometimes Lester visited Reubel, in hopes that one of his nine promiscuous daughters would help him, but they only laughed at him.

Lester had always been mean, but after he lost his farm, he seemed to go crazy. It was inevitable that he would get in trouble. One fall morning, while he was hunting, Lester found a woman lying on the ground, where she had evidently passed out drunk. They fought; then Lester ripped off the nightgown she was wearing and carried it away with him, leaving her naked. Later, the woman charged Lester with rape, and he was put in jail, where he spent nine rather pleasant days, eating his fill and enjoying the company of another inmate. After Lester was released, Fate warned him to stay out of Sevierville and out of trouble, predicting that if he did not change his attitude, Lester would end up murdering someone. Defiantly, Lester said that he did not care about the people of the town, or, he suggested, anyone else.

Lester still needed a woman. At a county fair, he shot a rifle so well that he won three stuffed animals and was chased away by the pitchman. Despite his skill and his trophies, the pretty girls in the crowd turned away from him. Lester went home alone, carrying two toy bears and a tiger.

Hoping to win the favor of one of the girls in the area, Lester captured a live robin and, despite her mother's objections, gave it as a toy to the girl's retarded child. When the child chewed off the bird's legs, the two women were annoyed and disgusted, and Lester left their house.

One December morning, Lester found the solution to his frustrations. He happened upon a car in which a man and a woman were lying dead, victims of carbon monoxide poisoning. Lester's first thought was to take their money, their whiskey, and the woman's makeup. Then he had an inspiration. Returning to the scene of the accident, he carried off the woman's corpse. At his house, he put her in the nightgown he had taken earlier from the drunk, and he hoisted her body into the attic. Later, in Sevierville, he bought sexy clothing for his find, and from that time on, whenever he needed a woman, he brought the corpse down from the attic and used it. Now Lester had money, as well as food and shelter, and even someone he could pretend was his wife. Since he had hidden the car and the man's body, Lester thought he was secure. One night, however, the house caught fire and burned to the ground. Lester was able to save some possessions, including his stuffed animals, but the body in the attic was totally consumed.

Still undefeated, Lester made his home in a cave. On one of his forays, he encountered Greer, but Lester made no threats. In fact, he even denied that he was the man whose property Greer now owned. His revenge could wait; he had more pressing needs. Finding the girl with the retarded child alone in her house, he made sexual advances to her. When she rejected him, he killed her and then burned down her house, with the child inside. Fate's prediction had come true; now Lester had become a murderer.

When Lester was arrested, however, it was merely for setting fire to the house where he had been living, and again he was released. Now Lester turned his attention to Greer. He took pleasure in stealing eggs from the man he believed had stolen so much from him, and he spent most of his time hiding near Greer's house, watching him and brooding upon revenge. So far, Lester had managed to cover his tracks. Even when Fate found the car in which the couple had died, he had no reason to connect Lester with the missing girl, and Lester remained free. Having given up on women who were alive, he now decided to procure dead ones. When he found a couple parked in a pickup truck, he killed them both and took the dead girl to his cave. Again, however, the cards seemed to be stacked against him. In the spring floods, he lost not only the girl's body, but most of his possessions, even the stuffed animals. The little he had left, Lester dragged farther up the mountain, depositing it in his new home, a sinkhole.

Then everything went wrong. When Lester tried to kill Greer, he succeeded only in wounding him. Greer shot back, and Lester awoke in the hospital with an arm missing. Certain that Lester was responsible for the other crimes, a mob seized him, and in order to keep from being lynched, Lester admitted his guilt and offered to take the men to the bodies. However, after he had led them into a cave, Lester got away and made his way safely back to the hospital. Judged insane, he was confined in a mental institution, where he died of pneumonia. One spring day, a farmer's team disappeared into a sinkhole, and, exploring the chamber below, the sheriff found the bodies of seven women. At last Lester's victims could be properly buried.

Critical Evaluation:

Although Cormac McCarthy has not won the fame or attained the financial success of many of his contemporaries, his works have received high praise from critics and from other writers. Technically, he has even been called superior to William Faulkner, another Southern writer, who in 1949 won the Nobel Prize in Literature. McCarthy's skills with spoken and written language are evident in *Child of God*, in which he moves easily from the laconic, colorful dialogue of his Tennessee mountaineers to descriptive passages whose lyricism is as often inspired by junked cars and moldy mattresses as by the beauty of the natural setting.

McCarthy's handling of narrative is as brilliant as his use of language. *Child of God* is on one level the story of a single man, Lester Ballard, during a relatively brief period of time. The narrator also reaches far into the historic past to describe the misdeeds of Lester's distant ancestors and of a whole troubled society; McCarthy thus gives his novel intellectual depth and thematic complexity. Similarly, the references to Lester's own history, whether they are presented through his dreams and reveries or through the narrator's vivid anecdotes, make Lester a more complicated character than might be assumed, given his appalling activities.

Lester's necrophilia, in particular, aroused the ire of some reviewers. Some who had praised McCarthy's previous work expressed disgust with *Child of God* and relegated its author to the ranks of those who peddle the grotesque with a Southern setting.

Other critics, however, have found much to interest them in *Child of God*. Some have even called the book a masterpiece. They point out that McCarthy is careful to emphasize Lester's humanity. One can understand the feelings of the boy who is abandoned by his mother, then deserted a second time when his father commits suicide, and of the man who is rejected whenever he reaches out to another human being. On a theological level, Lester's evil impulses can be explained by his being human. The question which must be asked is whether Fate's warnings constitute an offer of redemption, or whether, in Calvinistic terms, Lester was not born one of the elect but rather born damned.

Lester Ballard can also be viewed from a historical perspective. While murder, rape, and necrophilia would hardly have met the approval of any Jeffersonian democrat, it is true that Lester possesses many of the qualities that were admired on the frontier and that are still cherished by Americans with an agrarian leaning. He is an independent farmer, willing to fight to keep his land; when he is deprived of it, he remains independent, using his resourcefulness to live off the land. Clearly McCarthy does not intend to make of Lester a tragic hero; however, given the territorial imperative of an earlier time, it is not surprising that this man who makes his home in the wilderness sees the cars and trucks that invade his territory, and their inhabitants, as fair game. It could also be argued that although the way in which Lester expresses his territoriality is not acceptable in modern society, the impulse is simply another facet of human nature. After all, when Lester ventures outside of his own area, as when he sells the watches he has acquired, he is mocked, cheated, and expelled by the community. McCarthy does not equate the territorial impulse with depravity, but like a good Southerner he seems to understand it. He may be suggesting that the territorial impulse is as basic to human beings as is their desire to do evil.

If the real theme of *Child of God* is human nature, the author leaves readers with more questions than answers. Aside from his technical virtuosity, McCarthy's creation of Lester Ballard, a character who is at once despicable, pitiable, tragic, doomed, and damned, should assure McCarthy's place in Southern literature.

Rosemary M. Canfield Reisman

Bibliography:
Bartlett, Andrew. "From Voyeurism to Archaeology: Cormac McCarthy's *Child of God.*" *Southern Literary Journal* 24 (Fall, 1991): 3-15. Argues that the real focus of *Child of God* is not its sociopathic protagonist but the question of how he should be perceived. An incisive study of technique and theme.
Bell, Vereen M. *The Achievement of Cormac McCarthy*. Baton Rouge: Louisiana State University Press, 1988. The first book-length study of McCarthy. Devotes one chapter to *Child of God*; the introduction is also helpful.
Grammer, John. "A Thing Against Which Time Will Not Prevail: Pastoral and History in Cor-

mac McCarthy's South." *The Southern Quarterly* 30 (Summer, 1992): 19-30. An important essay, showing how one of the major themes in Southern literature is basic to McCarthy's thought. Lester Ballard meets his doom because he is an anachronism.

Winchell, Mark Royden. "Inner Dark: or, The Place of Cormac McCarthy." *Southern Review* 26 (Spring, 1990): 293-309. An excellent introduction. Argues that although in some ways McCarthy surpasses even Faulkner, only *Child of God* is likely to endure.

CHILDE HAROLD'S PILGRIMAGE

Type of work: Poetry
Author: George Gordon, Lord Byron (1788-1824)
Type of plot: Picaresque
Time of plot: Middle Ages
Locale: Europe
First published: 1812-1818

Principal characters:
LORD BYRON, the author
CHILDE HAROLD, a young traveler
JULIA, Childe Harold's first true love

The Story:

Childe Harold, a young English nobleman, became despondent, because the only young woman he loved would not return that love. He had long been engaged in drinking and general idleness, and was generally seen as a very unpleasant character by almost everyone, including his parents. Desperate, he decided to embark on a journey in an attempt to find happiness, or at least to give some meaning to his life.

He left England by ship, with no clear destination. As he left, he sang a mournful song, bidding farewell to his homeland, to his parents, and especially to his young page. He landed on the shore of Portugal and found himself moved in strange and unexpected ways. He began exploring the land on horseback, moving aimlessly in search of his destiny. He wandered into the mountains northeast of Lisbon, a land called Cintra.

Harold found the land beautiful. At the same time, he found the people to be dirty and immoral. He lamented on the sorry state of such men and women blessed with such a beautiful land, and continued into France.

In France, as in Portugal, Childe Harold found a beautiful land but a decadent people. He lamented that everywhere it seemed that the ancient glories were gone, replaced by the ruins of once beautiful works and a people who could not live up to their glorious heritage. He moved on to Spain.

In Spain, he was again thrilled by the magnificence of the scenery but appalled at the depths to which the civilization had fallen. His first real understanding of human cruelty occurred in Spain, where he watched a bullfight. He watched the cruelty of the humans tormenting the bull and the courage of the beast, who clearly could not understand why anyone was trying to hurt him. The bullfight, as always, ended in the death of the bull but brought Harold no further in his quest to understand the meaning of his life.

Childe Harold's first real change of heart occurred as he traveled through Albania into Greece, where he met a great many people of a variety of nationalities and religions. He found the Albanians to be barbaric by his standards, but in some ways nobler than the more civilized people he had encountered thus far. His spirits began to rise as he realized that whatever the situation of civilization, there was still great hope in both the wonders of nature and the natural state of humanity.

The next great change came in Germany, along the banks of the Rhine. There, finally feeling a sense of hope and beginning to see some meaning in the human condition, he was able to fall in love for the first time since he had left home. While he still lamented his first lost love, he found a young woman named Julia and found once again true love, although it was a very different sort of love from the love he had known before.

For the first time, Childe Harold was able to accept a love without the physical rewards of sex. He sang love songs to Julia but did not feel himself worthy to be her lover, and he soon left, feeling better but still in need of answers to the basic questions of life.

The journey ended in Rome, after long journeys through the Italian countryside and the ancient cities that were once part of the Roman Empire. He died in Rome, still unfulfilled, but having learned much about the world, and about human nature.

Critical Evaluation:

George Gordon, Lord Byron, was one of the greatest poets of the Romantic Era of British literature. He was a rebel, a malcontent, and a traveler. While Byron was writing *Childe Harold's Pilgrimage*, he was himself traveling; he visited all of the places he described in the poem.

The poem is difficult in several ways. It was published in three sections, over a span of six years, and Byron wrote other works in between. Since the poem was written, critics have widely disagreed as to its meaning and even as to whether it should be considered as two separate poems, or even three.

The first two cantos (the equivalent of chapters in prose) were published in 1812 and are as much a travelogue as they are the story of a pilgrimage. Byron interrupts his narrative regularly to make political and sociological comments about his own time. Often, it is difficult to know when Harold is speaking and when the poet Byron is commenting.

According to his introduction to the first two cantos, Byron intended the poem to be a long narrative poem in the style (and even the meter) of Edmund Spenser, a sixteenth century English poet. The language of the first two cantos is deliberately archaic, as was Spenser's deliberately "medieval" sounding poem. Byron uses Middle English words such as "whilome" and "hight," and the very title is intended to lend a medieval flavor to the work: "Childe" was originally a term used to refer to a young man approaching knighthood, but it had taken on its current meaning (and spelling) centuries before Byron was born.

Many critics have insisted that in Childe Harold, Byron was merely fictionalizing his own life. While this is not literally true—the two have much in common—Harold is more of a literary device than a real human being. This becomes increasingly obvious in the third and fourth cantos.

In canto 3, published in 1816, Harold appears only briefly. This section is almost entirely dedicated to a description of Greece and its environs, with a lamentation that the ancient glory has been lost. References are made quite directly to the emperor Napoleon (who lived contemporaneously with Byron), to contemporary poets including John Keats, and even to Byron's personal friends.

In the introduction to canto 4 (1817), Byron virtually disowns Harold, explaining that since virtually everyone seemed to assume that he was Byron's alter ego, there was no longer any point to keeping up the pretense. The entire canto, by far the largest of the four, is dedicated to a description of Rome, historically and currently. Childe Harold makes only a very brief appearance at the end, essentially to die and end the original story.

Childe Harold's Pilgrimage is not very exciting as a romantic quest. On one level—the shallowest level of the poem, and the least satisfying—it is the story of Harold's journey, but "pilgrimage" is probably an inappropriate word for this journey. Harold is never searching for anything specific; rather, he is running away from his past and trying, in the process, to find some meaning in life.

Byron's own pilgrimage was of quite a different sort. He was a member of the nobility, a wealthy man, and a highly successful writer. He had domestic problems, and the divorce from his first wife was a scandal of sorts. He lived in various parts of Europe, rarely in England. He had very specific viewpoints, and he had no problem in making them known.

Suffusing *Childe Harold's Pilgrimage*, and many other of Byron's poems, is a love of nature, a sentiment characteristic of all the Romantic poets, of whom Byron was perhaps the most famous during his own time. There are also powerful political messages, most of them having to do with the decadence Byron perceived in his own times, as compared to the glorious past of ancient Greece and Rome. At a deeper level, there was the question of human identity itself.

The sections of the poem that directly relate to Childe Harold are rendered in the Spenserian meter and archaic language alluded to above, but at times both the meter and the language change considerably. Byron's dedications at the beginnings of the cantos, and the love poems interspersed throughout, are written in much more modern form. Finally, in the fourth canto, the medieval language is almost entirely gone, replaced by the language that Byron spoke himself, with only a few outmoded words to preserve some of the flavor of the earlier sections and try to give some coherence to the whole.

It is essential to view *Childe Harold's Pilgrimage* in its historical context. When it was written, the French Revolution had failed, and Napoleon had assumed the robes of emperor—deeply disappointing the idealistic Romantics, who had seen the French Revolution and Napoleon as beacons, leading the way to a bright new era of Republican liberty, equality, and brotherhood. Although Byron and many of his contemporaries longed for bygone days, they also emphasized the dignity of humankind and the importance of equality. The rise of Napoleon, his subsequent fall, and the return of the French monarchy were tragedies. So, too, was the destruction of many ancient works and the barbarism of the Reign of Terror.

The influence of this poem on later literature is great. There are no earlier or later versions of the specific tale, but its echoes are immense. In Childe Harold, the "Byronic hero" was born, a literary device that has lasted to the present day. The Byronic hero is essentially an antihero, alienated and rebellious. This is a very difficult type to portray effectively, because although the hero may be depicted as extremely unpleasant (as is Harold himself), the reader must sympathize with him.

The essential point is that although Childe Harold certainly changes during the narrative, his basic nature never changes. Even when he falls in love, even when he describes great beauty, the reader knows he can never be happy. For happiness, he would require an impossible world, an ideal which can never be achieved. Nevertheless, he will continue searching for that ideal, against all odds.

Ultimately, Byron's basic goal in *Childe Harold's Pilgrimage* is to explore the nature of humankind and humanity's relation to nature. The descriptions of natural and ancient architectural beauty are far more moving than the descriptions of Childe Harold and his journey. Byron's long forays into social criticism are even more fascinating.

A contemporary writer would probably make the central points of this poem in a political essay. Once the difficulties of language, and the sometimes confusing switches in personas, are overcome, however, Byron's method is far more effective. His long poem, written in deliberately outdated language and meter, is still strangely moving, even to a person living in a society far removed from Byron's. Even when it is uncertain whether the traveler is Childe Harold or Lord Byron, the journey is compelling, and the reader wants to join the pilgrimage.

Marc Goldstein

Bibliography:
Byron, George Gordon, Lord. *Works.* Edited by Ernest Hartley Coleridge. 13 vols. New York: Octagon Books, 1966. Originally published between 1898 and 1904 in thirteen volumes, this is a complete collection of all Byron's poetry and prose, along with extensive introductions and notes, both by the editor and by Byron himself. *Childe Harold's Pilgrimage* appears in volume 2.

Gleckner, Robert F. *Byron and the Ruins of Paradise.* Baltimore: The Johns Hopkins University Press, 1967. A critical discussion of Byron's viewpoint, as seen through his poetry. Byron's views of natural beauty and human failings are emphasized. Two chapters are dedicated to *Childe Harold's Pilgrimage*, an excellent example of these feelings.

Jump, John D., ed. *Byron: A Symposium.* New York: Barnes & Noble, 1975. A collection of essays on Byron and his poetical works, by various authors. "The Poet of Childe Harold," by Francis Berry, emphasizes the stylistic devices of *Childe Harold's Pilgrimage* and other works Byron wrote during the same period, in relation to the works of his contemporaries and of later writers.

Marchand, Leslie A. *Byron's Poetry: A Critical Introduction.* Boston: Houghton Mifflin, 1965. A general introduction to Byron's poetry, intended for twentieth century students and general readers. This book places Byron's work in the context of the literary tradition he followed, the works of his contemporaries, and the historical times in which Byron lived.

Thorslev, Peter L. *The Byronic Hero: Types and Prototypes.* Minneapolis: University of Minnesota Press, 1962. A study of the alienated antihero common in Romantic poetry, essentially created by Byron, especially in Childe Harold. Emphasis is placed on the historical background of Byron's times.

CHILDREN OF A LESSER GOD

Type of work: Drama
Author: Mark Medoff (1940-   )
Type of plot: Psychological realism
Time of plot: Late 1970's
Locale: A state school for the deaf
First performed: 1979; first published, 1980

> *Principal characters:*
> JAMES LEEDS, a speech teacher in his thirties
> SARAH NORMAN, deaf from birth, age twenty-six
> MRS. NORMAN, her mother
> ORIN DENNIS, a hearing-impaired student and campus activist
> LYDIA, a hearing-impaired student
> MR. FRANKLIN, the superintendent of the school

The Story:

James Leeds, a new speech teacher at a state school for the deaf, was working with Orin Dennis to improve his ability to pronounce English. The superintendent, Mr. Franklin, introduced James to Sarah Norman, a twenty-six-year-old deaf woman who did not read lips or use speech, preferring to communicate exclusively in American Sign Language (ASL). Even though James's charm intrigued her, she informed him, with deliberate rudeness, that speech therapy was a waste of time. Sarah's hearing mother, Mrs. Norman, chided James for trying to get Sarah to speak and read lips so that she could pass for a hearing person. James responded that he was only trying to help Sarah function in the hearing world.

In his next meeting with her, James tried reaching Sarah with humor. When she was not amused, James apologized for using hearing idioms and promised to remember that she was deaf. She was skeptical, but accepted his offer to go out for Italian food. In the restaurant James asked Sarah why she did not want speech therapy. She responded that ASL was just as good as English, but James countered that ASL was only good among the deaf. Sarah accused him of wanting to be God, making her over in his own image. The next day, James discovered that Orin knew everything about his date with Sarah. Orin complained that deaf students did not want to be changed simply because hearing teachers wanted to change them. Orin vowed that someday he would change the deaf education system.

Sarah and James were becoming attracted to each other. When Lydia, a teenage student, tried to join them by the duck pond, Sarah chased her away. James was oblivious to Lydia's infatuation with him. After Sarah left, Mr. Franklin appeared from the trees and warned James that having sex with a student would lead to dismissal. James learned from Mrs. Norman that Sarah had stopped trying to speak because she believed people would think she was retarded. James nevertheless tried again to convince Sarah to use her voice. Sarah retorted that the only successful "communication" she ever had with hearing boys was in bed. James realized that he wanted to communicate with her no matter what the language. He and Sarah began an affair in her dorm room. Orin was outraged. He wanted Sarah for his political agenda. Lydia was jealous and informed Mr. Franklin, who again threatened to terminate James, so James and Sarah decided to get married. She confided that she wanted to become a teacher for the deaf and to have deaf children. Orin tried to tell Sarah, and Mr. Franklin tried to tell James, why their marriage could not work. James proclaimed that communication would cause no problems, but immediately caught himself trying to censor the conversation for Sarah. He realized he had no right to decide what she could and could not "hear." The next day, alone, they were married. Sarah and James moved into faculty housing and Sarah began to enjoy life in the hearing world. When Orin visited her, he urged Sarah not to turn her back on the deaf and informed her that his lawyer was investigating injustices perpetrated by the school. Sarah was beginning to feel caught between the deaf and hearing worlds. Orin's lawyer decided to file a complaint with the Equal Employment Opportunity Commission because of the lack of deaf teachers at the school. Orin wanted Sarah to join his cause because she was "pure deaf." He argued that deaf rights were more important than her marriage. When the lawyer arrived, Sarah and James decided to support Orin's complaint. During their meeting, Sarah realized that James wanted to change her into a hearing person, that Orin wanted her to remain "pure deaf," and that the lawyer wanted her to be angry about her deafness so that the commission would feel sorry for her. Orin and Sarah were both unhappy when they read the lawyer's brief because it was written from a hearing perspective. James suggested that the deaf protesters be allowed to speak for themselves, but Orin wanted to speak for Sarah too. Outraged by the hypocrisy, Sarah stormed off to write her speech alone.

James found Sarah and tried to make up with her. She asked him to watch her speech, but James was devastated when Sarah told him he could not interpret for her before the commission because she could not say, through a hearing person, how she felt as a deaf person. Deeply hurt, James resorted to bitter accusations, finally goading Sarah into speaking—an eruption of passionate, unintelligible sounds that shocked and repulsed him. Humiliated by James's reaction to her voice, she exploded in ASL and ran away.

Even without Sarah's testimony, Orin won the grievance, but it was a hollow victory. When James found Sarah at home with her mother, Sarah explained that she finally realized that it was she who did not have the right to change him. She no longer wanted deaf children, believing that people did not have the right to create others in their own image. James left, hoping that someday they might be able to help each other.

Critical Evaluation:

Children of a Lesser God followed William Gibson's *The Miracle Worker*, the last Broadway play to include a major deaf character, by twenty years. The two plays can be seen as metaphors for the deaf cultures of their time. In 1960, America was becoming aware of the deaf community, just as Helen Keller became aware of language. The intervening years brought the National Theatre for the Deaf, improved educational opportunities such as the National Technical Institute for the Deaf, the cultural attention of such groups as the American Theatre Association which established the Program on Drama and Theatre by, with and for the Handicapped, and civil rights legislation which included protection for individuals with handicapping conditions. In 1980, deaf political activists, such as Orin in *Children of a Lesser God*, were beginning to have the impact that would lead to the 1988 Deaf President Now protest at Gallaudet University in Washington, D.C. Just as Sarah does in the play, the deaf community was demanding the right to represent and speak for itself.

Ostensibly a love story, one of *Children of a Lesser God*'s most significant contributions is the accurate portrayal of the complex issues facing the deaf community. Not all deaf people are the same. Two students are portrayed using residual hearing, reading lips and having the ability to speak. Sarah, on the other hand, refuses to use her voice, wear a hearing aid, or read lips, preferring American Sign Language (ASL), the language of the manual deaf community. There is a hearing-impaired hierarchy; the hard-of-hearing think they're better than the "pure deaf." The goal of hearing teachers is to force deaf students to speak so they will be able to function in the hearing world, whether they want to or not. Several scenes in the play, such as the depiction of Sarah responding to music, are included merely to inform the audience about deafness.

Mark Medoff's recurring theme of self-discovery is developed primarily through the character of Sarah. In the beginning, she proclaims that others do not have the right to re-create her in their image. She expresses her desire to have deaf children. Later she realizes that those around her want to re-create her for their own selfish purposes. James still wants her to function as a hearing person. Orin still wants to preserve her as a dependent "pure deaf" pawn in his political movement. The lawyer-activist still wants her to be an object of pity. In the end, Sarah's triumph is to recognize that oppressive trait within herself. She no longer wants to have deaf children, because not even she has the right to re-create someone in her own image.

When Mark Medoff decided to write this play for deaf actress Phyllis Frelich, he did not realize he would have to devise a new literary technique in order to communicate to both the play's theatrical and reading audiences. Like the actress, the play's main character, Sarah Norman, communicated exclusively in ASL. The theater audience would not be able to understand her signing; the reader would not be able to understand a direct substitution of English words for ASL (English: "I have nothing; no hearing . . . no language . . . I have me alone." ASL: "Me have nothing. Me deafy . . . English, blow away . . . Think myself enough"). The reader's problem was solved when Medoff decided to write Sarah's lines in English, instructing theaters to use sign language experts to develop their own appropriate ASL. The translation problem for performance was solved by having another character, usually James, repeat in English everything that was signed. (Sarah [ASL]: "What I really want is pasta." James [speaking]: "What you really want is p-a—-pasta. Now we're talking.") That Medoff was able to write this kind of double-speak without interfering with the natural flow or emotional build of the dialogue was remarkable. This device also succeeds because the story is told in flashback, as James's memory. Medoff uses a cinematic style of writing that blends one scene, one memory, with the next, without the need to stop the action to establish passage of time or locales. Some critics have labeled this a "feminist" play because the man who wants to help his wife becomes her oppressor. That argument can be made, but it is a rush to judgment, ignoring the author's intent and the richness of the play's depiction of deaf education and culture. If the gender of every character was reversed, the story would still be true, because it is a story of deafness and not one of feminism.

Gerald S. Argetsinger

Bibliography:
Brustein, Robert. "Robert Brustein on Theater." *The New Republic* 187, no. 23 (June 7, 1980): 23-24. Satirizes the play as part of a new genre, the politically correct disability play. Argues that one cannot dislike such plays without being labeled hearingist or sexist.
Gill, Brendan. "Without Speech." *The New Yorker* 56, no. 8 (April 14, 1980): 101-106. Proclaims *Children of a Lesser God* to be not only successful but also a work of art. Focuses on the honesty of a story that portrays a seemingly perfect union but that is destroyed by ingrained flaws that the passion of the moment had at first minimalized.
Guernsey, Otis L., Jr. *Curtain Times: The New York Theater, 1965-1987.* New York: Dodd, Mead, 1987. Focuses on the uniqueness of the point of view of a minority that does not want to become part of the mainstream.

Simon, John. "April on Broadway: Indoor Showers." *New York Magazine* 13, no. 15 (April 14, 1980): 85-86. Describes the play's attempt to deal with weighty issues as shallow, falling short of melodrama, and functioning as mere soap opera. Simon cannot accept that James would become involved with the deeply troubled Sarah.

Weales, Gerald. "Belatedly, the Tonies." *Commonweal* 107, no. 18 (October 24, 1980): 595-596. Accuses the play of being the standard didactic play with the hearing-impaired replacing blacks or homosexuals as the new misunderstood minority.

Wilson, Edwin. "Broadway: Two Openings and One Closing." *The Wall Street Journal*, April 1, 1980. Reprinted in *New York Theatre Critics' Reviews* 41, no. 6 (March 24, 1980): 303. Points out that the play is three stories: Sarah's life, the rights of deaf people, and the romance. Argues that the play is worthy of serious critical attention.

THE CHILDREN OF HERAKLES

Type of work: Drama
Author: Euripides (c. 485-406 B.C.E.)
Type of plot: Tragedy
Time of plot: The age of legend
Locale: Before the temple of Zeus at Marathon
First performed: Hērakleidai, c. 430 B.C.E. (English translation, 1781)

Principal characters:
IOLAUS, the aged friend of Herakles
COPREUS, the herald of Eurystheus
DEMOPHON, the king of Athens
MACARIA, Herakles' daughter
ALCMENE, Herakles' mother
EURYSTHEUS, the king of Argos

The Story:
Iolaus, the aged warrior friend of the dead Herakles, together with Alcmene and the Herakleidae, the children of Herakles, had for years been wandering over Greece seeking a refuge from Eurystheus, king of Argos. No city had dared to take them in against the command of the powerful Argive ruler. At last the wanderers arrived in Athens. There, while resting at the temple of Zeus, they were immediately confronted by Copreus, the herald of Eurystheus, who demanded that they proceed at once to Argos and submit to death by stoning. Iolaus staunchly refused, and when Copreus seized the children a violent conflict ensued and Iolaus was thrown to the ground.

The chorus of aged Athenians immediately summoned their king, Demophon, who was warned by Copreus that his refusal to surrender the Herakleidae to the Argives would surely result in war. In response to Iolaus' plea, Demophon offered his protection on the grounds that the children of Herakles were gathered around the altar of Zeus, that they were bound to him by ties of kinship, and that the honor and freedom of Athens were at stake. Copreus sullenly departed, after warning that he would return with an army and punish Athens for its insolence. The grateful Iolaus praised the Athenians for their willingness to aid the helpless in an honest cause, but he refused to leave the temple until the issue with Argos was settled.

The Argive host appeared, led by Eurystheus himself. Demophon, who had consulted a variety of public and private oracles, came to Iolaus with the news that victory depended upon the sacrifice of some royal maiden and that he could not in good conscience slay his own daughter. When the distraught Iolaus offered to surrender himself to Eurystheus, Demophon pointed out that the Argive king desired only the children.

Macaria, daughter of Herakles, emerged from the temple to offer herself, insisting that she be chosen even after Iolaus proposed that the victim be selected by lot. After she had been led away, a servant of Hyllus, son of Herakles, entered to announce that Hyllus had arrived with an army to aid the Herakleidae. The elated Iolaus summoned Alcmene from the temple to hear the good news. He was so overjoyed that in spite of his age he insisted on donning armor and setting off to take part in the battle.

Later a servant brought Alcmene tidings of victory and described how, after the cowardly Eurystheus had refused single combat with Hyllus, the rejuvenated Iolaus plunged into the fray and took Eurystheus prisoner. Alcmene was astounded that Iolaus had not killed him on the spot. When guards brought the bound Eurystheus before her, she demanded his immediate death.

The messenger of Demophon cautioned her that such an act would violate Athenian custom, but the vengeful Alcmene swore that she herself would kill Eurystheus if necessary. The Argive king explained that he had never had any personal quarrel with the Herakleidae and that he was merely forced to do as he did by the divine power of Hera, the deity of Argos. Nevertheless, he would not ask for mercy; in fact, since an old oracle had predicted it, he was quite willing to submit to death if his body would be buried at Pallene, where in the future his spirit could protect his former enemies. The bloodthirsty Alcmene then demanded that he be taken away from the city, slain, and cast to the dogs. The chorus, observing that so long as Eurystheus was not killed within Athens no stain of guilt would come upon the city, led him away to be executed.

Critical Evaluation:

There is so much awkwardness in the structure of *The Children of Herakles* that critics have suggested that important scenes must be missing or that it was not intended as a tragedy but as a substitute for a satyr play. Another suggestion is that since *The Children of Herakles* was presented in the early years of the Peloponnesian War and glorifies the virtues of the Athenian city-state, Euripides depended upon the high patriotism of the play to carry it.

The Children of Herakles has been generally more criticized than praised. One critic sees it as "all in all the least attractive of Euripides' plays," although others have approved of its rapid pace, which moves inexorably toward the powerfully ironic, even satirical ending. The content of the play cannot be divorced form its political context: the Peloponnesian War between Athens and Sparta, which had just begun at the time it was produced, probably in 430 or 429 B.C.E. Eurystheus' promise to defend the city of Athens at the end of the play may be connected with the Spartan invasions of Athenian territory in 431 and 430 B.C.E. Likewise, the illegal execution of Spartan envoys at Athens in the winter of 430-429 B.C.E. may have inspired Euripides to explore the themes of supplication and refuge in a tragedy. These ambassadors were put to death without trial, in flagrant violation of the custom that such persons are not to be harmed.

The play draws upon the large body of myth surrounding Herakles, a hero whose career is marked by misfortune and subjection to the will of sundry gods and mortals. Persecuted by Hera and her agent Eurystheus, Herakles ended his life in agony on a funeral pyre. After his death, his children become the target of Eurystheus, who hunts them down with the same determination that drove him on against their father. Euripides fashions from these traditional elements a play about suppliants seeking asylum, which enables him to make pronouncements about Athenian policy in the war and about war in general.

Plays about suppliants are quite common in Greek drama. They tend to follow a pattern: The suppliants arrive seeking asylum, the pursuer attempts to seize them, the local authorities hear their appeal for sanctuary, a struggle ensues between the providers of asylum and the pursuer, and the suppliants are eventually saved. This pattern can also be seen in Aeschylus' *The Suppliants* (463? B.C.E.), about the daughters of Danaus, or in Sophocles' *Oedipus at Colonus* (401 B.C.E.), in which the Athenians grant asylum to the outcast king of Thebes. In such stories, the city that provides asylum is rewarded by blessings.

The action of the play is fast and furious, giving an impression of the bustling city-state at war. Decisions are made rapidly and there is always some new crisis looming. No character remains the center of attention for very long. The children of Herakles themselves, although they are named in the title, do not say anything; they are silent observers of the action throughout. They represent the helpless victims of war, whose voices are not heard and who are powerless to influence events.

The play turns on the issue of right versus might: Demophon takes a stand against the threats of Copreus and decides to protect the suppliants, whatever the cost may be. He does so partly out of duty to Zeus and partly because his father Theseus was indebted to Herakles. Moreover, the reputation of Athens as a free and honorable city has to be upheld. The treatment of the captured Eurystheus at the end of the play, however, undercuts the glorification of Athens: He is brought before Alcmene to be humiliated, physically abused, and sentenced to death. She has exchanged places with him and is now herself the incarnation of vengeful violence. Eurystheus, by contrast, seeks protection from Athens. The city that earlier took a brave stand against the pursuer to protect the pursued now abandons the suppliant to his fate. The speech that Eurystheus makes in his own defense reveals him to be courageous in the face of death, generous in his praise of Herakles, and even understanding of Alcmene's position. The chorus, who represent the Athenian state, urge Alcmene to let Eurystheus go, but are not prepared to stand in her way when she works out a means of killing him while ensuring that Athens suffers no harm from the murder. In other words, Athens acquiesces in an unjust act. It has failed the test when it comes to dealing with a prisoner of war, just as it did when it killed the Spartan envoys. In time of war, the poet seems to be saying, it is the spirit of Alcmene—vengeful, cruel, and irrational—that prevails. The play can thus be seen as a protest against the Peloponnesian war and a warning to Euripides' fellow Athenians that the war should be brought to an end as soon as possible.

The sacrifice of Macaria, demanded by the gods in order to ensure victory for Athens over Argos, recalls the sacrifices of Iphigeneia in Aeschylus' *Agamemnon* (458 B.C.E.). It symbolizes the heroic gesture made by a noble soul in time of war. It is significant that women are the sacrificial victims in such stories: It is as if the killing of so many men on the battlefield requires a concomitant sacrifice by the women of the city. It is interesting therefore that the play also contains the miraculous rejuvenation of the male warrior Iolaus. Macaria's death also symbolizes the victimization of the innocent by war. The attention that Euripides pays to the women Macaria and Alcmene in this play is typical of his work; it illustrates his concern with the subject of how men and women are to live harmoniously together in the same city.

The myth of the Return of the Children of Herakles provides a coda to the action of the play and also has some political ramifications. After the death of Eurystheus, the children made their way down through the Peloponnese, conquering Argos, Sparta, and other cities. The myth has been linked by some with the invasion of southern Greece by Dorian tribes in the prehistoric era. The aristocrats of the Peloponnese at any rate regarded themselves as descendants of Herakles, and so, when the king of Sparta led his army against Athens, he was marching against the city that had granted asylum to his ancestors. This is the kind of ironic twist that Euripides could well appreciate.

"Critical Evaluation" by David H. J. Larmour

Bibliography:
Dumezil, Georges. *The Stakes of the Warrior*. Translated by David Weeks. Berkeley: University of California Press, 1983. Explains how the Herakles figure embodies attributes of both the monster-slayer and the monster itself. Provides a useful background against which to consider Euripides' tragedy.
Euripides. *The Children of Herakles*. Translated by Henry Taylor and Robert A. Brooks. New

York: Oxford University Press, 1981. A clear translation in modern English. The introduction discusses the main themes of the play.

_____. *Heraclidae*. Introduction and commentary by John Wilkins. Oxford, England: Clarendon Press, 1993. Suitable for more detailed study of the play.

Foley, Helene P. *Ritual Irony: Poetry and Sacrifice in Euripides*. Ithaca, N.Y.: Cornell University Press, 1985. An enlightening treatment of the issue of sacrifice in Euripides' plays. Provides a clearer understanding of the sacrificial elements in *The Children of Herakles*.

Zuntz, Gunther. *The Political Plays of Euripides*. Manchester, England: Manchester University Press, 1955. A good account of the political elements found in many of Euripides' plays, which need to be taken into consideration by modern readers. Deals in detail with *The Children of Herakles*.

THE CHILDREN'S HOUR

Type of work: Drama
Author: Lillian Hellman (1905-1984)
Type of plot: Problem
Time of plot: 1930's
Locale: Massachusetts
First performed: 1934; first published, 1934

Principal characters:

KAREN WRIGHT, a cofounder of Wright-Dobie school
MARTHA DOBIE, a cofounder of Wright-Dobie school
MARY TILFORD, a student at the school
AMELIA TILFORD, Mary's grandmother, a patron of the school
LILY MORTAR, Martha Dobie's aunt
JOSEPH CARDIN, Karen's fiancé, the school doctor
ROSALIE WELLS, a student at the school

The Story:

In the living room of the Wright-Dobie private girls' school, seven girls aged twelve to fourteen conjugated Latin verbs and read aloud from Shakespeare's *The Merchant of Venice.* Fussily trying to teach the girls elocution, decorum, and sewing—all at once, to the girls' amusement—was school cofounder Martha Dobie's aging aunt, former actress Lily Mortar. Student Mary Tilford, tardy for the study session, explained that she had been detained gathering April flowers for Lily. When grateful Lily sent "sweet" Mary for a vase for the flowers, Mary disdainfully stuck her tongue out at a classmate.

When twenty-eight-year-old Karen Wright entered, the girls' tone changed from amused tolerance of Lily to respect for Karen. Karen was clearly in charge. She quietly showed her disapproval for Lily's dramatics while demonstrating care for the girls, offering to repair Rosalie's poor haircut and inquiring about a bracelet lost by another student, Helen. Mary Tilford, returning with the vase and flowers, squirmed under Karen's suspicion that Mary did not pick them but merely retrieved the bouquet from the garbage. Unhappy that Karen would destroy her excuse for missing the study session, Mary insisted on her story. Karen, trying to break Mary's habit of lying, imposed punishment by grounding her. Mary, furious, threatened to complain of maltreatment to her grandmother, Amelia Tilford, a major school supporter. Mary then faked a faint to avoid being sent to her room. Karen calmly picked her up and carried her away.

Cofounder and friend Martha Dobie discussed school problems with Karen, including what to do about Mary's bad influence on the other girls and how gently to rid themselves of Martha's outdated Aunt Lily. Clearly, Martha was struggling with another problem—Karen's impending marriage to school physician Joe Cardin. Karen tried to reassure her that they would be a threesome and that nothing would change at the school. When cheerful Joe arrived, he and Karen left to examine Mary and her latest complaint.

In a heated argument, Martha persuaded Aunt Lily to leave the school and return to Europe, the scene of Lily's pleasant acting memories. Hurt because she felt unwanted, Lily accused Martha of harboring a lesbian attachment to Karen that aimed to exclude all others, including Joe. Suddenly, both women realized that they had been overheard by Mary's roommates, hiding outside the room. Indignant, Lily left.

Joe Cardin entered, assuring Martha that Mary's health was fine. When Joe sensed Martha's uneasiness about his marrying Karen, he promised Martha that the three would remain close friends. Karen, joining Joe and Martha, suspected that Mary's influence on her two roommates was responsible for their eavesdropping; to weaken Mary's control, she separated the girls' rooms. The adults left. Furious, Mary smashed an ornament and threatened to blame her violence on her roommates. Next, she intimidated them into revealing Lily's accusation against Martha. Resenting the punishment for her earlier lie, Mary forced the girls to supply cash so she could flee to her grandmother, Amelia Tilford, and beg for sanctuary against Martha and Karen's "abuse."

Grandmother Tilford, at first determined to send Mary back to the school, gradually was convinced that the girl's fears were justified. Annoyed, then horrified, by Mary's whisperings about her schoolmistresses' "unnatural" behavior, she sent her granddaughter to bed. Immediately, she placed a telephone call to Joe to come to her house after his hospital duties, then called parents of other school boarders.

Several hours later, Rosalie joined Mary at Mrs. Tilford's for the night, wondering why several other girls suddenly were spending the night away from school at their parents' hasty requests. Mary blackmailed Rosalie, who had taken Helen's bracelet, into supporting her secret about Karen and Martha's alleged unnatural relationship.

Alone with astounded Joe, Amelia Tilford warned him not to marry Karen. Martha and Karen exploded into the room, describing the chaos at school: Parents had been snatching their daughters home because Amelia had told them the two founders were lovers. Against Martha and Karen's furious denunciations and their threats of a libel suit, Mrs. Tilford calmly maintained her position of protecting young girls. She advised the young women to leave quietly.

Karen, Martha, and Joe realized that Mary was the source of the story, but Mrs. Tilford supported her granddaughter's accusations. Under Joe's interrogation, Mary repeated Lily's overheard accusation against Martha and embellished it with concocted incidents about having seen the women behaving improperly together. Pinned down with inconsistencies in her story, such as peeking through a nonexistent keyhole, she then lied that Rosalie was in fact the one who had seen them. Confused by her questioners and terrified by Mary's blackmail, Rosalie cried that she did, in fact, witness Karen and Martha kissing inappropriately.

Seven months later, in the dim, unkempt school living room, listless Martha and Karen refused to answer the telephone. They had been reclusive for more than a week. Lily entered, relating her nomadic theater tour of several months. Her refusal to testify for her niece in court was crucial in Martha and Karen's loss of the libel suit against Mrs. Tilford. Bitter, Martha banished Lily from the school.

Arriving with plans for the three to leave for Vienna to start a new life, Joe reported that he had sold his practice. His slight hesitation when Karen kissed him was fatal to their relationship. Karen realized that privately he would always wonder about the truth of the accusations against her and Martha. Tenderly, she sent him away to think for a few days, knowing he would probably never return.

After he left, the two women discussed the unfairness of Mary's lie. As she denied that her affection for Karen was unnatural, Martha quietly and slowly realized that the charges were true, after all, and that she had resented Karen's impending marriage because of jealousy, not because she feared for the school. In spite of Karen's protests, Martha confessed that she had ruined their lives. She felt soiled. Karen thought Martha was exhausted and gently sent her to lie down. Suddenly, a shot sounded in the next room. From upstairs, Lily dashed in, but both women realized that medical help for the suicidal Martha was too late. Mrs. Tilford arrived, admitting that she had discovered Mary's blackmail scheme that forced Rosalie's support for the lie. Deeply remorseful, she apologized and offered Karen financial reparation. Numbed, Karen provisionally accepted while bitterly sending her away. Karen was left utterly alone.

Critical Evaluation:

One of America's first and most successful female playwrights, Lillian Hellman began her dramatic career at the age of twenty-nine with *The Children's Hour.* With 691 performances, it was her longest-running play. A book reviewer and a reader for films and playscripts, Hellman read an account of an early nineteenth century Scottish trial, "The Great Drumsheugh Case," about a child's false accusations ruining reputations. This, Hellman's first play, contains nearly all the themes and dramatic devices used in her other eleven dramas. Hellman created many ambitious female characters who, by greedy overreaching, leave death and destruction in their wake. Mary Tilford's ruthless manipulation of her classmates and wealthy grandmother to wield power over them is echoed in many other Hellman characters who seek undeserved power or wealth. Amelia Tilford's family loyalty in believing her granddaughter's contrived distress (over her better judgment) leads to several deaths: of the girls' school, of Karen and Joe's relationship, and of Martha through her suicide. Other Hellman plays such as *The Little Foxes* (1939) trace how distorted family allegiances result in ethical compromise and devastation. Amelia Tilford's belief at the end that money will relieve her conscience and Karen's pain demonstrates Hellman's harsh criticism of the wealthy classes and capitalism.

Traits found in all other Hellman plays make their debut here: a fast-moving plot using secrecy and increasing suspense, sparse detail about the past, and deftly drawn characters who speak everyday language. In her first play, Hellman introduces blackmail, a device that resurfaces in all her drama. Mary blackmails Rosalie, a petty thief, into supporting her story about Karen and Martha inappropriately kissing. This is an example of the terror inflicted on victims in other Hellman plays.

The play has been called dated because of its typical Hellman melodramatic style—obviously evil characters wreak havoc on clearly good or well-intentioned innocents before being discovered. Unlike in characteristic melodrama, however, the "evil" character in *The Children's Hour*, Mary, is not banished but is left in her grandmother's care. "Good" characters are not given clearly happy endings as in melodrama. Martha is dead; Karen is left without friendship, career, or marriage; and even Amelia Tilford's remorseful recognition of her error is too late. She also faces a bleak future in caring for her morally warped granddaughter. Amelia's "good" sense of responsibility to the parents and children of the school results in the irresponsible destruction of the two school founders and an unwanted responsibility for Mary's future.

Some critics contend that the characters are flawed. For example, Amelia Tilford is too intelligent to believe such a contrived story by a young girl. The girl's youth is one reason why the grandmother believes her: Amelia cannot fathom that a young girl would make up so shocking an incident. Given Amelia's privileged class, to change her mind after so strong a decision would be uncharacteristically humble.

In melodrama, a heroic man usually rescues victimized women. Here, Joe tries to rescue the two women with his plan to move to Vienna, but Karen takes control of their relationship by sensing Joe's unconscious doubt about the women's sexual past and pressuring him to articulate it. Unlike in melodrama, the lovers are not reconciled in the end: Joe's ultimate decision is left in doubt.

Although Mary is closer to a melodramatic villain with her intentional malice, her excuse of self-protection introduces a much more complex character. Mary believes that the two women discipline her because they dislike her. The young girl's parents are absent, and misbehavior by children in order to gain attention, even negative attention, is not uncommon. The cycle of transgression-punishment-transgression does not necessarily have a clear beginning in the transgressor's perception.

The drama's last act has been criticized as anticlimactic: The lethargy of the two friends depletes the play's intensity for too long. Hellman realized after a few rehearsals that the last ten minutes should be cut, but because she could not find an appropriate alternative, she left the act alone.

The Children's Hour differs from other Hellman plays in its lesbian theme, which caused a sensation on Broadway. Today, the homosexuality might seem mild, tastefully handled, and ambiguous. The acts for which the women are ruined have been disproved for the audience, and Martha's sudden admission of harboring "unnatural" affections for Karen is not entirely convincing. The women have been isolated and disoriented by the months-long ordeal before Martha's guilt about her new self-evaluation drives her to suicide. With Karen's strong disagreement, Hellman leaves the truth unclear. By the time Martha shoots herself, however, the prejudice that caused her death seems more immoral than her socially unacceptable affections. Hellman declared in a 1952 interview that she considered the play's major theme to be not lesbianism but the power of lying.

Nancy A. Macky

Bibliography:

Bigsby, C. W. E. *1900-1940*. Vol. 1 in *A Critical Introduction to Twentieth Century American Drama*. New York: Cambridge University Press, 1982. A chapter on Hellman evaluates *The Children's Hour*'s themes and explores its relationship to Hellman's life.

Falk, Doris V. *Lillian Hellman*. New York: Frederick Ungar, 1978. Falk analyzes Hellman's characters functioning as outsiders and plunderers.

Lederer, Katherine. *Lillian Hellman*. Boston: Twayne, 1979. A clearly written biography with informative analysis of themes and characters in *The Children's Hour* and other works.

Moody, Richard. *Lillian Hellman, Playwright*. New York: Pegasus Press, 1972. Chapter 5, "*The Children's Hour*," supplies background on the writing and performance of the play as well as providing a photograph of the original production.

Reynolds, R. C. *Stage Left: The Development of the American Social Drama in the Thirties*. Troy, N.Y.: Whitston, 1986. Examines Hellman's literary world and the contribution made to it by *The Children's Hour*.

THE CHIMERAS

Type of work: Poetry
Author: Gérard de Nerval (Gérard Labrunie, 1808-1855)
First published: Les Chimères, 1854 (English translation, 1957)

In the series of the twelve sonnets he grouped together under the title *The Chimeras,* Gérard de Nerval exploits ambiguities that resemble the creatures of his title. The chimera, as a monster depicted in Greek mythology, is a hybrid creature combining elements of a lion, goat, and serpent. In its later derivation, the word refers to something fanciful or imaginary that does not really exist. Nerval plays on both senses of the word: His poems recall mythic past times, but they also produce a somewhat fictitious portrait of Nerval himself.

Nerval separately titled each of the first six sonnets and the last but grouped the remaining five into a sonnet sequence entitled "Christ on the Mount of Olives." An analysis of the work, however, shows it to be composed of four parts, with the first and the last poems forming separate units. According to that model, the opening sonnet, "El Desdichado," presents the persona of Nerval himself. The next five sonnets, each bearing as title a name from antiquity (Myrtho, Horus, Antéros, Delfica, and Artémis), evoke the gods and goddesses of pre-Christian times. "Christ on the Mount of Olives" portrays the new leader, to whom the pagan gods must yield their power, in extremely human terms. Finally, "Vers dorés" (golden lines) returns to a perception of humanity in the present.

The autobiographical "El Desdichado" draws on Nerval's personal crisis of mental illness, seen here as a descent into Hell, and Nerval's identification of himself, through the lineage of his family, with heroes from French history. The linking of the poet's descent into Hell with that of the mythic musician, Orpheus, sets up a contrast of pagan and Christian referents within the poem, a dualism that leads to the poet's question concerning his own identity.

The opening quatrain introduces the complexity of the poem and Nerval's multiple perceptions of his own persona with a large number of separate references. In the first line, he describes himself as "somber and widowed," by implication separated from the woman he loves, as Orpheus was separated from Eurydice. In the second line, however, he is "the prince of Aquitaine at the abolished tower," a figure from a period of French history.

In the following lines the words "star" and "sun" are written in italics to emphasize the affinity of these similar objects. Their symbolic references, however, differ. When Nerval says "My *star* is dead," he seems to refer to the woman whose absence causes his widowed state. Yet when his starry lute carries as a chivalric device "the *black sun* of *Melancholia,*" he refers to the engraving by Albert Dürer in which an angel meditates sadly on the passing of time.

The second quatrain remains much more unified, as Nerval cries out from the tomb in which he sees himself and desires the happiness he had known in the past on a trip to Italy. The symbolic flower (again italicized) that represents this experience anticipates the further flower imagery of "Artémis." Meanwhile, the rose growing together with grapevines, although it reflects a pattern of planting common in vineyards, parallels the combining of different elements in the rest of the poem.

The simple declarations in the quatrains become a question in the tercets, as multiple allusions reflect Nerval's confusion about his true identity as a character from pagan antiquity (Cupid or Phoebus) or from Christian France (Lusignan or Biron). In whichever guise he has undergone the descent into Hell, to which he has twice "crossed the Acheron river," he has in the process been marked by a woman because his "forehead is still red from the queen's kiss."

The identity of the woman remains ambiguous. Nerval, as Orpheus, sings alternately of "the saint" and "the fairy," mythic women who represent Christian and pagan cultures.

The ensuing five sonnets constitute an excursion through pagan antiquity. The first, "Myrtho," invokes the "divine enchantress" whose name recalls the myrtle plant and who is linked both with the Italian scene of "El Desdichado" and with the more distant "brightness of the Orient." The quatrains portray a seduction of the poet by the female spirit as muse. First he becomes drunk from the cup of wine she holds and worships the pagan Bacchus. Then he declares that "the Muse has made me a son of Greece." Perhaps Nerval meant simply that he wrote poetry based on Greek tradition, but given Nerval's propensity for identifying himself with figures from the past, this claim to kinship could also be taken quite literally. The tercets in this poem refer to an eruption of Vesuvius that Nerval sees as having resulted from a French conquest of Naples. Such a conquest brought the Christian culture of France into direct confrontation with the pagan culture of antiquity still associated with southern Italy. Thus "the pale Hydrangea is united with green Myrtle" as the plants, like the rose and the vines of "El Desdichado," symbolize the fusion of unlike elements.

With "Horus," Nerval returns to his earliest point in history, to ancient Egypt where the male god, Kneph, attempts to dominate the female Isis. She denounces him, however, and observes that he is dying. She declares that "the eagle has already passed, and a new spirit is calling me." This new spirit is that of the Greek gods who would replace those of Egypt. Isis, dressed in new garments, is transformed into Cybele, but for such gods as Kneph, there is no future. This passing of the legacy of divine power parallels stories told of the coming of Christ, who would similarly eclipse the Greek gods.

The triumph of the new gods does not lead to an era of peace. In "Antéros," Nerval returns to the first-person narrative that he abandoned in "Horus" to describe himself as "descended from the line of Antaeus," a son of Neptune who gained his strength from the earth. He is an angry figure devoted to revenge, the force that has "marked his forehead" just as the queen's kiss marked Nerval in "El Desdichado." Nerval claims that in this guise he again combines opposing forces, "the paleness of Abel" and the "redness of Cain." He resembles Abel in that he will be killed as the Greek gods yield to Jehovah, but he acts as Cain when he "plants the old dragon's teeth," a gesture through which Cadmus, in antiquity, was said to plant the seeds that would produce a crop of avenging warriors.

"Delfica" predicts the revenge of displaced gods. With another allusion to the dragon's teeth, Nerval affirms that "the Gods you weep for will return." The final tercet, however, sees the ancient sibyl "asleep under the arch of Constantine." For the moment, Christianity triumphs over pagan culture.

The imagery of "Artémis" is the most complex in *The Chimeras*. The rose, or hollyhock, held by the queen, could identify her with the queen in a deck of cards, thus justifying the sequence of thirteen in the first line, or with a figure of love or death. There appear, however, to be two female figures in conflict. The white rose representing the Christian saint will fade because, as Nerval affirms in the last line, "the saint of the abyss" is stronger. This must be the Artémis of the title, Apollo's sister, noted in Greek tragedy for her conflict with Aphrodite.

After five sonnets devoted to pagan gods, the subsequent five-sonnet sequence turns to Christ as the exponent of the religion that replaced the old gods. Yet the Christ shown on the Mount of Olives is himself facing death. According to Christian belief, his death is the essential sacrifice for the redemption of humanity, but the Christ readers see here, with his "thin arms" and his despairing cry, is a very human figure. Power may have passed to him, but at this tragic moment, he seems about to lose it again.

1115

Nerval did not create this humanized representation of Christ. In "Le Mont des Oliviers" (1844), Alfred de Vigny portrays Jesus in a similar state of despair. In both poems he is abandoned by his sleeping apostles, and in both he fears, as he does in Nerval's first sonnet, that "God no longer exists."

In the second and third sonnets, Nerval turns from the personal suffering of Christ to his attempt to ease human suffering. At first, Christ fails to find the reassuring presence of God in the vastness of the universe. Then, tormented by the harshness of his fate, he seeks God within himself. He sees his death not as a part of redemption but as the extinguishing of the last hope for religion. In the fourth sonnet, Christ desires death merely as an end to his personal suffering. Ironically, Judas appears as an ineffective figure, and the only one who can ease Christ's torment is Pontius Pilate, who condemns him.

The final sonnet of this sequence returns to figures from pagan mythology, comparing Christ with Icarus in his vain attempt to win heaven. Only "for a moment" Olympus tottered toward the abyss. With the reference to Cybele, the goddess of resurrection, it appears that the old gods may survive. Their oracle, however, remains silent. The last line affirms that only the transcendent God understands the divine mystery.

Neither Christ nor the pagan gods can have the last word in Nerval's *The Chimeras*. After each religion has come and perished, the work ends with "Vers dorés," in which a pantheistic spirit in nature dwarfs human understanding. This sonnet puts the flower imagery of "El Desdichado," "Myrtho," and "Artémis" in a new context. Animals, plants, and even stones contain souls that are hidden from human comprehension. This assertion leads Nerval to the view that humans must respect nature rather than putting it to "impious usage." Yet the power contained in nature may also be a threat to humanity. An eye hidden within a rock wall may be looking out, and all matter is capable of action. In the context of revenge established in some of the earlier sonnets, the nonhuman elements of the world may be ready for their own revenge.

Nerval's *The Chimeras* grew out of ambivalent feelings that haunted his life, but beyond that it crystallized a mood of religious incertitude prevalent in the nineteenth century. In the third sonnet of the sequence, Christ sees himself "between a dying world and another being born." Nerval's review of the past was also an attempt to foresee the future.

Dorothy M. Betz

Bibliography:
Jones, Robert Emmet. *Gérard de Nerval*. New York: Twayne, 1974. This standard biography provides a chronology of Nerval's life and a selected bibliography. Chapter 2 on Nerval the poet analyzes the elements of his earlier works that contributed to *The Chimeras* and offers a partial interpretation of the work.
Knapp, Bettina L. *Gérard de Nerval: The Mystic's Dilemma*. University: University of Alabama Press, 1980. Offers an extensive consideration of Nerval's life and earlier work. Chapter 20 gives a line-by-line reading of the twelve sonnets of *The Chimeras*, incorporating paraphrases that amount to an analytical translation of the work.
Nerval, Gérard de. *Selected Writings of Gérard de Nerval*. Translated and edited by Geoffrey Wagner. Ann Arbor: University of Michigan Press, 1957. Contains an introduction that provides information on aspects of Nerval's life that influenced his poetry. Discusses *The Chimeras* in the context of Nerval's other work. Also included are translations of the principal works including all of *The Chimeras* except "Christ on the Mount of Olives."
Sowerby, Benn. *The Disinherited: The Life of Gérard de Nerval, 1808-1855*. London: P. Owen,

1973. This biography, with its convenient chronology of Nerval's life, focuses on events rather than text. Includes some comments on *The Chimeras*, chiefly in the last chapter.

Winston, Phyllis Jane. *Nerval's Magic Alphabet*. New York: Peter Lang, 1989. Chapter 4 is devoted to *The Chimeras*, citing principally "Antéros" and "Delfica." Provides an intellectual context for the work but limited interpretation of the text.

CHITA
A Memory of Last Island

Type of work: Novel
Author: Lafcadio Hearn (1850-1904)
Type of plot: Impressionistic realism
Time of plot: Nineteenth century
Locale: Louisiana coastal waters
First published: 1889

Principal characters:
FELIU VIOSCA, a fisherman
CARMEN VIOSCA, his wife
CHITA, a foundling
DR. JULIEN LA BRIERRE, her father

The Story:
Southward from New Orleans, one passed settlements of many nationalities and races. Beyond lay an archipelago, the islands of which were Grande Pass, Grande Terre, and Barataria. More to the south lay Grande Isle, a modern bathing resort, the loveliest island in the Gulf of Mexico. Last Island, forty miles west of Grande Isle, lay desolate, but at an earlier time it had been the most popular of the group and a fashionable resort. The island's hotel had been a two-story timber structure with many apartments, a dining room, and a ballroom. One night, the sea destroyed it.

On the northwest side of each island were signs of the incessant influence of the wind and sea, for the trees all bent away from the water. All along the Gulf coast, and on the island beaches, were the ruins of hurricanes, skeletons of toppled buildings, and broken tree trunks. The land itself was being eaten away.

The innocent beauty of summer on these islands was impossible to express. Years before, Last Island had been immersed in the azure light of a typical July. It was an unusually lovely summer and the breathless charm of the season lingered. One afternoon, the ocean began to stir and great waves started to hurl themselves over the beaches, giving warning on Last Island that a hurricane was brewing. The wind, beginning to blow, continued for a few days to stir the water. A steamer, the *Star*, due that day, was not expected to arrive.

Captain Abraham Smith, an American, knew the sea, and he knew his ship. Sensing that he might be needed, he had sailed for Last Island. As he approached, he saw the storm rising. He ordered the excess weight of the *Star* tossed overboard to help her ride out the storm. On the island, however, the guests at the hotel continued to dance until they noticed water at their feet, and the building began to be buffeted by the waves. Captain Smith spent the night rescuing as many as he could. Buildings were ripped apart, the shores were lashed by wind and wave, lakes and rivers overflowed, and by daybreak countless corpses floated on the stormy sea. When the hurricane subsided, scavengers came to claim whatever plunder could be salvaged from the ruins and from the dead.

On a tiny volcanic island lived Feliu Viosca, a fisherman, and his wife Carmen. On the night of the terrible storm, Carmen was awakened by the noise. Afraid, she aroused her husband, whose calmness comforted her, and he ordered her to return to sleep. In her dreams, her dead child, dark-eyed Conchita, came to her.

The next day the fishermen, gathered at the shore, stood watching the wreckage and the bodies floating past. A flash of yellow caught Feliu's eye. In a moment, he had stripped and was swimming out toward a child, still alive, clinging to her drowned mother. Feliu managed to rescue the baby and swim back to shore.

The half-drowned child was taken to Carmen, whose skillful hands and maternal instincts nursed the little girl into a warm, sound sleep; there was hope she would survive. Her yellow hair had saved her, for it was the flash of sun on her tresses that had caught Feliu's eye.

Captain Harris, of New Orleans, along with several other men, was sailing up and down the coast in search of missing persons, dead or still alive after the storm. Ten days after the rescue of the girl, Harris came to Viosca's wharf. Hardly able to communicate with the men, Feliu told them the story of his heroism but cautioned them that if they wished to question the child, they must proceed gently, since she was still not fully recovered from shock.

The child's Creole dialect was not comprehensible to anyone there until Laroussel, a Creole, began to question her. In her broken speech, she told him that her Creole name was Zouzoune, her real one Lili. Her mother was called Adele and her father Julien. Nothing more could be determined. Realizing that the child's relatives might never be found, Harris decided to leave her with Feliu and Carmen, who promised to give her excellent care. Laroussel gave the little girl a trinket that had caught her eye. Although other searching parties stopped to see Feliu's waif, the child's identity remained a mystery. Meanwhile, near another island, a pair of bodies drifting in the sea had been identified as those of Dr. Julien La Brierre and his wife, Adele. The doctor had survived, however; six months later, he was in New Orleans looking at his own epitaph and that of his wife.

Dr. La Brierre had grown up in New Orleans. In maturity, to please his father, he had studied medicine in Paris. After his return to New Orleans, he had fallen in love and had been wounded in a duel with a rival named Laroussel. Following the death of his father and mother, Julien had married Adele, and their child Zouzoune was born.

On the lonely island, the small child, now called Chita, had become a member of the Viosca family. Gradually, she adapted herself to the ways of her foster parents.

Years later, Dr. La Brierre was practicing in New Orleans, a lonely and kindly physician. One year, an elderly patient of his, named Edwards, went to Viosca's Point, which Captain Harris had recommended for the sick man's recovery. While there, Edwards suffered a stroke. Hurriedly summoned, Dr. La Brierre arrived too late to help his patient.

Before the doctor could set out for home, he too became ill. Carmen nursed him. In the vague consciousness that accompanied his malady, the doctor saw Chita, whose resemblance to his dead wife greatly excited him. In his delirium, he called out to Zouzoune and Adele, while Carmen tried to calm him. Reliving the horror of the hurricane that had taken Adele and Zouzoune from him, the sick man died.

Critical Evaluation:

Despite its graphic rendering of a devastating hurricane, *Chita* is not a naturalistic novel with a storm as its hero. Although Lafcadio Hearn was attracted by Herbert Spencer's evolutionary philosophy and read Charles Darwin avidly, his destiny was not to join the rising school of American Naturalism descending from Stephen Crane and Frank Norris to Theodore Dreiser. Hearn followed that other great trend in late nineteenth century literature—aestheticism. His kindred spirits were John Keats, Walter Pater, and Oscar Wilde. He was a pursuer of beauty and a painter with words. Shortly after completing *Chita*, Hearn left for Japan and eventually became the most important literary interpreter of Japan's aesthetic culture to the English-speaking world.

Chita's sentimental plot—the lost child and her chance reunion with her dying father—is designed to arouse human emotions that will correspond in intensity to the turbulence of the storm. It is the dynamic impressionism of the storm itself that fascinates Hearn. After the deceptive calm of summer come the roaring breakers; the storm swirls houses and ships and leaves an incredible magnitude of refuse in its wake. Endless wreckage and bodies are strewn everywhere—including the body of the foundling, Chita.

The child is fished out of all this dying waste like a creature returned from the dead. Her rescue has all the aura of a miracle to the simple Vioscas, who see the child as having been sent to them by the Virgin Mary. At the end of the story, La Brierre's fevered imagination once more re-creates the chaotic horror of the storm, more impressionistic than ever because its setting is now an agonized brain. Once again, a miracle is performed: The lost child is tossed up by the seething wreckage of La Brierre's tortured memories. She is there in his mind and in actuality. The blurring of the two realities makes for the perfect impressionistic ending. The novel opens with the calm, summery hues of a painting by Pierre-Auguste Renoir and closes with the brilliant frenzy of one by Claude Monet.

Bibliography:
Bisland, Elizabeth. *The Life and Letters of Lafcadio Hearn.* 2 vols. Boston: Houghton Mifflin, 1906. Includes letters by Hearn to friends, including Bisland herself, clarifying the insights leading to *Chita* and his artistic intentions in writing the novel.
Colt, Jonathan. *Wandering Ghost: The Odyssey of Lafcadio Hearn.* New York: Alfred A. Knopf, 1991. Informal biographical reader, combining an affectionate account of Hearn's career and generous selections from his works. Comments that, although Hearn depicts the characters in *Chita* with overdone sentimentality, his poetic prose imitates hypnotic tides and waves and conveys an impressionistic sense of the sea's eternal mystery.
Kunst, Arthur E. *Lafcadio Hearn.* New York: Twayne, 1969. Solid introductory critical biography. Includes treatment of *Chita* in detailed summary with many quotations. Relates Hearn's poetic prose to structural elements of music.
Stevenson, Elizabeth. *Lafcadio Hearn.* New York: Macmillan, 1961. Thorough, beautifully written biography. Discusses *Chita* as a story of solitude, the sea, and loneliness, with its three parts moving from the sea as destroyer to the sea as deceptively calm to a finale of human loss.
Turner, Arlin. Introduction to *Chita: A Memory of Last Island.* Chapel Hill: University of North Carolina Press, 1969. Relates *Chita* to events in Hearn's professional life, accounts for his being influenced by Pierre Loti and Théophile Gautier, and discusses Hearn's handling of sources for details in *Chita*, particularly the August, 1856, Last Island storm. Reprints two of Hearn's stories that are preliminary studies for *Chita*.

THE CHOSEN

Type of work: Novel
Author: Chaim Potok (1929-   )
Type of plot: Domestic realism
Time of plot: 1940's
Locale: Williamsburg neighborhood of Brooklyn
First published: 1967

> *Principal characters:*
> REUVEN MALTER, a teenage Orthodox Jew
> DAVID MALTER, his father
> DANNY SAUNDERS, a teenage Hasid
> RABBI ISAAC SAUNDERS, his father

The Story:

Two fifteen-year-old boys, growing up during World War II and within five blocks of each other, met on a Brooklyn softball field one Sunday in June. Their ensuing baseball game took on warlike proportions. One team was led by Danny Saunders, the eldest son of a prominent Hasidic rabbi, Isaac Saunders, who had led his people out of Russia to America. This team, and all of Rabbi Saunders' followers, wore the traditional clothing corresponding with Hasidism's founding in the eighteenth century: black hats or skullcaps, long black coats, and fringed prayer garments called tzitzits. Their long earlocks also set them apart.

The other team was led by Reuven Malter, son of widowed university professor David Malter. Reuven's and Danny's teams attended yeshivas, Jewish parochial schools. The marked difference between the two teams was exemplified by their respective coaches. Mr. Galanter, a gym teacher from the public school system, moonlighted by teaching in Reuven's school. He wore modern clothing and was described as being "fanatically addicted to professional baseball." Danny's team's "coach" was a rabbi. He dressed in black and carried a book that seemed to interest him far more than the ball game. His sole advice to his team was: "Remember why and for whom we play."

Even though Danny's team seemed an unlikely victor, they won the game. One of Reuven's teammates warned him: "They're murderers." The truth of this observation became evident early in the game. Although the majority of Danny's teammates were unremarkable ballplayers, they played with a fierce intensity.

During the game, one of Danny's hits struck pitcher Reuven, shattering his glasses and injuring his left eye. Reuven was taken to the hospital and underwent surgery to remove glass splinters. Reuven learned that, in addition to having a concussion, he faced the possibility of having scar tissue form and causing blindness in that eye.

While in the hospital Reuven made several new friends. Two were fellow patients in the eye ward. Tony Savo, a professional boxer, had lost an eye in a boxing injury. Billy Merrit, a young boy, had been blinded in a car accident. The most surprising friend that Reuven made during his hospitalization, however, was Danny. When Danny first visited Reuven in the hospital, Reuven noted that "he looked a little like the pictures I had seen of Abraham Lincoln before he grew the beard." Danny tried to apologize to Reuven, but Reuven ordered him to leave.

When Mr. Malter visited his son and learned how Danny had been treated, he reprimanded Reuven, telling him that the Talmud commands listening and forgiveness when an apology is offered. During this visit Reuven and his father also discussed the war in Europe, including the Allied Powers' D day invasion. "It is the beginning of the end for Hitler and his madmen," Mr. Malter told his son. The next day Danny visited again. Reuven apologized for his behavior, and the two talked civilly. Danny admitted that he did not understand his feelings during the ball game: "I don't understand why I wanted to kill you." He also confessed, "I wanted to walk over to you and open your head with my bat." Reuven observed that Danny "dressed like a Hasid, but he didn't sound like one."

During their first sustained conversation, Reuven learned of Danny's photographic mind and phenomenal intelligence. Danny could recite from memory virtually anything he had ever read. Reuven was both awed and disturbed by Danny's amazing ability, noting: "He did it coldly, mechanically . . . I had the feeling I was watching some sort of human machine at work."

The boys discussed their professional aspirations. Reuven planned to become a rabbi, although his father hoped he would become a mathematician. Danny was expected to become a rabbi because the position was an inherited one. He admitted, however, that if he could choose otherwise he would rather become a psychologist.

The hospital visits continued. Reuven's eye healed, and full vision returned. Sadly, his hospital mates did not fare as well. Nothing could be done to help the boxer, Tony Savo, and the surgery to restore Billy's sight was unsuccessful. As Danny and Reuven's friendship developed, Danny was astonished to learn that he had already met Reuven's father. On surreptitious visits to the public library, Danny had approached Mr. Malter. Without exchanging names, Danny asked him for book recommendations. Mr. Malter obliged, and they discussed Danny's reading. Mr. Malter knew that he was dealing with the brilliant son of Rabbi Saunders and that nothing could stop Danny's quest for knowledge. He felt uneasy, however, knowing that Rabbi Saunders would not approve of Danny's reading.

Reuven was eventually introduced to Rabbi Saunders and to Danny's world. Reuven attended religious services in Rabbi Saunders' synagogue, which occupied one floor of the family home. While attending services, Reuven was drawn into an intense, public debate between Danny and his father. He and Danny passed Rabbi Saunders' strange test. Reuven did not understand what had happened. His suspicions and distrust of Rabbi Saunders grew. Reuven was accepted by Rabbi Saunders, however, and he continued to visit and worship with the family. Reuven learned that Danny and his father never spoke except when they discussed holy writings. This silence was mysterious to Reuven, and his resentment toward Rabbi Saunders grew. Danny did not understand the painful silence either; still, he trusted and respected his father.

The boys finished high school and continued their education at Hirsch College. Danny majored in psychology, and Reuven studied philosophy with an emphasis in symbolic logic. They also continued their religious studies and gained the respect and admiration of professors and students alike.

A crisis in the friendship occurred following the end of the war and the subsequent movement to establish a secular Jewish state. Reuven and his father supported Zionism wholeheartedly, but Rabbi Saunders and his followers were vehemently opposed to it, claiming it would be a denial of the Torah and their hope in the coming Messiah. When Rabbi Saunders learned of Mr. Malter's avid, public support of Zionism, Danny was forbidden to have any more contact with Reuven. A second silence began. Not only was Danny's relationship with his father still marked by silence, the best friends could no longer communicate.

Danny obeyed his father's wishes, although it caused both boys great pain. Reuven described the silence as "ugly . . . black, it leered, it was cancerous, it was death." Adding to Danny's misery was his disappointment with his college studies. His psychology professor stressed experimental psychology. Danny found himself studying rats and experiments when he really wanted to be studying Freud and psychoanalysis. Reuven's pain was heightened when his father was hospitalized with a second heart attack.

One day in their third year of college, Danny surprisingly broke the friends' two-year silence. Danny sat down at the lunch table at school and asked Reuven for some help with math. Rabbi Saunders had finally lifted the ban when the Jewish state moved from concept to reality. Reuven reassumed contact with the Saunders family and even attended Danny's sister's wedding. He learned that, in accordance with Hasidic custom, Danny's wife had been chosen for him in childhood.

Rabbi Saunders repeatedly asked Reuven to visit, but Reuven let many months pass before honoring the request. Reuven's father was again disappointed to learn that his son had been unresponsive to another's wishes. He reminded his son, "Reuven, when someone asks to speak to you, you must let him speak to you. You still have not learned that? You did not learn that from what happened between you and Danny?" He urged Reuven to support Danny in the inevitable confrontation with Rabbi Saunders. Danny had decided to reject the inherited position from his father; he would do graduate study at Columbia University and become a psychologist. Mr. Malter urged Reuven to help Danny plan how he would answer his father's questions.

Reuven visited the Saunders' home during Passover and together he and Danny met with Rabbi Saunders in his study. Rabbi Saunders spoke to Danny through Reuven, explaining how he himself was raised in silence by his father. He spoke also of Danny's uncle, who had an exceptional mind but essentially no soul. In childhood Danny showed early signs of being like his uncle—restless, impatient, disdainful of others with less intelligence. Rabbi Saunders knew that it was not enough to have a brilliant mind. His son's soul, that divine spark of God, must be cultivated. To develop his son's soul and prepare him to take on the suffering of his people, Rabbi Saunders decided to raise Danny as he had been raised—in silence.

This discussion took place during the Passover—the festival of freedom. Danny was in tears as his father released him from the inherited position. Danny's brother, Levi, would become the tzaddik ("righteous one"), thereby continuing the tradition. With a heavy but understanding heart, Rabbi Saunders accepted his son's wishes to become a psychologist, noting that "I have no more fear now. All his life he will be a tzaddik. He will be a tzaddik for the world. And the world needs a tzaddik." Rabbi Saunders asked his son for forgiveness: "A—a wiser father . . . may have done differently. I am not . . . wise."

Danny and Reuven were graduated summa cum laude from Hirsch College. That September, as Danny prepared to move out of his family's home and into a rented room near Columbia University, he and Reuven once again discussed Danny's upbringing. Reuven learned that normal conversation had finally resumed between Danny and his father. Danny also told Reuven that when Danny had a son of his own, he would raise him just as he had been raised, "If I can't find another way."

Critical Evaluation:

This novel, Chaim Potok's first, received the Edward Lewis Wallant Memorial Book Award and was nominated for the National Book Award. It presents a clear and compelling view of orthodox Jewish life in America in the war years. It broadens the reader's understanding of the wide spectrum of Judaism, which ranges from the most conservative to the liberal. It is invaluable in providing all readers, particularly young ones, with social, political, and religious history. The book explores the themes of friendship and silence. The eye is a central image. Characters are literally blind or threatened with blindness; other characters wrestle with figurative blindness. Perceptions and understanding grow as each comes to new self-awareness and learns how to see through another's eyes. An often-repeated idea is that things are not always as they seem. Certainly the main characters come to a profound acknowledgment of this observation. Also central is an idea voiced most often by Tony Savo: "Crazy world. Cockeyed." The novel portrays colossal unfairness and injustice on many levels, and stresses the importance of finding and creating one's own meaning. *The Promise*, published in 1969, continues the story of Danny and Reuven.

Beverly J. Matiko

Bibliography:
Abramson, Edward A. *Chaim Potok*. Boston: Twayne, 1986. Chapter 2, about *The Chosen*, discusses the Hasidim and the Orthodox Jewish and non-Jewish worlds, the value of education, fathers and sons, and form and content.
Bluefarb, Sam. "The Head, the Heart and the Conflict of Generations in Chaim Potok's *The Chosen*." *College Language Association Journal* 14 (June, 1971): 402-409. Explores the father-son relationships.
Leeper, Faye. "What Is in the Name?" *The English Journal* 59 (January, 1970): 63-64. Offers answers to the question, "Who or what is chosen in this novel?"
Sgan, Arnold D. "*The Chosen, The Promise*, and *My Name is Asher Lev*." *The English Journal* 66 (March, 1977): 63-64. Offers useful plot summaries and themes for each novel; discusses Potok's place in high school units on "Ethnic Literature" or "The Search for Identity."
Studies in American Jewish Literature 4 (1985). This issue, entitled "The World of Chaim Potok," contains various articles, including one by Potok, and an interview with him.

A CHRISTMAS CAROL

Type of work: Short fiction
Author: Charles Dickens (1812-1870)
Type of plot: Moral
Time of plot: Nineteenth century
Locale: London, England
First published: 1843

> *Principal characters:*
> EBENEZER SCROOGE, a miser
> JACOB MARLEY'S GHOST
> BOB CRATCHIT, Scrooge's clerk
> TINY TIM, Cratchit's son
> SCROOGE'S NEPHEW

The Story:

Ebenezer Scrooge was a miser. Owner of a successful countinghouse, he would have in his bleak office only the smallest fire in the most bitter weather. For his clerk, Bob Cratchit, he allowed an even smaller fire. The weather seldom mattered to Scrooge, who was always cold within, never warm—even on Christmas Eve. As the time approached for closing the office on Christmas Eve, Scrooge's nephew stopped in to wish him a merry Christmas. Scrooge only sneered, for he abhorred sentiment and thought only of one thing—money. To him, Christmas was a time when people spent more money than they should and found themselves a year older and no richer.

Grudgingly, Scrooge allowed Cratchit to have Christmas Day off; that was the one concession to the holiday that he made, but he warned Cratchit to be at work earlier the day after Christmas. Scrooge left his office and went home to his rooms in a building in which he was the only tenant. They had been the rooms of Scrooge's partner, Jacob Marley, dead for seven years. As he approached his door, he saw Marley's face in the knocker. It was a horrible sight. Marley was looking at Scrooge with his eyes motionless, his ghostly spectacles on his ghostly forehead. As Scrooge watched, the knocker resumed its usual form. Shaken by this vision, Scrooge entered the hall and lighted a candle; then he looked behind the door, half expecting to see Marley's pigtail sticking out into the hall. Satisfied, he double-locked the door. He prepared for bed and sat for a time before the dying fire. Suddenly an unused bell hanging in the room began to ring, as did every bell in the house.

Then from below came the sound of heavy chains clanking. The cellar door flew open, and someone mounted the stairs. Marley's ghost walked through Scrooge's door—Marley, dressed as always, but with a heavy chain of cash boxes, keys, padlocks, ledgers, deeds, and heavy purses around his middle.

Marley's ghost sat down to talk to the frightened and bewildered Scrooge. Forcing Scrooge to admit that he believed what he saw was real, Marley explained that in life he had never done any good for humankind and so in death he was condemned to constant traveling with no rest and no relief from the torture of remorse. The ghost said that Scrooge still had a chance to save himself from Marley's fate. Scrooge would be visited by three spirits who would show him the way to change. The first spirit would appear the next day at the stroke of one. The next would arrive on the second night and the last on the third. Dragging his chain, the ghost disappeared.

After Marley's ghost had vanished, Scrooge went to bed, and in spite of his nervousness, he fell asleep instantly. When he awoke, it was still dark. The clock struck twelve. He waited for the stroke of one. As the sound of the bell died away, his bed curtains were pulled apart, and there stood a figure with a childlike face, but with long, white hair and a strong, well-formed body. The ghost introduced itself as the Ghost of Christmas Past, Scrooge's past. When the ghost invited Scrooge to go on a journey with him, Scrooge was unable to refuse.

They traveled like the wind and stopped first at Scrooge's birthplace. There Scrooge saw himself as a boy, neglected by his friends and left alone to find adventure in books. Next, he saw himself at school, where his sister had come to take him home for Christmas. Scrooge recalled his love for his sister, who had died young. The ghost reminded him that she had borne a son whom Scrooge neglected. Their next stop was the scene of Scrooge's apprenticeship, where everyone made merry on Christmas Eve. Traveling on, they saw a young girl weeping as she told young Scrooge that she realized he loved money more than he loved her. The ghost showed him the same girl, grown older but happy with her husband and children. Then the ghost returned Scrooge to his room, where he promptly fell asleep again.

When the Ghost of Christmas Present appeared, he led Scrooge through the city streets on Christmas morning. Their first stop was at the Cratchit home, where Bob Cratchit appeared with frail, crippled Tiny Tim on his shoulder. In the Cratchit home, a skimpy meal was a banquet. After dinner, Bob proposed a toast to Mr. Scrooge, even though it put a temporary damper on the holiday gaiety. Then the ghost and Scrooge crossed swiftly through the city where everyone paused to wish one another a merry Christmas. As they looked in on the home of Scrooge's nephew, gaiety prevailed, and Scrooge was tempted to join in the games. There, too, a toast was proposed to Scrooge's health. As the clock began to strike twelve o'clock, the ghost of Christmas Present faded away.

With the last stroke of twelve, Scrooge saw a black-shrouded phantom approaching him, the Ghost of Christmas Yet to Come. The phantom extended his hand and forced Scrooge to follow him until they came to a group of scavengers selling the belongings of the dead. One woman had entered a dead man's room; she had taken his bed curtains, bedding, and even the shirt in which he was to have been buried. Scrooge saw a dead man with his face covered, but he refused to lift the covering. Revisiting the Cratchits, he learned that Tiny Tim had died.

After seeing his old countinghouse and his own neglected grave, Scrooge realized that it was he who had lain on the bed in the cold, stripped room with no one to mourn his death. Scrooge begged the spirit that it should not be so, vowing that he would change, that he would forever honor Christmas in his heart. He made a desperate grasp for the phantom's hand and realized that the ghost had shriveled away and dwindled into a bedpost. Scrooge bounded out of bed and thanked Jacob Marley's ghost for his chance to make amends. Dashing into the street, he realized that it was Christmas Day. His first act was to order the largest turkey available to be sent anonymously to the Cratchits. The day before, Scrooge had ordered a man from his counting-house for asking a contribution; now Scrooge gave him a large sum of money for the poor. Then he astounded his nephew by arriving at his house for Christmas dinner and making himself the life of the party.

Scrooge never reverted to his old ways. He raised Bob Cratchit's salary, improved conditions in his office, contributed generously to all charities, and became a second father to Tiny Tim. It was said of him thereafter that he truly knew how to keep Christmas well.

Critical Evaluation:

   A Christmas Carol is one of Charles Dickens' best-known and most popular books. A century after it was written, it was still required reading at Christmas for many families. It has been made into films, plays, and parodies. As a result of this wide popularity, the book has come to be considered as a simplistic morality play, and its original intent is often forgotten.

As literature, *A Christmas Carol* is not easy to categorize. At one level, it is a ghost story, complete with clanking chains and foggy nights. It can also be viewed as a moral lesson about the true meaning of Christmas and the proper manner of treating fellow human beings. There is also a sociological element: Dickens had much to say about poverty, and the pitiful condition of the Cratchit family and especially the crippled Tiny Tim are set up as an indictment against an uncaring society. Another interesting aspect of the book is its psychological dimension.

Ebenezer Scrooge begins the story as a man obsessed by money, with apparently no feelings of humanity or interest in human society. He detests Christmas not because of any lack of Christian faith, but because Christmas is an interruption of business. Christmas is a time for emotions, which Scrooge has abjured. Christmas is used as a device for depicting Scrooge's attitudes toward people. The religious meaning of the holiday is relatively unimportant to the story, except in an indirect sense about Christian charity and love of one's neighbor.

It is important in this regard to consider that Dickens uses the terms "ghost" and "spirit" interchangeably in *A Christmas Carol*. The word "spirit" had several meanings in Dickens' time. The spirits that visit Scrooge on Christmas Eve are spirits in the supernatural, religious, and emotional senses.

Marley's ghost is the first visitor of the night, and interestingly, the only one that Scrooge is able to banish by his own willpower. Marley represents Scrooge's present state of mind, acting as a sort of mirror. He is also the only one of the four spirits that represents a human being. At the beginning of the story, Scrooge is still capable of ignoring human beings, and can thus handle Marley's ghost with relative ease.

The Ghost of Christmas Past is a different case entirely. This spirit represents Scrooge's own youth, and readers see scenes of a lonely boy, spending Christmas alone. Christmas Past represents memory, especially suppressed memory. As the second spirit departs, Scrooge has begun to understand that he has shut out the human race because he himself was excluded as a child.

The Ghost of Christmas Present represents the outside world, the world of joy and love that Scrooge has denied himself. Readers see the lives of other people at Christmas, including the Cratchits, who despite their poverty have hope and joy. Bob Cratchit has been treated as merely a faceless employee by Scrooge. At this stage of Scrooge's night, Cratchit becomes a symbol of a world that Scrooge can enter if he will allow himself to do so.

The final spirit, the Ghost of Christmas Yet to Come, is clearly Death, silent and hooded. It represents, however, a probable future, not a necessary one. When Scrooge awakens, he is immediately aware of the fact that he is capable of changing that future, of increasing happiness for other people, and thereby increasing his own happiness.

Scrooge ends the story by treating the Cratchits to a prize turkey, by joining his nephew's family in their Christmas celebration, and by joining children in their games out in the street. The last act is particularly important. By accepting the possibility of happiness, Scrooge has managed to redeem his own lost childhood, and thereby becomes an adult.

There is some question as to how much Scrooge has really changed. He is still primarily interested in money. It is interesting that he decides to spread Christmas joy by sharing his wealth, as wealth is still central to his character. Even after his apparent changes, Scrooge is still basically a businessman, primarily interested in money; he is simply more willing to share that money.

Tiny Tim, a boy living in poverty and condemned to physical misery as well, is a very important device for showing the reader how callous Scrooge has become. The fact that Scrooge can ignore the existence of this pitiful little boy is central to his divorce from the human race. When he befriends the child, this is a clear sign that he has changed his ways.

A Christmas Carol is, above all, a story of the journey through life of a lonely man. Until the very end of the novel, the other characters exist only in Scrooge's visions, and are no more real than the ghosts who show him those images. When the old miser begins to notice people, those people finally become real. The book is often dismissed as overly sentimental. Much better ghost stories have been written, and social commentary about Victorian England is sometimes difficult for contemporary readers. Read as a psychological journey, however, *A Christmas Carol* is unique. It shows readers the innermost thoughts of an unhappy man, through the device of having him see himself in a series of supernatural mirrors.

"Critical Evaluation" by Marc Goldstein

Bibliography:

Donovan, Frank. *Dickens and Youth*. New York: Dodd, Mead, 1968. A discussion of Dickens' extensive use of children in his novels. *A Christmas Carol* is considered in detail, in two ways. Scrooge's unhappy childhood is considered as the major cause for his present loneliness and misanthropy. The children of Bob Cratchit, especially Tiny Tim, are examined as examples of innocents who are happy even when their circumstances are difficult.

Kaplan, Fred. *Dickens: A Biography*. New York: William Morrow, 1988. A comprehensive biography of the author, with more than 500 pages of text and more than 100 illustrations. The focus is on Dickens' psychological makeup, and how it affected his written works.

Prickett, Stephen. *Victorian Fantasy*. Bloomington: Indiana University Press, 1979. A study of fantasy writings in Victorian England. Chapter 2, "Christmas at Scrooge's," discusses the use of fantasy elements in *A Christmas Carol* and Dickens' other Christmas stories.

Slater, Michael, ed. *Dickens 1970*. Briarcliff Manor, N.Y.: Stein & Day, 1970. An anthology of essays on Dickens' works, on the occasion of the one hundredth anniversary of his death. Particularly of interest is Angus Wilson's article "Dickens on Children and Childhood," which focuses on Tiny Tim as a symbol of innocence, hope, and faith.

Stone, Harry. *Dickens and the Invisible World: Fairy Tales, Fantasy, and Novel-Making*. Bloomington: Indiana University Press, 1979. A treatment of Dickens' use of fantasy elements in his literary works. The fifth chapter focuses on five short works, including *A Christmas Carol*. The emphasis is on the emotions of the characters as reflected in their supernatural experiences.

CHRONICLES

Type of work: History
Author: Jean Froissart (1337?-c. 1404)
Time of work: 1316-1399
Locale: England and Western Europe
*First transcribed: Chroniques de France, d'Engleterre, d'Éscoce, de Bretaigne, d'Espaigne,
d'Italie, de Flanders et d'Alemaigne,* 1373-1410 (English translation, 1523-1525)

Jean Froissart, by being so much of his age, became a writer for all time. This unpriestly priest, this citizen celebrator of chivalry took such an intense joy in chronicling his times that he devoted an entire half-century to traveling, interviewing, writing, and rewriting. He interviewed more than two hundred princes in various courts from Rome and the Pyrenees to Edinburgh, and with such zest that he was a favorite of the nobles on both sides in the Hundred Years' War. In his own time his works were widely copied and illuminated.

Although he recorded the Hundred Years' War on a colorful and unprecedented scale, he is not a reliable historian. Born in Valenciennes, now a city in France but at that time in the Low Country countship of Hainaut, Froissart was a Fleming who shifted his allegiance from one side of the conflict to the other, depending on the court that offered him patronage at the moment. Relying mostly on hearsay evidence from partisan observers, he never consulted official documents, many of which are still extant. As a result his history abounds in anachronisms, erroneous dates, garbled names, and impossible topography. Froissart was also, understandably, unaware that the fourteenth century marked the waning of the Middle Ages, and that he was the last of the medieval innocents. The histories that follow his reflect a realism and disillusionment that are in startling contrast to Froissart's chivalric naïveté.

Froissart's purpose was clear: He wrote "in order that the honorable and noble adventures and feats of arms, done and achieved by the wars of France and England, should notably be registered and put in perpetual memory." His remarkable career was auspiciously launched in 1361 when he went to England as Queen Philippa's secretary and court historian. There he thoroughly ingratiated himself with the aristocracy and began a pro-English account of the wars from the time of Edward III in 1316 to the death of Richard II in 1399. Curiously enough, he makes no mention of Chaucer, a rival at court. Chaucer reciprocated the slight. After the queen's death in 1369, Froissart returned to Valenciennes, went into business, and completed book 1 of the *Chronicles* under the patronage of Robert of Namur, Philippa's nephew. A very large proportion of that version was directly plagiarized from his pro-English predecessor, Jehan le Bel, but Froissart's fame was such that Count Guy de Blois gave him first a prosperous living at Lestinnes and later a sinecure as a private chaplain. Under Count Guy's patronage Froissart traveled through France, making an especially fruitful trip in 1388 to Gaston de Foix in Orthez. During this period, he rewrote book 1 and completed books 2 and 3, adopting a pro-French perspective on the wars. "Let it not be said," he lies, "that I have corrupted this noble history through the favor accorded me by Count Guy de Blois, for whom I wrote it. No, indeed! For I will say nothing but the truth and keep a straight course without favoring one side or the other."

In 1397, Count Guy de Blois, a drunkard who had sold his patrimony, died. Froissart gained a new patron in the duke of Bavaria, who sent him again to England. Although Richard II, the new king, did not receive him cordially, it is interesting to note that the chronicles again took on a somewhat pro-English turn, whether subconsciously or by design, when Froissart retired to his hometown eighteen months later.

Froissart more than returned the favors of his patrons by immortalizing them as heroes and heroines of chivalry, and he took immense delight in doing so: "I have taken more pleasure in it than in anything else. The more I work on these things, the more they please me, for just as the gentle knights and squires love the calling of arms and perfect themselves by constant exercise, so I, by laboring in this matter, acquire skill and take pleasure in it." What Froissart loved most was the resplendent panoply and pageantry of jousts and battle, and the *Chronicles* are really a pastiche of anecdotes, great and small. His knights are invariably "noble, courteous, bold, and enterprising" and his ladies are eternally noble, beautiful, and gentle. It is no wonder that Sir Walter Scott said of Froissart, "This is my master!"

The *Chronicles* abound in dramatic vignettes: the Black Prince graciously submissive to his own prisoner, King John; the duke of Brabant's envoy sick almost to death of the treachery he has unwittingly performed; King Henry IV meditatively feeding his falcons as he deliberates on the murder of deposed Richard; Gaston de Foix discovering a purse of poison on his treacherous son's person and unwillingly killing him; the blind king of Bohemia found dead in battle surrounded by the bodies of loyal guardsmen. In these narratives Froissart's style occasionally soars above the conventional rhetoric of the medieval romance. Froissart can range from the crude language of peasants and soldiers to the lofty rhetoric of the bishop of St. Andrew's. A knight storming battlements in Spain leans over the wall to see the defenders, "ugly as monkeys or bears devouring pears." The Earl of Derby greets Pembroke after the battle of Auberoche: "Welcome, cousin Pembroke, you have come just in time to sprinkle holy water on the dead!" "Where is that son of a Jew's whore?" demands de Trastamara before the murder of Don Carlos.

Perhaps one of the finest little dramas concerns Edward III's love game of chess with the countess whom he has rescued from a Scottish siege:

> When the chessmen arrived, the King, who wished to leave some possession of his with the Countess, challenged her, saying: "My lady, what stakes will you play?" And the Countess replied: "And you, Sire?" Then the King placed on the table a very fine ring, set with a large ruby, which he was wearing on his finger. The Countess said: "Sire, Sire, I have no ring as valuable as that." "Lady," said the King, "put down such as you have, it is indeed good enough."

The countess, to please the king, took from her finger a gold ring, which was not of great worth. Then they played at chess together, the countess playing as well as she could, in order that the king should not consider her too simple and ignorant; and the king made wrong moves, and did not play as well as he might. There was scarce a pause between the moves, but he looked so hard at the countess that she lost countenance and fumbled her game. When the king saw that she had lost a knight, a rook, or whatever it might be, he lost too to keep the countess in play.

Froissart is by no means always so delicately perceptive. He can describe in gruesome detail the dismemberment of Hugh Despencer, the heart thrown into the fire, the head sent to London, and the pieces of his quartered body carried off to be displayed in other cities—and then calmly proceed with the narrative of the queen's joyous arrival for feasting in London. One feels a bizarre sense of the grotesque when Froissart asserts matter-of-factly that Galeas Visconti murdered his uncle "by bleeding him in the neck, as they are wont to do in Lombardy when they wish to hasten a person's end." He laments when captives are killed because they would have brought a good ransom. There are dozens of accounts of towns sacked and women and children murdered, all related without the least trace of compassion. Perhaps this detachment is explained by the fact that in Froissart's time, violence, death, and murder were common experience or by Froissart's evident commitment to the Boethian philosophy of the wheel of fortune, dramatically presented in one of the illuminated miniatures of an early manuscript.

Michel Eyquem de Montaigne, who was a touchstone of the Renaissance just as Froissart was of the Middle Ages, said of the *Chronicles* that they were the "crude and unshapen substance of history." If he meant that they lacked any profound philosophical perspective, he was right. The simplicity of Froissart's mind can be seen in his obtuse declaration that "Mankind is divided into three classes: the valiant who face the perils of war . . . , the people who talk of their successes and fortunes, and the clerks who write and record their great deeds." Froissart was a man who could report, without realizing the significance of his account, that French King John's Round Table of three hundred knights, who were to meet annually to tell their tales and have their heroism recorded, lasted only one year because all the knights perished.

Nevertheless, the *Chronicles* are rich in sheer entertainment value. Froissart's account of the blazing day when Charles VI went mad is illustrative. As the troupe rode along, a page accidentally struck another's helmet with his spear:

> The King, who rode but afore them, with the noise suddenly started, and his heart trembled, and into his imagination ran the impression of the words of the man that stopped his horse in the forest of Mans, and it ran into his thought that his enemies ran after him to slay and destroy him, and with that abusion he fell out of his wit by feebleness of his head, and dashed his spurs to his horse and drew out the sword and turned to his pages, having no knowledge of any man, weening himself to be in a battle enclosed with his enemies, and lifted up his sword to strike, he cared not where, and cried and said: "On, on upon these traitors!"

Of greater horror are the descriptions of Sir Peter of Be'arn haunted by the ghost of a bear; or of the king of France at a marriage feast almost burned to death when five of his squires dressed in pitch-covered linen for an entertainment brushed against a torchlight and were consumed in the flames.

Bibliography:
Ainsworth, Peter F. *Jean Froissart and the Fabric of History: Truth, Myth, and Fiction in the "Chroniques."* Oxford, England: Clarendon Press, 1990. Examines Froissart's *Chronicles* as a literary work. Explores how Froissart crafted his historical subject matter in literary terms to attempt to reconcile the realities of war with the ideals of chivalry.
Coulton, G. G. *The Chronicler of European Chivalry.* London: The Studio, 1930. Narrates Froissart's biography and utilizes the *Chronicles* to provide information about Froissart's life. Illustrations of illuminations from two manuscripts of Froissart's *Chronicles* add vivacity to the events that Froissart recounts.
Froissart, Jean. *Chronicles.* Rev. ed. Selected, translated, and edited by Geoffrey Brereton. Harmondsworth, Middlesex, England: Penguin Books, 1978. The most accessible English translation of Froissart's *Chronicles.* Contains a concise, informative introduction about Froissart, the composition of the *Chronicles,* and the manuscript versions of this work. Helpful glossary, map, and index of persons.
Palmer, J. J. N., ed. *Froissart: Historian.* Woodbridge, Suffolk, England: Boydell Press, 1981. A collection of essays by ten historians. Addresses aspects of Froissart's writings in the *Chronicles.* Evaluates his contribution as a source for modern historical study of the Hundred Years' War.
Shears, F. S. *Froissart, Chronicler and Poet.* London: George Routledge and Sons, 1930. A literary biography of Froissart. Focuses on the *Chronicles* in the context of Froissart's life and experiences of English and French culture in the late fourteenth century.

THE CID

Type of work: Drama
Author: Pierre Corneille (1606-1684)
Type of plot: Tragicomedy
Time of plot: Eleventh century
Locale: Seville, Spain
First performed: 1637; first published, 1637 as *Le Cid* (English translation, 1637)

> *Principal characters:*
> DON FERNAND, the king of Castile
> DOÑA URRAQUE, the infanta, daughter of Fernand
> DON DIÈGUE, the father of Rodrigue
> DON GOMÈS, the father of Chimène
> DON RODRIGUE, the accepted suitor of Chimène
> DON SANCHE, in love with Chimène
> CHIMÈNE, the daughter of Don Gomès, in love with Rodrigue

The Story:

Because she was the princess royal, the infanta felt she could not openly love Rodrigue, a nobleman of lower rank. She encouraged, therefore, the growing attachment between Chimène and Rodrigue. Chimène asked her father, Don Gomès, to choose either Rodrigue or Sanche to be his son-in-law. She awaited the choice anxiously; her father was on his way to court and she would soon hear his decision. Don Gomès chose Rodrigue without hesitation, chiefly because of the fame of Don Diègue, Rodrigue's father.

However, a complication soon arose at court. The king had chosen Don Diègue as preceptor for his son, the heir apparent. Don Gomès felt that the choice was unjust. Don Diègue had been the greatest warrior in Castile, but he was now old. Don Gomès considered himself the most valiant knight in the kingdom. In a bitter quarrel, Don Gomès unjustly accused Don Diègue of gaining the king's favor through flattery and deceit. He felt that the prince needed a preceptor who would be a living example of the proper virtues, not a teacher who would dwell in the past. In the quarrel, Don Gomès slapped his older rival. Don Diègue, too feeble to draw his sword against Don Gomès, upbraided himself bitterly for having to accept the insult. His only recourse was to call on his young son to uphold the family honor.

Torn between love and duty, Rodrigue challenged Don Gomès to a duel. After some hesitation because of Rodrigue's youth and unproved valor, Don Gomès accepted the challenge of his daughter's suitor. To the surprise of the court, Rodrigue, the untried novice, killed the mightiest man in Castile, piercing with his sword the man whom he respected as his future father-in-law.

Chimène now felt herself in a desperate plight because her love for Rodrigue was mixed with hatred for the murderer of her father. She finally decided to avenge her father by seeking justice from the king. Since she had the right to petition the king, Don Fernand was forced to hear her pleas. In the scene at court, Don Diègue made a strong plea in favor of his son, reminding the king that Rodrigue had done only what honor forced him to do—uphold the family name.

The king was saved from the vexing decision when fierce Moors assaulted the walls of Seville. Chimène awaited the outcome of the battle with mixed emotions. The army of Castile returned in triumph, bringing as captives two Moorish kings. The man who had inspired and led the Castilians by his audacity was Rodrigue. The grateful king gave the hero a new title, the Cid, a Moorish name meaning "lord." The infanta was wretched. Although her high position would not allow her to love Rodrigue, she could love the Cid, a high noble and the hero of Castile. She showed her nobility, however, by yielding to Chimène's prior right.

Chimène was still bound to seek redress. The king resolved to test her true feelings. When she entered the throne room, he told her gravely that Rodrigue had died from battle wounds. Chimène fainted. The king advised her to follow the promptings of her heart and cease her quest for vengeance.

Still holding duty above love, however, Chimène insisted on her feudal right of a champion. Sanche, hoping to win the favor of Chimène, offered to meet Rodrigue in mortal combat and avenge the death of Don Gomès. Chimène accepted him as her champion. The king decreed that Chimène must marry the victor. In private, Rodrigue came to Chimène. Indignant at first, Chimène soon softened when she learned that Rodrigue had resolved to let himself be killed because she wished it. Again wavering between love and duty, Chimène begged him to defend himself as best he could.

Sanche went bravely to meet Rodrigue, who easily disarmed his opponent and showed his magnanimity by refusing to kill Chimène's champion. He sent his sword to Chimène in token of defeat. As soon as Chimène saw her champion approach with Rodrigue's sword in his hand, she immediately thought that Rodrigue was dead. She ran in haste to the king and begged him to change his edict because she could not bear to wed the slayer of her lover. When the king told her the truth, that Rodrigue had won, Don Diègue praised her for at last avowing openly her love. Still Chimène hesitated to take Rodrigue as her husband. The king understood her plight. He ordered the Cid to lead an expedition against the Moors. The wise king knew that time would heal the breach between the lovers.

Critical Evaluation:

The neoclassical tragedies of seventeenth century France are especially in need of introductions for a modern audience; Pierre Corneille's *The Cid* only a little less than most. The Renaissance had seen, among other things, a growth of interest in the individual and in the self. This focusing of interest was in conflict with the medieval view, which perceived humanity more as members of a race than as individuals. The individual was perceived, to be sure, but perceived as a component of society, reproducing it and assuring its integrity by maintaining binding interrelationships with other members of society both alive and dead. In Corneille's time, the more romantic tenets of the Renaissance had been displaced by the neoclassical adoption of the life of reason and order within a cohesive community; and with this life there came, understandably, a high regard for honor.

The twentieth century does not easily understand the classical and neoclassical concern for "honor" because the twentieth century is essentially a romantic one; its concerns are primarily for the immediate future and for those who are physically alive. These are the concerns of the individual. Romantic love, concerning itself as it does with the immediate future, is of extreme importance in the twentieth century. Honor, however, is based not upon immediacy or subjectivity but upon loyalty to others (particularly those to whom one is related by blood ties, marriage, or a shared set of cultural traditions) and concern for the opinions of others. It is not merely a matter of respectfully but radically differing from one's peers on moral questions; one's peers are a part of oneself; to differ radically from them is to be out of order with oneself. The task then, in living a life of honor, is to live it so that others approve. For if others do not approve, no man or woman in such an age can approve of himself or herself.

This is the situation of *The Cid*. The infanta's dilemma is one of the keynotes of the play; she must choose between her romantic love for Rodrigue (to whom she is impelled by her feelings as an individual) and her honor (as demanded by her ties to her father and her attendant position in society). Love urges that she marry him, but honor insists that she not marry beneath her station. She chooses honor almost instinctively, even going so far as to take direct action to decrease her own romantic love; she brings Rodrigue and Chimène together so as to make him completely unavailable to herself as a lover. In Act V she almost succumbs to love, thinking Rodrigue's newly won glories and title bring him nearly to her social station, but her lady-in-waiting (acting as her visible conscience on the stage) dissuades her. She goes on to aid in the final reconciliation of the principal pair.

Rodrigue and Chimène each face a similar choice. While the infanta's problem has a simpler (though not easier) solution, that of not declaring her love, Rodrigue cannot expect a loving response from the daughter of the man he has killed, and Chimène cannot give such a response. Both are acting in a typically honorable fashion, maintaining their fathers' reputations and forgoing their personal desires. To do less would be to make themselves less than human. Honor threatens the love affair of Chimène and Rodrigue, while love threatens the honor of the infanta.

It will seem to some readers that love wins out over honor in the end, the honorable scruples of the principal pair having been overcome by reason and circumstances. However, love and honor are actually synthesized, neither force canceling the other. The infanta's moral position, being above reproach, is perfect for her role as a proponent of marriage for the pair. Had she surrendered to her own emotion, she could not have been nearly so effective a spokesperson on the part of love for others. Add to this Elvira's chiding and, indeed, the king himself in the role of matchmaker, and it will be seen that Corneille is at some pains to overcome excessive preoccupation with honor, but only in such a way as to leave real honor intact and alive.

Until the denouement—Chimène's admission of her love—the heroine sees herself primarily as the daughter of Don Gomès; her admission of her feelings to the king and the resolution of the play are made possible by her being persuaded to see herself primarily as a member of the Castilian community. As a result of this shift in her perception of her role, she no longer sees Rodrigue as an enemy and begins to see the Moors in that capacity. As the principal bulwark against the common enemy, Rodrigue both lays the groundwork for this change in Chimène and is in a unique position to enjoy the benefits of it. Thus, while upholding the concept of honor in a humanly achievable form, the play uses a typically romantic process as the underpinnings of its plot: Thesis and antithesis (honor and love) are synthesized.

Critics have seen in this play certain basic similarities to William Shakespeare's *Romeo and Juliet* (1595), foremost among which is the feud between the lovers' families. A more essential similarity, however, lies in the use of death by both dramatists as a threat to young love. Both Romeo and Rodrigue think of death (for themselves) as a solution to their problems, and both offer the solution with such alacrity as to give rise to speculations of a death wish on both their parts. Such speculations, however, have the distinct disadvantage of focusing attention entirely upon the characters, causing us to ignore the play's overall design. Death is not initially the preoccupation of either hero. Both want simply to marry the ladies they love. Death presents itself to them as a solution only when this desire becomes both undeniable and impossible to satisfy. This renders life impossible, and when life begins to seem impossible the natural impulse is to consign it to a state of nonexistence (the natural state for any impossibility). Death is the inevitable threat, but death becomes truly inevitable only when the character is convinced that life is indeed impossible, that there is no hope for change. Rodrigue repeatedly offers himself to Chimène for execution, believing there is no other solution.

Death, then, is not intrinsic to Rodrigue's character; it is a force from without, threatening a healthy love relationship with the ferocity of a tangible monster. There is a level at which most love comedies are fertility rites, celebrating and promoting the optimism and fecundity of a society. In such comedies the lovers' eventual wedding (or promise of one) affirms this social optimism. However, when optimism and fertility are seriously threatened by death, as they are in this play, a comedy is renamed as a tragicomedy. *The Cid* ends happily with the promise of a marriage, the protagonists having avoided death's many invasions into their happiness. Death's attempts, however, were persistent and were overcome by the slimmest of margins. *The Cid* is Corneille's first major play and is often considered his finest. His plays are often compared to those of his younger contemporary, Jean Racine. Both authors adhered strictly to the neoclassical unities (one action, one time, and one place), though Racine evidently worked more comfortably within those restrictions. Corneille reminds the reader throughout *The Cid* that the action occurs within one day but that the day is an unnaturally full one.

"Critical Evaluation" by John J. Brugaletta

Bibliography:
Abraham, Claude. *Pierre Corneille*. New York: Twayne, 1972. Geared for the general reader; all quotations are in English. Gives a short biographical sketch and discusses the structure, themes, and style in Corneille's plays. Shows the significance of *The Cid* in Corneille's works.
Bénichou, Paul. *Man and Ethics: Studies in French Classicism*. Translated by Elizabeth Hughes. Garden City, N.Y.: Doubleday, 1971. Treats the social and moral conditions of life during the seventeenth century. Brilliantly considers the relation between aesthetic and moral values in literature.
Cook, Albert Spaulding. *French Tragedy: The Power of Enactment*. Chicago: Swallow Press, 1981. Presents an interesting discussion concerning the style of the neoclassical play. The quotations are in both French and English.
Moore, Will Grayburn. *The Classical Drama of France*. Oxford, England: Oxford University Press, 1971. Provides information about the form of the French neoclassical play. Explains the background of *The Cid*.
Yarrow, P. J. *Corneille*. New York: Macmillan, 1963. A general study of Corneille's plays that presents their structure and relates them to their epoch. An excellent treatment of *The Cid*'s importance in the developing of seventeenth century French neoclassicism.

CINNA

Type of work: Drama
Author: Pierre Corneille (1606-1684)
Type of plot: Tragedy
Time of plot: c. 10 C.E.
Locale: Rome
First performed: 1640; first published, 1643 as *Cinna: Ou, La Clémence d'Auguste* (English translation, 1713)

Principal characters:
AUGUSTUS, the emperor of Rome
LIVIA, his wife, the empress
CINNA, the grandson of Pompey
MAXIMUS, his friend and fellow conspirator
AMELIA, engaged to Cinna
FULVIA, her confidante and companion
POLYCLITUS, once Augustus' slave, now a free man
EVANDER, Cinna's freedman
EUPHORBUS, Maximus' freedman

The Story:

Amelia, the daughter of Augustus' tutor, sought revenge against Augustus for her father's death. She had asked for vengeance as a provision of her marriage to Cinna, the grandson of Pompey, who had been more deeply wronged by Augustus than had Amelia. Her friend Fulvia believed that the plot against Augustus' life could be successful only if anger and hatred were not apparent; especially since Augustus held Amelia in such high esteem that courtiers often asked her to act as an intermediary in affairs at court. The two women debated the worth of Augustus as compared to the cruelties exercised to establish him in his high position. Amelia thought the winning of love through the destruction of a tyrant was worth all the risk involved, but self-glorification seemed to Fulvia to be more of the impetus behind the plot than either love or desire for vengeance—a thought which almost caused Amelia to waver in deference to her endangered and beloved Cinna.

Cinna, however, believed the plot had an excellent chance of success. All the conspirators seemed to him as desirous of vengeance and as eager for the rewards of love as he was, though their inspiration was the result of his oratorical eloquence in reciting his own as well as the historical grievances against the emperor. Cinna would, while bearing the sacrificial cup at the next day's ceremony of thanksgiving to the gods, stab Augustus to death. His friend Maximus would hold back the mob, while others would surround Cinna. Even though he proclaimed that he cared not whether he lived or died as long as honor were upheld—an honor not unlike that of Brutus and Cassius, the murderers of Julius Caesar, Amelia hastened to add—he believed that the people would then accept him as emperor. Evander, a freed servant of Cinna, brought news that Augustus wanted to see both Cinna and Maximus, an event which upset their plans and struck fear into Amelia's heart. After the lovers had sworn to die for each other, Amelia retired to Livia's side, while Cinna went to confront Augustus.

Augustus prefaced his remarks with a long history of human desire for the empty bauble of power and then asked the two young men to decide his fate, whether he should be the emperor or a private citizen. Both conspirators swore that Augustus, so much nobler than Julius Caesar, should remain supreme in power as the rightful ruler of a grateful empire. Although the sentiment redounded to Augustus' credit, neither felt it to be more than weakness to want a republic when a monarchy could be maintained. Augustus, however, was not convinced that five generations of struggle to eminence proved anything more than that the people wanted democracy. Cinna, disclaiming this idea, even citing his grandfather's claim on the throne as evidence, urged Augustus to name a successor who could carry on this Augustan age to posterity. Cinna was surprised to hear himself so named. Although Maximus wavered after such a noble act by their ruler, Cinna remained resolute in his bloody plan. He would kill Augustus, put his bloody hand in that of Amelia, and marry her on Augustus' tomb.

A short time later, Maximus revealed to his companion and confidant Euphorbus that he too loved Amelia; the freedman in turn urged his former master to kill Cinna and gain not only the girl but the emperor's gratitude. Maximus, after much argument, was repelled and yet intrigued by such a prospect. Just such a conflict existed in Cinna's breast as well; he loved the revenge but could not feel true hatred for the object, so dear was his own person to Augustus. Maximus suggested that these sentiments were enfeebling, though he felt the justice of their cause. Cinna, alone with his conscience, reasoned from cause to effect and decided to ask Amelia to release him from his promise of revenge.

Amelia greeted her lover with rejoicing, for she too had heard the news of Augustus' high regard for Cinna; she was, however, relentless in her desire for vengeance. When Cinna pleaded with her to return not only his love but that of Augustus as well, she replied that treason was the only answer to Augustus' tyranny. Finally, he agreed to her demands, though not without a commentary on female ruthlessness.

In the meantime, perhaps thinking to better his own low position, Euphorbus went to Augustus with news of the plot against him. Augustus was more shocked at Cinna's treachery than at that of Maximus, who at least gave warning of his feelings, and he would have pardoned the latter had not Euphorbus lied and said that Maximus had committed suicide. In a soliloquy, Augustus summarized the pity of it all. Maximus proposed flight to Amelia as the best solution to a bad situation. When she spurned his love as traitorous to his friend, he in turn lamented the counsel of Euphorbus.

Augustus summoned Cinna and spoke of the leniency with which he had allowed his traditional enemy to live as recompense for ancient wrongs. For this, he declared, Cinna had planned to kill him at a religious ceremony in the capitol. The emperor then offered all to Cinna, even though, without the help of Augustus, the young man could not succeed in his design. Cinna, unrepentant, refused to give Augustus satisfaction over his death.

Amelia and Livia then resolved the conflict, the former taking the blame on herself, even begging to die with Cinna; the lovers quarreled over the seeming break in love and honor. Maximus then hastened to reveal his betrayal, through Euphorbus, of the plot. These circumstances moved Augustus to ask the friendship of those whom he most admired and loved. Amelia, the first to respond, was followed by the others, all moved by royal clemency. Livia commended her husband's generosity as a bright example to future rulers. Augustus humbly wished it would be so and appointed the morrow as a day of joyous sacrifice, doubly so because of the plotters' remorse and the forgiveness of the man against whom they had conspired.

Critical Evaluation:

Credited by many critics to have written the first play exemplifying the neoclassical style introduced into France in 1630, Pierre Corneille was received into the French Academy in 1647. His career was highly prolific, including thirty-two plays. Although he became a lawyer, the playwright won accolades at an early age for his versification in Latin and published poems entitled *Mélanges poétiques* in 1632. Corneille studied Aristotle, the Greek and Roman classics, and Spanish history, producing the neoclassical play *Le Cid* (1637), which defined the rules of seventeenth century French drama. Influenced by the precepts of both Aristotle and Horace concerning decorum, verisimilitude, and the unities of time, place, and action, Corneille brought reason, order, and clarity to French plays, combining realism with the marvelous by means of the elegant Alexandrine twelve-syllable line. After defining the neoclassical style with *Le Cid*, Corneille began his series of plays taken from Roman history; his first Roman tragedy was *Horace* (1640).

In the Roman tragedy *Cinna*, Corneille distinguishes himself by showing that a tragedy consisting of mental conflicts can be as theatrical as a drama involving exterior actions. *Cinna* illustrated one of the greatest contributions that Corneille gave to the development of neoclassical French tragedy: the establishment of abrupt changes of situation during the drama, changes designated as *coups de théâtre*. In Act I of *Cinna*, Corneille established the conflict of the play as duty versus love. In order to be worthy of Amelia's love, Cinna has to fulfill her duty to avenge the death of her father through killing Emperor Augustus. Amelia ponders the threat to her lover's life upon achieving this duty, while Cinna plots enthusiastically with other conspirators to overthrow the tyrannical Augustus. The *coups de théâtre* occur when Cinna and Maximus are called to present themselves to the king. This concluding action cements the lovers' commitment to their duty and love, thus creating the suspense that Augustus might have already gained knowledge of the conspiracy. Corneille's implementation of abrupt changes of situation gave interest to *Cinna* and provided the background for the irony of the play, in which the monstrous tyrant of Act I is portrayed as a compassionate human being in the final act.

This humanization is foreshadowed by the play's subtitle, the mercy of Augustus, since it underscores the significance of the emperor's response to the assassination plot. Cinna's regeneration exemplifies the rule that a neoclassical play should take its background from a credible source. In fact, Corneille consulted several Roman sources, including Seneca's *De Clementia* (c. 55) and thw works of Cassius Dio. Seneca's essay on mercy in *De Clementia* related the story of Augustus' discovery of the plot of Pompey's grandson Cinna upon whom Augustus had bestowed various favors; his wife Livia suggested that he use clemency to quell the conspiracy. This suggested the political theme of Corneille's *Cinna*, which involved the decision of the Romans to choose between anarchy or absolute monarchy. Augustus' first monologue to Cinna and Maximus reflects this indecisiveness: "Augustus, Rome, the State are in your hands. . . . You'll place all Europe, Asia, Africa under a monarch's or republic's rule." Corneille's use of dramatic irony is seen in Augustus' statement in that the emperor does not know that Cinna, Maximus, and Amelia have already devised a plot to kill him.

Corneille's condensation of the historical events in Roman history concerning the emperor's rise to power and the establishment of his absolute monarchy allowed the French author to emphasize Octavian's change of name to Augustus. This change of name, taken from the works of Cassius Dio, not only suggests that the sacred king merited respect but also links the political theme to the moral one. The moral theme refers to the evolution of Augustus' character, since the king could, in the end, reconcile himself with the conspirators because he ascertained that they were motivated by either love or jealousy. In fact, the plot could be reduced to the following formula: Maximus loved Amelia, who loved Cinna. The king's realization of this love triangle coupled with his wife's proposal to act out of clemency allows the monarch to develop morally in a way that is reminiscent of Seneca's three levels of moral ascendancy: pity, pardon, and clemency. At the beginning of the play, Augustus expresses pity for the fate of the people if he were to yield the throne to another monarch; Cinna hypocritically encourages the king to continue his reign. Then, after learning about the murder plot, Augustus offers Maximus an unmerited pardon out of sorrow over the whole situation, for Maximus has been tempted to arrange the death of his friend Cinna in order to marry Amelia. Finally, because of Livia's suggestion of clemency to resolve Cinna's participation in the treasonous situation, the play ends with the monarch's authority augmented. The positive result of Augustus' clemency is summarized by Cinna, who declares that the monarch's unparalleled action makes his own crime greater and Augustus' power more just. Hence, the emperor sees himself as the master of himself and of the world.

Augustus' act of clemency completes the theme of moral development as well as the political theme, since it allows the acceptance of the absolute monarchy. Corneille thus established in his plays a respect for the royal standard of conduct, a standard that the playwright termed "generosity."

Corneille's fast-moving, compact style and his observance of the unities of a single time, place, and action in *Cinna* prefigured Jean Racine's tragedies, which were written during the epoch of Louis XIV's absolute monarchy. Similar to Racine, Corneille based his action on psychological decisions, thus enabling *Cinna* to present a dramatic concentration that he rarely achieved in his other works.

"Critical Evaluation" by Linda Prewett Davis

Bibliography:
Allentuch, Harriet R. "The Problem of Cinna." *French Review* 48, no. 5 (April, 1975): 878-886. A general article that presents certain psychological aspects of Cinna's character. Discusses Cinna's contradictory behavior and his relationship with the other main characters.

Broome, J. H. *A Student's Guide to Corneille: Four Tragedies.* London: Heinemann Educational Books, 1971. Provides an introductory chapter about the scope of Corneille's works and his dramatic theory. Treats the subject, the scheme of characters, the dramatic mechanism, and the themes. Gives an evaluation of possible interpretations of the tragedies.

Fogel, Herbert. *The Criticism of Cornelian Tragedy: A Study of Critical Writing from the Seventeenth to the Twentieth Century.* New York: Exposition Press, 1967. An excellent basic analysis of the history of Cornelian tragedy. Divided into four periods that designate marked contrasts or strict compliance with tradition.

Lough, John. *An Introduction to Seventeenth Century France.* New York: David McKay, 1969. An informative general depiction of seventeenth century France through the great literary works. Discusses the social and political history of the seventeenth century, including the absolutism of Louis XIV. Contains a section on the literary background, portraying the relationship between the writers and their public which influenced the development of language and literature.

Nelson, Robert J. *Corneille, His Heroes, and Their Worlds.* Philadelphia: University of Pennsylvania Press, 1963. Gives various analytical insights concerning the dramatic skills of Pierre Corneille. Concentrates especially on the themes of the Cornelian hero and his world.

CINQ-MARS

Type of work: Novel
Author: Alfred de Vigny (1797-1863)
Type of plot: Historical
Time of plot: Seventeenth century
Locale: France
First published: 1826 (English translation, 1847)

Principal characters:

HENRI D'EFFIAT, Marquis of Cinq-Mars and a conspirator against
Richelieu
CARDINAL RICHELIEU, Minister of State
LOUIS XIII, king of France
ANNE OF AUSTRIA, queen of France
MARIE DE GONZAGA, the beloved of Henri Cinq-Mars
FRANÇOIS AUGUST DE THOU, a fellow conspirator with Cinq-Mars

The Story:

One June day in 1639, at the chateau of Chaumont in Touraine, young Henri d'Effiat, Marquis of Cinq-Mars, took leave of his family and set out, at the request of Cardinal Richelieu, Louis XIII's chief minister, to join the king's forces at the siege of Perpignan. Shortly after he left, his mother's guest, the Marshal Bassompierre, was placed under arrest at Richelieu's order and sent in chains toward Paris and the Bastille. Young Cinq-Mars tried to release the marshal, but the haughty old soldier refused to be rescued. As if his flouting of the king's officers were not enough for one day, Cinq-Mars returned under cover of night to the chateau to bid good-bye again to Marie de Gonzaga, the beautiful duchess of Mantua, who was staying with Cinq-Mars' mother at the chateau. He returned to bid her farewell again, because the two, despite the differences of their stations, were very much in love.

Finally leaving Chaumont, Cinq-Mars, accompanied by a few servants, set out for Loudun. Upon his arrival, he found the town in a turmoil because a local clergyman, a monk named Urbain Grandier, was under trial as a magician. Charges against the monk had been made by order of Richelieu, who wished to do away with the independent cleric. The Abbé Quillet, Cinq-Mars' former tutor, had taken the clergyman's part and was about to leave Loudun in secret, fearful for his own life. At the execution of Grandier, Cinq-Mars discovered that the man's assassins, for they were but that, had given him a red-hot cross to kiss. Cinq-Mars seized the cross and struck the judge's face with it, thus earning the enmity of one of Richelieu's most trusted agents.

After the execution, Cinq-Mars hastened on his way to Perpignan. In the meantime, however, Cardinal Richelieu was making plans to use Cinq-Mars as a tool in undermining the authority of the king. The report of his agents about Cinq-Mars' actions with regard to the king's officers and Richelieu's agents made no difference to the cardinal, who believed he could shape the young man to his own ends.

Shortly after his arrival at Perpignan, Cinq-Mars was asked to represent the monarchist's side in a duel against a cardinalist sympathizer. Immediately after the duel, he found himself in the thick of an attack on the walls of the besieged city, along with the members of the king's own guard. He behaved so valiantly in the struggle that the captain of the guard introduced Cinq-

Mars to the king, much to the disgust of Cardinal Richelieu, who himself had planned to introduce Cinq-Mars to the monarch.

The king took an immediate liking to Cinq-Mars, who had suffered a wound in the battle, and he made the young man an officer in the royal guards. During the battle, Cinq-Mars had befriended the son of the judge whom he had struck with the cross at Loudun, and thereby he made a new friend, for the son was a bitter enemy of his father and hated all that his father and Richelieu represented. At Perpignan, Cinq-Mars also renewed a friendship with a young aristocrat named de Thou, who was later to stand as close to him as a brother.

Two years passed. At the end of that time, Cinq-Mars had become the confidant of Louis XIII, an important officer in the court, and the open and avowed enemy of Richelieu. He hated the minister of state for what Richelieu was doing to France; more important, however, was the fact that Cinq-Mars was ambitious to win for himself honors and posts that might allow him to marry Marie de Gonzaga, who was being prepared against her will to become the queen of Poland.

To accomplish his ends, Cinq-Mars had earned more and more of the king's confidence and had improved his influence with the nobility and the army. He also had gained the support of the duke de Bouillon, who had been estranged from the king by Richelieu. De Bouillon was a strong support, for he had an army of his own in southern France. Cinq-Mars also gained the support of Gaston d'Orleans, the king's brother and another of Richelieu's enemies, and of Anne of Austria, the queen, who wished to protect her children, including the future Louis XIV, from the hatred and ambitions of Richelieu. The success of the plan to depose the minister lay in gaining the king's support and in securing aid from Spain. Cinq-Mars and his fellow conspirators were forced to deal with Spain on their own initiative, for neither King Louis nor his queen could assume responsibility for bringing Spanish troops into France. In addition, Louis XIII had been under the influence of Cardinal Richelieu and his agents for so long that he had little mind of his own and knew almost nothing of the problems, great and small, which daily beset those who guided the kingdom of France in those turbulent years of the 1640's.

Taking his chances, Cinq-Mars signed a treaty with Spain and sent a copy, concealed in a hollow staff, with a trusted messenger to Spain. Then he approached the king and secured the royal permission to revolt against Richelieu, after convincing the king that the revolt was not against the crown. Immediately afterward, as he was leaving the monarch's apartments, Cinq-Mars realized that an agent of the cardinal was on his way to seek an audience with King Louis. All Cinq-Mars could do was hope that the king would hold to the promise he had given the conspirators.

In order to ensure his union with Marie de Gonzaga, Cinq-Mars had the duchess and himself affianced by a clergyman, an act which at that time was the equivalent of legal marriage. In so doing, however, Cinq-Mars revealed all of his plans to the girl in the presence of the priest. Soon afterward, he learned that the priest was not his own agent but was instead a spy for Richelieu. Realizing that his plans were endangered, Cinq-Mars immediately went to Perpignan, which was to be the scene of the revolt.

Richelieu had known all the time what was afoot and had made his plans. Having won over the armies, he knew he had nothing to fear in that quarter. He had also arranged for Marie de Gonzaga, in spite of her love for Cinq-Mars, to become queen of Poland. All that was left was to finish off Cinq-Mars and the other conspirators and prevent the treaty from reaching Spain. The messenger carrying the treaty was intercepted in the Pyrenees by the cardinal's agents and killed. In order to gain control of the conspirators, Richelieu pretended to resign his post as minister. King Louis realized within a few hours that he did not know enough about the affairs of the kingdom to rule France. He called back Richelieu and granted the minister's request to do as he pleased with the conspirators. Gaston d'Orleans was banished, while Cinq-Mars and de Thou were arrested at Narbonne, tried at Lyons by a secret court appointed by Richelieu, and beheaded. Marie de Gonzaga, pawn of the cardinal's political schemes, became queen of Poland.

Critical Evaluation:

Although critics have generally respected Alfred de Vigny's *Cinq-Mars* as one of the first important French historical novels, their judgments have varied wildly regarding its literary or artistic worth. One says that *Cinq-Mars* is Vigny's only mediocre work (his ranking as a poet has always been high); another holds that he did not know what he was doing; a third calls him ideologically confused; a fourth accuses him of distorting history and truth; and a fifth maintains that his plot lacks drama and that his characters are flat.

It is a fact, however, that upon publication in January, 1826, *Cinq-Mars* proved a high popular success by going through a dozen or more editions. It was translated into English by William Hazlitt (not the famous critic and essayist, but his second son, a lawyer and a specialist in French translations) in 1847, an American edition following in 1889. Two other English translations occurred, one by W. Bellingham in 1851 and another, under the title of *The Spider and the Fly*, by Madge Pemberton in 1925. As Edgar Allan Poe once pointed out, however, a book may prove exceedingly popular and yet have no legitimate literary merit.

The reasons for these contrary critical evaluations of Vigny's *Cinq-Mars* are not difficult to imagine. Biases regarding politics, religion, and scientism together with misunderstanding of Vigny's aim and of the generic tendencies of a prose romance are the culprits.

If Vigny's *Cinq-Mars* is to be judged fairly, Vigny's background and his political and moral positions must be understood and weighed in the balance. Likewise his philosophy of history and his execution of his narrative must be considered in terms of his aim and the attributes found in the genre of the prose romance.

Vigny came of a distinguished family of aristocrats dating from the *ancien régime* of prerevolutionary France. He did not regard the French Revolution of 1789-1799 as a progressive event, but as a gross error caused by the centralization policy of the royal administration guided by Cardinal Richelieu. To Vigny, this policy, first, impoverished the majority of the rural nobility; second, it contributed to the moral degeneracy of the few rich *gentilshommes champêtres* who were tempted to desert the land of their fathers and go to Versailles or Paris to purchase an appointment at court; and, third, it confused and unbalanced the social hierarchy because the state raised money by creating offices to be purchased by the increasingly rich bourgeoisie who thereby had "nobility" conferred upon them.

Hence, Vigny was a royalist and a legitimist; that is, from a liberal point of view, he was a conservative and a reactionary. So was his mentor, Sir Walter Scott, whose adventures were his way of reacting against the effects of the Industrial Revolution in the region around Birmingham, England. Like Baron de Montesquieu, Vigny believed in the political balance of the three governing powers represented by the clergy, the nobility, and the common people. He was convinced that Louis XIII and his first minister Richelieu were responsible for the gross errors that led to the French Revolution.

Therefore, Vigny intended his historical novel to be a thesis narrative, a feudal parable which would prove his moral conclusion. This narrative, however, is a romance and not a novel. That is, it tends toward divinity and the demoniac, dealing as it does with heroes and not with normal humans. The logic of this results in idealization on the one hand and in demonization on the other, but it moves beyond the ideal to sink into the morass of the actual in a tragic and ironic conclusion. Armed with his didactic motivation, Vigny tends to allegorize his characterizations and even his settings to dramatize his characters appropriately. In thinking out his plot, his politics drove him to accept the feudal myth as true and forced him to face up to the problem of the relation of history to fiction. Attacked for his manipulation of history, he defensively included a manifesto-like preface, "Réflexions sur la vérité dans l'art" ("Thoughts on Truth in Art"), to the 1829 edition of *Cinq-Mars*, and it remained in place in subsequent editions.

In this preface, he affirmed that the past existed only in the minds of living generations. History was a fabula and a romance originally created true and experienced by those who passed it on to later generations by word of mouth. Not knowing more than themselves and nature, there were gaps in their account of the chain of events which the imagination of contemporary people would have to complete. What was true in fact ("le Vraie dans le fait") had to be complemented by the truth in art ("la Vérité dans l'art"); the first belonged to the narration of events, whereas the second belonged to the explanation of the events. This philosophy accounted for the liberties which Vigny took with historical facts. To him, the value of history lay primarily in the moral lessons it taught.

The above items are the factors which must be taken into consideration if a fair evaluation of the literary worth of *Cinq-Mars* is to be given. Vigny was an honest and sincere man who wrote in terms of his true feelings. *Cinq-Mars* is his protest against the destruction of the feudal aristocracy. Although a pessimist, he was strongly idealistic. His romance is much more interesting and exciting than has been reported by some critics in the past; indeed, it is eminently worthwhile.

"Critical Evaluation" by Richard P. Benton

Bibliography:
Denommé, Robert T. "Alfred Victor de Vigny." In vol. 5 of *European Writers: The Romantic Century*, edited by Jacques Barzun and George Stade. New York: Charles Scribner's Sons, 1985. An excellent general account of Vigny and his work, including a fine discussion of *Cinq-Mars*.
Doolittle, James. *Alfred de Vigny*. New York: Twayne, 1967. Mainly a critical biography, with an acute and relatively balanced discussion of *Cinq-Mars*.
Jensen, Mark K. "The Relation of History to Literature in Vigny's Thought Before the Preface to *Cinq-Mars*." *French Forum* 18, no. 2 (May, 1993): 165-183. This investigation shows that Vigny was strongly interested in writing about historical subjects from his tragic dramas written in the period 1815-1817 (which he later destroyed) until the theoretical grounding of his position in the preface to *Cinq-Mars* in 1829.
Kushner, Eva. "Vigny's Vision of History." *Bulletin of the New York Public Library* 69 (1965): 609-617. A study of Vigny in the context of the historical consciousness of French Romanticism that shows him to have been "the most acutely curious inquirer" of all the Romantic writers.
Wren, Keith. "A Suitable Case for Treatment: Ideological Confusion in Vigny's *Cinq-Mars*. *Forum for Modern Language Studies* 18, no. 4 (October, 1982): 335-350. This study takes issue with Marxist interpretations that *Cinq-Mars* is a "straightforward threnody for the defunct second estate" (the nobility) when, on the contrary, the romance is ideologically confused and hence fails to demonstrate its thesis that the destruction of the nobility resulted in the collapse of the whole of society.

THE CITY OF GOD

Type of work: Religious
Author: Saint Augustine (Aurelius Augustinus, 354-430)
First published: De civitate Dei libri, 412-427 (English translation, 1610)

Saint Augustine is one of the most important theologians of the Christian church. He was born a Roman citizen in North Africa. Although he was trained as a classical scholar and was a teacher of rhetoric in Rome and Milan, he became a priest under the influence of St. Ambrose in Milan and then served as bishop of Hippo in North Africa. His extensive writings include commentaries on books of the Bible, sermons, letters, and his famous autobiographical *Confessions* (397-400), which recounts his spiritual journey from his youth to his full acceptance of Christian beliefs during his years in Milan. Among these works, *The City of God* stands out as the most complete exposition of St. Augustine's Christian theology.

Augustine wrote *The City of God* during the later years of his life. The work was begun in 412. The catalyst for writing *The City of God* was a key event in the history of the Roman Empire, the sack of Rome in 410 by the Visigoths, a barbarian Germanic tribe. This event shook the dwindling confidence of the civilized Roman Empire. The remaining pagan Romans blamed the Christian religion for this catastrophe, and Christians became insecure about their faith. In *The City of God*, Saint Augustine addresses these charges and fears.

The City of God is more than a defense of Christianity in response to a particular historical circumstance. Augustine had been planning to write a work that set forth his worldview in its entirety, and *The City of God* fulfills that goal. It is a lengthy work whose composition took about fifteen years. It contains twenty-two books, which can be divided into two thematic parts. The first ten books, books 1 through 10, are apologetic. Their primary purpose is to counter the accusations of pagans about Christianity, especially in view of the recent attack on Rome. In the second part, books 11 through 22, Augustine presents his view of Christian history and the history of salvation as epitomized in his account of the two cities, the heavenly and the earthly. Both parts contain sections that expressly refute pagan beliefs, and both parts develop Augustine's ideas about the two cities.

Book 1 serves as a preamble because it confronts the immediate issues that the sack of Rome raised and it introduces the concept of the two cities. Augustine believed that disasters indiscriminately befall the good and the bad; the important thing is the attitude that any individual assumes toward those circumstances. The true goal is the heavenly City of God, and its citizens, the righteous, are merely pilgrims as they sojourn through life in the earthly city.

Books 2 and 3 demonstrate that the pagan gods have never protected the Romans. By surveying the numerous wars, internal conflicts, and natural disasters that Rome has endured, Augustine reinforces the message that the Romans' pagan religion had never prevented these calamities. Augustine then discusses the character of the Roman Empire and its rulers in books 4 and 5. He points out that God ordains the rise and fall of kingdoms and their rule by just or unjust rulers. Under God's omniscience, Roman power arose because of the virtues of Roman citizens and their leaders under Roman law, reaching its zenith under Christian emperors such as Constantine and Theodosius in the fourth century. In book 5, Augustine's description of the character of the just Christian ruler became a model of conduct, perhaps not always upheld perfectly, for Christian kings.

Books 6 and 7 turn from the politically-oriented remarks about the Roman Empire to aspects of Roman religion. These passages provide an extensive catalogue of the Roman gods. Augustine exposes the contradictions in the polytheistic Roman religion and demonstrates their lack of spiritual fulfillment, which, he argues, only the true Christian God can offer through the promise of eternal life. The first part concludes in books 8 through 10 by examining the claims of classical philosophy, particularly Platonism and its heir Neoplatonism. While Augustine acknowledged that philosophers articulated concepts about a transcendent one or god, the primary flaws in pagan philosophy are its acceptance of pagan beliefs, particularly in demon powers, and its inability to recognize Christ as the mediator between God and humanity.

The second major section, books 11 to 22, explains the origin, history, and ultimate end of the two cities. These twelve books can be subdivided into three groups of four books each. The first four, books 11 to 14, discuss the rise of the two cities from the Creation through the fall of Adam and Eve. The earthly city (sometimes called Babylon) came about from two events: the fall of angels and the fall of humanity. In both cases, willful behavior is the agency of bad deeds, not the essential nature of angels or humans, which is good. Books 12 and 13 refute a cyclical view of history in favor of a linear concept beginning with the Fall and proceeding toward the ultimate end of time in the Last Judgment. Book 14 summarizes the consequences of this situation in the formation of the two cities: the earthly city "seeks glory from men"; for the heavenly city (City of God or Jerusalem), God is "the greatest glory."

Augustine continues the history of the two cities in the next four books, 15 to 18. His account primarily covers biblical history from Adam's children Cain and Abel, who represent the two cities, through the advent of Christ. Particularly in book 18, biblical history is related to world history including Assyria, Egypt, Greece, and Rome. The biblical narrative emphasizes prophecies about the coming of Christ, while the overview of world history takes additional opportunities to refute pagan beliefs.

With the coming of Christ, Augustine has reached his own age, and the last four books, 19 to 22, look toward the final destiny of the heavenly city. Book 19 is important because it contains most of Augustine's views about politics and society. Although true peace can only be achieved in the eternal City of God, he argues, society on earth can strive for peace and order through a well-administered state. The final three books deal with last things: the Last Judgment in book 20, the punishments of hell in book 21, and in book 22 perfect harmony of God in heaven for eternity. Thus, the two cities are a history of God's redemptive plan of salvation from the original Fall through the biblical history of God's people and other secular kingdoms until the final fruition of the City of God at the end of time. On earth, in historical time, the course of the two cities is intertwined. While the citizens of the earthly city act out of self-interest, the citizens of the heavenly city think of themselves as transient pilgrims in this world, whose actions are guided only by the love of God. Their final reward will come, not on earth, but in the City of God, "the kingdom which has not end" where they will "rest and see, see and love, love and praise."

The City of God articulates most definitively the change from the humanistic viewpoint of classical philosophy to the God-centered outlook of the Christian Middle Ages. Throughout this work, Augustine challenges and refutes the belief systems of classical Roman culture, including Roman religion, philosophy, and the political foundation of the Roman Empire. In its place, he puts forward the City of God, the eternal, heavenly city as the ultimate goal of righteous Christians. While it is a duty of citizens of the heavenly city to work for the greatest peace and order during their lifetime spent in the earthly city, their ultimate concern is not with matters in this world but in the next world of the City of God.

In addition to this fundamental shift in perspective, from the Middle Ages to the present, *The City of God* has often been utilized as a source of political ideas and to support particular political positions. Writing a treatise on political theory was not Augustine's purpose. In examining the character of the Roman Empire and its governance, however, particularly in the first part, and in confronting the reality of the earthly city in the second part, Augustine voices opinions on the way society should function. Augustine essentially believed in a separation between earthly political institutions whose concern was social needs and God's kingdom in heaven whose concern was with spiritual welfare and salvation. Even the Church as an institution of human agency was not to be equated with the heavenly city, and a Christian empire led by a Christian ruler was not God's agent on earth. The most that could be expected of human government was the maintenance of an ordered and relatively harmonious society that would facilitate the journey of the citizens of the heavenly city in their pilgrimage through earthly life. Many of Augustine's comments on political matters such as the discussion of the characteristics of the model Christian ruler in book 5 are designed as a guide to bring about this ideal of a peaceful existence in a troubled and tension-filled world.

One of Augustine's most original and influential contributions in *The City of God* was to articulate a new view of history. The idea of history in classical antiquity was primarily cyclical and historical writing tended to be an accumulation of facts and observations. Augustine, in contrast, emphasized a linear and progressive view of history which is developed in the second part of *The City of God*. The course of history begins with the Creation, but the defining event is the fall of humanity from God's grace. From that point, God's plan of redemption governs the course of history which proceeds to the final goal of the Last Judgment at the end of time. While *The City of God* was significant in redirecting the focus of the human viewpoint from the earth-centered world of classical antiquity to the God-centered universe of the Middle Ages, the most enduring influence of *The City of God* in Western culture was the establishment of the progressive and developmental concept of history. This concept remains pervasive in interpreting the meaning of historical events.

Karen Gould

Bibliography:
Battenhouse, Roy W., ed. *A Companion to the Study of St. Augustine.* New York: Oxford University Press, 1955. A collection of essays about Augustine's life and works. Contains an essay by Edward R. Hardy, Jr., on *The City of God* and other essays that help interpret *The City of God* in the context of Augustine's thought.
Brown, Peter. *Augustine of Hippo.* Berkeley: University of California Press, 1967. The most complete and authoritative biography of St. Augustine. *The City of God* is discussed in several chapters within the chronological context of Augustine's life.
Markus, R. A. *Saeculum: History and Society in the Theology of St. Augustine.* Cambridge: Cambridge University Press, 1970. A study of *The City of God* that examines Augustine's concept of history and the political place of society in history that he develops in this work.
van Oort, Johannes. *Jerusalem and Babylon: A Study into Augustine's "City of God" and the Sources of His Doctrine of the Two Cities.* Leiden, The Netherlands: E. J. Brill, 1991. A complete study of *The City of God*, its compositional structure, the meaning of the two cities, and its character as an apologetic and theological work. The sources of Augustine's ideas receive full examination.
Versfeld, Marthinus. *A Guide to "The City of God."* London: Sheed & Ward, 1958. A study of the second part of Augustine's *The City of God*. The interpretation is taken from the standpoint of moral philosophy.

THE CITY OF THE SUN

Type of work: Utopian
Author: Tommaso Campanella (1568-1639)
First published: Civitas solis, 1623 (English translation, 1885)

Tommaso Campanella composed *The City of the Sun* in Italian in 1602, as *La Città del Sole*. It was not until he translated it, with significant changes, into Latin, still the language of the learned, that it was published in 1623. The Italian version is generally regarded as truer to Campanella's thought.

The work is very much a product of its time and Campanella's life. The scientific world-view—that nature can be known by observing the actual things of this world—was developing, but the medieval view was still powerful. A member of the Dominican order and a learned man, Campanella had been trained in the medieval view that truth was largely to be sought through traditional logic and revelation, but he had reacted against too absolute a version of that view. As a result, Campanella suffered greatly for his religious and political ideas; he was imprisoned by the Inquisition. In this work, he offers a kind of order in which people like himself would have a real function.

The Englishman Sir Thomas More had published his *Utopia* in 1516, a Renaissance version of Plato's *Republic* (388-368 B.C.E.). Their ideas of the perfect state underlie Campanella's. Although Campanella's subtitle is "A Poetical Dialogue," the work is a prose dialogue, in which a Genoese traveler, supposedly a sailor with Columbus, is questioned by a knight of the Order of Hospitalers of Saint John. The Genoese describes his visit to the City of the Sun, a utopian state which Campanella locates in, probably, Ceylon (Sri Lanka). The Hospitaler has little to say, his role being simply to feed questions to the Genoese. There are almost no critical responses to the traveler's assertions of what this utopia is or what it values.

The Genoese begins by describing the city itself, an ordered city built on a hill. It is defended by a series of seven great circular walls. On these walls are paintings, an early visual aid for purposes of teaching. Each circle is named after one of the planets, for astrology plays an important part in this utopia. (Campanella, an astrologer himself, regarded astrology as a science.) On the top of the hill, in the center of the city, is a magnificent temple, also designed to teach. Everything in the city is intended to teach, even if delightfully. Most of what is taught is useful knowledge and the values of the City of the Sun.

After the physical description, the Genoese speaks of the city's organization, an organization in which everything is arranged so as to offer order, security, and companionship to all of its inhabitants. One can say that the impulse behind utopias is always the human need for community.

In both Campanella and Plato, the state absolutely controls the lives of all who live in it. To make the state more than just a tyranny, Plato developed the ideal of the philosopher-king, which was imitated by Campanella. That is, the man who is wise and knowledgeable should rule over, but in the interests of, those who are weaker and less able. There is an elite ruling class, but it is not hereditary, for a hereditary ruling class cannot guarantee ability and will soon decay.

The Genoese traveler admires the City of the Sun, where there is no poverty, almost no crime, and very little vice. Everyone serves the state and receives everything from the state. As there is no private ownership, no one can become rich, and no one is poor. Although some people receive honors for service to the community, including the right to wear better or distinctively marked clothing, they are not given private wealth. Most people dress alike. They live in dormitories; every six months, they are moved to new quarters. They eat communally; their food is simple and healthful. All the young, not just a few, must wait on the others. There is a slight inequality in that officials get better portions, but they can share these with other persons as a sign of honor. This healthy life enables the residents to live long lives, most to one hundred years of age, a few to two hundred years old.

Most of the people of the Sun, the Solarians, are presented as being happy with their existence, including the rules they must live by. They accept their officials, because these officials are the most knowledgeable and capable in their various fields. These men are not chosen by popularity or promises: Some are elected; the four top officials and some subordinates select the others. The only criterion is the ability to best fill the office. The four highest officials are self-selected, in that they agree to willingly step down if someone is found who knows their jobs better.

At the apex of the state and the state religion is a single man, called the "Sun" or the "Metaphysician," who must be almost universal in his knowledge. In Campanella's concept of the state, the secular and the religious should not be separated. The Solarians' religion is a kind of christianity without Christ. They know about and honor Jesus, as they know about all other religions. The Hospitaler, listening to the Genoese (and no doubt with Campanella's approval) suggests that when the Solarians become Christian, their state truly will be the perfect state.

Under the Sun are three other major officials, "Power," "Wisdom," and "Love," each in charge of a major concern of the state. (One should note that these titles are attributes of God in Christianity.) These people need not know everything, but each must know well the matters entrusted to him.

"Power" is the war leader, chosen, like his subordinates, from the most courageous and able. He and his authority are necessary, because no state is safe in which individuals make their own decisions about what they should do in war. The neighboring states are continual threats, so the Solarians, even if they wish peace, will have to fight, but always defensively. Physical courage and ability are rewarded, not by wealth or material goods, but by status and such symbols as a crown of oak leaves. Men and women are trained for war. The Genoese says that they would be trained for war even if they were not threatened, because such training keeps them from laziness. Idleness is a crime. The old and the infirm can serve, even in war, for if one is lame, that person still has eyes and can be a sentry.

"Wisdom" directs the sciences, as well as all practical matters. Practical life is of primary importance for all but the highest officials. The Solarians see labor as a communal activity, something everyone shares and from which everyone gains, not just a selected few. A craftsman is as important as anyone else. The Solarians laugh at the Europeans who esteem an idle upper class that is ignorant of crafts. The Solarians also honor agriculture, all going out to the fields in troops at the proper times, and value practical inventiveness. They are ahead of the Europeans in this regard: They have ships that move without oars or sails, and have even learned to fly.

Campanella suggests that love of labor can be taught. Although children are allowed to play, their play is physical so that their bodies are strengthened. The Solarians have no games that can be played sitting down. Children are observed so as to see what jobs they like and can do, so that the worker fits and is happy with his job. The system is efficient and labor is not wasted on luxuries, so the Solarians work only four hours a day. As in war service, there is an equality of the sexes, although the heavier physical tasks are assigned to men.

The official "Love" is in charge of matters of sex. Sex in the City of the Sun is not for the pleasure of individuals. Like labor, it is a social matter. Although the delights of sex are admitted, its primary purpose must be procreation, because the Solarians believe that the state, in order to last, must be concerned with the kind of citizens that it has. Only the fit should have children. There is a certain sexual freedom, but sex is rather strictly controlled. Men and women may cohabit with many others, but chastity is valued up to a certain age, because restraint is thought to produce better children. Men and women come together only when the astrological signs are right, so as to ensure strong offspring. To keep balance, weak men are paired with strong women, so that the children will be fit. As the Solarians regard height, liveliness, and strength as beauty, there are no foolish unions based upon what Europeans imagine as beauty.

There is a paradox here. The Sun and other high officials, although necessarily capable of many practical things, spend most of their time in speculative thought, and so lack "animal spirits," that is, sexual drive. In order for them to father strong children, they must choose only the most vital, active women.

There are no families in the usual sense. Here is the basis of Solarian communism. The Genoese traveler explains that the people of the Sun believe that when men set up families, with homes for their wives and children, egoism enters. The father wants to help his children, so he begins to acquire property. Therefore, to keep people from pursuing wealth, there are no permanent unions. The whole community becomes the family. That love that otherwise would be directed to a small group is directed toward the community. The Genoese remarks that the Solarians love their country in the way the ancient Romans did, giving up family, personal liberty, and life for the state.

Like Plato's state, Campanella's utopia is based upon a rather pessimistic concept of human nature. Human beings are capable of evil; therefore, to preserve the ideal community, the state must direct the fallible individual. There is crime, so there is punishment, even the death penalty, in this commonwealth, admittedly rare but necessary nevertheless.

Campanella's ideal state is not an equalitarian state, although that is supposedly because, without control by the wisest and the best, there is no order. Even if women get the same education as men, are apparently eligible for all offices, are almost equal to men in war, and, because there are no marriages, not controlled by one man, the state is still, in the end, patriarchal, for Campanella has only males in power.

L. L. Lee

Bibliography:
Bonansea, Bernardino M. *Tommaso Campanella: Renaissance Pioneer of Modern Thought.* Washington, D.C.: Catholic University of America Press, 1969. A generally difficult book, but the chapter on *The City of the Sun* is quite clear and useful. Notes, extensive bibliography.

Donno, Daniel J. Introduction to *La Città del Sole.* Berkeley: University of California Press, 1981. The introduction gives a sketch of Campanella's life and discusses the themes of *The City of the Sun.*

Eurich, Nell. *Science in Utopia: A Mighty Design.* Cambridge, Mass.: Harvard University Press, 1967. Examines Campanella's interest in and defense of science. This book's brief section on him is very helpful.

Manuel, Frank E., and Fritzie P. Manuel. *Utopian Thought in the Western World.* Cambridge, Mass.: The Belknap Press of Harvard University Press, 1979. An excellent chapter on Campanella and *The City of the Sun.* Notes, bibliography.

Negley, Glenn, and J. Max Patrick. *The Quest for Utopia: An Anthology of Imaginary Societies.* New York: Henry Schuman, 1952. Includes a partial translation of *The City of the Sun*; short, insightful introduction.

CIVILIZATION AND ITS DISCONTENTS

Type of work: Psychology
Author: Sigmund Freud (1856-1939)
First published: Das Unbehagen in der Kultur, 1930 (English translation, 1930)

Sigmund Freud's *Civilization and Its Discontents*, one of his last and most influential books, treats human misery in establishing ideas about repression and the place of humans in the world. The book's leading concepts can be traced back to Freud's earliest pronouncements on incest in his letters to Wilhelm Fliess from the late 1890's. A full analysis of the restrictions on the individual from external and internal forces that pave the way to civilization was not possible until Freud's investigations of ego-psychology had led him to his hypotheses on the superego in *The Ego and the Id* (1923). Only by clarifying the nature of the superego and the sense of guilt—which he later declared to be the maker of civilized humanity—could he begin to explore the clash of that sense of guilt with the aggressive instinct derived from the self-destructive death drive that he had first confronted in *Beyond the Pleasure Principle* (1920). Using the concepts of the superego, the sense of guilt, and the aggressive instinct, Freud formulated the main theme of *Civilization and Its Discontents*: the ineradicable antagonism between the demands of the individual's instincts and the restrictions of civilization.

The small book is divided into eight short chapters, each packed with complex ideas and analyses. Freud begins with a meditation on belief, discussing the "oceanic feeling"—a peculiar mood that he had found confirmed by many, in which the individual feels a sensation of "eternity," something limitless and unbounded, and of being one with the whole external world. Although Freud admits he has not discovered this feeling within himself, he uses the concept to discuss the nursing infant that initially does not distinguish between its own ego and the external world. Because of internal pain and response from the external world to that pain, the infant begins the process of differentiating between what is internal (what belongs to the ego) and what is external (what emanates from the external world). In so doing, he arrives at the influence of the reality principle, which dominates further development, and the constructed ego, which will maintain sharp lines of demarcation toward the outside. The mature ego-feeling as separate and defined is, in fact, a shrunken residue of the all-embracing primary ego-feeling of infancy.

When this primary ego-feeling of undifferentiation persists alongside the sharply demarcated ego-feeling of maturity, the result is the "oceanic feeling." Freud explains that what is primitive in the mind is preserved alongside the transformed. To further elucidate this concept, he uses one of his most famous analogies: As in twentieth century Rome, underneath which there are ancient cities, so in mental life everything is preserved and, given the appropriate circumstances, can be brought back to life.

In his critique of religion, Freud maintains that in childhood, there is no need as strong as the need for a father's protection. He traces the religious attitude in the adult back to the feeling of infantile helplessness. For the adult, likewise, a belief in God is the attempt to pacify the need for protection from the threatening dangers of the external world. The "oceanic feeling" becomes connected with religion because its recollection offers again the sense of protection and oneness and provides consolation for the imperiled ego. This throwback to infancy for consolation, Freud concludes, reveals that religion is patently infantile and foreign to reality.

Yet Freud concedes that life is hard, and that humans are faced with too many pains, disappointments, and impossible tasks. Humans therefore take palliative measures by drawing on the substitutive satisfactions offered by such deflections as art or intoxicating substances. Freud defines happiness as the absence of pain in combination with strong feelings of pleasure. In the quest for happiness, the purpose of life is the pleasure principle; however, all the rules of the universe run counter to it. Humans are threatened with suffering from three sources: the body, the external world, and the relations to others.

In opposition to the external world, humans have become members of a community within which individuals work for the good of all and for which the individuals attempt to control their instincts. The aim of the pleasure principle is not relinquished, but a measure of protection against suffering is secured by means of sublimating instincts. Work, both physical and intellectual, yields pleasure and provides security within the human community. Another method by which humans strive to gain pleasure is in loving and being loved, although it is in this state that humans are the most defenseless against suffering. Religion also offers a path to happiness and protection from suffering, but Freud sees it as doing so by restricting choice, decreasing the value of life, distorting the picture of the real world, and placing believers in a state of psychic infantilism that draws them into a mass delusion. Freud's critical analysis of religion seems particularly germane to the phenomenon of religious cults.

Freud goes on to suggest that happiness is so hard to achieve because of the superior power of nature, the feebleness of the human body, and the inadequacy of the artificial regulations that maintain relations in the family, state, and society. Civilization serves two purposes: to protect humans against nature and to regulate human relations. Some nevertheless argue that civilization is largely responsible for human misery. There are those, for example, who cannot tolerate the frustrations that society imposes in the service of cultural ideals. Civilization (like human activity) strives toward goals of utility and a measured yield of pleasure. Yet, because the power of the community is in opposition to the power of the individual, community is only possible when a majority is stronger than any separate individual. The final outcome of law is a sacrifice of the individual's instincts; members of a community restrict themselves in their possible satisfaction because justice demands that no one escape these restrictions. The struggle of humanity centers on the claim of the individual and the cultural claims of the group. Using suppression and repression, civilization is built on a renunciation of instinct. If, however, a deprived instinct of satisfaction is not compensated, Freud warns, disorders will ensue.

Freud states that although Eros (love) and Ananke (necessity) are the driving forces of civilization, the tendency of civilization is to restrict sexual life (the vital drive of Eros) as it expands the culture unit. The founding of families made genital eroticism central while also restricting it; humans made themselves dependent on a chosen love-object and, in so doing, exposed themselves to extreme suffering. Since, moreover, a community requires a single kind of sexual life, it is necessarily intolerant of deviation from the norm, which leads to potentially serious injustices when deviation is judged as perversion. Freud maintains that humans are organisms with a bisexual disposition but that the sexual life of civilized humans is severely circumscribed by heterosexuality. Civilization summons up aim-inhibited libido to strengthen the communal bond through friendship, but for this to be fulfilled, sexual restrictions are unavoidable.

Freud goes on to insist that the golden rule ("Thou shalt love thy neighbor as thyself") cannot be recommended as reasonable. Men are aggressive, not gentle, and one's neighbor is one who tempts, exploits, rapes, steals, humiliates, and even kills. Aggression is an instinctual disposition and forces civilization into a high expenditure of energy because instinctual passions are stronger than reason. It is, for example, possible to bind a number of people in love only as long as there are other people to receive their aggressiveness. The Jewish people, Freud observes, have served civilizations in this way for centuries. Civilization is a process in the service of Eros to combine individuals, families, races, peoples, and nations into greater unities, but the inclination to aggression constitutes the greatest impediment to such bonds. The evolution of civilization, the human species' struggle for life, is the struggle between Eros (life) and Thanatos (death).

Civilization inhibits aggressiveness that opposes it by sending that aggressiveness back where it came from—to the ego of the individual, where it is internalized as the superego. In the form of conscience or guilt, the superego then sets up an agency within the individual to disarm the dangerous desire for aggression. Threatened external unhappiness—loss of love or punishment by an external authority—is exchanged for a permanent internal unhappiness caused by the tension of guilt. Paradoxically, Freud points out, the instinctual renunciation imposed by the external world creates the conscience which then demands further instinctual renunciation. Remorse, he writes, presupposes that a conscience is already in place when a misdeed takes place.

The price paid for the advance in civilization is a loss of individual happiness through the heightening of guilt. The development of the individual is a product of the interaction of two urges, the urge toward happiness, called "egoistic," and the urge toward union with others in the community, called "altruistic." Because these two urges oppose each other, individual and cultural development are in hostile and irreconcilable opposition. The cultural superego develops its ideals under the heading of ethics, but the commandment "Love thy neighbor as thyself" is an excellent example, notes Freud, of the unpsychological proceedings of that cultural superego. The commandment is impossible to fulfill, and those who follow it only put themselves at a disadvantage toward those who disregard it.

Freud is skeptical of the enthusiastic affirmation of civilization as the most precious possession of human beings. In conclusion, he offers no consolation, predictions, or even speculations but merely poses two fateful questions: To what extent will cultural development succeed in mastering the disturbances to communal life caused by the human instincts of aggression and self-destruction; and will immortal Eros make a sufficiently powerful effort to assert himself in the struggle with that equally powerful adversary, Death. *Civilization and Its Discontents* represents the summing up of a lifetime of reflection and invention from one of the twentieth century's greatest thinkers.

Janet Mason Ellerby

Bibliography:
Bettelheim, Bruno. *Freud and Man's Soul.* New York: Vintage, 1984. Bettelheim argues that the erroneous translation of Freud's most important concepts has led us to view his work as primarily scientific. In fact, Freud is always deeply personal in his appeals to humanity, and he writes not of what has been mistakenly translated as "mind" or "intellect" but of the soul (*die Seele*).
Gay, Peter. *Freud: A Life for Our Time.* New York: Norton, 1988. In this important biography, Gay discusses in exhaustive detail the entire span of Freud's life, in the process revealing enough conundrums to pique the interest of any psychoanalyst. He devotes an entire chapter to *Civilization and Its Discontents*, including circumstances that precipitated the writing of the book such as the horrors of World War I and the nature of the Jewish diaspora.
Ricoeur, Paul. *Freud and Philosophy: An Essay on Interpretation.* Translated by Denis Savage. New Haven, Conn.: Yale University Press, 1970. Ricoeur provides an unusual survey of

Freudian thought, focusing on language and symbolism with an insightful reading of *Civilization and Its Discontents*, the primordial mutual hostility of humans, and the cultural function of guilt.

Rieff, Philip. *Freud: The Mind of the Moralist.* 3d ed. Chicago: University of Chicago Press, 1979. Rieff provides clarity to one of the more difficult concepts of *Civilization and Its Discontents*: the relationship between civilization and its treacherous ally, neuroses. Rieff analyzes Freud's ambivalence toward repressive culture and his regard for health at the expense of culture.

Volosinov, V. N. *Freudianism: A Critical Sketch.* Translated by I. R. Titunik. Bloomington: Indiana University Press, 1987. Volosinov provides a useful chapter, "Freudian Philosophy of Culture," in which he elaborates on such central issues of *Civilization and Its Discontents* as social solidarity and cultural creativity.

CLARISSA
Or, The History of a Young Lady

Type of work: Novel
Author: Samuel Richardson (1689-1761)
Type of plot: Sentimental
Time of plot: Early eighteenth century
Locale: England
First published: 1747-1748

> *Principal characters:*
> CLARISSA HARLOWE, a young woman of family and fortune
> WILLIAM MORDEN, her cousin
> ARABELLA, her older sister
> JAMES, her older brother
> ROBERT LOVELACE, her seducer
> JOHN BELFORD, Lovelace's friend

The Story:

Robert Lovelace, a young Englishman of a noble family, was introduced into the Harlowe household by Clarissa's uncle, who wished Lovelace to marry Clarissa's older sister, Arabella. The young man instead fell deeply in love with Clarissa, but he quickly learned that his suit was balked by Clarissa's brother and sister. James Harlowe had disliked Lovelace since they had been together at Oxford, and Arabella was offended because he had spurned her in favor of Clarissa. Both were jealous of Clarissa because she had been left a fortune by their grandfather.

Having convinced his mother and father that Lovelace was a profligate, James Harlowe proposed that Clarissa be married to Mr. Solmes, a rich, elderly man of little taste and no sensibility. When Solmes found no favor in the eyes of Clarissa, her family assumed she was in love with Lovelace, despite her protestations to the contrary. Clarissa refused to allow Solmes to visit with her in the parlor or to sit next to her when the family was together. Her father, outraged by her conduct, ordered her to be more civil to the man he had chosen as her husband. When she refused, saying she would never marry any man against her will, not even Lovelace, her father confined her to her room.

Lovelace, partly out of love for her and partly in vengeance for the insults heaped upon him by the Harlowe family, resolved to abduct Clarissa from her family. He was greatly aided in this scheme by the domineering personalities of Mr. Harlowe and his son, who had taken away Clarissa's trusted maid and replaced her with a young woman who was impertinent and insolent to her mistress. They also refused to let her see any of the family, even her mother. Clarissa's only trusted adviser was Miss Howe, a friend and correspondent who advised her to escape the house if she could, even if it meant accepting Lovelace's aid and his proposal of marriage.

One evening, Lovelace slipped into the garden where Clarissa was walking and entreated her to elope with him. After some protest, she agreed to go with him so as to escape her domineering father. Lovelace told her she would be taken to the home of Lord M——, a kinsman of Lovelace, who would protect her until her cousin, Colonel Morden, could return to England and arrange for a reconciliation between Clarissa and her family. Lovelace did not keep his word, however, and took her instead to a house of ill repute, where he introduced her to a woman he called Mrs. Sinclair. Inventing reasons why he could not take her to Lord M——'s house, he persuaded the bewildered girl to pose temporarily as his wife. He told Mrs. Sinclair that Clarissa was his wife with whom he could not live until certain marriage settlements had been arranged. Clarissa permitted him to tell the lie, believing that it would prevent her father and her brother from discovering her whereabouts.

In Mrs. Sinclair's house, she was almost as much a prisoner as she had been in her father's home. Her family had meanwhile disowned her and refused to send her either money or clothes. Her father further declared that she was no longer his daughter and that he hoped she would have a miserable existence in both this world and the next. This state of affairs was distressing to Clarissa, who was now dependent upon Lovelace for her very existence. He took advantage of the circumstances to press his love upon her without mentioning his earlier promises of marriage. Clarissa tried to escape and got as far as Hampstead before Lovelace overtook her. There, he had two women impersonate his cousins to convince Clarissa that she should return to her lodgings with them. Upon her return to Mrs. Sinclair's house, they filled her with drugs, after which Lovelace raped her. A few days later, Clarissa received a letter from Miss Howe in which she learned that she was in a house in which no woman of her station would be seen. Again, Clarissa tried to escape by calling for aid from a window. Lovelace finally promised to leave her unmolested until she could get aid from her cousin or from Miss Howe.

Lovelace left London for a few days to visit Lord M——, who was ill. While he was gone, Clarissa contrived to steal the clothes of a serving girl and escape from the house; but within a day or two, Mrs. Sinclair discovered Clarissa's whereabouts and had her arrested and imprisoned for debt. When John Belford, a friend of Lovelace, heard of the girl's plight, he rescued her by proving the debt a fraud. He found shelter for Clarissa with a kindly glovemaker and his wife. Worn out by her experiences, Clarissa's health declined, in spite of all that the apothecary and doctor secured by John Belford could do for her. She spent her time writing letters in an effort to secure a reconciliation with her family and to acquaint her friends with the true story of her plight. She refused to have anything to do with Lovelace, who was by that time convinced that he loved her dearly. He wished to marry her to make amends for the treatment she had suffered at his hands, but she refused his offer with gentle firmness.

Clarissa's friends did what they could to reunite her with her family. When her father and brother refused to receive her, she went to an undertaking establishment and bought a coffin that she had fitted as she wished, including a plaque that gave the date of her birth as the day on which she left her father's house.

On his return to England, Colonel Morden tried to raise her spirits, but his efforts failed because he, too, was unable to effect any change in the attitude of the Harlowe family. He also had an interview with Lovelace and Lord M——. The nobleman and Lovelace assured him that their family thought very highly of Clarissa. They wished her to marry Lovelace, and Lovelace wished to marry her; but even her cousin was unable to persuade Clarissa to accept Lovelace as a husband.

When the Harlowe family finally realized that Clarissa was determined to die, her father and brother lifted their ban. Her sister was sorry she had been cruel to Clarissa, and her mother was convinced that she had failed in her duty toward her daughter. They all wrote to Clarissa, begging the girl's forgiveness and expressing their hope that she would recover quickly and be reunited with her family. Their letters arrived too late, for Clarissa had died.

Clarissa's body was returned to her father's house and she was interred in the family vault at the feet of the grandfather whose fortune had been one of the sources of her troubles. Lovelace, who was quite distracted by grief, was persuaded by Lord M—— to go to the Continent. There he met Colonel Morden in France, and early one winter morning, Clarissa's cousin fought a duel with her betrayer. Lovelace was mortally wounded by a thrust through his body. As he lay dying, he expressed the hope that his death would expiate his crimes.

Critical Evaluation:

Few men would have seemed less likely than Samuel Richardson to be influential in the history of the novel. A successful printer, he did not publish his first work until after he was fifty years old. Because of a reputation as an accomplished letter writer, he was encouraged to write a book of sample letters. Even before the publication of this volume, *Familiar Letters* (1741), he turned his epistolary talent to didactic purposes in fiction with the publication of *Pamela* (1740-1741), which was greeted with popular approval and critical disdain. By 1744, he had prepared a summary of his epistolary masterpiece, *Clarissa*. The massive novel was published in three installments between December, 1747, and December, 1748, and was subsequently printed in eight volumes. The length of the novel (about one million words) was probably not a great impediment for the more leisurely reading class of the mid-eighteenth century, but *Clarissa* eventually came to be read mostly in an abridged version by George Sherburn.

Richardson's main literary contribution is his mastery of the epistolary style. The use of letters as a means of narration has obvious drawbacks. Certainly the flow of the narrative is repeatedly interrupted, and it takes all the strength of the reader's will to suspend disbelief concerning the writing of thoughtful and informative letters by characters during periods of extraordinary stress. Conventions aside, it is difficult to sustain a continuous and progressive narrative in this form. The method frustrated Samuel Johnson, a friend of Richardson, who concluded that the work should be read for its sentiment. Richardson himself worried that his narrative technique had let his characters do too much in too short a period of time.

Richardson did, however, capitalize on the correlative advantages of the epistolary method. The immediacy of writing at the moment in which events are occurring is an excellent means of creating concerned attention in the reader. Moreover, Richardson's talent for dialogue transforms many of the lengthier letters into poignant scenes, and the text of each letter is most decorously cast in a style appropriate to the correspondent. There is the further advantage, especially in a didactic novel such as this, of multiple points of view that add complexity and sympathy to the interpretation of events. Letters are not simply presented but copied, sent, received, discussed, answered, intercepted, stolen, altered, and forged. The whole process of correspondence comes alive as Richardson blends theater, moral discourse, courtesy book, and romance into a compellingly tense analysis of contemporary morals and manners.

As the use of the epistolary style would suggest, action is less important to Richardson's fiction than reflection on the moral significance of the action. It may be that the author was familiar with the life of the gentry only through the theater. Nevertheless, despite an apparent ignorance of the occupations of a rich country family, the focus is so much on the tenseness of the situations and the meaning of actions that little is lost by the absence of sociological verisimilitude. Although Richardson occasionally presents dramatically vivid details, he usually is less interested in setting than in what Sherburn calls, in the contemporary eighteenth century terminology, a "distress."

The main theme of the novel, as described by Richardson on the title page, is "the distresses that may attend the misconduct both of parents and children in relation to marriage." There is no doubt that the motives of the Harlowes are crassly materialistic: to improve the already comfortable family fortune by forcing Clarissa to marry the suitable, but elderly, Solmes. There is a striking lack of tenderness and family feeling toward Clarissa, to whom they soften only after it is too late. Clarissa, for her part, is also strong-willed. As Richardson explains, "The principal of the two young Ladies is proposed as an exemplar of her Sex. Nor is it any objection to her being so, that she is not in all respects a perfect character."

At first, Clarissa is attracted by the roguish but fascinating Lovelace. In fact, he occasionally seems not entirely a bad fellow. At least he is the most vivid character in the novel; yet in his egocentrism and his love of intrigue he is inconsiderate and cruel to others, sins he does not recant until his sentimental dying breaths. After his assault on Clarissa, practicality seems to demand that Clarissa turn virtue into its own reward, as Pamela had done, by marrying her seducer. *Clarissa*, however, is a more complex novel than *Pamela*, and Clarissa and Lovelace have already shown a moral incompatibility that makes acquiescence by Clarissa impossible (despite the impassioned pleadings of Richardson's sentimental readers before the last third of the novel appeared).

At the heart of the incompatibility is Clarissa's rigid idealism. Although a gentle person, she is unreserved in her commitment to virtue and to, as Sherburn puts it, decorous behavior. She is not so much a puritan as a devotee of what is morally fit, and she carries her commitment to the grave. When her friend Miss Howe suggests that she take the expedient way out by marrying the ostensibly repentant Lovelace, Clarissa cannot give in. Her sense of propriety would not allow such moral and personal compromise. Nevertheless, it must be admitted that she is less interesting for her idealism than for the distressing situations and dilemmas her idealism occasions.

Despite its narrative improbabilities, *Clarissa* became a revered example not only of the epistolary novel but also of the refined novel of sentiment and, by the end of the century, it had been imitated and acclaimed both in England and on the Continent.

"Critical Evaluation" by Edward E. Foster

Bibliography:
Castle, Terry. *Clarissa's Ciphers: Meaning and Disruption in Richardson's "Clarissa."* Ithaca, N.Y.: Cornell University Press, 1982. An influential book, which provides an interpretation from the points of view of feminism and reader-response criticism. On the alleged textual incoherence in *Clarissa*, Castle asks: How can one expect coherence from a violated woman?
Doody, Margaret Anne. Chapters V through IX in *A Natural Passion: A Study of the Novels of Samuel Richardson*. Oxford, England: Clarendon Press, 1974. Provides lively, informative, and authoritative discussion of themes and imagery in *Clarissa*. The source of much sympathetic interpretation of *Clarissa* and Richardson's other novels.
Goldberg, Rita. *Sex and Enlightenment: Women in Richardson and Diderot*. Cambridge, England: Cambridge University Press, 1984. Highly intelligent discussion of *Clarissa* as a "mythic" book—a model for young women to follow. Examines the consequences to young women and their society of attempting to adhere to the prescribed model.
Hill, Christopher. "Clarissa Harlowe and Her Times." In *Samuel Richardson: A Collection of Critical Essays*, edited by John Carroll. Englewood Cliffs, N.J.: Prentice Hall, 1968. The seminal account of the social background of the novel. Includes examination of the economy, Puritanism, and attitudes toward the individual, the family, and marriage.
Warner, William Beatty. *Reading Clarissa: The Struggles of Interpretation*. New Haven, Conn.: Yale University Press, 1979. Uses deconstructionist approach to question any supposed need to establish a single authoritative text to *Clarissa*. Argues for the aptness of the novel's conflicting texts. Claims that Lovelace is the hero of the novel.

THE CLAYHANGER TRILOGY

Type of work: Novel
Author: Arnold Bennett (1867-1931)
Type of plot: Domestic realism
Time of plot: 1870-1895
Locale: England
First published: Clayhanger, 1910; *Hilda Lessways,* 1911; *These Twain,* 1915

Principal characters:
EDWIN CLAYHANGER, a businessman
HILDA LESSWAYS, his wife
MAGGIE CLAYHANGER, Edwin's sister
MR. INGPEN, Edwin's friend
GEORGE CANNON, Hilda's first husband
DARIUS CLAYHANGER, Edwin's father

The Story:

In 1872, sixteen-year-old Edwin Clayhanger was forced to leave school to help his father in the Clayhanger printing shop. His father had disregarded Edwin's request that he be allowed to go to school and study to be an architect. Old Darius Clayhanger was a self-made man who had risen from a boyhood in the workhouse to the position of affluence he held in his Midland community. Since he was a complete tyrant in the home, no one dared to cross him when he insisted that his work be carried on by his only son.

Several years later, Darius Clayhanger built a new house in a more affluent part of town. Edwin became friendly with the Orgreave family, who lived next door. The elder Orgreave was an architect, with whom Edwin spent many hours discussing that profession. Unknown to Edwin, the oldest Orgreave daughter, Janet, fell in love with him. It was at the Orgreave home that Edwin met Hilda Lessways, an orphan living in Brighton with the sister of a former employer, George Cannon, who wished to marry her. Although she was attracted to Edwin, she returned to Brighton and soon after married Cannon, giving him her small patrimony to invest for her.

By the time Hilda returned to visit the Orgreaves a year later she had learned about her husband's previous marriage, which made her own marriage to him void. On this second visit, she admitted to her love for Edwin and promised to marry him, for no one knew of her marriage at Brighton. Discovering that she was to have a baby, however, she returned to Brighton and wrote to Janet Orgreave to tell her she was married and to ask her to inform Edwin. Deeply hurt, he threw himself into his father's business, for his father had become mentally ill.

Hilda bore her child and named him George Edwin, after his father and Edwin Clayhanger. She managed a rooming house owned by her husband's sister. Cannon, discovered by his first wife, was sentenced to serve a two-year prison term for bigamy. After his release, he was again imprisoned for ten years for passing a forged check. The money he had imprudently invested for Hilda was lost when the hotel corporation, whose shares he had bought, collapsed. Hilda was thereafter no longer financially independent.

After his father's death, Edwin and his sister Maggie continued to live alone in the Clayhanger house, and the printing business continued to prosper and grow. Both Maggie and Edwin became settled in their habits, although many young women, including Janet Orgreave, would gladly have married Edwin.

Edwin became quite fond of Hilda's son during the boy's visit with the Orgreaves. When George Edwin became ill with influenza, it was Edwin who sent for the doctor and notified Hilda. Although neither spoke openly of their feelings, Hilda and Edwin felt their affection for each other return when they met at the sick child's bedside. Nine years had passed since Edwin and Hilda had first met. Once the boy recovered, he and his mother went back to Brighton, where Hilda continued to struggle with the failing boardinghouse at Brighton.

Months later, when Edwin went to see Hilda, he found her penniless and about to be evicted. Edwin paid her bills, and Hilda told him all that had happened to her, explaining that her marriage was void and her child illegitimate. Edwin returned home but resolved to marry Hilda quietly in London. After marrying, they moved into the Clayhanger house and Maggie went to live with a maiden aunt. Edwin adopted Hilda's son and gave him his name.

Edwin, having had his own way for a long time, was accustomed to a certain routine in his home and to making his own decisions. Hilda had an equally strong personality, however, and Edwin believed that she was trying to make him conform too much to her own views and habits. Most of all he resented her attempts to influence Edwin in business affairs, a realm which he thought was solely his own.

A few months after Edwin and Hilda married, the aunt with whom Maggie Clayhanger was living became seriously ill. During her last days, Mr. Ingpen, Edwin's business friend, was injured in a factory accident. At Ingpen's request, Edwin went to his room to destroy some letters and pictures, so they would not be found if Ingpen died in the hospital. Edwin found a woman asleep there who was Ingpen's mistress; her husband was incurably insane. Edwin was disturbed for his friend, but Ingpen laughed and said that the situation was best as it was because he did not want to be trapped in a marriage.

When Edwin's aunt died, her estate was left to the children of Edwin's younger sister, Clara. Edwin and Maggie were pleased, but Hilda thought that she and Edwin should have received part of the estate. Her selfishness irked Edwin. He felt he was rich enough and that his nephews and nieces deserved the money. Nostalgically recalling his bachelor days, he began to consider that a divorce might be the answer to his situation. The only bright ray in his life seemed to be George Edwin, his stepson, who was studying architecture with the aid of John Orgreave. Edwin hoped that his adopted son might have the chance to become an architect.

On a visit to a nearby city, Hilda and Edwin were taken to inspect a prison. There they saw George Cannon. He was released soon afterward when he was found to be innocent of the forgery charge. When Cannon went to Edwin without Hilda's knowledge, Edwin gave him money to go to America. Edwin never expected to see the money again, but he wanted to get the man out of the country. He was also bothered by the fact that Hilda had been in correspondence with Cannon's other wife.

The climax of Edwin's unhappiness with Hilda came after she took him to see a house in the country on Christmas Day. She tried to force him to buy it by diplomatic moves and conversations with their friends and family that would leave Edwin appearing foolish if he did not buy the house. After a violent argument, in which he accused his wife of being grasping, underhanded, and dishonest, Edwin left the house in a rage. After a long walk in the cold winter night, he realized, however, that his marriage and his wife meant much to him. He realized that he had to make concessions and that they both had to contend with having married so late in life, when their habits were already fixed. Finally he recalled his friend Ingpen, who was unable to marry the woman he loved. He went back to the house to reconcile with Hilda. His faith in human nature was completely reestablished when he found a check from America in the mail for the money he had lent to George Cannon.

Critical Evaluation:

Arnold Bennett completed *Clayhanger*, the first novel of the trilogy concerning the life apprenticeship of Edwin Clayhanger, on June 23, 1910, two years after the publication of *The Old Wives' Tale*. At the height of his creative powers as well as of his critical reputation, Bennett ventured to write his most nearly autobiographical novel in a format popular with Edwardian readers. Compared to George Moore's *Confessions of a Young Man* (1888), Samuel Butler's *The Way of All Flesh* (1903), E. M. Forster's *The Longest Journey* (1907), and H. G. Wells's *Tono-Bungay* (1909), *Clayhanger* is a fairly typical *Bildungsroman*, or "education novel." The representative hero of this genre is an inexperienced, often confused, but generally likable young man who, after learning from a series of valuable adventures, develops a better understanding about himself and about life. Typically, the hero comes to terms with his weaknesses and strengths, discovers a proper vocation for his talents, and begins to understand the meaning and limitations of romantic love.

Unlike the typical *Erziehungsroman* hero, whose education is completed at the end of the book, Edwin Clayhanger undergoes an extended apprenticeship from youth to middle age, testing the dreams and values of his young manhood against the often harsher realities of life itself. Indeed, in the novels that follow *Clayhanger*—*Hilda Lessways* (1911) and *These Twain* (1915)—Bennett alters some of the conventions familiar to the genre. With a relentlessly deterministic philosophy, he pursues the romantic follies of Edwin and teaches him, at the last, a bitter lesson about his restricted place in the world.

It was a lesson Bennett well understood, for his own early life resembled that of his protagonist. His father, Enoch Bennett, the Darius Clayhanger of the novel, was a Victorian tyrant who demanded absolute respect from his dreamy son, though he usually failed to get it. One theme of the novel that appears also in later twentieth century fiction is that of the quest of a son for his spiritual father. Edwin hates Darius and longs for the old man's death. Yet he saves his father from financial ruin when, with astonishing presence of mind, he secures a cable to hoist a collapsing printing press; and when Darius dies of natural causes (a scene as harrowing as any deathbed drama in literature), the son is moved to thoughts not of vengeance but of pity. Other characters and locations in the novel are modeled after real people and places that Bennett knew intimately: Auntie Bourne becomes Auntie Clara Hamps; Absolom Wood becomes Osmond Orgreave; Cobridge becomes Bleakridge; and Waterloo Road becomes Trafalgar Road. Probably many characteristics of Marguerite Soule, Bennett's French wife, appear in Hilda Lessways. Above all, the trilogy is carefully crafted to simulate reality. Bennet reproduces all the details, trivia, and actual circumstances of life, and the reader has a sense both of place solidly rendered and of time remorselessly passing.

To be sure, time itself is a mysterious force, almost a metaphysical element of fate in the trilogy. Like such other twentieth century writers as Marcel Proust, James Joyce, Thomas and Heinrich Mann, and T. S. Eliot, Bennett is deeply concerned with both the nature and effects of time. His characters develop, change, and mature to the slow rhythm of time, and they are ultimately destroyed by it. Whether with tantalizing deliberation (as time plays with old Mr. Shushion, its "obscene victim") or with sudden brutal finality (as time fells Darius), it is the sole absolute, the single truth around which all life appears to revolve as an illusion.

Counterpoised to time is the rhythm of life. In the wild sensual delight of Florence Simcox, the "clog-dancer" of the Midlands, Edwin first perceives the beauty of woman. At the "Dragon," where the Burseley Mutual Burial Club holds a "free-and-easy," he responds to the vital warmth of friendship; and with a single kiss from Hilda Lessways, a woman he both fears and loves, he is turned for the first time from a shy, fussy bachelor into a man of passion. For her part, Hilda has ignored Edwin until he exclaims, in a moment of compassion and despair, "I'm ashamed of seeing my father lose his temper." In this moment of spiritual illumination, she begins to fall in love with him, touched by what she believes to be his confession of weakness. Brutalized throughout her life by men such as George Cannon, she senses that Edwin has the strength of his tenderness. Her judgment is flawed, however, because life has conditioned her to see Edwin not as he is but as she wants him to be. Nor can Edwin truly understand the real Hilda, who is not (as he believes) a woman of romantic mystery; yet the illusion of the moment becomes the pattern for life. For Bennett, it is the small moments of life that have their deepest effects on character. Magic is in the rhythm of life, and beauty also; but the magic is terribly brief.

The last two novels of the trilogy, considerably less autobiographical than *Clayhanger*, show a decline in Bennett's emotional powers but complete his architectonic design. *Hilda Lessways* is interesting from a technical point of view, because the novel describes Hilda's life in parallel with Edwin's. For each lover, the romantic partner is a projection of a dream, not the real person. Edwin and Hilda meet too late in their lives; their habits have been formed, and they are incapable of change. Indeed, the very qualities that they perceive in each other—willpower and assertiveness—are inimical to their happiness. In *These Twain*, Bennett details the inevitable results of their mismatch. Hilda becomes a shrew, and Edwin becomes a man very much like his father: intolerant, smug, and materialistic. His decision, at the end of the trilogy, to make the best of a marriage that has lost its charm, is a triumph of practicality over romance. To Bennett, life at best is imperfect, but it is best lived without illusion.

"Critical Evaluation" by Leslie B. Mittleman

Bibliography:
Anderson, Linda R. *Bennett, Wells and Conrad: Narrative in Transition*. London: Macmillan, 1988. Contains a chapter on the *Clayhanger* trilogy, which Anderson sees as the last novels in which Bennett managed to investigate his complicated relationship to his past honestly. Focuses on the theme of guilt and selfhood. Select bibliography and index.

Drabble, Margaret. *Arnold Bennett*. London: Weidenfeld & Nicolson, 1974. The most readable of the biographies on Bennett. Helps relate the complicated nexus that held Bennett to his past. Includes a detailed bibliography and index.

Hall, James. *Arnold Bennett: Primitivism and Taste*. Seattle: University of Washington Press, 1959. Contains a chapter on the *Clayhanger* novels, which Hall sees as the best example of the balance achieved between the two opposing forces of primitivism and taste. Select bibliography.

Hepburn, James, ed. *Arnold Bennett: The Critical Heritage*. Boston: Routledge & Kegan Paul, 1981. Includes a number of publication reviews of each of the *Clayhanger* novels, as well as a general introduction, a select bibliography of critical material from the years 1904 to 1931, and an index.

Lucas, John. *Arnold Bennett: A Study of His Fiction*. London: Methuen, 1974. Probably the best general introduction to Bennett. Includes a reasonably thorough discussion of the *Clayhanger* trilogy, which Lucas rates highly in Bennett's oeuvre. Index.

CLIGÉS
A Romance

Type of work: Poetry
Author: Chrétien de Troyes (c. 1150-c. 1190)
Type of plot: Romance
Time of plot: Sixth century
Locale: England, Brittany, Germany, and Constantinople
First published: Cligés: Ou, La Fausse morte, c. 1164 (English translation, 1912)

Principal characters:
ALEXANDER, the heir to the Greek Empire
SOREDAMORS, Sir Gawain's sister, King Arthur's niece
CLIGÉS, the son of Alexander and Soredamors
ALIS, Alexander's brother, later regent for Cligés
FENICE, a German princess, later empress of Greece
KING ARTHUR
QUEEN GUINEVERE
SIR GAWAIN, Cligés' uncle, a knight of King Arthur's court
THESSALA, a necromancer, Fenice's nurse
JOHN, an artisan in stone

The Story:

Alexander, the older son of the emperor of Greece and Constantinople, scorned to receive knighthood in his own country. Having heard of the famed King Arthur of Britain, the young prince was determined to emulate the brave and courteous knights of that monarch's court and to win knighthood by his own merits. Accordingly, he swore never to wear armor on his face or a helmet upon his head until King Arthur himself should gird his knightly sword on him. At last he was allowed to have his own way, in spite of the disapproval of his father and his mother's grief at being separated from her son, and he set sail at once for Britain. With him went twelve noble companions and a store of rich treasure.

When Alexander and his friends arrived at the royal court in Winchester, King Arthur and Queen Guinevere welcomed them with gracious speech. All who saw him were impressed by the young Greek, not only for his generosity but for his strong character and handsome appearance as well. Sir Gawain, a knight of great prowess and the nephew of the king, took him for his friend and companion, and King Arthur, about to make a journey into Brittany, included the young man in his retinue. On the trip, Alexander and the damsel Soredamors, sister of Sir Gawain, fell deeply in love. Since each felt that such a love was hopeless, they did nothing but grow pale and sigh and tremble, so that Queen Guinevere, observing them, mistook their lovesickness for the effects of the heaving sea.

King Arthur remained in Brittany through the summer, and during that time the young lovers were much perplexed and distressed by emotions they were unable to reveal to each other. At the beginning of October, messengers arrived with news that Count Angrès, who had been entrusted with the rule of the kingdom during the king's absence, was raising an army and preparing to withstand King Arthur on his return. Angered by this traitorous deed, the king transported a great host across the channel and prepared to lay siege to London, where Count Angrès had assembled his forces. Prince Alexander and his twelve companions were knighted while the king's army was encamped outside the city walls. Queen Guinevere's gift to the young

1162

knight was a white silk shirt on which Soredamors had embroidered strands of her own hair, indistinguishable from the golden thread of the design.

When Count Angrès and his army slipped away from the city under cover of night and retreated to the strong castle at Windsor, King Arthur and his troops pursued the traitors and besieged the fortress. During the siege Alexander displayed great bravery and prowess. One night, while he was in attendance on the queen, Guinevere noticed that the gold thread on his shirt was tarnishing but that the golden hair of Soredamors was as lustrous as ever. So the damsel's deed was disclosed and Alexander rejoiced to wear on his person a token of the lady to whom he had vowed undying devotion.

A short time later, Windsor Castle was taken through his wit and valor. He and several of his companions dressed in the armor of vanquished traitor knights and then went by a secret path into the fortress, where they killed many of the enemy and captured Count Angrès. For this deed Alexander was awarded a gold cup which the king had promised to the most valiant of his knights. In the meantime, believing Alexander killed during the fighting inside the castle, Soredamors had revealed her love for the young prince. After the battle, the knight received three joys and honors as the reward for his valor: the town he had captured, a kingdom in Wales, and, greatest of all, the hand of Soredamors. From this union was born a handsome son, Cligés.

Meanwhile, in Constantinople, the emperor died without hearing again from his older son, and Alis, the younger heir, assumed the rule of the empire after receiving a report that Alexander was also dead. Hearing that his brother had taken the crown, Alexander set out to reclaim his kingdom, accompanied by his wife, his small son, and forty valiant knights from King Arthur's court. When Alis learned that his older brother was alive, an amicable arrangement was made whereby Alis would rule in name only and the affairs of the kingdom would be entrusted to Alexander. Also, Alis promised never to marry or have heirs, so that Cligés would in time reign over Greece and Constantinople. Before Cligés had grown to adulthood, however, Alexander died of a pestilence and Soredamors of grief.

Not long afterward, advisers began to urge Alis to take a wife, with the result that the emperor was moved to break the oath made to his brother. The bride proposed was the daughter of the emperor of Germany, the Princess Fenice, prophetically named for the phoenix bird. The princess had previously been affianced to the duke of Saxony, however, and that incensed nobleman felt that he had a prior claim to her hand. While arrangements for the wedding were being made, Cligés and Fenice fell deeply in love. At about the same time, the duke of Saxony sent his nephew to proclaim that his uncle's claim to the princess would be defended against the Greeks. His defiant speech so angered Cligés that he challenged the young Saxon to trial by arms and, in the melee, unhorsed him and routed his followers. By this time, although Fenice loved Cligés dearly, she prudently decided that she would not yield herself to either the uncle or the nephew, and, with the help of her nurse Thessala, a sorceress, she planned to remain a virgin. A potion served unwittingly to the bridegroom by his nephew made it seem to the emperor that he possessed his bride, though he never did so in reality.

On the return trip to Constantinople, the nephew of the duke of Saxony set an ambush for the travelers. When Cligés killed the treacherous knight and the duke offered a reward for Cligés' head, that resourceful young knight cut off the head of an enemy and affected a disguise as his father had done before him. Fenice was abducted, however, during the battle that followed. Overtaking her captors, Cligés killed all but one, who survived to carry to the duke news of what happened. The conflict ended when Cligés, inspired by his love for Fenice, defeated the duke in single combat. The lovers then parted, Fenice going to Constantinople with her husband and Cligés traveling to England, there to fulfill his father's wish that he receive knighthood at the hands of King Arthur.

At a great tournament on the plain before Oxford, Cligés, changing his armor each day, defeated King Arthur's most valiant knights and bore himself so bravely that he became the subject of much speculation concerning his origin and whereabouts, for the young warrior retired to his lodgings every night and kept away from the feasting that followed each day's tourney. As the Black Knight, he defeated the mighty Sagremore; as the Green Knight, Sir Lancelot of the Lake; as the Vermilion Knight, Sir Perceval of Wales. On the fourth day, disguised as the White Knight, he would have defeated Sir Gawain, his uncle, if King Arthur had not intervened. Then Cligés appeared in his own person and at the royal banquet revealed his name and told his story to the pleasure and astonishment of all. King Arthur and Sir Gawain, in particular, were delighted to find their young kinsman so brave in conduct, so pleasing in modesty and knightly courtesy.

On his return to Greece, Cligés learned that Fenice had missed him as much as he had desired her. Since their great love could no longer be denied, they were able, with the help of Thessala and an artful stonecutter, to devise a plan that would ensure their happiness. From the artisan, John, Cligés got possession of a tower in which the builder had constructed hidden chambers with secret entrances and exits. Thessala then concocted a potion which put Fenice into a trance so deep that all except three skeptical physicians from Salerno believed her dead. The three doctors were slain by a mob of indignant women before they could restore Fenice to consciousness by acts of torture, and the body of the empress was placed, amid great mourning throughout the kingdom, in a sepulchre which John had built. From there she was taken in secret by Cligés, restored to life, and hidden in one of the secret chambers of the tower.

There, for a year and two months, they were free to take their pleasure with each other as they pleased. At the end of that time, Fenice began to pine for the out-of-doors, and John revealed a secret door which opened upon a walled garden filled with beautiful blooming trees and flowers. Cligés and Fenice had much joy in their hidden paradise until, one day, a hunter searching for his lost hawk climbed the wall and saw the lovers asleep in each other's arms. Although Cligés awoke and wounded the hunter, the man escaped to tell the emperor of what he had seen. Alis dispatched troops to the tower, but Cligés and Fenice had already fled. Arrested, John accused the emperor of having tried to wrong Cligés by marrying and expecting to produce an heir; then the artisan revealed how Alis had been tricked by the potion he had drunk on his wedding night, so that he had never possessed his wife except in his dreams. The emperor swore that he could never again be happy until he had taken his revenge for the shame and disgrace that had been put upon him.

In the meantime, Cligés and Fenice, with Thessala's aid, had eluded their pursuers and enlisted the aid of King Arthur, who promised to fill a thousand ships with knights and three thousand more with men-at-arms in order to help Cligés regain his rights. Before the mighty expedition could set sail, however, messengers arrived in Britain with word that Alis had died of rage and grief because the lovers had escaped him. With Fenice, Cligés returned to rule over Greece and Constantinople, and there the two lived happily in love, as husband and wife, lover and mistress.

Since that time, however, every emperor, remembering the story of Fenice and her potions, has had little confidence in his empress and has kept her closely guarded, attended by no man except one who has been a eunuch since his boyhood.

Critical Evaluation:

Chrétien de Troyes' *Cligés*, like his later *Lancelot: Or, The Knight of the Cart* (c. 1168), can be read as part of his analysis of and response to what scholars call "courtly love," though that is a modern, not a medieval, term. The twelfth century was the first point in recorded history in which the consensus did not hold amorous love in contempt. Both the Roman and the Germanic traditions regarded love as something that conflicted with higher passions—loyalty to Rome, in the first instance, and to the king in the second. When political conditions in Europe settled down after the long period of anarchy ensuing from the collapse of the Roman Empire, the troubadours, or minstrels of southern France, began to express a new idea. Peace had given women a new prominence in society, and these minstrels were eager to make a profit from it. They began to write love songs that extolled ladies for their charm, wit, and beauty. It did not matter if she returned the emotion; what was important was the analysis and experience of the emotion of desire itself. When the northern poets picked up the theme, it underwent a transformation. For such a love to be satisfactory, they argued, it must be mutual, and if it was mutual, it must be deserved on both parts. So, not only must the lady be charming, witty, and beautiful, but her lover (the knight, since the common people were not considered capable of fine emotion) must be brave, courteous, and utterly devoted to pleasing the lady. The story that some regard as the ultimate expression of courtly love is that of Tristan and Isolde. This was the story of the adulterous passion of Tristan, Cornwall's greatest knight, for Queen Isolde, the wife of his uncle.

Many have seen *Cligés* as a kind of anti-Tristan. We know from the prologue that Chrétien had already written a romance "of King Mark and Isolde the Blonde," but he also makes a number of other references to the story. Cligés suggests to Fenice that they run away together, but she refuses. She does not want others to speak of them "as they do of Isolde the Blonde and Tristan," for everyone will "blame our pleasures." Her solution is to feign her own death before the consummation of her marriage and to have Cligés hide her in an orchard. According to medieval custom, marriage was binding only if consummated, so technically they are not committing adultery. In addition, the potion which Alis is given to convince him that he is taking his pleasure with Fenice parallels an episode in the Tristan legend. When Tristan takes Isolde to Cornwall to marry King Mark, Isolde's mother concocts a love potion so that the marriage should not be unhappy. Unfortunately, Tristan and Isolde drink the potion by mistake, beginning the whole affair. Rather than using a love potion—which seems rather an artificial excuse for falling in love—Cligés and Fenice fall in love because of the respective qualities of each. It is, unlike Tristan and Isolde's, a genuine love naturally occurring. It is governed not by passion but by level-headedness, as Fenice's planning illustrates.

Another episode duplicating one in the Tristan legend is the deception of Alis. In order to preserve the illusion of her own virginity, Isolde has her maidservant, Brangane, stand in for her on the wedding night. Later, fearing lest she reveal her secrets, Isolde plots to have Brangane assassinated. For his romance, Chrétien designs the episode with the potion that gives Alis the illusion that he is sleeping with Fenice. This enables the author to avoid the rather uncomplimentary scene in which Isolde plots to have Brangane murdered. There are other parallels that help to clarify the similarity of the two stories. Cligés is Alis' nephew, just as Tristan is Mark's; Alexander and Soredamors (Cligés' parents) fall in love on board ship, as do Tristan and Isolde: and the orchard to which Fenice retires strongly resembles the idyllic paradise that Tristan and Isolde discover in the forest when they elope from the court. On the whole, however, the comparison is one of contrast rather than similarity.

In some ways, *Cligés* can be considered a manual for the perfect courtly love relationship. Both Alexander and Soredamors and Cligés and Fenice have the requisite personal characteristics for such a romance. However, the difference in their respective situations allows

Chrétien the opportunity to test the theory of courtly love against two different sets of standards. Alexander and Soredamors are both unattached. The only obstacle between them is their own sense of inadequacy—which is, in truth, simply an appreciation for the excellence of the other's very great worth. Once recognized, their love follows a relatively simple path through courtship to marriage, and trouble only arises when they meet with political treachery in the form of Alis the usurper. When one passes to the next generation, however, one can see immediately that the author is anxious to show a different situation in which courtly love can operate. The rules of southern courtly love required that the lady be unobtainable—preferably because married. This, of course, led to the idea that adultery was to be admired, a concept that Chrétien did not value. The question still persisted: What if married people fell in love? How could their love be resolved with moral conduct? The author's solution, of course, is that Fenice refrain from sleeping with Alis, but his allusions to the Tristan legend make it clear that the alternative is not something lovers should consider. The result of the morally correct conduct is a happy ending. Cligés and Fenice live happily ever after, reigning as Emperor and Empress of Constantinople until their extreme old age. The result of Tristan and Isolde's choice, however, is tragedy: the deaths of the hero and heroine. Here, Chrétien has revealed one of the essential elements of medieval romance. It is the opposite of tragedy, for where tragedy concerns the results of making a morally bad choice, romance takes the potentially tragic situation and explores the alternative route: the morally good choice and its consequences.

"Critical Evaluation" by C. M. Adderley

Bibliography:
Frappier, Jean. "Chrétien de Troyes." In *Arthurian Literature in the Middle Ages*, edited by Roger Sherman Loomis. Oxford, England: Clarendon Press, 1959. This is a good starting point for a study of Chrétien de Troyes, dealing mainly with sources and characterization.

Haidu, Peter. *Aesthetic Distance in Chrétien de Troyes: Irony and Comedy in Cligés and Perceval*. Geneva, Switzerland: Droz, 1968. This is an examination of the style and structure of two of Chrétien's romances. Haidu concludes that the major theme of *Cligés* is the difference between appearance and reality.

Loomis, Roger Sherman. *Arthurian Tradition and Chrétien de Troyes*. New York: Columbia University Press, 1949. Loomis shows how Chrétien's romances were influenced by Celtic mythology. Although his conclusions have been challenged, his work is very stimulating, especially when he deals with the Sword Bridge.

Noble, Peter S. *Love and Marriage in Chrétien de Troyes*. Cardiff: University of Wales Press, 1982. This book examines the theme of love and marriage in all of Chrétien's romances, concluding that he prefers in *Cligés* a more self-controlled love than that seen in the Tristan legend.

Polak, Lucie. *Chrétien de Troyes: Cligés*. Critical Guides to French Texts 23. London: Grant and Cutler, 1982. This is the best critical study on *Cligés*. Polak examines the themes of war and love, and she makes a detailed comparison of *Cligés* to the Tristan story. She points out that, according to Chrétien's epilogue, Fenice is not regarded with favor by posterity and argues that she had been overly obsessed with appearing to be blameless.

A CLOCKWORK ORANGE

Type of work: Novel
Author: Anthony Burgess (John Anthony Burgess Wilson, 1917-1993)
Type of plot: Dystopian
Time of plot: Indeterminate
Locale: England
First published: 1962

> *Principal characters:*
> ALEX, a violent young man
> GEORGIE, a member of Alex's gang
> PETE, another member of Alex's gang
> DIM, the fourth gang member, later a policeman
> PA, Alex's father
> MUM, Alex's mother
> F. ALEXANDER, a writer

The Story:

Alex, a young, English "ultra-violent" gang leader, led his three "droogs" (or companions) in campaigns of robbery, mayhem, rape, and torture. Alex celebrated gratuitous cruelty and carnality, allowing nothing to get in the way of his impulses. After leaving the Korova Milkbar (the milk was spiked with various drugs) and ducking in and out of a pub, his gang beat up a "doddery starry schoolmaster type veck" (the gang spoke a dialect particular to their violent subculture) and destroyed his books, assaulted a man and woman while robbing their shop, and brutally thrashed a singing drunk. Spying a rival gang about to rape a girl, Alex, Georgie, Pete, and Dim, although outnumbered, went on the attack until the police broke it up.

Their night was not yet over. In a stolen car they took a joyride into the country, wildly running over things. Stopping in a village, they attacked a cottage occupied by a writer and his wife, whose educated accents drove them to even greater viciousness. They raped the wife and left the husband permanently paralyzed. After returning to the Korova Milkbar, Alex bullied and insulted Dim, who protested, with the support of Georgie and Pete. Alex's authority over the gang was faltering. At this point they quit for the night. For Alex, such an active evening required music to make it complete. At Municipal Flatblock 18-A, where he lived with his parents, he enjoyed terrible fantasies of violence as he listened to Mozart and Bach.

The next morning, his counselor sternly warned him that the police suspected him. Alex was undeterred. He lured two girls he met at a record store back to his flat for an orgy of sex and Beethoven's Ninth Symphony. As he left the flatblock that evening, his gang intercepted him. Georgie asserted himself as the new leader, but Alex, in a quick display of ruthlessness, made them back down. Alex nevertheless went along with the robbery they had planned. They forced their way into the flat of a woman who called the police and aggressively defended herself. Alex unintentionally killed her in the struggle. On the way out, his companions betrayed him. Dim hit him with a chain, blinding him, and the police quickly arrested him. In two nights and a day, Alex had participated in three gratuitous assaults on strangers, a rape, a murder, a gang fight, and statutory rape, all committed in a spirit of joyful anarchy.

Alex felt threatened in the overcrowded, hostile prison. Determined to win his early release by being a model prisoner, he attached himself to the prison chaplain. His hopes turned to the

Ludovico Technique, a conditioning procedure that reformed criminals by blocking their antisocial impulses. A prisoner was killed in Alex's cell, so he was put into the therapy program. Unwittingly, he became a pawn in a struggle between administrators anxious to prove their new anticrime policies and the political opposition to those policies.

Alex underwent the Ludovico Technique. After receiving an injection, he was forced to view films of street violence and rape. The drug and the images created in him a powerful aversion against even thoughts of violence. Beethoven's Ninth Symphony, his particular favorite, happened to be on a sound track, and he was conditioned against that as well. At the end of two weeks, he was displayed before the Minister of the Interior and other officials. Deliberately humiliated, he proved unable to defend himself.

Having been "cured" of his criminal nature, Alex was released. Though his therapy took only two weeks, two years had elapsed since he entered prison. Meekly returning home to his Pa and Mum, he discovered that he was no longer welcome. The new boarder, Joe, declared that he was "more like a son to them than a lodger." Thoroughly rejected, he left the home of his parents. The old haunts, however, were no longer the same, and he began to wish that he were dead or back in prison. In a highly improbable set of coincidences that suggest that the story is more fabulous than realistic, he ran into several of his victims. In the library he was recognized by the man whom he had assaulted in the street and whose books he had destroyed. The two policemen who came to his rescue were his old friend Dim and Billyboy, the former leader of a rival gang, who took him into the country and beat him. Alex, now victimized as he had once victimized others, stumbled upon the cottage where he had raped the woman and crippled the husband. The man recognized Alex, from a picture in the paper, as the young man involved in the Ludovico Technique, which he opposed philosophically and politically. The man seized upon Alex's deplorable condition to embarrass the government. He also realized that Alex (who had worn a mask during the attack) was the same person who had crippled him and brutalized his wife.

As an appropriate punishment, Alex was locked in his room and subjected to an emotionally powerful symphony. Unable to stand it, he jumped from the window, intending suicide. Although Alex recovered, the conspiracy to make him a martyr succeeded. Alex was publicly celebrated as a victim of the reformers' inhumane policies. He was reconciled to his Mum and Pa, and his conditioning was reversed so that he could return to his old life.

Alex, however, was growing older and no longer felt the thrills of the ultra-violent. One evening he ran into his old friend Pete, who was now married, working respectably, and speaking standard English. Pete's wife laughed at Alex's language. Alex appeared old to himself, out of it. Now eighteen, he envisioned himself with a wife and son.

Critical Evaluation:

A Clockwork Orange is a dystopian novel, one that shows a seriously malfunctioning society. Dystopian stories contrast with the long tradition of visions of an ideal society, which began with Sir Thomas More's *Utopia* (1516). After World War II, the dystopian novel, expressing a deeply pessimistic view of human nature and social possibility, became a literary staple. Probably the most famous example remains George Orwell's *Nineteen Eighty-Four* (1949).

A Clockwork Orange became Anthony Burgess' most popular novel in a long and varied literary career, but he protested what he believed to be its gross misinterpretation in an introduction to a new American edition (1988). In all earlier American editions the last chapter had been omitted, though it had always been present in the English and other versions. That last chapter gives a more hopeful view of Alex's life, describing him as eventually abandoning violence and yearning for marriage and fatherhood. The truncated American version, however, became the basis for Stanley Kubrick's film (1971) of the same name, which gave the story a brilliant visual and dramatic edge and was largely responsible for its popularity. The movie presented a starkly nihilistic world in which all institutions were corrupt and no hope was offered.

What Burgess intended to emphasize, as he points out in his introduction, was the necessity of free will and moral choice in the human makeup. Alex is a highly intelligent and articulate young man who chooses an evil life and later chooses to move away from it. Alex is a human creature only to the extent that he retains his free choice; when conditioned, he is reduced to nothing. Evil, the book argues, is a better condition than blankness. Alex is not given the usual excuses for being a criminal. He is not poor. His parents, however ineffectual, show concern. He demonstrates himself as a gifted natural leader. The title, derived from a Cockney expression, expresses what Burgess intended to emphasize: "A clockwork orange" is something that is "queer to the limit of queerness," something with its essential nature missing. In general imagistic terms, a clockwork orange applies to the conditioned Alex as well: Though he appears natural from the outside, he is thoroughly unnatural within.

Many readers, however, find that the author's professed interpretation of his book is not entirely convincing. Should the interpretation of the whole book be changed on the relatively slight evidence of the last chapter? The author's images of social disintegration and gang violence appear to be the novel's most compelling aspects and lead quite naturally to their visualization in the film and in the reader's imagination. Most American readers, at least, have attached their interpretation to what appears to be an uncompromising, nihilistic posture against all authority, attitudes that were very popular in the 1960's and 1970's.

There is no such disagreement, however, about the novel's language. Alex's first-person narration, an elaborate patter filled with many Russian-derived words, gives the book a highly original and much-admired texture. The mock-Shakespearean cadence becomes part of Alex's aestheticism: "But where I itty now, O my brothers, is all on my oddy knocky, where you cannot go." Using more than two hundred distinct words and phrases, Alex speaks an apparently impenetrable dialect. Burgess' presentation is so skillful, however, that the attentive reader learns the vocabulary in the course of the narrative. If Alex's nightmare of "smecking malchicks doing the ultra-violent on a young ptitsa who was creeching away in her red red krovvy, her platties all razrezzed real horrorshow," is translated into "smiling guys viciously assaulting a young woman who was screaming while lying in her own blood, her clothes beautifully torn up," the masked violence becomes naked. Language both disguises and reveals. Its significance goes well beyond an external and superficial effect. The English, more than most other nationalities, are aware of dialect as a social identifier. In choosing his patois, Alex has declared who and what he is. Language is a more important assertion of his identity than his oddly mannered clothes. Drawn into Alex's language, the reader enters his world of images and values, where there is no word for pity or compassion, and the familiar is brutally truncated ("father" and "mother" become "pee" and "em"). Language also creates an aesthetic of violence, celebrating the terrible and disgusting. The repetition of "O my brothers" is a grotesque irony in the midst of nonstop violence. Alex also learns that his chosen dialect has no lasting value. After two years, his patter is outdated, something laughable to the younger nadsats (teenagers) who already have expressions of their own.

Bruce Olsen

Bibliography:
Coale, Samuel. *Anthony Burgess*. New York: Frederick Ungar, 1981. A general discussion of Burgess' work, including an examination of the philosophical issues in *A Clockwork Orange*.

Morris, Robert K. *The Consolations of Ambiguity*. Columbia: University of Missouri Press, 1971. Compares *A Clockwork Orange* to *The Wanting Seed* (1962), another of Burgess' dystopian novels.

Petix, Esther. "Linguistics, Mechanics, and Metaphysics: *A Clockwork Orange*." In *Anthony Burgess*, edited by Harold Bloom. New York: Chelsea House, 1987. Defines the author's dualistic worldview and relates it to the language and images of the novel.

Ray, Philip E. "Alex Before and After: A New Approach to Burgess' *A Clockwork Orange*." In *Critical Essays on Anthony Burgess*, edited by Geoffrey Aggeler. Boston: G. K. Hall, 1986. Argues that the three sections of the novel represent changes in Alex's inevitable development.

Tilton, John W. *Cosmic Satire in the Contemporary Novel*. Cranbury, N.J.: Bucknell University Press, 1977. Argues that the restoration of the last chapter greatly increases the depth of the novel.

THE CLOSED GARDEN

Type of work: Novel
Author: Julien Green (1900-)
Type of plot: Psychological realism
Time of plot: 1908
Locale: France
First published: Adrienne Mesurat, 1927 (English translation, 1928)

Principal characters:
ANTOINE MESURAT, a retired teacher
ADRIENNE, his daughter
GERMAINE, her invalid older sister
DR. DENIS MAURECOURT, a physician
MADAME LEGRAS, a neighbor

The Story:

Adrienne Mesurat lived with her father, a retired writing master, and Germaine, her invalid older sister, in a small, ugly villa in the country town of La Tour l'Eveque. The routine of the household was simple, for Antoine Mesurat lived only to indulge his own quiet tastes. Three meals a day, his morning and evening walks, his favorite newspaper, an occasional game of *trente-et-un*—these were his pleasures. In his tranquilly stubborn manner, he was a complete domestic tyrant, and the idea that his daughters might be unhappy with their lot never crossed his mind.

There had been a time when callers came to the villa, for the Mesurats owned enough property to attract young men of the district. Old Mesurat, however, considered his daughters superior to the sons of provincial tradesmen and lawyers and laughed complacently at their proposals of marriage. Finally, the visits ceased. In the uneventful round of Adrienne's days, a strange passerby in the street, local gossip her father brought back from his walks, and the succession of tenants who each summer rented the Villa Louise on the corner became items for speculation and comment. Matters might have gone on indefinitely if Adrienne had not, in the summer of her seventeenth year, fallen suddenly in love.

She had been gathering flowers beside a country road when a carriage passed her. She saw in it a slight man of middle age, who half lifted his hat as the vehicle went by. Adrienne recognized him as Dr. Maurecourt, a recent arrival in the town. A feeling of gratitude and adoration filled her, because he had noticed her. For the rest of the summer, she walked the same road every day, but the doctor never rode that way again.

At last, Adrienne hit upon another plan. Each night, after Germaine had gone to her room and Mesurat had settled himself in the parlor for his evening nap, she would steal out of the house. From the corner on which the Villa Louise stood, she could see the front of the Maurecourt dwelling, and the sight of its lighted windows gave her a deep feeling of happiness. Once she saw Maurecourt on the street. Later, she felt that she had to see him again at any cost. One day, while cleaning, she discovered that she could also watch his house from the window of Germaine's room. As often as possible, she went there and sat, hoping to see him enter or leave by his front door.

Germaine, surprising Adrienne in her bedroom, became suspicious. That night, the older sister was awake when Adrienne returned quietly from her evening vigil. Mesurat, informed of what had happened, ordered Adrienne to play cards with him after dinner the next day. Under her father's suspicious gaze, she played badly. He became enraged and accused her of stealing out nightly to meet a lover. From that time on, she was allowed to leave the house only when she went walking with her father. Again she saw Maurecourt on the street. Thinking that if she were hurt he would be called to attend her, she thrust her arms through the windowpane. Her father and sister bandaged her cuts, much to her despair.

Germaine's sickness grew worse. Refusing to acknowledge her serious condition, Mesurat insisted that she get up for her meals. One morning, after he had berated her at breakfast, Germaine confided her intention of leaving home, and she borrowed five hundred francs from Adrienne's dower chest to pay her fare to a convent hospital. Adrienne was glad to see her sister go; she hoped to occupy the room from which she used to watch Maurecourt's house. Mesurat, surprised and furious, was puzzled to know how Germaine had arranged for her flight and where she had secured money for her train fare.

In June, Madame Legras became the new tenant of Villa Louise. Adrienne and her father had met the summer visitor at a concert, and Madame Legras had invited the young girl to visit. After Germaine's flight, Adrienne went to see her new neighbor. Madame Legras was affable but prying. Confused by questions about a possible lover, Adrienne had a strange attack of dizziness.

That night, Mesurat angrily ordered her to produce her dower box. Seeing that five hundred francs were missing, he accused her of plotting with Germaine to outwit him. While he stood reviling her from the head of the stairs, Adrienne ran against him in the dark. He fell into the hall below. Dazed and frightened by her deed, Adrienne went to bed.

The cook stumbled upon Mesurat's body the next morning, and Madame Legras, aroused by the disturbance, summoned Maurecourt. Although there were some whispers that the old man's end might not be all it seemed, the verdict was one of accidental death. Germaine did not return for the funeral. Before long, Adrienne, to her dismay, found herself lonelier than ever. A feeling of lethargy possessed her much of the time. When the prioress wrote asking for money in Germaine's name or lawyers sent legal papers for her signature, she disregarded them. Nothing seemed to matter except the time she spent with Madame Legras, who had assumed a protective attitude toward the young woman. At last, however, Adrienne began to realize that Madame Legras suspected the truth about Mesurat's death, and her sly looks and pointed remarks seemed intended to lead the young woman into a trap.

One day, Adrienne decided to go to Montfort. There, walking the streets, she imagined that people were staring at her. She spent the night in Dreux, where a young workman accosted her. Later, frightened because she did not remember why she had gone away, she returned to La Tour l'Eveque after sending Maurecourt a card telling him of her unhappiness.

Shortly after her return, she collapsed and had to be put to bed at Villa Louise. While undressing her, Madame Legras found a love letter, which she gave to the doctor when he came in response to her summons. That night, Adrienne awoke and went back to her own home. Maurecourt went to see her there the next day. When she confessed her love, he told her that he was sick and soon to die. Overcome by his visit, she was barely able to rouse herself when Madame Legras appeared and demanded an immediate loan in order to pay some pressing debts. While she looked on helplessly, the woman emptied the dower chest of its gold coins. Then she removed the watch and chain Adrienne was wearing and dropped them into her purse.

A short time later, when the cook brought word that Madame Legras had left town very suddenly, Adrienne realized that the servant also knew her guilt. Dazed, she sat vacant-eyed when Maurecourt's sister called to reproach her for her shameless behavior. At nightfall, she left the house and wandered toward the lighted square, where a party was in progress. Suddenly she turned and ran toward the dark countryside. Some peasants found her there a few hours later. She could not tell them her name. She was mad.

Critical Evaluation:

Julien Green has said that his novels allow glimpses of "great dark stirrings," which he believes to be the deepest part of the soul. Quietly, but inevitably, this novel probes the deepest aspects of Adrienne Mesurat's being. Green believed from the beginning of his literary career that a novelist is "like a scout commissioned to go and see what is happening in the depth of the soul," who then comes back to report what has been observed. The writer never lives on the surface, but only inhabits the darkest regions. In his diary, Green observes: "The anguish and loneliness of my characters can almost always be reduced to what I think I called a manifold dread of living in this world." Although Green's characters rarely express ideas, his books hold a view of the world, a philosophy. *The Closed Garden* stands at the head of his works, both in form and implied statement.

It has been said that the inspiration for *The Closed Garden* was a painting by Maurice Utrillo: The novel has the sunlit yet melancholy dullness readers find in many of Utrillo's street scenes. Green has also been compared with Emily Brontë for the intensity of his atmosphere and with Honoré de Balzac for his realistic rendering of French provincial life. These comparisons, however, are true only in part. Green is himself first of all, with his own powers and compelling insights.

The characters in *The Closed Garden* try to preserve their lives as they are, but nothing can stay the same. Even passivity is a choice, an action that must have consequences; and these consequences can force one forward to the destiny waiting at the end. Monotony can lead as inevitably as more colorful events to tragedy—and perhaps more inescapably. People can tangle themselves in tragic fates without realizing until too late (if ever) what has happened. Green seems to imply in his tale that the inarticulate suffer as deeply as the more intelligent and sophisticated.

Adrienne Mesurat lives surrounded by quiet, but still deadly, selfishness. Her father thinks only of his own comfort, and her sister lives only for her illness. Adrienne is crushed beneath their wills—wretched and hardly knowing why. Green suggests that her condition is a metaphor for that of most of humanity. What happens when she wakes up and tries to break loose from her invisible bonds? Life does not have the happy ending of the fairy tale. There can be only one ending. It is not contrived tragedy: It emerges from the characters themselves. "The author creates characters," writes Green, "and the characters create the plot."

The style of *The Closed Garden* is typical of Green's elusive, subtle manner. His prose is quiet and unobtrusive. André Gide commented about Green's books that the pencil seems never to leave the paper; the line is unbroken to the end. Green has said that his intention in *The Closed Garden* and his other early works was to tell the story without ever allowing the reader to be "diverted by the style in which it was written, a sort of invisible style, good and strong, if possible, but not in any way noticeable." The complete effacement of the author is, for Green, one of the major requirements of literary perfection. He believes that it should be impossible for a reader to know what kind of person had written the book. He wants the characters to speak and act for themselves and never be interfered with by the author's personality.

Green's premise is that, although Adrienne appears commonplace at first glance, she is as mysterious as any human being and just as alone. She breathes and moves in an atmosphere of solitude that gradually becomes oppressive. Green believes that most people never succeed in breaking down the barriers that separate them from the rest of humanity. Although people make constant contact with others, the communication is imperfect, at best. "When we are about to speak," writes Green, "and reveal something about our inner life, who is in the mood to listen?" If one is heard, can the listener understand? This aloneness is the theme of *The Closed Garden* and of most of Green's fiction.

Green was born of American parents in Paris, in 1900. While in his teens during World War I, he drove an ambulance and served in the French artillery. He studied music and art before turning to literature and achieving early recognition with his first novels. His elder sister, Anne, is also a novelist, although she writes in English, while the body of his work is in French. He was a close friend of Gide and was influenced by the master's style. The fall of France in World War II forced Green's return to Virginia, where he previously had attended college. During this time, he wrote his autobiographical *Memories of Happy Days* (1942), his only book composed in English. In 1942, Green entered the United States Army and worked with the Office of War information. After the liberation of France in 1945, he returned to Paris.

A French critic has spoken of Green as a "pure" writer, explaining that he never has written a line except under absolute artistic compulsion. He lives and works under rigid self-discipline, which rules out all petty distractions. In 1939, after twenty years, Green returned to the Catholic faith. This is shown strikingly in the several volumes of his *Journal* (1938-1972). Critics have compared his later novels favorably with those of François Mauriac and André Gide.

Green makes no sentimental appeals. He creates horror in books such as *The Closed Garden* by cumulative value, not by yielding to sensational effects. The realism of this novel is that of a nightmare. The lean style avoids decorations and seems to photograph the tragedy dispassionately. The emotion is concentrated and intense. Green maintains a firm control over the novel, avoiding the capriciousness and predictability of some of the later novels. His debt to the early United States writers Edgar Allan Poe and Nathaniel Hawthorne is evident in *The Closed Garden*. The carefully constructed prose and the moral concern that rule the story are especially reminiscent of Hawthorne. At times, Green seems to suggest that sexuality is apart from the rest of life and, because apart, evil. Certainly, Adrienne Mesurat, as so many other of Green's characters, cannot cope with her own sexuality and is destroyed by it as much as by anything else. Green's characters seem to have a longing nostalgia for a peace and happiness that they have never known. Dreams and vague memories of bittersweet desires, however, are not enough, as Green artfully demonstrates.

Green received many awards and prizes during his long career and, in 1971, became the first United States citizen to be elected to the French Academy.

"Critical Evaluation" by Bruce D. Reeves

Bibliography:
Burne, Glenn S. *Julian Green*. New York: Twayne, 1972. Study of Green's literary achievement. Discusses the structure of *The Closed Garden*; comments on the development of the protagonist, a "solid young lady" who is subdued by fate.
Dunaway, John M. *The Metamorphoses of the Self: The Mystic, the Sensualist, and the Artist in the Works of Julien Green*. Lexington: University Press of Kentucky, 1978. Comments on the novel are included in a study that explores the biographical genesis of Green's major fiction.
Reck, Rima Drell. *Literature and Responsibility: The French Novelist in the Twentieth Century*. Baton Rouge: Louisiana State University Press, 1969. Characterizes Green as an iconoclast

whose impact on fiction has been limited but important. Focuses on the sense of isolation the novelist evokes in *The Closed Garden*.

Stansbury, Milton H. *French Novelists of Today*. Philadelphia: University of Pennsylvania Press, 1935. A chapter on Green emphasizes the importance of *The Closed Garden* on his career; notes how successful the novelist is in creating a portrait of his tortured heroine.

Stokes, Samuel. *Julian Green and the Thorn of Puritanism*. New York: King's Crown Press, 1955. Study of Green's novels, concentrating on the various intellectual influences that help explain the spiritual background of his work. Discusses Green's use of fiction to relate the lives of individuals to the society in which they live.

THE CLOUDS

Type of work: Drama
Author: Aristophanes (c. 450-c. 385 B.C.E.)
Type of plot: Social satire
Time of plot: Fifth century B.C.E.
Locale: Athens
First performed: Nephelai, 423 B.C.E. (English translation, 1708)

> *Principal characters:*
> STREPSIADES, an Athenian gentleman
> PHEIDIPPIDES, his son
> SOCRATES, a Sophist philosopher

The Story:

Strepsiades, a rich gentleman of Athens, was plunged into poverty and debt by his profligate son, Pheidippides. Hounded by his son's creditors, Strepsiades pondered ways to prevent complete ruin. Hearing reports that the Sophists taught a new logic which could be used to confuse one's creditors and so get one out of debt, Strepsiades saw in the Sophist teachings a possible solution to his problem. He pleaded with Pheidippides to enter the school of the Sophists and learn the new doctrines. When Pheidippides, more interested in horse racing than in learning, refused to become a pupil, Strepsiades denounced his son as a wastrel and decided to enroll himself.

He went to the Thoughtery or Thinking-School, which was the term used for the classroom of the Sophists, and asked to see Socrates, the philosopher. After Strepsiades had explained his purpose, Socrates proceeded to demonstrate several logical conclusions of the new school. More certain than ever that the new logic would save him from ruin and disgrace, Strepsiades pleaded until Socrates admitted him to the Thoughtery.

Unfortunately, Strepsiades proved too old to master the Sophist technique in the classroom. Socrates then decided that Strepsiades could learn to do his thinking outdoors. When Socrates put questions concerning poetry to Strepsiades, his answers showed such complete ignorance that Socrates finally admitted defeat and returned to the Thoughtery. Strepsiades, disgusted with his own efforts, decided that he would either make Pheidippides go to the Sophist school or turn him out of the house. Approached a second time by his father, Pheidippides again protested against enrolling in the school but finally yielded to his father's demands. Strepsiades felt that all now would be well.

Some time afterward Strepsiades went to learn what progress his son had made. Socrates assured him that Pheidippides had done well. At this news, Strepsiades felt sure that his plan had been a good one and that the new logic, as learned by his son, would soon deliver him from his creditors. He asked Socrates to call Pheidippides from the classroom. When Pheidippides emerged, Strepsiades greeted him between tears and laughter and said it was fitting that he should be saved by the son who had plunged him into debt.

He asked Pheidippides to demonstrate his new learning, and Strepsiades was amazed by the cunning of the new logic. At that moment one of Strepsiades' creditors appeared to demand money that was owed him for a horse. Strepsiades, confident that the Sophist-taught Pheidippides could turn the tables on any creditor in the law court, refused to pay, ignoring threats of court action. He treated a second creditor in the same way and went home convinced that the new logic, as argued by Pheidippides, would save him in the pending law suits.

It became a different matter, however, when Pheidippides proceeded to demonstrate the Sophist teaching at home. Arguing that Strepsiades had beaten him often for his own good, Pheidippides buffeted his father during a family argument and declared that he was beating Strepsiades for his own good. The old man protested, but with the new logic Pheidippides silenced his protests and threatened to beat his mother on the same principle.

Strepsiades realized that the Sophists could justify all manner of evil with their tricky logic. Thinking the teachings dangerous to the youth of Athens, he took a torch and set fire to the Thoughtery. As Socrates and the Sophist disciples screamed their objection, the Thoughtery went up in flames. Strepsiades watched it burn, certain that he had eliminated an evil.

Critical Evaluation:

The Clouds is one of the best known of Aristophanes' many comedies. In it, he attacks the use of logic to justify ridiculous or self-serving ends. Aristophanes rejects the school of Sophists, whom he considers irreverent and artificial, and he satirizes their teachings in *The Clouds*.

Largely because of its caricature of the philosopher Socrates, *The Clouds* is one of Aristophanes' best-known plays. The play's buffoonery and raillery is sometimes savage and biting. Through Socrates, Aristophanes satirizes the entire Sophist movement in education. Although the play won only third prize when it was presented in 423 B.C.E., a fact which vexed its author considerably, *The Clouds* must have given the Athenian audience moments of high entertainment.

Greek comedy is a mixture of song and dance, resembling satirical comic opera at least as much as it does a comedic play. Aristophanes' humor is bawdy and cutting. Stylistically, *The Clouds* follows a conventional structure known as Old Comedy. In Old Comedy, the prologue sets forth a problem and the comic idea by which it might be resolved. The play turns on one central satiric situation or conceit. In *The Clouds*, the problem is that Strepsiades has a mountain of debts incurred by his son, and the idea for the resolution is to send his son to learn the Sophist methods of argument. Failing that, he goes to learn from Socrates. The *parode*, or entrance song of the chorus, follows, in which Socrates' new divinities, the clouds, appear singing. Later, the playwright, Aristophanes, steps out and sings a *parabasis* on a theme of public interest, which tells the audience what a fine dramatist he is and how foolish the Athenians were to let Cleon have power. Next comes the *agon*, or debate, in which Right Logic and Wrong Logic, two characters, attack and defend sophistic teaching. Then a series of episodes follows in which the audience views the results of Strepsiades' original notion of sending his son to learn how to argue falsely. The episodes are often the funniest part of the comedy, as in this play. The *exode*, or final choral song, is unusually brief in *The Clouds* and occurs as Socrates' house is being burned. The plot hinges on Strepsiades' attempt to evade paying his creditors; but he is not wholly to blame, since his extravagant son, Pheidippides, incurred the debts.

The brunt of the satire, however, falls on the figure of Socrates (and through him the whole Sophist movement in Athenian education) rather than on Strepsiades. Plato's more famous representation of Socrates is quite different from that of Aristophanes. Aristophanes' portrait shows Socrates as completely amoral, a man who destroys traditional religion and morality and replaces these with nonsense supported by specious reasoning. A further discrepancy is that in *The Clouds* Socrates is farcically concerned with natural science, particularly astronomy and meteorology, but in Plato's works Socrates is only concerned with moral questions.

Some critics explain these divergences by saying that the comic Socrates was a composite figure of several Sophists, including Protagoras, the logic-twister; Anaxagoras, who was interested in natural phenomena; and Diogenes of Apollonia, who regarded air as the primal element. This view is inaccurate. The character of Socrates in *The Clouds* was meant to be Socrates, and there is enough agreement with Plato in this play to make the caricature ring true. Socrates did study the natural sciences as a young man. Further, there is his ugliness, his poverty, his bare feet, his unorthodox religion, his penchant for homely analogies, his dialectical reasoning, his poking fun at the knowledge of the old, and, above all, his tremendous influence on young aristocrats. These are all subjected to farcical representation. Socrates was well-known as a Sophist, even though he disclaimed the name. Furthermore, Aristophanes had learned that if one intends to lambast some social ill one always picks the chief exponent of it. He invariably went for the chief figures—Cleon in politics, Euripides in tragedy, and Socrates in education.

Aristophanes, after all, was a conservative in every area of life. Born of landowners, he detested the way Athens was deteriorating in the Peloponnesian War, and he felt that the new spirit of radical experimentation was ruining the city. There is some justification for his assault on Socrates, for young idlers were learning his mode of dialectical logic and using it to prove that their immoral behavior was perfectly right, and that the gods were no longer to be feared. It is likely that these young men would have done as they pleased regardless of whether they had specious arguments, borrowed from serious thinkers, to support their actions. On the core of the matter, Socrates' own integrity, Aristophanes is completely wrong. It is likely that he came to realize this, because he lampooned Cleon and Euripides as long as they lived, and even after, but once he had written *The Clouds* he more or less gave up making Socrates the butt of his jokes.

It is interesting that the charges brought against Socrates a quarter of a century later, in 399 B.C.E., were identical to those that Aristophanes lodges against him in *The Clouds*. He was accused of corrupting the youth and of replacing the traditional gods with gods of his own making. Many of the jurors had seen Aristophanes' play and had been prejudiced by it.

James Weigel, Jr.

Bibliography:
Aristophanes. *The Clouds*. Translated by William Arrowsmith with sketches by Thomas McClure. Ann Arbor: University of Michigan Press, 1962. Discusses the history of the play and how it was originally performed. Claims Aristophanes is exploiting Socrates as a convenient comic representative of sophistic corruption. Excellent notes and glossary.
Arnott, Peter. *An Introduction to the Greek Theatre*. London: Macmillan, 1959. Examines Aristophanes as a comic writer. Asserts the satire of *The Clouds* is lost to an audience with no understanding of sophistic philosophy.
Butler, James H. *The Theatre and Drama of Greece and Rome*. San Francisco: Chandler, 1972. Claims Aristophanes was the greatest master of Grecian Old Comedy. Says *The Clouds* shows the decadence of Athens as well as the Sophists who corrupted it. Places *The Clouds* in the context of Old Comedy.
Hadas, Moses. *A History of Greek Literature*. New York: Columbia University Press, 1953. Asserts that Aristophanes handles Socrates kindly compared to other Greek playwrights. Covers the history of *The Clouds'* production as well as modern audiences' reactions to the treatment of Socrates in the play.
Snell, Bruno. *Poetry and Society: The Role of Poetry in Ancient Greece*. Freeport, N.Y.: Books for Libraries Press, 1971. Claims Aristophanes sees most wise men as mere busybodies and fools, such as he portrays Socrates to be in *The Clouds*. Compares the play to other dramatic works.

THE CLOWN

Type of work: Novel
Author: Heinrich Böll (1917-1985)
Type of plot: Psychological realism
Time of plot: 1945-1960
Locale: Bonn, Germany
First published: Ansichten eines Clowns, 1963 (English translation, 1965)

Principal characters:

HANS SCHNIER, the protagonist, a professional clown
LEO SCHNIER, his brother
HENRIETTA SCHNIER, his dead sister
DR. AND MRS. SCHNIER, his parents
MARIE DERKUM, his former lover
MONIKA SILVS,
KINKEL,
SOMMERWILD, and
HERIBERT ZÜPFNER, members of a Catholic group

The Story:

Hans Schnier, a professional clown, returned to Bonn, his hometown, after he injured his knee performing his act while drunk. When Schnier arrived in Bonn, he had little money (his last employer had refused to pay his full fee), no savings, and little hope of future work. Only weeks before this injury, Schnier had been a highly paid, well-regarded performer earning enough to live in luxury hotels with Marie Derkum, his lover and companion. When Marie left him to marry Heribert Züpfner, a Catholic official and a member of a religious group to which Marie belonged, Schnier ceased to care about the quality of his work as a clown. He stopped practicing and started to drink more, which caused his performances to decline rapidly.

From his Bonn apartment, Schnier called friends and family members, hoping for monetary and emotional support. However, each of his actions, even his conversations, triggered painful memories. At first these flashbacks were brief recollections of Marie and her group of progressive Catholics, but the reveries increased in length. In one of his early flashbacks, Schnier remembered his sister, affectionately, who had often acted unconventionally, saying and doing what she felt. With her parents' encouragement, especially that of her mother, this sister had been sent on antiaircraft duty in February, 1945, on a mission that killed her. Schnier blamed his mother's nationalistic fervor for his sister's death, and when he called his mother, her official tone and her greeting phrase—"Executive Committee of the Societies for the Reconciliation of Racial Differences"—angered Schnier and reminded him of his mother's zeal when sending her daughter off to save German soil from "Jewish Yankees." Although Schnier was calling his mother to ask for her support, he cruelly answered her greeting by saying, "I am a delegate of the Executive Committee of Jewish Yankees, just passing through—may I please speak to your daughter?" Mrs. Schnier was momentarily hurt, but she recovered quickly and rebuffed her son with her severe, dogmatic manner.

After the conversation with his mother, Schnier thought of Marie, and that triggered the memory of an event that had occurred six years earlier and resulted in the consummation of

1179

their relationship. Hans had been twenty-one and Marie nineteen when he had gone boldly to her room and slept with her. After this, Marie dropped out of school, and Schnier left his family to begin his career as a clown, but his career had developed slowly and the two barely earned enough money to survive. They both wanted children, but Marie had a number of miscarriages. The final one had occurred just before she left. Schnier's memories of his life with Marie were occasionally interrupted by speculations about Marie's present relationship with Züpfner, a relationship Schnier considered adulterous even though Marie and Züpfner were married.

Schnier called other friends and relatives and held unpleasant conversations with each. Although he wanted money and psychological support from them, his manner ensured that even those who could have helped him did not. When he talked to Kinkel, a respected Catholic theologian and a member of the group to which Marie and Züpfner belonged, Schnier blamed Kinkel and the Catholic church for his loss of Marie: "That much I have grasped of your metaphysics: What she is doing is fornication and adultery, and Prelate Sommerwild is acting the pimp." Schnier attacked Kinkel throughout their conversation, and he asserted that his relationship with Marie constituted a marriage that Kinkel and others had destroyed.

While waiting for friends to return his telephone calls, Schnier bathed and read newspapers. This, too, caused him to remember Marie and her Catholic group. He recalled that at first he had refused to marry Marie because she insisted on a Catholic marriage that required him to swear that their children would be raised in the Catholic faith. Later, when he was willing to agree to these conditions, Marie refused to marry him because she did not accept his conversion as sincere. Schnier believed that his union with Marie constituted a marriage, whether condoned by the government and the church or not, but Marie needed Schnier's commitment to the church. When Schnier talked with Sommerwild, another Catholic priest who was a member of Marie's group, Schnier accused him of having furthered Marie's marriage to Züpfner, claiming that the priest had sent the couple to Rome "to make the whoring complete."

Still waiting for phone calls, Schnier was surprised by the unexpected appearance of his father, a wealthy German capitalist. The visit was awkward and unpleasant for both, since they had not seen each other for several years and had never had a meaningful conversation. The two discussed many painful issues, but Schnier junior felt his father was playing a role that he could not abandon even to help his son. Schnier junior referred to the needless hardships the family had suffered and the fact that, despite their wealth, they had never had enough food. Schnier also remembered that his father had twice during the war shown compassion: once when Schnier was accused of "defeatism" and once when two women were accused of fraternizing with the enemy. The father agreed to pay his son a monthly stipend, but Schnier knew he would never receive it.

After his father left, Schnier read in the evening paper that Herbert Kalick had received a federal cross of merit for "his services in spreading democratic ideas among the young." This was the same Herbert Kalick who led the local Hitler youth group during World War II. It was Kalick who had denounced Schnier as a "defeatist," and he was also responsible for the death of a young boy whom Kalick had forced to carry a loaded bazooka.

Schnier attempted many times to contact his brother, Leo, who was in a Catholic seminary. Leo, who had converted from Protestantism to Catholicism, had renounced most worldly possessions and refused to break the seminary's rules to help his brother. Schnier contacted Monika Silvs, a sympathetic member of the Catholic group who had helped him in the past, but Sommerwild had instructed her to avoid Schnier. When it became clear that he would receive no help or support, Schnier decided to sing, play the guitar, and beg at the train station. One

March evening, Schnier walked to the train station and sat on the steps, singing a song about "Poor Pope John."

Critical Evaluation:

Nine years after writing *The Clown*, a work that exemplifies the themes and methods employed in his other novels, Heinrich Böll received the Nobel Prize in Literature. As a post-World War II German writer from a Catholic, pacifist family, a writer who fought in the war and was wounded four times before being captured and taken to an American prisoner-of-war camp, Böll's life and fiction encapsulates the religious, moral, and political dilemmas of post-World War II Germany. *The Clown* is the personal narrative of a single person, one individual, Hans Schnier, who is the clown of the title. In focusing on the character's idiosyncratic view of the world and in particular on his love for Marie, the novel explores the problems of all humans in twentieth century societies.

On a political level, the book recounts Hans's involvement with a Nazi youth group, his sister's death for the Nazi cause, his mother's anti-Semitic, pro-Nazi views, his own condemnation by another youth as a "defeatist," and his father's tacit support of the Nazis. The focus of Böll's satire is on those hypocrites who blindly supported fascism as well as on those who impetuously shifted their allegiance after the war. Schnier's mother, for example, an ardent Nazi supporter before 1945, afterward became the president of a society for the reconciliation of racial differences. Böll accurately depicts and attacks the erstwhile Nazis who attained positions of power in Germany during the 1960's, but on a more universal level the author satirizes all humans who heedlessly pledge allegiance to any political cause.

The Clown also explores a religious schism in German society. Hans Schnier is from a Protestant family, but Marie is an ardent Catholic and belongs to an influential and powerful Catholic group. The clown's brother abandons his family's Protestant religion and trains to be a Catholic priest in a seminary, a decision that hurts his parents. On one level, Böll examines the split between German Protestants and Catholics, but on another level he looks at a more universal question that parallels the political dilemma: To what extent should an individual blindly accept the doctrine of a religion. Marie accepts the teachings of her group and leaves the clown. Leo abandons his parents' faith to join the Catholic church, but his decision appears no more thoughtful than had been his decision to enlist in the army. The religious and political themes ultimately reinforce the novel's discussion of marriage.

Who has the right to sanction a marriage? Hans learns that the state must issue a license before a church will perform the marriage. In his case, he would have had to sign a document swearing that he would raise his children in the Catholic church. In opposition to these conventional, institutional definitions of marriage, the clown, Hans Schnier, advocates a monogamous, common-law definition that allowed him to claim Marie as his wife. The issue of marriage moves the political and religious themes to a very personal level, forcing the reader to consider whether marriage is a private, personal commitment between two individuals or a public, religious matter.

These questions of politics, religion, and marriage are presented ironically through the eyes of Hans Schnier, whose interior monologue conveys his anger, suffering, headaches, depression, and grief. The reader can identify with him because in his suffering he exposes the failings of others, even though his persona as an alcoholic clown can elicit little empathy or compassion. His role as a clown symbolizes his inability to commit and to take life seriously, but despite his faults the clown represents the individual who locates morality and responsibility within himself and fears those who abdicate their responsibility to society at large. Through Hans

Schnier, Böll explores the harm done by those who dogmatically accept the beliefs of political parties or organized religions. *The Clown* ultimately exhorts individuals to contemplate their relationship with authority and other human beings.

Roark Mulligan

Bibliography:
Beck, Evelyn T. "A Feminist Critique of Böll's *Ansichten eines Clowns.*" *University of Dayton Review* 12 (Spring, 1976): 19-24. Beck analyzes Hans Schnier as a negative person who exploited Marie. Beck asserts that with Marie, Böll depicted a victim of male domination.
Böll, Heinrich. *What's to Become of the Boy? Or, Something to Do with Books.* Translated by Leila Vennewitz. New York: Knopf, 1984. Written just before his death, this is Böll's longest autobiographical work. In it, he reveals connections between his life and his novels.
Conard, Robert C. *Heinrich Böll.* Boston: G. K. Hall, 1981. A good introduction to Böll's life and works.
_____. *Understanding Heinrich Böll.* Columbia: University of South Carolina Presses, 1992. Includes a brief biography, a chronology, and a bibliography. In one chapter, Conard analyzes Böll's major novels, among them *The Clown.*
Reid, James Henderson. *Heinrich Böll: A German for His Time.* Oxford, England: Oswald Wolff, 1988. Reid's book explores the connections among Böll's fiction, his life, and his times.

THE COCKTAIL PARTY

Type of work: Drama
Author: T. S. Eliot (1888-1965)
Type of plot: Comedy of manners
Time of plot: Mid-twentieth century
Locale: London
First performed: 1949; first published, 1950

> *Principal characters:*
> EDWARD CHAMBERLAYNE, a lawyer
> LAVINIA, his wife
> JULIA SHUTTLETHWAITE, a meddling woman
> CELIA COPLESTONE, a sensitive young woman
> PETER QUILPE, in love with Celia
> ALEXANDER MACCOLGIE GIBBS, a meddling man
> SIR HENRY HARCOURT-REILLY, at first unidentified

The Story:

The Chamberlaynes were giving a cocktail party in their London flat. The atmosphere was somewhat strained because Lavinia, the hostess, was not there, and Edward, her bumbling husband, hastily invented a sick aunt to account for her absence. As usual, Alex had an exotic story to tell, for he traveled widely and knew everyone. Julia, a sharp-eyed and sharp-tongued family friend, missed the point of his tale and wondered why Alex and the Maharaja were up a tree. Julia usually missed the point of stories she heard.

The assembly demanded that Julia give her inimitable imitation of Lady Klootz and the wedding cake. They had all heard the story before, except possibly Edward, who forgot stories, and an unidentified and unintroduced guest. Somehow Julia got off on a family who had a harmless son, and the story never did get told. The harmless son was a fascinating person: He could hear the cries of bats. Then Peter had to tell of a scenario that he had written and that, unfortunately, never was produced.

To Edward's relief, the guests prepared to leave. Only the stranger remained. He drank gin with Edward for a while, and Edward was compelled to confide in him. Lavinia was not really at her aunt's house; she had simply left with no explanation. The stranger pointed out that her leaving might be a blessing, since she was demanding and practical, but Edward was uneasy, without knowing exactly why he wanted her back. The stranger promised that the erring wife would return within twenty-four hours if Edward would ask for no explanations. He warned also that both Lavinia and Edward might be greatly changed. The stranger, full of gin, broke into song as he left the apartment.

Julia, returning for her glasses, had Peter in tow. The glasses were in Julia's bag all the time, and she departed again, leaving an agitated Peter behind. The young man wanted to confide in Edward. He had fallen in love with Celia after attending many concerts with her, and she had been very friendly. Lately, however, she had been unresponsive. He asked if Edward would intercede for him. At this juncture, Alex came gaily back. Edward was irritated. He asked Peter and Alex to lock the door when they left so no one else would wander in. Alex archly went to the kitchen, intent on whipping up a meal for the lone Edward. He succeeded in using up all the fresh eggs in some outlandish concoction.

At last, after answering the phone several times, Edward settled down in solitary comfort to play patience. Then the doorbell rang and in came Celia. She had divined that Lavinia had left Edward, and now she thought it would be a good time for Edward to seek a divorce so that he and Celia could marry. Edward agreed, but despite his repeated assurances of continued love, Celia was uneasy, for she sensed a change in him. Edward then confessed that Lavinia was coming back and that he almost wanted her back. He scarcely knew why he did, for until his wife left he had wanted only Celia. Celia was discomfited at her faint-hearted lover. When Julia returned once more, this time to invite Edward to dinner, Celia escaped into the kitchen. There, under pretext of getting a lunch for the lone Edward, she ruined Alex's concoction completely.

The next day, the stranger returned. Again he warned Edward that by wanting Lavinia to return he had set in motion forces beyond his control. When she returned, she would be a stranger and Edward would be a stranger to her. Edward had made his choice, however, and would have to abide by it. After admonishing Edward to receive any visitors who might come, the mysterious stranger left by the back stairs.

Celia was the first to arrive. She had come at Julia's request, apparently in response to a telegram from Lavinia. While they were together, Celia had a chance to look at Edward carefully; he seemed to her only a rather comic middle-aged man. She could laugh now at her infatuation. Peter arrived in response to Alex's invitation. Alex had also received a wire, ostensibly from Lavinia. He had time for some reproachful remarks to Celia and then announced he was leaving for Hollywood.

Lavinia herself arrived next, surprised to find Peter and Celia and disclaiming any knowledge of telegrams to Alex and Julia, with whose arrival the mystery deepened. At length the guests departed and Lavinia turned expectantly to Edward. He had little to say beyond reproaching her for her overbearing ways, and she twitted him for being unable to make decisions. When she suggested that he was on the verge of a nervous breakdown, he was angered but interested in the possibility. He resolved stoutly not to visit any doctor Lavinia might recommend.

In Sir Henry's offices, preparations were being made to receive patients. The first was Edward, who was surprised to see that Sir Henry was his mysterious stranger. In the consultation, Edward revealed that he had wanted Lavinia back because she had dominated him so long that he was incapable of existence without her. Sir Henry then brought in Lavinia, so that the whole problem could be threshed out.

During the conversation it was revealed that Lavinia had left because of Edward's affair with Celia. Edward, somewhat shaken to learn that she had known of the affair, grew confident again when Lavinia confessed that she had been infatuated with Peter. Sir Henry diagnosed their trouble as mutual fear: Edward was afraid he could not make successful love to anyone and Lavinia was afraid she was completely unlovable. The doctor assured them that they had every requirement for a successful life together. They had a mutual fear and hatred of each other, and both were quite mediocre people. They left, moderately reconciled.

Julia arrived at the doctor's office to ask how successful her scheming had been. It had been she who had induced Sir Henry to step in, and Alex had abetted her. Celia also came in for a consultation. She had vague feelings of guilt and sin and wanted to take a rest cure. After talking with her, Sir Henry recognized that she was an outstanding person, that her destiny called her. He advised her to be at ease and do whatever she had to do.

Two years later, the Chamberlaynes were giving another cocktail party for many of the old crowd. They were smugly settled in their mediocrity and even made a pretense of being in love. To them, cocktail parties were their measure of social standing. Peter came in hurriedly. He had been a great success in America and now had money and renown of a sort. His destiny had been a material one. Alex arrived next. He was just back from bearing the white man's burden on a tropical island. He reported Celia's death. Celia had been a nurse on the island and had been killed in a native rebellion. Her destiny had called her to martyrdom for the love of humanity.

Critical Evaluation:

Ten years after T. S. Eliot presented *The Family Reunion* (1939) to mixed reviews, he completed his second verse drama, *The Cocktail Party*, which became more popular. In its first draft, sketched out in June, 1948, the play was in three scenes (or acts) with a projected epilogue, and was tentatively titled *One-Eyed Riley*. According to Elliott Martin Browne, producer of all Eliot's plays except *Sweeney Agonistes* (1932), the original draft with its revisions was based more closely than the completed work upon Euripides' *Alcestis* (438 B.C.E.). The "death" of Alcestis was to correspond with Lavinia's departure from Edward before the party begins in scene 1. The services performed by Heracles, who descends into Hades to restore to Admetus his sacrificing wife, were to parallel to some extent those of Sir Henry (or Harry) Harcourt-Reilly, the psychiatrist who later patches together the flawed Chamberlayne marriage. Celia Coplestone, whom Eliot later described as the major character of the play, was only a minor personality in the early drafts, and the roles of Julia Shuttlethwaite, Peter Quilpe, and Alexander MacColgie Gibbs (first called Alexander Farquhar-Gibbs) were unexpanded and mostly comic.

In the preliminary revisions of the manuscript, Alex does not appear between the party scene of the first act and the conclusion of the consulting-room scene, with its elaborate libation-ritual of the Guardians. That scene, however, had been much more fully developed in the manuscripts. In the final version of *The Cocktail Party*, produced at the Edinburgh Festival in August, 1949, the scene was simplified and its poetic values were sharpened; it was offered in its present form, in three acts, with Act I in three fully developed scenes, Act II in one scene (Sir Harry's office), and Act III in a brief scene at the Chamberlaynes' London flat.

Because *The Cocktail Party* changed so markedly during the early stages of its writing, the parts, which separately are effective, do not perfectly cohere as a whole work of stagecraft. The play is both a comedy of manners, much like the social satires of the eighteenth century, and a theological—specifically Catholic—drama of salvation. The lighter parts, especially the entire first act and most of the last, resemble the witty, tart, urbane plays of Richard Sheridan or the sophisticated comedies of Oscar Wilde, W. Somerset Maugham, and even Noël Coward. The serious parts—also "comic" in the sense that Dante Alighieri's epic may be called a *commedia*—resemble more closely the tragic farces of the novels of Evelyn Waugh. To satisfy the requirements of both light and serious comedy, Eliot's characters play two kinds of roles. The Julia of the first act is a meddlesome, scatterbrained old gossip, but in the second act, she is a sober and indeed sanctified Guardian of spiritual destiny. Alex in the first act is a bumbling froth, an incompetent who concocts outrageous dishes and pops in and out of the action, much to Edward's annoyance. Yet in the ritual scene at the end of Act II, he is another Guardian, perhaps even more mysterious than Julia, who has connections throughout the world—"even in California."

The most difficult character to understand, because of his double function in the play, is Sir Harry, the psychiatrist. In the first act, he is described simply as the Unidentified Guest. A secretive but enlightened visitor to the Chamberlayne party, he apparently understands the nature of the quarrel between Edward and Lavinia, pulls the strings, so to speak, to arrange for her return to her husband, yet never reveals his own position. A confessor figure, he is at the same time a drunken reveler. Before he departs, toward the end of the first scene, he sings a bawdy song (the verses in the play are quite decorous, but other stanzas are traditionally ribald). "One-Eyed Riley" may remind the audience of the fertility themes in *The Waste Land* (1922), or it may, as Eliot suggested, recall the heroic-absurd figure of Heracles from the Euripides play. Sir Harry is both savant and fool, gifted with insight but unsteady from too much gin.

The meaning of his actions is similarly ambiguous. In his professional activity as a psychiatrist, he becomes a parody of psychiatrists. Nobody lies on the analyst's couch but Sir Harry; he collects "information" about Lavinia and Edward, without their consent, as part of his investigation of their marital condition; and he prescribes, when necessary, a cure that may require the patient to visit a hotel or a sanatorium. The hotel, a half-way house or retreat between the sane and insane world, was Lavinia's first destination, before she returned to Edward. The sanatorium, still more mysterious, is intended to cure victims of illusion, unreality. Still other patients, like Celia, he urges to discover their own mental health by working out their proper salvation. No wonder Lavinia questions whether the psychiatrist is a devil or merely a practical joker. In fact, Sir Harry is called a devil several times in the play, but he more closely resembles a divine agent. Although he has no power to effect spiritual cures, he understands the maladies of human or spiritual deprivation and prescribes a course of action to remedy the problem. Those sick persons must, however, make a decision to reject or accept the psychiatrist's advice. Gifted with prescience, Sir Harry does not control the moral choices of his patients. They have free will, and although their destinies can be predicted, they must resolve whether to follow the example of Peter Quilpe, who chooses to go to Boltwell—earthly corruption—or Celia, who chooses martyrdom as a means of salvation.

Celia, the moral center of the play, is also a difficult person to understand. Unlike Sir Harry, she has no metaphysical function in the drama, but her character seems inconsistent. In the first scene of Act I, she is a vapid young socialite, who presses Julia to finish her inane story about Lady Klootz's wedding cake. In the second scene, the audience discovers that Celia has been Edward's mistress. Disappointed when her faint-hearted lover tells her that he is quite comfortable in his relationship with Lavinia and awaits his wife's return, she comes to understand that he is mediocre and unworthy of her affections. In the third scene, she is further estranged from Edward but no longer annoyed with him. Rather, she dismisses him as an amusing little boy, ludicrous but not vexing. Like Peter, she announces her decision to go abroad. The audience is not fully prepared for the change in Celia's character in Act II, where she appears to be intense, introspective, almost visionary. In her consultation with Sir Harry, the most touching and poetically effective part of the play, she reveals unexpected resources of strength and integrity. She is weary of herself, not because others have failed her, but because she has failed the world. Guilt-ridden for no specific cause, she confesses to sin. Her psychiatrist-metaphysician suggests a spiritual cure for her guilt. She must discover her own redemption—one that will lead to a kind of crucifixion on an anthill, an absurd but (from Eliot's viewpoint) purposeful death.

Because Celia's death, announced by Alex in Act III, usually comes as a shock to the audience, it should be understood in the light of Eliot's theme. Although *The Cocktail Party* is superficially an elegant comedy of manners, it is a morality play. The theme of the play is that reality takes many guises. All of the characters attempt to approach the real—or what is real for their needs, but most continue to play out roles of illusion. Edward, a Prufrock-like lawyer, reconciles with his practical but unimaginative wife. At the end of the play, just as at the beginning, the Chamberlaynes prepare a cocktail party to amuse other bored, lonely people like themselves. Their reconciliation to the "building of the hearth," the commonplace but necessary compromises of domesticity, is satisfactory for each partner. Edward cannot love anyone, but at least he does not have to dissemble his frailty to Lavinia. She, for her part, is unlovable, but her vanity will not suffer any insult from a complaisant husband like Edward. So each is content, understanding no other destiny.

For the few elect souls like Celia, reality is not a casual entertainment like a cocktail party but the narrow path of Christian service. Her martyrdom (and, presumably, sainthood) is earned at the cost of terrible suffering. In Eliot's first version of the play, her death was described even more terribly: She was a victim of devouring ants. The final version toned down most of the horror by alluding to a crucifixion "very near an ant-hill." Eliot's point, however, was to affirm, through the announcement of Celia's death, the reality of divine interference in a world of the commonplace. Similarly, the transformation of comic figures like Sir Harry, Julia, and Alex into spiritual Guardians of humankind reminds the audience that the real world itself is illusion, the unseen world real. It is significant to remember that the Guardians' final blessing for Edward, Lavinia, and Celia is taken from Buddha's deathbed exhortation to his followers: "Work out your salvation with diligence." That is the message of Eliot's play.

"Critical Evaluation" by Leslie B. Mittleman

Bibliography:
Arrowsmith, William. "Notes on English Verse Drama, II: *The Cocktail Party.*" *Hudson Review* 3 (Autumn, 1950): 411-430. The best available article on *The Cocktail Party*. Offers a lucid analysis of the play's rich Christian implications and its intricate internal structure. Arrow-smith ranks the work as highly for verse drama as he ranks *The Waste Land* for poetry.
Jones, David E. *The Plays of T. S. Eliot*. London: Routledge & Kegan Paul, 1960. In chapter 5, Jones analyzes the play's relationship to its Greek model, Euripides' *Alcestis*, and explains the strengths of a verse drama that is easy to follow and yet profound.
Kari, Daven Michael. *T. S. Eliot's Dramatic Pilgrimage: A Progress in Craft as an Expression of Christian Perspective*. Studies in Art and Religious Interpretation 13. Lewiston, N.Y.: Edwin Mellen Press, 1990. Examines Eliot's steadily improving use of characterization, verse techniques, and stagecraft as an expression of his movement from ascetic to communal models of Christian faith. An innovative and readable critique.
Lightfoot, Marjorie J. "The Uncommon Cocktail Party." *Modern Drama* 11 (1969): 382-395. A lucid and revealing article that analyzes the rhythms that make *The Cocktail Party* so successful on stage. Also discusses why Eliot's verse drama is seldom understood.
Tydeman, William. *"Murder in the Cathedral" and "The Cocktail Party."* Houndmills, Basingstoke, England: Macmillan, 1988. A simple and straightforward interpretation of the plays as dramas. A good choice for directors and actors wishing to perform the play.

COLD COMFORT FARM

Type of work: Novel
Author: Stella Gibbons (1902-1989)
Type of plot: Parody
Time of plot: Early twentieth century
Locale: London and Sussex, England
First published: 1932

Principal characters:
FLORA POSTE, a young lady of excellent manners
ADA DOOM STARKADDER, her aunt
AMOS STARKADDER, Ada's son
JUDITH STARKADDER, Amos' wife
SETH and
REUBEN, Amos' and Judith's sons
ELFINE, their daughter

The Story:

Flora Poste's parents died when she was nineteen, leaving her an income of one hundred pounds a year. They had provided her with an expensive education that had not prepared her to earn her living. She visited a friend near London to decide what to do and developed a warm relationship with her cousin, Charles Fairford. She wrote to various relatives to ask if she might stay with them and chose the Starkadders, an aunt and cousins who lived at Cold Comfort Farm in Howling, Sussex. Charles promised to rescue Flora in his plane whenever living on the farm became too much for her.

Adam Lambsbreath, the ninety-year-old farmhand, met Flora at the station. He told Flora that a curse on Cold Comfort Farm prevented it from flourishing and any of the family from leaving. Flora suspected, however, that Mrs. Ada Doom Starkadder, her deceased mother's sister, was the real curse. Aunt Ada Doom stayed in her room and ruled the family with a will of iron. She had not left the farm in twenty years. Appalled by the condition of the farm and by the many violent and brooding Starkadders, Flora determined to tidy up life at Cold Comfort Farm.

Flora glimpsed her seventeen-year-old cousin, Elfine, who had never attended school and spent most of her time wandering about the moors writing poetry. Flora heard Meriam, the hired girl, groaning while delivering her fourth illegitimate child by Seth. Conferring with Cousin Judith, Flora learned that Judith's husband, Amos, had done a great, secret wrong to Flora's deceased father. Coarse and filled with lust for the land, Reuben was the only true farmer among the Starkadders. He suspected that Flora wanted to take over the farm, but when she assured him that the farm was the last thing she wanted, she won him over. Seth made suggestive advances to her, but Flora discovered that his great love in life was not women, as she had assumed, but "the talkies." Though exhausted by her interaction with these family members, Flora decided she must become acquainted with the other Starkadders.

Flora dropped hints but she was not invited to meet Aunt Ada Doom Starkadder. Flora decided to work on Cousin Amos, a huge, rude, religious fanatic. She accompanied him to his sermon at the Church of the Quivering Brethren and twice proposed that he could do even more good by preaching throughout the country. Opposite the Majestic Cinema, Flora was reminded of Mr. Neck, a Hollywood producer she knew who would be flying to England in the spring to look for film actors.

Flora began to worry about Elfine, who was apparently in love with Richard Hawk-Monitor, the scion of country gentry who lived nearby. There was soon to be a ball in honor of Richard's twenty-first birthday, and Flora arranged an invitation for Elfine, with herself as chaperon. The Starkadders expected Elfine to marry Urk, a farm cousin. Flora secretly groomed the girl and gave her private instruction in good taste and deportment. Elfine made a grand entrance at the ball. Before the night was over, Richard Hawk-Monitor had announced their engagement.

Satisfied with her night's work, Flora returned to Cold Comfort Farm with Elfine. They found the entire family, including Aunt Ada, assembled downstairs for the annual counting, when the matriarch counted the Starkadders to see if anyone had died. Flora announced Elfine's engagement, which caused Urk to fall into the sandwiches. Judith introduced Flora to Aunt Ada, but the old woman only raved and thrashed. Amos announced to his mother that he had broken her chain and would leave that night to spread the Lord's word abroad. Ada grew wilder. Soon Urk dragged Meriam out the door, bellowing that since he had lost Elfine he would take Meriam.

The next afternoon, Flora discovered Mr. Neck, her friend from Hollywood, had arrived. Flora introduced Seth, whom Mr. Neck recognized as the sexually successful local bounder, a type of film actor who tends to be a big hit with women. Seth packed and left with the producer, accompanied by wild screams from Aunt Ada. Letters arrived from Amos, who was off to America to preach and who left the farm to Reuben.

When Richard Hawk-Monitor's mother decided to have the wedding reception at Cold Comfort Farm, Flora was dismayed. She installed the men's wives at the farm to prepare while she attended to Judith and Aunt Ada. A luncheon for Judith with a Viennese psychoanalyst was arranged, and Judith drove off with Dr. Mudel for six months of treatment, looking quite content. Back in Howling, Flora brought her aunt's lunch upstairs and conferred with her until late.

The day of the wedding dawned bright and beautiful. The remaining Starkadders watched the church ceremony with pleasure. At the farm, resplendent with garlands, lush gardens, and striped awnings, Aunt Ada Doom Starkadder astonished everyone by greeting guests in a black leather flying suit. Flora tried to discover the secret wrong done to her father, but Aunt Ada never had a chance to answer before the plane arrived to whisk her off to Paris. The honeymoon couple were next to fly off. Flora went to the village to call Charles, who landed his plane at the farm three hours later. He and Flora fell into each other's arms, declared their love, and flew off to London together.

Critical Evaluation:

Stella Gibbons was a prolific writer who started out as a journalist after attending the University of London. For ten years she worked as a drama and literature critic, special reporter, and fashion writer. Later, she produced more than thirty novels and collections of poetry and short stories. In quality, none of them rivaled *Cold Comfort Farm*, her first published novel, which won the prestigious Femina Vie Heureuse prize in 1933 and became a popular classic of English literature. A member of the Royal Society of Literature, Gibbons was elected a fellow in 1950. She hated publicity and politics and spent the last thirty years of her life as a recluse.

Cold Comfort Farm is generally considered to be a parody of the type of novel that British authors such as Thomas Hardy, D. H. Lawrence, and Mary Webb wrote in the early twentieth century. Their novels were usually characterized by crude, uneducated characters; brooding landscapes; dark mysticism that included a fatalistic view of life; and a pervasive atmosphere of violence, which occasionally erupted. Mary Webb's novel *Precious Bane* (1924) includes a semiliterate, harelipped heroine; a brother who murders his own mother; and a village of savage, superstitious people. Many of the characters of *Precious Bane* could have appeared in the pages of *Cold Comfort Farm*, yet while Webb's novel is tragic, Gibbons used her material to comic effect.

Gibbons sets the tone of *Cold Comfort Farm* in an opening letter to one Anthony Pookworthy, a fictional novelist. She tells him he has given her joy with his books, which are "records of intense spiritual struggles, staged in the wild setting of mere, berg, or fen. Your characters are ageless and elemental things, tossed like straws on the seas of passion." Yet Gibbons intends to write a book that is funny, for which she begs Pookworthy's forgiveness. The letter explains Gibbons' guidebook method of using asterisks to mark certain of the finer passages in the novel so that readers will be sure they are literature and not "flapdoodle." These marked passages are masterpieces of overwrought writing, full of long sentences teeming with lush adjectives and numerous clauses.

The vocabulary of *Cold Comfort Farm* adds to the novel's atmosphere, from the names of the characters, animals, and vegetation to the idiomatic country terms. There are fourteen men who live at the farm: Amos and his two sons, five distant cousins, two of Amos' half brothers, and four farmhands. The names include Urk, Ezra, Micah, Caraway, Harkaway, Luke, and Mark Dolour. Adam Lambsbreath is an ancient farmhand who enjoys a mystical connection to the beasts for which he cares: Graceless, Pointless, Feckless, and Aimless, the cows; Big Business, the bull; and Viper, the vicious carriage horse. One of Adam's tasks is to "cletter the dishes," and Reuben brags that he has "scranleted two hundred furrows." "Mommet" seems to be a word of endearment or disparagement (sometimes both at once). This vocabulary is typical of pastoral novels of the period, but here it is overdone and often incomprehensible to Flora Poste, the city cousin. Yet she finds her own speech lapsing into the same country idiom before she escapes from Cold Comfort Farm.

Part of the humor is Flora's ironic attitude toward the rough country ways of her cousins. She realizes that people of their temperament revel in misunderstandings, brooding, rows at mealtime, spying, skulking, and constant emotional turmoil. "Oh, they *did* enjoy themselves!" Flora concludes. By the end of the book she sees the family quietly enjoying a traditional wedding in an ordinary manner without violence, gloom, pride, or lechery, all due to her own good offices. Flora is of course herself a parody, with her reliance on her self-help books, *The Higher Common Sense* and *Pensees*, to which she frequently turns.

Geniuses and intellectuals—as exemplified by Mr. Mybug, a writer who stays in Howling while working on a revisionist biography of the Brontës—fare badly in this novel. Mybug's book is intended to prove that it was Branwell Brontë who wrote *Wuthering Heights* instead of Emily Brontë. Gibbons has much fun with this character, who is obsessed with sex and is later spied, drunk and dirty, trying to gate-crash Richard Hawk-Monitor's birthday ball.

Gibbons manages her large cast of characters well, integrating them into the many subplots involved in Flora's "tidying" of the Starkadders. The author tidies up her plot at the end with a literary device of *deus ex machina*, which in classic Greek drama ended a story by mechanically lowering a god onstage to resolve the plot (the term has come to mean any improbable device by which an author resolves the plot). In *Cold Comfort Farm* the *deus ex machina* is three airplanes that arrive to whisk off Aunt Ada Doom, the newly married Hawk-Monitors, and Flora. Here, Gibbons parodies the end of Thomas Hardy's *Tess of the d'Urbervilles* (1891).

Sheila Golburgh Johnson

Bibliography:

Dangerfield, George. *"Brilliant Satire: Cold Comfort Farm." Saturday Review of Literature* 9 (April 1, 1933): 513. This is a rave review of the novel. Dangerfield appreciates the broad satire, which he finds necessary, and calls *Cold Comfort Farm* a "masterpiece."

Moorman, Charles. "Five Views of a Dragon." *The Southern Quarterly* 16 (1978): 139-150. Moorman compares and contrasts five authors, including Stella Gibbons, who write about Wales. Gibbons, the only one of the five who is not Welsh, sees the humor in Welsh extravagances.

Paterson, Isabel. "Cold Comfort Farm." *Books* (March 12, 1933): 9. Paterson finds the novel a joy and recognizes that Gibbons is a novelist to watch in the future.

Vickers, Jackie. "Cold Comfort for Ethan Frome." *Notes and Queries* 40, no. 4 (December, 1993). A careful and balanced comparison of *Cold Comfort Farm* and Edith Wharton's *Ethan Frome* (1911). Traces some of the influences *Ethan Frome* may have had on Gibbons' work. Vickers also discusses the animal imagery in *Cold Comfort Farm.*

COLLECTED POEMS

Type of work: Poetry
Author: Marianne Moore (1887-1972)
First published: 1951

Even after her poems had been published and critically acclaimed, Marianne Moore continued to revise them; sometimes she rejected them altogether. Between her first book, *Poems*
(1921), and her last, *The Complete Poems of Marianne Moore* (1967), she published several
other volumes of poetry. Typically, a new book was made up of substantially revised poems
from the previous book together with a number of previously uncollected poems. *Collected
Poems* (1951), for example, begins with most of the poems from *Selected Poems* (1935), which
in turn contains many of the poems from *Observations* (1924). *Collected Poems* also contains
all but four poems from *What Are Years* (1941), a volume of previously uncollected work, and
the six new poems from *Nevertheless* (1944), to which Moore added nine new titles "Hitherto
Uncollected."

The *Complete Poems of Marianne Moore*, which claims to be the "Definitive Edition, with
the Author's Final Revisions," contains a section headed "Collected Poems (1951)." This
section omits the poem "Melanchthon" from the 1951 publication but contains two poems from
Observations, "The Student" and "To a Prize Bird," which were originally omitted from
Collected Poems; these poems were subsequently revised for *The Complete Poems of Marianne
Moore*.

Confusing as all this seems, it is necessary for serious students of Marianne Moore's work
to be aware that the different publications contain different collections of poems and that the
poems themselves are likely to differ from collection to collection. Perhaps the most striking
example of the changes undergone by a poem is "Poetry," which appears in *Poems* as a poem
of thirty lines in five stanzas. In *Observations*, the poem is changed drastically in form and in
length, retaining only phrases from the original. In *Collected Poems*, its form is restored to one
resembling the original, but the poem itself is significantly different. In *The Complete Poems
of Marianne Moore*, finally, it is reduced to three lines. It is important to note that all references
here will be to *Collected Poems* as published in 1951.

In the poem "Silence," there is the passage: "The deepest feeling always shows itself in
silence;/ not in silence, but restraint." The word "restraint" implies reserve, discipline, control,
and moderation, and, indeed, restraint is one of the principal characteristics of Moore's poems.
The overriding impression created by the book is that it consists of reasoned, intelligent
discourse.

Some poems, such as "New York" and "Marriage," are free verse, but more frequently the
forms of the poems show a concern for orderliness and control, with close attention to detail.
Moore can be compared to her own description of an octopus: "Neatness of finish! Neatness of
finish!/ Relentless accuracy is the nature of this octopus." She tends to use subtle, sometimes
almost hidden metrical patterns. Poems such as "Peter" and "Bird Witted" have precise forms,
repeated in each stanza; the forms are based on syllabic count but without regard to whether
syllables are stressed or unstressed. It is unlikely that even a careful reader would be conscious
of this type of form without actually counting syllables. Other syllabic forms, as in "Melanchthon," are more obviously crafted. The syllabic counts in the short lines are quite noticeable and
there is a clearly visible repeated form in each stanza of two short lines followed by two long
lines.

There is some use of end rhyme, as in "The Jerboa," but the rhyme is often unobtrusive. This can be because of uneven line length, as in "Those Various Scalpels" and "To a Steam Roller," or because the lines run on in such a way that a rhyming word is unstressed, as in "To Statecraft Embalmed." Sometimes, as in "The Fish," the rhyme is on unexpected words such as "an" or "the"; sometimes a word is broken up to rhyme just one syllable as when the first syllable of "accident" is rhymed with the word "lack": "ac/ cident—lack." Frequently, there is rhyme, partial rhyme, or assonance in random fashion over a number of lines. In "An Octopus" and "Sea Unicorns and Land Unicorns," such rhymes are easily apparent, but at times they are so concealed as to be virtually unnoticed, save possibly at an unconscious level.

Another area of restraint is in Moore's diction. Her tone can be conversational; often it is rather dry, with a cool formality. There is no hyperbole, no prettiness, little that is conventionally "poetic." A prominent feature of *Collected Poems* is a sizeable section of notes at the end, citing the sources of her quotes and allusions, which in the poems are generally set off by quotation marks. This is more the practice of the essayist than the poet.

A part of Moore's educational background included undergraduate experience in a biology laboratory. Her scientific training in careful observation of phenomena and in careful deductions from observation provides the basis for many of her poems. Her interest in the natural world surfaces frequently. *Collected Poems* is peppered with animals, including cats, monkeys, elephants, birds, a snail, a wood-weasel, and many others. Moore typically observes an animal's appearance and behavior, then sets her imagination the task of interpreting the meaning of the observed facts.

In "Peter," Moore observes a cat with close attention to detail:

> . . . —the detached first claw on the
> foreleg, which corresponds
> to the thumb, retracted to its tip; . . .

The poem becomes an occasion to celebrate the cat's uninhibited naturalness. He spends his time doing as he pleases, unconstrained by the human world that surrounds him but does not impinge on his consciousness unless he chooses. The cat's behavior is contrasted to the complexity of the human world, and the poem arrives at the conclusion that such instinctive behavior is good: "to do less would be nothing but dishonesty." Observation of the cat has been used as a means to make a subtle, seemingly casual comment on moral issues such as selfishness, hypocrisy, and frankness.

"Melanchthon" shares with "Peter" a similar movement from approval of animal nature to a broader moral statement. This time the focus of the poem is an elephant, who is also the narrator of the poem. The rhythm of the poem is slow and ponderous, evocative of the physical being of the subject, and the overall tone is serene, in keeping with the natural personality, which, unconcerned with intellectualizing its experience, basks in the sun, enjoying experience for its own sake. Like the river mud which encrusts the elephant's skin, the "patina of circumstance," the accumulation of life's experiences, enriches and strengthens what is inside. It is the soul that is the true seat of power, that will ". . . never// be cut into/ by a wooden spear; . . ." The strength of the soul is inexplicable, and the center of spiritual poise is unknown, but recognition of the supreme importance of the spiritual world allows the individual an entirely new dimension of perception: "My ears are sensitized to more than the sound of// the wind. . . ." This poem, less condensed and difficult than many in the book, deals with ideas central to Moore's moral world. To understand this poem can be an aid to understanding some of the others.

Naturalness is central not only to Moore's moral values but also to her aesthetic tastes. Artistic integrity is the theme of a number of poems. The much anthologized "Poetry" is a clear exposition of this theme, with its blunt, rather shocking opening statement: "I, too, dislike it: there are things that are important beyond all this fiddle." What emerges in the poem is that Moore dislikes "all this fiddle" rather than poetry itself, which can be genuine and natural. In "Picking and Choosing" and "In the Days of Prismatic Color," she tells the reader that she does not like the nonsense of poetry created by willful obscurity and lack of genuine feeling masked by heightened language: ". . . the opaque allusion—the simulated flight// upward—accomplishes nothing."

The spiritual underpinning of Moore's moral world is also a part of her aesthetics. In "When I Buy Pictures," she states that all art must be: ". . . 'lit with piercing glances into the life of things';/ it must acknowledge the spiritual forces which have made it." In "An Egyptian Pulled Glass Bottle in the Shape of a Fish," Moore contemplates an inanimate object in the way that she observes animals, using it as a concrete image from which to develop more abstract thoughts. The bottle is beautiful, pleasing to the eye, a work of art. Yet its beauty is derived from more than its outward appearance. Its making required "patience," a moral quality, and it was made in response to "thirst," a need, so it is functional. This combination of elements invests the bottle with perfection that should be celebrated.

The poems in the "What are Years" and "Nevertheless" sections of the book were written during World War II and are in many cases responses to that great crisis in the history of civilization. The poems encompass such themes as courage, heroism, and endurance. The final poem in these sections, "In Distrust of Merits," is a direct and uncharacteristically emotional testimony to the poet's feelings of horror, outrage, fear for the outcome. But responsibility for the war lies, at least in part, with the individual:

> There never was a war that was
>   not inward; I must
> fight till I have conquered in myself what
> causes war, but I would not believe it.

In other poems in these sections, contemplation of the ostrich, the mother mockingbird, and the nautilus leads to the understanding that naturalness includes a nurturing that requires courage and love and patience. "Elephants" illustrates strength hand-in-hand with philosophical resignation. In "The Pangolin," that unattractive animal is used, surprisingly, as an exemplar of physical grace which leads to contemplation of humans—flawed, ambiguous, and fearful, but the recipient of grace in the theological sense.

When *Collected Poems* was published, Marianne Moore's work had already attracted the attention and acclaim of such literary giants of her generation as Ezra Pound, T. S. Eliot, W. H. Auden, and William Carlos Williams. She was already the recipient of numerous awards when *Collected Poems* gained her additional accolades: the Bollingen Prize, the Pulitzer Prize, and the National Book Award. Moore's poetic voice is admired for its distinctive, even eccentric qualities, her vision for its acuity and its integrity. Her use of form is inventive, her craftsmanship meticulous, and her subject matter displays a wide range of interest and knowledge. The poems are sometimes oblique, their meanings elusive, but they reward persistent and repeated readings.

Susan Henthorne

Bibliography:
Costello, Bonnie. *Marianne Moore: Imaginary Possessions*. Cambridge, Mass.: Harvard University Press, 1981. This book demonstrates how to read Moore's poems by investigating recurrent themes, images, and forms. Examines in detail individual lines and phrases as well as whole poems.
Lentfoehr, Therese. *Marianne Moore: A Critical Essay*. Grand Rapids, Mich.: William M. Eerdmans, 1969. A lucid and sensitive analysis of Moore's work from a specifically Christian perspective. Without laboring the point, it concludes that there are religious meanings latent throughout Moore's poetry.
Nitchie, George W. *Marianne Moore: An Introduction to the Poetry*. New York: Columbia University Press, 1969. A useful introduction that traces the evolution of Moore's poetic voice and the complex history of the poems. Praises the poet's originality and intelligence. Includes an interesting and varied "List of Works Consulted."
Schulman, Grace. *Marianne Moore: The Poetry of Engagement*. Urbana: University of Illinois Press, 1986. Analyzes the poetry by tracing the poet's thought processes. In many cases, this is achieved by relating the dialectic of the poems to the visual perception that inspired and informed them.
Tomlinson, Charles, ed. *Marianne Moore: A Collection of Critical Essays*. Englewood Cliffs, N.J.: Prentice-Hall, 1969. Perhaps the best starting point for the serious student, this book provides an excellent, varied overview of the entirety of Moore's work. Contains essays by her contemporaries such as Pound and Eliot, as well as by later critics.

THE COLLECTOR

Type of work: Novel
Author: John Fowles (1926-   )
Type of plot: Psychological realism
Time of plot: c. 1960
Locale: London and Sussex, England
First published: 1963

>Principal characters:
>FREDERICK CLEGG, a butterfly collector
>MIRANDA GREY, an art student

The Story:

Frederick Clegg, a government clerk in his middle twenties, won seventy-three thousand pounds in the football pools, which enabled him to act out his secret fantasy. Just as he collected butterflies in the past, he stalked and kidnapped Miranda Grey, an art student in her early twenties who was studying at the Slade School in London. Clegg had recently purchased an expensive home in the Sussex countryside, with an underground room that he secured and prepared for his kidnapped guest, as he called her.

When Miranda was chloroformed and taken to Clegg's house, she discovered that he had made extensive preparations for her, including the purchase of clothing and other items. In the beginning he treated her deferentially, served her the food she wished, and brought her anything she desired. It quickly became clear to Miranda that, although Clegg apparently was not interested in sex or violence, he did not plan to allow her to leave. The two characters, of approximately the same age but from very different worlds, became acquainted with each other.

Clegg, of working-class origin, resented his lower social position and had not had access to the privileged, artistic world that Miranda inhabited. In addition, his mental problems became more pronounced as his conversations with Miranda continued, just as her idealism and naïveté were revealed. Her naïveté was particularly evident when she believed he would make good on his promise to release her at the end of four weeks, for Clegg had no intention of doing this.

During the four weeks, more differences between the two emerged, particularly between her artistic, politically liberal worldview and Clegg's disturbed, repressed mind. In his spare time, Clegg was a butterfly collector who killed and photographed his collections, activities that Miranda abhorred. She made clear her disgust with his narrowness and lack of culture and usually criticized him sharply. Clegg accepted her verbal abuse and continued to defer to her wishes, telling her he had abducted her because he was in love with her.

Shortly before the four weeks were to end, Clegg purchased an expensive dress and diamond necklace for Miranda. They pretended to have a party, and he permitted her to come upstairs into the house. She refused his proposal of marriage, one that he specified would be in name only, and afterward he made it clear he would not release her as promised. She attempted to escape, but he caught her and again gave her chloroform to subdue her. While she was unconscious, Clegg removed all her clothing except for her underclothes and took photographs, the first time he had violated her physically since her arrival.

Several days later Miranda, after being taken upstairs by Clegg to bathe, struck him in the shoulder and head with an ax he had left lying around. The blow only slightly injured him, and he was able to bind, gag, and lock her up once again in the underground room. Miranda, desperate to be released, again asked to be taken upstairs for a bath. She then attempted to seduce Clegg. When he proved to be impotent, he lied that an army psychiatrist had told him that he would never be able to perform the sexual act.

Clegg's response to his sexual failure was humiliation and rage, and he blamed all his subsequent actions on Miranda's attempted seduction. He claimed he no longer respected her, and when she asked to live in an upstairs bedroom he pretended to prepare it for her. He then asked permission to photograph her nude, which she angrily refused. It was at this point that Clegg's anger and the depths of his perversion began to surface as his earlier ostensible fondness for Miranda disappeared. When she taunted him that he was "not a man," he bound and gagged her, removed her clothing, and photographed her tied to her bed.

The next day, the cold she had caught from Clegg worsened, and she told him she had pneumonia. Although her temperature was 102 degrees and she was unable to eat, he refused to take her symptoms seriously. As her condition worsened, Clegg began to understand that she was very ill, but he could not bring himself to get her medical attention. When he finally went to a doctor's office to ask advice, he was overwhelmed by fear and paranoia, and right after this incident he was terrified when a policeman began asking him questions.

After he returned to Miranda, it was clear that she was dying, but Clegg still refused to get her any help. After her death he considered suicide, but instead buried her body, which he referred to as "the deceased," under the apple trees. Clegg then began to follow another young woman and to dry out the underground room in preparation for another guest. The next experience, he promised himself, would be different because Marian, his next victim, would be someone he could teach, someone who would not place herself above him.

Critical Evaluation:

John Fowles's fiction has met with a popular and commercial success that is unusual for a novelist who has also received such serious critical attention. *The Collector*, his first novel, was followed by *The Magus* (1965, revised 1977), *The French Lieutenant's Woman* (1969), *Daniel Martin* (1977), *Mantissa* (1982), and *A Maggot* (1985). The first three novels were made into successful films, and both the novel and film version of *The French Lieutenant's Woman* were critically praised. Fowles enjoys experimenting with narrative technique, and with each new novel he attempts to find different forms and structures for his fiction.

In *The Collector*, Fowles tells the story from two points of view. Fred Clegg narrates the first half of the novel in an unimaginative, flat-footed style that underscores the horror and the realism of his tale. The second half of the novel is narrated by Miranda in the form of a journal she keeps during her captivity, which is found by Clegg after her death. Her voice, completely different from Clegg's, reveals her artistic, idealistic, and sometimes pretentious personality, and gives the reader an entirely different perspective on the incidents recounted earlier by Clegg. Her journal entries end just before her death, when Clegg returns for a brief final section that recounts her death and burial, and his ominous plans for the future.

Like many post-war British novels, *The Collector* focuses on issues of social class. Clegg's deprived background and lack of education have stunted him emotionally, intellectually, and spiritually, just as Miranda's privileged upper-middle-class upbringing has provided her with opportunities to develop herself personally and artistically. This is revealed in both the form and content of their speech in the novel. Clegg, resentful and hesitant because of his social inferiority, is always bested verbally by Miranda, whose spirited assertiveness and self-confidence attract and later enrage him. Fowles has said that Clegg's environment has played a major role in shaping him, and that the relationship between Clegg and Miranda is representative of the problems of social class in England.

The difficulties between the two characters go much deeper than social class. *The Collector*, like so many of Fowles's later novels, is profoundly concerned with the nature of power and its abuses. Fowles, who was himself at one time a collector of butterflies, has talked at length about the connections among power, fascism, and collecting. Clegg's psychological problems are related to his desire for complete power over another person. Unable to have any kind of loving, living, interdependent relationship with Miranda, he forces her into an environment over which he has complete control and subjects her to a variety of humiliations.

After his inability to respond to her sexual overtures, he reduces her to the status of a pornographic photograph, a photograph he can pose and later view as a voyeur with no fear of its talking back to him. Just as collectors must kill their specimens in order to capture, mount, and preserve them, Miranda must eventually die so that Clegg's collection of her can be complete. His desire for power is rooted in his inability to connect with the world of free, living, protean human beings. Fowles, a strong believer in individualism and the individual's potential for growth and development, posits Clegg as emblematic of the person who can only resort to the abuses of power in order to feel anything at all.

The Collector is also concerned with another issue important to Fowles, the distinction between what he calls "The Many" and "The Few." Clegg is a representative of The Many, a group who are dulled to the real significance of life by their lack of emotional and intellectual sensitivity and their need to acquire more and more material possessions. Having no aesthetic sense, Clegg is instead at the mercy of what he considers to be proper opinions and popular taste. His leaden, cliché-filled language reflects this, just as Miranda's quirky, fragmented, questioning verbal style identifies her with The Few, those who refuse to be compromised by bourgeois values and instead embody liberal-humanist, aesthetic ideals that privilege tolerance, skepticism, and open-mindedness. Although Fowles has accused Miranda of being a "liberal-humanist snob" and sometimes treats her ironically, she does indeed represent a true alternative to the intellectual and emotional void that is Frederick Clegg.

In spite of the fact that *The Collector* is a starkly realistic novel, Fowles inserts references to William Shakespeare's play *The Tempest* (1611) that help mitigate the intensely claustrophobic world that is created. In Shakespeare's play, Ferdinand is the young, handsome hero who falls in love with the beautiful young heroine Miranda. Caliban, a monstrous creature, has earlier unsuccessfully attempted to rape Miranda, but is prevented by her magician-father, Prospero. Clegg, who dislikes his real name, Fred, lies to Miranda that his name is Ferdinand, but she refers to him in her journal as Caliban. Unlike *The Tempest*, in which Prospero is able to save his daughter, Fowles's novel has no magician, and Miranda's death is the prelude to another, perhaps more brutal, abduction. *The Collector* is an important novel about the nature of obsession and perversion, one that seems to become more relevant as time goes by.

Angela Hague

Bibliography:
Laughlin, Rosemary M. "Faces of Power in the Novels of John Fowles." *Critique: Studies in Modern Fiction* 13, no. 3 (1972): 71-88. Focuses on issues of power in Fowles's fiction, particularly how power operates to violate, annihilate, or perhaps help another person achieve a more complete humanity. Asserts that Fowles's depiction of power in *The Collector* is simplistic in light of his later novels.
Olshen, Barry N. *John Fowles.* New York: Frederick Ungar, 1978. Discusses the narrative structure of *The Collector* and focuses on issues of social class and opportunity. Maintains,

however, that the most significant distinction is between life- and freedom-loving individuals and those who can only attempt to possess and destroy.

Rackham, Jeff. "John Fowles: The Existential Labyrinth." *Critique: Studies in Modern Fiction* 13, no. 3 (1972): 89-103. Asserts that class conflict is of minor significance in *The Collector*, and that the novel is a metaphorical exploration of existentialism. The novel is a "minor allegory of existence," in which people who believe that they have an insight into life are in reality at the mercy of their own smugness.

Wolfe, Peter. *John Fowles, Magus and Moralist*. Cranbury, N.J.: Bucknell University Press, 1976. Excellent introduction to Fowles's philosophical and aesthetic ideas. Discusses *The Collector* specifically in light of his attitudes about "collecting," the dichotomy between The Many and The Few, and the social and cultural milieu that produces a Frederick Clegg.

Woodcock, Bruce. *Male Mythologies: John Fowles and Masculinity*. Brighton, England: The Harvester Press, 1984. Suggests that Clegg is "the prototype of masculinity," both perpetrator and victim of male power, and also the representative for the novelist himself, who can collect his characters and subject them to his own male fantasies.

COLOR OF DARKNESS
Eleven Stories and a Novella

Type of work: Short fiction
Author: James Purdy (1923-   )
First published: 1957

Color of Darkness, James Purdy's first book, is a collection made up of eleven short stories and a novella. In the course of the work, ordinary human experiences are purposely exaggerated to reveal a covert truth.

Purdy went on to write novels, more short stories, and plays. Yet if a writer's first book can be thought to serve as a signpost to the road of his intention, *Color of Darkness* points the way to a very personal arena that Purdy was marking out as his own, and in it he dealt with the sort of problem, and the types of people, with which he continued to concern himself in his later oeuvre. From the time of his first work, Purdy showed a penchant for unusual and often bizarre situations that his characters, by contrast, seem hardly to notice. In Purdy's work, the outlandish is handled with nonchalance, and the mundane contains the outlandish.

Each story, like a candle, would guide readers through the darkness, but some burn more and others less intensely. In the more skillful stories, "Sound of Talking," "Cutting Edge," and the title story, "Color of Darkness," readers are inescapably confronted with one of the most hidden of human secrets: Contact with one another makes people the helpless victims of ambivalence. The lifelong precept that there should be no hate for those who are closest and dearest forces people into concealing the truth when it is at variance with the precept. In *Color of Darkness*, Purdy tries courageously to explore that hidden passageway and to shine his light on the unreasoning, frightening ambivalence that causes a child to brutalize his pet and then to hug it lovingly and tearfully.

In "Sound of Talking," probably the best story in the collection, Purdy demonstrates how surely he can implicate his reader in the situation he draws. In a kitchen, a woman is talking to her husband, Vergil, who is paralyzed and in a wheelchair; he is in pain. Mrs. Farebrother, who knows her husband well, counters his steady flow of bilious expletives with a loquacity designed to distract him from his pain. By the time they realize that the deceptively innocent kitchen is really Mrs. Farebrother's wheelchair and that she is irrevocably locked into her husband's ebbing life, readers have already witnessed and sympathized with her impotent flutterings of chatter. By allowing themselves to welcome her to the fire, Purdy's readers must recognize that her ambivalence, when it reveals itself, is a reflection of their own. At that point, the readers too need respite from the responsibility of caring for a helpless fellow human being.

It is small wonder that Mrs. Farebrother comes to admire a bird, a bird that not only can fly but can talk as well. The raven that called her into the seed store keeps readers focused upon that one point of concentration, Mrs. Farebrother's paralytic ambivalence, so that all seemingly independent strands of thought or conversation are ultimately seen as a careful release from this single spool.

The woman first speaks of desire: She would like a bird, a raven. As she describes to her paraplegic husband the events that led up to that desire, she remembers her former attraction to a boy who was called The Raven, and that the bird talks of someone who is dead. Both thoughts are seen to be repetitions of her nighttime speculations. In the dark, in her need, she can safely wish Vergil dead, but during the daylight hours, when such thoughts have scurried to their hiding place, she must sheathe herself in solicitous redress. This has been her life's condition since Vergil's release from the hospital.

The raven is a perfect solution. It would amuse her husband, she hopes, and signify the achievement of a mutual desire; both will have made the decision to have the bird. That there would be an even greater profit is known to the reader by implication. The bird's presence would give brazen, corporeal expression to her more timid, ambivalent, hidden thoughts. Vergil's refusal to accept any responsibility for the pet, however, eliminates all possibility of their ever sharing a desire again. The story ends with this realization, and both continue to manipulate their wheelchairs. For the reader, having sympathized with Mrs. Farebrother, there is a recognition that her love-hate ambivalence is an exaggeration of something familiar.

Also familiar is the situation in the title story, "Color of Darkness," which concludes uncomfortably, like a long unfulfilled desire nakedly exposed. The faintly dreamlike quality that suffuses this story may be attributed to the pensive nature of the father who is preoccupied with the exploration of his identity. He is out of touch with the people around him, the victim of his inappropriate responses to them. Purdy designates him "the father," which is a most suitable epithet in its paradoxical implications. He is, indeed, the actual father of the boy, Baxter, for which he will be punished, but he has long ago delegated his parental responsibilities to his housekeeper-"mother," Mrs. Zilke. It is she who at the conclusion of the story has learned with the reader that the boy is already corrupted, that he knows the ways of the world and is a sinister member of the community. From its hiding place within the half-truth of love and affection expressed in the boy's snuggling close and suddenly and surprisingly kissing his father, leaps forth the other half to complete the truth, his protestations of hate, culminating with a kick in the groin and an obscene word for that same bewildered father. Baxter allows himself to expose his ambivalence because his father is weak. Purdy recognizes in human beings an animal aversion to weakness and sickness that leads to brutality.

Most people handle their ambivalence more gracefully but must recognize that an intensification of the circumstances that evoke such unwelcome feelings could weaken the check on their manifestations. Purdy has intensified and exaggerated to denote a truth, and the reader must identify his own properly.

In the novella "63: Dream Palace" and in the story "Why Can't They Tell You Why?" the truth that Purdy overstates remains hidden in the exaggeration. It is hidden because the distortion allows readers to deny the relevance to themselves of a boy who murders the brother he loves in an abandoned house, or of a mother who drives her son into a hysterical state, apparently beyond recall. Readers may sense the horror of it, the disgust of it, but those "abnormalities" are the acts of distant relatives. There is a saving aura of unreality here for the readers, a dreamlike quality through which they may escape our responsibility of recognition.

The novella's exposition would have readers believe that Fenton Riddleway, a boy who is possessed of what Sigmund Freud called brutal egotism, is extremely important to the interlocutors, Grainger and Parkhearst. Their intimacy and boredom, conveyed by what feebly attempts to pass for provocative conversation, suggest that the boy is the subject of frequent discussion and considerable thought. The story's energy is dispersed among the lives of Parkhearst, Grainger, and Fenton, settling finally on the Fenton fragment.

The boy has neither charm nor grace; he demonstrates no wit, nor is he particularly intelligent. His interests are personal, and his learning understandably little. In fact, the most interesting thing about him is the situation in which he finds himself. He is unfamiliar with the city in which he is stranded and is waiting for someone to guide him from the abandoned house to which he was directed. His ability to fascinate seems locked with him within the story, and the reader must accept Fenton as the protagonist of a homosexual daydream. Fenton fails to make the reader dream, however; he is inordinately cruel to his brother Claire, and he abuses everyone whose interest in him indicates a weakness. Those who are willing to indulge his predatory nature resemble some flat-toothed creatures who happily embrace the beautiful tiger. Physical beauty is the quality that Fenton possesses, and those who meet him once may never recover from the encounter.

The novella insists that the handsome boy brings havoc to all who seek him out. Why he is considered so valuable a possession cannot be understood easily. The victims' willingness, therefore, to be oppressed, and to share oppression with their friends—Parkhearst brings the tormentor to Grainger and Bruno brings him to Hayden—seems to be an indulgence in homosexual fantasy. This, however, is not the nightmare of a Franz Kafka story that well might be the daylight experience of a nighttime adventure; rather, it is as if the reader were eavesdropping on someone else's fantasy.

Bibliography:
Adams, Stephen D. *James Purdy*. New York: Barnes & Noble Books, 1976. Provides detailed interpretations of Purdy's work. Analyzes his use of character and theme, as well as his distinctive characteristics of symbol and style, placing him in the tradition of Herman Melville and Nathaniel Hawthorne. Describes Purdy as a Christian existentialist.
Chupack, Henry. *James Purdy*. Boston: Twayne, 1975. Excellent introductory source. Presents Purdy's use of gothic devices to portray a cold, barren world centered around loveless families. Clear analysis of each story, discussing character and exploring the collection's basic theme of tragic incompatibility. Extremely helpful annotated bibliography.
Malin, Irving. *New American Gothic*. Carbondale: Southern Illinois University Press, 1962. Discusses Purdy's use of misfits as heroes, analyzing the symbolism with which he illustrates the horror in his characters' everyday lives. Focuses on "63: Dream Palace," "Why Can't They Tell You Why?" and "Man and Wife."
Peden, William Harwood. *The American Short Story: Continuity and Change, 1940-1975*. 2d ed. Boston: Houghton Mifflin, 1975. Evaluates Purdy's ruthlessly honest portrayal of emotional or physical grotesques. Discusses his use of paradox and contrast in "63: Dream Palace," "Color of Darkness," "Why Can't They Tell You Why?" and "Cutting Edge."
Schwarzschild, Bettina. *The Not-Right House: Essays on James Purdy*. Columbia: University of Missouri Press, 1968. Interesting collection of essays discussing Purdy's use of setting and atmosphere and his uniquely accurate portraits of physically or psychically wounded characters. Good analysis of "63: Dream Palace" and "Don't Call Me by My Right Name."

THE COLOR PURPLE

Type of work: Novel
Author: Alice Walker (1944-   )
Type of plot: Social realism
Time of plot: 1920's-1940's
Locale: Georgia, Tennessee, and Africa
First published: 1982

Principal characters:
CELIE, the novel's narrator-protagonist
MR. _____, Celie's husband
SHUG AVERY, Mr. _____'s longtime mistress
NETTIE, Celie's younger sister
HARPO, Mr. _____'s eldest son by a previous marriage
SOFIA, Harpo's wife

The Story:
Celie, a poor, barely literate black woman living in rural Georgia, was raped and impregnated by the man she assumed was her father when she was fourteen years old. A short time later, Celie's mother died, and Pa, her stepfather, took Celie's children away, removed her from school, and had her married to a poor farmer she called Mr. _____. She became the stepmother of his four children by a previous marriage, and she became his slave. When his son, Harpo, asked him why he beat his wife, he said that he did it because she was his wife and because she was stubborn.

Far from rebelling against her treatment by Mr. _____, Celie accepted her abuse and neglect. Having been called ugly and worthless so often by both her stepfather and her husband, Celie came to accept their view of her. Whatever hope she had possessed early in life was directed outward in two directions: toward God and toward her sister, Nettie. By writing letters to both, Celie was asserting that she was still alive. Her real hope for life lay in Nettie, to whom she was very devoted and whom she helped escape when Mr. _____ made advances to her and threatened to have someone marry her. While Celie felt that her own life was over, she hoped that Nettie—who had a similar intelligence and a love of learning—could escape; then she could live vicariously through Nettie. Nettie moved to Africa to become a missionary, and the sisters vowed to write to each other; however, Mr. _____ intercepted Nettie's letters for many years.

Harpo married Sofia and, modeling his behavior after his father, attempted to dominate her in the same way his father dominated Celie. Sofia was too strong and independent, however, to submit to his abuse. Though she later felt guilty for having betrayed Sofia by telling Sofia's husband that if he wanted to keep her in line he should beat her, Celie was actually jealous of Sofia's strength.

When Mr. _____ brought his mistress, Shug Avery, home to be nursed through an illness, Shug joined him in mocking Celie's looks and submissive behavior. A growing closeness emerged between Celie and Shug, however; Shug was a strong, independent woman with a career as a blues singer. She taught Celie many things: to stand up to Mr. _____, to believe in her self-worth and to appreciate her own beauty, and to experience the joys of sexuality. Shug was the first person, besides the absent Nettie, to love Celie for who she was, and Shug and Celie banded together to make Mr. _____ end his abuse of Celie. With Shug's encouragement, Celie defied Mr. _____ and eventually cursed him when she discovered that he had kept Nettie's letters from her. She left him, just as Sofia had previously left Harpo.

Shug took Celie to her home in Memphis, and Celie began a business making men's trousers. Later, when Celie discovered that her stepfather had left her and Nettie a house and a dry goods store in Georgia, she returned to Georgia as an independent woman.

Nettie's letters from Africa indicated that the relationship between African men and women paralleled the relationship between men and women in the American South. The social structure of the Olinka tribe was rigidly patriarchal; the men ruled, and the women were wives and mothers. Nettie's life in Africa was full of fulfillment and frustration. Unlike Celie, she had been able to escape the rural South, and she had been educated by books and by the experience of a wider world. A sincerely religious person, she felt that she was doing important work as a missionary, but she was frustrated by her lack of success. Nettie, her family, and Celie's children had to return to the American South to find integration into a true community. Like Celie, Nettie was frustrated by her lack of communication with her sister, but she developed a meaningful relationship with Samuel, another missionary. She later married him.

At the conclusion of the novel, Nettie, her husband, and Celie's long-lost children returned to Georgia to live in the home that had been left to Celie. The novel ended with a Fourth of July celebration which signified the absorption of all the characters of the novel into a living, vital community.

Critical Evaluation:

The Color Purple won the American Book Award and the Pulitzer Prize in fiction in 1983. Alice Walker's novel is unique in its preoccupation with spiritual survival and with exploring the oppressions, insanities, loyalties, and triumphs of black women. Walker's major interest is whether or how change can occur in the lives of her black characters. All the characters except Nettie and Shug lead insular lives, unaware of what is occurring outside of their own small neighborhood. They are particularly unaware of the larger social and political currents sweeping the world. Despite their isolation, however, they work through problems of racism, sexism, violence, and oppression in order to achieve a wholeness, both personal and communal.

In form and content, *The Color Purple* is a slave narrative, a life story of a former slave who has gained freedom through many trials and tribulations. Instead of black oppression by whites, however, in this novel there is black oppression by blacks. It is also a story by a black woman about black women. Women fight, support, love, and heal each other—and they grow together. The novel begins in abject despair and ends in intense joy. To discover how this transformation occurs, it is important to examine three aspects of the novel: the relationships between men and women; the relationships among women themselves; and the relationships among people, God, and nature. At the beginning of the novel, alienation and separation are evident in all of these relationships, but by the conclusion of the novel, an integration exists among all elements of life. In terms of the relationship between men and women, no personal contact between the sexes is possible at the beginning of the novel, since the male feels that he must dominate the female through brutality.

The correspondence between Celie and Nettie is the novel's most basic example of the alienation of women from women. Sometimes the alienation is caused by the men, as when Mr. _____ keeps Nettie's letters from Celie, but often it results from the attitudes of the women themselves. For the first half of the novel, the women are against one another, often because of jealousy, as when Shug mocks Celie and flaunts her relationship with Celie's husband. Walker presents numerous examples of women in competition with one another, frequently because of men, but, more important, because they have accepted the social code indicating that women define themselves by their relationship with the men in their lives.

The first indication that this separation between women will be overcome occurs when the women surmount their jealousy and join together. Central to this development is the growing closeness of Celie and Shug. Shug teaches Celie much about herself: to stand up for herself to Mr. _____, about her own beauty and her self worth, and about the enjoyment of her own body. The love of Celie and Shug is perhaps the strongest bond in the novel; the relationship between Celie and her sister is also a strong bond.

While the men in the novel seem to have no part in the female community, which, in essence, exists in opposition to them, they, too, are working out their salvation. As a result of the way the women have opposed them, they reevaluate their own lives and they come to a greater sense of their own wholeness, as well as the women's. They develop relationships with the women on a different and more fulfilling level. The weakness of the men results from their having followed the dictates of their fathers, rather than their having followed their own desires. Mr. _____, for example, wanted to marry Shug, but in the face of his father's opposition, he married another woman and made her miserable because she was not Shug. Harpo tries to model his relationship with Sofia on the relationship between his father and Celie. Ultimately, both men find a kind of salvation because the women stand up to them and because the men accept their own gentler side. The men, by the end of the novel, become complete human beings just as the women do; therefore, the men are ready for relationships with women. Near the end of the novel, Mr. _____ is content to sew trousers alongside Celie. By the end of the novel, Celie and Mr. _____, whom she at last calls Albert, find a companionship of sorts. Harpo is content doing housework and caring for the children while Sofia works outside the home. Each individual becomes worthy in his or her own eyes—and in the eyes of others. The separation between men and women is shattered, and fulfilling human relationships can develop.

Alienation is also present in Nettie's letters from Africa. The relationship between African men and women is presented as similar to that of men and women in the American South. The social structure of the Olinka tribe is rigidly patriarchal; the only roles available to women are those of wife and mother. At the same time, the women, who frequently share the same husband, band together in friendship. Nettie debunks the myth that Africa offers a kind of salvation for African Americans searching for identity.

In Walker's view, God and nature are inextricably intertwined; therefore, alienation from one implies alienation from the other. Celie writes to God for much of the novel, but she writes out of despair, not hope; she feels no sustaining connection with God. Through her conversations with Shug, she comes to believe that God is in nature and in the self, and that divinity is found by developing the self and by celebrating everything that exists as an integrated whole. Celie also comes to believe that joy can come even to her; she learns to celebrate life's pleasures, including the color purple.

That spirit of celebration is embodied in the conclusion of the novel. At the Fourth of July celebration, all the divisions between people—divisions that had plagued and tormented the characters throughout the novel—have been healed. The characters' level of consciousness has been raised, and the seeds of feminism and liberation have been planted.

Genevieve Slomski

Bibliography:
Butler-Evans, Elliott. *Race, Gender, and Desire: Narrative Strategies in the Fiction of Toni Cade Bambara, Toni Morrison, and Alice Walker*. Philadelphia: Temple University Press, 1989. Insightful comparative study of the relationship between narrative technique and politics in three African American women writers. Bibliography.

Evans, Mari, ed. *Black Women Writers (1950-1980): A Critical Evaluation*. Garden City, N.J.: Anchor Press, 1984. Three excellent essays on the novels of Alice Walker. Includes a biography and selected bibliography. Discusses Walker's work in the context of African American women's writing.

Gates, Henry Louis, Jr., and K. A. Appiah, eds. *Alice Walker: Critical Perspectives Past and Present*. New York: Amistad Press, 1993. The most comprehensive and well-written collection of essays on Walker. Contains reviews, essays, and interviews. Includes chronology and bibliography.

Harris, Trudier. "From Victimization to Free Enterprise: Alice Walker's *The Color Purple*." *Studies in American Fiction* 14 (Spring, 1986): 1-17. Focuses on the movement from domination to liberation in Walker's female characters.

Hite, Molly. *The Other Side of the Story: Structures and Strategies of Contemporary Feminist Narrative*. Ithaca, N.Y.: Cornell University Press, 1989. Discusses Walker's fiction as an attempt to create an opposing view to the dominant stories of culture. Analyzes her relationship to language and her relationship to narrative tradition.

THE COMEDY OF ERRORS

Type of work: Drama
Author: William Shakespeare (1564-1616)
Type of plot: Farce
Time of plot: First century B.C.E.
Locale: Greece
First performed: c. 1592-1594; first published, 1623

> *Principal characters:*
> SOLINUS, duke of Ephesus
> AEGEON, a merchant of Syracuse
> ANTIPHOLUS OF EPHESUS and
> ANTIPHOLUS OF SYRACUSE, twin brothers, sons of Aegeon and Aemilia
> DROMIO OF EPHESUS and
> DROMIO OF SYRACUSE, twin brothers, attendants of above twins
> AEMILIA, Aegeon's wife
> ADRIANA, wife to Antipholus of Ephesus
> LUCIANA, Adriana's sister
> A COURTESAN

The Story:

According to the laws of the lands of Ephesus and Syracuse, it was forbidden for a native of one land to journey to the other; the penalty for the crime was execution or the ransom of a thousand marks. Aegeon, a merchant of Syracuse who had recently traveled to Ephesus, was to be put to death because he could not raise the thousand marks. When Solinus, duke of Ephesus, heard Aegeon's story, he gave the merchant one more day to raise the money.

It was a sad and strange tale Aegeon told. He had, many years earlier, journeyed to Epidamnum. Shortly after his wife joined him there she was delivered of identical twin boys. Strangely enough, at the same time and in the same house, another woman also bore identical twin boys. Because that woman and her husband were so poor that they could not provide for their children, they gave them to Aegeon and his wife Aemilia, to be attendants to their two sons. On the way home to Syracuse, Aegeon and his family were shipwrecked. Aemilia and the two children with her were rescued by one ship, Aegeon and the other two by a different ship, and Aegeon did not see his wife and those two children again. When he reached eighteen years of age, Antipholus, the son reared by his father in Syracuse, grew anxious to find his brother, so he and his attendant set out to find their twins. Aegeon had come to Ephesus to seek them.

Unknown to Aegeon, Antipholus and his attendant, Dromio, had just arrived in Ephesus. There a merchant of the city warned them to say that they came from somewhere other than Syracuse, lest they suffer the penalty already meted out to Aegeon. Antipholus, having sent Dromio to find lodging for them, was utterly bewildered when the servant returned and said that Antipholus' wife waited dinner for him. What had happened was that the Dromio who returned to Antipholus was Dromio of Ephesus, servant and attendant to Antipholus of Ephesus. Antipholus of Syracuse had given his Dromio money to pay for lodging, and when he heard a tale of a wife about whom he knew nothing he thought his servant had tricked him and asked for the return of the money. Dromio of Ephesus had been given no money, however, and when he professed no knowledge of the sum Antipholus of Syracuse beat him soundly for dishonesty. Antipholus of Syracuse later heard that his money had been delivered to the inn.

A short time later, the wife and sister-in-law of Antipholus of Ephesus met Antipholus of Syracuse and, after berating him for refusing to come home to dinner, accused him of unfaithfulness with another woman. Not understanding a word of what Adriana said, Antipholus of Syracuse went to dinner in her home, where Dromio was assigned by her to guard the gate and allow no one to enter. Thus it was that Antipholus of Ephesus arrived at his home with his Dromio and was refused admittance. So incensed was he that he left his house and went to an inn. There he dined with a courtesan and gave her the gifts he had intended for his wife.

In the meantime, Antipholus of Syracuse, though almost believing that he must be the husband of Adriana, fell in love with her sister Luciana. When he told her of his love, she called him an unfaithful husband and begged him to remain true to his wife. Dromio of Syracuse was pursued by a kitchen maid whom he abhorred but who mistook him for the Dromio of Ephesus who loved her.

Even the townspeople and merchants were bewildered. A goldsmith delivered to Antipholus of Syracuse a chain meant for Antipholus of Ephesus and then tried to collect from the latter, who in turn stated that he had received no chain and accused the merchant of trying to rob him.

Antipholus and Dromio of Syracuse decided to leave the seemingly mad town as soon as possible, and the servant was sent to book passage on the first ship leaving the city. Dromio of Syracuse brought back the news of the sailing to Antipholus of Ephesus, who by that time had been arrested for refusing to pay the merchant for the chain he had not received. Antipholus of Ephesus, believing the servant to be his own, sent Dromio of Syracuse to his house to get money for his bail. Before Dromio of Syracuse returned with the money, however, Dromio of Ephesus came to Antipholus of Ephesus, naturally without the desired money. Meanwhile Dromio of Syracuse took the money to Antipholus of Syracuse, who had not sent for money and could not understand what his servant was talking about. To make matters worse, the courtesan with whom Antipholus of Ephesus had dined had given him a ring. Now she approached the other Antipholus and demanded the ring. Knowing nothing about the ring, he angrily dismissed the woman, who decided to go to his house and tell his wife of his betrayal.

On his way to jail for the debt he did not owe, Antipholus of Ephesus met his wife. Wild with rage, he accused her of locking him out of his own house and of refusing him his own money for bail. She was so frightened that she asked the police first to make sure that he was securely bound and then to imprison him in their home so that she could care for him.

At the same time Antipholus and Dromio of Syracuse were making their way toward the ship that would carry them away from this mad city. Antipholus was wearing the gold chain. The merchant, meeting them, demanded that Antipholus be arrested. To escape, Antipholus of Syracuse and his Dromio fled into an abbey. To the same abbey came Aegeon, the duke, and the executioners, for Aegeon had not raised the money for his ransom. Adriana and Luciana also appeared, demanding the release to them of Adriana's husband and his servant. Adriana, seeing the two men take refuge in the convent, thought they were Antipholus and Dromio of Ephesus. At that instant a servant ran in to tell Adriana that her husband and Dromio had escaped from the house and were even now on the way to the abbey. Adriana did not believe the servant, for she herself had seen her husband and Dromio enter the abbey. Then Antipholus and Dromio of Ephesus appeared before the abbey. Aegeon thought he recognized the son and servant he had been seeking, but they denied any knowledge of him. The confusion increased until the abbess brought from the convent Antipholus and Dromio of Syracuse, who instantly recognized Aegeon. Then all the mysteries were solved. Adriana was reunited with her husband, Antipholus of Ephesus, and his Dromio had the kitchen maid once more. Antipholus of Syracuse was free to make love to Luciana, and his Dromio too was freed. Still more surprising, the abbess turned out to be Aegeon's wife, the mother of the Antipholus twins. So the happy family was together again. Lastly, Antipholus of Ephesus paid his father's ransom and brought to an end all the errors of that unhappy day.

Critical Evaluation:

William Shakespeare was not always the master playwright that he became in his later life. When he first began writing plays, he did not have the mastery of plot, character, concept, and language for which he was to be universally praised. In 1592, he was a young playwright with a historical trilogy and a classical tragedy to his credit; he was just beginning to explore and perfect his craft. *The Comedy of Errors* is an early experiment with comedy, and his enthusiasm for the experiment is clear in his writing.

Shakespeare followed the example of most playwrights of the Elizabethan era by adapting other plays and sources to make his dramas. This in no way detracts from his genius because what he adapted he made distinctively his own.

Most of *The Comedy of Errors* derives from *Menaechmi* (*The Twins Menaechmi*) by the classical Roman playwright Plautus, who lived from c. 254 B.C.E. to 184 B.C.E. Act III, scene i of the play originates from another work by Plautus, *Amphitruo* (*Amphitryon*). Both of these plays concern mistaken identity, which Shakespeare adapted for the crux of his plot as well. Just as Shakespeare adapted Plautus, Plautus apparently drew from an unknown Greek playwright. It was said of Plautus that his special genius was for turning a Greek original into a typically Roman play with typically Roman characters. Similarly, Shakespeare, like Plautus, set the play in ancient Ephesus, and used some of Plautus' situations, but Shakespeare's characters are typically and recognizably of Shakespeare's Elizabethan age.

Shakespeare changed the framework of the plot, making it much more romantic and accessible to popular tastes. In Shakespeare's version, the twins' father, Aegeon, is introduced in the midst of his search for his wife and other son, separated from him by shipwreck. This story line, demonstrating husbandly and paternal devotion, was appealing to the audience. Shakespeare then created the servant twins (Dromios) to add to the fun of the mistaken identity plot. In so doing he doubled the amount of action. He also introduced Luciana, sister of the wife of Antipholus of Ephesus, and thus provided a love interest for Antipholus of Syracuse. Out of the Plautine cast of nine, Shakespeare retained six of the original characters and developed many more of his own.

In addition, Shakespeare changed the characters to fit the tastes of his audience. Plautus' twins are extremely one-dimensional characters. Both are self-centered, callous young men whose only interest was in the gratification of their animal appetites. It is difficult to feel any sympathy or empathy for them. In Shakespeare's play, however, the twins are simply callow youths whose characters are not yet completely formed. They are not amoral, as are Plautus' twins. They are simply naïve.

The relationship between Shakespeare's Antipholus of Ephesus and his wife was much more appealing to Elizabethan audiences than that relationship, as depicted by Plautus, would have been. Shakespeare's Antipholus does not steal his wife's jewelry and gowns to give to a courtesan. In fact, he dines with the courtesan and gives her his wife's presents only out of revenge at being shut out of his house and being given the impression that his wife was entertaining another man. There is a moral dimension to Shakespeare's play that is lacking in Plautus'.

Like Plautus', Shakespeare's play is a farce, filled with fast-paced action and dialogue, peopled with eccentric characters, and developed by improbable, exaggerated situations. It was the most elementary of the comic arts—the comedy of situation, rather than the comedy of character or theme. Shakespeare's later comedies would develop the more difficult styles.

Even in this elementary comedy, Shakespeare shows talent enough to draw some basic characterization and suggest polarities of characters. The younger twin from Syracuse is, stereotypically, more timid than his arrogant older brother. Luciana is gentler and shier than her sister. The eccentrics, the courtesan and Doctor Pinch, are each separately and strikingly developed.

Shakespeare's experiments with language and poetry betray his apprenticeship. There is a noticeable simplicity and repetition of diction. The play's accomplishment and fluency augur what the mature Shakespeare would later produce. The poetic passages of wooing that he created for the Syracuse twin and Luciana anticipate *Romeo and Juliet* (1594-1595). Dromio of Ephesus' punning description of his twin's wife, the slattern Nell, in geographic terms, is a masterpiece of comic overstatement, as is the bawdy, double entendre that enriches the scene in which Ephesus is denied access to his home and wife. All of these touches are strokes of genius and wit.

Shakespeare's later romantic comedies are foreshadowed by the dignified characters of Aegeon and Aemilia: Their lifelong devotion and eventual reunion elevate the farce to a higher level of comedy. Their plot resolution not only incorporates the plot and subplots but also unites all the characters. This plot development anticipates the festive communion that is the goal of all of Shakespeare's later romantic comedies.

Shakespeare probably set out to write the perfect Roman-style play. It observes two of Aristotle's unities. It is set in one locale, and it takes place in the span of a day's time. Shakespeare added subplots, however, to complement and complicate the main plot. Plautus would never have broken the third unity. Shakespeare also handles his exposition tritely (Solinus asks Aegeon what brought him to Ephesus), and as a result, the first act moves slowly. Once the playwright moves into the plot complications of Act II, the action and humor never slow until the conclusion.

The characters are shallowly developed, the plot is improbable, and the comedy is developed primarily through situation, but *The Comedy of Errors* has proved to be a play that delights audiences. Shakespeare wrote more thought-provoking plays than this one, plays that were more sensitive and profound, and plays peopled with better-developed characters, but *The Comedy of Errors* remains a fun romp, written in excellent pentameter.

"Critical Evaluation" by H. Alan Pickrell

Bibliography:
Baldwin, Thomas Whitfield. *On the Compositional Genetics of "The Comedy of Errors."* Champaign: University of Illinois Press, 1965. Likens Shakespeare to the Dromios, awed by their change from the rural to the urban.
Berry, Ralph. *Shakespeare and the Awareness of the Audience.* New York: St. Martin's Press, 1985. Discusses the "dark underside" of the play, which enriches and compliments the comedy. Argues that Aegeon may be more important to the plot structure than he seems to be.
Colie, Rosalie L. *Shakespeare's Living Art.* Princeton, N.J.: Princeton University Press, 1974. Colie sees the plays as experiments with the craft of writing plays. Discusses Shakespeare's improving on Plautus.

Dorsch, T. S., ed. *The Comedy of Errors*, by William Shakespeare. Cambridge: Cambridge University Press, 1988. This edition features a comprehensive introductory essay, with a brief look at history, sources, characters, and plot.

Tillyard, E. M. W. *Shakespeare's Early Comedies*. New York: Barnes & Noble Books, 1965. One of the most noted of Shakespeare's commentators points out that Shakespeare probably did not read the Roman original for the play; the commentator focuses on a translated manuscript.

COMMENTARIES

Type of work: History
Author: Julius Caesar (100-44 B.C.E.)
First transcribed: Commentarii de bello Gallico, 52-51 B.C.E.; *Commentarii de bello civili*, 45 B.C.E. (English translation, 1609)

Principal personages:
JULIUS CAESAR, the Roman governor and general in Gaul
VERCINGETORIX, the rebel leader of the Gauls
ORGETORIX, a chieftain of the Helvetii
DIVITIACUS, a Gaul loyal to the Romans
ARIOVISTUS, a chieftain of the Germanic tribes

In 59 B.C.E., after the Roman Empire had expanded north and westward into the area now known as France and Germany, Julius Caesar, already famous as a general and administrator, was appointed to govern the Roman territories inhabited by the Gauls. Here a strong, active government was required, and from the start Caesar kept records of the events of his governorship. The record eventually came to be known as Caesar's *Commentaries* and to be regarded as an important record for posterity. Indeed, scholars and general readers have wished that Caesar had left a more complete record than he did. To expect a detailed history in the *Commentaries* is, however, to misunderstand the writer's purpose. His intention was not to write a definitive history of the period of the Gallic Wars but rather to put down in writing what he, the Roman general and administrator, considered most important.

No one can understand the *Commentaries* without having some concept of the flux of migration and its consequent pressures in Europe during the first century before Christ. The Gallic peoples were under pressure from the Germanic peoples across the Rhine River who coveted the rich lands of the Gauls and were, in their turn, under pressure from migrations still farther to the east. Rome faced a double threat from the Germanic tribes: They were pressing constantly southward (and would eventually invade and dismember the Roman Empire) and they threatened Rome indirectly by the unrest they created in Gaul. Being a man of action and a clear analyst of the situation confronting Rome, Caesar took war into the German territory.

In his *Commentaries*, he gives a chronological account of his activities in Gaul from the time of his succession to the governorship of Gallia Narbonensis in 59 B.C.E. to the end of the Gallic revolt led by Vercingetorix late in the same decade. During those years, Caesar and his Roman legions confronted first one group of tribes, then another. Most of the sections of the book carry such headings as "Campaign Against Ariovistus," "Expedition Against the Unelli," "First Expedition into Germany," and "Siege and Sack of Avaricum." Only two sections, the first section of book 1 and the second section of book 6, are not about actual battle operations or preparations. The former is a description of Gaul and its inhabitants; the latter, an account of customs of the Gauls and Germans.

In his comments about the Gauls, Caesar stirs the imagination and stimulates curiosity by giving only enough information to make the reader wish more had been written. An account of the druids' place in Gallic culture, for example, and of the religious rites at which the druids officiated would have been welcome. In other cases, however, Caesar taxes credulity, as in reporting certain kinds of animals as existing in the Hyrcanian Forest. One such animal, according to Caesar, was an elk captured by partly cutting trees against which the elk leans to rest; because the animal has no joints in its legs, it cannot rise once it is down. Caesar also reports a fabulous ox with but one horn growing from the middle of the forehead. Such reports resemble other natural histories of the period and do not detract from the value of the *Commentaries*, for in Caesar's time such reports were generally taken seriously.

Caesar's account of the Gallic Wars is a reminder that war has been a continual factor in human affairs. As one example of the fury and effectiveness of war in ancient times, Caesar comments at the end of his account of the battle with the Nervii: "This battle being ended, and the name and nation of the Nervii almost reduced to annihilation, their old men, together with the boys and women whom we have stated had been collected together in the inlets and the marshes, when this battle had been reported to them, convinced that nothing was an obstacle to the conquerors, and nothing safe to the conquered, sent ambassadors to Caesar with the consent of all who survived, and surrendered themselves to him; and in recounting the calamity of their state, they said that their senators were reduced from six hundred to three; that of sixty thousand men who could bear arms, scarcely five hundred remained." Another example of the character of these ancient wars is the siege of Avaricum, at which, according to Caesar, scarcely eight hundred people of all ages and both sexes escaped the city when it was taken, out of a population of forty thousand; the rest were killed.

Caesar the Roman administrator is apparent throughout the *Commentaries*. He writes in an impersonal fashion, however, much as though he were preparing a favorable report to the Roman senate. Only rarely does an individual come through to the reader as a real personality. Even Caesar himself, whose name figures more largely than any other, remains an official and a general rather than emerging as a clearly visualized person. The Gallic and Germanic chieftains who opposed him are little more than names, and the same is true of the lieutenants who served under him. The only outstanding exception to this general statement is the passage concerning Sextius Baculus who, sick though he was, arose from his bed and saved the day for the Romans by rallying their forces when they were attacked in a camp at Aduatuca; he fought bravely until he had to be carried back to rest.

Of particular interest to English-speaking readers are those portions of the *Commentaries* that deal with Britain and Caesar's invasions of Britain. Caesar's account of the early history of that part of the world is the earliest of the Roman documents. Caesar tells of his first expedition, an abortive one, made in 55 B.C.E., and his second and more successful attempt the following year, an invasion that paved the way for the Roman occupation that lasted until the fifth century C.E. For his second invasion, he ordered a fleet of more than eight hundred vessels built and assembled, a logistical success noteworthy in any era of history. This fleet carried two thousand cavalrymen with their mounts and five Roman legions, each consisting at that time of about five thousand men.

Caesar was a remarkable man, one of the greatest in human history, in the sense that greatness may be defined as leaving an indelible mark on the pages of history. Few such men have lived; fewer still have left written records for posterity; and none has left a document to compare with Caesar's *Commentaries*. The book occupies a unique place in the written records of the Western world. In addition to its value as history, it deserves to be read as an example of a concise report presented with an idiosyncratic style and flavor.

Bibliography:
Adcock, Frank E. *Caesar as a Man of Letters*. Cambridge, England: Cambridge University Press, 1956. A brief biography that focuses exclusively on Caesar's literary style. Valuable as a supplement to other historical works that deal primarily with Caesar's military and political achievements.

Balsdon, John Percy Vyvian Dacre. *Julius Caesar and Rome*. London: English Universities Press, 1967. A political biography by one of the twentieth century's most influential Roman historians. Scholarly but accessible to the general reader, this work gives more treatment to Caesar's triumphs than to his literary works, but it reveals much about the background and origin of the *Commentaries*.

Gelzer, Matthias. *Caesar: Politician and Statesman*. Translated by Peter Needham. Cambridge, Mass.: Harvard University Press, 1968. Unquestionably the most comprehensive and scholarly biography of Caesar available in English. Contains copious notes and an analysis of nearly every detail of Caesar's life and literary work.

Grant, Michael. *Caesar*. London: Weidenfeld and Nicolson, 1974. An accurate account of Caesar and his *Commentaries*. Combines biographical information with literary analysis. Extensively illustrated and easy to read.

Kahn, Arthur David. *The Education of Julius Caesar*. New York: Schocken Books, 1986. Both a biography and a reconstruction of the educational forces that influenced Caesar's life. Useful both for its background on the literary style of the *Commentaries* and for its information on pedagogical values of Roman society in the first century B.C.E..

Yavetz, Zvi. *Julius Caesar and His Public Image*. London: Thames and Hudson, 1983. A detailed account of Caesar's use of propaganda, of which his published *Commentaries* were a major part.

THE COMPANY OF WOMEN

Type of work: Novel
Author: Mary Gordon (1949-   )
Type of plot: Social realism
Time of plot: 1963-1977
Locale: New York City and western New York State
First published: 1981

> *Principal characters:*
> FELICITAS
> CHARLOTTE, Felicitas' mother
> FATHER CYPRIAN
> MARY ROSE,
> ELIZABETH,
> CLARE, and
> MURIEL, friends of Father Cyprian
> JOE, Mary Rose's friend
> ROBERT, Felicitas' lover
> SALLY and
> IRIS, Robert's other women
> RICHARD, Robert's neighbor
> LINDA, Felicitas' child
> LEO BYRNE, Felicitas' husband

The Story:

Part 1, 1963. Fourteen-year-old Felicitas Maria Taylor traveled with her mother, Charlotte, to Orano, in western New York State to meet Elizabeth, Clare, Mary Rose, and Muriel for a summer retreat. Since meeting in 1932, the women had made this retreat every year under the guidance of the Roman Catholic priest, Father Cyprian, who conducted retreats for working women.

Felicitas believed she had to lie to her friends about how she spent her summer vacations because her friends were interested in "TV doctors" and would not understand the pleasure she had in being the center of attention for three of the four childless women and for Father Cyprian, who called Felicitas the group's "only hope." Of the women who followed "Cyp," as Charlotte called him, only Muriel detested the child Felicitas and considered her as a threat. The other women did not regard Muriel as one of them. She was excluded from Felicitas' baptism, when Charlotte's daughter was given not one but three godmothers—Mary Rose, Elizabeth, and Clare. Father Cyprian was the focus for the women, each of whom characterized "Cyp" in a different way. He in turn had his own characterizations for them. For example, Charlotte was "down to earth," Clare a wealthy and genteel lady, Mary Rose the divorced and wronged woman, and Muriel "an extraordinary soul" who did not fit with the other women and whom Father Cyprian always admonished to fight against bitterness.

On a ride with Cyprian to inspect the family property that he had recently acquired, thanks to Clare's generosity, the car went out of control and Felicitas suffered a concussion. She shared a hospital room with another fourteen-year-old, Gidget, who was smart-mouthed and worldly.

1215

Although she despised the girl, Felicitas found herself betraying her relationship with Father Cyprian and the women by telling Gidget that the only reason she put up with the constant attention from the adults was because her mother promised to buy her a car when she turned sixteen as long as she continued to come on the group vacations. Felicitas' guilt over this betrayal was increased by the loving attention that Father Cyprian and the women gave to Gidget. When Felicitas was released from the hospital, she learned that Gidget was dying of Hodgkin's disease, but this knowledge did not soften her heart.

Each woman reflected on the gifts she had given to Felicitas while the child was in the hospital. Felicitas' favorite gift was a copy of Jane Austen's *Pride and Prejudice* (1813) given to her by Elizabeth. Her least favorite gift, a collection of inspirational religious pamphlets, had come from Muriel.

Part 2, 1969-1970. Felicitas transferred to Columbia University from the Catholic college she had attended. She was very concerned about the Vietnam War and took a political science class in addition to the Latin and Greek courses in which she was majoring. At first sight, Felicitas fell in love with her political science professor, Robert. He advised her to drop the class so that they could become lovers. Completely under his spell, Felicitas not only dropped the course but also moved into Robert's "free love" household, where two of Robert's other women, Sally and Iris, lived in an uneasy equilibrium. Sally, who hated Felicitas purely, had had a son, Mao, by Robert but refused to tell Robert that he was the father.

Felicitas found herself very involved in training the dogs of Robert's neighbor, Richard, who spent most of his time in Robert's apartment. Felicitas gave the dogs dog food, as opposed to the vegetarian meal they had been getting, and within a week she had house-trained them. During the time that Felicitas lived at Robert's apartment, Clare, Mary Rose, and Joe Seigel all visited her. They were all concerned about her, but only Joe had the worldly experience to see what was actually going on in the house. He warned Felicitas that men do not want what they can have easily, and he suggested that Felicitas move out.

Robert tired of Felicitas quickly and advised her to make love with other men as well. To please Robert, Felicitas slept with Richard, who fell in love with her. When Felicitas became pregnant, she could not be sure who the father was. After seriously considering abortion, Felicitas decided instead to have the baby. She took the dogs, Ho, Che, and Jesus from Richard's apartment and went back to her mother's home.

Part 3, 1977. Felicitas, her mother, Clare, Muriel, and Elizabeth had all gone to live near Father Cyprian after learning of Felicitas' pregnancy. Father Cyprian, the women admitted, was magnificent. When he learned of Felicitas' pregnancy, he said merely that perhaps the pregnancy had saved her from greater sin. Each of the women built a house near Father Cyprian's. On the way to Cyprian's, they renamed the dogs Joe, Jay, and Peaches. Felicitas did not have any say in the matter of the move, which, she felt, was just as well.

When her child was born, she gave her the common name of "Linda" in hopes that she would have a "normal" upbringing. Several years later, Felicitas planned to marry a very quiet, slow man named Leo Byrne, who was close to the earth and its workings. Felicitas had tried to give her daughter the most ordinary upbringing she could. By marrying Leo, she hoped to assure her girl an "ordinary childhood," something she thought she herself had missed.

Charlotte continued to work to maintain herself, her personality, and her equilibrium. She felt lucky to be near her daughter—"As if that explains it," she says at the end. Elizabeth was content to remain near her friends and Father Cyprian, to whom she was especially devoted; it seemed that Felicitas' child gave her a sound reason to position herself closer to those she loved best. Muriel, who felt "inconvenienced" by the other women's descent on Cyprian, believed that eventually her own self would be lost in the vision of God and that she would die as the "first beloved of no soul." Clare's voice articulated the beauty of their surroundings. In her old age, she turned her attention to the house she had built.

Father Cyprian, who had a heart attack and suffered from failing health, ended his days believing he had been a failure as a priest. He felt that he had not been true to the perfection of the Mass. He recalled his love for Felicitas and having felt during the years of her rebellion "the bitterest of Jesus' sorrows," likening his intolerance to Christ's agony in Gethsemane.

Linda in her childish understanding knew that Cyprian would die. She knew death, she said, from having seen dead animals along the road, and she compared herself and her mother and grandmother to Cyprian: "We are not dying," she said.

Critical Evaluation:

Mary Gordon's second novel, *The Company of Women*, followed the first, widely acclaimed, *Final Payments* (1978). In both novels, Gordon dealt with the theme of being the offspring of a deeply religious Roman Catholic family in a secularized American society. In both novels, daughters must come to grips not only with their strict religious upbringing but with the issues of "choice"—whether to remain virginal, to use contraceptives, or to consider abortion.

In *The Company of Women*, Gordon set up two spheres of womanhood, each centered on charismatic yet domineering males. In the early sections, the "company of women" centers on the austere and commanding figure of Father Cyprian, who sees the main character, the child Felicitas, as the group's only hope for the future. Father Cyprian's influence over Felicitas is broken by her youthful rebellion against his authority and, by extension, that of the Church. However, Felicitas leaves one "company of women" only to find herself in another, that of Sally and Iris around Robert.

The novel suggests that any company of women centered around a patriarchal male figure will succeed only insofar as the women form their own independent "company." It is the women who hold one another together in both "companies," and by holding together they attain a collective authority that enables them to survive the conditions under which they find themselves.

The main theme of the novel concerns the regaining of matriarchal strength. While the liaisons formed in consequence of the domination and direction, spiritual or carnal, of a single male personality consists initially of the women orbiting around that male, in the end it is the force of maternity that determines the lives of Felicitas, her mother, and her mother's friends. Linda is, as her mother puts it, the daughter of "one of two men who live very far away." While Linda has little knowledge of her paternity, she knows well who her mother and grandmother were. With the last words of the novel—Linda's "We are not dying"—Gordon indicates that matriarchy is, in the present age, a well-kept but powerful secret to longevity.

The use of varied narrative voices in the novel reveals the author's strength as a stylist. The earliest parts of the novel are written in a well-tempered but fairly omniscient voice. Much of the imagery is taken from the beauty of Roman Catholic ritual and relates to the women's adherence to Roman Catholic teachings. Later, in part 2, following Felicitas' rebellion, the narrative voice shifts to a sardonic yet subtly comic voice. In part 3, each one of the original "company of women" is allowed to speak. Cyprian's voice, which until this point has often been the "last word," is superseded by the voice of the daughter, Linda.

An underlying theme of the novel—that the Old World seems to be crumbling under the impact of the New—is both played out and subverted in the novel. The "Old World" patriarchy, the novel makes clear, is near extinction. To a great extent, this failure of Old World values is encapsulated in Felicitas' rebellion, which is directed not so much against the Church but against the male-dominated government that sends young men to die in a senseless war.

Susan M. Rochette-Crawley

Bibliography:
Clark, Diana Cooper. "An Interview with Mary Gordon." *Commonweal* 107 (May 9, 1980): 270-273. Gordon responds to questions about her interest as a novelist in exploring the limits and potential of religious belief.

Gray, Francine du Plessix. "A Religious Romance." *The New York Times Book Review*, February 15, 1981, 1, 24, 26. Gray focuses on the religious themes in *Final Payments* and in *The Company of Women* and notes Gordon's conclusion in both novels that friendship is the most important requirement for human happiness.

Lardner, Susan. "No Medium." *The New Yorker* 57 (April 6, 1981): 177-180. In this review of *The Company of Women*, Lardner compares Gordon's second novel to her first, *Final Payments*, and notes that the overriding theme in both is the question of whether female self-sacrifice is a form of self-indulgence.

Perry, Ruth. "Mary Gordon's Mothers." In *Narrating Mothers*, edited by Brenda O. Daly and Maureen T. Reddy. Knoxville: University of Tennessee Press, 1991. Perry explores the nature of what she calls the "motherlessness" of the mothers in Gordon's fiction. The discussion centers primarily on *Men and Angels* (1985) but can be applied as well to *The Company of Women*.

THE COMPLEAT ANGLER

Type of work: Philosophy
Author: Izaak Walton (1593-1683)
First published: 1653

The Compleat Angler is a practical guide to the art of angling, or fishing. The work has a nominal plot: Piscator (a fisherman), Venator (a hunter), and Auceps (a falconer) meet by chance and fall to discussing the merits of each man's preferred sport. Piscator's eloquent description of the joys and virtues of fishing convinces Venator to accompany him for several days of fishing. The bulk of the work, however, consists of practical advice to fishermen, as told by Piscator to Venator, about such topics as bait and fishing equipment, the habits of different kinds of fish, and methods of catching and cooking various fish.

The Compleat Angler was by no means the only fishing handbook of its day. It was certainly the most popular, however, and by the middle of the twentieth century, The Compleat Angler had been reprinted and translated nearly four hundred times. What sets The Compleat Angler apart from other practical handbooks and puts it firmly in the realm of literature is a delightful style that is technically polished and charming to read, and an abundance of insight into human nature.

Being a fishing handbook, The Compleat Angler does not fit neatly into any traditional literary category. It has at times been described as a pastoral (that is, an idealized description of country life), a georgic (a poem dealing with rural concerns, not usually as idealized as a pastoral), or an eclogue (a poetic dialogue between shepherds or other rural characters), and has even been credited with originating a category of its own, the "piscatory." The difficulty in categorizing The Compleat Angler and in separating the voluminous practical information from its more "literary" aspects may be one of the reasons that the work has historically suffered from critical neglect. From a critical point of view, however, The Compleat Angler is interesting for its structure (which owes much to plays and other dramatic pieces of its day), its witty and rhetorically complex style, and its political and historical underpinnings.

To understand fully the subtle themes of The Compleat Angler, it is necessary to understand the historical era in which Izaak Walton wrote. Walton published The Compleat Angler in 1653, when he was sixty years old, and when England was in social upheaval. With the English Civil War, Walton was alive at the time that Cromwell's army overthrew the monarchy, and in 1649 executed King Charles I. The Puritan movement, with its austerity and religious fanaticism, was in full swing. Persecution of Anglican and Catholic believers was widespread. The struggle of the Royalists (supporters of the monarchy and the king's son Charles) against the theocratic rule of Cromwell and his successors would soon succeed, resulting in a hedonistic backlash against Puritanism during the Restoration. It was a time of social, religious, and political extremes.

Walton was not an extremist by nature. A successful merchant and biographer, Walton had during the course of his life befriended many leading Anglican thinkers, including John Donne and Richard Hooker. In the gentle, intelligent theology of these friends and colleagues, Walton saw an ideal "middle path" between the extremes of Puritan and Royalist. One of the themes of The Compleat Angler centers on finding this ideal (and theologically based) compromise between two extremes of thought. Early in the work, Piscator and his student Venator encounter a hunter pursuing otters. Although Piscator and the hunter enjoy a pleasant enough exchange, Piscator later confides to Venator that he does not care much for the company of the hunter, because he swears excessively and is given to sacrilegious and lewd jests. Piscator is not a prude, however; he explains that he does not enjoy the company of serious and overly grave men, of "sowre complexion" and "anxious care," any more than he enjoys the company of the foul-mouthed hunter. Piscator describes the qualities of the type of company he prefers: "learned and humble, valiant, and inoffensive, vertuous, and communicable."

Walton's belief in the middle way is not confined simply to questions of personality, however; it encompasses a wider theological view. Piscator expounds at length on the relative virtues of the two traditional paths of religious life, the active and the contemplative. Piscator ultimately argues for a "via media" (middle way) that reconciles action and contemplation. And what better emblem of the via media, he argues, than the art of angling: time spent peacefully enjoying nature but still accomplishing something worthwhile. Walton embraces a naturalistic theology that finds God through contemplation of His creation; Walton's praise of the country-side and country life is often couched in religious terms. Walton's religious beliefs require action, too, and specifically acts of charity. The bounty of fish that Piscator catches allows him to make charitable offerings of food to poorer characters such as the milkmaid and her mother, and the group of beggars.

While the opposing attractions of the active and contemplative lives are nothing new to literature or theology, for Walton and others of his day they had a special meaning. With the tensions inherent in the religious and political extremes of the Civil War and Restoration eras, many prominent men chose to retire from public life to a life of seclusion in the country, rather than take sides with the Puritans or the Royalists. While Walton's religious views seemed to incline him to reject worldliness and involvement in political affairs, his active social conscience made him acutely aware that running from the pressing issues of the day was socially and politically irresponsible. Walton's paean to angling can thus be seen as a wider social and political analogy for the importance of reconciling quiet, inostentatious retirement with productive, benevolent activity.

The art of fishing has another religious significance for Piscator (and Walton). One of Piscator's lectures to Venator describes the many fishermen in the Old Testament. Walton, through the voice of Piscator, makes the New Testament parallels clear: The apostles, after all, were all fishermen, whom Christ proposed to make fishers of men. The brother that Piscator meets at the inn (it is unclear whether Walton uses the term "brother" in its genealogic sense or in the wider sense of belonging to what he calls "the brotherhood of the angle") is named Peter.

Walton's themes are not purely religious, however; he also expresses very definite political views. For example, the social class of Piscator and Venator is deliberately left undefined. It seems clear that they are neither very rich nor very poor; however, they are definitely not snobbish or class-conscious. When they meet the lowly milkmaid and her mother, Piscator and Venator do not talk down to them or treat them as inferiors; instead they jovially offer the trade of fish for songs and milk. It is interesting to note Walton's choice of songs for the milkmaid and her mother. The milkmaid sings Christopher Marlowe's "The Passionate Shepherd to His Love" ("Come live with me and be my love") a romantic verse about idealistic pastoral love. Her mother replies by singing Sir Walter Raleigh's "The Nymph's Reply to the Shepherd" ("If all the world and love were young"). Once again, Walton contrasts opposing views, this time extreme romanticism and cynicism about love, suggesting that extreme views can tell only part of the story.

Piscator's story of his meeting with the gypsies and beggars is illustrative of his political view. Piscator describes how the gypsies got into an argument over how to divide a sum of money. Likewise, the beggars argued over the answer to a riddle about whether it was easier to rip or to "unrip" a cloak. In each case, the dispute was resolved peacefully and diplomatically by the "government" of each group. Instead of looking down on these traditional outcasts as inferiors, Piscator seems to admire the democracy of their way of life, using the favorable terms "commonwealth," "government," and "corporation" to describe their social organization. In Piscator's other encounters with men who may be his social superiors, equals, or inferiors, (the hunter, innkeeper, brother, and friend) all are treated with exactly the same courtesy and frankness.

No study of Walton's work could be complete without a discussion of his style. By choosing a dialogue as the structure of his work, Walton is able to maintain an informal, conversational tone. He constantly lightens the lengthy technical passages with humorous verses or observations, and his philosophical and theological observations are neither pedantic nor belabored. Walton uses devices such as Piscator's seeming to lose his train of thought or wander from the subject, and his crediting things like recipes and bits of fishing lore to friends (who are sometimes named and sometimes not), to make the dialogue seem as if it were really spoken by a living person, rather than formally composed by an author. This apparent artlessness is a very careful construction used by Walton to give the dialogue a warm, intimate, and often humorous tone. It is this easy and pleasant tone, along with Walton's intelligent observations on a wide variety of political and religious subjects, that makes *The Compleat Angler* more than a sportsman's handbook. It is also a finely crafted work of literature that for centuries has been enjoyed by fishermen and lovers of literature alike.

Catherine Swanson

Bibliography:
Bevan, Jonquil. *Izaak Walton's "The Compleat Angler."* New York: St. Martin's Press, 1988. This critical volume provides a thorough discussion of the religious and political underpinnings of *The Compleat Angler*, placing the work in its social and historical context. Bevan also demonstrates the relation of *The Compleat Angler* to other literature of its time. Extensive bibliography.
Bottrall, Margaret. *Izaak Walton.* London: Longmans, Green, 1955. Discusses his religious and political beliefs and offers some general criticism on *The Compleat Angler*. Walton's biographical works are also discussed.
Cooper, John R. *The Art of "The Compleat Angler."* Durham, N.C.: Duke University Press, 1968. Cooper's study of Walton's technique focuses on his form, style, and sources. Provides an in-depth discussion of the different traditions that influenced Walton's work, and an interesting section detailing Walton's borrowings from other authors.
Keynes, Geoffrey. *The Compleat Angler.* New York: Random House, 1945. This edition of Walton's work is of interest for its textual variations section, which shows some of the major differences between successive editions of the work. It also contains a biography of Walton and detailed bibliographical notes.
Walton, Izaak. *The Compleat Angler.* Edited by Jonquil Bevan. Oxford, England: Clarendon Press, 1983. Offers two different editions of *The Compleat Angler* (1653 and 1676) in their entirety, along with an extensive introduction covering Walton's life, his literary sources, and a comprehensive discussion of the many different editions of *The Compleat Angler*. Includes reproductions of the original illustrations.

THE COMPLETE POEMS OF EMILY DICKINSON

Type of work: Poetry
Author: Emily Dickinson (1830-1886), edited by Thomas H. Johnson
First published: 1960

After Emily Dickinson's death in 1886, her sister Lavinia found forty-nine fascicles, or packets, of poems that Dickinson had sewn together during the late 1850's and early 1860's. Lavinia enlisted the help of Mabel Loomis Todd, the wife of an Amherst professor, to transcribe them. With the assistance of the literary editor Thomas Wentworth, they altered the rhyme scheme, regularized the meter, and revised unconventional metaphors for the 115 poems they published in 1890. These were well received and led to the publication in 1891 of 161 additional poems and, in 1896, of 168 more.

In 1914, Dickinson's niece and literary heir, Martha Dickinson Bianchi, compiled other poems. She kept alterations to the verse to a minimum, as was also the case with additional volumes in 1929 and 1935. Millicent Todd Bingham in 1945 published the remaining 688 poems and fragments. When Dickinson's literary estate was transferred to Harvard University in 1950, Thomas H. Johnson began to arrange the unreconstructed and comprehensive body of Dickinson's poetry chronologically. *The Poems of Emily Dickinson* appeared in 1955; *The Complete Poems of Emily Dickinson* appeared in 1960. Aside from correcting misspellings and misplaced apostrophes, Johnson let Dickinson's original punctuation and capitalization stand. To the previously editorialized publications, Johnson restored the original dashes and other nonconformist usage, listing for each poem both the approximate date of the earliest known manuscript and the date of first publication. There is also a helpful "Index of First Lines" (Dickinson did not title her poems) and a fairly comprehensive subject index based on key words or images in the poems, the three most prominent being life, death, and love.

Of those poems which celebrate life, a substantial number are about nature, the inhabitants of which Dickinson frequently praises. Dickinson describes her mission to reveal nature in #441: "This is my letter to the World/ That never wrote to me—/ The simple News that Nature told—/ With tender majesty." In #111, "The Bee is not afraid of me," butterflies, brooks, and breezes are among her dearest friends. She often pays tribute to these friends, nature's creatures, as in "A fuzzy fellow, without feet" (#173), which catalogs the glorious transformation of caterpillar into a butterfly, or "A narrow Fellow in the Grass" (#986), a multisensory description of a sleek but frightening snake. In "An awful Tempest mashed the air" (#198), nature is personified. In #214, nature is a "liquor never brewed" that inebriates the speaker with joy. The sunset is a "Housewife" who has swept the west with color in "She sweeps with many-colored Brooms" (#219). Nature assumes the role of "Gentlest Mother" in #790, bestowing "infinite Affection—/ And infiniter Care" on all the world. Likewise the "Juggler of Day," the sun, blazes in gold and quenches in purple (#228). In "These are the days when Birds come back" (#130), Dickinson uses sacred—Sacrament, Last Communion—diction to welcome the holy return of spring. In "An altered look about the hill" (#140), she likens the return of spring to the resurrection with a biblical allusion to Nicodemus.

Nature is the focus of Dickinson's spiritual life, as well. Her play with custom is seen in her subverting of religious ceremonies. In "The Gentian weaves her fringes" (#18), Dickinson reveres nature, which pools her resources to memorialize "departing blossoms." She joins with Bobolink and Bee, Gentian and Maple in this commemoration service, which she closes with a sacrilegious play on the Trinity:

> In the name of the Bee—
> And of the Butterfly—
> And of the Breeze—Amen!

Refreshingly, these are the entities with which Dickinson is most comfortable: In #19, the Bee and the Breeze enable her transformation into a Rose; and in #111, the reader learns that her reverence of them is not based in fear, nor is it founded upon not knowing the Other. Rather, they share a mutual knowledge and comfortable relationship:

> The Bee is not afraid of me.
> I know the Butterfly.
> The pretty people in the Woods
> Receive me cordially—
>
> The Brooks laugh louder when I come—
> The Breezes madder play;
> Wherefore mine eye thy silver mists,
> Wherefore, Oh Summer's Day?

Her communion with nature is a voluntary ritual, a genuine connection that makes her misty-eyed. Equally significant, she implies that it is a reciprocally nurturing relationship.

Dickinson resents the dominance of nature by predominantly male scientists and is "mad" about its co-optation, as she writes in #70:

> "Arcturus" is his other name—
> I'd rather call him "Star."
> It's very mean of Science
> To go and interfere!
> . . . .
> I pull a flower from the woods—
> A monster with a glass
> Computes the stamens in a breath—
> And has her in a "class"!
>
> Whereas I took the Butterfly
> Aforetime in my hat—
> He sits erect in "Cabinets"—
> The Clover bells forgot.

She has contempt for the scientists, whom she mocks for thinking they can objectively know nature through detached analysis. She fears that such objectification of an entity that she reverences will destroy or endanger its spiritual aspect, "What once was 'Heaven'." Poems #97, #108, and #185 are among others that indict science's "advances" and its preoccupation with subduing nature, suppressing its playfulness, and interfering with its course.

Dickinson likewise makes a farce of militarism and its threat to life and the world; in #73 she criticizes the hypocrisy of militarism, first camouflaging her satire with the interrogative form, then affirming her disgusted sarcasm with exclamation points.

> Who never lost, are unprepared
> A Coronet to find!
> . . . .

How many Legions overcome—
The Emperor will say?
How many *Colors* taken
On Revolution Day?

How many *Bullets* bearest?
Hast Thou the Royal scar?
Angels! Write "Promoted"
On this Soldier's brow!

She concludes that what makes "sense" to society is "Madness" (#435), whereas what society, with its undiscerning eye, would deem "mad" makes the most sense:

Much Madness is divinest Sense—
To a discerning Eye—
Much Sense—the starkest Madness—
'Tis the Majority
In this, as All, prevail—
Assent—and you are sane—
Demur—you're straightway dangerous—
And handled with a Chain—

Dickinson knows the cost of being labeled mad yet risks it, for she can discern the value of her genius and—in a society of one—it matters not whether anyone else can discern that value. The poet understands the price exacted for nonconformity or originality, but nature allows her to balance the risk with her sense of hope, ". . . the thing with feathers—/ That perches in the soul—" (#254). The creator in "He fumbles at your Soul" (#315) stuns "by degrees" until he "Deals-One-imperial-thunderbolt—/ That scalps your naked Soul—." Dickinson reveals her pantheism in "Some keep the Sabbath going to Church" (#324), wherein the speaker stays at home "With a Bobolink for a Chorister—/ And an Orchard, for a Dome—." Here, a choir of sextons makes for a heavenly service. Heaven is as accessible as our "Capacity" to imagine, according to poem #370, one of 366 poems written during Dickinson's marathon poetry year of 1862. This seems quite understandable if one agrees with #383 that "Exhilaration—is within—" and is among the divine feelings "the Soul achieves—Herself—."

Two other soul poems, #303 and #306, are thematically linked: "The Soul selects her own Society," which embodies willful solitude and seclusion, and "The Soul's Superior instants." One of her most well-known "soul" poems is #512, which delineates the soul's varied dimensions, such as "Bandaged moments" when healing from a blow; "moments of Escape" when it "dances like a Bomb, abroad," testing the limits of its liberty, and "retaken moments" of caution. The soul is also "an imperial friend" to itself (#683), a theme Dickinson resumes in "There is a solitude of space" (#1695), wherein the soul enjoys a "polar privacy" and, with itself, experiences the paradox of "Finite infinity." In "A Thought went up my mind today," the soul even facilitates so-called déjà-vu experiences. The integral connection between the soul and Dickinson's poetry is encapsulated in "There is no Frigate like a Book" (#1263), wherein ". . . a Page/ Of prancing Poetry—" can bear the soul "Lands away."

This transport may be necessary when grieving the loss of loved ones to death, another of Dickinson's subjects. One of the most prominent of these poems is "I felt a Funeral, in my Brain" (#280) wherein the mourners pace and the service drones on to the point that "My Mind was going numb—." Along similar lines, in "After great pain, a formal feeling comes" (#341), grief reduces the narrator to disorientation and mechanical, routine functioning. Also mournful in tone is #258, "There's a certain Slant of light," in which "Winter Afternoons," like "Cathedral tunes," are oppressive. Even "the Landscape listens" to what is like ". . . the Distance/ On the look of Death—."

Similarly, in #389, the House wherein "There's been a Death" has a "numb look" as it prepares for the "Dark Parade" of mourners. It is in just such a house that the speaker of "I heard a Fly buzz—when I died—" (#465) met her death. The tenuous "Stillness" that pervades the atmosphere of anticipated death is broken only by the "Blue—uncertain stumbling Buzz—" of a carrion insect, oblivious to the exhausted tears of loving relations. This deceased speaker, in turn, could inhabit "I died for Beauty" (#449) wherein she converses with a kindred "One who died for Truth," "until the Moss had reached our lips." Or, she could become one of those who are "Safe in their Alabaster Chambers" (#216), awaiting the Resurrection, unable to experience the light of day before that moment. The undercurrent of finality also surfaces in "'Twas warm—at first—like Us" (#519), a graphic and sobering delineation of the stages of rigor mortis and burial, and in "All but Death, can be Adjusted" (#749), a brief poem about death's irrevocability and incapacity for change.

Personification enables another view of death in one of Dickinson's most famous poems: "Because I could not stop for Death" (#712). In one of several lyrical poems that correspond to the rhythm and meter of the hymn "Amazing Grace," Death stops for the speaker in a carriage wherein they pass a figurative panorama of her life and her gravesite on the way to "Eternity." The redemptive quality of death also surfaces in "A Death blow is a Life blow to Some" (#816), a one-stanza paradox wherein death is described as a wake-up call, as a prerequisite to "Vitality." In #501, life on earth is merely a way station to what scholars and the faithful can only conjecture. Death, therefore, is to be welcomed rather than feared. Beyond riddle and bordering conundrum are Dickinson's poems about pain, in which Dickinson undercuts dualities by conflating opposites. Perhaps most poignant among these is #125:

> For each ecstatic instant
> We must an anguish pay
> In keen and quivering ratio
> To the ecstasy.
>
> For each beloved hour
> Sharp pittances of years—
> Bitter contested farthings—
> And Coffers heaped with Tears!

Even in her earliest poems, Dickinson demonstrates the fun she has with experimental language, particularly with wordplay that reverses meaning, as in #33:

> If recollecting were forgetting,
> Then I remember not.
> And if forgetting, recollecting,
> How near I had forgot.
> And if to miss, were merry,
> And to mourn, were gay,
> How very blithe the fingers
> That gathered this, Today!

In #67, those who can define or know a thing such as success or victory are those most removed from it: "Success is counted sweetest/ By those who ne'er succeed." Here, Dickinson again explores notions of identification through opposites and explodes the duality of language as found, for example, in the oxymoron saved for the final line of #1695:

> There is a solitude of space
> A solitude of sea
> A solitude of death, but these
> Society shall be
> Compared with that profounder site
> That polar privacy
> A soul admitted to itself—
> Finite infinity.

In society, people experience the loneliness of death and of vastness; true solitude is that found by the soul that admits only itself but, strangely, has limitless potential—infinity—within the finite bounds it sets itself. Interestingly, in #303, the soul—significantly gendered as feminine—"selects her own Society—"

> Then—shuts the Door—
> To her divine Majority—
> Present no more—

In her society of "One" (which she chooses, as we learn in the third stanza), the poet is free to exercise any choice and free to play with the language of religion, custom, or ceremony. To demonstrate the former, Dickinson in #172 realizes that concepts and words are just that: They have no power beyond themselves. As she says in stanza 2:

> Life is but Life! And Death, but Death!
> Bliss is, but Bliss, and Breath but Breath!
> And if indeed I fail,
> At least to know the worst, is sweet!
> Defeat means nothing *but* Defeat,
> No drearier, can befall!

Even defeat and death lose their force. The only threat lies in what can be imagined, not in what simply is. Demonstrative of her play with language's dictates, too, is her use of the exclamation points in this poem and others. Having discovered the limits of language, the poet cannot only (ex)claim revelatory/revolutionary discoveries but sustain whatever degree of emphasis she wishes.

In #165 ("A *Wounded* Deer—leaps highest"), Dickinson combines these techniques to address the subject of disguising pain by suggesting the unexpected or something seemingly disparate. In another poem referring specifically to female deer (#754), Dickinson dissociates herself from those, especially women, who would defer to powerful forces. Instead, she defines her life as a "Loaded Gun" in search of the doe. Every time she speaks, "The Mountains straight reply—," thus satisfying her desires both to be heard (for she incurs an echo) and to have, like a bullet, an impact. Only then can she experience pleasure, as we learn in stanza 3:

> And do I smile, such cordial light
> Upon the Valley glow—

It is as a Vesuvian face
Had let its pleasure through—

Dickinson's persona in this poem is both madly at play and enjoying the pleasures of play.

As these poems illustrate, Dickinson's language is highly compressed and disjunctive. The compression accounts for the multiplicity of meaning and the often anomalous, riddling quality of her poems, though it is not clear whether her intention is to speak subversively, to disguise her power or pain, or to express through form her personal ethic of renunciation. Disjunction in punctuation, syntax, action, and tone disrupts the expected patterns of style and meaning. Disjunctive poetry disallows a single "correct" interpretation. Dickinson's surface features of often inexplicable punctuation, inverted and elliptical syntax, occasional metrical irregularity, off-rhyme, and ungrammaticality rest on the acceptance of an underlying regularity of meter, rhyme, and stanza forms. A similar interplay is found in the juxtaposition of singular nouns with plural verbs and vice versa, as well as in singular versions of plural reflexive pronouns (as in "ourself"). While Dickinson primarily uses the lyric present tense, the subjunctive mood often connotes conditionality or universality. In similar fashion, her figurative language reinforces the nonconventional.

Dickinson believed that language's potential for meaning exceeds the individual's control of it. She manipulates punctuation to reflect the resulting flux. Her use of the dash, for example, represents a resistance to definiteness, definition, or closure, as does her irregular vocabulary. Her use of exclamation points and question marks expresses emotional urgency and self-doubt. She also draws on an ironic tone, negation, qualification, and challenges to authority.

Dickinson was reluctant to publicize her rich, nontraditional work, and she was adamant about not selling out. "Publication—is the Auction/ Of the Mind of Man—" she contends in #709, wherein she reluctantly concedes that only poverty could justify "so foul a thing." She cautions readers not to reduce their souls "To Disgrace of Price—." Not surprisingly—as in "I'm Nobody! Who are you?" (#288)—she prefers the privacy and dignity that come from being unknown, to the dreariness of being ". . . Somebody!/ How public—like a Frog—" a simile that captures her disdain for those who crave fame and recognition. This poem, like countless others about the subject of poetry (#1212, #1261, #754, #657), demonstrates the integrity of her philosophy and the quiet genius of her poetics, shaped as it is by her age.

As a female literary genius born into a male writing and publishing world in a region where late Calvinist and Puritan theology manifests itself in ideal conventional feminine behavior, Dickinson had few options. Her art expresses an attempt to transcend the patriarchally imposed limits on prose (#613), heaven (#947), and her own sexual identity (#908), limits that she felt deprived her of purpose or place. As she wrote early in her career, in the poem #613 of approximately 1862:

They shut me up in Prose—
As when a little Girl
They put me in a Closet—
Because they liked me "still"—

Still! Could themself have peeped—
And seen my Brain—go round—
They might as wise have lodged a Bird
For Treason—in the Pound—
Himself has but to will

And easy as a Star
Abolish his Captivity—
And laugh—No more have I—

The negative images of the first line suggest that Dickinson did not regard prose highly. In a letter, Dickinson wrote, "We please ourselves with the fancy that we're the only poets, everyone else is prose." Stating that she had the madness of a poet who would not stay shut up in convention, Dickinson will break out of this outer-imposed prison and reveal the true singer. The very fact that this inhibition is outer-imposed rather than chosen leaves the persona speechless (that is, "shut up"). Only by creating her own self-initiated and self-chosen style can she abolish her captivity, similar to the "Patriarch's bird" as female explorer in poem #48. The captive's dream of freedom found in #613 and #48 also surfaces in #661, when the bee escapes the authoritative chase of police and exclaims: "What Liberty! So Captives deem/ Who tight in Dungeons are." In another poem, #657, poetry and possibility provide more freedom than prose: "I dwell in Possibility—/ A fairer house than Prose—."

Prose, specifically as it was conventionally practiced at the time, was not a form of expression conducive to Dickinson's art, for most of its forms would have required a plot— typically a romance plot whose end restricts female characters either to marriage or death, and in any case a linear progression of events. Dickinson is aware that her mind does not follow such a path and that it is, instead, cyclic, circular, and concentric. In pursuing the nonlinear nature of her thinking and writing, Dickinson created her new aesthetic. She may also have found the prose with which she was familiar to be static, final, and lacking in affect. Its syntax and grammar represent the rational structures she wished to undercut.

The imagination can enact simultaneously both needed sequestration and escape. Dickinson hoped through words to assert autonomy and independence. She mocked social efforts to control and negate her adult liberating self-expression. Through laughter, Dickinson overcame confinement and transformed into success the futility she felt in poems such as #77:

I never hear the word "escape"
Without a quicker blood,
A sudden expectation,
A flying attitude!

I never hear of prisons broad
By soldiers battered down,
But I tug childish at my bars
Only to fail again!

This poem, written in 1859, during a year of self-initiated and symbolic changes that Dickinson made in her life—she began, for example, to wear white—indicates her conscious affirmation of her own emancipatory poetry and her decision to ignore external pressures and follow on her own artistic independence and convictions, as she writes in so many subsequent poems.

Dickinson became a stylistic innovator and modern experimentalist so as to voice her sense of autonomy. At the same time, she recognized the tension this innovation would necessarily entail. She discovers, for example, the inevitable discontinuity of her thought in #937:

I felt a Cleaving in my Mind—
As if my Brain had split—
I tried to match it—Seam by Seam—
But could not make them fit.

The thought behind, I strove to join
Unto the thought before—
But Sequence ravelled out of Sound
Like Balls—upon a Floor.

Perhaps the split is a result of the agonistic relation between her poetic aesthetic and conventional writing. Even though sequential thought decomposes and ruptures cognition, incoherence attests Dickinson's use of paradoxes to explode binarism and enable multiplicity and disunity.

If, therefore, Dickinson is to tell the truth, she must tell it "slant," "in circuit" (#1129):

Tell all the Truth but tell it slant—
Success in Circuit lies
Too bright for our infirm Delight
The Truth's superb surprise

As Lightning to the Children eased
With explanation kind
The Truth must dazzle gradually
Or every man be blind—

Dickinson reveals truth gradually, so as not to blind its recipients with its dazzling light. Dazzled by her own discoveries, she experiences a splitting that leads to loneliness and possibly even insanity, as indicated by the final two stanzas of #410:

My Brain—begun to laugh—
I mumbled—like a fool—
And tho' 'tis Years ago—that Day—
My Brain keeps giggling—still.

And Something's odd—within—
That person that I was—
And this One—do not feel the same—
Could it be Madness—this?

Again laughter accompanies this splitting and multiplicity, as it liberates the speaker to the space of madness in which to create and to exercise poetic license. In her attempts to dissociate self, mind, and world, Dickinson in her multiplicitous project tries to speak for those who do not have the language, to see for those who are less conscious, and to create a poetry of extreme states that allows others to go further into their awareness and consciousness.

Dickinson's poetry focuses meaning even as it scatters, disperses, undoes, and disrupts it. Dancing, spinning, and weaving, even of webs, serve as metaphors for her poesis: She is the performing artist and craftswoman in a sharply defined world. The poet artistically adopts several roles but settles for none. Dickinson believed that the female, like the male, poet would be able to dance freely and fiercely, like the lillies and daisies liberated from toil into ecstasy. Her poetry offers readers the same opportunities.

Roseanne L. Hoefel

Bibliography:

Bennett, Paula. *Emily Dickinson: Woman Poet*. Iowa City: University of Iowa Press, 1990. A probing, instructive discussion of feminine creativity, sexual imagery, and themes of desire.

Pollak, Vivian R. *Dickinson: The Anxiety of Gender*. Ithaca, N.Y.: Cornell University Press, 1984. A psychobiographical, feminist study of the poetry's intensity and resonance in Dickinson's relations with family, friends, and literary acquaintances.

Sewall, Richard B. *The Life of Emily Dickinson*. New York: Farrar, Straus & Giroux, 1980. Winner of the National Book Award for biography, this interpretive biography brilliantly discusses Dickinson's poetry in the context of her life, family, region, and historical setting.

Stonum, Gary Lee. *The Dickinson Sublime*. Madison: University of Wisconsin Press, 1990. Analyzes Dickinson's idiosyncratic style. Uses literary theory to assess topics such as reading, writing, language, intention, fame, power, knowledge, imagination, the resistance to closure, and the suspension between trauma and sublimation.

Wolosky, Shira. *Emily Dickinson: A Voice of War*. New Haven, Conn.: Yale University Press, 1984. Examines Dickinson's poetic forms and syntax, as well as martial imagery and historical and metaphysical issues.

COMUS

Type of work: Drama
Author: John Milton (1608-1674)
Type of plot: Allegory
Time of plot: Antiquity
Locale: Kingdom of Neptune
First performed: 1634; first published, 1637

> *Principal characters:*
> ATTENDANT SPIRIT, later disguised as Thyrsis
> COMUS, an evil magician who beguiles travelers
> THE LADY,
> THE ELDER BROTHER and
> THE SECOND BROTHER, children traveling to meet their father Neptune
> SABRINA, a river nymph

The Story:

The Attendant Spirit came into a wild wood, far from his usual abode outside Jove's court, far above the dirt and hubbub of the world. He was on earth only to show the rare mortals before him some of the ways to godly virtue. He spoke of the plight of three children who were traveling to visit their father Neptune, ruler of many island kingdoms. Their path lay through a dark and treacherous wood where their lives would have been in danger if Jove had not sent the Spirit to protect them. The chief danger was Comus, son of Bacchus and Circe. He lived in the wood and possessed a magic wine which, when drunk by thirsty travelers, gave them the heads and inclinations of wild animals. The Spirit disguised himself as a shepherd to guide the children of Neptune. He left when he heard Comus and his band of bewitched travelers approaching.

Comus, invoking joy and feasting, drinking and dancing, declared that the night was made for love and should be so used before the sun revealed the revels of his band and turned them to sinfulness. His followers danced until he stopped them, sensing the approach of a young woman whom he immediately wished to enchant.

The Lady entered, drawn to the scene by the noise of the revelers. Unwilling as she was to meet such people, she nevertheless felt that they were the only hope she had of finding her way out of the wood. Because she had been tired by her walking, her brothers had left her to find wild fruit for refreshment, but night had fallen before they could return and they were unable to find her again. Meanwhile, a dark cloud had covered the stars. The Lady called and sang to the nymph, Echo, to guide her to her brothers.

Comus, delighted with the song she sang, decided that the Lady should be his queen, and, in the disguise of a village boy, he greeted her as a goddess. The Lady reproved him and said that she wanted help to find her companions. After questioning her about them, he said that he had seen two such young men gathering fruit and that it would be a delight to help her find them. Comus added that he knew the woods perfectly and that he would therefore lead the Lady to her brothers. She replied that she would trust him. They left the clearing together.

The two brothers arrived and the elder called to heaven for the moon and stars, so that they might see their way. Failing this, he wished to see the lights of someone's cottage. The Second Brother, adding that even the sound of penned-up flocks would help them, expressed great fear for his sister's fate. The Elder Brother insisted that the Lady's perfect virtue would protect her. The Second Brother said that beauty such as hers needed to be guarded and that she could easily be in danger in such a place. The Elder Brother repeated that he had great hope for her safety as she was armed by chastity. Nothing could violate this; the very angels in heaven would protect her.

Hearing someone approaching, the brothers called out to him. When the Attendant Spirit greeted them, they thought they recognized him as their father's shepherd, Thyrsis. He anxiously asked where their sister was and, hearing that she was lost, told them that Comus dwelt in the wood. He added that he had overheard Comus offer to escort a lady to her companions. Fearing that she was their sister, he had himself left to find the brothers. That news plunged the Second Brother into complete despair. The Elder Brother, maintaining that virtue could be attacked but not injured, declared that they must find Comus and fight him for their sister, but the Attendant Spirit warned them that swords would not help them against Comus. He said, however, that he had been given a magic herb that was effective against all enchantments. He instructed the brothers to break the glass in Comus' hand when they found him and to seize his wand.

In Comus' palace, meanwhile, the Lady refused his wine and attempted to leave, but she was restrained by a threat to transfix her in her chair. When she declared that Comus could not control her mind, he propounded his hedonistic philosophy, saying that she should enjoy her youth and beauty, not cruelly deny them. She replied that she would never accept anything from him, since only the good man can give good things. Comus argued that in rejecting him she was denying life and the plentiful gifts of nature by her abstinence; beauty should be enjoyed, not left to wither like a dying rose. The Lady decided that she must refute these arguments with her own. She stated that nature's gifts are for the temperate to use well and that excess of luxury only breeds ingratitude in men. She feared that Comus could never understand this doctrine, and she felt that if she attempted to explain, her conviction would be so strong that his palace would tumble around him. Comus was impressed by her argument, which seemed to him inspired by Jove himself, yet he determined to try again to persuade her. As he began to speak, the brothers rushed in, broke his glass on the ground, and overwhelmed his followers.

Comus himself escaped because they had not captured his wand. The Attendant Spirit despaired of freeing the Lady until he remembered that he could summon Sabrina. This river nymph would help them, since she loved the virtue that the Lady personified. By song, he summoned her in the name of Neptune and Triton to save the girl. As Sabrina rose from the river, she sang of the willows and flowers that she had left. She freed the Lady by sprinkling on her the pure and precious water from her fountain. The Attendant Spirit gave Sabrina his blessing and prayed that the river should always flow in good measure and that its banks would be fertile.

The Attendant Spirit then told the Lady that he would lead them to Neptune's house, where many friends were gathered to congratulate him. In Ludlow Town, at the President's castle, country dancers led the Lady and her two brothers before the Earl and the Countess, who impersonated Neptune and his Queen. There the Attendant Spirit praised the young people's beauty, patience, and honesty, and their triumph over folly; then he announced his return to his natural home in the Gardens of Hesperus, for his task was done. If any mortal would go with him, however, his way was the path of virtue.

Critical Evaluation:

Milton's *Comus* was first published in 1637 as *A Maske Presented at Ludlow Castle*. The title *Comus*, derived from the name of the evil magician in the masque, became the normal designation during the eighteenth century and has replaced the original title. The work—written as dramatic entertainment for the installation of John Egerton, Earl of Bridgewater, as Lord President of Wales—was performed at Ludlow Castle on September 29, 1634. Written primarily in blank verse, with rhymed lyrics interspersed, the drama extends to 1,023 lines, exceptionally brief for a play but above average length for a masque. The work was a collaboration between Milton and his friend Henry Lawes, a tutor to the Egerton children. Lawes wrote the music for the songs, staged the production, and acted the part of Thyrsis.

Much critical attention has centered upon *Comus* as a masque and its resemblance to other masques of the period. A popular form of aristocratic entertainment, the masque was a relatively short drama featuring simple conflict, static characters, song and dance, and pageantry. The actors were usually amateurs, often members of a noble family, who felt free to take part in private dramatic productions but would not have ventured onto the public stage. The plot of *Comus* features a simple journey through a wood at whose end the three young actors are presented to their parents. The masque pits the three children of the Egerton family, who acted the parts of the Lady and her two brothers, against the evil magician Comus and his deformed rout of followers, whose dances form the antimasque.

Milton draws upon the classics, early English literature, and folk tradition to present an elemental conflict between good and evil. Overall, the tone of the poem, despite its philosophical speeches and theme of rigid morality, suggests a fairy tale. Spirits intervene at the appropriate times; evil magic is countered by good magic; and the creatures with supernatural powers exercise them within conventional limits. Thyrsis, the spirit who becomes a shepherd, cannot intervene directly to protect the Lady but must serve as instructor and guide to her brothers, who attack the magician with drawn swords. Their failure to carry out all of their instructions, to seize Comus's wand, means that Sabrina must be summoned to release the Lady. Spells and incantations are as much a part of the masque as is Comus's seductive, transforming chalice.

A few critics have suggested that Milton's strong ethical theme and limited use of singing and dancing mean that the work is not really a masque but a type of ethical debate. Passages like the somewhat formal speeches of the Elder Brother, the Lady's refutation of Comus's arguments in support of immediate pleasures, and the concluding speech of Thyrsis represent examples of extended moralizing. Most critical opinion, however, while acknowledging that Milton presses the limits of the genre, accepts its classification as a masque. The original title suggests that Milton believed he was writing a masque; in addition, he had earlier produced another example of the genre in Arcades, for the countess of Derby, the stepmother of the earl of Bridgewater.

Exploration of Milton's connection with the Egerton family has unearthed some hints of a scandal that had little direct effect on the family. These discoveries were sufficient, however, to fuel critical speculation that the ethical emphasis in Milton's drama was adopted as an effort to enhance their reputation.

A more likely explanation for the moral theme arises when one places the masque within the context of Milton's major poetry. Along with *Paradise Lost* (1667), *Paradise Regained* (1671), and *Samson Agonistes* (1671), it forms a fourth major poetic work on the theme of temptation. All four present an ethical conflict marked by the fundamental contrast between right and wrong, occurring within the context of a Providential view of history and human life. In *Comus*, the Lady must preserve her chastity by rejecting the sensual life that Comus urges upon her. She recognizes that the values espoused by Comus and his followers are incompatible with both temperance and chastity. Her ethical understanding and strong will enable her to overcome his arguments and defeat his purpose. While her character remains unblemished, however, her body is imprisoned by Comus, whose magical power forces her to sit immobile in an alabaster chair.

Humanity's dependence upon Providence is demonstrated when Sabrina, symbolizing grace, arrives to release the Lady through sprinkling drops of water over her, an allegorical representation of Christian baptism. The Lady emerges triumphant over evil, and her brothers demonstrate their courage in putting Comus and his followers to flight.

Among numerous poetic elements in the masque, Milton draws heavily on myth and on the pastoral tradition. He develops an ethic based upon willful choice through the speeches of the Lady, the Elder Brother, and the guardian spirit Thyrsis. As the Elder Brother explains, throughout life one rises to ever greater spirituality by making right choices, and each correct choice leads to a higher level of ethical being. Conversely, each wrong choice causes one to become progressively more immoral. In the end, evil is self-defeating, and good is triumphant. In *Comus*, as in other poems, however, Milton portrays ethical behavior as a simple choice between right and wrong, and the Lady's decision is neither complex nor subtle.

To mirror and reinforce his ethical theme, Milton makes elaborate use of the idea of metamorphosis or transformation, borrowed from the Roman poet Ovid but imbued with Christian overtones. The followers of Comus, with their animal faces, have been partially transformed to a lower life because they failed to resist his blandishments. Other transformations are self-imposed. Thyrsis is able to transform himself into the likeness of a shepherd on a mission to help the two brothers free the Lady. For the purpose of deception, Comus transforms himself into the appearance of a country person. Providence also intervenes to transform the virtuous. Sabrina, who represents grace, has been made into a river goddess that she might escape pursuit by a cruel stepmother. It remains for the Lady and the Brothers to retain the virtue they possess, not to be led astray by evil. Their most important transformation will occur at the end of life as a confirmation of their virtue.

"Critical Evaluation" by Stanley Archer

Bibliography:

Diekhoff, John, ed. *A Mask at Ludlow: Essays on Milton's "Comus."* Cleveland: Case Western Reserve University Press, 1968. Diekhoff's work assembles previously published essays by eminent Milton critics. The selections deal with all major critical issues concerning the masque.

Hanford, James Holly, and James G. Taaffe. *A Milton Handbook*. New York: Meredith, 1970. A mine of information about Milton's life, works, and critical reputation, this book offers synopses of individual works and comprehensive critical assessments. An excellent beginning point for the general reader and student.

Hunter, William B., ed. *Milton's English Poetry*. Lewisburg, Pa.: Bucknell University Press, 1986. Hunter's book assembles entries on Milton's poetry. The essay on *Comus*, listed under its original title, provides an introductory overview of the masque and a detailed survey of critical opinion.

Lovecock, Julian, ed. *Milton: "Comus" and "Samson Agonistes."* New York: Macmillan, 1975. In his casebook, Lovecock reprints five of the most significant twentieth century studies of Milton's masque. Five additional selections include significant criticism from the eighteenth and nineteenth centuries.

McGuire, Maryann Cale. *Milton's Puritan Masque*. Athens: University of Georgia Press, 1983. In an extended analysis of the masque, McGuire places *Comus* within the Puritan tradition. In a genre that was usually Royalist, she finds Puritan values reflected in its style, ethical themes, and historical contexts.

THE CONCUBINE

Type of work: Novel
Author: Elechi Amadi (1934-   )
Type of plot: Tragedy
Time of plot: Precolonial times, mid-nineteenth century
Locale: Eastern Nigeria
First published: 1966

> *Principal characters:*
> EMENIKE, a fine wrestler and a favorite son of the village
> IHUOMA, his young, beautiful wife, the village model of ideal womanhood
> NWONNA, Ihuoma's son
> NNADI, Ihuoma's brother-in-law
> MADUME, the "big eyed," quarrelsome land grabber
> WOLU, his unfortunate wife
> EKWUEME, an accomplished singer and trapper
> WIGWE and
> ADAKU, his parents
> AHUROLE, Ekwueme's immature, moody girl bride
> WODU WAKIRI, the village wag, a gifted singer and comic
> ANYIKA, village medicine man (*dibia*), diviner of Omokachi
> AGWOTURUMBE, a rival, powerful *dibia* from Aliji village

The Story:

Emenike died suddenly, after a full recovery from injuries he suffered during a fight with Madume, his neighbor and adversary, over some disputed farmland. Although the villagers were uncertain about the cause of death, and even though they suspected that Madume had a hand in Emenike's death, they said Emenike died from "lock chest." Ignoring the arbitration on the land dispute which the village elders and priests had made in favor of Emenike, and with Emenike out of the way, Madume decided to stake his claim on the disputed farmland. While at it, he claimed Ihuoma, whom he alleged Emenike had snatched from him. In a show of power, Madume embarked on assaults on Ihuoma and her brother-in-law, Nnadi, as they tried to protect Emenike's land and crops from Madume's "big eyes." A series of misfortunes, brought on by personal ill will, inordinate greed, and insensitivity, befell Madume until excessive cockiness and a final act of brazenness brought him face-to-face with a spitting cobra, which blinded him as he reached in defiantly to harvest a plantain tree on Emenike's farm. Blinded and miserable, Madume hanged himself. The villagers agreed that his abominable death was retributive justice from the ever-watchful, powerful gods. Though finally rid of Madume, Ihuoma characteristically bemoaned the loss of two village men in a two-year span, fearing that there would be "too few left to organize village activities."

Young, already a mother of three children, and widowed at the tender age of twenty-two, Ihuoma continued to live out her widowhood in her dead husband's compound, devoted to his memory and care of her children. More attractive than ever even in her misfortune, Ihuoma commanded great respect from the village women, especially Madume's wife, Wolu. Ekwueme, the gifted song composer and singer, although betrothed to Ahurole, was irrepressibly taken by Ihuoma's exceptional beauty of character and looks. In a bind, aware of his obligation to filial obedience and to the propriety of Omokachi tradition, Ekwueme gave up his personal desires and married Ahurole, his immature, neurotic child bride, whose unpredictable mood swings and incessant sobbing tested their marriage sorely. Although Ekwueme reconciled himself to his marriage to Ahurole, he could not repress his desire for Ihuoma, his ideal of a wife. As his half-hearted interest in Ahurole waned, his repressed feelings for Ihuoma emerged stronger. Suspecting this, and upon her mother's advice, Ahurole sought the help of a diviner to renew Ekwueme's diminishing conjugal interest. Unfortunately, Ahurole's effort to recapture Ekwueme's love interest, by way of a love potion, only succeeded in bewitching him and temporarily bringing on madness.

After being relieved of Ahurole, Ekwueme openly declared his intentions to marry Ihuoma, who was responsible for curing him of his madness. The diviner-priest Anyika, however, revealed to Ekwueme's parents the ill-fatedness of an Ihuoma-Ekwueme union because, contrary to physical appearances, Ihuoma was not an ordinary human being but a goddess-human, a mermaid in human form, betrothed to the powerful, malevolent Sea-King. Only the series of bizarre events toward the end of the novel revealed the truth of an identity of which she herself was unaware. Her husband's sudden death and Madume's blindness and subsequent suicide after he assaulted her were all explained by her secret godlike status.

Unequivocal in his resolve, and secretly hoping that the cause of the ill-fatedness of the proposed marriage to Ihuoma could be mediated, Ekwueme and his parents sought a second opinion of a rival diviner, the renowned Agwoturumbe of Iliji village. Unlike Anyika, Agwoturumbe, perhaps in a bid to outdivine his rival Anyika, assured Ekwueme and his parents that Agwoturumbe had the power to bind the Sea-King and render him powerless through appropriate sacrifice. Preparations for the elaborate and costly sacrificial mediation were well under way when a sudden turn of events during the search for the lizard, the final item called for on the list of items for the sacrifice, hastened the end of Ekwueme's life. Ekwueme's bizarre, premonitory dream of being lured away to the land of the dead by Emenike, Ihuoma's dead husband, came true tragically and ironically at the hands of Nwonna, Ihuoma's son. Ekwueme had instructed Nwonna in the art of lizard-shooting moments before the young man loosed the arrow that, intended for the desired "big coloured male lizard," felled Ekwueme.

Critical Evaluation:

Unlike Chinua Achebe's *Things Fall Apart* (1958) and *Arrow of God* (1964), which infuse the elements of the tragic into the themes of the impact of colonialism on traditional African cultures, Elechi Amadi's lesser-known *The Concubine* focuses on the private, the social, and the supernatural. Notably lacking the fanfare of color, ritual, rhetoric, and ceremony characteristic of many West African novels of the 1960's, Amadi's novel's central concern is with the notion of cosmic totality, the precarious nature of man's relationship to the supernatural—a relationship in which unseen forces manipulate human life and control human thought and action in the painful and tragic human drama. From its opening chapters to the end, the novel teems with omens, its pages pervaded by fatalism. Divine authority predominates; the presence of the gods is felt long before the story of Ihuoma's status begins to unfold. Its plot and structure are controlled by supernatural forces. The remarkably simple plot describes a complex situation in which the fortunes and misfortunes of four key characters are set against a background of communal peace and harmony, an idyllic setting governed by a traditional propriety. Good behavior is applauded, excessive and fanatical feelings are frowned upon, and personal feelings are controlled almost to a fault. Except for Madume, the quarrelsome and greedy land grabber, the generous villagers of Omokachi live peacefully with one another. The good-natured humor, the constant bantering, and the profuse singing and dancing that characterize this seemingly perfect community is disrupted by implacable gods. In their hands it appears humans are like puppets, goaded by fate into the gods' wily snares.

The tragedy of *The Concubine* is centered on the dual character of Ihuoma, the almost flawless embodiment of Omokachi's ideal of propriety, a goddess-human who, unbeknown to her and the villagers, was fated to be the wife of the Sea-King even before birth. Reincarnated into the Omokachi community, Ihuoma becomes a death-snare for men, the bait to lure those with amorous intentions to a deadly rivalry with the Sea-King. Given this femme fatale's winning personality and looks, it is not surprising that the cream of the village manhood is attracted to her. While the villagers readily gave plausible explanations for Emenike's and Madume's deaths ("lock chest" and "big eyes" respectively), they are particularly stunned by the cruel and mysterious circumstances of Ekwueme's death on the eve of his impending marriage to Ihuoma and on the day that his life is especially sweet.

When the two rival diviners—Anyika and Agwoturumbe—enter the scene, each with his own explanation and vision of the potency of the superior power at work and how to "bind" it, the action of the tragedy shifts to a blatant contention between man and god on two counts: Ekwueme's unequivocal, often-repeated love for Ihuoma and his intentions to marry her, and Agwoturumbe's presumptuous claim to power and knowledge strong enough to fetter the Sea-King. Moreover, Ekwueme's well-intentioned but proud quip that "if Ihuoma was a sea-goddess, then he could very well be a sea-god himself," combined with Agwoturumbe's equally boastful reassurance that all will be well, even if it means making a journey to the bottom of the river himself, inevitably hasten the tragic denouement of the story.

The role of mystery, though downplayed through twenty-eight of the novel's thirty chapters, is crucial in sustaining the plot and structure of the story. For example, even the most discerning reader, though vaguely suspicious of Emenike's and Madume's sudden deaths, does not discover the mystery of Ihuoma's true identity and the nature of her unusualness until Anyika divulges it in fragments in chapter 28. Mysterious as Ihuoma's goddess-human nature might be, the reader's surprise at its revelation is short-lived because the reader recognizes the novel's implicit belief in the coexistence of the natural and supernatural worlds.

Once made in light of Ihuoma's "almost perfect" nature, Anyika's revelation makes sense and is therefore credible because no human can be "quite so right in everything, almost perfect." Emenike's "lock chest" death, Madume's "big eye" death and Ekwueme's young lover's death are now fully explained because the jealous Sea-King husband, after highly involved rites, can be persuaded to tolerate concubinage but not marriage. For this reason, Ekwueme was marked, destined to die from the moment he expressed amorous interests in Ihuoma. Ekwueme, like the grasshoppers which Ihuoma's second son was feeding limb by limb to some ants, is helpless in the web of the relentless Sea-King. He is felled by an errant arrow meant for a lizard, the final, perhaps least consequential item on the list of materials for the rite that would ensure the future Ekwueme and Ihuoma were preparing for optimistically.

Amadi's achievement in his first novel is his controlled narrative and sustained dialogue. Although not given to rendering the rhythms of traditional speech with the same flair with which Achebe captures Ibo oratory, Amadi successfully combines narrative simplicity with conversational language of everyday realities. Without being idealistic, Amadi paints an idyllic picture of village life, including the aesthetic and artistic, using the language of good-natured bantering, humor, singing and dancing. *The Concubine* ranks as one of the most successful, realistic West African village novels.

Pamela J. Olubunmi Smith

Bibliography:

Banyiwa-Horne, Naana. "African Womanhood: The Contrast Perspectives of Flora Nwapa's *Efuru* and Elechi Amadi's *The Concubine*." In *Ngambika: Studies of Women in African Literature*, edited by Carole Boyce Davies and Anne Adams Graves. Trenton, N.J.: Africa World Press, 1986. Gives a strictly feminist reading of the writers' contrasting portrayal of their female protagonists. Concludes that Amadi's perspective is male oriented and therefore limiting.

Gikandi, Simon. "Myth, Language and Culture in Chinua Achebe's *Arrow of God* and Elechi Amadi's *The Concubine*." In *Reading the African Novel*. London: Heinemann, 1987. Suggests a reinterpretation of the narrowly held view that, in Achebe's and Amadi's novels, myth is simply an expression of a community's fears, hopes, or expectations.

Obiechina, Emmanuel. *Culture, Tradition and Society in the West African Novel*. New York: Cambridge University Press, 1975. Discusses *The Concubine* as one of ten major West African novels. This classic study gives a comprehensive analysis of many aspects of the novel—characterization, setting, language, and aesthetics.

Osundare, Niyi. "As Grasshoppers to Wanton Boys: The Role of the Gods in the Novels of Elechi Amadi." *African Literature Today* 11 (1980): 97-109. An insightful essay on Amadi's preoccupation with fatalism. It examines how supernatural forces shape human action and control the plots of Amadi's novels.